STATE AND LOCAL GOVERNMENT IN A FEDERAL SYSTEM

CONTEMPORARY LEGAL EDUCATION SERIES

CONTEMPORARY LEGAL EDUCATION SERIES

EDITORIAL ADVISORY BOARD

Murray L. Schwartz, Chairman
James E. Krier
A. Kenneth Pye
Maurice Rosenberg
Stephen A. Saltzburg
Roy L. Steinheimer, Jr.

State and Local Government in a Federal System

CASES AND MATERIALS

SECOND EDITION

DANIEL R. MANDELKER

Stamper Professor of Law
Washington University

DAWN CLARK NETSCH

Professor of Law
Northwestern University

PETER W. SALSICH, JR.

Professor of Law and Associate Dean
Saint Louis University

THE MICHIE COMPANY
Law Publishers
CHARLOTTESVILLE, VIRGINIA

COPYRIGHT © 1977 BY THE BOBBS-MERRILL COMPANY, INC.
COPYRIGHT © 1983 BY THE MICHIE COMPANY
Library of Congress Catalog Card No. 83-61345
ISBN 0-87215-663-X

The publisher gratefully acknowledges permission to reprint from the following copyrighted material:

Borchard, Government Liability in Tort. Reprinted by permission of The Yale Law Journal Company and Fred B. Rothman & Company from The Yale Law Journal, Vol. 34, pp. 1-5, 41-43, 45, 132-34.

Phillips, Development in Water Quality and Land Use Planning: Problems in the Application of the Federal Water Pollution Control Act Amendments of 1972. Reprinted by permission from The Urban Law Annual, Vol. 10, pp. 101-04.

Report of the California Commission on the Law of Preemption. Reprinted by permission from The Urban Law Annual, Vol. [1969], pp. 131, 133-34, 138.

Comment. Reprinted by permission from The Urban Law Annual, Vol. 8, pp. 229, 231-34.

H. Aaron, Who Pays the Property Tax? A New View. Copyright © 1975 by the Brookings Institution, Washington, D.C.

R. Reischauer & R. Hartman, Reforming School Finance. Copyright © by the Brookings Institution, Washington, D.C.

Payne, From the Legislatures: The Unhappy Job of Revaluing Property. Reprinted by permission from the Real Estate Law Journal, Vol. 9, No. 3, Winter 1981. Copyright © 1981, Warren, Gorham & Lamont Inc., 210 South Street, Boston, Mass. All rights reserved.

Note, An Evaluation of Municipal Income Taxation. Reprinted by permission from the Vanderbilt Law Review, Vol. 22, pp. 1317, 1318, 1320, 1321, 1323, 1324, 1348, 1349, 1353. Copyright the Vanderbilt Law Review.

J. Coons, W. Clune & S. Sugarman, Private Wealth and Public Education. Reprinted by permission of the publishers: The Belknap Press of Harvard University Press, Copyright © 1970 by the President and Fellows of Harvard College.

A. Adden & J. Augenblick, School Finance Reform in the States: 1981, pp. 1-5, 41. Reprinted by permission of the Education Commission of the States.

McDermott & Klein, The Cost-Quality Debate in School Finance Litigation: Do Dollars Make a Difference? Reprinted, with permission, from a symposium on Future Directions for School Finance Reform appearing in Law & Contemporary Problems (Vol. 38, No. 3, Winter/Spring 1974), published by the Duke University School of Law, Durham, North Carolina. Copyright © 1974 by Duke University.

A. Cox, The Role of the Supreme Court in American Government, pp. 95, 96. Copyright © 1976 by Oxford University Press, Inc.

Barnett, The Foundations of the Distinction Between Public and Private Functions in Respect to the Common-law Tort Liability of Municipal Corporations. Reprinted by permission from the Oregon Law Review, Vol. 16, pp. 259, 268-69. Copyright © 1937 by University of Oregon.

S.B. Warner, ed., Planning for a Nation of Cities, p. 210. Reprinted by permission of the MIT Press.

Comment, An Analysis of Authorities: Traditional and Multicounty. Reprinted by permission from the Michigan Law Review, Vol. 71, pp. 1429, 1432-34.

Pressman, Political Implications of the New Federalism, and Inman, Grants in a Metropolitan Economy — A Framework for Policy, in W. Oates, Financing the New Federalism, pp. 37, 88, 89. Published for Resources for the Future by Johns Hopkins University Press. Copyright © 1975 by Resources for the Future, Inc.

J. Richard Aronson & Eli Schwartz, eds., Management Policies in Local Government Finance, Washington, D.C.: International City Management Association, 1975, pp. 193-95.

J. Rodgers, Sales Taxes, Income Taxes, and Other Revenues, in Management Policies in Local Government Finance, ed. Aronson & Schwartz (Washington, D.C.: International City Management Association, 1981).

To John and Amy
To Walter
To Denise

Preface to the Second Edition

The preface to the first edition of this casebook by the two co-authors of that edition states our purpose in publishing these classroom materials:

> It is reasonable to assume that every casebook has a point of view; it is an equally safe assumption that no casebook could satisfy the point of view, needs, or objectives of every teacher of state and local government law. Within these boundary conditions we have constructed a casebook which has a modest and frequently unobtrusive point of view and which at the same time attempts to provide materials adequate to satisfy the needs and objectives of other teachers.
>
> This point of view is relatively simple and essentially structural. The study of state and local government for law students should be built on a framework of the tri-partite distribution of powers, both vertically and horizontally: the federal-state-local levels of government and their interrelationship, the legislative-executive-judicial branches of government and their interaction.
>
> The objective is to identify and begin to understand (a) the kinds of issues that arise as a result of the exercise of state and local government powers in a federal system and how those issues get resolved, and (b) the participants in the process — who they are and how they play their roles. "They" are often, perhaps most of the time, a unit of government disputing with another unit of government or with an individual. But government also operates through individuals; it does not have an existence of its own. And so the participants are also legislators, judges and the executive — mayors, or governors, or administrative officers. Moreover, government is a political process as well as a legal one — indeed some would say rather than. As a result, more than most casebooks in this area, the materials call attention to the interaction of these three major participants in governmental decision-making. We call this intra-governmental distribution of powers. Its roots, of course, lie in the American separation of powers.
>
> Students will also find a good deal more state government law and somewhat less municipal law than is traditional in courses in this area. That also reflects our structural preoccupation. Despite the faded grandeur of state government during the middle half of the 20th Century, states are living and breathing entities and continue to occupy a pivotal role in our multi-level structural system.
>
> The book is designed for the generalist in state and local government law rather than for the municipal law practitioner. The reasons are twofold. First, and we concede that this is a complaint heard from every law teacher, the time allotted is inadequate: rarely more than three hours, sometimes only two hours. The pressure has been somewhat relieved by the practice in some law schools in recent years of creating a separate course for land use issues and sometimes also for state and local taxation. On the other hand, while some of the content may have moved on to other offerings, new problems have more than replaced them — metropolitan government, reapportionment, school finance, etc. Even by our standard of selectivity, there are more materials than a three-hour course will comfortably contain — which allows room for free choice. We feared that if we expanded coverage the doctrines would pass by so fast that what remained for the student would be a blur.
>
> Secondly, more than is true for most public law courses, the students who elect state and local government law do not usually intend to practice in this area and probably do not expect even to confront a state or local governmental problem, except perhaps for an occasional land use question. Teachers of state and local government courses are nevertheless accustomed to hearing from former students that there was more "practical use" for clients from the course

than they would have guessed. A substantial number are also likely to find that their extracurricular professional activities — as school board members, combatants in a neighborhood zoning or highway or environmental dispute — require a legal understanding of local, state and federal governments. It is important for the course to meet their needs also.

The decision to write for the generalist meant that we do not purport to include all of the subjects and issues which might be covered, or to cover topics which we have included exhaustively (with perhaps a few exceptions). We have omitted such areas as internal state and local government problems in personnel, the duties and rights of office holders, government contract powers, rights of access to government records and state legislative reapportionment. Neither do we deal directly with the various roles which lawyers play in the governmental setting, such as city attorney, elective office holder, appointed officer, lobbyist, or attorney for private litigants. Nevertheless, we believe that our materials offer an opportunity to the instructor to bring out these varied roles.

The second edition is thoroughly updated and includes major revisions. A new chapter on governmental liability includes materials on liability in tort, liability under § 1983 of the federal Civil Rights Act, and liability under the antitrust laws. A new chapter on federalism examines relationships between state and local governments and the federal government in federal grant-in-aid and other programs. It also reviews limitations on federal power imposed by the tenth amendment to the federal constitution. A new chapter on officers and employees examines hiring, employee dismissal and labor relations problems as they arise in government service. The chapter on public finance is expanded to include new developments in this area. The chapter on metropolitan government has been shortened, reflecting the authors' belief that problems of metropolitan reorganization have become a regional rather than a national issue.

A special word is in order on the chapter on the role of the judiciary. This chapter considers problems of licensing, voting rights and school finance that either are not treated in state and local government casebooks or are considered in separate chapters — an approach that we chose not to adopt. We believe that each of these substantive areas is characterized by varying degrees of judicial intervention that have important consequences for the scope and exercise of state and local governmental functions. Our purpose in this chapter is to examine the exercise of judicial power both for its own sake and for its impact on substantive programs. In this edition, the chapter omits the materials on housing discrimination and zoning, which are treated fully in other courses.

The first edition co-authors are pleased to welcome Professor Peter W. Salsich, Jr. as a co-author of this edition. He has made an invaluable contribution to this book.

Only selected footnotes from the cases and other reprinted materials have been reproduced. These footnotes have not been renumbered. Statutes cited in the text were current as of the date of publication.

The authors were assisted by a number of students. We acknowledge particularly the assistance of Jeanmarie Beisel, research assistant to Professor Mandelker; Thomas M. Lynch, Jeanne E. Bishop, Karin A. Gerlach, and Michael J. Klinker, research assistants to Professor Netsch; and Robin Bennett and Patricia Shapiro, research assistants to Professor Salsich. Thanks are also due to the library staffs at our schools, who were most helpful in meeting our many requests for research materials. We also acknowledge a deep debt of gratitude for the patience and skills of Virginia C. Autry, Dianna L. Nunn, and Mary Ann Jauer, our secretaries and manuscript assistants.

> Daniel R. Mandelker
> Dawn Clark Netsch
> Peter W. Salsich, Jr.
>
> June 1, 1983

Summary Table of Contents

	Page
Preface	vii
Table of Contents	xiii
Table of Cases	xxiii

PART ONE. THE GOVERNMENTAL SYSTEM

CHAPTER 1. AN OVERVIEW OF THE GOVERNMENTAL SYSTEM ... 3
   A. Trends and Perspectives ... 3
   B. State Government ... 6
   C. Local Government ... 25

CHAPTER 2. LOCAL GOVERNMENT INCORPORATION AND ANNEXATION ... 41
   A. The Judicial Review Problem ... 41
   B. Municipal Incorporation and Annexation ... 52
   C. Special Districts ... 65
   D. Boundary Commissions ... 71

CHAPTER 3. LOCAL GOVERNMENT POWERS ... 79
   A. The Local Autonomy Problem ... 79
   B. Statutory Powers ... 83
   C. Home Rule ... 101
   D. State Preemption and Standards ... 131

CHAPTER 4. GOVERNMENTAL INTEGRATION ... 153
   A. Interlocal Conflict ... 153
   B. Intergovernmental Cooperation and Transfer of Function ... 163
   C. Consolidation, Federalism and Councils of Government ... 173

CHAPTER 5. STATE AND LOCAL FINANCE ... 185
   A. Fiscal Trends ... 185
   B. Constitutional Limitations ... 192
   C. Revenues ... 211
   D. Borrowing ... 273
   E. Tax and Expenditure Limitations ... 311
   F. State Assistance to Local Governments ... 345
   G. Expenditures ... 347

CHAPTER 6. SERVING THE PUBLIC SECTOR: OFFICERS AND EMPLOYEES ... 375
   A. Limiting Entry to Government Service ... 376
   B. Removal from Government Service: Patronage and Politics ... 384
   C. Integrity in Government Service: Conflicts of Interest ... 397
   D. Unions, Strikes and Collective Bargaining ... 406

	Page
CHAPTER 7. GOVERNMENTAL LIABILITY	427
A. State Courts and Legislation	428
B. Federal Law	463
CHAPTER 8. FEDERALISM	495
A. The Federal System	495
B. Federal Standards for State and Local Programs	533
C. The Federal Grant-in-Aid System	555

PART TWO. INTRA-GOVERNMENTAL DISTRIBUTION OF POWER

CHAPTER 9. THE STATE LEGISLATURE	581
A. Special Legislation	581
B. Delegation of Power	598
CHAPTER 10. THE ROLE OF THE JUDICIARY	617
A. In Ordinary State and Local Government Issues: Licensing and Regulation	617
B. In Major Policy Decisions	634
CHAPTER 11. THE CHIEF EXECUTIVE	731
A. Executive Orders	731
B. Veto Powers	750
CHAPTER 12. CITIZEN CONTROL OF GOVERNMENTAL ACTION	767
A. Through the Courts	767
B. Through Initiative and Referendum	808
Index	825

Table of Contents

	Page
Preface	vii
Summary Table of Contents	xi
Table of Cases	xxiii

PART ONE. THE GOVERNMENTAL SYSTEM

CHAPTER 1. AN OVERVIEW OF THE GOVERNMENTAL SYSTEM	3
A. Trends and Perspectives	3
B. State Government	6
1. The Reform of State Government	6
2. Constitutional Limitations on State and Local Authority	8
State v. Ludlow Supermarkets, Inc.	10
Comments	15
3. Legislative Power: Grant Versus Limitation	16
Oakland County Taxpayers' League v. Board of Supervisors	16
Comments	20
Independent School District, Class A, No. 1, Cassia County v. Pfost	21
Comments	23
C. Local Government	25
1. Local Government Structure	25
Comments	29
2. The Constitutional Status of Local Government	29
Hunter v. City of Pittsburgh	30
Comments	33
Gomillion v. Lightfoot	35
Comments	38
CHAPTER 2. LOCAL GOVERNMENT INCORPORATION AND ANNEXATION	41
A. The Judicial Review Problem	41
Superior Oil Co. v. City of Port Arthur	42
Comments	45
Town of Beloit v. City of Beloit	47
Comments	50
B. Municipal Incorporation and Annexation	52
1. Incorporation	52
Comments	54
2. Annexation by Municipalities	55
In re Char	57
Comments	60
Racial Discrimination in Annexations and the Federal Voting Rights Act	63

		Page
C.	Special Districts	65
	Phillips, Developments in Water Quality and Land Use Planning: Problems in the Application of the Federal Water Pollution Control Act Amendments of 1972, 10 Urban Law Annual 43, 101-04 (1975)	65
	City of Scottsdale v. McDowell Mountain Irrigation & Drainage District	67
	Comments	69
D.	Boundary Commissions	71
	City of Wood Village v. Portland Metropolitan Area Local Government Boundary Commission	72
	Comments	75

CHAPTER 3. LOCAL GOVERNMENT POWERS 79

A.	The Local Autonomy Problem	79
	Tribe v. Salt Lake City Corp.	81
	Comments	82
B.	Statutory Powers	83
	Dillon, Municipal Corporations (1st ed. 1872)	83
	Comments	84
	Early Estates, Inc. v. Housing Board of Review	85
	Comments	89
	State v. Hutchinson	91
	Comments	97
	Problem	100
C.	Home Rule	101
	1. The Home Rule Issue	101
	Comments	103
	2. Home Rule Powers in the *Imperio* States	103
	United States Elevator Corp. v. City of Tulsa	105
	Comments	107
	City of Miami Beach v. Fleetwood Hotel, Inc.	109
	Comments	111
	A Note on the Comparative Autonomy of Local Governments in Home Rule and Non-Home Rule States	113
	Weekes v. City of Oakland	115
	Comments	119
	3. Legislative Home Rule	121
	Comments	122
	State *ex rel.* Swart v. Molitor	124
	Comments	127
	A Note on the Discretionary Authority of Local Governments	130
D.	State Preemption and Standards	131
	Miller v. Fabius Township Board	131
	Comments	135
	Plaza Joint Venture v. City of Atlantic City	137
	Comments	141
	Public Service Co. v. Town of Hampton	144
	Comments	146
	Report of the California Commission on the Law of Preemption, 1969 Urban L. Ann. 131, 133-34, 138	148
	Comments	149
	A Note on State Standards for Local Regulatory Programs	150

TABLE OF CONTENTS

Page

CHAPTER 4. GOVERNMENTAL INTEGRATION 153
  A. Interlocal Conflict 153
      Township of Washington v. Village of Ridgewood 153
      Comments 158
      A Note on the Condemnation of the Property of One Governmental
          Unit by Another 161
  B. Intergovernmental Cooperation and Transfer of Function 163
      1. Intergovernmental Cooperation 163
          Constitutional and Statutory Authority for Interlocal
            Cooperation 164
          Advisory Commission on Intergovernmental Relations, State
            Legislative Program #2, Local Government Modernization
            Interlocal Contracting and Joint Enterprise, 2.204 (1975) .. 164
          Comments 165
          Goreham v. Des Moines Metropolitan Area Solid Waste Agency 166
          Comments 169
      2. Transfer of Function 172
  C. Consolidation, Federalism and Councils of Government 173
      1. Consolidation and Federation 173
          Advisory Commission on Intergovernmental Relations, State and
            Local Roles in the Federal System 395-404 (1982) 173
          Comments 176
          A Note on Neighborhood Government and Citizen Participation 178
          Comments 180
      2. Councils of Government and Regional Agencies 181
          Comments 182

CHAPTER 5. STATE AND LOCAL FINANCE 185
  A. Fiscal Trends 185
      Advisory Commission on Intergovernmental Relations, Significant
        Features of Fiscal Federalism, 1980-81 Edition: Highlights 7-9
        (1981) 185
      Advisory Commission on Intergovernmental Relations, State and
        Local Roles in the Federal System 133, 137, 144, 168-70 (1980) 188
  B. Constitutional Limitations 192
      1. Due Process and Equal Protection 193
          City of Pittsburgh v. Alco Parking Corp. 193
          Comments 197
          Helton v. City of Long Beach 199
          Comments 201
      2. Public Purpose 201
          Wilson v. Connecticut Product Development Corp. 201
          Comments 205
          Idaho Water Resource Board v. Kramer 205
          Comments 209
      3. The Commerce Clause 210
          Comment 211
  C. Revenues 211
      1. The General Ad Valorem Property Tax 211
          H. Aaron, Who Pays the Property Tax?, 6-17 (1975) 212
          Comment 214

	Page
R. Netzer, Impact of the Property Tax: Its Economic Implications for Urban Problems 30, 31 (Research Rep. No. 1, National Commission on Urban Problems, 1968)	214
Comment	215
a. Fractional Assessments	216
Hellerstein v. Assessor of Islip	216
Comments	221
b. Differential Assessments and Classifications	224
Payne, From the Legislatures: The Unhappy Job of Revaluing Property, 9 Real Estate Law Journal 227 (1981)	224
Comments	227
A Note on the Constitutionality of Differential Property Tax Assessment	228
Comments	231
c. Tax Increment Financing	232
Richards v. City of Muscatine	232
Comments	237
2. Special Assessments and Special Benefit Taxation	238
S. Shinn, Special Assessments: City and County of Honolulu 28-29, 32-35 (Thesis on file at University of Hawaii, 1974)	240
McNally v. Township of Teaneck	242
Comments	247
Heavens v. King County Rural Library District	250
Comments	255
Bair v. Central & Southern Florida Flood Control District	255
Comments	257
3. Local Income Taxes	258
International City Management Association, Management Policies in Local Government 165-68 (1981)	258
Note, An Evaluation of Municipal Income Taxation, 22 Vanderbilt Law Review 1313, 1348-49, 1353 (1969)	260
Comment	261
4. User Charges and Other Taxes	262
Apodaca v. Wilson	262
Comments	265
City of Texarkana v. Wiggins	266
Comments	270
5. Sales Taxes	271
International City Management Association, Management Policies in Local Government Finance 152-65 (1981)	271
D. Borrowing	273
1. Types of Issues	273
a. General Obligations Bonds	274
Flushing National Bank v. Municipal Assistance Corp.	274
Comments	277
b. Revenue Bonds	278
State ex rel. Warren v. Nusbaum	279
Comments	281
A Note on Industrial and Commercial Development and Pollution Facilities Bond Financing	283

TABLE OF CONTENTS

Page

        A Note on the Tax Equity and Fiscal Responsibility Act of 1982 (Pub. L. 97-248) 288
        Tax Equity and Fiscal Responsibility Act of 1982 288
        Comments 290
    2. Debt Limitations 294
        Advisory Commission on Intergovernmental Relations, City Financial Emergencies: The Intergovernmental Dimension 63, 70-71 (1973) 294
        Comments 296
        Bulman v. McCrane 298
        Comments 301
        Board of Supervisors v. Massey 302
        Comments 307
        Advisory Commission on Intergovernmental Relations, State Technical Assistance to Local Debt Management 20, 21 (1965) 309
        Comments 310
E. Tax and Expenditure Limitations 311
    Federation of Tax Administrators, State Revenue and Spending Limits Since Proposition 13, at 7-8 (1980) 313
    Amador Valley Joint Union High School District v. State Board of Equalization 314
    Comments 324
    Los Angeles County Transportation Commission v. Richmond 326
    Comments 330
    Roberts v. McNary 332
    Comments 335
    Property Tax Relief Provisions 339
    Massachusetts Teachers Ass'n v. Secretary of Commonwealth 340
F. State Assistance to Local Governments 345
G. Expenditures 347
    1. State Mandates 347
        Advisory Commission on Intergovernmental Relations, State and Local Roles in the Federal System 157, 162, 166-68 (1982) .. 347
    2.. The Budgeting Process 349
        a. Operations 349
            Advisory Commission on Intergovernmental Relations, State & Local Roles in the Federal System 121-23 (1982) 349
        b. Capital Improvements 351
            Golden v. Planning Board of Ramapo 352
            Comments 355
            Hawkins v. Town of Shaw 356
            Comments 359
    3. Appropriations 361
        Krahmer v. McClafferty 362
        Comments 365
        Shapp v. Sloan 366
        Comments 372

CHAPTER 6. SERVING THE PUBLIC SECTOR: OFFICERS AND EMPLOYEES 375
A. Limiting Entry to Government Service 376
    Wardwell v. Board of Education 376

			Page
		Comments	379
		A Note on Federal Employment Discrimination Legislation	382
B.		Removal from Government Service: Patronage and Politics	384
		Branti v. Finkel	384
		Comments	394
C.		Integrity in Government Service: Conflicts of Interest	397
		Dana-Robin Corp. v. Common Council	397
		Comments	401
		A Note on Post-Employment Restrictions on Government Officers, Employers and Attorneys	403
D.		Unions, Strikes and Collective Bargaining	406
	1.	The Scope of Collective Bargaining	407
		City of Beloit v. Wisconsin Employment Relations Commission	407
		Comments	416
	2.	Strikes and Strike Injunctions	419
		Timberland Regional School District v. Timberlane Regional Education Ass'n	420
		Comments	423

CHAPTER 7. GOVERNMENTAL LIABILITY ... 427

A.		State Courts and Legislation	428
	1.	The Governmental-Proprietary Distinction and Tort Immunity	428
		Comments	437
		A Note on the Governmental-Proprietary Distinction in Other Contexts	438
	2.	The Discretionary-Ministerial Distinction	440
		Lipman v. Brisbane Elementary School District	440
		Comments	442
		Commercial Carrier Corp. v. Indian River County	443
		Comments	452
		A Note on the Immunity of Public Officials	454
	3.	Inverse Condemnation	455
		V. T. C. Lines, Inc. v. City of Harlan	456
		Comments	460
B.		Federal Law	463
	1.	The Eleventh Amendment	463
	2.	Civil Rights Cases: Suing Government and Its Officials Under the Civil Rights Act of 1871, 42 U.S.C. § 1983	464
		Owen v. City of Independence	465
		Maine v. Thiboutot	475
		Comments	477
	3.	Federal Antitrust Statutes	484
		Community Communications Co. v. City of Boulder	484
		Comments	491

CHAPTER 8. FEDERALISM ... 495

A.		The Federal System	495
	1.	Tenth Amendment Problems	495
		National League of Cities v. Usery	496
		Comments	507
		Walker Field v. Adams	512

TABLE OF CONTENTS xix

	Page
Comments	516
Equal Employment Opportunity Commission v. Wyoming	517
Comment	523
2. Supremacy: Preemption and Borrowing of Power	523
DeCanas v. Bica	524
Comments	529
A Note on the Borrowing of Federal Substantive Powers by State and Local Governments	531
B. Federal Standards for State and Local Programs	533
1. In General	533
2. Mental Disability	536
Pennhurst State School & Hospital v. Halderman	538
Comments	546
In re Schmidt	548
Comments	552
C. The Federal Grant-in-Aid System	555
1. In General	555
Advisory Commission on Intergovernmental Relations, Categorical Grants: Their Role and Design 5-6 (1978)	555
Executive Office of the President, Strengthening Public Management in the Intergovernmental System 9-10, 12 (1975)	556
Pressman, Political Implications of the New Federalism, in Financing the New Federalism 37-38 (W. Oates ed. 1975)	558
2. The General Revenue Sharing Program	559
Statement by John Shannon, Assistant Director, Advisory Commission on Intergovernmental Relations, in Revenue Sharing with the States, Hearing Before the Subcomm. on the City, House Comm. on Banking, Finance and Urban Affairs, 96th Cong., 1st Sess. 53, 54-57 (1979)	561
Comments	563
State *ex rel.* Conger v. Madison County	565
Comments	570
3. Block Grants	572
Senate Report No. 139, 97th Cong., 1st Sess. 868-72 (1981)	573
Comments	575

PART TWO. INTRA-GOVERNMENTAL DISTRIBUTION OF POWER

CHAPTER 9. THE STATE LEGISLATURE	581
A. Special Legislation	581
Comments	582
Gaca v. City of Chicago	583
Comments	589
Harvey v. Clyde Park District	592
Maloney v. Elmhurst Park District	594
Comments	596
B. Delegation of Power	598
1. Delegation to Administrative Agencies and Officials	599
Stofer v. Motor Vehicle Casualty Co.	600
Department of Business Regulation v. National Manufactured Housing Federation, Inc.	605
Comments	608

			Page
		Miller v. Covington Development Authority	610
		Comments	613
	2.	Delegation to the Judiciary	614
	3.	Delegation to Local Governments	614
		State ex rel. City of Charleston v. Coghill	614
		Comments	615

CHAPTER 10. THE ROLE OF THE JUDICIARY 617
  A. In Ordinary State and Local Government Issues: Licensing and Regulation 617
     Watchmaking Examining Board v. Husar 620
     State ex rel. Whetsel v. Wood 622
     Comments 625
     Independent Electricians & Electrical Contractors' Ass'n v. New Jersey Board of Examiners of Electrical Contractors 628
     Comments 629
     A Note on Licensing Boards and Administration 631
     Comments 633
  B. In Major Policy Decisions 634
    1. Reapportionment and Voting Rights 634
      a. The One Person-One Vote Principle in Legislative Apportionment 635
      b. Application of "One Person-One Vote" to Local Governments 638
        Avery v. Midland County 638
        Comments 643
        Salyer Land Co. v. Tulare Lake Basin Water Storage District 645
        Comments 650
      c. Voting Rights in Local Elections 652
        Town of Lockport v. Citizens for Community Action at the Local Level, Inc. 652
        Comments 657
        Holt Civic Club v. City of Tuscaloosa 658
        Comments 663
        A Note on the Quality of Representation 667
    2. School Finance 670
      a. *McInnis* and Educational Needs 676
        McInnis v. Shapiro 676
      b. *Serrano* and District Wealth 680
        Serrano v. Priest 680
        Comments 688
        A Note on Remedial Alternatives 689
      c. *Rodriguez* and Local Control 691
        San Antonio Independent School District v. Rodriguez ... 692
      d. State Constitutional Challenges: Thorough and Efficient 703
        Comments 705
        A Note on State Constitutional Challenges 706
        Board of Education, Levittown Union Free School District v. Nyquist 711
        Comments 718

TABLE OF CONTENTS

Page

    A Note on the Legislative Response to *Serrano, Rodriguez* and Thereafter 720
    A Note on the Cost-Quality Issue and Equality of Educational Opportunity 724

CHAPTER 11. THE CHIEF EXECUTIVE 731
A. Executive Orders 731
    1. Governor's Powers of Administration: Reorganization 733
        Martin v. Chandler 733
        Attorney General of California 736
        Comments 738
    2. Governor's Power to Make Policy Through Executive Agencies 740
        Rapp v. Carey 740
        Comments 748
B. Veto Powers 750
    Welden v. Ray 752
    State *ex rel.* Kleczka v. Conta 757
    Comments 761
    A Note on Executive Impoundment 765

CHAPTER 12. CITIZEN CONTROL OF GOVERNMENTAL ACTION 767
A. Through the Courts 767
    1. Mandamus 767
        Cartwright v. Sharpe 767
        Comments 772
        A Note on Mandamus Against the Chief Executive 775
    2. Prohibition 776
        Family Court v. Department of Labor & Industrial Relations 776
        Comments 780
    3. Quo Warranto 781
        State *ex rel.* Cain v. Kay 781
        People *ex rel.* Gordon v. City of Naperville 783
        Comments 786
    4. Injunction 789
        Bechak v. Corak 789
        Brent v. City of Detroit 792
        Comments 793
    5. Taxpayer Standing 796
        St. Clair v. Yonkers Raceway, Inc. 797
        Comments 800
        Blair v. Pitchess 801
        Comments 804
        A Note on the Standing of Citizens and Citizen Organizations 806
B. Through Initiative and Referendum 808
    Norlund v. Thorpe 809
    Comments 812
    Rauh v. City of Hutchinson 814
    Comments 820
    A Note on the Constitutionality of the Referendum in the Federal Courts 822

Index 825

Table of Cases

A

Abate v. Mundt, 644
Accacia Park Cemetery Ass'n v. Southfield Township, 258
Adams v. City of Colorado Springs, 657
Addiego v. State, 626
Agins v. Tiburon, 461, 463
Agnew v. City of Culver City, 609
Albemarle Paper Co. v. Moody, 383
Albuquerque Metropolitan Arroyo Flood Control Auth. v. Swinburne, 308
Allen v. State Bd. of Elections, 668
Allstate Leasing Corp. v. Board of County Comm'rs, 301
Altman v. City of Lansing, 804
Amador Valley Joint Union High School Dist. v. State Bd. of Equalization, *314*
American Distilling Co. v. Sausalito, 788
American Fed'n of State, County & Mun. Employees v. County of Lancaster, 419
American Federation of State, County & Municipal Employees, AFL-CIO v. State Dep't of Roads, 24
American Motor Sales Corp. v. New Motor Vehicle Bd., 632
American Nat'l Bank & Trust Co. v. Indiana Dep't of Highways, 308
American Nat'l Bldg. & Loan Ass'n v. City of Baltimore, 143
Ampersand, Inc. v. Finley, 108
Anchorage Educ. Ass'n v. Anchorage School Dist., 419
Anderson v. Baehr, 209
Anderson v. City of Boston, 793
Anderson v. City of Olivette, 98
Anderson v. Department of Real Estate, 625
Anderson v. Wagner, 596
Anderson Fed'n of Teachers v. School City of Anderson, 423
Angell v. City of Toledo, 119
Antonio v. Kirkpatrick, 381
Apartment Ass'n of Los Angeles County, Inc. v. City of Los Angeles, 266
Apartment House Council v. Mayor & Council, 99
Apodaca v. Wilson, *262*
Appeal of Radnor Township School Auth., 160
Application of Anamizu, 147
Application of McGlynn, 764
Archer v. City of Indianapolis, 309
Arkansas Pub. Serv. Comm'n v. Pulaski, 232
Armstrong Educ. Ass'n v. Armstrong School Dist., 424
Arnel Dev. Co. v. City of Costa Mesa (Cal.), 821
Arnel Dev. Co. v. City of Costa Mesa (Cal. App.), 821
Arnett v. Kennedy, 396
Aronoff v. Franchise Tax Bd., 781
ASARCO, Inc. v. Idaho State Tax Comm'n, 211
Ashley v. Rye School Dist., 366
Assessors of Weymouth v. Curtis, 223
Associated Enterprises, Inc. v. Toltec Watershed Improvement Dist., 650
Associated Homebuilders v. City of Livermore, 821
Atkins v. City of Tarrant City, 135
Atlantic City Hous. Action Coalition v. Deane, 821
Atlantic City Parking Auth. v. Atlantic County, 590
Attorney General of Cal., *736*
Austin Indep. School Dist. v. City of Sunset Valley, 160
Avery v. Midland County, *638*
Avis Rent-A-Car Sys., Inc. v. Romulus Community Schools, 590
Ayala v. Philadelphia Bd. of Pub. Educ., 438
Ayres v. City Council, 115

B

Babcock v. Kansas City, 788
Bachtell v. City of Waterloo, 301
Backman v. Salt Lake County, 83
Baffoni v. State, 626
Baggett v. Gates, 108
Bagley v. City of Manhattan Beach, 813
Bailey v. Mayor of New York, 431
Bair v. Central & S. Fla. Flood Control Dist., *255*
Bair v. Layton City Corp., 170
Baker v. Carr, 635
Ball v. James, 650
Bankhead v. McEwan, 597
Barbara Realty Co. v. Zoning Bd. of Review, 401
Barr v. First Taxing Dist., 271
Barsky v. Board of Regents, 631
Barto v. Felix, 455
Basehore v. Hampden Indus. Dev. Auth., 209
Bates v. State Bar, 618
Bayside Timber Co. v. Board of Supervisors, 632

xxiii

Beard v. Town of Salisbury, 128
Bechak v. Corak, *789*
Begin v. Inhabitants of Sabbattus, 128
Belford v. City of New Haven, 805
Bell v. Planning & Zoning Comm'n, 805
Belovsky v. Redevelopment Auth., 82
Bennett v. Garrett, 54
Berberian v. Housing Auth., 89
Berry v. Bourne, 665
Berry v. Costello, 192
Bettigole v. Assessors of Springfield, 222
Biloon's Elec. Serv., Inc. v. City of Wilmington, 453
Birge v. Town of Easton, 113
Birkenfeld v. City of Berkeley, 129
Bishop v. City of San Jose, 142
Blackhawk Teachers' Fed'n Local 2308 v. Wisconsin Employment Relations Bd., 416
Blades v. Genesee Drain Dist. No. 2, 257
Blair v. Pitchess, *801*
Blalock v. Johnston, 775
Bledsoe v. Watson, 796
Blue Cross v. Ratchford, 599
Blue Hills Cemetery v. Board of Registration, 15
Board of Educ. v. Board of Educ., 589
Board of Educ., Levittown Union Free School Dist. v. Nyquist, *711*
Board of Educ. of City School Dist. v. Walter, 707
Board of Supervisors v. Duke, 52, 54
Board of Supervisors v. Horne, 84
Board of Supervisors v. Massey, *302*
Board of Supervisors v. Moland Dev. Co., 90
Board of Trustees v. Foster Lumber Co., 121
Board of Trustees of Policemen's & Firemen's Retirement Fund v. City of Paducah, 80
Bond v. Floyd, 787
Bonnet v. State, 361
Boone County v. State, 337
Bopp v. Spainhower, 583
Borom v. City of St. Paul, 794
Borough of West Caldwell v. Borough of Caldwell, 170
Boryszewski v. Brydges, 800
Boswell v. Board of Medical Examiners, 781
Bowie Inn, Inc. v. City of Bowie, 85
Boyd v. Board of Trustees, 795
Bozung v. Local Agency Formation Comm'n, 76
Bradner v. Hammond, 382

Brann v. State, 597
Branti v. Finkel, *384*
Brent v. City of Detroit, *792*
Breslow v. School Dist., 297
Bright v. Baesler, 795
Bristol Township Educ. Ass'n v. School Dist., 425
Britt v. City of Columbus, 113, 162
Broadrick v. Oklahoma, 394
Brouillard v. Governor & Council, 775
Brown v. Barkley, 739
Brown v. Firestone, 763
Brown v. Heymann, 738
Bruce v. Riddle, 479
Buckley v. Valeo, 402, 580
Buettell v. Walker, 748
Bullock v. Carter, 381
Bulman v. McCrane, 298
Burlington N., Inc. v. City of McCook, 249
Burton v. Furman, 776
Burton v. Whittier Regional Vocational Technical School Dist., 644
Buse v. Smith, 721
Butz v. Economou, 478

C

Cabell v. Chavez-Salido, 380
Cahill v. Board of Educ., 795
Cairl v. State, 443
Caldis v. Board of County Comm'rs, 63
Callaway v. City of Overland Park, 121
Canavan v. Messina, 112
C & H Enterprises, Inc. v. Commissioner of Motor Vehicles, 625
Capella v. City of Gainesville, 667
Capitol Cable, Inc. v. City of Topeka, 112
Carlisle v. Bangor Recreation Center, 309
Carman v. Alvord, 331
Carter v. Beaver County Serv. Area No. One, 82
Carter Carburetor Corp. v. City of St. Louis, 119
Carter County v. City of Elizabethton, 170
Cartwright v. Sharpe, *767*
Cascade Tel. Co. v. Tax Comm'n, 764
Caserta v. Village of Dickinson, 38
Casey v. South Carolina State Hous. Auth., 282
Caso v. District Council 37, 425
Cauley v. City of Jacksonville, 452
Centennial Land & Dev. Co. v. Township of Medford, 478
Central Mich. Univ. Faculty Ass'n v. Central Mich. Univ., 418
Chang v. University of Rhode Island, 749
Chapman v. Meier, 637, 668

TABLE OF CASES

Chappell v. City of Springfield, 454
Charles v. Diamond, 355
Charles City Community School Dist. v. Public Employment Relations Bd., 417
Charles Gabus Ford v. Iowa State Highway Comm'n, 774
Chastain v. City of Little Rock, 54
Chesser v. Buchanan, 667
Choudhry v. Free, 651
CHR Gen., Inc. v. City of Newton, 129
Christiaan's Inc. v. Chobanian, 626
Cities Serv. Co. v. Governor, 597
Citizens Against Forced Annexation v. Local Agency Formation Comm'n, 665
Citizens Comm. to Oppose Annexation v. City of Lynchburg, 665
Citizens Counsel Against Crime v. Bjork, 781
Citizens to Preserve Overton Park v. Volpe, 162
Citizens to Save Our Land v. McKee Creek Watershed Conservancy Dist., 644
City & County of Denver v. Duffy Storage & Moving Co., 121
City & County of Denver v. Sweet, 120
City & County of San Francisco v. Farrell, 331
City & County of San Francisco v. Pace, 627
City Council v. Naturile, 627
City of Albuquerque v. New Mexico State Corp. Comm'n, 123
City of Aurora v. Bryant, 52
City of Beloit v. Wisconsin Employment Relations Comm'n, 407
City of Birmingham v. Community Fire Dist., 39, 666
City of Birmingham v. Mead Corp., 56
City of Bloomington v. Chuckney, 129
City of Bowie v. Board of County Comm'rs, 182
City of Brookfield v. Wisconsin Employment Relations Comm'n, 417
City of Cambridge v. Commissioner of Pub. Welfare, 34
City of Camden v. Byrne, 301, 359, 366
City of Carbondale v. Van Natta, 114
City of Ceres v. City of Modesto, 76
City of Chester v. Commonwealth, 163
City of Clive v. Iowa Concrete Block & Material Co., 249
City of Coral Gables v. Burgin, 176
City of Corbin v. Kentucky Utils. Co., 114
City of Creve Coeur v. Braume, 60
City of Dania v. Central & S. Fla. Flood Control Dist., 161
City of Dearborn v. Michigan Turnpike Auth., 177
City of Des Moines v. Lampart, 46
City of Des Moines v. Public Employment Relations Bd., 418
City of Dover v. International Ass'n of Firefighters, Local No. 1312, 424
City of Eastlake v. Forest City Enterprises, 823
City of Ecorse v. Peoples Community Hosp. Auth., 170
City of Erie v. Northwestern Pa. Food Council, 150
City of Evanston v. Create, Inc., 112
City of Fairfield v. Superior Court, 401
City of Fargo v. Hardwood Township, 160
City of Hallandale v. Meekins, 249
City of Highland Park v. Fair Employment Practices Comm'n, 80
City of Hitchcock v. Longmire, 821
City of Houston v. Blackbird, 257
City of Houston v. Fore, 258
City of Huntsville v. Smartt, 793
City of Kansas City v. Robb, 591
City of Kodiak v. Jackson, 128
City of Lafayette v. Louisiana Power & Light Co., 440, 484
City of La Grande v. Public Employees Retirement Bd., 109
City of Logansport v. Public Serv. Comm'n, 439
City of Los Angeles v. City of Artesia, 590
City of Louisville v. Coulter, 630
City of Louisville v. Fiscal Court, 62
City of Louisville v. Munro, 460
City of Loveland v. Public Utils. Comm'n, 82
City of Macon v. Anderson, 781
City of Meridian v. Town of Marion, 55
City of Mesa v. Salt River Project Agricultural Improvement & Power Dist., 161
City of Mesquite v. Aladdin's Castle, Inc., 9
City of Miami Beach v. Fleetwood Hotel, Inc., 109
City of Miami Beach v. Forte Towers, Inc., 129
City of Miami Beach v. Sunset Islands 3 & 4 Property Owners Ass'n, 775
City of Mobile v. Bolden, 669
City of Mobile v. Salter, 232
City of Newark v. New Jersey, 33
City of New Haven v. Connecticut State Bd. of Labor Relations, 418
City of New Orleans v. Dukes, 629
City of New Orleans v. State, 160
City of Newport v. Fact Concerts, Inc., 454, 481
City of New York v. New York Tel. Co., 440

City of North Miami Beach v. Metropolitan Dade County, 176
City of Oakland v. Williams, 170
City of Olivette v. Graeler, 60
City of Osceola v. Whistle, 84
City of Palm Springs v. Ringwald, 308
City of Phoenix v. Phoenix Civic Auditorium & Convention Center Ass'n, 297
City of Pipestone v. Madsen, 284
City of Pittsburgh v. Alco Parking Corp., 193
City of Pittsburgh v. Allegheny Bank, 143
City of Pompano Beach v. Oltman, 270
City of Port Arthur v. United States, 668
City of Pueblo v. Flanders, 114
City of Racine v. Town of Mt. Pleasant, 170
City of Richmond v. United States, 63
City of Rome v. United States, 63, 668
City of Roseburg v. Roseburg City Firefighters Local No. 1489, 109
City of St. Louis v. Brune, 90
City of St. Petersburg v. Collom, 452
City of S. Burlington v. Vermont Elec. Power Co., 146
City of Scottsdale v. McDowell Mountain Irrigation & Drainage Dist., 67
City of Scottsdale v. Municipal Court, 159
City of Scottsdale v. Superior Court, 813
City of Shreveport v. Curry, 135
City of South Bend v. Krovitch, 80
City of Sparks v. Best, 237
City of Spokane v. Portch, 143
City of Stuttgart v. Strait, 98
City of Tacoma v. Taxpayers of Tacoma, 532
City of Tempe v. Prudential Ins. Co. of Am., 143
City of Texarkana v. Wiggins, 266
City of Trenton v. New Jersey, 33
City of Urbana v. Paley, 209
City of Walnut Creek v. Silveira, 308, 591
City of Warren v. State Constr. Code Comm'n, 609
City of Wichita v. Board of County Comm'rs, 50
City of Wilmington v. Lord, 805
City of Wood Village v. Portland Metropolitan Area Local Gov't Boundary Comm'n, 72
Clark v. City of Overland Park, 121
Clarke v. City of Wichita, 46
Cleveland ex rel. Neelon v. Locher, 775
Coffey v. Milwaukee, 454
Cole v. Richardson, 382
Colegrove v. Green, 635
Collins v. Town of Goshen, 360

Colonial School Bd. v. Colonial Affiliate, 417
Colt Indus. v. Finance Adm'r, 222
Commercial Carrier Corp. v. Indian River County, 443
Commercial Fisheries Entry Comm'n v. Apokedak, 15, 630
Commercial Nat'l Bank v. City of Chicago, 121
Committee for Washington's Riverside Parks v. Thompson, 407
Common Cause v. State, 801
Commonwealth v. Barnett, 763
Commonwealth v. County Bd., 89
Commonwealth v. Town of Andover, 227
Commonwealth Edison Co. v. Montana, 210
Commonwealth ex rel. Carroll v. Tate, 774
Commonwealth ex rel. Parks v. Wherry, 787
Community Builders, Inc. v. City of Phoenix, 493
Community Communications Co. v. City of Boulder, 484
Concerned Citizens v. Pantalone, 820
Concerned Taxpayers v. Commonwealth, 808
Connecticut v. Teal, 383
Connor v. Finch, 637
Conrad v. City of Pittsburgh, 307
Continental Bank & Trust Co. v. Farmington City, 198
Contractors & Builders Ass'n v. City of Dunedin, 265
Coomey v. Board of Assessors, 222
Cooper v. Henslee, 793
Cooperrider v. San Francisco Civil Serv. Comm'n, 380
Corning Hosp. Dist. v. Superior Court, 436
Corporation of Collierville v. Fayette County Election Comm'n, 55
Cottonwood City Electors v. Salt Lake County Bd. of Comm'rs, 46
Cottrell v. City & County of Denver, 608
County Comm'rs v. County Executive, 764
County Executive v. Doe, 750
County of Alameda v. City & County of San Francisco, 261
County of Fresno v. Malmstrom, 331
County of Los Angeles v. Marshall, 517
County of Oneida v. Berle, 765
County of Ramsey v. Stevens, 151
County of Rockingham v. City of Harrisonburg, 61
Crawford v. Board of Educ., 823
Cunningham v. Exon, 800

Curtis v. Board of Supervisors, 657
Custer v. Bonadies, 772

D

Dail v. City of Phoenix, 804
Dalehite v. United States, 435
Daly v. Town Plan & Zoning Comm'n, 401
Dana-Robin Corp. v. Common Council, 397
Danson v. Casey, 707
Danville Fire Protection Dist. v. Duffel Fin. & Constr. Co., 149
Datisman v. Gary Pub. Library, 80
Davidson Baking Co. v. Jenkins, 99
Davies v. City of Lawrence, 249
Davis v. City of Seattle, 821
Davis v. City of Westland, 248
Dean v. Kuchel, 20
Dearden v. City of Detroit, 160
DeCanas v. Bica, 524
DeFraties v. Kansas City, 248
Delany v. Badame, 596
DeLong v. City & County of Denver, 108
Delong v. United States, 394
DePalma v. Rosen, 455
Department of Business Regulation v. National Manufactured Hous. Fed'n, Inc., 605
Department of Licenses & Inspections v. Weber, 147
Department of Pub. Works & Bldgs. v. Ellis, 161
Department of Transp. v. Nelson, 452
Detroit Police Officers Ass'n v. City of Detroit, 418
Detz v. Hoover, 480
De Vigil v. Stroup, 786
Dieruf v. City of Bozeman, 820
Dinsky v. Town of Framingham, 453
Doan v. City of Ft. Wayne, 62
Dodge v. Prudential Ins. Co. of America, 237
Doenges v. City of Salt Lake City, 667
Donnelly v. City of Manchester, 380
Dooley v. City of Detroit, 119
Doremus v. Board of Educ., 801
Dortch v. Lugar, 176
Dothard v. Rawlinson, 383
Douglas v. Seacoast Prods., Inc., 529
Dowdell v. City of Apopka, 361
DuBree v. Commonwealth, 455
Duncan Dev. Corp. v. Crestview Sanitary Dist., 255
Dunellen Bd. of Educ. v. Dunellen Educ. Ass'n, 417
Dwyer v. Omaha-Douglas Pub. Bldg. Comm'n, 309, 590

E

Eagle Nest Corp. v. Carroll, 806
Early Estates, Inc. v. Housing Bd. of Review, 85
East Carroll Parish School Bd. v. Marshall, 668
East Ohio Gas Co. v. City of Akron, 143
East Peoria Waterworks Improvement Project v. Board of Trustees, 255
East Suburban Press v. Township of Penn Hills, 610
Eaton v. Boston, C. & M.R.R., 460
Eckl v. Davis, 141
Ector v. City of Torrance, 379
Edelman v. Jordan, 463, 464
Edelstein v. Ferrell, 773
Edmonds School Dist. No. 15 v. City of Mountlake Terrace, 160
Edwards v. Bridgeport Hydraulic Co., 461
Edwards v. California, 529
Edwards v. Housing Auth., 616
Eggert v. City of Seattle, 379
Elias v. City of Tulsa, 590
Elfbrandt v. Russell, 382
Elgin v. District of Columbia, 433
Elk City v. Johnson, 776
Enourato v. New Jersey Bldg. Auth., 301
Equal Employment Opportunity Comm'n v. Wyoming, 517
Essex County Bd. of Taxation v. City of Newark, 365
Estate of Carey v. Village of Stickney, 121
Evans v. Carey, 748
Evans v. Just Open Gov't, 461
Eways v. Board of Road Supervisors, 66
Ex parte Young, 463
Extension of Boundaries of Ridgeland, 61
Exxon Corp. v. Governor of Md., 529

F

Fair Assessment in Real Estate Ass'n v. McNary, 228, 481
Family Court v. Department of Labor & Indus. Relations, 776
Fasano v. Board of County Comm'rs, 479
Federal Energy Regulatory Comm'n v. Mississippi, 509
Federal Reserve Bank v. Metrocentre Improvement Dist., 258
Ferguson v. City of Keene, 461
Ferzacca v. Freeman, 787
Firemen's Pension & Relief Fund v. Sudduth, 776
Fiscal Court v. City of Louisville, 99
Fiser v. City of Knoxville, 401
Fitzpatrick v. Bitzer, 463, 508

Fladung v. City of Boulder, 66
Flast v. Cohen, 801
Florida E. Coast Ry. v. City of Miami, 161
Florida Real Estate Comm'n v. McGregor, 627
Fluckey v. City of Plymouth, 248
Flushing Nat'l Bank v. Municipal Assistance Corp., 274
Fort v. Civil Serv. Comm'n, 394
Fort Howard Paper Co. v. Town Bd., 309
Forwood v. City of Taylor, 113
Four-County Metropolitan Capital Improvement Dist. v. Board of County Comm'rs, 177
Franciscan Hosp. v. Town of Canoe Creek, 34
Frank v. City of Cody, 169
Frazer v. Carr, 176, 590
Freeman v. City of Norfolk, 436
Friedman v. Rogers, 617, 618, 631
Friends of Mount Diablo v. County of Contra Costa, 813
Frost v. City of Chattanooga, 591
Frothingham v. Mellon, 801
Fry v. United States, 496
FTC v. Gibson, 738
Fullerton Joint Union High School Dist. v. State Bd. of Educ., 664
Fullilove v. Carey, 750
F.W. Woolworth Co. v. Taxation & Revenue Dept., 211

G

Gaca v. City of Chicago, 583
Gaffney v. Cummings, 637
Garden City Educators' Ass'n v. Vance, 418
Gardner v. City of Dallas, 439
Garono v. State Bd. of Landscape Architects, 630
Gates Co. v. Housing Appeals Bd., 90
Georgia v. United States, 668
Georgia Pub. Serv. Comm'n v. City of Albany, 439
Gerner v. State Tax Comm'n, 229
Giacopelli v. Clymer, 780
Gibbs v. City of Napa, 813
Gibson v. Berryhill, 618, 631
Gibson v. Smith, 281
Gifford v. State ex rel. Lilly, 788
Gilbert v. State, 381
Golden v. Planning Bd. of Ramapo, 352
Gismondi Liquor License Case, 807
Goldfarb v. Virginia State Bar, 618
Gomillion v. Lightfoot, 35
Gordon v. Mayor & City Council, 805
Goreham v. Des Moines Metropolitan Area Solid Waste Agency, 166

Gorman Towers, Inc. v. Bogoslavsky, 479
Grace v. Howlett, 596
Grant v. Kansas City, 120
Grassman v. Minnesota Bd. of Barber Examiners, 626
Green v. Cox Cable of Omaha, Inc., 805
Griggs v. Duke Power Co., 383
Gumbhir v. Kansas State Bd. of Pharmacy, 609

H

Hack v. City of Salem, 434
Hadley v. Junior College Dist., 643
Halderman v. Pennhurst State School & Hosp., 533
Halvorson v. Dahl, 454
Hames v. Polson, 793
Haney v. City of Lexington, 460
Hans v. Louisiana, 463
Harang v. State ex rel. City of West Columbia, 53
Hardin v. City of Devalls Bluff, 437
Hargrove v. Town of Cocoa Beach, 435
Harlow v. Fitzgerald, 478
Harper v. Schooler, 285
Harper v. Virginia Bd. of Elections, 822
Harrington & Co. v. Tampa Port Auth., 609
Harris v. McRae, 547
Harrison v. Board of Supervisors, 248
Hart v. Columbus, 176
Harvey v. Clyde Park Dist., 437, 592
Hatley v. Lium, 781
Hawkins v. Town of Shaw, 356
Haymart v. Freiberger, 773
Hays v. Wood, 402
Hayward v. Clay, 665
Heavens v. King County Rural Library Dist., 250
Hedrick v. County Court, 582
Hellerstein v. Assessor of Islip, 216
Helton v. City of Long Beach, 199
Henderson v. McCormick, 804
Heritage Homes of Attleboro, Inc. v. Seekonk Water Dist., 481
Hermer v. City of Dover, 455
Hernandez v. City of Lafayette, 479
Hicklin v. Orbeck, 379
Hill v. Stone, 651
Hillman v. Northern Wasco County Util. Dist., 609
Hinds County Democratic Executive Comm. v. Muirhead, 773
Hodel v. Virginia Surface Mining & Reclamation Ass'n, 508
Holt v. City of Richmond, 63

TABLE OF CASES

Holt Civic Club v. City of Tuscaloosa, *658*
Holtz v. Superior Court, 460
Holversten v. Minnesota Water Resources Bd., 67
Home Builders League v. Township of Berlin, 807
Homeowners v. Countryside Sanitary Dist., 788
Homes Unlimited, Inc. v. City of Seattle, 625
Hopkins Fed. Sav. & Loan Ass'n v. Cleary, 508
Horgan v. Dauphin Island Water & Sewer Auth., 257
Horner's Market, Inc. v. Tri-County Metropolitan Transit Dist., 177
Horton v. Meskill, 709
Hortonville Joint School Dist. No. 1 v. Hortonville Educ. Ass'n, 425
Hosclaw v. Stephens, 176
Hotel Dorset Co. v. Trust for Cultural Resources, 583
Housing Auth. v. Fetzik, 33
Howard v. City of Boulder, 805
Howe v. City of St. Louis, 598
Hubbard v. City of San Diego, 112
Hughey v. Cloninger, 210
Humane Society of the U.S. v. New Jersey State Fish & Game Council, 632
Hunt v. Washington State Advertising Comm'n, 808
Hunter v. City of Pittsburgh, *30*
Hunter v. Erickson, 822
Hutchinson Human Relations Comm'n v. Midland Credit Management, Inc., 114
Hutton Park Gardens v. Town Council, 99

I

Idaho Water Resource Bd. v. Kramer, *205*
Ieva v. Grabowski, 481
Illinois Broadcasting Co. v. City of Decatur, 805
Illinois Polygraph Soc'y v. Pelicano, 597, 625
Incorporation of East Bridge v. City of Aurora, 45
Independent Electricians & Elec. Contractors' Ass'n v. New Jersey Bd. of Examiners of Elec. Contractors, *628*
Independent School Dist., Class A, No. 1, Cassia County v. Pfost, *21*
Independent School Dist. No. 700 v. City of Duluth, 108
Indian Towing Co. v. United States, 434
Indiana Univ. v. Hartwell, 614
Industrial Union Dep't v. Amercian Petroleum Inst., 598

Inganamort v. Borough of Fort Lee, 97
Ingham v. State Dep't of Transp., 452
In re Certain Petitions for a Binding Referendum, 813
In re Char, *57*
In re Denial of Approval to Issue $30,000,000.00, 283
In re Di Brizzi, 739
In re Esler v. Walters, 652
In re Extension of Boundaries of Glaize Creek Sewer Dist., 667
In re Hubbard, 142
In re Incorporation of Elm Grove, 53
In re Lane, 142
In re Lappie, 807
In re Opinion of Justices, 763
In re Petition for Find du Lac Metropolitan Sewerage Dist., 51
In re Petition of Idaho State Fed'n of Labor, 24
In re Pub. Serv. Elec. & Gas Co., 146
In re Request for Advisory Opinion, 23
In re Sandia Conservancy Dist., 616
In re Schmidt, *548*
In re State Bd. of Professional Ethical Misconduct, 781
In re Validity of Maintenance Dist. No. 5A, 332
In re Village of Burnsville, 249
Isaacs v. Oklahoma City, 591
Isbrandtsen-Moller Co. v. United States, 738
Itzen & Robertson v. Board of Health, 90

J

Jackson Redevelopment Auth. v. King, Inc., 590
Jacobberger v. Terrey, 108
Jacobs v. City of Chicago, 121
James v. Valtierra, 822
J & B Dev. Co. v. King County, 454
Jefferson v. State, 127
J. G. Cryan v. State, 626
J. M. Mills, Inc. v. Murphy, 616
Johnson v. City of Inkster, 249
Johnson v. City of Louisville, 170
Johnson v. Elkin, 625
Johnson v. Hamilton, 381
Johnson v. Lewiston Orchards Irrigation Dist., 651
Johnson v. Railway Express Agency, 382
Johnson v. Roberts, 609
Johnson v. State, 439, 443
Joint School Dist. No. 1 v. Wisconsin Rapids Educ. Ass'n, 424
Jones v. Packel, 775

TABLE OF CASES

Jones v. Rath Packing Co., 529
Jones v. State Bd. of Medicine, 15
Julian v. City of Liberty, 788

K

Kahn v. Shevin, 228
Kane v. Fortson, 795
Kansas City v. City of Raytown, 170
Kansas City S. Ry. v. City of Shreveport, 56
Kaufman v. Swift County, 165
Kelley v. Mayor & Council, 666
Kelly v. Curtis, 776
Keniston v. Board of Assessors, 223
Kenny v. Byrne, 748
Kentucky Inst. for Educ. of the Blind v. City of Louisville, 159
Kevelin v. Jordan, 775
King v. Smith, 553
Kirpatrick v. Preisler, 637
Kliks v. Dalles City, 266
Kollar v. City of Tuscon, 663
Konfal v. Charter Township of Delhi, 249
Kopff v. District of Columbia Alcoholic Beverage Control Bd., 180
Kovalik v. Planning & Zoning Comm'n, 401
Krahmer v. McClafferty, *362*
Kremer v. City of Plainfield, 402
Kugler v. Yocum, 812

L

Laborer's Int'l Union, Local 1029 v. State, 419
Lake Country Estates, Inc. v. Tahoe Regional Planning Agency, 479
Lamphere Schools v. Lamphere Fed'n of Teachers, 425
Lanier v. Overstreet, 229
Lap v. Thibault, 795
Larson v. Independent School Dist. No. 314, 443
Latham v. Board of Educ., 589
Laufenberg v. Cosmetology Examining Bd., 626
Lawrence v. Beermann, 814
Laxalt v. Cannon, 787
Lee v. State, 609
Leek v. Theis, 382
Leonardson v. Moon, 361
Levine v. Whalen, 609
Liberati v. Bristol Bay Borough, 85
Lipman v. Brisbane Elementary School Dist., *440*
Lincoln County v. Johnson, 160
Litten v. City of Fargo, 123
Local 1485, Am. Fed'n of Teachers v. Yakima School Dist. No. 7, 615

Lockport v. Citizens for Community Action, 651
Long v. City of Charlotte, 461
Los Angeles County Transp. Comm'n v. Richmond, *326*
Lovequist v. Conservation Comm'n, 91
Lujan v. Colorado State Bd. of Educ., 708
Lund ex rel. Wilbur v. Pratt, 787
Lunding v. Walker, 396
Lynn v. Commonwealth Dep't of Pub. Welfare, 570

M

Maceluch v. Wyson, 627
MacLeod v. City of Takoma Park, 455
Madeiros v. Kondo, 454
Madsen v. Oakland Unified School Dist., 170
Mahan v. Howell, 637
Maher v. Gagne, 480
Maine v. Thiboutot, *475*
Maloney v. Elmhurst Park Dist., *594*
Mandelkern v. City of Buffalo, 380
Mangold Midwest Co. v. Village of Ridgefield, 136
Marbury v. Madison, 273, 776
Marshal House, Inc. v. Rent Review & Grievance Bd., 129
Marshall v. Kansas City, 114
Marston v. Superior Court, 793
Martin v. Chandler, *733*
Martin v. North Carolina Hous. Corp., 282
Maryland v. Wirtz, 495
Mason City Center Ass'n v. City of Mason City, 492
Massachusetts Hous. Fin. Agency v. New England Merchants Nat'l Bank, 281
Massachusetts Teachers Ass'n v. Secretary of Commonwealth, *340*
Mathews v. Massell, 560
Mayle v. Pennsylvania Dep't of Highways, 464
Mayor, Councilmen & Citizens v. Beard, 56
Maywood Bd. of Educ. v. Maywood Educ. Ass'n, 417
Maywood Proviso State Bank v. City of Oakbrook Terrace, 62
McCamant v. City & County of Denver, 788
McCarthy v. Philadelphia Civil Serv. Comm'n, 379
McCormick v. Edwards, 395
McCoy v. Commonwealth Bd. of Medical Educ. & Licensure, 627
McDaniel v. Thomas, 708
McGinley v. Hynes, 781
McInnis v. Shapiro, *676*

McKee v. City of Louisville, 813
McKee v. Likins, 800
McManus v. Love, 372
McManus v. Skoko, 45
McNally v. Township of Teaneck, *242*
Meadowlands Regional Redevelopment Agency v. State, 177
Memphis Power & Light Co. v. City of Memphis, 439
Menzer v. Village of Elkhart Lake, 135
Merchantile Incorporating Co. v. Junkin, 23, 192
Meyer v. State of New Jersey, 483
Miami Shores Village v. Cowart, 176
Middlesex County Sewage Auth. v. National Sea Clammers Ass'n, 481
Midwest Employers Council, Inc. v. City of Omaha, 114
Milford School Dist. v. Whitley, 780
Millar v. Barnett, 301
Miller v. Covington Dev. Auth., *610*
Miller v. Fabius Township Bd., *131*
Millis v. Board of County Comm'rs, 70, 666
Mills v. County of Trinity, 330
Mills v. Porter, 763
Mills v. Rogers, 555
Mitchell v. North Carolina Indus. Dev. Fin. Auth., 284
Mlikotin v. City of Los Angeles, 360
Mobil Oil Corp. v. Commissioner of Taxes, 210
Mobil Oil Corp. v. Town of Westport, 250
Mohland v. State Bd. of Equalization, 229
Mohrhusen v. McCann, 781
Molbreak v. Village of Shorewood Hills, 249
Molitor v. Kaneland Community Unit Dist. No. 302, 436
Monell v. New York City Dep't of Social Servs., 465
Monier v. Gallen, 382
Monroe v. Pape, 465
Montgomery v. Daniels, 596
Montgomery Citizens League v. Greenhalgh, 113
Montgomery County v. Califano, 516
Moore v. City of Boulder, 115
Moore v. School Comm., 820
Moorman v. Wood, 663
Morrison Homes Corp. v. City of Pleasanton, 62
Morrissette v. De Zonia, 772
Moses Lake School Dist. No. 161 v. Big Bend Community College, 34
Moshier v. City of Romulus, 793
Mt. Healthy School Dist. Bd. of Educ. v. Doyle, 395, 483
Mulligan v. Junne, 143
Municipality of Metropolitan Seattle v. City of Seattle, 177, 590
Murphy v. Kansas City, 667
Music Plus Four, Inc. v. Barnet, 141
Muskopf v. Corning Hosp. Dist., 436
Myles Salt Co. v. Board of Comm'rs, 257

N

National Asphalt Pavement Ass'n v. Prince George's County, 141
National Educ. Ass'n-Fort Scott v. Board of Educ., 20
National Educ. Ass'n of Shawnee Mission, Inc. v. Board of Educ., 417
National League of Cities v. Usery, 290, 482, *496*
National Soc'y of Professional Eng'rs v. United States, 618
Neal v. Donahue, 438
Nebbia v. New-York, 617
Needham v. County Comm'rs, 161
Nelson v. City of Seattle, 115
New Hampshire v. Maine, 171
New Hampshire Dep't of Employment Security v. Marshall, 517
New State Ice Co. v. Liebmann, 617
New York Cardiac Center v. Kondzielaski, 258
New York City Hous. Auth. v. Foley, 171
New York Tel. Co. v. City of Binghamton, 440
New York Tel. Co. v. New York Labor Dep't, 529
New York Times v. Sullivan, 454
Nicholson v. State Comm'n on Judicial Conduct, 781
Non-Resident Taxpayers Ass'n v. Municipality of Philadelphia, 261
Norlund v. Thorpe, *809*
North Carolina ex rel. Morrow v. Califano, 517
Northcutt v. State Rd. Dep't, 461
Northern Pac. Ry. v. City of Grand Forks, 250
Northshore School Dist. No. 417 v. Kinnear, 709
NRDC v. EPA, 535
Nueces County Drainage & Conservation Dist. No. 2 v. Bevly, 794
Nueces County Water Control & Improvement Dist. v. Wilson, 257
Nugent v. City of East Providence, 112

O

Oakland County Taxpayers' League v. Board of Supervisors, *16*

xxxii TABLE OF CASES

O'Fallon Dev. Co. v. City of O'Fallon, 794
Ohio Motor Vehicle Dealer's & Salesmen's Licensing Bd. v. Memphis Auto Sales, 625
Oklahoma v. United States Civil Serv., 546
Oklahoma City Hotel & Motor Hotel Ass'n v. Oklahoma City, 266
Olsen v. Oregon, 703, 707
Omaha Parking Auth. v. City of Omaha, 177
O'Neill v. Kallsen, 781
Opinion of Attorney General, 739, 749
Opinion of Justices, 738, 739, 763, 766
Oswald v. City of Blue Springs, 338
Owen v. City of Independence, *465*

P

Pacific Legal Found. v. Brown, 20, 419
Pacific Legal Found. v. State Energy Resources Conservation & Dev. Comm'n, 531
Pacific Tel. & Tel. Co. v. Redevelopment Agency, 440
Packer v. Board of Behavioral Science Examiners, 630
Paper Supply Co. v. City of Chicago, 121
Parcell v. State, 749
Parish v. Pitts, 437
Parker v. Brown, 440, 484
Parker v. City of Highland Park, 438
Parks v. Alexander, 800
Parnell v. State *ex rel.* Wilson, 53
Parratt v. Taylor, 480
Patsy v. Board of Regents, 483
Patterson v. City of Bismarck, 250
Pauley v. Kelly, 710
Paulson v. Civil Serv. Comm'n, 396
Pease v. Board of County Comm'rs, 170
Pennhurst State School & Hosp. v. Halderman, 481, *538*
Penn Parking Garage v. City of Pittsburgh, 807
Pennsylvania State Bd. of Pharmacy v. Pastor, 9
People v. City of Los Angeles, 161
People v. Cook, 616
People v. Doe, 228
People v. Johnson, 625
People v. Llewellyn, 135, 142
People v. Tremaine, 763
People *ex rel.* Adamowski v. Wilson, 589
People *ex rel.* Bd. of Park Comm'rs v. Common Council, 79
People *ex rel.* Brooks v. Lisle, 788
People *ex rel.* City of Canton v. Crouch, 237, 764
People *ex rel.* City of Salem v. McMackin, 114, 776
People *ex rel.* County of Du Page v. Smith, 589
People *ex rel.* Des Plaines v. Village of Mt. Prospect, 788
People *ex rel.* Dixon v. Community Unit School Dist., 162
People *ex rel.* Gordon v. City of Naperville, *783*
People *ex rel.* Hanrahan v. Caliendo, 257
People *ex rel.* Holland v. Bleigh Constr. Co., 379
People *ex rel.* Hopf v. Barger, 775
People *ex rel.* Illinois State Dental Soc'y v. Sutker, 627
People *ex rel.* Kirk v. Lindberg, 762
People *ex rel.* Klinger v. Howlett, 764
People *ex rel.* Knaus v. Village of Hinsdale, 789
People *ex rel.* Lignoul v. City of Chicago, 108
People *ex rel.* McCarthy v. Firek, 788
People *ex rel.* Newdelman v. Swank, 805
People *ex rel.* Sanitary Dist. v. Schlaeger, 438
People *ex rel.* Sutherland v. Governor, 776
People *ex rel.* Thomson v. Barnett, 813
People *ex rel.* Turner v. Lewis, 786
People *ex rel.* Younger v. County of El Dorado, 171, 644, 772
Perkins v. Matthews, 64
Perry v. Lawrence County Election Comm'n, 23
Personnel Adm'r v. Feeney, 381
Peters v. City of Springfield, 128
Petition of Lower Valley Water & Sanitation Dist., 67
Philadelphia v. New Jersey, 529
Philadelphia Fed'n of Teachers v. Ross, 425
Pinchback v. Stephens, 591
Piscataway Apartment Ass'n v. Township of Piscataway, 266
Plantation Datsun, Inc. v. Calvin, 625
Plaza Joint Venture v. City of Atlantic City, *137*
Plumfield Nurseries, Inc. v. Dodge County, 51
Pomeroy v. Riley, 763
Ponzio v. Anderson, 633
Port Arthur Indep. School Dist. v. City of Groves, 160
Port of Longview v. Taxpayers of Longview, 287
Powell v. McCormack, 787
Procunier v. Navarette, 478

TABLE OF CASES

Property Appraisal Dept. v. Ransom, 229
Proprietors of Mt. Hope Cemetery v. City of Boston, 162
Protsman v. Jefferson-Craig Consol. School Corp., 297
Pruett v. City of Rosedale, 436
Public Serv. Co. v. Town of Hampton, *144*
Public Util. Dist. v. Town of Newport, 616
Pueblo Aircraft Servs., Inc. v. City of Pueblo, 493

Q

Quick Chek Food Stores v. Township of Springfield, 15

R

Railroad Comm'n v. Riley, 763
Ranjel v. City of Lansing, 821
Rapp v. Carey, *740*
Rauh v. City of Hutchinson, *814*
Ray v. Atlantic Richfield Co., 529
Rayco Inv. Corp. v. Board of Selectmen, 91
Reagan v. City of Sausalito, 820
Real Estate Dev. Co. v. City of Florence, 795
Reardon v. Riley, 763
Redevelopment Agency v. Malaki, 237
Redevelopment Authority v. State Corp. Comm'n, 591
Rees v. Department of Real Estate, 625
Regents of Univ. of Cal. v. City of Los Angeles, 258
Region 10 Client Management, Inc. v. Town of Hampstead, 147
Reilly Tar & Chemical Corp. v. City of St. Louis Park, 67
Residents of Beverly Glen, Inc. v. City of Los Angeles, 808
Resource Defense Fund v. Santa Cruz Local Agency Formation Comm'n, 76
Reynolds v. Sims, 635
Rice v. Draper, 776
Richards v. City of Muscatine, *232, 307,* 615
Richards v. City of Tustin, 46
Richardson v. Brunelle, 630
Ringwood Solid Waste Management Auth. v. Borough of Ringwood, 795
Rivera v City of Fresno, 143
Rivergate Residents Ass'n v. Land Conservation & Dev. Comm'n, 75
Riverside City v. Idylwild County Water Dist., 258
Roberts v. McNary, *332*
Robertson v. Zimmerman, 177
Robin v. Incorporated Village of Hempstead, 98

Robinson v. Cahill, 703
Rochlin v. State, 307
Rock v. Thompson 776
Rogers v. Herman Lodge, 670
Rogers v. Medical Ass'n, 632
Rollow v. West, 170
Rosenthal v. Board of Educ., 644
Rosewell v. LaSalle Nat'l Bank, 228, 482
Ruberoid Co. v. North Pecos Water & Sanitation Dist., 257
Ruel v. Rapid City, 255
Rutgers v. Piluso, 159
Ryans v. New Jersey Comm'n for the Blind & Visually Impaired, 548

S

Saenz v. Lackey, 788
Saffioti v. Wilson, 764
Sailors v. Board of Educ., 643
St. Charles City-County Library Dist. v. St. Charles Library Corp., 301
St. Clair v. Yonkers Raceway, Inc., *797*
St. Louis Police Comm'rs v. St. Louis County Court, 337
Salt Lake City Fire Fighters Local 1645 v. Salt Lake City, 380
Salyer Land Co. v. Tulare Lake Basin Water Storage Dist., *645*
San Antonio Indep. School Dist. v. Rodriquez, *692*
San Bernardino County Flood Control Dist. v. Superior Ct., 161
San Diego Gas & Elec. Co. v. City of San Diego, 461, 462
San Ysidro Irrigation Dist. v. Superior Court, 788
Save a Valuable Env't Bothell, 401
Scheuer v. Rhodes, 478
Schmidt v. Department of Resource Dev., 50
Schmoll v. Housing Auth., 171
School Dist. No. 351 Oneida County v. Oneida Educ. Ass'n, 423
Schroeder v. Binks, 625
Schumacher v. City of Bozeman, 255
Schwanda v. Bonney, 128, 142
Schware v. Board of Bar Examiners, 631
Scroggs v. Kansas City, 301
Seattle Newspaper-Web Pressmen's Local No. 26 v. City of Seattle, 141
Seattle School Dist. No. 1 v. State, 709, 710
Security Life & Accident Co. v. Temple, 131
Seibel v. Kemble, 454
Serian v. State, 703

TABLE OF CASES

Serrano v. Priest (Cal. 3d), *680*
Serrano v. Priest (Cal.), 689
Seward County Bd. of Comm'rs v. City of Seward, 159
Sharp v. Commonwealth, 483
Shapp v. Sloan, *366*
Sheridan Drive-In Theatre, Inc. v. State, 461
Shofstall v. Hollins, 707
Shoup Voting Mach. Corp. v. Board of County Comm'rs, 301
Sibert v. Garrett, 24
Sierra Club v. Morton, 806
Sigma Tau Gamma Fraternity House Corp. v. City of Menomonie, 237
Silverbrook Cemetery Co. v. Department of Finance, 781
Simpson v. Municipality of Anchorage, 142
Skafte v. Rorex, 529
Skehan v. Board of Trustees, 464
Slebodnik v. City of Indianapolis, 257, 258
Smith v. City of Riverside, 107
Snow v. City of Memphis, 228
S.O.L. Club v. City of Williamsport, 255
Solvang Mun. Improvement Dist. v. Board of Supervisors, 257, 331
Sosna v. Iowa, 380
South Bend Community School Corp. v. National Educ. Ass'n-South Bend, 418
Southern Burlington County NAACP v. Township of Mt. Laurel [I], 808
Southern Ocean Landfill, Inc. v. Mayor & Council, 147
Spencer v. General Hosp., 434
Spokane County Fire Protection Dist. v. Spokane County Boundary Review Bd., 77
Square Parking Sys., Inc. v. Jersey City Business Adm'r, 199
Stanley v. Department of Conservation & Dev., 285
State v. Boynton, 616
State v. City of Riviera Beach, 114
State v. City of Spokane, 439
State v. City of Sunrise, 128
State v. Crawford, 787
State v. Crawley, 149
State v. Jacobson, 141
State v. Jones, 787
State v. Hall, 483
State v. Hickey, 787
State v. Hutchinson, *91*
State v. Julson, 610
State v. Lewis, 807
State v. Lombardo, 781
State v. Ludlow Supermarkets, Inc., *10*
State v. McPhail, 776
State v. Orange County, 308
State v. Orton, 789
State v. Rodriguez, 610
State v. State Supervisory Employees Ass'n, 417, 419
State *ex inf.* Danforth *ex rel.* Farmers' Elec. Coop. v. State Environmental Improvement Auth., 20
State *ex rel.* Abercrombie v. District Court, 787
State *ex rel.* Althouse v. City of Madison, 775
State *ex rel.* Anaya v. McBride, 786
State *ex rel.* Armstrong v. Davey, 775
State *ex rel.* Barker v. Manchin, 616
State *ex rel.* Beck v. City of York, 209
State *ex rel.* Becker v. Common Council, 820
State *ex rel.* Brown v. City of Canton, 774
State *ex rel.* Brown v. Ferguson, 762
State *ex rel.* Cain v. Kay, *781*
State *ex rel.* Capitol Addition Bldg. Comm'n v. Connelly, 23
State *ex rel.* Card v. Kaufman, 814
State *ex rel.* Cason v. Bond, 762, 776
State *ex rel.* City of Charleston v. Bosely, 590
State *ex rel.* City of Charleston v. Coghill, *614*
State *ex rel.* Cole v. City of Hendersonville, 53
State *ex rel.* Collier v. City of Pigeon Forge, 55
State *ex rel.* Conger v. Madison County, *565*
State *ex rel.* Douglas v. Marsh, 583
State *ex rel.* Fatzer v. Redevelopment Auth., 591
State *ex rel.* Fatzer v. Urban Renewal Agency, 591
State *ex rel.* Finnegan v. Dammann, 763
State *ex rel.* Flaxel v. Chandler, 616
State *ex rel.* Gebhardt v. City Council, 439
State *ex rel.* Gralike v. Walsh, 781
State *ex rel.* Grand Bazaar Liquors, Inc. v. City of Milwaukee, 15, 625, 630
State *ex rel.* Gray v. Martin, 814
State *ex rel.* Greenberg v. Florida State Bd. of Dentistry, 780
State *ex rel.* Grimes County Taxpayers Ass'n v. Texas Mun. Power Agency, 169
State *ex rel.* Haberkorn v. DeKalb Circuit Court, 806
State *ex rel.* Harvey v. Wright, 24
State *ex rel.* Helena Hous. Auth. v. City Council, 439

State ex rel. Jardon v. Industrial Dev. Auth., 209
State ex rel. Kern v. Arnold, 439
State ex rel. Kleczka v. Conta, 757
State ex rel. McCormack v. Foley, 24
State ex rel. Mueller v. Thompson, 99
State ex rel. Northern Pump Co. v. So-Called Village of Fridley, 53
State ex rel. Ohio City v. Samol, 209
State ex rel. Patterson v. Tucker, 776
State ex rel. Pickrell v. Downey, 54
State ex rel. Pike v. Bellingham, 821
State ex rel. Repay v. Fodeman, 787
State ex rel. Robb v. Stone, 776
State ex rel. Sayad v. Zych, 337
State ex rel. Sayre v. Moore, 776
State ex rel. Schneider v. City of Topeka, 237
State ex rel. Sego v. Kirkpatrick, 762
State ex rel. S. Monroe & Son Co. v. Baker, 740
State ex rel. State Highway Comm'n v. Board of County Comm'rs, 162
State ex rel. State Highway Comm'n v. Hoester, 161
State ex rel. Stephan v. Martin, 230
State ex rel. Turner v. Earle, 780
State ex rel. Turner v. Iowa Highway Comm'n, 763
State ex rel. Wagner v. St. Louis County Port Auth., 786
State ex rel. Whetsel v. Wood, 622
State ex rel. W. Va. Bd. of Educ. v. Miller, 775
State ex rel. Swart v. Molitor, 124
State ex rel. Taft v. Campanella, 209
State ex rel. Thompson v. Morton, 396
State ex rel. Ulrick v. Sanchez, 396
State ex rel. Wagner v. St. Louis County, 614
State ex rel. Warren v. Nusbaum, 279
State ex rel. Wehe v. Frazier, 396
State ex rel. White v. City of Cleveland, 439
State ex rel. Wood v. City of Memphis, 39
State ex rel. Woodahl v. Straub, 721
State Highway Comm'n v. Haase, 740
State of Utah by & through Road Comm'n v. Salt Lake City Pub. Bd. of Educ., 163
State Tax Comm'n v. Wakefield, 230
State Water Pollution Control Bd. v. Salt Lake City, 82
Stauffer v. Town of Grand Lake, 492
Stein v. Highland Park Indep. School Dist., 460
Sterling v. Constantin, 776
Stephens v. Synder Clinic Ass'n, 597
Steup v. Indiana Housing Fin. Auth., 281
Stewart v. Schmeider, 454
Stocks v. City of Irvine, 807
Stofer v. Motor Vehicle Casualty Co., 600
Strickland v. City of Wichita, 249
Strickland v. Richmond County, 591
Strutwear Knitting Co. v. Olson, 776
Sugarman v. Dougall, 380
Summer v. Township of Teaneck, 147
Superior Oil Co. v. City of Port Arthur, 42, 45
Sussex Woodlands, Inc. v. Mayor & Council, 80
Sutfin v. State, 460
Sutherlin Educ. Ass'n v. Sutherlin School Dist. No. 130, 417
Swann v. Adams, 637
Swayne & Hoyt v. United States, 738
Sweeney v. Bond, 395
Sweetwater County Planning Comm. for the Org. of School Dists. v. Hinkle, 711
Switzer v. City of Phoenix, 308

T

Tabler v. Board of Supervisors, 85
Tabor v. Moore, 804
Tally & Jade, Inc. v. City of Detroit, 113
Tangen v. State Ethics Comm'n, 401
Tanner v. McCall, 395
Tate v. Antosh, 365
Taylor v. Abernathy, 775
Taylor v. Township of Dearborn, 38
Temple Terrace v. Hillsborough Ass'n for Retarded Citizens, Inc., 160
Tennessee v. Louisville & Nashville R.R., 231
Territory of Hawaii ex rel. County of Oahu v. Whitney, 615
Texas Antiquities Comm. v. Dallas County Community College Dist., 34
Texfi Indus., Inc. v. City of Fayetteville, 666
Thibodeaux v. Comeaux, 257
Thomas v. State ex rel. Cobb, 23
Thompson v. Engelking, 707
Thompson v. Schmidt, 633
Thornburg v. Port of Portland, 461
Thorne v. Roush, 626
Tiegs v. Patterson, 787
Timberlane Regional School Dist. v. Timberlane Regional Educ. Ass'n, 420
Toms River Affiliates v. Department of Environmental Protection, 614
Torres v. Village of Capitan, 667
Town of Arlington v. Board of Conciliation & Arbitration, 507

TABLE OF CASES

Town of Beloit v. City of Beloit, *47*
Town of Conover v. Jolly, 98
Town of Godfrey v. City of Alton, 29
Town of Hallie v. City of Chippewa Falls, 493
Town of Lockport v. Citizens for Community Action at the Local Level, Inc., *652*
Town of Milton v. Civil Serv. Comm'n, 379
Town of North Hempstead v. Village of North Hills, 401
Town of Ouita v. Heidgan, 53
Town of Pleasant Prairie v. City of Kenosha, 61, 795
Town of Sudbury v. Commissioner of Corps. & Taxation, 222
Town of Terrell Hills v. City of San Antonio, 270
Town of Wickenburg v. State, 33
Township of Cascade v. Cascade Resources Recovery, Inc., 147
Township of Jefferson v. City of W. Carrollton, 657
Township of Midland v. Michigan State Boundary Comm'n, 75
Township of Washington v. Village of Ridgewood, *153*
Towse v. State, 454
Train v. City of New York, 765
Tregor v. Board of Assessors, 223
Tribe v. Salt Lake City Corp., *81,* 237, 307
Trustees of Dartmouth College v. Woodward, 431
Tucker v. Crawford, 129
Tucson v. Commissioner, 292
Tucson Community Dev. & Design Center, Inc. v. City of Tucson, 804
Turnpike Auth. v. Wall, 282
Tweed v. City of Cape Canaveral, 128
Tyson v. Lanier, 230

U

Unified School Dist. No. 1 v. Wisconsin Employment Relations Comm'n, 33
Union Elec. Co. v. Land Clearance for Redevelopment Auth., 440
Union Mut. Life Ins. Co. v. Emerson, 625
United Constr. Workers v. Laburnum Constr. Corp., 425
United Illuminating Co. v. City of New Haven, 223
United Mine Workers of Am. v. Miller, 773
United Pub. Workers v. Mitchell, 394
United States v. Causby, 461
United States v. Carmack, 161
United States v. United Mine Workers, 424
United States Civil Serv. Comm'n v. National Ass'n of Letter Carriers, 394

United States Elevator Corp. v. City of Tulsa, *105*
United States Steel Corp. v. Multistate Tax Comm'n, 171
United States Steel Corp. v. Save Sand Key, Inc., 807
United States Trust Co. v. New Jersey, 279
United Tavern Owners v. School Dist., 143
United Transp. Union v. Long Island R.R. (F. Supp.), 509
United Transp. Union v. Long Island R.R. (F.2d), 509
United Transp. Union v. Long Island R.R. (U.S.), 508
Utah Hous. Fin. Agency v. Smart, 281

V

Vail v. City of Bandon, 249
Valley Forge Christian College v. Americans United for Separation of Church & State, Inc., 801
Van Dissel v. Jersey Power & Light Co., 531
Van Ootehgem v. Gray, 395
Vansickle v. Shanahan, 739
Vap v. City of McCook, 171
Vermont Home Mortgage Credit Agency v. Montpelier Nat'l Bank, 283
Village House, Inc. v. Town of Loudon, 91
Village of Amityville v. Suffolk County, 161
Village of Arlington Heights v. Metropolitan Housing Dev. Corp., 38
Village of Arlington Heights v. Regional Transp. Auth., 33
Village of Bloomingdale v. LaSalle Nat'l Bank, 249
Village of Blue Ash. v. City of Cincinnati, 162
Village of Burnsville v. Onischuk, 177
Village of Dennison v. Martin, 170
Village of Farmington v. Minnesota Mun. Comm'n, 75
Village of Richmond Heights v. Board of County Comm'rs, 161
Village of Riverwoods v. Untermyer, 360
Village of Sherman v. Village of Williamsville, 165
Virginia v. Tennessee, 171
Virginia State Bd. of Pharmacy v. Virginia Citizens Consumer Council, 618
Volunteers of Am. Care Facilities v. Village of Brown Deer, 147
V.T.C. Lines, Inc. v. City of Harlan, *456*

W

Wagner v. Salt Lake City, 307
Walker v. Junior, 787

Walker Field v. Adams, *512*
Wall v. Board of Elections, 667
Wallace v. Commissioner of Taxation, 610
Waller v. Florida, 143
Waller v. State, 143
Wambat Realty Corp. v. State, 109
War Memorial Hosp. v. Board of County Comm'rs, 309
Wardwell v. Board of Educ., *376*
Warth v. Seldin, 806
Washakie County School Dist. No. One v. Herschler, 711
Washington v. Commissioner, 293
Washington v. Davis, 38, 382, 823
Washington v. Federal Power Comm'n, 531
Washington v. Seattle School Dist. No. 1, 823
Washington Ass'n of Apartment Ass'ns v. Evans, 764
Washington Pub. Power Supply Sys. v. Pacific Northwest Power Co., 533
Watchmaking Examining Bd. v. Husar, 609, *620*
Watkins v. Fugazzi, 238
Watson v. McGee, 480
Weber Basin Home Builders Ass'n v. Roy City, 265
Weekes v. City of Oakland, *115*
Wein v. City of New York, 282
Welden v. Ray, *752*
Wells v. Edwards, 644
Westborough Mall, Inc. v. City of Cape Girardeau, 493
Western Amusement Co. v. City of Springfield, 257
Westervelt v. National Resources Comm'n, 608
West Mead Township v. City of Meadville, 60
Westring v. James, 51

West Side Org. Health Servs. Corp. v. Thompson, 765
Wheeler v. District of Columbia Bd. of Zoning Adjustment, 181
Whitaker v. Arizona Real Estate Bd., 627
Whitcomb v. Chavis, 637, 668
White v. Lorings, 53
White v. Regester, 637, 668
White v. Weiser, 637
Wilkerson v. City of Coralville, 34
Wilkinsburgh-Penn Joint Water Auth. v. Borough of Churchill, 159
Williams v. Eastside Mental Health Center, Inc., 553
Williams v. Mayor & Council, 33
Williams v. Starr, 591
Williamson v. Lee Optical Co., 617
Willits v. Askew, 775
Wilson v. Board of Comm'rs, 285
Wilson v. City of Waynesville, 597
Wilson v. Connecticut Prod. Dev. Corp., *201*
Wilson v. Hidden Valley Mun. Water Dist., 69
Wilt v. Commonwealth, 396
Wing v. City of Eugene, 250
Wirin v. Parker, 804
Wisconsin Elec. Power Co. v. City of Milwaukee, 258
Wisconsin Solid Waste Recycling Auth. v. Earl, 285
Withrow v. Larkin, 618, 632
Wood v. State Admin. Bd., 763
Wood v. Strickland, 478
Wright v. Rockefeller, 38
Wunderlich v. City of St. Louis, 308

Y

Youngberg v. Romero, 547
Youngstown Sheet & Tube Co. v. Sawyer, 749

PART ONE

THE GOVERNMENTAL SYSTEM

Chapter 1
AN OVERVIEW OF THE GOVERNMENTAL SYSTEM

A. TRENDS AND PERSPECTIVES

State and local governments are entering a time of change. Federal assistance and the federal role are declining. States are assuming or reassuming new functions as federal assistance is decentralized, while local governments face increasing responsibilities in a time of fiscal stress. These changing governmental roles provide essential background for the study of state and local government in a federal system.

The past decade has also seen a substantial change in migration and settlement patterns, both within metropolitan areas and in the nation generally. Older cities, especially in the northeast, continue to decline. The suburbs now hold the largest share of the metropolitan population, while national migration has shifted to nonmetropolitan areas. These changes have occurred as the legal, political, and territorial structures of local governments have remained much the same.

An overview of the political, fiscal, and population changes which affect the intergovernmental system indicates the following major trends:

The declining federal role. Federal assistance to state and local governments rose dramatically to thirty-two percent of state and local expenditures in 1978. With federal assistance came federal limitations and controls in the form of conditions attached to federal grants. Federal assistance affected state and local governments in a number of ways. At the state level, the common federal legislative requirement for the designation of a single state agency to administer federal assistance shaped the organization of state government. Similar changes occurred at the local level, where special local government units were formed to match federal assistance with borrowing authority that escaped state constitutional debt limitations. Federal assistance also affected the state and local budgeting and appropriation process, and shaped spending priorities. Conditions attached to federal assistance imposed federal requirements ranging from civil rights and equal opportunity responsibilities to minimum wage and maximum hour requirements. New state legislation and local ordinances were required to provide the enabling authority to undertake federally authorized programs.

Federal aid to states and local governments has now stabilized and is declining. Congress has also enacted new "block" grants which place the power to distribute federal funds with the states, subject only to minimal federal limitations. These trends, if they continue, will reduce the federal role at the same time that new responsibilities are conferred on state governments.

Reform in state government. State government had long been the weak link in the intergovernmental system. Reforms in recent decades have improved state government capability. Constitutions have been modernized, state legislatures reapportioned, and state administrations reorganized.

Whether these changes will bring a heightened concern for the welfare of cities is another matter. State legislatures often ignored city problems in the days before reapportionment, but the suburban shift in population has decreased big city representation despite the reapportionment mandate.

Changes in national migration patterns. The migration of population nationally from rural to metropolitan areas brought about a major demographic shift in the postwar years. Migration to metropolitan areas now appears to be moderating. A noted geographer has summarized this change.

2. Decreasing migration flows from the south and west to the north and east and increasing flows in the other direction have resulted in growing net migration from snowbelt to sunbelt. The receiving regions have a younger population, whereas those losing people have the progressive disabilities that characterize all places and people left behind.

3. Similar migration reversals in favor of nonmetropolitan areas, together with acceleration of suburbanization and exurbanization within metropolitan regions, have produced (a) absolute population declines in the majority of the nation's largest central cities; (b) a slowing of the growth and the onset of decline in some of the metropolitan regions of the northeastern snowbelt; (c) continued growth of smaller and intermediate-sized sunbelt metropolitan regions; and (d) the onset of new growth in nonmetropolitan regions throughout the nation, approximately one-third due to urban overspill beyond metropolitan boundaries and two-thirds due to new development outside the daily commuting areas of metropolitan regions that currently have metropolitan recognition.

4. Absolute industrial job losses in the Northeast's former manufacturing belt — 1.7 million between 1969 and 1977 — have been matched by an equivalent magnitude of industrial employment growth in the former peripheral sunbelt.

5. Regional income convergence in nominal terms by the mid-1970s and significant reversals, in real terms, have led to former high-income regions', for example, New England, slipping beneath former poverty regions, for example, the South.

Berry, *Urbanization and Counterurbanization in the United States,* 451 ANN. ACAD. POL. SCI. 13, 15, 16 (1980).

These trends have important implications for local government. Slowed growth in metropolitan areas and growth declines in older cities mean declines in tax base and greater fiscal constraints. In the sunbelt and nonmetropolitan areas, rapid growth creates a different kind of pressure for government facilities and services. In rural areas, local governments are more primitive and may be less able to meet these demands. For additional discussion see Advisory Commission on Intergovernmental Relations, Regional Growth (1980).

The suburbanization of metropolitan areas. Within metropolitan areas, declines in the growth of the core, or "central" cities, have been accompanied by a continuing increase in suburban population. Forty-five percent of the metropolitan population lived in suburban areas in 1970, and the 1980 census will probably show an even higher proportion. Jobs have decentralized to the suburbs along with the population, although some studies question the impact on employment opportunities in core city areas. Jobs appear to be suburbanizing more slowly than population.

Suburban growth has been selective:

Many empirical studies show that generally the young, the employed, the well-to-do, the white move to the suburbs leaving the aged, the unemployed, the poor, and the blacks in the central cities. In fact, one of the most striking features of the suburban movement has been its racial selectivity. Because of this selectivity, the racial composition of central cities has undergone a significant change . . . . In 1970, in all metropolitan areas of 1 million or more, nearly 80 per cent of the blacks but only 36 per cent of the whites lived in central cities.

Solomon, The Emerging Metropolis in the Prospective City 3, 11 (A. Solomon ed. 1980).

Metropolitan suburbanization has created what are known as "disparities" in central city and suburban taxation and expenditure levels:

> In the 85 largest [metropolitan areas], the per capita expenditures of central cities exceeded those of their suburbs by 35%. The gap was largely due to the higher outlays for noneducational purposes in central cities — 77% greater than in the [suburban] areas. Cities were spending relatively more than in the past on education, but in 1977 they still devoted only 35% of their budgets to this purpose, as compared to 59% in the suburbs.
>
> Overall, per capita taxes in 1977 were 25% higher in the central cities than in the [suburban] areas. Intergovernmental aid was also greater — by 46%. A considerable share of the aid difference was due to the substantially larger portion of federal aid directed to central cities . . . . [P]er capita educational aid was 5% greater in the suburbs, but noneducational aid was 124% larger in the central cities.

Advisory Commission on Intergovernmental Relations, Central City-Suburban Fiscal Disparity and City Distress, 1977, at 20 (1980).

Declining federal aid can only weaken the fiscal condition of central cities in metropolitan areas. *See What the Budget Cuts Mean for Cities — Lean Years, With Less for the Poor,* 13 Nat'l J. 960 (1981). For a discussion of contemporary suburbia see P. Muller, Contemporary Suburban America (1981).

The fiscal crisis. All of these trends add up to a growing fiscal crisis in many older central cities. New York's near default may be a forecast of what will happen elsewhere. Federal guarantees helped solve the New York crisis, but they are not likely to be available on a large scale if other cities face municipal insolvency.

A recent congressional survey of urban fiscal distress reports the following findings:

> For all cities, the average increase in both revenues and expenditures was below the rate of inflation in 1979-80 . . . . More than 50 percent of the cities reported operating deficits . . . . Operating deficits were not confined to the largest cities . . . .
> For all cities, three main trends are apparent concerning changes in revenue: less Federal aid, little growth in state aid and large increases in fees . . . .
> Capital outlays have increased by an average of 19.4 percent for all the cities . . . .
> Debt outstanding, particularly tax-supported general obligation debt, continues to grow very slowly. The emphasis in borrowing continues to be in the self-supporting enterprise activities . . . . In the face of decreasing Federal aid for capital purposes, capital spending plans will increasingly rely on access to the credit markets, a process that is difficult and costly in view of high interest rates and city fiscal pressures . . . .
> Wage and salary increases for police, fire and sanitation workers were frequently below the rate of inflation . . . . [I]n the largest cities, the shortfall was dramatic.

Joint Economic Committee, Congress of the United States, Trends in the Fiscal Condition of Cities: 1979-81, at 3-8, 97th Cong., 1st Sess. (1981). *See also* Cities Under Stress (R. Burchell & D. Listokin eds. 1981).

Local governments often face a fiscal "Catch-22." Property tax limitations in some states limit the revenue local governments can generate from local taxes, and lowered tax collections limit borrowing power. The flood of special borrowing for industrial facilities, housing, and related revenue-producing enterprises limits accessibility to the municipal bond market for general municipal borrowing. Reductions in municipal wages, services, and capital spending become unpleasant but necessary realities.

The impact on local government. Changes in the distribution of population nationally and in metropolitan areas have shifted population into areas where local governments are not well developed and have fewer capabilities. Most of the larger and older cities are unable to take in new suburban population through annexation. Older suburban municipalities also have limited expansion possibilities. Metropolitan areas have become a complex of fragmented suburban governments.

Counties have assumed urban governmental functions in some areas. They close the governmental gap by providing a full range of services to residents in unincorporated areas. New incorporations have provided new governmental entities in some areas, but services are often provided in outlying areas by special districts established to provide a single or a limited number of governmental functions. Special districts are the fastest growing local government unit. Their proliferation, especially in metropolitan areas, has complicated the local government problem.

These changes affect the availability of local governments in metropolitan areas which can provide a comprehensive set of governmental functions. Constitutional home rule, for example, is often limited to cities above a certain size, and has not been extended to counties in all states. Although some counties have acquired urban functions, county as well as municipal governments in outlying metropolitan areas often belong to a lower governmental "class," and have limited governmental powers.

The concluding sections of this chapter examine state and local governments more closely. They review state government and local government patterns, the constitutional limitations on state legislatures, and the status of local governments in the constitutional system.

B. STATE GOVERNMENT

1. THE REFORM OF STATE GOVERNMENT

The reform of state government which has occurred over the past thirty years is one of the most unknown yet important changes in American governmental structure in recent years. These reforms have substantially modified the legal and political structure which affects the implementation of state government responsibilities. The following excerpts capture the essence of the state government reform movement:

> Since 1950, four-fifths of the states have modernized their constitutions. Though there are some exceptions, most of the rewritten documents conform to the principles of brevity and simplicity, strengthen the powers of the governor, unify court management, enlarge legislative powers and flexibility and make amendments easier to effect than in the past. To a lesser extent, they extend home rule and increase tax authority of local governments.
>
> The executive offices of the governors have been strengthened, noted Temple University's Daniel Elazar, "in a manner reminiscent of the strengthening of the President's office in the 1920s and 1930s." Appointment powers were broadened, partly through a significant reduction in the number of statewide elective offices between 1964 and 1978 . . . .
>
> Twenty-three states underwent major executive branch reorganization between 1964 and 1979; 36 currently have cabinet forms of government in place

of the antiquated systems of dozens or even hundreds of independent departments, agencies, boards and commissions.

Beneath the governors and their cabinet directors is a vast state bureaucracy of 3.6 million people, compared with the federal government's 2.8 million. About three-fourths of state employees are covered by some form of merit system, compared with half in 1950, when only 1.5 million people worked for the states.

. . . .

Few disagree that the legislatures have come a long way in 20 or 30 years. They are no longer the "sometimes governments" of yore, meeting a few weeks every other year, grossly malapportioned, devoid of adequate staff support, paid paltry sums and controlled by narrow leadership cliques or powerful economic interests.

Thanks to the courts, equally apportioned districts are nearly universal . . . .

[A]ll states now have their own legislative reference libraries, bill analysis, legal research services and fiscal and policy review and analysis.

Professional staffing of committees and legislative service units, previously sporadic in some states and non-existent in others, has spread to include virtually all the legislative reference services and standing committees in both houses in 36 states.

Pierce, *The States Can Do It, But Is There the Will?*, 14 NAT'L J. 374 (1982).

These changes are detailed more fully in a report of the Advisory Commission on Intergovernmental Relations, State and Local Roles in the Federal System ch. 3 (1982). The Report also notes the dominant role states play in the provision of government services:

States are the dominant service providers, providing more than 55% of the expenditures in most states in highways, state-local public welfare, hospitals, health, natural resources, and corrections. In addition, they now pay most of the court and school costs. In other areas, such as water transportation, they often provide most of the financing . . . and they have become increasingly important in mass transit services.

Id. at 62. The Report also notes "the major state responsibilities in the provision of criminal justice and the regulation of business," pointing out that "[s]tate responsibilities for the regulation of business encompass almost every phase of business activity" from the licensing of professions to the control of financial institutions and utility companies.

Local governments have long been dominant in health and safety and land use regulation, although there are state incursions even here. State public health legislation regulates a wide variety of health problems. States also enact and enforce occupational safety codes and have adopted state housing and building codes. Some states have adopted state land use control programs. Coastal zone management programs are an example.

The role of the state as the "architect" of local government is critical. As the Advisory Commission report, *supra,* noted:

As decisionmakers for local governments, states determine — either through the state constitution, or by statute or charter — what local governments there will be; the proper allocation of powers to and among them; their functional assignments; their internal structure, organizations, and procedures for local operations; their fiscal options in regard to revenue, expenditures, and debt; the extent of the interlocal cooperation; how their boundaries can be expanded or contracted; and to some degree their land-use patterns. When one government exercises this kind of influence over others, its decisions affect those subordinate governments critically.

Id. at 151.

Much of the first part of this casebook considers the role of the state, and especially the state legislature, in determining local government organization, powers, and fiscal authority. The role of the state in the intergovernmental fiscal system is especially critical. In general, it is the state which imposes the broad-based taxes that generate large revenues, such as the income tax and the sales tax. This preemption of revenue sources leaves local governments in many states with the property tax as their principal revenue source. In addition, the revenue and borrowing powers of local governments depend primarily on the state legislature. Local taxes and local borrowing authority must be authorized by the state legislature, even in most home rule states.

2. CONSTITUTIONAL LIMITATIONS ON STATE AND LOCAL AUTHORITY

Like the federal constitution, the state constitution contains limitations on state and local authority, but its role in setting limits on state authority is very different. As one commentator has noted:

> State constitutions differ from the federal constitution in scope and effect. The federal constitution is a document of grant and delegation, for in spite of its enormous powers, the federal government must trace all of its powers to one of several constitutional grants made to it by the original states. The states have plenary powers simply by virtue of their original sovereignty; they retain all the powers it is possible for government to have except insofar as these powers have either been delegated to the federal government, or have been limited by the state constitution.

Grad, *The State's Capacity to Respond to Urban Problems: The State Constitution,* in THE STATES AND THE URBAN CRISIS 27 (A. Campbell ed. 1970).

Like the federal constitution, most state constitutions also contain due process or equal protection clauses, or their equivalents, which limit state and local regulatory authority. Due process and equal protection limitations on government regulation may have seen their day in the United States Supreme Court, but they often are more rigorously enforced at the state level. The following excerpt from a state court decision summarizes the Supreme Court view and indicates why a more rigorous application of the due process clause may be warranted at the state level. The Pennsylvania Supreme Court was considering a state law prohibiting the advertising of drugs, which it held unconstitutional:

> Our adjudication begins with an acknowledgement that the day has long passed when the Due Process Clause of the Fourteenth Amendment could be used to indiscriminately strike down state economic regulatory statutes. It is certainly clear that the "vague contours" of due process, see *Adkins v. Children's Hospital,* 261 U.S. 525, 567, 568 . . . (1923) (Holmes, J., dissenting), cannot be employed to engulf a State's efforts to, for example, set minimum hours for work, see *Lochner v. New York,* 198 U.S. 45 . . . (1905), or set minimum wages for children, see *Adkins v. Children's Hospital, supra,* or prohibit employment agencies from collecting fees from employees, see *Adams v. Tanner,* 244 U.S. 590 . . . (1917). In a long line of cases, see *Day-Brite Lighting v. Missouri,* 342 U.S. 421, 423 . . . (1952) (citing cases), the Supreme Court of the United States has "returned to the original constitutional proposition that courts do not substitute their social and economic beliefs for the judgment of legislative bodies, who are elected to pass laws." *Ferguson v. Skrupa,* 372 U.S. 726, 730 . . . (1963). "Deference to the legislative judgment" is now the federal watchword, see *Daniel v. Family Security Life Insurance Co.,*

336 U.S. 220, 224 n.4 ... (1949); *United States v. Carolene Products Co.,* 304 U.S. 144, 152 ... (1938). "It is enough that there is an evil at hand for correction, and that it might be thought that the particular legislative measure was a rational way to correct it." *Williamson v. Lee Optical of Oklahoma, Inc.,* 348 U.S. 483, 488 ... (1955). ...

While this test may mean that in the federal courts the "due process barrier to substantive legislation as to economic matters has been in effect removed," the same cannot be said with respect to state courts and state constitutional law. This difference between federal and state constitutional law represents a sound development, one which takes into account the fact that "state courts may be in a better position to review local economic legislation than the Supreme Court. State courts, since their precedents are not of national authority, may better adapt their decisions to local economic conditions and needs. ... And where an industry is of basic importance to the economy of a state or territory, extraordinary regulations may be necessary and proper." Hetherington, State Economic Regulation and Substantive Due Process of Law, 53 Nw.U.L.Rev. 226, 250 (1958) (footnote omitted).

Thus Pennsylvania, like other state "economic laboratories," see *New State Ice Co. v. Liebmann,* 285 U.S. 262, 280, 311 ... (1932) (Brandeis, J., dissenting), has scrutinized regulatory legislation perhaps more closely than would the Supreme Court of the United States. We have held unconstitutional, for example, an act regulating car rental agencies as a public utility, see *Hertz Drivurself Stations, Inc. v. Siggins,* 359 Pa. 25, 58 A.2d 464 (1948), an act forbidding gasoline stations from displaying price signs in excess of a certain prescribed size, see *Gambone v. Commonwealth,* 375 Pa. 547, 101 A.2d 634 (1954), an act forbidding the sale of carbonated beverages made with sucaryl, see *Cott Beverage Corp. v. Horst,* 380 Pa. 113, 110 A.2d 405 (1955), an act forbidding the sale of ice-milk milk shakes, see *Commonwealth ex rel. Woodside v. Sun Ray Drug Co.,* 383 Pa. 1, 116 A.2d 833 (1955), and an act forbidding nonsigners from selling fair traded items below the price specified in price maintenance contracts, see *Olin Mathieson Chemical Corp. v. White Cross Stores, Inc.,* 414 Pa. 95, 199 A.2d 266 (1964).

Through all these cases we have been guided by the proposition that "a law which purports to be an exercise of the police power must not be unreasonable, unduly oppressive or patently beyond the necessities of the case, and the means which it employs must have a real and substantial relation to the objects sought to be attained." *Gambone v. Commonwealth,* 375 Pa. at 551, 101 A.2d at 637. It is with this test, and the above principles, in mind that we now move to consider the constitutionality of the instant statute.

Pennsylvania State Board of Pharmacy v. Pastor, 272 A.2d 487, 490-91 (1971).

More rigorous application of state constitutional guarantees was advocated by a Supreme Court Justice in an article which has been influential. Brennan, *State Constitutions and the Protection of Individual Rights,* 90 Harv. L. Rev. 489 (1977). The Supreme Court cited Brennan in a case that recognized this state court option:

As a number of recent state court decisions demonstrate, a state court is entirely free to read its own constitution more broadly than this Court reads the federal Constitution, or to reject the mode of analysis used by this Court in favor of a different analysis of its corresponding constitutional guarantee.

City of Mesquite v. Aladdin's Castle, Inc., 455 U.S. 283, 293 (1982).

The following case illustrates the more rigorous application of a state constitutional provision:

STATE v. LUDLOW SUPERMARKETS, INC.

Supreme Court of Vermont
448 A.2d 791 (1982)

Before BARNEY, C. J., HILL and UNDERWOOD, JJ., and SHANGRAW, C. J., and DALEY, J. (Ret.), Specially Assigned.

BARNEY, CHIEF JUSTICE.

This opinion deals with the validity of the so-called Sunday closing law, 13 V.S.A. §§ 3351-3358, as tested against the Constitutions of the United States and of Vermont. The law is set out in its entirety in an appendix to this opinion.

The issue before the Court is whether the statutory prohibition, quoted below, passes constitutional muster as an enforceable criminal enactment, or indeed whether it would do so even as a regulatory enactment, carrying only civil penalties. The law declares at 13 V.S.A. § 3353 that:

> It shall be unlawful on Sundays, January 1, July 4, Labor Day, Thanksgiving, except for the Sundays between Thanksgiving and Christmas, for any person, firm, or corporation:
> (1) to engage in or conduct business or labor for profit in the usual manner and location, or to operate a place of business open to the public; or
> (2) to cause, direct, or authorize any employee or agent to engage in or conduct business or labor for profit in the usual manner and location, or to operate a place of business open to the public.

In 13 V.S.A. § 3355, there are listed a great many exceptions to this prohibition of business operation hardly consistent with the thesis that this is a "common day of rest" act. Central to the issue raised in this case is 13 V.S.A. § 3355(a)(6), which says the law shall not apply to "stores which have no more than 5,000 square feet of interior customer selling space, excluding back room storage, office and processing space." Further on, in 13 V.S.A. § 3355(b), this exception is withdrawn from stores in enclosed shopping malls of more than 20,000 square feet. This last provision was of concern in the case of *State v. Grand Union Co.,* 141 Vt. —, 449 A.2d 984 (1982), from Washington Superior Court, but does not affect the result reached in this opinion.

The issue has been raised in several procedural ways by three lawsuits heard on appeal at the same term of Court. The instant case raises on report by agreement, under V.R.A.P. 5(a), the following question:

> As applied to Ludlow Supermarkets, Inc., d/b/a Clark's Bennington IGA, a supermarket containing approximately 9,000 square feet of interior customer selling space that was open to the public on Sunday, May 17, 1981 and that was not exempted under 13 VSA Section 3355(a)(2) through (a)(7), does Title 13 Chapter 74 violate the United States or Vermont constitutions?

State v. Ames Big N Department Store, 141 Vt. —, 449 A.2d 984 (1982), from Vermont District Court, Windsor Circuit, comes to us on interlocutory appeal pursuant to V.R.A.P. 5(b), after the lower court granted, then stayed, its order dismissing the prosecution as unconstitutional under the Vermont Constitution. The third case, *State v. Grand Union Co., supra,* commenced as a civil action and proceeded to trial. The trial court upheld the law's constitutionality with the exception of subsection 3355(b), which excepted stores located in enclosed malls from the general exemption for small stores. The parties each appealed that portion of the judgment against them. Although the disposition of each of these cases will vary depending on the procedure followed and the result reached below, none presents a factual dispute and all are determined by our resolution of the common question.

At the outset we must set one matter to rest. The State makes the statement that there is no constitutional right to shop on Sunday. This stands constitutional law on its head. Our constitutions are restraints on governmental powers. The rights of citizens are not conditioned on grants given by constitutional fiat, but exist without the aid of expressed governmental permission, subject only to properly authorized circumscription where the public welfare requires. Since the citizens have long since chosen to be governed through a limited grant of authority to each branch of government, it is their right, and this Court's duty, to see that any legislative action prohibiting as a crime otherwise lawful activity is bottomed on the proper exercise of a constitutional power assigned to the legislative branch. *State v. Dodge,* 76 Vt. 197, 201-02, 56 A. 983, 983-84 (1904); see also *Vornado, Inc. v. Hyland,* 77 N.J. 347, 364 et seq., 390 A.2d 606, 615 et seq. (1978) (Pashman, J., dissenting). Specifically we are concerned here with the propriety of the legislature's exercise of its general police power, and whether that power has been exercised so as to affect all citizens equally.

Almost all regulatory legislation, particularly when the concern is economic, tends to be uneven in its impact. Such inequalities are not fatal with respect to constitutional standards if the underlying policy supporting the regulation is a compelling one, and the unbalanced impact is, as a practical matter, a necessary consequence of the most reasonable way of implementing that policy.

Although Vermont formerly had in place a Sunday closing law held to pass muster under these standards in the case of *State v. Giant of St. Albans, Inc.,* 128 Vt. 539, 268 A.2d 739 (1970), relying on federal equal protection standards enunciated in *McGowan v. Maryland,* 366 U.S. 420 ... (1961), the Vermont legislature has seen fit to amend the Sunday closing law twice since that case was decided. Thus we are called upon to review the enactment as presently constituted.

This new statute, like its predecessors in *State v. Rockdale Associates,* 125 Vt. 495, 218 A.2d 718 (1966), *State v. Giant of St. Albans, Inc., supra;* and *State v. Shop and Save Food Markets, Inc.,* 138 Vt. 332, 415 A.2d 235 (1980), contains a list of exemptions, grouped in the present law under some twenty-five headings rather than the longer previous lists, that encompass most, if not all possible commercial activities which are thereby allowed on Sunday, in spite of any supposed need for a day of rest or energy conservation. These activities range from engaging in the real estate business to merchandising any commercial item at all, if the store it is sold in is small enough.

In our cases we have not so far chosen to follow the lead of some states in setting such statutes aside on the ground that they lack a cohesive scheme as a basis for their implementation, because they are riddled with exceptions. See *People v. Abrahams,* 40 N.Y.2d 277, 353 N.E.2d 574, 386 N.Y.S.2d 661 (1976); *Caldor's, Inc. v. Bedding Barn, Inc.,* 177 Conn. 304, 417 A.2d 343 (1979); *Kroger Co. v. O'Hara Township,* 481 Pa. 101, 392 A.2d 266 (1978). Compare *City of Warwick v. Almac's, Inc.,* R.I., 442 A.2d 1265 (1982).

It should be said, however, that whatever our duty to give validity and credit to stated legislative purposes, we are not required to accept as underpinning for any law a purpose that, through wide-ranging exceptions or other emasculating devices, the legislature has reduced to a sham or deceit. See *State v. Shop and Save Food Markets, Inc., supra,* 138 Vt. at 343, 415 A.2d at 241 (Daley and Hill, JJ., concurring). The language of Justice Pashman, dissenting in *Vornado, Inc. v. Hyland, supra,* is particularly apt:

> Irrespective of whether the statutory classification satisfies any of the current Equal Protection tests, it fails abysmally when subjected to scrutiny under a

standard too frequently ignored by judges attracted by the intellectual allure of legal niceties incomprehensible to the public — the test of common sense. When examined from that perspective, the idyllic scenario wistfully conjured by the majority to provide the "rational basis" justifying the statutory classification is patently at odds with the realities of the commercial and consumer worlds of 1978. Assuming any "Sunday Closing" legislation with the purpose ascribed to Chapter 119 can be valid, the unreasonableness of this particular statutory manifestation should earn it the condemnation of this Court.

77 N.J. at 365, 390 A.2d at 615-16.

However, there is a different and more critical vulnerability in the Sunday closing law under review here that requires it to be invalidated. It violates Chapter I, Article 7 of the Vermont Constitution. The basis for that conclusion becomes evident in the analysis that follows.

Each amendment to our law since *State v. Giant of St. Albans, Inc., supra,* was decided has directed itself to defining restraints and exceptions to those restraints that result, among other consequences, in forcing large grocery stores to close one day a week, while small grocery stores may remain open. In the 1976 amendment this purpose went unstated, but was advanced in support of the enactment during argument before us in *State v. Shop and Save Food Markets, Inc., supra.* By 1981, when the amendment as it now appears before us was passed, that objective was expressly set out as "to promote the economic health of small business enterprises." 13 V.S.A. § 3352.

It can hardly be questioned today that benefit to small stores is the most crucial of the legislative objectives behind the Sunday closing law, stated or otherwise, or that this purpose, being selectively beneficial by design and not as a mere incident to its operation, must be tested by appropriate constitutional standards.

In *McGowan v. Maryland, supra,* the United States Supreme Court measured a state law by the standards of the United States Constitution. If the states are to have any meaningful separate sovereign existence, this consideration is of great importance, for the concept of judicial restraint, and its exercise, is involved. Federal examination of a state's exercise of state police power, absent restraints of a suspect character, such as race, sex, religion or national origin, or of basic constitutional concern expressly provided for in the Constitution itself, should certainly be undertaken with a view toward recognizing and respecting properly exercised state authority. Indeed, a recurring theme indicates that the United States Supreme Court recognizes that generalized restraint on state action may unnecessarily restrict the right of the states to attempt individualized responses to particular legislative concerns. *City of Mesquite v. Aladdin's Castle, Inc., . . .* (citing Brennan, *State Constitutions and the Protection of Individual Rights,* 90 Harv.L. Rev. 489 (1977)). Hence, great deference is given to the presence of any rationally related legislative objective undergirding a state statute when it is being reviewed by our highest federal court.

State courts likewise have a duty of judicial restraint which encompasses, similarly, deference to legislative exercise of the sovereign power allocated to that body by the state constitution. It includes the presumption that the legislative action is taken in good faith, and in accordance with constitutional standards. . . .

But it should be noted that a state court reviewing state legislation is in a very different posture from the United States Supreme Court when it undertakes the parallel task. Rather than disposing of a case on the premise that its impact will presumably affect more than fifty varying jurisdictions, a state court reaches its result in the legal climate of the single jurisdiction with which it is associated, if federal proscriptions are not transgressed. *Developments in the Law — The*

Interpretation of State Constitutional Rights. 95 Harv.L.Rev. 1324, 1349 (1982). It has access to specific legislative history and all other proper resources to evaluate the aim and intent of the statutory enactments, as well as the precise expressions of its own state constitutional equivalents.

The federal question is only whether the state law can, in any rational way, be justified under federal constitutional standards. The state issue is whether the enactment is valid under the combination of state and federal requirements.

This is the complicating concern with the law under review. Chapter I, Article 7 of the Vermont Constitution declares:

> That government is, or ought to be, instituted for the common benefit, protection, and security of the people, nation, or community, and not for the particular emolument or advantage of any single man, family, or set of men, who are a part only of that community; . . . .

Somewhat similar to the equal protection test of the fourteenth amendment, this language only allows the statutory classifications involved in a Sunday closing law if a case of necessity can be established overriding the prohibition of Article 7 by reference to the "common benefit, protection, and security of the people."

Given the breadth of the police power, described as another name for sovereignty itself, its exercise, even in the presence of other generalized restraints on state action, may be supported if premised on an appropriate and overriding public interest. . . . This protective concern for the citizenry supports regulation of utilities to prevent wasteful and destructive competition, and to assure safe and adequate service; regulation of common carriers for customer protection and traffic safety; imposition of product quality standards for consumer protection; graduated income tax schedules; professional licensing, and so on down a lengthy list founded on like concerns for public welfare. . . .

In the present case, however, the statute under consideration uses as its justification and policy the very preferential purpose that our constitution says is improper in Article 7. Even though that preference is premised on a declaration that small business enterprises "are essential and fundamental to the economy of the state," 13 V.S.A. § 3352, without more, this objective of favoring one part of the community over another is totally irreconcilable with the Vermont Constitution. It is the very kind of benefit prohibited as an improper purpose by Chapter I, Article 7. The purpose of the preferential legislation must be to further a goal independent of the preference awarded, sufficient to withstand constitutional scrutiny. Justice Stevens would go so far as to say that "When Congress creates a special preference, or a special disability, for a class of persons, it should identify the characteristic that justifies the special treatment." *Fullilove v. Klutznick,* 448 U.S. 448, 553 (Stevens, J., dissenting). When the state legislature in this case made that identification, it was clearly on the basis of an unconstitutional purpose.

We must then turn to the other stated purposes put forward in support of the statute: (1) the establishment of a common day of rest and (2) energy conservation. The inquiry is whether they both, or either of them, justify resort to the police power in the form this statute takes, to the point of overriding the constitutional prohibition of preference.

Both objectives are certainly legislatively valid, but as is the case with other constitutional concerns relating to due process, equal protection, and the commerce clause, there is a duty on the State to demonstrate that any impingement on the right of citizens to engage in otherwise lawful activities, resulting from pursuit of these objectives, is a mere incident, and that the objectives cannot be otherwise reached.... Even accepting for the purpose of this examination that the legislative judgment, however questionable, that the day of rest and energy conservation objectives are critical enough to risk some constitutional infringement on Article 7, it certainly cannot be said that it has in any way been demonstrated that those same purposes cannot be achieved without this particular law.... We have only to look to previous legislation to refute that contention....

Indeed, as already noted, the whole recent history of legislation in this area is a demonstration that the core purpose of these laws, confirmed by legislative language, is the special protection of the economic health of small, locally owned, retail stores. Chapter I, Article 7, cannot thus be legislatively repealed. We hold, therefore, that 13 V.S.A. §§ 3351-3358 are invalid under the Constitution of Vermont.

Our disposition of these statutes on this basis does not require us to examine the troublesome criminal aspects of the law, but we note our previously stated position that where otherwise harmless activity is made subject to criminal penalties, the enactment must be carefully scrutinized. *State v. Shop and Save Food Markets, Inc., supra.* ...

The question on report by agreement is answered in the affirmative and the cause remanded for further proceedings consistent with the views expressed herein.

Appendix

[The Appendix, which contains the text of the statute, is omitted. — Eds.]

RUDOLPH J. DALEY, JUSTICE (Ret.), Specially Assigned.

I concur with the views and the result reached by my associates in the main opinion.

I would point out that the legislative act in question is constitutionally infirm inasmuch as it impacts upon areas of personal privacy and freedom. Though directed toward the conventional police power concerns of the public health and welfare, the act trenches upon areas ordinarily reserved for individual autonomy, i.e., what people should be free to do with themselves on Sunday....

Sunday is a shopping day for a great many people, and for those who are so minded this activity, depending upon individual circumstances, is necessitous, convenient, diversionary and recreational, at bottom reflecting the myriad of personal wishes and subjective choices of individuals....

The effect of the Common Day of Rest Act is to allow Sunday shopping provided it is done in a limited group and type of stores, during forty-eight Sundays of the year. This to me is an unwarranted, unjustified regulatory act. It transgresses the proper role of the police power, of protecting the public safety, health and welfare. The police power is not a license to organize individuals by governmental fiat.

The public should not be restricted in their freedom of choice — to relax or to shop in the absence of an adequate governmental justification in the face of public need. Such justification and need has not, in my opinion, been demonstrated.

Comments: 1. The standard United States Supreme Court equal protection and due process tests require a "rational basis" for regulatory legislation and a "rational relationship" between the classification adopted in the statute and a legitimate state purpose. Many state courts still follow these Supreme Court "minimal review" standards. *See, e.g., Blue Hills Cemetery v. Board of Registration,* 389 N.E.2d 471 (Mass. 1979) (upholding statute prohibiting funeral directors from engaging in any other business).

The Supreme Court also has adopted a more stringent "strict scrutiny" standard of equal protection review that requires a "compelling state interest" to justify a legislative classification. The Court applies this standard to justify suspect classifications such as those based on race and national origin, and classifications affecting fundamental rights such as the right of privacy and the right to vote. State courts do not usually have an opportunity to apply this more stringent review standard, as cases of this type are usually litigated in federal court. The state cases usually consider objections to economic regulation, to which the minimal judicial review standard usually applies. *See Commercial Fisheries Entry Commission v. Apokedak,* 606 P.2d 1255 (Alaska 1980) (classification adopted in licensing statute).

The Supreme Court also applies an intermediate "means-focused" equal protection test, as in cases considering legislative classifications based on gender. *See* Gunther, *In Search of Evolving Doctrine on the Changing Court: A Model for a Newer Equal Protection,* 86 HARV. L. REV. 1 (1972). Some state courts apply the means-focused test to "obviously discriminatory classifications." *See Jones v. State Board of Medicine,* 555 P.2d 399 (Idaho 1976) (remanding to determine whether statute limiting malpractice actions was constitutional). *See also Commercial Fisheries, supra.* Which review standard did the court apply in *Ludlow Supermarkets*?

2. Some state courts apply a "less-restrictive alternative" analysis to due process objections to regulatory legislation. This test derives from another influential article, Struve, *The Less-Restrictive Alternative Principle and Economic Due Process,* 80 HARV. L. REV. 1463 (1967).

In *Quick Chek Food Stores v. Township of Springfield,* 416 A.2d 840 (N.J. 1980), the court upheld an ordinance requiring retail establishments in residential neighborhoods to close between the hours of 9:00 p.m. and 6:00 a.m. The dissenting opinion made the following comments on the constitutionality of the ordinance:

> [C]ontrol of noise pollution is a legitimate purpose of a municipal ordinance .... No amount of liberal construction, however, should convert this delegation into a license to control noise indirectly by closing retail establishments in certain areas .... The present case, however, is not a direct attempt to control the noise of the business — it is an indirect attempt to control the noise of customers .... The majority's validation of Springfield's closing ordinance reflects a total failure to consider existing less restrictive alternatives which are more appropriately tailored to noise control.

Id. at 850. In a footnote, and as a "less restrictive" alternative, the dissenting opinion quoted from a township ordinance prohibiting loitering and disturbances. What other alternative controls might the municipality adopt? Did *Ludlow Supermarkets* apply a less-restrictive alternative analysis?

3. Some courts will strike down state legislation and local ordinances even under the minimal due process and equal protection tests. In *State ex rel. Grand Bazaar Liquors, Inc. v. City of Milwaukee,* 313 N.W.2d 805 (Wis. 1982), the court invalidated a local ordinance limiting Class "A" liquor licenses to establishments receiving no less than half of their income from liquor sales. The court noted that the purpose of the ordinance was to prohibit grocery stores from selling liquor. The court held:

> [The city] argues that the 50 percent classificatory scheme promotes the observance of liquor regulations by limiting Class "A" licenses to those to whom the threat of revocation presents a greater financial loss. We find this argument unpersuasive. First, a licensee attaining a 5 percent income from sales of liquor amounting to a million dollars would appear equally, if not more, protective of the license as a licensee receiving 50 percent income from sales of liquor amounting to several thousand dollars .... Second,

we note that liquor licenses are reviewed annually to ensure control and adherence to the liquor laws.... While we have recognized the presumption of constitutionality and the rather easily accommodated rational-basis test, we should not blindly rubber stamp legislation enacted under the guise of the city's police power when careful review has revealed no logical link between the legislation and the objective it was enacted to effect.

Id. at 810, 811, 813.

4. A student article suggests a revised state substantive due process review. The article first proposes an "ends analysis." "[C]ourts should employ a typology based on the functional categorization of state ends traditionally used by economists: allocation, stabilization, and redistribution." Allocative measures correct market failure. Stabilization measures ensure full employment and other "aggregate goals." Redistribution accomplishes wealth transfer. Which of these ends should courts approve?

The article then suggests a "means analysis," and suggests that the "less drastic alternative" and "heavy presumption of validity" rules are "workable" methods for carrying out this analysis. The article concludes that "the burden of proof should be put on the state to establish a means-ends nexus." Note, *State Economic Substantive Due Process: A Proposed Approach,* 88 YALE L.J. 1487 (1979).

Do you agree with this approach? Is it consistent with the approach taken in any of the cases in this section? Should it apply to the equal protection clause? If not, how should the analysis differ? For additional discussion see Note, *Counter-revolution in State Constitutional Law,* 15 STAN. L. REV. 309 (1962).

5. The *Developments* article cited in *Ludlow Supermarkets* also attempts to rationalize the more assertive state due process cases. The article makes the comment that assertive substantive economic review in state courts may be justified by the judicial need to protect widely shared values. The article then gives the following example:

> Many state court opinions reflect the belief that the statute at hand does no more than benefit one group at the expense of another. The redistribution of economic or other interests from A to B, with no larger purpose than that legislators prefer B to A, is generally considered an improper use of legislative power.

Id. at 1484. Does this analysis explain the holding in *Ludlow Supermarkets?* Do you agree with it?

3. LEGISLATIVE POWER: GRANT VERSUS LIMITATION

The equal protection and due process clauses act as a limitation on the regulatory power of state legislatures. State constitutions also contain other provisions establishing the structure of local government, providing the power to tax and borrow, and conferring other substantive powers on the state and its local governments.

This second set of constitutional provisions operates differently at the state level than it does at the federal level. Congress can only exercise powers granted by the federal constitution. State legislatures are plenary, except as limited by the state constitution. This section develops this concept.

The "plenary power" rule is critical, among other things, to the authority of the state legislature to establish the organizational structure of local government and the powers local government may exercise, as the following case illustrates:

OAKLAND COUNTY TAXPAYERS' LEAGUE v. BOARD OF SUPERVISORS

Supreme Court of Michigan
355 Mich. 305, 94 N.W.2d 875 (1959)

KELLY, JUSTICE.

The Oakland county board of supervisors decided on a site and commenced plans for the construction of a new and adequate court house. No one challenges the fact that a new court house was necessary.

Plaintiff, a voluntary, nonpartisan association of taxpayers and electors of Oakland county, filed its bill of complaint asking the court to decree:

. . . .
C. That amounts in excess of constitutional and statutory limitations for the purchase of land and the construction of public buildings without the approval of the electors, have been heretofore included by defendants in various county budgets. . . .

In its bill of complaint, plaintiff does not by this action impugn the personal honesty or integrity of the members of defendant board, but does question any legal authority for their official action.

An extensive hearing was held and Hon. Herman Dehnke, circuit judge sitting in Oakland county, ruled: . . . 3) that the moneys belonging to the general fund were unlawfully placed in the building fund.

Defendant, board of supervisors, and defendant-intervenor, South Oakland County Bar Association, appealed from the ruling that . . . moneys belonging to the general fund were unlawfully placed in the building fund. . . .

The attorney general, as plaintiff-intervenor and appellee, files a brief stating that the people are only concerned with the following problems: 1) Does article 8, section 10, of the Michigan Constitution, which limits raising of money by taxation or borrowing, for the construction or repair of public buildings or bridges to 1/10 of a mill also limit the amount that can be spent or accumulated from sources that properly should be used to reduce the tax revenue; and 2) are [the statutes quoted below] unconstitutional?
. . . .

Question No. 4: "Does article 8, section 10, of the Michigan Constitution, which limits raising of money by taxation or borrowing 'for the construction or repair of public buildings or bridges' to 1/10 of a mill, also limit the amount that can be spent or accumulated from sources other than direct taxation?"

August 3, 1954, a special election, pursuant to a resolution of the board of supervisors, was held and the following proposals were submitted:

1.—Shall the county borrow $4,500,000 to pay the cost of erecting a county building in the city of Pontiac to house the courts and general county offices?

2.—Shall the limitation on the total amount of taxes be increased by 1/20 of 1% for the purpose of paying principal and interest on bonds to pay the cost of erecting a county building in the city of Pontiac, Michigan, to house the courts and county offices?

Oakland county voters approved the bond issue, but defeated the increase of millage.

The board again submitted the question of increasing the millage at the general election of November 2, 1954, but again the millage proposal was defeated.

The board considered the creation of a county authority and a revenue bond issue but, on advice of the county financial expert, abandoned the plan.

The board of supervisors then decided to proceed toward the construction of the court house, using the balance in the building fund, allocating to the building fund miscellaneous county revenues, and continuing the 1/10 mill property tax, and the board employed an architect. The county's plan of financing is described by appellant county as "a pay-as-you go, piecemeal plan which would be financed with the surpluses on hand plus current receipts." This plan, however, was brought to a halt on the 20th day of November, 1956, when appellee instituted this action.

During the past 10 years, out of an appropriated surplus on hand, the board of supervisors has erected the following county buildings: an addition to the infirmary, two juvenile cottages, an office building, social service building, medical center, dog pound, a market, and a children's clinic, at a cost of $2,192,716.70. Appellee admits all of these buildings were necessary.

During this 10-year period only $528,303.70 was derived from the 1/10 mill tax, and the board of supervisors met the needed moneys, approximately 1½ million dollars, by using the unexpended balance that remained at the end of each year. Appellee claims this financial plan does not change the fact that it was derived from taxation; that continued annual underestimate of miscellaneous revenue was to increase the county tax levy by the amount of the annual surplus; that the surplus miscellaneous revenues could not be expended by the board without authority of the electors.

. . . .

Article 8, section 10, of the Constitution, reads:

> The board of supervisors of any county may in any 1 year levy a tax of 1/10 of 1 mill on the assessed valuation of said county for the construction or repair of public buildings or bridges, or may borrow an equal sum for such purposes; . . . but no greater sum shall be raised for such purposes in any county in any 1 year, unless submitted to the electors of the county and approved by a majority of those voting thereon.

Similar limitations are found in the statutes. . . .

Appellants, endeavoring to justify the use of funds accumulated from sources other than direct taxation, contend that the word "raised" as used in article 8, section 10, of the Constitution, means "raised by taxation," and cites from 36 Words and Phrases, p. 79, as follows:

> Words "to raise money," as applied to municipality, commonly mean to raise by taxation. *Dowling v. Board of Assessors of City of Boston,* 168 N.E. 73, 75, 268 Mass. 480.

. . . .

Appellants contend that neither article 8, section 10, nor any other section, of the Constitution places any limitation upon the expenditure of miscellaneous or nontax derived revenues, and, therefore, the legislature had the right to provide for use of said funds for county building and that the legislature so provided by P.A. 1943, No. 177, . . . and, also, by P.A. 1923, No. 118. . . .

Some portion of these transferred funds came from surpluses in other tax-raised brackets, but the great bulk of these miscellaneous receipts consisted of the statutory fees paid to the county clerk, treasurer, register of deeds, sheriff, probate and circuit courts, and receipts of other county departments or activities, including children's center, contagious hospital and juvenile home, all in very substantial amounts. . . .

[The supreme court then reversed the trial court on the statutory issue and held that the legislation gave the county the right to use accumulated surplus for building purposes. — Eds.]

The main question, therefore, centers down to this: Did the legislature have the constitutional right to grant this power to the board of supervisors?

In the early case of *Attorney General v. Preston,* 1885, 56 Mich. 177, 22 N.W. 261, this Court established that the legislative power of the people through their agent, the legislature, is limited only by the Constitution, which is not a grant of power, but a limitation on the exercise of power; and, secondly, that this Court will not declare a statute unconstitutional unless it is plain that it violates some provisions of the Constitution and the constitutionality of the act will be supported by all possible presumptions not clearly inconsistent with the language and the subject matter.

In *Huron-Clinton Metropolitan Authority v. Boards of Supervisors,* 300 Mich. 1, 1 N.W.2d 430, we stated: 1) That the State legislature is the repository of all legislative power subject only to limitations and restrictions imposed by the State or Federal Constitutions as constitutional provisions are to be regarded as limitations on State legislatures and not a grant of power to them; 2) That in passing upon the constitutionality of State legislation, it is necessary to point out in the Constitution of the State the limitations which have been placed by the people through the Constitution upon the power of the legislature to act, before our Court will declare the enactment unconstitutional; 3) That the advisability or wisdom of statutory enactments, which are not violative of the constitutional provisions, is a matter for legislative consideration and not for this Court.

Do the words of article 8, section 10, of the State Constitution, authorizing the board of supervisors to in any one year levy a tax of 1/10 of 1 mill for the construction or repair of public buildings prevent the legislature from enacting that the board, without submitting the same to a vote of the electors, has the right and power to authorize annually the expenditure from any funds on hand not raised by taxation a sum not in excess of 1 mill of the assessed valuation of the county for the purpose of constructing public buildings, and that the board is authorized and empowered to create and establish a fund for setting aside and accumulating moneys to be used for acquiring, constructing, extending, altering and repairing public buildings?

This question has been presented to this Court for the first time. We agree with Judge Dehnke that our opinion will have far-reaching results for other counties besides Oakland. We set forth the following paragraph from his opinion:

> The problem is one that has become acute because of the pressure from every side for appropriations to support numberless good causes out of limited funds, and pressure from other directions to keep tax burdens within reason. But we must reckon also with the human tendency which sometimes causes public officials, confident that their own means of information and judgment are superior, to come to look upon legal and constitutional limitations on official power, such as having to ask the voters for specific authorization or approval, as irksome shackles, tending only to impede the efficient administration of public business, which should therefore be ignored so far as possible, and must otherwise be endured with as much patience and forbearance as can be mustered. Nothing said in this opinion should be construed as reflecting on the motive and intentions of defendant boards. What the case turns on is the question of authority — were the actions complained of within the limits of legal and constitutional powers.

. . . .

Applying principles from the earliest decision to the latest, we conclude that there is no constitutional inhibition preventing the legislature from allowing the board of supervisors to use the surplus accumulated from what the trial court aptly described as "miscellaneous receipts." However, moneys cannot be used for building purposes which were raised or accumulated through direct taxation beyond the 1/10 of 1 mill constitutional limitation and we, therefore, order that the board refrain from using any of said funds for the contemplated purpose of building the court house.

....

Reversed in part and affirmed in part. No costs, a public question being involved.

DETHMERS, CARR and EDWARDS, JJ., concurred with KELLY, J.

[Black, Smith and Voelker, JJ., concurred except with respect to question no. 4.]

Comments: 1. The principle of plenary state legislative power is so basic that the litany of which it is a part is recited in countless decisions: the state constitution, unlike the federal, is a limitation on, not a grant of power to the state legislature; the state legislature possesses all powers not specifically denied it by the federal or state constitution; legislative enactments are presumed valid unless clearly shown to violate a constitutional proscription. Much of the time the recitation appears to be primarily background and orientation but does not directly affect the outcome of the case. *See, e.g., State ex inf. Danforth ex rel. Farmers' Electric Cooperative v. State Environmental Improvement Authority,* 518 S.W.2d 68 (Mo. 1975). In upholding the validity of the Missouri act creating a pollution control financing agency, the court set the stage by repeating the limit-not-grant series of principles; but the real challenge to the statute was not a lack of power to legislate but rather a conflict with specific constitutional provisions (such as the prohibition on the lending of public credit to a private entity). In some cases, however, the fact that constitutional language does not describe the full extent of the legislature's power is critical to the result. The *Oakland County* case appears to be one.

2. Constitutional provisions often are ambiguous and incomplete. A familiar rule of statutory construction, *expressio unius est exclusio alterius,* holds that a delegation of power must be found within the statute: the mention of one thing implies the exclusion of another.

This strict construction rule may not apply to constitutional delegations of authority. *Dean v. Kuchel,* 230 P.2d 811 (Cal. 1951). The constitution authorized the legislature to delegate fish and game powers to a constitutionally created Fish and Game Commission. The legislature adopted a statute creating a separate board to manage a coordinated fish and game conservation program.

The statute was upheld. An argument that the constitution only authorized the delegation of authority over fish and game to the commission was rejected. The "limitation versus grant" rule was cited, and the court added that any doubts about the legislature's authority should be resolved in its favor. The doctrine of *expressio unius* did not apply to constitutional language.

Later chapters review the traditional rule that authority delegated to municipal corporations by the legislature must be strictly construed. Why the difference? Is the municipal power strict construction rule consistent with the legislative plenary power rule?

3. The limitation versus grant analysis has been applied to conflicts in jurisdiction between state agencies. In *National Education Ass'n-Fort Scott v. Board of Education,* 592 P.2d 463 (Kan. 1979), the legislature assigned negotiation and mediation responsibilities in teacher strikes to the state Secretary of Human Resources. The board claimed that the statute violated a constitutional provision which delegated to it the "general supervision" of the schools.

The court rejected this argument. It applied the limitation versus grant doctrine to hold that it need not find constitutional authority for a statute but need only determine whether it "clearly violates" a constitutional prohibition:

> The authority granted to the secretary in no way conflicts with the basic mission of the State Board of Education. The board's mission is to equalize and promote the quality of education for the students of this state by such things as statewide accreditation and certification of teachers and schools.... The functions of the Secretary of Human Resources under the act are limited and confined to professional negotiations, an area not considered by this court to be within the basic mission of the public schools of this state.

Id. at 466.

Compare *Pacific Legal Foundation v. Brown,* 624 P.2d 1215 (Cal. 1981), holding that a statute conferring collective bargaining authority on the governor did not conflict with the state's merit civil service system, which was required by the constitution. The court relied on the limitation versus grant principle in its decision. How could the collective bargaining statute conflict with a merit civil service? Why is the limitation versus grant rule relevant to a resolution of this conflict?

In cases involving the state's fiscal powers — the power to tax or to issue debt — the principle that legislative power is limited, not granted, by the constitution can play an important role. Many state constitutions, particularly those that were adopted in the last half of the nineteenth century when distrust of state legislatures was widespread, contain specific and occasionally detailed provisions describing the power to tax and issue debt. As the need for additional and new forms of revenue arose, the effect of these constitutional revenue provisions took on importance.

INDEPENDENT SCHOOL DISTRICT, CLASS A, NO. 1, CASSIA COUNTY v. PFOST

Supreme Court of Idaho
51 Idaho 240, 4 P.2d 893 (1931)

McNaughton, J.

In this case the school district seeks to enjoin the commissioner of law enforcement of the state of Idaho and Burley Home Oil Company from collecting from it the gasoline tax provided for in chapter 172 of the 1923 Session Laws and amendatory acts.

The defendants demurred to the complaint. The demurrer was overruled. The defendants not desiring to plead further, judgment in conformity with the allegations and prayer of the complaint was entered against them. They appeal.

. . . .

The purpose of the law and the character of the tax are disclosed by the following excerpts from the act as amended:

> Section 2. . . . That in addition to the taxes now provided for by law, each and every dealer, as defined in this Act, who is now engaged or who may hereafter engage in his own name, or in the name of others, or in the name of his representatives or agents in this State, in the sale of motor fuels herein defined, shall, not later than the fifteenth day of each calendar month beginning with the second calendar month after this Act has become effective, render a statement to the Commissioner of Law Enforcement of the State of Idaho of all motor fuels sold and/or used by him or them in the State of Idaho during the preceding calendar month, and pay a license tax of five cents per gallon on all motor fuels as shown by such statement in the manner and within the time hereinafter provided. . . .

. . . .

Section 4, chapter 172, of the Session Laws of 1923, as amended by section 1, chapter 68, of the Session Laws of 1931, provides that the taxes collected under the act shall be paid into the state highway fund.

The points raised involve the construction of the following provisions of the state Constitution:

Sec. 2, art. VII. The legislature shall provide such revenue as may be needful, by levying a tax by valuation, so that every person or corporation shall pay a tax in proportion to the value of his, her, or its property, except as in this article hereinafter otherwise provided. The legislature may also impose a license tax (both upon natural persons and upon corporations, other than municipal, doing business in this state); also a per capita tax: Provided, The legislature may exempt a limited amount of improvements upon land from taxation.

[The court first addressed the question of whether a school district was exempted from paying the gas tax in light of the constitutional provision that authorized the imposition of license taxes on natural persons and corporations but not on municipal corporations. The court's answer was that the tax, although denominated a license tax by the legislature, was in reality an excise tax. — Eds.]

In Idaho the Legislature was confronted with this condition. It found a demand for better roads incident to the use of rapid motor-driven vehicles. It found an extensive use of gasoline on its highways in this traffic. Without affecting the legality of that use, it imposed a tax upon the use, and adopted a method of collecting the tax without exacting any license or permit. The tax having no relation to any license granted or required, it is in no sense a license tax limited by the Constitution to persons and corporations doing business in the state.

3. In imposing taxes, is the Legislature limited to property taxes, license taxes, and per capita taxes? It is sometimes said that the constitutional methods of taxation are those mentioned in section 2, art. 7, of the Constitution, but this is misleading, for the Legislature is not limited by the Constitution to the methods mentioned.

This court in *Idaho Power & Light Co. v. Blomquist,* 26 Idaho 222, 141 P. 1083, 1088, Ann. Cas. 1916E, 282, said: "The Constitution of the state of Idaho is a limitation upon the legislative power in all matters of legislation, and is not a grant of power. The Legislature has plenary power in all matters of legislation, except as limited by the Constitution."

In *Williams v. Baldridge,* 48 Idaho 618, 284 P. 203, 206, the court said: "The power of the Legislature to tax or to exempt from taxation is plenary, save only as it may be limited by the Constitution of this state or of the United States. Unless, therefore, this right has been limited by either the Constitution of this state or the Constitution of the United States, the Legislature unquestionably had a right to exempt from taxation certain property of power companies in this state," and in *Achenbach v. Kincaid,* 25 Idaho 768, 140 P. 529, 533, said: "As to the question of taxation: The Legislature possesses plenary power, except as such power may be limited or restricted by the Constitution. It is not necessary that the Constitution shall contain a grant of power to the Legislature to deal with the question of taxation. It is sufficient proof of its power if there be found in the Constitution no prohibition against what the Legislature has attempted to do."
. . .

The tax in question is by a method other than those mentioned in section 2, art. 7, of the Constitution, but is not on that account unconstitutional, because it is not necessary that the Constitution expressly authorize the Legislature to enact each and every kind of tax adopted by it. An act is legal when the Constitution contains no prohibition against it. . . .

It follows that the judgment must be reversed, with directions to sustain the demurrer.

Lee, C.J. and Budge, Givens, and Varian, JJ., concur.

Comments: 1. *See also Mercantile Incorporating Co. v. Junkin,* 123 N.W. 1055 (Neb. 1909). The State constitution authorized the state legislature to tax sixteen designated occupations. The Nebraska legislature had enacted a statute requiring all corporations doing business in the state to obtain a state occupation permit and to pay an annual occupation fee. The court rejected the argument that "the enumeration of 16 occupations upon which the Legislature is authorized to impose an occupation tax 'by the universal rule of interpretation excludes by necessary implication all occupations not enumerated.' " *Id.* at 1055. It found the better rule to be that "in the absence of constitutional limitations, every species of property within the jurisdiction of the state, all privileges and franchises existing, and every trade or vocation exercised therein may be taxed by the Legislature for the support of the state." *Ibid.*

2. Constitutional debt limitations for both state and local governments are frequently written in the language of negative command, e.g., "no debt shall be issued except . . .". The exceptions are usually referendum approval or a requirement that the debt not exceed a stated percentage of local assessed valuation for property taxation. When debt limitations prove unduly burdensome, as they frequently do, state legislatures have sometimes sought ways to avoid them. The principle that state legislative power is plenary except for specific constitutional prohibitions has often served to support the validity of financing methods that do not precisely fit the constitutional mold.

In *In re Request for Advisory Opinion,* 254 N.W.2d 544 (Mich. 1977), a statute authorized the state to lease property from a state building authority and to contract for the "true rental value" of the property. This type of financing arrangement is common. Lease payments are used to retire debt issued to finance the property.

The constitution provided that "[n]o evidence of state indebtedness shall be issued except for debts authorized pursuant to this constitution." The court held that the lease payments did not fall within this provision, holding that the only purpose of the constitutional debt limitation was "to limit the power of the Legislature to borrow money and issue evidence of the debt thereby incurred."

In *State ex rel. Capitol Addition Building Commission v. Connelly,* 46 P.2d 1097 (N.M. 1935), the issue was the validity of a state debenture to finance an addition to the state capitol, to be financed by an additional fee on civil actions filed in the state courts. The New Mexico constitution provided that no debt could be issued by the state unless supported by an annual tax levy and submitted to referendum. The court decided that the constitutional provision clearly contemplated a debt repayable by resort to general property taxation. Because the debenture in issue was payable solely from a special fund, the court upheld the statute despite the negative command of the constitutional language.

3. Application of the principle of plenary legislative power may be more troublesome than is sometimes acknowledged. Some state constitutions set out qualifications for holding office, such as age and residence qualifications. May the state legislature, in the exercise of its plenary power, impose additional qualifications? In *Thomas v. State ex rel. Cobb,* 58 So. 2d 173 (Fla. 1952), the court answered that question in the negative. The Florida constitution required the legislature to provide for the election of a county superintendent of public instruction. No qualifications were specified. The Florida legislature enacted a statute requiring that every candidate for that office, as a condition of eligibility, hold a Florida graduate certificate based on graduation from a four-year course of higher education. The court, while conceding that the constitution is a limitation on power rather than a grant of power, nevertheless held that the legislature was prohibited from adding to the qualifications for the office of county superintendent. It relied on another rule of construction that when the constitution prescribes the manner in which a thing shall be done, it impliedly prohibits its being done in a different manner.

Did the court apply a strict construction rule? Can this rule be reconciled with the more traditional limit — not grant doctrine? For a contrary holding see *Perry v. Lawrence*

County Election Commission, 411 S.W.2d 538 (Tenn.), *cert. denied,* 389 U.S. 821 (1967).

4. The virtually unchallenged proposition that the state legislature possesses all powers not specifically prohibited by the national or state constitution leaves several questions unanswered. For one, does the legislature's plenary power extend only to those matters traditionally legislative — e.g., taxation, police power, maintenance of schools — and do the presumptions favoring existence of legislative power fade when the legislature begins to encroach on executive or judicial matters? If that is so, what is the line between the three reservoirs of power? For example, in *State ex rel. McCormack v. Foley,* 118 N.W.2d 211 (Wis. 1962), the question was the assignment of a nonconstitutional judge to a constitutional court. When the court found no express constitutional prohibition against the legislature's authorization of the assignment, it upheld the act. But why should the assignment of judges be considered a legislative matter at all? The Wisconsin constitution provided that the judicial power was vested in designated courts, including the circuit courts, and the determination of who was entitled to hear circuit court cases could well have been considered part of the judicial power. (It should be noted, however, that several constitutional provisions dealing with the judiciary contemplated legislative action to implement so that it is probably not surprising that the question of whether this assignment was a legislative or judicial matter did not occur to the court.)

In *American Federation of State, County, & Municipal Employees, AFL-CIO v. State Department of Roads,* 263 N.W.2d 643 (Neb. 1978), a state Court of Industrial Relations was granted jurisdiction over collective bargaining in state agencies. An argument was made that the state statute authorizing the court violated the constitutional provision granting the heads of state executive departments the power to appoint and remove all employees. The court upheld the legislation, noting that the statute creating the court did not change "the character of control by the executive branch." Why not?

Compare *Sibert v. Garrett,* 246 S.W. 455 (Ky. 1922), in which the court invalidated a statute authorizing the legislature to appoint members of the state highway commission. It held that the plenary power rule applied only to legislative acts. The legislature "may not perform . . . executive or judicial acts, except in such instances as may be expressly or by necessary implication directed or permitted by the Constitution." Any other holding, the court said, would "destroy the separation of the powers of government into the three great departments."

5. Is the state constitution a limitation rather than a grant of executive power to the executive officers, and of judicial power to the courts? In *State ex rel. Harvey v. Wright,* 158 S.W. 823 (Mo. 1913), a case in which the legislature had created an office and attached specific qualifications to the governor's appointments to the office, the court said: "Our Constitution by its provisions may be said to be a limitation upon the powers of the legislative department, but a grant of powers to the executive branch." *Id.* at 825. The office in this case being one created by the legislature and the governor's power to appoint the members being one conferred by the legislature, the legislature also had the power to attach such conditions and qualifications as it saw fit.

Compare *In re Petition of Idaho State Federation of Labor,* 272 P.2d 707 (Idaho 1954) (dissenting opinion of Justice Taylor). The issue in the case was whether the state supreme court could take an appeal from the attorney general's designation of a title to be used on the election ballot to describe a "right-to-work" initiative proposal. The majority concluded that the statutes establishing its appellate jurisdiction did not include this matter, but that it could review it on writ of certiorari. Justice Taylor disagreed that the court had no jurisdiction to hear the matter as an appeal. Noting that the judicial power is vested in the courts "without any limitation or reservation whatever," *id.* at 713, he said:

> "The judicial power" means all the judicial power and cannot be construed to mean only a part thereof. Nor can it mean all of the power, subject to reservations or restrictions nowhere expressed. The word "vested" must be given its commonly accepted meaning. It cannot be construed to mean that the power referred to, or any part of it, is suspended, withheld, or reserved. Accordingly the courts are free to exercise any power properly belonging to the judicial department, subject only to the limitations contained in the federal and state constitutions.

Is there any reason to distinguish between the three branches of government?

6. Does the principle of plenary legislative power apply to units of local government? "Inherent powers, such as are conceded to appertain to the state legislature, are usually denied to the local legislative body." 4 McQuillin, Municipal Corporations § 13.03 at 510 (3d ed. 1979 rev. vol.). *See also* Chapter 3.

C. LOCAL GOVERNMENT

1. LOCAL GOVERNMENT STRUCTURE

A basic fact about local governments in the United States is their great diversity with respect to such matters as legal nature, size, area, functions, and organizations, both within and among states. . . . [Local governments] may be divided between municipal corporations and quasi-municipal corporations. Or, on the basis of the number of functions, a differentiation may be made between general-purpose governments, such as municipalities and counties, providing a range of services and special-purpose governments, such as school districts, limited to one or a few services.

Advisory Commission on Intergovernmental Relations, State and Local Roles in the Federal System 227 (1982).

A brief primer on local government types and functions will help provide a sense of orientation. Note that the "quasi-municipal" versus "municipal" distinction made in the Advisory Commission report is widely used but does not always have legal significance. Cities and other incorporated local governments are called "municipal" corporations because they exercise local functions. Counties and townships are called "quasi-municipal" because they carry out state functions at the local level as well as exercising local government powers. For discussion of these concepts see O. Reynolds, Local Government Law § 6 (1982).

Counties. The county was well established in seventeenth century England and was brought to the United States as a governmental form by the colonists. As the Advisory Commission points out, counties are "first of all local units for state purposes." *Id.* at 236. Practically all counties nationwide provide a number of essential statewide services at the local level. These services include property tax assessment and collection, courts of general jurisdiction, elections, road maintenance, and detention and police services.

In recent decades, counties have expanded their functions to include urban services, especially in metropolitan areas. These services include public health, social services, fire protection, airports, and land use controls. Counties also had traditionally provided services only in their unincorporated areas. This pattern also is changing. Especially in metropolitan areas, counties provide services throughout their area, including incorporated municipalities. This expansion has occurred because counties provide an attractive alternative source of urban services in a time when municipalities face serious problems in meeting constantly expanding needs generated by urbanization. Counties also provide economies of scale, and have a more extensive and varied tax base. Over 125 counties in metropolitan areas are "urban" counties serving large populations.

Most counties have an elected board or commission, which also serves as the executive body. Urban counties may have an elected or appointed chief executive. *See* H. Duncombe, Modern County Government (1977).

Municipalities. "A municipality is defined . . . as a political subdivision within which a municipal corporation has been established to provide general local government for a specific population concentration in a defined area." Advisory Commission, *supra,* at 240. Municipal corporations are usually termed a city or village, but may be called towns (except in New England) or boroughs (except in Alaska).

Municipalities are the units of local government which are authorized to provide the most comprehensive set of services. They dominate local government expenditure in highways, police and fire protection, parking and libraries, housing and urban redevelopment, and sewerage and sanitation. In practice, many municipalities are quite small, and may provide a limited number of services. Counties may provide more extensive services than municipalities in some metropolitan areas.

Municipalities have three common types of organization. Under one form, voters elect a municipal commission which also serves as the executive body. The mayor-council form also is common, although mayors have less executive power than state governors. Another form retains the mayor and council but confers administrative responsibility on a city manager. Under this form, the mayor does not have significant executive power.

Townships. Twenty states in the northeast and north central states have 17,000 local governments organized as townships. Townships are not incorporated. Where they exist, they usually cover all of the county area outside the incorporated municipalities, and in some states they also overlap incorporated areas. They include rural areas as well as unincorporated settlements. Townships are known as "towns" in New York and the New England states.

The northeastern and some north central states are "strong township" states. Townships in these states have powers and functions not unlike those conferred on municipalities. The other north central states are "rural township" states in which townships have limited functions, such as road maintenance and police protection, and do not usually have legislative powers. The rural townships have been declining in importance.

Special districts. The special district is the most rapidly expanding local government type. Special districts are organized to perform one or at most a few public functions, and are usually established by local action under state enabling legislation. Two thirds of all special districts are in rural areas. Special districts have been popular because they provide an alternative to municipal incorporation, can provide services where they are needed, and have independent fiscal powers. Multipurpose special districts in metropolitan areas can also provide a more acceptable alternative to metropolitan government, and many serve an entire metropolitan area. Special districts usually raise revenue through user fees or special assessments. They do not usually have the power to tax, or legislative powers.

Most special districts are single-function districts. Fire protection, water supply, soil conservation, housing and urban renewal, and drainage are the services most usually provided.

Special districts are either independent or dependent. Independent districts are governed by appointed or elected boards. Dependent special districts are organized by a parent municipality, which also appoints its board. A local public housing authority is an example.

School districts. School districts are a form of special district, but are considered separately because they are universal and because of the importance of the educational function in local government. Their importance is underlined by their share of local expenditure. School districts account for over one third of all governmental expenditure at the local level.

Like other special districts, school districts are either independent or dependent. The vast majority of school districts are independently organized, and may serve more than one municipality. Dependent school districts are agencies of other local governments, such as counties or municipalities, and serve only their local government jurisdiction. In metropolitan areas, the central city is usually served by a single school district while several school districts may cover the suburban areas. These separate identities may reinforce fiscal and other disparities in metropolitan areas.

Unlike other special districts, school districts have declined rapidly in recent years, from 108,500 in 1942 to 15,000 in 1982. This decline has been the result almost entirely of school district consolidations in rural areas.

Local government trends. The table that follows indicates trends in local government numbers in recent years. The significant trend is the stability in numbers of most local government units. The exception is the continuing and rapid growth in special districts. Local government incorporations have been moderate in numbers, although 1,000 municipal governments incorporated between 1962 and 1982.

LOCAL GOVERNMENT UNITS: 1962 TO 1982

	1982	1977	1962
Local governments	82,637	79,862	91,186
County	3,041	3,042	3,043
Municipal	19,083	18,862	18,000
Township	16,748	16,822	17,142
School district	15,032	15,174	34,678
Special district	28,733	25,962	18,323

Source: U.S. Bureau of Census, 1982 Census of Governments, Preliminary Rep. No. 1, Governmental Units in 1982 (1982).

Local government patterns. The historical development of local government in this country provides an important perspective on local government patterns. This country entered the twentieth century with a simple local government model. Counties were the basic building block, and provided essential but minimum governmental services throughout the state. Municipalities organized to provide a more complete range of urban services as rural areas urbanized. Municipalities expanded through annexation as their fringe areas urbanized.

This simple pattern changed with extensive suburbanization. Central cities in metropolitan areas could not annex quickly enough to keep up with urbanization, and in some states annexation statutes imposed legal impediments to extensive annexation programs. Permissive municipal incorporation laws led to the extensive incorporation of new municipalities in suburban areas. The central city became surrounded by a checkerboard of suburban municipalities that cut off all opportunities of growth through annexation. Annexation was possible only by suburban municipalities on the urban edge. In many metropolitan areas, the county organized as an urban government to provide urban services in outlying unincorporated areas.

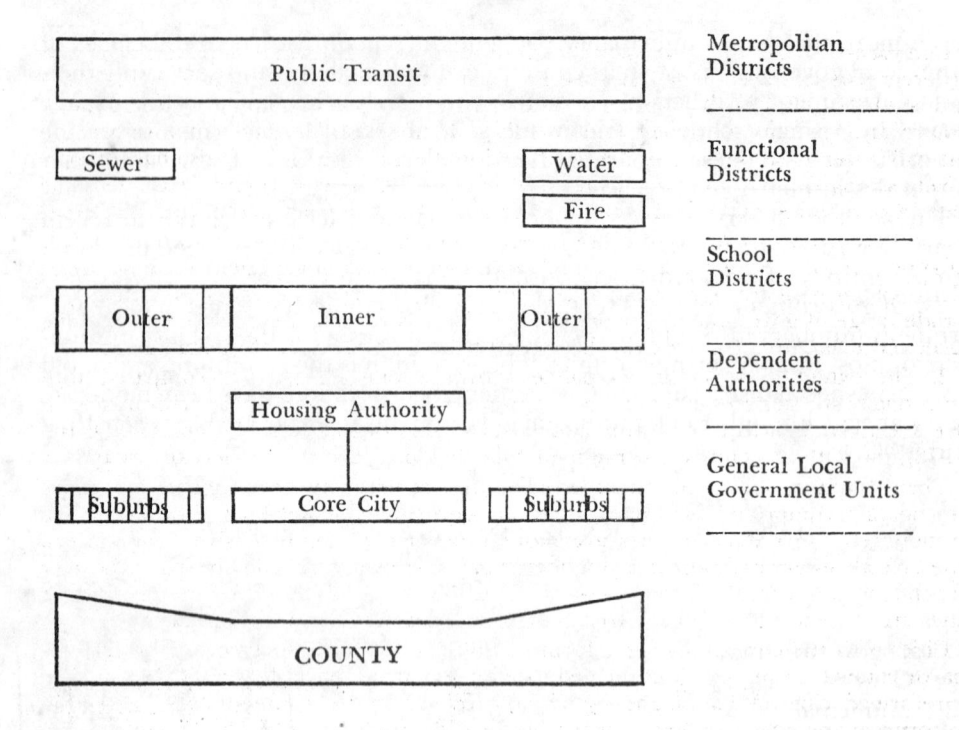

```
┌─────────────────────────────────────┐     Metropolitan
│          Public Transit             │     Districts
└─────────────────────────────────────┘     ─────────────

  ┌────────┐                  ┌────────┐    Functional
  │ Sewer  │                  │ Water  │    Districts
  └────────┘                  └────────┘
                              ┌────────┐
                              │  Fire  │
                              └────────┘    ─────────────

                                             School
  ┌──────┬──────────────┬──────┐             Districts
  │Outer │    Inner     │Outer │
  └──────┴──────────────┴──────┘             ─────────────

              ┌──────────────┐               Dependent
              │Housing Authority│            Authorities
              └──────┬───────┘
                     │                       ─────────────
  ┌──────┐    ┌──────────────┐    ┌──────┐   General Local
  │Suburbs│    │  Core City   │    │Suburbs│  Government Units
  └──────┘    └──────────────┘    └──────┘
                                             ─────────────

  ┌─────────────────────────────────────┐
  │              COUNTY                 │
  └─────────────────────────────────────┘
```

This balkanization pattern is portrayed in schematic form in the diagram. Although the diagram is oversimplified, it illustrates the distribution of local government entities which is typical in metropolitan areas around the country. The critical point made by the diagram is the absence of horizontal linkages among governmental units at the local level.

This fragmented local government structure is reinforced by the strong vertical links between local governments and the federal and state agencies which provide assistance for local programs. Each state and federal assistance program is functionally specialized. Assistance is provided by a functional agency at the federal or state level to a comparable functional agency at the local level. A special district organized to provide wastewater treatment facilities, for example, receives construction grants from the federal Environmental Protection Agency. Regional planning organizations required by federal assistance legislation can coordinate federal assistance programs, but they have not been remarkably effective.

Problems in intergovernmental coordination at the local level have prompted a governmental reform movement that calls for the integration and consolidation of local government in metropolitan areas. The reform movement has had some successes in some metropolitan areas, but it has not led to the wholesale reform of local government structure.

Comments: 1. As the discussion has indicated, local government patterns vary in different parts of the country. The local government pattern is least complex in the south and southwest, and in the southern middle Atlantic region beginning with Maryland. County governments are strong, and townships do not exist. Metropolitan areas also are less balkanized in some parts of the south and southwest. The midwest also has comparatively strong county government, but the intermediate township layer exists in some states. Counties are not as well organized in the border area from Kentucky to Arkansas.

Local government patterns are more complicated in the northeast and upper middle Atlantic region. Counties are not important units of local government in these areas. Metropolitan areas are highly balkanized. The towns and townships, as noted earlier, have a wide range of government functions. These local government entities are often quite small and make up a complex checker-board pattern in many metropolitan areas.

2. The extent to which municipalities provide comprehensive as compared with functionally specialized services is an important indicator of municipal performance. In Dye & Garcia, *Structure, Function, and Policy in American Cities,* 14 URB. AFF. Q. 103 (1978), the authors contrast the range of functions provided by a variety of city types.

Their findings show, not unexpectedly, that central city governments are more functionally comprehensive than suburban governments. Regional differences are pronounced. Northeastern cities are more functionally comprehensive than western cities. Northeastern cities also have higher per capita expenditures and taxes and a heavier dependency on federal aid than western cities. Why would this be so? Older and larger cities are also more functionally comprehensive than newer and smaller cities.

Cities with the council-manager form of government are reformed. Cities with the mayor-council form are unreformed. Reformed cities have fewer functions than unreformed cities. What might explain the difference? The authors also note that "reformism and specialization appear to reduce the responsiveness of aggregate taxing and spending levels to the social and ethnic character of the city's population."

3. When reviewing the materials in this book, consider the extent to which local government structure and performance should influence court decisions. For instance, on the issue of delegation of power to local governments, should a court take a strong or weak approach toward delegation of power in states where local governments in metropolitan areas are balkanized? In a state without counties where townships have important government powers? In states where local governments are "unresponsive" to social and ethnic demands?

2. THE CONSTITUTIONAL STATUS OF LOCAL GOVERNMENT

The doctrine of plenary state legislative power means that the state legislature possesses full authority to provide for the organization and allocation of power to local government units. Legislative plenary power is limited only by particular provisions of the state constitution and, of course, by the federal constitution, notably the equal protection and due process clauses. An important inquiry in state and local government law is to explore how this theory is applied in practice as well as to ask whether local governments can make constitutional claims against state legislation. The cases and materials that follow begin this inquiry.

Town of Godfrey v. City of Alton, 338 N.E.2d 890 (Ill. App. 1975), illustrates a typical case in which these questions arose. A statute required the consent of an existing municipality before a new municipality could incorporate within one and a half miles of the existing municipality's limits. The court held:

> We do not find such requirement repugnant to either our Constitution or the United States Constitution . . . . Rather, we find the consent requirement to be constitutionally permissible under the well recognized power of the state to control the formation of political subdivisions within its boundaries.

Id. at 895.

HUNTER v. CITY OF PITTSBURGH

United States Supreme Court
207 U.S. 161 (1907)

. . . .

MR. JUSTICE MOODY . . . delivered the opinion of the court.

The plaintiffs in error seek a reversal of the judgment of the Supreme Court of Pennsylvania, which affirmed a decree of a lower court, directing the consolidation of the cities of Pittsburgh and Allegheny. This decree was entered by authority of an act of the General Assembly of that State, after proceedings taken in conformity with its requirements. The act authorized the consolidation of two cities, situated with reference to each other as Pittsburgh and Allegheny are, if upon an election the majority of the votes cast in the territory comprised within the limits of both cities favor the consolidation, even though, as happened in this instance, a majority of the votes cast in one of the cities oppose it. The procedure prescribed by the act is that after a petition filed by one of the cities in the Court of Quarter Sessions, and a hearing upon that petition, that court, if the petition and proceedings are found to be regular and in conformity with the act, shall order an election. If the election shows a majority of the votes cast to be in favor of the consolidation, the court "shall enter a decree annexing and consolidating the lesser city . . . with the greater city." The act provides, in considerable detail, for the effect of the consolidation upon the debts, obligations, claims and property of the constituent cities; grants rights of citizenship to the citizens of those cities in the consolidated city; enacts that "except as herein otherwise provided, all the property . . . and rights and privileges . . . vested in or belonging to either of said cities . . . prior to or at the time of the annexation, shall be vested in and owned by the consolidated or united city," and establishes the form of government of the new city. This procedure was followed by the filing of a petition by the City of Pittsburgh; by an election in which the majority of all the votes cast were in the affirmative, although the majority of all the votes cast by the voters of Allegheny were in the negative, and by a decree of the court uniting the two cities.

Prior to the hearing upon the petition the plaintiffs in error, who were citizens, voters, owners of property and taxpayers in Allegheny, filed twenty-two exceptions to the petition. These exceptions were disposed of adversely to the exceptants by the Court of Quarter Sessions, and the action of that court was successively affirmed by the Superior and Supreme courts of the State. The case is here upon writ of error, and the assignment of errors alleges that eight errors were committed by the Supreme Court of the State. This assignment of errors is founded upon the dispositions by the state courts of the questions duly raised by the filing of the exceptions under the provisions of the Act of the Assembly.

. . . .

After thus eliminating all questions with which we have no lawful concern, there remain two questions which are within our jurisdiction. There were two claims of rights under the Constitution of the United States which were clearly made in the court below and as clearly denied. They appear in the second and fourth assignments of error. Briefly stated, the assertion in the second assignment of error is that the Act of Assembly impairs the obligation of a contract existing between the City of Allegheny and the plaintiffs in error, that the latter are to be taxed only for the governmental purposes of that city, and that the legislative attempt to subject them to the taxes of the enlarged city violates Article I, section 9, paragraph 10, of the Constitution of the United States. This assignment does not rest upon the theory that the charter of the city is a contract with the State, a proposition frequently denied by this and other courts. It rests upon the novel proposition that there is a contract between the citizens and taxpayers of a municipal corporation and the corporation itself, that the citizens and taxpayers shall be taxed only for the uses of that corporation, and shall not be taxed for the uses of any like corporation with which it may be consolidated. It is not said that the City of Allegheny expressly made any such extraordinary contract, but only that the contract arises out of the relation of the parties to each other. It is difficult to deal with a proposition of this kind except by saying that it is not true. No authority or reason in support of it has been offered to us, and it is utterly inconsistent with the nature of municipal corporations, the purposes for which they are created, and the relation they bear to those who dwell and own property within their limits. This assignment of error is overruled.

Briefly stated, the assertion in the fourth assignment of error is that the Act of Assembly deprives the plaintiffs in error of their property without due process of law, by subjecting it to the burden of the additional taxation which would result from the consolidation. The manner in which the right of due process of law has been violated, as set forth in the first assignment of error and insisted upon in argument, is that the method of voting on the consolidation prescribed in the act has permitted the voters of the larger city to overpower the voters of the smaller city, and compel the union without their consent and against their protest. The precise question thus presented has not been determined by this court. It is important, and, as we have said, not so devoid of merit as to be denied consideration, although its solution by principles long settled and constantly acted upon is not difficult. This court has many times had occasion to consider and decide the nature of municipal corporations, their rights and duties, and the rights of their citizens and creditors.... It would be unnecessary and unprofitable to analyze these decisions or quote from the opinions rendered. We think the following principles have been established by them and have become settled doctrines of this court, to be acted upon wherever they are applicable. Municipal corporations are political subdivisions of the State, created as convenient agencies for exercising such of the governmental powers of the State as may be entrusted to them. For the purpose of executing these powers properly and efficiently they usually are given the power to acquire, hold, and manage personal and real property. The number, nature and duration of the powers conferred upon these corporations and the territory over which they shall be exercised rests in the absolute discretion of the State. Neither their charters, nor any law conferring governmental powers, or vesting in them property to be used for governmental purposes, or authorizing them to hold or manage such property, or exempting them from taxation upon it, constitutes a contract with the State within the meaning of the Federal Constitution. The State, therefore, at its pleasure may modify or withdraw all such powers, may take without compensation such property, hold it itself, or vest it in other agencies, expand or contract the territorial area, unite the whole or a part of it with another municipality, repeal the charter and destroy the corporation. All this may be done, conditionally or unconditionally, with or without the consent of the citizens, or even against their protest. In all these respects the State is supreme, and its legislative body, conforming its action to the state constitution, may do as it will, unrestrained by any provision of the Constitution of the United States. Although the inhabitants and property owners may by such changes suffer inconvenience, and their property may be lessened in value by the burden of increased taxation, or for any other reason, they have no right by contract or otherwise in the unaltered or continued existence of the corporation or its powers, and there is nothing in the Federal Constitution which protects them from these injurious consequences. The power is in the State and those who legislate for the State are alone responsible for any unjust or oppressive exercise of it.

Applying these principles to the case at bar, it follows irresistibly that this assignment of error, so far as it relates to the citizens who are plaintiffs in error, must be overruled.

It will be observed that in describing the absolute power of the State over the property of municipal corporations we have not extended it beyond the property held and used for governmental purposes. Such corporations are sometimes authorized to hold and do hold property for the same purposes that property is held by private corporations or individuals. The distinction between property owned by municipal corporations in their public and governmental capacity and that owned by them in their private capacity, though difficult to define, has been approved by many of the state courts (1 Dillon, Municipal Corporations, 4th ed., sections 66 to 66a, inclusive, and cases cited in note to 48 L.R.A. 465), and it has been held that as to the latter class of property the legislature is not omnipotent. If the distinction is recognized it suggests the question whether property of a municipal corporation owned in its private and proprietary capacity may be taken from it against its will and without compensation. Mr. Dillon says truly that the question has never arisen directly for adjudication in this court. But it and the distinction upon which it is based has several times been noticed. . . . Counsel for plaintiffs in error assert that the City of Allegheny was the owner of property held in its private and proprietary capacity, and insist that the effect of the proceedings under this act was to take its property without compensation and vest it in another corporation, and that thereby the city was deprived of its property without due process of law in violation of the Fourteenth Amendment. But no such question is presented by the record, and there is but a vague suggestion of facts upon which it might have been founded. In the sixth exception there is a recital of facts with a purpose of showing how the taxes of the citizens of Allegheny would be increased by annexation to Pittsburgh. In that connection it is alleged that while Pittsburgh intends to spend large sums of money in the purchase of the water plant of a private company and for the construction of an electric light plant, Allegheny "has improved its streets, established its own system of electric lighting, and established a satisfactory water supply." This is the only reference in the record to the property rights of Allegheny, and it falls far short of a statement that that city holds any property in its private and proprietary capacity. Nor was there any allegation that Allegheny had been deprived of its property without due process of law. The only allegation of this kind is that the taxpayers, plaintiffs in error, were deprived of their property without due process of law because of the increased taxation which would result from the annexation — an entirely different proposition. Nor is the situation varied by the fact that, in the Superior Court, Allegheny was "permitted to intervene and become one of the appellants." The city made no new allegations and raised no new questions, but was content to rest upon the record as it was made up. Moreover, no question of the effect of the act upon private property rights of the City of Allegheny was considered in the opinions in the state courts or suggested by assignment of errors in this court. The question is entirely outside of the record and has no connection with any question which is raised in the record. For these reasons we are without jurisdiction to consider it, ... and neither express nor intimate any opinion upon it.

The judgment is

Affirmed.

Comments: 1. In the New Jersey stream litigation, the cities of Trenton and Newark challenged a New Jersey statute which imposed a charge on the diversion of water from streams in excess of the amount being diverted by these cities on a named day. Trenton urged against the statute a prior grant from the state to take free and without limitation to quantity all the water it required, and claimed that the statute violated the contract clause of the federal constitution. The United States Supreme Court held that municipalities possess no inherent right of local self-government. They are merely departments of the state, which can grant or withdraw powers and privileges as it sees fit. The contract clause did not apply. *City of Trenton v. New Jersey,* 262 U.S. 182 (1923). Newark argued that the basis for allocation of stream water constituted an unreasonable classification. For the reasons given in the *Trenton* case, the equal protection clause was held inapplicable. *City of Newark v. New Jersey,* 262 U.S. 182 (1923).

See also *Williams v. Mayor & City Council,* 289 U.S. 36 (1933). In this case the City of Baltimore challenged, as invalid under the equal protection clause, a state law that had exempted a railroad from general property taxation by the city. Writing for the Court, Justice Cardozo stated clearly that a municipal corporation may assert no privileges or immunities against the state as its creator.

2. Does the *Hunter* case and its progeny cover all varieties of municipal corporations? See *Housing Authority v. Fetzik,* 289 A.2d 658 (R.I. 1972), in which the court held that the housing authority had standing as a "person" to challenge on constitutional grounds a state statute creating a Board of Tenants' Affairs for each housing authority and giving that board the power to hear and determine tenant complaints. "The housing authority is not a political subdivision of the state [but] is one of a large class of corporations created by the government to undertake public enterprises in which the public interests are involved [but is not an instrument] of the government created for its own uses or subject to its direct control." *Id.* at 662. Is this reasoning consistent with the holding in the *Hunter* case?

Compare § 1983 of the Federal Civil Rights Act, which authorizes suits against "persons." Should a local government be considered suable as a "person" under this act? See Chapter 7.

See also *Village of Arlington Heights v. Regional Transportation Authority,* 653 F.2d 1149 (7th Cir. 1981). The court held that the village and other constitutional home rule municipalities could not bring a fourteenth amendment challenge to a tax levied by the authority. The court rejected an argument by the municipalities that the *Hunter* rule did not apply to them because "they are no longer creatures of the state legislature but derive their powers directly from the Constitution."

3. *Hunter* rule problems arise frequently:

Town of Wickenburg v. State, 565 P.2d 1326 (Ariz. App. 1977). The town challenged a state statute requiring cities to adopt standards of financial disclosure for its officers. The mayor and members of the town council were later added as plaintiffs. Citing *Williams* and *Trenton,* see Comment 1, the court held that the town could not challenge the statute on federal constitutional grounds. It noted that a municipality may not "bring a lawsuit in court to protect personal rights guaranteed to its citizens as individuals."

Compare *Unified School District No. 1 v. Wisconsin Employment Relations Commission,* 259 N.W.2d 724 (Wis. 1974). The court applied the Wisconsin rule, which allows municipalities to question the constitutionality of a statute "involving issues of great public concern." The municipality claimed that a state statute violated the one person-one vote principle of the fourteenth amendment to the federal constitution.

Franciscan Hospital v. Town of Canoe Creek, 398 N.E.2d 413 (Ill. App. 1979). The hospital sued the town under the state's aid to the medically indigent program to recover payment for services given to a resident of the town. The town challenged the statute as an improper delegation of power, and the court considered but rejected this objection. The court refused, however, to consider a fourteenth amendment objection to the state's action, holding that under the *Hunter* rule the town was precluded from making this objection because it did not come within the constitutional protection of due process and equal protection.

4. The *Hunter* opinion suggested in dictum that municipalities might be able to invoke constitutional protections when property held by them in their proprietary as distinguished from their governmental capacity was taken from them by the state without compensation. This kind of property transfer usually occurs in governmental reorganization proceedings, when one governmental unit is merged with another. State legislation may then provide that property owned by the governmental unit being merged is to be transferred to the consolidated unit without compensation.

The proprietary property argument was raised in the *Trenton* case but rejected. Noting the *Hunter* dictum, the Court nevertheless there said, with reference to the cases relied upon by *Hunter* to support its dictum, that "[i]n none of these cases was any power, right or property of a city or other political subdivision held to be protected by the contract clause or the Fourteenth Amendment. This Court has never held that these subdivisions may invoke such restraints upon the power of the State." 262 U.S. at 188. The Supreme Court has not reconsidered this question.

Most state courts have followed the Supreme Court's lead on the property compensation issue. *See Moses Lake School District No. 161 v. Big Bend Community College,* 503 P.2d 86 (Wash. 1973). The school district challenged the statutory transfer of its property to a community college district without compensation. Its challenge was rejected in an opinion which relied on the *Hunter* case. The court held that a provision in the state constitution prohibiting the taking of property without compensation applied to private and not public property. An admitted exception to the rule was noted in the case of holders of school district general obligation bonds, who possessed a "legally enforceable right." These individuals were not a party to the lawsuit.

A few states follow the rule that compensation must be paid when the property transferred is held by the municipality in its proprietary capacity. Even this rule has its harsh effects. In *City of Cambridge v. Commissioner of Public Welfare,* 257 N.E.2d 782 (Mass. 1970), a state statute decreed the release of all public assistance liens held by municipalities within the state. These liens had in the past been foreclosed upon to provide funds to reimburse the municipality for the cost of public assistance paid to the owners of property made subject to the liens. The court held that as the public welfare function was governmental and not proprietary no compensation was payable.

Compare Texas Antiquities Committee v. Dallas County Community College District, 554 S.W.2d 924 (Tex. 1977). The court held that an order by the committee prohibiting the district from demolishing buildings owned by it was an unconstitutional diversion of school property to noneducational purposes. The court refused to apply the *Hunter* rule, holding that "[o]ne agency of the state does not possess powers to divest vested property and contract rights of another state agency 'unrestrained by the particular prohibitions of the constitution.'" The court also felt that *Gomillion, infra,* had closely restricted *Hunter*'s plenary power doctrine.

What distinguishes these cases? Does *Hunter* hold only that a municipality is not a "person" under the fourteenth amendment, as the Illinois appellate court seemed to say? Is there any justification for making an exception of cases in which a municipality challenges a statute as an unconstitutional delegation of power? See also the discussion of § 1983 of the federal Civil Rights Act in Chapter 7.

5. As the *Moses Lake* case suggested, other rights asserted in local government organizational, annexation, and consolidation proceedings may indeed require constitutional protection. Consider *Wilkerson v. City of Coralville,* 478 F.2d 709 (8th Cir. 1973). Residents of a settled but unincorporated area sought relief in federal court on the grounds that the city, when carrying out an annexation program, had refused to annex them because of their poverty. Plaintiff's case was dismissed:

From a search of the constitution, statutes, cases, and Iowa laws, this Court cannot find the right which residents assert. We find no right of annexation available to anyone, owners or residents, regardless of economic status. Whether Coralville, in the exercise of its powers relating to the annexation of territory, should be permitted to encircle and exclude an impoverished area is a matter of legislative policy for the State of Iowa.

Id. at 711. As the next case indicates, the courts may react differently when racial issues are raised.

GOMILLION v. LIGHTFOOT

United States Supreme Court
364 U.S. 339 (1960)

Mr. Justice Frankfurter delivered the opinion of the Court.

This litigation challenges the validity, under the United States Constitution, of Local Act No. 140, passed by the Legislature of Alabama in 1957, redefining the boundaries of the City of Tuskegee. Petitioners, Negro citizens of Alabama who were, at the time of this redistricting measure, residents of the City of Tuskegee, brought an action in the United States District Court for the Middle District of Alabama for a declaratory judgment that Act 140 is unconstitutional, and for an injunction to restrain the Mayor and officers of Tuskegee and the officials of Macon County, Alabama, from enforcing the Act against them and other Negroes similarly situated. Petitioners' claim is that enforcement of the statute, which alters the shape of Tuskegee from a square to an uncouth twenty-eight-sided figure, will constitute a discrimination against them in violation of the Due Process and Equal Protection Clauses of the Fourteenth Amendment to the Constitution and will deny them the right to vote in defiance of the Fifteenth Amendment.

... We brought this case here since serious questions were raised concerning the power of a State over its municipalities in relation to the Fourteenth and Fifteenth Amendments. ...

... Prior to Act 140 the City of Tuskegee was square in shape; the Act transformed it into a strangely irregular twenty-eight-sided figure as indicated in the diagram appended to this opinion. The essential inevitable effect of this redefinition of Tuskegee's boundaries is to remove from the city all save only four or five of its 400 Negro voters while not removing a single white voter or resident. The result of the Act is to deprive the Negro petitioners discriminatorily of the benefits of residence in Tuskegee, including, *inter alia,* the right to vote in municipal elections.

These allegations, if proven, would abundantly establish that Act 140 was not an ordinary geographic redistricting measure even within familiar abuses of gerrymandering. If these allegations upon a trial remained uncontradicted or unqualified, the conclusion would be irresistible, tantamount for all practical purposes to a mathematical demonstration, that the legislation is solely concerned with segregating white and colored voters by fencing Negro citizens out of town so as to deprive them of their pre-existing municipal vote.

It is difficult to appreciate what stands in the way of adjudging a statute having this inevitable effect invalid in light of the principles by which this Court must judge, and uniformly has judged, statutes that, howsoever speciously defined, obviously discriminate against colored citizens. "The [Fifteenth] Amendment nullifies sophisticated as well as simple-minded modes of discrimination." *Lane v. Wilson,* 307 U.S. 268, 275.

The complaint amply alleges a claim of racial discrimination. Against this claim the respondents have never suggested, either in their brief or in oral argument, any countervailing municipal function which Act 140 is designed to serve. The respondents invoke generalities expressing the State's unrestricted power — unlimited, that is, by the United States Constitution — to establish, destroy, or reorganize by contraction or expansion its political subdivisions, to wit, cities, counties, and other local units. We freely recognize the breadth and importance of this aspect of the State's political power. To exalt this power into an absolute is to misconceive the reach and rule of this Court's decisions in the leading case of *Hunter v. City of Pittsburgh,* 207 U.S. 161, and related cases relied upon by respondents.

The *Hunter* case involved a claim by citizens of Allegheny, Pennsylvania, that the General Assembly of that State could not direct a consolidation of their city and Pittsburgh over the objection of a majority of the Allegheny voters. It was alleged that while Allegheny already had made numerous civic improvements, Pittsburgh was only then planning to undertake such improvements, and that the annexation would therefore greatly increase the tax burden on Allegheny residents. All that the case held was (1) that there is no implied contract between a city and its residents that their taxes will be spent solely for the benefit of that city, and (2) that a citizen of one municipality is not deprived of property without due process of law by being subjected to increased tax burdens as a result of the consolidation of his city with another. Related cases, upon which the respondents also rely, such as *City of Trenton v. State of New Jersey,* 262 U.S. 182, ... are far off the mark. They are authority only for the principle that no constitutionally protected contractual obligation arises between a State and its subordinate governmental entities solely as a result of their relationship.

In short, the cases that have come before this Court regarding legislation by States dealing with their political subdivisions fall into two classes: (1) those in which it is claimed that the State, by virtue of the prohibition against impairment of the obligation of contract (Art. I, § 10) and of the Due Process Clause of the Fourteenth Amendment, is without power to extinguish, or alter the boundaries of, an existing municipality; and (2) in which it is claimed that the State has no power to change the identity of a municipality whereby citizens of a pre-existing municipality suffer serious economic disadvantage.

Neither of these claims is supported by such a specific limitation upon State power as confines the States under the Fifteenth Amendment. As to the first category, it is obvious that the creation of municipalities — clearly a political act — does not come within the conception of a contract under the *Dartmouth College* case. 4 Wheat. 518. As to the second, if one principle clearly emerges from the numerous decisions of this Court dealing with taxation it is that the Due Process Clause affords no immunity against mere inequalities in tax burdens, nor does it afford protection against their increase as an indirect consequence of a State's exercise of its political powers.

Particularly in dealing with claims under broad provisions of the Constitution, which derive content by an interpretive process of inclusion and exclusion, it is imperative that generalizations, based on and qualified by the concrete situations that gave rise to them, must not be applied out of context in disregard of variant controlling facts. Thus, a correct reading of the seemingly unconfined dicta of *Hunter* and kindred cases is not that the State has plenary power to manipulate in every conceivable way, for every conceivable purpose, the affairs of its municipal corporations, but rather that the State's authority is unrestrained by the particular prohibitions of the Constitution considered in those cases.

The *Hunter* opinion itself intimates that a state legislature may not be omnipotent even as to the disposition of some types of property owned by municipal corporations, 207 U.S. at pages 178-81. Further, other cases in this Court have refused to allow a State to abolish a municipality, or alter its boundaries, or merge it with another city, without preserving to the creditors of the old city some effective recourse for the collection of debts owed them.... For example, in *Port of Mobile v. United States ex rel. Watson* the Court said:

> Where the resource for the payment of the bonds of a municipal corporation is the power of taxation existing when the bonds were issued, any law which withdraws or limits the taxing power, and leaves no adequate means for the payment of the bonds, is forbidden by the constitution of the United States, and is null and void.... [116 U.S. 289, 305 (1886).]

This line of authority conclusively shows that the Court has never acknowledged that the States have power to do as they will with municipal corporations regardless of consequences. Legislative control of municipalities, no less than other state power, lies within the scope of relevant limitations imposed by the United States Constitution. The observation in *Graham v. Folsom,* 200 U.S. 248, 253, becomes relevant: "The power of the state to alter or destroy its corporations is not greater than the power of the state to repeal its legislation." In that case, which involved the attempt by state officials to evade the collection of taxes to discharge the obligations of an extinguished township, Mr. Justice McKenna, writing for the Court, went on to point out, with reference to the *Mount Pleasant* and *Mobile* cases:

> It was argued in those cases, as it is argued in this, that such alteration or destruction of the subordinate governmental divisions was a proper exercise of legislative power, to which creditors had to submit. The argument did not prevail. It was answered, as we now answer it, that such power, extensive though it is, is met and overcome by the provision of the Constitution of the United States which forbids a state from passing any law impairing the obligation of contracts.... 200 U.S. at pages 253-54.

If all this is so in regard to the constitutional protection of contracts, it should be equally true that, to paraphrase, such power, extensive though it is, is met and overcome by the Fifteenth Amendment to the Constitution of the United States, which forbids a State from passing any law which deprives a citizen of his vote because of his race. The opposite conclusion, urged upon us by respondents, would sanction the achievement by a State of any impairment of voting rights whatever so long as it was cloaked in the garb of the realignment of political subdivisions. "It is inconceivable that guaranties embedded in the Constitution of the United States may thus be manipulated out of existence." *Frost & Frost Trucking Co. v. Railroad Commission of California,* 271 U.S. 583, 594....

MR. JUSTICE WHITTAKER, concurring.

I concur in the Court's judgment, but not in the whole of its opinion. It seems to me that the decision should be rested not on the Fifteenth Amendment, but rather on the Equal Protection Clause of the Fourteenth Amendment to the Constitution. I am doubtful that the averments of the complaint, taken for present purposes to be true, show a purpose by Act No. 140 to abridge petitioners' "right ... to vote," in the Fifteenth Amendment sense. It seems to me that the "right ... to vote" that is guaranteed by the Fifteenth Amendment is but the same right to vote as is enjoyed by all others within the same election precinct, ward or other political division. And, inasmuch as no one has the right to vote in a political division, or in a local election concerning only an area in which he does not reside, it would seem to follow that one's right to vote in Division A is not abridged by a redistricting that places his residence in Division B *if* he there enjoys the same voting privileges as all others in that Division, even though the redistricting was done by the State for the purpose of placing a racial group of citizens in Division B rather than A.

But it does seem clear to me that accomplishment of a State's purpose — to use the Court's phrase — of "fencing Negro citizens out of" Division A and into Division B is an unlawful segregation of races of citizens, in violation of the Equal Protection Clause of the Fourteenth Amendment, *Brown v. Board of Education,* 347 U.S. 483....

Comments: 1. *Gomillion* has had a substantial impact on local government law, although the decision leaves many questions unanswered. Justice Frankfurter avoided fourteenth amendment problems by placing the decision on the fifteenth amendment, but subsequent court decisions have frequently treated *Gomillion* as a fourteenth amendment case.

Nor was it clear whether the decision was based on proof of discriminatory effect or discriminatory intent. The Supreme Court now requires proof of discriminatory intent in fifteenth amendment cases, *Wright v. Rockefeller,* 376 U.S. 52 (1964), and in fourteenth amendment cases, *Washington v. Davis,* 426 U.S. 229 (1976). In *Village of Arlington Heights v. Metropolitan Housing Development Corp.,* 429 U.S. 252 (1977), the Court cited *Gomillion* for the following proposition: "Sometimes a clear pattern, unexplainable on grounds other than race, emerges from the effect of state action even when the governing legislation appears neutral on its face."

2. Would the *Hunter* principle permit the Alabama legislature to abolish the city of Tuskegee altogether?

How might the *Gomillion* case apply to incorporations? Assume that the Alabama statutes included the typical municipal incorporation process. Incorporation is initiated by a petition signed by a stated percentage of the property owners in the area seeking to incorporate. Could the incorporation of Tuskegee as a "strangely irregular twenty-eight-sided figure" be successfully challenged?

In *Caserta v. Village of Dickinson,* 491 F. Supp. 500 (S.D. Tex. 1980), *aff'd,* 672 F.2d 431 (5th Cir. 1982), plaintiff argued that the village boundaries were "consciously drawn . . . to impermissibly exclude . . . Black, Mexican-American and poor citizens who have historically been deemed an integral part of the 'natural community of Dickinson.'" The court found no constitutional violation. It noted that the size and population of the village were limited by the Texas incorporation statutes. A number of other considerations also influenced the size of the village. Earlier attempts to incorporate as a city had failed, and the incorporators decided to incorporate as a village to avoid another defeat. State law limited village tax rates, and defused opposition based on a fear of high taxes.

Other considerations included a desire to take in the heart of "old downtown Dickinson," an attempt to include the most heavily populated areas, and a decision to plan along natural and topographic boundaries. The court held:

> The facts . . . are a far hue and cry from the Tuskegee gerrymander presented in *Gomillion*. Absent a pattern as stark as that presented in *Gomillion,* impact alone is not determinative, and action by the State or its political subdivision racially neutral on its face violates the Fourteenth and Fifteenth Amendments only if motivated by discriminatory purpose.

Id. at 506. The court added in a footnote that "[l]ack of a preexisting right to vote as existed in *Gomillion* is only one of the glaring distinguishing features." For another incorporation case in which no *Gomillion* violation was found see *Taylor v. Township of Dearborn,* 120 N.W.2d 737 (Mich. 1963), *noted,* 48 Minn. L. Rev. 604 (1964).

3. *Gomillion* may affect the judicial treatment of boundary change issues even when racial issues are not present. This problem is treated in Chapter 10, which considers cases in which claims were made that annexation and similar statutes impaired voting rights which have been protected under the fourteenth amendment. See also *State ex rel. Wood v. City of Memphis,* 510 S.W.2d 889 (Tenn. 1974), dismissing on *Hunter* grounds a claim that an annexation was unconstitutional because it brought an area into an unconstitutional school system. The claim of "unconstitutionality" was not clear, but may have referred to racial segregation in the school system of the annexing municipality.

4. Compare *City of Birmingham v. Community Fire District,* 336 So. 2d 502 (Ala. 1976). The city gerrymandered the boundaries of an area it proposed to annex so that voters it had polled and who opposed the annexation were excluded. The exclusions were quite arbitrary. For example, a densely populated black community was split in half and residents of the community opposing the annexation were excluded from the annexed area. "The divisions between those allowed to vote and those excluded were sometimes merely lot lines in the same block." People living in the excluded residences were entirely surrounded by the city.

The court held the gerrymander unconstitutional. It relied in part on the United States Supreme Court's voting rights cases, see Chapter 10. It also held that "[t]he facts in this case show rank discrimination." It added the following comments on the *Hunter* rule:

> That was the law when eight of the present members of this Court were law students. But it is not now the law and has not been since 1960, when the U.S. Supreme Court modified its stance in *Gomillion* . . . .

Id. at 507. Has the court overstated the effect of *Gomillion* on *Hunter?* Again, see the cases in Chapter 10.

Chapter 2

LOCAL GOVERNMENT INCORPORATION AND ANNEXATION

Despite the existence of 80,000 local governments in the nation, municipalities continue to incorporate, and existing municipalities continue to expand through annexation. The most recent statistics show that 440 municipalities incorporated between 1970 and 1979. In the same period, municipalities throughout the country carried out 61,350 annexations totalling 8,770 square miles and containing a population of over three million. United States Department of Commerce, Boundary and Annexation Survey 1970-1979, at 1, 2 (1980).

Municipal incorporation and annexation through an act of the legislature no longer is common. The statutory procedure used in the *Gomillion* case is available primarily in the south and in New England. Elsewhere, incorporation and annexation occur through procedures at the local level authorized by general enabling legislation. This legislation usually imposes minimal conditions. Incorporation statutes, for example, usually contain incorporation procedures and minimal incorporation requirements, such as population and area minimums. Judicial review under this legislation is limited to whether these minimal statutory requirements were observed. Annexation statutes are similar.

When statutes have authorized the courts to review the reasonableness and desirability of incorporations or annexations, some courts apply the political question doctrine to hold that the statute improperly confers legislative power on the judiciary. Some courts avoid this result by holding that the power to review the "reasonableness" of an incorporation or annexation is a proper exercise of judicial power, at least when the standards themselves are reasonably objective. In these states, the courts can review incorporations and annexations on the merits. A few states have created local boundary review commissions to carry out an administrative review of local government incorporation and boundary changes.

This chapter examines local government organization and expansion problems. It first reviews the prevailing "political question" doctrine, and then considers municipal incorporations and annexations. The chapter concludes with a discussion of special district problems, and a discussion of local boundary commissions which have the authority to make local government organization and expansion decisions.

A. THE JUDICIAL REVIEW PROBLEM

The majority rule holds that local government organization and boundary changes do not raise judicially reviewable questions. This rule reflects a number of influences in local government law. One important influence is the nature of the organization and boundary change process. This process usually provides, in the case of incorporations, for the filing of an incorporation petition with a local governing body, usually the county board. Under many statutes, the board orders an election once it determines that the statutory requirements for incorporation are satisfied. These requirements usually are minimal. The delegation of authority to order an election to a political body, the necessity for an election, and the narrowly circumscribed basis on which incorporation petitions may be reviewed, all argue for an interpretation that limits judicial review.

The Utah municipal incorporation statute illustrates the process:

> The registered voters of any contiguous territory not included within the boundaries of another municipality may initiate organization towards municipal status by filing a written petition for incorporation with the board of county commissioners.... The petition shall bear signatures equal in number to 25% of all votes cast from the unincorporated area ... at the last congressional election, or 1,000 signatures, whichever is less.... The petition for incorporation shall:
> (1) Describe the territory to be embraced in the city;
> (2) Have annexed an accurate map or plat thereof;
> (3) State the name proposed for the city; and
> (4) Be accompanied with reasonable proof of the number of inhabitants within the proposed city's boundaries....
>
> When the petition for incorporation is presented ... the board of county commissioners shall ... cause the proposal to incorporate to be placed on all ballots ... at the next county-wide election, or at a special election....

Utah Code Ann. §§ 10-2-101, 10-2-102. On what requirements for an incorporation does the statute imply a possibility for judicial review?

Annexation proceedings also are politically controlled. They are initiated under many statutes by the municipality seeking to annex. The following case illustrates the application of the majority nonreviewability rule to an annexation proceeding:

SUPERIOR OIL CO. v. CITY OF PORT ARTHUR

Texas Court of Appeals
628 S.W.2d 94 (1981), *appeal dismissed,* 103 S. Ct. 481 (1982)

CLAYTON, JUSTICE.

Appellant, Superior Oil Company, filed this suit against the City of Port Arthur, attacking the validity of an annexation ordinance and to enjoin the City from attempting to collect any ad valorem taxes from appellant on its property in question, and in the alternative seeking a declaration that the "discriminatory failure of Defendants to include Plaintiff's property in an industrial district is an unconstitutional denial of the equal protection of the laws" and that "Plaintiff is entitled to have its property taxed on the same basis as property included in industrial districts by the City...." The trial court granted the City's motion for summary judgment, upholding the validity of the questioned annexation ordinance.

The City of Port Arthur, a home rule city, by the process of several sequential annexation ordinances, annexed an area extending three marine leagues into the Gulf of Mexico, encompassing a drilling platform, five oil, gas, and mineral leases (leased from the State) and various other production facilities owned by appellant. The last of such ordinances, Ordinance No. 79-116, adopted December 10, 1979, annexed the territory in which appellant's property is situated. An area of a mile in width and 10½ miles in length, extending into the Gulf of Mexico, has been annexed by seven separate ordinances. The City began its southward expansion and annexation in 1969. Originally, it did so to permit it to buttress levies in order to prevent property damage to city residents from rising water and storms.

In reaching its present boundary lines, the City annexed southward down the Sabine River until it reached the mouth thereof, then proceeded in a southwesterly direction along the Texas coastline, and then out into the Gulf of Mexico to the three marine league line. This was done by separate annexation ordinances, all of which complied with the provisions of the Municipal Annexation act, *Tex.Rev.Civ.Stat.Ann. art. 970a* (1963). Appellant attacks the validity of the last ordinance No. 79-116.

Appellant, by its fourth, fifth, and sixth points of error complain of the granting of the motion for summary judgment upon the grounds that the annexation ordinance, and the tax assessed against its property, was void "because it constituted a violation of the due process clause of the Fourteenth Amendment to the Constitution of the United States," and that the annexation ordinance is void "because it was done solely for purposes of taxation."

Appellant has grouped these three points under its argument, and we will consider them in the same manner. The sole argument made under the three points is that the Annexation Ordinance No. 79-116 is void because the annexed area, within which appellant's property is located, was annexed solely for taxation purposes, and the City cannot provide any municipal services to the annexed territory. We disagree and, accordingly, overrule these points of error.

The City of Port Arthur enacted the questioned annexation ordinance pursuant to and in full compliance with the provisions of *Article 970a*. Appellant's only complaint is that the annexation and taxation of its property violates the due process clause and the equal protection clause of the Fourteenth Amendment of the United States Constitution. These contentions do not present a justiciable matter under such constitutional amendment, and cannot form a basis for rendering void the annexation of appellant's property.

The United States Supreme Court in *Hunter v. City of Pittsburgh,* 207 U.S. 161 ... (1907), ... held that annexation of territory by political subdivisions of the states does not present a justiciable matter under the Fourteenth Amendment. The Court states ...

> Municipal corporations are political subdivisions of the state.... The number, nature, and duration of the powers conferred upon these corporations and the territory over which they shall be exercised rests in the absolute discretion of the state.... Although the inhabitants and property owners may, by such changes, suffer inconvenience, and their property may be lessened in value by the burden of increased taxation, or for any other reason, they have no right, by contract or otherwise, in the unaltered or continued existence of the corporation or its powers, and there is nothing in the Federal Constitution which protects them from these injurious consequences. The power is in the state, and those who legislate for the state are alone responsible for any unjust or oppressive exercise of it.

Although the *Hunter* decision has been limited in some voting right cases, the Supreme Court has made it clear that the case is still viable today. In *Holt Civic Club v. City of Tuscaloosa,* 439 U.S. 60 ... (1978), the Supreme Court stated:

> [W]e think that the [*Hunter*] case continues to have substantial constitutional significance in emphasizing the extraordinarily wide latitude that states have in creating various types of political subdivisions and conferring authority upon them.

On numerous occasions, the *Hunter* decision has been applied to municipal annexations. The courts have consistently held that annexations do not present a justiciable matter under the Fourteenth Amendment. In *Hammonds v. City of Corpus Christi,* 226 F.Supp. 456, 458-9 (S.D.Tex. 1964), affirmed, 343 F.2d 162 (5th Cir.), cert. denied, 382 U.S. 837 ... (1965), the Court states: "The annexation of lands to a city or town has been held without exception to be purely a political matter, entirely within the power of the Legislature of the State to regulate.... Although we may disagree with the mode of annexation or annexations themselves, the remedy of those aggrieved is not in the courts, but in the State Legislature."...

This has also been the holding of the courts of Texas.... In *State ex rel. Pan American Production Co. v. Texas City,* 157 Tex. 450, 303 S.W.2d 780, 782 (1957), appeal dism'd per curiam, 355 U.S. 603 ... (1958), our Supreme Court states:

> [T]he conclusion of petitioners here that the annexation ordinance was unreasonable and arbitrary is only to say that it was unreasonable and arbitrary because the land was not suitable, and had no relation to the City's needs, and it was for the purpose only of acquiring additional revenue and could afford no benefit to the owners of the property annexed. The decisions of this State have repeatedly held that such facts do not warrant intervention or review by the courts.

Appellant's attack upon the validity of the annexation ordinance in the case at bar for the reason that the annexation was for the sole purpose of raising revenue and not offering municipal services has been rejected in numerous cases. Texas courts have consistently held that they will not look to the purposes of an annexation to determine its validity. Assuming appellant established that its property was within an area annexed by the City solely for purposes of raising additional revenue, we find such fact would not render the annexation ordinance void. In *City of Wichita Falls v. State ex rel. Vogtsberger,* [533 S.W.2d 927 (Tex. 1976)] our Supreme Court states: "Traditionally, the courts of this State have not scrutinized the purpose of annexation ordinances or the use or character of the occupation of the annexed territory."...

Appellant relies on *Myles Salt Co. v. Board of Commissioners,* 239 U.S. 478 ... (1916). However, our Texas Supreme Court in *State ex rel. Pan American Production Co. v. Texas City,* ... distinguished the *Myles* case by stating:

> A valid distinction is to be made, however, between a special tax or assessment to finance special improvements designed to benefit property or persons located within the particular taxing district, and on the other hand an ad valorem tax on all property within the taxing jurisdiction of the general welfare of the entire community.... [I]t is constitutionally sufficient if the taxes are uniform and are for public purposes in which the City has an interest. [*Morton Salt Co. v. City of South Hutchinson,* 177 F.2d 889 (10th Cir. 1949)].

Based upon the foregoing authorities, we hold the City's Ordinance No. 79-116 is not void, and we follow the long established rule that the determination of the boundaries of a municipality, as to the grounds of attack made by appellant in the case at bar, is ordinarily a political function, entirely within the power of the legislature of this State to regulate, and the remedy of those aggrieved is not in seeking relief in the courts, but in the State Legislature. Furthermore, the mere fact that the annexation was for taxation and revenue raising purposes and that no municipal services were provided does not render the annexation ordinance void.

....

Affirmed.

KEITH, JUSTICE, concurring. [Omitted.]

Comments: 1. Why is the *Hunter* decision relevant to the scope of judicial review in annexation cases? Didn't that decision simply determine the status of municipalities under the fourteenth amendment of the federal Constitution? For discussion of the voting rights cases that qualify the *Hunter* rule see Chapter 10.

The oil company also argued that the annexation was "for the sole purpose of raising revenue." Could this argument be read as an objection that its property was being taken without due process through taxation? Is *Hunter* relevant to this issue?

The court in *Port Arthur* distinguished special assessments from general ad valorem property taxes, suggesting that a special assessment could raise a due process issue. A special assessment can be levied only for benefits received. *See* Chapter 5. Is this distinction relevant to the basis on which a court can review an annexation?

A federal district court reached a different result and invalidated the annexation in *Superior Oil Co. v. City of Port Arthur*, 553 F. Supp. 511 (E.D. Tex. 1982). The court held that the Texas court decision that the claim was not justiciable was not a decision on the merits and did not bar the federal court suit. Noting that the Supreme Court had "never interpreted *Hunter* as a complete bar to suits challenging municipal annexations," the federal court held that Superior Oil's claim was justiciable:

> [I]t presents a straightforward question of interpretation of the fourteenth amendment, a traditional function of the federal judiciary . . . . There is no textually demonstrable constitutional commitment of this issue to the states; there are manageable judicial standards to resolve this conflict; there is no need for any initial policy determination that this Court is not well-equipped to make; a decision by this Court will not demonstrate a lack of respect for a coordinate branch of government; there is no unusual need for unquestioning adherence to Port Arthur's annexation; and there is no potential for embarrassment from conflicts between various departments.

The court then invalidated the annexation as "a land grab, motivated solely by a lust for tax revenue and having no relation to the traditional purposes of municipal government and its legitimate powers." It held that the disparity between the tax imposed and the benefits received was so flagrant that it was a taking of property without compensation. This holding is distinctly the minority view in annexation cases.

2. The incorporation cases have reached the same result. *McManus v. Skoko*, 467 P.2d 426 (Or. 1970), considered an incorporation law similar to the Utah law quoted above. The statute also authorized the county board to alter the boundaries of a proposed city, and to exclude any land that would not be benefited. The board refused to approve a petition to incorporate because it was inconsistent with good governmental practices and not in the best interest of the general public or the general welfare. It interpreted the provision just summarized to mean that a petition for incorporation could be disapproved if it found that none of the land within the proposed boundaries of the city would be benefited by the incorporation.

This interpretation was rejected by the court, which relied on legislative policy indicating that an election was mandatory once a petition was filed. It construed the boundary alteration provision to give the board control over the boundaries of the city but not to give the board the power to refuse an incorporation on "political" grounds.

3. Of course, the political question doctrine does not disable a court from interpreting a statute that governs incorporation and annexation proceedings. In *Incorporation of East Bridge v. City of Aurora*, 601 P.2d 1374 (Colo. 1979), the statute authorized the incorporation of "any territory not embraced within the limits of any existing municipality." Inhabitants of an unincorporated area completely surrounded by a city filed a petition for incorporation. The court held that the phrase "embraced within the limits" was ambiguous and did not authorize the incorporation of municipal enclaves. "This type of incorporation results in a duplication of governmental facilities, frustrates area-wide coordination and uniformity of regulations, complicates governmental structure, often circumvents legitimate zoning controls, frequently leads to an avoidance of city tax burdens, and thus creates an inequitable distribution of the costs of municipal services." *Id.* at 1375. Do you agree that the statute was ambiguous?

4. Even though the *Port Arthur* case found no objection to a boundary change that would raise property taxes, courts and legislatures have been sensitive to the inequities that result when a municipality annexes an area but does not provide services. Landowners in the annexed area pay the higher city taxes but do not receive benefits from the annexation. To avoid this problem, some legislatures have enacted provisions requiring municipalities to extend services to an annexed area within a reasonable period of time after annexation.

When court review of the annexation is required these statutes have been upheld as providing adequate standards, *Clarke v. City of Wichita,* 543 P.2d 973 (Kan. 1975), or as presenting factual questions for the court to determine, *City of Des Moines v. Lampart,* 82 N.W.2d 720 (Iowa 1957). The *Clarke* decision hastened to add "that all municipal services and facilities are subject to economic and other vicissitudes, too numerous to mention, over which a municipality has no absolute and complete control." It required only that the annexation be done in good faith, and that substantial compliance with the statute be shown. Will a court intervene if a municipality refuses to provide services subsequent to annexation? *See Richards v. City of Tustin,* 37 Cal. Rptr. 124 (Cal. App. 1964) (no, in absence of fraudulent abuse of discretion).

5. A few courts have interpreted legislative authority to incorporate to allow judicial review of the merits of an incorporation. In *Cottonwood City Electors v. Salt Lake County Board of Commissioners,* 499 P.2d 270 (Utah 1972), a group of residents adjoining a shopping center near Salt Lake City filed a petition to incorporate as a town. The town incorporation law authorized the electors of an unincorporated town with a population of not less than 100 and no more than 7,000 to file a petition to incorporate with the county board. The statute provided that "[o]n approval of such petition by the said board ... such town shall constitute a body corporate." Only 153 residents lived in the area proposed for incorporation. The board rejected the petition and the incorporators appealed, claiming that the board had a ministerial duty under the statute to approve the incorporation.

The court disagreed. It pointed out that the function of the board was "to so govern the county as to best provide for the general welfare and good order," and that it "must necessarily be allowed a reasonable latitude of discretion." The statutory language supported this holding. If the legislature had intended to deny any discretion to the board, "it could have simply said that upon such filing ... the town was thus established, or that the town 'shall' or 'must' be established." The court added:

> In this connection it should also be observed that if the County Commissioners had no discretion at all in such a matter, then any area whatsoever, of whatever shape or size, or for whatever purpose, and regardless of how discordant or disruptive it may be of an overall plan, or however impractical any aspect of such a proposal might be, if it but met the technical specifications of a petition, it would have to be established as an incorporated town. Based on what we have said above, it is our opinion that this does not comport with the fair and reasonable meaning to be divined from the statute.

Id. at 272.

For discussion of the *Cottonwood* case see Comment, *Utah's Future Municipalities — Incorporation by Chance or Design?,* 1972 UTAH L. REV. 597. A city over 100,000 in population has since incorporated in western Salt Lake County. What does this incorporation say about local political control of the incorporation process?

The *Cottonwood* case rejected a delegation of power objection to the town incorporation law, enigmatically noting that the law conformed with the constitutional mandate that the legislature provide for incorporation through general laws. More serious separation of power problems may arise when an incorporation or annexation law bypasses the local political process and confers the power to incorporate on a local court, as the next case indicates.

TOWN OF BELOIT v. CITY OF BELOIT

Supreme Court of Wisconsin
37 Wis. 2d 637, 155 N.W.2d 633 (1968)

This action was commenced by the City of Beloit, respondent, in compliance with sec. 66.021 (11) (b), Stats., for a determination by the court that its annexation of certain lands was in the public interest. The Towns of Beloit, Rock, and Turtle, in which part of the land lay, intervened to contest the annexation. The City of Beloit reserved the right and raised the question of whether the requirement of sec. 66.021 (11) (b), Stats., was constitutional. The trial court held it had no jurisdiction to make a determination of whether the annexation was or was not in the public interest and that sec. 66.021 (11) (b), conferring on the court such power was unconstitutional but its invalidity did not affect the rest of sec. 66.021 relating to annexations. From the order dismissing the action, the Towns of Beloit, Rock, and Turtle appeal. . . .

HALLOWS, CHIEF JUSTICE. The facts are simple and undisputed. On February 6, 1967, the city council of the City of Beloit enacted an ordinance under sec. 66.021, Stats., for the annexation to the city of certain lands situated in the Towns of Beloit, Rock, Turtle, and La Prairie. Since the area annexed was in excess of one square mile, the city was required by sec. 66.021 (11) (b) to immediately petition the circuit court for a determination that the annexation was in the public interest. The question on appeal is whether this requirement is constitutional.

In 1957 the legislature enacted revised statutes relating to annexations. In sec. 66.021 it provided that territory contiguous to a city or village could be annexed either by (a) direct annexation, or (b) referendum. The details of these methods were set forth. In 1959 by sec. 66.021 (11) (a) additional requirements were provided for annexations in a county having a population of over 50,000. The state director of the planning function in the department of resource development must be notified of the proposed annexation and within 20 days the director may give his opinion that the annexation is against public interest. His reasons therefor must be given within the next 10 days. Public interest for this purpose is defined in paragraph (c) [2] in terms of governmental services to be supplied, the shape of the proposed annexation, and the homogeneity of the territory. The annexing municipality is required to review this advice before taking final action on the annexation.

In 1959, sec. 66.021 (11) (b), Stats., was also added to sec. 66.021 and requires "Whenever a village or city adopts an ordinance annexing an area of one square mile or more, it shall immediately petition the circuit court of the county in which the village or city is situated for a determination that the annexation is in the public interest and the ordinance shall not be in effect until the court so deter-

---

[2] 66.021(11) Review of Annexations. . . .

(c) *Definition of public interest.* For purposes of this subsection public interest is determined by the director of the planning function in the department of resource development after consideration of the following:

1. Whether the governmental services, including zoning, to be supplied to the territory could clearly be better supplied by the town or by some other village or city whose boundaries are contiguous to the territory proposed for annexation which files with the circuit court a certified copy of a resolution adopted by a two-thirds vote of the elected members of the governing body indicating a willingness to annex the territory upon receiving an otherwise valid petition for the annexation of the territory.

2. The shape of the proposed annexation and the homogeneity of the territory with the annexing village or city and any other contiguous village or city.

mines." This section also provides the court shall receive an advisory report from the state director of regional planning on whether or not the annexation is in the public interest as defined in paragraph (c).

The trial court in holding sec. 66.021 (11) (b) was unconstitutional as an unauthorized delegation of legislative power to the judiciary, relied on *Scharping v. Johnson* (1966), 32 Wis. 2d 383, 145 N.W.2d 691, and *In re Incorporation of Village of North Milwaukee* (1896), 93 Wis. 616, 67 N.W. 1033. The trial court was of the opinion the delegation was clearly unconstitutional because the circuit court was granted an unlimited power to determine what constituted public interest and this power was not limited by the definition of public interest in paragraph (c), nor was such a term a codification of or to be equated with the "rule of reason" of juridical origin.

We reach the same conclusion as did the trial court but with less alacrity and confidence. But we hasten to add that in this day of restless technical and social change this court is alert to the necessity of guarding against a well-meaning fusion of judicial and legislative power. . . .

But even considering the construction contended for by the Towns we are unable to find that the section only prescribes the conditions necessary for an annexation and all that is delegated to the courts is the power to determine whether those conditions exist. Many years ago in *In re Incorporation of Village of North Milwaukee,* supra, 93 Wis. at p. 624, 67 N.W. at p. 1036, we held, "The question as to whether incorporation is for the best interest of the community in any case is emphatically a question of public policy and statecraft, not in any sense a judicial question; and in attempting to submit that question to the decision of the circuit court the legislature has undoubtedly done that which the constitution forbids." While the case involved incorporation of a village, the principle is fundamental and has been followed both in this state and elsewhere. Its latest recognition was in *Scharping v. Johnson,* supra, also an incorporation case, and we now apply the principle to annexation cases.

There is no question that if we consider public interest as an unrestricted term or concept, as did the trial court, the determination of what political and economic expediency constitute public interest is a legislative function. What is "desirable" or "advisable" or "ought to be" is a question of policy, not a question of fact. What is "necessary" or what is "in the best interest" is not a fact and its determination by the judiciary is an exercise of legislative power when each involves political considerations and reasons why there should or should not be an annexation. This is the general and universal rule which sharply draws the differentiating line between legislative power and judicial power and by which the validity of the delegation of functions to the judiciary by the legislature is determined. . . .

The appellants correctly argue the broad definition of public interest is not applicable in this case because the statute confines public interest for the purpose of this type of annexation to three factors: government service, shape and homogeneity. It is further argued these three factors have often been used by the courts under the rule of reason to review annexations and in effect all the section does is to codify this concept and make its application a mandatory part of the annexation process. This is a two-phased argument. We think the determination of public interest is restricted to the consideration of the factors enumerated and both the state director of regional planning and the circuit court are so limited. The legislative history of the section would indicate the concept of public interest is limited and the legislature intended to avoid the *North Milwaukee* Case in providing for a court's determination of public interest on designated factors.

The purpose of subsection (11) is stated in notes which were a part of Bill 226, A, creating the subsection. The belief is therein expressed that the advisory report of the state administrative officer would supply a sufficient foundation to avoid the proscription of the *North Milwaukee* Case. Perhaps the legislature intended to leave only a question of the existence of certain facts for the court to decide without having to consider political factors, but the question is, does the statute as enacted avoid the *North Milwaukee* Case?

We pointed out in *Nash v. Fries* (1906), 129 Wis. 120, 108 N.W. 210, relied on by the appellants, there was a distinction between the function of deciding a question of legislative policy and the ascertainment of existence of certain facts and conditions upon which the legislature had decided and declared the policy. In that case the court was considering the phrase "in its discretion," which was used in a statute providing the procedure for the organization of a town. The court took the view of favoring constitutionality and found the only discretion in the court was as a trier of facts to determine whether the conditions for organization required by the statute in fact existed and the section did not compel the court to pass upon the advisability of the incorporation after the facts had been so determined. . . .

However, we have difficulty applying this reasoning to sec. 66.021, Stats. This section does not require the ascertainment of facts as the word "fact" is normally understood but requires the determination of public interest. This narrow concept of public interest still leaves the court with too much discretion to determine whether such public interest requires the annexation. Nor is there any standard provided by which to determine which governmental services are "better supplied" or what the "shape" of the annexed territory should be. If the court were to determine these three factors as facts and end there, perhaps we would have a different question. But, they are not found by the court as facts upon which the annexation necessarily stands or falls, but constitute elements considered by the court in the process of determining public interest, i.e., the advisability and desirability of the annexation after receiving an advisory opinion on the subject by a legislative agent.

A court cannot substitute its judgment for that of an administrative agency determining a legislative matter within its province. . . . *A fortiori* a court cannot form its own judgment of legislative policy even upon the advice of an administrative agency. The determination required by the statute is not by way of review but is a condition precedent to the validity of the annexation. While this is not controlling, it is of some significance.

[The Wisconsin court then turned to a discussion of its so-called "rule of reason." This rule was derived from a provision of the Wisconsin constitution placing a duty on the legislature to provide for the incorporation of cities and villages. From this general provision the court at an early date implied a substantive standard to be applied to the incorporation of municipalities, *Smith v. Sherry,* 6 N.W. 561 (Wis. 1880). — Eds.]

We think, too, the argument that the definition of "public interest" is a codification of the rule of reason is not persuasive. We pointed out in *Town of Fond Du Lac v. City of Fond Du Lac* (1964), 22 Wis. 2d 533, 126 N.W.2d 201, the rule of reason had its roots in *Smith v. Sherry* (1880), 50 Wis. 210, 6 N.W. 561. The rule of reason there applied concerned the application of a constitutional requirement (sec. 3, Art. XI) to a legislative enactment relating to the creation and change of boundaries of cities and villages. In the *Fond Du Lac* Case the court was not advancing its own ideas of the advisability or feasibility of the annexation when it struck down the annexation. It was not the fact that a hole in the area or an island was left unannexed, but it was the reason for leaving the island which was important and stamped the action of the municipality as arbitrary and capricious. We used the rule of reason to review the method by which the municipality exercised its legislative function, not to determine the merits of the legislative choice.

In *Town of Brookfield v. City of Brookfield* (1957), 274 Wis. 638, 80 N.W.2d 800, in applying the rule of reason to the annexation there involved, we pointed out that facts proper for a determination of legislative policy such as reasonable suitability and adaptability of the territory for annexation and the reasonable necessity for the proper growth development and welfare of the city may be reviewed, but "Upon a review the courts cannot disturb the council's determination unless it appears that it is arbitrary and capricious or is an abuse of discretion." 274 Wis. at p. 646, 80 N.W.2d at p. 804....

We think therefore that the judicial determination of public interest in sec. 66.021 (11) (b) is not the same function as applying the rule of reason. If the intention of the legislature was to have the court apply the rule of reason, it should not have provided for a determination of public interest but for a review of the action of the municipality to determine whether that action of the municipality was arbitrary or capricious....

This opinion requires no change in the order of dismissal of the lower court but does affect the scope of its decision because the ordinance of the City of Beloit does not result in a valid annexation.

Order affirmed.

Comments: 1. The "rule of reason" is similar to the holding of some courts that they may review an incorporation or annexation to determine whether it is "reasonable," or whether it is "arbitrary or capricious." In these states, this limited scope of judicial review of the merits is not based on a constitutional clause. Where do the courts get this authority? Why doesn't it violate the separation of powers? How would you rewrite the Wisconsin statute to comply with the *Beloit* decision?

Judicial review under the "arbitrary and capricious" standard may be limited. In *City of Wichita v. Board of County Commissioners,* 632 P.2d 717 (Kan. 1982), a county board approved the incorporation of an area adjacent to the city. The trial court reversed, but the supreme court upheld the incorporation. The statute contained extensive standards for incorporation. They included consideration of the effect of the incorporation "on the local government structure of the entire community" and the effect of the incorporation on a city located within five miles.

The supreme court applied the "arbitrary and capricious" standard of review to the board's decision. It held that "substantial, convincing and compelling" evidence submitted by Wichita showing that annexation by the city was preferable was "not the test." "The Board, in an incorporation proceeding, is not bound by the weight of the evidence and, in fact, may grant or deny incorporation even though the evidence favors a contrary result." The court also held that the weight to be given by the board to the statutory incorporation factors was "a matter left solely to the Board in the performance of its legislative functions." Wichita had the burden to show "a reversible impropriety." *Id.* at 725.

2. Would it make a difference if the decision on incorporation or annexation were delegated to an administrative agency, subject to the usual judicial review? Shortly after the *Beloit* case, the Wisconsin Supreme Court upheld the constitutionality of its municipal incorporation law. This law authorized the state director of planning to review proposed municipal incorporations which met specified statutory standards. *Schmidt v. Department of Resource Development,* 158 N.W.2d 306 (Wis. 1968). As quoted in the supreme court's opinion, the standards were as follows:

Standards to be applied by the director. (1) The director may approve for referendum only those proposed incorporations which meet the following requirements:

Characteristics of territory. The entire territory of the proposed village or city shall be reasonably homogeneous and compact, taking into consideration natural boundaries, natural drainage basin, soil conditions, present and potential transportation facilities, previous political boundaries, boundaries of school districts, shopping and social customs. An isolated municipality shall have a reasonably developed community center, including some or all such features as retail stores, churches, post office, telephone exchange and similar centers of community activity.

(b) *Territory beyond the core.* The territory beyond the most densely populated square mile . . . shall have in an isolated municipality an average of more than 30 housing units per quarter section or an assessed value, . . . for real estate tax purposes, more than 25 per cent of which is attributable to existing or potential mercantile, manufacturing or public utility uses; but the director may waive these requirements to the extent that water, terrain or geography prevents such development. Such territory in a metropolitan municipality shall have the potential for residential or other land use development on a substantial scale within the next 3 years.

(2) In addition to complying with each of the applicable standards set forth in sub. (1) . . . any proposed incorporation in order to be approved for referendum must be in the public interest as determined by the director upon consideration of the following:

(a) *Tax revenue.* The present and potential sources of tax revenue appear sufficient to defray the anticipated cost of governmental services at a local tax rate which compares favorably with the tax rate in a similar area for the same level of services.

(b) *Level of services.* The level of governmental services desired or needed by the residents of the territory compared to the level of services offered by the proposed village or city and the level available from a contiguous municipality which files a certified copy of a resolution. . . .

(c) *Impact on the remainder of the town.* The impact, financial and otherwise, upon the remainder of the town from which the territory is to be incorporated.

(d) *Impact on the metropolitan community.* The effect upon the future rendering of governmental services both inside the territory proposed for incorporation and elsewhere within the metropolitan community. There shall be an express finding that the proposed incorporation will not substantially hinder the solution of governmental problems affecting the metropolitan community.

After reviewing the *Beloit* and its early cases, the court held the statute constitutional and commented:

> We are dealing here not with a delegation of legislative power to the judiciary but with a delegation of that power to an administrative agency or administrative director. The legislative agency or director is, in fact, an arm or agent of the legislature itself. The very existence of the administrative agency or director is dependent upon the will of the legislature; its or his powers, duties and scope of authority are fixed and circumscribed by the legislature and subject to legislative change. An administrative agency does not stand on the same footing as a court when considering the doctrine of separation of powers. An administrative agency is subject to more rigid control by the legislature and judicial review of its legislative authority and the manner in which that authority is exercised.

Id. at 312.

The court later noted that the statute in the *Schmidt* case was not as "broad" as the statute in the *Beloit* case, and did not require the same type of policy decision. *Compare Plumfield Nurseries, Inc. v. Dodge County,* 167 N.W.2d 560 (Neb. 1969), upholding against delegation of power objections a statute which gave to the court the authority to determine whether lands annexed to a city were "urban or suburban in character." In its later pronouncement on the delegation issue, the Wisconsin court held unconstitutional a statute which conferred on a county court the authority to determine whether an area would be "best" served by organization of a metropolitan sewerage district. *In re Petition for Fond du Lac Metropolitan Sewerage District,* 166 N.W.2d 225 (Wis. 1969).

The Wisconsin legislature has since amended the annexation statute under consideration in the *Beloit* case by repealing subsection (b) of Section 66.021 (11). 1969 Wis. Laws, ch. 21. Does this change meet all of the objections of the *Beloit* case, considering the court's further views on delegation of power as expressed in the *Schmidt* case? See *Westring v. James,* 238 N.W.2d 695 (Wis. 1976) (reaffirming *Schmidt*).

3. The Indiana Supreme Court passed on the delegation of power question in *City of Aurora v. Bryant,* 165 N.E.2d 141 (Ind. 1960). In holding the statute valid, and answering a delegation of power objection, it noted:

> However, the power and duties of the court are, under the remonstrances in the case at bar, limited to ascertaining whether the annexation will be for the interest of the city and will cause no manifest injury to the persons owning property in the territory. [These were the statutory standards. — Eds.] If the court is satisfied that these two conditions are met it "shall so find"; and "said annexation shall take place." The judgment of the court merely establishes the fact that the conditions of the statute, necessary to overcome a remonstrance, have or have not been met, and if they have been met the statute *ex proprio vigore,* annexes the territory.

Id. at 145. Can you distinguish the "facts" to be considered under the Indiana statute from the "factors" to be considered under the statute held invalid in the *Beloit* case?

4. The holding of the *Beloit* opinion applies equally to other proceedings in which organizational and boundary issues are important, *e.g.,* incorporation of municipalities, detachment from municipalities, and organization and reorganization of special districts such as school districts and drainage districts. In these proceedings, four types of issues can be isolated:

a. Procedural issues, *e.g.,* a notice of hearing requirement;

b. Factual substantive issues, *e.g.,* a requirement that a new village contain a minimum of 250 inhabitants;

c. Mixed factual and legal issues arising under statutes isolating the substantive elements that are a condition to organization or annexation, *e.g.,* a requirement that the annexed area be urban in character;

d. Issues requiring an exercise of discretion on generic questions of policy, *e.g.,* a requirement that the incorporation or annexation be in the "public interest."

Judicial willingness to accept jurisdiction and pass judgment on the questions raised in organizational and annexation proceedings decreases as we move down this list. While almost all courts would pass on issues raised in the first three categories, it is at the fourth category, in which issues relating to the expediency and propriety of the incorporation are raised, that most courts balk.

5. A few courts extensively review municipal incorporations and boundary changes on their merits. Virginia is almost unique in extending the scope of judicial inquiry to include almost all issues, and in practically abandoning the separation of powers requirement. *See Board of Supervisors v. Duke,* 73 S.E. 456 (Va. 1912).

B. MUNICIPAL INCORPORATION AND ANNEXATION

1. INCORPORATION

Municipal incorporations now present a major problem only in rural and suburban areas. Municipal incorporation laws, which are usually limited to minimum population requirements, are inadequate to deal with suburban incorporation problems. They may actually encourage suburban municipal balkanization because the population minimums are so small.

A few statutes impose additional statutory requirements which allow some judicial review of incorporations. Some require that an incorporation must be "right and proper," or "reasonable." Other statutes require the presence of a "community." Some states authorize the incorporation of "villages," or "towns," and the courts have interpreted these statutes to mean that the area seeking incorporation must be a town or village in the ordinary sense of the term. *See* Mandelker, *Standards for Municipal Incorporation on the Urban Fringe,* 36 TEX. L. REV. 271 (1958).

Although the courts may not review the desirability of an incorporation under statutes of this type, they do impose some substantive criteria on incorporation proposals. The following categories are illustrative:

a. *Urban territory.* The courts regularly put a limit on the amount of non-urban or "agricultural" land that may be included in a new municipality. Usually the new municipality attempts to include undeveloped rural land along with the developed portions of the territory that are to be included in the new incorporation. Judicial reluctance to allow too much undeveloped land in a new incorporation may indicate judicial sensitivity to the taxes and benefits issue, whatever the constitutional limitations on municipal incorporations that arguably do not confer sufficient benefits on those property owners who are included.

The Arkansas Supreme Court had interpreted the "right and proper" language in its incorporation law to require the exclusion of excessive agricultural land. *Town of Ouita v. Heidgan,* 448 S.W.2d 631 (Ark. 1970). *But see White v. Lorings,* 623 S.W.2d 837 (Ark. 1981) ("[t]here has never been such a provision in the statutes governing ... incorporation").

When development is scattered, the courts may have difficulty deciding how much undeveloped land may permissibly be included. *State ex rel. Northern Pump Co. v. So-Called Village of Fridley,* 47 N.W.2d 204 (Minn. 1951) was a case decided before enactment of a statute creating a state boundary review commission and modifying the incorporation law. The court reviewed an incorporation of a suburban area north of Minneapolis, which was in the course of development. The court looked to growth trends in the metropolitan area and the probability that the entire area would be developed in the near future to justify the inclusion of a substantial amount of undeveloped land. The case was decided under a statutory requirement that the area to be incorporated must be "so conditioned as to be properly subjected to village government." The decision is typical, although some courts have also required that the undeveloped areas have an adaptability to and a community of interest with the built-up portion of the community. How restrictive would such a test be in practice?

b. *Narrow "community" standard.* This test has social and economic as well as physical dimensions. If the test is applied only to the area to be incorporated, it will often lead to a splintering of the metropolitan area into an excessive number of municipalities. For a case raising similar issues see *In re Incorporation of Elm Grove,* 64 N.W.2d 874 (Wis. 1954). A built-up area on the outer fringe of Milwaukee sought incorporation as a village. One objection was that the incorporators had not included all the territory that was eligible for inclusion under the community characteristics standard. This and related objections were dismissed by the court, which noted that the community characteristics requirement was only a minimum. The court had no discretion to determine the proper size of the community. This question was a matter for the electors.

In some fringe incorporations in which the population nucleus is not compact and population density is low, the courts have denied incorporation on the ground that no community exists. *See Parnell v. State ex rel. Wilson,* 206 P.2d 1047 (Ariz. 1949), in which the court disallowed the incorporation of an area near Tucson, largely open range or desert land, which was sparsely populated. This point of view has led some courts to deny incorporation for new municipalities that do not have any apparent community identity. *See Harang v. State ex rel. City of West Columbia,* 466 S.W.2d 8 (Tex. Civ. App. 1971). *Contra, State ex rel. Cole v. City of Hendersonville,* 445 S.W.2d 652 (Tenn. 1969).

The Arizona incorporation law now defines a community as "a locality in which a body of people reside in more or less proximity having common interests in such services as public health, public protection, fire protection, and water which bind together the people of the area, and where the people are acquainted and mingle in business, social, educational and recreational activities." Ariz. Rev. Stat. Ann. § 9-101E. This statute was applied in *State ex rel. Pickrell v. Downey,* 430 P.2d 122 (Ariz. 1967). An objection was made that the community did not meet the statutory test because it included no businesses, offices or transportation facilities, and because the boundaries of the new municipality were drawn to exclude certain residential, business, and other areas, including "religious" areas. The court replied that "[c]ertainly a body of several hundred people residing within an area of 2.85 square miles 'reside in more or less proximity.' The people of the area have common interests in such services as public health, public protection, fire protection and water. The fact that some or most of these services may come from without the area or be available to others who are without the area sought to be incorporated does not make the interests in such services any less common to people within the area. We believe the statute does not contemplate that all such services be in existence at the time a community seeks incorporation." *Id.* at 128. It appears that the community was in the Phoenix metropolitan area, but the court did not discuss this point.

[margin note: Permitted]

c. *Broad "community" standard.* This standard was adopted by the Virginia court in an interpretation of its incorporation statute that contained best interest and general good of the community, reasonableness, and non-excessive area standards. *See Board of Supervisors v. Duke,* 73 S.E. 456 (Va. 1912). That case denied incorporation of a small and thickly settled area on the outer fringe of Norfolk. The rule of this case was also applied to prevent any incorporation in populous Arlington County, adjacent to Washington, D.C. *Bennett v. Garrett,* 112 S.E. 772 (Va. 1922). These cases have been evaded in recent years by the incorporation of entire counties.

[margin note: Denied]

d. *Need and ability to pay for governmental services.* Few cases consider this factor, except in a self-serving sense, to justify a new incorporation. *See* the *Fridley* case, *supra.* Some lower court Pennsylvania cases have considered the impact of the incorporation on the township from which it is to be carved, but the cases are conflicting.

A court wishing to take a broad perspective on the "community" affected by the incorporation is limited in the initiatives it can take because it cannot redraw proposed municipal boundaries to make the proposed municipality more viable. To do so would be to improperly assume a legislative function. Any attempt to judicially arbitrate between competing incorporation petitions, or competing incorporation and annexation petitions, is further limited by a usual rule of procedure that gives preference to the petition that is first filed. *Contra, Chastain v. City of Little Rock,* 185 S.W.2d 95 (Ark. 1945). *Cf.* Tenn. Code Ann. § 6-5-110, giving priority as among competing annexation petitions to the petition filed by the largest municipality.

Comments: 1. PROBLEM: A foreign manufacturer of automobiles has acquired 200 acres of land on which it proposes to build an assembly plant. The plot is about one-half mile from a small unincorporated settlement of 500. The settlement consists of a main street with a few stores, surrounded by residential dwellings. About one-quarter mile outside of the settlement a developer has built a large subdivision of 200 single-family homes. All of the surrounding area is agricultural, but some of the agricultural land near the settlement is held by developers who plan to build residential subdivisions.

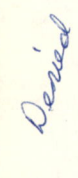

Residents of the settlement propose to incorporate and to include the settlement, the automobile assembly plant land, the nearby subdivision, and agricultural land extending about one-half mile out from the perimeter of the settlement. Under what statutes and court decisions reviewed in this section would incorporation be allowed by a county board, assuming the board has the authority to authorize incorporation? Under what statutes could incorporation be disallowed by a court, assuming the board decides to authorize incorporation?

2. Several states have established so-called "growth zones" around major cities in order to deal with the problem of fringe incorporations and to provide room for the natural expansion of major cities. These statutes usually prevent the incorporation of any new municipality within a three- to six-mile distance of the protected city, unless that city has consented to the incorporation. *E.g.,* Ariz. Rev. Stat. Ann. § 9-101.1. Under the Mississippi version of the growth zone statute the protected city is simply entitled to become a party to any incorporation proceeding within the protected area. In a case in which a petition for incorporation was filed for a new municipality one-half mile east of the City of Meridian, the supreme court allowed the incorporation to proceed because the area to be incorporated had a critical water and sewer problem and there was evidence that it would be fifteen or twenty years before Meridian could annex it. *City of Meridian v. Town of Marion,* 255 So. 2d 906 (Miss. 1971). *See generally* Mandelker, *Municipal Incorporations on the Urban Fringe: Procedures for Determination and Review,* 18 LA. L. REV. 628 (1958).

In *Corporation of Collierville v. Fayette County Election Commission,* 539 S.W.2d 334 (Tenn. 1976), an area proposed to incorporate in violation of a growth zone statute. The city protected by the statute sued to challenge the proposed incorporation. The court held that the city had standing, although private citizens could not sue to challenge incorporations. A contrary holding, the court said, would make the growth zone statute unenforceable.

2. ANNEXATION BY MUNICIPALITIES

Annexation continues in full strength. More than three million Americans were annexed to municipalities between 1970 and 1979. The reasons for annexation are summarized in the following excerpt:

> Annexation is a mechanism which cities can employ to deal with decreasing tax bases, suburbs unwilling or unable to provide adequate services to their residents, governmental fragmentation which prevents comprehensive and organized planning for the development of metropolitan areas, and inequities and disparities in taxes and resources among communities. It is argued that if a city annexes fringe areas before they can incorporate, then the exodus of the original city residents and commercial interest will not affect the city tax base since they will be moving within the political boundaries of the city. Further, government fragmentation and tax inequities will not arise since, as part of the cities, these annexed areas will be subject to the same tax rates. This situation supposedly would eliminate disparities in school quality and services by allowing the government to decide where to spend its revenue. Since only one government would exist, comprehensive planning and adequate services could be provided without costly duplication and intergovernmental conflict.

A. Mushkatel, Citizen Response to Annexation 15, 16 (1975) (Ph.D. thesis on file at University of Oregon Library). *See also State ex rel. Collier v. City of Pigeon Forge,* 599 S.W.2d 545, 547 (Tenn. 1980).

Like incorporations, annexations occur in rural areas and on the outer fringe of metropolitan areas, where municipalities are not surrounded and still have room to grow. To a very large extent, much annexation activity occurs in medium-sized freestanding cities which are growing and which are not surrounded by incorporated suburbs. Lincoln, Nebraska is one example. Texas, where the statute provides virtually no limitation on annexation within a designated extraterritorial area, provides some typical contrasts. Dallas is ringed with suburbs while Houston and Austin have largely prevented the formation of suburban municipalities through active annexation programs.

Annexation Conflicts

Annexation often is a strategic move to acquire "turf" in a contested "turf battle." Two municipalities may want to annex the same territory. A county or township may be threatened by the withdrawal of territory by an annexing municipality. Municipalities sometimes annex industrial or commercial development in a move that opponents call a "tax grab."

Annexation may also be triggered by a zoning controversy. A developer denied a necessary zoning by a county or municipality may seek annexation by a friendlier municipality. These rival claims for turf often trigger judicial review if the annexation succeeds.

Methods and Mechanics

Annexation law may authorize the initiation of annexation proceedings by the annexing municipality, by adjacent property owners or residents, or may authorize both methods. Voter approval may be required in the annexing municipality, in the area to be annexed, in both areas, or in none. Voting issues in annexation are discussed in Chapter 10.

Annexation by special act of the legislature is available in a few states, and is an incident of home rule in Texas and Missouri. Judicial review and approval are required in Virginia and Missouri, and in some states is required following a protest by a specified number of objectors. Most states provide for more than one method of annexation, and may authorize different methods of annexation for different classes of cities. For a detailed review of annexation methods and statutes see Advisory Commission on Intergovernmental Relations, State and Local Roles in the Federal System 360-83 (1982).

Judicial Review Under the Rule of Reason

Courts in several states provide some review of annexations under the rule of reason. The rule is constitutional in Wisconsin, see the *Beloit* case, *supra,* and is mandated by statute in Missouri. Mo. Rev. Stat. § 71.015(5)(b) ("reasonable and necessary to the proper development of the city").

How much judicial review the rule of reason allows is not clear. The following definitions may help:

> "[A] case of reasonableness is made where it appears that the land annexed is so situated as to be adaptable to urban purposes and necessary or convenient to a reasonable exercise of the city government." . . . "[R]easonableness" and "necessity" are closely related concepts and . . . the need to the city for annexation is encompassed within the whole concept of reasonableness.

Mayor, Councilmen & Citizens v. Beard, 613 S.W.2d 642, 651, 652 (Mo. App.), aff'd, 613 S.W.2d 641 (Mo. 1981).

> Reasonableness in enlargement of municipal boundaries is determined by a number of factors such as a substantial increase in population; a need for additional area for construction of homes, mercantile, manufacturing or industrial establishments; a need for additional land area to accommodate the present or reasonably anticipated future growth of the municipality; and the extension of police, fire, sanitary protection or other municipal services to substantial numbers of residents of adjacent areas. [A case-by-case analysis applies.] The court considers generally the benefits and detriments to both the municipality and the area to be annexed.

Kansas City Southern Railway v. City of Shreveport, 354 So. 2d 1362 (La. 1978). See also City of Birmingham v. Mead Corp., 372 So. 2d 825 (Ala. 1979).

Reconsider the automobile plant incorporation problem in the Comment, *supra*. Now assume that the developed part of the small settlement is incorporated. It plans to extend its boundaries to include all of the land proposed in that problem for incorporation. Would this annexation be allowed under the rule of reason?

Reread the last sentence in the excerpt from the *Kansas City Southern* case. That sentence appears to apply a "balancing test" to annexation that considers both the interests of the annexing municipality and the area to be annexed. The application of the balancing test may be critical. Some other municipality, or the county, may better be able to serve the needs of the area to be annexed than the annexing municipality. A court could apply the balancing test to disapprove the annexation. Would this application of the balancing test violate separation of powers? *See* the *Beloit* case, *supra*. The following case considers these problems:

IN RE CHAR

Court of Appeals of Ohio
59 Ohio App. 2d 152, 392 N.E.2d 1312 (1978)

WILEY, JUDGE.

The appeal herein is from the judgment of the Common Pleas Court of Montgomery County, whereby the decision of the Board of County Commissioners of Montgomery County denying the annexation of 63.754 acres of land in Butler Township to the city of Dayton was reversed and the petition for annexation was granted.

The petition for annexation herein was filed with the Montgomery County Board of Commissioners by the three owners of the territory sought to be annexed — namely, Inland Steel Development Corporation, Frederick E. Gagel, and O. B. Scharrer. Anthony B. Char was appointed by the petitioners as their appointed agent, as required by R.C. 709.02. On August 26, 1976, the board adopted resolution No. 2661 denying the annexation, which reads in pertinent part as follows:

Now, Therefore, Be It Resolved by the Board of County Commissioners of Montgomery County, Ohio, that it finds:

1. There are 3 owners of real estate in the territory sought to be annexed, of which 3 signed the petition.
2. A full description and accurate map or plat of the area was submitted.
3. A statement of the total number of owners of real estate in the area was submitted.
4. The name of a person, or persons, to act as Agent was submitted.
5. Proper notice, as required by law, was given.
6. That the names on the petition are owners or (*sic*) real estate in the territory sought to be annexed and at the time of filing the number of valid signatures did constitute a majority of the owners of real estate in the territory sought to be annexed.
7. The area sought to be annexed is not unreasonably large.
8. The description and map or plat are accurate.
9. The general good of the territory sought to be annexed would not be served pursuant to the petition inasmuch as there was no evidence before the Board of County Commissioners that would indicate that the City of Dayton could better serve the area sought to be annexed than Butler Township is presently serving.

Thereafter, a timely appeal was filed in the Common Pleas Court of Montgomery County, pursuant to R.C. Chapter 2506. Twenty-three persons, twelve of whom reside in an apartment complex located within the territory in question and 11 of whom reside upon land adjacent thereto, sought by motion to intervene in the appeal. This motion was granted as to the 12 residents within the territory sought to be annexed and were considered by the trial court as appellees in that they were opposed to disturbing the decision of the commissioners.

In an appeal brought under R.C. Chapter 2506, the trial court may determine whether the order appealed from is unconstitutional, illegal, arbitrary, capricious, unreasonable, or unsupported by the preponderance of substantial, reliable and probative evidence. Prior to the enactment of R.C. 709.033, in 1967, County Commissioners were given broad and practically unlimited discretion by the state legislature to grant or deny a petition for annexation.... By amendment to the Revised Code sections dealing with annexations in 1967 and 1969, the discretion to be exercised by Boards of County Commissioners in such proceedings was substantially curtailed. R.C. 709.033, *Lariccia v. Board of Commrs.* (1974), 38 Ohio St.2d 99, 310 N.E.2d 257. It is also noted that prior to 1967, R.C. 709.02 referred to the fact that the *"inhabitants* residing on territory adjacent to municipal corporations may, at their option, cause such territory to be annexed...." (Emphasis added.) The wording as to *inhabitants* was retained in the 1967 amendment; however, by further amendment effective November 21, 1969, R.C. 709.02 was amended to read in this respect "the *owners of real estate* adjacent to...."

In the case at bar, the County Commissioners found all the substantive and procedural statutory prerequisites for annexation to be present, except it found that the general good of the territory would not be served if annexation were approved. Particular reference is made to item 9 of the resolution of the Board of County Commissioners of Montgomery County, to wit: "The general good of the territory sought to be annexed would not be served pursuant to the petition inasmuch as there was no evidence before the Board of County Commissioners that would indicate that the city of Dayton could better serve the area sought to be annexed than Butler Township is presently serving." The trial court stated in its detailed decision and entry, which we quote with approval, to wit:

> The Court is unable to sustain such a finding. Within the record there is evidence that, (1) The City will, upon annexation, provide a higher level of certain existing governmental services, (2) certain additional services not heretofore available within the territory will be available by annexation, and (3) annexation is commercially advantageous to all of the petitioning owner-appellants.

The trial court proceeded to point out that the fire chief of the city of Dayton testified regarding the fire services available upon annexation and indicated that the high rating of the Dayton Fire Department was superior to the rating of the Butler Township Volunteer Fire Department. The trial court further referred to the informal resolution of the city of Dayton detailing the various services it would provide to the area upon annexation. Representatives of the city also testified before the Board of County Commissioners of Montgomery County concerning the other numerous services that would be provided, including waste collection, street lighting and maintenance, water and sanitary sewerage, engineering, parks and recreation, and 24-hour police service. Upon our consideration of the record of the proceedings before the Board of County Commissioners of Montgomery County, we find that the record sustains the trial court's findings that the general good of the territory in question will be served by annexation.

As noted by the trial court, we also call attention to the recent case of *In re Char,* unreported, Second Appellate District, No. 5472, rendered in 1977, wherein the Court of Appeals of Montgomery County affirmed a Common Pleas Court decision reversing a denial of annexation of property to the city of Dayton. This court stated:

> In considering this question we cannot minimize the fact that the Commissioners failed to recognize the petitioners as the owners and as owners of all the territory involved (*sic*). These owners by affidavits stated that annexation would serve the general good of the territory and that services available thereby would enhance the value of their property. Since they represented all owners, no property owner was opposed and no property owner spoke against the issue.

Continuing, this court stated:

> In *Lariccia v. Board of County Commissioners,* 38 Ohio St.2d 99 [310 N.E.2d 257], the Supreme Court considered this new statute and provided a determinative guide as to its meaning and purpose. The good of the territory to be annexed is identified as a significant factor. The effect upon other territory is not an element in the statutory mandate to the Commissioners. Here and in all annexations there is the ever present effort of a municipality to enlarge and the anguish of the subdivision encroached. However, the good or evil to either is not one of the statutory considerations for annexation. This is interesting because in *Lariccia,* other than the customary benefits of improved services, the specific good to the single owner of the territory was the opportunity to obtain a license from the State Liquor Board which in turn would enhance the value of the owner's business operation. This novel personal benefit was sufficient, though not necessarily alone, to qualify as general good of the territory under the statutory language and to require the mandated annexation.

Likewise in the case at bar, the personal benefit to the sole owners of the territory to be annexed is sufficient, though not necessarily alone, to qualify as general good of the territory under the statutory language and to require the mandated annexation.

There is one factual difference in the case at bar from the facts in *Lariccia* and the unreported *Char* case, to wit: In both cases there were no residents who were opposing the annexation, whereas in the case at bar there are residents of the territory to be annexed who are opposing the annexation although *these residents are not owners.*

The trial court addressed this very issue as to how much weight and significance is given by law to the intervening appellees, the lessee-residents, within the affected acreage. This court adopts the reasoning and the statement of the trial court in this regard, as follows:

> Although these appellees were, upon motion, properly permitted to intervene in this appeal as "interested persons" the court concludes that their interests are substantially outweighed by the interests of the petitioning landowners.
>
> ....
>
> Although the implications for the community to which the property in question would be annexed may well be of some consequence, the clear statement of the General Assembly in R.C. 709.033 cannot be ignored. That statute directs that the ultimate focus of annexation proceedings be on "the

general good of the territory sought to be annexed," and requires granting of the petition when it is shown that such benefit will result.

. . . .

The legislature, by specifically amending, in 1969, the wording of R.C. 709.02 to read "owners" instead of "inhabitants" indicates the legislative intent to give great preference to *owners of real estate* adjacent to a municipal corporation rather than to the *inhabitants of real estate* adjacent to municipal corporations, in respect to annexation proceedings.

Arguably, when the amendments by the legislature were made in 1967 and 1969 to correct, in part, the inadequacies, the inequities, and the ambiguities existing under the former statutes relating to annexation, the legislature went too far and has disregarded totally the equities in regard to the inhabitants of the territory to be annexed as well as disregarding the welfare of the inhabitants of areas adjacent to the territory to be annexed. On balance, if this is actually the case, and if in correcting one situation the legislature has created other inequities, it is desirable that the legislature correct these inequities rather than for this court to attempt to do so.

. . . .

Judgment affirmed.

KERNS, P.J., and MCBRIDE, J., concur.

Comments: 1. Do you agree with the court's reading of the statute? Consider the following cases:

West Mead Township v. City of Meadville, 294 A.2d 600 (Pa. Commw. 1972). The city planned to annex a multifamily development. The court applied the annexation law, whose guiding "polestar" was whether the annexation served the public interest. A "threat of piecemeal annexation township suicide" was raised by the township but rejected by the court. Although large blocs of township acreage and tax revenue had been taken from the township in recent years, neither township debt nor tax rate had increased.

City of Olivette v. Graeler, 338 S.W.2d 827 (Mo. 1960), 369 S.W.2d 85 (Mo. 1963), *noted,* 1961 WASH. U.L.Q. 159. A suburban city in St. Louis County, which had almost 100 incorporated suburban municipalities, planned to annex land intended for industrial development. The court disapproved the annexation. It took note of the metropolitan setting of local government in the area and indicated that it would weigh the interests of the county as a viable unit of local government against the interests of the annexing city. The Missouri intermediate appellate courts have since allowed suburban annexations in St. Louis County. *See City of Creve Coeur v. Braume,* 446 S.W.2d 173 (Mo. App. 1969). See the Missouri statute, *supra.*

2. Virginia has long been noted for its annexation system, in which annexations are subject to approval by an annexation court. The court applies a "best interests" test which requires consideration of the best interests of the annexing city, the county from which the annexed area is taken, and "the best interests of the State in promoting strong and viable units of government." Va. Code § 15.1-1041(b).. The Virginia courts have approved this use of the judicial power in annexations. Cities pursued annexation aggressively, with court approval, and their annexation programs eventually led to strained relationships with the counties. The city-county problem is aggravated in Virginia because the cities are governmentally separate from the counties. Annexation can remove tax-rich and highly developed areas from county jurisdiction.

The legislature responded in 1971 by imposing a moratorium on city annexations and by creating a Commission on City-County Relationships to report on annexation problems. The committee reported in 1975. It noted that, as counties have increasingly provided urban services, city justifications for annexation have changed. Cities now justify annexations on a "community of interest" between the city and residents of the annexed area, the economic and social viability of the city, and the need to extend to suburban residents the operating costs of the cities on which they depend. *See* the Advisory Commission report, *supra*, at 374-75; *County of Rockingham v. City of Harrisonburg*, 294 S.E.2d 825 (Va. 1982) (quoting report recommendations).

The legislature adopted many of the Commission's recommendations. These include an immunity from annexation for densely populated counties, authority to counties to incorporate as cities, and a right to share in the economic growth of the county as an alternative to annexation. The legislature also created a Commission on Local Government, with authority to investigate and report on proposed annexations and other boundary changes. Annexation reports are admissible in annexation court proceedings. The annexation statute was amended to define in detail the criteria to be used in applying the "best interests" test.

These statutory changes were considered in the *County of Rockingham* case, *supra*. The annexation area contained about thirteen percent of the county's taxable value. The area almost surrounded the city, and had been developed for major commercial and industrial uses including the county's only shopping mall, all of the county's major hotels, and ninety-eight percent of the county's water customers.

The county argued that "the law no longer recognizes the proposition that urban areas must be governed by cities," but the court approved the annexation. It found a need for city services, noting that this need was justified by the "planning context." The county's master plan anticipated the urbanization of most of the annexed area. The court also noted that many businesses had left the city's downtown for the shopping mall, which was now the area's principal shopping center, that vacant storefronts remained in the city, and that the city would "soon need a larger tax base." The county did not qualify for annexation immunity under the statute. To what extent did the court accept the justifications for city annexation which were noted above? What does the Virginia experience indicate about the role of annexation in the urban growth and development process? In resolving claims for territory between competing local governments?

3. What if a developer planning to build an industrial facility approaches the county in which the land is located for a rezoning of her property. The county declines to rezone because water and sewer services are not available. The developer then approaches a contiguous city. Several meetings are held, and city officials tell her that a rezoning is likely. The developer petitions for annexation as provided under state law. She owns all of the land which is the subject of the annexation petition. One day later she petitions the city for a rezoning. One month later the city approves the annexation and proceeds with the rezoning.

A court approved an annexation under facts similar to these in *Town of Pleasant Prairie v. City of Kenosha*, 249 N.W.2d 581 (Wis. 1977). The court noted:

> The Ganglers' purpose was to develop their land, preferably for industrial use, which required zoning and municipal services not available in the Town. It cannot be doubted that a purpose to develop one's land is legitimate, and this court has stated that property owners may seek annexation in pursuit of their own perceived best interest.

Id. at 586. The court also held that the annexation was proper "with respect to . . . sound land use, management and urban planning."

Should personal interest be relevant to an application of the rule of reason? What if the rezoning was "bad" land use planning? Should the court adjudicate this issue in an annexation case, or leave it to neighbors to challenge the rezoning?

4. What about a "turf" fight between two municipalities? In *Extension of Boundaries of Ridgeland*, 388 So. 2d 153 (Miss. 1980), the city, which is a suburb of Jackson, sought to annex a developing area. Jackson claimed that the area was more properly within its "path of growth." The court dismissed this objection by upholding the following findings by the trial chancellor:

> I take no issue with the argument that Tract III is within Jackson's path of growth. The truth is that all areas immediately surrounding Jackson are in its path. While the path

of growth factor is not the only one to be considered . . ., I do feel that Tract III is in a less definite way also in Ridgeland's path of growth . . . .

The fears of Jackson in being ultimately restricted from future annexation through encirclement by small municipalities is understandable. . . . However, Ridgeway itself stands to have its growth thwarted by both natural and political barriers.

Id. at 156. If the court disapproved the Ridgeway annexation, could it compel Jackson to act?

5. *Annexation agreements.* Many annexations occur through annexation agreements between landowners and municipalities. They often are used when a developer wishes to develop land that requires city services or needs a rezoning which the local government in which the land is located is not willing to give. The agreement usually provides that the developer will not protest annexation in return for the municipality's promise to provide necessary services and, if necessary, to rezone the developer's land. The agreement may also provide for fees and site improvements to be provided by the developer.

If the annexation agreement is not authorized by statute, a court may declare it invalid as a circumvention of the annexation law. *Doan v. City of Ft. Wayne,* 252 N.E.2d 415 (Ind. 1969). Some states authorize annexation agreements. *See* Ill. Ann. Stat. ch. 24, § 11-15.1-2 et seq. (agreement may cover zoning of land).

Statutory authority does not necessarily protect an annexation agreement from all legal objections. Assume a group of property owners protests an annexation. The city settles the protest by executing an annexation agreement which includes, among other provisions, a promise to "assist and cooperate fully" with the property owners in securing any necessary zoning changes. Is there an invalid bargaining away of the municipality's legislative power? The court thought so in *City of Louisville v. Fiscal Court,* 623 S.W.2d 219 (Ky. 1981):

> [T]he city is required to cooperate . . . in matters which fall within the duty and responsibility of the city . . . . It is very conceivable, (and even likely) that the obligations of the City under the agreement would create a conflict between the constitutional and statutory duties of the City and its contractual obligations.
>
> . . . [T]he contract . . . also creates an obligation to legislate in the future. . . . A contract which binds a legislative body, present or future, to a course of legislative action is void against public policy.

Id. at 225.

See also Maywood Proviso State Bank v. City of Oakbrook Terrace, 214 N.E.2d 582 (Ill. App. 1966). The city agreed in the annexation agreement to give the landowner a five-year liquor license. The court held that the agreement was contrary to state law, which authorized only a one-year license.

The court upheld an annexation agreement in *Morrison Homes Corp. v. City of Pleasanton,* 130 Cal. Rptr. 196 (Cal. App. 1976). The agreement provided that the city would extend water and sewer services in return for a promise by the corporation to make street and other improvements on its land and to pay sewer connection fees. Both sides performed under the agreement until additional sewer service was prohibited by a regional water quality agency because the city's treatment plant was inadequate.

The court ordered the city to continue to provide services. The agreement had been executed, and the court held that it did not "surrender" the city's annexation powers or sewer authority. The agreement recited that the corporation would carry out its development in accordance with the city's master plan and ordinances, and the trial court had found the agreement "just, reasonable, fair and equitable." For these reasons, the appellate court held that the agreement was not void because some of its executory features might extend beyond the term of office of city council members who made the agreement. Should the "bargaining away" problem disappear if the agreement is partially executed?

6. Voters brought into a municipality after a contested annexation may oppose municipal programs by voting against bond issues and tax increases needed to provide municipal services in the municipality and the annexed area. *See* Mushkatel, Wilson & Mushkatel, *A Model of Citizen Response to Annexation,* 9 URB. AFF. Q. 139 (1977). Some states have attempted to defuse opposition by agricultural landowners who object to higher city taxes by adopting legislation provided for the taxation of agricultural land at agricultural value following annexation. See *Caldis v. Board of County Commissioners,* 279 N.W.2d 665 (N.D. 1979), upholding a statute of this type against equal protection objections. The court held that "when the market value of a specific parcel of annexed agricultural land increases because of a change in its potential 'highest and best use,' the increase in assessment is a burden to the owner warranting a more lenient tax treatment of the property." *Id.* at 672. Is legislation of this type a response to the rule that landowners cannot object to an annexation because of an increase in their property taxes?

RACIAL DISCRIMINATION IN ANNEXATIONS AND THE FEDERAL VOTING RIGHTS ACT

Annexation usually has been regarded favorably by local government experts as an orderly method for extending municipal boundaries when areas adjacent to municipalities are urbanized and require urban services or regulation. *Gomillion, supra,* foreshadows another issue in annexation proceedings. Just as the municipal deannexation in that case substantially reduced the black vote in Tuskegee, municipal annexations of adjacent white-populated areas will dilute the black vote in municipalities that have or are approaching black voting majorities. The question is whether annexations brought with this purpose or effect are actionable under the fourteenth amendment, and whether they violate the voting abridgement provisions of the Federal Voting Rights Act.

These issues surfaced in a series of cases considering a major annexation to the city of Richmond, Virginia. This annexation was initiated in 1962, but lingered for several years until it was settled in 1969. There was some evidence that the compromise was spurred by the growing black voting strength in the city. As a result of the settlement, a substantial white population was added to the city, reducing what was previously a marginal black majority to a minority that, after the annexation, made up 42 percent of the city's population. While a federal district court found that the annexation had an illegal racial purpose, the court of appeals reversed. *Holt v. City of Richmond,* 334 F. Supp. 228 (E.D. Va. 1971), *rev'd,* 459 F.2d 1093 (4th Cir.), *cert. denied,* 404 U.S. 998 (1972), *noted,* 51 N.C.L. Rev. 573 (1973).

The court of appeals appeared to require a showing of impermissible legislative purpose before it could invalidate the annexation on racial grounds, and was unwilling to find such a purpose. There were compelling reasons for the annexation at the time it was initiated, including a desire to expand the social and demographic population mix in the city. The improper motives of some councilmen that arose after the increase in black voting strength became apparent could not be attributed to the entire council. *Gomillion* was distinguished as a case whose "sole or clearly dominant purpose was both obvious and constitutionally impermissible." *Id.* at 1097.

An action was then brought by the city to have the annexation validated under the federal Voting Rights Act. *City of Richmond v. United States,* 422 U.S. 358 (1975), *noted,* 54 N.C.L. Rev. 206 (1976). This Act, 42 U.S.C. § 1973c, requires that any change "in any voting qualification or prerequisite to voting, or standard, practice, or procedure with respect to voting" must be approved by the United States Attorney General, or by the District Court of the District of Columbia in a declaratory order that finds that this change "does not have the purpose and will not have the effect of denying or abridging the right to vote on account of race or color." The Act requires proof only of discriminatory effect rather than a discriminatory purpose. *City of Rome v. United States,* 446 U.S. 156 (1980). Compare the voting rights cases, *infra* Chapter 10.

An earlier United States Supreme Court case, *Perkins v. Matthews,* 400 U.S. 379 (1971), brought annexations within the Voting Rights Act because they had a "sufficient potential" for denying or abridging the right to vote because of race or color. In the *Richmond* case, an argument was made that the single-member ward system for electing city council members, proposed by the city and approved by the Attorney General after the annexation to replace at-large elections of the council, denied or abridged the right to vote under the Voting Rights Act. The annexation reduced the black population from 52% to 42%. In pre-annexation elections three of the nine council members were black endorsed. In the proposed plan four wards were over 64% black; four were heavily white; the ninth was 41% black.

The Supreme Court first considered whether the adoption of the single-member ward system following the annexation had the effect of denying or abridging the right of blacks in Richmond to vote:

> We cannot accept the position that such a single-member ward system would nevertheless have the effect of denying or abridging the right to vote because Negroes would constitute a lesser proportion of the population after the annexation than before and, given racial bloc voting, would have fewer seats on the city council. If a city having a ward system for the election of a nine-man council annexes a largely white area, the wards are fairly redrawn, and as a result Negroes have only two rather than the four seats they had before, these facts alone do not demonstrate that the annexation has the effect of denying or abridging the right to vote. As long as the ward system fairly reflects the strength of the Negro community as it exists after the annexation, we cannot hold, without more specific legislative directions, that such an annexation is nevertheless barred by § 5. It is true that the black community, if there is racial bloc voting, will command fewer seats on the city council; and the annexation will have effected a decline in the Negroes' relative influence in the city. But a different city council and an enlarged city are involved after the annexation. Furthermore, Negro power in the new city is not undervalued, and Negroes will not be underrepresented on the council.
>
> As long as this is true, we cannot hold that the effect of the annexation is to deny or abridge the right to vote. To hold otherwise would be either to forbid all such annexations or to require, as the price for approval of the annexation, that the black community be assigned the same proportion of council seats as before, hence perhaps permanently overrepresenting them and underrepresenting other elements in the community, including the nonblack citizens in the annexed area. We are unwilling to hold that Congress intended either consequence in enacting § 5.

Id. at 370-71.

The Supreme Court then considered whether the annexation had the purpose of denying or abridging the right to vote. While adopting a "plain" statement that any annexation having this impermissible purpose violates the Act, the Court also adopted a justification test. An alleged racially discriminatory purpose could be rebutted by proof of countervailing economic or administrative benefits that supported the annexation. These justifications could be advanced after the fact, at the time the annexation is challenged, a self-justifying opportunity available to the municipality that led Justice Brennan, in dissent, to a conclusion that the "prophylactic purpose" of the Voting Rights Act had been negated. Note that the Voting Rights Act had attempted to overcome the difficulties of proof faced by plaintiffs in cases such as *Richmond* by shifting the burden of proof under that Act to the municipalities. To what extent does the *Richmond* case undercut this congressional intent? For a case upholding a refusal to approve annexations of predominantly white areas by a predominantly white city see *Rome, supra.*

The preclearance requirement of the Voting Rights Act was extended by Congress in 1982. It is applicable to selected southern states and areas and to some areas outside the south. For a discussion of the application of the Act to southern annexations see Cotrell & Steven, *The 1975 Voting Rights Act, Annexation Policy and Urban Growth in the Sunbelt,* 3 [Tex.] Urb. L. Rev. 1 (1979). For case studies of racial issues in annexations in the St. Louis metropolitan area see Dubrow, *Municipal Antagonism or Benign Neglect: Racial Motivations in Municipal Annexations in St. Louis County, Missouri,* 53 J. Urb. L. 245 (1975). The Voting Rights Act is discussed further in Chapter 10.

C. SPECIAL DISTRICTS

PHILLIPS, DEVELOPMENTS IN WATER QUALITY AND LAND USE PLANNING: PROBLEMS IN THE APPLICATION OF THE FEDERAL WATER POLLUTION CONTROL ACT AMENDMENTS OF 1972, 10 Urban Law Annual 43, 101-04 (1975)

Nature and Functions of Special Districts

Special districts are generally considered to be distinct, limited-purpose units of local government. Because of disparities in size, function and organizational framework, they are incapable of precise definition, but all special districts exhibit the same basic characteristics. They are organized to perform one or more governmental services or functions, are governed by a board of directors who possess administrative independence from other units of local government, have independent financial and revenue powers similar to those of other local government units, and are separate corporate entities, with a perpetual existence, created by state enabling legislation.

The modern special district is an outgrowth of the drainage and flood control districts that were created to encourage and facilitate development of the Northwest Territory. Although originally formed as a service mechanism for existing communities, special districts are once again being utilized to provide urban services to unincorporated fringe areas. The reasons for the present resort to the special district form of government are varied and reflect both the historical growth and current decline of urban areas.

Special districts are utilized primarily because of the unsuitability of other units of local government for dealing with specific metropolitan problems. Often the territorial jurisdiction of an existing governmental unit does not conform to the area in need of assistance. This problem of inadequate geographic size is particularly acute in the field of water management. Demands for water supply and sewage disposal are most efficiently met when planned on a watershed basis. Municipalities and counties are often ineffective in providing such services because their territory is delineated by political rather than geographic boundaries. By contrast, special districts have the necessary geographic flexibility to coordinate service area and function.

Financial restrictions often dictate the creation of special districts. Most state constitutions impose a limitation upon the debt and taxing powers of general governments. When such limits are attained, the general government is prevented from expanding or providing new services. These financial restrictions, however, do not prevent residents from forming a new unit of government and endowing it with powers to incur debts or levy taxes throughout the same approximate area. Thus special districts are created as a means of circumventing restrictive tax and debt limitations. The special district can "incur revenue bond debt, secured by user charges and special assessments which are excluded from debt limitations of cities and counties."

Another financial incentive fostering the creation of special districts is that the majority of the districts' revenue is generated from non-tax sources, such as service charges and sales. Since they are generally single-functional and geographically flexible, most districts are financed by those who are directly benefited by the service. The financial pool of the special district usually covers a larger area, encompassing several local governments. It remains an attractive service mechanism, however, because "the financing process rarely directly affects the public at large, which does not have to pay taxes or guarantee the bonds of those authorities."

Special districts may also be created in response to a desire for autonomy and independence by those who have an interest in the peculiar function or service of the district. This interest may be reflected by a desire among residents of the unincorporated fringe areas to share only a single service with the urban center; it may be a reaction to the perceived effectiveness of the local governing unit; or it may be manifested by a desire to keep the function "out of politics." Since the special district is independent of local government, it is often claimed that creation of the district will promote functional efficiency and operational expertise. Although there are numerous other reasons and conditions that prompt the formation of special districts, they are usually created in response to the insufficiency and inadequacy of the existing unit of local government to provide the needed service or function. Furthermore, due in part to the peculiarities of state enabling legislation and partly to general political inertia, it is often easier to form a new unit of government than it is to pressure the existing government into assuming a new function. For all of these reasons, the special district device is often the most efficient means of securing a service for an area with a minimal disruptive influence on the existing local government structure.

Organization of Special Districts

Statutes authorize the organization of special districts through a variety of methods. A special act of the legislature is one alternative, although most legislation authorizes the formation of a special district on the filing of a petition by residents or taxpayers living in the area proposed as a special district. An election may or may not be required. Municipalities and counties may be authorized to organize dependent special districts, and some legislation authorizes the formation of special districts by state agencies.

Judicial review of the organization of special districts is even more limited than judicial review of municipal incorporations. Some statutes provide no criteria for organization, and judicial review is not available. *See Fladung v. City of Boulder,* 417 P.2d 787 (Colo. 1966). Judicial review of special district decisions to undertake projects also is limited. See *Eways v. Board of Road Supervisors,* 220 A.2d 840 (Pa. 1966), limiting judicial review to fraud and bad faith. For discussion see M. POCK, INDEPENDENT SPECIAL DISTRICTS: A SOLUTION TO THE METROPOLITAN AREA PROBLEMS (1962).

When criteria for the formation of a special district are provided by statute, they may be limited to the purposes to be served by the district. A Washington statute, for example, provides that a county board of commissioners may "activate" an air pollution control district if:

(1) Air pollution exists and is likely to occur; and
(2) The city or town ordinances or county resolutions or their enforcement, are inadequate to prevent or control pollution . . . .

Wash. Rev. Code Ann. § 70.94.055. On what basis could a court disapprove a district organized under this statute?

Some statutes provide broader criteria. A Minnesota statute authorizes the state water resources control board to organize watershed districts. These districts perform flood control, water supply, drainage and conservation functions. The board must find that the organization of the district "would be for the public welfare and public interest, and that the purpose of this chapter would be subserved." Minn. Stat. Ann. § 112.39(3). The purposes of the statute are carrying out "conservation of the natural resources of the state through land utilization, flood control and other needs upon sound scientific principles for the protection of the public health and welfare and the provident use of natural resources." *Id.* § 112.34.

A court is likely to uphold a "health and welfare" finding of this type. See *Holversten v. Minnesota Water Resources Board,* 188 N.W.2d 923 (Minn. 1971), upholding the organization of a district against objections that "the landowners in the watershed area have no substantial water problems." What if the statute authorized formation of a watershed district only if "substantial water problems" were present? See *Reilly Tar & Chemical Corp. v. City of St. Louis Park,* 121 N.W.2d 393 (Minn. 1963). A statute authorized a city to organize a housing and redevelopment authority if it found "blighted" areas within a city. The court held that organization of a district would be in "excess" of the city's powers if blighting conditions did not exist.

More rigorous judicial review may be available when a statute requires a "benefit" to included landowners before a district may be organized. See *Petition of Lower Valley Water & Sanitation District,* 632 P.2d 1170 (N.M. 1981), in which landowners argued that they had no need for sewer improvements to be provided by a proposed sewer and sanitation district. The court upheld a lower court decision excluding their land for sewer but retaining it for water improvement purposes.

What if a district is organized for purposes not authorized by the statute? The following case raises this problem:

CITY OF SCOTTSDALE v. McDOWELL MOUNTAIN IRRIGATION & DRAINAGE DISTRICT

Supreme Court of Arizona
107 Ariz. 117, 483 P.2d 532 (1971)

WILLIBY E. CASE, JR., JUDGE OF THE COURT OF APPEALS.

This is an appeal from an order granting appellees' motion for summary judgment in an action wherein appellants sought to test the validity of the organization of the McDowell Mountain Irrigation and Drainage District (hereinafter referred to as the District).

Two issues are presented on appeal. First, do any or all of the appellants have standing to test the validity of the District's organization? Second, did the jurisdictional prerequisites exist for the Board to authorize the organization of the District?

The facts necessary for a determination of these issues are as follows.

In the summer of 1968 a petition was filed with the Maricopa County Board of Supervisors, (hereinafter referred to as the Board), pursuant to Title 45, Chapter 6, A.R.S., seeking the organization of certain described land into the McDowell Mountain Irrigation and Drainage District. The land consisting of 11,420 acres was located within Maricopa County and part thereof was situated within six miles of the Scottsdale city limits. [The city appeared in opposition to the formation of the district, but the board granted the petition for organization. The city appealed, the board moved to dismiss, and the trial court granted the motion. The city then appealed to the supreme court. It held that the city had standing to appeal. The state had a growth zone statute which prohibited the formation of new cities and towns within five miles of cities over 5,000, such as Scottsdale. This statute indicated a legislative intent to allow cities of this size to expand without conflicts from newly created municipalities. — Eds.]

2. Did the Jurisdictional Prerequisites Exist for the Board to Authorize the Formation of the District?

The Court's role in the creation of cities, towns or irrigation districts is limited to determining whether the jurisdictional facts necessary for the Board to act existed. . . .

The statutes defining the jurisdictional prerequisites pertinent herein are as follows:

§45-1503. Organization of district

A. When a majority of the holders of title or evidence of title, including receipts or other evidence of the rights of entrymen on lands under any law of the United States or of this state, to lands in a designated area desire to provide for the irrigation of lands in the area, they may propose the organization of an irrigation district under the provisions of this chapter. When organized the district shall have all powers conferred by law upon irrigation districts.

§45-1505. Petition for organization; inclusion of power of drainage

A. For the purpose of organizing an irrigation district as provided by this chapter, a petition signed by a majority of the resident owners of real property to which they hold title or evidence of title in the proposed district shall be filed with the board of supervisors of the county in which the greater portion of the proposed district is located. Each signer of the petition shall describe the lands to which he holds title or evidence of title in the proposed district.

. . . .

The final issue to be decided is whether an irrigation district can be formed wherein the primary intent is not to irrigate arid lands but to develop a planned urbanized community.

In *Post v. Wright,* 37 Ariz. 105, 289 P. 979 (1930), this Court stated:

. . . Petitioners for the organization of districts must always indicate the purpose of the organizers to be to provide water for the irrigation of their lands. . . .

The Court further declared:

It goes without saying that an irrigation district may not enter into business of laying out and promoting townsites. Such business is foreign to any of the purposes for which it is organized. . . .

Appellees indicate that *Post* would control had it not been abrogated by a statutory amendment to what is presently Section 45-1578 A.R.S. Appellees cite the 1931 Amendment to Section 3341, Rev. Code 1928, ... which added to the District's delineated powers the power "to engage in any and all activities, enterprises and occupations within the powers and privileges of municipalities generally." This language, adopted after *Post,* persists today.

Appellees' reliance on the above amendment is misplaced as they fail to appreciate the significance of the language which prefaces the above delegation of power and all other powers of the District. The preface recites: "In order to accomplish the purposes of the district the board may:" (then follows the individual powers). Obviously, the power to engage in activities of municipalities generally is proper only when acting pursuant to the purpose of irrigating arid lands.

Appellees further urge that irrigation be interpreted so as to encompass providing water for city needs such as watering lawns. The cases cited by appellees for this proposition do not deal with irrigation districts and accordingly are inapplicable. In *Post* this Court quoted at length from the California case of *In re Central Irrigation District,* 117 Cal. 382, 49 P. 354 (1897), which discussed the Wright Act. That case indicated that a drugstore owner, a blacksmith or a town resident could not "desire" to irrigate their lands in the sense the word was used in the Wright Act. That Court further noted that the purpose of the Irrigation District Act was to improve agricultural and farming lands by conveying an adequate supply of water to the soil.

. . . .

Accordingly, we reverse and remand for proceedings not inconsistent with this opinion.

Comments: 1. What is the basis for the court's decision? Why is the decision "jurisdictional"? Note that the "intent" of the district was to "develop a planned urbanized community." The developer probably decided to organize the district so that it could issue tax exempt bonds to provide improvements for the community. Should this fact be relevant to the decision on whether the statute authorized the formation of the district?

2. The question of what powers may be exercised by a special district is closely linked to the question of whether a district may be organized at all. *See Wilson v. Hidden Valley Municipal Water District,* 61 Cal. Rptr. 889 (Cal. App. 1968). This district had been formed to prevent the introduction of water and thus the urbanization of the valley. Certain landowners sought to be excluded from the district, but their petition was denied without reasons by the district board of directors. The board's decision was upheld in an opinion which characterized its decision (as is usually the case) as quasi-legislative. Whether the petition should be granted raised "political" questions, and was part of an ongoing struggle between an overwhelming majority and a very small minority over the district's basic policies.

Landowners petitioning for exclusion argued that the district was fraudulent, illegal, and an abuse of the legislative power to form districts as it was illegally performing land use control rather than water supply functions. They claimed that the district had never provided water, although the court noted in a footnote that the district stood ready to provide water whenever a "general demand" existed for this service. It also noted that a special district could be formed for negative as well as positive purposes, in this case the prevention of the importation of water and the urbanization of the valley.

3. Some states provide more extensive control over the organization of special districts. For example, a Colorado law requires the petitioners for any proposed special district to file a service plan with the board of county commissioners.

The board of county commissioners shall disapprove the service plan submitted by the petitioners of a proposed special district upon satisfactory evidence to the board on any of the following:

(a) There is insufficient existing and projected need for organized service in the area to be serviced by the proposed district;

(b) The existing service in the area to be serviced by the proposed district is adequate for present and projected needs;

(c) Adequate service is, or will be, available to the area through municipal annexation by other existing municipal or quasi-municipal corporations within a reasonable time and on a comparable basis;

(d) The proposed special district is incapable of providing economical and sufficient service to the area within its proposed boundaries;

(e) The area to be included in the proposed district does not have, or will not have, the financial ability to discharge the proposed indebtedness on a reasonable basis;

(f) The facility and service standards of the proposed district are incompatible with the facility and service standards of adjacent municipalities and special districts;

(g) The proposal is not in substantial compliance with a [local] master plan;

(h) The proposal is not in compliance with any duly adopted county, regional, or state long-range water quality management plan for the area.

Colo. Rev. Stat. § 32-1-203.

What problems may have prompted the adoption of this law? Does it address the problem in the *Scottsdale* case? In the *Hidden Valley* case? *See Millis v. Board of County Commissioners*, 625 P.2d 652 (Colo. 1981). The court held that a board's finding that a proposed water district's service plan was economically feasible was not an abuse of discretion.

4. Special districts should not always be looked upon as undesirable intruders on the governmental scene. In some places, as in rural areas, they may be the only entity available to provide needed public services. Some states have authorized the formation of multifunctional special districts to provide a wide range of governmental services as an alternative to municipal incorporation. The special district form also is used to provide for metropolitan special districts and authorities that can integrate the provision of one or more public services on the metropolitan level. Several arguments have been advanced for multicounty metropolitan districts serving large areas:

[T]he strengths of multicounty authorities lie in increased efficiency and flexibility of jurisdiction. Among the services that are best suited for administration by this kind of body are those that require accumulated expertise and technological sophistication in their management. Continuity of management, attraction of superior personnel, and corporate powers and decision-making will be most beneficial in such areas as transportation, water supply and sewerage, port direction, and pollution control. Services in which area-wide administration and planning would result in significant economies of scale and integration of separate facilities are also likely to benefit from administration by multicounty authorities. An area-wide policy is mandatory, for instance, if a transportation plan is effectively to coordinate bus, train, and subway services with auto travel on the roads, ferries, and bridges, and through tunnels.

Comment, *An Analysis of Authorities: Traditional and Multicounty*, 71 Mich. L. Rev. 1376, 1429 (1973).

5. Accountability is a major problem in the administration of special district affairs. Special districts collect and disburse vast sums of money, yet their directors may be appointed and not subject to elector control. Even when elections are provided, voter turnout may be low. The Michigan Law Review Comment quoted above addresses this problem:

The greatest cause for concern about the increasing impact of authorities is the lack of public supervision of their activities. However, although the policies of most authorities are not subject to electoral approval, their activities are subject to some legal checks. State legislatures have the final power over authorities in that they may dissolve them once their bonds are discharged. Similarly, as an ultimate check on mismanagement, there are various statutory, and possibly common law, remedies for the bondholder constituency should an authority default. Other provisions to deter misconduct include the powers possessed by governors to remove directors for cause or, more rarely, to veto authority activities. Some authorities are empowered or required to hold public hearings before taking certain actions, and a majority of authorities are required to submit annual reports to executive officials or state legislatures. The presence of state or locally elected officials as ex officio members of an authority's governing body may also keep authority policies in harmony with those of general governments. There have been scattered attempts to provide for supervision of authorities by other government units through such means as the Advisory Board of the Massachusetts Bay Transportation Authority. Such an arrangement is now unique but may well become more common.

Direct accountability to the public remains a major problem. In one sense, this problem arises from the relative anonymity of authorities. An authority may only rarely embark upon major new projects, and its routine duties are seldom considered newsworthy by the press. Moreover, the information released about those large authorities that are in the public eye frequently comes from within the authority itself.

Id. at 1432-34. For an illuminating review of accountability and policy-making problems in one major metropolitan district see Hughes, *Realtors, Bankers and Politicians in the New York/New Jersey Port Authority,* 11 SOCIETY No. 4, at 63 (1974).

6. Special districts may also annex land. Legislatures which create districts by special act may expand them in the same manner. Legislation authorizing annexation through local initiative follows the municipal annexation pattern. Few standards are provided or none are provided, judicial review is minimal, and voter consent usually is necessary. *See* M. POCK, *supra,* at 164-78.

Municipalities may annex land within special districts. This type of annexation creates unique problems. Annexation may not leave the district as a viable unit, or the municipality may annex the capital facilities of the district but leave service lines within the remaining district boundaries. For a discussion of judicial and statutory solutions to this problem see Note, *Problems Created by Municipal Annexation of Special District Territory,* 1967 WASH. U.L.Q. 560.

D. BOUNDARY COMMISSIONS

Several states have created boundary review commissions to provide more adequate and orderly controls over local government organization and boundary change problems. Michigan and Minnesota are midwestern examples, and boundary commissions have been created in all three Pacific coast states. *See* the Advisory Commission Report, *supra,* at 375-81.

The boundary commissions are either state- or county-level agencies, and usually have a broad jurisdiction over all local government organization and boundary problems. Special districts may be included along with municipalities. The commissions are administrative agencies with the power to review the merits of an incorporation or annexation proposal. The statutes usually provide a set of factors which the commissions are to apply in their decisions. These factors usually authorize a comprehensive review of local government organization and boundary change applications. Judicial review is provided on the record developed by the commission. Approval of the commission's decision in an election may be required.

The boundary commission legislation substitutes an agency with expertise and continuing jurisdiction over local government incorporations for bodies like a county board, which considers incorporation petitions infrequently and has no expertise on incorporation problems. For annexations, the commission is a substitute for an annexation process which would otherwise be initiated by a municipality or adjacent property owners for reasons that may be self-serving. Because the commission is an administrative agency with original jurisdiction, it is not restricted by the limitations most state courts impose on their courts when they consider or review incorporation and annexation proceedings.

The following case illustrates the scope of authority exercised by a boundary commission under typical boundary commission legislation. Compare this decision with those in *Caserta* and *Char, supra.*

CITY OF WOOD VILLAGE v. PORTLAND METROPOLITAN AREA LOCAL GOVERNMENT BOUNDARY COMMISSION

Court of Appeals of Oregon
48 Or. App. 79, 616 P.2d 528 (1980)

Before GILLETTE, P.J., and ROBERTS and CAMPBELL, JJ.
GILLETTE, PRESIDING JUDGE.

This is a petition for judicial review of a decision of the Portland Metropolitan Area Local Government Boundary Commission (Boundary Commission) which approved a proposed annexation to the City of Gresham. The petition was initiated by the owner of the property, Peter McGill, pursuant to ORS 222.170 (the so-called "Triple Majority" rule) and proposed the annexation of approximately 278.88 acres located on the north edge of the present city boundaries, which property is also contiguous to the cities of Troutdale and Wood Village. The Gresham City Council adopted a resolution supporting the annexation and the Boundary Commission approved it. The City of Wood Village appeals that decision. We reverse and remand.

The subject property is agricultural land used for growing nursery stock. It contains five agricultural buildings and one single family residence. The owner intends to continue his nursery operations indefinitely. He has no immediate plans to develop the property and is not seeking city services at the present time. He sought annexation to the City of Gresham because he felt that Gresham can best serve his property in the future. The property is identified as urban on the Regional Plan and "future urban" on Multnomah County's Plan. The City of Wood Village included the McGill property in its Comprehensive Plan and claims that the annexation of the property to Wood Village is necessary to maintain Wood Village's financial integrity as a functioning city unit. The nearby cities of Troutdale and Fairview agree.[1]

Petitioner raises a number of assignments of error on appeal; three of these assignments are interrelated and we deal with them together. Petitioner claims that the Boundary Commission's final order did not adequately consider the required statutory criteria, that the Commission failed to make adequate findings of fact and statements of reasoning, and that its findings and reasons are not supported by reliable, credible and substantial evidence.

Petitioner first focuses on the lack of certain findings. It maintains that the Boundary Commission's final order failed to adequately consider the effect annexation to Gresham of the McGill property would have on the continued viability and financial integrity of Wood Village as a city; that there is no finding that Wood Village cannot adequately service the area or that Gresham can better service the area; that the order fails to adequately consider the effect annexation

---

[1] The issue, in part, before the Boundary Commission was whether Gresham should be allowed to continue to grow at the expense of these smaller cities. The hearing on this proposed annexation, # 1467, was combined with the hearing on a proposed annexation, # 1447, to the City of Fairview. The City of Gresham expressed an interest in the property involved in that annexation, # 1447, also. The hearing demonstrated the different interests involved, *viz.,* the interests of the cities of Wood Village, Troutdale and Fairview on one hand and the interests of Gresham on the other.

would have on the financial integrity of Fire District # 10; and that the Boundary Commission fails to adequately discuss the effect annexation would have on the people in the "island" area created by the annexation. Petitioner also takes note of the fact that the property owner does not plan to develop his property at the present time and does not desire further city services. This suggests, in petitioner's view, a lack of need for annexation now.

We first consider whether the matters about which petitioner claims the findings are inadequate are, in fact, relevant statutory criteria which the Boundary Commission is required to consider. ORS 199.410(2) sets forth the function and purpose of local Boundary Commissions. They are:

> to provide a method for guiding the creation and growth of cities and special service districts in Oregon in order to prevent the illogical extensions of local government boundaries and to assure adequate quality and quantity of public services and the financial integrity of each unit of local government.

In implementing these purposes, the Boundary Commission, when reviewing a petition for a boundary change, is to

> consider economic, demographic and sociological trends and projections pertinent to the proposal, past and prospective physical development of land that would directly or indirectly be affected by the proposed boundary change and, except as provided in ORS 197.275, the state-wide planning goals adopted under ORS 197.255. ORS 199.462(1).

We turn first to petitioner's contention that Wood Village would be an adequate provider of services. This contention misses the mark, inasmuch as the issue before the Boundary Commission was whether annexation of the McGill property to the *City of Gresham* would be appropriate. The Boundary Commission did not have to consider whether Wood Village could service the area as well or better than Gresham could or whether, in fact, Gresham was a better service provider. It was required to determine whether Gresham would be an *adequate* service provider. We note, however, that the findings do compare the two cities' ability to provide certain city services.

Turning next to the question of petitioner's continuing viability, we agree with petitioner that the findings do not consider the effect this annexation will have on Wood Village as a city. ORS 199.462(1) states that the Boundary Commission is to consider economic, demographic and sociological trends and projections pertinent to the proposal. It is also to consider the past and prospective physical development of land that would be affected directly or indirectly by the annexation. Certainly, the term "pertinent to the proposal" is as broad as the phrase "land directly or indirectly affected by the proposed annexation" and would include a consideration of the effect this annexation would have on surrounding cities, where evidence is offered on the subject. Moreover, we note that one purpose of the Boundary Commission is to guide the extension of boundaries in a manner that insures the financial integrity of local government units. ORS 199.410(2).

The question is whether there was evidence offered on the subject of the financial integrity of Wood Village which would require the Boundary Commission to address the matter in its final order. There was. Wood Village included the McGill property in its Comprehensive Plan. The mayor of Wood Village testified that this annexation would devastate the financial integrity of Wood Village and its chance to become an economically viable community in the future. Wood Village's planning consultant testified that if Wood Village cannot expand to the south, in the direction of the McGill property, then it cannot expand at all and, if it cannot grow in population, then it can never reach a full level of urban services and fully maintain itself as a city. The three cities of Troutdale, Fairview and Wood Village submitted a letter to the Boundary Commission outlining the growth pattern of their cities and Gresham. They indicated that the economic viability of the smaller cities is at stake and that, if they cannot expand, they will not be able to develop a full range of city services.

The Boundary Commission may not believe that the ability of Wood Village to survive as a viable city unit will be affected by this annexation or that, if affected, this would be a reason to deny annexation. However, sufficient evidence was presented to raise the issue, and as it is a relevant criterion, the Boundary Commission must at least address the matter of its findings.... Failure to do so was error.

A more glaring deficiency in the Boundary Commission's order is the lack of consideration given to the effect this annexation will have on the people and land in the "island" area. It is undisputed that this proposed annexation creates an island area which appears from the maps in evidence to be completely surrounded by the City of Gresham. The area contains seventy-five residential homes. There was testimony from various sources, including the Multnomah County Planning Department, regarding the problems that would arise because of the creation of this "island" area. Concern centered on the inefficiency of providing services to this area, the jurisdictional problems, and the fact that the people in this area would, in effect, be subject to annexation against their wishes. Some of the residents in this area testified and others submitted letters stating their opposition to the annexation and their concern that the cost of services to them would increase and that ultimately they would be paying for services from the City of Gresham that they did not want.

The Boundary Commission found that this proposal creates an island and that the residents of the island do not desire annexation. There is no indication that they considered the interests of these people or the problems that would arise because of creation of this "island" area. This lack of consideration seriously undermines the conclusion that this boundary extension is a logical one. We are not saying that the proposed annexation is illogical because an "island" is created. This is a matter for the Boundary Commission's judgment. We are saying that the question must be recognized and dealt with as such in the final order. The Boundary Commission did not do so.

We turn now to the question of the fire district. Evidence was introduced by the chairman of the fire district; he claimed that the district and the people it served would be adversely affected by the withdrawal of the McGill property from its coverage: the cost of service would increase and service to the area would decrease in efficiency. Others supported his testimony. The Boundary Commission's findings and reasons recognize the fire district's interests and the fact that it might experience problems as a result of this annexation. They do not, however, deal with the effect this annexation will have on the fire district and thus on the people and land area it serves. This is a relevant consideration under ORS 199.162(1), and must be addressed.

Petitioner next attacks the Boundary Commission's order as being speculative, inasmuch as the applicant does not desire city services at the present time. It suggests that annexation is thus not necessary. Our review of the Boundary Commission's action is to determine if the correct procedures and law were followed and whether its order is supported by substantial evidence. ORS 183.482(7), (8). It is not our function to judge whether the annexation is appropriate or necessary; that is a matter for the Commission. We cannot say that, because services are not now desired, the annexation is inappropriate. The Boundary Commission considered the matter and found otherwise.

Petitioner further claims that the order of annexation furthers the improper goals of some of the commissioners and reflects consideration of "political" motives. It specifically points to the statements of two of the commissioners made prior to casting their votes. One statement relates to where the boundary of Gresham should be; the other expresses the opinion that small cities should be required to consider consolidation. Without deciding whether these are proper considerations, we find no indication in the record or in the Boundary Commission's order that these were factors in its decision.

Petitioner also notes that there is no finding concerning the fact that the applicant was experiencing problems with Multnomah County over development of his property. Petitioner does not tell us the significance of this fact, assuming it is a fact; the suggestion is that this was the real reason McGill desired annexation to the City of Gresham. We fail to see how this is a relevant consideration under ORS 199.462(1).

. . . .

Reversed and remanded.

Comments: 1. What authority over annexations does the boundary commission have that a court in a "rule of reason" state is not likely to have? How would you resolve the intergovernmental conflict in the *Wood Village* case?

The "state-wide planning goals" referenced in the opinion are goals adopted by a state Land Conservation and Development Commission. Local government comprehensive plans and land use controls must conform to the state goals. What weight did the court give to local comprehensive plans in *Wood Village*? See also *Village of Farmington v. Minnesota Municipal Commission,* 170 N.W.2d 197 (Minn. 1969), reversing the Commission for failing to consider the merits of annexation as compared with consolidation.

The state planning goals provide policies applicable to annexation. Goal No. 11 requires the planning and development of "a timely, orderly and efficient arrangement of public facilities and services to serve as a framework for urban and rural development." *See Rivergate Residents Ass'n v. Land Conservation & Development Commission,* 590 P.2d 1233 (Or. App. 1979), applying Goal No. 11 and related state planning goals to uphold approval of an annexation.

Are there any constitutional objections to boundary commissions? *See Township of Midland v. Michigan State Boundary Commission,* 259 N.W.2d 326 (Mich. 1977) (held constitutional under *Hunter* doctrine).

2. Some of the boundary commission laws contain more elaborate factors to guide commission decisions. California legislation authorizes Local Agency Formation Commissions (LAFCO) at the county level. The legislation contains the following factors:

(a) Population, population density; land area and land use; per capita assessed valuation; topography, natural boundaries, and drainage basins; proximity to other populated areas; the likelihood of significant growth in the area, and in adjacent incorporated and unincorporated areas, during the next 10 years.

(b) Need for organized community services; the present cost and adequacy of governmental services and controls in the area; probable future needs for such services and controls; probable effect of the proposed incorporation, formation, annexation, or exclusion and of alternative courses of action on the cost and adequacy of services and controls in the area and adjacent areas. As used in this subdivision, "services" is to be construed as referring to governmental services whether or not the services are such as would be provided by local agencies subject to this chapter, and as including the public facilities necessary to provision of services.

(c) The effect of the proposed action and of alternative actions, on adjacent areas, on mutual social and economic interests and on the local governmental structure of the county.

(d) The conformity of both the proposal and its anticipated effects with both the adopted commission policies on providing planned, orderly, efficient patterns of urban development and the policies and priorities set forth in . . . this code.

(e) The effect of the proposal on maintaining the physical and economic integrity of lands in an agricultural preserve in open-space uses.

(f) The definiteness and certainty of the boundaries of the territory, the nonconformance of proposed boundaries with lines of assessment or ownership, the creation of islands or corridors of unincorporated territory, and other similar matters affecting the proposed boundaries.

(g) Conformity with appropriate city or county general and specific plans.

(h) The "sphere of influence" of any local agency which may be applicable to the proposal being reviewed.

Cal. Gov't Code § 54796. What factors does the California legislation add to the factors contained in the Oregon legislation? Would a California boundary revision commission reach a different result in the *Wood Village* case?

3. The "sphere of influence" mentioned in the California law refers to authority to given to the commissions to determine plans "for the probable ultimate physical boundaries and service area of a local government agency." *Id.* § 54774. When adopting spheres of influence, the commissions are to consider a number of factors, including available services, population growth, planned development, and "[t]he existence of social and economic interdependence and interaction."

A study of spheres of influence indicated that the policy was not always effective, and that the spheres of influence varied from county to county. J. Eells, LAFCO Spheres of Influence: Effective Planning for the Urban Fringe? (Cal. Inst. of Gov't'l Studies, 1977). The author notes:

> Fresno County LAFCO allocates land to the various zones depending on when urban services are expected. There are no specific policies indicating where development should be actively discouraged . . . . Santa Clara County combines the concept of timing for urban services with policies specifying where urban development should be prohibited.

Id. at 21.

Is the "sphere of influence" enforceable? In *City of Ceres v. City of Modesto,* 79 Cal. Rptr. 168 (Cal. App. 1969), Modesto proposed to extend sewer lines into an area within the Ceres sphere of influence. The court held that the sphere of influence did not absolutely deprive Modesto of the authority to extend its sewer lines into the area. It also held that a Modesto taxpayer had standing to contest the sewer line extension as statutory "waste" if he could show that the area would ultimately be annexed to Ceres and that the sewer line extension was intended to "thwart" the LAFCO.

A court of appeal has held that a LAFCO must adopt a sphere of influence before it can approve an annexation. *Resource Defense Fund v. Santa Cruz Local Agency Formation Comm'n,* 188 Cal. Rptr. 499 (Cal. App. 1983). The decision may be reversed by a statutory amendment.

Minnesota's boundary commission law contains a similar procedure. Municipalities may designate areas for "orderly annexation." Minn. Stat. Ann. § 414.0325. They may annex land within these areas if approved by the state boundary review commission. The state commission is to consider factors similar to those contained in the California law, *supra* Comment 2. It may then order annexation, inter alia, if the area "is now or is about to become urban or suburban in character and that the annexing municipality is capable of providing the services required by the area within a reasonable time."

4. The boundary commission laws specify "factors" for the commissions to consider. They do not dictate how local governments shall be organized, even though they may encourage "the orderly formation and development of local government agencies." Cal. Gov't Code § 54774.

Consider *Bozung v. Local Agency Formation Commission,* 529 P.2d 1017 (Cal. 1975). A complaint was made that a LAFCO sphere of influence plan indicated that all of the area in a county should be included within an existing city or should eventually be organized as a city. The court held:

> There is simply nothing in [the legislation] which positively enjoins wall-to-wall cities in a county .... What the legislation does seek to accomplish is that at every step along the way the public agencies to whom it is addressed keep the enumerated considerations in mind.

Id. at 1034.

5. In California and Washington, annexations fall under state counterparts of the National Environmental Policy Act (NEPA), and environmental impact statements must be filed on annexations. See *Bozung, supra.* The state NEPA legislation requires "consideration" of environmental impacts. What "environmental" concerns must be considered under this legislation? See *Spokane County Fire Protection District v. Spokane County Boundary Review Board,* 618 P.2d 1326 (Wash. App. 1980), in which the court approved a board decision annexing agricultural land. The court held that the board had considered "independent environmental concerns, [including] population growth, proximity to other populated areas, soil conditions, drainage, water supply, air pollution, sewerage problems and topography." Could a California LAFCO consider these factors under the factors listed in the LAFCO legislation, *supra* Comment 2?

6. The record of the boundary commissions is difficult to assess. The Advisory Commission report, *supra,* found that most annexations were approved and that in some states, such as California, the formation of special districts had been slowed. The report concluded:

> The overall record, then, suggests that boundary commissions have proven to be somewhat successful in preventing further increases or slowing down the rate of growth in ... local governments .... This modest success has been primarily the product of reacting to proposals brought before them. Statutory controls and/or political factors dictate a go-slow attitude.

Id. at 380.

7. Having reviewed the structure and functioning of boundary commissions, how would you evaluate the differences between commissions and courts in the management of the boundary change process? What are the advantages and disadvantages of each? Note that some commissions may initiate boundary changes and may redraw boundary proposals. Do courts have these powers? See also the *Farmington* case, *supra* Comment 1, holding that the Minnesota commission was not bound by the usual rule that annexations first in time have priority.

Chapter 3
LOCAL GOVERNMENT POWERS

A. THE LOCAL AUTONOMY PROBLEM

Earlier chapters established that state legislatures have plenary power over local governments, except as qualified by the Supreme Court's restrictions on the *Hunter* doctrine, or by limitations contained in their own state constitutions. These doctrines mean that local governments, in some way, must receive all the powers they exercise from the state. State legislatures have conferred extensive powers on local governments through what is known as "enabling" legislation. Local governments may also exercise "home rule" powers in states whose constitutions contain a home rule provision. Many states now authorize municipal home rule, and half of the states authorize county home rule. Constitutional home rule may expand local government powers, but home rule powers are not unlimited and are defined by the home rule grant of authority.

Whether a local government exercises power through a statutory or home rule grant, a state legislature may "preempt" the exercise of local power by adopting legislation covering an area of concern also covered by a local ordinance. Preemption may occur even though a local government enjoys constitutional home rule. One difference is that a legislature may not preempt powers which are "exclusively" local under a constitutional home rule clause. The home rule powers which are exclusively local are limited in scope.

This chapter considers statutory and home rule grants of power and statutory preemption. This section reviews the local autonomy problem. It considers the "inherent right" to local self-government and the limitations on state power over local governments imposed by a constitutional "special commission" clause adopted in some states.

The "Inherent Right" to Local Self-Government

At one time, local governments were thought to have an "inherent right" to local self-government that provided autonomy from state interference and presumably gave them inherent governmental powers. The inherent right issue arose when state legislatures in the nineteenth century attempted to intervene in local government affairs. State-appointed commissions were given authority in areas of local concern.

The most notable of these incidents occurred in Michigan. The state legislature created a commission to control a Detroit public park and at the same time appointed the commissioners who were to exercise this function. C. ANTIEAU, MUNICIPAL CORPORATION LAW § 2.11 (1975). The Michigan Supreme Court invalidated this legislation in an opinion that recognized an inherent right of local government, in this case to be free of state intervention in the control of municipal facilities. *People ex rel. Board of Park Commissioners v. Common Council,* 28 Mich. 228 (1873).

Subsequent decades have not been kind to the inherent right doctrine. Repudiation of the doctrine in almost every jurisdiction in which it was accepted is now practically complete, but its persistence in the romantic literature of local government law requires strong contrary citations. The Kentucky court refused to strike down an act establishing a new retirement and pension system for police and fire departments and stated: "We have concluded that the time has come for this Court to reject, positively and unequivocally, the theory that a right of local self-government inheres in Kentucky municipalities." *Board of Trustees of Policemen's & Firemen's Retirement Fund v. City of Paducah,* 333 S.W.2d 515, 518 (Ky. 1960).

In Indiana, the teeth of the inherent right doctrine were drawn in *Datisman v. Gary Public Library,* 170 N.E.2d 55 (Ind. 1960). An act of the legislature provided for the appointment of the library board by local officials, and this was claimed to violate the inherent right to local government. The court pointed out:

> The right of local self-government in towns and cities of Indiana is vested in the people of the respective municipalities, and while the Legislature has no right or power to appoint municipal officers, it does, however, have the power to enact laws prescribing the manner of selection and the duties of such officers.

Id. at 59-60. An earlier inherent right case was distinguished because it provided for the appointment of local officers by the governor — a state officer.

In Michigan, where the inherent right doctrine originated, it has lost its vitality. In *City of Highland Park v. Fair Employment Practices Commission,* 111 N.W.2d 797 (Mich. 1961), the city claimed that to apply the fair employment law to it would invade "the rights of self-government granted municipalities under the provisions of the Constitution." The court found no such provisions, assumed that the reference was to the constitutional home rule clause, but noted that Michigan municipalities under that provision were subject to the "general laws" of the state. *See also Sussex Woodlands, Inc. v. Mayor & Council,* 263 A.2d 502 (N.J.L. 1970).

The rejection of the inherent right doctrine is the basis for the well accepted rule that local governments enjoy only those powers expressly or impliedly granted, either by statute or by a constitutional home rule provision. In *City of South Bend v. Krovitch,* 372 N.E.2d 288 (Ind. App. 1971), the mayor established, by press conference and memorandum, a public safety program in which certain firemen would be trained as policemen and would perform certain police duties. No power to adopt this program was found by the court: "There was a time when local autonomy was the rule in Indiana .... As appellant correctly points out, there is no later case specifically overruling the above cited cases, however, the bulk of the decisions have eroded the local autonomy theory into a state of practical nonexistence." *Id.* at 291. The common law power to abate nuisances is an exception to the rule that municipalities have no inherent powers.

The "Special Commission" Problem

Arising out of and closely linked to the inherent right doctrine was the adoption in several states of a constitutional provision providing that "[t]he Legislature shall not delegate to any special commission, private corporation or association, any power to make, supervise or interfere with any municipal improvement, money, property or effects, . . . to levy taxes, . . . or to perform any municipal functions." Utah Const. art. VI, § 28. The link to the Detroit public park incident is clear; the problem there was that the state created and appointed a "special commission" to supervise a park in the Detroit park system. The broad language of this constitutional provision may be applicable in a modern context, as the following case interpreting the Utah provision indicates:

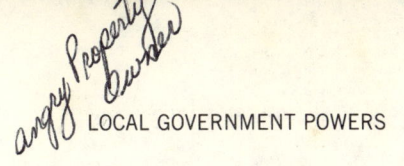

TRIBE v. SALT LAKE CITY CORP.

Supreme Court of Utah
540 P.2d 499 (1975)

MAUGHAN, JUSTICE:

Here on appeal is the decision of the district court declaring the Utah Neighborhood Development Act constitutional, and that actions taken and proposed to be taken pursuant to those statutory provisions are constitutionally permissible.

Plaintiffs commenced a declaratory judgment action in the court below with the alleged purpose of having the foregoing statutes and actions declared unconstitutional. On appeal plaintiffs raise seven points, any one of the first five of which, if valid, would be sufficient to reverse the action of the lower court, and defeat the proposed project. In summary, the points raised by plaintiffs are:

1. That the Redevelopment Agency proposed is in fact a special commission and contravenes the provisions of Article VI, Section 28, Utah Constitution.
. . . .

In June of 1969, Salt Lake City Corporation created the Redevelopment Agency of Salt Lake City, (hereinafter referred to as the Agency) pursuant to the provisions of the Utah Neighborhood Development Act (hereinafter referred to as the Act). The Board of Commissioners of Salt Lake City Corporation was designated as the Redevelopment Agency of the City. In February of 1971, the City duly adopted an ordinance approving a redevelopment plan for the project area with which we are here concerned, viz., the blocks and streets adjacent thereto, of the two-block area bounded on the north by First South Street, on the east by Main Street, on the south by Third South Street, and on the west by West Temple Street.

The plan recognized that in this project area there were a number of substandard buildings and substandard land use; and that through rehabilitation, in some cases, or acquisition, clearance and rebuilding in other cases, the project area could be improved, with the result, among other things of strengthening the tax base and ameliorating the economic health of the entire community. Within this area the plan called for the construction and operation of a parking facility, to be financed by the issuance of $15,000,000 of tax allocation and parking revenue bonds. These bonds are to be retired by parking revenues and from an allocation of taxes, the formula for which is given in the Act. . . .

. . . .
Are the Agency, and its methods for implementing its objects constitutionally permissible? The answer to this question hinges on whether the objects and purposes of the Act are statewide or local; and whether the Agency, as structured by the Act, is such a one as can concurrently exist with municipal corporations and assessment units.

The concept of redevelopment was enacted by the state legislature, its area of operation is statewide, and deals with a statewide problem, viz., blight. To be sure, the present project area would appear to have only local operation, but it must be remembered that it is a local operation of an act of general statewide scope; and that its local operation hinges on a contingency — the decision of the legislative body of the Agency. A decision motivated by the existence of a condition of statewide concern.

It appears clear that the Agency here concerned is a quasi-municipal corporation, and not a special commission. A quasi-municipal corporation has been defined as a public agency created by the legislature to aid the state in some public work for the general welfare, other than to perform as another community government. A municipal corporation is a body politic and corporate, created to administer the internal concerns of the district embraced within its corporate limits, in matters peculiar to such place and not common to the state at large. A special commission is some body or group separate and distinct from municipal government. Such a commission is not offensive to the constitution by its creation, but only when such a commission is delegated powers which intrude into areas of purely municipal concern.

The success of plaintiff's challenges depends upon the character of the agency created by the legislature. If the legislative enactment authorizes the performance of activities, which qualify as a function appropriately performed by a state agency, the constitutional interdiction of Article VI, Section 28, is not applicable. This section applies only to *municipal* functions, the performance of which are constitutionally limited to the units of local government. The problem of "urban blight" we recognize as one of statewide concern, and not merely a local or municipal problem. The agency for that reason does not run counter to Article VI, Section 28. The agency is a quasi-municipal corporation, a public agency created for beneficial and necessary public purposes. It is not a true municipal corporation, having power of local government, but an agency of the state designed for state purposes. Since it is a quasi-municipal corporation, formed for public purposes, it is within the discretion of the legislature to grant it any powers, not expressly prohibited by the constitution, to further such purposes, including the power of taxation. The public purposes for which the agency is organized inures [sic] to the benefit of the public generally, therefore the public may be charged for such benefits through general taxation. The agency is separate and apart from the city government, and yet is administered by a legislature [sic] body responsible to the local electorate.

Comments: 1. If the redevelopment authority was created by the city, why was there a special commission problem? Does every statute authorizing a municipality to create a department or appoint an officer create a special commission problem? The courts usually exempt special districts and authorities from the special commission prohibition. See *Belovsky v. Redevelopment Authority,* 54 A.2d 277 (Pa. 1947).

Compare *Carter v. Beaver County Service Area No. One,* 399 P.2d 440 (Utah 1965). A county service district was created with the authority to undertake an expansive list of governmental functions, including almost every function that could be undertaken by cities. The court invalidated the district, in part under the special commission prohibition, as the large number of functions vested in the district would "emasculate the performance of municipal functions" vested by the Utah constitution in local governments.

2. Municipalities sometimes invoke the special commission prohibition to prevent state regulation of local utilities. In *State Water Pollution Control Board v. Salt Lake City,* 311 P.2d 370 (Utah 1957), the court held that the city's sewage disposal facility was not subject to state regulation. It rejected a governmental-proprietary approach to the special commission provision which would have held the city subject to state regulation in the exercise of its proprietary functions.

A court may distinguish the provision of extraterritorial services. In *City of Loveland v. Public Utilities Commission,* 580 P.2d 381 (Colo. 1978), the court held that the state commission had jurisdiction to regulate electrical services which the city provided in its extraterritorial jurisdiction. The court had previously held that the special commission prohibition prevented utility commission regulation of municipal electricity rates within the city limits. Commission supervision was unnecessary in that case because "the customers are citizens of the municipality and can protest oppressive rates or poor management by recalling city officials or voting them out of office at an election." *Id.* at 384. Extraterritorial customers did not have this option. Is this distinction relevant to the purpose of the special commission prohibition?

The Utah court has held that the special commission prohibition limits the authority of the state legislature to authorize special districts. In *Backman v. Salt Lake County,* 375 P.2d 756 (Utah 1962), the court invalidated a statute requiring a referendum in Salt Lake County to establish a special district to build and operate a sports arena, and to levy a tax for this purpose.

3. The state-local and governmental-proprietary distinctions used in the special commission cases are typical of the two-sided classifications courts frequently use in local government law cases. This type of analysis reappears in the home rule cases, where the state-local distinction sometimes is used to delineate the scope of local home rule authority. The governmental-proprietary distinction also reappears in a number of contexts, including municipal liability in tort. Municipalities were historically liable in tort only in the exercise of proprietary functions.

Commentators have generally been critical of this kind of two-sided analysis in local government law. Did the state-local distinction help explain the court's decision in the *Tribe* case? What kind of analysis would you have used to decide that opinion?

4. The special commission prohibition may soon become a matter of historic interest. California, for example, has eliminated the special commission limitation, and now only prohibits the delegation of municipal functions to a "private person or body." Calif. Const. art. XI, § 11.

B. STATUTORY POWERS

State courts frequently apply a strict construction rule, known as "Dillon's Rule" after its author, to the statutory powers of local governments. Dillon's Rule appeared in the following form in the first published text on local government law, which was authored by Judge Dillon of the Iowa Supreme Court:

DILLON, MUNICIPAL CORPORATIONS (1st ed. 1872)

Sec. 55. It is a general and undisputed proposition of law that a municipal corporation possesses, and can exercise, the following powers, and no others: First, those granted in *express words;* second, those *necessarily or fairly implied* in, or *incident* to, the powers expressly granted; third, those *essential* to the declared objects and purposes of the corporation—not simply convenient, but indispensable. Any fair, reasonable doubt concerning the existence of power is resolved by the courts against the corporation, and the power is denied. . . . These general principles of law are indisputably settled, but difficulty is often experienced in their application.

The meaning of the Dillon Rule must be understood against the pattern of statutory enabling authority for local government which was common in Dillon's day. State legislatures typically enacted a list of local government powers which were quite specific. A licensing enabling law, for example, might have authorized municipalities to license peddlers, candle-makers, and a number of other occupations. Dillion apparently concluded from this typical enumeration of powers that any powers not clearly conferred by the legislation were not granted.

Modern enabling legislation for local governments often takes a different form. The legislature may adopt a comprehensive enabling act authorizing the exercise of local powers in an area of regulatory concern. A number of examples come to mind, including enabling legislation for zoning, special assessments for public facilities, and housing and community development programs. Although comprehensive enabling legislation also specifies the powers to be exercised by municipalities, it avoids the specific listing of enumerated powers which may have prompted Dillon's Rule. The strict construction rule may also owe its origin to *Kent's Commentaries,* Kent having made it applicable both to private and public corporations. The rule no longer applies to private corporations.

A fascinating article, Frug, *The City As a Legal Concept,* 93 HARV. L. REV. 1057 (1980), provides additional insight on the problem of municipal autonomy and Dillon's Rule. Professor Frug argues that municipalities originally had full legal autonomy, and that the concept of subordination to the state developed only in the nineteenth century. He traces the origins of Dillon's Rule to Dillon's concept of local government. Dillon believed that cities were not managed by those "best fitted" by intelligence, experience, capacity and moral character. Municipal management often was unwise and extravagant. A major change in city government was needed to achieve local governments dedicated to the public good. *Id.* at 1111.

Dillon believed that these goals could be achieved through state control of cities, a restriction of cities to "public" functions and a strict judicial construction of municipal powers. *Id.* at 1112. Frug adds that "[i]t is hard for us to comprehend fully Dillon's confidence in noblesse oblige and in the expectation that state and judicial control would help ensure the attainment by cities of an unselfish public good." *Id.* Frug also notes that "Dillon's vision of society may be gone forever." *Id.*

Dillon's Rule may also reflect his conservative view of government regulation of private property. *See* Dillon, *Property — Its Rights and Duties in Our Legal and Social Systems,* 29 AM. L. REV. 161 (1895).

Comments: 1. The Dillon Rule is still applied full-blown by some courts. In *Board of Supervisors v. Horne,* 215 S.E.2d 453 (Va. 1975), the court applied the rule to hold that an Interim Development Order adopted by Fairfax County, substantially freezing all development permission pending a comprehensive revision of the zoning ordinance, was unauthorized by its enabling legislation. It noted:

> In Virginia the powers of boards of supervisors are fixed by statute and are limited to those conferred expressly or by necessary implication. This rule is a corollary to Dillon's Rule that municipal corporations have only those powers expressly granted, those necessarily or fairly implied therefrom, and those that are essential and indispensable. . . .

The Commission on Constitutional Revision recommended inclusion of a provision to reverse Dillon's Rule as to cities and certain counties in order to relax the constraints on local government. Report of the Commission on Constitutional Revision (1969), at 228-231. This recommendation, however, was rejected by the General Assembly, and was not incorporated in the revised Constitution which became effective July 1, 1971. We must conclude, therefore, that, regardless of its fate in other jurisdictions, Dillon's Rule remains in effect in this state. Accordingly, the Board could not enact the IDO under its general police power.

Id. at 455-56. For another explicit application of Dillon's Rule see *City of Osceola v. Whistle,* 410 S.W.2d 393 (Ark. 1966).

2. The application of Dillon's Rule often is inconsistent, both within the same state and among different state courts. Compare the following cases considering the question of statutory authority for an ordinance requiring a cash deposit on soft drink containers:

Bowie Inn, Inc. v. City of Bowie, 335 A.2d 679 (Md. 1975). The court held that the ordinance was authorized. The court quoted Dillon's Rule, and noted that it had "repeatedly" been applied by the court. It then held that the ordinance was "expressly" authorized by a state statute enabling municipalities "[t]o regulate or prevent the throwing or depositing of any dirt, garbage, trash, or liquids in any public place and to provide for the proper disposal of such material."

Tabler v. Board of Supervisors, 269 S.E.2d 358 (Va. 1980). The court held that a similar local ordinance was not authorized by similar enabling legislation, noting that "Virginia follows the Dillon Rule." *See* Comment 1, *supra.* The court also relied on the refusal of the state legislature to adopt legislation expressly authorizing local ordinances of this type.

3. The ambiguities inherent in Dillon's Rule give considerable latitude to the courts:

> If the Court wants to restrict municipal power, adherence to the express language of the statute is a convenient means of doing so. [If] the Court wants to find an implicit grant of municipal power behind the statutory language, it must assume a quasi-legislative stance, because there will be little to guide its search. This purely result-oriented jurisprudence, however, defies principled reconciliation with Dillon's Rule of strict construction.

Note, *Dillon's Rule: The Case for Reform,* 68 VA. L. REV. 693, 703, 704 (1982).

4. Some states have repealed Dillon's Rule. The Alaska Constitution, art. X, § 1, provides that "[t]he purpose of this article is to provide for maximum local self-government." The court read this section as a repeal of Dillon's Rule in *Liberati v. Bristol Bay Borough,* 584 P.2d 1115 (Alaska 1978). The court quoted a statement at the constitutional convention that the purpose of the article was "to provide the maximum powers to the legislature and to the local government." Does the constitutional provision, and its contemporary interpretation, provide a clearer rule for interpreting the statutory enabling authority granted to local governments? How would you apply the Alaska rule in the "bottle bill" cases discussed in Comment 2?

Under some enabling legislation it is clear that a power has been granted to local governments; the question is the extent of the power granted, and the authority of the local government to elaborate on the statutory grant. The following case illustrates this problem:

EARLY ESTATES, INC. v. HOUSING BOARD OF REVIEW

Supreme Court of Rhode Island
93 R.I. 227, 174 A.2d 117 (1961)

PAOLINO, JUSTICE. This is a petition for certiorari to review the decision of the housing board of review of the city of Providence denying the petitioner's appeal from a compliance order of the director of the division of minimum housing standards pursuant to the provisions of chapter 1040 of the ordinances of said city, entitled the Minimum-Standards Housing Ordinance. Pursuant to the writ the board has certified the pertinent records to this court.

The petitioner owns a three-tenement house. Public Laws 1956, chap. 3715, is the enabling act which authorizes the city of Providence to enact a minimum standards housing ordinance. The question presented by this petition is whether the act as written vests the city with power to enact an ordinance requiring petitioner to provide a rear hallway light in its premises and to install hot water facilities in the third-floor tenement, and, if so, whether such requirements are valid.

Sections 7 and 8 of article 4 of the act delegate to the city council power to enact minimum housing standards. Section 7 provides that: "The city council of the city of Providence is authorized to pass, ordain, establish and amend ordinances, rules and regulations for the establishment and enforcement of minimum standards for dwellings." In defining this general grant of power the legislature provided as follows in sec. 8:

> Without limiting the generality of the foregoing, such ordinances, rules and regulations may include:
> (a) Minimum standards governing the conditions, maintenance, use and occupancy of dwellings and dwelling premises deemed necessary to make said dwellings and dwelling premises safe, sanitary and fit for human habitation.

Pursuant to the provisions of the enabling act the city council enacted chapter 1040, the Minimum-Standards Housing Ordinance. The provisions involved in the instant proceeding are subsecs. 8.8, entitled "Lighting of Public Spaces," and 6.4, entitled "Hot Water." Subsection 8.8 provides that:

> Every public hall and common stairway used primarily for egress or ingress in connection with two or more dwelling units shall be supplied with a proper amount of natural or electric light at all times; provided that such public halls and common stairways in structures containing not more than three dwelling units shall be deemed to have fulfilled such requirement if they are properly supplied with conveniently located switches, controlling an adequate electric lighting system which may be turned on when needed; and provided that all common stairways not used primarily for egress or ingress in all dwellings shall be properly supplied with such switches.

Subsection 6.4 provides that:

> Within three (3) years following the effective date of this Ordinance every kitchen sink, lavatory basin, and bathtub or shower bath required under the provisions of Subsections 6.1, 6.2 and 6.3 of this section shall be properly connected to hot as well as cold water lines.

The petitioner concedes that subsecs. 8.8 and 6.4, if valid, apply to its premises. However, with respect to the requirements of 8.8, it contends that under the common law of this state as declared in *Capen v. Hall,* 21 R.I. 364, 43 A. 847, and followed by other later cases, there is no duty on a property owner to provide artificial light or switches in common hallways and stairways. The petitioner also contends that the council, absent legislative authority, is without power to change the common law relating to hallway lights; that the act as written contains no language vesting the council with such power; and that consequently subsec. 8.8 is invalid and the director's compliance order requiring such hallway light is null and void.

After careful consideration it is our opinion that the enabling act clearly vests the council with power to legislate on the subject of lighting for common hallways and stairways. The legislature therein declared in art. 2, sec. 2, that "the establishment of minimum standards for dwellings is essential to the protection of the public health, safety, morals and general welfare." Such language clearly indicates a legislative intent to vest in the council power to require minimum standards dealing with factors relating to safety.

Again, in carrying out such intent, the legislature provided in art. 4, sec. 8, that the ordinances which the council was empowered to enact might include, without limiting the generality of the language in sec. 7, minimum standards governing the conditions, maintenance, use and occupancy of dwellings and dwelling premises deemed necessary to make said dwellings and dwelling premises safe, sanitary and fit for human habitation. The use of such language makes it abundantly clear that the legislature clearly intended to vest the council with power to require hallway lights as a safety measure. We are satisfied that the council had legislative authority to enact subsec. 8.8 and that the requirements therein are reasonable and therefore are a proper exercise of the police power. See *Palombo v. Housing Board of Review,* R.I., 169 A.2d 613. The cases cited by petitioner are not in point and require no discussion.

We come now to a consideration of the provisions of subsec. 6.4 requiring the installation of hot water facilities in the third-floor tenement of petitioner's property. Its principal contentions with respect thereto are that the act is silent on the subject of hot water; that there is no language therein vesting the council with power to legislate on the subject; and that therefore the council acted in excess of its jurisdiction.

At this point we are not concerned with the wisdom or desirability of the requirements in question. It may very well be that hot water facilities in a dwelling are convenient and desirable, but the only question before us is whether the act as written vests the council with power to require the installation of such facilities. The act contains no express grant of such power.

In art. 2 the legislature declares that it has found that there exist in the city of Providence numerous dwellings which are substandard due to "uncleanliness" and lack of adequate "sanitary facilities," and that the establishment of minimum standards for dwellings is essential to the protection of the public health, safety, morals and general welfare. Under sec. 8 the council is vested with power to enact minimum standards governing the conditions, maintenance, use and occupancy of dwellings deemed necessary to make said dwellings safe, sanitary and fit for human habitation.

In the absence of an express grant of legislative authority, the determination of the issue raised by petitioner's instant contentions depends wholly upon the question whether the statutory language discussed in the preceding paragraph indicates a clear legislative intent to delegate the power in question. In other words, is the use of such language equatable to a grant of power to the council empowering it to require the installation of hot water facilities? Is the requirement of hot water facilities related to the "uncleanliness" of dwellings and dwelling premises? Is such requirement related to sanitation or public health and welfare?

Keeping in mind that chap. 3715 involves a delegation of power relating to *minimum* housing standards, can it reasonably be said that by empowering the council to enact minimum standards necessary to make dwellings and dwelling premises "fit for human habitation," the legislature meant that the installation of hot water facilities is necessary to achieve the desired purpose? Can it be said that dwellings and dwelling premises lacking such facilities are unfit for human habitation?

Prior to the enactment of chap. 3715, in the absence of contractual obligations to the contrary there was no duty on a property owner to provide hot water facilities under the law of this state. After careful consideration it is our opinion that the act contains no language indicating a legislative intent to create such a duty or to vest the council with power to enact an ordinance requiring the installation of hot water facilities. The requirement of those facilities is not necessarily related to sanitation or public health and welfare, nor is such requirement reasonably necessary to make dwellings and dwelling premises fit for human habitation. We cannot read into the act that which is not there.

From what we have stated, it is clear that in enacting subsec. 6.4 the council exceeded its jurisdiction. That portion of the ordinance is therefore invalid and the decision of the board based thereon is in error. In view of this result it becomes unnecessary to discuss or consider the petitioner's other contentions.
. . . .

ROBERTS, JUSTICE (dissenting). . . .

The enabling act confers upon the city council authority to establish by ordinance minimum standards for dwellings. In art. 4, sec. 8 thereof, after expressly stating it to be the legislative policy that the generality of the grant of such authority is not limited thereby, the legislature provided that such an ordinance could set out certain specific provisions, among which were included "Minimum standards governing the conditions, maintenance, use and occupancy of dwellings and dwelling premises deemed necessary to make said dwellings and dwelling premises safe, sanitary and fit for human habitation."

Clearly, it was the intention of the legislature to confer upon the city council comprehensive authority to provide minimum standards for dwelling premises. The subsequent enumeration of norms to be observed by the city council in its exercise of the police power thus delegated to it was not intended to diminish the scope of that authority. Because the legislature intended to bestow upon the city council such a broad power to provide for minimum dwelling standards, I am persuaded that the legislature also intended to leave to the discretion and judgment of the local legislature the nature of the precise minimum standards to be established. If the specific requirements thus prescribed as minimum standards by the city council bear a reasonable relationship to the public health, morals, and welfare, the enactment thereof constituted a valid exercise of the police power delegated to it.

I am unable to perceive that the action of the city council requiring the connecting of kitchen sinks, lavatory basins, and bathing facilities to hot water lines was violative of the norms set out in art. 4, sec. 8(a), of the enabling act. Nor do I think it reasonable to conclude that the providing of lines which would serve to give the occupant of the dwelling access to an appliance that would, if utilized, make available to him a supply of hot water may not be deemed necessary to promote sanitation in dwelling premises or to render such premises fit for human habitation.

That a definite relationship exists between the maintenance of an adequate condition of sanitation in a community and the availability of access to a supply of hot water in the dwelling units in that community has been given judicial recognition in *City of Newark v. Charles Realty Co.,* 9 N.J. Super. 442, 74 A.2d 630. In that case, on the basis of the evidence adduced, the court found that where a supply of hot water is not readily available in dwellings by reasons of a failure to have access to facilities for supplying such hot water, the danger of production and spread of disease in the community tends to increase. Without intending to unduly extend this dissenting opinion, I quote in part from that case at page 452 of 9 N.J. Super., at page 635 of 74 A.2d: "For instance, as to gastro-intestinal diseases, there have been 'outbreaks of that disease because hot water was not available for that purpose,' the testimony instancing as typical, the spread of such disease throughout the city from a restaurant, an employee of which fails to properly wash his hands due to the lack of hot water at home, and thus spreads this diarrheal disease." While it may be possible to maintain adequate sanitation in a community where there is a lack of readily available supplies of hot water for use in personal hygiene by the residents thereof, it is manifestly clear that a high degree of sanitation would be promoted and more effectively maintained when access to adequate supplies of hot water is provided for in the dwellings in that community.

Neither do I believe that the requirement of subsec. 6.4 for the connecting of hot water lines to kitchen sinks, lavatory basins, and bathing facilities may not reasonably be deemed necessary to render a dwelling fit for human habitation. To attribute to the legislature an intention to use the phrase "fit for human habitation" as meaning any structure that suffices to give one shelter from the elements so as to survive the vicissitudes and hardships of life in a climate such as ours is to attribute to the legislature an intent to have its enactment result in an absurdity. It is my belief that a dwelling fit for human habitation within the contemplation of the legislature was a dwelling so built and equipped as to afford the occupants thereof access to those conveniences and amenities that, in this day of social enlightenment, are considered as the responsibility of the property owner to the welfare of the community. When the city council included within the ordinance provisions requiring the connecting of kitchen sinks, lavatory basins and bathing facilities with hot water lines, it was acting well within the norm inherent in the legislative phrase "fit for human habitation."

Comments: 1. Municipal housing codes apply to existing housing, and are viewed as an essential strategy in housing conservation efforts. They generally require the maintenance of buildings, specify minimum facilities (such as hot water), and impose minimum occupancy space requirements. They came into vogue in the late 1960s under prompting from a requirement then contained in the federal urban renewal legislation that required the adoption of local housing codes as a condition to the receipt of federal urban renewal assistance. Perhaps for this reason, most states did not have enabling legislation for local housing codes and most did not provide the necessary statutory authority.

Early Estates poses an important dilemma. A court may interpret a broadly stated grant of authority to exclude necessary powers of implementation. The alternative is detailed specification in the statute, which the legislature may not wish to undertake.

The Rhode Island legislature took the second approach in an amendment to the housing code statute adopted after the *Early Estates* decision. R.I. Gen. Laws § 45-24.2-3. How far the amended statute stretched was litigated in *Berberian v. Housing Authority*, 315 A.2d 747 (R.I. 1974):

> The petitioner further contends that The Code of the City of Cranston, Rhode Island, article X, sec. 14-71, is invalid because it goes beyond the scope of the authority delegated to municipalities pursuant to the enabling legislation, G.L. 1956 (1970 Reenactment) §§ 45-24.2-1 and 45-24.2-3. As has been stated, one of the purposes of § 45-24.2-1 is to prevent blight. Section 45-24.2-3 states that city or town councils have the power to enact ordinances to establish minimum standards for dwellings: "Without limiting the generality of the foregoing, such ordinance, rules and regulations may include . . . (3) Minimum standards relating to the healthful, safe and sanitary maintenance of parts of dwelling and dwelling units including, but not limited to, provisions relating to weathertight, watertight and rodent proof foundations, floors, walls, ceilings, roofs, windows and doors, condition and repair of stairs and porches, condition of plumbing fixtures, imperviousness of floor surfaces to water and functioning of supplied facilities, pieces of equipment, and utilities." It cannot be seriously contended that this enabling act did not delegate the power to Cranston to provide in sec. 14-71(b): "All exposed surfaces which have been adversely affected by exposure or other causes shall be repaired and coated, treated or sealed so as to protect them from serious deterioration."

Id. at 749.

2. Are "detail" cases like *Early Estates* an application of Dillon's Rule, or does this rule not apply to this problem? The Virginia Supreme Court provided one answer in *Commonwealth v. County Board*, 232 S.W.2d 30 (Va. 1977). The court held that the county did not have the authority to recognize local bargaining agents or to bargain collectively with them. The statutes did not confer this power, but did confer general powers such as the power to "manage the affairs of the county." The court noted a contention by the local public agencies

> that the extent of their powers is to be determined not only by application of the Dillon Rule, but also by resort to another rule, *viz.*, that a general grant of power implies the necessary means for carrying into execution the power granted, and, accordingly, where a power is granted expressly but no mode or manner is specified for its execution, the public body, in its discretion, may select any reasonable method of exercising the power.

Id. at 39.

The court harmonized the "reasonable selection of method" rule with the Dillon Rule as follows:

> [T]he "reasonable selection of method" rule always is stated in terms that there must be an express grant of power silent upon its mode or manner of execution before the rule comes into play. We perceive no reason, however, that the rule should not apply also, in a proper case, to a power which has been implied from an express grant. Given this application, the "reasonable selection of method" rule can be made to harmonize with, rather than contradict, the Dillon Rule.

Id. at 40-41. The court has apparently adopted a two-step analysis in the application of the "reasonable selection of method" rule. What is it? How would the Virginia court apply this analysis to the *Early Estates* problem?

3. Constitutional questions often lurk behind statutory power questions. Some courts, for example, have struck down housing code provisions requiring hot water facilities as an unconstitutional taking of property. They hold that these facilities are a matter of convenience, not necessity. See *City of St. Louis v. Brune,* 515 S.W.2d 471 (Mo. 1974); *Gates Co. v. Housing Appeals Board,* 225 N.E.2d 222 (Ohio 1967). The court's decision in *Early Estates* avoided the constitutional problem. This judicial response is typical, as courts will not decide constitutional questions unless they are necessary to a resolution of the litigation.

See also *Itzen & Robertson v. Board of Health,* 215 A.2d 60 (N.J.L. 1965), *aff'd,* 222 A.2d 769 (N.J. App. Div. 1966). The court held unauthorized an ordinance requiring septic tank installers to post a one-year maintenance bond. The court noted that the installer might be liable on the bond for acts of homeowners or third parties over which she had no control. What constitutional problem does this contingency raise? Is the "reasonable relationship" standard adopted in the *Early Estates* dissent a camouflage for substantive due process review?

4. An interesting statutory authority problem arises when a municipality attempts to avoid limitations imposed under one statutory power by relying on another. Mobile home regulation is an example. Some courts have limited the authority of municipalities to restrict mobile homes under their zoning powers. A municipality may then attempt to accomplish the same result under its general "police" power.

In *Board of Supervisors v. Moland Development Co.,* 339 A.2d 141 (Pa. Commw. 1975), a township passed a "Regulation of Lot Size and Sewage Disposal Ordinance." It contained a series of requirements for dwelling units including a minimum lot size of 31,250 square feet, and minimum street frontage, lot depth, and front, side and rear yard requirements. Moland, who desired to build a planned mobile home community, brought an action attacking the ordinance.

The township argued that the ordinance was a proper exercise of its police power to pass ordinances for the public health, safety, and welfare, as authorized by state legislation. The court disagreed: "We will not stretch the language of these basic enabling clauses dealing with health, fire prevention, sanitation and building lines to permit what the lower court found to be, and what we agree are, essentially zoning regulations." *Id.* at 143. The court also noted that to uphold the enactment of the ordinance under the police power would permit a circumvention of the protections built into the zoning legislation, such as the requirement that the zoning ordinance be based on a comprehensive plan. It held the ordinance unconstitutional as an improper exclusion of mobile homes from the community. For a similar holding see *Rayco Investment Corp. v. Board of Selectmen,* 331 N.E.2d 910 (Mass. 1975).

In these cases, the municipalities had also adopted zoning ordinances. *Compare Village House, Inc. v. Town of Loudon,* 314 A.2d 635 (N.H. 1974). This town did not have a zoning ordinance, but did have a building code with minimal requirements. It was a small town of 2,000 inhabitants, and prior to plaintiff's application for a mobile home park had already allowed three mobile home parks with spaces for 260 mobile homes. Fifty-eight mobile homes had located in these parks, and an additional 64 mobile homes were located elsewhere in the town. Shortly after the plaintiff applied for a permit to build another mobile home park the town enacted an ordinance prohibiting the establishment of additional mobile home parks within its limits. This ordinance was enacted as a police power ordinance under the appropriate enabling statute.

An earlier New Hampshire case had held that a police power ordinance enacting "comprehensive" land use regulations had to be adopted under the provisions of the zoning enabling act. In this case, "the mobile home park ordinance itself was a simple, direct and narrow addition to the ordinances in that it dealt solely with mobile homes. It apparently was not intended to be integrated into previous enactments as part of an overall, regulatory scheme and apart from the banning of additional parks, no ordinance regulates the use of land or the types of structures placed on land. The building code is lenient and imposes on the right of property owners in only the most unobtrusive way. The handful of rules comprising the building code cannot be said, in either intention or effect, to be regulating land usage, construction of buildings or location of businesses in any 'comprehensive' way...." *Id.* at 637. The court also held that the ordinance served a valid public purpose and was not an unconstitutional taking. Is this case distinguishable from *Moland*?

Are the courts holding that municipalities may not avoid constitutional problems by evading statutory authority requirements? *Compare Lovequist v. Conservation Commission,* 393 N.E.2d 858 (Mass. 1979). The court held that an ordinance regulating land use in wetlands, which are transitional marshy areas, was not a zoning law subject to the procedures required by the zoning statute. The court distinguished *Rayco, supra,* noting that the municipality did not have a comprehensive zoning ordinance. "*Rayco,* moreover, nowhere suggests that municipal regulations that simply overlap with what may be the province of a local zoning authority are to be treated as zoning enactments." *Id.* at 863. Is *Lovequist* perhaps distinguishable because the environmental land use regulation considered there was viewed favorably by the court?

In addition to specific enabling legislation, some states have also adopted legislation authorizing municipalities to adopt ordinances necessary to serve their "general welfare." Whether a statutory delegation of this kind expands local government authority is considered in the next case.

STATE v. HUTCHINSON

Supreme Court of Utah
624 P.2d 1116 (1981)

STEWART, JUSTICE:

Defendant, a candidate for the office of Salt Lake County Commissioner, was charged with having violated § 1-10-4, Revised Ordinances of Salt Lake County, which requires the filing of campaign statements and the disclosure of campaign contributions. That section provides:

Campaign Statements.

1. Every candidate for election or his designated committee secretary shall file with the county clerk on forms furnished by the clerk, full, correct and itemized statements of all monies and things of monetary value received and expended in the furtherance of said candidacy in accordance with the schedule set forth in this section.

. . . .

5. All statements shall be dated and signed by the candidate and the committee secretary.

Failure to comply with those provisions is a misdemeanor.

A complaint charged defendant in two counts: (1) failure to report the name and address of a $6,000 contributor to his election campaign, and (2) failure to file supplemental campaign disclosures of the discharge of campaign debts and obligations.

Defendant filed a motion in a city court to dismiss the complaint on the ground that the ordinance was in violation of the Utah Constitution. The court granted the motion and held that Salt Lake County was without constitutional or statutory authority to enact the ordinance under which defendant was charged and dismissed the complaint.

An appeal was taken to a district court which affirmed the dismissal. That court wote a memorandum decision observing that ". . . it may be true that our Utah Supreme Court has not been completely consistent in every case on this issue, [but] the majority of the [Utah Supreme Court] cases have indicated that grants of powers to cities or counties are to be strictly construed to the exclusion of implied powers not reasonably necessary in carrying out the purposes of the expressed powers granted." The court noted that, on the other hand, *Salt Lake City v. Kusse,* 97 Utah 113, 93 P.2d 671 (1938), and *Salt Lake City v. Allred,* 20 Utah 2d 298, 437 P.2d 434 (1968), "suggest that a county has fairly broad power to enact ordinances . . . under the general welfare clause of § 17-5-77 [Utah Code Annotated.]" Nevertheless, the court held that there is no express authority in state statutes authorizing the enactment of § 1-10-4 and that there was nothing that could be "implied from any express power that would justify the enactment of these ordinances." Accordingly, the court held the ordinance unconstitutional, and the State appeals.

Defendant contends that because the Legislature has not specifically authorized counties to enact ordinances requiring disclosure of campaign contributions in county elections, Salt Lake County had no power to enact the ordinance in question. . . .

Concededly, the district court was correct in holding that the Legislature has not expressly authorized enactment of an ordinance requiring disclosure of campaign contributions in county elections. However, the Legislature has conferred upon cities and counties the authority to enact all necessary measures to promote the general health, safety, morals, and welfare of their citizens. Section 17-5-77, U.C.A. (1953), as amended, provides:

> The board of county commissioners may pass all ordinances . . . not repugnant to law . . . *necessary and proper to provide for the safety, and preserve the health, promote the prosperity, improve the morals, peace and good order, comfort and convenience of the county and the inhabitants thereof,* . . . and may enforce obedience to such ordinances . . . by fine in any sum less than $300 or by imprisonment not to exceed six months, or by both such fine and imprisonment . . . . [Emphasis added.]

The Legislature has made a similar grant of power to the cities.

The specific issue in this case is whether § 17-5-77 by itself provides Salt Lake County legal authority to enact the ordinance for disclosure of campaign contributions, or whether there must be a specific grant of authority for counties to enact measures dealing with disclosures of campaign financing to sustain the ordinance in question. Defendant claims that the powers of municipalities must be strictly construed and that because Salt Lake County did not have specific, delegated authority to enact the ordinance in issue, the ordinance is invalid.

The rule requiring strict construction of the powers delegated by the Legislature to counties and municipalities is a rule which is archaic, unrealistic, and unresponsive to the current needs of both state and local governments and effectively nullifies the legislative grant of general police power to the counties. Furthermore, although the rule of strict construction is supported by some cases in this State, it is inconsistent with other cases decided by this Court—a situation that permits choosing between conflicting precedents to support a particular result.

Dillon's Rule, which requires strict construction of delegated powers to local governments, was first enunciated in 1868. The rule was widely adopted during a period of great mistrust of municipal governments and has been viewed as "the only possible alternative by which extensive governmental powers may be conferred upon our municipalities, with a measurable limit upon their abuse."

The courts, in applying the Dillon Rule to general welfare clauses, have not viewed the latter as an independent source of power, but rather as limited by specific, enumerated grants of authority.... More recently, however, reasoned opinion regarding the validity of the rule has changed. One authority has noted the harmful effects that the rule of strict construction has had upon the effective exercise of appropriate municipal authority:

> Any vestige of inherent powers or liberality in construing delegated powers was soon swept away by the Dillon Rule. This rule was formulated in an era when farm-dominated legislatures were jealous of their power and when city scandals were notorious. It has been the authority, without critical analysis of it, for literally hundreds of subsequent cases.
>
> As it arose, the strict construction doctrine applied to municipal corporations but it has been extended to local government generally and it must be faced in any approach to liberalizing local powers. This rule sends local government to State legislatures seeking grants of additional powers; it causes local officials to doubt their power, and it stops local governmental programs from developing fully. The strict construction rule stimulated home rule efforts and is largely responsible for the erosion of home rule. Because of its importance the rule should be examined critically from time to time. [Footnotes omitted.] [6]

As pointed out in Frug, *The City As A Legal Concept,* 93 Harvard L.Rev. 1059, 1111 (1980):

> Most troubling of all to Dillon, cities were not managed by those "*best fitted* by their intelligence, business experience, capacity and moral character." Their management was "too often both *unwise* and *extravagant.*" A major change in city government was therefore needed to achieve a fully public city government dedicated to the common good. [Footnotes omitted.] [Emphasis in original.]

---

[6] Advisory Commission on Intergovernmental Relations, State Constitutional and Statutory Restrictions Upon the Structural, Functional, and Personnel Powers of Local Government, 24 (1962) (hereinafter cited as Advisory Commission).

If there were once valid policy reasons supporting the rule, we think they have largely lost their force and that effective local self-government, as an important constituent part of our system of government, must have sufficient power to deal effectively with the problems with which it must deal. In a time of almost universal education and of substantial, and sometimes intense, citizen interest in the proper functioning of local government, we do not share the belief that local officials are generally unworthy of the trust of those governed. Indeed, if democratic processes at the grassroots level do not function well, then it is not likely that our state government will operate much better. . . .

But the Court has also ignored the rule on occasion without attempting to distinguish it or overrule it. . . .

The fear of local governments abusing their delegated powers as a justification for strict construction of those powers is a slur on the right and the ability of people to govern themselves. Adequate protection against abuse of power or interference with legitimate statewide interests is provided by the electorate, state supervisory control, and judicial review. Strict construction, particularly in the face of a general welfare grant of power to local governments, simply eviscerates the plain language of the statute, nullifies the intent of the Legislature, and seriously cripples effective local government.

There are ample safeguards against any abuse of power at the local level. Local governments, as subdivisions of the State, exercise those powers granted to them by the State Legislature, . . . and the exercise of a delegated power is subject to the limitations imposed by state statutes and state and federal constitutions. A state cannot empower local governments to do that which the state itself does not have authority to do. In addition, local governments are without authority to pass any ordinance prohibited by, or in conflict with, state statutory law. . . . Also, an ordinance is invalid if it intrudes into an area which the Legislature has preempted by comprehensive legislation intended to blanket a particular field.

In view of all these restraints and corrective measures, it is not appropriate for this Court to enfeeble local governments on the unjustified assumption that strict construction of delegated powers is necessary to prevent abuse. The enactment of a broad general welfare clause conferring police powers directly on the counties was to enable them to act in every reasonable, necessary, and appropriate way to further the public welfare of their citizens.

. . . .

In short, we simply do not accept the proposition that local governments are not to be trusted with the full scope of legislatively granted powers to meet the needs of their local constituents. On the contrary, the history of our political institutions is founded in large measure on the concept—at least in theory if not in practice—that the more local the unit of government is that can deal with a political problem, the more effective and efficient the exercise of power is likely to be.

. . . .

The wide diversity of problems encountered by county and municipal governments are not all, and cannot realistically be, effectively dealt with by a state legislature which sits for sixty days every two years to deal with matters of general importance. Thus the manner in which the Legislature operates militates in favor of a rule of judicial construction which permits localities to deal with their problems by local legislative action.

The general welfare provision, § 17-5-77, grants county commissioners of each county two distinct types of authority. In the first instance, power is given *to implement specific grants of authority.* Second, the counties are granted *an independent source of power to act for the general welfare of its citizens.* Thus § 17-5-77 provides authority to "pass all ordinances and rules and make all regulations, not repugnant to law, necessary for carrying into effect or discharging the powers and duties conferred by this title . . . ." The second part of that section empowers counties to pass ordinances that are "necessary and proper to provide for the safety, and preserve the health, promote the prosperity, improve the morals, peace and good order, comfort and convenience of the county and the inhabitants thereof, and for the protection of property therein."

Nothing in § 17-5-77 or in Title 17 suggests that the general welfare clause should be narrowly or strictly construed. Its breadth of language demands the opposite conclusion. Moreover, the Constitution does not allow the Legislature unlimited discretion to deal with local government. The broad delegation of power by the Legislature to the counties is consistent with constitutional provisions which establish counties as governmental entities and place certain aspects of county government beyond the power of the Legislature. Article XI, § 1 gives constitutional status to the counties as they existed at the time of adoption of the Constitution, and they are "recognized as legal subdivisions of this State . . . ." Sections 2 and 3 of that article restrict the Legislature with respect to the changing of county seats and county lines. In addition, it should be noted that charter cities have been endowed with even more wide-ranging powers by Article XI, § 5 of the Constitution. See also Article I, § 25 which provides that those rights enumerated in the Constitution "shall not be construed to impair or deny others retained by the people."

The grant of general welfare power to counties is duplicated by a similar grant to the cities, and this Court has on several occasions squarely sustained city ordinances solely on the basis of the general welfare clause. . . .

The Supreme Court of Pennsylvania adopted a similar position in *Adams v. City of New Kensington,* 357 Pa. 557, 55 A.2d 392 (1947). In that case, the plaintiff brought an action to enjoin enforcement of a city ordinance which required the licensing of music boxes, juke boxes, and mechancial vending machines on the ground that the city did not have the authority to pass the ordinance. In upholding the ordinance, the court stated: "It is at once obvious that this provision constitutes a grant of extremely broad powers, and such 'general welfare clauses' have always been liberally construed to accord to municipalities a wide discretion in the exercise of the police power." [*Id.,* 55 A.2d at 395.]

Closely in point with the facts of the instant case is *Lehrhaupt v. Flynn,* 140 N.J. Super. 250, 356 A.2d 35 (1976), which dealt with the validity of a financial disclosure ordinance adopted by a township without express authority for such action. The court stated: "[A]lthough there is no specific statutory authorization for municipal enactment of official financial disclosure ordinances, general power to adopt such local legislation is inherent in the broad delegation of police power . . . ."

These cases state the rule which we adopt in this case. When the State has granted general welfare power to local governments, those governments have independent authority apart from, and in addition to, specific grants of authority to pass ordinances which are reasonably and appropriately related to the objectives of that power, i. e., providing for the public safety, health, morals, and welfare. . . . And the courts will not interfere with the legislative choice of the means selected unless it is arbitrary, or is directly prohibited by, or is inconsistent with the policy of, the state or federal laws or the constitution of this State or of the United States. Specific grants of authority may serve to limit the means available under the general welfare clause, for some limitation may be imposed on the exercise of power by directing the use of power in a particular manner. But specific grants should generally be construed with reasonable latitude in light of the broad language of the general welfare clause which may supplement the power found in a specific delegation.

Broad construction of the powers of counties and cities is consistent with the current needs of local governments. The Dillon Rule of strict construction is antithetical to effective and efficient local and state government. The complexities confronting local governments, and the degree to which the nature of those problems varies from county to county and city to city, has changed since the Dillon Rule was formulated. Several counties in this State, for example, currently confront large and serious problems caused by accelerated urban growth. The same problems however, are not so acute in many other counties. Some counties are experiencing, and others may soon be experiencing, explosive economic growth as the result of the development of natural resources. The problems that must be solved by these counties are to some extent unique to them. According a plain meaning to the legislative grant of general welfare power to local governmental units allows each local government to be responsive to the particular problems facing it.

Local power should not be paralyzed and critical problems should not remain unsolved while officials await a biennial session of the Legislature in the hope of obtaining passage of a special grant of authority. Furthermore, passage of legislation needed or appropriate for some counties may fail because of the press of other legislative business or the disinterest of legislators from other parts of the State whose constituencies experience other, and to them more pressing, problems. In granting cities and counties the power to enact ordinances to further the general welfare, the Legislature no doubt took such political realities into consideration.

We therefore hold that a county has the power to preserve the purity of its electoral process. The county was entitled to conclude that financial disclosure by candidates would directly serve the legitimate purpose of achieving the goal that special interests should not be able to exercise undue influence in local elections without their influence being brought to light.

. . . .

In sum, the Dillon Rule of strict construction is not to be used to restrict the power of a county under a grant by the Legislature of general welfare power or prevent counties from using reasonable means to implement specific grants of authority. County ordinances are valid unless they conflict with superior law; do not rationally promote the public health, safety, morals and welfare; or are preempted by state policy or otherwise attempt to regulate an area which by the nature of the subject matter itself requires uniform state regulation. Of course a specific power delegated to municipalites may imply a restriction upon the manner of exercise of that power, but the restriction on the exercise of such power is to be construed to permit a reasonable discretion and latitude in attaining the purpose to be achieved.

. . . .

CROCKETT, C.J., and HALL, J., concur.

MAUGHAN, JUSTICE (dissenting): [Most of the dissenting opinion is omitted, but the following comments indicate the dissenting justice's viewpoint on state-local relations as it applies to the exercise of local powers:]

For the following reasons, I dissent. . . .

The analysis of the majority opinion utilizes the familiar technique of erecting a straw man, in this case, the abstract principle of law identified as Dillon's Rule, and throttling it with the evocative shibboleth of local control. The majority then interprets Section 17-5-77 as a carte blanche delegation of the state police power to local government, unless there be a specific and direct conflict between state and local law. This interpretation is inconsistent with the multiple statutes, wherein the legislature confers specific powers and duties on local government, and distorts the nature of the police power.

The State is the sole and exclusive repository of the police power, neither the federal nor local government has any such inherent power. The police power is awesome, for it confers the right to declare an act a crime and to deprive an individual of his liberty or property in order to protect or advance the public health, safety, morals, and welfare. The decision of whether a problem should be deemed one of local concern and should be regulated under the police power should initially be decided by the legislature representing all the citizens of this state. The legislature may then elect to delegate the power to local government to deal with the specific area of concern. It is equally a legislative judgment to deny delegating this power to local government.

The palliative suggested by the majority opinion that local citizens can change the law by electing new officials provides no relief for the individual previously convicted and avoids the basic issue of whether the police power has, in fact, been delegated under the specific circumstance. All exercise of the police power by local government is derivative, none is inherent, and it is the exclusive prerogative of the State to establish the conditions under which it will be exercised. If local government discerns a condition which merits control through the police power, this matter should be submitted to the legislature so that representatives of the entire state may resolve whether the problem should be addressed on a local level.

It is within the context of the foregoing principles that the specific delegation of the police power in Section 17-5-77 should be interpreted in this case.

Comments: 1. Does the court place any limitations on the exercise of local power under a general welfare clause, other than constitutional limitations and the possibility that a local ordinance may be preempted by state legislation? How would the court have decided the problem posed in *Early Estates*? The court in *Hutchinson* states that the general welfare clause may be relied upon to "implement" a specific granted power. Was this the *Early Estates* problem?

2. Other courts have also taken an expansive view of the authority granted by a general welfare clause. In *Inganamort v. Borough of Fort Lee,* 303 A.2d 298 (N.J. 1973), the court held that a local rent control ordinance was authorized by a general welfare clause. The statute authorized municipalities to adopt ordinances as they "may deem necessary and proper for the good government, order and protection of persons and property, and for the preservation of the public health, safety and welfare of the municipality and its inhabitants." The court held, as did the Utah court, that the general welfare grant was an independent source of municipal power, broad enough to confer the power to enact a rent control ordinance.

The court did, however, suggest some limitations on the exercise of delegated municipal authority:

> There is a limitation upon the power to delegate . . . . [S]ome matters must be dealt with at the state level . . . . For example, the law of wills or the law of descent and distribution

may not be left to local decision. Nor could the State leave it to each municipality to say what shall constitute robbery or whether it shall be punished. The reason is evident. "The needs with respect to those matters do not vary locally in their nature or intensity. Municipal action would not be useful, and indeed diverse local decisions could be mischievous or even intolerable." *Summer v. Teaneck,* .... 251 A.2d 761, 763 (1969).

Id. at 302. New Jersey also has a constitutional provision requiring that laws "concerning" municipal corporations should be "liberally construed in their favor," an apparent repeal of the Dillon Rule.

These qualifications suggest an area of exclusive state competence in which municipalities may not act, even under a general welfare clause. What is the source of this limitation? Could a municipality adopt its own divorce law? Could the legislature, if it chose to do so, specifically delegate to a municipality the power to adopt its own divorce law? What in the state constitution prohibits it?

The New Jersey "local intensity and hurt" rule was applied in the *Teaneck* case to uphold a local ordinance aimed at "blockbusting" by real estate agents. The ordinance required agents to register with the municipality before carrying out real estate solicitations. What is the "local intensity and hurt" here? *See* Note, *Legal Control of Blockbusting,* 1972 URB. L. ANN. 145. Is the control of campaign expenditures, which was at issue in the *Hutchinson* case, a matter of "local intensity and hurt"?

3. In *Robin v. Incorporated Village of Hempstead,* 285 N.E.2d 285 (N.Y. 1972), a state statute authorized abortions under stated circumstances. The town adopted an ordinance requiring all abortions to be performed in a duly licensed and accredited hospital. This ordinance was invalidated because it was held preempted by state law in the absence of clear and express statutory authority to deal with the subject of abortions. No such authority was found in a state statute authorizing the enactment of local ordinances "deemed expedient or desirable for the ... health of its inhabitants." The New York court had previously held that local health regulations could be enacted despite state regulations only if they were based on "special conditions" existing in the municipality. In this case it remarked that it was "hardly necessary" to note that no special conditions concerning the performance of abortions distinguished Hempstead from the rest of the state.

4. Some states follow the familiar ejusdem generis rule of statutory construction. This rule states that the grant of specific powers excludes any powers not specifically granted. These states hold that a "general welfare" grant of power cannot add to specific enabling grants of power appearing elsewhere in the statutes. *See City of Stuttgart v. Strait,* 205 S.W.2d 35 (Ark. 1947) (no power to establish setback lines).

In *Anderson v. City of Olivette,* 518 S.W.2d 34 (Mo. 1975), the city relied on a general welfare delegation authorizing it to enact ordinances for the "good government" of the city to pass a municipal fair housing ordinance applicable to real estate brokers and aimed at preventing discrimination in the sale or rental of housing. The court found that the ordinance was not authorized by this statute. It noted that cities of this class had been authorized to license and regulate certain businesses, but real estate brokers were not among the businesses that the city was authorized to regulate. For other classes of cities the power to regulate real estate brokers was expressly granted. It then took note of this legislative classification of powers and held that the specific grant to Olivette, which did not include the power to regulate, "may not be expanded to authority to license and regulate by reference to the general police power statutes." *Id.* at 39. Reference was also made to the strict construction rule applicable to municipal powers, which is still recognized in Missouri. How would the New Jersey courts react to this ordinance? If the regulation of blockbusting is a "local" affair what about a fair housing ordinance?

Other courts have placed implicit restrictions on the exercise of the general welfare power. *See Town of Conover v. Jolly,* 177 S.E.2d 879 (N.C. 1970). The town, "with a population of approximately 3,000 persons and containing within its limits residential areas, general business areas, neighborhood trading areas, manufacturing areas and minor farming areas" enacted an ordinance totally excluding mobile homes from the town. The ordinance was not part of a zoning ordinance. For statutory enabling authority the town relied in part on a statutory general welfare clause, which was held not to confer the necessary authority. A well constructed mobile home connected to public facilities cannot be held to be per se detrimental to the general welfare, "without regard to the nature and use of the surrounding properties."

5. The dissenting opinion in *Fort Lee* believed that the majority had gone too far. It read the majority as holding that "*any* power which is constitutionally delegable to a municipality . . . is *automatically* deemed in fact delegated" by the general welfare clause in the absence of state preemption. Is this comment applicable to the holding in *Hutchinson*?

The rent control ordinance upheld in *Fort Lee* inevitably affected housing market problems which are more than local in scope. This point was made by the dissent:

> 1. The jurisdiction affects freedom to contract with respect to a very common and important commodity in general commerce—apartment units of every price description and price range . . . .
> 2. The public need for and constitutionality of rent control regulation depends upon the existence of a shortage of housing accommodations of emergency dimensions. This is typically a concomitant of general cyclical inflationary trends of regional if not national importance . . . .
> 4. Chaotic conditions can be foreseen in relation to the interests of both owners and tenants if only a municipal boundary line can separate apartment houses subject to no rent controls whatever from those where an infinite variety of kinds of control may exist, none conformable to any state regulation.

Id. at 310-11.

A few months before *Fort Lee*, a lower New Jersey court upheld an ordinance requiring owners of apartments to post security with a local commission. The commission was authorized to spend money from this fund to make emergency repairs which the owners of the apartments refused to make after due notice. *Apartment House Council v. Mayor & Council*, 301 A.2d 484 (N.J.L. 1973), *aff'd*, 319 A.2d 507 (N.J. App. Div. 1974). The court commented that this ordinance was a "precisely intended" use of the general welfare clause. Is this case consistent with *Fort Lee*? Would the dissenting opinion in *Fort Lee* hold this ordinance unauthorized?

In *Hutton Park Gardens v. Town Council*, 350 A.2d 1 (N.J. 1975), the New Jersey Supreme Court upheld the constitutionality of local rent control ordinances against claims that they violated substantive due process and were confiscatory. It rejected the "emergency" doctrine that had been advanced by the United States Supreme Court and numerous state court decisions as the basis for upholding such ordinances. *See* Baar & Keating, *The Last Stand of Economic Substantive Due Process — The Housing Emergency Requirement for Rent Control*, 7 URB. LAW. 447 (1975). Is this decision relevant to the grant of power problems?

6. Home rule proponents have been suspicious of legislative home rule delegations, partly on the ground that "what the legislature gives it can take away." Consult the materials below on state preemption in constitutional home rule states. A legislative home rule delegation may also be unconstitutional. The early cases on this issue were divided, and there have been few decisions since the turn of the century. But see *Fiscal Court v. City of Louisville*, 559 S.W.2d 478 (Ky. 1977), partially invalidating a "home rule" statute granting "all rights, powers, franchises, and privileges" to counties. The court's opinion is a fascinating struggle to attempt to explain why the home rule grant was invalid as overly broad. In some of the adverse decisions, the legislature had simply delegated to municipalities the power to make their own charters. *See State ex rel. Mueller v. Thompson*, 137 N.W. 20 (Wis. 1912). Is this grant the same as a general welfare statute; if not, what is the difference? On the subject of legislative grants see Etter, *General Grants of Municipal Power in Oregon*, 26 OR. L. REV. 141 (1947).

For an example of a statutory delegation of power which approximates a home rule delegation see Or. Rev. Stat. § 221.410(1): "Except as limited by express provision or necessary implication of general law, a city may take all action necessary or convenient for the government of its local affairs." In *Davidson Baking Co. v. Jenkins*, 337 P.2d 352 (1959), the court relied on this provision to uphold a local ordinance licensing bakeries and bakery distributors.

A PROBLEM

REPORT OF THE STATE OF METRO JOINT
LEGISLATIVE COMMITTEE ON MUNICIPAL POWERS

(The report is fictitious)

Your committee was formed at the request of the governor and the chief justice of the supreme court following the now-famous *Wyckham* decision, and the widespread disturbances following the abortive attempt to introduce corrective legislation. In *Wyckham v. Metro City Housing Authority,* the supreme court of our state, after an agonizing appraisal, held that the housing authority did not have the implied statutory power to acquire land for the purposes of constructing low-income housing units in the suburbs and outside its jurisdiction, which is coterminous with the city limits of Metro City. Legislation conferring this power was introduced in the General Assembly, but hearings on the bill brought mutually antagonistic groups to the state capital, and resulted in a series of disturbances lasting several days when hearings on the bill were adjourned. The bill was never reported out of committee.

We have been asked to review the entire problem of delegation of power to municipalities and authorities in this state, putting aside the home rule possibility, which has been soundly rejected by the voters on two occasions and which has been adamantly opposed by a variety of organizations. It has not been an easy task to collect and organize the wide variety of measures which together add up to a collective statutory charter for local authorities in our state. But we have been convinced after a thorough review that the problems lie less with the specifics of individual measures than with the organizing concepts that underlie the delegation of statutory authority.

What seems to be the case is that decisions about the scope of local powers have been made under hierarchical linear principles which assume that all legal authority is centralized in the state, which delegates power downward at will to local units of government. It is this assumption which has led to limiting judicial interpretations of municipal powers, such as the decision in the *Wyckham* case. Your committee feels that current attitudes toward delegation of statutory power, and judicial interpretations of those delegated powers, have been unnecessarily inhibited by too close adherence to these concepts. What we must recognize is that the state government, and its local counterparts, are equal partners in the solution of our metropolitan area problems. State legislation conferring powers on local government units must be analyzed from this perspective. By setting limits on what local units can and cannot do, state enabling legislation sets limits on how and in what capacity these local units can intervene to aid in solutions to our urban crisis. For example, whether or not a municipal housing authority can or cannot build housing in the suburbs has a direct impact on the development of metropolitan strategies for dispersal of our big city ghettos. . . .

(a) This report is incomplete. Consider what other factors might be considered by the committee in making recommendations for a reworking of statutory delegations to municipal units. For example, if most of the local tax burden in this state is borne by local property taxes, would this fact have influenced the decision in the *Wyckham* case? Should distinctions be made between "enterprise" powers and regulatory "coercive" powers?

(b) Can the committee "solve" the problems it has raised without recommending explicit and comprehensive enabling legislation? What about the following proposal: Local units of government would be authorized by legislation to "claim" implied powers not expressly delegated but "reasonably inferred" from delegated powers. Claiming resolutions would be laid before the appropriate legislative committee at the general session of the legislature. Exercise of the claimed power would be deferred until the conclusion of that legislative session,

C. HOME RULE

1. THE HOME RULE ISSUE

The legislative "plenary power" rule and the problems inherent in legislative grants of power led many states to adopt constitutional home rule provisions. These provisions are intended to delegate autonomous power to local governments through a constitutional grant not dependent on state legislative action. Missouri adopted the first municipal home rule provision in 1875, and a substantial majority of states now authorize home rule for municipalities. One half of the states also authorize home rule for counties. In some states, the home rule clause merely authorizes the state legislature to adopt legislation conferring local home rule powers.

Constitutional home rule clauses take two forms. The original form, dubbed "imperium in imperio" — a "state within a state" — grants a defined scope of power to local governments. This form of home rule usually grants local governments powers over "municipal" affairs, or over their "property, affairs and government." The courts play an important role under this form of home rule, as they must determine the granted scope of local power. Many commentators have been critical of *imperio* home rule, claiming that the courts have unduly restricted the scope of power granted to local governments.

A more recent form of constitutional home rule, which can be called "legislative" home rule, was first proposed by Dean Jefferson Fordham. This proposal was adopted by national municipal organizations, and has since been adopted in several states. Under this form of home rule, the constitution grants local governments all powers the legislature is capable of delegating, but the legislature is authorized to withdraw or limit home rule powers by statute. This form of home rule is intended to shift control over home rule municipalities from the courts to the legislature. Dean Fordham proposed this reform to reduce the role of the courts in interpreting home rule provisions, and to expand the powers of home rule municipalities.

Preemption by the state legislature also is possible under the *imperio* form of home rule. The constitutional home rule clause often states that the exercise of local home rule is subject to "general" laws adopted by the state legislature, and courts imply this limitation even if it is not express. This exception allows state legislatures to preempt home rule municipalities through "general" legislation unless the home rule power is exclusively of local concern, in which case, at least in theory, the local law prevails.

Home Rule as Initiative and Protective

In a classic article, Dean Sandalow distinguished the initiative and the protective roles of the *imperio* form of constitutional home rule. Home rule confers an initiative on local governments to exercise autonomy in local affairs. Home rule also protects local governments from state legislation which preempts the exercise of local powers. Sandalow, *The Limits of Municipal Power Under Home Rule: A Role for the Courts,* 48 MINN. L. REV. 643 (1964).

Dean Sandalow believes that the courts have construed the initiative power broadly:

Analysis of the decisions reveals that, with the possible exception of a single state, the grant of municipal initiative in home rule provisions has been broadly construed by the courts. There are, of course, in almost every jurisdiction a few decisions limiting the scope of municipal initiative [but in most jurisdictions they] have not resulted in denying municipalities power to legislate concerning those matters which even the staunchest advocates of local autonomy consider appropriate for local control.

Id. at 663.

These two issues are combined in practically all of the home rule cases. The state legislature has usually enacted a statute covering a problem on which the home rule municipality has also legislated under its constitutional home rule powers. The court may concentrate on the "protective" issue raised by the state preemption problem and not consider the "initiative" problem directly. Even when the legislature has not acted, the court may confuse the two sides of home rule.

Sources of Local Power

A non-home rule government has only one source of power: the state enabling statute. For a home rule unit there are typically at least two sources: enabling statutes and the constitutional home rule grant. States have adopted enabling legislation that covers most of the areas in which municipalities function, and the courts have held that a home rule municipality may rely on a statutory as well as a home rule grant of power. A more difficult question, which has not been answered decisively, is whether a home rule municipality may rely on its home rule powers as an alternative to statutory authority. This problem usually arises when a home rule municipality attempts to modify a statutory power, or to add implementation powers not conferred by the enabling legislation.

Source of power problems also arise because most constitutional home rule provisions require the adoption of a charter as a condition to the exercise of home rule. Courts must then determine the source of a power claimed by the municipality under its charter. In states which treat the charter as a limitation on authority rather than a grant of authority, the courts are more likely to favor the municipality's exercise of the claimed power even though it is not explicitly "granted" in the charter. A majority of states, however, treat the charter as a grant, and failure of the charter to include the claimed power will be fatal. O. REYNOLDS, LOCAL GOVERNMENT LAW § 49 (1982).

Home Rule, The State's Role And Metropolitanism

The home rule movement is far from dead. The number of home rule states has more than doubled since 1953, with most recent states adopting the legislative rather than the *imperio* model. The growth of home rule raises questions about the role of the states and their local governments in determining the scope of local government powers. Legislative will to act may be the critical question here. Except for taxing powers, most courts have not seriously restricted the home rule initiative power, even in the *imperio* states. Sandalow notes that the court decisions "have not resulted in denying municipalities power to legislate concerning those matters which even the staunchest advocates of local autonomy consider appropriate for local control." *Id.* at 663.

This conclusion requires some qualification. Court decisions may be favorable generally, but doubts and uncertainties remain. Municipalities that decide to exercise home rule powers not expressly upheld by their state courts always face a possible court challenge. Concern about the outcome may lead to a conservative use of home rule authority. This problem is especially serious in fiscal matters, such as bond issues, since local debt obligations not backed by a clear holding of authority may be unmarketable. *See* Chapter 6.

How home rule affects the resolution of metropolitan area problems is another issue. Strengthening the powers of balkanized suburban governments by conferring home rule authority may complicate solutions to metropolitan problems. This possibility is mitigated, to some extent, by the limitation of home rule powers under some constitutions to municipalities over a certain size. Neither may low-profile suburbs in metropolitan areas elect to adopt home rule charters. In the end, the balkanization problem may also help to explain, and even justify, some court decisions which otherwise seem unduly restrictive.

Comments: Although some forty states by now have constitutional home rule provisions, one study indicated that home rule powers were vigorously exercised only in about a dozen states. Vanlandingham, *Constitutional Municipal Home Rule Since the AMA (NLC) Model,* 17 WM. & MARY L. REV. 1 (1975). For an excellent review of municipal home rule see Vanlandingham, *Municipal Home Rule in the United States,* 10 WM. & MARY L. REV. 269 (1968). On county home rule, see Glauberman, *County Home Rule: An Urban Necessity,* 1 URB. LAW. 170 (1969). Seventy-five of the nation's 3,000 counties have adopted home rule charters.

2. HOME RULE POWERS IN THE *IMPERIO* STATES

The critical home rule issue in the *imperio* states is the scope of the delegated local home rule power. The representative state constitutional home rule provisions that follow indicate typical *imperio* home rule language, and the tendency of these constitutional provisions to delegate home rule power in areas of "local" concern. Courts usually impose this limitation even where the constitution does not expressly provide it.

Most of the home rule constitutional provisions reproduced below are self-executing. The Connecticut provision is not self-executing. Do you see the difference?

NEW YORK CONSTITUTION, ART. 9, § 2.

(b) Subject to the bill of rights of local government [see art. 9, § 1] and other applicable provisions of this constitution, the legislature:

(1) Shall enact . . . a statute of local governments granting to local governments powers including but not limited to those of local legislation and administration in addition to the powers vested in them by this article . . . .

(c) In addition to powers granted in the statute of local governments or in any other law, (i) every local government shall have the power to adopt and amend local laws not inconsistent with the provisions of this constitution or any general law relating to its property affairs or government, and (ii) [may adopt local laws on subjects specified in this subsection, including financial obligations, its legislative body, local taxes, and the "government, protection, order, conduct, safety, health and well-being of persons or property therein."]

CONNECTICUT CONSTITUTION, ART. X, § 1.

The General Assembly shall by general law delegate such legislative authority as from time to time it deems appropriate to towns, cities, and boroughs relative to the powers, organization, and form of government of such political subdivisions.

OHIO CONSTITUTION, ART. XVIII.

Sec. 3. Municipalities shall have authority to exercise all powers of local self-government and to adopt and enforce within their limits such local police, sanitary and other similar regulations, as are not in conflict with general laws.

Sec. 7. Any municipality may frame and adopt or amend a charter for its government and may, subject to the provisions of section 3 of this article, exercise thereunder all powers of local self-government.

WASHINGTON CONSTITUTION, ART. XI, § 11.

Any county, city, town or township may make and enforce within its limits all such local police, sanitary and other regulations as are not in conflict with general laws.

CALIFORNIA CONSTITUTION, ART. XI.

Sec. 5(a). It shall be competent in any city charter to provide that the city governed thereunder may make and enforce all ordinances and regulations in respect to municipal affairs, subject only to restrictions and limitations provided in their several charters and in respect to other matters they shall be subject to general laws. City charters adopted pursuant to this Constitution shall supersede any existing charter, and with respect to municipal affairs shall supersede all laws inconsistent therewith.

(b) It shall be competent in all city charters to provide, in addition to those provisions allowable by this Constitution, and by the laws of the State for: (1) the constitution, regulation, and government of the city police force (2) subgovernment in all or part of a city (3) conduct of city elections and (4) plenary authority is hereby granted, subject only to the restrictions of this article, to provide therein or by amendment thereto, the manner in which, the method by which, the times at which, and the terms for which the several municipal officers and employees whose compensation is paid by the city shall be elected or appointed, and for their removal, and for their compensation, and for the number of deputies, clerks and other employees that each shall have, and for the compensation, method of appointment, qualifications, tenure of office and removal of such deputies, clerks and other employees.

Sec. 7. A county or city may make and enforce within its limits all local, police, sanitary, and other ordinances and regulations not in conflict with general laws.

The delegation of home rule power over "local" affairs, and the implicit limitation that power over "state" affairs is not delegated, creates a three-part taxonomy of local home rule powers:

(a) Some powers are exclusively of state concern. Home rule municipalities may not act.

(b) Some powers are shared between the states and local governments. Home rule municipalities may act, but they may also be preempted by the state. Most home rule powers fall in this category.

(c) Some powers are exclusively of local concern. Home rule municipalities may act, and may not be preempted by the state. The cases and comments that follow illustrate these three home rule power categories.

The category of home rule powers classified as exclusively local is narrow. There also is some indication that courts tend to find exclusively local powers in states, such as California, where the constitutional home rule provision contains express language of preemption making local home rule powers "subject to general law." A court can avoid preemption by placing a home rule power in the exclusively local category.

UNITED STATES ELEVATOR CORP. v. CITY OF TULSA

Supreme Court of Oklahoma
610 P.2d 791 (1980)

Appeal from the District Court, Tulsa County; Richard V. Armstrong, District Judge.

Appellants appeal from an order of the District Court enjoining the City of Tulsa from complying with the terms of a contract between it and Otis Elevator Company and declaring such contract invalid because of the failure of the City of Tulsa to comply with the provisions of the Public Competitive Bidding Act of 1974, 61 O.S. 1974 Supp., §§ 101 et seq., in letting such contract.

. . . .

IRWIN, VICE CHIEF JUSTICE.

The issue presented is whether the Public Competitive Bidding Act of 1974 (61 O.S. §§ 101 *et seq.*), insofar as it relates to the advertising, receiving bids and awarding public improvement contracts, applies to a "Home Rule" municipality which has charter provisions for competitive bidding on public improvement contracts. If the Act is applicable we must then determine if the contract involved here is within its terms.

We hold the Act is not applicable and reverse the judgment of the trial court.

The City of Tulsa (City), a "Home Rule" city, followed its charter provisions instead of the Act in advertising, receiving bids and awarding a contract for elevator maintenance service for two public buildings. Otis Elevator Company (Otis) was the successful bidder, and United States Elevator Company (USEC) was an unsuccessful bidder. After the contract was awarded to Otis, USEC brought an action seeking an injunction enjoining City from complying with its contract with Otis. In turn, City sought to have its contract with Otis declared invalid in the event USEC was granted its requested relief.

USEC's action is based upon its contention that public improvement contracts are of statewide concern, and City should have followed the Act instead of its charter provisions in advertising, receiving bids and awarding the service contract. On the other hand, City and Otis contend that since City (Tulsa) is a "Home Rule" city, and its charter provides for competitive bidding on contracts such as the one involved here, the Act was not applicable and the charter provisions were properly followed.

The parties stipulated that if the Act is applicable, its provisions were not followed. USEC does not contend that the charter provisions were not followed if they are applicable.

The trial court granted summary judgment to USEC and declared the contract between City and Otis invalid. City and Otis appealed.

The parties recognize that municipalities may adopt charters containing provisions not in accord with the general law, and insofar as such charter provisions conflict with the state law on subjects relating to purely municipal matters, the state law is thereby suspended. *City of Muskogee v. Senter*, 186 Okl. 174, 96 P.2d 534 (1939). Under this rule, the conflict between the supremacy of the state law and the exercise of municipal power under its charter is resolved by determining "whether such law pertains to general matters of the state and its government or pertains to municipal affairs." *Lackey v. State*, 29 Okl. 255, 116 P. 913 (1911).

The application of this principle in the light of the various decisions has been likened to cutting a path through a jungle. Merrill, "Constitutional Home Rule for Cities Oklahoma Version", 5 Okl.L.Rev. 139, 159 (1952). Professor Merrill said that in searching for the "harmonizing principle" to be applied in determining which items are "municipal affairs", we may not simplify the process by concluding that matters of general concern, and hence not "municipal affairs", are those which concern the state at large or affect the people generally. Nearly every function of any local government may be said to affect "the people generally" in this mobile society. Practically any action of a city will have an impact upon persons not permanent residents of that municipality.

There are no constitutional guidelines for awarding public improvement contracts by a municipality that are comparable to those involving municipal bonded indebtedness over which the state maintains its complete sovereignty. *Sublett v. City of Tulsa,* Okl., 405 P.2d 185 (1965). However, USEC urges that this case may be resolved by resort to such constitutional provisions and other statutory provisions which arguably evidence an overriding state concern in the "economic" welfare of the municipalities of this state.

We do not find this argument persuasive. Article X, §§ 26, 27, and 35 of the Oklahoma Constitution, cited in this regard by USEC, relate to limitations on municipal indebtedness and procedures for incurring such indebtedness. They do not speak to the manner in which municipalities may carry on ordinary business affairs or for letting public building contracts. And we are not concerned here with how the contract in question will be paid or financed. Nor does the fact that the legislature has enacted numerous statutes concerning the financial affairs of a municipality, and the procedures to be used in providing for payments from certain funds dictate a finding that the Act pertains to general matters of state wide concern. We are concerned with a public improvement contract of a municipality and must determine whether the power which the City exercised in providing for its own bidding procedure "is purely municipal, or whether there is a wider public interest." *City of Wewoka v. Rodman,* 172 Okl. 630, 46 P.2d 334 (1935). Professor Merrill (5 Okl.L.Rev. 139, 161) in discussing the term "a wider public interest" said by using the phrase, attention was focused upon the true nature of the problem. That the term is

> ... not any single thing upon which we are to concentrate our attention. Rather, we are to take into account all the factors which center around the particular exercise of power and strike a balance to determine whether we can say there is a public interest "wider" than a purely municipal interest. This we can not do by rule of thumb, but by a balancing of the interests affected by the matter under consideration. It is this overall consideration of factors involved which offers the best way to a satisfactory explanation of the otherwise oft perplexing course of decision.

Other cases decided by this court are instructive in determining whether this involves a "municipal affair". In what seems to be in conflict with USEC's contention that matters affecting the "economic" well being of a municipality are not "municipal affairs", the court in *Bodine v. Oklahoma City,* 79 Okl. 106, 187 P.209 (1919) held that a county excise board could not second-guess the city government's discretion as to municipal needs. More recently, in *Moore Funeral Homes, Inc. v. City of Tulsa,* Okl., 552 P.2d 702 (1976) we held that the formation of a street improvement district, the levy of special assessment, and the procedure used in doing so were "municipal affairs".

USEC places great emphasis upon the dollar amount of the service contract, and urges that when all municipal contracts of this type are aggregated it involves a substantial amount of taxpayer funds. What is at issue here is not the amount of the contract, i. e. City's "indebtedness" and how it will be financed, but under which law (state or municipal) was City required to follow in letting the public improvement contract. In *City of Muskogee v. Senter, supra,* we said that in the absence of a charter provision prescribing the manner in which the City of Muskogee (a Home Rule city) could make contracts for professional services, the authority to make such contracts was governed by the general law of the state.

We need not determine whether the Act would be applicable to a "Home Rule" city whose municipal "law" did not provide for any "competitive bidding" procedure, or which expressly provided for some other method of letting contracts. We are satisfied that the specific procedures to be followed in advertising and accepting competitive bids on public improvement contracts is a "municipal affair" and outside the scope of that "wider public interest" which would allow the state law to supersede the municipal provisions of a "Home Rule" city. The particular manner in which a "Home Rule" municipality may let and approve public contracts based upon competitive bidding has no overriding impact beyond the municipality so as to authorize state interference in the conduct of such business affairs of the municipality.

Accordingly, we need not determine whether the service contract involved in this case would be otherwise covered by the provisions of the Act. Since it is not contended that the procedures followed by City in letting this contract did not comply with the requirements of the applicable law, i. e. the municipal law, the judgment of the trial court must be reversed, and the case remanded with instructions to deny USEC injunctive relief and enter judgment for City.

Reversed and remanded with instructions.

All the Justices concur.

Comments: 1. The court apparently applied a "balancing" test to resolve the municipal affairs problem. Did the court specify the factors to considered in the balancing test? If so, what are they? Is this approach to the problem of determining the scope of municipal affairs helpful or justified?

If Tulsa's charter, or home rule ordinance, had specifically provided that public improvement contracts were to be let by negotiated award rather than competitive bidding, would the court's decision have been different? If so, hasn't the court circumscribed a very narrow range of "home rule" power: the city may go its own way so long as it is not far afield from what the state requires?

2. As the *Tulsa* case suggests, internal contracting, structural and governmental process functions are usually held exclusively municipal, although the cases are not unanimous on this point. For a similar case *see Smith v. City of Riverside,* 110 Cal. Rptr. 67 (Cal. App. 1973), upholding the city's right to act under a charter provision requiring the use of city employees on public works construction as a proper exercise of home rule power over municipal affairs. A state statute required that all work on public projects be let to the lowest possible bidder.

In his summary of the California home rule cases, Professor Sato lists the following examples of internal functions held to be municipal affairs:

> [T]he information required in a recall petition; the method of enacting an ordinance; the procedure for the issuance of bonds for public park acquisition and the election with respect thereto; the place of deposit of municipal funds; the use of sewer charges for sewer improvements; the establishment of a city board of health; the procedure to be followed for municipal library site selection; street opening procedure; park abandonment procedures; and specification of funding for street improvement.

Sato, *"Municipal Affairs" in California,* 60 CALIF. L. REV. 1055, 1080 (1972). California ranks among the more liberal home rule states.

With Professor Sato's list compare *Baggett v. Gates,* 649 P.2d 874 (Cal. 1982). The court held that a Bill of Rights Act applicable to police officers applied to home rule municipalities. The Act granted a number of rights, including the right to political activity and the right to an administrative appeal of punitive actions taken against them. Although noting that it had invalidated legislation regulating local employee compensation and residency, the court distinguished the Bill of Rights Act even though it affected the removal of municipal employees:

> [T]he maintenance of stable employment relations between police officers and their employees is a matter of statewide concern. The consequences of a breakdown in such relations are not confined to city borders. These employees provide an essential service . . . . Our society is no longer a collection of insular local communities. Communities today are highly interrelated.

Id. at 880. How much does this opinion appear to limit "municipal affairs" in California?

Likewise, although local elections are usually a matter of local concern, the court upheld a statute mandating single-member districts in city council elections in *Jacobberger v. Terrey,* 320 N.W.2d 903 (Neb. 1982). The court noted that the purpose of the statute "was to insure proportionate representation in every socioeconomic segment of the population" and protect the "fundamental human and civil right" to vote.

3. When a matter is exclusively of state concern, the home rule municipality has no power to act at all. Illinois cases interpreting the home rule provision adopted in the 1970 constitution have provided guidance on the scope of matters which are exclusively state concern. The Illinois home rule provision was intended as an enactment of the legislative home rule model. For the text of the provision see Section 3, *infra.*

In *Ampersand, Inc. v. Finley,* 338 N.E.2d 15 (Ill. 1975), a county ordinance levied a county law library fee to be collected on the filing of a first pleading in a civil action. The court found the fee unauthorized. It held that "[t]he administration of justice under our constitution is a matter of statewide concern and does not pertain to local government or affairs."

In *People ex rel. Lignoul v. City of Chicago,* 368 N.E.2d 100 (Ill. 1977), the court struck down a local ordinance which authorized branch banking. The court relied on a constitutional provision giving control over banking to the state legislature and the history of the constitutional home rule provision to hold that "home rule units are without jurisdiction over such predominantly State and national matters as banking." For a discussion of Illinois home rule see Michael & Norton, *Home Rule in Illinois: A Functional Analysis,* 1978 U. ILL. L.F. 559.

4. The courts usually hold that incorporation and annexation are not within the home rule grant. *See Independent School District No. 700 v. City of Duluth,* 170 N.W.2d 116 (Minn. 1969). The court held that "because annexation procedures by their very nature involve land outside of the territorial limits of the annexing city, such procedures cannot be spelled out in a home rule charter." *Id.* at 122. On what basis is a court likely to hold that incorporation is exclusively a matter of state concern?

5. Probably the largest number of matters are of shared state and local concern. The Colorado Supreme Court articulated this concept in *DeLong v. City & County of Denver,* 576 P.2d 537 (Colo. 1978), in which it held that a local ordinance waiving governmental immunity in tort was not preempted by state tort liability legislation:

> This court has long recognized that certain matters are not exclusively of local or statewide interest, but are properly of concern to both. Examples of such concurrent areas of interest are: policemen's and firemen's pensions . . . ; assault and battery . . . ; shoplifting . . . ; disturbance of the peace . . . ; gambling . . . ; and speeding . . . . If a subject matter is of both local and statewide concern, then a home-rule charter provision or ordinance and a state statute may coexist if they do not conflict.

Id. at 540. Do these examples have any characteristics in common? Most of them are examples of criminal misconduct. Why should this area be shared?

Environmental regulation has usually been held to be a shared matter of state and local concern. In *Wambat Realty Corp. v. State,* 362 N.E.2d 581 (N.Y. 1977), *noted,* 16 URB. L. ANN. 389 (1978), the court upheld the state Adirondack Park Agency Act against claims that it infringed on local planning and zoning powers. The court noted that "preserving the priceless Adirondack Park through a comprehensive land use and development plan is most decidedly a substantial State concern . . . ."

6. Obviously, no bright line separates the home rule categories, and commentators have not been able to find a principled and universally applicable basis for distinguishing them. Dissatisfaction with the traditional state-local distinction led the Oregon Supreme Court to formulate an entirely different principle in *City of La Grande v. Public Employees Retirement Board,* 576 P.2d 1204, *aff'd on reh'g,* 586 P.2d 765 (Or. 1978). The court held that police and fire employees of home rule cities were brought within the state's employee retirement system. It rejected the traditional state-local distinction because "the court's decision must be derived from a constitutional standard, not from the court's own view of competing public policies." The court then held:

> When a statute is addressed to a concern of the state with the structure and procedures of local agencies, the statute impinges on the powers reserved by the [home rule] amendments to the citizens of local communities. Such a state concern must be justified by a need to safeguard the interests of persons or entities affected by the procedures of local government.
> Conversely, a general law addressed primarily to substantive social, economic or other regulatory objectives of the state prevails over contrary policies preferred by some local governments if it is clearly intended to do so, unless the law is shown to be irreconcilable with the local community's freedom to choose its own political form.

Id. at 1215. In a footnote, the court emphasized that its decision applied to the limitations on state statutes affecting home rule governments, not to the powers granted to these governments.

That the new formula has not been easy to apply is indicated by *City of Roseburg v. Roseburg City Firefighters Local No. 1489,* 639 P.2d 90 (Or. 1981). A widely split court held that home rule governments were subject to the state public employees collective bargaining act. For discussion of *La Grande,* see Andersen, *Resolving State/Local Governmental Conflict — A Tale of Three Cities,* 18 URB. L. ANN. 129 (1980).

Home rule power questions may also turn on the scope of authority contained in a local charter, as affected by the court's view of the local home rule initiative. The following case considers these problems:

CITY OF MIAMI BEACH v. FLEETWOOD HOTEL, INC.
Supreme Court of Florida
261 So. 2d 801 (1972)

ROBERTS, CHIEF JUSTICE.

We here review by direct appeal a decision of the Circuit Court, Dade County, holding unconstitutional an Ordinance of the City of Miami Beach purporting to regulate rents. In rendering his opinion and making his decision the trial judge construed a controlling provision of the Constitution, namely, Section 2, Article VIII, Constitution of Florida, F.S.A. Ordinance No. 1791, entitled "Housing and Rent Control Regulations," provides for regulation of rents in all housing with four or more rental units except for hospitals, nursing homes, retirement homes, asylums or public institutions, college or school dormitories or any charitable or educational or non-profit institutions, hotels, motels, public housing, condominiums and cooperative apartments, and any housing accommodations completed after December 1, 1969.

The City Council enacted the Ordinance in October, 1969 after making a determination that an inflationary spiral and a housing shortage existed in the City which required the control and regulation of rents. The City contends that it acted with the intent and purpose of protecting its residents from exorbitant rents.

Several lessors, who were directly affected, filed a complaint seeking declaratory judgment and injunctive relief and attacking the validity on constitutional grounds. After considering motions for summary judgment filed by both parties, the Circuit Court, Dade County, declared the Ordinance invalid, holding, inter alia that the Ordinance was an unlawful delegation of legislative authority by the City Council and construed Section 2, Article VIII, *supra*. This appeal followed and we affirm.

. . . .

The legal issues involved in this case are as follows:
(1) Whether or not the City of Miami Beach has the power to enact this rent control ordinance? . . .

The first issue must be answered in the negative. The City of Miami Beach does not have the power to enact the ordinance in question. This Court recognizes that the language in the Florida Constitution which governs the powers exercisable by municipalities has been changed by Article VIII, Section 2(b), 1968 Florida Constitution.

Article VIII, Section 8 of the Constitution of 1885 reads,

The Legislature shall have power to establish, and to abolish, municipalities to provide for their government, to prescribe their jurisdiction and powers, and to alter or amend the same at any time . . . .

Section 2, Article VIII of our *new 1968* Constitution provides,

(a) Establishment. Municipalities may be established or abolished and their charters amended pursuant to general or special law. . . .
(b) Powers. Municipalities shall have governmental, corporate and proprietary powers to enable them to conduct *municipal* government, perform *municipal* functions and render *municipal* services, and may exercise any power for *municipal* purposes except as otherwise provided by law. (Emphasis supplied.)

Although this new provision does change the old rule of the 1885 Constitution respecting delegated powers of municipalities, it still limits municipal powers to the performance of *municipal* functions.

That the paramount law of a municipality is its charter, (just as the State Constitution is the charter of the State of Florida,) and gives the municipality all the powers it possesses, unless other statutes are applicable thereto, has not been altered or changed. . . . The powers of a municipality are to be interpreted and construed in reference to the purposes of the municipality and if reasonable doubt should arise as to whether the municipality possesses a specific power, such doubt will be resolved against the City. . . . "Municipal corporations are established for purposes of local govenment, and, in the absence of specific delegation of power, cannot engage in any undertakings not directed immediately to the accomplishment of those purposes." *Hoskins v. City of Orlando, Florida* (5th Cir., 1931) 51 F.2d 901. The aforestated holding of the United States Fifth Circuit Court is entirely consistent with the 1968 change in our Constitution.

The Charter of the City of Miami Beach does not authorize the City of Miami Beach the power to enact a rent control ordinance. Section 6 of the Code contains no mention of such a power. The only possible source of such a power is Section 6 (x) which permits the City "to adopt all ordinances or do all things deemed necessary or expedient for promoting or maintaining the general welfare, comfort, education, morals, peace, health and convenience of said city, or its inhabitants and to exercise all of the powers and privileges conferred upon cities or towns by the General Law of Florida when not inconsistent herewith."

The weight of authority is that without specific authorization from the state, the cities cannot enact a rent control ordinance either incident to its specific municipal powers or under its General Welfare provisions. . . . *Wagner v. Mayor and Municipal Council of City of Newark* (1957), 24 N.J. 467, 132 A.2d 794.

Local governments have not been given omnipotence by home rule provisions or by Article VIII, Section 2 of the 1968 Florida Constitution. "Matters that because of their nature are inherently reserved for the State alone and among which have been the master and servant and landlord and tenant relationships, matters of descent, the administration of estates . . . and many other matters of general and statewide significance, are not proper subjects for local treatment. . . ." *Wagner v. Mayor and Municipal Council of City of Newark, supra* at 800. Mr. Justice Cardozo, in *Adler v. Deegan,* 251 N.Y. 467, 167 N.E. 705, 713 (Ct. App. 1929) made the following statement which is in support of the above-stated proposition,

> There are other affairs exclusively those of the state . . . . None of these things can be said to touch the affairs that a city is organized to regulate, whether we have reference to history or to tradition or to the existing forms of charters.

Furthermore, since the inception of federal controls after the beginning of World War II, legislative history and the development of case law shows a recognition that rent control was not a matter within the realm of municipal power without express authority from the state and the existence of an emergency—as hereinafter discussed. *Wagner v. Newark, supra.* The Supreme Court of Errors of Connecticut has held that a city charter conferring police power in general terms did not empower the city to adopt a rent control ordinance. *Old Colony Gardens, Inc., et al. v. City of Stamford, et al.,* 147 Conn. 60, 156 A.2d 515 (1959).

The State of Florida through legislative action has enacted statutory provisions to regulate the landlord-tenant relationship. Chapter 83, Fla. Stat. F.S.A. Absent a legislative enactment authorizing the exercise of such a power by a municipality, a municipality has no power to enact a rent control ordinance.

[The court then reaffirmed the rule, that rent control ordinances must be founded on emergency conditions, and refused to find an emergency condition in this case.—Eds.]

Comments: 1. Is the Florida court simply holding that the Miami Beach charter does not confer the authority to enact the rent control ordinance, or is it holding that the charter could not even be amended to confer this power? Is its holding that a "legislative enactment" is needed to confer the power on Miami Beach to regulate rents by implication a holding that the power to regulate rents is not included in the home rule grant? Or is the reference to the state landlord and tenant law by implication a holding that the power to regulate rents has been preempted by that statute?

2. *Fleetwood* may also be read as holding that the rent control ordinance was unauthorized, not because the state had not specifically delegated it, but because rent control is not a matter which can be delegated to municipalities. The same thought was expressed but rejected in *Inganamort v. Borough of Fort Lee,* discussed *supra,* Section B, which then held that the authority to adopt a rent control ordinance was conferred by a statutory general welfare clause. *Fort Lee* also reinterpreted the earlier *Wagner* case, which was relied on in *Fleetwood.*

Fleetwood quotes *Wagner* for the proposition that landlord and tenant relationships also are outside the scope of local home rule. In *City of Evanston v. Create, Inc.,* 421 N.E.2d 196 (Ill. 1981), the city adopted an ordinance extensively regulating landlord and tenant relationships. The court held that the ordinance was within the scope of the Illinois constitutional home rule grant.

The court rejected an argument that the ordinance was an improper interference with the substantive law of contracts. "[T]he Ordinance does not alter any basic principle of contract law. The State has always had the right under police powers to impose conditions on private contractors as long as it was necessary for the public good." *Id.* at 202.

The court also held that a home rule government "possesses the same power as the State." This statement could be read as a holding that the home rule provision grants plenary power, except for the court's treatment of the *Ampersand* case, which is discussed, *supra.* The court distinguished *Ampersand* because the Evanston ordinance placed no "condition or barrier ... upon a citizen's access to the State's court system." In *Ampersand,* the court invalidated a local filing fee for civil actions, holding that control of the judiciary was a matter of state concern. Do you agree with the distinction? How might a local landlord and tenant ordinance affect the state court system? What if the ordinance created new defenses to a tenant eviction action?

The Illinois constitution has a provision requiring the grant of home rule power to be liberally construed, and the history of the clause indicates that it was intended as a repeal of the Dillon Rule. Does this background help explain the *Evanston* case? Did the *Fleetwood* case implicitly apply the Dillon Rule?

Compare *Nugent v. City of East Providence,* 238 A.2d 758 (R.I. 1968). The court held that a constitutional home rule provision delegating authority over "property, affairs and government" did not authorize a local ordinance licensing cable TV systems. The constitutional provision did not delegate powers "reserved to the general assembly," and the court held that the power to license businesses was a reserved power. It did indicate that the licensing power could be delegated to municipalities by statute. *Contra, Capitol Cable, Inc. v. City of Topeka,* 495 P.2d 885 (Kan. 1972) (constitution delegated power over "local affairs and government").

3. *Fleetwood* may be an application of the rule that a constitutional home rule clause and a municipal charter are a grant, not a limitation, of authority. Municipal authority must be found within the grant.

The grant theory may especially be strong in statutory home rule states. In *Canavan v. Messina,* 334 A.2d 237 (Conn. Super. 1973), the court held that the home rule municipality did not have the power to establish a minimum age for its mayor in its charter. The home rule statute listed fifty-six powers specifically granted to home rule municipalities, and also authorized these municipalities to "make all lawful regulations and orders in furtherance of any of said powers." Conn. Gen. Stat. § 7-194. The court held that all powers possessed by home rule municipalities are "specifically derived" from the state, and found no express power to establish a minimum age requirement. It refused to imply one from the general grant of power just quoted, especially as the state by statute had established its own minimum age requirement for local officers.

The stronger home rule states are "limitation" states. Home rule municipalities have all powers within the home rule initiative unless the exercise of these powers is limited by the constitution, by a statute, or by the municipal charter. *See Hubbard v. City of San Diego,* 127 Cal. Rptr. 587 (Cal. App. 1976).

A constitutional home rule provision that might be construed as a grant of power can be converted by a favorably disposed court into a "limitation" home rule provision. The Texas constitutional home rule provision, following the early Missouri model, provides that "Cities ... may ... adopt or amend their charters, subject to such limitations as may be prescribed by the Legislature ...." Texas Const. art. XI, § 5. This provision was interpreted as authorizing home rule municipalities to exercise any power the legislature could have authorized them to exercise. Statutes are only limitations on and not grants of power to home rule cities. *See Forwood v. City of Taylor,* 214 S.W.2d 282 (Tex. 1948).

The California and Texas view has been adopted even under statutory home rule grants. In *Tally & Jade, Inc. v. City of Detroit,* 220 N.W.2d 778 (Mich. App. 1974), the court upheld a municipal ordinance regulating topless go-go dancers under a statutory home rule provision authorizing the "regulation of trades, occupations and amusements." The statute implemented a constitutional home rule provision. Although the ordinance was arguably supported by the grant of power in the statute, the court reaffirmed the Michigan rule that municipalities act as agents of the state when they exercise powers under the home rule act. It noted that this act conferred a general police power except as limited by constitution or statute. See also *Montgomery Citizens League v. Greenhalgh,* 252 A.2d 242 (Md. 1969), upholding the authority of the county to enact a fair housing ordinance under a general welfare clause contained in the statutory home rule grant. Compare the discussion of the grant versus limitation rule as applied to state legislatures, *supra* Chapter 1, Section B3.

A NOTE ON THE COMPARATIVE AUTONOMY OF LOCAL GOVERNMENTS IN HOME RULE AND NON-HOME RULE STATES

This discussion raises the question whether local governments have more autonomy in self-government under home rule constitutional provisions than they have in states where all local powers are conferred by enabling legislation. To answer this question, this Note examines two areas of local authority which are highly controversial — authority over extraterritorial areas and the enactment of local civil rights ordinances. A related question is whether municipalities in home rule states may enlarge upon their statutory enabling authority in particular areas by relying instead on their home rule authority.

Extraterritorial powers. Because the exercise of extraterritorial controls brings nonresidents within the ambit of local home rule powers, an argument can be made that the exercise of extraterritorial powers is not a local affair. The problem has arisen in cases in which a municipality sought to extend its electric and other utilities to extraterritorial areas.

Britt v. City of Columbus, 309 N.E.2d 412 (Ohio 1974). The court held that the condemnation of land extraterritorially to expand municipal public utilities was not authorized by the Ohio constitutional home rule clause. "It is self-evident that the exercise of a power to condemn beyond a municipality transcends matters of 'purely local nature.'" *See* N. LITTLEFIELD, METROPOLITAN AREA PROBLEMS AND MUNICIPAL HOME RULE 33-42 (1962).

Birge v. Town of Easton, 337 A.2d 435 (Md. 1975). A charter amendment of the town authorizing the acquisition of land extraterritorially was held to be within the Maryland constitutional home rule provision. The court noted that the power to purchase land outside municipal limits is usually implied from the express power to operate publicly owned utilities, and that the acquisition in this case was necessary in order to meet the town's energy needs. "Considering the nature and needs of the Town's electric utility, its limited service area, its overall regulation by the State through the [Public Service Commission], and the negligible effect upon nonresidents of the Town, we think the power granted by the charter amendment with respect to the Town's electric system is in the sense contemplated by [the constitutional home rule provision] a local matter involving the 'incorporation, organization, government, or affairs' of the municipality." *Id.* at 441.

Can the Ohio and Maryland cases be explained by the fact that one involved a condemnation, the other an acquisition of extraterritorial property? What difference should that make? Compare *People ex rel. City of Salem v. McMackin,* 291 N.E.2d 807 (Ill. 1972) (dictum, home rule municipalities may exercise extraterritorial proprietary powers), *with City of Carbondale v. Van Natta,* 338 N.E.2d 19 (Ill. 1975) (contra, extraterritorial zoning).

In statutory authority states, most courts will imply a statutory power to extend services extraterritorially, although they are less willing to imply extraterritorial powers than they are to imply powers exercised within municipal limits. See *City of Pueblo v. Flanders,* 225 P.2d 832 (Colo. 1950), implying a power to furnish extraterritorial fire service. *Compare City of Corbin v. Kentucky Utilities Co.,* 447 S.W.2d 356 (Ky. 1969). The court held that the sale of electricity to nonresident consumers served no legitimate purpose as service was available from a private utility. The extension was not related to the development of the city. For a liberal view of the exercise of extraterritorial authority under statutory powers see *State v. City of Riviera Beach,* 397 So. 2d 685 (Fla. 1981).

Civil rights ordinances. Possibly because of their controversial nature and their impact on private businesses and individuals, civil rights ordinances have sometimes had tough sledding under constitutional home rule provisions, although the cases are divided.

Marshall v. Kansas City, 355 S.W.2d 877 (Mo. 1962), upheld a local public accommodations ordinance applicable to hotels, motels, and restaurants. The court relied on a series of provisions in the charter which added up to the power to regulate businesses for the public welfare. From these provisions it found the power to enact the ordinance. The court dismissed an objection that the ordinance improperly regulated private relationships. *See also Hutchinson Human Relations Commission v. Midland Credit Management, Inc.,* 517 P.2d 158 (Kan. 1973) (municipal human relations ordinance authorized by Kansas home rule provision).

A contrary view was taken in *Midwest Employers Council, Inc. v. City of Omaha,* 177 Neb. 877, 131 N.W.2d 609 (1964), which held a local FEPC ordinance unconstitutional. The court said in part: "The home rule charter adopted by the city of Omaha is a grant as distinguished from a limitation of power. Being a grant of power the charter is to be construed according to the same rules as a legislative act containing the same provisions in determining what authority is thereby granted the city government. . . . [W]e are unable to find any express authority which granted the city council power to pass legislation pertaining to fair employment practices or civil rights. Neither does the city charter fairly imply that the city council is vested with the power to pass such an ordinance. . . . The matters of fair employment practices and civil rights are matters of statewide and not of local concern." *Id.* at 613-14.

Few cases have considered the implied authority to adopt local civil rights ordinances under statutory grants. But see the *Olivette* case, discussed *supra,* which held that a statutory general welfare clause did not confer the authority to adopt a local civil rights ordinance. *See* Note, *Municipal Civil Rights Legislation — Is the Power Conferred by the Grant of Home Rule?,* 53 MINN. L. REV. 342 (1968).

Reliance on home rule rather than statutory powers. Statutes confer extensive powers on local governments through comperehensive enabling legislation. One example is the Standard Zoning Enabling Act, which is in force in most states and provides the basis for the exercise of the local zoning power. This act was first proposed more than fifty years ago, and often is not extensive enough to authorize procedural and substantive innovations in the exercise of the zoning power that municipalities may wish to adopt. May municipalities rely on their home rule powers as an alternative basis for the zoning function?

Ayres v. City Council, 207 P.2d 1 (1949). The City of Los Angeles imposed a series of conditions concerning street dedications and other matters on a subdivider. The court held that the city as a home rule city had a general power to impose these conditions because they were not prohibited by the statutes, city charter, or ordinances. This holding appears consistent with the California "limitation" theory of home rule.

Moore v. City of Boulder, 484 P.2d 134 (Colo. App. 1971). A local zoning ordinance authorizing low-cost housing was a "question of purely local concern" and could be adopted by a home rule municipality under its home rule authority. Any argument that the ordinance did not comply with the state zoning enabling act must be resolved in favor of the municipality.

Compare Nelson v. City of Seattle, 395 P.2d 82 (Wash. 1964). The court held that reliance on the zoning enabling act was optional with the home rule city, which had taken "no action" to use the powers conferred by the statute. For discussion see Note, *Land-Use Control, Externalities, and the Municipal Affairs Doctrine,* 8 Loy. L.A.L. Rev. 432 (1975).

How would you now answer the question posed at the beginning of this Note? Do home rule municipalities necessarily have more autonomy in self-government than municipalities in states where all local powers are conferred by enabling legislation?

Courts are less likely to find a power to levy taxes under constitutional home rule than they are to find other powers authorized by the home rule provision. The problem arises most frequently when home rule municipalities adopt income taxes. The state may also be levying an income tax, and this attempt by a home rule municipality to tap the same revenue source may lead to a negative home rule decision.

WEEKES v. CITY OF OAKLAND

Supreme Court of California
21 Cal. 3d 386, 146 Cal. Rptr. 558, 579 P.2d 449 (1978)

BY THE COURT.

May a chartered city, in the exercise of powers conferred by the home rule provision of the California Constitution . . . , levy upon all persons employed within the city a tax measured by the compensation received from employers, notwithstanding an express statutory prohibition against municipal taxes "upon income"? [The city adopted] an "employee license fee" upon the "privilege of engaging in or following any business, trade, occupation or profession as an employee." The fee is measured by the employee's "gross receipts" for services performed in Oakland and consists generally of 1 percent of Oakland-derived earnings.

[The court did not reach the constitutional home rule question, but held that the tax was an occupation tax expressly authorized by statute.]

RICHARDSON, JUSTICE, concurring.

[Justice Richardson considered the constitutional home rule question. He noted that the power to tax was within the home rule grant but was limited by the concept of "municipal affairs." He then concluded that the power to levy the local tax was not foreclosed by the adoption of a constitutional provision authorizing the state to levy an income tax. California has adopted a state income tax. He held that the purpose of this constitutional provision was to "establish the legitimacy of the income tax as a permissible levy." He then noted that the constitutional home rule amendment was adopted seventeen years later, and that its history did not indicate an intent to exclude the power to levy local income taxes.

[Justice Richardson then turned to the "municipal affairs" question. He noted that the court had not formulated an "exact definition" of this term, and continued:] On the specific issue of taxation for revenue only, numerous cases declare without equivocation or qualification that "the power of municipal corporations operating under a freeholder's charter to impose taxes for revenue purposes is strictly a municipal activity authorized by the state Constitution and subject only to those limitations appearing in the Constitution or the charter itself." ...

Past adherence to the principle of local autonomy in tax matters, however, is neither conclusive nor dispositive as to the issue before us. Matters once entirely local in nature may, in a society rapidly increasing in both complexity and interdependence, lose their "strictly local" character and become "matters of statewide concern." ... Plaintiffs argue that the unprecedented mobility of contemporary society, the prevalence of the commuter who works in one community while maintaining his home in another, and the growing disposition of businesses to treat local tax burdens as a key factor in location decisions will all combine to spread, distort and magnify the effect of a local income tax, necessarily producing considerable impact at the state level. The Legislature, it is asserted, has a significant interest in preventing the emergence of a series of separate and competitive "economic enclaves" with varying tax rates and overlapping jurisdictions.

We have on occasion suggested that to be a "municipal affair," a particular matter must be "solely" or "exclusively" of local interest. ... Literal application of that standard would compel termination of the present inquiry at this point, for it certainly cannot be said that the state interests urged herein are wholly fictitious. Judicial characterization of a particular matter as either a "municipal affair" or "of statewide concern," however, has always and necessarily been less a practical description of raw fact than a legal conclusion. The briefest reflection will confirm that virtually anything touching upon the welfare and management of a municipality will also be of some concern to the state. (See *Bishop v. City of San Jose,* ... 460 P.2d 137, dis. opn. of Peters, J.) But article XI, section 5, by committing one class of affairs to local government and the other to the Legislature, compels a dichotomy when state and local enactments conflict. Classification, then, is unavoidable; how is it to be accomplished?

In *Bishop,* we stated quite plainly that the Legislature may not arrogate to itself a particular area of activity merely by asserting an interest. ... That course would "return us to the time of the pre-1896 constitution when all general laws prevailed over charter provisions . . . . The only virtue of [such an approach] . . . is the ease of resolving the problem, but this would be accomplished at the expense of historical development and the clear import of the constitution." (Sato, *"Municipal Affairs" in California,* supra, 60 Cal.L.Rev. [1055], at pp. 1074-1075.) Our examination cannot cease once some legitimate but perhaps tenuous or overly broad state interest has been identified. If the home rule provision is not to be excised from the Constitution virtually at the will of the Legislature, as we have said it is not, then the only reasonable and practicable means of distinguishing matters committed to local control from areas in which the Legislature is free to assert supremacy is to weigh, in each case, the city's interest against the state's need to require uniformity, or to prohibit, control or coordinate the extraterritorial impact of the challenged municipal activity. . . .

Applying this principle to the case before us, we must acknowledge that the Legislature's attempt to appropriate the field of income taxation is certainly an indication of the seriousness with which it views the potential statewide impact of local income taxes. (Cf. Stats.1968, ch. 559, § 3, pp. 1226-1227, declaring the mobility of California citizens a matter of statewide interest insofar as it may be affected by "discriminatory" local taxes.) However, the Legislature's evaluation is not conclusive . . . , and in the present instance I am not persuaded that the problems potentially generated by municipal income taxes are so sweeping that they can be resolved by nothing less than an absolute proscription of this type of tax.

Plaintiffs contend with some force that municipal income taxes, particularly a network of municipal income taxes that vary in their structure and comprehensiveness from city to city, pose the very real danger of unfair distribution of tax burdens flowing from the commuter situation. While it undoubtedly is true that the raising of revenue for municipal purposes is a vital and traditional local concern, it is equally indisputable that the state has a right to prevent what one commentator has described as the exportation of "spillover costs," whether those costs be measured in money or otherwise. (Sato, supra, at pp. 1074-1075.) When a local tax measure threatens serious extraterritorial effects, those consequences rise to the level of a substantial state concern, and the Legislature may properly assert its supremacy to prevent or minimize them. But the sweep of the state's protective measures may be no broader than its interest.

Here, it is the "spillover" effect, not the local revenue ordinance itself, that is the proper concern of the Legislature. If a number of sister cities follow Oakland's lead, it is perhaps conceivable that the resulting network of uncoordinated local income taxes might cause such a heavy impact upon the ubiquitous California commuter as to impede intermunicipal business activities. None of the recitation of facts or arguments presented to us, however, suggests that such external difficulties, present or potential, cannot be adequately controlled by means less stringent and intrusive than total prohibition. For example, there is available a mandatory credit and allocation system comparable to provisions of the Bradley-Burns Uniform Local Sales and Use Tax Law. (§§ 7200-7209; see also *Legislative Developments, The Limits of Municipal Income Taxation: The Response in Ohio* (1970) 7 Harv.J.Leg. 271; Sato, supra, at pp. 1101, 1103-1104. I note in passing that the terms of the Bradley-Burns Act, which now purport to preempt the field of local sales and use taxes (§ 7203.5, added by Stats.1968, ch. 1265, § 1, p. 2388), do not dictate the absolute uniformity claimed to be essential with respect to local income taxes. Any local entity enacting a sales tax must adopt a standard percentage rate; the decision to tax, however, is not compelled. Theoretically, a particular city and the county in which it is located could choose to forego that source of revenue and so create a substantial imbalance with respect to neighboring counties and municipalites levying the tax. It may be assumed that such eventuality was thought unlikely, but apparently the possibility was not considered intolerable.

Similarly, it is urged that businesses may be heavily influenced by the existence or nonexistence of a local income tax; however, the variation in total tax burden created by differences in local property, special district and business taxes has approximately the same effect at present. I am not persuaded that this danger so expands the state interest as to justify a flat prohibition of the city tax. Nor can I discern any potential impact upon the state income tax system, except insofar as the addition of local income tax liability increases the citizens' overall burden. However, an increase in property and business taxes, the traditional resort of financially troubled local governments, would have the same result.

Although I hasten to acknowledge that neither the economic wisdom nor the social propriety of a municipal tax measured by "income" lies within our purview, I cannot say that the mere existence of a tax such as the Oakland employee license fee threatens to disrupt a state legislative scheme or produce serious *and uncontrollable* adverse consequences outside the bounds of the taxing jurisdiction. Accordingly, an absolute prohibition of a particular type of revenue-raising tax is neither warranted nor tolerable under the home rule doctrine. . . .

The foregoing analysis is not novel. . . . As long as the Legislature retains reasonable control over those features of the matter which are its legitimate concern, local governments remain free to exercise their legitimate and independent powers as to the local aspects.

CLARK, J., concurs.

MOSK, JUSTICE, dissenting. [Omitted.]

HOMER B. THOMPSON, JUSTICE, dissenting.

[Most of this dissent is omitted, except for the following discussion of the statewide concern problem:]

Finding preemption evidences a strong indication that the subject matter is of statewide concern. Here the field has been occupied by a comprehensive statute, and local legislation has been specifically prohibited. . . .

The extraterritorial effect of the Oakland tax is obvious. This court has taken judicial notice of the rapid growth of suburban areas in California and the high rate of mobility of the citizens of the state. . . .

In the 1968 reaffirmance of the intent to preempt set forth in Government Code, section 50026, the Legislature declared: "The Legislature finds and declares that the right of citizens of California to move freely about the state in search of employment is a matter of statewide interest and concern. Any unnecessary barriers which impede the mobility of citizens of this state or limit their choice of employment are contrary to state policy." (Stats.1968, ch. 559, § 3.)

Other factors evidencing statewide concern include: (1) the effect of the tax on out-of-county workers regarding free inter-city travel; (2) the effect on nonresident work decisions; (3) the redirection of business market forces; and (4) the effect on nonresident residential decisions. All these factors demonstrate extraterritorial impact.

It appears that large numbers of commuters are subject to the Oakland tax. These person have no voice in the adoption of such tax, the level of tax imposed, the duration of the levy, or even the expenditure of the tax proceeds thus extracted. It is taxation without representation, a matter of evident statewide concern.

If the subject tax were held to be a municipal affair, the entire municipal field would be opened to creation of a crazy quilt of overlapping taxing jurisdictions. Drawing from the federal-state parallel: "If fifty independent economic units within the United States are undesirable, 387 economic enclaves within California would be intolerable." (Sato, . . . 53 Cal.Law Rev. 801, 818 (1965) . . . . Such taxation problems are indeed matters of grave statewide concern.

The issue before us should not be encapsulated. Viewed from outside its geographic boundaries, it is apparent Oakland is not a law unto itself. Other communities will be affected by and react to the Oakland tax—in some the tax may well spark retaliation. These two are matters of statewide concern.

Neither the economic wisdom nor the social propriety of a municipal income tax is within our purview. These are, however, matters of concern to the Legislature; and to the degree such taxing decisions affect nonresident citizens and other taxing structures, such matters are of statewide concern.

Local income taxes, such as at issue here, have been criticized as regressive, imposing the greatest proportionate burden on those whose income is lowest. Excluding interest, dividends, and capital gains also favors the rich. The tax fails to recognize that gross income is not always an accurate measure of taxpaying abilities. . . . Proponents argue that the low rate reduces the inequities. There is no guarantee such rates will remain low, especially in view of rising costs and increased reluctance to raise property taxes.

The license tax form creates arbitrary results. Neighbors, one working within the city and one without, are taxed at different levels—yet receive identical services. Non-residents do not receive the same benefits as residents, yet both are taxed at the same rate. The tax is also thought unfair to those commuters who may live in a community without income taxes but with resultingly high property taxes. Such commuters could be required to pay both taxes. All of these alleged inequities are not for us to evaluate, but they are matters of statewide concern, once one's perspective exceeds the geographic boundaries of Oakland.

For all of these reasons, I respectfully conclude that the subject matter is of general or statewide concern and the instant tax is invalid. The judgment of the trial court should be affirmed.

Comments: 1. What makes the income tax problem different from other local home rule authority problems? Can other home rule ordinances have "spillover" effects and an adverse effect on population mobility? What about a home rule ordinance regulating the landlord-tenant relationship? Imposing rent control?

A holding that the power to levy an income tax is a home rule power also affects the distribution of revenue sources in metropolitan areas and creates double taxation problems. All home rule municipalities will be able to levy the tax, not just older cities like Oakland which face heavier fiscal burdens. Employees might also be taxed by the municipality where they live as well as the municipality where they work. Would Justice Richardson uphold a state statute limiting the income tax to the core city in metropolitan areas? Providing offsets to avoid double taxation? For more discussion of the local income tax see Chapter 5.

2. Court decisions on the authority to levy local income taxes under an *imperio* home rule grant are divided. In *Dooley v. City of Detroit,* 121 N.W.2d 724 (Mich. 1963), the court held that a local income tax was authorized under a home rule statute that authorized "excise taxes." The statute implemented a constitutional home rule provision. *See also Angell v. City of Toledo,* 91 N.E.2d 250 (Ohio 1960).

Carter Carburetor Corp. v. City of St. Louis, 203 S.W.2d 438 (Mo. 1947), is a leading case holding that a city charter did not confer the power to levy a municipal income tax. The city charter provided that the city could "assess, levy and collect taxes for all general and special purposes on all subjects or objects of taxation." The Missouri constitution conferred the taxing power on the legislature, authorized it to grant the power to tax to local governments and provided that "the power to tax shall not be surrendered . . . except as authorized by this Constitution." The city claimed the right to levy a municipal income tax under the charter clause quoted above.

Missouri then had the *imperio* form of constitutional home rule, but the home rule clause did not expressly grant authority over municipal affairs. The court held:

> [T]he power to tax is an extraordinary one, which does not inhere in municipal corporations, and will not be implied unless the implication be necessary and the grant unmistakable. . . . A constitutional grant of power to a city to frame and adopt a special charter, is a grant to the *people* of that city. But the city's people may not deem it desirable to delegate to the city in its charter *all* of the powers they could have granted under the constitutional sanction. Therefore, the city's power to impose taxes is *not* the uncontrolled power to impose *any* tax *except* as limited by its charter, or general law. On the contrary, it is only the power to impose such taxes as have been *authorized* by the General Assembly in a general law, or by the people in its charter—if not in conflict with the Constitution.
>
> . . . .
>
> Now as to the instant case, there admittedly is no specific authorization in the statutes or the St. Louis charter for an "earnings" tax. And the General Assembly has more than once forbade *all* cities to impose certain kinds of taxes. . . . The General Assembly has never authorized municipalities to impose an income tax—which would diminish pro tanto the state's revenue from the state income tax—and no city has ever tried to do it so far as appears. As a basis for the proposed earnings tax the appellants are forced to rely here on the single abstract provision in art. 1, Sec. 1, Par. 1 of the charter which merely provides the city may "assess, levy and collect taxes for all general and special purposes on all subjects or objects of taxation."
>
> If that authorization alone is sufficient, the City of St. Louis needs no other sanction for *any* tax it may desire to impose. Yet the city charter does not commit itself to that view. Art. XX thereof specifically authorities [sic] license and perhaps some excise taxes, and enumerates a great number of specified "objects" of taxation. And the statutes for years have authorized (but limited in amount) the imposition of ad valorem taxes. . . . It may be inquired: if the people of St. Louis *did* really intend by their charter to give the board of aldermen free rein to impose any and all taxes in any amount on any and all objects of taxation, how could it have been better said than it was stated in art. 1, Sec. 1, Par. 1 of the charter? But on the other hand, can it be believed that the people of the city when they voted for the charter in 1914 thought it would give the board that unlimited power over them? Such a construction would have been unprecedented and contrary to the general rule of law. We hold the charter provision relied on by appellants is too indefinite to support the tax, which is novel in this State. . . .

Id. at 441-44 (emphasis in original).

Statutory authority to levy a municipal income tax was provided following the *Carter Carburetor* case. The statute applicable to Kansas City limited the municipal income tax to a rate of one half of one percent. A charter amendment to the Kansas City charter was submitted to the voters which would have increased the municipal income tax rate to one percent. In *Grant v. Kansas City,* 431 S.W.2d 89 (Mo. 1968), the court held that the city did not have the power to increase the tax rate by amending the charter. It noted that the constitution required municipal charters to be "consistent" with state law, and pointed out that the limitation would nullify the grant if every charter provision had to be consistent with every state law. The court reconciled the difficulty by holding that consistency was required only in the case of governmental, as distinguished from corporate, powers. The power to tax was a governmental power. A concurring opinion held that the statutory authorization would not have been required in the first instance, and that if the enabling law had not been passed, Kansas City could have increased the tax rate through a charter amendment. These cases allow the state legislature to designate the municipalities authorized to levy an income tax. In the St. Louis metropolitan area, for example, only the City of St. Louis has been authorized to levy the tax. *See* Comment 1.

Missouri has now adopted the legislative home rule model, which is discussed in the next section. Consider, when reviewing that model, whether the Missouri Supreme Court might now reach a different result in the *Carter Carburetor* case.

3. Another leading case holding that a local income tax is not a home rule power is *City & County of Denver v. Sweet,* 329 P.2d 441 (Colo. 1958). The court invalidated a charter amendment authorizing an income tax. It relied, in part, on the adoption of a constitutional amendment authorizing a state income tax, which was held to limit the home rule power. The court wrote a heavily rhetorical opinion, in which it held that "[t]he United States Constitution provides for a national government with a federal system of states . . . . Clearly our federal system does not envisage as a part thereof city-states." (Emphasis in original.)

Later, in *City & County of Denver v. Duffy Storage & Moving Co.,* 450 P.2d 339 (Colo.), *appeal dismissed,* 396 U.S. 2 (1969), the court held that the city charter authorized an ordinance levying a business occupational privilege tax. The tax imposed a fixed levy of two dollars a month on owners, partners and employees receiving in excess of $250 per month. See also *Board of Trustees v. Foster Lumber Co.,* 548 P.2d 1276 (Colo. 1976), holding that an occupation tax authorized by statute cannot be levied on gross receipts or income. Compare the Oakland tax upheld in *Weekes.*

4. Home rule constitutional provisions can authorize local taxes subject to legislative control. The Illinois home rule provision expressly includes the power to tax and incur debt, excluding the power to license for revenue and to impose income, earnings or occupation taxes. §§ 6(a), 6(c). State preemption of home rule taxing power requires an extraordinary vote of 3/5 of each house of the legislature. § 6(g).

The supreme court has considered home rule taxing powers in several cases. In *Paper Supply Co. v. City of Chicago,* 317 N.E.2d 3 (Ill. 1974), a Chicago employer's expense tax of three dollars a month per employee on businesses employing fifteen or more persons was held not to be a prohibited occupation tax or a license for revenue and was held to fall within the home rule grant. See also *Jacobs v. City of Chicago,* 292 N.E.2d 401 (Ill. 1973), upholding a parking tax as a tax on the privilege of using parking facilities, not a prohibited license for revenue. But see *Estate of Carey v. Village of Stickney,* 411 N.E.2d 209 (Ill. 1980), holding that a ten cent tax imposed on any licensee operating a race track for every person entering the grounds on an admission ticket was a prohibited occupation tax.

The interpretive problems presented by these distinctions are illustrated by the lengthy majority and dissenting opinions in *Commercial National Bank v. City of Chicago,* 432 N.E.2d 227 (Ill. 1982). The court held that a "service tax" levied at a rate of one percent on all purchasers of service in the city was a prohibited tax on occupations.

The Illinois home rule provision was intended as an alternative to a "laundry list" designation of home rule powers. Has this objective been accomplished in the taxation field? The home rule provision also was intended to expand home rule taxation powers subject to limited legislative control. Has this objective been accomplished?

See also Kan. Const. art. 12, § 5(b), authorizing home rule governments to levy "taxes, excises, fees, charges and other exactions except when . . . limited or prohibited by enactment of the legislature applicable uniformly to all cities of the same class." See *Callaway v. City of Overland Park,* 508 P.2d 902 (Kan. 1973), holding that this provision authorized the levy of a business occupation tax. For the complicated legislative treatment of local sales taxes see *Clark v. City of Overland Park,* 602 P.2d 1292 (Kan. 1979).

5. A comprehensive review of home rule powers of taxation found, at that time, that home rule taxing powers were limited, except in California and Ohio. Cohn, *Municipal Revenue Powers in the Context of Constitutional Home Rule,* 51 Nw. U.L. Rev. 27 (1956). *See also* Note, *An Evaluation of Municipal Income Taxation,* 22 Vand. L. Rev. 1313 (1969). For a discussion of home rule in California see David, *California Cities and the Constitution of 1879: General Laws and Municipal Affairs,* 7 Hastings Const. L.Q. 643 (1980).

3. LEGISLATIVE HOME RULE

States recently adopting constitutional home rule provisions have followed the legislative home rule model. This form of home rule grants all powers to home rule governments that the legislature would be capable of granting, subject to legislative restriction. The following excerpts illustrate the legislative model as adopted by the two national municipal organizations, and as adopted in Illinois, South Dakota and Pennsylvania.

NATIONAL LEAGUE OF CITIES MODEL

A municipal corporation which adopts a home rule charter may exercise any power or perform any function which the legislature has power to devolve upon a nonhome rule charter municipal corporation and which is not denied to that municipal corporation by its home rule charter, is not denied to all home rule charter municipal corporations by statute and is within such limitations as may be established by statute.

NATIONAL MUNICIPAL LEAGUE ALTERNATIVE MODEL

Sec. 8.02. *Powers of Counties and Cities.* A county or city may exercise any legislative power or perform any function which is not denied to it by its charter, is not denied to counties or cities generally, or to counties or cities of its class, and is within such limitations as the legislature may establish by general law. This grant of home rule powers shall not include the power to enact private or civil law governing civil relationships except as incident to an exercise of an independent county or city power, nor shall it include power to define and provide for the punishment of a felony.

ILLINOIS CONSTITUTION, ART. VII, § 6.

[A] home rule unit may exercise any power and perform any function pertaining to its government and affairs, including but not limited to, the power to regulate for the protection of the public health, safety, morals and welfare; to license; to tax; and to incur debt.

SOUTH DAKOTA CONSTITUTION, ART. X, § 5 [prior to amendment].

A municipal corporation which adopts a home rule charter may exercise any power or perform any function which the Legislature has power to grant to nonhome rule charter municipal corporation by statute and is within such limitations as may be established by statute. . . . [Grant] does not include the power to enact private or civil law governing civil relationships except as an incident to exercise of an independent municipal power. . . .

Charter provisions with respect to municipal executive, legislative and administrative structure, organization, personnel and procedure are of superior authority to statute. . . . [Grant of power to be liberally construed.]

PENNSYLVANIA CONSTITUTION, ART. 9, § 2.

Municipalities shall have the right and power to frame and adopt home rule charters . . . . A municipality which has a home rule charter may exercise any power or perform any function not denied by this Constitution, by its home rule charter or by the General Assembly at any time.

Comments: 1. The legislative home rule model was intended to avoid or at least dilute the judicial role in interpreting the "imperio" home rule provisions by eliminating the option to invoke the state-local distinction used to define home rule powers. Legislative home rule also requires a denial of home rule power by the legislature or the home rule charter, a reversal of the presumption usually applied under the imperio model. The imperio home rule provisions interpreted as limitations, not grants, of authority could have been given this interpretation, but the drafters of the legislative model apparently believed that the courts had not adopted this view.

Even the legislative model does not fully delegate all powers to home rule municipalities. If a home rule unit under the legislative model were to attempt to legislate on divorce, for example, the courts probably would not allow it, even in the absence of a civil relationships clause. The courts must also determine what is denied by state law. They may rely on the state-local distinction in making this decision, although they should be less restrictive than courts in imperio states if they respect the intent of the legislative home rule model.

2. The drafters of the Illinois home rule provision offered the following explanation of their intent:

> [The home rule clause] is designed to be the broadest possible description of the powers that the receiving units of local government may exercise. It is clear, however, that the powers of home-rule units relate to their own problems, not to those of the state or the nation. Their powers should not extend to such matters as divorce, real property law, trusts, contracts, etc. which are generally recognized as falling within the competence of state rather than local authorities. Thus the proposed grant of powers to local governments extends only to matters "pertaining to their government and affairs."

Record of Proceedings, Sixth Illinois Constitutional Convention 1621 (1972).

See the Illinois cases, such as the *Ampersand* case discussed *supra*, which find no home rule power to legislate on matters of statewide concern. Is this holding consistent with the drafters' intent? With the theory of legislative home rule?

3. The New Mexico court has held that the state versus local distinction still applies under its legislative home rule provision. The home rule clause provides that "[a] municipality may exercise all legislative powers and perform all functions not expressly denied by general law or charter." In *City of Albuquerque v. New Mexico State Corporation Commission,* 605 P.2d 227 (N.M. 1980), the court held that a constitutional provision giving the commission authority over the regulation of common carriers was superseded by the legislative home rule provision. The city claimed that the commission did not have authority over a contract the city had executed for airport limousine services. The court held:

> [W]e hold that the proposed limousine service is a proprietary rather than a governmental function and therefore within the Home Rule Authority of the City. This court reasoned in *Apodaca v. Wilson,* . . . 525 P.2d 876 (1974), that the term "general law," as used in the Home Rule Amendment, means a law that applies generally thoughout the state, or is of statewide concern, as contrasted to a "local" or "municipal" law. The Home Rule Amendment applied in that case to service charges for municipally owned sewer and water facilities and the use of funds received therefrom. Such matters are of local concern. In the instant case, transportation of passengers between points and places within the City is not of any more statewide concern than the operation of the municipally owned sewer and water facilities of Albuquerque.

Id. at 229-30. The court then held that the governmental-proprietary distinction could be applied to determine whether an activity was of state or local concern, and concluded that a limousine service was proprietary. What if the airport had been located outside the city?

In the *Apodaca* case, the city increased its water and sewer service charges and appropriated the increase in revenue to its general fund. The court rejected an argument that the increase and fund transfer were prohibited by a statute providing that a municipality operating a water utility "may levy . . . a just and reasonable service charge." Are the New Mexico decisions consistent with the "spirit" of legislative home rule despite the application of the state versus local distinction?

4. Some states have modified the legislative home rule model to convert it into a home rule provision requiring a legislative grant of authority. The North Dakota home rule provision states that the legislature "may authorize [home rule governments] to exercise all or a portion of any power or function which the legislative assembly has power to devolve." In *Litten v. City of Fargo,* 294 N.W.2d 628 (N.D. 1980), the court noted that the "constitutional provision in itself does not grant any powers to home rule cities. Whatever powers home rule cities may have are based upon statutory provisions."

The following case illustrates the interplay between the plenary grant of authority and the statutory authority to limit home rule powers in states which have adopted the legislative home rule model as proposed by its drafters:

STATE EX REL. SWART v. MOLITOR

Supreme Court of Montana
___ Mont. ___, 621 P.2d 1100 (1981)

SHEEHY, JUSTICE.

Charles R. Swart, a registered land surveyor, appeals from a ruling by the District Court, Fifth Judicial District, Madison County, refusing mandamus against Lorraine P. Molitor, county clerk and recorder, and David Bowman, county examining land surveyor, and requiring them to approve and record a certificate of survey prepared by Swart. We affirm the District Court.

Swart had prepared a certificate of survey of a parcel of land containing 102,409 acres in Madison County and tendered it to Lorraine P. Molitor, county clerk and recorder, on December 7, 1979. Lorraine P. Molitor refused to file the certificate of survey because the county examining land surveyor, David Bowman, had not certified that the certificate of survey was free from errors and omissions in calculation and drafting.

Before he tendered the certificate of survey to the county clerk and recorder, Swart had taken the survey to David Bowman for his inspection. At that time, Swart informed Bowman that he would not pay a separate fee to Bowman for examining the certificate of survey. Because Swart refused to pay the separate fee, Bowman refused to examine the certificate of survey and refused to certify it as free from errors and omissions. Since the certificate had not been approved by Bowman, the county clerk and recorder refused to accept the certificate of survey for recording in her office.

Swart sought a writ of mandate in the District Court, either directing Bowman to examine the certificate of survey, or directing Lorraine P. Molitor to record the document. After a show cause hearing, the court refused to issue a writ of mandamus. This appeal followed.

As permitted by 1972 Mont.Const., Art. XI, § 5, Madison County has adopted a self-government charter. As such, it has these powers under 1972 Mont.Const., Art. XI, § 6:

> *Self-government powers.* A local government unit adopting a self-government charter may exercise any power not prohibited by this constitution, law, or charter . . . .

Prior to the 1972 Montana Constitution, and during the period that the 1889 Montana Constitution controlled, counties in this state could exercise only such powers as were expressly granted to them by the state, together with such implied powers as were necessary for the execution of the powers expressly granted. . . . Under the 1889 Montana Constitution, legislative control over counties was supreme. . . .

The 1972 Montana Constitution, in addition to providing for the continuance of the county, municipal, and town governmental forms already existing, opened to local governmental units new vistas of shared sovereignty with the state through the adoption of self-government charters. Whereas the 1972 Montana

Constitution continues to provide that existing local governmental forms have such powers as are expressly provided or implied by law (to be liberally construed), 1972 Mont.Const., Art. XI, § 4, a local government unit may act under a self-government charter with its powers uninhibited except by express prohibitions of the constitution, law, or charter, 1972 Mont.Const., Art. XI, § 6.

The broad expanse of shared sovereignty given to self-governing local units is illustrated by section 7-1-103, MCA, which provides:

> A local government unit with self-government powers which elects to provide a service or perform a function that may also be provided or performed by a general power government unit is not subject to any limitation in the provision of that service or performance of that function except such limitations as are contained in its charter or in state law specifically applicable to self-government units.

And again in section 7-1-106, MCA:

> The powers and authority of a local government unit with self-government powers shall be liberally construed. Every reasonable doubt as to the existence of a local governmental power or authority shall be resolved in favor of the existence of that power or authority.

Acting under its charter, the Madison County Commission, on September 27, 1977, adopted the following ordinance:

> 1. That pursuant to Section 11-3867, R.C.M.1947 [now section 76-3-301, MCA], the Chief Executive of Madison County shall, with the approval of the Commission appoint an examining land surveyor. All final subdivision plats and certificates of survey shall be reviewed for errors or omissions in calculation or drafting by the examining land surveyor before recording with the County Recorder. When the survey data shown on the plat or certificate of survey meet the conditions set forth by or pursuant to this ordinance, the examining land surveyor shall so certify in a printed or stamped certificate on the plat or certificate of survey; such certificate shall be signed by him.
>
> No land surveyor shall act as an examining land surveyor in regard to a plat or certificate of survey in which he has a financial or personal interest. In such case, the Chief Executive shall delegate the duties of the examining land surveyor under this ordinance to a registered land surveyor of his choice. In such case, the delegatee shall serve as examining land surveyor for all purposes with regard to that review.
>
> 2. Upon completion of review by the examining land surveyor, but before recording with the County Recorder the subdivider shall pay to the examining land surveyor all reasonable and necessary costs and expenses necessary to defray the expense of reviewing final subdivision plats and certificates of survey.

It is the position of Swart, and the principal issue in this case, that the provision foregoing for the payment of expenses to the examining land surveyor is illegal and in excess of the authority of Madison County. Swart also contends that the failure of the examining land surveyor to deposit such fees in the Madison County treasury is in violation of the county's charter.

There is no dispute between the parties that Madison County may require that final subdivision plats and certificates of survey be reviewed for errors and omissions by an examining land surveyor. That is permitted by section 76-3-611(2)(a), MCA. Swart's contention is that the requirement of a fee to be paid to the examining land surveyor is in excess of the authority granted to Madison County, even considering its self-government charter provisions.

Swart's contention is principally based upon section 7-1-114, MCA, which provides that a local government with self-government powers is subject, among others, to "all laws which require or regulate planning or zoning;" and that the examining land surveyor's fee in this case is not one of those enumerated as proper to be charged by a county clerk in section 7-4-2631, MCA. His further contention is that the examination of a plat or certificate of survey for filing is a part of "planning and zoning" and as such is controlled by state law; in effect, that the concept of shared sovereignty for self-governing local governmental units does not extend to fees to be charged by Madison County for the services of the examining land surveyor. The fee in this case was a charge of $20.

Swart also contends that this case is controlled by our prior holding in *State ex rel. Swart v. Stucky* (1975), 167 Mont. 171, 536 P.2d 762. In that case, we approved the issuance of a writ of mandate against a county clerk and recorder who had refused to record a certificate of survey from Swart because the survey had not first been submitted to the city county planning board for review, accompanied by a $20 reviewing fee. However, the issues presented in *Stucky* were not the same as we face here. In *Stucky,* the pertinent statute did not provide for a review of certificates of survey, as distinguished from subdivision plats. We therefore held that a review of a certificate of survey was not necessary for its recording and that a charge for such review was improper. In this case, section 76-3-611(2)(a), MCA, provides that the governing body may require that certificates of survey be reviewed before recording. We have the additional problem of the effect of the extension of shared powers to self-governing local units.

In capsule, we have a statute that permits local governing bodies, whether operating under general powers or self-governing powers, to require review of subdivision plats and certificates of survey before recording. We have a self-governing unit that has required review of subdivision plats and certificates of survey before recording, and has provided that a fee be paid for such review. Further, we have a state statute which makes it mandatory that self-governing units be subject to all laws which require or regulate planning or zoning.

The question becomes, does the fact that a self-governing unit is mandatorily subject to laws which regulate planning and zoning preclude the unit from prescribing a fee for reviewing certificates of survey where the state statutes are silent on that subject.

We are told by section 7-1-113, MCA, that a local government with self-government powers is prohibited from exercising any power inconsistent with state law. We are further told, in the same statute, that the exercise of a power is inconsistent with state law "if it establishes standards or requirements which are lower or less stringent than those imposed by state law or regulation."

The state standard that permits the review of certificates of survey, from a statutory viewpoint, is found in section 76-3-611(2)(a), MCA, which states that such certificates may "be reviewed for errors and omissions in calculation or drafting by an examining land surveyor before recording." Madison County's ordinance does not prescribe a lower standard than that required by the state statute, nor is it less stringent. Therefore, under the statutory definition of inconsistency found in section 7-1-113(2), MCA, Madison County's ordinance is not the exercise of a power inconsistent with state law. If it is not inconsistent, it is not the exercise of a prohibited power by a self-governing unit under section 7-1-111, MCA.

This is the first case we have had in which we examine the powers of a self-governing local unit vis-a-vis mandated state laws. In the construction of self-government powers, we are commanded to resolve all reasonable doubts in favor of the existence of such powers. Section 7-1-106, MCA. Had Madison County been acting as a general power jurisdiction, we should perforce be required to hold that Madison County had only such powers as were expressly or impliedly delegated to it. Section 7-1-2101(2), MCA. As a self-governing unit, Madison County has shared powers of legislative, executive and administrative authority. A self-governing unit which elects to provide a service or perform a function that may also be provided or performed by a general power government unit is not subject to any limitation in the provision of such service or performance of that function, except such limitations found in its charter or in state law specifically applicable to self-government units. Section 7-1-103, MCA, supra. Madison County is not limited in this respect by its charter, and there is no state statute specifically forbidding self-government units from assessing a fee for the review of certificates of survey, Madison County's prescribed fee is therefore valid. This means that Madison County in prescribing such a fee is merely exercising a legislative power that as a self-governing unit, it shares with the state. It means that or it means nothing.

The parties spent considerable time in their briefs and in oral argument discussing whether the review of certificates of survey was a planning or zoning function. In view of our holding that Madison County is exercising a shared legislative power with the state in prescribing a review fee, and that such exercise of power is not prohibited, it makes no difference to this decision whether the review of subdivision plats or certificates of survey is a function of planning or zoning.

Swart also contends that denying Madison County the power to prescribe a fee for reviewing certificates of survey would make for uniformity among the several counties with respect to this subject. We find in the statutes, however, that governing bodies may establish fees to be paid by subdividers for reviewing subdivision plats (certificates of survey are not mentioned). Sections 76-3-602 and 76-4-105(1), MCA. We find it more compatible with uniformity among the several counties to determine that a fee charge for such reviews, whether of subdivision plats or certificates of survey, and whether levied by general power governments or self-governing units, be recognized as valid.

. . . .

Affirmed.

Comments: 1. Has the court held that a grant of statutory authority which is silent on a claimed home rule power is not a limit on that power? Must the state legislature expressly limit the exercise of the home rule authority? Some of the legislative home rule provisions, as in New Mexico and Illinois, require an express legislative denial.

This question was considered by the Alaska Supreme Court under a constitutional provision identical to the Montana provision. In *Jefferson v. State*, 527 P.2d 37 (Alaska 1974), one municipality attempted to take over the control and operation of the sewer system of another, an act expressly prohibited by state statute. The court held that the municipality did not have this power:

> However, to say that home rule powers are intended to be broadly applied in Alaska is not to say that they are intended to be preeminent. The constitution's authors did not intend to create "city states with mini-legislature." They wrote into Art. X, § 11 the limitation of municipal authority "not prohibited by law or charter." The test we derive from Alaska's constitutional provisions is one of prohibition, rather than traditional tests such as statewide versus local concern. A municipal ordinance is not necessarily

invalid in Alaska because it is inconsistent or in conflict with a state statute. The question rests on whether the exercise of authority has been prohibited to municipalities. The prohibition must be either by express terms or by implication such as where the statute and ordinance are so substantially irreconcilable that one cannot be given its substantive effect if the other is to be accorded the weight of law.

In this case we find the prohibition to be express. The statutes established a procedure by which certain city powers could be transferred to a second class borough and precluded a city from exercising a power once that power was being exercised areawide.

Id. at 43. Would the Alaska court reach the same result as the Montana court in the *Molitor* case? *See* Sharp, *Home Rule in Alaska: A Clash Between Constitution and the Court,* 3 U.C.L.A.-ALASKA L. REV. 1 (1973). Compare the concurring opinion in the *Weekes* case, *supra.*

2. The legislative limitation on home rule powers authorized by the legislative home rule model raises statutory restriction problems similar to the statutory preemption problems considered in the next section. The cases decided so far seem to place slightly more emphasis on legislative intent under this model than they do in preemption cases not decided under legislative home rule provisions.

The Maine statutory home rule provision, based on the legislative home rule model, authorizes a denial of home rule power "either expressly or by clear implication." The court held that a municipality had the authority to adopt an ordinance limiting the number of permits issued annually in mobile home parks. *Begin v. Inhabitants of Sabbattus,* 409 A.2d 1269 (Me. 1979). The statute had previously required growth control ordinances of this type, but this statute was repealed. The statutes presently contain language authorizing but not requiring such ordinances. The court held that the repeal of the provision meant that the enactment of such ordinances was no longer mandatory, "but it does not necessarily or '*clearly*' imply that [such an ordinance] is no longer allowed." (Emphasis in original). *See also Schwanda v. Bonney,* 418 A.2d 163 (Me. 1980) (ordinance making minimum sentence mandatory not authorized when statute makes it discretionary); *City of Kodiak v. Jackson,* 584 P.2d 1130 (Alaska 1978) (ordinance may not add to statutory requirements for gun license).

One of the preemption provisions in the Illinois home rule clause authorizes the legislature to "specifically limit" the concurrent exercise of power by a home rule unit or to "specifically declare the State's exercise to be exclusive." Ill. Const. art. VII, § 6(i). The Illinois Supreme Court has interpreted this provision to require an explicit limitation.

In *Peters v. City of Springfield,* 311 N.E.2d 107 (Ill. 1974), the court upheld a home rule ordinance setting a lower mandatory retirement age for municipal firemen and police than the state municipal code. The court found no preemption, and required the legislature to act explicitly when it intended to limit an otherwise valid exercise of the home rule power.

3. Although Florida did not adopt a pure constitutional home rule provision, the courts have given it a general interpretation. The constitution grants municipalities "governmental, corporate and proprietary powers," and also provides that they "may exercise any power for municipal purposes except as otherwise provided by law." Fla. Const. art. VIII, § 2(b). In *Tweed v. City of Cape Canaveral,* 373 So. 2d 408 (Fla. 1979), the court held that a long-term contract with an employee performing a governmental function was binding on a new city council. Referring to the constitutional home rule provision and implementing legislation, the court said that "[w]e cannot take these words lightly and merrily ignore the obvious legislative intent to leave the cities alone and let them conduct their own affairs." See also *State v. City of Sunrise,* 354 So. 2d 1206 (Fla. 1978), holding that "[m]unicipalities may issue bonds to finance any capital or other project permitted by the state Constitution."

The Massachusetts court has indicated that the legislative home rule model may contain some implied limitations. In *Beard v. Town of Salisbury,* 329 N.E.2d 832 (Mass. 1979), the town adopted an ordinance prohibiting the removal of any sand, loam or gravel from the town. The court held that the ordinance regulated "intermunicipal" traffic and concluded that "[a]lthough the Home Rule Amendment confers broad powers on municipal governments, . . . it does not appear to be so expansive as to permit local ordinances . . . that, as here, regulate areas outside a municipality's geographical limits." The court also noted that the power to regulate traffic was vested in the legislature, and that "it is inconsistent with the present statutory scheme for a town to assume this power on its own." For a discussion of extraterritorial powers see the Note on the Comparative Autonomy of Local Governments in Home Rule and Non-Home Rule States, *supra.*

4. As this chapter has indicated, the enactment of local laws affecting civil relationships has been a troublesome problem. Recall that in the *Fleetwood Hotel* case, *supra,* the Florida Supreme Court held that a rent control ordinance was not authorized by the traditional version of constitutional home rule then in effect in that state. Shortly after that decision, the Florida legislature enacted a statutory home rule provision patterned after the National Municipal League model which provides that municipalities may "exercise any power for municipal purposes, except when expressly prohibited by law." The court held that this statutory home rule provision authorized the enactment of a local rent control ordinance. *City of Miami Beach v. Forte Towers, Inc.,* 305 So. 2d 764 (Fla. 1975). This opinion noted that bringing a rent control ordinance under the "municipal purposes" clause presented no "judicial problem."

The National Municipal League model prohibits the enactment of "private or civil law governing civil relationships except as an incident to an exercise of an independent municipal power." This clause has been included in some state constitutions adopting this model, including Massachusetts. In *Marshal House, Inc. v. Rent Review & Grievance Board,* 260 N.E.2d 200 (Mass. 1970), the court held that this clause barred the enactment of a local rent control ordinance by the municipality. The court, after noting that the civil relationships clause was vague, admitted that it had upheld an ordinance passed under a statutory grant of power in which the municipality had fixed taxicab rates as an incident to licensing:

> The fixing of rates in that case, however, was incidental to the exercise of a clearly defined, delegated power to regulate a transportation service having some aspects of a carrier or public utility. The rate fixing was at most a regulation of a temporary relationship between the taxi operator and his customer. The by-law before us, . . . at least as a matter of degree, more directly intervenes in the continuing landlord-tenant relationship. This it does by efforts to restrict the rent which may be charged to the tenant in leases and tenancies of a type frequently granted by owners of residential real estate. The by-law thus purports to control the principal incentive to the landlord for entering into the relationship at all.

Id. at 205. For similar reasons, the court rejected an argument that the ordinance was a "public law" governing economic relationships as a substitute for temporarily distorted market forces. The court admitted that a municipality could adopt ordinances protecting the public health, such as building and housing codes, that might affect "the circumstances of a tenancy." Rent control was an objective in itself, and could not be viewed as an incident of some other municipal power. Local rent control in Massachusetts was subsequently authorized by statute. *Contra, Birkenfeld v. City of Berkeley,* 550 P.2d 1001 (Cal. 1976), the court noting that there was no private law exception in the California constitutional home rule provision. The Massachusetts court relied on *Marshal House* to strike down a local ordinance regulating condominium conversions. *CHR General, Inc. v. City of Newton,* 439 N.E.2d 788 (Mass. 1982).

Compare *Tucker v. Crawford,* 315 A.2d 737 (Del. Super. 1974). A city ordinance created a warranty running in favor of the buyer of any dwelling which was sold in violation of the requirements of the city housing code. A seller failed to have the dwelling inspected as provided by the code and the buyer sued on the warranty for the cost of bringing the dwelling into compliance with the code. Delaware has enacted a statutory home rule law practically identical to the Massachusetts constitutional home rule provision. No violation of the civil relationship clause was found. The court noted that no authority had been cited indicating that a municipality could not expand civil liability between its citizens when so authorized by the legislative body. The ordinance merely codified the increasingly recognized warranty of habitability. *But see City of Bloomington v. Chuckney,* 331 N.E.2d 780 (Ind. App. 1975) (city ordinance adopting model landlord-tenant code violates civil relationships clause in statutory home rule provision). For an excellent discussion of the civil relationship problem see Schwartz, *The Logic of Home Rule and the Private Law Exception,* 20 U.C.L.A. L. Rev. 671 (1973).

A NOTE ON THE DISCRETIONARY AUTHORITY OF LOCAL GOVERNMENTS

The home rule materials indicate continuing interest in an expansion of local autonomy. The legislative home rule model was intended as a step in this direction, and also as a limitation on the role of the courts in delineating the scope of home rule. How successfully these objectives have been accomplished by this model is a matter of conjecture. Judicial interpretation has been necessary on the limitations imposed by legislatures on home rule municipalities. Where it exists, the "civil relationship" clause also requires judicial interpretation.

Discretionary home rule powers also vary by type of municipality, and by function. Cities are more likely to have home rule than counties. Courts are less likely to find taxing powers included within home rule provisions than non-taxing powers.

The following excerpt is from a study by the Advisory Commission on Intergovernmental Relations. The study used a questionnaire to local governments to determine the extent of discretionary authority delegated under home rule provisions and statutory enabling authority. The study's conclusions are of interest:

> Based both on the knowledge and judgment of experienced observers in the 50 states and extensive legal research, Prof. Joseph Zimmerman developed indices of the amount of local discretionary authority possessed by each of the various types of general-purpose unit of local government found among the 50 states. One index was developed for each type of local unit for each of four kinds of authority: structural, functional, fiscal, and personnel. . . . Examination of those tables highlights that:
>
> Nationwide, . . . cities have about an equal amount of discretionary authority in regard to their structure of government, functions, and personnel . . . . The greatest variations are found in the structural area, with cities in Arkansas, Georgia, Indiana, and Vermont having no discretionary authority relative to their structure . . . , in contrast to cities in 20 states with complete authority in this area . . . .
>
> Cities in 38 states possess the least discretionary authority in the area of finance. The major exceptions—those where financial discretion is relatively broad—are cities in Arizona, Illinois, Maine, and Texas.
>
> Counties nationwide have been granted significantly fewer powers by state constitutions and statutes than have cities, relative to all four types of authority examined. The greatest differences are in the areas of structure and functions, where, with certain exceptions, counties have little discretionary authority, while cities desiring to change their structure or expand their functions have relatively fewer state-imposed restraints in most states.
>
> Towns seem to have discretionary powers identical, or nearly identical, to those of cities—with the major exceptions of Oklahoma, Texas, and Wisconsin, where cities have relatively broad powers and towns have relatively narrow ones. A similar pattern exists with respect to villages in comparison with cities—with the exceptions of Maine, Missouri, Nebraska, New Hampshire, and Texas, where village powers are substantially weaker than city powers.
>
> Townships generally possess relatively little discretionary authority in the nine Midwestern states with so-called "rural" townships. These units are controlled tightly by the state government and are allowed to exercise few discretionary powers.

Advisory Commission on Intergovernmental Relations, Measuring Local Discretionary Authority 6 (1981).

D. STATE PREEMPTION AND STANDARDS

Even though a municipality may have the power to adopt a regulatory ordinance or impose a tax, state legislation may preempt the municipal power, or the local ordinance may be held to conflict with the state statute. State legislation may preempt without limit in statutory power states. Home rule municipalities may be preempted except when they exercise powers exclusively of local concern in those states which recognize exclusively local powers. See *Security Life & Accident Co. v. Temple,* 492 P.2d 63 (Colo. 1972), holding that the levy of a local sales and excise tax was exclusively of local concern and could not be preempted. Note also that courts will, not infrequently, confuse preemption or conflict with the power to act, denying the latter because of the presence of a state statute on the same subject.

Preemption and conflict problems arise constantly. Enabling legislation is rarely complete, and municipalities often enact regulations and requirements that supplement the state statute. Neither does most state legislation clearly indicate an intent to preempt. Whether preemption was intended must be determined by a judicial reading of the statute, and many preemption cases turn on judicial interpretations of statutory intent. Some legislation such as the Uniform Motor Vehicle Code, which has been widely adopted, contains a statutory declaration of uniformity which often leads courts to find against local supplementary regulation.

The cases that follow illustrate three common preemption problems. The first case illustrates the statutory conflict problem where the conflict is not direct. The state statute regulates some aspects of the regulatory problem but is silent on whether additional regulation is preempted. If the statutory scheme is incomplete, does this mean (a) that municipal regulation of unregulated problems is preempted, or (b) that municipal regulation is permissible? And how do you know whether the statutory scheme is complete?

The next case illustrates the preemption problem that arises when a state statute comprehensively regulates an area of concern, and the local ordinance imposes additional requirements. The question is whether the state legislation has adopted a comprehensive regulatory system that precludes any municipal initiative in the subject area.

In the third case, the state more affirmatively asserts its interest by providing a licensing program for an activity or facility. A municipality attempts to restrict the state licensee in some way. The question is whether the state interest as expressed through the licensing program preempts the municipal action.

MILLER v. FABIUS TOWNSHIP BOARD

Supreme Court of Michigan
366 Mich. 250, 114 N.W.2d 205 (1962)

KAVANAGH, JUSTICE. Plaintiff filed a bill of complaint in chancery in the circuit court for the county of St. Joseph naming the Fabius township board as defendant under the Michigan declaratory judgment statute, Comp. Laws 1948, § 691.501 et seq. He sought a decree finding the following ordinance adopted by defendant board to be void and unconstitutional:

> Effective August 25, 1959, powerboat racing and water skiing shall be prohibited on Pleasant lake in Fabius township, St. Joseph county, Michigan each day after the hour of 4:00 p.m. until the following day at 10:00 a.m. Any person who violates, disobeys or refuses to comply with or who resists the

enforcement of the provisions of this ordinance shall upon conviction, be fined not less than $25 nor more than $100 for such offense, or imprisonment in the county jail until such fine and costs shall be paid and such imprisonment shall be for a period not to exceed 30 days.

Defendant board appeared and filed an answer to the bill of complaint alleging that the ordinance in question was valid and praying for dismissal of the bill of complaint.

Plaintiff claims he is one of a number of people who own land or cottages on the shores of Pleasant Lake and who enjoy the sport of water skiing during the summer months.

Plaintiff alleges that he, like many other summer lake vacationers, due to employment, is unable to arrive at his property on Pleasant Lake until after 5:00 p.m. He desires to take advantage of the recreational facilities of Pleasant Lake and participate in the sport of water skiing during the daylight hours, which last until approximately 9:00 p.m.

Plaintiff claims he is deprived of water skiing by reason of the ordinance adopted by the local township board.

In 1959 the Michigan legislature enacted Act 55, P.A. 1959, amending Act 246, P.A. 1945, the title of which reads as follows:

> An act to authorize the township boards of certain townships to adopt ordinances and regulations to secure the public peace, health, safety, welfare and convenience; to provide for the establishment of a township police department; to provide for policing of townships by the county sheriff; to provide penalties; and to repeal all acts and parts of acts in conflict therewith.

Section 1 of the act, as amended, reads in pertinent part as follows:

> The township board of any township may, at any regular or special meeting by a majority of the members elect of such township board, adopt ordinances regulating health and safety of persons and property therein....

The case came on for hearing in the circuit court for St. Joseph county. After proofs and briefs, the trial court in his opinion found the ordinance constitutional and valid and entered an order dismissing the bill of complaint.

Plaintiff appeals claiming the ordinance is void because the statutes—Act 215, P.A. 1931 and Act 310, P.A. 1957—have preempted the field of regulating motorboating and water skiing on Michigan's inland lakes.

Plaintiff alleges the ordinance is void because it prohibits that which the state statutes permit and exceeds the powers granted townships by Act 246, P.A. 1945, as amended. Plaintiff also claims the ordinance is void because it treats motorboating and water skiing as a local regulatory problem when, in fact, such activities are not local but are state-wide in scope and require uniform state-wide regulation.

Plaintiff argues that in 1931 the legislature undertook regulation of motorboating and water skiing activities on inland lakes when it enacted section 1 of Act 215, P.A. 1931. The act required motorboats and other watercraft to be equipped with mufflers and other devices to deaden the sound. It also purported to regulate the speed and use of motorboats on inland lakes.

Plaintiff further alleges that 26 years later a second statute—Act 310, P.A. 1957—was enacted by the legislature which recognized the need for more comprehensive regulation of boating and water activities on our inland lakes. This statute made certain changes in the regulation of motorboating and provided limitations on water skiing activities.

Section 3 of the 1957 act relates to persons operating watercraft under the influence of intoxicating liquor or narcotic drugs. Section 4 of the act relates to the speed of watercraft. Section 5 of the act as amended by Act 208, P.A. 1958, for the first time took recognition of the problem of water skiing and other water surface sports, and provides as follows:

> Any person who operates any watercraft, or who navigates, steers or controls himself while being towed on water skis, water sleds, surfboards or similar contrivances, upon any of the waterways of this state carelessly and heedlessly in disregard of the rights or safety of others, or without due caution and circumspection and at a speed or in a manner so as to endanger or be likely to endanger any person or property, shall be guilty of reckless operation of a watercraft and upon conviction shall be punished as provided in section 16 of this act.

Section 8 of the act specifically relates to restrictions on the periods when water skiing is prohibited and reads as follows:

> No operator of any watercraft shall have in tow or shall otherwise be assisting in the propulsion of a person on water skis, water sled, surfboard, or other similar contrivance during the period 1 hour after sunset to 1 hour prior to sunrise. Any person permitting himself to be towed on water skis, water sleds, surfboards or similar contrivances in violation of any of the provisions of this act shall be guilty of a misdemeanor.

It is contended the 1957 act was to cover on a state-wide basis the entire field of prohibitory regulation of motorboating and water skiing on our inland lakes.

The trial court rejected plaintiff's claim in this regard. On appeal we are asked to determine whether the ordinance conflicts with the state statutes.

Concerning this problem, 37 Am. Jur., Municipal Corporations, § 165, p. 790, states the following:

> It has been held that in determining whether the provisions of a municipal ordinance conflict with a statute covering the same subject, the test is whether the ordinance prohibits an act which the statute permits, or permits an act which the statute prohibits. . . .
>
> The mere fact that the state, in the exercise of the police power, has made certain regulations does not prohibit a municipality from exacting additional requirements. So long as there is no conflict between the two, and the requirements of the municipal bylaw are not in themselves pernicious, as being unreasonable or discriminatory, both will stand. The fact that an ordinance enlarges upon the provisions of a statute by requiring more than the statute requires creates no conflict therewith, unless the statute limits the requirements for all cases to its own prescription. Thus, where both an ordinance and a statute are prohibitory and the only difference between them is that the ordinance goes further in its prohibition, but not counter to the prohibition under the statute, and the municipality does not attempt to authorize by the ordinance what the legislature has forbidden or forbid what the legislature has *expressly* licensed, authorized, or required, there is nothing contradictory between the provisions of the statute and the ordinance because of which they cannot coexist and be effective. Unless legislative provisions are contradictory in the sense that they cannot coexist, they are not deemed inconsistent because of mere lack of uniformity in detail. (Emphasis supplied.)

This court has followed the above rule holding portions of a field not covered by state law are open to local regulation. See *City of Howell v. Kaal*, . . . 67 N.W.2d 704; . . . *People v. McGraw*, . . . 150 N.W. 836.

The rule has long been recognized that municipalities are not divested of all control even where the legislature has enacted laws.

This Court said in *People v. McGraw, supra*. . . :

> . . . the municipality retains *reasonable control* of its highways, which is such control as cannot be said to be unreasonable and inconsistent with regulations which have been established, or may be established, by the state itself with reference thereto. This construction allows a municipality to recognize local and peculiar conditions, and to pass ordinances, regulating traffic on its streets, which do not contravene the state laws. The congested condition of traffic on many of the streets of the city of Detroit is a matter of common knowledge, and these conditions make it absolutely necessary, for the protection of pedestrians and the drivers of vehicles, to enact rules and regulations peculiarly adapted to the conditions there found, and to enact ordinances to diminish the danger. . . .

The question we have to determine, then, is whether the state has so preempted the field that it would be unconstitutional for the township to attempt to regulate water skiing by ordinance.

The legislation relied upon by plaintiff merely relates to various phases of the operation of watercraft, including its speed and use upon inland lakes. Section 8 of the 1957 statute only prohibits water skiing during the period 1 hour after sunset to 1 hour before sunrise. It, therefore, certainly cannot be said that the legislature intended to preempt the entire field or activity of water skiing. If the legislature so intended, it could have expressly stated preemptive control. It logically follows, then, that the portions of the township ordinance which endeavor to regulate water skiing, if not in conflict with the state law, are valid so far as the preemption doctrine is concerned.

It is obvious the ordinance was enacted to prevent the many dangers and alleviate the congested local conditions that existed on Pleasant lake.

In *City of Howell v. Kaal, supra* this court held that an ordinance may not invade a field completely occupied by statute but may enter an area not preempted by the state act, and further held that what the state law *expressly* permits an ordinance may not prohibit.

Since the cited statutes do not expressly control the period of regulation covered by the ordinance, it must be concluded there is no conflict. The ordinance speaks only where the statutes are silent. . . .

The remaining question deals with the subject of whether the ordinance can be sustained on the reasoning it deals with a local regulatory problem which the township has the authority to regulate under the 1959 amendatory act relating to "health and safety of persons and property" if the activity is in fact not local but state-wide. Plaintiff cites several cases in other states which seem to indicate support of his position. However, the cited cases do not deal with acts similar to the ones we are here asked to construe.

While the general problem with reference to water skiing and motorboating and the use of our inland lakes by different classes of sportsmen are state-wide problems, there are peculiar circumstances that are local in character—such as the number of boat users on the lake; the amount of fishing on the lake; the congestion and conflict between fishermen and water skiers; the location of the lake to densely populated areas—which the 1959 amendment authorizes townships to deal with under the "health and safety of persons and property" clause.

A comparison might be made between traffic ordinances of a city and the state traffic statutes. Densely populated cities with large numbers of automobiles require more local regulation, even to a greater reduction in speed, than do rural communities. The state prescribes by its statutes the general provisions with respect to problems, and this court has upheld the right of municipalities to further regulate as long as there is no conflict between the state statute and the municipal ordinance. We believe this rule of law equally applicable to the regulation of boating and water skiing on inland lakes.

The trial court reached a correct conclusion in finding the ordinance was valid as having a reasonable relation to the health and safety of persons and property of the area involved.

Under the facts in this particular case, we do not find the ordinance unconstitutional or invalid for the reasons claimed by plaintiff.

The decree of the lower court is affirmed. A public question being involved, no costs are allowed.

DETHMERS, CARR, KELLY, BLACK and ADAMS, JJ., concurred with KAVANAGH, J.

SOURIS, JUSTICE (for reversal). I read the township ordinance to *prohibit* from 4:00 p.m. until one hour before sunset and from one hour after sunrise to 10:00 a.m. that which the state statute *permits* to be done during a period which includes those hours. The ordinance conflicts with the statute and, therefore, necessarily is invalid. . . .

I would reverse, but would not award costs.

SMITH, J., concurred with SOURIS, J.

Comments: 1. Over thirty-five states have now enacted legislation authorizing state or local regulation of recreational activities on local waters. Note, *State Land Use Regulation—A Survey of Recent Legislative Approaches,* 56 MINN. L. REV. 869, 877-81 (1972). Legislation enacted in Michigan subsequent to the principal case allows the state resources agency to adopt rules governing the use of vessels, water skis and similar contrivances, but these rules are subject to local approval. Mich. Stat. Ann. § 18.1287(14) (15).

The Michigan Supreme Court recently stated that "examination of relevant Michigan cases indicates that where the nature of the regulated subject matter calls for regulation adapted to local conditions, and the local regulation does not interfere with the state regulatory scheme, supplementary local regulation has generally been upheld," citing several cases including *Fabius. People v. Llewellyn,* 257 N.W.2d 902 (Mich. 1977). Does this statement explain the *Fabius* holding?

2. When a state statute prohibits some but not all types of conduct without indicating whether the legislative prescription is complete, the inference to be drawn from legislative failure to specify its intent is not clear. Consider the following cases:

City of Shreveport v. Curry, 357 So. 2d 1078 (La. 1978). A city ordinance allowed the taking of frogs near a lake through mechanical devices — frog gigging — during June, but disallowed frog gigging during other months of the year. A state statute allowed frog gigging during the months prohibited by the ordinance. The court held that the ordinance was valid if it did not "forbid what the state legislature has explicitly or implicitly authorized." The court upheld the ordinance, finding that its intent was not to prohibit the taking of frogs, but to discourage this activity near the lake.

Atkins v. City of Tarrant City, 369 So. 2d 322 (Ala. Crim. App. 1979). A local ordinance made it a crime to ride in a motor vehicle while intoxicated. A state statute made it a crime to travel along the public roads while intoxicated, but expressly exempted passengers in motor vehicles. The court found the ordinance preempted, holding that it prohibited an act which was permitted by state law.

See also Menzer v. Village of Elkhart Lake, 186 N.W.2d 290 (Wis. 1971). The court held that a local ordinance prohibiting motorboating on lakes on Sundays during the summer was not preempted by a state statute authorizing local ordinances not "contrary to or inconsistent with this chapter, relative to the equipment, use or operation of boats or relative to any activity regulated" by the state law. Because the statute did not prohibit boat operation the argument was made that the clear intent of the statute was to permit the operation of any boat conforming to state regulations. This argument was rejected, the court noting that the argument "confuses a safe boat with the safe operation of a boat." *Id.* at 79, 186 N.W.2d at 295.

3. The Minnesota court set forth comprehensive guidelines on the statutory conflict problem in *Mangold Midwest Co. v. Village of Ridgefield,* 143 N.W.2d 813 (Minn. 1966). The state had a Sunday closing law which, among other things, flatly prohibited the sale of groceries. The village adopted an ordinance permitting the sale of groceries on Sundays in stores with less than four employees. The court found no conflict, and set forth the following general principles for conflict cases:

> (a) As a general rule, conflicts which would render an ordinance invalid exist only when both the ordinance and the statute contain express or implied terms which are irreconcilable with each other.
> (b) More specifically, it has been said that conflict exists where the ordinance permits what the statute forbids . . . .
> (c) Conversely, a conflict exists where the ordinance forbids what the statute *expressly* permits . . . .
> (d) It is generally said that no conflict exists where the ordinance, though different, is merely additional and complementary to or in aid and furtherance of the statute.

Id. at 816-17. (Emphasis in original.) The court then held:

> [T]he ordinance does not permit, authorize, or encourage violation of the statute. It might be termed a complementary regulation which simply fails to make sales of groceries by certain establishments an additional offense under the ordinance.

Id. at 819. The court also noted that the ordinance was adopted in the "best interest" of the municipality. If the sale of groceries by stores with four and fewer employees continues to be a violation of the state statute, what had the city accomplished by excepting it from the local ordinance? Wasn't the city's purpose, despite what the court said, to authorize the small grocery stores to operate? Is there an equal protection issue here?

How helpful are the tests for conflict stated in *Mangold*? Do you agree with the court's holding? Would a court find a conflict under these tests in *Fabius*? In the cases discussed in Comment 2?

The court in *Mangold* next considered an argument that the ordinance had been "preempted." The court noted:

> Although some cases have confused the two and even used them interchangeably, it is our opinion that preemption and conflict are separate concepts and should be governed by separate doctrines. The preemption doctrine has also been known as the "occupation of the field" concept, and is familiar in drawing the line between state and Federal powers.

Id. at 819. The court found no preemption in this case, although it was "a fairly close question."

The following case illustrates an application of the "preemption-by-occupation" concept:

PLAZA JOINT VENTURE v. CITY OF ATLANTIC CITY

Superior Court of New Jersey
174 N.J. Super. 231, 416 A.2d 71 (App. Div. 1980)

The opinion of the court was delivered by BISCHOFF, P. J. A. D.

The issue presented by this appeal is whether the state has preempted the power of the City of Atlantic City to enact "an ordinance regulating the conversion of rental units to condominiums" and declaring a "moratorium on the conversion of any rental unit into a condominium for a period of one year" from passage of the ordinance.

Plaintiffs Plaza Joint Venture and Edward Cantor hold an option to purchase Plaza Apartments, a 159-unit apartment building in Atlantic City, and are obligated to pay the sum of $850,000 for the option. They intend to purchase the premises and convert the apartments into condominiums. In pursuit of their intention to convert, plaintiffs have incurred expenses of $382,500. On August 24, 1979 plaintiffs filed an application for registration and a public offering statement with the State Department of Community Affairs under the Planned Real Estate Development Full Disclosure Act, *N.J.S.A.* 45:22A-21 *et seq.*

In order to preserve the availability of rental housing, Ordinance 69-1979 declared a moratorium on the conversion of rental units in the following terms:

(a) There is hereby declared a moratorium on the conversion of any rental unit into a condominium for a period of one (1) year commencing upon the passage of this Ordinance.

(b) During the existence of this moratorium no sales, or contracts for sale can be entered into; no prospectus issued; and no notice of intent is to be sent to tenants; and no one can request a tenant to vacate a unit as a consequence of conversion of a unit to a condominium.

(c) If the vacancy rate at the time when the aforesaid moratorium would have otherwise expired is less than five percent (5%), then this moratorium shall automatically be extended for six (6) additional months, but shall not be extended further.

(d) The Notice of Eviction, pursuant to *N.J.S.A.* 2A:18-61.2(g), shall not be given until the termination of the aforesaid moratorium.

The ordinance also provides for the appointment of a committee to study and "assess the impact of conversion on local housing needs" and "formulate a plan for maintaining and or increasing the number of rental units available." Finally, the ordinance requires registration of notices of conversion and provides for relocation assistance by evicting landlords.

Ordinance 70-1979, adopted the same day, prohibits any conversion, unless one parking space is provided on the premises for each condominium unit.

On November 9, the day after the ordinances were adopted, plaintiffs filed a complaint in lieu of prerogative writs against the City of Atlantic City, challenging the validity of the ordinances and seeking a restraint against their enforcement. The city filed an answer and the trial judge granted appellant tenants leave to intervene. Following a hearing on an order to show cause, the judge issued a letter opinion dated January 3, 1980, granting an interlocutory injunction against enforcement of the ordinances because the subject matter of Ordinance 69-79 appeared to be "preempted by state statutes," and Ordinance 70-79 appeared to be "barred by *N.J.S.A.* 40:8B-29 [46:8B-29], which prohibits zoning ordinances that discriminate on the basis of the form of ownership." Defendant's application for a stay of the injunction pending appeal was denied.

On November 8, 1979 the Board of Commissioners of the City of Atlantic City adopted Ordinances 69-1979 and 70-1979 which regulate the conversion of rental units into condominiums. In enacting Ordinance 69-1979 the board found "that an emergency exists within the ... City with respect to the unavailability of rental space" and that "the advent of casino gambling has escalated property values ...," contributing to "the trend toward the conversion of rental units to condominiums ...." The conversion of existing rental units to condominiums, the board continues, would remove them from the rental housing market, "forcing the displacement of a large number of residential tenants, many of whom are senior citizens or persons of low or moderate income levels." The board concluded that the acute housing shortage in Atlantic City and nearby municipalities will make it impossible for the displaced tenants to find decent housing at a price they can afford; that these tenants were unable to have anticipated or prepared to meet the radical changes in housing demands created by casino gambling, and that a "need exists for legislation to afford tenants relief from the situation without unnecessarily infringing on the property rights of the owner."

The board determined that "the maintenance of the current numbers of rental units available will foster and improve the health, safety and welfare of its residents by insuring the availability of a minimum number of residential rental units. ..."

Defendants and intervenors moved in this court for leave to appeal and for a stay of the injunction pending appeal. We denied the motion for a stay but granted leave to appeal to consider plaintiffs' challenge to Atlantic City Ordinance 69-1979 on constitutional grounds and on the grounds that the subject of the ordinance had been preempted by state action. We accelerated disposition, electing to determine the appeal on the papers submitted on the motion pursuant to R. 2:11-2 and giving all parties opportunity to submit additional papers and be heard at oral argument.

On this appeal defendant City of Atlantic City and the intervenors contend:

(1) The enactment of Ordinance 69-1979 is a valid exercise of the police power of the city, and

(2) The Legislature has not preempted the subject matter of the ordinance.

It is now firmly established that N.J.S.A. 40:48-2 [the general welfare clause] constitutes an abundant reservoir of police power granted municipalities by the Legislature. ... Ordinances enacted in support of this police power carry a presumption of validity and there is a heavy burden on anyone seeking to overturn such ordinances. ... Moreover, legislative bodies enacting ordinances are presumed to act on the basis of adequate factual support and their enactments are presumed to rest upon some rational basis within their knowledge and experience. ... And, it is now well settled that municipalities have power to enact a reasonable moratorium on certain land uses while studying a problem and preparing permanent regulations. ...

However, an ordinance properly enacted and within the police power of the municipality will be invalid if it intrudes upon a field preempted by the Legislature. When the Legislature has preempted a field by comprehensive regulation, a municipal ordinance attempting to regulate the same field is void if the municipal action adversely affects the legislative scheme. ... And

> A legislative intent to preempt a field will be found either where the state scheme is so pervasive or comprehensive that it effectively precludes the coexistence of municipal regulation *or* where the local regulation conflicts with

the state statutes *or* stands as an obstacle to state policy expressed in enactments of the Legislature. [*Garden State Farms, Inc. v. Bay,* 77 *N.J.* 439, 450, 390 *A.*2d 1177 (1978); emphasis supplied].

Justice Schreiber, in *Overlook Terrace Mgmt. Corp. v. West New York Rent Control Bd.,* 71 *N.J.* 451, 366 *A.*2d 321 (1976), stated that pertinent questions for consideration in determining whether preemption had occurred, were:

1. Does the ordinance conflict with state law, either because of conflicting policies or operational effect? . . .
2. Was the state law intended, expressly or impliedly, to be exclusive in the field? . . .
3. Does the subject matter reflect a need for uniformity? . . .
4. Is the state scheme so pervasive or comprehensive that it precludes coexistence of municipal regulation? . . .
5. Does the ordinance stand "as an obstacle to the accomplishment and execution of the full purposes and objectives" of the Legislature?

Our review of pertinent statutes leads us to the conclusion that the subject of Ordinance 69-1979 has been preempted.

The Legislature recently enacted comprehensive legislation regulating condominiums. The Planned Real Estate Development Full Disclosure Act, *N.J.S.A.* 45:22A-21 *et seq.,* regulates the development, offering and sale of various forms of real estate development in which owners share common facilities or property interests, including condominiums. *N.J.S.A.* 45:22A-23(h). This act requires a developer to file a detailed registration with the Division of Housing and Urban Renewal before offering or disposing of any interest in a planned real estate development, and to provide a purchaser with an extensive public offering statement, *N.J.S.A.* 45:22A-29, and the Division is given broad enforcement powers. *N.J.S.A.* 45:22A-32 to 35. The Disclosure Act further provides for private, double damage actions to remedy any violations of the disclosure requirements. *N.J.S.A.* 45:22A-37. The Division of Housing and Urban Renewal, the administrative agency responsible for regulation under the act *(N.J.S.A.* 45:22A-24), promulgated comprehensive and detailed regulations. *N.J.A.C.* 5:26-1.1 *et seq.* Moreover, while the Disclosure Act provides a uniform means for regulating, investigating and monitoring planned developments, the Condominium Act, *N.J.S.A.* 46:8B-1 *et seq.,* provides detailed structural guidelines for the creation of condominiums.

In 1976 the Legislature amended the Anti-Eviction Act, *N.J.S.A.* 2A:18-61.1 *et seq.,* to afford residential tenants substantial procedural safeguards and the opportunity to obtain comparable housing when an owner converts an apartment building to a condominium. *N.J.S.A.* 2A:18-61.1(k); *L.*1975, *c.* 311 (effective February 19, 1976). As amended, the act requires an owner who intends to convert an apartment building into a condominium to give tenants 60 days' notice of his intent to convert and to provide the tenant the full plan of conversion prior to serving notice. The notice of intention must inform the tenant of his right to purchase ownership in the premises at a specified price, including his exclusive right of purchase within 90 days, and of his other rights secured by the Act. *N.J.S.A.* 2A:18-61.8.

If a tenant decides not to purchase a condominium, the owner must give him three years' notice prior to instituting an action for eviction, and no action shall be instituted prior to the expiration of a written lease. *N.J.S.A.* 2A:18-61.2(g). The owner is further obligated to offer the tenant comparable rental housing when the tenant so requests within 18 months after receiving notice of eviction. *N.J.S.A.* 2A:18-61.11. Moreover, when an action for eviction is filed, the court must authorize up to five one-year stays of eviction with reasonable rent increases until the tenant is offered and provided a reasonable opportunity to examine and rent comparable housing. After the first of these stays is entered, however, the owner may prevent the entry of any further stays by paying the tenant hardship relocation compensation equal to five months' rent. *Id.*

In order to ensure compliance with its provisions, the amended Anti-Eviction Act vests the Department of Community Affairs with the authority to adopt rules and regulations setting forth the procedures to be followed by evicting landlords, the rights and duties of tenants, and the types of real estate transactions subject to the act. *N.J.S.A.* 2A:18-61.12. Pursuant to this authority the Department has adopted extensive rules governing condominium and cooperative conversions. See *N.J.A.C.* 5:24-1.1 *et seq.*

Since the adoption of the casino gambling amendment to the New Jersey Constitution in 1976, *N.J.Const.* (1947), Art. IV, § 7, par. 2 D, the Legislature has adopted the Casino Control Act, *N.J.S.A.* 5:12-1 *et seq.*, which imposes stringent controls over that industry and created a special agency to license and regulate casinos. *N.J.S.A.* 5:12-50 *et seq.* The Legislature has continued to maintain close contact and scrutiny over problems developing within the industry and in Atlantic City, the only city where gambling is legally permissible. This appears quite clearly from the 1978 amendments to the Anti-Eviction Act, *N.J.S.A.* 2A:18-61.13 *et seq.*; *L.*1978, c. 139. That statute was the Legislature's specific response to the developing housing crisis created by the advent of casino gambling, and provided additional substantial protection for tenants in Atlantic City in danger of eviction by the owner of an apartment house retiring the premises from the rental market.[2]

It is clear from these statutes that the Legislature has viewed the housing crisis in Atlantic City, including the conversion of rental units to condominiums, and casino gambling as an integrated problem and provided a comprehensive solution by amending the Anti-Eviction Act. Moreover, viewing the problems facing tenants apart from the impact of casino gambling, the Legislature has provided a broad integrated plan to balance the rights of tenants with the rights of owners and potential purchasers of condominiums. It is clear that preemption of the field has occurred. . . .

It is appropriate to note that there is a presumption that enactment of state legislation creating a state agency preempts municipal control over that agency and the field it regulates. . . . Here, the Legislature has vested the Division of Housing and Urban Renewal and the Department of Community Affairs with broad powers to regulate the conversion of rental units into condominiums and to protect tenants evicted as a result of conversion.

We conclude the legislative scheme regulating the creation, conversion and operation of condominiums and the eviction of tenants from rental units intended for conversion with special consideration for Atlantic City tenants similarly circumstanced is so comprehensive as to clearly evidence a legislative intent to preempt the field, protect condominiums from discrimination and proscribe municipal regulation based on the form of ownership. *N.J.S.A.* 46:8B-29 . . . . The conflict between the state legislation and municipal Ordinance 69-1979 is patent. The Anti-Eviction Act provides in specific terms that conversion of rental

---

[2] We have been informed that there is additional legislation proposed before the State Assembly which, if enacted, will establish a two-year statewide moratorium on the conversion of rental housing into cooperatives or condominiums. *Assembly Bill* 1032 (1980) (referred to Committee on Commerce, Industry and Professions).

units into condominiums is a ground for eviction. The ordinance before us effectively—albeit temporarily—eliminates conversion as a ground for eviction. The ordinance is therefore "invalid as having been preempted by state enactments." *Brunetti v. New Milford,* 68 N.J. 576, 603, 350 A.2d 19, 33 (1975). Ordinance 69-1979, by prohibiting the conversion of rental units to condominiums for the stated time period, clearly obstructs the state policy of permitting conversion to proceed while affording protection to tenants.

We affirm the judgment entered in the Law Division holding Ordinance 69-1979 invalid and remand the matter for the entry of a judgment permanently enjoining its enforcement and for further proceedings on other pending issues not here considered.

Comments: 1. Why didn't the court analyze the preemption problem in *Atlantic City* as a conflicts case? The state statute neither authorized nor prohibited local moratoria. Isn't this like the problem raised by the motorboating and waterskiing ordinance in *Miller*?

2. Whether a state statute enacts a comprehensive code preempting local regulation is always a matter of statutory interpretation and produces conflicting results:

Mangold Midwest Co. v. Village of Richfield, supra. The court held that a local ordinance exempting small grocery stores from the state Sunday closing law was not preempted. The ordinance was not likely to have an adverse effect on the populace of the entire state. Neither had Sunday closing been "impliedly declared by the legislature to be solely of state concern." The legislature had not dictated "the specific regulation of an area as . . . the tax and traffic provisions do."

National Asphalt Pavement Ass'n v. Prince George's County, 437 A.2d 651 (Md. 1981). The court held that a local employment discrimination ordinance applying to employers with fifteen employees or less was not preempted by the state employment discrimination legislation, which applied to employers with fifteen employees or more. The court noted that "employment discrimination is dealt with by five relatively brief [statutory] sections . . . which do not comprehensively cover the entire field." *See also accord, Seattle Newspaper-Web Pressmen's Local No. 26 v. City of Seattle,* 604 P.2d 170 (Wash. App. 1979).

Is statutory brevity relevant to the preemption problem? Would the court in *Atlantic City* have found preemption if some of the sections in the state law had been omitted? Which ones?

3. Courts sometimes handle statutory preemption problems by comparing the purpose of the local regulation with the purpose of the state statute. A court may not find preemption if the local ordinance serves a different purpose:

State v. Jacobson, 588 P.2d 358 (Ariz. App. 1978). A local ordinance required a permit for signs on motor vehicles. The state motor vehicle code specified the types of equipment which were allowed or prohibited on motor vehicles. The only connection between the statute and the ordinance was the motor vehicle as a "common element," and this was not enough to find preemption.

Eckl v. Davis, 124 Cal. Rptr. 685 (Cal. App. 1975). A local ordinance prohibiting nudity on public beaches was held not preempted by a state statute covering the same subject matter which had been limited to sexually-motivated nudity. The purpose of the ordinance was "to insure the peaceful and undistracted enjoyment of the parks and public beaches of the city." *See also Music Plus Four, Inc. v. Barnet,* 170 Cal. Rptr. 419 (Cal. App. 1981). A local ordinance excluding minors from rooms where drugs were sold was held not preempted by a statute making it a crime to induce minors to use drugs. The ordinance regulated "the operation of local retail businesses frequented by minors."

How could it be argued that the ordinance in *Atlantic City* had a different purpose from the state statute? Did the statute regulate the impact of conversions on tenants while the ordinance regulated the impact of conversions on the local housing market?

4. The need for statewide uniformity is another factor courts sometimes consider in preemption cases. The Uniform Motor Vehicle Code adopted by many states clearly indicates that statewide uniformity in the control of motor vehicles is an important statutory purpose. For a case relying on this statutory purpose to hold that a local ordinance modifying the statutory definition of drunk driving was preempted see *Simpson v. Municipality of Anchorage,* 635 P.2d 1197 (Alaska 1981). *See also Schwanda v. Bonney,* 418 A.2d 163 (Me. 1980) (gun registration requires uniform statewide regulation).

Did the ordinance in *Atlantic City* violate the uniformity requirement? Don't the housing conditions which require conversion moratoriums differ around the state?

5. The factors which determine whether a local ordinance has been preempted may be similar to the factors which determine whether a matter is of statewide or local concern under local home rule powers in *imperio* states. The court noted this relationship in *In re Hubbard,* 396 P.2d 809 (Cal. 1964), holding that a local ordinance regulating gambling was not preempted by the state gambling law.

Defendants were convicted of playing a game of chance that was prohibited by a city ordinance. They claimed that the ordinance was preempted by the state penal code, which prohibited playing "for money, checks, credit, or other representative of value," as well as betting at or against any of twelve expressly enumerated games. The code also prohibited any banking or percentage game. The game for which the defendants were convicted was not among the games listed in the state code.

The court held that "[s]ince the question whether the subject is of state concern is often determined by whether or not the state has enacted legislation, preemption or full occupation of the field may become one, but only one, test of whether the given subject is a municipal affair." The court then held that home rule governments have full power to regulate concerning municipal affairs unless:

> (1) the subject matter has been so fully and completely covered by general law as to clearly indicate that it has become exclusively a matter of state concern; (2) the subject matter has been partially covered by general law couched in such terms as to indicate clearly that a paramount state concern will not tolerate further or additional local action; or (3) the subject matter has been partially covered by general law, and the subject is of such a nature that the adverse effect of a local ordinance on the transient citizens of the state outweighs the possible benefit to the municipality.

Id. at 815. Compare this formulation with the comparable statement in *Atlantic City.* See also *Bishop v. City of San Jose,* 460 P.2d 137 (Cal. 1969), holding that the adoption of state legislation is "not determinative" on the state-local affairs issue.

6. In the criminal area, local ordinances may attempt to ease problems of proof and conviction by modifying the elements of a crime as defined by a state statute. This tendency has been criticized. "[A] shift in power from the courts and the legislature to municipal government could work a substantive change in the criminal law and in the powers of law enforcement agencies." Blease, *Civil Liberties and the California Law of Preemption,* 17 HASTINGS L.J. 517, 563 (1966).

A state court may apply a strict preemption test in order to prevent municipalities from making substantive changes in the criminal law. In *In re Lane,* 372 P.2d 897 (Cal. 1962), defendant was convicted of violating a city ordinance that prohibited "resorting" in hotels, motels and other places for the purpose of engaging in sexual intercourse. The purpose of the ordinance was to enact a less stringent substantive test for the crime of prostitution. The court held the ordinance was preempted by state penal code provisions covering the criminal aspects of sexual activity. It held that these provisions were so extensive that they constituted a general scheme for the regulation of sexual activity that preempted any local supplementation. With this case compare the *Hubbard* case, *supra.*

Constitutional issues also underlie the criminal prohibition problem. The obscenity problem is a good example. In *People v. Llewellyn,* 257 N.W.2d 902 (Mich. 1977), the court held that the state obscenity statute preempted a municipality from providing its own definition of obscenity. The court noted:

> [A] balkanized system of obscenity definition and prohibition would, through the resultant confusion and provocation of endless appeals, both threaten important individual rights and undermine efficiency in the control of obscenity .... [T]he

uncertainty created by local definitions of obscenity would effectively chill the right to free expression, and raise serious due process problems . . . .

Id. at 907. *Accord, City of Spokane v. Portch,* 596 P.2d 1044 (Wash. 1979). What is the assumption underlying a holding that the state legislature is better able to resolve delicate constitutional issues in the definition of a crime?

7. Double jeopardy problems also arise from dual criminal prohibitions enacted by statute and by local ordinance. In *Waller v. Florida,* 397 U.S. 387 (1970), defendant stripped a canvas mural from a city hall wall in the course of a demonstration. He was convicted under municipal ordinances prohibiting the destruction of city property and a disorderly breach of the peace, and was then indicted under a state statute for grand larceny. Defendant moved for a writ of prohibition to prevent prosecution for the state offense.

On the assumption that the municipal violations included offenses within the grand larceny charge, the Supreme Court found double jeopardy. It noted the traditional rule that state political subdivisions are not sovereign entities but are subordinate governmental instrumentalities created by the state. On remand, defendant was convicted on the grand larceny charge. The Florida District Court of Appeal refused to find double jeopardy, holding that it had only assumed but had never decided that the municipal offenses were included within the state crime. *Waller v. State,* 270 So. 2d 26 (Fla. App. 1972), *cert. denied,* 414 U.S. 945 (1973). See also Texas Penal Code Ann. § 1.08: "No governmental subdivision . . . may enact or enforce a law that makes conduct covered by this code an offense subject to a criminal penalty."

8. Local taxes also raise statutory preemption problems. Courts may find preemption because state and local taxes are levied on the same revenue source. See *East Ohio Gas Co. v. City of Akron,* 218 N.E.2d 608 (Ohio 1966), holding that a home rule city's net income tax levied on public utilities was preempted by a state gross receipts tax on utilities. The court found a clear example of double taxation. Compare *American National Building & Loan Ass'n v. City of Baltimore,* 224 A.2d 883 (Md. 1966), holding that a state franchise tax on savings and loan associations was a fee imposed to raise revenue for regulatory purposes, and did not preempt a city privilege tax levied on these associations.

Concerns about double taxation often prompt the state legislature to specify the limits of state and local taxing authority. The decision whether or not the local power to tax is preempted becomes a matter of statutory interpretation. In *City of Tempe v. Prudential Insurance Co. of America,* 510 P.2d 745 (Ariz. 1973), a statute authorized a state tax on the premium income of insurance companies and prohibited all other taxes levied on these companies except for taxes on their real and tangible personal property. The statute was held to preempt a local transaction privilege tax levied on the income from rental properties owned by an insurance company. *Cf. United Tavern Owners v. School District,* 272 A.2d 868 (Pa. 1971). A state statute prohibited a local tax on any "transaction" subject to a state tax. The district was held to be preempted from levying an over-the-counter sales tax on liquor as the state had levied a sales tax on the sale of liquor by the state distributing agency to retail liquor stores.

The state statute may expressly authorize supplementary local taxes. In *Rivera v. City of Fresno,* 490 P.2d 793 (Cal. 1971), the state sales and use tax act authorized cities and counties to levy a tax "substantially different" from the state sales and use tax. The court held that a city telephone, gas, and electricity services tax was not preempted as this tax was substantially different from the state sales and use tax on tangible personal property.

Extensive state regulation may preempt local taxation. See *City of Pittsburgh v. Allegheny Bank,* 412 A.2d 1368 (Pa. 1980), holding that the extensive regulation of banking by the state preempted a local business privilege tax as applied to banks. The state did not levy a comparable tax, and the state legislation did not expressly prohibit local taxation. Contra, *Mulligan v. Junne,* 338 N.E.2d 6 (Ill. 1975), upholding a home rule liquor tax despite the state's regulation of the liquor industry.

State legislation may do more than merely regulate or tax. States license numerous businesses and professions, and comprehensively regulate public utility businesses as an alternative to market competition. These statutes confer licensing and regulatory authority on state agencies. Comprehensive and agency-directed regulation in licensing and public utility legislation may provide a strong case for preemption, as the following case indicates:

PUBLIC SERVICE CO. v. TOWN OF HAMPTON

Supreme Court of New Hampshire
___ N.H. ___, 411 A.2d 164 (1980)

PER CURIAM.

The issue we decide in this interlocutory transfer is whether the defendant towns may require the plaintiff to use underground transmission lines after the public utilities commission has issued to the plaintiff a certificate of site and facility authorizing above-ground transmission lines for the Seabrook Nuclear Electric Generating Station, in compliance with RSA ch. 162-F. We hold that the towns lack power to require underground transmission lines.

In this petition for declaratory judgment and injunctive relief brought by the Public Service Company of New Hampshire against the town of Hampton and other towns, the plaintiff seeks an order declaring void, as applied to it, certain votes of the towns purporting to require underground construction of electric transmission lines above a rated capacity of 69 kilovolts. The Seabrook transmission lines have a rated capacity of 345 kilovolts. The Court (*Goode,* J.) transferred, without ruling, the following questions of law in advance of trial:

1. Do the votes purportedly adopted by the defendant towns endow them with any legal authority to interfere with the construction of overhead transmission lines associated with the Seabrook Project, in light of RSA 162-F, the Certificate and the other permits held by the plaintiff?

2. Do the votes purportedly adopted by the defendant towns endow them with any legal authority to interfere with the construction of overhead transmission lines by the plaintiff in connection with the Seabrook Project, in light of the requirements of the Zoning Enabling Act (RSA 31:60 et seq.) or other provisions of law relating to actions taken by Town Meetings?

The plaintiff holds a certificate of "site and facility" authorizing the construction of the Seabrook Nuclear Power Plant and the necessary transmission lines. This certificate, issued by the public utilities commission (PUC) on January 29, 1974, after compliance with RSA ch. 162-F, specifically authorizes the erection of overhead transmission lines within the boundaries of the defendant towns. Incorporated into the certificate are permits issued by the water resources board, and by the department of public works and highways authorizing the erection of overhead transmission lines within the defendant towns.

The plaintiff also holds a construction permit from the United States Nuclear Regulatory Commission authorizing the construction of the Seabrook Nuclear Station with associated overhead transmission lines within the defendant towns. The plaintiff claims to have already invested over two million dollars in preparing for the construction of overhead lines in accordance with the certificate and permits.

In March 1979, the defendant towns voted to adopt certain ordinances requiring all electric transmission lines over 69,000 volts to be buried underground. The plaintiff's lines have a capacity much in excess of this voltage.

Enacted in 1971, the declared purpose of RSA ch. 162-F is to provide a resolution, in an "integrated fashion," of all issues involving the selection of sites and routing of associated transmission lines. RSA 162-F:1. It establishes a site evaluation committee composed of certain officials from specified State agencies. RSA 162-F:3. The committee is required to review all plans for the siting and construction of bulk power plants and the routing of transmission lines as defined in the statute. The statute requires joint public hearings to be held by the committee, the PUC and such other agencies as have jurisdiction over the subject matter. The initial hearing and every fourth hearing thereafter must be held in the county where the facility is to be located. RSA 162-F:7 I. It provides that no additional application shall be required to satisfy the requirements of individual agencies and departments. RSA 162-F:7 IV. The committee is required to give due consideration to the views of municipal and regional planning commissions and municipal legislative bodies in determining the effect of such a project on esthetics, historic sites, air and water quality, the natural environment and the public health and safety. RSA 162-F:8 I. It is provided that the findings of the committee shall be conclusive on all questions of siting, land use, air and water quality. RSA 162-F:8 II.

In the instant case, the site evaluation committee followed all the procedural and substantive requirements of RSA ch. 162-F. After thirty-two days of hearings lasting almost a year, the committee approved the plaintiff's application for a certificate of site and facility on July 27, 1973. During the hearings, the committee considered both overhead and underground transmission lines and heard evidence regarding both methods. In its report, the committee approved overhead lines over specific routes. Incorporating the report of the committee, the PUC issued a "certificate of site and facility" on January 29, 1974. After rehearings were denied, an appeal was brought to this court. On April 23, 1975, we upheld the decision of the committee. *Society for Protection of N. H. Forests v. Site Evaluation Commission,* 115 N.H. 163, 337 A.2d 778 (1975).

A fair reading of RSA ch. 162-F reveals a legislative intent to achieve comprehensive review of power plants and facilities site selection. The statutory scheme envisions that all interests be considered and all regulatory agencies combine for the twin purposes of avoiding undue delay and resolving all issues "in an integrated fashion." By specifically requiring consideration of the views of municipal planning commissions and legislative bodies, the legislature assured that their concerns would be considered in the comprehensive site evaluation. Thus, the committee protects the "public health and safety" of the residents of the various towns with respect to the siting of power plants and transmission lines falling under the statute.

We regard it as inconceivable that the legislature, after setting up elaborate procedures and requiring consideration of every imaginable interest, intended to leave the regulation of transmission lines siting to the whim of individual towns. Towns are merely subdivisions of the State and have only such powers as are expressly or impliedly granted to them by the legislature. . . . Whatever power towns may have to regulate the location of transmission lines within their borders, that power cannot be exercised in a way that is inconsistent with State law. . . .

Local regulation is repugnant to State law when it expressly contradicts a statute or is contrary to the legislative intent that underlies a statutory scheme.

... The action by the defendant towns in this case is repugnant to RSA ch. 162-F because it is contrary to the legislative intent that all matters regarding the construction of bulk power plants and transmission lines covered by the statute be determined in one integrated and coordinated procedure by the site evaluation committee whose findings are conclusive.... By enacting RSA ch. 162-F, the legislature has preempted any power that the defendant towns might have had with respect to transmission lines embraced by the statute, and the actions by the defendant towns with regard to transmission lines is of no effect....

. . . .

Accordingly, we hold that the lines here in question are within the jurisdiction of the committee and cannot be regulated by the town. Our view is buttressed by the fact that in its original proposal for the Seabrook transmission lines, the plaintiff desired to locate a much greater proportion of the lines over new routes. Only after consultation with the defendant towns and the committee did the plaintiff agree to locate a greater portion of the lines over routes already occupied by transmission equipment. That decision, motivated in part to satisfy the affected towns, should not later be used to divest the committee of site review authority.

In view of our answer to the first question, we need not answer the second.

Remanded.

Comments: 1. Note the nature of the competing state and local interests in the principal case. The municipality asserts a local interest in the maintenance of its visual environment through undergrounding. The state agency asserts the interests of the state in the efficient provision of utility service, which transcends local boundaries. The court held that the required consideration of the local interest by the state agency was a factor tending toward preemption. Do you agree? Is the state utility agency likely to find against the utility? Was the court perhaps influenced by the "soft" environmental interest of the municipality as compared with the need to provide utility service at least cost? See accord, under similar legislation, *City of South Burlington v. Vermont Electric Power Co.,* 344 A.2d 19 (Vt. 1975) (local zoning preempted).

Most courts have found for the utility interest in the undergrounding cases. In some of the cases, the statutes did not provide a specific transmission line siting authority. The state commission authorized a transmission line as part of its general regulatory authority. The court found a local undergrounding ordinance preempted by relying on the comprehensive authority of the state agency to regulate the utility business. *In re Public Service Electric & Gas Co.,* 173 A.2d 233 (N.J. 1961), is a leading case. The court noted:

> Were each municipality through which a power line has to pass free to impose its own ideas of how the current should be transmitted through it, nothing but chaos would result, and neither the utility nor the state agency vested with control could be assured of ability to fulfill its obligations of furnishing safe, adequate and proper service to the public in all areas.

Id. at 239. Some state utility legislation expressly authorizes the state utility agency to preempt local zoning. Mass. Gen. Laws ch. 40A, § 3.

2. Preemption problems also arise when municipalities exclude facilities licensed by state agencies. Examples are landfills for the disposal of solid waste and private treatment centers for the care of the mentally disabled, drug addicts and similar groups. The courts tend to override local exclusions and give the state licensing power a preemptive effect.

In the group home cases, the state agency has licensed a group home at a designated location. The local zoning ordinance does not allow the group home at this location as a permitted use. The cases hold the local ordinance preempted because it infringes on and "thwarts" a general policy of the state. *See Region 10 Client Management, Inc. v. Town of Hampstead,* 424 A.2d 207 (N.H. 1980) (physically impaired adults); *Volunteers of America Care Facilities v. Village of Brown Deer,* 294 N.W.2d 94 (Wis. 1980). What factors may influence these decisions? Is there a valid local public policy that supports the exclusion? Many courts hold local zoning ordinances that exclude group homes invalid even in the absence of state licensing.

Some states have adopted legislation covering the group home zoning problem. Some of these statutes authorize group homes as a permitted use in all residential districts. Other statutes allow group homes in residential districts as a special use, require state licensing, and require the dispersal of group homes throughout residential areas. *See* Hopperton, *A State Legislative Strategy for Ending Exclusionary Zoning of Community Homes,* 19 URB. L. ANN. 47 (1980).

The waste disposal site cases arise under similar facts. The state agency has again licensed a facility at a designated site and the municipal zoning ordinance excludes it. *Southern Ocean Landfill, Inc. v. Mayor & Council,* 314 A.2d 65 (N.J. 1974), is a leading case holding a local exclusionary ordinance preempted. The court noted:

> The disposition of solid waste in this state has reached crisis proportions. [The state legislation contains] a declaration of legislative policy that ... the health, safety and welfare of the people of this State require efficient and reasonable solid waste collection, disposal and utilization service.... In addition, such operation is subject to the supervision of the Department of Environmental Protection which is empowered to adopt codes, rules and regulations related to solid waste collection and disposal.

Id. at 66, 67.

The court suggests that the state agency can regulate the nuisance aspects of waste disposal sites. Is this enough to meet local objections and justify a preemption holding? *See accord, Township of Cascade v. Cascade Resources Recovery, Inc.,* 325 N.W.2d 500 (Mich. App. 1982). In holding that the state Solid Waste Management Act preempted a local ordinance, the court noted that the state agency must consider the impact on the municipality where the facility proposes to locate. The court also held that the regulation of waste management required statewide treatment.

3. Premption problems also arise under state occupational licensing legislation. Some courts follow standard preemption doctrine and allow local ordinances containing health regulations that supplement the state law. *See Department of Licenses & Inspections v. Weber,* 147 A.2d 326 (Pa. 1959) (beauty parlors). Courts also apply the rule that local ordinances are not preempted if they serve a different purpose than the state licensing legislation. See *Summer v. Township of Teaneck,* 251 A.2d 761 (N.J. 1961), holding that a local ordinance requiring the registration of real estate agents planning real estate solicitations was not preempted by the state real estate agents licensing law. The ordinance was intended to limit racial blockbusting by real estate agents. The court noted that the state licensing statute "is not intended to exhaust the police power with respect to all misbehaviors of a licensee."

A local ordinance may be struck down if it interferes with the purposes of a state licensing system. In *Application of Anamizu,* 481 P.2d 116 (Hawaii 1971), a local ordinance limited electrical contractors' licenses to full-time electricians, even though part-time electricians were eligible for licenses under the state licensing law. Finding that the state statute had enacted a comprehensive and pervasive licensing system, the court held the local ordinance preempted because it interfered with the right of a state licensee to pursue his occupation throughout the state.

4. For discussion of statutory preemption problems see D. MANDELKER, LAND USE LAW §§ 4.32-4.36, 516 (1982); Note, *Conflicts Between State Statutes and Municipal Ordinances,* 72 HARV. L. REV. 737 (1969); Note, *Transmission Line Siting: Local Concerns Versus State Energy Interests,* 19 URB. L. ANN. 183 (1980).

The ambiguities and uncertainties in state preemption doctrine suggest the need for a principled basis for deciding statutory preemption problems. The following report is one effort in this direction:

REPORT OF THE CALIFORNIA COMMISSION ON THE LAW OF PREEMPTION, 1969 Urban L. Ann. 131, 133-34, 138

III.

The State Constitution is not neutral in the allocation of regulatory power between the State Legislature and local governments. It is true that cities and counties have been given constitutional authority to adopt regulatory measures, *but only* if the local measures do not conflict with general (i.e., state) laws. Thus, it rests with the State Legislature to determine whether it desires to regulate specific types of conduct, and, once having done so, whether it desires to permit any additional regulation of similar conduct by local governments. The latter function, it should be emphasized, calls for legislative judgment based upon a thorough consideration of competing policies. What are those policies?

The central inquiry implicit in the concept of pre-emption is whether there should be statewide uniformity in the regulation of specific conduct. If there is no need for statewide uniformity, there is no need for state law to preempt local power to regulate. If it appears desirable that there be statewide uniformity, the legislative decision to preempt or not preempt should be based on whether the need for statewide uniformity outweighs the need of local government regulation. We thus emphasize the need of local government to be permitted to respond quickly and adequately to the varied types of local problems which continually arise throughout the state; for, in general, a problem must be of statewide magnitude before it reasonably can be expected that the Legislature will respond to it. This is the core of the preemption question—to consider, on the one hand, the need for statewide uniformity of regulation of a specific type of conduct, and, on the other hand, the need of local governments to be able to respond to local, as distinguished from statewide, problems.

There are two basic factors either of which creates a need for state-wide uniformity of regulation of specific conduct:

(1) *The desirability of freedom of movement of persons or goods within the State.* . . .

(2) *The desirability of a statewide consensus.*

We refer here to an examination of the nature of the conduct sought to be regulated and the desirability that, if such conduct is to be regulated, the regulation be based upon a statewide rather than a local consensus. Thus regulation of some types of conduct should reflect a broader consensus than the regulation of other types of conduct which can more appropriately be left to a local viewpoint. For example, conduct which does not pose a substantial threat, direct or indirect, to the health, safety or welfare of others should be regulated on the basis of a statewide consensus. We refer here to such conduct as recreational gambling in one's home or wearing the attire of the opposite sex in public (where not done for the purpose of committing a crime), and describe such conduct in this report as conduct "within the realm of individual privacy." . . .

The following is the text of the statute which we recommend for adoption:

A local, police, sanitary or other regulation authorized by Section 11 of Article XI of the Constitution shall be permitted notwithstanding a state statute on the same or a related subject except only in the following cases:

1. When the regulation duplicates general law.
2. When the regulation authorizes that which is expressly prohibited by general law.
3. When the regulation prohibits that which is expressly permitted by general law.
4. When general law expressly prohibits that type of regulation.
5. When the need for statewide uniformity in regulation is greater than the need for the city or county to impose such regulation.

(a) There shall be considered to be a need for statewide uniformity in reguation of the conduct if

(i) the city or county regulation would have a significant adverse affect [*sic*] upon the movement of persons or goods within the state, or

(ii) the conduct involved poses no substantial threat, direct or indirect, to the safety, health or welfare of others, or

(iii) the city or county regulation is a regulation of speech or expression.

(b) In evaluating the need for the city or county to impose the regulation there shall be considered

(i) the degree to which the nature and magnitude of the harm which is sought to be prevented by the regulation vary from place to place within the State, and

(ii) the imminence and gravity of the harm which is sought to be prevented by the regulation.

Comments: 1. The principles of the California report were applied in *Danville Fire Protection District v. Duffel Financial & Construction Co.*, 129 Cal. Rptr. 882 (Cal. App. 1976). The district adopted a requirement for the installation of heat, smoke, and sprinkler systems that was more widely applicable than those of the Uniform Building Code that had been adopted by a county having concurrent jurisdiction with the district. The court quoted the two "basic factors" contained in the Commission report and held that their application required preemption of the district regulation:

> The regulation of building codes fits exceptionally well into either of these categories. A patchwork of varying code regulations would be extremely costly for the construction industry, particularly in metropolitan areas. Second, building codes are technical matters based on the opinions of experts who are not always available to local entities. The Uniform Codes specified by [the state statute] represent at least a statewide, if not a national consensus.

Id. at 887.

2. Some states have adopted legislation expressly providing a rule of preemption. N.J. Stat. Ann. § 2C:1-5(d) prohibits the enactment and enforcement of any local ordinance "conflicting with any ... policy of this State ... whether that policy be expressed by inclusion of a provision in the code or by exclusion of that subject from the code." In *State v. Crawley*, 447 A.2d 565 (N.J. 1982), this statute was applied to a claim that a municipal loitering ordinance was preempted. The court noted that the preemption provision "requires us to determine the Legislature's will without reference to a specific statutory test. Courts must infer legislative intent from the overall structure of the Penal Code and its legislative history." *Id.* at 567.

The court then reviewed a number of provisions in the state penal code covering similar conduct. It concluded that "the absence of a loitering prescription from the Code reflects a state policy to decriminalize such activity." *Id.* at 568-69. Does this method of analysis differ from typical preemption analysis?

See also City of Erie v. Northwestern Pennsylvania Food Council, 322 A.2d 407 (Pa. Commw. 1974). A state statute provided that local ordinances dealing with food storage, distribution, and sale must be "uniform in all respects with . . . Commonwealth laws and regulations." A local ordinance requiring fresh and frozen meat packaging in colorless and transparent material was held preempted under this provision by a state law containing detailed packaging requirements but omitting a comparable regulation. *See also* Hawaii Rev. Stat. § 70-105.

A NOTE ON STATE STANDARDS FOR LOCAL REGULATORY PROGRAMS

Some state legislation provides more detailed control over local regulatory programs by mandating the adoption of regulatory ordinances that meet statutory standards and requirements. State mandating legislation is most advanced in the environmental and land use field. Some state coastal management legislation, for example, contains coastal policies that states are to follow in adopting local coastal plans. Coastal governments then administer a land development permit requirement under which development may be approved if it is consistent with the local coastal plan. The California Coastal Act is one example of this technique. *See* Finnell, *Coastal Land Management in California,* 1978 A.B.F. RESEARCH J. 647.

Some of the midwestern states have adopted legislation for floodplain and shoreland management that provides for state-mandated local controls in compliance with state standards and criteria. *See* Note, *State Land Use Regulation — A Survey of Recent Legislative Approaches,* 56 MINN. L. REV. 869 (1972).

The regulatory system adopted by this legislation is typified by the Minnesota shoreland management act. Minn. Stat. Ann. § 105.485. This statute, which originally applied only to unincorporated areas, has now been extended to municipalities. The statutory requirements applicable to unincorporated areas will indicate how the management program operates. The legislation applies to "shoreland," which is defined as land within 1,000 feet from the normal high watermark of a lake, pond, or flowage, and land within 300 feet of a river or stream or the landward side of a delineated floodplain on a river or stream, whichever is greater. The statute contained a timetable for state adoption of:

> model standards and criteria for the subdivision, use, and development of shoreland in unincorporated areas, including but not limited to the following: (a) the area of a lot and length of water frontage suitable for a building site; (b) the placement of structures in relation to shorelines and roads; (c) the placement and construction of sanitary and waste disposal facilities; (d) designation of types of land uses; (e) changes in bottom contours of adjacent public waters; (f) preservation of natural shorelands through the restriction of land uses; (g) variances from the minimum standards and criteria; and (h) a model ordinance.

The statute then provides for state enforcement of these standards and criteria as follows:

> If a county fails to adopt a shoreland conservation ordinance [by a stated date], or if the commissioner of natural resources at any time [after that date], after notice and hearing . . . finds that a county has adopted a shoreland conserva-

tion ordinance which fails to meet the minimum standards established pursuant to this section, the commissioner shall adapt the model ordinance to the county. ... This ordinance is effective for the county on the date and in accordance with such regulations relating to compliance as the commissioner shall prescribe.

If a municipality does not adopt the model shoreland ordinance, a court may issue a writ of mandamus to compel it to act. *County of Ramsey v. Stevens,* 283 N.W.2d 918 (Minn. 1979).

The statute also authorizes the adoption of local controls "more stringent" than the state standards and criteria. Local planning and controls within the vicinity of the shoreland shall, to the maximum extent practicable, be "compatible" with the shoreland ordinance. What kinds of uses are likely to be compatible with a shoreland area? Incompatible? Do the cases on statutory preemption in this section provide any guide in answering these questions?

For discussion of state-mandated local environmental regulations see J. KUSLER, REGULATING SENSITIVE LANDS (1980); Note, *Minnesota's Flood Plain Management Act — State Guidance of Land Use Control,* 55 MINN. L. REV. 1163 (1971).

Chapter 4

GOVERNMENTAL INTEGRATION

The integration and consolidation of local governments in metropolitan areas has been an important reform agenda in American politics for decades. Reformers believe that fragmented local governments are inefficient, more costly, unaccountable, and that fragmentation creates disparities in the availability of fiscal resources. Declining central cities face growing fiscal burdens as fiscal sources wither. Population has moved to the suburbs, where fiscal burdens are less and fiscal resources greater. *See* Chapter 1.

The primary aim of governmental reformers has been the creation of integrated governments in metropolitan areas which can consolidate existing governmental units. Consolidation has been achieved in a few areas, primarily in the south and midwest, but the consolidation movement has not caught on nationally. Other integration techniques, which are less complete but which are considered useful, have a wider acceptance. These techniques include the use of interlocal agreements for the provision of governmental services, the creation of metropolitan districts and authorities for particular purposes, and the establishment of regional councils of government with planning functions and the authority to consider applications for state and federal financial assistance.

This chapter reviews governmental integration and consolidation reforms and the techniques that have been used to accomplish reform objectives. The chapter opens with a review of interlocal conflict problems in the control of land use and development by public agencies. These interlocal conflicts illustrate the governmental integration problems that fragmented governments in metropolitan areas create.

A. INTERLOCAL CONFLICT

TOWNSHIP OF WASHINGTON v. VILLAGE OF RIDGEWOOD

Supreme Court of New Jersey
26 N.J. 578, 141 A.2d 308 (1958)

WEINTRAUB, C. J. The Chancery Division of the Superior Court entered a judgment directing the Village of Ridgewood to dismantle and remove an elevated steel water tower it erected upon Van Emburgh Avenue, partially within the village and partially within the Borough of Ho-Ho-Kus. 46 N.J. Super. 152, 134 A.2d 345 (1957). Ridgewood appealed and we certified the appeal on our own motion prior to consideration of it by the Appellate Division.

Ridgewood operates a water supply system serving itself, the Boroughs of Glen Rock and Midland Park and the Township of Wyckoff, and meeting the needs of the inhabitants and municipalities, including fire fighting. The water is obtained from deep-rock wells. There are no reservoirs; storage to meet the increased demands of certain days or portions thereof is provided by tanks.

The pressure being inadequate, Ridgewood engaged a consulting engineer, Mr. Crew, to devise a plan for additional storage. He recommended three tanks, all elevated, one at the Van Emburgh site here involved, another on Goffle Road in Ridgewood, and the third on the Cedarhill site in Wyckoff. The anticipated total cost was $1,701,000.

In view of the sum involved, Ridgewood solicited the opinion of another expert, Mr. Capen. Mr. Capen, then some 1,200 miles away, was familiar with the Goffle site, and on the basis of his recollection of it, said in his report:

> In areas where elevated tanks have been established (and particularly where such installation has been made prior to nearby residential developments) repetition of the practice may well be in order. A very serious question is raised, however, in regard to placing an elevated tank in the Goffle area, near Goffle Road. There are a number of substantial residences in the vicinity which will probably be adversely affected in value by such a structure. It is therefore recommended that the entire matter of this storage be carefully reviewed and that an underground or ground level storage tank be substituted. This procedure is not a new trend but has been adopted in various residential communities.

This recommendation was explored and a decision made to shift from the Goffle site to another on Lafayette Avenue in Wyckoff, where a tank could be installed partially below ground level. The change was profitable. Instead of the Goffle tank, designed to provide storage of two million gallons at an estimated cost of $499,000, Ridgewood obtained storage of 2¼ million gallons at Lafayette at a cost of $243,672.84.

With respect to the proposed Cedarhill tank, the Board of Adjustment of Wyckoff refused approval because of objections to an elevated structure. Ridgewood thereupon selected another site where as of the time of trial a ground level tank was to be installed without increase in cost and with an increase in capacity from one million to 2¼ million gallons.

Thus as to two of the sites, objections to elevated tanks led to their abandonment in favor of tanks at or below ground level.

Mr. Capen's report was received in February 1955. In September 1955 Mr. Crew approached the governing body of Ho-Ho-Kus with respect to the Van Emburgh improvement. The testimony is not harmonious, but it is clear that the officials of Ho-Ho-Kus understood the tank would be at ground level, the same as the existing water tanks of Ho-Ho-Kus, and as such would be shielded by trees. In the light of Mr. Capen's report, Mr. Crew should have been explicit, but was not. The board of adjustment and planning board approved, and a permit issued. The approvals were granted informally; Ridgewood concedes that the statutory requirements for a variance or exception were not met, and that if the zoning ordinance of Ho-Ho-Kus applies, it can claim no benefit from the wholly irregular grant.

When the work got under way, it was realized that an elevated structure was involved. It in fact would tower to the height of 160 feet. Ho-Ho-Kus immediately adopted a resolution rescinding the permit, and Ho-Ho-Kus and the abutting Township of Washington and residents affected instituted these actions promptly. About 75 to 85% of the structure itself was completed by the time of trial, representing a cost of some $80,000.

Three issues are involved: (1) whether the improvement violates the zoning ordinance of Ridgewood; (2) whether it violates the zoning ordinance of Ho-Ho-Kus, and (3) whether the action of Ridgewood in any event constitutes an unreasonable and arbitrary exercise of delegated power.

I

We are satisfied that neither zoning ordinance applies.

In *Thornton v. Village of Ridgewood,* 17 N.J. 499, 111 A.2d 899 (1955), a question involved was whether Ridgewood could acquire property within its one-family district for use as an administrative building and assembly hall. It was held that the zoning statute does not restrain the power of a municipality to determine where to locate municipal facilities within its borders, and hence the issue became whether the zoning ordinance itself accomplished a restriction. As the ordinance then read, "any governmentally owned or operated building" was authorized in the one-family district. It was concluded that the proposed use came within the quoted phrase.

In the course of *Thornton,* it was indicated that the phrase "governmentally owned or operated" would "seem to bar governmental buildings devoted to industrial or proprietary use" (17 N.J. at page 514, 111 A.2d at page 906). For the obvious purpose of meeting that view, Ridgewood amended its ordinance to substitute "Any *municipally* owned or operated building, structure or use" for the phrase quoted above. There can be no doubt that the amendatory expression embraces the storage tank, and hence there is no violation by Ridgewood of its own ordinance.

With respect to so much of the site as is situate in Ho-Ho-Kus, it is conceded that the zoning ordinance of that municipality by its terms forbids the improvement and, as pointed out above, that the informal variance cannot be sustained. The issue accordingly is whether Ridgewood is bound by the ordinance of Ho-Ho-Kus in the use of property as part of a water supply system. We think it is not.

We see no difference between this case and *Aviation Services, Inc. v. Board of Adjustment of Hanover Township,* 20 N.J. 275, 119 A.2d 761, 765 (1956) in which it was held that a municipality's power to establish and maintain an airport was not subject to the zoning ordinance of another municipality in which the airport was situate. In *Aviation Services,* the municipality was authorized to acquire and establish airports "within or without" its boundaries, with power to condemn. Here R.S. 40:62-49, N.J.S.A., provides:

> Any municipality may provide and supply water, or an additional supply of water, ... in any one or more of the following methods: ....
> (g) Any municipality may purchase, condemn or otherwise acquire the necessary lands, the rights or interests inlands, water rights and rights of flowage or diversion, within or without the municipality, for the purpose of a water supply, or an additional water supply, and for the connection thereof with the municipality, and in case of highway or other public or quasi public structures, may require the same to be abandoned as far as necessary for such purposes, and to be relaid, if necessary, by some other route or in some other location. ...

The lands necessary for "a water supply" must include lands necessary for facilities required to meet the needs of the consumer. The consent of such other municipality is required only with respect to the laying of pipes or mains "in and under any and all streets, highways, alleys and public places" in that municipality, subject to the power of the Superior Court to direct the terms of such laying if consent should be refused. N.J.S.A. 40:62-65.

This result has a baneful potential, but so does a contrary holding. The problem invites a legislative solution committing the final decision to a body other than the interested municipalities themselves, but if *Aviation Services* correctly found the legislative will in that case, the same considerations dictate the same answer here.

Plaintiffs urge that the supply of water is a "proprietary" rather than a "governmental" function and hence should be subject to the Ho-Ho-Kus ordinance.

We cannot agree that the distinction between governmental and proprietary functions is relevant to this controversy. The distinction is illusory; whatever local government is authorized to do constitutes a function of government, and when a municipality acts pursuant to granted authority it acts as government and not as a private entrepreneur. The distinction has proved useful to restrain the ancient concept of municipal tort immunity, not because of any logic in the distinction, but rather because sound policy dictated that governmental immunity should not envelop the many activities which government today pursues to meet the needs of the citizens. *Cloyes v. Delaware Township,* 23 N.J. 324, 129 A.2d 1, 57 A.L.R.2d 1327 (1957). We see no connection between that classification and the problem before us. Surely the supply of water cannot be deemed to be a second-class activity in the scheme of municipal functions. Nor is it significant that the municipality serves areas in addition to its own, for from the nature of the subject, cooperative action among municipalities is imperative and consonant with the governmental nature of the activity.

II

But Ridgewood was required to act reasonably in the exercise of its authority, *Aviation Services, supra* (20 N.J. at page 285, 119 A.2d at page 766), and the circumstance that its own interests conflicted with those of Ho-Ho-Kus and Washington emphasized that obligation. Among the considerations which Ridgewood should have weighed but in fact ignored were the zoning schemes of the municipal plaintiffs and the land uses abutting and near the site.

Mr. Crew was concerned solely with the engineering aspects. Despite Mr. Capen's *caveat* and the confirmation of it by experience with respect to the Goffle and Cedarhill sites recited above, Ridgewood made no effort to reevaluate its plan for an elevated tank on the Van Emburgh property. The testimony shows without contradiction that the residential development there was equal or superior to that at either of the other sites and that Mr. Capen had not adverted to the interest of property owners at the Van Emburgh location only because he was not aware of that development.

Mr. Crew and Mr. Capen agreed a ground level tank could be used at Van Emburgh Avenue if pumping facilities were added. Mr. Crew stated that a gravity flow system would yield a better quality of water, but conceded that a satisfactory, wholesome supply would be furnished by ground level storage tanks. Mr. Capen made no reference to that subject and in fact had suggested pumping at the Goffle site if a ground level tank were used. The difference between the two approaches is one of cost. If the elevated tank should be used, the estimated cost for the complete installation is $226,026, whereas if the tank is placed at ground level the pumping facilities would increase the outlay to a total of $272,700. Mr. Capen would prefer to add an inlet pipe costing another $60,000 but agreed the improvement could be engineered to operate without it. The annual bill for pumping would be $5,000, less a saving of the higher maintenance costs of an elevated structure.

It appears further that immediately before trial consideration was given to alternate sites, and that one permitting a ground level tank with gravity flow operation is available at an estimated expenditure of $292,600. This exceeds the original proposal by some $66,000, part of which is attributable to the increase in costs in the intervening period (and perhaps also to the inclusion of land costs;

it is not clear whether the figure of $226,026 for the elevated tank installation includes the value of the land which Ridgewood had acquired back in 1940).

Hence Ridgewood could have placed the tank at ground level either at the Van Emburgh site or the alternate site. The difference is one of cost described above. Under the circumstances, Ridgewood should have assumed that cost rather than visit the burden of an elevated structure of 160 feet upon the other municipalities. We agree with the trial court's finding that Ridgewood acted arbitrarily.

The judgment is accordingly affirmed.

For affirmance: CHIEF JUSTICE WEINTRAUB and JUSTICES WACHENFELD, BURLING and FRANCIS — 4.

For affirmance and remandment: JUSTICES HEHER, JACOBS and PROCTOR — 3.

HEHER, J. (for affirmance) . . . . But under the Ho-Ho-Kus zoning ordinance, Ridgewood's land ownership extending into the Borough is within a zone restricted to the highest residence use, an area where dwellings range in value between $25,000 and $50,000; and Ridgewood's planned municipal or corporate use is by its nature within the interdiction of the Ho-Ho-Kus use regulation.

. . . .

. . . Ridgewood's land in Ho-Ho-Kus is bound by the use-restriction to residences of the highest class laid down in the Borough's zoning ordinance. We are not here concerned with a water source vital to the essential public welfare, but rather the storage of water for distribution by the pressure of gravity, the alternative, for reasons of cost alone, to underground or ground-level distribution that in structure and mechanism would not be so violent in its intrusion upon the character of the zone district and the essential rights of those who had established their dwellings there in reliance on the reserved use.

[The opinion then discussed cases from other jurisdictions holding that a municipality is bound by its own zoning ordinance when it acts in a municipal or corporate capacity.—Eds.]

Thus it is that, in this activity, Ridgewood is engaged in a municipal or corporate function, and in the pursuit of the endeavor it is bound equally with all others, individual or corporate, by the terms of the Ho-Ho-Kus zoning ordinance. There is no statutory exemption, either express or implied, from the operation of the Ho-Ho-Kus use limitation. R.S. 40:62-65, as amended by L. 1953, c. 37, N.J.S.A., merely authorizes the extension of pipes and mains in and under the streets of another municipality "for the purpose of connecting its waterworks with the pipes and mains so laid or to be laid" for the supplying of water "in one or more of the methods" provided by the statute, but only with the consent of the other municipality. There is provision for a review in case such consent is refused in the Superior Court, and affirmative action on terms.

There is not here an exertion of delegated state power that by the legislative will is not subject to the local use-zoning process, as in *Town of Bloomfield v. New Jersey Highway Authority*, 18 N.J. 237, 113 A.2d 658 (1955), and *Hill v. Borough of Collingswood*, 9 N.J. 369, 88 A.2d 506 (1952). . . .

. . . There is no showing of need for land in Ho-Ho-Kus for the given purpose, much less the land in question; presumably, the motivating consideration is the economic advantage of using land now in Ridgewood's ownership, even though in part beyond its borders in an area restricted against such use. R.S. 40:62-65, N.J.S.A., requiring the consent of the other municipalities for the extension of pipes and mains, is significant in this regard. Why this particular provision if there be the claimed broad power to condemn? Can it be that, though consent be required for the mere extension of pipes and mains, Ridgewood may, ex proprio vigore, store and distribute water to other municipalities through a plant maintained in Ho-Ho-Kus' highest class residence district? It is to be borne in mind that Ho-Ho-Kus has no interest whatever in the operation; neither it nor its inhabitants are to have water service from Ridgewood. Ridgewood may undertake to supply water to other municipalities, but not by subverting Ho-Ho-Kus' zone plan, and thus to lay the burden on its neighbor, *in invitum*. Simple justice so ordains. . . .

Local use-zoning and water power derive from the Legislature, and they are to be reconciled accordingly to advance the essential public interest; and one predominates over the other only when and to the extent directed by the over-all legislative authority. And the statute itself provides the means of modifying zoning rules and regulations. Zoning is a major constitutionally-secured public policy that is not to be sacrificed save in the service of an imperative public need recognized as such by the legislative authority.

I submit that there is no jurisdiction in equity, nor at law, for that matter, to enjoin submission by Ho-Ho-Kus (and such is a postulate of the majority opinion) to this invasion of its first-class residence zone by an alien use deemed by the court to be "reasonable" in its exercise as compared with other more conspicuous means of accomplishing the same end. And if the given use of its lands in Ho-Ho-Kus is not subject to the established use-restrictions, then is it reasonable thus to outlaw a much less expensive mechanism, both as to capital outlay and cost of operation, and in the face of expert opinion evidence that "a gravity flow system would yield a better quality of water"? Compare *Wallerstein v. Westchester Joint Water Works,* 166 Misc. 34, 1 N.Y.S.2d 111 (Sup. Ct. 1937). There, also, the water tower had been almost completed. And if the whole of the land so used were situated in Ridgewood, could the gravity-flow use be enjoined in equity as arbitrary on the hypothesis that since the ground-level mechanism is feasible, Ridgewood "should have assumed [the greater] cost rather than visit the burden of an elevated structure of 160 feet upon the municipalities"? The choice of means would then rest in the discretion and judgment of the local authority. It is, I would suggest, the zoning restriction established by Ho-Ho-Kus that alone restrains Ridgewood's use of the lands in question.

We have here the problem of a local political boundary dividing an expanse of land area peculiarly suitable for the highest residence use, and so zoned by the adjoining municipalities save that in one a variant use is allowable that is denied in the other, a border conflict involving something more than the mere nonconforming use of Ridgewood's land in Ho-Ho-Kus. Ho-Ho-Kus may assert its sovereignty over lands within its limits, except as otherwise ordained by the Legislature, but it cannot oppose a different use of adjacent lands in Ridgewood unless such use constitutes a nuisance—a clash of interests that suggests the wisdom of coordinate inter-municipal action for the essential common good.

I would affirm the judgment and remand the cause with direction to stay execution until plaintiff is afforded an opportunity to take such further action in the light of the foregoing considerations as it may be advised.

PROCTOR, J., joins in this opinion.

Comments: 1. The lesson of the *Ridgewood* case is that the courts decide interlocal conflict problems in the absence of statutory direction. The balancing test for resolving these conflicts is a recent judicial innovation. As the majority opinion indicates, the courts traditionally use more mechanical tests which require less exercise of judicial discretion once the test is applied. The conventional tests adopted to resolve interlocal conflicts are the following:

(a) *Government versus proprietary.* This test appears elsewhere in local govenment law, and the majority opinion is critical of its application to interlocal zoning problems. For an application of this test see *City of Scottsdale v. Municipal Court,* 368 P.2d 637 (Ariz. 1962). The court held that the operation of the Scottsdale sewage disposal plant was a governmental function which was not subject to the municipal zoning ordinance of Tempe.

(b) *Eminent domain rule.* Under this rule, a governmental authority having the power of eminent domain is deemed superior in status and therefore immune from local zoning. See *Seward County Board of Commissioners v. City of Seward,* 242 N.W.2d 849 (Neb. 1976) (airport authority). This rule is self-serving. The local government planning to build a facility almost always has the power of eminent domain. The zoning power is not an eminent domain power.

(c) *Superior policy rule.* The concurring judge applied this rule in the *Ridgewood* case, and found that the zoning policy was superior. See also *Wilkinsburgh-Penn Joint Water Authority v. Borough of Churchill,* 207 A.2d 905 (Pa. 1965). A court impressed with the necessities of planning and zoning will probably find that the zoning power is superior.

(d) *Superior power rule.* The concurring judge in *Ridgewood* indicated that both zoning and the power to provide water facilities derived from legislative authorization. He implied that they were equal in stature, but must be reconciled whenever possible. If not, the court must determine which of the two powers is superior.

(e) *Legislative intent rule.* Some courts resolve interlocal conflicts by determining the legislative intent. The *Rutgers* case, discussed in the next Comment, is an example.

(f) *Superior entity rule.* Other courts decide interlocal conflict cases by giving priority to the superior governmental entity. This view has been adopted in cases in which the state was one of the governmental entities. The leading state case is *Kentucky Institute for Education of the Blind v. City of Louisville,* 97 S.W. 402 (Ky. 1906). The court found an absolute immunity based on sovereign immunity principles. It held that the Institute did not have to comply with the city's fire safety code.

(g) *Most inclusive power rule.* Some courts give priority to the most inclusive power. In *Wilkinsburgh-Penn Joint Water Authority v. Borough of Churchill,* 207 A.2d 905 (Pa. 1965), the authority planned to construct a water tower in an area where it was prohibited by the borough zoning ordinance. The court held that "the objectives of zoning regulation are more comprehensive than and, in fact, include the objectives of the water Authority . . . . [T]he objectives of both statutes can be secured only if the Authority's land is subject to the Borough's zoning power." *Id.* at 910.

2. Courts may be shifting to the balancing test because the priorities in interlocal zoning conflict cases are not always clear. Planning and zoning are important local powers, and public agencies as well as private developers should be required to comply with zoning ordinances. Zoning can also be used to exclude important public facilities, such as waste disposal landfills, which communities do not want in their neighborhoods. A court may preempt a local zoning ordinance if the facility is licensed by a state agency. See Chapter 3, Section D. In the absence of state licensing, the public facility will be protected only if the court sets the local zoning aside. The balancing test allows the court to make this decision on a case-by-case basis.

Subsequent to the *Ridgewood* case, the New Jersey Supreme Court adopted a more elaborate version of the balancing test in *Rutgers v. Piluso,* 286 A.2d 697 (N.J. 1972). This case was a conflict between the state university and a municipality. A dormitory for married students violated a zoning ordinance limiting the number of university married student dormitories. The court found the university immune, and held that the "true test" of immunity was to determine the legislative intent as revealed by a number of "obvious and common" factors. These factors included —

> the nature and scope of the instrumentality seeking immunity, the kind of function or land use involved, the extent of the public interest to be served thereby, the effect local land use regulation would have upon the enterprise concerned and the impact of legitimate local interest.

Id. at 702. The court stressed that state agency immunity was not absolute, and that the state agency must not assert immunity in an unreasonable and arbitrary manner. The court found no legitimate local interest served by the zoning regulation. Avoiding the cost of educating children living in married university housing was not a legitimate zoning concern. Recall that most courts hold that state agencies are absolutely immune.

A somewhat different version of the balancing test was adopted in *Temple Terrace v. Hillsborough Ass'n for Retarded Citizens, Inc.,* 322 So. 2d 571 (Fla. App. 1975), *aff'd,* 332 So. 2d 610 (Fla. 1976). In this case, a zoning ordinance excluded a home for the mentally retarded operated under a state agency contract. The court did not adopt the *Rutgers* legislative intent rule, but held that when the statute is silent a public agency has "the burden of proving that the public interests favoring the proposed use outweigh those mitigating against a use" not allowed by the zoning ordinance. Which version of the balancing test favors the local zoning ordinance most?

For additional decisions adopting the balancing test in interlocal zoning conflict cases see *City of Fargo v. Hardwood Township,* 256 N.W.2d 694 (N.D. 1977); *Lincoln County v. Johnson,* 257 N.W.2d 543 (S.D. 1977). For cases rejecting the balancing test *see City of New Orleans v. State,* 364 So. 2d 1020 (La. 1978); *Dearden v. City of Detroit,* 269 N.W.2d 139 (Mich. 1978).

3. School districts present special problems. Schools must locate where they can serve adjacent neighborhoods, but local residents may object and the city may zone schools out of their optimum locations. The school district may cover several municipalities, and may be subject to local political pressures in some of the municipalities it serves.

Most courts recognize this necessity and hold that school districts are immune from local zoning regulations. *Appeal of Radnor Township School Authority,* 252 A.2d 597 (Pa. 1969), is a typical case. The school authority planned an elementary school on land within an A-2 Zoning District in which the school use was not permitted by special exception or otherwise. The township refused to rezone or to grant a variance. The court compared the very general power of the township to enact zoning regulations with the specific power of the school authority to choose the location of schools, and held that the township had no authority to regulate the location of school buildings. The court noted additionally that a school district of the first class (at that time Philadelphia and Pittsburgh) had complete and plenary power over its physical plant, and that the ordinance in question did not involve school construction but location.

Municipalities may also apply their building code requirements to the construction of school buildings. In the absence of comprehensive regulation of school construction at the state level, courts may hold that the local building code applies. *See Edmonds School District No. 15 v. City of Mountlake Terrace,* 465 P.2d 177 (Wash. 1970). The courts may distinguish the local building code from the zoning ordinance. *Compare Port Arthur Independent School District v. City of Groves,* 376 S.W.2d 330 (Tex. 1964) (school district compliance with city building ordinance required), *with Austin Independent School District v. City of Sunset Valley,* 502 S.W.2d (Tex. 1973) (city zoning ordinances cannot prevent location of school within city by school district). Is the distinction valid?

4. In an article generally favoring the jurisdiction of defending municipal governmental units over the prerogatives of invading governmental entities, the authors make the following comments about the building code and zoning cases:

> [In the building code cases the] courts assumed that the responsibility of establishing construction standards that would take into account the needs of governmental facilities would remain with the municipalities, unless there was some indication that the special government was capable of exercising that function. This theory has gained increasing acceptance in recent cases involving school districts subject to the authority of a state education agency.... While in the building code cases both governments were basically interested in the safe construction and maintenance of facilities and neither had standards likely to cause substantial harm to the other, zoning cases involve conflicts over the location of facilities that are difficult to locate anywhere and impossible to locate without causing considerable damage to residents of whatever area is chosen as the site. ... In such a situation, the traditional view of municipalities as protectors of private, parochial interests will often be persuasive.

Levi, Gehring & Groethe, *Application of Municipal Ordinances to Special Purpose Districts and Regulated Industries: A Home Rule Approach,* 12 URB. L. ANN. 77, 92, 97, 98 (1976). Is this analysis consistent with the *Ridgewood* decision?

5. Some state statutes provide that local zoning ordinances shall apply to publicly owned property, Or. Rev. Stat. § 227.280, or contain a provision found in the Standard State Zoning Enabling Act, that the local zoning ordinance shall prevail over other statutes and regulations when the zoning ordinance is more restrictive. *E.g.,* N.C. Gen. Stat. § 160A-390.

6. For discussion of intergovernmental immunity problems see D. MANDELKER, LAND USE LAW §§ 4.37-4.43 (1982); Ross, *Intergovernmental Zoning Disputes: A Continuing Problem,* 32 LAND USE L. & ZONING DIG., No. 7, at 6 (1980); Note, *Government Immunity From Local Zoning Ordinances,* 84 HARV. L. REV. 869 (1971); Note, *Governmental Immunity from Zoning,* 22 B.C.L. REV. 783 (1981).

A NOTE ON THE CONDEMNATION OF THE PROPERTY OF ONE GOVERNMENTAL UNIT BY ANOTHER

Intergovernmental conflicts also arise when one governmental unit seeks to condemn land for a public project when the land is owned by another governmental entity. In this situation, the courts are inclined to apply a method of analysis that differs somewhat from the doctrines they apply when a public project is blocked by the zoning ordinance or building code of another governmental unit, although there are similarities in the analytical devices applied.

Federal supremacy usually insulates federal agencies exercising the power of eminent domain from any limitations on that power that may be imposed at the state or local level. *See, e.g., United States v. Carmack,* 329 U.S. 230 (1946). The states also have a broad power of eminent domain; the state or one of its agencies, in general, can condemn successfully the property of a governmental subdivision of the state. *See, e.g., People v. City of Los Angeles,* 4 Cal. Rptr. 531 (Cal. App. 1960) (state condemnation of city park for construction of state highway); *State ex rel. State Highway Commission v. Hoester,* 362 S.W.2d 519 (Mo. 1962) (state condemnation of property of fire district). *But see Department of Public Works & Buildings v. Ellis,* 179 N.E.2d 679 (Ill. 1962).

As a general rule, one governmental unit or subdivision of a state does not have the power to condemn the public property of another unit or subdivision without either an express grant of power or a power which arises by necessary implication. *See, e.g., City of Dania v. Central & Southern Florida Flood Control District,* 134 So. 2d 848 (Fla. App. 1961) (flood control district attempted to condemn land owned by city); *cf. Florida East Coast Ry. v. City of Miami,* 321 So. 2d 545 (Fla. 1975) (city attempted to condemn waterfront land owned by railroad). When the two governmental units are of comparable status and powers, there is a split of authority. *Compare Needham v. County Commissioners,* 86 N.E.2d 63 (Mass. 1949) (unsuccessful county attempt to condemn city park land), *with Village of Richmond Heights v. Board of County Commissioners,* 166 N.E.2d 143 (Ohio App. 1960) (successful county condemnation of municipal land when city had acquired land only to prevent construction of county airport).

Courts have developed exceptions to the general rule. The prior public use doctrine permits intergovernmental condemnation when the proposed use would not interfere with or be inconsistent with the public use to which the property is presently devoted. *See, e.g., San Bernardino County Flood Control District v. Superior Court,* 75 Cal. Rptr. 24 (Cal. App. 1969); *Village of Amityville v. Suffolk County,* 132 N.Y.S.2d 845 (Sup. Ct. 1954). Another exception has been recognized when the proposed use is a higher or more necessary use than the present one. *See, e.g., City of Mesa v. Salt River Project Agricultural Improvement & Power District,* 373 P.2d 722 (Ariz. 1962), *appeal dismissed,* 372

U.S. 704 (1963). Some courts refuse to make such determinations and rely exclusively upon the construction of relevant constitutional and statutory authority. *See, e.g., Village of Blue Ash v. City of Cincinnati,* 182 N.E.2d 557 (Ohio 1962). *Cf. Britt v. City of Columbus,* 309 N.E.2d 412 (Ohio 1974). *See generally* Dau, *Problems in Condemnation of Property Devoted to Public Use,* 44 TEX. L. REV. 1517 (1966). The federal-aid highway act presently places limitations on the authority of state highway agencies to condemn public parks, natural resource areas, and historic sites. 23 U.S.C. § 138. *See Citizens to Preserve Overton Park v. Volpe,* 401 U.S. 402 (1971).

When property already devoted to a public use is authorized to be taken by another public agency, is the condemnor required to pay compensation? Most state constitutional provisions require that just compensation be paid only for the taking of private property. Courts generally acknowledge that there is no resulting constitutional right to compensation for a taking of public property. Invoking the familiar governmental-proprietary distinction, some courts will nevertheless award compensation for the taking of property held in a proprietary capacity, but deny it when the property is used for governmental purposes. In one of the early and leading decisions taking this approach, the city's "proprietary" property (a cemetery) was analogized to private property entitled to constitutional protection. *Proprietors of Mt. Hope Cemetery v. City of Boston,* 158 Mass. 509, 33 N.E. 695 (1893). The governmental-proprietary distinction continues to be invoked, see Parr, *State Condemnation of Municipally Owned Property: The Governmental-Proprietary Distinction,* 11 SYRACUSE L. REV. 27 (1959), but it appears less frequently as the basis for decision and it seems also to have lost some of its constitutional character.

Just as the governmental-proprietary standard does not serve well to resolve the issue of right to compensation, neither does the equally venerable theory that the state has absolute dominion over its creatures, the subunits of government. *See, e.g., People ex rel. Dixon v. Community Unit School District,* 118 N.E.2d 241 (Ill. 1954). The "taking" in that case came about through annexation by one school district, acting in accordance with state law, of much of the territory and the only school building belonging to a second school district. The court denied relief to residents of the second district, saying, "With or without the consent of the inhabitants of a school district, over their protests, even without notice or hearing, the State may take the school facilities in the district without giving compensation therefor, and vest them in other districts or agencies." *Id.* at 246. As a result some courts have read general eminent domain statutes, or a combination of statutory and constitutional provisions, to demonstrate a legislative intent that compensation be paid for a public taking of publicly held property. For example, in *State ex rel. State Highway Commission v. Board of County Commissioners,* 380 P.2d 830 (N.M. 1963), the court found that the state statute establishing procedures for condemnation of public or private property for highway purposes contemplated payment whether the property taken was used for proprietary or governmental purposes.

The court held that "any other conclusion would lead to incongruous results." It noted that local governments must provide local facilities through taxation or bond issues. "If the state took the buildings and did not compensate the county, replacement would have to be made through new bond issues or by other means . . . ." This burden "would be intolerable." Because state highways were financed by state and sometimes by federal funds, "it is only just and proper that the legislature in its wisdom should provide for compensation when public property is taken for highway purposes as they have clearly done [here]." *Id.* at 835.

Accord, State of Utah by & through Road Commission v. Salt Lake City Public Board of Education, 368 P.2d 468 (Utah 1962). *See also City of Chester v. Commonwealth,* 434 A.2d 695 (Pa. 1981). For discussion see Note, *The Sovereign's Duty to Compensate for the Appropriation of Public Property,* 67 COLUM. L. REV. 1083 (1967).

B. INTERGOVERNMENTAL COOPERATION AND TRANSFER OF FUNCTION

Interlocal zoning conflicts illustrate the intergovernmental problems that can arise from a lack of governmental integration. Voluntary measures that realign governmental responsibilities provide an opportunity to integrate governmental functions at the local level. One or more local governments may contract for the provision of a service function, or to exercise regulatory powers. Governmental functions may also be transferred from a lower to a different or higher governmental level. This section reviews these voluntary governmental integration techniques.

1. INTERGOVERNMENTAL COOPERATION

Intergovernmental cooperation is most common in the provision of governmental services. Intergovernmental service agreements can take several forms:

(1) A contractual agreement — that is, one locality hires another local government to provide the service to its citizens, similar to the local government contracting with a private firm.
(2) When two or more local governments jointly perform the service, provide support facilities or operate a public facility.
(3) When a service is run by a jointly created separate organization which aids all jurisdictions party to the agreement.

Advisory Commission on Intergovernmental Relations (ACIR), State and Local Roles in the Federal System 327 (1982).

Intergovernmental cooperation has many advantages. It can improve services, lower service costs and promote service coordination. Cooperation also has disadvantages. It is voluntary, and can lead to intergovernmental conflict if the participating governments disagree. Cooperation may also create a patchwork provision of services because it is voluntary and ad hoc. One study also suggests that intergovernmental cooperation may not eliminate disparities in fiscal capacity in metropolitan areas. A study in the Philadelphia area found that "cooperation occurs among municipalities with similar social rank and tax resources, in that order." O. WILLIAMS, H. HERMAN, C. LIEBMAN & T. DYE, SUBURBAN DIFFERENCES AND METROPOLITAN POLICIES 264 (1965).

Intergovernmental cooperation is widespread, and has been stimulated by the adoption of constitutional provisions and enabling legislation based on models suggested by national organizations such as the ACIR. One survey showed that sixty percent of all local governments responding had at least one intergovernmental agreement. These agreements were usually used when high capital costs made it difficult for one government to undertake the function, when there was no existing service provider, and when the function was specialized and did not affect governmental control. An example is the creation of a specialized crime laboratory. Cooperation was used most frequently in metropolitan areas, and between intersuburban and urban-rural governments. *See* State and Local Roles, *supra,* at 330.

Practically all the states now have general enabling legislation authorizing intergovernmental cooperation, and may also have legislation authorizing cooperation for designated governmental functions. A few states also have constitutional provisions authorizing intergovernmental cooperation. Adoption of a constitutional provision can eliminate some of the constitutional problems that an intergovernmental agreement can raise. Constitutional provisions are usually implemented through the adoption of statutory authorization.

The materials that follow review some of the legal problems that arise under intergovernmental agreements. The recurring questions are whether the creation of a joint entity or the exercise of governmental powers jointly through an intergovernmental agreement violates constitutional limitations on state and local government authority. The extent of the powers conferred by state legislation and the limitations on governmental discretion imposed by intergovernmental agreements also raise important legal questions.

CONSTITUTIONAL AND STATUTORY AUTHORITY FOR INTERLOCAL COOPERATION

NEW YORK CONSTITUTION ART. 9, § 1(c).

Local governments shall have the power to agree, as authorized by act of the legislature, ... to provide cooperatively, jointly or by contract any facility, service, activity or undertaking which each participating local government has the power to provide separately....

ILLINOIS CONSTITUTION ART. VII, § 10(a).

Units of local government and school districts may contract or otherwise associate among themselves [and with the State, other states and their local governments and school districts, and the United States] to obtain or share services and to exercise, combine, or transfer any power or function, in any manner not prohibited by law or ordinance. [They may also contract or associate unless prohibited with individuals, associations, and corporations.] Participating units of government may use their credit, revenues, and other resources to pay costs and to service debt related to intergovernmental activities.

ADVISORY COMMISSION ON INTERGOVERNMENTAL RELATIONS, STATE LEGISLATIVE PROGRAM #2, LOCAL GOVERNMENT MODERNIZATION INTERLOCAL CONTRACTING AND JOINT ENTERPRISE, 2.204 (1975)

Section 4. Interlocal Agreements. (a) Any power or powers, privileges or authority exercised or capable of exercise by a public agency of this state may be exercised and enjoyed jointly with any other public agency of this state (having the power or powers, privilege or authority), and jointly with any public agency of any other state or of the United States to the extent that laws of such other state or of the United States permit such joint exercise or enjoyment. Any agency of the state government when acting jointly with any public agency may exercise and enjoy all of the powers, privileges and authority conferred by this act upon a public agency.

(b) Any two or more public agencies may enter into agreements with one another for joint or cooperative action pursuant to the provisions of this act. Appropriate action by ordinance, resolution, or otherwise pursuant to law of the governing bodies of these participating public agencies shall be necessary before any such agreement may enter into force.

(c) Any such agreement shall specify the following:
(1) its duration;
(2) the precise organization, composition and nature of any separate legal or administrative entity created thereby, together with the powers delegated thereto, which is hereby authorized to be created with its governing body composed solely of local elected officials *ex officio* unless otherwise provided by law;
(3) its purpose or purposes;
(4) the manner of financing the joint or cooperative undertaking and of establishing and maintaining a budget therefor, and of accounting and keeping records thereof;
(5) the permissible method or methods to be employed in accomplishing the partial or complete termination of the agreement and for disposing of property upon such partial or complete termination; and
(6) any other necessary and proper matters.

Comments: 1. Does the ACIR model act authorize interlocal cooperation if only one of the contracting governments had the authority to exercise the power which is the subject of the contract? Does the statute authorize a simple joint contract for the provision of services or other functions, or does it require a formal joint agreement?

Compare Minn. Stat. Ann. § 471.59(1), authorizing local governments to "cooperatively exercise any power common to the contracting parties." This statute was interpreted to mean that both a city and a county contracting to build a joint hospital must have the power to do so singly. *Kaufman v. Swift County,* 30 N.W.2d 34 (Minn. 1947). On the authority to enter into debt compare Cal. Gov't Code § 6508, authorizing an agency created by an interlocal agreement "to incur debts, liabilities, or obligations."

The Advisory Commission model act, *supra,* which some states have adopted, authorizes interlocal agreements providing for the joint exercise of "[a]ny power . . . exercised or capable of exercise by a public agency." *E.g.,* Okla. Stat. Ann. tit. 74, § 1004(a). Does this statute allow the joint exercise of a power delegated to only one of the contracting municipalities? If so, isn't it really a form of statutory home rule?

The Illinois constitutional provision, *supra,* has received a liberal interpretation. It has been interpreted as a repeal of Dillon's Rule, see Chapter 3, and as removing "the necessity of obtaining statutory authority for cooperative ventures." *See Village of Sherman v. Village of Williamsville,* 435 N.E.2d 548 (Ill. App. 1982). On the Illinois experience see Hall & Wallack, *Intergovernmental Cooperation and the Transfer of Powers,* 1981 ILL. L. REV. 775.

2. Consider this description of an interlocal agreement for sewer facilities which is taken from U.S. Department of Housing and Urban Development, Cooperative Ventures in Urban America 65 (1967):

BATTLE CREEK, MICHIGAN
The City of Battle Creek, the core city of a metropolitan area surrounded by five units of government, was the only unit which had a modern sewage treatment plant. Because of a peculiar combination of three industrial wastes, sewage treatment in the area did not come up to State standards and the State ordered the surrounding communities to correct this problem. The five communities considered building their own plants, but subsequently four townships entered into forty year contracts and one township a three year contract with Battle Creek for sewage treatment service and water supply service. The Battle Creek plant was therefore established as a metropolitan area sewage plant.

In view of the constitutional and statutory provisions quoted above, just how would you implement this arrangement legally? Which provisions would be most helpful, and which might limit your efforts?

GOREHAM v. DES MOINES METROPOLITAN AREA SOLID WASTE AGENCY

Supreme Court of Iowa
179 N.W.2d 449 (1970)

LARSON, JUSTICE.

This is a declaratory judgment action involving the validity of a contract and the constitutionality of chapter 28E, Code of Iowa 1966, and chapter 236, Acts of the Sixty-third General Assembly, submitted upon an agreed stipulation of facts.

Plaintiffs, who are residents, property owners, and taxpayers of the cities of Des Moines and West Des Moines, Iowa, brought this action at law against the Des Moines Metropolitan Area Solid Waste Agency (hereafter called the Agency) and its members asking an interpretation of chapter 28E, Code of Iowa 1966, and chapter 236, Acts of the Sixty-third General Assembly, First Session, with reference to the power and authority of the Agency under those laws. The vital question presented is whether under these statutes and the Iowa Constitution the Agency can issue bonds to finance the planned functions of the Agency in the collection and disposition of solid waste, and pay the interest and principal from fees legally collectible from its members for this service. The trial court held that the Agency was properly created, that due authority was properly delegated to it, that the submitted agreement between the members was valid, and that it could issue such revenue bonds and fix and collect fees from those using these services including interest and principal on the bonds . . . . Plaintiffs appeal as to the creation of the Agency, the propriety of the authority delegated, and the legality of the agreement. . . .

Appellants further contend that the defendant Agency is invalid and has no legal character as a "public body corporate and politic" for the reason that chapter 28E of the 1966 Code of Iowa and Senate File 482 (also known as chapter 236, Acts of the 63rd General Assembly, First Session) under which said Agency was created is in violation of Article III, Section 1, of the Constitution of the State of Iowa, as an improper delegation of legislative authority, and that as a result the creation of said Agency by the "Intergovernmental Agreement, Exhibit A," is ultra vires and of no force and effect, and that as a consequence thereof said defendant Agency is without authority to issue revenue bonds pursuant to Senate File 482 enacted by the 63rd General Assembly of Iowa.

Fairly summarized, the Stipulation of Facts filed herein on March 30, 1970, states as follows:

[The stipulation recites the serious solid waste disposal problems that existed in the City of Des Moines. An application for federal funds and a study and report led to an intergovernmental agreement between the city and thirteen other governments in the metropolitan area creating the Metropolitan Area Solid Waste Agency. — Eds.]

Pursuant to said agreement the Agency was duly organized, officers were elected and a director was hired to manage the affairs of the Agency under the direction of the Agency board which was composed of one representative from the governing body of each member of the Agency, each having one vote for every 50,000 or fraction thereof population in his area of representation.

. . . .

I. Perhaps before discussing these contentions [discussed below—Eds.] we should set out the provisions of the law in question.

Chapter 28E entitled "Joint Exercise of Governmental Powers" purports to authorize any political subdivision of the State of Iowa and certain agencies of the state or federal government to join together to perform certain public services and by agreement create a separate legal or administrative entity to render that service. Its worthy purpose is clearly expressed in section 28E.1. Section 28E.2 provides definitions, and section 28E.3 purports to define the limitations upon the participants as follows:

>28E.3. *Joint exercise of powers.* [This section enacts § 4(a) of the model act, *supra*.—Eds.]

Sections 28E.4 and 28E.5 provide for the agreement and its contents as follows:

>28E.4. *Agreement with other agencies.* Any public agency of this state may enter into an agreement with one or more public or private agencies for joint or co-operative action pursuant to the provisions of this chapter, *including* the creation of a separate entity to carry out the purpose of the agreement. Appropriate action by ordinance, resolution or otherwise pursuant to law of the governing bodies involved shall be necessary before any such agreement may enter into force. (Emphasis supplied.)
>
>28E.5. *Specifications.* [This section enacts § 4(c) of the model act, which is substantial as set forth *supra*.—Eds.]

II. Although appellants contend the creation of a separate legal entity or public body is solely a function of the legislature, we find no unconstitutional delegation of legislative power involved in this law providing for the creation of the Des Moines Metropolitan Area Solid Waste Agency. It is not the mere establishment or creation of such an agency or entity that causes trouble, but the functions to be performed by that agency in the legislative field which must be examined closely to determine whether there has been an unlawful delegation of legislative authority. See *Lausen v. Board of Supervisors,* 204 Iowa 30, 214 N.W. 682; . . . .

In *Lausen,* in upholding the constitutionality of what is known as the "Bovine Tuberculosis Law," this court stated at page 34 of 204 Iowa, page 685 of 214 N.W., "We think that the state has the power to select any reasonable means and methods it may choose, to establish these (area-eradication) districts, so long as they are in the interest of public health; . . . ."

In this connection it must also be noted that administrative agencies may be delegated certain legislative functions by the legislature when properly guidelined, and that when this is done, the distinction between such agencies and public bodies, corporate and politic, which have been delegated proper legislative functions, has largely disappeared. Ordinarily the latter body is created by an act of the legislature and the former by an already-established public body with legislative authority. However, the power and authority of each must be measured by the legality of the delegation thereof. If such power is derived from the State Legislature, is adequately guidelined, and does not violate the separation-of-powers provision of the State Constitution set forth in Article III, Section 1, the exercise thereof should be sustained.

Thus, our primary problem here is whether the authority provided in chapter 28E of the 1966 Code and chapter 236, Acts of the Sixty-third General Assembly, constitutes a lawful delegation of legislative power.

III. Regularly-enacted statutes are presumed to be constitutional, and courts exercise the power to declare such legislation unconstitutional with great caution. It is only when such conclusion is unavoidable that we do so. . . .

Thus, while the provisions of section 28E of the 1966 Code leave much to be desired as to the extent of the authority granted to such a newly-created entity, the presumption of constitutionality operates strongly in its favor.

It is also well to remember that our function is not to pass upon the feasibility or wisdom of such legislation, but only to determine whether the power here exercised exceeds that which the legislature could or did delegate to the newly-created entity. . . .

In this regard it is also well to note the importance of the expressed or recognized purpose or policy to be achieved by the legislation. Generally, when the legislature has adequately stated the object and purpose of the legislation and laid down reasonably clear guidelines in its application, it may then delegate to a properly-created entity the authority to exercise such legislative power as is necessary to carry into effect that general legislative purpose. . . .

The purpose of this legislation, as recognized in chapter 28E, is to provide a solution to the growing problems of local government including the problem of collection and disposal of solid wastes by public bodies and to cooperate with the Office of Solid Waste of the United States Department of Health, Education and Welfare to accomplish that purpose by joint efforts. We further observe that this purpose may soon be made a legal requirement for all communities throughout the entire land under federal law. We are satisfied that this is health and general welfare legislation and that the legislative policy and purpose for chapter 28E is sufficiently stated. It amounts to this, that public agencies or governmental units may cooperate together to do anything jointly that they could do individually.

True, if chapter 28E is examined without reference to the powers granted the various governmental units by other legislation, the factors constituting sufficient guidelines might well be said to be insufficient. But this legislation must be interpreted with reference to the power or powers which the contracting governmental units already have. The pre-existing powers contain their own guidelines. The legal creation of a new body corporate and politic to jointly exercise and perform the powers and responsibilities of the cooperating governmental unit would not be unconstitutional so long as the new body politic is doing only what its cooperating members already have the power to do. This would be true under the above-recognized general rule that a statute is presumed to be constitutional until shown otherwise beyond a reasonable doubt.

Chapter 28E does not attempt to delienate the various governmental or proprietary functions which the individual governmental units may be implementing. While such a broad approach may be unwise, as appellants argue, it is not unconstitutional so long as the cooperating units are not exercising powers they do not already have.

With this in mind, it appears that chapter 28E supplies sufficient guidelines for the purposes necessary to the chapter. That is, the units are authorized to handle what might be called the mechanical details of implementing the joint project either by the creation of a separate entity or by using a joint administrator or board for the purpose of implementing the agreement reached. The agreement itself, of whatever nature, must have its specific contents delineated in section 28E.5 and specifically prohibits governmental units being involved in the new entity, except insofar as the new entity is in fact performing the same responsibilities as the units involved.

. . . .

IV. [The statute authorized revenue bonds to finance the construction of projects authorized by the act, the bonds to be paid off by revenues from the project. The court held that the bonds fell within the special fund doctrine and did not constitute debt of the contracting municipalities. Although the statute did not allow these municipalities to withdraw from the project, and although they were committed to the payment of the bonds, no financial obligation was imposed as charges for the use of project services would be passed on to the users. Any obligation on the part of the contracting municipalities to make up project revenues out of general taxation was contingent and speculative. The debt limitation problem is discussed in Chapter 5.—Eds.]

. . . .

IX. Appellants further contend that the agreement creating the Agency is contrary to public policy to the extent that it permits elected officials of the member municipalities to serve on the governing board of the Agency. They argue that the integrity of representative government demands that the administrative officials should be able to exercise their judgment free from the objectionable pressure of conflicting interests. We agree with that proposition, but do not believe it appears here that these members of the Agency board are in such a position. It is conceded that here there is nothing to indicate a personal pecuniary interest of those representatives is involved such as appears in *Wilson v. Iowa City,* Iowa, 165 N.W.2d 813, 820.

Although the members of the board understandably will want to keep the rates their constituents must pay as low as possible, they are well aware that rates must be maintained sufficient to meet the Agency's cost for such services. This is not such a conflict of interest as to be contrary to public policy or fatal to the agreement.

In passing on this question the trial court said, "Inasmuch as each representative is on the board primarily to serve as spokesman for the particular municipality or political subdivision he represents, (it could) . . . see no conflict of interest such as would likely affect his individual judgment by virtue of his status as an elected official." It pointed out no compensation is provided for such service and the representative serves at the pleasure of his municipality or political subdivision. We agree with the trial court.

In the recent case of *Wilson v. Iowa City, supra* we discussed the issue of conflict of interest and held, where it appeared the official had a personal interest, either actual or implied, he would be disqualified to vote on a municipal project—in that case, urban renewal. No such interest would appear in connection with this project unless some litigation would occur between the municipality he represents and the Agency, in which event the contract itself provides for arbitration procedures. We conclude there is no merit in this assignment. . . .

All justices concur except BECKER and LEGRAND, who dissent.

BECKER, JUSTICE.

I respectfully dissent. [Omitted.]

Comments: 1. Is the court in the principal case concerned about the *vertical* delegation of power by the legislature to create the intergovernmental unit, with the horizontal *delegation* of power by the contracting municipalities to the intergovernmental unit, or with the *exercise* of powers through the interlocal contract which have not previously been delegated to the contracting units? For more on delegation see Chapter 9.

The courts have usually rejected delegation of power and similar objections to interlocal cooperation legislation. For cases rejecting a number of constitutional objections to joint agencies created by intergovernmental agreements see *State ex rel. Grimes County Taxpayers Ass'n v. Texas Municipal Power Agency,* 565 S.W.2d 258 (Tex. Civ. App. 1978); *Frank v. City of Cody,* 572 P.2d 1106 (Wyo. 1977). Why do you suppose the courts struggle to find ways to uphold these agreements? Is the delegation of power analysis in the *Goreham* case convincing?

The inference would appear to be clear that the general interlocal cooperation act does not confer additional powers on the contracting municipalities. *See, e.g., Rollow v. West,* 479 P.2d 962 (Okla. 1971), holding that a voluntary association created by an interlocal agreement does not have eminent domain powers when these have not been independently conferred by statute. *Accord, Carter County v. City of Elizabethton,* 287 S.W.2d 934 (Tenn. 1956) (method for distributing school aid as provided by interlocal contract may not conflict with applicable statutory provision). *Compare City of Racine v. Town of Mount Pleasant,* 213 N.W.2d 60 (Wis. 1973), holding that a city contracting to provide sewage treatment under an interlocal contract is not subject to the same duties and obligations as a public service system or utility. Can these cases be reconciled?

2. The Iowa statute provided that the joint contract was nonterminable during the life of the joint project. A judicial disposition antagonistic to the termination of a joint contract is also evident in *Kansas City v. City of Raytown,* 421 S.W.2d 504 (Mo. 1967). The development of a joint sewer facility was contingent on the approval of a successful bond issue in one of the contracting municipalities by a certain date. Although the bond issue was not approved until the date had passed, the court was not troubled. It held that the cutoff date was inserted for the protection of the other contracting municipality which had raised no objection.

In a case in which one municipality sought to withdraw from a long-standing interlocal contract for the provision of sewage facilities, the court held that the contract would be allowed to run for a reasonable time but that governmental power to provide sewage services could not be surrendered indefinitely. *Borough of West Caldwell v. Borough of Caldwell,* 138 A.2d 402 (N.J. 1958). A fifty-year interlocal contract was upheld as reasonable in *Bair v. Layton City Corp.,* 307 P.2d 895 (Utah 1957).

Non-terminable interlocal contracts may create political problems if subsequent local administrations object to the bargain that was struck by their predecessors. *Village of Dennison v. Martin,* 210 N.E.2d 912 (Ohio 1964). The court found that the joint board created by contract to manage a joint waterworks system had sole management responsibility over the system, to the exclusion of the village board of one of the contracting municipalities.

3. When an interlocal contract requires one governmental unit to pay money over to another, problems may arise under the provision common to many constitutions that prevents one governmental unit from lending its credit to another. For the most part, this provision has not been an obstacle. *See* Antieau, *Some Legal Aspects of Municipal Finance,* 20 U. KAN. CITY L. REV. 15, 42 (1952). The court in *Johnson v. City of Louisville,* 261 S.W.2d 429 (Ky. 1953), held that the city could issue bonds to finance construction of a sewage disposal plant by a metropolitan sewer district. The district covered the city and some areas outside the city, although only six percent of the system's users resided outside the city limits. The court noted that the system would be a substantial benefit to city residents. In addition, the city had retained title to its portion of the system and had only turned over the management and operation of the system to the district. *See also Pease v. Board of County Commissioners,* 550 P.2d 565 (Okla. 1976), holding that county contributions to a council of governments created by an interlocal agreement were for local purposes and did not violate a constitutional provision prohibiting the expenditure of local funds for state purposes.

If the interlocal contract creates an independent authority to operate the facility, the constitutional provision prohibiting an appropriation of funds may not apply if appropriations to public authorities are not within the constitutional prohibition. *Opinion of the Justices,* 319 So. 2d 699 (Ala. 1975). For a case holding that an appropriation by a city to a school district covering most of the city's area was within the city's home rule powers see *Madsen v. Oakland Unified School District,* 119 Cal. Rptr. 531 (Cal. App. 1975).

4. Claims that an interlocal cooperation act infringed on the inherent right to local self-government were laid at rest in *City of Ecorse v. Peoples Community Hospital Authority,* 58 N.W.2d 159 (Mich. 1953). Interlocal agreements may also raise home rule objections. They were rejected in *City of Oakland v. Williams,* 103 P.2d 168 (Cal. 1940), holding that there was a state interest in regional cooperation for the purpose of studying sewage problems in the San Francisco Bay area.

5. Interlocal agreements are sometimes used for regulatory purposes. One example occurs under the federal public housing act, which requires cooperation agreements between municipalities and their public housing authorities to assist the construction of public housing projects. A model agreement provided by the U.S. Department of Housing and Urban Development required municipalities "to make such changes in any zoning of the site and surrounding territory of such [public housing] project as are reasonable and necessary for the development and protection of such project and the surrounding territory."

This agreement clearly raises objections that the municipality has bargained away its zoning power. See *Schmoll v. Housing Authority,* 321 S.W.2d 494 (Mo. 1959), holding that the agreement does not bargain away the zoning power in advance of a zoning change. The court relied on a clause in the agreement, which is common, and which limits zoning changes to those the municipality may "lawfully" make. Compare *New York City Housing Authority v. Foley,* 223 N.Y.S.2d 621 (Sup. Ct. 1961), interpreting an agreement providing that the city was to "endeavor to maintain [existing] zoning without variance" in the area adjacent to a public housing project. The agreement was construed not to prohibit the city's board of adjustment from granting a zoning variance in the adjacent area to allow a gasoline filling station. The court suggested that a contrary interpretation would deny the board of adjustment the powers granted to it under the zoning act.

Compare *Vap v. City of McCook,* 136 N.W.2d 220 (Neb. 1965). The municipality and the state highway agency entered into a contract under which the city agreed to prohibit parking on a federal-aid highway which was being improved through the city. The contract was upheld against a contention that it was an improper bargaining away of the municipality's police power. A statute authorized contracts between municipalities and the highway department. The court appeared to rely on the plenary power of the state to allocate state and local powers. It noted that the contract was necessary for the administration of the state highway system and to secure federal funds. Can you reconcile these cases?

6. *Interstate compacts.* State and local governments in interstate areas have used the interstate compact to create transportation, water planning and other authorities with regional responsibilities. Most interlocal contracting enabling legislation authorizes interstate agreements, but the consent of Congress may be required under art. I, § 10 of the federal constitution. Where it is, Congress must either consent to each individual contract or provide consent in advance. Advance consent has been given in several federal laws, including the Clean Air Act and the Coastal Zone Management Act.

In the planning area, one important regional agency created by interstate compact is the Lake Tahoe Regional Planning Agency. *See* Comment, *Nationalizing Lake Tahoe,* 19 SANTA CLARA L. REV. 681 (1979). In *People ex rel. Younger v. County of El Dorado,* 487 P.2d 1193 (Cal. 1971), the court rejected home rule objections to the interstate compact. It held that the compact served important state and regional concerns in the protection of the environmental quality of the region.

For discussion of the use of the interstate compact in the formation of interstate agencies see Advisory Commission on Intergovernmental Relations, Multistate Regionalism ch. 5 (1972); M. RIDGEWAY, INTERSTATE COMPACTS: A QUESTION OF FEDERALISM (1971).

Read literally, the compact clause prohibits any interstate compact or agreement unless Congress consents, but the Supreme Court has not adopted this interpretation. In *United States Steel Corp. v. Multistate Tax Commission,* 434 U.S. 452 (1978), the court held that a multistate tax compact agreed to by a large number of states did not require congressional approval. The purpose of the compact was to resolve interstate taxation problems, including the taxation of multistate taxpayers. The Court reaffirmed the early holding in *Virginia v. Tennessee,* 148 U.S. 503 (1893), where the Court held that the application of the compact clause is limited to agreements that are "directed to the formation of any combination tending to the increase of political power in the States, which may encroach upon or interfere with the just supremacy of the United States." *Id.* at 519. See also *New Hampshire v. Maine,* 426 U.S. 363 (1976), upholding an interstate compact which did not receive congressional assent and which located an ancient boundary.

The application of the *Tennessee* doctrine to interstate compacts providing for joint intergovernmental regulation is not clear. For example, what about an interstate compact providing for the joint administration of traffic laws in an interstate metropolitan area? *See* Engdahl, *Interstate Urban Areas and Interstate "Agreements" and "Compacts": Unclear Possibilities,* 58 GEO. L.J. 799 (1970). The Court in *United States Steel* did hold that congressional consent was not required just because the compact created an interstate administrative body. For studies of interstate compacts that include case studies of interstate compact organizations see M. RIDGEWAY, INTERSTATE COMPACTS: A QUESTION OF FEDERALISM (1971); R. LEACH & R. SUGG, THE ADMINISTRATION OF INTERSTATE COMPACTS (1959).

2. TRANSFER OF FUNCTION

A few state constitutions and statutes provide a method for authorizing the transfer of functions from one governmental unit to another. The Pennsylvania constitutional provision authorizing interlocal cooperation, *supra,* also contains transfer of function authority. These statutes and constitutional provisions are divided between those that require voter approval of the transfer and those that do not. None contain explicit provisions making the transfer permanent. Additional examples follow:

CALIFORNIA GOVERNMENT CODE § 51330.

If authorized by the city charter and approved by resolution of the board of supervisors, a city organized under a freeholders' charter may transfer any of its functions and any of the functions of an officer, board, or commission to an officer, board, or commission of the county in which the city is situated.

NEW YORK CONSTITUTION ART. 9, § 1(h)(1).

[Counties adopting alternative form of government] by act of the legislature or by local law, may transfer one or more functions or duties of the county or of the cities, towns, villages, districts or other units of government wholly contained in such county to each other or when authorized by the legislature to the state ... provided, however, that [no such transfer] shall become effective unless approved on a referendum by a majority of the votes cast thereon in the area of the county outside of cities, and in the cities of the county, if any, considered as one unit.

About one third of the local governments responding to an ACIR survey reported transfers of functions during a preceding ten-year period. State and Local Roles, *supra,* at 337. Functions were transferred to meet regional service demands, to meet regional environmental and other problems, and to alleviate fiscal problems of cities affected by inflation. The larger central cities most frequently transferred functions, and functions were most often reassigned to counties.

Functional transfers can also occur under intergovernmental agreements. A massive transfer of functions through intergovernmental agreement has occurred in Los Angeles County, California under what is known as the Lakewood Plan. To forestall annexations and incorporations that would impair the county's ability to provide services at scale economies, a plan was implemented under which new cities would incorporate but would contract with the county for the provision of most of their services.

Although the Lakewood Plan has been hailed by government reformers as an innovative step, a recent study indicates that it has served other purposes. "Minimal" cities have been incorporated by upper income homeowners who view the

Lakewood Plan as an opportunity to protect themselves from higher taxes by financially pressed cities. A "Lakewood" incorporation also preserves local control over zoning while providing for municipal services without the need for a local bureaucracy. G. MILLER, CITIES BY CONTRACT (1981). *See also* Kuyper, *Intergovernmental Cooperation: An Analysis of the Lakewood Plan*, 58 GEO. L.J. 777 (1970).

C. CONSOLIDATION, FEDERALISM AND COUNCILS OF GOVERNMENT

1. CONSOLIDATION AND FEDERATION

The following excerpts from an ACIR report explain how consolidation and federation work, and give some examples of recent consolidation and federation reforms. The Report begins by contrasting city-county consolidation with a "comprehensive urban county." Earlier, the report noted three characteristics of a comprehensive urban county:

> (1) an administrative structure capable of delivering services efficiently and accountably, (2) the authority to undertake the necessary functions, and (3) the fiscal capacity to finance these functional responsibilities.

Id. at 383. Counties have been modernized along these lines in many urban areas.

ADVISORY COMMISSION ON INTERGOVERNMENTAL RELATIONS, STATE AND LOCAL ROLES IN THE FEDERAL SYSTEM 395-404 (1982)

City-County Consolidation

City-county consolidation, going several steps beyond the comprehensive urban county, continues to intrigue metropolitan reformers because of its potential to reduce structural fragmentation and produce functional consolidation. A city-county consolidation has been defined as the "unification of the governments of one or more cities with the surrounding county. As a result of the consolidation, the boundary lines of the jurisdictions involved become coterminous. However, certain incorporated jurisdictions may opt to be excluded from the consolidation."

. . . .

Consolidation is generally a phenomenon of medium-sized metropolitan areas, ranging from 150,000 to nearly 800,000 population. The largest consolidated government ever formed in the post-World War II period was Indianapolis/Marion County and it was established by the state legislature without a local referendum. Some of the more recent mergers have involved smaller populations and been in rural, western areas of the country. Furthermore, although most consolidation referenda attempts have occurred in areas of from 100,000 to 249,999 the approval rate has been better in jurisdictions of under 25,000. . . . The success of these smaller consolidations, chiefly in the South and West, can be attributed to their generally less fragmented structural environment and fewer political conflicts. The 14 referenda in cities over 250,000 all failed—including the two largest in Cleveland and St. Louis.

City-county consolidation rarely means a total structural and functional merger. In several consolidations, certain small municipalities were not included. For instance, in the Jacksonville/Duval County consolidation, four municipalities were not merged into the consolidated government. . . . School districts in four of the six major consolidations were excluded, although in some cases the school function had already been consolidated before the city and the county merged.

Citizens often are unwilling to surrender local control of schools to a unified county system, but other functional assignments can experience considerable change when a city-county consolidation occurs, particularly in the more urbanized areas. Services have been expanded and improved in both central and suburban areas. A review of Nashville/Davidson County ten years after consolidation substantiated the fact that there were major improvements in education, police, fire, recreation, water, and sewerage services: Duplication was reduced, programs expanded, and services professionalized. Citizens found education and police services to be adequate or more than adequate. Yet, functional assignment problems can still plague consolidated governments, particularly when they fail to provide services on a countywide basis or extend basic services to fringe areas.

Federative Governments

. . . .

The comprehensive urban county is a modified two-tiered, federated government. In this form, municipalities retain their existence and continue to perform many functions. At the same time, the county provides services in unincorporated areas and most importantly assumes responsibility for areawide services. While Dade County, FL, is viewed by some as the only county with a truly federated system, many other urban counties have essentially become federated systems through structural reorganization and the piecemeal transfer of functions from municipalities.

The difference between Dade County and other modernized counties is that Dade County made a conscious decision to set up a two-tier system when it approved a new charter in 1957. The new charter retained 26 cities and preserved their right to perform local services. Substantial changes, however, were made in the structure and functional powers of the county government, expanding its ability to perform areawide and urban services. The county government was changed from the traditional commission form to a commission of eight members elected at large with residency requirements. A mayor is elected at large and is a member of and presides over commission meetings. A manager is appointed by the commission and is the chief administrator.

The county was assigned functional responsibility for many areawide and urban functions: health and welfare, enforcement of the building code, comprehensive planning, pollution control, social action programs, the courts, and areawide aspects of traffic control and highways. The county also became the prime provider of local services to unincorporated areas that were rapidly urbanizing. The charter also gave the county the power to assume operating responsibility for a municipal service if authorized to do by a two-thirds vote of the governing body of the municipality or by a majority of those voting within the municipality. Because Dade County—or Metro, as it is called—is the only government in unincorporated areas, and because of numerous transfers by the municipalities Metro is the major service provider in the area. The county now furnishes fire protection to the unincorporated areas and 19 cities. In contrast, no municipal police department has been transferred to Metro. Certain police activities—such as the crime lab, bomb squad, and central accident records—have been consolidated; but those which are vital—such as communications—have not, despite numerous attempts. Metro also handles most waste disposal, public housing, and community development activities and has a strong comprehensive land-use plan, but it has not been very successful at enforcing it. Whether Dade County remains a two-tiered, federated system is debatable. Some predict that, as more and more functions are transferred by the cities to the county level, the cities will be left with only a few very localized services such as routine police patrol.

Another federated form of reorganization is the multifunctional metropolitan service district. Although a few states—notably California, Oregon, Washington, and Colorado—have enacted legislation which enables metropolitan areas to establish these districts, the range of functions is usually limited. Even in the states which have authorized this form, very few metropolitan areas have established them, and when they have done so these units have tended to have few functional responsibilities.

One of most notable is the Municipality of Metropolitan Seattle (Metro). Established in 1958, its 37-member governing body is composed of representatives from the local units of government. All nine Seattle city council members and the Mayor of Seattle are automatically members of the Metro council. Also included are the nine King County council members, the county executive, and six additional representatives from unincorporated areas. In addition, there is representation from other cities in the county. One member represents the sewer districts and votes only on actions related to water quality. The enabling authorization permits any regional service corporation to perform six functions: sewage disposal, water supply, public transportation, garbage disposal, parks and parkways, and comprehensive planning. Yet, the Seattle Metro has assumed responsibility for only two of these functions: sewage disposal and public transportation. Metro also was designated as the agency to develop water quality planning for the area's four river basins. . . .

Summary

Major reorganizations or mergers of local units of government are not a common occurrence in the U.S. Few city-county consolidations have been established in the postwar period and none has been in big metropolitan areas. Most have taken place in medium-sized or small metropolitan and nonmetropolitan areas—usually in the South and most recently in the West—suggesting that consolidation may be most useful in preventing future fragmentation problems in jurisdictionally uncomplicated areas. City-county consolidation rarely solves all servicing assignments, since some local units are not merged and the consolidated government usually does not encompass the entire metropolitan population. Yet, where established, they have been generally successful.

The other major form of multijurisdictional reorganization—federative government—is even less common. Comprehensive, reorganized urban counties have been achieved through ad hoc structural, functional, and financial modifications; but only one county—Dade—has officially established a two-tier system, and the trend there is toward centralization. A few multifunctional metropolitan service districts have not fulfilled their potential. Thus, on the basis of the record to date, large-scale restructuring of government at the local level is the least likely method of realigning functional responsibilities, regardless of its ability to broaden the tax base, reduce duplicative services, improve administrative capacity, and provide a structural format for areawide service performance.

Comments: 1. Consolidation and federation can create complex legal problems. They may superimpose a new governmental authority on existing units, or add authority to an existing governmental unit which then becomes the consolidated or federated government for the area. Constitutional provisions eliminate or mitigate these legal problems in some states. A constitutional challenge is likely if the consolidation or federation is authorized by a statute.

Most of the cases have considered questions based on specific provisions in the state constitution affecting the structure of local government in the state. The decisions have upheld consolidation and federation when it has been challenged. The following examples are typical:

Hosclaw v. Stephens, 507 S.W.2d 483 (Ky. 1973). The court considered a challenge to a merger of the City of Lexington and Fayette County into an urban county form of government. The merger was carried out under statutory authority. The court held that the creation of the consolidated government did not violate the constitution. The legislature could create new forms of local government not limited to existing cities and counties.

A delegation of power objection also was rejected. The court found that the statute only delegated the authority to alter the structure of the affected governments, not their powers. The statute could not abolish the county executive agency, which was established by the constitution, but it could limit its powers.

Miami Shores Village v. Cowart, 198 So. 2d 468 (Fla. 1968). This case considered the Dade County federated government, which was created through adoption of a county charter authorized by a constitutional provision. The court interpreted a set of ambiguous provisions in the charter defining the powers of the federated county government. It held that the charter authorized the county to carry out functions that were metropolitan in character. *See also City of North Miami Beach v. Metropolitan Dade County,* 317 So. 2d 110 (Fla. App. 1975) (county may impose moratorium on sewer hook-ups); *City of Coral Gables v. Burgin,* 143 So. 2d 859 (Fla. 1962) (city may not impose more stringent standards on county plumbing license). *See* Gustely, *The Allocational and Distributional Impacts of Governmental Consolidation: The Dade County Experience,* 14 URB. AFF. Q. 349 (1977).

Dortch v. Lugar, 266 N.E.2d 25 (Ind. 1971). The court rejected a series of constitutional challenges to the consolidation of Indianapolis and Marion County, which had been carried out by statute. One argument was that an unconstitutional evasion of the constitutional debt limitation had occurred because the consolidation transferred the control of special districts to the consolidated government. The court held that the independent status of the districts was not destroyed by the transfer.

2. When local governments are consolidated over entire county areas, tax equity questions will arise if the entire area of the consolidated government is subjected to the property tax rate of the major city that becomes part of the consolidation. Undeveloped areas of the consolidated government will be subject to an urban tax rate that does not reflect the limited level of services they receive after consolidation.

To remedy this problem, some consolidated governmental structures have provided for the creation of two or more service districts within the consolidated government within which the level of taxes reflects the level of services that is provided. For discussion see White, *Differential Property Taxation in Consolidated City-Counties,* 63 NAT'L CIVIC REV. 301 (1974). The creation of these districts creates problems under constitutional uniformity clauses because they produce a tax rate that is not uniform for the entire area of the consolidated government.

Differential service districts have been upheld when they are created by the constitutional provision authorizing the consolidated government. *Frazer v. Carr,* 360 S.W.2d 449 (Tenn. 1962). In some consolidations, the differential service districts were created without the benefit of constitutional provision. *Hart v. Columbus,* 188 S.E.2d 422 (Ga. 1972). Four differential taxing districts were created for the City of Columbus-Muscogee County consolidated government. A different level of services was provided in each service district, and tax rates in the service districts were based on the level of services rendered. No attack on the differential service districts was made under the uniformity of taxation clause of the state constitution. The court applied a "reasonableness" test to uphold the districts, finding that the benefits conferred in each district were commensurate with the tax burden imposed. An equal protection attack also was rejected.

3. Property tax inequities and disparities in metropolitan areas can be handled through tax sharing or tax pooling plans. Minnesota has experimented with this approach in its Metropolitan Fiscal Disparities Act, Minn. Stat. Ann. ch. 473F, upheld against a challenge based on uniformity of taxation grounds in *Village of Burnsville v. Onischuk,* 222 N.W.2d 523 (Minn. 1974), *appeal dismissed,* 420 U.S. 916 (1976). The sharing formula is complicated but generally distributes a share of the increase in taxes on commercial and industrial property on an areawide basis. As the tax is redistributed under a formula that considers population and fiscal capacity, the formula provides a disincentive to zone property for commercial and industrial purposes. Some of the increased revenues from these properties are redistributed areawide based on the formula, and the formula may not return all of the revenue increase to the municipality in which the new commercial and industrial development is located. For discussion see Note, *Minnesota's Metropolitan Fiscal Disparities Act — An Experiment in Tax Base Sharing,* 59 MINN. L. REV. 927 (1975). The Act is limited to the Minneapolis-St. Paul metropolitan area.

For a case upholding a similar tax sharing scheme applied to the Hackensack Meadowlands redevelopment area in New Jersey, see *Meadowlands Regional Redevelopment Agency v. State,* 304 A.2d 545 (N.J. 1973). *See generally* Lyall, *Tax-Base Sharing: A Fiscal Aid Towards More Rational Land Use Planning,* 41 J. AM. INST. PLANNERS 90 (1975).

4. Constitutional objections have also been made to the creation of metropolitan authorities and districts, and these objections also have been dismissed.

Horner's Market, Inc. v. Tri-County Metropolitan Transit District, 471 P.2d 798 (Or. 1970). A statute authorized the City of Portland to create the district, and this authority was challenged as an unconstitutional delegation of power. The court disagreed. It held that the legislature could have created the district, but that it had no "practical" way to know what effect it would have on the metropolitan districts in the state. "[T]he most feasible method of providing the necessary flexibility in carrying out the legislative policy is to delegate the decision to those whose interests are most seriously involved and who are best equipped" to activate the district.

The court also rejected arguments that the statute violated the United States Supreme Court's voting rights cases, see Chapter 10. The court also held that the power to levy taxes could be vested in an appointive rather than an elective body. *See* Tobin, *The Metropolitan Special District: Intercounty Metropolitan Government of Tomorrow,* 14 U. MIAMI L. REV. 333 (1960) (supports holding in decision).

Municipality of Metropolitan Seattle v. City of Seattle, 357 P.2d 863 (Wash. 1960). The court rejected an argument that the creation of the metropolitan district violated local home rule powers. It noted that home rule municipalities were subject to "general laws." Home rule powers would have to yield had the state decided to deal with the problems the metropolitan district was intended to solve. Home rule must also yield when the state provides the "machinery whereby these problems might be remedied on the local level." *Contra, Four-County Metropolitan Capital Improvement District v. Board of County Commissioners,* 369 P.2d 67 (Colo. 1962).

Most cases dealing with the creation of metropolitan special districts have avoided home rule and related objections by classifying the special district as a state "agency" serving a state purpose. This characterization is not difficult to apply when the district is dealing with environmental problems that transcend municipal boundaries. *See City of Dearborn v. Michigan Turnpike Authority,* 73 N.W.2d 544 (Mich. 1955); *Omaha Parking Authority v. City of Omaha,* 77 N.W.2d 862 (Neb. 1956); *Robertson v. Zimmerman,* 196 N.E. 740 (N.Y. 1935) (Buffalo sewage authority). These state or single-purpose authorities were limited to a single municipality.

5. The literature on governmental consolidation and federation is extensive. *See* H. HALLMAN, SMALL AND LARGE TOGETHER: GOVERNING THE METROPOLIS (1977); Frisken, *The Metropolis and the City: Can One Government Unite Them?,* 8 URB. AFF. Q. 395

(1973) (growing disparities in metropolitan areas hamper consolidation efforts); Grant, *Metropolitan Problems and Local Government Structure: An Examination of Old and New Issues,* 22 VAND. L. REV. 757 (1969); Note, *The Urban County: A Study of New Approaches to Local Government in Metropolitan Areas,* 73 HARV. L. REV. 536 (1960).

One perceptive review of governmental reorganization problems suggests that the reasons for governmental integration and the likelihood of success may vary with the metropolitan area affected:

> Most metropolitan reorganization in this country has been concerned with such issues as fiscal equity between jurisdictions within a region, technical efficiency in the allocation of governmental functions, and the quality-of-life gains afforded by centralized planning and zoning. But all these concerns are related to the internal affairs of a single region. Some of the mature (we might say, simply, older) cities in this country face a problem of an entirely different dimension: the region taken as a whole is in decline—in some cases an accelerated decline—and there seems to be no strong empirical basis for saying that metropolitan government will impede this trend. But there are some impressionistic bases for suggesting that reorganization can make a difference.

Campbell, *Metropolitan Governance and the Mature Metropolis* in THE MATURE METROPOLIS 203 (C. Leven ed. 1978). For a review of the experience with consolidated governments in several metropolitan areas see J. HORAN & G. TAYLOR, EXPERIMENTS IN METROPOLITAN GOVERNMENT (1977).

A NOTE ON NEIGHBORHOOD GOVERNMENT AND CITIZEN PARTICIPATION

Governmental integration has a centralizing tendency: Local government becomes more removed from the people. Developments in citizen participation at the local level in the past decades provide a counterpoint to this centralizing trend. Stimulated by requirements in federal programs adopted in the 1960s, citizens began to take a more active role in local government, usually through participation in decision-making for local utilization of federal assistance. Citizens also demanded a voice in the administration of local programs such as elementary and secondary education.

The citizen participation movement has declined with the weakening of participation requirements in federal programs and the weakening of citizen groups devoted to social change. *See* M. GITTEL, LIMITS TO CITIZEN PARTICIPATION: THE DECLINE OF COMMUNITY ORGANIZATIONS (1980). A related citizen participation movement — the establishment of neighborhood advisory councils and neighborhood governments — continues to flourish. Neighborhood governments and advisory councils can provide an opportunity for decentralizing the management of local government.

Structural forms for decentralized neighborhood governments are reviewed in Schmandt, *Decentralization: A Structural Imperative,* in NEIGHBORHOOD CONTROL IN THE 1970's, at 17 (G. Frederickson ed. 1973). Schmandt isolates what he calls five simplified models of decentralization. Each of these will be reviewed in turn.

1. *The exchange model.* "This model encompasses the decentralization devices for informing, advising, and interacting; in short, for communicating. Ideally, the process represents a two-way flow. Information about city plans, programs, and opportunities is made available to neighborhood residents through field offices, and feedback is passed upward to the relevant points in the bureaucratic structure. The same is true with respect to advice...." *Id.* at 19. Schmandt notes that this method works well with groups and classes that identify with established agency goals, but that it is not useful with lower class

neighborhoods whose residents suspect manipulation by the bureaucratic structure.

2. *The bureaucratic model.* "The bureaucratic model involves the delegation of authority to subordinate civil servants in the neighborhood. This delegation may take two forms: functional and territorial. In the first instance, power is vested in locality-based officials along functional lines.... In the second instance, authority over a mix of functions is placed in a district or neighborhood manager, with personnel administering the individual services or programs reporting to him." *Id.* at 20-21. Schmandt points out that several difficulties impede the effectiveness of this model. It interferes with the depersonalization demanded by bureaucratic systems, it gives the neighborhood managers no direct ties to the neighborhood, and it leads these managers into protective and defensive positions when faced with a hostile lower class neighborhood constituency.

3. *Modified bureaucratic model.* Under this model the responsibilities of the neighborhood manager flow in two directions, to his superiors and to a neighborhood council representative of neighborhood residents. For example, the council might be given limited powers to pass on personnel appointments and to decide on the level of neighborhood services. Again, there are difficulties. "One of the more evident and typical problems is the difficult position of the neighborhood manager under such an arrangement. An administrator invariably operates within a set of varying expectations. His superiors, his subordinates, and the organization's clientele all perceive his role in different ways.... In the case of the bureaucratic official assigned to a neighborhood, the divergent expectations of the resident council and the service personnel could lead to severe role conflict." *Id.* at 23.

4. *The development model.* Schmandt notes that minority group leaders convinced "that the poor cannot win over city hall and the established bureaucracy ... have turned to approaches that bypass the regular political and administrative institutions of the community and look at the neighborhood itself as a framework for control. One such approach is represented by the community development or neighborhood corporation chartered by the state, or federal government, and controlled by the residents. Incorporating physical and civic development, the new structural mechanism encompasses both economic activities and service delivery functions." *Id.* at 24. For example, the corporation may sponsor housing and business projects, and may also contract with the city to assume the administration of certain public functions, such as health centers.

While the neighborhood corporation is free of some of the contradictions and weaknesses of some of the other forms, it imposes new constraints. By taking on business and service functions the residents become producers as well as consumers of public and private services. "The assumption of this responsibility necessarily places constraints on their freedom of action. For as board members and managers, they must relate not only inwardly to the constituents they serve but also outwardly to the established bureaucracies and funding agencies on whom they are dependent for cooperation and resources." *Id.* at 24. For additional discussion of neighborhood corporations see TWENTIETH CENTURY FUND: CDCS: NEW HOPE FOR THE INNER CITY (1971).

5. *Governmental model.* Under this model, the most radical of the five, legal powers are delegated to newly created political subunits of large central cities. This model does not eliminate bureaucratization. It simply reduces its scale and permits the replacement of existing personnel with those better oriented toward the neighborhood. Otherwise, the neighborhood government faces the same problems as a traditional bureaucracy, and has the same needs for organizational

maintenance, integration, adaptability, goal achievement, and stability and predictability in its operations. It must also set policy and develop program expertise.

Schmandt comments: "[Over time] a neighborhood government will become more concerned with its survival and enhancement needs and more bureaucratic. ... Similarly, whatever innovative potential the new structure may have, it is likely to be quickly submerged in the task of maintaining the enterprise. The inability of citizen self-help organizations of recent years to develop approaches to service needs and problems essentially different from the more traditional agencies attests to this likelihood." *Id.* at 26. Schmandt does see some advantages in the governmental model, including the capacity to develop indigenous leadership and the provision of a governmental structure that is legitimate in neighborhood eyes.

Comments: 1. The legislation creating the consolidated Indianapolis-Marion County government contained innovative provisions authorizing the creation of neighborhood community councils. Ind. Code § 15-5-15.5-14 et seq. (1976). This option was not exercised, and the statutory authority for the community councils has expired. The councils were delegated fairly extensive powers, including the power to participate in the city planning process and to enact local traffic regulations. They were not granted fiscal powers.

2. The "home rule" act for the District of Columbia adopted by Congress in 1973 provides for the creation of Advisory Neighborhood Commissions. The Commissions have the following powers:

(a) Each advisory neighborhood commission ... may advise [the council, mayor and agencies, boards and commissions] with respect to all proposed matters of District government policy including decisions regarding planning, streets, recreation, social services programs, education, health, safety and sanitation which affect that commission area....
(b) [Thirty days notice of "such District government actions or proposed actions" to be given to affected commissions.]
....
(c)(2) [Alcoholic Beverage Control Board to give commissions notice of applications for liquor licenses.]
(d) [Commission to forward "written recommendations with respect to the proposed actions" to the appropriate body.] ... The issues and concerns raised in the recommendations of the commission shall be given great weight during the deliberations by the governmental agency and those issues shall be discussed in the written rationale for the governmental decision taken.

D.C. Code § 1-261. The clear purpose of the statute is to give the commissions a participatory role in agency decision making. Where do the commissions fit in Schmandt's categories?

The "great weight" requirement was considered in *Kopff v. District of Columbia Alcoholic Beverage Control Board*, 381 A.2d 1372 (D.C. App. 1977). The commission argued that an agency should give the same weight to a commission's recommendations that it gives to its construction of its own enabling statute. The court rejected this interpretation. It held that the commission role was advisory and that to adopt this interpretation would interfere with "the established pattern of governmental relationships" and would come "perilously close to, if not cross into, the realm of improper delegation of governmental authority to a private party." For more on this delegation problem see Chapter 9.

The court then interpreted the "great weight" requirement: It means ... that an agency must elaborate, with precision, its response to the ANC [neighborhood commission] issues and concerns. It is a statutory method of forcing an agency to come to grips with the ANC view — to deal with it in detail, without slippage. An agency must focus particular attention not only on the issues and concerns as pressed by an ANC, but also on the fact that the ANC, as a representative body, is the group making the recommendation. That is, the agency must articulate why the particular ANC itself, given its vantage point, does — or does not — offer persuasive advice under the circumstances.

Id. at 1384. What must an agency do to meet this requirement? May an agency finding be reversed if it declines to follow an ANC recommendation? Does this interpretation fatally dilute the role of the commissions in agency decision making?

For a case indicating that an agency need only articlate its response to a commission recommendation but need not follow it see *Wheeler v. District of Columbia Board of Zoning Adjustment,* 395 A.2d 85 (D.C. App. 1978) (zoning variance).

3. There is substantial literature on decentralization and neighborhood government. See H. HALLMAN, NEIGHBORHOOD GOVERNMENT IN A METROPOLITAN SETTING (1974); M. KOTLER, NEIGHBORHOOD GOVERNMENT: THE LOCAL FOUNDATION OF POLITICAL LIFE (1969); S. LANGTON, CITIZEN PARTICIPATION IN AMERICA (1978); IMPROVING THE QUALITY OF URBAN MANAGEMENT pt. III (W. Hawley & D. Rogers eds. 1974).

2. COUNCILS OF GOVERNMENT AND REGIONAL AGENCIES

Political resistance to governmental consolidation has stimulated other approaches to governmental integration at the regional level. Voluntary councils of government (COG) and regional planning agencies are the best example, and they are now well established throughout the country. Regional planning agencies are usually organized under state enabling legislation, and are usually authorized to adopt an advisory regional plan. Councils of government are organizations voluntarily formed by local governments in the region, although most of their funding has come from federal sources. COGs may be organized under state legislation or through intergovernmental agreements. They carry out regional planning responsibilities in many areas.

The COG experiment was an innovation in regional governance prompted by federal legislation beginning in the 1960s. Federal planning legislation provided funding for the COGs, and a number of federal statutes give them important planning responsibilities. Transportation planning under the federal highway and urban mass transportation acts is one example. 23 U.S.C. § 134.

Until recently, COGs and regional planning agencies also performed an important "clearinghouse" function under federal assistance legislation. The basis for this function was Circular A-95, issued by the federal Office of Management and Budget (OMB). This circular required state and regional Clearinghouse review of state and local government applications for federal assistance. The circular was authorized by the Intergovernmental Cooperation Act of 1968, which requires OMB to "establish rules and regulations governing the formulation, evaluation and review of federal programs and projects having a significant impact on area and community development, including programs providing Federal assistance to the States and localities." 42 U.S.C. § 4233.

President Reagan revoked Circular A-95. Exec. Order 12372, 47 Fed. Reg. 30959 (1982). The order shifts the initiative for establishing federal assistance review procedures and priorities to states and localities. They may decide to continue the clearinghouse review system as it existed prior to the Executive Order. Federal agencies are required to make every effort to accommodate state and local government recommendations on federal program decisions. If a federal agency disagrees with a state or local recommendation, it must explain why in a timely manner. For a discussion of regional organizations see State and Federal Roles, *supra,* ch. 5.

Comments: 1. Regional clearinghouses were supposed to coordinate applications for federal assistance, it was hoped, in accordance with regional plans. This clearinghouse function was weakened by a number of factors. These included weak regional plans or the failure to adopt a plan; the failure to bind federal agencies to the regional clearinghouse decision; opposition from the state level; and the threat of local government withdrawal if the decisions of the regional agency are politically unpopular.

An early review of clearinghouse performance, which is still relevant, pointed out that "[t]he image of the COG we mean to convey is one of a beleaguered organization, surrounded by unsure federal partners, unwilling local members and a barely awakening state government." M. MOGULOF, GOVERNING METROPOLITAN AREAS 16 (1971). The author continues:

> [T]he relative independence of various federal actions from each other (and at times the relative independence of actions within a federal agency) confront the COG with a regional terrain which can seem also impossible to put in order. These various federal planning grants go to a variety of forces in local and state government, as well as to independent and quasi-governmental agencies. Important client/constituency lines develop between federal agencies and local grantees which impose serious constraints on the COG as, and if, it attempts to become the super comprehensive planner for the metropolitan area.

Id. at 28. For discussion of the COG experience see N. WILKSTROM, COUNCILS OF GOVERNMENT: A STUDY OF POLITICAL INCREMENTALISM (1977). *See City of Bowie v. Board of County Commissioners,* 271 A.2d 657 (Md. 1970). This case was a suit to enjoin the county from taking any steps to proceed with the construction of a proposed airport. As federal aid was involved, two preliminary applications "of some sort" had been submitted to the regional COG, and had been approved. A third application was pending before the COG. The injunction was not allowed, and the court commented: "We see no reason to suppose the COG, which found 'no conflict with metropolitan planning' in the preliminary applications, would do otherwise than comment favorably on any subsequent application. Even if its comments should turn out to be unfavorable it is unlikely the federal grant would be withheld." *Id.* at 659.

2. The classic example of a regional agency with comprehensive planning powers is the metropolitan council in the Twin Cities area in Minnesota. The council is not a voluntary COG. It was created by state legislation, and council members are elected rather than appointed.

The metropolitan council has been given planning and implementation powers far in excess of those possessed by comparable agencies elsewhere. The exercise of these powers affects the relationship of the council to local units of government. The enabling legislation authorizes the council to prepare a development guide, which "shall consist of a compilation of policy statements, goals, standards, programs, and maps prescribing guides for an orderly and economic development, public and private, of the metropolitan area." Minn. Stat. Ann. § 473.145. It is also to adopt policy plans for metropolitan commissions, such as the waste control and transit commission, as well as an open space and solid waste plan. Council approval of all metropolitan commission development programs and budgets also is provided. The council may also review and suspend if inconsistent with the development guide any comprehensive plan of an independent commission, board or agency within the area if the plan will have a metropolitan effect. *Id.* §§ 473.161-165. Highway projects must also be approved by the council. *Id.* § 473.167. The council reviews all applications by local government units within its area for federal or state aid, thus establishing its clearinghouse review function. *Id.* § 473.171.

Two other important powers of the metropolitan council should be noted. The council may review any privately or publicly proposed "matters of metropolitan significance" for consistency, among other criteria, with the development guide, and may suspend action on the matter of metropolitan significance for twelve months. *Id.* § 473.173. The council reviews the comprehensive plans of local government units and the capital improvement programs of school districts to determine their consistency with the metropolitan system plans. *Id.* § 473.175. If a local government unit fails to adopt a local comprehensive plan consistent with the system plans the metropolitan council may take appropriate action in court. *Id.* The system plans cover airports, metropolitan waste control, transportation, and regional recreation open space. *Id.* § 473.852(8).

As the council's powers of review operate in practice, the plans and projects submitted for review are evaluated for consistency with its development guide, which contains the various system plans required by the statute. It also contains a development framework which specifies a metropolitan urban service area within which urban services will be made available, and which determines where new growth is to occur. For discussion of the metropolitan council see Note, *State Intervention into Local Land Use Regulation — A Proposal for Reform of Minnesota Legislation,* 63 MINN. L. REV. 1259 (1979).

3. Some states have delegated powers to their regional planning agencies which are not as substantial as the powers of the metropolitan council but which do give the agencies a role in the planning and land use control process. Under Florida legislation, developers of major developments known as developments of regional impact (DRI) must submit development applications to local governments for review and approval. As part of the review process, the regional planning agency provides comments on the environmental and other impacts of the legislation. These comments are taken into account by the local government when it makes its decision on a DRI. Appeals from local DRI determinations may be taken to a state agency. Fla. Stat. Ann. §§ 380.03-380.06.

The regional agencies adopt a comprehensive regional policy plan which provides a planning basis for reviewing DRI applications. They also adopt a list of regional planning issues to be used in DRI review. DRI developers must have a pre-application conference with the regional agency to define the issues which are relevant in the DRI review.

Like regional agencies elsewhere, the Florida agencies were also subject to pressures from local governments in carrying out their DRI review functions. Their independence was strengthened by amendments to the legislation which authorized the governor to appoint one third of their members, subject to confirmation by the Senate. For a discussion of the Florida DRI process see Pelham, *Regulating Developments of Regional Impact: Florida and the Model Code,* 29 U. FLA. L. REV. 789 (1977).

Chapter 5
STATE AND LOCAL FINANCE

A. FISCAL TRENDS

One of the major political issues likely to occupy the attention of the nation during the balance of the twentieth century is the question of how to finance government. Government activities, and corresponding costs, have risen enormously in the past twenty years. One of the consequences of this growth is a major taxpayers' revolt which has been gathering steam and appears to be on a collision course with increasing demands for government services.

This chapter will examine legal issues concerning state and local government finance. After a review of major constitutional limitations on the power of government to raise and spend money (due process, equal protection and public purpose), we will explore in detail major revenue raising activities (taxation and borrowing) as well as new forms of tax and expenditure limitations. The chapter will conclude with a review of the budget and appropriations process.

Legal issues, of course, must be studied in a context of economic, political and social concerns. Important trends in federal, state, and local expenditures, revenues, and fiscal affairs are detailed in the following reports:

ADVISORY COMMISSION ON INTERGOVERNMENTAL RELATIONS, SIGNIFICANT FEATURES OF FISCAL FEDERALISM, 1980-81 Edition: Highlights 7-9 (1981)

The Great Slowdown

Between 1942-76, the state and local public sector was a high growth industry. During this 34-year period, state-local spending (including federal aid) grew almost three times as fast as the economy — rising from 7.5% of personal income in 1942 to 20.3% by 1976. During a similar period (1939-76) per capita expenditures in constant dollars increased by 2.9 times . . . .

Since 1976, state-local government has become a static if not declining industry in most parts of the country. While spending continues to increase, it has neither kept pace with the growth of a sluggish economy nor the high rates of inflation . . . .

This great transition from fast growth to slow decline is clearly a grass roots development. The growth in "real" spending stopped first at the local level (1974), then at the state level (1976), and federal aid topped off in 1978. Of special note is the fact that state and local spending from own sources peaked well before the approval of Proposition 13 in 1978 and federal aid flows began to decline (in real terms) two years before President Reagan presented his cutback budget . . . .

Two developments were primarily responsible for this remarkable fiscal turnaround — state legislators stopped raising taxes and started to cut them, and

Congress applied the brakes to federal aid growth. During most of the post World War II period, the states did a very brisk business in new and used taxes — an activity that came to an abrupt halt in the late 1970s . . . .

The possibility of a strong revenue resurgence in the near future is extremely slim for most of our 50 state-local systems. The 1970s left in its wake a wide variety of fiscal restrictions on state and local authorities. Moreover, falling school enrollments now make it extremely difficult for the once powerful school lobbies to run political interference for tax increases. Without the help of periodic increases in state sales and income taxes, most of our 50 state-local systems cannot generate sufficient "automatic" revenue growth to keep pace, much less exceed the growth of the economy . . . .

All indicators now point to a continued decline in federal aid flows over the next several years. Aid to states and localities is bound to be curtailed for some time to come as federal policymakers return "to the basics" — strengthening national defense, bolstering social security finances, and stimulating the economy through tax cuts and balanced budget strategies . . . .

State and local employment and payrolls follows the same general pattern of decline. After a fairly steady increase in state-local payroll in relation to state personal income, from 5.6% in 1957 to 9.2% in 1975, the percentage decreased to 8.5% in 1978 and to 8.3% in 1980. The average annual increase in state-local employment per 10,000 population dropped to less than 1% between 1972 and 1980 after increasing by an average of 3.3% between 1957 and 1972 . . . .

Even though state and local governments managed to keep the average increase in state-local indebtedness below the average increase in GNP during the last decade, state and local interest payments are taking an increasingly larger share of state and local general revenue. State interest payments in relation to "own source general revenue" increased from 2.9% in 1971 to 4.0% in 1980. For local governments, the increase for this same period was from 5.8% to 6.1% . . . .

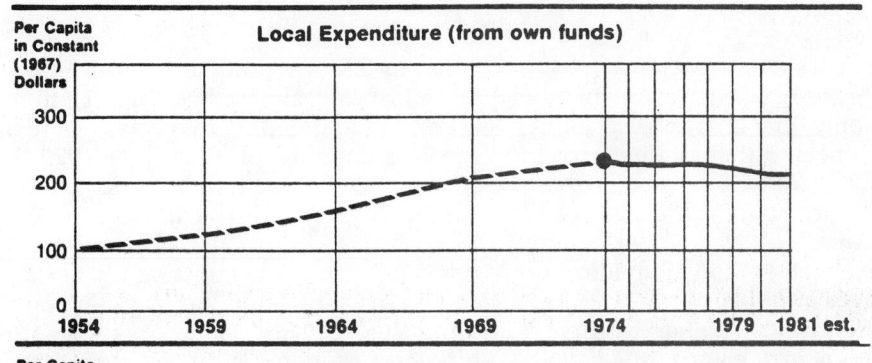

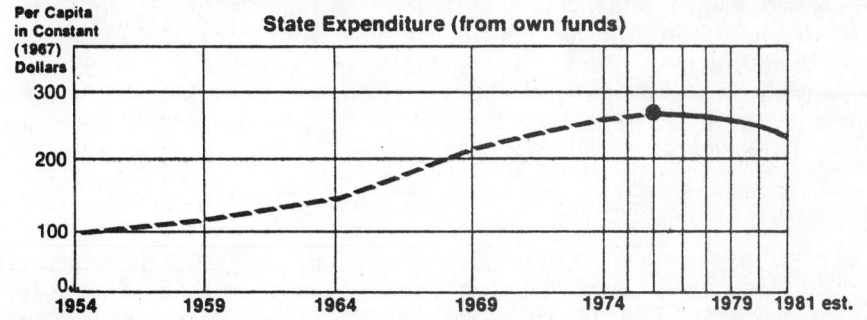

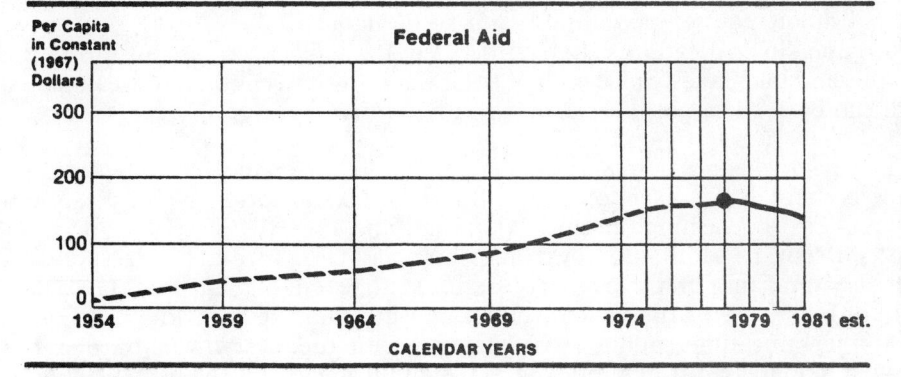

The Decline In "Real" State-Local Spending
(Decline in Local Spending Commencing 1975, State Spending 1977, Federal Aid Flows 1979)

Sources: Tables 1 and 3

● High points.

ADVISORY COMMISSION ON INTERGOVERNMENTAL RELATIONS, STATE AND LOCAL ROLES IN THE FEDERAL SYSTEM 133, 137, 144, 168-70 (1980)

State Finances

State financial systems have recently undergone, and are continuing to undergo, marked transformations. After growing almost twice as fast as the economy for a quarter of a century, state and local spending in the aggregate has fallen behind the nominal growth in the gross national product since 1975. Per capita state-local expenditures have declined as well. The result is the "transformation of the state and local sector from a fast-growth to a no-growth industry." . . .

Many factors contributed to the slowdown. Probably the most significant were changes in public opinion, economic conditions, and demographics. The public attitude appears to have shifted from support, or at least tolerance, of increased spending to demands for a halt. The shift in the economy from a situation of real growth to one of little or no growth, coupled with high rates of inflation, dampened enthusiasm for government expansion. Moreover, the steadily rising school enrollments of the post-World War II era have now declined, reducing the pressures for more funds for education. As a consequence of these changes, the states have entered an era of fiscal restraint.

State Revenue System Changes

State revenue systems have undergone transformation as well. In many ways they differ widely, even from what they were ten years ago. Many states have moved toward a higher quality system that provides greater revenue diversification, equity, moderation, and accountability.

Revenue diversification can be provided by a balanced use of property, income, and sales taxes. Since each of these has its own strengths and weaknesses, each can be used to provide balance in the tax structure. . . .

. . . .

[The major changes noted are an increase in reliance on income and sales taxes (only six states do not have some type of income tax — Florida, Nebraska, South Dakota, Texas, Washington, and Wyoming, and only five lack sales taxes — Alaska, Delaware, Montana, New Hampshire, and Oregon) and a corresponding decrease in reliance on the property tax for state revenues. State sales taxes now account for 50.9% of state tax revenues and income taxes provide 35.9%.

[At the same time, public dissatisfaction with the overall tax burden has resulted in increased use of indexed personal income taxes, roll back provisions requiring reductions in tax rates to offset large increases in assessments, as well as tax and expenditure limitations. — Eds.]

State Indebtedness

State debt continues to grow, although it has leveled off and started a decline as a percent of the gross national product (GNP). The percent of increase appears to be on the decline as well; nonetheless, it quadrupled in the last 20 years. . . .

[The ACIR report concludes that states appear to be holding their own financially, while at the same time emerging as the senior partners in state-local finance. By 1979, states were financing more than 50% of state-local expenditures from nonfederal sources in 46 states, up from 28 in 1966 and 23 in 1957. Major increases in state shares occurred in education, health care, and public welfare finance. — Eds.]

A number of trends have altered the state and local financial picture. The trends include increasing financial stress in many cities, the effects of inflation, the relative decline in federal assistance as compared with the growing affluence of energy-rich states with taxable energy resources, and the worst recession and the highest rate of unemployment in forty years.

As the following chart listing tax resources available to Colorado local governments indicates, these governments have a wide variety of tax sources open to them. Nevertheless, the property tax remains the mainstay of local government finance, at least for all local governments except special districts.

Although the amount collected through the property tax doubled between 1970 and 1980, the percentage of general revenue for local governments raised by property taxation declined during that same period from forty percent to twenty-eight percent. The following chart from the Tax Foundation illustrates the growth and composition of local government revenue. In fiscal year 1980, intergovernmental aid topped $100 billion for the first time. Tax Foundation, Incorporated, Monthly Tax Features, Vol. 26, No. 8, at 1 (1982).

Composition and Growth of Local Government Revenue by Source

Fiscal Years 1970 and 1980

Source	Amount (billions) 1970	Amount (billions) 1980	Percent of total 1970	Percent of total 1980	Percent change 1970-1980
Total general revenue, all sources	$80.9	$232.5	100.0	100.0	187.3
Total, own sources	51.4	130.0	63.5	55.9	153.0
Total, taxes	38.8	86.4	48.0	37.2	122.5
Property tax	33.0	65.6	40.7	28.2	99.0
Sales and gross receipts	3.1	12.1	3.8	5.2	293.5
Other taxes and licenses	2.8	8.7	3.5	3.7	210.8
Charges and miscellaneous	12.6	43.6	15.5	18.8	247.5
Total, intergovernmental aid	29.5	102.4	36.5	44.1	246.9
From states	26.9	81.3	33.3	35.0	202.0
From Federal	2.6	21.1	3.2	9.1	711.4

Source: Bureau of the Census, Department of Commerce; and Tax Foundation computations.

Revenue Alternatives For Colorado Local Governments

	GENERAL SALES TAX	SELECTIVE SALES TAX	USE TAX	AD VALOREM PROPERTY TAX	GENERAL OCCUPATION TAX	SPECIFIC OCCUPATION TAX
DESCRIPTION	Excise tax levied on retail sales of tangible personal property (sometimes services) made inside the taxing jurisdiction.	Excise tax levied on retail sales of certain products inside taxing jurisdiction. Most common are tobacco, alcoholic beverages, motor fuel, public utilities, insurance, and parimutuels.	Tax on the privilege of storing, distributing, using, or consuming articles of tangible personal property in the taxing jurisdiction and on which no sales tax has been paid. It is generally complementary to sales tax.	Ad valorem tax computed on the assessed valuation of all property, real and personal, located within the territorial limits of the authority levying the tax.	Tax imposed for the privilege of carrying on any of a broad range of occupations within the taxing jurisdiction. Denver's head tax is an example.	Tax imposed for the privilege of carrying on certain occupations within a taxing jurisdiction. Utility occupation (franchise) taxes and beer and liquor occupation taxes are common in Colorado.
LEGALITY	Legal for home rule cities, counties, statutory cities and towns. Election required in all but home rule cities (unless charter requires election). 4% maximum cumulative levy for all cities and counties in any one location.	Legal for home rule cities. No statutory authority for counties, statutory cities/towns. Localities with cigarette taxes do not receive cigarette tax distribution from the state.	Legal for home rule cities and statutory cities/towns. No authority for counties. 4% maximum cumulative levy for all cities and towns in any one location.	Legal for home rule cities, counties, and statutory cities/towns subject to extensive charter, constitutional and statutory limitations.	Legal for home rule cities within charter limits. Legal for statutory cities/towns. No authority for counties, districts.	Legal for home rule cities within charter limits. Legal for home rule cities/towns. No authority for counties, districts.
ELASTICITY	Unit elastic (range 0.8-1.3)	Strongly inelastic (range 0.0-0.8)	Unit elastic (range 0.8-1.3)	Moderately inelastic (range 0.4-1.4). Property tax base in Garfield and Rio Blanco counties will be dominated by oil shale facilities, not by local economic conditions.	Strongly inelastic as typically used. Can be structured to be less inelastic.	Strongly inelastic as typically used. Can be structured to be less inelastic.
INCIDENCE	Regressive to income. Neutral to household size. Taxes non-resident visitors. Relief programs can *reduce* regressivity.	More regressive to income than general sales tax. Neutral to household size. Taxes non-residents and visitors.	Same as general sales tax. Particularly hits purchasers of motor vehicles and construction and building materials.	Regressively similar to general sales tax. Neutral to household size. Relief programs can reduce regressivity. Oil shale facilities will dominate tax bases in Garfield and Rio Blanco. Much of the tax would be exported out of the region.	Where taxes are levied on firms doing business locally, same as general sales tax. Where tax is on exporting industry, it is exported outside of the region. A flat rate is regressive to individual income above any exemption level. Government employees exempt.	Same as general occupation tax.

Source: Briscoe, Maphis, Murray, and Lamont, Inc., **Oil Shale Tax Lead Time Study**, prepared for Regional Development and Land Use Planning Subcommittee of the Governor's Committee on Oil Shale Environmental Problems, Denver, Colorado, 1974. This chart is a summary of Section 3 of that study. [Some elements of the chart have been omitted—Eds.]

Revenue Alternatives For Colorado Local Governments—Continued

	USER FEES	SEVERANCE TAX	LOCAL INCOME TAX	REAL ESTATE TRANSFER TAX	SITE VALUE TAX	LAND VALUE INCREMENT TAX
DESCRIPTION	Prices charged the consumers of various public services such as water and sewer charges or recreation program charges. Fees may include charge for capital facilities as well as operating costs.	Tax on the production or extraction of certain minerals. Colorado's oil and gas production is a form of severance tax. It is levied on gross incomes derived from the production of certain types of oil and gas from Colorado deposits.	Tax on the income of resident individuals, estates, and trusts and income of non-residents derived from local sources. Also would apply to the incomes of corporations located in or doing business in the local area.	Tax levied on the conveyance of real property. The tax is analogous to a sales tax on real property.	Ad valorem tax on assessed valuation of land but not improvements.	Tax imposed on the net gain in the value of a given parcel of land or land with improvements between two points in time.
LEGALITY	Legal for all types of local governments.	No existing authority for this tax. The General Assembly could enable such a tax at the state, regional, or local level.	A local income tax, levied by the General Assembly at the request of local political subdivisions, may be constitutional but unauthorized by statute.	Counties, statutory cities and towns, and special districts do not have express authority to levy a real estate transfer tax. The tax may be legal for home rule cities, but no court test has been made.	No authorization for statutory political subdivisions. May be legal for home rule cities. Does not appear to be prohibited by constitution.	Same as income tax.
ELASTICITY	Strongly inelastic with respect to inflation. Unit elastic with respect to population growth and real income growth.	Changes in revenue from severance taxes are not correlated with changes in local economic conditions.	Strongly elastic (range 1.3-2.0).	Generally elastic, yet subject to strong influence of money market conditions.	Same as property tax.	Highly elastic but subject to strong influence of money market conditions.
INCIDENCE	Paid by the beneficiary of the service or facility. User fees ignore citizens' ability to pay. User fees can insure growth pays its own way.	Mining companies faced with severance taxes attempt to pass them along to customers or their labor force. In tight labor markets, more taxes will be passed on to consumers, thus exported from the region.	Graduated income taxes (State of Colorado) are strongly progressive with respect to income. Corporate income taxes are exported by export base industries. Income taxes bear lightly on elderly and low income people.	Conditions in real estate markets determine tax incidence. In a soft buyers market, the seller will bear more tax burden than in a tight sellers market.	Landowners of all types. Less burden on occupants of high density residences.	Landowners in areas experiencing rapid increases in land values.

Source: Briscoe, Maphis, Murray, and Lamont, Inc., **Oil Shale Tax Lead Time Study**, prepared for Regional Development and Land Use Planning Subcommittee of the Governor's Committee on Oil Shale Environmental Problems, Denver, Colorado, 1974. This chart is a summary of Section 3 of that study. [Some elements of the chart have been omitted.—Eds.]

B. CONSTITUTIONAL LIMITATIONS

A major theme of this book is the limitations placed on state and local governments by the federal and state constitutions. We have already reviewed a number of important constitutional limitations. In this chapter, we focus specifically on limitations on the taxing and spending powers. Some state constitutions, such as Vermont's, have no grant or limitation of state taxing power of any kind. Constitutions of most states speak to the state taxing power and place limits on that power. Most at least provide that taxation must be uniform, a limitation that led some states to provide explicitly for state income taxation on the assumption that a graduated income tax would not be uniform throughout the state. An example of a specific grant-sounding constitutional provision is the old Nebraska Revenue art. IX, § 1 (1909):

> The Legislature shall provide such revenue as may be needful, by levying a tax by evaluation, so that every person and corporation shall pay a tax in proportion to the value of his, her or its property and franchises the value to be ascertained in such manner as the Legislature shall direct, and it shall have power to tax peddlers, auctioneers, brokers, hawkers, commission merchants, showmen, jugglers, innkeepers, liquor dealers, toll bridges, ferries, insurance, telegraph and express interests or business, venders of patents, in such manner as it shall direct by general law, uniform as to the classes upon which it operates.

This provision was construed in *Mercantile Incorporating Co. v. Junkin,* 123 N.W. 1055 (Neb. 1909). The Nebraska legislature enacted a statute requiring all corporations doing business in the state to obtain a state occupation permit and to pay an annual occupation fee. The court rejected the argument that "the enumeration of 16 occupations upon which the Legislature is authorized to impose an occupation tax 'by the universal rule of interpretation excludes by necessary implication all occupations not enumerated.'" *Id.* at 1055. It applied the limit-not-grant theory to hold that "in the absence of constitutional limitations, every species of property within the jurisdiction of the state, all privileges and franchises existing, and every trade or vocation exercised therein may be taxed by the Legislature for the support of the state." *Id., see also* Chapter 1, Section B3.

Illinois expressly adopted the limitation theory:

> The General Assembly has the exclusive power to raise revenue by law except as limited or otherwise provided in this Constitution.

Ill. Const. art. IX, § 1. This provision was given a broad interpretation along the intended lines in *Berry v. Costello,* 341 N.E.2d 709 (Ill. 1976), upholding a "privilege tax" on mobile homes. The constitution then adds a series of limitations on the state's taxing power. Some of these are framed in general terms, such as the uniformity provision:

> Section 2. In any law classifying the subjects or objects of non-property taxes or fees, the classes shall be reasonable and the subjects and objects within each class shall be taxed uniformly. Exemptions, deductions, credits, refunds and other allowances shall be reasonable.

Some limitations are more specific:

> Section 3(a). A tax on or measured by income shall be at a non-graduated rate. At any one time there may be no more than one such tax imposed by the State for State purposes on individuals and one such tax so imposed on corpora-

tions. In any such tax imposed upon corporations the rate shall not exceed the rate imposed on individuals by more than a ratio of 8 to 5.

Some state constitutions simply place limitations on the way in which state taxes shall be imposed:

No tax shall be levied except in pursuance of law; and every law imposing a tax shall state distinctly the object of the same to which only it shall be applied.

Wash. Const. art. 7, § 5. Some states have also imposed restrictive limitations on some forms of taxation. For example, some states have given constitutional status to their highway trust fund, providing that all motor vehicle and motor vehicle fuel taxes shall be used only for highway purposes. *See* Or. Const. art. IX, § 3.

Some of these more specific constitutional limitations address problems specific to the state. Thus Nebraska Const. art. VIII, § 1, provides that "[t]he Legislature may provide that livestock shall constitute a separate and distinct class of property for purposes of taxation."

1. DUE PROCESS AND EQUAL PROTECTION

Most litigation, other than questions of authority to enact by local governments (that is, enabling legislation or home rule grant), turns on broader limitations of state uniformity clauses, state or federal equal protection, due process and occasionally federal commerce clause or supremacy questions. The following case indicates that federal due process challenges to state and local taxes generally have been set to rest:

CITY OF PITTSBURGH v. ALCO PARKING CORP.

United States Supreme Court
417 U.S. 369 (1974)

MR. JUSTICE WHITE delivered the opinion of the Court.

The issue in this case is the validity under the Federal Constitution of Ordinance No. 704, which was enacted by the Pittsburgh, Pennsylvania, City Council in December 1969, and which placed a 20% tax on the gross receipts obtained from all transactions involving the parking or storing of a motor vehicle at a nonresidential parking place in return for a consideration. The ordinance superseded a 1968 ordinance imposing an identical tax, but at the rate of 15% which in turn followed a tax at the rate of 10% imposed by the city in 1962. Soon after its enactment, 12 operators of offstreet parking facilities located in the city sued to enjoin enforcement of the ordinance, alleging that it was invalid under the Equal Protection and Due Process Clauses of the Fourteenth Amendment, as well as Art. VIII, § 1, of the Pennsylvania Constitution, which requires that taxes shall be uniform upon the same class of subjects. It appears from the findings and the opinions in the state courts that, at the time of suit, there were approximately 24,300 parking spaces in the downtown area of the city, approximately 17,000 of which the respondents operated. Another 1,000 were in the hands of private operators not party to the suit. The balance of approximately 6,100 was owned by the Parking Authority of the city of Pittsburgh, an agency created pursuant to the Parking Authority Law of June 5, 1947, Pa. Stat. Ann., Tit. 53, § 341 *et seq.* (1974). The trial court also found that there was then a deficiency of 4,100 spaces in the downtown area.

The Court of Common Pleas sustained the ordinance. Its judgment was affirmed by the Commonwealth Court by a four-to-three vote, on rehearing, . . .;

but the Pennsylvania Supreme Court reversed, also four to three. 453 Pa. 245, 307 A.2d 841 (1973). That court rejected challenges to the ordinance under the Pennsylvania Constitution and the Equal Protection Clause, but invalidated the ordinance as an uncompensated taking of property contrary to the Due Process Clause of the Fourteenth Amendment. Because the decision appeared to be in conflict with the applicable decisions of this Court, we granted certiorari, 414 U.S. 1127 (1974), and we now reverse the judgment.

In the opinion of the Supreme Court of Pennsylvania, two aspects of the Pittsburgh ordinance combined to deprive the respondents of due process of law. First, the court thought the tax was "unreasonably high" and was responsible for the inability of nine of 14 different private parking lot operators to conduct their business at a profit and of the remainder to show more than marginal earnings. . . . Second, private operators of parking lots faced competition from the Parking Authority, a public agency enjoying tax exemption (although not necessarily from this tax) [3] and other advantages which enabled it to offer offstreet parking at lower rates than those charged by private operators. The average all-day rate for the public lots was $2 as compared with a $3 all-day rate for the private lots. *Ibid.* The court's conclusion was that "[w]here such an unfair competitive advantage accrues, generated by the use of public funds, to a local government at the expense of private property owners, without just compensation, a clear constitutional violation has occurred. . . ." "[T]he unreasonably burdensome 20 percent gross receipts tax, causing the majority of private parking lot operators to operate their businesses at a loss, in the special competitive circumstances of this case constitutes an unconstitutional taking of private property without due process of law in violation of the Fourteenth Amendment of the United States Constitution." *Id.,* . . . at 863, 864.

We cannot agree that these two considerations, either alone or together, are sufficient to invalidate the parking tax ordinance involved in this case. The claim that a particular tax is so unreasonably high and unduly burdensome as to deny due process is both familiar and recurring, but the Court has consistently refused either to undertake the task of passing on the "reasonableness" of a tax that otherwise is within the power of Congress or of state legislative authorities, or to hold that a tax is unconstitutional because it renders a business unprofitable.

In *Magnano Co. v. Hamilton,* 292 U.S. 40 (1934), the Court sustained against due process attack a state excise tax of 15¢ per pound on all butter substitutes sold in the State. Conceding that the "tax is so excessive that it may or will result in destroying the intrastate business of appellant," *id.,* at 45, the Court held that "the due process of law clause contained in the Fifth Amendment is not a limitation upon the taxing power conferred upon Congress," that no different

---

[3] The ordinance on its face applies to all nonresidential parking transactions. The following, however, appears in n. 9 of the opinion of the Pennsylvania Supreme Court, 453 Pa., at 265, 307 A.2d, at 862:

As of this writing, the Allegheny County Court of Common Pleas has ruled that the Public Parking Authority is exempt from payment of the challenged gross receipts tax. Public Parking Authority of Pittsburgh v. City of Pittsburgh, No. 687, July Term, 1972. . . . An appeal is presently pending before the Commonwealth Court.

However, whether the Public Parking Authority is subject to the tax seems to make little real difference in the context of this present dispute. Even if the Authority had to pay the tax to the City it would mean only in reality an accounting transaction, transferring dollars from one pocket of an instrumentality of City government to another. Thus although appellants' argument would be strengthened by the common pleas court's decision, we need not presently rest our decision upon Public Parking Authority of Pittsburgh v. City of Pittsburgh, supra.

rule should be applied to the States, and that a tax within the lawful power of a State should not "be judicially stricken down under the due process clause simply because its enforcement may or will result in restricting or even destroying particular occupations or businesses." *Id.,* at 44. The premise that a tax is invalid if so excessive as to bring about the destruction of a particular business, the Court said, had been "uniformly rejected as furnishing on juridical ground for striking down a taxing act." *Id.* at 47. *Veazie Bank v. Fenno,* 8 Wall. 533, 548 (1869); *McCray v. United States,* 195 U.S. 27 (1904); and *Alaska Fish Salting & By-Products Co. v. Smith,* 255 U.S. 44 (1921), are to the same effect.

In *Alaska Fish,* a tax on the manufacture of certain fish products was sustained, the Court saying, *id.,* at 48-49: "Even if the tax should destroy a business it would not be made invalid or require compensation upon that ground alone. Those who enter upon a business take that risk.... We know of no objection to exacting a discouraging rate as the alternative to giving up a business, when the legislature has the full power of taxation." ...

Neither the parties nor the Pennsylvania Supreme Court purports to differ with the foregoing principles. But the state court concluded that this was one of those "rare and special instances" recognized in *Magnano* and other cases where the Due Process Clause may be invoked because the taxing statute is "so arbitrary as to compel the conclusion that it does not involve an exertion of the taxing power, but constitutes, in substance and effect, the direct exertion of a different and forbidden power, as, for example, the confiscation of property." 292 U.S., at 44.

There are several difficulties with this position. The ordinance on its face recites that its purpose is "[t]o provide for the general revenue by imposing a tax ...," and in sustaining the ordinance against an equal protection challenge, the state court itself recognized that commercial parking lots are a proper subject for special taxation and that the city had decided, "not without reason, that commercial parking operations should be singled out for special taxation to *raise revenue* because of traffic related problems engendered by these operations." ... 307 A.2d at 858 (emphasis added).

It would have been difficult from any standpoint to have held that the ordinance was in no sense a revenue measure. The 20% tax concededly raised substantial sums of money; and even if the revenue collected had been insubstantial, *Sonzinsky v. United States,* 300 U.S. 506, 513-514 (1937), or the revenue purpose only secondary, *Hampton & Co. v. United States,* 276 U.S. 394, 411-413 (1928), we would not necessarily treat this exaction as anything but a tax entitled to the presumption of the validity accorded other taxes imposed by a State.

Rather than conclude that the 20% level was not a tax at all, the Pennsylvania court accepted it as such and merely concluded that it was so unreasonably high and burdensome that, in the context of competition by the city, the ordinance had the "effect" of an uncompensated taking of property.... 307 A.2d, at 864. The court did not hold a parking tax, as such, to be beyond the power of the city but it appeared to hold that a bona fide tax, if sufficiently burdensome, could be held invalid under the Fourteenth Amendment. This approach is contrary to the cases already cited, particularly to the oft-repeated principle that the judiciary should not infer a legislative attempt to exercise a forbidden power in the form of a seeming tax from the fact, alone, that the tax appears excessive or even so high as to threaten the existence of an occupation or business....

Nor are we convinced that the ordinance loses its character as a tax and may be stricken down as too burdensome under the Due Process Clause if the taxing authority, directly or through an instrumentality enjoying various forms of tax exemption, competes with the taxpayer in a manner thought to be unfair by the judiciary. This approach would demand not only that the judiciary undertake to separate those taxes that are too burdensome from those that are not, but also would require judicial oversight of the terms and circumstances under which the government or its tax-exempt instrumentalities may undertake to compete with the private sector. The clear teaching of prior cases is that this is not a task that the Due Process Clause demands of or permits to the judiciary. We are not now inclined to chart a different course.

In *Veazie Bank, supra,* a 10% tax on state bank notes was sustained over the objection of the dissenters that the purpose was to foster national banks, instrumentalities of the National Government, in preference to private banks chartered by the States. More directly in point is *Puget Sound Power & Light Co. v. Seattle,* 291 U.S. 619 (1934), where the city imposed a gross receipts tax on a power and light company and at the same time actively competed with that company in the business of furnishing power to consumers. The company's contention was that "constitutional limitations are transgressed ... because the tax affects a business with which the taxing sovereign is actively competing." *Id.,* at 623. Calling on prior cases in support, the Court rejected the contention, holding that "the Fourteenth Amendment does not prevent a city from conducting a public waterworks in competition with private business or preclude taxation of the private business to help its rival to succeed." *Id.,* at 626. See also *Madera Water Works v. Madera,* 228 U.S. 454 (1913). The holding in *Puget Sound* remains good law and, together with the other authorities to which we have already referred, it is sufficient to require reversal of the decision of the Pennsylvania Supreme Court.

Even assuming that an uncompensated and hence forbidden "taking" could be inferred from an unreasonably high tax in the context of competition from the taxing authority, we could not conclude that the Due Process Clause was violated in the circumstances of this case. It was urged by the city that the private operators would not suffer because they could and would pass the tax on to their customers, who, as a class, should pay more for the services of the city that they directly or indirectly utilize in connection with the special problems incident to the twice daily movement of large number of cars on the streets of the city and in and out of parking garages. The response of the Pennsylvania Supreme Court was that competition from the city prevented the private operators from raising their prices and recouping their losses by collecting the tax from their customers. On the record before us, this is not a convincing basis for concluding that the parking tax effected an unconstitutional taking of respondents' property. There are undisturbed findings in the record that there were 24,300 parking places in the downtown area, that there was an overall shortage of parking facilities, and that the public authority supplied only 6,100 parking spaces. Because these latter spaces were priced substantially under the private lots it would be anticipated that they would be preferred by those seeking parking in the downtown area. Insofar as this record reveals, for the 20% tax to have a destructive effect on private operators as compared with the situation immediately preceding its enactment, the damage would have to flow chiefly, not from those who preferred the cheaper public parking lots, but from those who could no longer afford an increased price for downtown parking at all. If this is the case, we simply have another instance where the government enacts a tax at a "discouraging rate as the alternative to giving up a business," a policy to which there is no constitutional objection. *Alaska Fish Salting & By-Products Co. v. Smith,* 255 U.S., at 49; *Magnano Co. v. Hamilton,* 292 U.S., at 46.

The parking tax ordinance recited that "[n]on-residential parking places for motor vehicles, by reason of the frequency rate of their use, the changing intensity of their use at various hours of the day, their location, their relationship to traffic congestion and other characteristics, present problems requiring municipal services and affect the public interest, differently from parking places accessory to the use and occupancy of residences." By enacting the tax, the city insisted that those providing and utilizing nonresidential parking facilities should pay more taxes to compensate the city for the problems incident to offstreet parking. The city was constitutionally entitled to put the automobile parker to the choice of using other transportation or paying the increased tax.

The judgment of the Pennsylvania Supreme Court is reversed.

. . . .

MR. JUSTICE POWELL, concurring.

The opinion of the Court fully explicates the issue presented here, and I am in accord with its resolution. I write briefly only to emphasize my understanding that today's decision does not foreclose the possibility that some combination of unreasonably burdensome taxation and direct competition by the taxing authority might amount to a taking of property without just compensation in violation of the Fifth and Fourteenth Amendments.

To some extent, private business is inevitably handicapped by direct governmental competition, but the opinion of the Court makes plain that the legitimate exercise of the taxing power is not to be restrained on this account. It is conceivable, however, that punitive taxation of a private industry and direct economic competition through a governmental entity enjoying special competitive advantages would effectively expropriate a private business for public profit. Such a combination of unreasonably burdensome taxation and public competition would be the functional equivalent of a governmental taking of private property for public use and would be subject to the constitutional requirement of just compensation. As the opinion of the Court clearly reveals, . . . no such circumstance has been shown to exist in the instant case.

Comments: 1. While leaving open the possibility that an application of the "special instances" rule might lead to the invalidation of a tax on due process grounds, the *Alco* case nevertheless reflects the usual reluctance of the Supreme Court to examine the constitutional basis for the exercise of taxation powers. There are exceptions:

> The Constitution of the United States grants certain basic rights which may not be interfered with or encroached upon by governmental activity. When the government imposes a tax which may impinge upon a substantive constitutional right, the courts have exhibited a greater willingness to look beyond the face of the tax to its actual effect. Illustrative of the scope of judicial review in these cases is the treatment the courts have given the taxation of the rights to freedom of religion, speech, and press embodied in the First Amendment. As to these rights, the courts have held that the imposition of a tax which serves to discourage their exercise directly is invalid.
>
> When a tax adversely affects a substantive constitutional right, the courts will invalidate it to the extent of the adverse effect. In *Marchetti v. United States,* [390 U.S. 39 (1968)] for example, the constitutionality of the tax on gambling was challenged as violative of the Fifth Amendment's prohibition against self-incrimination. This tax scheme required each person engaged in wagering to register with the district collector of revenue and to pay a tax. The revenue officers were then required to submit a registration list to any state or local prosecuting officer who requested it. The Supreme Court held that to the extent the accused was forced to incriminate himself, the tax was unconstitutional.

Note, *Constitutional Limitations on the Power to Tax: Alco Parking Corp. v. Pittsburgh,* 26 HASTINGS L.J. 215, 220-21 (1974).

The Court's willingness in *Alco* to allow the use of taxing powers that accomplish a regulatory purpose should be contrasted with the care with which courts examine direct delegations of regulatory power to municipalities, both in home rule and statutory grant states. Of course, all taxes have an incidental regulatory effect. Should courts consider invalidating taxes that are clearly passed only for a regulatory purpose? What would be the basis for such a ruling? How should such a distinction be made, if at all? Several criteria are suggested in the student note quoted above: A tax should be considered regulatory as the number of people subject to the tax increases; if the tax is not traditionally revenue-raising; if the tax is on businesses rather than people; if the revenue to be raised is excessive; and if the statement of purpose indicates that the tax is regulatory. *Id.* at 230. What kind of a tax would fit the regulatory mode?

Note that courts are also reluctant to review the excessiveness of a tax levy, at least in considering taxes other than special benefit taxes on property. This reluctance has been attributed to "the institutional inability of the judiciary to review the legislature's judgments on which the tax is based." *Id.* at 226. It will be of interest to consider why the judiciary considers itself more competent to review these questions in the special benefit taxation category.

2. *With Alco Parking compare Continental Bank & Trust Co. v. Farmington City,* 599 P.2d 1242 (Utah 1979). The city levied a two percent license tax against Lagoon, a large, and the only, amusement park within the city limits. The court invalidated the tax. It noted that Lagoon provided a number of services usually provided by municipalities. It also noted that the contribution of Lagoon to city revenues from a number of city taxes was considerable, and that Lagoon's proportionate share of city revenues had nearly doubled in the past five years. The court's rationale for striking down the tax was as follows:

> Closely related is the question of the oppressiveness of the licensing tax imposed by Farmington upon Lagoon. Whenever a class is singled out for taxation, the amount of which is unduly burdensome, the question of abuse of taxing power is raised. Evidence is uncontradicted that Lagoon operates on a low margin of profit, traditionally pays no dividends, and has recently indebted itself in the installation of Pioneer Village on the east end of the park. Despite these facts, Farmington has seen fit to impose a tax on gross receipts, which makes no provision for high overhead. Moreover, the license tax adds to an already stiff tax burden imposed on Lagoon. Were the license tax permitted to stand, Lagoon would sustain a staggering ten-fold increase in taxation since 1975. In none of the cases to which Farmington directs us, where a tax of 2 percent or more of gross income has been sustained, was such a tax load already in existence.
>
> We are not unmindful of the fact that the action of Farmington in this matter is entitled to broad deference by a reviewing court, nor of the fact that any legislative enactment is entitled to a presumption of constitutionality. As was stated by this Court in the case of *Salt Lake City v. Christensen Co.,* . . . "[w]here neither the Constitution nor the statute imposes absolute restrictions, the courts may not arbitrarily impose any unless it clearly appears that the tax imposed is oppressive, or clearly and unreasonably discriminatory, and thus is an abuse of the [tax paying] power." The conclusion is inescapable that a situation such as the one at hand, where a municipality imposes a potentially crippling tax on a single business for the benefit of the community as a whole, coupled with vague promises of improved services which the business has not been guaranteed, and to a large extent, does not need, presents such a case of abuse of taxing power. We therefore hold the Farmington license tax invalid.

Id. at 1246.

How does this opinion compare with the majority opinion in *Alco Parking*? The concurring opinion? Note that a license tax may be levied in Utah solely for revenue-raising purposes. Since this is so, was the concurring and dissenting opinion in the *Farmington* case justified when it commented that the tax does not "rise to any such level that it can be characterized as so oppressive and burdensome that the court can declare it to be confiscatory and therefore invalid." *Id.* at 1248. As in *Alco Parking,* why didn't the Utah court simply conclude that Lagoon could pass the license tax on to its customers? Note that the Lagoon amusement park had no competition.

3. In *Square Parking Systems, Inc. v. Jersey City Business Administrator,* 449 A.2d 559 (N.J.L. 1982), the court considered a city ordinance, similar to that in *Alco,* which exempted residential tenants of multiple dwelling units from a fifteen percent tax on parking fees. In upholding the tax against equal protection challenges, the court relied upon the Supreme Court's language in *Alco* to find a rational basis in the city's exclusion of residential tenants from the tax (although that was not the issue addressed by the Supreme Court). The city advanced four main arguments, in support of the tax and the exclusion: (a) raise revenue; (b) extract payment from nonresidents for city services such as road maintenace, fire and police protection, and emergency medical services; (c) relieve heavily taxed residents of an additional burden; and (d) administrative convenience. How persuasive is the argument that residents should be exempted because they already pay substantial real estate taxes?

The following case, which considers without really examining an equal protection objection to a local non-property tax, is typical of judicial approaches to these broader limitations on the taxing power.

HELTON v. CITY OF LONG BEACH
Court of Appeal of California
55 Cal. App. 3d 840, 127 Cal. Rptr. 737 (1976)

THOMPSON, ASSOCIATE JUSTICE.

This is an appeal from a judgment enjoining enforcement of Long Beach Ordinance C-5106 as amended by Ordinance C-5145. It raises the issue of the constitutionality of a city business license tax surcharge differing by region imposed to implement a municipal parking and business improvement area plan adopted pursuant to Streets and Highway Code sections 36000 et seq. We conclude that: (1) the validity of the surcharge must be determined by the "rational basis" rather than "suspect classification" test of equal protection; (2) that a legislative classification of businesses based upon a reasoned conclusion of anticipated benefits to be derived from a municipal project is a rational basis for differences in taxes; (3) the City of Long Beach has applied such a reasoned conclusion in the ordinances here involved; and (4) the ordinances, therefore, do not deny equal protection of the law and are valid. Accordingly, we reverse the judgment.

The California Parking and Business Improvement Area Law of 1965 was enacted "to authorize cities to impose a tax on businesses within a parking and business improvement area . . . in addition to the general business license tax, if any, in the city, and to use such proceeds for the following purposes: [¶] (a) The acquisition, construction or maintenance of parking facilities for the benefit of the area. [¶] (b) Decoration of any public place in the area. [¶] (c) Promotion of public events which are to take place on or in public places in the area. [¶] (d) Furnishing of music in any public place in the area. [¶] (e) The general promotion of retail trade activities in the area." (Sts. & Hy. Code, § 36000.)

City councils are authorized to designate parking and business improvement areas by following procedure prescribed by the act. (Sts. & Hy. Code, § 36020.) The statute provides that the municipality "may make a reasonable classification of businesses, giving consideration to various factors, including the degree of benefit received from parking only" in determining any additional tax to be imposed. (Sts. & Hy. Code, § 36040.) The special tax levied pursuant to the authority of The Parking and Business Improvement Area Law of 1965 must be used for the purposes of the areas established by the authority of the act. (Sts. & Hy. Code, § 36063.)

The City of Long Beach imposes a business license tax in the traditional form, classifying businesses by their specific type of activity and imposing tax upon them at varying amounts depending upon the classification. Long Beach adopted a parking and improvement area ordinance conforming to the procedural and substantive requirements of the state enabling legislation. The amended ordinance which encompasses the plan includes a special business license tax as permitted by the state law. The amount of the tax is determined by classification of business and "benefit zone." Two benefit zones, designated "Zone No. 1" and "Zone No. 2," are included within the parking and business improvement area. Zone 2 apparently encompasses an area surrounding a core segment consisting of Zone 1. Businesses are classified by their type of activity in classes "A" through "G." The rate of special parking and business improvement tax varies from one-fourth of the regular business license tax for class A businesses in Zone 1 to four times the regular business license tax for class F businesses in Zone 1. Class G businesses in Zone 1 pay a tax based upon gross receipts. Except for class A businesses in Zone 2, which are exempt from the tax, businesses in Zone 2 are taxed at one-half the rate of those in Zone 1. Long Beach businesses outside both Zones 1 and 2 are not subject to the tax.

Plaintiffs filed the action at bench seeking to enjoin the Long Beach parking and business improvement ordinances and contended that the taxing scheme denied them equal protection of the law. Concluding that "the imposition of greater license taxes upon businesses located in one area of the City than are imposed upon the same or similar businesses located in other parts of the City" violates equal protection of the law, the trial court permanently enjoined enforcement of the amended ordinance. This appeal followed.

"Two tests are applied ... in examining ... statutory classifications for violations of the constitutional guarantees of equal protection. In ordinary equal protection cases not involving suspect classifications or the alleged infringement of a fundamental interest, the classification is upheld if it bears a rational relationship to a legitimate state purpose. [Citations.] But if the statutory scheme imposes a suspect classification, such as one based on race [citations] or a classification which infringes on a fundamental interest, such as the right to pursue a lawful occupation [citations] or the right to vote [citations] the classification must be closely scrutinized and may be upheld only if it is necessary for the furtherance of a compelling state interest. [Citations.]" (*Weber v. City Council,* 9 Cal. 3d 950, 958-959, 109 Cal. Rptr. 553, 558, 513 P.2d 601, 606.)

Where a suspect classification or fundamental interest is not involved, "[a] legislative classification may satisfy the traditional equal protection test without being the most precise possible means of accomplishing its legislative purpose. Only a reasonable relationship to that purpose is required." (*Weber v. City Council, supra* ...). Legislative classifications drawn in a taxing scheme are subject to the "ordinary-traditional" test of equal protection.... The power of the legislative branch to classify for the purposes of taxation is a broad one....

A municipality may thus impose license taxes at different rates upon different classes of taxpayers so long as the classification is founded on a reasonable basis.... It may create subclasses of businesses engaged in the same type of activity for the purpose of imposing different rates of tax if the classification "is founded on natural, intrinsic, or fundamental distinctions which are reasonable in their relation to the object of the legislation ..." (*Fox, etc., Corp. v. City of Bakersfield,* 36 Cal. 2d 136, 142, 222 P.2d 879, 883) rather than on a fanciful difference or one designed to afford an advantage to local business competing with outsiders.

The classification drawn by Long Beach Ordinances C-5106 and C-5145, creating subclasses of businesses located in Zone 1, Zone 2, and outside the parking and business improvement area, is founded upon a natural and intrinsic distinction reasonable in relation to the objective of the ordinances. The purpose of the Parking and Business Improvement Law and ordinances enacted to implement it is to prevent flight of businesses from the core area of cities, to prevent further deterioration of the areas, and to rehabilitate the deteriorating business districts. (Stats. 1965, ch. 241, § 2, p. 1230.) The rehabilitative function necessarily improves the financial prospects of existing businesses within the rehabilitated area. Their prospects of improvement are related to the proximity to the improvements made by the municipality with the funds derived from the special taxes used to finance the project. In sum, the classification of businesses governing the differences in tax rates found by the trial court to deny equal protection of the law is based upon the prospects of economic benefit from the use of the tax funds to the businesses taxed. That is a rational basis and one particularly related to the purpose of the legislation.

We thus conclude that the ordinances here involved do not deny plaintiffs the equal protection of the law.

The judgment is reversed.

LILLIE, ACTING P.J., and HANSON, J., concur.

Comments: 1. Note that the municipality in this case might have proceeded by creating a "special benefit" district for the parking improvement and then levying a special benefit or special assessment tax to cover the cost of the improvements. Had it done so it would have been subject to the rules governing special benefit taxes, see *infra,* which look generally to the benefit conferred on the property as a justification for the assessment that is levied. The court was apparently willing to take the municipality on faith, nonetheless, and treat the tax on the terms under which it was enacted.

2. One of the anchors of equal protection jurisprudence is the requirement that, in those cases not involving suspect classifications or fundamental interests, the particular classification has some rational basis to it. In the principal case, what was the classification? Are you persuaded that the classification met the rational basis test? Does the court even discuss the test, or simply draw a conclusion?

2. PUBLIC PURPOSE

Some specific constitutional limitations do limit the taxing power. One of these, the public purpose doctrine, is either expressly included in state constitutions or is read in judicially by implication. The public purpose doctrine limits the purposes for which public funds may be spent. This doctrine, and a related constitutional limitation prohibiting the lending of credit to private entities, also limits the purposes for which public debt may be incurred.

WILSON v. CONNECTICUT PRODUCT DEVELOPMENT CORP.

Supreme Court of Connecticut
167 Conn. 111, 355 A.2d 72 (1974)

COTTER, ASSOCIATE JUSTICE.

The plaintiffs seek a declaratory judgment to determine the constitutionality of Public Act No. 248, adopted by the 1972 General Assembly, now chapter 581,

§§ 32-32 through 32-46 inclusive of the General Statutes. The plaintiffs bring this action in their capacity as citizens, residents, and taxpayers of Connecticut....

Under 1972 Public Acts, No. 248, the state may provide direct financial assistance to private enterprises for the development and exploitation of products and inventions in Connecticut. The act establishes a quasi-public instrumentality designated the "Connecticut Product Development Corporation" (hereinafter refered to as "corporation" or "C.P.D.C.") to implement its provisions. General Statutes § 32-35. Its purpose is "to stimulate and encourage the development of new products within Connecticut by the infusion of financial aid for invention and innovation in situations where such financial aid would not otherwise be reasonably available from commercial sources...." General Statutes § 32-39. The corporation determines on a case-by-case basis which applicants are eligible to receive financial assistance to develop qualifying products and projects after instituting a staff investigation and reviewing its report. General Statutes §§ 32-39, 32-40. The corporation's powers are enumerated in § 32-39, subsections (1) through (14) inclusive.

The creation of the C.P.D.C. resulted from proposals emanating from a study conducted by the governor's strike force for full employment. The strike force, authorized by executive order number 8 (November 16, 1971) was charged to prepare a legislative program that will facilitate full employment and economic development in Connecticut. In the summer of 1972, the strike force submitted an action plan designed to deal with what it described as "Connecticut's growing job crisis." The plan called for legislation creating seven wholly innovative programs to respond to the overall economic and employment problems facing Connecticut in the 1970's. The C.P.D.C. proposal was one of the recommended programs.

The act provides for funding by authorizing the state bond commission to issue bonds not exceeding an aggregate amount of ten million dollars to carry out its provisions. General Statutes § 32-41. The defendants Barnes Engineering Company and Kurtz Diecraft, Inc., applied to the C.P.D.C. for financial aid under the act; upon the application of the C.P.D.C., the defendant state bond commission authorized the issuance of bonds with which to provide the requested aid.

Upon a stipulation of facts by the parties, the superior court has reserved the matter for the advice of this court.

The plaintiffs have launched a constitutional attack upon the act. They claim, first, that contrary to the command of article first, § 1, of the Connecticut constitution that "no man or set of men are entitled to exclusive public emoluments or privileges from the community" it authorizes the use of public funds for a private benefit and not for a public purpose....

I

This court has long held that every presumption will be made in favor of the constitutionality of a legislative act.... Parties challenging the constitutionality of an act in a proceeding seeking declaratory relief have the burden of showing its invalidity beyond a reasonable doubt.... When the thrust of the challenge is that the act violates article first, § 1, of the state constitution, the plaintiffs have demonstrated such invalidity if they can show beyond a reasonable doubt that the legislation "directs the granting of an emolument or privilege to an individual or class without any purpose, expressed or apparent, to serve the public welfare thereby." *Warner v. Gabb,* 139 Conn. 310, 313, 93 A.2d 487, 488 . . . .

Confusion as to the precise meaning of such concepts as "public purpose" has often thwarted a quick determination of whether a plaintiff has met his burden in an attack upon a legislative act under article first, § 1. The modern trend, both in Connecticut and in other states with similar constitutional provisions, has been to expand and construe broadly the meaning of "public purpose." . . . As one court has stated, "[a] slide-rule definition to determine public purpose for all time cannot be formulated; the concept expands with the population, economy, scientific knowledge, and changing conditions." *Mitchell v. Financing Authority,* 273 N.C. 137, 144, 159 S.E.2d 745, 750. . . . Generally, if an act will promote the welfare of the state, it serves a public purpose. . . . In deciding whether an act serves such a purpose this court has traditionally vested the legislature with wide discretion and suggested that the latter's determination should not be reversed unless "manifestly and palpably incorrect." *Barnes v. New Haven, supra.* . . .[2]

The plaintiffs argue that any benefit to the public in the way of increased employment and tax revenue sought to be achieved through the creation and operation of the C.P.D.C. is too remote and speculative to survive what they believe to be the demands of article first, § 1. In support of this claim, they call attention to the fact that before the state can receive any return on the money it advances to finance the risk ventures contemplated by the act, those ventures must ultimately prove their success in the marketplace; yet they contend that such success is unlikely since the projects that are eligible for the state's assistance under the act are the kind which most businessmen would characterize as commercially unattractive. They also claim that although the act requires assurances by appellants that the benefits of increased employment and revenues remain in Connecticut, there is no statutory guarantee that such assurances will be enforced. Since the appropriation of public funds to support such projects will produce no direct benefit to the people of Connecticut, the plaintiffs conclude the act must fail as an "exclusive public emolument" lacking a genuine "public purpose" contrary to the requirements of article first, § 1.

The presence of a direct benefit to the state from the expenditure of public funds is a useful factor in aiding the court's determination of whether a legislative act serves a public purpose. . . . But other factors serve a similar function. This court has found that an act serves a public purpose under article first, § 1, when it "promote[s] the welfare" of the state; . . . or when the "principal reason" for the appropriation is to benefit the public. . . . "The test of public use is not how the use is furnished but rather the right of the public to receive and enjoy its benefit." *Barnes v. New Haven, supra.* . . . The governor's strike force for full employment and the legislature which followed its recommendations in enacting 1972 Public Acts, No. 248, believed that the capital program envisioned as operating under the auspices of the C.P.D.C. would stimulate business in Connecticut by promoting the development of new kinds of products, technologies,

---

[2] The legislative enactment need not "contain a specific statement of the public purpose sought to be achieved by it." Roan v. Connecticut Industrial Building Commission, 150 Conn. 333, 339, 189 A.2d 399, 402. Legislative findings, however, purporting to establish the existence of a public purpose should be considered when the text of the act itself incorporates these findings, as does General Statutes § 32-33. This is not to say, of course, that the legislature can, by mere fiat or finding, make "public" a truly "private" purpose so as to authorize an appropriation of public funds surreptitiously. Its findings and statements about what is or is not "public" cannot be binding upon the court. Lyman v. Adorno, 133 Conn. 511, 517, 52 A.2d 702.

and projects, which ordinarily do not attract conventional forms of financing. It was their considered opinion that the support of enterprises eligible for assistance under the act would result in an improved economy for the people of Connecticut by helping to keep new business in the state, to provide increased employment opportunities, and to establish a new source of public revenues. In claiming that the success of such enterprises is only "speculative," such that the ultimate benefits to be realized by the state are "remote," the plaintiffs merely dispute the business judgment of the legislature; they have not demonstrated that in exercising its judgment the general assembly violated the principle underlying the constitutional requirement that the act serve a public purpose. The strong presumption of the act's constitutionality will not be overcome simply because the plaintiffs' economic forecasts differ from those of the legislature. . . .

The plaintiffs' claim that the act unlawfully entitles a limited class of persons to "exclusive public emoluments" falls short of its mark for another reason. They rightly suggest that the danger against which article first, § 1, seeks to protect the people of Connecticut is the possibility that the legislature will indulge in uncontrolled "giveaways" of public monies to specific persons or classes of individuals. . . . Yet 1972 Public Acts, No. 248, counteracts this threat to the integrity of the public treasury. The act establishes a quasi-public corporation, the C.P.D.C., as a buffer between the legislature and the recipients of the financial support. The act seeks to benefit neither named individuals nor specific industries or enterprises, but, rather, types of projects, technologies, inventions, and products sponsored by persons whose assistance this corporation determines would most likely redound to the public good. The corporation is authorized to funnel out and withhold funds from those projects whose development it does not feel would fulfill the ultimate goals of the act, and it may enter into contractual arrangements or agreements whereby it may obtain rights from or in an invention or product, or proceeds in exchange for the granting of financial aid. In addition, the state bond commission acts as a further restraining influence. Section 32-41 of the General Statutes provides that only the bond commission may authorize the issuance of bonds to fund the application in accordance with the provisions of § 3-20. Section 3-20(g) of the General Statutes provides that the commission is empowered to authorize bonds whenever it "finds that the authorization of such bonds will be in the best interests of the state." These provisions in their totality comprise a system of barriers preventing any automatic flow of public funds to preferred persons or groups.

The plaintiffs have failed to sustain the burden of overcoming the presumption in favor of the act's constitutionality by showing beyond a reasonable doubt that it entitles successful applicants to exclusive public emoluments without any purpose to serve the public welfare thereby. . . .

Based upon the stipulated facts reserved for consideration by this court, we cannot find that the plaintiffs have sustained their burden of proving the unconstitutionality of 1972 Public Acts, No. 248. This is not to say, of course, that no remedies are available for any possible actions undertaken pursuant to the administration of the act, which may be unconstitutional or otherwise unlawful. But it is hardly necessary to point out that the act cannot be held invalid on the mere possibility that such actions will be taken. . . .

Comments: While the "emoluments" clause of the Connecticut state constitution is unusual, forty-five states have a related clause in their constitutions which typically provides that the credit of the state and its political subdivisions "shall not in any manner be given or loaned to or in aid of any individual, association or corporation." This limitation on taxing and spending arose out of the railroad scandals of the later nineteenth century. State legislatures authorized their municipalities to issue bonded debt in aid of railroad construction, and there were massive defaults when many of these enterprises failed. The so-called "lending of credit" provision was an attempt to foreclose this kind of public borrowing and spending.

The purpose of the "lending of credit" clause is detailed in Pinksy, *State Constitutional Limitations on Public Industrial Financing: An Historical and Economic Approach,* 111 U. Pa. L. Rev. 265, 280 (1963):

> The term "lending of credit," so popular in the nineteenth century but now relatively obsolete, is significant. A basic element of the railroad-aid schemes was the marketing of state and municipal obligations, without direct government control, by the corporation which was to receive the proceeds. The common pattern involved delivery to the railroad of governmental bonds payable to the corporation or bearer, either as a donation or in exchange for shares; the corporation in turn disposed of the bonds as it saw fit....
>
> In addition, there was practically no public control over the planning of the railroad project or over the actual expenditures of publicly contributed funds. These functions were completely delegated to private corporate officials. To phrase it more dramatically, but no less accurately, there was a total abdication of public responsibility.

Apparently the majority of state courts treat the public purpose and lending of credit limitations as fungible; the lending of credit objection is overcome if a public purpose is found. This approach to the issues is strenuously protested in Comment, *State Constitutional Provisions Prohibiting the Loaning of Credit to Private Enterprise — A Suggested Analysis,* 41 U. Colo. L. Rev. 135 (1969). The author of the comment suggests that the lending of credit provision was directed to a "critical problem" not subsumed within the public purpose limitation, and that analysis of the lending of credit issue should focus on the relationship of the parties, the nature and extent of the public funding commitment, and the classification of the transaction as a loan or a donation. *Id.* at 139, 140.

In *Common Cause v. State,* 455 A.2d 1 (Me. 1983), the court held that state borrowing for a port development project served a proper public purpose but rejected an argument that it violated a constitutional lending of credit provision. The court treated the lending of credit provision as a separate limitation but held that it was limited to cases in which the state agreed to provide surety for private debt.

Both the public purpose limitation and the lending of credit provision were intended as restrictions on state and local borrowing powers, and as a method of limiting public debt. These restrictions are often used to challenge projects in which public borrowing powers are utilized to secure funding for privately owned and operated projects in which there is nevertheless a distinct public interest. The next case illustrates this situation.

IDAHO WATER RESOURCE BOARD v. KRAMER

Supreme Court of Idaho
97 Idaho 535, 548 P.2d 35 (1976)

[This case was a challenge to a state statute authorizing joint ventures between the Board and private companies for the construction of a dam and hydroelectric power generating facility in the Grandview-Guffey Reach of the Snake River.

The statute is reproduced in full in the opinion. It authorized the Board to sell revenue bonds to finance the construction of the facility, and to enter into joint venture agreements with a privately owned electric utility under which the facility is to be leased to the utility, all revenues from the lease to be pledged to the retirement of the bonds. Any surplus revenues from the facility were to be held in the custody of the Board in a special development fund and used by the Board "in the development of water and related land resources" in the state. Any agreements authorizing a joint venture were to be submitted to an interim committee, apparently of the legislature, if one was appointed, and in any event were subject to veto by the legislature at its next regular session.

[The intervenor in this case, a private electric utility, proposed to enter into a joint venture with the Board pursuant to the statute under which the utility would reconstruct a dam and power plant and construct a new dam and power plant in the Grandview-Guffey Reach, pursuant to and in order partly to implement a comprehensive water, land and related resources plan for southwestern Idaho that had been prepared prior to 1969 by the United States Bureau of Reclamation. This joint venture followed the terms of the statute. The dams were to be constructed by the state Board and leased to the utility, which would make payments to the Board to cover the cost of constructing the dams. Power generating facilities at the dam sites were to be constructed, owned, and operated by the utility. Any surplus payments made to the Board were to be applied by it for future irrigation development. — Eds.]

Appellant next argues that [the statute], and the agreement, . . . constitute a violation of the due process clause provision of art. I, § 13 of the State Constitution because the proposed joint venture arrangement is not for a "public purpose." [Courts often assimilate the public purpose requirement to due process limitations. — Eds.] Appellant contends that this provision of the Constitution requires that any activity engaged in by the state be for some public purpose. In appellant's view, the proposed undertaking does not effectuate a public purpose because the state is being placed in a position of constructing dams for the sole purpose of leasing them to a privately owned and operated company, with no showing that the state must construct the dams and lease them to the intervenor in order to adequately provide for its inhabitants. We do not agree with this argument.

It is a fundamental constitutional limitation upon the powers of government that activities engaged in by the state, funded by tax revenues, must have primarily a public rather than a private purpose. A public purpose is an activity that serves to benefit the community as a whole and which is directly related to the functions of government. The development and conservation of the state's water resources has long been recognized as constituting a necessary public purpose. Such a public purpose is evident in this case.

In addition, the Legislature in enacting chapter 265, as amended declared:

> SECTION 1. The legislature finds and declares that the development of the Grandview-Guffy Reach of the Snake River by the Idaho water resource board is in the public interest and that it is a public purpose that the Idaho water resource board exercise the powers authorized in sections 2, 3, 4, 5 and 6 of this act to:
>
> (a) maximize the recreational potential, development of fish and wildlife habitat, and uses of the water resources of Idaho;
>
> (b) facilitate irrigation of the arid lands of Idaho by providing means of utilizing the water resources of Idaho; and

(c) by contributing to the development of necessary electrical energy for use in the Ada-Canyon County area of southwest Idaho, achieve economy in the generation of electricity through the use of water resources thereby meeting the future power needs of the state of Idaho and its inhabitants.

This declaration by the Legislature of public purpose is normally afforded great deference, although it is by no means binding or conclusive upon this Court. It will not be overturned, however, unless it is found to be arbitrary or unreasonable. We are not convinced that such is the situation in the present appeal.

Appellant next argues that the state in this proposed undertaking is loaning its "credit" to the intervenor, and that this is contrary to the prohibition contained in art. VIII, § 2 of the Idaho Constitution. Appellant places primary reliance upon this Court's decision in *Village of Moyie Springs, Idaho v. Aurora Mfg. Co.*[, 353 P.2d 767 (Idaho 1960). — Eds.] We believe appellant's reliance upon that case is misplaced.

Art. VIII, § 2 of the State Constitution provides in pertinent part:

> 2. *Loan of state's credit prohibited — Holding stock in corporation prohibited — Development of water power.* — The credit of the state shall not, in any manner, be given, or loaned to, or in aid of any individual, association, municipality or corporation; ....
>
> ....

In the case of *Engelking v. Investment Bd.,* [458 P.2d 213 (Idaho 1969). —Eds.] this Court construed art. VIII, § 2 of the State Constitution as follows:

> The word "credit" as used in this provision (art. VIII, § 2) implies the imposition of some new financial liability upon the State which in effect results in the creation of State debt for the benefit of private enterprises. This was the evil extended to be remedied by Idaho Const. art. 8 § 2, and similar provisions in other state constitutions.

The Court later on in the opinion added:

> The credit clause of Idaho Const. art. 8 § 2 is intended to preclude only State action which principally aims to aid various private schemes.

We have previously decided that no state "debt" or "liability" for the benefit of a private enterprise will be created by respondent's proposed bond issuance. On the contrary, the bonds themselves clearly show that the state is *not* placing its faith or credit behind their payment. The bonds are to be retired out of revenues generated from the project only. Under no circumstances can a tax be levied or public property be encumbered to help pay any part of the bond issue. Prospective bond purchasers are put on notice that they have no payment recourse against any public entity. Furthermore, not only is the proposed issuance of revenue bonds by respondent not a loaning of the state's credit, as that term has been interpreted, but the contemplated bond issue is not "... in aid of any ... corporation ..." within the meaning of that prohibition contained in art. VIII, § 2. The principal benefits of the project inure to the public. Any benefit to the intervenor is secondary and incidental. We therefore hold that the joint venture arrangement does not contravene the prohibition on the loaning of state credit expressed in art. VIII, § 2.

We do not believe the *Moyie Springs* case compels us to reach a contrary conclusion. There are significant distinctions between the facts of that case and the circumstances of the present appeal which make the *Moyie Springs* decision inapposite.

In *Moyie Springs,* at issue was a state statute which authorized municipalities to issue revenue bonds for the purpose of financing the cost of acquiring land and constructing facilities which were to be sold or leased to private enterprises. The village of Moyie Springs acting pursuant to this statute, passed an ordinance providing for the issuance of revenue bonds to defray its cost of acquiring a site, and constructing an industrial plant which it planned to lease to the Aurora Manufacturing Company for a term of thirty years. When Aurora Manufacturing Company questioned the legality of the proposed arrangement and refused to perform its part of the agreement, the village brought an action for a declaratory judgement, to adjudicate both the rights of the parties, and the constitutionality of the statute and ordinance.

This Court found both the statute and ordinance to be invalid. It ruled that the proposed revenue bond issue was violative of the constitutional restriction against a municipality loaning its credit in aid of a private corporation. In addition, the proposed venture was found to have only an incidental or indirect benefit to the public. In reaching its conclusion, the Court was particularly concerned with the spectre of a state or one of its subdivisions promoting, sponsoring or regulating one private commercial or industrial enterprise to the detriment of others in the field, and the effect such a dangerous precedent would have upon the free enterprise system:

> It is obvious that private enterprise, not so favored, could not compete with industries operating thereunder. If the state-favored industries were successfully managed, private enterprise would of necessity be forced out, and the state, through its municipalities, would increasingly become involved in promoting, sponsoring, regulating and controlling private business, and our free private enterprise economy would be replaced by socialism.

In the situation before us, there is no effort by the state to single out one private commercial or industrial enterprise in competition with several others in the field for preferential treatment or favored tax exemption status. Rather, what is involved is a joint cooperative effort between a state agency, and a public utility subject to state regulation, to enhance the production and availability of electrical power, essential to the welfare of all the citizenry of the state. The state is not proposing to engage in or sponsor a project traditionally left to the private domain, as was the situation in *Moyie Springs,* but instead is participating in an activity with a quasi-public entity, to produce a service necessary for the well being of the public. Unlike the *Moyie Springs* case, where the village sought to purchase the industrial land site and construct the entire facility for the private entity's commercial exploitation, here the state is only financing the cost of its part of the undertaking. The intervenor is responsible for financing the cost of the power generation facilities which it will use at the dam sites. In *Moyie Springs,* the state legislation pursuant to which the village was acting, authorized the municipalities to sell or otherwise dispose of any project upon such terms and conditions as it deemed advisable. There is no comparable provision in the enabling legislation providing for the Swan Falls-Guffey Project, nor is there any section in the agreement, as amended, which allows for the state's interest in the project to be sold or otherwise disposed of. For all of the above-mentioned reasons, we cannot agree with appellant's assertion that there is no real distinction between the present Swan Falls-Guffey Project and the project contemplated in *Moyie Springs.* We have carefully reviewed the additional authority cited by appellant from other jurisdictions and find them to be distinguishable.

Comments: 1. In the principal case, did the court find the public and private features of the project to be severable? Clearly, the construction of the dam was essential to the viability of the private power generating facility. Many courts will dismiss public purpose objections to this kind of project by holding the private benefit "incidental." Note also that, given the nature of the project, a company default on the dam payments does not affect the public interest as the dam remains in public ownership and available for the public purposes for which it was constructed. Thus, the public risk is minimized. Compare the industrial and commercial financing schemes discussed below. Those schemes force the courts to weigh less tangible public benefits against clearly private advantages.

2. In *State ex rel. Ohio City v. Samol,* 275 S.E.2d 2 (W. Va. 1980), the court faced a challenge to a West Virginia statute which authorized counties and municipalities to issue revenue bonds for commercial projects. The Ohio County Commission sought to compel its administrator to sign $1.575 million in revenue bonds to finance acquisition and expansion of a shopping plaza. The court upheld the bond issuance, finding that the project would serve the public purpose by providing an increase in employment opportunities and tax revenues.

In his concurring opinion, Chief Justice Neely pressed for a distinction between bond financing for commercial and industrial development.

> At the national level the distinction between industrial and commercial projects may not be distinct, but in state court the distinction is overwhelming. To analogize for a moment to international trade, one can say that industrial projects in West Virginia are designed to generate foreign exchange by providing export goods while commercial projects merely reallocate existing wealth. Not all commercial projects, of course, are so devoid of public purpose as to be invalid; parking garages and housing developments are examples of projects which are both in competition with private enterprise *and* serve a legitimate public goal. However, in order for government subsidization of any *commercial* project to be legitimate it is necessary to demonstrate that there is an unfulfilled need in the *project market* which has been determined by the political process to be so urgent that government support to the purveyors of the needed product is required to meet the demand. Traditionally housing, parking, and transportation have been included in this class. Employment (i. e., the production of wages) may also fulfill a "public purpose," when only state constitutional provisions are considered, but it is necessary to demonstrate that *total* employment is significantly increased. I have no quarrel with the general proposition that government may elect to use private enterprise to meet public needs, but the key there is the "public needs" requirement.

Id. at 6.

3. The origins of the public purpose and lending of credit provisions in a desire to limit public debt generally have exempted private projects constructed with the proceeds from revenue bonds from these limitations. See *Basehore v. Hampden Industrial Development Authority,* 248 A.2d 212 (Pa. 1968). Contra, *State ex rel. Beck v. City of York,* 82 N.W.2d 269 (Neb. 1957); *Anderson v. Baehr,* 217 S.E.2d 43 (S.C. 1975). A similar position has been taken in the interpretation of state constitutional limitations on the amount of debt that can be incurred at the local level. *See infra.* While revenue bonds are payable solely from the proceeds of the project, a default may nevertheless still affect the general credit position of the municipality.

For further discussion of the public purpose issue in bond financing see *City of Urbana v. Paley,* 368 N.E.2d 915 (Ill. 1977) (holding that the city's urban redevelopment plan satisfied the public purpose doctrine and that the issuance of bonds to finance the program did not constitute an objectionable loan of credit to private parties); *State ex rel. Taft v. Campanella,* 364 N.E.2d 21 (Ohio 1977) (holding that the use of over ten million dollars in hospital improvement revenue bonds to retire the outstanding debt of a hospital did not violate the public purpose doctrine); *State ex rel. Jardon v. Industrial Development Authority,* 570 S.W.2d 666 (Mo. 1978) (holding that revenue bonds issued by industrial development authorities for commercial and industrial use served a public purpose and that the issuance of the bonds did not violate the prohibition against lending public credit).

4. Public purpose arguments often turn on competing philosophies of government spending. Should government spending be limited to programs and projects that affect all of the public, such as public buildings and public safety? Should the test be public use or public benefit? A majority of the public? Some of the public? Who are the appropriate recipients of government largess?

In *Hughey v. Cloninger,* 245 S.E.2d 543 (N.C. 1978), the court saw the end (education) as serving a public purpose but concluded that the means chosen (appropriations to private entities) did not meet the test. Does this mean that all appropriations to private entities are per se unconstitutional?

Commentators disagree on whether useful criteria may be specified to determine whether or not the public purpose test has been satisfied. One author lists several factors to be used to determine whether a proposed expenditure meets the public purpose test: Prior characterization of the expenditure by the courts; legislative or voter approval; general economic benefit; competition with private enterprise; number of beneficiaries; and necessity because of infeasibility of private performance. Van Wert, *Determining Permissive Municipal Expenditures: The Public Purpose Doctrine Revived,* 7 U. MICH. J.L. REF. 225, 227-32 (1973). *Compare* Note, *State Constitutional Limitations on a Municipality's Power to Appropriate Funds or Extend Credit to Individuals and Associations,* 108 U. PA. L. REV. 95, 96 (1959): "In any case, few objective, relatively measurable standards — economic feasibility, number of persons benefited, necessity for government action — are available for determining the proper scope of municipal power to use public funds."

3. THE COMMERCE CLAUSE

The commerce clause of the United States Constitution is an additional limitation on state-local taxing powers. An example may be found in the Supreme Court's approach to the common state desire to force nonresidents to contribute to state revenues through a variety of taxes. Severance taxes, general sales and use taxes, net income taxes and property taxes are examples of typical state efforts to export a portion of their tax burden to nonresidents. In addition to due process problems of apportionability discussed in *Mobil Oil Corp. v. Commissioner of Taxes,* 445 U.S. 425 (1981), upholding Vermont's decision to include Mobil's "foreign source" dividend income from subsidiaries and affiliates doing business abroad in calculating Mobil's apportionable Vermont income tax, the Court has examined tax exportation schemes under the commerce clause.

In *Commonwealth Edison Co. v. Montana,* 453 U.S. 609 (1981), the Court held that a Montana coal severance tax, which was as high as thirty percent of the contract sales price, did not impose a discriminatory burden on interstate commerce even though ninety percent of the coal was shipped to out-of-state purchasers. The Court declared that there is

> no real discrimination in this case; the tax burden is borne according to the amount of coal consumed and not according to any distinction between in-state and out-of-state consumers. Rather, appellants assume that the Commerce Clause gives residents of one State a right of access at "reasonable" prices to resources located in another State that is richly endowed with such resources, without regard to whether and on what terms residents of the resource-rich State have access to the resources. We are not convinced that the Commerce Clause, of its own force, gives the residents of one State the right to control in this fashion the terms of resource development and depletion in a sister State.

Id. at 619.

Mobil and *Commonwealth Edison* suggest that the present attitude of the Court toward state tax exportation is permissive. Has the Court contracted the scope of commerce clause protection by reducing the constitutional limitations on state taxing powers? For a more detailed discussion of recent Court decisions in this area see Golden, *The Constitutionality of State Taxation of Energy Resources,* 46 ALB. L. REV. 805 (1982); Hellerstein, *Constitutional Limitations on State Tax Exportation,* 1 AM. B. FOUND. RESEARCH J. 1 (1982); DuMars, *Evaluating Congressional Limits on a State's Severance Tax Equity Interest in Its Natural Resources: An Essential Responsibility for the Supreme Court,* 22 NAT. RESOURCES J. 673 (1982); Note, *Commonwealth Edison Co. v. Montana,* 10 ECOLOGY L.Q. 97 (1982). The DuMars article is part of a valuable symposium on the Taxation of Natural Resources.

Comment: In the 1982 term, the Supreme Court again faced the due process problem of apportionability discussed in *Mobil Oil.* In *ASARCO, Inc. v. Idaho State Tax Commission,* 102 S. Ct. 3103 (1982), the Court held that the due process clause prohibited Idaho from including dividends and interest that ASARCO had received from its subsidiaries in apportioning ASARCO's Idaho tax. In *F.W. Woolworth Co. v. Taxation & Revenue Department,* 102 S. Ct. 3128 (1982), the Court again found that dividends received from subsidiaries could not be included in the parent company's apportionable tax basis without violating the due process clause. For a discussion of the *ASARCO* and *Woolworth* cases see Hellerstein, *State Income Taxation of Multijurisdictional Corporations, Part II: Reflections on ASARCO and Woolworth,* 81 MICH. L. REV. 157 (1982).

C. REVENUES

1. THE GENERAL AD VALOREM PROPERTY TAX

Numerous studies have noted the decline of the property tax as a percent of personal income and total state and local government taxes. The following table illustrates graphically the shifts in sources of municipal revenue over the past twenty-five years:

The Shifting Significance of Municipal Finance Sources[1]

1957-77 vs. 1977-80

FEDERAL AID	Rising Rapidly (from 1.0% to 24.2%)	Falling Slowly (from 24.2% to 22.8%)
STATE AID	Rising Rapidly (from 19.8% to 38.5%)	Falling Moderately (from 38.5% to 33.4%)
PROPERTY TAX	Falling Steadily (from 57.1% to 42.7%)	Falling Sharply (from 42.7% to 35.3%)
NON-PROPERTY TAXES	Rising Steadily (from 21.4% to 28.5%)	Rising Moderately (from 28.5% to 30.1%)
USER CHARGES	Rising Steadily (from 12.7% to 18.6%)	Rising Rapidly (from 18.6% to 20.7%)
SPECIAL ASSESSMENT	Falling Steadily (from 2.9% to 1.4%)	Holding Steady (from 1.4% to 1.5%)

---

[1] The totals exceed 100% because all components are expressed as percent of own-source municipal revenues.

Source: Cline & Shannon, Municipal Revenue Behavior After Proposition 13, Intergovernmental Perspective, Vol. 8, No. 3, at 22, 23 (1982).

| OTHER MISCELLANEOUS REVENUES | Rising Slowly (from 6.0% to 8.8%) | Rising Sharply (from 8.8% to 12.4%) |

Why, then, is the tax still so controversial (Proposition 13 and school finance reform are but two examples)? Professor Bahl, in an excellent monograph, PROPERTY TAXATION IN THE 1980s (Lincoln Institute of Land Policy, 1979), argues that the property tax, while continuing to decline in relative importance, will remain in the forefront of fiscal issues because it is still the most important local government revenue source and the actual dollar amount raised by the property tax continues to increase.

Property Tax Trends
1962, 1970, 1977

	1962	1970	1977	Percent Change 1962-70	1970-77
Property Taxes as a percent of personal income	4.3	4.3	4.1	-1.6	-3.8
Property Taxes as a percent of total State and Local Government Taxes	45.9	39.2	35.6	-14.4	-9.4
PerCapita Property Tax revenues (current dollars)	102.54	167.09	289.07	63.0	73.0
Per Capita Property Tax revenues (in real 1972 dollars)	145.34	182.89	204.17	25.8	11.6

Id. at 1.

H. AARON, WHO PAYS THE PROPERTY TAX?, 6-17 (1975)*

One can imagine a perfectly uniform national property tax, levied periodically on the value of all property in existence. It would fall on land, including natural resources, structures, machinery, consumer durables and nondurables, business inventories, government bonds, and cash. To avoid double counting, it would exclude stocks and corporate bonds, since these pieces of paper represent claims on tangible assets that are already taxed. Such a base would come close to matching what economists have in mind by the term "capital." To levy such a tax at an equal ad valorem rate would require ascertaining the market value of all assets and setting the nominal tax equal to the product of the effective tax rate and market value. In practice the property tax is not so neat. First, all states exempt some real property from taxation because it is owned by governments, or by religious, nonprofit, philanthropic, or educational organizations. However, the breadth of these exemptions varies, and an organization or person whose real property in one jurisdiction is exempt may be taxed on some or all of it in another. Second, the effort to tax business property other than land and struc-

---

* Copyright © 1975 by the Brookings Institution, Washington, D.C. Reprinted by permission.

tures differs widely. An increasing number of states exempt part or all of business inventories. In some states new plants are exempt, often for ten years or more, and in some so is property used to abate or control pollution. Third, the market value of property used by railroads and other utilities, banks, and mines is particularly hard to ascertain. Taxes on these properties are handled differently in the various states and are often calculated by methods different from those applied to other real properties. Fourth, the coverage of personal tangible and intangible property differs widely among the states. Only [a few] states claim to tax personal property (including motor vehicles) of households, businesses, and agriculture in full at normal rates. All others fully or partially exempt one or more of these classes of property. Some jurisdictions claim authority to tax intangible property such as stocks, bonds, and cash. Finally, tax rates vary widely, from less than 1 percent of market value to 5 percent or more. Beyond all this, the procedures used in assessing property and the efficiency with which they are applied differ widely, so that the accuracy of appraisals is uneven. Thus, the ratio of tax to market value varies widely across and within jurisdictions.

As a result of such variations in law and administration, the property tax is far from uniform. In practice, it is very nearly a tax on real property only: 86 percent of the assessed value of locally assessed property is real estate. Not all real property is covered, however; perhaps one-third is exempt.

Trends in Property Tax Collections

Before World War II, the property tax had the largest yield of any tax in the United States. In 1934 its proceeds were more than double those of all other state and local taxes combined and exceeded total receipts of the federal government. The subsequent growth of the federal and state governments, both of which relied on other taxes, reduced the importance of the property tax relative to other sources of revenue. As a fraction of gross national product, property tax collections fell from just under 5 percent during the 1920s to 2.6 percent in 1950.
....

The foregoing statistics [omitted — Eds.] make several points. First, property tax collections are an important indicator of the relative importance of local government and, more specifically, of local responsibility for education. While logic does not require that local governments depend on property taxes or that all property taxes flow to local governments, any major shift in responsibilities for public education to higher governmental levels would probably signal the relative decline of property taxes. Second, less property taxation means more of other taxes or fewer public expenditures or both. Third, property taxes have become less important in state and local finance at the same time that they have maintained their position in the national revenue system and grown relative to national product. The stabilization of the school-age population and the possibility of absolute declines make it extremely likely that the relative importance of the property tax will drop from the peaks reached around 1970 until at least the early 1980s.

Administration

The impact of the property tax depends on the vagaries of administration more than does that of any other tax.... [T]he property tax is levied on estimated values, not on values reported in actual sales; consequently, changes in property values lead to changes in property tax liabilities only after an assessor changes his estimate of taxable value, a process that may occur virtually instantly or only after decades. Furthermore, effective rates and coverage differ widely not only among, but within, states.

The conventional measures of administrative efficiency are based on the ratio of assessed values, used for apportioning property taxes, to market values, expressed in prices of arm's-length sales. If the ratio of assessed values to market prices is uniform within a taxing jurisdiction, the effective tax rate will be the same on all properties. . . .

. . . [A]ctual administration falls far short of both the ideal and the achievable. The most commonly used index of nonuniformity is the "coefficient of intra-area dispersion." This statistic is equal to the average percentage difference between the assessment-sales ratio of each property and the median assessment-sales ratio in the jurisdiction. It is not the only possible measure, but, as the one most commonly reported in ratio studies, it will be used here.

Official statistics suggest that property tax administration in the United States, as measured by coefficients of dispersion, improved sharply between 1956 and 1966, but not since then. . . . Roughly half of all jurisdictions had "acceptable" administration by these standards in 1971, though only one in sixteen (and even fewer of large jurisdictions) had "excellent" administration. At the other extreme, large numbers of jurisdictions had atrocious administration, as measured by coefficients of dispersion. . . .

Since administrative inaccuracy has greater consequences when tax rates are high than when they are low, it is reassuring that jurisdictions with high property taxes tend to administer them somewhat more equitably than do jurisdictions with low tax rates.

Comment: As Aaron suggests, there are wide regional variations in the extent to which local governments rely on the property tax as a source of revenue. Property taxes provide less than one third of total local general revenues in the South Atlantic and South Central states. In the North Central states, property taxes provide one half and in the New England states about two thirds of all local general revenues. Since some local general revenue comes from non-tax sources, the share of total tax collections represented by the property taxes is usually higher than these figures indicate. For example, in the New England and North Central states property taxes make up more than ninety-five percent of all local tax revenues. *See* L. MOAK & A. HILLHOUSE, CONCEPTS AND PRACTICES IN LOCAL GOVERNMENT FINANCE 122-24 (1974).

R. NETZER, IMPACT OF THE PROPERTY TAX: ITS ECONOMIC IMPLICATIONS FOR URBAN PROBLEMS 30, 31 (Research Rep. No. 1, National Commission on Urban Problems, 1968)

Urban Development and Land Use

The argument thus far is that the property tax does have one important class of effects on urban development and land use; by reducing consumer demand for housing in central cities, it tends to retard central city rebuilding and may very well make surburban areas appear relatively more attractive for households in a position to choose suburban residential locations as an alternative to central city locations....

Central City Economics

There has been much discussion of the effects of taxes on the location of economic activity in recent years. Most analysts have come up with negative findings, to the effect that State-local tax differentials have little impact on location, largely because tax differentials are so small, relative to the differentials in other costs of doing business, expecially labor and transport costs.

However, most such studies have been done on a statewide or inter-regional basis, using States or regions as the units of observation. Nontax costs do differ greatly among widely separated locations, so the usual findings are not surprising. But within a single metropolitan area, nontax cost factors are likely to differ only slightly; indeed, in some cases, local taxes may be the only costs of doing business which differ among alternative locations. An analysis of tax differentials for manufacturing in the New York area in the late 1950's indicated very large differentials in State-local tax burdens, with the older central cities having markedly unfavorable positions. A more recent study of New York City's finances provides fairly clear evidence that these major business tax differentials actually have stimulated decentralization of economic activity away from the central city.

Moreover, if the tax differentials are unfavorable to central city locations, this reinforces rather than works against the powerful economic forces making for decentralization of economic activity from central cities to suburbs. The central cities have been losing out relatively (and in some cases absolutely) with respect to manufacturing and wholesale distribution of goods and with respect to population-serving activities (which follow population out to the suburbs). Tax differentials may trigger decisions to move away from the central city which might have occurred in any case, but at a later date. But this acceleration of locational shifts is a loss to the central cities.

Of course, not all economic activities are equally susceptible to tax differentials. For one thing, some kinds of activities have heavy requirements for special types of public services, which higher central city taxes may buy. Then, too, there will be no effect on location if the tax disadvantages do not exceed the special advantages of central city locations — for example, for corporate headquarters in large-city central business districts — or if there is no choice at all, typically the case for banks, public utilities and newspapers.

Are actual property taxes on business property enough higher in central cities so that they do in fact stimulate or contribute to migration of economic activity from central cities to the outlying parts of metropolitan areas? It is difficult to assemble conclusive evidence on this, but there is some fragmentary evidence which supports a positive answer to the question.

[Netzer's data indicates that property tax rates are generally higher in central cities than in their neighboring suburban areas. — Eds.]

Comment: For additional literature on the property tax see N. GOLD, PROPERTY TAX RELIEF (1979); INTERNATIONAL CITY MANAGEMENT ASS'N, MANAGEMENT POLICIES IN LOCAL

GOVERNMENT FINANCE ch. 6 (1981); PROPERTY TAXATION USA (R. Lindholm ed. 1967); THE PROPERTY TAX AND ITS ADMINISTRATION (A. Lynn ed. 1969); PROPERTY TAX REFORM (G. Peterson ed. 1973).

a. Fractional Assessments

State constitutional provisions requiring uniformity of taxation vary, and the uniformity required in any state will depend on the wording of the constitutional provision. The materials that follow concentrate especially on uniformity within geographic jurisdictions, and on uniformity of taxation among different types of property.

The language of constitutional uniformity provisions is summarized in Matthews, *The Function of Constitutional Provisions Requiring Uniformity in Taxation,* 38 KY. L.J. 31, 54-55 (1949):

> On the face of the constitutional provisions the major differences in phraseology occur in the modifiers which describe the system of taxation required, or how taxes must be levied. The terms used include uniform, uniform rule, uniform rate, levied according to value, and assessed in proportion to value.... Many provisions combine the descriptive terms used in a single clause, and also have different modifiers in different clauses.

Examples of constitutional uniformity clauses follow:

MAINE CONST. ART. IX, § 8.

All taxes upon real and personal estate, assessed by authority of this State, shall be apportioned and assessed equally, according to the just value thereof. [The constitution then authorizes the valuation of certain lands, such as farm and agricultural lands, "in accordance with a valuation based upon the current use thereof."]

ARIZONA CONST. ART. IX. § 1.

All taxes shall be uniform upon the same class of property within the territorial limits of the authority levying the tax . . . .

INDIANA CONST. ART. 10, § 1(a).

The General Assembly shall provide, by law, for a uniform and equal rate of property assessment and taxation and shall prescribe regulations to secure a just valuation for taxation of all property, both real and personal. [Specific exemptions from property taxation are then authorized.]

For a comprehensive review of the uniformity question see W. NEWHOUSE, CONSTITUTIONAL UNIFORMITY AND EQUALITY IN STATE TAXATION (1959). *See also* M. BERNARD, CONSTITUTIONS, TAXATION AND LAND POLICY (1979).

HELLERSTEIN v. ASSESSOR OF ISLIP

Court of Appeals of New York
37 N.Y.2d 1, 332 N.E.2d 279 (1975)
Noted, 27 SYRACUSE L. REV. 1045 (1976)

WACHTLER, JUDGE.

Petitioner, an owner of real property located on Fire Island, claims that the entire assessment roll for the Town of Islip is void. The argument has been raised in a proceeding instituted pursuant to article 7 of the Real Property Tax Law Consol. Laws, c. 50a, which permits court review of an assessment upon a complaint of illegality, overvaluation or inequality (see Real Property Tax Law, § 706). There is no claim of overvaluation or unequal treatment in the assessment of petitioner's property. She argues only that the assessments are illegal because they were not made in accordance with section 306 of the Real Property Tax Law which states: "All real property in each assessing unit shall be assessed at the full value thereof." This, we have held, means market value, unless that cannot be established "and then other tests of full value must be used." (*People ex rel. Parklin Operating Corp. v. Miller,* 287 N.Y. 126, 129, 38 N.E.2d 465, 466.) Here it is conceded that all assessments throughout the township are based on a *percentage* of market value.

The Supreme Court, Suffolk County, in an opinion, dismissed the petition. The Appellate Division, Second Department, affirmed, without opinion. Justices Hopkins and Latham concurred on constraint of *McAlevey v. Williams,* 41 A.D.2d 971, 344 N.Y.S.2d 193 but cited cases from other States in which the highest court has held that "full value," or similar language, prohibits fractional assessments. The case has come to our court by leave of the Appellate Division.

Section 306 of the Real Property Tax Law has an ancient lineage. [The court then discusses the origins of this statutory requirement. — Eds.]

Although the statute is one of the oldest in the State there does not appear to be any extant legislative history indicating what the full value requirement was intended to accomplish. And despite the fact that the custom of fractional assessments appears to be at least as old as the statute (see Kilmer, Legal Requirements for Equality in Tax Assessments, 25 Albany L. Rev. 203, 210), it has prompted very little litigation. In several of the older cases the problem can be seen lurking in the background; but it is only during the last 10 years that we find the practice being directly challenged in the courts. [The court then discusses early New York cases in which the practice of fractional assessment was criticized. — Eds.]

In the case now before us, the lower courts made no reference to these early decisions. They relied instead on *C. H. O. B. Assoc. v. Board of Assessors of County of Nassau,* 257 N.Y.S.2d 31, affd. . . . 256 N.Y.S.2d 550, affd. 209 N.E.2d 820 and its progeny. . . . In *C. H. O. B.,* the trial court stated: "Section 306 provides that all real property shall be assessed at full value thereof. Although full value has been held to be synonymous with market value . . . the courts have uniformly held that this section does not mandate assessments at 100% of full or market value. It requires merely that the assessments be at a uniform rate or percentage of full or market value for every type of property in the assessing unit. . . . The Legislature through Section 720(3) of the Real Property Tax Law has acknowledged and apparently sanctioned this statewide practice."

When the case reached our court in 1965, we affirmed without opinion . . . . Thus the custom of fractional assessments, once roundly condemned as a flagrant violation of the statute, has endured and acquired a new life through a kind of legislation by violation.

The *C. H. O. B.* decision assumes that fractional assessment is an ancient custom, never before challenged, which has, over the years, acquired recognition and, by implication, legal status from the courts and the Legislature. As the township notes, it involves two basic arguments: (1) By holding in "numerous cases" that "assessments [must] be at a uniform rate or percentage of full or market value for every type of property in the assessing unit" we have decided, *sub silentio,* "[that] Section 306 does not mandate assessments at 100% of full or market value" and thus fractional assessments are legal; (2) by establishing the State Board of Equalization the Legislature has indicated that section 306 of the Real Property Tax Law does not require assessment at 100% of market or full value but only that assessments be made at a uniform percentage of full value for every type of property within the assessing unit. Neither argument bears up under close analysis.

Regarding the first point we note that historically an assessment which was at or below full value, but above the average rate, presented a dilemma to the courts. On the one hand there was a rather obvious violation of equal protection. But on the other hand the requirements of the statute had been met and if the court ordered a reduction from full value, it would be compelling the assessors to "do an unlawful act" . . . . Thus many courts "held themselves precluded by the letter of the law from doing more than advise the complainant that he had the theoretically satisfactory privilege of suing out a writ of mandamus to compel the assessors to revalue every other piece of property in the jurisdiction" (1 Bonbright, Valuation of Property, p. 501).

The Supreme Court felt that this approach denied the taxpayer an effective remedy. They put an end to the practice and resolved the dilemma, by holding that "where it is impossible to secure both the standard of the true value, and the uniformity and equality required by law, the latter requirement is to be preferred" (*Sioux City Bridge Co. v. Dakota County,* 260 U.S. 441, 446 . . .). Now that the courts have been forced to choose equality over the full value standard — when it appears that one or the other must be violated — the respondent draws the type of conclusion the courts originally sought to avoid.

Viewed against this background it is obvious that these inequality decisions, reducing assessments to the uniform rate, are not premised on the legality of fractional assessments . . . and it is ironic that the township has inferred that they are.

. . . .

One of the most peculiar aspects of the township's case is the narrowness of their defense of the practice of fractional assessments. They are satisfied to rest on the theory "thus it has been, thus it always must be," without making any effort to explain how the custom began, whether it serves any useful purpose, and what would happen if the assessors complied, or were made to comply, with the strict letter of the law. Our own cases do not discuss these points; but they have been extensively reviewed and debated by scholarly commentators and by the courts in other jurisdictions.

The vast majority of States require assessors, either by statute or constitutional prescription, to assess at full value, true value, market value or some equivalent standard. (See Note, 68 Yale L.J. 335-387.) Two States have expressly provided by statute that this requires assessment at 100% of value (see 13 Ariz. Rev. Stat. Ann., § 42-227; California Revenue & Taxation Code, §§ 401, 408). Several States have specifically authorized fractional assessments, and this seems to be the modern trend. In 1917 there were four States in this latter category (*see Greene v. Louisville Interurban R.R. Co.,* 244 U.S. 499, 516 . . .); by 1958 there were eight (see Note, 68 Yale L.J. 335, 387); and, as of 1962 15 States had enacted legislation providing for fractional assessments, either at a fixed percentage or according to local option (Note, 75 Harvard L. Rev., 1374, 1377, n. 28).

Where full value is required, the standard has been almost universally disregarded. A 1957 study by the United States Census Bureau placed the average assessment ratio in the country at 30% of actual value (see Bird, The General Property Tax: Findings of the 1957 Census of Governments 40).

No one seems to know exactly how the practice of fractional assessment began. In an early case the Supreme Court suggested that: "If we look for the reason for this common consent to substitute a custom for the positive rule of the statute, it will probably be found in the difficulty of subjecting personal property, and especially invested capital, to the inspection of the assessor and the grasp of the collector. The effort of the land-owner, whose property lies open to view, which can be subjected to the lien of a tax not to be escaped by removal, or hiding, to produce something like actual equality of burden by an underevaluation of his land, has led to this result" (*Cummings v. National Bank,* 101 U.S. 153, 163 . . .).

This may well explain the origin of the rule, but it does not account for its remarkable powers of endurance, especially in a State like New York, which has removed personal property from the tax rolls (Real Property Tax Law, § 300). Its survival depends on other factors none of which are particularly commendable.

Bonbright, in his treatise *(op. cit.),* lists (p. 498) "several reasons for the persistence of partial valuation." Gullible taxpayers associate a larger valuation with a larger tax, or at any rate are less contentious about a relatively excessive assessment if it does not exceed their estimate of true value. The ability to maintain a stable rate and to increase revenue by tampering with the tax base — a change which calls for less publicity and less opposition — is naturally desired by the party in power. Occasionally, partial valuation is intended as a substitute for a varied system of rates; i.e., different forms of property, while nominally taxed at the same rate, are in fact taxed at differing rates by being assessed at different proportions of full values. Undervaluation of realty is sometimes justified as compensating for the elusiveness of personalty; but even if the latter is assessed fully when caught, experience has shown that the net result is to furnish an additional incentive for evasion.

> Another inducement to undervaluation has been that, since the state relies on the property tax for part of its revenue, the county assessors seek to lighten their constituents' burden at the expense of the rest of the state by assessing the local property at a lower percentage than is applied elsewhere. This process has often resulted in a competition between counties as to which could most nearly approach the limit of nominal valuation. With the increasing trend in some states toward reserving the property tax for the support of the local communities, and in other states toward the creation of state boards of equalization, the enthusiasm for percentage valuation has been dampened.

Most of these considerations have probably served to perpetuate the custom in New York; but there may be other factors at work.

This State, of course, does not depend on real property taxes as a source of State revenue. However the State does supply financial aid to communities based primarily on assessed valuation . . . and this undoubtedly furnishes "another inducement to undervaluation." The activities of the State Equalization Board are meant to correct this problem but as one commentator observes "possibly local tax officials believe that there is no harm in trying" (Johnson, Fractional Ratios and Their Effect on Achievement of Uniform Assessment, the Property Tax: Problems and Potentials, Tax Institute of America, p. 210).

Since the State Constitution provides that "[a]ssessments shall in no case exceed full value" (N.Y. State Const. art. XVI, § 2) assessing at a percentage of value discourages claims of unconstitutional overvaluation. Then the taxpayer is left with the far more difficult task of proving comparative inequality.

Obviously these reasons are all good reasons for abolishing the custom (see, e.g. Note, 68 Yale L.J. 335, op. cit.; Note, 75 Harvard L. Rev. 1374; Kilmer, Legal Requirements for Equality in Tax Assessments, 25 Albany L. Rev. 203, *op. cit.*). As Bonbright observes (*op. cit.,* pp. 497-498): "Theoretically the taxpayer's pocket is not in the least affected by uniform undervaluation or overvaluation. Systematic undervaluation diminishes the tax base and the tax rate must therefore rise in order to supply the required government revenue.... The objections to the practice of undervaluation are patent. In the first place, except where sanctioned by statute, it involves a generally known and sanctioned disregard by officials of the law requiring them to assess property at its full and fair value. The other great vice is that the percentage of undervaluation is rarely a matter of common knowledge, so that it is extremely difficult to ascertain whether there is uniformity in the proportion or whether, through incompetence, favoritism, or corruption of the assessors, some portions of the taxpaying body are bearing the others' burdens, as between either individuals or local groups."

In recent years the high courts in several States, noting the mounting criticism, have held that full value means what it says and that the practice of fractional assessments is illegal (see, e.g., *Switz v. Township of Middletown,* 23 N.J. 580, 130 A.2d 15; *Ingraham v. Town & City of Bristol,* 144 Conn. 374, 132 A.2d 563; *Russman v. Luckett,* 391 S.W.2d 694 [Ky.]; *Bettigole v. Assessors of Springfield,* 343 Mass. 223, 178 N.E.2d 10; *Walter v. Schuler,* 176 So.2d 81 [Fla]; *Southern Ry. Co. v. Clement,* 57 Tenn. App. 54, 415 S.W.2d 146).

In sum, for nearly 200 years our statutes have required assessments to be made at full value and for nearly 200 years assessments have been made on a percentage basis throughout the State. The practice has time on its side and nothing else. It has been tolerated by the Legislature, criticized by the commentators and found by our own court to involve a flagrant violation of the statute. Nevertheless the practice has become so widespread and been so consistently followed that it has acquired an aura of assumed legality. The assessors in Islip inherited the custom and it is conceded that they have continued it. Throughout the years taxes have been levied and paid, or upon default, tax liens have arisen, followed by foreclosure and ultimate transfer of title, all on reliance on the apparent legality of fractional assessments. Now we have before us a petition directly challenging the practice and seeking an order "declar[ing] the entire assessment roll of the Town of Islip for the year 1968-1969 as illegal, null and void." In the alternative the petitioner requests that we direct the township to "make future assessments of all property on the assessment rolls of said town at the full value."

[In order to avoid fiscal chaos in the Town, the court then decided not to hold the "settled" assessment roll void but directed prospective relief only. — Eds.]

Accordingly, the order of the Appellate Division should be modified to the extent of directing that, within a reasonable time, but in no event later than December 31, 1976, the respondent shall assess the real property within the township at full value.

JONES, JUDGE (dissenting).

[The dissent would not have overruled a practice of 200 years standing, and doubted the authority of the court to give prospective relief. — Eds.]

Comments: 1. Professor Hellerstein, attorney for one of the plaintiffs in the *Islip* case, summarized the results of the case in the following testimony:

Testimony of Jerome R. Hellerstein on Full Value Assessment of Real Property in Hearings Before N.Y. Sen. Comm. on Cities (1980).

B. *The Results of the Town of Islip Case*

....
1. Reassessments
   (a) The first result has been that many taxing districts in which for decades there had been no general reassessment, have been prodded into reassessing their properties on a full value basis. The Department of Equalization and Assessment or (DEA) has reported that in the three years following the Town of Islip decision, 1976-1978, 233 towns and cities in the State were conducting, or had completed, general reassessment on a full value basis, 128 of which had been completed.... The DEA estimated that by 1981 about one-third of the approximately 1,000 towns and cities in the State will have reassessed on a full value basis....
   The importance of reassessment is reflected in a decision directing a reassessment at full value in Nassau County. There had been no general reassessment in that rapidly growing county of some 400,000 parcels in over 40 years (*Forte v. Board of Assessors of Nassau County,* ... 395 N.Y.S.2d 212 [2d Dept.] 1977). The resulting inequalities in assessments as between the older and the new properties had to be very great indeed. To take merely single family and two family houses, in view of the rapid increases in property values and construction costs since the mid 30's, a disproportionately high property tax burden was undoubtedly being borne by younger families, which had bought houses in new subdivisions constructed in recent years, while the long time owners of property built 20-30 or 40 years ago were greatly underpaying their portion of the tax.
   (b) There is one other highly significant aspect of these reassessments, and that is that they are being carried out under the DEA computerized program, under which year by year data as to sales prices, construction costs and the like, will be fed into the computers. It is hoped by the architects of this program that, as a consequence, for the first time in the history of the property tax, we shall be able to keep ad valorem assessments abreast with changing values. If that prognostication proves anything like true, science will have accomplished a tax miracle.
   2. Improvement in the Equality of Assessments
   Turning to the effects of the reassessments, we now have the results of a DEA study of the impact of revaluation on the 2 cities and the 29 towns that completed their reassessments on a full value basis in 1978. While the shifts in tax burden vary markedly depending on the mix of properties and other factors, and we have had no full value reassessment by a large city, nevertheless, the DEA's study tends to confirm what had been anticipated.
   The DEA found that in the great majority of municipalities — 25 out of 31 — the share of the overall tax load on residential properties, which includes apartment houses as well as one and two family residences, increased as a result of the reassessment; there was a decrease in the remaining 6 municipalities.... In most of the districts (16 out of 25) the increase was less than 10%, and in a number (8) the increase was less than 5%....
   Commercial property experienced the opposite result. In practically all the municipalities studied, reassessment resulted in a decrease in the tax load borne by commercial property as a class.... In the case of utility and industrial property, there was likewise a reduction of the share of the tax borne in over 3 out of 4 municipalities....
   Predictably, the DEA study shows that vacant lands, which had been notoriously underassessed, had their share of the tax increased in more than 4 out of 5 districts....
   Farm land showed a much closer division as between municipalities in which that class of property experienced an increase or decrease in their share of the municipality's tax bill as a result of full value reassessment. In 12 out of the 22 municipalities containing farm properties (55%), the tax share of farms increased, whereas in the remaining 10 municipalities, their share decreased....
   Turning to the effect of the full value reassessments on intra-class inequalities within the residential class, the DEA study again bears out the expected results. It concluded that "intra-class changes far outweigh the overall shift in tax burdens between the

residential and other classes of property" . . . . As the Executive Director of the DEA has put the matter, the study shows that "the primary reason for tax shifts in the residential class is the elimination of relative assessment inequities *among homeowners* and not a result of reductions in the tax burdens of other classes." . . .

There is one other finding of the DEA study to which I should like to advert, and that is that the prior assessment practice had tended to favor residential properties of the affluent segment of the population, at the expense of more modest residential properties. The DEA found that "in most municipalities, the greatest proportion of residential parcels incurring the decreases of greater than 25% [as a result of the revaluation on a full value standard] were of less than average residential taxable value (after revaluation) . . . .

2. In 1981, the New York legislature adopted, over the governor's veto, a new assessment law, L. 1981, ch. 1057, which essentially opted for the status quo. For a critical analysis of the new statute with a pessimistic conclusion, see Payne, *From the Legislatures: The Unhappy Job of Revaluing Property,* 11 REAL EST. L.J. 165 (1982). Alternative assessment systems, based on classifications of property, are provided for New York City and Nassau County (four classes — residential three-family or less, all other residential, utility property and all other property), and for the rest of the state (two classes — residential three-family or less and all other property). Apparently, assessing units may choose to continue the status quo or to elect the new system. The classification principle for the new systems provides for a uniform tax rate to be applied to differentially classified assessment ratios (dubbed a "share of the pie" system by local commentators).

Professor Payne argues that the system of classification by assessment ratios falls somewhere in between the "existing assessing functions" so severely criticized in *Hellerstein* and a full value assessment system with differential tax rates applied for differential classes of property.

3. In the case of *Colt Industries v. Finance Administrator,* 430 N.E.2d 1290 (N.Y. 1982), taxpayers challenged assessments on inequality grounds. The taxpayers attempted to introduce state equalization rates as evidence to support their claim. However, the court found that the 1981 statute distinguished municipal units on the basis of size and limited the use of state equalization rates to "all assessing units other than special assessing units" [New York City and Nassau County. — Eds.]. The court upheld this limitation finding that:

> The Legislature had a rational basis for designating the City of New York and Nassau County special assessing units and restricting the admissibility of State equalization rates in such units. This legislation which was designed to overrule this court's decision in *Matter of Hellerstein v. Assessor of Town of Islip,* . . . which required full value assessment for all property, recognized the unique nature of those communities with their high density of population and diversity of property.

Id. at 1293.

4. For another case enforcing a constitutional and statutory duty to assess at full cash value see *Town of Sudbury v. Commissioner of Corporations & Taxation,* 321 N.E.2d 641 (Mass. 1974). In this case, the town successfully attacked unequal fractional assessment of property among the various municipalities in the state. *See also* Note, *Equality in Property Taxation — The Law, Practice and Prospects,* 11 NEW ENG. L. REV. 617 (1976).

In *Bettigole v. Assessors of Springfield,* 178 N.E.2d 10 (Mass. 1961), the Massachusetts court interpreted the state constitutional provision requiring "proportional and reasonable assessments" to require the invalidation of the differential fractional assessment policy that had been adopted by the municipality. The court invalidated the assessment roll and required an immediate reassessment. It noted that if the assessment were not enjoined the alternative would be a multiplicity of tax abatements for unequally treated taxpayers, creating unnecessary work, congestion in the courts and the appellate tax board, and delays. *Compare Coomey v. Board of Assessors,* 329 N.E.2d 117 (Mass. 1975), in which the plaintiffs, who had alleged that their property had been overvalued in relation to comparable properties, were given the opportunity to ask for an abatement in taxes that would make their assessment proportional to other assessments. There was an allegation in this case that the town had intentionally assessed all the property in the town at less than its fair cash value.

5. What is the appropriate remedy for a taxpayer victimized by a disproportionate assessment? Should the assessment be allowed to stand if the property, in fact, has been assessed at full cash value (or appropriate fraction) under the law even though the assessment is disproportionately higher than similar property? Or should assessments and taxes be abated to some lower level? If so, what level — a municipal average of all classes of property in the city, the average of assessments for the particular class of property, or the average for the most favored class?

In *Tregor v. Board of Assessors,* 387 N.E.2d 538 (Mass. 1979), the court was faced with a "pattern of assessment in the city of Boston in flagrant disregard of constitutional and statutory mandates." *Id.* at 540. In 1976, assessments of various classes of property ranged from 26.8% to 100%. The Appellate Tax Board, applying a recently established rule of lowest percentage of fair cash value, *Assessors of Weymouth v. Curtis,* 378 N.E.2d 655 (Mass. 1978), reduced the assessment of land and an office building from $320,000 to $87,904.

The court affirmed the board's decision, holding that the decision to choose the lowest percentage of value (26.8%) instead of a municipal average (50%) was a reasonable approach to the problem of remedying unlawful discrimination and not an invalid penalty. "The remedy may provide some incentive to the assessors to comply with laws they have blatantly violated for many years, but that fact does not render it punitive." *Id.* at 544.

Responding to *Tregor,* the Massachusetts legislature enacted a law limiting the remedy for disproportionate assessments to the municipal average for all taxable property during the years the new Massachusetts classification plan is being implemented (November 1979 to June 30, 1983). In *Keniston v. Board of Assessors,* 407 N.E.2d 1275 (Mass. 1980), the court upheld the statute as a "constitutionally permissible legislative response to the potential erosion of municipal revenues mandated by the most favored class remedy . . ., and to a need for a more stable distribution of local property tax burdens pending statewide revaluation of real property to full and fair cash value." *Id.* at 1276. The court stressed that the temporary nature of the remedy was an important factor in its decision.

6. *United Illuminating Co. v. City of New Haven,* 427 A.2d 830 (Conn. 1980), addresses the question of how a state can fairly reassess property values without placing an undue burden on specific groups of property owners. Many times a substantial increase in a residential assessment presents a liquidity problem for a homeowner. Legislatures may provide some relief to these individuals through a tax phase-in statute.

In *United Illuminating Co.,* three Connecticut companies claimed that the tax phase-in statute violated the equal protection clause of the United States and Connecticut Constitutions. The phase-in statute in part provided:

> (1) In the event the October 1, 1978 assessment list results in an increase in the total assessed value of all real property in excess of thirty percent (30%) over the October 1, 1977 assessment list, all of such excess assessment on any piece of residential* real property shall be divided into five (5) equal increments, and each of said increments shall be effective on each of the succeeding five list years, thereby successively increasing each such residential* real property assessment increase until the full assessment originally fixed in October 1, 1978 is implemented.

Id. at 833-34 n.7.

Plaintiffs claimed that the statute violated the equal protection clause because it provided for " 'systematic and intentional underassessment' of certain property within a class of like property." *Id.* at 835. Plaintiffs also contended that the thirty percent increase qualification was "arbitrary and irrational." The court rejected the plaintiffs' arguments finding that:

> Several rational bases are conceivable for the classification regarding the 30 percent increase in real property assessments which triggers the act and ordinance.

---

*The word "residential" was deleted by an amendment "An Ordinance Amending a Previous Ordinance Concerning Staged Increases in Certain Real Property Tax Assessments."

... [T]he use of the act is confined to those municipalities in which the potential of significantly enlarged tax burdens on real property owners or the possible disruption of the real estate market is sufficiently substantial to justify the administrative costs of the phase-in program. Further, the requirement of a 30 percent increase helps ensure that the phase-in process is equitable....

As to the second classification, the real property-personal property distinction, a conceivable rational basis likewise exists. The legislature may have drawn this line because it considered that there was a potential for a sudden and dramatic increase in the assessment of realty because revaluation of such property for assessment purposes may occur at intervals as far apart as ten years. General Statutes §12-62. The previous revaluation of a piece of real property revalued in 1978 may have occurred in 1968. The legislature may well have feared that although the appreciation in the value of that property may have been gradual over the years, the cumulative appreciation may have been so substantial that when reflected in the subsequent assessment, forced sales, foreclosures, and other conceivable hardships might result. Such a dramatic increase in assessment may have been thought not to exist for personal property which is revaluated annually. With annual revaluation there would be no cumulative appreciation accruing over a period of years which would be compressed into one revaluation. The real property-personal property distinction certainly is not irrational.

Id. at 839.

7. The "full value" movement and the inequities in assessments which spawned it are discussed in more detail in Lesnick, *Does Full Value Mean Full Value? Prospects for Assessment Reform in New York in Light of the Experiences of Other States with Hellerstein's Progenitors,* 5 HOFSTRA L. REV. 235 (1977); Baar, *Property Tax Assessment Discrimination in Low-Income Neighborhoods,* 13 URB. LAW. 333 (1981) and 1 PROP. TAX J. 1 (1982).

---

b. Differential Assessments and Classifications

The practice of fractional assessment highlights the potentiality that lies in the property tax for unequal treatment of property owners short of outright classification. Indeed, Professor Hellerstein's testimony, *supra,* highlighted both the inter- and intra-class inequities that resulted from fractional assessment practices. In view of the uniformity provision in most state constitutions, a question arises concerning the validity of classifications of real property where the rate of tax or the assessment ratio is varied for each class. Whatever the answer to that question, the response to the full value movement was a heightened interest in classification, as the following comment suggests.

PAYNE, FROM THE LEGISLATURES: THE UNHAPPY JOB OF REVALUING PROPERTY, 9 Real Estate Law Journal 227 (1981)

Judicial Activism Leads to Legislative Reassessment

With inflationary pressures all around, and the dollar amount of tax bills rising, more and more property owners have found it worth their while to challenge local taxing practices, and they have been winning. In all three jurisdictions, local taxing authorities had, for many years, allowed assessments on individual properties to slip out of line with each other, thus violating either constitutional or statutory mandates that properties be valued at "true value," "full and fair cash value," or some equivalent phrase. Such was the case in New Jersey's largest city, Newark, where a revaluation had not occurred for more than twenty years, during which time a vast commercial and industrial deterioration had weakened the city's business-property base. Revaluation was resisted, because of a reasonable fear that it would throw a significantly higher portion of the city's tax burden onto residential properties. Similarly, a 1976 Boston study demonstrated assessment ratios varying from less than 17 to 100 percent, with residential properties generally, enjoying the lowest ratios. On the basis of studies such as this, the Massachusetts Supreme Judicial Court authorized substantial rebates to overassessed business properties.

. . . .

The Massachusetts Classification Scheme

Some insight into the prospects for sensible reform of property tax assessment practices can be gleaned from the Massachusetts experience. Coincident with the judicial pressures described earlier, the Massachusetts voters approved, in 1978, a state constitutional amendment that permitted classification [Mass. Const. Part II, c. 1, § 1, art. 4, as amended by Art. 112 of Articles of Amendment, approved 1978. — Eds.], and a statutory classification scheme was ready to be put into effect.[10] The legislation, Chapter 580 of the Laws of 1978, provided for a fourfold division of properties: residential, commercial, industrial or manufacturing, and open space. Although all property in each classification was to be assessed at full value, the statute then provided that a percentage of this value be taken as the "taxable value" of the property; these percentages ranged from 25 percent for open space to 55 percent for manufacturing and industrial, with residential property pegged at 40 percent and commercial at 50 percent. In addition, a $5,000 exemption from value was provided for each residential unit, "unit" being defined to include individually owned condominiums but not individual rental apartments. As an inducement to comply with the legislative and judicial mandate that all properties be valued initially at "fair cash value," the legislation provided that no jurisdiction be permitted to classify until it came into compliance with the full value assessment rule; thus, invidious variations that might occur if fractional assessments were applied to the prior system of already fractionalized ad hoc valuations would be prevented.

Before the dawn of the first tax year covered by the new legislation, it was repealed by the legislature, and a substantially modified classification system was substituted. The four classes of property were retained, but instead of the provision for fractional "taxable values," which locked each town into an inflexible

---

[10] . . . .

The Massachusetts legislation was sustained against constitutional attack in a comprehensive decision of the Supreme Judicial Court. Associated Indus. of Mass. v. C.I.R., 393 N.E.2d 812 (Mass. 1979). The challengers relied on language of the new constitutional amendment requiring proportionality "within the same class," and contended that the actual tax burden borne by any class of property would vary from municipality to municipality. This occurs since the effective tax rate in any given municipality would depend on whether that class of property was a large or small percentage of the jurisdiction's tax base. The court, however, construed the constitutional language to permit such local variations. It noted that the property tax has been recognized as "intensely local [in] character," *Id.* at 816, for hundreds of years, with great judicial deference to be given to rationally based dividing lines drawn by the legislature in the tax area. The court similarly deferred to the legislative judgment in permitting the residential exemption, finding that rental and condominium housing have different legal incidents, and implying that these legal differences result in generally higher valuations for condominium buildings, thus justifying the exemption to bring their taxable value more into line with other forms of residences. *Id.* at 819. As a matter of tax policy, it may be doubted whether more valuable properties, whatever the cause, ought to be given preferential tax treatment.

yield for any given class of property at any given rate, the new law permits the adjustments to the tax rate applicable to each class of property. This is accomplished through an incredibly cumbersome procedure involving local determination (within the state-determined limits) of a "residential factor," a percentage that can serve as a weighting factor, reducing the effective tax rate on residential properties (and also open space lands) in relation to the two "business" classes. The statute on its face requires establishment of a residential factor that would provide a substantial reduction in the effective residential rate, but local jurisdictions are authorized to modify this factor in such a way that the disparity could be reduced or even eliminated. The new law also requires that tax rates for commercial and industrial properties be identical, in effect reducing the number of classifications from four to three, and changes the residential exemption from a flat dollar amount to a percentage (no more than ten) of the average assessed value of all residential properties in the jurisdiction. These legislative amendments, although in slightly different form, were given advance judicial approval in *Opinion of the Justices,* [393 N.E.2d 306 (Mass. 1979)] which concluded that the discretionary power to adjust tax rates could be constitutionally delegated to local jurisdictions. Barring further challenges, the revised law went into effect for fiscal years beginning on or after July 1, 1980. Massachusetts seems at last to have a classified tax.

How to Reconcile Inconsistent Interests

The Massachusetts experience illustrates the difficulties that will beset New York, New Jersey, and other jurisdictions trying to curb the neglect of decades in the administration of a fair property tax system. In New York, one commentator observed that "it takes three to tango," referring to the governor and the two houses of the state legislature. The Massachusetts experience suggests more accurately that the three partners, not necessarily in dancing harmony, are residential property owners, commercial and industrial owners, and local financial officials. The residentials have the most to gain from a system of classification, since it will confer legality on time-honored practices working generally to their benefit. Moreover, as the Newark experience reminds, sound public policy may be served by a system that allows what are, in effect, tax incentives that will stimulate an appropriate land use mixture in that most endangered of public species, the central city. And the public at large is undoubtedly served by a system that operates in the open, rather than through indirect, poorly supervised, and potentially corrupt mechanisms as in the past.

The competing interests (and the political power) of both the business community and local taxing officials are demonstrated by the revisions to the Massachusetts system, although these interests are not necessarily consistent with each other. By obtaining some tax rate flexibility, local officials have regained a measure of tax policy discretion lost in the initial classification scheme, while the business property owners who stand to bear the heaviest rates gained what they undoubtedly hope will be an opportunity to influence local policy in their favor on a case-by-case basis. These gains are limited, however, since the legislation (as administered by the state commissioner of revenue) places close outer limits on local discretion; these limited gains, moreover, are purchased at a substantial and undesirable increase in the complexity of the state's property tax legislation.

Comments: 1. In *Commonwealth v. Town of Andover,* 391 N.E.2d 1225 (Mass. 1979), reassessment under the new classification system in the absence of local municipal cooperation was considered. Assessors for a number of municipalities submitted plans for reassessment to the State Commissioner of Revenue. The plans were approved, but no funds were appropriated by the municipalities to carry out the plans. Massachusetts sought to have the commissioner contract with commercial appraisal firms to revalue the real estate in each noncomplying city. The state treasurer would then deduct the cost of the contract from the amount of state aid to be dispersed to that municipality. The court concluded that the state commissioner did not have independent authority to reassess property because that was a function of local assessors but could obtain a court order to do so under appropriate circumstances.

Although there is no express authority, in the absence of an appropriation, for a board of assessors or the Commissioner to incur obligations on behalf of a municipality, none of the defendants seriously contends that a city or town may effectively thwart its assessors and the Commissioner in their efforts to achieve a result that is required by the constitution and by statute....

. . . .

Under the court's general equity power, judgments may be fashioned to assure the completion of necessary revaluations.... In particular instances, orders might be fashioned that would permit a city or town, if it wished, promptly to appropriate the funds necessary for a revaluation of its real property. The municipality would thus have the opportunity to determine the source from which appropriations would be met and to have a role in selecting the procedures to be followed in revaluing its real property. Any plan for revaluation must, however, be a reasonable one calling for final results in a timely manner. The Commissioner's views on the adequacy of any program of revaluation and her directions to local assessors will be entitled to great weight in determining what orders should be entered. Municipalities that have not performed their statutory and constitutional duties should not expect a sympathetic judicial reception....

If the local assessors and the local appropriating body do not respond promptly and fully, the single justice may conclude that more drastic relief is required, resulting in some loss of local control by the city or town and its officials. Thus, for example, the court might authorize the Commissioner to contract for revaluation services and direct that the cost of the contract be imposed on the city or town, perhaps by directing the State Treasurer to withhold funds otherwise distributable to the municipality....

We reluctantly reach the conclusion that there must be judicial participation in the process, because we see no reasonable alternative, in the absence of a legislative solution.

Id. at 1231-32.

2. An excellent discussion of full cash value as compared with classified property tax assessment, and the distributive consequences of each system, is contained in Farr, *The Property Tax as an Instrument for Economic and Social Change,* 9 URB. LAW. 447 (1977). Farr points out that the distributive consequences of tax assessment systems depend on a number of factors, including the mix of taxable property in a municipality and the extent to which each class of property contributes to the tax base.

Distributive effects occur because property taxes are capitalized into land and building prices. Relatively low property tax assessments and rates are reflected in relatively higher prices. Farr argues that uniform property tax assessment in exclusionary suburbs, to take one example, will not have a dramatic effect on prices. Nonresidential property values will fall if their taxes increase. Impacts on residential property values from property tax increases will be negligible if residential property makes up a large portion of the municipality's tax base; the tax increase will be spread over a large number of residential properties.

In large cities, tax increases and property value declines for residential property might be substantial. In these cities, residential property makes up a much smaller portion of the property tax base. The consequence may be an accelerated flight of upper income families from the city.

Farr concludes:

> Since no change is without cost, continuance of the existing flawed system deserves another look. While the present system has developed largely as a result of neglect and historical accident, it is maintained because it has some advantages and because it works. ... Given the political convulsions that accompany any tax change, it is easy to understand why government officials favor the status quo.

Id. at 494.

A NOTE ON THE CONSTITUTIONALITY OF DIFFERENTIAL PROPERTY TAX ASSESSMENT

State constitutional and statutory mandates that are interpreted to require uniform assessment may effectively foreclose any attempt at the local level to adopt different assessment ratios for different classes of property. Nevertheless, de facto classification became widespread, and along with less-than-full valuation, was part of the almost universal pattern of unequal assessment which confronted the courts when they began to play a more active role in the 1960s. As one close observer said of the effect of court-ordered adherence to the law:

> Confronting such decrees or the threat of them, many states changed their laws to bring them into accord with prevailing practice rather than vice versa. This is the primary explanation for adoption of nearly all of the classification laws of the past two decades.

GOLD, THE CHANGING SHAPE OF PROPERTY TAX RELIEF SINCE THE LATE 1960's, at 24 (Natl. Conf. of State Legislatures 1982). Some ten states, the District of Columbia and Cook County, Illinois, now have formal classification systems, and several others classify some category of property. *Id.* at 13-14.

As some of the above cases have indicated, classifications within property tax systems have not generally presented serious federal constitutional problems. In *Snow v. City of Memphis,* 527 S.W.2d 55 (Tenn. 1975), a constitutional amendment was challenged that classified real property into four classes and required that rental property containing two or more rental units be defined as commercial property. Rental property was assessed at a forty percent assessment ratio while single-family and two-family dwellings and farms were assessed at a twenty-five percent ratio. The court upheld the classification under the equal protection clause, relying on United States Supreme Court cases according considerable discretion to states and local governments in enacting tax classification schemes. See also *Kahn v. Shevin,* 416 U.S. 351 (1974), upholding a five hundred dollar property tax exemption for widows. The exemption was attacked by a widower. Moreover, as recent Supreme Court decisions indicate, taxpayers are faced with a number of obstacles in attempting to use federal courts to challenge inequities in their property tax system. *See Rosewell v. LaSalle National Bank,* 450 U.S. 503 (1981); *Fair Assessment in Real Estate Ass'n v. McNary,* 454 U.S. 100 (1981).

More difficult constitutional hurdles may be faced in the state courts where especially difficult questions have been presented by attempts to differentiate property for assessment according to its use. For example, the manner in which land is laid out and held may be claimed to affect its value. Thus it can be argued that land platted into residential lots has a higher value than land which is not so platted. Would this distinction justify a higher assessment for platted lots, or a higher tax rate? See *People v. Doe,* 174 N.E.2d 830 (Ill.), *cert. denied,* 368 U.S. 890 (1961), upholding under the uniformity clause a higher increase in assessments for platted lots than for unplatted lots. All platted lots were subjected to the greater tax assessments, whether improved or not. See also *Property Appraisal Department v. Ransom,* 506 P.2d 794 (N.M. 1973), upholding a state statute that limited preferential assessment of farmland to "unsubdivided" as distinguished from subdivided land.

What if a municipality decides to recapture speculative value in land by assessing at a higher assessment ratio all open, unplatted land that is sold and held for speculative purposes, while assessing at a lower ratio all unplatted land not sold or held on speculation? The argument would be similar to that made in the platted land cases, that holding for speculation leads to higher market values, and that these should be reflected in the higher assessment. For a case indicating that a classification of this kind would be unconstitutional see *Gerner v. State Tax Commission,* 378 P.2d 619 (N.M. 1963) (land was allegedly held for speculation in oil). How would the municipality get probative evidence of the fact that the land was being held for speculative purposes?

Differential assessment of land based on use is often attempted for just the opposite purpose. Urban planners and experts frequently allege that farmland adjacent to urbanized areas is assessed at high land values reflecting the higher values on nearby land which is already in urban use. As a result, farmers unable to bear the increased tax burden are forced to sell their land for urbanization prior to the time when it is ready to be urbanized, or prior to the time a local plan indicates it should be urbanized, with negative effects on urban development patterns.

In the absence of preferential assessment legislation or comparable assessment practices at the local level, agricultural land located near urbanized areas will be assessed at its market value and this value will reflect the possibility that the agricultural land may be put to urban use. *See Mohland v. State Board of Equalization,* 466 P.2d 582 (Mont. 1970). Plaintiff's agricultural land was located "within the expanding commercial interests" of the city, and was assessed at market value. Plaintiff complained that the assessment did not reflect the "actual use" to which the land was put, but the court disagreed and held that market value was a proper assessment standard. "There obviously is a present demand for the land under consideration for a use that justifies a higher value than can be economically justified in agricultural use." *Id.* at 584.

Over forty states and many municipalities have adopted tax abatement programs for agricultural land under which, in one way or another, primarily through lowered assessments, agricultural land is taxed at its value for agricultural, or current, use. This value is usually lower than the market value at which land is ordinarily assessed. While some states have now amended their constitutions to allow this kind of differential taxation, the acceptability of this kind of differential taxation under conventional uniformity clauses led to conflicting responses from the courts. *See generally* PROPERTY TAX PREFERENCES FOR AGRICULTURAL LAND, LINCOLN INSTITUTE OF LAND POLICY (N. Roberts & H. Brown eds. 1980); ECONOMIC RESEARCH SERVICE, U.S. DEP'T OF AGRICULTURE, STATE PROGRAMS FOR THE DIFFERENTIAL ASSESSMENT OF FARM AND OPEN SPACE LAND (1974); Note, *Property Taxation of Agricultural and Open Space Land,* 8 HARV. J. LEG. 158 (1970).

Thus a Florida law provided that "All lands being used for agricultural purposes shall be assessed as agricultural lands upon an acreage basis." The constitutionality of this law was upheld in *Lanier v. Overstreet,* 175 So. 2d 521 (Fla. 1965). The court dealt shortly with the constitutional objections as follows:

The appellants' contention that [this law] provides, in effect, for an unconstitutional partial exemption of this particular class of property, is without merit. The argument here is that property currently used for agricultural purposes may have a potential value far in excess of its value as agricultural land, attributable to other uses to which it is reasonably susceptible; that other classes of property — residential, commercial, recreational, etc. — have not been singled out by the Legislature and required to be assessed according to their current use without regard to their value for other reasonably susceptible uses, and that to sustain the legislative directive as to agricultural lands would, in effect, grant a partial exemption to such lands, commensurate with such additional potential value, and would also unjustly discriminate against all other classes of taxable property.

The short answer to this contention is that there is nothing in the legislative regulations respecting the "just valuation" of taxable property to authorize the assessment of property in accordance with a *potential* use which *might* be made of the property at some future time.

Id. at 523. *See also Elwell v. County of Hennepin,* 221 N.W.2d 538 (Minn. 1974), in which the court upheld a similar law with a minimum of discussion on the ground that the classification of property according to use for assessment purposes is constitutional, and indicated that there was a "trend" toward the adoption of such legislation.

A dissenting judge in the *Overstreet* case adopted his earlier dissent in *Tyson v. Lanier,* 156 So. 2d 833 (Fla. 1963), which had considered a statutory construction question arising under the preferential farm assessment law. There he had written:

The classification effected by the statute here involved is not, in fact, a classification of land on the basis of any inherent characteristic but instead is a "classification" of taxpayers or owners of taxable realty so as to single out those who choose or are able to subject their land to agricultural use and accord to that group alone the right to have the "just value" of their property determined on the basis of actual use rather than on the basis of the same criteria controlling the valuation of other property.

Whatever might be the validity of an act which classified taxable realty generally on the basis of actual use, an inequality is obvious when a law requires, as does this statute, a different assessment basis for parcels of land having identical salable or market value, whenever one parcel may be subjected to agricultural use. In any event, nowhere in the voluminous record at bar is there any effort to justify the classification attempted by demonstrating that the purpose of the act, i. e., to prevent consideration of potential uses in addition to actual use, has a unique relationship to the particular class affected, or that no other property shares the need for protection from market considerations for assessment valuation purposes.

Id. at 839. The leading case invalidating preferential farm assessment is *State Tax Commission v. Wakefield,* 161 A.2d 676 (Md. 1960). Maryland subsequently authorized legislation providing for such taxation by constitutional amendment. See also *State ex rel. Stephan v. Martin,* 608 P.2d 880 (Kan. 1980), invalidating under the Kansas constitutional uniformity provision a statute which in effect reduced by twenty percent the assessed valuation of farm machinery and equipment. The court called the statute a partial exemption of property directed to the economic condition of the owners, not the economic factors affecting the value of the property. Kansas has a 1976 constitutional amendment permitting valuation of agricultural land on the basis of its agricultural income or productivity. Kan. Const. art. 11, § 12.

Comments: 1. Classification systems that pass muster under uniformity requirements of state constitutions face a potentially serious federal challenge under recently enacted legislation to protect railroads and motor carriers from discrimination. Section 306 of the Railroad Revitalization and Regulatory Reform Act of 1976, 49 U.S.C. § 11503 (4R Act), and § 31 of the Motor Carrier Act of 1980, 49 U.S.C. § 11503(a), prohibit the assessment of rail transportation and motor carrier property at a value which has a higher ratio to true market value than other commercial and industrial property. Also prohibited is the levy or collection of taxes at a higher rate than that applicable to commercial and industrial property. Federal courts are given jurisdiction to enjoin state classification systems that discriminate in the prohibited manner as undue burdens on interstate commerce.

In *Tennessee v. Louisville & Nashville Railroad,* 478 F. Supp. 199 (M.D. Tenn. 1979), aff'd, 652 F.2d 59 (6th Cir. 1981), the court enjoined an assessment of railroad property by the State of Tennessee contrary to the terms of the statute. The court upheld the constitutionality of the statute under the power of Congress to regulate interstate commerce. In dismissing tenth amendment objections (discussed in Chapter 8 *infra*), the court applied a balancing test and concluded that Congress's effort to revitalize the railroad industry by implementing the 4R Act outweighed the state's interest in a property tax classification system. The court reasoned that section 306 of the 4R Act did not affect state policy choices with respect to its sources of revenues but only restricted those tax collection practices which discriminated against railroad companies. For critical analyses of the 4R Act provisions, see Shelton, *A System Under Fire,* Assessment Dig., at 2 (Mar./Apr. 1982); Fisher, The Four-R Act and the Taxation of Transportation Property (paper prepared for delivery at 48th International Conference on Assessment Administration, Kansas City, Missouri, October 1982).

2. Much of the commentary on the preferential farm assessment laws has been critical. For example, a study of the operation of such a law in New Jersey found that it conferred substantial benefits on land speculators, who bought and held farm land for development in order to take advantage of the preferential assessment. J. Kolesar & J. Scholl, Misplaced Hopes, Misspent Millions (1972). Another purpose of these laws is to prevent premature development and contain urban sprawl through the conferment of preferential taxation benefits at the urban fringe, where it is expected to encourage farmers to keep their land in agricultural production. However, a massive study of preferential farm tax assessment laws by the federal Council on Environmental Quality indicates that these laws are not likely to achieve this objective:

> Except for a few specific situations, which account for a small fraction of potential sales of farmland, differential assessment is not likely to be effective in achieving land use objectives. Whether or not a particular farm is sold and converted to a non-open use depends on three sets of considerations: supply factors, demand factors, and governmental approval of the proposed development. Differential assessment operates primarily on one of the supply factors, by reducing the income squeeze which farmers in rural-urban fringe areas experience as a result of rising real property taxes. It has a secondary impact on the demand side because it permits farmers-buyers, speculators and developers either to offer somewhat more for the land or to buy more land at the same price because their carrying costs are reduced. This latter effect is difficult to appraise, but is likely to be marginal because the buyer will normally be simply exchanging tax costs on the land for interest costs on the money he has to borrow either to pay the higher price or to buy additional land.

Council on Environmental Quality, Untaxing Open Space 77-78 (1976). *See also* Keene, *Differential Assessment and the Preservation of Open Space,* 14 Urb. L. Ann. 11 (1977). In view of this evaluation of the preferential farm tax assessment laws, how would you judge the reasons given for and against the constitutionality of these laws in the Florida opinions quoted above? Is there any way to achieve the stated objective? *See* H. Aaron, Who Pays the Property Tax? 95 (1975):

The practice of granting a variety of tax concessions to owners of rapidly appreciating farmland surrounding expanding metropolitan areas is particularly questionable. This device provides an additional boon to the owners of a valuable and appreciating asset at the expense of other, perhaps less lucky, taxpayers. While deferral of taxes on such land may be desirable to protect those who wish to continue farming from experiencing unfavorable cash flow, the deferred taxes, accumulated at market interest rates, should be recovered when the farmland is sold.

3. Some states have passed legislation either deferring for a period of time the imposition of property taxes on areas newly annexed to municipalities or providing some other form of tax relief. Thus in Arkansas, all annexed agricultural lands are to be taxed as such whether or not they are subdivided and no matter how they are zoned. Ark. Stat. Ann. § 84-479.

See, however, *Arkansas Public Service Commission v. Pulaski,* 582 S.W.2d 942 (Ark. 1979), invalidating an Arkansas statute which provided that agricultural and timber land be assessed on the basis of current use. The constitution requires current market value, according to the court. Does this decision affect the annexation statute? Minnesota provides a five-year phase-in for newly annexed lands in order to bring them up to the tax rate for land in the annexing municipality. Minn. Stat. Ann. § 414.032(4).

In *City of Mobile v. Salter,* 255 So. 2d 5 (Ala. 1971), a special act applicable to the city provided that no city property taxes could be levied against annexed property until the city provided a specified list of city services. This statute was upheld against a challenge that it violated a constitutional provision requiring all property to be taxed at the same rate. The court noted that the property was not subject to city taxation prior to annexation, and that the act merely continued that status until certain specified services were provided. These statutes should be compared with the judicial approach to the due process taxation rights of landowners annexed to municipalities, *supra* Chapter 2.

c. Tax Increment Financing

Property tax differentials of a sort also occur under an innovative technique for financing local projects and improvements known as tax increment financing. For example, local bonds are issued to provide the local share of urban renewal projects. To finance these bonds, assessments in the urban renewal area existing prior to the adoption of the official urban renewal plan are frozen, and existing government entities are guaranteed all taxes levied on these assessments for the life of the urban renewal project. However, all revenues from any subsequent increases in tax assessments from the project are allocated to pay for the retirement of urban renewal bonds. The constitutionality of tax increment financing was considered in the following case:

RICHARDS v. CITY OF MUSCATINE

Supreme Court of Iowa
237 N.W.2d 48 (1975)

[The statutes quoted in the opinion are not reproduced in full. — Eds.]
En banc.
Uhlenhopp, Justice.

In this appeal we pass upon the validity of the tax increment plan for urban renewal which the legislature authorized in §§ 403.9 and 403.19 of the Iowa Code.

Chapter 403 of the Code, the urban renewal law, empowers Iowa cities to take specified steps "to eliminate slums and prevent the development or spread of slums and urban blight and to encourage needed urban rehabilitation. . . ." § 403.3. In 1969, the General Assembly amended the urban renewal law to provide a new method of financing urban renewal projects; it added § 403.19 to allow a city to allocate to a special fund the increment in state, city, county, school, and other taxing district taxes resulting from the increase in valuation of an urban renewal area brought about by an urban renewal project. 63 G.A. ch. 237, § 2. In addition, the General Assembly amended § 403.9 to provide for the payment of urban renewal bonds out of the tax increment fund. *Id.* § 1. The portions of amended § 403.9 relevant to our inquiry provide:

1. A municipality shall have power to periodically issue bonds in its discretion to pay the cost of carrying out the purposes and provisions of this chapter.... Said bonds shall be payable solely from the income and proceeds of the fund and portion of taxes referred to in subsection two of section two (2) of this Act, and revenues and other funds of the municipality derived from or held in connection with the undertaking and carrying out of urban renewal projects under this chapter. The municipality may pledge to the payment of the bonds the fund and portion of taxes referred to in subsection two (2) of section [403.19] of this Act....

Section 403.19 provides:

A municipality may provide by ordinance that taxes levied on taxable property in an urban renewal project each year by or for the benefit of the state, city or town, county, school district, or other taxing district after the effective date of such ordinance, shall be divided as follows:

1. That portion of the taxes which would be produced by the rate at which the tax is levied each year by or for each of the taxing districts upon the total sum of the assessed value of the taxable property in the urban renewal project, as shown on the assessment roll used in connection with the taxation of property by the taxing district, last equalized prior to the effective date of the ordinance ... shall be allocated to and when collected be paid into the fund for the respective taxing district as taxes by or for said taxing district into which all other property taxes are paid....

2. That portion of the taxes each year in excess of such amount shall be allocated to and when collected be paid into a special fund of the municipality to pay the principal of and interest on loans, moneys advanced to, or indebtedness ... including bonds issued under the authority of section 403.9, subsection 1, incurred by the municipality to finance or refinance, in whole or in part, the redevelopment project, except that taxes for the payment of bonds and interest of each taxing district must be collected against all taxable property within the taxing district without limitation by the provisions of this subsection. Unless and until the total assessed valuation of the taxable property in an urban renewal project exceeds the total assessed value of the taxable property in such project as shown by the last equalized assessment roll referred to in subsection 1 of this section, all of the taxes levied and collected upon the taxable property in the urban renewal project shall be paid into the funds for the respective taxing districts as taxes by or for said taxing districts in the same manner as all other property taxes. When such loans, advances, indebtedness, and bonds, if any, and interest thereon, have been paid, all moneys thereafter received from taxes upon the taxable property in such urban renewal project shall be paid into the funds for the respective taxing districts in the same manner as taxes on all other property.

3. The portion of taxes mentioned in subsection two (2) of this section and the special fund into which they shall be paid, may be irrevocably pledged by a municipality for the payment of the principal and interest on loans, advances, bonds issued under the authority of section four hundred three point nine (403.9), subsection one (1) of the Code, or indebtedness, incurred by a municipality to finance or refinance, in whole or in part, the urban renewal project.

4. As used in this section the word "taxes" includes, but is not limited to, all levies on an ad valorem basis upon land or real property.

On July 18, 1974, acting under chapter 403 of the Code, the City of Muscatine, Iowa, adopted Resolution 74067 which approved an urban renewal plan for a one-block downtown area as Urban Renewal Project No. 2. (The present litigation does not involve Muscatine's Project No. 1, which was federally funded.) The plan called for acquisition and clearance of this area and redevelopment into a multi-story office building. Also on that date, Muscatine adopted Ordinance 74070 which directed the division and allocation of the taxes levied on the property within Project No. 2 in the manner provided by § 403.19. On August 15, 1974, Muscatine adopted Resolution No. 74185 which authorized issuance under § 403.9 of $800,000 of urban renewal bonds, to be paid from the tax increment fund created by Ordinance 74070.

On October 1, 1974, plaintiffs commenced the present action for a declaration that the resolutions, the ordinance, and §§ 403.9 and 403.19 of the Code are invalid. On February 5, 1975, the trial court upheld the validity of the resolutions, ordinance, and sections in all respects. Plaintiffs appealed and in this court attack the validity of §§ 403.9 and 403.19 and Muscatine's actions thereunder on a number of grounds. We consider the grounds in a different order than plaintiffs present them....

III. *Substantive Due Process.* Plaintiffs claim that §§ 403.9 and 403.19, and Muscatine's resolutions and ordinance, deprive them of property without due process of law. Iowa Const. art. 1, § 9; U.S. Const. Amend. XIV, § 1.

Here as elsewhere on their claims of unconstitutionality, plaintiffs have a heavy burden. "It is a well-settled rule that one who attacks a statute on constitutional grounds must negate every reasonable basis upon which it could be sustained.... [T]he provisions of amendment 14 ... do not prohibit the state from exercising its police power to pass and enforce laws as will benefit the health, morals, and general welfare of the people." *Green v. Shama,* 217 N.W.2d 547, 553, 554 (Iowa). We must uphold §§ 403.9 and 403.19 unless we can say no rational basis exists for believing that those sections further the public health, safety, morality, and general welfare....

A. In divisions IV and X of their brief, plaintiffs argue that by reducing the amount of property which would otherwise be taxable to meet the general expenses of the various taxing districts involved, § 403.19 increases the taxes of the property owners of those districts and reduces the ability of the taxing districts other than the city to raise revenue and incur indebtedness — all of which, plaintiffs say, amounts to deprivation of property without due process of law. We place the last of these claims aside — that § 403.19 reduces the ability of other taxing districts to incur indebtedness — as contrary to the plain language of § 403.19(2) ("taxes for the payment of bonds and interest of each taxing district must be collected against all taxable property within the taxing district without limitation by the provisions of this subsection").

An argument can be made that no tax increment would exist had Muscatine not created the urban renewal project — so that the urban renewal project itself does not deprive any person or district of property. Yet the real issue is whether the allocation of taxes under § 403.19 deprives any person or district of property without due process *with the urban renewal project carried out.* Viewed in this light, plaintiffs may be correct that § 403.19 deprives them and affected taxing districts of property. But are they right that such deprivation is without "due process"?

The tax increment scheme in § 403.19 is extraordinary. The various taxing districts will levy taxes for particular purposes — such as a levy of two mills by the county for court expenses in a given year just ahead. That levy will be imposed on the increased value (as well as on the frozen value) of the developed urban renewal property. But the taxes collected from that levy on the increased value will not be used for court expenses for which they were levied, but rather for urban renewal bond principal and interest — as though the city had made the levy for such purpose.

We can readily see that individuals of good will might differ about the wisdom of the scheme. But the wisdom of legislation is not for us to decide. We must confine our inquiry to whether the legislation lacks a rational basis. . . .

Urban renewal itself serves a valid public purpose and relates to the general welfare. . . . The tax increment plan appears to be a feasible method of financing such projects. It is more advantageous to the city than ordinary general obligation bonds, since the plan places the direct burden on the urban renewal property. We cannot say that the tax division scheme in § 403.19 is without a rational basis. . . .

A. Uniform Operation of the Law; Special Privileges. Section 6 of article I of the Iowa Constitution states, "All laws of a general nature shall have a uniform operation; the General Assembly shall not grant to any citizen, or class of citizens, privileges or immunities, which, upon the same terms shall not equally belong to all citizens."

(1) In divisions VI and VIII of their brief, plaintiffs argue that allocation of taxes under § 403.19 violates the quoted constitutional section because the allocation uses tax revenues to enable the urban renewal developer to obtain property at a cost lower than he would otherwise have to pay.

Plaintiffs' argument is contrary to the rationale of *Webster Realty Co. v. City of Ft. Dodge,* 174 N.W.2d 413 (Iowa). There the plaintiff claimed that chapter 403 gave special privileges to those who lived in the urban renewal area. This court rejected the claim, saying the fact that one class incidentally benefits more than another does not "destroy the public character of urban renewal or make it vulnerable to the attack that it is a special privilege law." 174 N.W.2d at 416. . . .

The leading case construing § 6 of article I is *Dickinson v. Porter,* 240 Iowa 393, 35 N.W.2d 66. This court there upheld a statute which gave a property tax credit to the owners of agricultural land in school districts where the millage for the general school fund exceeded 15 mills. In doing so the court stated, "If there is any reasonable ground for the classifications in this law and it operates equally upon all within the same class, there is uniformity in the constitutional sense and no violation of [§ 6 of article I].". . .

. . . .

We think a reasonable ground and a public purpose exist for any special benefits § 403.19 incidentally creates. The legislature must have thought — and we cannot say without reason — that urban renewal benefits a city, not just a developer. As this court said in *Dickinson,* "A law may serve the public interest although it benefits certain individuals or classes more than others.". . .

In arguing that § 403.19 results in lack of uniformity in the operation of laws of a general nature, plaintiffs rely upon Wisconsin cases. Section 1 of article VIII of the Wisconsin Constitution states, "The rule of taxation shall be uniform." The Wisconsin Supreme Court held that this provision permits only one class of property in the taxation of real estate and prohibits partial exemptions for certain types of property. *Ehrlich v. City of Racine,* 26 Wis.2d 352, 132 N.W.2d 489. Plaintiffs in the instant case argue § 403.19 creates a partial exemption and we should follow *Ehrlich* and hold § 403.19 invalid on that basis.

We decline to do so. First, § 403.19 can hardly be said to create a partial exemption for the urban renewal developer. He will pay taxes at the same rate as everyone else; § 403.19 only affects the use of taxes after collection.

Second, even if § 403.19 could be said to create a partial exemption, it would not necessarily violate our constitutional requirement of uniform operation of the laws. As we have indicated, this court's interpretation of § 6 of article I is quite different from the Wisconsin court's interpretation of its somewhat dissimilar section. Contrast *Dickinson v. Porter,* ... with *Gottlieb v. City of Milwaukee,* ... 147 N.W.2d 633.

We hold that a reasonable ground exists for the classification created by § 403.19 and that the section operates equally upon all within the class. Section 6 of article I requires no more. The trial court properly rejected plaintiffs' claim in divisions VI and VIII....

C. Appropriations for Private Purposes. In divisions VI and XII plaintiffs argue that § 403.19, by benefiting the developer and causing other taxpayers to carry a greater share of the general costs of government, violates § 31 of article III of the Iowa Constitution, which states in part that "no public money or property shall be appropriated for local, or private purposes, unless such appropriation, compensation, or claim, be allowed by two-thirds of the members elected to each branch of the General Assembly." We again assume arguendo that the quoted clause applies to cities.

In order to prevail on their claim, plaintiffs must show "there is an absence of all possible public interest in the purposes for which the appropriation here is used...." *Dickinson v. Porter, supra.* ... The appropriation in question is the allocation of the tax increment fund to the payment of urban renewal bonds. We have held that urban renewal itself serves a legitimate public purpose, ... and we thus reject plaintiffs' claim that § 403.19 violates § 31 of article III.

D. Equal Protection. As their final argument concerning improper classification, plaintiffs assert that §§ 403.9 and 403.19 deny equal protection of the laws in several ways. U.S. Const. Amend. XIV, § 1.

If a classification is not based upon race, sex, alienage, or national origin and does not involve a fundamental right, it must be sustained "unless it is patently arbitrary and bears no rational relationship to a legitimate governmental interest." *Lunday v. Vogelmann,* 213 N.W.2d 904, 907 (Iowa)....

(1) In division VII in their brief, plaintiffs argue that the allocation of taxes under § 403.19 denies them equal protection because it causes property owners such as plaintiffs to pay a greater share of the general costs of government than the project developer. Section 403.19 does cause the developer to pay a proportionately smaller amount to the general funds of the local taxing districts than owners of other property pay. We have already indicated, however, that the classification of § 403.19 has a rational relationship to the legitimate governmental purpose of having the urban renewal project pay for itself, in a sense, rather than spreading the cost throughout the city. We therefore reject plaintiffs' argument.

[The court held, however, that the urban renewal bonds constituted debt within the constitutional debt limit provision and were thus valid only in an amount which, together with the city's other indebtedness, came within that debt limitation. — Eds.]

Comments: 1. Tax increment financing for urban renewal was also upheld in *Tribe v. Salt Lake City,* 540 P.2d 499 (Utah 1975), reproduced *supra.* An argument was again made that equal protection was violated because diversion of increased taxes in the urban renewal area to urban renewal bond retirement would lead to the shifting of a disproportionate share of the tax burden on other taxpayers. This argument was answered in the concurring opinion as follows:

> But in looking at the overall picture, any such inequity may be minimized or perhaps eliminated if it is the taxation on *the assessed valuation of the property in the project area,* which is pegged down as of 1970, and if the total fair assessed evaluation is subject to taxation, including any increased mill rate of taxes levied in subsequent years, and it is *only the extra taxes generated from the amount of increased valuation over the base year, 1970,* that is diverted into a special fund and used to pay on the bonds.

Id. at 506. (Emphasis in original.)

Tax increment financing legislation now has been upheld by several courts against uniformity of taxation and other objections. *See, e.g., People ex rel. City of Canton v. Crouch,* 403 N.E.2d 242 (Ill. 1980); *State ex rel. Schneider v. City of Topeka,* 605 P.2d 556 (Kan. 1980); *City of Sparks v. Best,* 605 P.2d 638 (Nev. 1980); *Sigma Tau Gamma Fraternity House Corp. v. City of Menomonie,* 288 N.W.2d 85 (Wis. 1980). For an excellent discussion of tax increment financing see Davidson, *Tax Increment Financing as a Tool for Community Development,* 56 U. DET. J. URB. L. 405 (1979).

2. Recall that in the principal case the Iowa court contrasted the agricultural tax credit, which it had upheld in *Dickinson v. Porter,* with the interpretation of a comparable uniformity clause by the Wisconsin Supreme Court, as illustrated by *Gottlieb v. City of Milwaukee.* In the *Gottlieb* case the Wisconsin court had invalidated a related tax preference feature which is often urged for urban renewal projects, a real property tax freeze which exempts any private development in the urban renewal area from any increase in taxation for a given period of time. The Wisconsin court noted:

> While it may be conceded [that] new building may be stimulated and the tax base broadened to the extent that at some time in the future other taxpayers not covered by the freeze might be benefited, nevertheless, the fact remains undisputed and undisputable that, if redevelopment corporations are assessed at a figure less than that which would be assigned to other taxpayers holding equally valuable property, other taxpayers will be paying a disproportionately higher share of local property taxes. This is not uniformity.

Id. at 645. The Wisconsin court had invalidated the tax freeze as a prohibited partial exemption from taxation. *Contra, Dodge v. Prudential Insurance Co. of America,* 179 N.E.2d 234 (Mass. 1961), relying in part on the contribution that the urban renewal project would make to the elimination of blight. Is the tax increment financing upheld in the principal case really comparable with a freeze on tax increases?

3. Tax increment financing presents some difficult constructional problems concerning what property goes into the frozen and into the augmented tax base. Assume that as part of an urban renewal project several acres of land are to be devoted to a public library; the library is exempt from property taxation, but the land on which the library is to be built and the then standing improvements are technically part of the tax base that is frozen as of the date of the project. Can an argument now be made that a share of the augmented taxes collected in the project should be diverted from payment of the bonds in a sum sufficient to represent the tax that would have been levied on the library site had the library not been built? Or is the building of the library to be attributed to the project with the result that the previously assessed land and improvements will not be considered in determining the guaranteed revenues on the property assessments frozen when the urban renewal project was started? For a case taking the former view under the complicated California constitutional provision authorizing tax increment financing see *Redevelopment Agency v. Malaki,* 31 Cal. Rptr. 92 (Cal. App. 1963). *See* Calif. Const. art. XVI, § 16.

Assume that the facts are that private redevelopers would have developed the area included in the urban renewal project anyway, even if the project had not been adopted, but that the project is established so that the city may engage in the necessary planning to make the project compatible with the city plan. If augmented project property tax revenues are then diverted to pay off bonds used to finance municipal improvements in the project, is the tax increment financing still valid under the strictures of the concurring opinion in the *Tribe* case? See *Watkins v. Fugazzi*, 394 S.W.2d 594 (Ky. 1965). This case interpreted a Kentucky statute which authorized the pledging to the payment of urban renewal project bonds "such occupational license fees . . . by reason of employment in or directly related to" the project. This statute was interpreted to allow the city to pledge all subsequent occupational license fees derived from a shopping area to bond payments.

Tax increment financing can be used for municipal projects other than urban renewal projects. For example, a municipality could finance the construction of a new municipal parking garage on a similar basis. Tax increment financing also can create debt limitation problems under constitutional debt limitation provisions, as it did in the Iowa case. These are discussed *infra*.

4. Tax increment financing (TIF) is not without its critics:

Fundamental issues unresolved by experience gained with TIF to date are numerous. Given the magnitude of the accounting fictions behind the suggestion that such programs pay for themselves within reasonably short time spans, are there compelling reasons to link massive development programs to property taxation if inflexibility results for such other governmental units as school boards? If the fiction is thought to be worth perpetuating, might it be better modified to permit pooling of increments across separate projects or division of the increments along lines other than those now followed? Given such flexibility, would not cheaper general revenue bonds be preferable to TIF bonds? Should the definition of blighted areas be broadened to encompass economic obsolescence as well as physical deterioration, and, if so, how should the former be operationalized? To what extent does TIF result in suboptimal rationing or dissipation of redevelopment potential, with only the most lucrative projects being attempted while other properties are left to languish? Finally, ought not the limitations of such practices to be better understood by the voters who may have to approve such projects or the reporters who are lauding the arrival of a new nonfederal, nonsubsidized technique to rejuvenate cities?

Denne, *Explict Property Tax Policies and the Promotion of Specific Land-Use and Economic Development Objective: A Review,* 11 Assessors' J. 13, 27 (1976).

In view of these criticisms, consider the Minnesota statutes authorizing tax increment financing. In 1979, Minnesota consolidated five statutory sections and special laws authorizing tax increment financing (all with different standards and procedures) into a uniform system. Minn. Stat. Ann. §§ 273.71-273.86. Three kinds of TIF districts are authorized: redevelopment, housing and economic development, with varying requirements and lengths of duration. All TIF developments must comply with certain disclosure, planning and reporting requirements. Greater local control is instituted and more of the risk of noncompletion is shifted from the municipality to the developer. See generally Note, *The 1979 Minnestoa Tax-Increment Financing Act,* 7 Wm. Mitchell L. Rev. 627 (1981).

5. Property tax differential schemes affecting city redevelopment should be appraised in view of their impact on central city property tax burdens. In view of his anlaysis, would Netzer, *supra,* approve all of the differential schemes discussed above? Some of them? Which ones? Tax differential schemes create intra-city shifts in property tax burdens, and these are not discussed by Netzer. How would he evaluate these intra-city shifts in tax burden?

2. SPECIAL ASSESSMENTS AND SPECIAL BENEFIT TAXATION

While conceptually the general ad valorem property tax is not based on special benefit principles, a variety of related taxes are predicated on the conferment of a special benefit on the property that is taxed. These taxes provide a method for escaping the uniformity of taxation requirements that have been discussed above, and are attractive to local governments as a method of financing municipal improvements while at the same time avoiding general ad valorem property tax rates increases. In addition, as a subsequent section will indicate, benefit-related taxes confer some advantages under state constitutional debt limitation provisions. This section opens with a discussion of special assessments, which are the precursor of more sophisticated special benefit taxation techniques.

Special assessments are described as

> [S]pecial and local impositions upon the property in the immediate vicinity of municipal improvements, which are necessary to pay for the improvement, and are laid with reference to the special benefit which the property is supposed to have derived therefrom.... The foundation of the power to levy a special assessment ... is the benefit which the object of the assessment or tax confers on the owner of the abutting property ... which is different from the general benefit which owners enjoy in common with the other citizens of the municipal corporation.

E. McQuillin, The Law of Municipal Corporations 10, 18 (3d ed. 1970).

Use of special assessments financing was more prevalent in the first half of this century than it has been since World War II. The following report discusses the relative decline in the use of special assessments from 1957 to 1977 and suggests certain conditions which may reverse this trend:

> Prior to World War II, special ... assessments [were] widely used to facilitate the financing of capital improvements deemed to be of direct benefit to adjacent property....
>
> [During the Depression] defaults were rampant as the assessments derived from speculative real estate development ... failed to materialize.
>
> ....
>
> With the oncoming of the FHA mortgages and developments associated therewith, the financing of improvements incident to the development of raw land came in for a new approach. Namely, the new developments ... were obliged to furnish a wide range of public improvements as an incident to being able to secure permission to develop new land [resulting in a significant lessening of the reliance upon special assessments to finance improvements].
>
> [Special assessment] still provides one of the few automatic devices for reconciling demands for public expenditures with the willingness of the citizen to pay.
>
> Despite the difficulties and occasional gross inequalities created by the system, it does afford a means of equitable financing for a number of types of benefits. Moreover, it also acts to forestall some of the unjust windfall in ... public expenditures being broadly financed by the moneys provided by all.
>
> ... [W]hen the pressures derived from limitations upon taxation are broadly felt, this alternative is likely to become more attractive.

L. Moak, *The Revenue Source with Vitality,* in Cities Under Stress 475, 488-89 (R. Burchell & D. Listokin eds. 1981).

Recent census data suggest that such a reversal may now be taking place.

	1957	1967	1976	1977	1978	1979
Total taxes ($ bill.)	$ 5.86	$10.45	$23.34	$26.07	$27.83	$28.76
Spec. Asmts. ($ bill.)	$ .22	$ .31	$ .53	$ .53	$ .59	$ .68
(% of t. tax)	3.8%	2.9%	2.3%	2.0%	2.1%	2.4%

Sources: U.S. Dep't of Commerce, Bureau of the Census, *City Government Finances in 1978-1979,* at 5 (1980), ... *in 1966-67,* at 5 (1968), ... *in 1957,* at 7 (1958).

The benefit theory of special assessments is used by municipalities in determining proper and equitable assessments. In practice, however, municipalities are confronted with numerous problems. The author of a study of special assessments in the city and county of Honolulu describes typical municipal approaches to these problems.

S. SHINN, SPECIAL ASSESSMENTS: CITY AND COUNTY OF HONOLULU 28-29, 32-35 (Thesis on file at University of Hawaii, 1974)*

The approach taken by many municipalities has been to divide the problem into three areas:

1. The Allocation of Costs — The allocation of costs requires a sharing of costs between the public and private sector. The sharing of costs should be based on the amount of public and special benefit received.
2. The Method of Assessment — The method of assessment determines the allocation of private sector costs among the private property owners.
3. The Zone of Benefit — The zone of benefit is the geographical area composed of properties which are thought to receive special benefit. It is commonly called an improvement district.

The Allocation of Costs

The allocation of costs between government and the private sector is usually accomplished through the use of one of the following formulas:

1. The estimated total cost of the project minus public benefit equals private benefit; or
2. The estimated total cost minus private benefit equals public benefit.

There are several problems implicit in the use of these formulas:

1. They assume that either private or public benefit can be ascertained. In practice, this has not been done.
2. They assume that total cost equals total benefit. In actuality, total cost may exceed or be less than total benefit. This can not be determined unless special benefit can be measured.

. . . .

Due to the difficulties involved in determining special benefit, many cities have allocated costs by use or the opportunity to use an improvement. This assumes that the increase in property value is a result of the availability and utility of the improvement. Properties or property owners who have access to the improvement are held to be the recipients of special benefits. When utility is used as a criterion, the focus is on the design and/or purpose of the improvement. For example, cost-sharing for streets is determined by the width or design of the street, as this influences the capacity and use of the street. The properties assessed are the properties served by the street. . . .

---

* The excerpts that follow have been edited and somewhat revised by the casebook editors.

Assessment Methodology

Common Assessment Methods

The methods of assessment used by most cities are not based on the dollar increase in property value or special benefit. The actual value of the special benefit accruing to individual properties is as difficult to determine as the aggregate value of private benefit.

Some alternative indicator of special benefit must be employed to determine the special benefit received. The indicator should reflect the benefit-producing characteristics of the improvement and the increase in property value. Various assessments methods employ different indicators. The most common assessment methods use front footage, property area, assessed valuation of property, assessed benefit, benefit zone, actual cost, and standard lot benefit as indicators. A discussion of the methods employing these indicators follows. These methods often take the name of the indicators used:

1. *Front footage* — This method is the most commonly used. It is employed in the assessment of improvements such as streets, sidewalks, curbs and gutters. "The rate per front foot is derived by dividing the total private benefit by the total assessable footage. The individual assessment is determined by multiplying the rate per front foot by the frontage of the lot. This method disregards such factors as area and shape of lot."
2. *Property area* — The rate per square foot is determined by dividing the total private cost by the total amount of assessable square footage. The individual assessment is determined by multiplying the assessable square footage of the lot by the rate per square foot.
3. *Valuation of property* — The assessment is determined by dividing the assessed value of the lot by the total value of assessable lots and multiplying this quotient by the total private benefit. "Valuation of land is generally not considered a very good method of determining benefit, especially if assessed valuation is used. Some of the arguments against the use of assessed valuation are:
    a. there are likely to be inequities in the assessed valuation even in the best tax system;
    b. assessed value does not usually represent current market value, but rather some hypothetical and historical 'average' value; and
    c. enhancement of value resulting from an improvement may not be proportional to assessed value."
4. *Benefit zone method* — This method is based upon the theory that the land closest to the improvement receives the greatest benefit from the improvement and that land not directly abutting the improvement also benefits in some degree from the improvement. The main disadvantage of the benefit zone method is that the zones are often arbitrary, as it is very difficult to establish zones that actually correspond to benefit.
5. *Actual cost* — Under this method, the individual property owners are assessed according to the actual cost of improvements adjacent to their properties. The obvious shortcoming of this method is that benefit does not necessarily have any relationship to the actual cost of work done. The benefit may be less than or greater than the costs of the project.
6. *Lot benefit method* — Under this method, all standard lots are assessed at the same rate. The underlying assumption . . . is that every standard lot receives the same benefit whether the lot has 60 feet or 85 feet of frontage.

7. *Assessed benefit* — This method involves the assessment of benefit through appraisal.... It is probably the most flexible, as peculiarities of the area can readily be taken into account. However, because it is based primarily on human judgment, it is often subjected to the questionings and criticism of protesting property owners.

[Shinn next points out that the same problems that are faced in determining special benefit must also be faced in determining the zone of benefit. Most local governments only assess those properties abutting the improvement, but a few extend the zone of benefit to include non-abutting properties. *Id.* at 36-37.]

McNALLY v. TOWNSHIP OF TEANECK

Supreme Court of New Jersey
75 N.J. 33, 379 A.2d 446 (1977)

SCHREIBER, J.

The Township of Teaneck, pursuant to N.J.S.A. 40:56-1, which authorizes a municipality to assess lands benefited by a local improvement, levied special assessments against 313 residential properties for reimbursement of the costs of paving streets and installing curbs. Owners of 74 properties appealed asserting that the criteria used in determining the amounts of the assessments were improper. The Superior Court vacated the assessments and remanded the matter to the Township for reassessment. 132 N.J.Super. 442, 334 A.2d 67 (Law Div. 1975). On appeal the Appellate Division, while retaining jurisdiction, remanded the cause to the trial judge to reassess each property. The matter is before us by virtue of our having granted motions for leave to appeal by the plaintiff landowners and defendant Township.

The detailed facts are set forth in the trial court's decision. For purposes of this opinion a summary of the pertinent facts is in order.

In March 1971 the Township adopted an ordinance providing that new paving and new curbs would be installed on parts of eleven streets located in three residential areas. These were designated as local improvements, the cost to be assessed upon the lands in the vicinity of the improvement in accordance with N.J.S.A. 40:56-1 *et seq.* The ordinance also stated that the assessments "shall in each case be as nearly as may be in proportion to and not in excess of the peculiar benefit, advantage or increase in value which the respective lots and parcels of real estate shall be deemed to receive by reason of such improvement. The total amount of the assessments so levied shall not exceed the cost of said improvement. The portion of such cost which shall not be so assessed shall be paid by the Township as in the case of a general improvement which is to be paid for by general taxation."

Upon completion of the project the Township appointed three residents of the municipality as commissioners to assess property owners for such improvement. N.J.S.A. 40:56-22. The chairman, Norman F. Sirianni, had previously served on eight to ten assessment commissions. He was a businessman and was president of a company which mined and marketed industrial sand. Julian Jerome Case, a member of the bars of New York and New Jersey, had 35 years experience in the real estate field as an owner, attorney, and instructor in real estate assessments and taxation. James R. Wynn, who did not testify at the trial, was an attorney and an accountant.

The total project costs consisted of $331,280 for the street paving, $12,105 for the curbing, and 7% overhead. These costs were itemized by streets and were furnished to the commissioners by the Township Engineer, Milton Robbins. The respective street costs varied depending upon such factors as the soil condition and size of the street. The accuracy and reasonableness of these figures are not in dispute.

Proposed assessments were calculated on a front-foot basis, that is, the total cost on a particular street was divided by the total foot frontage and the resultant figure multiplied by the foot frontage of each property. [Each commissioner visually inspected the improvements and the property. The commissioners also met on numerous occasions and held two public hearings with property owners. They submitted their report to the council, which confirmed the report after holding a hearing at which some property owners appeared. — Eds.]

. . . .

In their complaint the landowners asserted that the assessments were improper because "there was no attempt made to assess for the peculiar benefits" to each property as a result of the improvement. They sought the return of any monies which had been paid and a restraint to enjoin the Township from assessing the plaintiffs on any basis other than the peculiar benefits or increased value received. In the pretrial order the plaintiffs' factual and legal contentions were that the assessment commissioner did not attempt to identify precisely the peculiar benefit, advantage or increase in value which accrued to each property and that N.J.S.A. 40:56-27, which restricts each individual assessment to the benefit, advantage or increase in value received, had been violated.

. . . .

The trial judge, holding that use of a front-foot formula dependent on a cost basis is improper, rejected the method utilized by the assessment commissioners, asserted that there was unlawful discrimination among property owners, and remanded the assessments appealed from to the Township for reassessment. The Appellate Division, holding that the amount of a special assessment may not exceed the quantum of the enhanced value, was not certain as to the standards the trial judge would impose in fixing the assessments. Apprehensive that the assessment commissioners would be unable to comply with the trial court's order, the Appellate Division, while retaining jurisdiction, remanded the cause of the trial judge to reassess each property.

Municipalities are authorized to undertake the paving or repaving of a street and the curbing of a sidewalk along a street as local improvements. N.J.S.A. 40:56-1d. and e. By definition a local improvement is one the cost of which the whole or in part "may be assessed upon the lands in the vicinity thereof benefited thereby." N.J.S.A. 40:56-1. The governing body may in the ordinance authorizing a local improvement provide that a part of the costs be paid by the municipality. N.J.S.A. 40:56-12. Particular assessments may be made either by the tax assessor or board charged with the duty of making general assessments or by a board created for that purpose. N.J.S.A. 40:56-21. In the absence of a board, the governing body may appoint by resolution "three discreet freeholders, residents of the municipality, in no way interested in the improvement, as commissioners to make the assessments for benefits for such improvement." N.J.S.A. 40:56-22.

Upon completion of any local improvement, whoever is in charge "shall certify" to the commissioners a statement showing in detail the cost of improvement and the amount, if any, paid or contributed by the municipality. N.J.S.A. 40:56-24. If the assessments do not equal the cost less the contribution, the balance must be paid by the municipality. *Id.*

The commissioners are charged with examining the improvement and viewing all lands and real estate "upon the line and in the vicinity thereof benefited thereby ...." N.J.S.A. 40:56-25. They must also hold a public hearing, after notifying the affected property owners by mail and by publication in a newspaper. *Id.* Witnesses may be examined under oath and the commissioners may "make a just and equitable assessment of the benefits conferred upon any real estate by reason of such improvements having due regard to the rights and interests of all persons concerned, as well as to the value of the real estate benefited." N.J.S.A. 40:56-26.

Certain guidelines are statutorily mandated. The total amount of the assessment levied cannot exceed the total project cost less any municipal contribution. N.J.S.A. 40:56-24. Further, all assessments are to be "as nearly as may be in proportion to and not in excess of the peculiar benefit, advantage or increase in value which the respective lots and parcels of real estate shall be deemed to receive by reason of such improvement." N.J.S.A. 40:56-27. If the total cost exceeds the assessments, the municipality must pay the difference. N.J.S.A. 40:56-37.

The commissioners then submit a report in which the assessments are itemized to the governing body of the municipality. N.J.S.A. 40:56-30. Before approving the assessments, the governing body must consider the report at a public meeting, notice having been given by mail to the affected property owners and by newspaper publication. *Id.* After considering the report, the governing body is empowered to adopt and confirm the assessments with or without alterations. *Id.* Within 30 days thereafter a property owner may appeal to the Superior Court. N.J.S.A. 40:56-54. Upon review the court presumes that the assessments were regularly made and confirmed. N.J.S.A. 40:56-33, and determines whether the assessment is "just and fair." N.J.S.A. 40:56-54. If not, the court "shall make an order correcting the same ...." *Id.* The commissioners then are required to assess anew the benefits which become a lien upon the property. N.J.S.A. 40:56-34. If an assessment has been illegally made and paid, and the new assessment is for a lesser amount, the municipality must refund the difference. *Id.*

The key issue in this case is whether utilization of cost per front-foot basis, when employed in conjunction with the judgment of commissioners based upon their visual observations and examinations of each property and their individual experiences, is appropriate in fixing assessments for paving streets and installing curbs in a residential neighborhood.

Use of the cost per foot frontage formula has been constitutionally sustained.... It has long been embedded in our history as an appropriate tool for commissioners to use. See *State, Kohler, pros. v. Town of Guttenberg*, 38 N.J.L. 419 (Sup. Ct. 1876), where Justice Dixon wrote that:

> It is their [commissioners'] duty to consider, specifically, the advantage accruing to each plot, but on such consideration, they may judge that because of the uniform condition of the land, every foot of frontage is equally increased in value. Upon such a conclusion, the frontage would, of course, fix the proportion of burden. [*Id.* at 422-423.]

In *Wilson v. Ocean City*, 112 N.J.L. 97, 170 A. 56 (E. & A. 1934), aff'g *per curiam* o. b. 11 N.J.Misc. 325, 165 A. 880 (Sup. Ct. 1933), the Court of Errors and Appeals adopted the opinion of the former Supreme Court, which, rejecting an attack on cost per foot frontage assessments, wrote:

> The law is settled that an assessment on a frontage basis will not be set aside if that basis appears to be a fair test for the estimation of benefits. [11 N.J.Misc. at 326, 165 A. at 880.]

... It has likewise been sanctioned in many other jurisdictions. *See* Annot., *"Assessments for improvements by the front-foot rule,"* 56 A.L.R. 941 (1928) (listing 23 states other than New Jersey which have upheld the validity of assessments in which the cost per foot frontage has been utilized).

Whether the property subject to assessment has been benefited and, if so, the extent thereof are factual issues. The ultimate test is, of course, the difference between the market value of the land before and after the improvement.... That difference, the incremental value, may be established by the conventional method of expert testimony or by some other reliable proof....

The cost of the new pavement and curb is evidence of its value to the abutting property owner. In the absence of any proof to the contrary the enhancement in value presumably would be equated with that cost. That is comparable to the use of cost to ascertain increased market value for general tax assessments when an improvement is made to an existing structure. In that case, in the absence of other evidence, the value increase would usually be presumptively equivalent to the cost. Where the value of personal property has decreased, use of the cost of repairs has been held to be sufficient in itself to establish damages.... This principle has been applied in ascertaining damages to realty.... We envision no reason why the same principle should not be applied to measure increases in value. This approach is sensible and practical. Moreover, this approach in the context of special assessments for street pavements and curbs where the commissioners have made the necessary inspections and determinations operates effectively to bring about fair and equitable results.

Exaction of more than the special benefit to the property owner would constitute a taking of private property for public use without compensation.... So, if it is shown that the market value enhancement is less than cost, then the assessment must be reduced accordingly. This is somewhat analogous to the situation involving property damages where the difference between market value before and after the event acts as a recoverable ceiling even though the cost of repair may exceed that amount....

The two statutory ceilings that the total assessments may not exceed the total costs and that the individual assessment must not be in excess of the enhanced value assure property owners that they will not be charged more than a fair share of the improvement costs.... In this manner the assessments will not be in excess of the peculiar benefit to a particular property, N.J.S.A. 40:56-27, even though as a result property owners may pay, *inter se,* varying amounts. The statute, N.J.S.A. 40:56-27, refers to the relationship of the betterment to each owner's property and not to the relationship among property owners.

The special assessment is not a tax which comes within the constitutional provision requiring that property be assessed for taxation under general laws and by uniform rules.... The purpose of a special assessment is to reimburse the municipality in whole or in part for a particular expenditure. The scheme of the local improvement law makes it abundantly clear that its function is not to raise funds for revenue purposes.... The ordinance, authorized by statute promulgated under the State's police power, simply created a method of levying assessments on those who have received a special benefit from the expenditure....

The commissioners here were well qualified to perform their functions. Their collective experiences included service on prior commissions, operation of a business, practice as an attorney and accountant, ownership and operation of realty holdings, and instruction in courses on real estate appraisal and taxation. Judge Mountain in *In re South Orange,* [2 N.J.Misc. 867, 869 (Cty. Civ. Ct. 1924)], approvingly quoted a judicial pronouncement that: "They [commissioners] are expected to act on their own opinion as citizens of experience and intelligence with the aid of such information as they are able to gather." These commissioners complied with all the statutory requisites. They viewed the properties affected to determine whether there were any circumstances which would warrant a different treatment of any particular property or whether they were all substantially the same. They afforded the property owners an opportunity to be heard and to present evidence, expert or otherwise, to demonstrate the lack of uniformity or unusual nature of their property as well as proof that the assessment exceeded the difference between the market value before and after completion of the project. The property owners adduced no such evidence, expert or otherwise.

The record reveals that the commissioners certified and reported that the assessments were as nearly as may be in proportion to and not in excess of the peculiar benefit, advantage or increase in value which the respective parcels of real estate received by reason of the improvements. The contents of the report are presumptively correct and the taxpayers had the burden of overcoming that presumption by clear and convincing evidence. . . .

The expert Burek's testimony, accepted by the trial court, established that the enhancement in market value for certain properties was less than the assessed proportionate cost. We conclude that it therefore satisfied those taxpayers' burdens of overcoming the presumption. However, the presumption was not overcome as to the remaining properties. As indicated above, use of the cost per front-foot formula for pavement and curbs by the commissioners who viewed the improvements and each of the properties and applied their own judgment and expertise adequately established the incremental values, there being no indication in the record that the parcels on a per street basis lacked substantial uniformity. Those findings are buttressed by the expert's testimony that the increased values and benefits to each of these properties were equal to or exceeded the assigned costs of the pavement and curbs.

The trial court invalidated these assessments (even though the benefits exceeded those assessments) because of the widely differing percentages among the 73 properties of the ratios of their respective assessments to incremental value and assessments to value of the real estate before the improvement. 132 N.J.Super. at 458, 334 A.2d 67. This rationale raised *sua sponte* by the trial court rests upon some underlying misconceptions.[3] First, imposition of the special assessment is not a general tax which constitutionally requires uniformity. N.J. Const. (1947), Art. VIII, § 1, par. 1. The special assessment is a means of reimbursing a municipality for a capital expenditure which was specially advantageous to certain properties. Second, the statute does not call for a comparison of benefits among property owners. N.J.S.A. 40:56-27. Third, the costs of the improvement allocable to each property do not necessarily result in the same percentage of increased value of each parcel. Each example, assume pavement costs of $2500 each for a $25,000 and a $50,000 home on comparable adjoining lots. Though the value increase of both properties may be the same, the percentage increase in value of one would be 10% as compared to 5% for the other. So long as neither owner is required to pay more than the benefit received and the method of determining the amount of that benefit is reasonable and applied uniformly to all property owners, the statutory mandate has been satisfied.

---

[3] The plaintiffs' theory at trial was twofold. First, that the cost per foot frontage method was erroneous and, second, that paving a road created no benefit to the properties. The plaintiffs never

Contrary to the trial court's expectation the ratios of the assessment to the realty value before betterment and of the assessment to the incremental value may vary widely. Elimination of the divergence among plaintiffs in their assessment to before improvement value ratios, as suggested by the trial court, would require application of the lowest ratio of assessment to before improvment value to each of the 313 properties. This would effectively thwart the municipality's efforts to obtain reimbursement, result in a bonanza to many property owners who would be paying a lower percentage of the pro rata costs, and thrust the additional burden on all the municipality's taxpayers. Neither the statute nor the constitution calls for this.

Attempts to equalize the varying ratios of assessment to enhancement among plaintiffs might also produce anomalous effects. If one were to apply the lowest ratio to each property the same results as described above would occur. Or, if one were to assess at full benefit, certain property owners would be called upon to pay more than their allocable cost of the improvement whereas others would pay less than their proportionate share. The commissioners applied the same front-foot formula to all properties, with due regard to any special circumstances affecting any particular parcel. There is no evidence that different ratios of allocated costs were applied. The same standards and criteria were applied to every property and the resulting special assessments arrived at did not violate any rights in an equal protection sense. Thus the method results in a balancing of costs and is a practical workable device for assessment commissioners.

Accordingly, the matter is remanded to the trial court to enter appropriate judgments directing reduction of assessments in those cases where the total assessment exceeded the enhancement value. The remaining assessments shall be confirmed.

Affirmed in part and reversed in part and remanded.

Comments: 1. In the lower court opinion, standards for determining the amount of assessment were discussed:

> It is also clear that special benefit in this context has a well-settled meaning. Special benefit is the actual increase in the value of the property which results from the local improvement or, more particularly stated, the difference in the fair market value immediately before and immediately after the making of the improvement. This definition of special benefit is not only currently accepted, . . . but has also been recognized in our jurisprudence on this subject for at least 50 years; . . . . Thus, the task of the commissioners is to devise and implement a method of determining the assessment which is reasonably calculated both to reflect the before and after value of the benefited property and to fairly apportion the burden of payment for the improvement among all the affected property owners. In performing this task the cost of the improvement has relevance — it is not, however, both as a matter of constitutional requirement and statutory mandate, dispositive as the commissioners here seemed to think. That is to say, the cost of the improvement constitutes a ceiling on the total assessments, so that even if the total dollar amount of the special benefits exceeds the improvement cost, the total assessments cannot exceed that cost and will be, consequently, less than the enhancement value. On the other hand, if the cost of the improvement exceeds its enhancement value, the amount of the assessment cannot exceed the enhancement and the municipality must itself pay the difference between the cost and the assessment. This is the express provision of N.J.S.A. 40:56-24, which thereby recognizes the economic reality that cost and enhancement are not equal, equitable or interchangeable concepts. Thus an assessment calculation method, such as the front-foot formula here

---

claimed that their respective assessments were too high because of the inadequacy of other assessments.

employed, which is exclusively dependent upon the cost of the improvement and is obviously designed primarily to recoup for the municipality the cost of the improvement on a simplistic mathematical basis, prima facie fails to meet the statutory requirements unless the commissioners have made an initial determination, first, that the total cost does not exceed the total enhancement value, and second, that the formula fairly apportions the burden among all the property owners in accordance with their respective benefits.

334 A.2d at 67, 72 (N.J. App. Div. 1975).

With reference to the cost allocation question, it seems apparent that most local improvements that are linear facilities, such as streets and sewers, should provide some benefit to adjacent properties. But the presumption is not irrebuttable. Is the court's analysis consistent with the cost-allocation formulas discussed by Shinn, *supra*? Did the New Jersey Supreme Court resolve the objections to the front-foot formula raised by the lower court?

Courts sometimes find that no special benefit was conferred. *Harrison v. Board of Supervisors,* 118 Cal. Rptr. 828 (Cal. App. 1975), was a challenge to a storm sewer special assessment. "The amount of the assessment was calculated upon a rainfall runoff coefficient based wholly upon the zoning of the units in question." After noting that "the validity of the formula will of necessity depend upon just what the special benefit is," the court found that no special benefit existed:

> The benefit to be derived from the drainage system in the case at hand is the prevention of street flooding which occurs during the rainy season in certain spots of the area. There was no testimony of floodings on the private properties themselves and much testimony from people who claimed there was no excess water problem at all in their immediate vicinity even in the streets.
>
> The theory on which the benefit was presented at the administrative hearings was that the general area would benefit by relief of the traffic problems and that those who contribute to the problem should contribute to the solution. . . . The fact that the traffic problems are seen as caused, not by the rain, but by the property from which the rainwaters drain, is not a basis for levying a special assessment according to the special benefit rule.

Id. at 831-32.

Similar problems arise in road widening cases. Assume that a county wishes to upgrade an existing, two-lane, paved road so that it can carry the heavier traffic that is being generated by development in the surrounding area. Accordingly, the road is widened, paved to its widened length, and strengthened. It is clear that after the improvement the adjacent residential properties lining the widened highway will be detrimentally affected by the increased noise, dirt, and soot arising from the heavier highway use. May they nevertheless be specially assessed for at least part of the improvement? Since *Fluckey v. City of Plymouth,* 100 N.W.2d 486 (Mich. 1960), the Michigan courts have not allowed assessments in such cases, the court there noting that "[i]n frontier days, and even today, in some areas, the mere location of a road to or near one's property may confer a real benefit. This not such a case." *Id.* at 489. *Accord, DeFraties v. Kansas City,* 521 S.W.2d 385 (Mo. 1975). Under Shinn's analysis, is the special assessment disallowed because the widened highway is a public good, because there is no special benefit, or for both reasons? Does a finding of no special benefit necessarily mean that the improvement is a public good? *See also* the *Heavens* case, *infra.*

It should be noted that assessments on a front-foot basis have usually been approved when they reflect the true benefit resulting from the improvement. For discussion see *Davis v. City of Westland,* 206 N.W.2d 750 (Mich. 1973).

2. Assessments for facilities serving large areas, such as sewer systems, may sometimes be saved if the court is willing to treat benefits accruing to the future use of the property as justifying the assessment. Note that the special assessment is against the land and not the improvements, and to this extent differs from the general ad valorem property tax. Thus the rule, generally, is that future uses of the land may be taken into account in justifying the assessment.

For example, in *City of Hallandale v. Meekins,* 237 So. 2d 318 (Fla. App. 1970), the sewer for which the assessment was levied was sized at a capacity substantially in excess of what was needed to serve existing uses. One property, which was vacant and was being used as a dog track, was assessed 10.4 percent of the cost of the improvement even though it had a projected flow of only 4.9 percent of the sewer's designed capacity. Nevertheless, the assessment was upheld:

> Clearly, there is no necessary correlation between the special benefit conferred upon property by a sanitary sewer system servicing the property and the present use being made of such property. The special benefit is the availability of the system and is permanent, but the use to which the property is put is usually temporary and changes from time to time. . . . [With reference to the dog track] such continued special use of the property is purely voluntary on the part of the owner. . . . However, if the owner should find it to his best interests to do so, he would convert the property to another use.

Id. at 322.

See also *Konfal v. Charter Township of Delhi,* 283 N.W.2d 677 (Mich. App. 1979) (sewer project); *Burlington Northern, Inc. v. City of McCook,* 283 N.W.2d 380 (Neb. 1979) (special assessment upon industrial property is void where the sewer improvement is solely for residential use).

Similarly, the Minnesota Supreme Court held that improvements may confer too speculative a future benefit upon property to justify an assessment when a lot receives no present benefit and future enhancement in value is uncertain. *In re Village of Burnsville,* 287 N.W.2d 375 (Minn. 1979) (sewers); *see also Village of Bloomingdale v. LaSalle National Bank,* 387 N.E.2d 416 (Ill. 1979) (there must be either a present or assured future use of the improvement which can be enforced). A special assessment, on the other hand, may be found to provide greater benefit to unimproved than to improved land because of the greater potential for appreciation in the former. *Vail v. City of Bandon,* 630 P.2d 1339 (Or. 1981).

Zoning is one indicator of future use. Yet, in *Strickland v. City of Wichita,* 457 P.2d 162 (Kan. 1969), the court struck down an assessment for sewer construction based entirely on existing zoning classifications on the ground that no attention was given to the extent to which the existing zoning reflected actual land values. On the other hand, it is not necessary to rely on existing zoning classifications if there is a reasonable probability that the zoning will be changed to allow a use that will benefit from the improvement. For discussion see *Molbreak v. Village of Shorewood Hills,* 225 N.W.2d 394 (Wis. 1975) (street widening). If the special assessment can be based on a probable future use of the land why isn't this a tax on speculative value of the kind apparently prohibited under the general ad valorem tax cases, *supra*?

3. Special assessments on non-abutting owners often come under attack. In *Davies v. City of Lawrence,* 545 P.2d 1115 (Kan. 1976), the city set up a benefit district for a "skeletal" system of sidewalks. These sidewalks were to be built only on some of the streets in the benefit district. Noting that "property lying many hundreds of feet from a sidewalk could conceivably pay more of the cost of the sidewalk than a property located directly on an abutting sidewalk," the court struck down the assessment on the grounds that it did not impose a "substantially equal" burden on the property included within the district.

See also *Johnson v. City of Inkster,* 258 N.W.2d 24 (Mich. 1977), where the court held that the assessment of non-abutting properties for improvements to a major road were designed to benefit the general public and that no special benefit was conferred on the assessed lots. The court reversed a lower court decision finding that the non-abutting properties were specially benefited because the road improvement would allow policemen and firemen to reach these properties more easily, residents of non-abutting properties would be benefited by the use of the safer and faster-moving improved road, and property values would be enhanced by the improved ingress and egress provided by the road. *Accord, City of Clive v. Iowa Concrete Block & Material Co.,* 298 N.W.2d 585 (Iowa 1980) (street widening from two to four lanes held to be a "major transportation corridor").

Assessment of non-abutting property owners presents what Shinn calls a zone of benefit problem. Consider how this problem should be handled in the following special assessment context: Metro City wishes to revive its downtown business district, and decides to construct several parking lots throughout the district, the cost to be recovered by special assessment on all property within the district. Several problems are presented. Do the parking lots confer a private benefit for which the assessments may be levied? *See Wing v. City of Eugene,* 437 P.2d 836 (Or. 1968) (held yes). How wide should the district be drawn? May lots presently used for residential purposes be included in the assessment on the grounds that they may eventually be used for commercial purposes? See the *Wing* case, *supra,* holding that future use may be considered. What method of assessment should be used? The *Wing* case upheld a zoned system under which assessments varied with the distance from the parking lots. *Accord, Mobil Oil Corp. v. Town of Westport,* 438 A.2d 768 (Conn. 1980) (and basing fifty percent of assessment on number of parking spaces needed for the property). *See also Patterson v. City of Bismarck,* 212 N.W.2d 374 (N.D. 1973). *Compare Northern Pacific Railway v. City of Grand Forks,* 73 N.W.2d 348 (N.D. 1955) (unqualified front foot assessment disapproved).

In the cases and materials reviewed so far, the special assessment was levied on a one-time basis by the local government making the improvement. State legislation may also allow the formation of special districts for the purpose of carrying out a single improvement, which is then financed throughout the district by a tax on real property. In these situations, the zone of benefit has clearly been expanded to include property non-abutting the improvement. If an attempt is made to characterize the tax that is levied as a special assessment or special benefit tax, questions may then arise, as the next case indicates, concerning the propriety of using this taxing device for the improvement in question.

HEAVENS v. KING COUNTY RURAL LIBRARY DISTRICT

Supreme Court of Washington
66 Wash. 2d 558, 404 P.2d 453 (1965)

WEAVER, JUDGE. Fundamentally, this action, commenced under our Uniform Declaratory Judgments Act (RCW 7.24), challenges the constitutionality of Laws of 1961, chapter 162, which authorizes local improvement districts for public libraries.

After trial, the court dismissed plaintiffs' complaint with prejudice but continued a temporary injunction in force against defendants, the King County Rural Library District and its trustees, pending appeal, providing plaintiffs file a $5,000 bond. The bond was filed....

Defendant King County Rural Library District was created January 4, 1943. RCW 27.12.040. Its management is vested in a board of library trustees. RCW 27.12.190. Except for the issue involved in the instant case, rural libraries are financed by *general taxation.* Based upon a budget submitted by the board of library trustees to the county commissioners, the commissioners may levy a tax of not more than two mills a year upon the property in the district for libarary service. RCW 27.12.050. Additional funds may be made available to library districts by taxation by a vote of the people pursuant to RCW 27.12.222, RCW 84.52.052 and RCW 84.52.056. It is not necessary to detail the manner and method by which additional funds may be made available. It is sufficient to point out that

> ... Such levies shall be a part of the *general tax roll* and shall be collected as a part of the *general taxes* against the property in the district. RCW 27.12.050 (Italics ours.)

Laws of 1961, chapter 162 introduced into the tax structure of this state a new concept for financing library districts. It permitted library districts to form local improvement districts within all or part of the library districts. Section 2 of the act provides:

> In any instance where the acquisition of land, buildings or capital equipment, or the construction of library buildings are of special benefit to part or all of the lands in the district (we note the legislature did not find that a library *is* of special benefit to land), the governing board of the library district shall have authority to include such lands in a local improvement district, and to levy special assessments under a mode of annual installments extending over a period not exceeding twenty years on all property specially benefited by any local improvement, on the basis of the special benefits to pay in whole or in part the damages or costs of any such improvements ordered in such library district.... Laws of 1961, chapter 162, § 2, p. 1759 et seq. (Italics ours.) ...

June 6, 1962, pursuant to the 1961 statute, the board of the King County Rural Library District adopted Resolution No. 1962-4. The resolution announced the board's intention to form a local improvement district (hereafter called "LID") to be known as the "Shoreline Library District No. 1." The boundaries of the LID were defined to include the area between the northern Seattle city limits (145th Street) and the King-Snohomish County line (205th Street) and between Puget Sound and Lake Washington and a line extending north from the lake. We take judicial notice of the fact that the proposed district is extensive in area.

The property upon which the King County Rural Library District sought to complete a library building is located at approximately the geographic center of the proposed library LID district. Plaintiffs are owners of property within the proposed district....

This case brings into sharp focus the constitutional difference between special assessments for local improvements inuring to the benefit of specific land and general ad valorem taxes levied for the benefit of the entire taxing district. A special assessment for local improvements is not a tax within the constitutional limitations upon the amount of taxation; nor is it a tax subject to the constitutional provision requiring uniformity and equality of taxation....

Special assessments to pay for local public improvements benefiting specific land are of ancient lineage. They have been held valid for the construction and improvement of streets, curbs, gutters, sidewalks, and for the installation of sanitary and storm sewers, drains, levees, ditches, street lighting, and water mains.... All such assessments have one common element: they are for the construction of local improvements that are appurtenant to specific land and bring a benefit substantially more intense than is yielded to the rest of the municipality. The benefit to the land must be actual, physical and material and not merely speculative or conjectural.

In *In re Shilshole Avenue,* 85 Wash. 522, 537, 148 P. 781 (1915), the court said:

> It is the basic principle and the very life of the doctrine of special assessments that there can be no special assessment to pay for a thing which has conferred no special benefit upon the property assessed. To assess property for a thing which did not benefit it would be *pro tanto* the taking of private property for a public use without compensation, hence unconstitutional. Though the right to levy special assessments for local improvements is referable solely to the sovereign power of taxation, our state Constitution, art. 7, § 9, expressly limits its exercise to assessments of property benefited....

In the last analysis a valid special assessment for a local improvement is merely compensation paid by the property owner for the improved value of his land. If there is no benefit, there can be no assessment. To hold otherwise would be to deprive the owner of property without due process of law in contravention of the fourteenth amendment to the federal constitution.

We accept counsel's statement that no other state has attempted to authorize the construction of a public library financed by local improvement district special assessments. We find, however, that other jurisdictions have held special assessments invalid when applied to analogous situations. The following are illustrative: a war memorial plaza, a public auditorium, a court house, public school buildings, water works.... They were held to be general improvements that should be financed by general taxation; they were not "local" improvements which added a unique and peculiar benefit to land, so that they could be financed by special assessment.

The closest analogy to a public library LID is an LID for a public auditorium. Without dispute, both contribute to the culture of the members of the community. Can it be said that they create a public improvement which attaches to and increases the value of land adjacent to the improvement or within the confines of a large district? We do not believe so.

In *Lipscomb v. Lenon,* 169 Ark. 610, 276 S.W. 367 (1925), the Arkansas Supreme Court held unconstitutional an act authorizing the formation of a local improvement district in order to build a public auditorium. Paraphrasing the language of the Arkansas court, we believe it is plain that a public library is for the benefit of the members of the whole community individually and collectively who may be served by it; the library cannot and does not confer any peculiar or special benefit upon the land to be subjected to an LID special assessment. The Arkansas court continued:

> ... If it could be said that such an improvement is essential to the progress and prosperity of the city and suburban communities, the contribution which an auditorium makes to such prosperity is general to the entire community and not peculiar and special to the real property in the city and outlying contiguous territory. Whether the building of an auditorium would be beneficial rather than harmful to the real property immediately contiguous thereto would be wholly problematical and dependent upon many contingencies, notably the character of the architecture and construction and the nature of the assemblies gathered there, etc. Certain it is there is no such similarity between an improvement district for the construction of an auditorium and improvement districts for the construction of roads, bridges, wharves, levees, drains, etc., as would bring the former in the category of the latter. In the former the benefit, at most, to the real property, can only be incidental and of the most remote and general character, while in the latter, it must be, and is, a peculiar and special benefit to the real property taxed for its construction.

In *Wilson v. Lambert,* 168 U.S. 611 ... (1898), the court refused to strike down a special assessment about to be levied in order to establish a public park in the District of Columbia. We find the case neither persuasive nor controlling. The argument based upon it is answered in *Lipscomb, supra:*

> ... Then, too, a city park is a wholly different character of improvement from a city auditorium. A city park, properly kept and maintained, adds decidedly to the attractiveness of, and hence, enhances the value of the real property immediately contiguous thereto, and to the beauty of the whole city, considered as a corporate entity....

We believe the difference is obvious. A public park might well enhance the value of adjacent property.

In conclusion, we agree with plaintiffs that:

> The construction of public libraries is a legitimate and laudable exercise of governmental power for the general education of the community at large, but libraries are not constructed primarily to enhance the value of the real estate surrounding them. For this reason their construction cannot constitutionally be financed by assessing the cost thereof against the adjacent real estate.

Were our conclusion otherwise, the rationale of Laws of 1961, chapter 162 and defendants' argument in support thereof, would result in revolutionary changes in the constitutional tax structure of this state.

In view of our conclusion it is not necessary for us to discuss the remaining assignments of error.

The judgment dismissing plaintiffs' complaint is reversed and the case remanded to the trial court with directions to enter judgment consistent with this opinion.

It is so ordered.

ROSELLINI, C. J., and HILL, DONWORTH, OTT, HUNTER, and HAMILTON, JJ., concur.

FINLEY, JUDGE (dissenting):

The decision arrived at by the majority herein is not inevitably directed or absolutely required either by provisions of the state constitution or the constitution of the United States. Viewed realistically, the decision involves a policy judgment, or a matter of judgment as to values.

The issue in this case is clear cut: If utilized for the establishment of a library, where does the local improvement district concept, device or mechanism fall on the legal spectrum of permissible and nonpermissible special assessments? The early case of *Wilson v. Lambert,* . . . identified the poles of the spectrum. On the one end of the span are the clearly permissible uses of special assessments to cover the cost of installing roads, sewers, et cetera. There is no argument those improvements add value to the adjacent land. On the other hand, there are certain improvements which have been held to be too general for assessment against property in the LID format. *Wilson v. Lambert* identified examples of the latter category as courthouses and post offices. My difference with the majority is that I believe a library is amenable to classification on the permissible side of the spectrum insofar as LID financing is concerned.

The use of local improvement districts to finance needed projects has not been limited to streets and sewers. *Wilson v. Lambert, supra* upheld assessments for a park in Washington, D.C. Other state courts have also upheld assessments for parks. *In re Improvement of Lake of the Isles Park,* 152 Minn. 29, 188 N.W. 54 (1922); *Brightwell v. Kansas City,* 153 Mo. App. 519, 134 S.W. 87 (1911). Even more recently, local improvement districts have been created to deal with modern problems. In *Northern Pacific Ry. Co. v. City of Grand Forks,* 73 N.W.2d 348 (N.D. 1955), and *Thomson v. City of Dearborn,* 349 Mich. 685, 85 N.W.2d 122 (1957), the courts upheld assessments for the creation of off-street parking lots in the business district. See also, *Whittier v. Dixon,* 24 Cal. 2d 664, 151 P.2d 5, 153 A.L.R. 956 (1944).

I do not think the closest analogy to the present case is an LID for a public auditorium. It appears to me that the example of a public auditorium is somewhat in the category of a straw man envisioned or created and then decried argumentatively by the majority opinion. Among other things, an auditorium is generally located in a business district, or at least removed from good residential property. Realistically, the validity of an LID for a public auditorium would seem to depend upon its location. If the auditorium was placed in a business section, then by analogy to the parking lot cases it would seem that an argument could even be made for sustaining the LID, because the auditorium conceivably could add value to the adjacent property. However, if the auditorium is placed in a surrounding of residential property, or near it, then it is highly likely that the resulting congestion of traffic and people will not add value to the property, and in fact the auditorium might reduce values.

Thus, to me the analogy of the public auditorium is not convincingly apt. I see a modern library as akin to a park, which has been repeatedly upheld as a proper subject for the LID approach and format. A library can fit aesthetically into a quiet neighborhood. The architecture, landscaping and parklike setting of modern library facilities compel the conclusion that the surrounding property is benefited by the improvement. I am convinced that any qualified appraiser of urban real estate, if asked whether an attractively constructed library facility would add appreciably to the market value of the reasonably adjacent real estate, would most likely answer in the affirmative.

Thus, for me the crucial test — *i.e.*, benefit to the reasonably adjacent land — is satisfied. The majority opinion obliquely remarks that the local improvement district involved here is quite large. Since this appeal from a declaratory judgment does not deal with the reasonableness of the assessment, the size of the district is immaterial. The majority opinion correctly states that the issue here is the constitutionality of any assessment, but, as herein pointed out, the opinion still includes the size of the district as an important consideration in its decision. Since I can see direct, substantial monetary value added to the property of residents within at least walking distance, and, perhaps, even moderate driving distance, I would hold the purpose of the local improvement district constitutional.

In summary, let me stress that the initial sanctioning or fundamental authority for the creation of this local improvement district is traceable, in fact is based upon, a 1961 enactment of the Washington legislature. This fact, I think, should be accorded greater judicial respect and weight, policy-wise, by this court. The majority asserts or concludes that the use of a local improvement district to finance library construction "would result in revolutionary changes in the constitutional tax structure of this state." This, I think, overstates the case. While the law and our Anglo-American jurisprudence are more idealistically describable in terms of evolution rather than revolution, the distinction between the two terms in this particular context is perhaps the rate of change or growth rather than no change or no growth as an essential characteristic of law and the jurisprudence of our times. It seems to me that legislative approval of the use of local improvement districts to finance libraries is a natural and appropriate step or development in the utilization of that financing mechanism, especially when the legislature had before it the examples of the past use of the mechanism to finance parks and off-street parking lots. Once again, I stress that this purported new use or adaptation of the LID was born in the legislative halls — the place at least preferable to most traditionalists (if there is a choice) and acceptable to realists respecting innovations to meet contemporary social needs and problems. I cannot say this statute is an unconstitutional use of the LID plan, that it should be judicially exorcised or struck down, any more than I can say the new spring growth of a tree is repugnant to the rest of the tree, and, therefore, the new growth is to be lopped off.

For the reasons indicated, I dissent.

HALE, J., concurs in JUDGE FINLEY's dissent.

Comments: 1. In *Ruel v. Rapid City,* 167 N.W.2d 541 (S.D. 1969), the city attempted to levy a special assessment throughout the city for a convention center. Only residential property was exempted from the special assessment. Holding that a special assessment could not be levied for this purpose, the court noted:

> A public convention hall of the type contemplated would undoubtedly on occasion attract large groups of people to Rapid City. It is easy to visualize that it could be a boon to the economy of that city as well as to neighboring areas.... Nevertheless, in our opinion, the benefit conferred by such a structure is general to the community and cannot be translated into a specific benefit to commercial and other nonexempt real estate within the city. The benefit to land to qualify for special assessment must be actual, physical and material and not merely speculative or conjectural.

Id. at 545.

Compare Duncan Development Corp. v. Crestview Sanitary District, 125 N.W.2d 617 (Wis. 1964). The sanitary district covered an area about one-half mile square in a township. Part of the district was already receiving water service. The district then decided to construct an elevated water tower, primarily in order to provide water service to the rest of the district. Special assessments to pay for the tower were levied throughout the district. Holding that the tower was a local and not a general improvement, for which special assessments could be levied, the court commented:

> The underlying principle determining the method of financing the cost of the public improvement is one of equity and fairness to be determined by the commissioners of the sanitary district. Although an improvement confers a general benefit on all the property in a town sanitary district if in addition and primarily it enhances the value of all the property in the district but in different degrees, such improvement may be financed by the special assessment.... What may be called a local improvement under one set of facts may well constitute a general improvement in the context of different facts.

Id. at 620. *See also East Peoria Waterworks Improvement Project v. Board of Trustees,* 434 N.E.2d 781 (Ill. 1982).

2. Cash-poor cities have increasingly turned to special assessments to finance central business district revitalization projects. In *S.O.L. Club v. City of Williamsport,* 443 A.2d 410 (Pa. Commw. 1982), the city levied a special assessment to fund the rehabilitation of properties within its central business district. The court upheld the assessment, noting that it could be justified by its "aesthetic" purposes. *See also Schumacher v. City of Bozeman,* 571 P.2d 1135 (Mont. 1977). The court rejected a contention that off-street parking facilities only provided a general public benefit and could not be funded through special assessments.

BAIR v. CENTRAL & SOUTHERN FLORIDA FLOOD CONTROL DISTRICT

Supreme Court of Florida
144 So. 2d 818 (1962)

DREW, JUSTICE. This is an appeal from a decree of the Circuit Court for Martin County dismissing with prejudice an amended complaint seeking an injunction against the appellee District. The questioned decree passed directly upon and sustained the validity of Chapter 25270, General Acts, Laws of Florida 1949, F.S.A. § 378.01 note, which was attacked on constitutional grounds hereinafter detailed.

The amended complaint recited the formation of the 17 county District by the above cited act, the levy of an annual uniform ad valorem tax on all real property therein pursuant to Section 3 of that act, and alleged that certain lands in Martin County were owned by appellants, plaintiffs below who sued "for themselves and for the benefit of all other similarly situated owners" who were "so numerous that it is impractical to bring all of said owners of such property before this Court as individual party-plaintiffs." It was asserted that plaintiffs' lands were not in fact benefited by the District's operations which, on the contrary, "accumulated large amounts of surplus water which the District has discharged through the St. Lucie Canal into the waters of the St. Lucie River and Estuary which has had the effect of depreciating and lowering the market value of plaintiffs' lands." Plaintiffs' prayer was to enjoin further assessments or expenditures on behalf of the District, to require refund of monies on hand, and for "such other and further relief as the Court in its conscience may deem meet and just." The complaint as amended was dismissed upon the ground, among others, of failure to state a cause of action.

The contention here and in the trial court was, first, that the levy authorized by Chapter 25270 is, under the circumstances not in proportion to benefits and therefore constitutes a taking of private property without just compensation in violation of Section 12, Declaration of Rights, and Article XVI, Sections 28 and 29, Florida Constitution. The ruling of the court below against plaintiffs on this point is fully sustained by the rationale of earlier cases before this Court. These cases treat at length the distinctions between "an assessment against abutting property to pay for a street improvement that should be special, peculiar, and direct benefit to the abutting property at least equal to the assessment" and "an ad valorem assessment upon all the lands in a taxing district formed by statute to provide for a public improvement that is a general and common benefit to the district as an entirety." The allegations of the complaint in the instant case are clearly insufficient to overcome the legislative determination of such benefit inherent in the enactment of the provision here in question. The imposition of a levy uniformly throughout the district necessarily and, we think, properly upon this record implies a finding of benefits accruing in some fashion either direct or indirect to all real property located therein, and the cited cases clearly control the question of valid relationship between such benefits and the levy on the particular parcels here involved, more properly characterized as an ad valorem tax for special purposes rather than a special assessment on an ad valorem basis: "For a general, common, public benefit to a taxing unit as a whole, lands in the taxing unit may be reasonably assessed [on an ad valorem basis] by legislative authority, even though the lands as such are not immediately or directly benefited by the public improvement, when the assessment is not an abuse of authority."

Appellants next allege infraction of the 1940 amendment to Article IX, Sec. 2, Florida Constitution, which proscribes ad valorem taxes upon real property for the state purposes. This question may be decided upon the same reasoning which sustain the creation of the district in the first instance, *i.e.* a determination that the constituent area is differentiated from that excluded, or from the state at large, with respect to benefits resulting from operations under the act. In distinguishing district from state purposes this controlling question of benefit is one of degree, incidental effects beyond the confines of the district being often inevitable and by no means fatal. On this point we therefore conclude that the purposes for which the levy in this case is authorized are by nature district or local as opposed to state and refrain from further debate upon the affirmative definition of state purposes in this area of potential constitutional transgression.

Comments: **1.** *People ex rel. Hanrahan v. Caliendo,* 277 N.E.2d 319 (Ill. 1972), was a challenge to the constitutionality of an urban transportation district created under statutory authority by the City of Chicago. As the tax to be levied by the district was a general ad valorem property tax, the court held that no showing of special benefit was necessary. *See also Slebodnik v. City of Indianapolis,* 412 N.E.2d 854 (Ind. 1980) (levy for sewer service held an ad valorem tax); *Horgan v. Dauphin Island Water & Sewer Authority,* 409 So. 2d 1359 (Ala. 1982) (character of improvement determines whether the charge is a special assessment or a tax).

Similar problems arise when property owners attempt to have their land excluded from special districts. In *Ruberoid Co. v. North Pecos Water & Sanitation District,* 408 P.2d 436 (Colo. 1965), the court rejected an argument that land should be excluded from the district because it would not be benefited. "Unlike special improvement districts, which do have as their objective improvement of the respective properties and which are financed by a special assessment on each by reason of the relationship to the improvement bestowed, a water and sanitation district is directly concerned with the public health and welfare." *Id.* at 437.

A California appellate court provided a nice overview of the distinctive qualities of these two very different kinds of levies in *Solvang Municipal Improvement District v. Board of Supervisors,* 169 Cal. Rptr. 391 (Cal. App. 1980).

> [A] special assessment is not, in the constitutional sense, a tax at all. It is a compulsory charge placed by the state upon real property within a predetermined district, made under express legislative authority for defraying in whole or in part the expense of a permanent public improvement....
>
> ....
>
> In practical application, the two types of taxation ... to some extent overlap, and we cannot always differentiate between them with precision.... Yet in spite of ambiguities encountered in practice, the base distinction between general ad valorem taxation and special assessment to meet the cost of a local improvement remains reasonably clear.

Id. at 396.

2. When a special assessment or special benefit tax is levied, there must be a finding that benefits sufficient to support the levy have been conferred. The leading case is *Myles Salt Co. v. Board of Commissioners,* 239 U.S. 478 (1916), which held that an island consisting of high land and which would not benefit from the drainage project could not be included within a drainage district. See also *Nueces County Water Control & Improvement District v. Wilson,* 304 S.W.2d 281 (Tex. Civ. App. 1957), in which the court excluded an area which received no benefit from a water improvement.

The special benefit requirement is constitutional, but some courts exercise judicial restraint when reviewing to determine whether a special benefit has been conferred. The point was made in a special assessment case, *Western Amusement Co. v. City of Springfield,* 545 P.2d 592 (Or. 1976):

> There are probably several reasons why the court, including this court, have adopted this policy of restraint. While making special assessments is correctly classified as a quasi-judicial function, it also has aspects of an exercise of the legislative function.... The local government imposes a tax when it specially assesses. The imposition of a tax is the exercise of a legislative function. The decision to tax is not subject to judicial review.

Id. at 594.

Other courts have taken a close look at special benefit findings. *E.g., Blades v. Genesee Drain District No. 2,* 135 N.W.2d 420 (Mich. 1965) (establishment of district); *City of Houston v. Blackbird,* 384 S.W.2d 929 (Tex. Civ. App. 1964) (assessment for street paving). See also the more expansive statement of judicial review in *Thibodeaux v. Comeaux,* 145 So. 2d 1 (La. 1962), *cert. denied,* 372 U.S. 914 (1963) (objection to bond issue and specialty tax). *See also* Note, *New Developments in Special Assessment Law,* 11 U.C.D.L. Rev. 43 (1978) (discussing changing standards of judicial review in California).

The property owners in the principal case were unsuccessful in their argument that their land was not benefited by the district. What explains this result?

3. The Supreme Court has held that special assessments require notice and hearing "reasonably calculated" to inform affected property owners. *Wisconsin Electric Power Co. v. City of Milwaukee,* 352 U.S. 948 (1956). Notice by publication is not sufficient if some method of personal notice by mailing or otherwise is possible. This holding also is based on the special benefit requirement. Why do you suppose this is so? For the application of procedural due process reqirements in the state courts see, e.g., *Slebodnik v. City of Indianapolis,* 412 N.E.2d 854 (Ind. App. 1980); *City of Houston v. Fore,* 412 S.W.2d 35 (Tex. 1967).

4. Nonprofit and charitable organizations and public entities exempt from property taxation may claim that the exemption extends to special assessments, but the courts do not always agree. A New York court, for example, held that an organization exempted from all property taxes was liable for special assessments levied against its properties even though a frontage charge for water main improvements was labeled a "tax" and the organization did not use city water. *New York Cardiac Center v. Kondzielaski,* 443 N.Y.S.2d 748 (N.Y. App. Div. 1981); *see also Accacia Park Cemetery Ass'n v. Southfield Township,* 268 N.W.2d 373 (Mich. 1978) (despite public policy of preserving burial places, a cemetery is not exempt from special assessments when the burial place is not the property's sole asset).

In another decision, however, a California appellate court ruled that a property tax exemption extended to special assessments. *Regents of University of California v. City of Los Angeles,* 160 Cal. Rptr. 925 (Cal. App. 1980). The court noted that while the university may benefit from the sewer improvements, the "sewage facilities charge" was not a service fee, but "little more than a disguised special assessment." *Id.* at 927. Since "state and local government property is specifically exempt from property taxation" the court reasoned, "such property is also exempt from special assessments." *Id.* at 926-27. *See also Riverside City v. Idylwild County Water District,* 148 Cal. Rptr. 650 (Cal. App. 1978) (unless the legislature provides otherwise, public property is exempt from special assessments).

The immunity enjoyed by federal agencies and instrumentalities from state and local taxation extends to special assessments, notwithstanding the liability of some agencies for property taxes under 12 U.S.C. § 531. *Federal Reserve Bank v. Metrocentre Improvement District,* 657 F.2d 183 (8th Cir. 1981).

3. LOCAL INCOME TAXES

Local income taxes have attracted wide attention as a potential local revenue source, but have so far been extensively used only in relatively few cities and metropolitan areas. The following selections document the history as well as some of the major problems in developing a local income tax, including double taxation problems that arise when the same individual is subject to tax in more than one local jurisdiction.

INTERNATIONAL CITY MANAGEMENT ASSOCIATION, MANAGEMENT POLICIES IN LOCAL GOVERNMENT 165-68 (1981)

Local income taxes were levied by over 4,000 cities, counties, and school districts in the late 1970s. Use of the tax, however, was not uniformly distributed over the country. Except for the 1.0 percent employee license tax in Oakland, California, the local income tax was levied only by localities in the eastern half of the United States. Producing about 3.7 percent of overall local general revenues, the income tax ranked just behind the local general sales tax, which generated 5.4 percent. However, as discovered by the man who almost drowned trying to wade across a lake having an average depth of only two feet, averages or aggregate percentages often fail to tell the whole story. Local governments in

Kentucky, Maryland, and Pennsylvania derived a sixth or more of all locally raised general revenues from the tax, and for some municipalities (e.g., Philadelphia), it provided well over half of such revenues.

... The first modern income tax was adopted by the city of Philadelphia in 1938 under authority from the state (the 1932 Sterling Act) permitting the city to tax any nonproperty sources not taxed by the state. In 1939 the Philadelphia tax was declared unconstitutional by the state supreme court for violating the uniformity requirement of the Pennsylvania constitution, which was interpreted to preclude a progressive income tax. The Philadelphia flat-rate tax was progressive because of an exemption of the first $1,000 of income. The following year the city adopted a flat-rate tax on all earned income (i.e., wages, salaries, and net income of professions, partnerships, and unincorporated businesses) within its boundaries, with no personal deductions or exemptions. Major features of this tax — its flat rate, exclusion of property income and capital gains from its base, and lack of personal exemptions and deductions — have been retained, and it has served as a model for localities in Alabama, Kentucky, Missouri, Pennsylvania, and Ohio.

Between 1940 and 1962 the income taxes adopted by localities were all essentially "earned income taxes" of the Philadelphia type. In 1962 Detroit introduced the first change by levying an income tax on all forms of income, including dividends, rental income, interest, and capital gains. Two years later Michigan adopted the Uniform City Income Tax Ordinance incorporating the provisions of the Detroit tax. The tax base was essentially adjusted gross income as defined in the federal Internal Revenue Code.

The next major innovation occurred in 1966 when New York City introduced a personal income tax very similar to the federal levy. Like the tax in Michigan cities, the resident tax base was essentially the same as the federal base and personal exemptions were allowed. In addition, however, income was taxed at graduated rates (ranging from 0.4 percent to 2.0 percent), and the taxpayer was permitted to take personal deductions. (Married couples were allowed to file separately and assign their combined deductions to the spouse with the higher income.)

A final major development occurred in Maryland in 1967, when the state enacted a law under which Baltimore City and each county must levy a local income tax on residents at not less than 20 percent nor more than 50 percent of the state income tax liability. Increases or decreases in rates between these limits had to be in increments of 5 percent. Nonresidents could not be taxed.

... If the income tax is defined very broadly to include not only taxes on the income of individuals and corporations but also payroll taxes paid by employers (because this tax is probably shifted to the workers), by the late 1970s local income taxes were authorized for use by localities in fifteen states and were actually being used in thirteen.

....

Tax rates Localities in all states but Maryland and New York impose income taxes with a flat rate, frequently 1.0 percent. Philadelphia has the highest rate of any locality (4.3125 percent), even when the highest rates of the graduated taxes in Maryland localities and New York City are included in the comparison. Prior to 1980 the highest rate applied to the top bracket ($25,000 and over) in New York City was 4.3 percent; effective in 1980, the New York rates ranged from 0.4 percent to 2.0 percent. In Maryland counties and Baltimore City, which generally apply a tax consisting of 50.0 percent of the state liability, effective rates range from 1.0 percent to 2.5 percent (for taxable incomes of $3,000 and over); the state income tax rates range from 2.0 percent to 5.0 percent.

In most localities, the same rate applies to the taxable income of residents and of nonresidents earning income in the local taxing jurisdiction. However, Indiana counties are permitted to tax nonresidents at a rate of only 0.25 percent, one-quarter of the resident rate. Michigan cities tax nonresidents at half the rate (0.5 percent) applied to residents; localities in Maryland do not tax nonresidents at all.

New York City has a unique structure: nonresidents pay a flat-rate earnings tax (no exemptions or deductions allowed), with a sliding scale of exclusions for the tax base. A nonresident's total tax liability is not permitted to exceed the liability that would be incurred if the nonresident were treated as a resident. The nonresident rates in the late 1970s were 0.45 percent and 0.65 percent of wages and self-employment net earnings, respectively. Beginning in 1980 these rates fell to 0.25 percent and 0.375 percent.

. . . .

Tax base In most states the tax base for the local income tax differs considerably from that of federal and state income taxes on individuals. The two major differences are that local taxes often (1) exclude property income (rental income, capital gains, dividends, and interest) from the tax base, and (2) disallow personal exemptions, deductions, and employee business expense allowances. These two differences make the income tax in these localities essentially a tax on earned income (wages, salaries, and the net income of unincorporated businesses). The major exceptions to this general pattern are the taxes in Michigan cities, Maryland counties, and New York City, all of which essentially use the federal tax base and therefor include property income. All three also allow personal exemptions, and New York City and Maryland localities permit personal deductions.

Property income has been excluded from the tax base in most localities primarily because of the greater administrative costs of collecting and enforcing a tax on this income source. Whereas the almost universal practice of employer withholding from wages and salaries keeps collection and enforcement costs low, the administrative costs for processing returns for business and professional income (where there is no withholding for salaries and wages) are much higher. The high administrative costs for processing business and professional income returns would seem to indicate similar high administrative costs for other types of nonwithheld property income (rent, dividends, interest, and capital gains).

NOTE, AN EVALUATION OF MUNICIPAL INCOME TAXATION, 22 Vanderbilt Law Review 1313, 1348-49, 1353 (1969)

[*Uniformity Problems—Due Process and Equal Protection*]

1. *Classification Problems.* — (a) *Distinctions between residents and non-residents.* From the early days of its existence, municipal income taxation has been subjected to constitutional challenge on the ground that the taxation of non-residents amounts to a taking of property without due process of law. One of the first cases to consider the problem of the taxation of non-residents was *Kiker v. City of Philadelphia,* [31 A.2d 289 (Pa. 1943)]. The court upheld the tax as applied to a non-resident federal employee, a citizen of New Jersey, working at a federal installation in Philadelphia. The court reasoned that since the non-resident worked in Philadelphia, he received the benefits and protection of the city during his working hours. These benefits and protections were held to justify the taxation of his income because the city had a right to expect the non-resident to render some payment in return for the services it provided.

Thus, the tax was not held to constitute a deprivation of property without due process of law since the taxpayer received tangible benefits in return. In the more recent Missouri case of *Arnold v. Berra* [361 S.W.2d 321 (Mo. 1963)], the St. Louis income tax was upheld on similar reasoning, over the objection of an Illinois resident that he was being deprived of property without due process of law, and that such a tax placed an undue burden on interstate commerce.

In a closely related group of cases, courts have considered due process challenges to the municipal income tax liability of persons who are residents of the taxing city but earn all or part of their income outside of the city. Once again, the courts have upheld the tax on the ground that the taxpayer receives tangible benefits, protection, services, and opportunities from the city of his residence. Consequently, the taxpayer should contribute to the city's support by paying the income tax, even though his income may have been earned elsewhere....

An excellent example of an "unfortunate taxpayer" was presented in *Thompson v. City of Cincinnati,* [208 N.E.2d 747 (Ohio 1965)]. That case involved a declaratory judgment action brought by a resident of Loveland, Ohio, who worked in Cincinnati, to determine his liability with respect to the payment of municipal income taxation. Both cities had enacted income tax ordinances. The court held that the plaintiff was subject to the taxes of both cities and determined, with respect to the Cincinnati tax, that a city may levy a tax on wages derived from work performed within its boundaries by a non-resident of that city. With regard to the Loveland tax, the court indicated that the city of residence could levy a tax on wages resulting from work done in another city. The court concluded that the plaintiff could be taxed by both cities because the burden of supplying necessary revenue to maintain municipalities must be shared by those who are provided with substantial benefits by municipalities. Thus, it appears that a benefit theory of taxation, which has been used to uphold the municipal income tax against due process contentions, also supports taxation by the city of residence as well as the city of employment.

[The Note then discusses two alternative methods of administering local income taxes that can avoid some of these inequities. One method requires intergovernmental coordination with state and federal taxing authorities. The other requires the administration of the local income tax on a metropolitan basis, either by a metropolitan government or by a central administrative agency.—Eds.]

Comment: What if a municipality imposes a local income tax solely on nonresidents and exempts residents? A tax of this kind was held unconstitutional in *County of Alameda v. City & County of San Francisco,* 97 Cal. Rptr. 175 (Cal. App. 1971), noted, 48 A.L.R.3d 343 (1973). The court decided that the tax had to fall under a line of California cases that prohibited arbitrary discrimination by a city against nonresidents. It noted that "economic enclaves within California would be intolerable." *Id.* at 177. See Note, *The Validity of San Francisco Commuter Tax,* 20 HASTINGS L.J. 813 (1969).

An attempt was made to justify the tax because it was set at a level requiring commuters to pay their fair share of services provided by the city. Since nonresidents made up 19.9% of the "population" of the city, they were charged with 19.9% of service costs. This formula was found to be faulty as nonresidents were only in the city during working hours. For a case dismissing a challenge to the taxation of nonresident income when residents were also taxed see *Non-Resident Taxpayers Ass'n v. Municipality of Philadelphia,* 341 F. Supp. 1139 (D.N.J. 1971), aff'd, 406 U.S. 951 (1972). For additional discussion see Note, *Suburbia Lost — Constitutional and Other Challenges Regarding the*

Municipal Income Tax on Nonresidents, 5 WILL. L.J. 295 (1969). Compare *Austin v. New Hampshire,* 420 U.S. 656 (1975), in which the Supreme Court struck down under the federal privileges and immunities clause a nonresident commuter income tax imposed by the State of New Hampshire.

4. USER CHARGES AND OTHER TAXES

User and service charges are discussed in INTERNATIONAL CITY MANAGEMENT ASSOCIATION, MANAGEMENT POLICIES IN LOCAL GOVERNMENT FINANCE 184-203 (1981). This text points out that user charges have grown over the past years as municipalities sought alternatives to the property tax. Between 1973 and 1977, revenues from user charges increased 57% while those from the property tax increased 31.8%. An even greater increase in user fees occurred in California and other states in the wake of voter-approved tax and expenditure limitations discussed *infra.* San Francisco's user fee revenues increased by more than 27% in fiscal year 1979. Cline & Shannon, *Municipal Revenue Behavior After Proposition 13,* Intergovernmental Perspective, Vol. 8, No. 3, at 27, 28 (1982).

Service and user charges can be levied for government services that are similar to private goods. These services have the following characteristics: they can be provided in divisible units; their benefits are not interrelated; and users can be excluded from the benefits of the service without unduly increasing their costs. User and service charges are justified in order to provide greater equity in fiscal burdens among users; those who use the service will pay for what they get. In addition, these charges are claimed to increase economic efficiency, as goods and services will be supplied by the community in conformity with user preference, as indicated by a willingness to pay for the service.

How service and user charges should be set is another matter. Since municipal suppliers of services have a monopolistic hold on the market, they will not be constrained by market pressures to set prices at a level that will maximize demand for the service. Charges for municipal services are set instead by public decision or regulation. What limits the courts place on municipal pricing of services are indicated by the following case.

APODACA v. WILSON

Supreme Court of New Mexico
86 N.M. 516, 525 P.2d 876 (1974)

Opinion

MONTOYA, JUSTICE.

On August 2, 1971, the Albuquerque City Commission adopted Ordinance 102-1971 which increased sewer and water service charges over those charged under the superseded ordinance. On the same day, the City Commission adopted Budget Resolution No. 2, where by its terms, the City requests approval by the Attorney General and the Department of Finance and Administration for budget transfers and increases enumerated in schedules attached to the resolution. The schedules indicated that water and sewer revenues increased by the amount of $1,505,233, and that from such amount $1,129,903 was to be appropriated to the general fund of the City and appropriated from the general fund to cover budget increases for various departments of the municipality.

Plaintiffs Apodaca, Ames and Edmon filed a complaint against the City of Albuquerque and its agents (City) on January 14, 1972, on behalf of themselves and all others similarly situated, seeking to enjoin the City from collecting increased sewer and water service charges under the city ordinance. The plaintiffs also sought an order invalidating City Ordinance 102-1971 as being in violation of state law and the New Mexico Constitution, and directing the refund of any service charges previously collected under the ordinance. Subsequently, the Albuquerque Consumer Federation and New Mexico Taxpayers Association intervened as party-plaintiffs, seeking the same relief as the original plaintiffs.

On May 12, 1972, the court, sitting without a jury, dismissed plaintiffs' complaint and entered judgment for the City. This appeal ensued.

. . . .

Plaintiffs argue that §§ 14-26-4 and 14-25-2, N.M.S.A., 1953 (Repl. Vol. 3, 1968), set out the limitations which are to be adhered to by the City in the formulation of any service charge rates. Section 14-26-4, *supra,* states in pertinent part that:

> A municipality owning and operating a water utility may:
> A. A municipality, for the purpose of maintaining, enlarging, extending, constructing and repairing water facilities, and for paying the interest and principal on revenue bonds issued for the construction of water facilities, may levy, by general ordinance, a just and reasonable service charge, . . .[.]

Section 14-25-2 (A), supra, provides that:

> A. A municipality, for the purpose of maintaining, enlarging, extending, constructing and repairing sewage facilities, and for paying the interest and principal on revenue bonds issued for the construction of sewage facilities, may levy, by general ordinance, a just and reasonable service charge, . . .[.]

. . . .

Plaintiffs also contend that "the City's sewer and water rate increase is not a just and reasonable service charge," arguing that the charges in order to be so classified must be measured in terms of what is required for maintaining, extending, enlarging the systems, and paying principal and interest on revenue bonds, as provided in §§ 14-25-2 and 14-26-4, *supra.* We have already discussed the effect of the home rule amendment on those statutes and how they contain no express denial of authority to the City to fix water and sewer rates based only on the criteria provided by those statutes. We do, however, agree that the rates must be reasonable.

Admittedly, here the rates fixed by the ordinance produced more revenue than needed to satisfy the cost of operating the system and the requirements for the payment of principal and interest on revenue bonds issued. The proper general rule to be applied here is that the City, by owning and operating its water and sewer system, is acting in a business or proprietary capacity rather than in a governmental capacity. Therefore, the obligations resting upon it are identical to those of a private utility company operating under a municipal franchise, insofar as the determination of the reasonableness of its rates is concerned. In *Holton Creamery Co. v. Brown,* 137 Kan. 418, 420-421, 20 P.2d 503, 504-505 (1933), the Supreme Court, in a case involving the excessiveness of rates imposed by the city operating its own utility, quoted the following with approval:

> In 5 McQuillin's Municipal Corporations (2d Ed.) 64, 65, it is said: "Where a municipality owns its water or light works, it is settled that it has the right to charge rents against consumers who make use of its service. However the rates must be reasonable, although the municipality may charge a rate which will yield a fair profit, and need not furnish the supply or service at cost; and the same rules in regard to the reasonableness of rates apply as in case of the rates of private companies owning a public utility. Otherwise stated, where the

municipality owns its plant, the rates for water, light or any other product, furnished by it must be fair, reasonable and just, uniform and nondiscriminatory." ...

There was evidence at trial as to the reasonableness of the rate increases and as to the fact that Albuquerque rates compared favorably with amounts received by private utility companies. We note that § 14-17-1(H), N.M.S.A., 1953 (Repl. Vol. 3, 1968, 1973 Pocket Supp.), specifically gives a municipality power to —

> H. establish rates for services provided by municipal utilities and revenue-producing projects, including amounts which the governing body determines to be reasonable and consistent with amounts received by private enterprise in the operation of similar facilities.

Although the instant case was filed prior to June 1972, the effective date of this statute, it expresses current legislative policy and is consistent with our holding as to the City's power to set reasonable rates in excess of actual expenditures in furnishing municipally-owned utility services, if such rates compare favorably with those received by private utility companies. The trial court, in its finding No. 23, stated:

> The City's water and sewer rates as increased by Ordinance 102-1971 are just and reasonable, fair and equitable.

This finding is supported by substantial evidence.

We next consider plaintiffs' second contention, that the sewer and water service charge increase is a tax and, as such, is in violation of law and the New Mexico Constitution. The home rule amendment provides that the City may not impose a tax until approved by a majority vote, excepting therefrom a tax authorized by general law. In addition, the Charter Municipality Tax Act, § 14-14-1, N.M.S.A., 1953 (Repl. Vol. 3, 1968, 1973 Pocket Supp.), under its temporary provisions in force when Ordinance 102-1971 was adopted, prohibited any charter municipality from adopting any tax to become effective July 1, 1973, unless such tax was authorized by general law. We have heretofore made reference to the provisions of § 72-4-1.1 limiting the tax powers of home rule cities. The question to be resolved is whether the increased sewer and water charges can be construed to be a tax. In *City of Clovis v. Crain,* [357 P.2d 667, 671, 88 A.L.R.2d 1250, 1259 (N.M. 1960)], where the collection of garbage and sewer assessments was in question, we said:

> Rhyne, Municipal Law, § 20-5, p. 462, states the rule as follows:
>
> . . . .
>
> "It is the majority rule that sewer service charges are neither taxes nor assessments, but are tolls or rents for benefits received by the user of the sewer system; . . . ."

Here, plaintiffs again rely on *City of Cincinnati v. Roettinger*[,137 N.E. 6 (Ohio St. 1922)—Eds.], *supra* in support of their position, contending that water or sewer charges become a tax when the revenues or a portion thereof are used for general governmental purposes. We disagree with the conclusion reached in the *Roettinger* case, and agree with the Ohio Supreme Court's later decision in *City of Niles v. Union Ice Corporation, supra* when it said [12 N.E.2d at 488-489]:

> Appellants further contend that if a municipal utility is permitted to charge a rate in excess of the cost of furnishing the service or product, and if such excess were used to finance the cost of municipal government, that such excess,

so used, would assume the nature and be used in lieu of taxes and the municipality would thereby be enabled to evade the constitutional limitations upon its power of taxation, and that municipalities would be free to impose the cost of municipal government upon the consumers of light and power.

This contention proceeds on the theory that a municipality has no right to charge for its utility service or product a rate in excess of cost, *i.e.*, that it has no right to make a profit. Nevertheless, we are not referred to any statute or constitutional provision denying this right. In the absence of such prohibition, a municipality, no less than a private corporation engaged in the operation of a public utility, is entitled to a fair profit. In the operation of a public utility, a municipality acts, not in a governmental capacity as an arm or agency of the sovereignty of the state, but in a proprietary or business capacity. 9 Ruling Case Law 1232, § 38. In its proprietary capacity it occupies the same "posture" as that occupied by a private corporation engaged in business [citations omitted].

. . . .

The rate charged in excess of cost is not a tax or in the nature of a tax, regardless of how the fund derived therefrom is ultimately used. A municipality, acting in a proprietary capacity, cannot impose taxes. While thus engaged, it is engaged in business but not in the business of government. A municipality may impose and collect taxes only when acting as an arm or agency of the state, but when engaged in business, it does not so act. A tax is a tribute levied for the support of government. 38 Ohio Jurisprudence 714, § 3. A rate charged for a public utility service or product is not a tax, but a price at which and for which the public utility service or product is sold [citations omitted]. . . .

Since the rate charged is not a tax in its inception, ultimate use of surplus funds derived therefrom for the support of municipal government will not convert it into taxes or cause it to assume the nature of taxes.

. . . .

We therefore hold that the water and sewer charges in the instant case are not "taxes" irrespective of the application of the revenues derived from such charges.

Comments: 1. The principal case appears to state the usual rule. *See* ANTIEAU, MUNICIPAL CORPORATION LAW § 19.06 (1973). However, there is some authority indicating that profits from utility charges must be "modest," and that an unreasonable reliance on utility revenues for general government purposes imposes unfair burdens on rate payers. *See Contractors & Builders Ass'n v. City of Dunedin*, 329 So. 2d 314, 318, 319 n.5 (Fla. 1976). The problem also arises in connection with building permits and similar licensing charges. Compare *Weber Basin Home Builders Ass'n v. Roy City*, 487 P.2d 866 (Utah 1971), in which the court struck down on equal protection grounds an increase in building permit fees concededly made to obtain additional revenues for the city's general fund. This increase was found to weigh unequally on new residents, and was not justified even though each new resident increased the cost of city government. Service charges increases falling equally on new and old residents were suggested as a method of meeting increased service costs without violating equal protection restrictions.

2. Has the city in the principal case set the increased rate at an amount sufficient to cover marginal cost, or at a greater amount? If the rate exceeds marginal cost, to what extent will it affect different income groups within the city, and what effect will it have on the use of sewer and water services? Is there an argument for shifting part of the cost of utility operation to the general ad valorem property tax? Why do you suppose the city preferred a rate increase instead?

3. One problem that frequently arises is whether apartments, motels, hotels, and mobile home parks are to be charged for services such as water services on the basis of the number of units in the structure or whether a single charge must be made for the entire building. If each dwelling unit is charged separately the rate in the aggregate is likely to be higher. Since these users generally have only one meter for each building, and are billed only once, and since service charges are based to some extent on the cost of providing the service, it can be argued that only one charge should be made to the building as a single customer. For discussion see *Kliks v. Dalles City,* 335 P.2d 366 (Or. 1959) (separate dwelling unit charge may not be made for apartments when units not separately charged in hotels and rooming houses).

Some courts, however, use an "ultimate consumer" theory to justify separate dwelling unit charges for apartments and hotels, which has the effect of treating them like single family residences and differentiating them from other commercial users. These are charged bulk rates based on the use by the business as a whole. See *Oklahoma City Hotel & Motor Hotel Ass'n v. Oklahoma City,* 531 P.2d 316 (Okla. 1974). The separate dwelling unit charge was sustained for apartment houses and mobile home parks, the court noting that apartments were an "aggregation of dwellings" comparable to single-family homes. However, the separate units charge was struck down for hotels and motels, the court noting that "[t]he mere fact that people sleep in motels and hotels does not place them in the same class as single-family dwellings." *Id.* at 320. The court justified its reliance on the ultimate consumer theory by noting that the increased rate would be passed on to the tenant.

User charge classifications raise an equal protection problem. The equal protection standard applicable is the relaxed "substantial relationship" standard, and some courts apply this standard to uphold user charge classifications. See *Apartment Ass'n of Los Angeles County, Inc. v. City of Los Angeles,* 141 Cal. Rptr. 794 (Cal. App. 1977) (upholding sewer service charge applied only to apartment projects with five or more dwelling units); *Piscataway Apartment Ass'n v. Township of Piscataway,* 328 A.2d 608 (N.J. 1974) (rejecting argument that sewerage charge for apartments should be lower than charge for single-family dwellings because apartments have lower sewerage flow). *See generally* Annot., 61 A.L.R.3d 1236, 1263-87 (1975).

Does the problem change when the rate differential is based on residence or nonresidence in the municipality providing the utility? The next case deals with this question.

CITY OF TEXARKANA v. WIGGINS

Supreme Court of Texas
151 Tex. 100, 246 S.W.2d 622 (1952)

SMITH, JUSTICE. Respondents, all nonresidents of the City of Texarkana, Texas, filed this suit against petitioner, the city, seeking to enjoin it in the operation of its municipally-owned water and sewer systems from charging nonresidents higher water and sewer rates than those paid by persons residing within the corporate limits of the city.

The trial court rendered judgment for petitioner, the judgment reciting that the court heard sufficient evidence to determine the case on its merits. This judgment was reversed and the cause remanded by the Court of Civil Appeals. 239 S.W.2d 212. The case is before us on writ of error.

Prior to August, 1948, the City of Texarkana, Texas, and surrounding territory, was served by the American Water Works, Inc., a privately-owned utility corporation. At that time the petitioner purchased from this utility corporation all its property serving the city and surrounding territory, payment being made with proceeds derived from the sale of revenue bonds previously authorized by vote of the citizens of the city. An ordinance of the city, enacted on August 27, 1948, adopted for the municipally-owned utility the schedule of rates theretofore charged by the American Water Works; this schedule of rates remained in effect until August 8, 1950. The system of rates charged by the American Water Works was, of course, non-discriminatory in that both residents and nonresidents were charged the same rate for service.

On August 8, 1950, petitioner passed an ordinance providing that water service to nonresident consumers would be furnished at one and one-half times the rate which applied within the corporate limits of the city. The ordinance further provided that sewer service to nonresident users would be furnished "at a rate double the rate applying within the city limits." A water tapping charge for all connections to the water system for residential use outside the city was fixed at $50; the water tapping charge for users within the city was set at $10 on unpaved streets, and $15 on paved streets.

Respondents are all residents of the City of North Texarkana, Texas, which adjoins the petitioner on the north. The east-west streets in the City of Texarkana, Texas, are numbered consecutively, beginning with 1st Street in the business district of the City of Texarkana, Texas, and continuing to 36th Street in the City of North Texarkana. The line marking the corporate limits of the City of Texarkana, Texas, lies in the center of 29th Street. The north-south streets, which continue through both cities, bear the same names throughout their entire lengths. In short, the geographical line upon which the rate differentiation is based is an arbitrary line marking the limits of a political subdivision.

Petitioner contends that it is under no legal duty to furnish water and sewerage disposal service to the respondents; that if it does furnish such service to respondents it is under no legal duty to charge the respondents the same rate as is charged residents, but that it may make such charge as appears to be for the best interest of the City of Texarkana, Texas. This latter contention is based upon the provisions of Article 1108, section 3, R.C.S. of Texas, Vernon's Ann. Civ. St. art. 1108, subd. 3, which provides:

> Any town or city in this state which has or may be chartered or organized under the general laws of Texas, or by special act or charter, and which owns or operates waterworks, sewers, gas or electric lights, shall have the power and right: . . . .
> 3. To extend the lines of such systems outside of the limits of such towns or cities and to sell water, sewer, gas, and electric light and power privileges or service to any person or corporation outside of the limits of such towns or cities, or permit them to connect therewith under contract with such town or city under such terms and conditions as may appear to be for the best interest of such town or city; provided that no electric lines shall, for the purposes stated in this section, be extended into the corporate limits of another incorporated town or city.

Respondents contend that the city in operating its water and sewer systems is acting in its proprietary capacity, that it is subject to the same rules and regulations as privately-owned utility corporations engaged in the same or similar business, and that the rates established by the ordinance of August 8, 1950, being discriminatory, are void and their collection should be enjoined.

We cannot agree with petitioner's contention that this statute is sufficient to authorize it to charge a discriminatory rate for utilities furnished to nonresidents than to its residents. Under the facts in this case, the city has dealt with the residents and nonresidents as one class or unit. The ordinance under consideration recites that the city has purchased and is now maintaining and operating within and without the limits of said city a municipal water system. Since 1948 the same rates have been charged consumers living within and without the city. No other utility exists within the area to furnish water and sewer service.

The common-law rule that one engaged in rendering a service affected with a public interest or, more strictly, what has come to be known as a utility service, may not discriminate in charges or service as between persons similarly situated is of such long standing and is so well recognized that it needs no citation of authority to support it. The economic nature of the enterprise which renders this type service is such that the courts have imposed upon it the duty to treat all alike unless there is some reasonable basis for a differentiation. Statutes have been enacted in almost every state making this common-law rule a statutory one. Pond, Public Utilities (4th ed. 1932) sections 270-275. Hence, the American Water Works was required to, and did, render service to respondents at the same rate as was charged within the corporate limits of petitioner.

It is settled in this state that the petitioner, upon the purchase by it of the property of the privately-owned utility, was subject to this same rule prohibiting unreasonable or unjustified discrimination in rates and service.... This same rule prevails in many other states....

Admittedly these cases do not settle the particular question before us; they announce the broad common-law principle that a municipality may not unreasonably discriminate in rates and charges and they do not determine the further question whether or not different rates based on nothing more than the limits of a municipal corporation are unreasonably discriminatory. These cases are authority, however, for at least this much: in the absence of (1) a showing that the discrimination has a reasonable basis or (2) a statute to the contrary, a municipality may not discriminate in charges or service as between those similarly situated. Many decisions have transported the concept of proprietary capacity, as distinguished from governmental capacity, from the cases involving the liability of a governmental unit for the torts of its agents to these decisions involving the duty of a municipality to offer its utility service at nondiscriminatory rates and have found in this concept a basis for the rule set out above. The concept of proprietary capacity is, however, hardly helpful in this situation. The real reason for the rule that, in so far as treatment of consumers is concerned, the municipally-owned utility is no different from the privately-owned utility is that the economic nature of the business has not changed; it remains a monopoly in spite of the change in ownership.

The change from private to public ownership may, in theory at least, eliminate or lessen the profit motive, but the consumer of utility services still cannot pick and choose his supplier of water as he does his grocer. The utility consumer is thus at the mercy of the monopoly and, for this reason, utilities, regardless of the character of their ownership, should be and have been, subjected to control under the common-law rule forbidding unreasonable discrimination....

The petitioner being subject to the rule prohibiting unjustified discrimination between consumers of utility service, the question presents itself whether there is in fact any justification for treating the respondents differently from the residents of the petitioner city. The ordinance complained of contains, on its face, no such justification. The difference in rates, so far as is shown by the ordinance, is based entirely upon the location of the corporate limits. The petitioner does not contend that the costs of supplying the service to respondents vary so as to justify the difference in charges and the record is devoid of any evidence upon which to base such a contention. As was pointed out by the Court of Civil Appeals in its opinion below, the discrimination cannot be justified on the ground that the residents of the City of Texarkana, Texas, are liable to taxation to pay for acquisition of the water system. We are brought again, then, to what is apparent from the record of this case: the only difference between consumers who pay more and those who pay less for petitioner's utility service lies in the fact that the former reside north of 29th Street while the latter reside south of 29th Street. The limits of a municipal corporation, of themselves, do not furnish a reasonable basis for rate differentiation....

[The court then turned to an analysis of the statute.]

We think the effect of the statute is that when a city decides to exercise this power to provide its utility service to customers outside the city limits it may then fix such service charges as it decides the situation requires; if it requires a higher charge than is fixed against residents of the city for the same service, the city may exact the higher rate. But whatever it fixes, a rate status between the city and its outside customers is thereby established and the city cannot thereafter arbitrarily change the rate so as to discriminate, or further discriminate, between them and customers residing in the city. This conclusion is certainly in line with well-established principles of public utility law.

For these reasons we hold that the statute did not change the common-law rule prohibiting unreasonable discrimination. The ordinance is therefore void unless the petitioner can show, on another trial of the cause, that there is some reasonable basis for the difference in rates which it establishes. In order that the petitioner may have an opportunity to make such a showing the judgment of the Court of Civil Appeals reversing and remanding the cause is affirmed.

SMEDLEY, GARWOOD, GRIFFIN and CALVERT, JJ., dissent.

CALVERT, JUSTICE. I dissent.

The conclusion reached by the majority is contrary to the overwhelming weight of authority as evidenced by the decisions in those states in which the question has been decided under applicable common-law rules....

The citizens of North Texarkana do not occupy the same relationship toward the City of Texarkana as do its own citizens. "The primary purpose of a municipal corporation is to contribute towards the welfare, health, happiness, and public interest of the inhabitants of such city, and not to further the interests of those residing outside of its limits." *City of Sweetwater v. Hamner,* Tex. Civ. App., 259 S.W. 191, 195. The City of Texarkana owes to its own citizens a duty to see that their health and welfare are protected through the continuing availability of water and sewer lines and facilities. It owes no such duty to the citizens of North Texarkana. It may furnish water and sewer services and facilities to residents of North Texarkana so long and only so long as the residents of that municipality contract for such services and the authorities of that municipality permit; but being under no duty to furnish in the first instance it may discontinue such services, on reasonable notice, with or without cause. Being entitled to discontinue the services according to its want, it follows that the city can continue them on its own terms and conditions. This was its common-law right. It is now its statutory right....

The conclusion of the majority that the language of the statute is not sufficiently broad to authorize the City of Texarkana to charge higher rates to nonresidents is contrary to a decision of the Supreme Court of South Carolina in the case of *Childs v. City of Columbia,* 87 S.C. 566, 70 S.E. 296, 34 L.R.A., N.S., 542 and contrary to a decision of the Supreme Court of Colorado in the case of *Englewood v. City and County of Denver,* Colo., 229 P.2d 667, the two latter decisions involving construction of statutes highly similar to the Texas statute....

The majority fear that to construe the statute so as to uphold the ordinance here "would return us to the primitive state of development in utility control when rates were determined by friendship and political power or pressure." I doubt that such a consequence is reasonably to be expected, but it is not enough to defeat the plain wording of the statute to say that it may lead to unjust or unsound results. It is our duty to enforce the statute as written, leaving to the legislature the right and the duty to effect a change if a change is needed.

Comments: 1. With the principal case compare *Town of Terrell Hills v. City of San Antonio,* 318 S.W.2d 85 (Tex. Civ. App. 1958). San Antonio charged residents of Terrell Hills about one third more for water than it charged its own residents. Terrell Hills is an incorporated community lying in the northern portion of San Antonio and completely surrounded by San Antonio, which extends as much as four miles beyond.

Differential rates outside the city were justified by the following factors: (1) The cost of meter reading outside the city was substantially greater. (2) The standby water demand outside the city was substantially greater. (3) Rates outside the city should be based on a higher return on plant value. (4) Rates outside the city included a substantial charge for fire protection, which is not made inside the city.

Upholding the rate differential, the court in the *Terrell Hills* case distinguished *Texarkana* on the ground that the San Antonio rate differential was historical and had been recognized when the city acquired the water utility from a private company. The court also noted that "[c]ity areas which have utility connections have higher valuations than areas which do not have the utility. The city levies and collects its taxes upon this enhanced value. Nonresident areas, however, not being taxable at all, receive the same benefits of enhanced value from utility connections but bear no part of this additional burden." *Id.* at 88. What about property taxes paid to Terrell Hills? The court accepted the charge for fire protection as proper, and held that the difference in the rate of return was not unlawful if the rate was not unreasonable. Is either the *Terrell Hills* or the *Texarkana* case inconsistent with the opinion in *Apodaca, supra*?

In *City of Pompano Beach v. Oltman,* 389 So. 2d 283 (Fla. App. 1980), the court reversed an adverse decision against the city for charging nonresidents double what city residents were charged for use of the city's water system with the comment that the city "has no duty to explain or justify its actions in setting rates until . . . establishment of a prima facie case of invalidity based on competent evidence." *Id.* at 286. Florida law permits cities to charge higher rates to nonresident utility users so long as these are reasonable and nondiscriminatory. The court concluded that testimony focusing on an alleged excess rate of return did not establish unreasonableness because cities are entitled to a reasonable profit from their utility operations.

2. Consider the following hypothetical dissenting opinion to the *Terrell Hills* case:

JONES, JUSTICE [after reviewing the facts:] No doubt there are fiscal disparities in urban areas, but the inequities do not lie only on one side. Core cities, for example, may face greater demands, but they also have the lion's share of the tax base. In this confused imbalance of externally inflicted costs and externally appropriated benefits, judgment is difficult. But it does seem to me that differential pricing plans such as the plan employed by San Antonio will only create a distorted set of relative prices for intergovernmental exchanges. What happens is that the monopoly power wielded by the core city will only reduce the real income of the whole urban area by working against economic efficiency. Sewer and water services will be underconsumed unless they are highly price inelastic.

Problems of equity also trouble us. Core cities, faced with severe economic problems, will seek fiscal surcease by overcharging for utility services for which payment is easily collected. But the result may only be that suburban developers will hold back on the capital investments in utility services which are necessary if we are to avoid severe health and amenity problems. Excessive use of private water and sewer systems may only impose external diseconomies back on the central system through increased pollution of streams, uncontrolled drainage, and the like. We would do better to provide service facilities at cost, and make user charges for streets and roads, which are presently available free once the initial capital investment has been made. Unfortunately, central cities often turn to excessive extraterritorial charges for services because they cannot impose user charges on suburbanites who use their streets. We cannot judicially alter this imbalanced trade-off, but we can at least take a step in the right direction by invalidating the charges that have been imposed here. [This fictional dissent is based on W. THOMPSON, A PREFACE TO URBAN ECONOMICS 283-86 (1965). *See also* Sax, *Municipal Water Supply for Nonresidents: Recent Developments and a Suggestion for the Future,* 5 NAT. RES. J. 54 (1965).]

3. *Barr v. First Taxing District,* 192 A.2d 872 (Conn. 1963), raised the question of the validity of a rate differential based on the additional cost of serving suburban customers. The district comprised the "old" city of Norwalk prior to its consolidation. Plaintiffs, who challenged the district's rate, lived in the city of Norwalk but outside the district's area. Water was supplied to plaintiffs, in what can be called the outer area, at twice the usual rate. This differential was approved by the court. Of some interest is the fact that about two thirds of the district's customers lived in the outer area in 1958, although this area had included less than half of the customers in 1933. The court noted:

> In addition to the facts stated, it was found also that the customers in the inner district are in what constitutes a compact area, where the customer density is much greater than in the outer district. The latter is spread over a much larger terrain, and while there are more customers in the outer district, they are located much farther apart than those in the inner district.... The result is that the increased costs of installation, the additional lengths of mains between customers, and the need of pumping facilities make it more expensive to provide and maintain the system and the service in the outer district.

Id. at 874. In commenting on a consultant's report, which recommended a rate reduction in the outer area, the court also noted: "His report indicates the problem to be more practical than legal."

5. SALES TAXES

Like local income taxes, local sales taxes have attracted widespread attention as an alternative to the property tax, particularly in metropolitan areas. Actual use has been spotty, though, with little absolute growth since a period of rapid expansion during the 1960s. The following excerpt summarizes the history of the local sales tax movement and highlights some of the limitations of this revenue source.

INTERNATIONAL CITY MANAGEMENT ASSOCIATION, MANAGEMENT POLICIES IN LOCAL GOVERNMENT FINANCE 152-65 (1981)

The first local general sales taxes were adopted in the 1930s, a time when significant reductions had occurred in local revenues as a result of the Great Depression. New York City adopted a sales tax in 1934, followed by New Orleans in 1938. In 1950 Mississippi adopted a system of state-administered local sales taxes, an innovation that significantly enhanced the feasibility of the tax for a large number of local governments. The most rapid period of expansion in the use of local sales taxes occurred in the 1960s, when the number of states authorizing local sales taxes increased from twelve in 1963 to twenty-five in 1970.

In the mid-1970s general sales taxes were authorized for use by local governments in twenty-nine states and the District of Columbia, although in three states (Kentucky, Oregon, and Wisconsin) none of the local governments authorized to levy a sales tax had chosen to do so. Authorization for the tax may derive from home rule charter powers, general licensing powers, or specific state legislation. The latter is the source of sales tax authority in most localities.

Among the twenty-six states where local governments actually use the local sales tax, the rate ranges from 0.25 percent to 1.0 percent in every state except Alaska, where the local rate can go as high as 5.0 percent (Alaska does not have a state sales tax). The number of governments using the tax ranges from a high of more than thirteen hundred cities and counties in Illinois to one city in Arkansas.

In 1976-77 general sales tax revenue amounted to $5.472 billion, or about two-thirds of the $8.278 billion raised by local governments from all sales and gross receipts taxes. General sales tax receipts represented 5.4 percent of the general revenues for all local governments; however, for municipalities the percentage was almost twice as great, 9.6 percent.

[The report discusses the general characteristics of local sales taxes. Virtually all general sales taxes are ad valorem rather than per unit taxes (e.g., cigarette and gasoline taxes): the tax is computed as a percentage of the value of the transaction. Sales taxes are imposed on retail purchasers. Since the tax is imposed at the retail level, sales for resale generally are not taxed.

[The report also discusses several problems which occur in administering sales taxes, suggesting that local sales tax administration often results in higher costs of administration and vendor compliance. Moreover, when sales taxes are administered at both the local and state level, a duplication of administrative and compliance costs may result. Other serious issues are revenue allocation, locational effects and equity problems.

[The report concludes with the following observations. — Eds.]

From the foregoing examination of local sales taxes, it is possible to draw some conclusions about what appear, on balance, to be desirable features for such a tax.

First, successful operation of a local sales tax is more likely under state rather than local administration. State administration brings greater efficiency in operation and greater coordination in the tax rates and tax bases in different locations using the tax.

Second, to avoid complicating compliance and auditing, the base of the local tax should be the same as that of the state sales tax (if a state tax exists, as it does in forty-five states).

Third, compliance is greatly facilitated by locating the tax liability with the vendor rather than at the place of delivery and limiting use taxes to out-of-state purchases.

Fourth, the best insurance against adverse locational effects is to prevent sales tax rate differentials among jurisdictions; tax rates should be uniform over as large a geographic area as possible (i.e., countywide is better than citywide).

Fifth, the allocation of local sales tax revenue between counties and municipalities should be sensitive to the division of local government functions (and hence relative expenditures of each), taking account of the revenues available to the respective local governments from other sources.

Even if these conditions were fulfilled, there remains the fundamental question of whether it is wise to use local sales taxes at all. Considered in the context of this chapter, however, local sales taxes are an important revenue source for many localities. They offer localities some extra degree of autonomy in setting local revenue and expenditure levels. In addition, the local sales tax offers a way (albeit imperfect) for localities to collect taxes for services provided to nonresidents; and the local sales tax may be (in the absence of a food exemption or credit) in rough correspondence with the benefit-received principle.

On the negative side, the tax, unless applied uniformly over a wide geographic area, has adverse effects on locational decisions. It also is not in accord with widely held views of horizontal and vertical equity, though this problem could be remedied at least in part by special credits or rebates for taxes paid on food. Finally, tax proceeds are almost always distributed by sales location and hence may not match the demands of constituents for provision of public services. The first and third problems have led some observers to conclude that when additional revenues are to be provided to local government, allowing increases in local sales tax rates would be distinctly inferior to increasing the state sales tax rate and redistributing the extra revenue to localities on the basis of a formula embodying various criteria of local need, such as population and average income. This argument could be carried further to recommend eliminating all local sales taxes and substituting increases in state sales tax rates, or even replacing all state sales taxes with a national sales tax. Such sweeping changes, however, would likely result in a loss in the ability of local governments to satisfy local constituents and an increase in income redistribution among geographic areas and ultimately individuals.

D. BORROWING

Many American municipalities face a deepening financial crisis. Of the three traditional sources of state and local revenue (taxation, federal aid and borrowing), the latter has grown enormously in the past decade as the taxpayers' revolt and the curtailment of federal spending have forced state and local governments to rely increasingly on borrowing to meet their expenditures. One survey finds new issues of municipal debt doubling from 1970 to 1978, from approximately thirty-five to sixty-eight billion dollars. During this same period, outstanding corporate debt remained in the twenty-five billion dollar range. By the end of 1977, total outstanding state and local debt had risen to approximately 265 billion dollars, four times the amount of debt in 1960. *A Decade of Municipal Financing,* The Daily Bond Buyer, July 6, 1979, p. 5 [as reported in R. LAMB & S. RAPPAPORT, MUNICIPAL BONDS 7-8 (1980).] These developments suggest that an analysis of local borrowing and debt limitations must be put in the context of recent trends of federal, state and local fiscal affairs, as noted at the beginning of this chapter.

1. TYPES OF ISSUES

A major reason for the growth of municipal borrowing has been the attractiveness of the investment vehicle — the tax exempt bond. As a result of the federalism principle suggested in *Marbury v. Madison,* 1 Cranch 137 (1803), and codified in I.R.C. § 103, holders of securities issued by state and local governments do not have to pay federal income taxes on interest income. Interest income also is frequently exempt from state and local taxes. While the largest holders of tax exempt bonds have been commercial banks and insurance companies, the federal income tax exemption is of substantial benefit to high bracket individual investors. For example, a person in the fifty percent tax bracket with $100,000 to invest will have a $5,000 tax liability on $10,000 interest income if the money is invested in taxable corporate securities, but will realize the full $10,000 income if tax exempt municipal bonds are purchased instead. Because of the substantial tax advantage, investors normally have been willing to accept a lower rate of return, often as much as one third, on municipal bonds than they would require for taxable investments. This, in return, has lowered the cost of borrowing to municipalities, thereby increasing the attractiveness of borrowing as a source of funds. The combined effect of these factors has produced an attitude in some sectors of "everybody wins but the federal government and what's wrong with that!"

Municipal bonds have been used to finance everything from airports to student loans. They come in all sizes and shapes, but generally take two basic forms.

> While all Municipal securities are debt obligations, having fixed maturities and paying fixed rates of interest, they exhibit a large and somewhat fluid spectrum of security, that is, the amounts and kinds of resources pledged to meet the debt service charges vary. Alternative systems of classification are available, but the convention of the market is to divide all bonds into two broad categories of security:
> (1) general obligations, which are secured by the full faith credit and taxing power of a government;
> (2) revenue or special fund obligations which are secured on the revenues or on receipts of a project or special fund and which are not backed by the full taxing power of a borrower.

Doty & Peterson, *The Federal Securities Law and Transactions in Municipal Securities,* 71 Nw. U.L. Rev. 283, 304-05 (1976). *See also* L. Moak, Municipal Bonds: Planning, Sale, and Administration (1982).

a. General Obligations Bonds

As noted, general obligation bonds are backed by the full faith and credit of the issuing government with the guarantee of repayment based on its taxing ability. While the full faith and credit provision does limit investor risk, it does not remove it altogether. The following case, arising out of New York City's fiscal crisis, is illustrative.

FLUSHING NATIONAL BANK v. MUNICIPAL ASSISTANCE CORP.

Court of Appeals of New York
40 N.Y.2d 731, 358 N.E.2d 848 (1976)

Breitel, Chief Judge.

This is an action by a holder of New York City short-term anticipation notes to declare unconstitutional the New York State Emergency Moratorium Act for the City of New York (L. 1975, ch. 874, as amd. by ch. 875). Special Term and the Appellate Division held the act constitutional under both the Federal and State Constitutions.

[At the height of the fiscal crisis, the state legislature enacted emergency legislation imposing a three-year moratorium on actions to enforce the city's outstanding short-term obligations. Holders of these obligations, which were backed by the city's faith and credit as required by the state constitution (N.Y. Const., art. VIII, § 2), were given the opportunity to exchange their notes for an equal principal amount of long-term bonds issued by a new state entity, the Municipal Assistance Corporation for the City of New York. These bonds were not backed by the faith and credit of either the state or the city, but were supported by revenues the city anticipated receiving. About $4 billion in outstanding notes were exchanged. Holders of approximately $1 billion refused the offer of MAC bonds. The moratorium applied to the notes that were not exchanged. — Eds.]

A pledge of the city's faith and credit is both a commitment to pay and a commitment of the city's revenue generating powers to produce the funds to pay. Hence, an obligation containing a pledge of the city's "faith and credit" is secured by a promise both to pay and to use in good faith the city's general revenue powers to produce sufficient funds to pay the principal and interest of the obligation as it becomes due. That is why both words, "faith" and "credit" are used and they are not tautological. That is what the words say and that is what courts have held they mean when rare occasion has suggested comment....

A "faith and credit" obligation is, therefore, entirely different from a "revenue" obligation, which is limited to a pledge of revenues from a designated source or fund.... It is also in contrast to a "moral" obligation, which is backed not by a legally enforceable promise to pay but only by a "moral" commitment....

The constitutional requirement of a pledge of the city's faith and credit is not satisfied merely by engraving a statement of the pledge in the text of the obligation. The last is a strange argument made by respondents. It is difficult to understand the financial value of such a commitment as contrasted with a "moral" obligation, wisely prohibited by the Constitution for municipalities (N.Y.Const. art. VIII, § 2). Instead, by any test, whether based on realism or sensibility, the city is constitutionally obliged to pay and to use in good faith its revenue powers to produce funds to pay the principal of the notes when due. The effect of the Moratorium Act is, however, to permit the city, having given it, to ignore its pledge of faith and credit to "pay" and to "pay punctually" the notes when due. Thus, the act would enable the city to proceed as if the pledge of faith and credit had never been.

It is argued that the city has insufficient funds to pay the notes and cannot in good faith use its revenue powers to pay the notes. The city has an enormous debt and one that in its entirety, if honored as portions become due, undoubtedly exceeds the city's present capacity to maintain an effective cash flow. But it is not true that any particular indebtedness of the city, let alone the outstanding temporary notes, is responsible for any allocable insufficiency. In short, what has happened is those responsible have made an expedient selection of the temporary noteholders to bear an extraordinary burden. The invidious consequence may not be justified by fugitive recourse to the police power of the State or to any other constitutional power to displace inconvenient but intentionally protective constitutional limitations.

The constitutional prescription of a pledge of faith and credit is designed, among other things, to protect rights vulnerable in the event of difficult economic circumstances. Thus, it is destructive of the constitutional purpose for the Legislature to enact a measure aimed at denying that very protection on the ground that government confronts the difficulties which, in the first instance, were envisioned....

It is not only the faith and credit clause of the State Constitution which marks out the constitutional plan for performance of municipal financial obligations. Other parts of article VIII control the debt-incurring or spending power of municipalities and yet also provide exception in order that outstanding debt obligations may be paid (§§ 2-a —6, 7, 7-a, applicable to New York City). Thus, for example, real estate taxes which the city may levy are limited, with certain exceptions, to 2½% of the average full valuation of taxable real estate (§§ 10, 11). The limit, however, may be exceeded to provide for all debt service (§ 10). So, too, although the Legislature is given the duty to restrict municipalities in order to prevent abuses in taxation, assessment, and in contracting of indebtedness, it may not constrict the city's power to levy taxes on real estate for the payment of interest on or principal of indebtedness previously contracted (§ 12)....

While phrased in permissive language, these provisions, when read together with the requirement of the pledge of faith and credit, express a constitutional imperative: debt obligations must be paid, even if tax limits be exceeded. A Constitution is no less violated because one would undermine only its prevailing spirit, and, arguably, not its letter.... However, in this case there is no split; spirit and letter speak in unison.

Thus, it is disingenuous to contend that, since the constitutional language allowing the city to exceed tax limits to pay its indebtedness is in form permissive, it may be disregarded. Similarly disingenuous is the argument that the Legislature has not unconstitutionally restricted the power of the city to levy taxes to pay its indebtedness because the city is "free" under the Moratorium Act to pay the notes if it wishes. The problem is not that, but that the city is free under the questioned legislation not to pay them.

. . . .

The point is that the Moratorium Act, if it were valid, would bar all remedies for a period of three years. For this there is no warrant. And the city's position on the appeal and the discussions publicized in connection with the exchange offers of MAC bonds for the temporary notes make quite clear that the noteholders would have to have a life expectancy of longer than three years if they expect the city voluntarily to redeem the notes. In short, if a three-year moratorium be valid, then one for a longer period should be valid, and perhaps too, one so long until all the noteholders take MAC bonds "voluntarily" in exchange for their notes.

It is not without significance that although Special Term and the Appellate Division treated the many Federal constitutional issues, neither offered any analysis to overcome the crux of the case — the faith and credit clause and its implications. As for the respondents they offer only a chimera.

In sum, to hold, as respondents would have the court do, that the operative effect of the faith and credit clause is exhausted when the indebtedness has been incurred would result in an economic and legal chimera. The only practical significance of a pledge of faith and credit with respect to an indebtedness must be in relation to its payment here on earth and on its due day. To interpret the constitutional provision otherwise would be to honor it as a form of window-dressing but to deny it substantive significance.

. . . .

Emergencies and the police power, although they may modify their applications, do not suspend constitutional principles. It is not merely a matter of application to interpret the words of the Constitution and obligations issued subject to the Constitution to mean exactly the opposite of what they say. The notes in suit provided that the city pledged its faith and credit to pay the notes and to pay them punctually when due. The clause and the constitutional mandate have no office except when their enforcement is inconvenient. A neutral court worthy of its status cannot do less than hold what is so evident.

The city and State, and to some extent the National Government, for almost two years have been engaged in a most difficult struggle to resolve the city's grave fiscal and economic problems. For well over a year many financial transactions have occurred on the assumption, however strained, that the moratorium would be constitutionally acceptable. In order to minimize market and governmental disruptions which might ensue it would be injudicious at this time to allow the extraordinary remedies in the nature of injunction and peremptory mandamus sought by plaintiff. Plaintiff and other noteholders of the city are entitled to some judicial relief free of throttling by the moratorium statute, but they are not entitled immediately to extraordinary or any particular judicial measures unnecessarily disruptive of the city's delicate financial and economic balance.... It is significant too that the Legislature will shortly meet in regular annual session and will be in a position once again to treat with the city's problems and to seek a fiscal solution in the light of the holding in this case.... It would serve neither plaintiff nor the people of the City of New York precipitately to invoke instant judicial remedies which might give the city no choice except to proceed into bankruptcy. The strenuous and valiant efforts by the city and State administrations, with the aid of the National Government, should be given as much leeway as constitutional decency permits. Yet none of this means that remedy can be denied to plaintiff or to noteholders beyond the short period necessary to prepare for the consequences of the determination to be made in this case.

Accordingly, the order of the Appellate Division should be reversed, with costs, the moratorium statute declared unconstitutional, and the proposed remittitur settled on 30 days' notice.

. . . .

COOKE, JUDGE (dissenting).

The New York City Emergency Moratorium Act of 1975, is, I submit, constitutional.

[In Judge Cooke's opinion, the Act was a valid exercise of the state's police power and one that had been explicitly authorized by a 1963 constitutional amendment requiring the legislature to provide for continuity of government during periods of emergency. — Eds.]

A faith and credit pledge simply means that the issuing government *agrees* to be generally obligated to pay the indebtedness out of all the government's revenues, rather than restrictively obligated only from specific revenues; it expresses an *undertaking* by the government to be irrevocably obligated in good faith to use such of its resources and taxing power as may be authorized or required by law for the full and prompt payment of the obligation according to its terms.

. . . .

The faith and credit pledge, as the words imply, requires no more than that the city make a good faith effort to use its resources, credit and powers to pay its indebtedness. This effort must be measured in the light of the city's over-all financial condition and its over-all obligations to its citizens and others....

[The dissent concluded that a good faith effort had been made as evidenced by the imposition of hiring and wage freezes, adoption of a crisis budget, increases in numerous city taxes, establishment of the Municipal Assistance Corporation, approval of a three-year financing plan calling for a balanced budget and the closing of numerous public facilities including fire stations and schools. — Eds.]

Comments: 1. Despite the setback, MAC (or in some quarters, "Big Mac") was able to carry out its mandate because of an agreement reached with trustees of the city's retirement systems to invest about $2.5 billion from the pension funds in city or MAC obligations. With the substantial assistance of the federal government, the New York City fiscal crisis was eased. By 1979, New York City was able to reenter the municipal securities markets (successfully marketing $125 million in short-term notes). Although the financial problems of New York City are far from resolved, the experience demonstrated to one group of analysts that "the untapped and largely disguised resources inherent in the structure of the nation's public finance systems have the resiliency to turn a likely mammoth fiscal disaster into a much more stable financial situation within a relatively short time." R. LAMB & S. RAPPAPORT, MUNICIPAL BONDS 359 (1980).

Federal assistance came in two stages. The New York City Seasonal Financing Act, 31 U.S.C. § 1501 (Supp. 1976) authorized the Secretary of the Treasury to lend the city up to $2.3 billion annually for three years. This was replaced in 1978 by the New York City Loan Guarantee Act of 1978, 31 U.S.C. § 1521, which authorized federal loan guarantees for up to $1.65 billion in city securities which would be sold only to city or state agency employee pension funds. The fiscal problems were so deep-seated, however, that even this assistance did not take the city out of danger. The comptroller general called for additional budget cuts after reviewing the city's approved plan in 1979 which projected budget deficits of $464 million for fiscal 1981, $830 million for 1982, and $854 million for 1983.

> The projected 1981-83 budget deficits do not represent the totality of the budget imbalance which the City will have to overcome to arrive at a balanced budget for 1982 and future years under generally accepted accounting principles, because the 4-year plan does not adequately recognize two significant uncertainties which can reasonably be expected to have a major impact upon it. The plan
>
> — does not make adequate provision for future labor costs, and
> — is based on economic assumptions which may be overly optimistic.

Comptroller General of the United States, New York City's Fiscal Problems: A Long Road Still Lies Ahead 10 (1979).

2. One of the major concerns that surfaced in the aftermath of the financial crises in New York was the adequacy of disclosure in an essentially unregulated market. Numerous commentators have pointed out that New York City's financial statements indicated that its budgets were balanced at a time when the city had several billion dollars of outstanding short-term debt. Municipal securities have been exempt from regulation under the Securities Exchange Act of 1934, although an amendment in 1975 required brokers and dealers trading municipal securities to register with the Securities and Exchange Commission. That same legislation established the Municipal Securities Rulemaking Board to set standards for tighter self-regulation of the industry. But because municipal securities are authorized by state and local law, questions regarding federal regulatory power have hindered efforts to tighten disclosure requirements. *See generally* R. LAMB & S. RAPPAPORT, MUNICIPAL BONDS 273-305 (1980). In commenting on the disclosure problem, the authors note an increasing trend toward more informative and more sophisticated disclosure of material information by this issuing entities. When New York City reentered the market in 1979, its offering statement contained more than 200 pages.

See also Steinberg, *Municipal Issues Liability Under the Federal Securities Laws*, 6 J. CORP. L. 277 (1981); Doty & Petersen, *The Federal Securities Laws and Transactions in Municipal Securities*, 71 Nw. U.L. REV. 283 (1976).

3. For a history of New York City's fiscal crisis and an argument that it resulted from a failure to share responsibilities and resources in a satisfactory way and to plan for growth so that social infrastructure does not decay in one area while vast sums are expended to duplicate it elsewhere, see W. TABB, THE LONG DEFAULT (1982).

b. Revenue Bonds

As noted earlier, revenue bonds are secured by revenues or receipts of a particular project and do not enjoy the backing of governmental taxing powers. A number of different types of bonds have been developed. One type involves a state or local governmental entity which issues bonds to fund a state or local project. Examples include tollway bonds, water and sewer bonds and public university dormitory bonds. Another type requires the creation of a separate entity, often a not-for-profit, "quasi-governmental" agency, that issues bonds to finance projects carried out by private organizations. Housing bonds, private hospital bonds, pollution control facility bonds and student loan bonds are examples of this category. Because investors in revenue bonds do not have the protection of governmental taxing powers, they normally demand a higher rate of return than do investors in general obligation bonds. In addition, revenue bond purchasers will be particularly concerned about the enforceability of the agreements the borrower makes with respect to the use of revenues generated by the project being financed.

In *United States Trust Co. v. New Jersey,* 431 U.S. 1 (1977), the Supreme Court, in a 4-3 decision, used the contract clause, U.S. Const. art. I, § 10, cl. 1, to strike down a 1974 New Jersey statute repealing a 1962 statutory covenant made by New Jersey and New York that had limited the ability of the Port Authority of New York and New Jersey to subsidize rail passenger transportation from revenues and reserves. The 1962 covenant grew out of bondholders' concerns that active involvement in commuter trains and other forms of mass transit (essentially deficit operations) could jeopardize the security of the outstanding revenue bonds on the four bridges and two tunnels owned by the Authority. Renewed interest in mass transportation developed in the wake of the energy crisis, resulting in the 1974 legislative repeal. In striking down the 1974 statute, the court concluded that while mass transportation, energy conservation, and environmental protection were important public goals, they were not new goals and circumstances had not changed so drastically in the twelve-year interval between the covenant and its repeal as to justify the impairment of the bondholders' contracts that occurred. The dissent argued that the court had turned its back on a century-old doctrine that "lawful exercises of a State's police powers stand paramount to private rights held under contract." *Id.* at 33.

A hybrid form of bond is the moral obligation bond. These bonds have been extensively used at the state level to finance a variety of state programs, especially housing assistance programs undertaken by state agencies. They first came to prominence in New York State, where they were invented by John Mitchell, formerly United States Attorney General, after a series of successive defeats of public housing bond issues in public referenda. The theory of the moral obligation bond is that the state legislature will be called upon to make an appropriation to pay any deficiency that may occur should the reserve fund maintained to make principal and interest payments fall below the maximum amount of principal and interest that could become due in any one year.

When a moral obligation is included in legislation authorizing revenue bonds, the question arises whether the moral obligation converts the revenue bond into debt because of the implied obligation to make up any deficits in project revenues. This issue is considered in the following case.

STATE EX REL. WARREN v. NUSBAUM

Supreme Court of Wisconsin
59 Wis. 2d 391, 208 N.W.2d 780 (1973)

[This case considered a broadside challenge to the constitutionality of the Wisconsin state housing finance authority. The Authority was empowered to issue notes and bonds, and to make the proceeds of these obligations available to the housing industry for a variety of housing projects. That part of the opinion which is reproduced here considers the constitutionality of the moral obligation provision included in the statute, which is paraphrased in the opinion.—Eds.]

Connor T. Hansen, Justice.

....

Does ch. 234, Stats., create state debt in violation of sec. 4 and sec. 7, art. VIII, or constitute a pledge of the state's credit in violation of sec. 3, art. VIII?

Sec. 4, art. VIII, forbids the state from contracting any debt except in the manner and amount provided by that article.

The word "debt," as used in the constitution, means all absolute obligations to pay money or its equivalent. This court in *State ex rel. Owen v. Donald* (1915), 160 Wis. 21, 59, 151 N.W. 331, 342, defined "debt" in the following manner:

> There is nothing particularly technical about the meaning of the word "debt" as used in the constitution. It includes all absolute obligations to pay money, or its equivalent, from funds to be provided, as distinguished from money presently available or in process of collection and so treatable as in hand. . . .

This court has heretofore consistently held that no state debt is created unless the state itself is under a legally enforceable obligation. . . .

Ch. 234, Stats., contains an express negation of the Authority's power to incur state debt or pledge the credit of the state. Sec. 234.14 provides:

> . . . The state shall not be liable on notes or bonds of the authority and such notes and bonds shall not be a debt of the state. All notes and bonds of the authority shall contain on the face thereof a statement to such effect.

The initial appropriation of $250,000; sec. 234.19, Stats., which pledges the noninterference of the state in the contractual relationship between the Authority and the holders of its notes and bonds; sec. 234.26, which provides that the state may legally invest any sinking funds, moneys or other funds belonging to it or within its control in any notes or bonds issued by the Authority; and sec. 234.30, which commands all state departments and agencies to extend their full cooperation to the Authority, do not indicate the contracting of state debt as that term has been defined by this court. No absolute obligation is created to be satisfied or discharged out of future appropriations.

However, sec. 234.15(4), Stats., directs the governor and the secretary of administration to include in the biennial budget in odd-numbered years the amount certified by the chairman of the Authority as necessary to maintain the Authority's capital reserve fund. The capital reserve fund, among other things, services the payment of the principal and interest of the Authority's notes and bonds. This section further requires the governor to recommend to the legislature in even-numbered years the Authority's additions to the budget for servicing its debt.

Future legislative approval is necessary before appropriations are to be made into the Authority's capital reserve fund. Thus, sec. 234.15, Stats., creates no presently binding legal obligation on the part of the state but merely constitutes an expression of future intention or aspiration.

Other jurisdictions, construing similar legislative acts, have held that provisions similar to sec. 234.15, Stats., are intended only to express to succeeding legislatures an expectation and aspiration that the project might be found worthy of financial assistance, if later needed. . . .

It is argued that, despite the express negation of state debt contained in sec. 234.14, Stats., sec. 234.15 creates an expectation of financial assistance from the state to the Authority, and that investors will feel that the state is giving its credit to the Authority even though there is no binding legal obligation on the part of the state.

Similar argument was raised and rejected in [earlier Wisconsin cases]. In *State ex rel. Thomson v. Giessel* [60 N.W.2d 763 (Wis. 1953)] this court stated:

> Respondent argues that the bond buying public will feel that the state is giving its credit to the turnpike corporation bonds even though there is no legal obligation on the part of the state, because it will be reasoned that the state could not afford to allow the project to fail. Obviously, this cannot be the test to be applied. The test of a "legally enforceable obligation" . . . is the only sound one.

No enforceable legal obligation is created on the part of the state to subsidize the debts of the Authority even though good judgment may dictate that it do so voluntarily. No state debt can be created where payment of state funds is to be made solely at the state's option. . . .

Respondents contend that ch. 234, Stats., evidences a moral obligation on the part of the state to insure the Authority's debts, and that such moral obligation is sufficient to create state "debt" within the meaning of sec. 4, art. VIII. The term "moral obligations" recognizes the absence of any legally enforceable claim. It is generally held that the state is not compelled to recognize moral obligations, but it is free, through appropriate legislation, to satisfy that which it recognizes as its moral debt. It is stated in 63 Am. Jur. 2d, Public Funds, pp. 457, 458, sec. 70:

> The essence of a moral obligation is that it arises out of a state of facts appealing to a universal sense of justice and fairness, even though upon such facts no legally enforceable claim can be based. A "moral obligation" justifying the enactment of a statute providing for the payment of compensation in a case in which no legal liability exists on the part of the state or its subdivisions is such an obligation as would be recognized by men with a keen sense of honor and with a real desire to act fairly and equitably without compulsion of law. However, it is generally recognized that a moral obligation is more than a mere desire to do charity or to appropriate money in acknowledgment of a gratitude. It is an obligation which, though lacking any foundation cognizable in law, springs from a sense of justice and equity which an honorable person would entertain, but not from a mere sense of doing benevolence or charity.

Even if a moral obligation on the part of the state exists, the fact is that ch. 234, Stats., does not create a legally enforceable claim against the state by the holders of its notes and bonds. Whether future appropriations are made pursuant to sec. 234.15, depends upon the exercise of legislative wisdom of each successive legislative session when and if such requested appropriations are submitted to it for its consideration. Ch. 234 does not create a state debt within the meaning of Sec. 4, art. VIII.

[The court then held that as the moral obligation clause did not create a legally enforceable obligation there had been no unconstitutional lending of credit in aid of an individual or corporation.—Eds.]

Comments: 1. If moral obligation bonds are not legally enforceable, why do the parties bother to include the provision? Most of the courts that have passed on this issue have agreed with the Wisconsin court. *See, e.g., Steup v. Indiana Housing Finance Authority,* 402 N.E.2d 1215 (Ind. 1980); *Utah Housing Finance Agency v. Smart,* 561 P.2d 1052 (Utah 1977); *Massachusetts Housing Finance Agency v. New England Merchants National Bank,* 249 N.E.2d 599 (Mass. 1969); Griffith, *"Moral Obligation" Bonds: Illusion or Security?,* 8 URB. LAW. 54, 70-93 (1976). *Contra, Gibson v. Smith,* 531 P.2d 724 (1975).

The court noted that the constitutional provision limiting state debt applied as well to liabilities of the state, and that the moral obligation provision attempted to do indirectly what was prohibited directly and "so would bear characteristics of misrepresentation which could eventually result in an indirect legal defeat of the positive direct proscription." *Id.* at 728.

Compare Turnpike Authority v. Wall, 336 S.W.2d 551 (Ky. 1960), invalidating a statute under which the state highway department was obligated from its general revenues to make up any deficiency between turnpike project revenues and turnpike bond debt service requirements. The court held that this obligation was debt within the constitutional provision "for the reason that the state could not disengage itself therefrom by discontinuing the levy of taxes and appropriation of funds for such an unavoidable function of government as the construction and maintenance of public highways." *Id.* at 557. No referendum on this obligation was provided in the legislation, as required by the constitutional state debt provision.

2. What can happen when the moral obligation authority is overused is illustrated by the situation in New York State. By 1974, the long-term moral obligation debt of New York state authorities was 6.5 billion, almost twice the amount of the state's long-term full faith and credit debt. Statement of Sheldon H. Elsen, Chief Counsel, to Moreland Act Commission on the Urban Development Corporation and other State Financing Agencies, October 14, 1975, at 4. One bond rating organization has questioned whether any state could raise taxes in an amount sufficient to meet such a staggering moral obligation, and noted:

> The analysis of obligations secured by revenues associated with a project must look first and primarily to those revenues. Where the issue is secondarily secured by an opinion that the state may legally appropriate funds to fill a reserve deficiency, that element of security can at best, in our opinion, be regarded as a rating floor in which elements of speculation remain.

Backups, Makeups, and Moral Obligations, Moody's Bond Survey, September 17, 1973, at 568-69. *See also* Hochberg & Taylor, *Public Authority Bond Issues: The Need for Legislative Reform,* 21 N.Y.L.F. 183 (1975); Quirk & Wein, *A Short Constitutional History of Entities Commonly Known as Authorities,* 56 CORNELL L. REV. 521 (1971). Both articles concentrate on New York State.

3. New York City's fiscal crisis also stimulated the creation of a public service corporation which was temporarily to assist the city in providing needed public services, and the legislation creating this corporation also contained a moral obligation provision. In *Wein v. City of New York,* 331 N.E.2d 514 (N.Y. 1975), an action was brought challenging the constitutionality of the legislation creating the corporation on various grounds, including an allegation that the moral obligation provision had created an indebtedness of the city. The problem arose because the corporation was authorized to issue bonds, to be paid out of a capital reserve fund to be replenished annually. A provision in the legislation required the city to pay annually into the fund an amount necessary to assure its maintenance. The court held, in a 4-3 decision, that city payments into the fund would constitute a constitutionally proper gift and so did not constitute an indebtedness of the city.

4. That the lending of credit provision still has some vitality is indicated by *Casey v. South Carolina State Housing Authority,* 215 S.E.2d 184 (S.C. 1975). This case held unconstitutional a state housing authority act that authorized the Authority to issue state bonds, the proceeds to be used for direct loans to lending institutions, direct mortgage loans, and mortgage purchases. A guaranty fund was created out of which any defaults on these loans were to be met. The court held that the act violated the lending of credit provision. "We are of the opinion that the Act commits the State of South Carolina and, by so doing, pledges its credit to make good any deficit arising because of default under both the Direct Mortgage Loan Program and the Mortgage Purchase Program." *Id.* at 187.

A large number of states have now enacted state housing authority laws. Most have been held constitutional when attacked on public purpose grounds. The cases are summarized in *Martin v. North Carolina Housing Corp.,* 174 S.E.2d 665 (N.C. 1970) (statute limited to low-income housing). Courts have not usually had difficulty in finding a public purpose when the program is limited to lower income families, who cannot compete effectively in the housing market. The Vermont court sustained a similar law which was not explicitly so limited, although a ceiling was placed on the mortgage amount of loans that qualified under the act. *Vermont Home Mortgage Credit Agency v. Montpelier National Bank,* 262 A.2d 445 (Vt. 1970). The court noted the purpose of the act to stimulate economic growth in the state and expand employment opportunities, and commented that the need for adequate housing was created by the state's growing population and industrial development. It also took notice of the fact that the rising cost of money had placed capital funds for home construction in critically short supply.

The North Carolina court has upheld a statutory expansion of the state housing program authorizing the sale of bonds to finance single-family and multifamily housing for persons of moderate incomes. *In re Denial of Approval to Issue $30,000,000.00,* 296 S.E.2d 281 (N.C. 1982). Noting that mortgage interest rates had climbed to seventeen percent for single-family homes and nineteen percent for multifamily in the state, the court had little difficulty in finding a valid public purpose.

> Any casual observer knows that the present economy is drastically different from that existing at the time the Act was originally enacted. Such an observer is equally aware of the serious problems facing those with moderate incomes who wish to acquire decent housing for their families. We agree with the appellee that issuance of the proposed bonds would benefit all the citizens of our State. The infusion of low interest mortgage money into the private construction industry should inevitably lead to more jobs, increased local and state tax revenues, more stable neighborhoods and an enhanced economy generally. The supply of available residential housing ultimately would be increased, thus generally improving the opportunities for our people to obtain better housing. Moreover, ... the acquisition of houses by people otherwise unable to afford them provides those same people with a stake in the preservation of our society that they would not have were it not for the Agency's assistance.... A lack of adequate housing inevitably engenders slum-like conditions, a situation the legislature obviously sought to eliminate with its proposed bond proceeds.

Id. at 286.

A NOTE ON INDUSTRIAL AND COMMERCIAL DEVELOPMENT AND POLLUTION FACILITIES BOND FINANCING

Shades of the railroad era have arisen in recent years under widely adopted state legislation authorizing state and local bond financing in aid of industrial and commercial development and to assist private companies to acquire pollution abatement equipment in order to comply with pollution control legislation. The industrial development programs have been operational longest, and while they may take the form of direct loans a common form of this program is for the state or locality to issue general obligation or revenue bonds to construct or expand an industrial plant, or even a commercial facility, which is then leased to a private company. The bonds are retired from the rental payments made by the private company, which owns the facility once the bonds are paid off. These programs ordinarily are quite opportunistic; they are adopted to attract industry, with little thought usually given to planning for that industry or to the impact the industry might have on the community or on the added need for public services.

The private benefits in the bond program may be substantial, as leasehold terms may be favorable and the tax-exempt status of governmental securities means lower financing costs and lower rentals. Nevertheless, there is substantial risk for the community if the firm subsequently quits business, possibly leaving the community with an unuseable plant.

Industrial Development Bonds

Industrial development bonds were initially limited to some of the southern states, but as interest in this financing device increased their use spread and the number and size of these bonds grew rapidly, ultimately leading to a congressional reform which withdrew the income tax exemption for interest on these issues except for two categories of bonds: (a) Industrial Development Bonds (IDBs) unlimited in size but restricted to public projects such as airports, convention centers, housing for low- and moderate-income persons, pollution control projects, ports and sports stadiums; and (b) "Small Issue" Industrial Development Bonds (single bond issues of one million dollars or less, or issues up to ten million dollars if the recipient company does not spend more than ten million dollars in a six-year period beginning three years prior to the date of issue) limited in size but unrestricted in use. I.R.C. § 103(c).

I.R.C. § 103(b) defines a security as an IDB if the proceeds are to be used in a trade or business by someone other than a governmental unit or a tax-exempt organization (I.R.C. § 501(c)(3)), and payment of principal or interest is secured by interests in, or derived from payments with respect to, property or borrowed money used in a trade or business. This change in the tax-exempt status of these bonds had an immediate effect on their popularity, as the amount of industrial development bonds issued fell dramatically shortly after the tax exemption was withdrawn. For discussion see Note, *The Limited Tax-Exempt Status of Interest on Industrial Development Bonds Under Subsection 103(c) of the Internal Revenue Code,* 85 HARV. L. REV. 1649 (1972).

Industrial development bond issues with a face value of one million dollars or less are still entitled to the exemption of interest, and the exemption is also available for bonds that finance certain specified projects, such as residential family housing, sports facilities, airports, mass commuting facilities, and sewage and solid waste treatment plants. In addition, interest on bonds financing air or water pollution control facilities remains exempt from federal income taxation. The result of this differential tax treatment has been a rapid growth in bond issues whose proceeds are used by private companies for the construction of air and water pollution control facilities. The rest of this Note will discuss the constitutional problems arising out of the use of both industrial and pollution control bonds; the legal issues involved are roughly similar. *See, e.g.,* Friedman, *Pollution Control Bonds: Developing Case Law in the States,* 5 ENV. AFF. 333 (1976).

The principal advantage and primary purpose of industrial development financing is the economic stimulation of underdeveloped areas. In theory, at least, the economic growth stimulated by new or expanded industrial activity will affect the general public in the form of a higher standard of living, increased employment opportunities, curtailment of nongovernmental investment in manufacturing plants, and a higher tax base. There are disadvantages as well. Public credit is being used to finance private industrial expansion and may hamper the ability of state and local governments to improve other community services by glutting the market and making general obligation bonds for necessary public improvements less attractive. The decision making must also enter into an evaluation of these programs.

In spite of the potential pitfalls in these programs, the overwhelming majority of the courts that have considered their constitutionality under the public purpose doctrine have held them constitutional. *See City of Pipestone v. Madsen,* 178 N.W.2d 594 (Minn. 1970) (held constitutional). *Contra, Mitchell v. North Carolina Industrial Development Financing Authority,* 159 S.E.2d 745 (N.C. 1968) (reviewing authorities). The reasons given by the Minnesota court for upholding the program are typical:

> The development of industrial enterprises in the Pipestone area will substantially overcome the deteriorating economy affecting the community.... Providing gainful employment for our people will increase their purchasing power, improve their living conditions, and relieve the demand for unemployment and welfare assistance. New or modernized buildings will add properties to the tax lists and increase the tax base. There is little doubt that the establishment of new and improved industry will measurably increase the resources of the community, promote the economy of the state, and thereby contribute to the welfare of its people. These benefits are clearly public in nature.

Id. at 603. For discussion see Note, *Some Legal and Economic Aspects of Industrial Development Financing,* 22 VAND. L. REV. 159 (1968). Some commentators suggest that these programs be built on comprehensive economic planning, and include safeguards such as prohibitions against employment discrimination and against the conversion of public-aided plants to nonmanufacturing uses. See Pascarella & Raymond, *Buying Bonds for Business: An Evaluation of the Industrial Revenue Bond Program,* 18 URB. AFF. Q. 73 (1982) (suggesting that these programs generate insufficient social benefits to offset real social costs).

Pollution Abatement Bonds

Public pollution bond financing to aid private industries in the construction of pollution abatement facilities, prompted by the heightened adoption and enforcement of pollution control programs in recent years, follows the same pattern as industrial bond financing. Revenue bonds are again issued by the state or local authority, the pollution facility constructed with the proceeds of the bond issue is leased to the private company, and the rental payments secure the retirement of the bonds. Often there is an important economic benefit to the community issuing the bonds, as the plant benefited by the bond issue might have closed down because of its inability to meet air or water pollution requirements unless the facility had been built. It was this possibility that prompted the issuance of pollution facility bonds in the North Carolina case, to be discussed below.

Courts willing to sustain the constitutionality of pollution facility bonds have stressed that the elimination, mitigation, or prevention of air or water pollution is a proper public purpose for which public bonds may be issued. *See,* especially, *Wilson v. Board of Commissioners,* 327 A.2d 488 (Md. 1974). Accord, *Harper v. Schooler,* 189 S.E.2d 284 (S.C. 1972). Cf. *Wisconsin Solid Waste Recycling Authority v. Earl,* 235 N.W.2d 648 (Wis. 1975).

Nevertheless, contrary considerations led the North Carolina Supreme Court to invalidate pollution facility bonds in *Stanley v. Department of Conservation & Development,* 199 S.E.2d 641 (N.C. 1973). It should first be noted that the North Carolina court has taken a strict view of the public purpose doctrine. As the court noted, an "incidental advantage to the public" will not save the program in that state, and it added that "[i]t is only when private enterprise has demonstrated its inability or unwillingness to meet a public necessity that government is permitted to invade the private sector." *Id.* at 653. The court then continued:

> Does the State serve a public purpose when it assists a private industry in financing the abatement and control of the pollution the industry creates? Beyond any doubt air and water pollution have become two of modern society's most urgent problems, and noise pollution is likewise a major modern evil. Such pollution knows no boundaries, for it cannot be contained in the area where it occurs.... Regardless of where it occurs, the abatement and control of environmental pollution are immediately necessary to the public health,

safety, and general welfare; and, in the exercise of the State's police power, the legislature has plenary authority to abate and control pollution of all kinds. . . .

The power of the State to regulate private institutions and industries under its police power, however, is more extensive than the authority to accomplish the same purpose by use of its taxing power. . . . It does not follow, therefore, that because the State has power to order an industry to abate a nuisance or cease operations it may constitutionally assist the industry in financing the abatement.

Pulp and paper mills are recognized to be among the major industrial pollutants . . . and Albemarle is no exception. In their briefs defendants pose this question with reference to the pollution which Albemarle is creating: "Does the public in common benefit from the elimination of the dumping of tons of solid waste every day into the Roanoke River, the reduction of odors emitted into the air, the drastic reduction of suspended solids in the air, the elimination of the necessity to breathe air containing various sulphur compounds, the control of slime bacteria in the Roanoke River, the elimination from the air of chemicals so strong that they cause the paint to come off houses and cars, and the general improvement and cleaning up of the total environment?"

To ask this question is, of course, to answer it. Certainly the elimination of the terrible condition described above will benefit all the people. Furthermore, they are entitled to its elimination, and the State is now using its police power to abate the nuisance and halt the damage to the environment which this pollution has caused.

It is stipulated that Albemarle's air and water pollution emissions are and have been in violation of the laws and regulations of the State; that it is and has been operating under temporary, conditional permits; and that if Albemarle is to continue its operations it must reduce its air and water emission to the legal limits. . . . There is no finding that Albemarle is unable to provide the required facilities at its own expense and without outside assistance. Indeed, upon the argument of these cases, defendants conceded that Albemarle is able to correct the pollution it creates and that construction of the necessary facilities is in progress.

It is recognized that the net result of revenue bond financing such as the Act authorizes "is that the municipality lends its tax-free bond issuing power to the private corporation or organization so that the interest on what would otherwise be a private bond issue becomes free of income tax and a low interest rate on borrowed money is obtained". . . . Thus the Act would permit the Authorities to do indirectly for Albemarle that which the constitution forbids Albemarle to do for itself, that is, to issue tax-free revenue bonds to finance construction of an integral part of its plant. The cost of such construction is just one of the many expenses which a manufacturing enterprise must take into account in fixing the price of its product.

The conclusion is inescapable that Albemarle is the only direct beneficiary of the tax-exempt revenue bonds which the Halifax and Northampton Authorities propose to issue and that the benefit to the public is only incidental or secondary. It cannot be said that a benefit results to the public when the State assists a private industry in financing facilities the law requires the industry to construct without such aid. . . . This is especially true when, as here, the industry is able to do its own financing. . . .

Were the State to aid Albemarle by tax-free revenue bond financing, to that extent it would subsidize a particular pulp and paper mill which is in competition with other and unsubsidized pulp and paper mills, a violation of N.C. Const. art. V, § 2(1). We take judicial notice that competing pulp and paper mills are located in different counties in widely separated parts of this State. Under the Act the governing body of a county creates a Pollution Abatement and Industrial Facilities Financing Authority in the exercise of its own discretion. Obviously, therefore, the Act does not purport to give any assurance that all competing private industries (taxpayers in the same classification) would receive the same benefits from the Act. Moreover, once any industrial polluter receives the subsidy provided by tax-free revenue bond financing, all others—chemical producers, iron and steel mills, petroleum refineries, smelters, energy producing utilities, et cetera—would be equally entitled to the same subsidy. Incidentally, it can reasonably be anticipated that, were all their demands to be met, industrial revenue bonds would flood the bond market to the detriment of old fashioned municipal bonds backed by the full faith and credit of the municipality seeking to finance schools, sewerage disposal systems, fire equipment and other public ventures.

Pollution control facilities are single-purpose facilities, useful only to the industry for which they would be acquired and to which they would be leased. If that industry were to become insolvent or, for any reason, default in its rental payments and guarantee of the bonds which an authority had issued to finance the facilities, those bonds would soon be in default. A few such defaults would certainly adversely affect the revenue-bond market and, almost certainly, also the credit rating of the county whose governing body had created the defaulting authority. These economic dangers demonstrate the wisdom of N.C. Const. art. V, § 2(1).

The only benefit which could inure to the public from State aid to an industry under mandate to abate its pollution would be the general benefit to the community's economy from the retention of the industry in the event the industry was unable or unwilling to comply with the State's mandate without State aid, and the alternative was to cease operations. Undeniably the consequences of any wholesale lay-off or substantial unemployment for whatever cause is detrimental to a community. . . ."

Id. at 655-57. The North Carolina court then noted that in the *Mitchell* case, *supra*, it had rejected the argument that public aid for the purpose of attracting or retaining industry in the state served a public purpose. Are any supportable distinctions to be made, then, between industrial development and pollution facility bonds? Don't industrial development bonds also have the same pricing effect to which the North Carolina court took objection? For a case invalidating pollution facility bonds under a lending of credit provision see *Port of Longview v. Taxpayers of Longview,* 527 P.2d 263 (Wash. 1974), *modified,* 533 P.2d 128 (Wash. 1975), *noted,* 50 WASH. L. REV. 440 (1975).

Clearly the public purpose spending and lending of credit limitations, although adopted to restrain public borrowing, have provided the courts with a legal basis to review and invalidate innovative public programs when they happen to rely on the spending or borrowing power. The kinship of the public purpose requirement with the due process clause, and the relaxed view which the federal courts have taken toward due process objections in the economic regulation field, make us at least wonder whether or not judicial invalidation of public spending programs on public purpose or lending of credit grounds is wise. Should decisions on what are and what are not proper arena for public spending be left to the legislature to decide? Should we not rely on political resolution of these issues through the legislative process? Note that the North Carolina decision is distinctly a minority view.

Is it of some bearing on the continuing vitality of the public purpose and lending of credit limitations that thirty-eight states have held industrial development and pollution facility bonds constitutional under such provisions? *See* 50 WASH. L. REV. at 447, *supra*. That several states have amended their constitutions to allow such programs? *See id.* at 451 n.43. That Nebraska and Idaho expressly overruled adverse court decisions through constitutional amendments? *See* Neb. Const. art. XIII, §§ 1-3; Idaho Const. art. VIII, § 3(A). Or does this history suggest that major innovations in public spending policies should occur through changes in the basic charter for state government rather than through judicial decision?

A NOTE ON THE TAX EQUITY AND FISCAL RESPONSIBILITY ACT OF 1982 (Pub. L. 97-248)

In response to concerns about the enormous growth of the tax-exempt bond market and perceived abuses of the concept, Congress imposed restrictions on the use of tax-exempt bonds in 1980 and additional restrictions as part of a major tax increase and reform effort in 1982. The following excerpts from the 1982 Conference Committee report summarize the changes and the rationale:

TAX EQUITY AND FISCAL RESPONSIBILITY ACT OF 1982

H.R. Rep. No. 4961, 98th Cong., 2d Sess. 166-69, 178-79 (1982)

REPORT OF THE COMMITTEE ON FINANCE, UNITED STATES SENATE

8. Tax-Exempt Obligations

a. Restrictions on tax-exempt bonds for private activities (secs. 221, 222, and 223 of the bill and secs. 103 and 168 of the Code)

. . . .

Reasons for Change

In General

The committee is concerned with the use of tax-exempt bonds used for private activities. There has been a tremendous increase in recent years in the volume of such bonds. In 1976 the volume of private activity bonds was about $8.5 billion, or about 25 percent of the long-term tax-exempt bond market. The volume of private activity bonds rose to more than $25 billion in 1981, representing 48 percent of the tax-exempt bond market. The Treasury Department estimates that over $35 billion of private activity bonds will be issued in 1982, consuming over 55 percent of the entire long-term tax-exempt bond market.

The proliferation of private activity bonds has contributed to a significant narrowing of the difference in interest rates between tax-exempt and taxable bonds. While the tax-exempt rate historically has been about 65 to 75 percent of the taxable rate, tax-exempt bonds are now generally yielding about 80 to 85 percent of the taxable rate. This erosion of the relative advantage of tax-exempt financing has made it more costly for state and local governments to finance essential public projects such as schools, roads and prisons. It also has made tax-exempt financing even less cost effective as a subsidy for private activities, since more of the benefit is siphoned off for bond investors as tax-exempt rates grow closer to taxable rates. The increasing volume of private activity bonds has also caused mounting Federal revenue losses. The Treasury Department estimates that the total Federal revenue loss from private activity tax-exempt bonds outstanding in fiscal year 1981 was $3.2 billion and will be $4.2 billion for private purpose obligations outstanding in fiscal year 1982.

While the growth of private activity bonds in recent years has been large, information concerning the specific uses is incomplete. Accordingly, in order to enable the Congress and others to monitor the use of tax-exempt bonds for private activities and to help in enforcing other restrictions on industrial development bonds [IDBs], the committee bill requires issuers to make quarterly reports to the Internal Revenue Service on private activity tax-exempt obligations issued by them.

. . . .

Industrial Development Bonds

The committee believes that new restrictions are needed on IDBs to help eliminate inappropriate uses and to help restore the benefit of tax-exempt financing for traditional governmental purposes. However, the committee believes that, in general, State and local governments are best suited to determine the appropriate uses of IDBs. The committee believes that providing tax exemption for the interest on certain IDBs may serve legitimate purposes in some instances provided that the elected representatives of the State or local governmental unit determine after public input that there will be substantial public benefit from issuance of the obligations and provided that the affected public has had an opportunity to comment on the use of tax-exempt financing for particular facilities. In order to achieve this goal, the committee bill requires notice and a public hearing and approval by an elected representative of the issuer before issuance of any IDBs.

The committee is also concerned with the combined subsidies provided for investment from the tax rules for cost recovery, investment tax credit and tax-exempt financing. In most cases, the committee believes that the combined subsidies are too generous. Consequently, the committee believes that new restrictions in cost recovery deductions taken by private taxpayers for property financed by IDBs are necessary. Therefore, the committee bill requires taxpayers to choose between (1) ACRS and conventional financing and (2) tax-exempt financing and a slower rate of cost recovery than that provided by ACRS. The committee does not believe such a requirement will reduce the use of IDBs in appropriate circumstances, but will simply eliminate an unnecessary portion of the total subsidy available to the user of the bond proceeds. [The Accelerated Cost Recovery System, introduced by the Economic Recovery Tax Act of 1981 (ERTA), 26 U.S.C. §§ 1-9033, provides incentives for business investment through substantial increases in the deductions allowed for depreciation of property used in a trade or business. This is accomplished by sharply reducing the number of years allowed to write off investment costs. For example, real property under the ACRS can be depreciated generally in fifteen years; previous guidelines were thirty to fifty years.—Eds.]

The committee believes that extraordinary levels of subsidy are necessary in the case of certain types of property. In those cases, both tax-exempt financing and the full ACRS deductions should be available. The committee believes that additional levels of subsidy are appropriate for low income rental housing, municipal solid waste disposal facilities, air and water pollution control facilities installed in existing plants, and projects financed in part with a UDAG grant. [Urban Development Action Grants pursuant to section 119 of the Housing and Community Development Act of 1974.—Eds.]

Small Issue Industrial Development Bonds

The committee is also particularly concerned with the extraordinarily rapid growth in the volume of small issue IDBs. In 1976, according to the Treasury Department, the volume of new, small issue IDBs was $1.4 billion. In 1981, that volume had grown to $10.5 billion, an annual rate of growth of 50 percent. By contrast, public activity bonds grew at an annual rate of approximately 1 percent during the same period. Continued growth in the use of small-issue tax-exempt bonds for private purposes is expected unless actions are taken to limit their use. Under present law, for instance, the annual volume of new small issues by 1987 is estimated to be $31.3 billion.

In addition to its concern with the increasing volume of small issue bonds, and the impact of that volume on the market for public purpose tax-exempt securities, the committee is concerned with (1) the use of small issue IDBs by large companies that are able to raise funds readily in capital markets without a federal subsidy, (2) the use of small issue IDBs to finance a variety of types of facilities, from private recreational facilities to fast food restaurants, that generally may be less deserving of a Federal credit subsidy than other types of facilities, and (3) the lack of any substantial targeting of the use of small issue IDBs to economically distressed or otherwise needy areas.

[To encourage the development and use of steam and hot water heating and cooling systems as an energy-conservation measure, the bill added these facilities to the list of tax-exempt IDB activities.—Eds.]

Comments: 1. In general, the penalty for noncompliance with the restrictions on IDBs in the 1982 Act is loss of tax exemption on interest income received by investors. 26 U.S.C. § 103(b)(1). This is, obviously, a very serious penalty and one that would make any investor think twice about the risks. For a number of the requirements on IDBs (public hearing, approval by elected public official), the investor retains some control because these requirements must be met before the bonds are issued. But what about the reporting requirement for bonds issued by not-for-profit organizations? Reports must be filed quarterly (no later than the fifteenth day of the second following month). Property must be identified on an asset-by-asset basis and by a general description of the facility or project. 26 U.S.C. § 103(L) (1982). Since the money will have been advanced several months prior to the reporting deadline, the investor will have no control over the risk of noncompliance. Is this a serious problem?

2. To what extent do the requirements for public hearing and approval by the chief elected official (or elected designee) raise federalism issues under the tenth amendment? Suppose state law mandates a different approach to public accountability? Is this an unwarranted interference with state government of the type proscribed in *National League of Cities v. Usery*, 426 U.S. 833 (1976)? Do the new requirements preempt the states from considering other forms of public accountability, e.g., approval by an appointed official or a blue ribbon citizens' panel? Federalism questions of this type are discussed in Chapter 8, *infra*.

3. The use of tax-exempt bonds to stimulate the housing market has generated considerable controversy. Techniques for using tax-exempt bonds to purchase single-family mortgages were developed by state housing finance agencies in the mid-1970s as a response to a federal freeze on multifamily housing subsidies and the first of a series of sharp increases in interest rates on single-family mortgages. The state programs developed along two lines. The first approach was to sell bonds and lend the proceeds from those bonds to local lenders who agreed to make first mortgage loans to qualified low- and moderate-income purchasers at below market interest rates. The second and more popular approach was to use the bond proceeds to purchase from local lenders mortgages on single-family residences that those lenders had obtained by financing the purchase of the residences. Some states, notably Minnesota and Kentucky, also developed second mortgage purchase programs to finance rehabilitation of existing residences.

National attention was focused when individual cities and counties began issuing tax-exempt bonds to purchase local mortgages for middle- and upper-income housing, including expensive condominiums. Dubbed the "Chicago plan" because of its origin, the new type of issue combined elements of the state mortgage purchase program with the corporate sector mortgage-backed bonds and pass-through securities (devices for pooling funds and passing mortgage payments directly through to the investor). The combination of tax-free interest income and good security because of the more expensive type of housing being financed made the Chicago plan housing bond extremely popular. It was viewed as a possible savior of the real estate industry. For a discussion of the Chicago plan, see R. LAMB and S. RAPPAPORT, MUNICIPAL BONDS, *supra,* at 172. However, an intense debate developed over the "public purpose" of the Chicago plan, culminating in sharp restrictions built into the Mortgage Subsidy Bond Tax Act of 1980. In general, tax-exempt status is still available, but only if the housing will benefit low- and moderate-income persons, as defined in the Act.

The 1980 restrictions limited mortgages financed from bond proceeds to mortgages for first-time home buyers defined as persons without a present ownership interest in a principal residence for three years prior to the execution of the mortgage. 26 U.S.C. § 103A(e)(1). Exceptions were made for home improvement loans, rehabilitation loans and loans in targeted areas (generally, central cities). 26 U.S.C. § 103A(e)(2). The acquisition cost could not exceed 90% (110% in targeted areas) of the applicable average area purchase price. 26 U.S.C. § 103A(f). The restrictions were relaxed somewhat in 1982. The three-year requirement was reduced to 90% of the lendable proceeds and the purchase price limit was increased to 110% (120% in targeted areas) of the average area purchase price. Pub. L. 97-248, § 220(c)-(d). The Act imposed annual limits on the amount of tax-exempt mortgage subsidy bonds that can be issued. The state ceiling is the greater of 9% of the previous three-year average of single-family mortgages executed for residences within the state, or $200,000,000. State housing agencies are allocated 50% of the ceiling, with the balance going to local issuing authorities on a pro rata basis of mortgage activity. Constitutional home rule cities ("Chicago plan" cities issuing bonds under home rule authority) share in the allocation based on 100% of the state ceiling. 26 U.S.C. § 103A(g).

Under the 1980 Act, single-family mortgage subsidy bonds will lose their tax-exempt status after December 31, 1983 unless Congress extends their status. 26 U.S.C. § 103A(c)(1)(B). Arguments that tax-exempt housing bonds are an unwarranted drain on the federal treasury and a subsidy to the well-off persist. The debate was dramatized by a Marin County, California (San Francisco Bay area) plan to assist the "middle class" by issuing bonds to purchase below market interest rate loans made by persons earning up to $58,000 a year to acquire houses costing as much as $160,000. St. Louis Globe-Democrat, Dec. 2, 1982, at 7 A, col. 3. This is possible because the restrictions in the Mortgage Subsidy Bond Tax Act are geared to average area purchase price. 26 U.S.C. § 103A(f). Marin County, one of the wealthiest counties in the nation, has one of the highest average purchase prices. Two Chicago-area bond issues (one in the city, the other in Cook County, Ill.) in late 1982 had purchase price limits of $90,310 ($98,520 targeted) for new and $78,430 ($85,560) for existing homes. Purchasers with annual gross incomes of $50,000 could qualify. 10 Hous. & Dev. Rep. (BNA) 532-33 (1982). The figures noted represent maximum allowable limits. Actual prices will usually be much lower. The Missouri Housing Development Commission reports an average purchase price of $30,000 for approximately 10,000 mortgages purchased between 1976 and 1982. Missouri Housing Development Commission, Eleventh Annual Report, at 4 (1982).

4. Decentralization of housing bond activity from state to local government raises important questions of state-local relationships. How, for example, should a dispute be resolved between a state housing finance agency that has sold bonds at a lower interest cost than similar bonds sold by a city? Should the state agency agree not to purchase mortgages within that city's boundaries so the city can market the proceeds from its bonds? Should the state share its proceeds with the city? The timing of the bond sale in a volatile market can have significant consequences. Can a 13% home loan (city rate) compete with an 11% home loan (state rate) in the above example?

5. High interest rates and increased competition for the investment dollar have reduced the attractiveness of municipal bonds. The then-record 7.38% municipal bond yield of October 1979 was viewed as an exceptional bargain in the wake of 12-13% yields in 1981-1982. In addition, new savings devices (tax-exempt All Savers Certificates, tax-deferred Individual Retirement Accounts, etc.) and reduced tax rates on capital gains as well as personal income for upper bracket individuals have made alternatives attractive. Finally, the explosion of private activity bond issues (discussed *supra*) has made life uncomfortable for state and local governments seeking funds for traditional public projects such as bridges, streets and sewers. *See generally* Galper, *The State and Local Bond Market,* Intergovernmental Perspective, ACIR, Vol. 8, No. 3, at 12 (1982).

6. Another source of concern to Congress and the Internal Revenue Service has been the potential use of the tax-exempt feature of municipal securities to realize profits through arbitrage. A tax-exempt entity issuing bonds paying 9% interest could realize a tidy profit if it invested the funds received from the bond issue in taxable securities paying twelve percent. To forestall this practice, Congress added a provision to § 103 in 1969 denying tax-exempt status to "arbitrage" bonds. Section 103(c) defines an "arbitrage bond" as an obligation which a state or local government issues for which all or a major portion of the proceeds will be used for investment in securities which will generate a materially higher yield of interest than the tax-exempt obligations.

Administration of this relatively simple concept has become quite complicated. For example, in Treas. Reg. § 1.103-13(g) the Treasury interpreted the provision as meaning that "[a]mounts held in a sinking fund for an issue . . . are treated as proceeds of the issue." Section 1.103.03(g) defines a sinking fund to include "a debt service fund . . . or any similar fund, to the extent that the issuer reasonably expects to use the fund to pay principal or interest on the issue." The city of Tucson, Arizona, proposed to issue bonds to provide for certain public improvements, intending to pay the debt service on the bonds from a sinking fund. The city expected to use the sinking fund to invest in non-exempt obligations while the bonds were outstanding. In *Tucson v. Commissioner,* 78 T.C. No. 52, 78.52 PH T.C. (1982), the city sought a declaratory judgment that the bonds would qualify for tax-exempt treatment, arguing that the bonds were not arbitrage bonds and that the Treasury regulation conflicted with § 103(c).

In upholding the regulation, the Tax Court reasoned as follows:

> The . . . history of the sinking fund regulations shows they were adopted in response to efforts by borrowing municipalities to circumvent section 103(c) by using invested sinking funds to realize profits on the difference between the interest paid on tax-exempt obligations and the interest received from taxable obligations. The municipalities could achieve this result by accumulating a sinking fund expected to be used for the repayment of bonds, holding the annually increasing fund until the entire (or most of the) bond issue became due at the end of a 20-year period, for example, and in the meantime investing the funds in Federal government (or other) securities paying higher interest rates. Such use of a sinking fund produces the same undesirable consequences of arbitrage as section 103(c) was intended to cure—the issuance of an abnormally large volume of bonds in relation to municipal needs for improvements, increased public borrowing costs, the crowding of weaker borrowers out of the market, and a loss of Federal revenues. The sinking fund regulations designed to control this "relatively new" and "ingenious way of circumventing the arbitrage rules" . . . are thus clearly consistent with the broad objectives and purposes of section 103(c).
>
> . . . .
>
> If a municipality accumulates funds (from sources other than bonds) to finance a public project, but then uses those funds to acquire high yielding taxable obligations and sells its own tax-exempt bonds expecting to use the proceeds for the public project, it seems clear that the accumulated funds have been indirectly replaced by bond proceeds and, for the purposes of section 103(c), should be "treated as proceeds" of the bonds. Economically, the municipality is in the same position it would have been had it used the accumulated funds for the public project and issued bonds to acquire the higher yielding taxable securities.
>
> We perceive no reason why a municipality which issues bonds to be used for a particular purpose, reasonably expecting to collect funds which otherwise would be used for that purpose but which will be invested pending the retirement of the bonds,

should be treated differently from a municipality which collects and invests the funds before issuing bonds. It seems unlikely that Congress would have given the broad discretion to the Secretary in section 103(c)(6) to issue regulations "to carry out the purposes" of the subsection had it intended the language to be taken as literally and narrowly as petitioner reads it; none of the legislative history suggests that the time sequence of events producing arbitrage was to be decisive.

Id. at 411-13.

How does a municipality avoid an arbitrage charge?

The practice of refunding bonds to take advantage of more favorable interest rates by issuing new bonds whose proceeds are used to retire outstanding issues can raise arbitrage issues. In *Washington v. Commissioner,* 692 F.2d 128 (D.C. Cir. 1982), the court was faced with the question whether expenses incurred (approximately $40,000) as well as the discount given (1½), for refunding bonds should be taken into consideration in determining the yield of those bonds. The question came up because the proceeds from the new bonds were going to be invested in direct obligations of the United States until the outstanding bonds could be retired.

Internal Revenue Service regulations excluded expenses and discounts from yield calculations. In the *Washington* case, the IRS ruled that yield should be based on the price paid by the public (par) upon resale by the original bond purchasers (underwriters) who had purchased at a discount and that issuance costs should not be included. The effect of this ruling was to decrease the effective yield on the bonds and increase the spread between the bond yield and the state's return on its investment of the bond proceeds to the point that the bonds would become taxable as arbitrage bonds.

In ruling for the state that the refunding bonds were not arbitrage bonds under I.R.C. § 103(c)(2), the court reasoned:

1. *Discount.*

The State and the Tax Court present the better construction of the statutory term. "Yield" has a common and accepted meaning: it is the economic return on a debt instrument.

The Treasury regulation that defines the term "yield" accepts this common meaning by defining it to be the rate "which, when used in computing the present worth of all payments of principal and interest to be paid on the obligation, produces an amount equal to the purchase price." Treas.Reg. § 1.103-13(c)(1) (1978). "Yield" therefore changes whenever a different purchase price is paid. But whenever a bond is sold—from state to underwriter or from underwriter to public—a different purchase price is paid, and a different yield must result. Yield can be consistently determined only by using the purchase prices in the transactions to which the State was a party—the purchase price paid to the State for its bonds and the purchase price paid by the State for the U.S. Treasury certificates. It is the State that borrows money, and it is the State that buys Treasury certificates; only the State can earn arbitrage profits, and only the State can eliminate those profits by restricting the yield of its investment. By interpreting the relevant purchase prices to be those in the transactions to which the State was a party, the Tax Court used the same parameter in calculating the permissible yield, and thus applied one (not two) interpretation(s) of the statutory term.

The Commissioner's argument—that the relevant purchase price of the State's issuance is the one paid by the public—makes sense only if the price at which an underwriter resells the bonds to the public can be attributed to the State. If attribution is possible, then the effective price would not be a discounted one and the effective yield to the State would be higher. But attribution is not possible in this case: The proposed bond sale is to be undertaken pursuant to sealed bids, the purchaser will be the one making the best offer, and the purchaser will have no continuing obligation to the State. The important incidents of ownership—especially the risk that the value of the bonds may rise or fall—shifts to the underwriter, and the discount on par is a genuine reduction in the purchase price. Thus, the discount should be taken into account in computing the rate that makes the present worth of the future principal and interest payments equal to that purchase price.

The most natural reading of the statute supports the Tax Court's and the State's interpretation. To begin with, the statute expressly contemplates that discounts should be taken into account in calculating "yield." Congress specifically provided that arbitrage bonds would exist only if the proceeds available from the sale of the bonds were invested in taxable obligations with a yield materially higher than the yield on the bonds themselves, "taking into account any discount" incurred. 26 U.S.C. § 103(c)(2)(A) (1976).

Second, the statute uses the term "yield" both for bonds issued by the State and for securities acquired by the State. The key denominators in the statute are the purchase prices in transactions to which the State was a party; the determination of whether the State will make arbitrage profits can be comfortably made only by using these purchase prices. The Commissioner encourages the awkward construction that would require the State to compute "yield" by reference to two transactions, one in which the State *is* a party, and one in which it *is not*.

2. Issuance expenses.

Deciding whether the Tax Court permissibly allowed the State to include issuance costs in the yield calculation is, however, a more difficult issue. While the term "discount" explicitly appears in Section 103(c), the term "issuance expenses" does not. Thus, Congress may intentionally have drawn a distinction between "discount" and "issuance expenses" in identifying precisely which costs the State could take into account in determining the permissible reinvestment yield. But such a congressional intent is unlikely. Issuance expenses—legal fees, printing costs, advertising expenses, and so on—are outlays made to procure money, are incurred directly in connection with the bond issuance, and effectively reduce the money available from the issuance. They thereby reduce the real economic value of the debt instrument to its issuer. When Congress required states and municipalities to restrict their reinvested proceeds to "yields" not materially higher than the "yields" on their Section 103 issuances, there had been a long and consistent practice of requiring issuance expenses to be treated the same as discounts.

Id. at 132-33.

2. DEBT LIMITATIONS

The financial emergency in New York sparked renewed interest in state supervision of municipal borrowing and finance. Excerpts from the following report provide a valuable perspective.

ADVISORY COMMISSION ON INTERGOVERNMENTAL RELATIONS, CITY FINANCIAL EMERGENCIES: THE INTERGOVERNMENTAL DIMENSION 63, 70-71 (1973)

[State supervision of municipal borrowing and finance is one possible method of avoiding municipal financial emergencies. The report notes that a few states exercise substantial control over municipal financial matters, some states exercise none at all, while the great majority exercise some controls that fall short of providing any method of reasonably complete state supervision. These alternative modes of state control are then discussed in turn.—Eds.]

No Substantive Administrative Control by States

One alternative is that substantive State involvement in local financial matters be kept to a minimum. Municipal taxing and borrowing would be governed by constitutional and statutory delegation of these powers to the municipalities, and by whatever statutory controls of a self-executing nature might be necessary. In addition, there would need to be provisions for State action by the attorney general or another appropriate State authority in the case of criminal acts by municipal officials. Although financial reports might be required, the action of the State would be limited to statistical compilation of the information submitted and examination of the reports for criminal violations. Underlying this approach is the assumption that in the event a municipality has a financial emergency that cannot be resolved without State involvement, the legislature, by special act will determine what role the State is to play.

Arguments for this alternative are primarily based on the home-rule concept. ... By giving cities protection from interference by State officials in day-to-day affairs, it is hoped that cities will arrive at innovative solutions to their financial problems.

Arguments against a policy of non-involvement by States center primarily on the need for States to guarantee that their subdivisions will handle their finances in a responsible fashion. Financial irresponsibility in municipalities may endanger the local economy and local citizens and threaten the credit rating and the reputation of other municipalities in the State and the State itself. ...

Limited State Administrative Controls

In contrast to a passive State role, a State agency may be charged with an active but limited responsibility to supervise and control municipal financial management. Under this alternative, uniform forms and procedures for accounting, budgeting, and financial reporting might be required of all municipalities, and the annual financial reports required by municipalities would be reviewed by a responsible State agency to determine the presence of any management deficiencies. Specifically, the State agency might be on the lookout for tell-tale signs like: expenditures that exceed revenues by more than 5 percent; expenditures that have exceeded revenues for two consecutive years with the second year deficiency being larger than the first year; short-term debt outstanding at the end of the fiscal year; interfund loans outstanding at the end of the fiscal year; a substantial increase in accounts payable or unpaid bills; an increase of 1 percent or more in the delinquency rate of current property tax collection; and failure to provide full funding for currently incurred pension liabilities—all factors indicative of potential financial emergency. ... In cases in which the review of financial reports reveals such deficiencies, the State agency would have the powers necessary to require correction in subsequent years.

An argument in favor of this alternative is that although it provides a basis for State supervision and control to insure good financial management in cities, the controls that are exercised are after the fact, and they become operative only when there is a problem at the local level, or when a municipality attempts to violate a State law or regulation. ...

Arguments against this alternative are based on the premise that the creation of a State agency with powers to require action by local officials to correct management deficiencies will lead to State involvement in substantive affairs at the local level and may also inject State political considerations into local affairs. ...

Complete State Control

The concept of complete control of all aspects of municipal financial management by a State agency developed first in the 1930's when a substantial number of local governments were forced by the Depression to default. Although a number of States instituted complete control as a last resort in cases in which specific cities were experiencing financial emergencies, some States such as New Jersey and West Virginia had such extensive municipal default problems that they instituted a State control system over all municipalities. In a complete control system, State officials begin their scrutiny of local financial affairs with a review of the proposed budgets prior to their adoptions; they have authority to require local officials to make substantive changes in such budgets to avoid a deficit or to improve fiscal management. State officials closely follow the course of local budgets during the year and give approval for any major modifications. At the conclusion of the fiscal year, the municipal finances are audited, and the audit reports are compared to originally adopted budgets. Short- and long-term debt can be incurred only after careful review and approval by a State agency. The review not only determines that the debt meets legal requirements but that it is prudent for the municipalities to undertake such an obligation in view of their present and prospective financial conditions.

The argument for such a control system is that it allows a State to keep municipalities out of trouble and provides ample opportunity for correction of any financial problems before they become serious or chronic. . . .

Although there is little quarrel with the need for such extensive control in cases of actual financial emergency, it can be contended that this type of State control makes effective local administration very difficult because most decisions involving financial matters must be approved at the State level before they can be initiated.

Comments: 1. *Nature and extent of debt limitation restrictions.* Statutory and constitutional limitations on municipal borrowing are widespread in the United States, dating largely from that period in the middle and late nineteenth century when restrictive constitutional limitations on local government powers were first adopted. All states have either constitutional or statutory limitations on municipal debt for either some or all of their local government units. Advisory Commission on Intergovernmental Relations, Federal-State-Local Finances: Significant Features of Fiscal Federalism 143-52 (1974). In addition, almost all states have constitutional or statutory provisions requiring referendum approval for general obligation long-term debt. *Id.* at 153-54. Practically all states also have constitutional or statutory restrictions on local taxes. Advisory Commission on Intergovernmental Relations, State Constitutional and Statutory Restrictions on Local Taxing Powers (1962).

We will concentrate here on the debt limitation provisions, although it is clear that it is these along with the referendum provisions that create problems of compliance for municipalities seeking to embark on local borrowing programs. Unless the debt obligation issued by the local government is found to fall outside the debt limitation or referendum requirement it will be found to violate the applicable constitutional or statutory restriction unless (a) the amount of that obligation together with all other outstanding obligations does not exceed the debt limit and (b) voter approval has been obtained. Both conditions may often be difficult to satisfy. Debt limitations are being pressured as municipal debt increases and voter approval for new obligations is increasingly harder to obtain.

The structure and character of debt limitations is explained in Bowmar, *The Anachronism Called Debt Limitation*, 52 Iowa L. Rev. 863, 865-67 (1967):

> Many state constitutions make no provision for political subdivision indebtedness; but at least some of these states have enacted statutes which limit municipal indebtedness by various formulae. Many, by the terms of their constitutions, leave such limitations to the legislature, while others allow a unit to incur unlimited indebtedness with voter approval. By far the most common constitutional standard for debt restriction is the debt-to-property ratio, usually articulated in terms of indebtedness as a fixed percentage of assessed valuation of the subdivision's taxable property. There also are variations on this general theme. One variation provides a limitation based on the usual standard of debt-to-property ratio, but with a higher percentage limitation where there is qualified voter approval. Another coordinates the current revenue and percentage

of assessed property limits: the unit is limited to an indebtedness not in excess of current annual revenue, but, upon approval of the qualified voters, it is permitted additional indebtedness up to a fixed percentage of assessed valuation.

2. *The impact of financial restrictions.* General obligation bonds are traditionally funded by the general ad valorem real property tax, i.e., a tax collected on the value of real property within the limits of the municipality. This is the tax which is meant when reference is made to the "real property tax." How much general obligation debt can be issued depends upon the real property tax base. The debt limitation is computed on the assessed property valuation, and the municipality may borrow up to that limit. Thus, if the assessed value of real property within Metro City is—

$10,000,000,
and the applicable debt limitation is—
five percent
then the borrowing capacity of Metro City is—
$500,000.

How restrictive the debt limitation is depends on the borrowing capacity of the community, which is a function of its assessed valuation for taxation purposes and the applicable debt limitation. The assessment ratio is another important factor. No problems are presented if the borrowing capacity is ample, but with the pressures for public improvements that have been characteristic of the postwar years many municipalities have reached or exceeded their debt limits and have had to look to other methods of borrowing long-term funds. One recent effort is to pass statutory enactments which permit the debt limitation to be calculated on market value rather than on assessed value as reported for taxation purposes. In one state, such a statute was struck down as an evasion of the constitutional limitation. *Breslow v. School District, 182 A.2d 501 (Pa. 1962).*

3. *Debt avoidance techniques.* A series of debt avoidance techniques have been adopted for local government financing and have been accepted by some courts as not creating debt that comes within the debt limitation. One such technique has been used in school financing. Under this method, a state statute is passed authorizing the creation of a special agency to build and hold title to a school building. The agency may be organized as a nonprofit corporation or simply as a separate state agency. Bonds for construction are issued by the agency, which is empowered by the statute to lease the school building back to the school district for an annual rent. At the end of the lease term, the title to the school building passes to the school district.

Obviously, this arrangement can be challenged as a subterfuge. If the cumulative rentals are equivalent to the initial cost of the building, and if the school district is obligated to take the building at the end of the lease term, it is difficult to argue that the school district has not been obligated from the very beginning of the lease. Nevertheless, many courts have been willing to ignore all of these objections and to hold that the school district has merely leased the building. *See Protsman v. Jefferson-Craig Consolidated School Corp.,* 109 N.E.2d 889 (Ind. 1953). *Contra, City of Phoenix v. Phoenix Civic Auditorium & Convention Center Ass'n,* 408 P.2d 818 (Ariz. 1965) (excellent review of the cases). The result is that the only debt incurred by the school district is the annual rental, which becomes a successive annual obligation in each year of the lease. If the municipality has funds sufficient to meet each rental payment as it falls due and without having to borrow, no problems are raised under the constitutional debt limitation. This technique has also been used extensively to build state office buildings and other state facilities. *See* Morris, *Evading Debt Limitations with Public Building Authorities: The Costly Subversion of State Constitutions,* 68 YALE L.J. 234 (1958).

The debt limitation problem also arises at the state level because many states also have debt limitation requirements, although these are often expressed as monetary ceilings rather than related to the property tax base.

The following case dealing with the leasing technique must thus be read in the context of the state debt limitation, although its reasoning is also persuasive at the local level.

BULMAN v. McCRANE

Supreme Court of New Jersey
64 N.J. 105, 312 A.2d 857 (1973)

CONFORD, P. J. A. D., Temporarily Assigned.

The Chancery Division struck down as offensive to our constitutional debt limitation provision, Const. of 1947, Art. VIII, Sec. II, Par. 3, a proposed arrangement by the State to take a 25 year lease on a building to be erected by a developer on state-owned land and to be used by the State as a records storage center and printing facility. 123 N.J.Super. 213, 302 A.2d 163 (1973). We certified the case prior to its consideration by the Appellate Division. 63 N.J. 505, 308 A.2d 669 (1973).

The State was to have the option to purchase at fixed, progressively declining figures during the 10th, 15th and 20th years of the lease, failing which, title to the building would revert to the State at the end of the term. The terms and conditions of the integrated transaction for construction of the building and lease thereof to the State, to be effected on behalf of the State by the Division of Building and Construction and the Division of Purchase and Property, both in the Department of the Treasury, are accurately summarized in the reported Chancery Division opinion and need not be repeated here. . . .

We thus turn to the primary subject of the appeal—the holding of the Chancery Division that the transaction in substance creates a debt of the State and not a lease, the court having correctly conceded . . . that a true lease would not offend the prohibition of "debts" or "liabilities" not qualifying under the constitutional requirements for the enabling statute and for approval of the people by referendum (the text of the constitutional section is found in 123 N.J. Super. at 217-218, 302 A.2d 163). After an extensive examination of cases in other jurisdictions, some involving leases for public uses by independent public authorities and others by private lessors, as here, the court concluded "that the arrangement in this case is an installment contract of purchase and not a lease" and therefore violates the debt clause . . . . Found influential were the circumstances (a) that the State retained ownership of the land, with the "incongruous result if, at the expiration or earlier termination of the lease, the builder-developer should own a building on land title to which was in the State"; . . . (b) the fact that the proposed building would have value at the end of the term, of which the State would get the benefit without further cost . . . ; (c) the builder-developer would be recapturing during the period of the lease his total cost of construction, profit and financing expense . . . ; and (d) formal opinions by the Attorney General in the past that transactions like this constituted a debt subject to the debt limitation clause . . . .

A reading of the trial court's opinion in this matter and the cases from other jurisdictions cited therein, as well as of the opinions of this court in such cases as *McCutcheon v. State Building Authority,* 13 N.J. 46, 97 A.2d 663 (1953); *Clayton, et al. v. Kervick, et al.,* 52 N.J. 138, 244 A.2d 281 (1968); *Holster v. Bd. of Trustees of Passaic County College,* 59 N.J. 60, 279 A.2d 798 (1971); and *N.J. Sports & Exposition Authority v. McCrane,* 61 N.J. 1, 292 A.2d 545 (1972), reveals that the varying approaches by courts to assertions of violation of debt limitation clauses have been largely dependent upon the differing views of judges as to the scope of the evils sought to be abated by such clauses and as to the degree of flexibility in methods of financing publicly needed facilities which should be accorded modern legislatures and public officials where such methods do not seem to entail the conditions which begot the debt limitation provisions but may yet, on analytical scrutiny, be strongly argued in substance to offend the letter thereof. The *McCutcheon* and *Clayton* cases, both *supra,* although partly distinguishable from the instant situation in that independent authorities were implicated in the financing plans in those cases, are pertinent in respect of the contrasting treatment in the respective prevailing opinions of the question whether leases by such agencies to state operating departments were truly leases, or rather, to the contrary, installment contracts to purchase, creating present debts within the constitutional provisos. The decisions are also demonstrative of the evolution of the current attitude of this court in the general area.

In *McCutcheon* the Legislature had created a State Building Authority and empowered it to issue bonds to acquire, construct and operate building facilities, and to lease them only to the State or any of its agencies and departments. The bonds expressly stated that they were not to "be deemed to constitute a debt or liability of the State or of any political subdivision thereof or a pledge of the faith and credit of the State or of any such political subdivision." Since the income of the Authority was solely from rentals and the Authority could rent only to a governmental division, payments for the bonds would be indirectly made out of the State Treasury. The majority of the Court felt that the statute impermissibly evaded the debt limitation because upon the payment of the bonds the Authority could be dissolved and the State acquire the building. Justice Jacobs, joined by Justice (now Mr. Justice) Brennan, dissented. . . . He was of the view that the bonds were not obligations of the State but only of the Authority. The State's only obligation was to pay the annual rental. It was pointed out that the great weight of authority indicated that future rents were not debts in violation of such a constitutional debt limitation. . . .

As significant as the differing conclusions of the majority and the dissenters in *McCutcheon* as to the specific holding involved was the broadly sympathetic approach to flexibility in public financing manifested by the dissenting opinion of Justice Jacobs, which in essence was repeated by him, this time for the court majority, in the later case of *Clayton, et al. v. Kervick, et al., supra.* . . .

In *Clayton, et al. v. Kervick, et al., supra* . . ., the Legislature had enacted a statute creating an Educational Facilities Authority for the purpose of constructing projects and leasing them to participating educational institutions. The financing of the operation was accomplished by a bond issue of the Authority. But unlike *McCutcheon,* where the State would eventually pay for all the rentals, here the rentals would come substantially from sources other than legislative appropriations. While, therefore, in approving the arrangement, *Clayton* did not expressly overrule *McCutcheon,* it was obviously the purpose of the court in *Clayton* radically to revise the *McCutcheon* approach of readiness to find constitutional evasion to one of broad tolerance to permit public financing devices of needed facilities not constituting on their face present, interest-bearing obligations of the State itself or involving the danger of public reproach consequent upon widespread default of formal state-funded indebtedness such as motivated adoption of the original constitutional provision in 1844. . . .

With the foregoing guidelines as to the general approach which should govern us, we proceed to direct examination of the controversy before us and the *ratio decidendi* of the trial judge in invalidating the instant transaction. Concededly, there is no prior New Jersey case directly in point on the facts. We begin with the fact that the agreement here is in form a lease and with the normal assumption that those who challenge the validity of actions of public officials apparently within their statutory powers must carry the burden of demonstrating such invalidity. If the concept of a lease here is defensible theoretically, then, under *Clayton,* there is no present debt, and no constitutional violation. In such event, it should surely make no difference, under the approach of the recent line of decisions of this court cited above, that the parties could have formulated this transaction as an installment purchase had they wished to do so.

Putting to one side, for the moment, the terminal reversion of title to the lessee, the lease terms generally are harmonious with the theory of a lease as opposed to a sale. The lessor pays the taxes (not exceeding those levied in the third lease year). See *West Jersey Grove Camp Ass'n v. Vineland,* 80 N.J.Super. 361, 365, 193 A.2d 785 (App. Div. 1963). As customary, the lessor repairs and maintains the exterior, the lessee the interior. And most significantly, damage to the building impairing useability for the lessee's purposes suspends the rent, and if repairs are not completed within six months the lessee has the option to terminate the lease. *Cf.* N.J.S.A. 46:8-6, 7. While the trial judge adverted to the fact that there is no reserved right of termination and entry by the lessor in event of a default by lessee, this is at best a neutral factor, since, contemplating the alternative position that the transaction is an installment sale, there would ordinarily be a provision for acceleration and forfeiture for nonpayment of installments—a stipulation absent here. See *Dorman v. Fisher,* 31 N.J. 13, 155 A.2d 11 (1959). Realism suggests that the lessor's failure to demand a reentry clause is attributable to total confidence that the State will pay the rents as due.

The heart of the Chancery Division decision lies in the circumstances that the developer-builder recaptures his whole investment, costs and profit during the term of the lease, and, inferentially, at any option stage, and that a building inferably still usable at the end of the term goes to the State at that time without additional consideration if a purchase option is not exercised earlier by the State as lessee. . . .

. . . [H]ere . . . the State owns the land. At the end of the 25 year term, absent a clause for reversion of the structure to the lessee, the lessor would own a building of no value to him without title to the land. He would be economically compelled to leave the building on site since the cost of removal and relocation would be prohibitive even if otherwise economically practicable. His situation in that regard is comparable to that of the lessor . . . who would have been left with a special purpose building at the end of the term with no value to anyone but the city. . . .

Thus, entirely consistently with the lease theory . . . there is nothing anomalous in the present builder-developer being permitted to collect as rental sufficient to recover his total investment including the depreciation inherent in his reversion as a wasting asset destined to become devoid of economic value at the end of the term. The fact that the State may be advantaged by ultimately acquiring title to a potentially useful building as the residue of a transaction otherwise faithful to the theory of a lease (certainly so from the viewpoint of the lessor) represents no good reason for judicial assiduity in laying hold of that circumstance to destroy the transaction as an unconstitutional debt. The sole obligation of the State here is for future installments of rent. They will presumably be paid out of current revenues as annually appropriated for the purpose. Under settled principles, there is no present debt in the constitutional sense. . . .

Comments: 1. An alternative procedure is for the state to establish a public agency which issues bonds to construct buildings and then leases those buildings to state agencies. Does the fact that the bonds are payable from rents which in turn are paid by state-appropriated funds make the bonds debts of the state? In *Enourato v. New Jersey Building Authority,* 440 A.2d 42 (N.J. App. Div. 1981), the court held that the statute establishing the New Jersey Building Authority did not violate the debt limitation provision because of the leasing arrangement. Citing *Bulman,* the court held that the only appropriations contemplated were for the rent payments (not bond payments) and even those future appropriations were subject to the express reservation that they might not be made. *See also St. Charles City-County Library District v. St. Charles Library Corp.,* 627 S.W.2d 64 (Mo. App. 1981) (upholding one-year lease-purchase agreement with twenty-four successive options to renew between library district and not-for-profit corporation to finance new library building, after voters defeated two separate proposals to finance the building through general obligation bond and tax increases).

2. Why aren't future rent installments debt under a long-term lease? What happens if the state fails to pay rent? For discussion of the effect of a failure by the legislature to appropriate funds, see *City of Camden v. Byrne,* 411 A.2d 462 (N.J. 1980), discussed *infra.*

The cases on lease financing are divided, and seemingly contradictory opinions may be handed down in the same state, as the principal case indicates. Note that the building financed in the principal case was a comparatively modest building to be used for ordinary governmental purposes. In some of the recent leasing cases the technique has been used to finance the convention centers that many municipalities are now rushing to build. Consistent with outstanding authority, the cases on the use of the leasing technique in this context are also divided. For recent cases invalidating this technique in this situation see *Bachtell v. City of Waterloo,* 200 N.W.2d 548 (Iowa 1972); *Scroggs v. Kansas City,* 499 S.W.2d 500 (Mo. 1973). In both cases the courts cut through the formalities of the transaction and found the lease to constitute installment debt. *Contra, Millar v. Barnett,* 221 N.W.2d 8 (S.D. 1974).

Similar issues arise when a state or local government acquires equipment to be used and paid for over an extended period. In *Allstate Leasing Corp. v. Board of County Commissioners,* 450 F.2d 26 (10th Cir. 1971), the court upheld county leases of heavy road equipment for periods of thirty-four and sixty months; the lease contract did not constitute a debt. The court, however, distinguished an earlier New Mexico case, *Shoup Voting Machine Corp. v. Board of County Commissioners,* 256 P.2d 1068 (N.M. 1953), in which the county had contracted to purchase voting machines and to pay for them over a ten-year period. Because the purchase contract constituted an unconditional obligation to pay, it was held to constitute a debt.

With the analysis of the leasing transaction in the principal case contrast the following:

Magnusson, *Lease-Financing by Municipal Corporations as a Way Around Debt Limitations,* 25 Geo. Wash. L. Rev. 377, 392 (1957):

> Annual rent payments are indistinguishable in fact from annual debt service on bonds. Under lease-financing legislation, rent is never related to any market value for the property (in most cases there is no such value because of the unique purpose for it) but is always the exact amount needed to pay for debt service (annual principal and interest) on long-term bonds or notes of the lessor to finance the improvement, plus a proportionate share of the lessor's administrative overhead, plus an amount sufficient to build up a reserve of, usually, one year of debt service on the lessor's bonds, plus the

cost of any maintenance, repair, replacement and insurance borne by the lessor and plus an amount for "the fulfillment of the terms and provisions of any agreements made with the purchasers or holders of any such bonds." The latter might include attorneys' fees and an annual fee of a trustee to supervise the relation between lessor and the lessee. The rent is the amount that would be paid as debt service on the lessee's own bonds (if any could be issued) plus the additional expense of a one-year reserve, a trustee's fee, and insurance.

If the leasing arrangement is upheld as not in violation of the debt limitation no difficulties are created so long as the annual lease payments can be met out of current revenues. This analysis provides the basis for another debt avoidance technique known as contingent financing. Many municipal obligations are contingent in the sense that they are met annually, out of annual appropriations, even though the obligation may extend over several years. An example would be a long-term contract for services or supplies. This concept has been used in some cases to guarantee the financing of capital improvements through contingent pledges of municipal support in guarantee of possible default. Again, this technique has met a varied response from the courts.

BOARD OF SUPERVISORS v. MASSEY

Supreme Court of Appeals of Virginia
210 Va. 253, 169 S.E.2d 556 (1969)

Before EGGLESTON, C.J., and BUCHANAN, SNEAD, I'ANSON, CARRICO, GORDON, and HARRISON, JJ.

I'ANSON, JUSTICE.

These cases are before us under the original jurisdiction of the court upon separate petitions for writs of mandamus filed by the Board of Supervisors of Fairfax County (County) and the City of Falls Church (City), petitioners, pursuant to § 17-96, Code of 1950, 1960 Repl. Vol., to compel Carlton C. Massey, County Executive, and Harry E. Wells, City Manager, respondents, to execute on behalf of their respective County and City a contract designated "Transit Service Agreement" (Agreement), to which Washington Metropolitan Area Transit Authority (Authority) and other public bodies of Virginia, Maryland, and the District of Columbia are also parties.

The Authority was created as a body corporate and politic by the Washington Metropolitan Area Transit Authority Compact (Compact), an interstate agreement between Virginia, Maryland, and the District of Columbia, as an agency and instrumentality of each of the signatory parties thereto, to plan, develop, finance, and provide improved transit facilities and service for the Washington Metropolitan Area Transit Zone (Zone). The Zone encompasses the District of Columbia; the counties of Arlington and Fairfax, and the cities of Alexandria, Falls Church and Fairfax in Virginia and Montgomery and Prince George's counties in Maryland.

In contemplation of the Compact the General Assembly of Virginia adopted the Transportation District Act of 1964 (ch. 631, Acts of 1964, p. 935, codified as §§ 15.1-1342 through 15.1-1372, Code of 1950, 1964 Repl. Vol.). It authorizes the creation of transportation districts to cooperate and participate with an agency such as the Authority in planning and financing an interstate regional transit system. In order to take advantage of this Act, the Northern Virginia

Transportation District, consisting of the counties of Arlington and Fairfax and the cities of Alexandria, Fairfax and Falls Church, was created by Chapter 630, Acts of 1964, p. 933.

The Authority has adopted a mass transit plan for the Zone. It proposes to construct a combination subway and surface rapid rail system, 97.7 miles in length, with stations to serve the most densely populated areas of the Zone.

The estimated cost of constructing the transit system is $2,494,600,000. Funds are to be obtained from the following sources: The Authority will issue tax-exempt gross revenue bonds in the amount of $835,000,000; the federal government will contribute $1,147,044,000; and political subdivisions in the Zone will contribute the sum of $573,522,000. Of this amount, $149,900,000 will come from political subdivisions in Virginia. The shares of the County and City are $61,900,000 and $800,000, respectively. The County and City have authorized the issuance of general obligation bonds in these amounts, and have entered into a capital contributions agreement with the Authority for the payment of these sums during the estimated ten-year construction period.

Article VII, § 16, of the Compact declares as a policy that, "as far as possible, the payment of all costs shall be borne by the persons using or benefiting from the Authority's facilities and services, and any remaining costs shall be equitably shared among the federal government, the District of Columbia, and the participating local governments in the Zone."

Article VII, § 18(a), of the Compact, and Code § 15.1-1357(b)(3) of the Transportation Act authorize the County and City to enter into contracts with the Authority to contribute to the capital for construction and/or acquisition of facilities, and for meeting expenses and obligations *in the operation of such facilities.* See also, Code § 15.1-1359, as amended, 1968 Cum. Supp.

The Transit Service Agreement states in its preamble, *inter alia,* that the Authority's engineering studies estimate that fare box receipts and other transit system revenues will be more than sufficient to pay debt service and reserves on the Authority's transit revenue bonds as well as to meet operating and maintenance expenses, but it is nevertheless considered that the financing of the transit system on favorable terms requires each of the political subdivisions to agree to make payments for services to be provided by such transit systems.

Under the Agreement, the County and City will underwrite their proportionate shares of any deficits incurred in the operating expenses of the transit system by making monthly service payments in advance to the Authority, beginning with the first day of the fiscal year next succeeding the initial operation date and ending June 30, 2040. The Agreement defines "operating deficiency requirement" and "operating expenses" as follows:

> Operating Deficiency Requirement shall mean, for any Fiscal Year, the amount, if any, by which Operating Expenses for such Year exceed the Revenues for such Year remaining after provision is made for the debt service and reserve requirements for such year with respect to Transit Bonds.
>
> Operating Expenses shall mean all the expenses of operating and maintenance of the Transit System, including but not limited to, renewals and replacement of the facilities of the Transit System and interest on temporary borrowings to meet expenses of operation and maintenance of the Transit System, and payments to reserves for such expenses as may be required by the terms of any contract of the Authority with or for the benefit of the holders of Transit Bonds.

Each year the Authority is required to make a complete review of its financial condition, rate and fare structure, and the procedures, schedules and standards of transit service. On the basis of such data the Authority shall determine the transit service to be provided and the rate and fare structure for the ensuing year. The Authority is also required to determine whether the estimated revenues of the transit system, after making provision for debt service and reserve requirements for that year on the Authority's transit revenue bonds, will be sufficient to cover the cost of operation and maintenance incurred. The extent to which the revenues are insufficient for this purpose is the "operating deficiency requirement" for the ensuing year. There is then added to or subtracted from the estimated "operating deficiency requirement" such amounts as are required to adjust for the difference between results of operations for the preceding year. The "operating deficiency requirement" as thus adjusted constitutes the aggregate service payment.

The aggregate service payment is allocated among the political subdivisions in the Zone in accordance with a prescribed formula. The amounts thus allocated constitute the service payment to be made by each political subdivision. The Authority is required to advise each political subdivision of its monthly service payment at least nine months before the beginning of the Authority's fiscal year. After the end of each year an adjustment is made to reflect the obligation of each political subdivision on the basis of the actual operating deficiency. If there is no operating deficiency for a particular year, the service payments are returned.

The obligation of each political subdivision to make its service payment is conditioned upon transit service being rendered to it. If no transit service is rendered in any particular year, no service payment is required for that year. And if the Authority furnishes any political subdivision less than 85 percent of the service, measured in train miles or number of trains, previously determined by the Authority for a particular year, the amount of the service payment is reduced in accordance with the service actually furnished for that year. Service payments shall be applied by the Authority only to the payment of its operating expenses and temporary borrowings to meet operating expenses, and shall not be applied to any other purposes.

Under the financial plan of the Authority, gross revenue derived from the operation of the transit system will be pledged to secure the payment of the principal and interest to the holders of transit bonds in accordance with the terms of the bond indenture. See also § 44 of the Compact.

The questions presented are:

(1) Will the obligations of the County and City under the Agreement constitute debt or indebtedness within the meaning of §§ 115a or 127 of the Constitution of Virginia, or §§ 7.03 or 7.06 of the charter of the City of Falls Church? . . .

I

Sections 115a and 127 of the Constitution of Virginia are designed to control indebtedness of localities, but each approaches the problem in a different way. Section 115a limits county debt by requiring a referendum approved by the qualified voters. Its pertinent language follow:

> No debt shall be contracted by any county . . . except in pursuance of authority conferred by the General Assembly by general law; and the General Assembly shall not authorize any county . . . to contract any debt except to meet casual deficits in the revenue, a debt created in anticipation of the collection of the revenue of the said county . . . for the then current year, or to redeem a previous liability, unless in the general law authorizing the same provision be

made for the submission to the qualified voters of the proper county ... for approval or rejection by a majority vote of the qualified voters voting in an election ... and such approval shall be a prerequisite to contracting such debt.

Section 127 limits the indebtedness of cities and towns to eighteen percent of local taxable real estate values. Its pertinent provisions follows:

No city or town shall issue any bonds or other interest-bearing obligations for any purpose, or in any manner, to an amount which, including existing indebtedness, shall, at any time, exceed eighteen per centum of the assessed valuation of the real estate in the city or town subject to taxation, as shown by the last preceding assessment for taxes ... and provided further, that in determining the limitation of the power of a city or town to incur indebtedness there shall not be included the following classes of indebtedness:

(a) Certificates of indebtedness, revenue bonds or other obligations issued in anticipation of the collection of the revenues of such city or town for the then current year; provided that such certificates, bonds or other obligations mature within one year from the date of their issue, and be not past due, and do not exceed the revenue for such year;

(b) Bonds authorized by an ordinance enacted in accordance with section one hundred and twenty-three, and approved by the affirmative vote of the majority of the qualified voters of the city or town voting upon the question of their issuance, at the general election next succeeding the enactment of the ordinance, or at a special election held for that purpose for a supply of water or other specific undertaking from which the city or town may derive a revenue. ...

Section 7.03 of the Falls Church charter applies the limitation of § 127 of the Constitution to the issuance of "bonds and notes." Section 7.06 of the charter prescribes the procedure for the issuance of bonds and requires that bond ordinances be approved by a referendum.

Petitioners recognize that while § 127 refers to "bonds or other interest-bearing obligations," the language includes any unconditional obligation requiring the payment of money and has the same meaning as "debt" as used in § 115a, and that the Falls Church charter provisions rest upon the same determination. See, *Button v. Day,* 205 Va. 629, 642, 139 S.E.2d 91, 100 (1964).

Hence the paramount inquiry here is whether by executing the contract designated "Transit Service Agreement" the County and City will incur debts in violation of the constitutional limitations.

Petitioners say that to constitute a debt within the meaning of constitutional limitations, there must be a present obligation; and that since the Agreement requires the County and City to make the service payments when, as, and if transit service is rendered, and then only if available revenues of the transit system are inadequate, this creates nothing more than a contingent liability and not a present indebtedness.

Petitioners rely on the principle that a local government may lawfully contract for necessary services such as water, electricity, or sewerage, over a period of years and agree to pay therefor in periodic installments as the services are furnished. In such cases the amounts to be paid as the services are rendered under such contracts do not give rise to a present indebtedness of such local governments, and such contracts are not rendered invalid by the fact that the aggregate of the installments exceeds the debt limitation. ...

We do not think, however, that the principle relied on is applicable in the present cases. Our examination of the authorities cited by the petitioners did not reveal a single case in which the local governments underwrote or guaranteed the deficit incurred in the operation of the facilities furnishing the services under their contracts.

Petitioners give much weight to the dictum in *Button, supra* ... supporting their contention that where the obligations of the County and City are contingent upon the furnishing of essential services they would not constitute a present debt. There a tripartite agreement between the City of Newport News, the Peninsula Ports Authority of Virginia and the Cheaspeake & Ohio Railway Company, which was to lease and operate the port facilities, provided that the authority would "urgently request" the General Assembly to appropriate an amount equal to fifty percent of the annual amortization of the authority's bonds; but, in the absence of such appropriations, the city would pay such amount. We held that by the tripartite agreement the city became primarily obligated for payments on the authority's bonds and a present debt was created, though it was payable in future installments; and that this debt, not authorized by a referendum, would exceed the debt limitation of § 127, thereby making the agreement invalid.

It is true that in *Button* we said: "It is not a contract to furnish water, electricity or other public service utilities to the City, the furnishing of which is a condition of the obligation." This dictum was a mere recognition of the general rule that a continuing service contract, for which the municipality agrees to pay in installments as the service is furnished, does not create a present debt for the aggregate amount of all the installments throughout the term of the contract within the meaning of constitutional limitations of municipal indebtedness. However, it cannot be concluded from the dictum in *Button* that all contracts which are called service agreements are in fact such, irrespective of the provisions contained therein.

Although the County's and City's contract is designated a "Transit Service Agreement," the label placed upon it does not necessarily make it such. The obligations of the County and City under the Agreement are for more than just payments for transit service. They agree to pay that amount by which the "operating expenses" exceed the revenues from the transit system after provision is first made for debt service and reserve requirements for the revenue bonds issued by the Authority. The "operating expenses" include all the expenses of operation, maintenance, renewals and replacement of the facilities of the system, interest on temporary borrowings to meet expenses of operation, and payments to reserves for such expenses as may be required by the terms of any contract of the Authority with or for the benefit of the transit bond holders. The payments to be made by the County and City guarantee the continued operation of the transit system during the life of the contract, which expires June 30, 2040, since the operating revenues are pledged to the payment of the transit bonds. While it is true that the payments required of the County and City do not go directly to the payment of debt service, their obligations to pay the "operating expense" deficit in effect amount to making payments on the Authority's bonds. The obligations of the County and City to underwrite and guarantee an unknown "operating expense" deficit of the transit system are fixed and absolute and constitute a present debt within the meaning of the constitutional limitations on County and City debt or indebtedness.

There are no facts in the record, by stipulation or evidence, to show that the County's obligation under the Agreement can be paid out of current revenues or that there has been an election by the people of the County authorizing the obligation to be incurred. In the case of the City, there is nothing showing the value of its taxable property, or what is the aggregate amount of its indebtedness, or the amount of its constitutional debt limit.

Thus we hold that the obligations of the County and City under the Agreement constitute debt or indebtedness within the meaning of the constitutional prohibitions of §§ 115a and 127 and under the charter provisions of the City of Falls Church.

Comments: 1. Was it the uncertainty of the "deficit" that was fatal in this case, or was it the "certainty" of having to make up a deficit? How does this arrangement differ from a long-term contract to purchase coal or oil with an annual consumer price index adjustment in price?

2. How could the agreement in the principal case have been drafted to avoid the adverse holding?

Following the *Massey* decision, new agreements were entered into providing for Fairfax County and the City of Falls Church to make payments to the Transit Authority for transit services based on the number of train miles operated within the county and the city and the number of their residents using the system. In *Board of Supervisors v. Massey,* 173 S.E.2d 869 (Va. 1970), the court approved the arrangement as a valid service contract. Did the change in the method of calculating the charge really justify the reversal in the court's opinion?

Compare Conrad v. City of Pittsburgh, 218 A.2d 906 (Pa. 1966), which considered a contract between the city and its stadium authority which was entered into in connection with the construction of a major league baseball stadium. A provision of the enabling legislation under which the stadium was built authorized the city "to make annual grants from current revenues ... to assist in defraying the costs of operation, maintenance and debt service of the project and enter into long term agreements providing for the payment of the same." This authority to make contingent payments was held not to be debt under the applicable debt limitations because the statute provided that the payments were to be made from current revenues.

See also Rochlin v. State, 540 P.2d 643 (Ariz. 1975). Here the argument was made that the obligation of political subdivisions in the state to meet unfunded liabilities under a state pension system constituted debt. The argument was rejected on the ground that the liability was mandated by the state and not voluntarily incurred. Is this holding consistent with the purposes of debt limitation provisions?

3. A third debt avoidance technique involves the so-called special fund doctrine. Numerous bonds, as noted earlier, are retired from project revenues or other funds instead of general tax revenues. Under the special fund doctrine, these bonds are not considered debt under debt limitation provisions, on the ground that they do not commit the full faith and credit of the municipality. The classic instance is the municipal obligation that is funded by a special assessment on real property. Street paving has traditionally been financed by special assessments levied against abutting property owners, a technique which is the ancestor of the special district financing methods which we have already discussed. The assessment is not considered a tax as it is based on the benefit which has been received by the adjoining landowner. Since assessments are ordinarily collected over a period of time, funds for paving have to be obtained by issuing municipal bonds. These bonds in turn are funded by the special assessment levy. Often the bonds will be "bought" by the contractor on the project, who thus provides its financing as well. See *Wagner v. Salt Lake City,* 504 P.2d 1007 (Utah 1972), upholding the use of the special assessment to finance bonds used to bury overhead utility lines. *See also Tribe v. Salt Lake City Corp.,* 540 P.2d 499 (Utah 1975). The court held that the bonds issued to finance an urban renewal project did not fall under the debt limitation because they were payable only from revenues from the project and from the specially allocated tax increment revenues. *Contra, Richards v. City of Muscatine,* 237 N.W.2d 48 (Iowa 1975). The court noted:

> Clearly the urban renewal bonds would constitute a constitutional debt if they were payable from the general revenues of the city without limitation. We think the result is not different because [the statute] carves out a certain portion of a city's general revenues and limits the liability of the city to those revenues. If the result were otherwise, a city could divide its general revenues into several special funds, each with a bond issue restricted to recourse against its own fund—and thus commit large por-

tions of the city's revenues without regard to [the constitutional debt limitation which] could thus be virtually nullified.

Id. at 64. See also *Wunderlich v. City of St. Louis,* 511 S.W.2d 753 (Mo. 1974), in which bonds issued to finance a convention center were found not to be revenue bonds because they were to be paid off in part with proceeds from city taxes.

Does the special fund doctrine require the creation of a separate corporate entity to operate the project and issue the bonds? In *American National Bank & Trust Co. v. Indiana Department of Highways,* 439 N.E.2d 1129 (Ind. 1982), the court, in a 3-2 decision, ruled that a governmental reorganization that consolidated the Indiana Toll Road Commission, the State Highway Commission and several other independent agencies into the newly created Department of Highways constituted an assumption by the state of the debt obligations of the consolidated agencies, even though the bonds were being retired by project revenues. The court reasoned:

> Although the special fund is present in the case before us, the separate entity that was originally the Toll Road Commission is not. The state of Indiana, through its Highway Department, is responsible for the maintenance and operation of the Toll Road and it is the one obligated on and issuing the bonds of indebtedness as to the $259,500,000 now extant and the completion bonds needed for further work. For this Court to provide that the legislation involved here is constitutional merely upon the existence of a special fund doctrine, would be to provide that any and every agency of the state could issue bonds of indebtedness so long as that authorization provided for special funds from which to pay that indebtedness. This would be nothing short of once again opening the floodgates of authorizing unlimited state indebtedness.

Id. at 1135.

The dissenting judges emphasized that most courts that have considered the question have concluded that a separate entity is not necessary so long as the statutes authorizing the bonds and the bond covenants themselves specifically provide that the bonds are not obligations of the state (or municipality) and do not constitute a debt or pledge of faith and credit of the state (or municipality). In their opinion, the separate entity is an artificial device without significance to the determination of debt.

> The question of constitutionality must be answered not by a determination of the funds from which they are payable but by a determination of the funds from which they are *not* payable. Whether or not they are ever paid is of no moment, under the constitution, so long as payment cannot be compelled from the general revenues.

Id. at 1136.

4. As state constitutional limitations on local government debt are expressed in terms of a proportion of assessed property valuation for general ad valorem tax purposes, the assumption usually is that the debt limitation is tied to the tax rate, and in particular to the general ad valorem property tax rate. The question then arises whether an obligation funded by a tax other than the general property tax would come under the debt limitation. See *Switzer v. City of Phoenix,* 341 P.2d 427 (Ariz. 1959), holding that the city's share of motor vehicle fuel and gasoline taxes remitted to it by the state could be pledged to the payment of street improvement bonds without creating debt under the constitutional limitation. California is one state that has now held to the contrary. Compare *City of Palm Springs v. Ringwald,* 342 P.2d 898 (Cal. 1959), with *City of Walnut Creek v. Silveira,* 306 P.2d 453 (Cal. 1957). Cf. *State v. Orange County,* 281 So. 2d 310 (Fla. 1973). A non-charter county issued capital improvement bonds to be paid from the proceeds of race track and jai alai funds allocated to the county by the state. The majority (4-3) held that the state constitution and statutes did not preclude the county from issuing bonds without the required referendum so long as ad valorem taxes were not pledged.

5. *Special districts and fiscal limitations.* For a variety of reasons, the special district is a favored device for escaping fiscal limitations. It may be useful to review the ways in which debt limitations make the use of the special district advantageous.

(a) If the special district is independently organized, it may escape the constitutional debt limitation altogether if it is found not to be among the governmental units to which the constitutional provision applies. *Albuquerque Metropolitan Arroyo Flood Control*

Authority v. Swinburne, 394 P.2d 998 (N.M. 1964). Even if the constitutional debt limitation applies, the special district will be entitled to its own debt limit. That is, the district will be able to issue its own obligations independently of any debt restrictions that may be placed on other governmental units with which it overlaps territorially. The creation of overlapping special districts may be challenged in court, however. For a case taking the position that the creation of additional special districts overlaying existing units of government is not reviewable see *Carlisle v. Bangor Recreation Center,* 103 A.2d 339 (Me. 1954). In other cases the issue turns on whether there has been an "evasion" of the debt limitation. *Fort Howard Paper Co. v. Town Board,* 63 N.W.2d 122 (1954). *See also Dwyer v. Omaha-Douglas Public Building Commission,* 195 N.W.2d 236 (Neb. 1972). The court held that an act creating a joint city-county building commission did not violate a constitutional provision limiting county tax levies; the commission was authorized to make its own tax levy for building purposes. The court held that it was permissible to assign county functions to an independent governmental authority to carry out joint governmental purposes.

Finally, the "governmental" distinction was picked up in *War Memorial Hospital v. Board of County Commissioners,* 279 P.2d 472 (Wyo. 1955). Hospital, cemetery, and fire protection districts were created, overlaying the boundaries of an existing town. The court approved the creation of the first two districts, but disapproved the creation of the fire protection district on the ground that this was a governmental function which the town must perform.

(b) The district is usually created to perform a service function which can be made the basis for a service charge or a special assessment levy. If the court is willing to extend the theory underlying the special assessment, the bonds of the district which are funded by the special assessment will not be counted as debt under the constitutional debt limitation. The Indiana court has gone farther than most in its willingness to accept this extension. This court recognizes an entity known as a taxing district, which levies a uniform tax on real property throughout its area even though the proceeds of the tax are used to pay for an improvement in only part of the district. Yet the tax is considered to be a special assessment tax. *Archer v. City of Indianapolis,* 122 N.E.2d 607 (Ind. 1954). "The special tax which is authorized to be levied upon property within the territorial limits of said sanitary district is declared to be and constitutes the amount of benefits resulting to said property." *Id.* at 610. And, "[t]here is no constitutional provision limiting the number or amount of bonds that may be issued in anticipation of special benefit taxes by a special taxing district." *Id.* at 612.

(c) In many instances, the special district is a convenient way of avoiding the impact of constitutional uniformity of taxation clauses. If the district levies a special assessment tax then the tax does not fall under the uniformity clause, which again applies only to general ad valorem property taxation.

ADVISORY COMMISSION ON INTERGOVERNMENTAL RELATIONS, STATE TECHNICAL ASSISTANCE TO LOCAL DEBT MANAGEMENT 20, 21 (1965)

[The Report offers the following criticisms of debt limitations and of bond referenda, which it characterizes as the "traditional legalistic approach" to problems of local debt management.—Eds.]

1. [The traditional legalistic approach] pertains to present or past conditions, rather than those of the future when long-term debt will be subject to servicing, and thus takes no account of divergent trends for various governments and communities.

2. It deals with separate layers of local governments rather than the aggregate of local government for a particular area.

3. It purports to measure economic capacity by reference to only one revenue source, the property tax, which provides less than half of the revenue of most local governments in most States.

4. This type of limit is, in most States, imprecise and potentially discriminatory because of the nature of the property tax base to which it refers. The real level of limitation is determined by local assessment practices rather than being closely governed by the legal provisions.

5. Being commonly applicable only to full faith and credit debt, this type of limitation offers no assurance that aggregate local debt will be kept within prudent bounds.

6. Debt restrictions have probably restrained the total volume of local government borrowing to some extent, but the extent to which this is true cannot be definitely measured.

7. The restrictions have been an important factor in the rapid recent growth of nonguaranteed local debt, as against full faith and credit borrowing. This development has a differential effect among various purposes of local borrowing and various types of local governments. It tends to increase the cost of borrowing, through higher interest rates and more extended bond maturities. It also is likely to impose more rigidity on local governments' future budgeting than would full faith and credit borrowing.

8. Debt restrictions have tended to impair the public accountability and responsiveness of local governments in various ways, including the promotion of special districts and various kinds of financing authorities, and the complication and obfuscation of financial arrangements.

9. The restrictions have affected governmental relations in various ways. They may artificially increase the need and demand for Federal and State grants to local governments. In some States they have contributed to urban-rural and local-State frictions.

Comments: 1. With this analysis compare Pogue, *The Effect of Debt Limits: Some New Evidence,* 23 NAT'L TAX J. 36 (1970), reporting an empirical study indicating that debt limits have been effective in inhibiting debt levels, primarily by inhibiting local spending rather than inducing the substitution of tax revenues for debt finance. Pogue also notes that debt limits have their greatest effect in metropolitan areas, and that there and generally they lead to lower public service levels. For these reasons, Pogue also argues that debt limitations should be revised or eliminated.

Compare Wagner, *Optimality in Local Debt Limitation,* 23 NAT'L TAX J. 297, 304 (1970):

> Although it is probably correct that debt limits have been circumvented sufficiently to make them ineffective, this empirical observation does not refute the conceptual rationale for debt limitation, nor does it deny that debt limitation can be made more effective. We noted earlier that the primary means of circumventing debt limits are through the creation of special districts, the use of nonguaranteed revenue bonds, and the development of special lease-purchase arrangements. Each of these loopholes can be tightened. Lease-purchase arrangements can be handled by considering the capitalized value of long-term rental contracts as debt. Nonguaranteed bonds can be counted within the debt limits, or, alternatively, local governments can be prohibited from acting to prevent default. Finally, incentives to the creation of special districts can be reduced by setting debt limits on some alternative basis, as, for example, by establishing maximum ratios of debt to per capita income within any county, which would make debt limits invariant to changes in governmental organization.

2. A variety of reforms of the constitutional debt limit approach to local government finance have been urged for decades, ranging all the way from repeal of the constitutional debt limit, to state technical assistance on financial matters to local governments, to state supervision and approval of local government debt. Some of these proposals are reviewed in the Advisory Commission report, which also contains the text of a model act on state technical assistance for local debt management.

One question is whether the emphasis on reform of the constitutional debt limit provisions is not misplaced. First, concentration on debt limitations ignores the role of the federal government in the financing of local capital improvements. Second, increasingly sophisticated budgeting and budget management procedures at the local level have improved the decision-making capability of local government units in debt and financial management. Proper capital budgeting and capital programming ought to be part of any decent program of comprehensive local planning. *See generally* So, *Finance and Budgeting* in THE PRACTICE OF LOCAL GOVERNMENT PLANNING 115 (F. So, I. Stollman, F. Beal & D. Arnold eds. 1979).

3. Detailed regulation of local debt limits is contained in N.Y. Const. Art. VIII. Among other restrictions, section 3 of that article provides that no municipal corporation or district other than a county, city, town, village, school district, fire district, river improvement, or drainage district may be created with power to contract indebtedness and to levy ad valorem taxes or benefit assessments. An improvement district may be created in a county or town with such powers if the indebtedness of the district is included in the indebtedness of the county or town. A South Carolina constitutional provision which attempts to limit the aggregate indebtedness of local government units covering the same territory has not been notably successful. *See* Sinkler, *Constitutional Limitations on Public Finance in South Carolina,* 3 S.C.L.Q. 303 (1951).

4. Consider the policy decisions implicit in the following newly adopted constitutional provision on municipal debt limits:

Pennsylvania Const., art. IX, § 10: "Subject only to the restrictions imposed by this section, the General Assembly shall prescribe the debt limits of all units of local government including municipalities and school districts. For such purposes, the debt limit base shall be a percentage of the total revenue, as defined by the General Assembly, of the unit of local government computed over a specific period immediately preceding the year of borrowing. . . . [Debt limit to exclude indebtedness for self-liquidating project or] which has been approved by referendum held in such manner as shall be provided by law. The provisions of this paragraph shall not apply to the City or County of Philadelphia."

This constitutional provision has now been implemented in the Local Government Debt Unit Act, Pa. Stat. Ann. tit. 53, § 6780-1 et seq. *See* Comment, 46 TEMP. L.Q. 322 (1973). The statute sets a debt limit based on total revenues for all local governments in the state, ranging from 100 percent for school districts to 250 percent for all other local governments except for counties, whose rate is set at 300 percent. *Id.* § 6780-52(a). "Subsidies or reimbursements" from the state or the federal government are not included in the revenue base, but the statute also appears to exclude obligations financed by these intergovernmental revenues from the debt obligations that fall under the Act. *See id.* §§ 6780-2(b)(2), 6780-2(c)(16). The effect of this set-off is that any debt obligation supported in whole or in part by state or federal subsidy is excluded from the debt limit, a result more favorable to the local government than the inclusion of intergovernmental subsidy in the revenue base. *See* Comment, *supra,* at 336. Debt approved by a majority of the voters in a referendum is excluded from the debt limit. *Id.* § 6780-51. Debt secured by leasing arrangements is included in the debt limit when lease payments are made from taxes and general revenues and when title to the property vests in the governmental unit at the termination of the lease. *Id.* § 6780-4.

E. TAX AND EXPENDITURE LIMITATIONS

Many states have had state and local government tax and expenditure limitations since the nineteenth century. While these limits placed some restraint on state and local government finance, only with the "tax revolt" of the past decade have states imposed limitations that substantially curtail the taxing and spending powers of state and local governments. The origins and nature of this new tax limitation movement are explained in the following excerpt:

> The most common limitation on local government taxing power is restriction of the real estate tax rate. Local government tax limits initially appeared

in state statutes in the 1870s and 1880s. Alabama in 1875 and New York in 1884 became the first states to constitutionalize these local government real estate tax limits. Although the principal concern characterizing this era was the limitation of local government debt powers, some saw tax limits as an adjunct remedy necessary to prevent an increase in taxes to pay for capital projects previously financed by public debt. Early property tax limits, like the debt ceilings, were thus aimed at reducing the growth of public expenditures. Since nearly all local government revenues were derived from the property tax at that time, a property tax rate limit was believed to be the most effective means for controlling current expenditures. In addition, the limits were aimed at the narrower interest of protecting property owners from an undue rise in their tax burden in the wake of the panic of 1870 and the depression that followed.

The next group of constitutional tax limitations emerged during the depression of the 1930s. As individual income and property values declined, tax delinquency rose. Property owners and real estate groups pressured state legislatures and the electorate to lower assessments and impose new or tighter tax limitations. They successfully persuaded three states to adopt new overall constitutional limitations and two more to reduce the rate permitted by pre-existing constitutional limits. Unlike earlier tax limits, which were intended to prevent a rise in taxes, the primary purpose of tax restrictions imposed in the 1930s was to force reductions in then current tax levels.

Beginning in 1970, several states have employed a slightly different approach to the restriction of property taxes—the levy limit. Unlike earlier limits, which restricted the tax rate that could be applied to assessed (or full) real property values, levy limits establish the maximum revenue that a jurisdiction's property tax can generate in a particular year. Levy limits, which have uniformly been statutory rather than constitutional, generally allow the total real estate tax levy to rise by only a specified percentage each year. The principal purpose of levy limits has been to provide property tax relief, primarily for home owners faced with rising assessments caused by inflation. These limits can generally be exceeded by referendum or by approval of a state agency. State-mandated cost increases often are excluded from the levy limits.

The Jarvis-Gann initiative (Proposition 13), adopted by California voters in June, 1978, was the first of a new wave of constitutional and statutory property tax rate limits that have swept the country. This development was referred to in the popular press as "the tax revolt of 1978." In November of that year, voters in seven states considered proposals for new limits on real estate taxes. Although there were overtones of distrust of government and concern about state and local government expansion, the principal purpose and effect of these new limits, like those imposed in the 1930s and early 1970s, was property tax relief.

. . . .

A third method of regulating local government finance has been direct restriction on the level of spending. The first such expenditure lid was imposed by statute on Arizona counties and municipalities in 1921. Subject to certain exclusions, it prohibits local budgets from rising more than ten percent over those of the prior year. New Jersey adopted a similar spending limit in 1976, which restricted local government budget increases to five percent per year. Although subsequent attempts to impose local government expenditure limits have generally been unsuccessful, several state government spending lids have been adopted.

Gelfand, *Seeking Local Government Financial Integrity Through Debt Ceilings, Tax Limitations, and Expenditure Limits: The New York City Fiscal Crisis, the Taxpayers' Revolt, and Beyond,* 63 Minn. L. Rev. 545, 551-55 (1979). *See also* Tax and Expenditure Limitations (J. Rose ed. 1982).

In the five-year period from 1977-1982, twenty states enacted an additional twenty-nine tax and expenditure lid laws. Some measures were defeated, though, and the rate of adoption slowed considerably with only two new limit laws imposed in 1982. Cline & Shannon, Municipal Behavior After Proposition 13, Intergovernmental Perspectives, Vol. 8, No. 3, at 23, 24 (1982). *See also* Gold, Results of Local Spending and Revenue Limitations: A Survey (National Conference of State Legislatures, 1981). The following selection describes the general features of recently enacted local limits on taxation and spending.

FEDERATION OF TAX ADMINISTRATORS, STATE REVENUE AND SPENDING LIMITS SINCE PROPOSITION 13, at 7-8 (1980)

The Form of the Limits

With only a few exceptions, the limits on local governments are specifically limits on the taxation of property. The measures in effect in Massachusetts and Nevada limit both local taxation and local budgets, and the measures in California (Proposition 4), Nebraska, and New Jersey (now expired) govern local budgets. Nevertheless, as far as taxation goes, local governments depend heavily on the property tax; when their use of that source of revenue is restricted, their budgets must be limited as well, and vice versa.

The local limits may be divided into four categories: (1) those which impose certain procedural requirements on local governments which raise property taxes, (2) those which provide for a rollback of property taxes, either for particular years or in particular circumstances, (3) those which combine a rollback with limits on future taxes or spending (Proposition 13 in California is such a measure), and (4) those which limit increases in local taxes or budgets.

Procedural requirements. Only one state's measure falls into this category: the 1978 Texas amendment requires local governments which contemplate raising property taxes to hold public hearings and to give notice to property owners.

Rollbacks. The provisions in Alabama, Arizona, Iowa, and Missouri fall into this class. The Arizona and Iowa provisions, which have expired, applied only to specific years. Both reduced the assessed value of all the property in the state for purposes of taxation. The Alabama amendment reduced the property tax rate and the assessment ratio on residential property and provided for a tax credit in the event of a county-wide reassessment. The Missouri provision also provides for a rollback in rates in the event a reassessment results in valuation increases over a certain amount.

Proposition 13 and similar measures. California's Proposition 13 rolled property assessments back to 1975 levels and limited future tax rates to 1 percent of full cash value, with a 2 percent annual allowance for inflation. Property which is newly constructed or which changes hands after the 1975 assessment may be reassessed up to current levels, but the 1 percent rate still applies. Idaho voters approved a similar, statutory measure at the 1978 general election. This has been extensively amended by the legislature, but retains much of the force of Proposition 13. . . .

Limits on future increases. The other twelve measures impose limits on future local taxes or appropriations. Six of these limits provide that a local government's taxes or spending may rise only a certain percentage a year: In Massachusetts, local taxes and spending may rise only 4 percent a year. Local tax levies in Indiana, for years after 1980 (in which no increases are permitted), may rise 5 percent, which was the limiting percentage in New Jersey's measure (now expired). The Colorado and Nebraska statutes allow increases of 7 percent a year, with Nebraska permitting adjustments for growth in population as well. The earlier of the two New Mexico provisions limits increases in the valuation of property to 10 percent a year. (The later measure in New Mexico, however, limits revenue increases to at most 5 percent.)

The remaining six limits prohibit local revenues or spending from increasing faster than certain specified indices. The measures in California (Proposition 4) and Nevada prevent local budgets from increasing faster than the cost of living and local population. The Michigan amendment uses the cost of living alone, while the Utah provision uses population and personal income. Wisconsin permits local property tax levies to grow only as fast as the valuation of all property in the state, with adjustments for changes in local population. Local revenues in New Mexico are limited by a general business indicator index, but may not rise more than 5 percent in a year.

Other Features

Exclusions and overrides. Most of the limits on local taxation and spending, like those on state governments, exclude certain categories of revenues or appropriations from the limit, funds for debt service being perhaps the most common. The limits do not usually apply to funds required to be spent by subsequent state or federal laws. Finally, the limits commonly specify some procedure by which they may be overridden.

California's Proposition 13 remains the model of the "new" tax limit measures. Since it has been in effect for a few years it has received judicial interpretation, and the state and its local governments have had some experience in adjusting to its requirements. The nature of Proposition 13 and the constitutional problems it raised are indicated in the following decision by the California Supreme Court, which upheld Proposition 13 against a number of constitutional objections. Only those parts of the opinion dealing with the home rule and equal protection objections are reproduced here. Proposition 13 is reproduced in full in the Appendix to the opinion.

AMADOR VALLEY JOINT UNION HIGH SCHOOL DISTRICT v. STATE BOARD OF EQUALIZATION

Supreme Court of California
22 Cal. 3d 208, 149 Cal. Rptr. 239, 583 P.2d 1281 (1978)

RICHARDSON, JUSTICE.

In these consolidated cases, we consider multiple constitutional challenges to an initiative measure which was adopted by the voters of this state at the June 1978 primary election. This measure, designated on the ballot as Proposition 13 and commonly known as the Jarvis-Gann initiative, added article XIII A to the California Constitution. Its provisions are set forth in their entirety in the appendix to this opinion. . . . As will be seen, the new article changes the previous system of real property taxation and tax procedure by imposing important limitations upon the assessment and taxing powers of state and local governments.

Petitioners, and the amici supporting them, are various governmental agencies and concerned citizens, each of whom has alleged actual or potential adverse effects resulting from the adoption and ultimate operation of the article. (Hereafter we refer jointly to all petitioners and their amici as petitioners, and refer to all respondents herein and those amici urging the validity of XIII A as respondents.) The issues herein presented are of great public importance and should be resolved promptly. Under well settled principles petitioners, accordingly, have properly invoked the exercise of our original jurisdiction. . . .

We stress initially the limited nature of our inquiry. We do not consider or weigh the economic or social wisdom or general propriety of the initiative. Rather, our sole function is to evaluate article XIII A legally in the light of established constitutional standards. We further emphasize that we examine only those principal, fundamental challenges to the validity of article XIII A as a whole. . . . As will appear, we have concluded that, notwithstanding the existence of some unresolved uncertainties, as to which we reserve judgment, the article nevertheless survives each of the serious and substantial constitutional attacks made by petitioners.

It is a fundamental precept of our law that, although the legislative power under our constitutional framework is firmly vested in the Legislature, "the people reserve to themselves the powers of initiative and referendum." (Cal. Const., art. IV, § 1.) It follows from this that, "[t]he power of initiative must be liberally construed . . . to promote the democratic process." (*San Diego Bldg. Contractors Assn. v. City Council* (1974) 13 Cal. 3d 205, 210, fn. 3, 118 Cal. Rptr. 146, 148, 529 P.2d 570, 572, and cases cited. . . .) Bearing in mind the foregoing interpretive aid, we briefly review the basic provisions of article XIII A. We caution that, save only as to the specific constitutional issues resolved, our summary description and interpretation of the article and of the implementing legislation and regulations do not preclude subsequent challenges to the specific meaning or validity of those enactments.

The new article contains four distinct elements. The first imposes a limitation on the *tax rate* applicable to real property: "The maximum amount of any ad valorem tax on real property shall not exceed one percent (1%) of the full cash value of such property. . . ." (§ 1, subd. (a).) (This limitation is made specifically inapplicable, under subdivision (b), to property taxes or special assessments necessary to pay prior indebtedness approved by the voters.) The second is a restriction on the *assessed value* of real property. Section 2, subdivision (a), provides: "The full cash value means the County Assessors valuation of real property as shown on the 1975-76 tax bill under 'full cash value', or thereafter the appraised value of real property when purchased, newly constructed, or a change in ownership has occurred after the 1975 assessment. . . ." Subdivision (b) permits a maximum 2 percent annual increase in "the fair market value base" of real property to reflect the inflationary rate.

The third feature limits the method of changes in *state* taxes: "From and after the effective date of this article, any changes in State taxes enacted for the purpose of increasing revenues collected pursuant thereto whether by increased rates or changes in methods of computation must be imposed by an Act passed by not less than two-thirds of all members . . . of the Legislature, except that no new ad valorem taxes on real property, or sales or transaction taxes on the sales of real property may be imposed." (§ 3.) The fourth element is a restriction upon *local* taxes: "Cities, Counties and special districts, by a two-thirds vote of the qualified electors of such district, may impose special taxes on such district, except ad valorem taxes on real property or a transaction tax or sales tax on the sale of real property within such City, County or special district." (§ 4.) (The remaining sections relate to the effective dates (§ 5) and severability (§ 6) of the provisions of the new article.)

We examine petitioners' specific contentions.

1. *Constitutional Revision or Amendment*

The petitioners' primary argument is that article XIII A represents such a drastic and far-reaching change in the nature and operation of our governmental structure that it must be considered a "revision" of the state Constitution rather than a mere "amendment" thereof. [The court held that, viewed both qualitatively and quantitatively, Proposition 13 was not a constitutional revision.—Eds.]

Petitioners insist, however, that the new article also will have far reaching *qualitative* effects upon our basic governmental plan, in two principal particulars, namely, (1) the loss of "home rule" .... A close analysis of XIII A convinces us that its probable effects are not as fundamentally disruptive as petitioners suggest.

a.) *Loss of home rule.* The principle of home rule involves, essentially, the ability of local government (technically, chartered cities, counties, and cities and counties) to control and finance local affairs without undue interference by the Legislature.... It is undeniably true that a constitutional limitation upon prevailing local taxation rates and assessments will have a potentially limiting effect upon the management and resolution of local affairs. Reduced taxes may be expected to generate reduced revenues, inevitably resulting in a corresponding curtailment of locally financed services and programs. To conclude, however, that the mere imposition of tax limitations, per se, accomplishes a constitutional revision would in effect bar the people from ever achieving *any* local tax relief through the initiative process. Petitioners have cited to us no authorities which support such a broad proposition, and our own research, disclosing only one case, indicates a contrary rule. (*See School Dist. of City of Pontiac v. City of Pontiac* (1933) 262 Mich. 338, 247 N.W. 474, 477 [initiative measure adopting a 1½ percent tax limitation on assessed value, and requiring two-thirds approval of electorate to increase taxes, was a constitutional amendment, not a revision].)

Petitioners insist, however, that article XIII A has an additional effect beyond the mere limitation of tax revenues, namely, the vesting in the Legislature of the power to allocate to local governmental agencies the revenues derived from real property taxation. It is suggested that, by reason of the operation of section 1, subdivision (a), of article XIII A (allocating the revenues from the 1 percent maximum tax "according to law"), the Legislature is thereby empowered, at its whim, and upon whatever conditions it may impose, to pick and choose among the local agencies, rewarding "deserving" agencies with substantial amounts while penalizing others by reduced awards. Certainly nothing on the face of the article, however, abrogates home rule to this extent, or discloses any intent to undermine or subordinate preexisting constitutional provisions on that subject (Cal. Const., art. XI, §§ 3-7). Indeed, present legislative implementation of article XIII A reveals that such a result has not ensued. For several reasons, petitioners' fears in this connection seem illusory and ill-founded.

First, it is clear that even prior to the adoption of article XIII A, the Constitution authorized the Legislature to "provide maximum property tax rates and bonding limits for local government" (art. XIII, § 20), to provide similar limits for school districts (*id.*, § 21), and to grant exemptions from real property taxation in favor of certain specified classes of property (*id.*, § 4). Thus, from the standpoint of legislative control, the new article appears potentially no more threatening to home rule than these preexisting constitutional limitations.

Second, . . . article XIII A neither destroys nor annuls the taxing power of local agencies. Although revenues derived from real property taxes may well be substantially reduced by reason of the new tax rate and assessment restrictions (§§ 1, 2), local agencies retain full authority to impose "special taxes" (other than certain real property taxes) if approved by a two-thirds vote of the "qualified electors." (§ 4.) Although the interpretation of the foregoing quoted provisions is not presently before us, it seems evident that section 4 assists in preserving home rule principles by leaving to *local* voters the decision whether or not to authorize "special" taxes to support *local* programs.

Third, article XIII A does not by its terms empower the Legislature to direct or control local budgetary decisions or program or service priorities, and we have no reason to assume that the Legislature will attempt to exercise its powers in such a manner as to interfere with local decision-making. Certainly, local agencies retain the same constitutional and statutory authority over municipal affairs which they possessed and exercised prior to the adoption of the new article. The mere fact of reduction in local revenues does not lead us necessarily to the conclusion that local agencies have forfeited control over allocations and disbursements of their remaining funds.

Finally, recent implementing legislation (Stats. 1978, chs. 292, 332) confirms the Legislature's present intention to preserve home rule and local autonomy respecting the allocation and expenditure of real property tax revenues. Although this legislation is, of course, subject to future change and, accordingly, is not conclusive on the point, the present pattern of legislative implementation of article XIII A appears to refute petitioners' premise that the article *necessarily and inevitably* has resulted or will result in the loss of home rule. Among other provisions, the Legislature has enacted Government Code section 26912 which contains the formulae whereby county auditors must allocate to various local agencies and school districts within county boundaries the revenues to be derived from the 1 percent maximum real property tax during the fiscal year 1978-1979. Although these formulae are somewhat complex, in general they aim at allocating these funds on a *pro rata basis,* without imposing any condition whatever regarding their ultimate use. Each "local agency" (city, county, city and county, and special district) is to receive a proportionate share based upon its average property tax revenues during the previous three fiscal years. (Gov. Code, § 26912, subds. (a), (b)(1). Similarly, each school district, county superintendent of schools, and community college district, is to receive a proportionate share based upon the entity's average property tax revenues for the 1977-1978 fiscal year. (*Id.,* subd. (b)(2).)

The foregoing tax allocation scheme is evidently intended to assure that each local agency and school district will receive approximately the same percentage of the total tax revenues as it had previously received. Thus, contrary to petitioners' fears and assumptions, the adoption of XIII A need not *necessarily* result either in abrogation of home rule in this state or in the delegation to the Legislature of the power to make those revenue and budgetary decisions formerly left to local discretion and control. (Other sections of the new legislation contain formulae for allocating the state's surplus tax funds. These provisions do not relate to the distribution of revenues from real property taxation and, accordingly, they are not relevant to our present discussion, except insofar as the availability of these funds may minimize the impact of the reduction in local tax revenues.)

. . . .

3. Equal Protection of the Laws

Petitioners' equal protection argument against article XIII A is directed at two aspects of the article. They contend that (1) the "rollback" of assessed valuation (§ 2, subd. (a)) assertedly will result in invidious discrimination between owners of similarly situated property, and that (2) the two-third voting requirement for enacting "special taxes" by local agencies (§ 4) unduly discriminates in favor of those voters casting negative votes. As will appear, we hold that neither contention has merit.

a.) *1975-1976 Assessment Date.* As we have noted, section 2, subdivision (a), of article XIII A provides that "The full cash value [to which the 1 percent maximum tax applies] means the County Assessors valuation of real property as shown on the 1975-76 tax bill under 'full cash value', or thereafter, the appraised value of real property when purchased, newly constructed, or a change in ownership has occurred after the 1975 assessment. All real property not already assessed up to the 1975-76 tax levels may be reassessed to reflect that valuation." (Section 2, subdivision (b), permits an annual 2 percent maximum increase on the "fair market value base" of property, to reflect the inflationary rate.) Petitioners emphasize that, by reason of the "rollback" of assessed value to the 1975-1976 fiscal year, two substantially identical homes, located "side-by-side" and receiving identical governmental services, could be assessed and taxed at different levels depending upon their date of acquisition. Such a disparity in tax treatment, petitioners claim, constitutes an arbitrary discrimination in violation of the federal equal protection clause (amend. XIV, § 1).

Preliminarily, we note that petitioners' equal protection challenge, arguably, is premature. As a general rule, courts will not reach constitutional questions "unless absolutely necessary to a disposition" of the case before them . . . and we could decline to consider the issue in the abstract and instead await its resolution within the framework of an actual controversy wherein the disparity is pivotal.

Nevertheless, we have elected to treat the equal protection issue as constituting an attack upon the face of the article itself, because the assessors throughout this state must be advised whether to follow the new assessment procedure. As will appear, we will conclude that the essential demands of equal protection are satisfied by a rational basis underlying section 2 of the new article.

The general principles applicable to the determination of an equal protection challenge to state tax legislation were recently summarized by the United States Supreme Court as follows: "We have long held that '[w]here taxation is concerned and no specific federal right, apart from equal protection, is imperiled, the States have large leeway in making classifications and drawing lines which in their judgment produce reasonable systems of taxation.' [Citation.] A state tax law is not arbitrary although it 'discriminate[s] in favor of a certain class . . . if the discrimination is founded upon a reasonable distinction, or difference in state policy,' not in conflict with the Federal Constitution. [Citation.] This principle has weathered nearly a century of Supreme Court adjudication . . . ." (*Kahn v. Shevin* (1974) 416 U.S. 351, 355-356 . . . .)

Consistent with the foregoing expression of broad liberality, the high court has recognized the wide flexibility permitted states in the enforcement and interpretation of their tax laws, holding that "The latitude of discretion is notably wide *in the classification of property for purposes of taxation and the granting of partial or total exemptions upon grounds of policy." (Royster Guano Co. v. Virginia* (1920) 253 U.S. 412, 415 . . ., italics added. . . .) There exists no "iron rule of equality, prohibiting the flexibility and variety that are appropriate" to reasonable schemes of taxation. (*Allied Stores of Ohio v. Bowers* (1959) 358 U.S. 522, 526. . . .) So long as a system of taxation is supported by a rational basis, and is not palpably arbitrary, it will be upheld despite the absence of "a precise, scientific uniformity" of taxation. (*Kahn v. Shevin,* supra, 416 U.S. at p. 356, fn. 10. . . .)

Petitioners, in response, rely upon a line of cases which hold, as a general proposition, that the intentional, systematic *under-valuation* of property similarly situated with other property assessed at its full value constitutes an improper discrimination in violation of equal protection principles. . . .

The foregoing cases, however, involved constitutional or statutory provisions which *mandated* the taxation of property on a *current value* basis. These cases do not purport to confine the states to a current value system under equal protection principles or to state an exception to the general rule accepted both by the United States Supreme Court and by us, as previously noted, that a tax classification or disparity of tax treatment will be sustained so long as it is founded upon some reasonable distinction or rational basis.

By reason of section 2, subdivision (a), of the article, except for property acquired prior to 1975, henceforth all real property will be assessed and taxed at its value *at date of acquisition* rather than at current value (subject, of course, to the 2 percent maximum annual inflationary increase provided for in subdivision (b)). This "acquisition value" approach to taxation finds reasonable support in a theory that the annual taxes which a property owner must pay should bear some rational relationship to the original cost of the property, rather than relate to an unforeseen, perhaps unduly inflated, current value. Not only does an acquisition value system enable each property owner to estimate with some assurance his future tax liability, but also the system may operate on a fairer basis than a current value approach. For example, a taxpayer who acquired his property for $40,000 in 1975 henceforth will be assessed and taxed on the basis of that cost (assuming it represented the then fair market value). This result is fair and equitable in that his future taxes may be said reasonably to reflect the price he was originally willing and able to pay for his property, rather than an inflated value fixed, after acquisition, in part on the basis of sales to third parties over which sales he can exercise no control. On the other hand, a person who paid $80,000 for similar property in 1977 is henceforth assessed and taxed at a higher level which reflects, again, the price he was willing and able to pay for that property. Seen in this light, and contrary to petitioners' assumption, section 2 does not unduly discriminate against persons who acquired their property after 1975, for those persons are assessed and taxed in precisely the same manner as those who purchased in 1975, namely, on an acquisition value basis predicated on the owner's free and voluntary acts of purchase. This is an arguably reasonable basis for assessment. (We leave open for future resolution questions regarding the proper application of article XIII A to involuntary changes in ownership or new construction.)

In addition, the fact that two taxpayers may pay different taxes on substantially identical property is not wholly novel to our general taxation scheme. For example, the computation of a sales tax on two identical items of personalty may vary substantially, depending upon the exact sales price and the availability of a discount. Article XIII A introduces a roughly comparable tax system with respect to real property, whereby the taxes one pays are closely related to the acquisition value of the property.

In converting from a current value method to an acquisition value system, the framers of article XIII A chose not to "roll back" assessments any earlier than the 1975-1976 fiscal year. For assessment purposes, persons who acquired property prior to 1975 are deemed to have purchased it during 1975. These persons, however, cannot complain of any unfair tax treatment in view of the substantial tax advantage they will reap from a return of their assessments from current to 1975-1976 valuation levels. Indeed, the adoption of a uniform acquisition value system without some "cut off" date reasonably might have been considered both administratively unfeasible and incapable of producing adequate tax revenues. The selection of the 1975-1976 fiscal year as a base year, although seemingly arbitrary, may be considered as comparable to utilization of a "grandfather" clause wherein a particular year is chosen as the effective date of new legislation, in order to prevent inequitable results or to promote some other legitimate purpose. . . . Similar provisions are routinely upheld by the courts. . . .

Petitioners insist, however, that property of equal *current* value must be taxed equally, regardless of its original cost. This proposition is demonstrably without legal merit, for our state Constitution itself expressly contemplates the use of "a value standard other than fair market value . . .." (Art. XIII, § 1, subd. (a).) Moreover, the Legislature is empowered to grant total or partial exemptions from property taxation on behalf of various classes (e.g., veterans, blind or disabled persons, religious, hospital or charitable property; see art. XIII, § 4), despite the fact that similarly situated property may be taxed at its full value. In addition, homeowners receive a partial exemption from taxation (art. XIII, § 3, subd. (k)) which is unavailable to other property owners. As noted previously, the state has wide discretion to grant such exemptions. . . .

Finally, no compelling reason exists for assuming that property lawfully may be taxed only at current values, rather than at some other value, or upon some different basis. As the United States Supreme Court has explained, "The State is not limited to *ad valorem* taxation. It may impose different specific taxes upon different trades and professions and may vary the rate of excise upon various products. In levying such taxes, the State is not required to resort to close distinctions or to maintain a precise, scientific uniformity with reference to composition, use or value." (*Ohio Oil Co. v. Conway*, . . ., 281 U.S. 146 . . ..) We cannot say that the acquisition value approach incorporated in article XIII A, by which a property owner's tax liability bears a reasonable relation to his costs of acquisition, is wholly arbitrary or irrational. Accordingly, the measure under scrutiny herein meets the demands of equal protection principles.

b.) *Two-Thirds Voting Requirement.* Petitioners have also questioned whether the requirement of a two-thirds vote to approve "special" local taxes (§ 4) denies to voters the equal protection of the laws. We may quickly dispose of the contention. Petitioners rely upon our decision in *Westbrook v. Mihaly*, . . . 2 Cal. 3d 765, 87 Cal. Rptr. 839, 471 P.2d 487, wherein we held that a two-thirds requirement for approval of county general obligation bonds violated federal equal protection principles. However, our *Westbrook* opinion was vacated by the United States Supreme Court (*Mihaly v. Westbrook* (1971) 403 U.S. 915, . . .) and the cause was remanded for our reconsideration in the light of *Gordon v. Lance* (1971) 403 U.S. 1 . . ., a case which upheld a 60 percent vote requirement primarily because no "discrete and insular minority" was singled out for special treatment by application of the voting requirement. Thus, *Westbrook* no longer represents the controlling law on the subject. . . . Because persons who vote in favor of tax measures may not be deemed to represent a definite, identifiable class, equal protection principles do not forbid "debasing" their vote by requiring a two-thirds approval of such measures.

. . . [W]e have concluded that article XIII A survives each of the substantial challenges raised by petitioners. The orders to show cause previously issued in these cases are discharged, and the respective petitions are denied.

TOBRINER, MOSK, CLARK, MANUEL and NEWMAN, JJ., concur.

APPENDIX
ARTICLE XIII A

"Section 1.(a) The maximum amount of any ad valorem tax on real property shall not exceed one percent (1%) of the full cash value of such property. The one percent (1%) tax to be collected by the counties and apportioned according to law to the district within the counties.

"(b) The limitation provided for in subdivision (a) shall not apply to ad valorem taxes or special assessments to pay the interest and redemption charges on any indebtedness approved by the voters prior to the time this section becomes effective.

"Section 2.(a) The full cash value means the County Assessors valuation of real property as shown on the 1975-76 tax bill under 'full cash value', or thereafter, the appraised value of real property when purchased, newly constructed, or a change in ownership has occurred after the 1975 assessment. All real property not already assessed up to the 1975-76 tax levels may be reassessed to reflect that valuation.

"(b) The fair market value base may reflect from year to year the inflationary rate not to exceed two percent (2%) for any given year or reduction as shown in the consumer price index or comparable data for the area under taxing jurisdiction.

"Section 3. From and after the effective date of this article, any changes in State taxes enacted for the purpose of increasing revenues collected pursuant thereto whether by increased rates or changes in methods of computation must be imposed by an Act passed by not less than two-thirds of all members elected to each of the two houses of the Legislature, except that no new ad valorem taxes or real property, or sales or transaction taxes on the sales of real property may be imposed.

"Section 4. Cities, Counties and special districts, by a two-thirds vote of the qualified electors of such district, may impose special taxes on such district, except ad valorem taxes on real property or a transaction tax or sales tax on the sale of real property within such City, County or special district.

"Section 5. This article shall take effect for the tax year beginning on July 1 following the passage of this Amendment, except Section 3 which shall become effective upon the passage of this article.

"Section 6. If any section, part, clause, or phrase hereof is for any reason held to be invalid or unconstitutional, the remaining sections shall not be affected but will remain in full force and effect."

BIRD, CHIEF JUSTICE, concurring and dissenting.

Initiatives by their very nature are direct votes of the people and should be given great deference by our courts. Judges should liberally construe this power so that the will of the people is given full weight and authority. However, if an initiative conflicts with the federal Constitution, judges are duty bound to hold the offending sections unconstitutional.

When these principles are applied to the cases before this court, it is clear that article XIIIA is constitutional in all respects save one. I endorse the majority opinion's view that there has not been a violation of the one subject rule, an impermissible revision of the Constitution, or a curtailment of the right to travel. Further, it is correct in holding that the question of impairment of contract is not properly before this court and is not ripe for decision.

One issue remains which troubles me deeply. As judges we must be devoted to the preservation of the great constitutional principles which history has bequeathed to us. In article XIIIA, one of those principles has been violated—the equal protection clause. No one mindful of this nation's colonial history can seriously question the right of the people to act to redress tax grievances. However, our citizens also have a right to be treated equally before the law. The right to equality of taxation is as basic to our democracy as is the right to representation in matters of taxation. Under article XIIIA property taxpayers are not treated equally, and those sections which promote this disparity must fall.

I

Consider these facts. John and Mary Smith live next door to Tom and Sue Jones. Their houses and lots are identical with current market values of $80,000. The Smiths bought their home in January of 1975 when the market value was $40,000. The Joneses bought their home in 1977 when the market value was $60,000. In 1977, both homes were assessed at $60,000, and both couples paid the same amount of property tax. However, under article XIIIA in 1978, the Joneses will pay 150 percent of the taxes that the Smiths will pay. Should a third couple buy the Smiths' home in 1978, that couple would pay twice the taxes that the Smiths would have paid for the *same* home had they not sold it. Today, this court holds that such disparity is not only equitable, but that it does not violate the equal protection clause of the Constitution.

The basic problem with this position is that it upholds the adoption of an assessment scheme that systematically assigns different values to property of equal worth. By pegging some assessments to the value of property at its date of purchase and other assessments to the value of property as of March 1, 1975, article XIIIA creates an irrational tax world where people living in homes of identical value pay different property taxes. Thus, instead of establishing an assessment scheme with one basis by which all property owners are taxed, article XIIIA utilizes two bases, acquisition date and 1975 market value, to impose artificial distinctions upon equally situated property owners.

Article XIIIA divides the property taxpaying public into two classes, pre- and post-1975 purchasers. Section 2(a) rewards those owners who purchased their property before March 1, 1975, by constitutionally fixing their tax assessments at lower figures than those who buy property of similar or identical value at a later date. This "roll back" provision confers substantial benefits upon one group of property owners not shared by other similarly situated owners. This provision raises the ugly specter of a race for tax savings in which the players start at different points, weighed down by different "handicaps."

Inequalities in state taxation have been held to be constitutional so long as they "rest upon some ground of difference having a fair and substantial relation to the object of legislation . . . ." (*Royster Guano Co. v. Virginia* (1920) 253 U.S. 412, 415. . . .)

However, even minimal scrutiny requires that the statutes of the Legislature and the initiatives of the people be defensible in terms of a shared public good, not merely in terms of the purposes of a special group or class of persons. (*See* Tribe, American Constitutional Law (1978) p. 995.) The law should be something more than just the handmaiden of a special class; it must ultimately be the servant of justice.

Respondents fail to establish the general public benefit to be found in giving some, but not all, individuals a "roll back" to 1975 assessments. To be eligible for the full "roll back," article XIIIA requires that an individual have owned continuously his or her property since a date prior to March of 1975. This requirement makes it literally impossible for persons purchasing property in 1978 or thereafter to qualify for benefits granted fully to pre-1975 owners (and less fully to 1975-78 owners). In so doing, article XIIIA transgresses the constitutional guarantee of equal protection under the law.

Respondents defend the rationality of the 1975 date by characterizing it as a cut-off date or "grandfather" clause. Although its arbitrariness is conceded, they argue that it is defensible as a matter of administrative convenience. This contention lacks merit. It merely acknowledges that "it is difficult to be just, and easy to be arbitrary." (*Stewart Dry Goods Co. v. Lewis* (1935) 294 U.S. 550, 560 . . . .) Administrative convenience is wholly inadequate to warrant preferred treatment of a closed class of property owners. . . .

The fact that the former property tax system allowed inequalities through exemptions for charitable, religious, nonprofit and educational institutions is no answer to the questions raised by article XIIIA. Those exemptions benefitted the general public since the public received specific benefits from the exempted organizations. No one has yet established what benefits the general public derives from the systematic under-valuation of the property of pre-1975 purchasers, and this court should decline to hypothesize rationales. . . .

[Chief Justice Bird then discussed United States Supreme Court and California decisions that support her conclusions. She also added the following observations on the inequities of Proposition 13.—Eds.]

Section 2(a) mandates reassessment to current market value not only for voluntary purchasers but any time there is a "change in ownership." Thus, as previously noted, the person who inherits the family home or the spouse who gains title to property after a divorce may find that the assessment on the property suddenly skyrockets for property tax purposes. There is no rationality to the jump in valuation that accompanies these occurrences. Similarly, those persons who must move often because of the nature of their employment (for example, military families) will find that section 2(a)'s mandated reassessments bear little relation to their financial situation. Even more perplexing is the situation of persons who find that new construction must be done to their property after a natural disaster. Section 2(a) once more requires reassment to "full cash value." The arbitrariness of article XIIIA's assessment scheme could not be more apparent.

Finally, the arbitrariness of the acquisition date valuation as a tax standard can be demonstrated by considering the plight of the taxpayer whose property has actually *decreased* in value since 1975. Under the previous tax system, such a person's property tax assessment would eventually reflect the decline in market value. However, under article XIIIA the assessment remains fixed at the acquisition date value since section 2(b) allows for a reduction in assessment only on the basis of a downward turn in the consumer price index.

Comments: 1. The opinions in the principal case consider possible equal protection violations arising out of the assessment "rollback" provided by Proposition 13. Is the classification upheld in this case more, or less, justified than the preferential farm assessment laws discussed *supra*? Do the United States Supreme Court decisions discussed by the majority opinion support its holding?

2. In the period immediately after the adoption of Proposition 13, "[l]ibrary services, parks and recreation services, and cultural activities were the most severely affected county and city programs on a State-wide basis." Comptroller General of the U.S., *Proposition 13—How California Governments Coped with a $6 Billion Revenue Loss* 19 (1979). School districts were minimally affected because a state "bail out" law, enacted soon after the adoption of Proposition 13, distributed $4.2 billion in state surplus to local governments in fiscal 1979. *Id.* at 5. What does this experience indicate about the distributive effects of a tax limitation? The "bail out" helped ease the burden of transition but the surplus did not last long. By the end of 1982, the state was confronted with a potential deficit of more than $1 billion. Time, Dec. 20, 1982, at 27. For discussion of the immediate aftermath of Proposition 13, see *Lincoln Institute of Land Policy Conference—Proposition 13: A First Anniversary Assessment,* 53 S. CAL. L. REV. 75 (1979). See also Lefcoe & Allison, The Legal Aspects of Proposition 13: The Amador Valley Case, 53 S. CAL. L. REV. 173 (1980).

3. The expectations of California voters in adopting Proposition 13 are relevant to an assessment of its restrictions and its impact. The following article summarizes the circumstances leading up to Proposition 13 and its adoption. It summarizes a longer article written by Frank Levy, a senior research associate at the United States Urban Institute. See Levy, *On Understanding Proposition 13,* 56 PUB. INTEREST 66 (1979).

Levy found that California's total perceived taxes equaled 9.2 percent of its total revenues, a rate higher than that of all other states except Alaska, Hawaii, and New York and nearly 3 percentage points above the nationwide average. His estimates revealed that perceived property taxes in California amounted to 3.9 percent of personal income in the state, a rate higher than that of all but five other states and 1.7 percentage points above the nationwide average.

The Burden on Homeowners

Not only were Californians' property taxes high, they were escalating rapidly. In many areas of the state, rising assessments caused homeowners' property tax bills to increase by as much as or more than 100 percent between 1973 and 1977.

Homeowners' property taxes rose sharply during this period because housing values in the state were increasing steeply while commercial property values were increasing only weakly. The cost of housing in the Los Angeles and San Francisco metropolitan areas rose at an average rate of 14-15 percent per year between 1973 and 1977, a rate significantly higher than in most other areas of the nation.

Because of the rigidity of the state's property tax system, California tax assessors had little discretion to act as buffers between rising housing prices and homeowners' property tax assessments. A tax reform measure enacted in 1967 required that all property — both residential and commercial — be assessed at 25 percent of its full value and that reassessments be conducted frequently. "In a world of 'unreformed' property taxes," says Levy, "tax assessors might have reacted to the housing inflation by looking the other way or only increasing assessments slowly." But the requirement that all property be reassessed frequently ensured that assessed values kept pace with market values.

Where Were the Local Governments?

High assessments need not necessarily lead to high tax bills: tax rates can be lowered to counteract the effect of rising assessments. In California, however, a combination of factors—the composition of the property tax rolls, general economic conditions, and a provision of the state constitution—made it impossible for localities to lower tax rates without jeopardizing their revenue bases.

In 1973, single-family homes represented less than 40 percent of the value of California's property tax rolls. The remainder — about 60 percent — consisted of commercial property.

While housing prices and residential assessments soared in the early and mid-1970s, business was caught in a period of stagnation. Business income lagged, and commercial assessments, which are based on business income, grew slowly in relation to residential assessments.

Because the California constitution requires that a jurisdiction tax all property at the same rate, a locality that wanted to cut taxes for homeowners would have had to apply the same cut to slower-growing commercial property, thereby sharply reducing total revenues.

Where Was the State Government?

Unlike local governments, California's state government did have the means to alleviate homeowners' mounting property tax burden. In 1968, the legislature passed a measure that exempted from taxation the first $750 of assessed value of an owner-occupied home. In 1972, the legislature passed a bill that increased this exemption to $1,750, limited city and county tax rates, and limited school district expenditures.

Both the 1968 and 1972 bills were last-minute responses by Governor Reagan and the state legislature to more comprehensive property tax relief initiatives on the election ballots in those years. In mid-1977, however, before Proposition 13 had yet been presented to the public by Howard Jarvis and Paul Gann, several moderate tax relief measures were before the legislature, but none cleared both houses before the end of the session.

Levy attributes the state's failure to act in 1977 to (1) internal disagreement over the form tax relief should take—in particular, whether relief should be focused solely on low- and moderate-income households — and (2) uncertainty over the size of the state surplus, which led to uncertainty over how much relief the state could afford to give.

Soon after the September adjournment of the 1977 legislative session, Jarvis and Gann began circulating a petition to put Proposition 13 on the June 1978 election ballot. Within a month, Proposition 13 had qualified.

When the state legislature reconvened in 1978, it passed a compromise property tax relief measure, but according to Levy, the bill's passage appeared to be little more than an attempt to ward off the impending threat of Proposition 13. Furthermore, the compromise measure called for separate tax rates on residential and commercial property, a provision which required voter approval of a constitutional amendment. The proposed amendment, listed on the ballot as Proposition 8, made no mention of property tax relief per se. As a result, Levy surmises, some voters may have viewed Proposition 8 as a vague promise of future relief rather than as a tool for implementing a relief bill that had already been enacted.

The fates of Propositions 8 and 13, however, were not sealed until May 1978. In that month, Los Angeles County received its fiscal 1979 property tax assessments. Although only one-third of the county's properties had been reassessed, the property tax rolls had grown in value by 17.5 percent, and assessments on many single-family homes had increased by as much as 50-100 percent. The next month, Proposition 13 was approved by 65 percent of California's voters.

Proposition 13: Harbinger of Nationwide Tax Revolt? URB. INST. POL'Y & RESEARCH REP., Vol. 9, No. 1, at 15, 16 (1979).

Are the restrictions imposed by Proposition 13 consistent with voter expectations? Its impact? Levy also notes that "[w]hat Californians will see in the aftermath of Proposition 13 . . . is a substantial shift in power from local governments to the state government." Why? Is this shift in power consistent with voter expectations? Other evaluations of Proposition 13 have noted that it is slowing the growth in local government spending and that it is basically a tax reform measure—one which shifts the emphasis from the property tax to the income tax. Are these results consistent with voter expectations?

A major criticism of tax and spending limitations such as Proposition 13 is the resulting inflexibility and corresponding restrictions imposed on the ability of state and local governments to respond to changing public needs. Perhaps in recognition of this criticism, the California Supreme Court has gone to great lengths to uphold attempts by state and local officials to respond to particular public needs. Recent California Supreme Court cases construing specific provisions of Proposition 13 illustrate this trend.

LOS ANGELES COUNTY TRANSPORTATION COMMISSION v. RICHMOND

Supreme Court of California
31 Cal. 3d 197, 182 Cal. Rptr. 324, 643 P.2d 941 (1982)

Mosk, Justice.

The issue in this case is whether the Los Angeles County Transportation Commission (LACTC) may, consistent with the provisions of section 4 of article XIIIA of the California Constitution, impose a "retail transaction and use tax" in Los Angeles County with the consent of a majority of the voters, but less than two-thirds of their number.

In 1976, the Legislature created LACTC in order to meet a demand for an efficient public transportation system in the Southern California region. (Pub.Util.Code, § 130301 et seq.) To finance such a system, LACTC was authorized to adopt a "retail transaction and use tax" (*id.*, §§ 130350-130355) [1] limited to one-half of one percent on the sale, storage, or use of tangible personal property in Los Angeles County (Rev. & Tax.Code, §§ 7261, 7262; Pub.Util.Code, § 130350). The tax could not be imposed, however, unless the measure received the approval of a majority of the county's voters who voted in the election. (*Id.*, § 130350.) Any revenues received were to be used for "public transit purposes." (*Id.*, § 130354.) LACTC was not authorized to levy a property tax.

On June 6, 1978, the voters approved Proposition 13 by initiative (now Cal.Const., art. XIIIA). Section 4 of article XIIIA provides, "Cities, Counties and special districts, by a two-thirds vote of the qualified electors of such district, may impose special taxes on such district, except ad valorem taxes on real property or a transaction tax or sales tax on the sale of real property within such City, County or special district."

Following adoption of Proposition 13, LACTC enacted a sales tax in accordance with the requirements of the Public Utilities Code, and the voters of the county approved the measure by a 54 percent majority in November 1980. . . .

. . . This case involves the application of section 4 to the sales tax enacted by LACTC and adopted by a majority of the voters of Los Angeles County. We must decide whether imposition of the tax violates the prohibition against the levy of a "special tax" by a "special district" without a two-thirds vote of the electors. We shall conclude that the tax was validly adopted by a majority vote because LACTC is not a "special district" within the meaning of section 4. As we explain below, the goal of article XIIIA is real property tax relief, and a governmental

---

[1] This tax will hereinafter be referred to as a sales tax.

body like LACTC, which does not have the power to levy a property tax, is not the type of "special district" governed by the section.

. . . .

In our analysis of section 4, we begin, as we must, with the language of the provision. The exception at the end of the section provides the first indication that the "special districts" referred to are those which have the power to levy a tax on real property. The fact "special districts" are prohibited, even with the consent of two-thirds of the voters, from levying "ad valorem taxes on real property or a transaction tax or sales tax on the sale of real property" implies that the "special districts" referred to are those which may levy a tax on real property. Although this construction is not compelled, it is an appropriate interpretation of the language of the provision because ordinarily the subject matter of an exception is the same as that to which the exception applies.

The material set forth in the voter's pamphlet also provides support for our conclusion. The description of the background and effect of Proposition 13 by the Legislative Analyst strongly suggested to the voters that the term "special districts" in section 4 refers to entities authorized to levy a tax on real property. The analysis begins with "some basic facts" about California property taxes; the first item of information under this heading is that "[u]nder existing law cities, counties, schools and special districts are permitted to levy local property taxes." (Ballot Pamp. Proposed Amends. to Cal.Const. with arguments to voters, Primary Elec. (June 6, 1978) p. 56.) The analysis then states that because under the Constitution certain types of local entities, including "special districts," must receive legislative approval in order to impose "special taxes," the ability of such districts, even with local voter approval, "to *replace* property tax losses resulting from the adoption of this initiative" would be limited. (Emphasis added, *id.* at pp. 57, 60.) In a similar passage, the analysis tells the voters that "the initiative would restrict the ability of local governments to impose new taxes in order to *replace* the property tax revenue losses." (Emphasis added, *id.* at p. 60.) Since only those "special districts" which levied property taxes could "replace" the "loss" of such taxes, these statements imply that the "special districts" referred to are those which are authorized to levy a property tax.

. . . .

The third prong of our inquiry in assessing the intention of the electorate is the interpretation of the term "special districts" by the Legislature following the enactment of Proposition 13.

We can derive no plain guidance from these measures. As we have seen, some statutes enacted following adoption of Proposition 13 exclude entities which do not levy property taxes from the term "special districts." (E.g., Gov.Code, § 16271, subd. (d); Rev. and Tax.Code, § 2215.)[9] On the other hand, section 50077 of the Government Code employs the term "district" without the qualifying word "special," but it is clear from its context that it was intended to implement article XIIA. Perhaps this statute is most favorable to Richmond's position, since it is designed to implement article XIIIA (Gov.Code, § 50075) and defines a "district" broadly as "an agency of the state, formed pursuant to general law or special act, for the local performance of governmental or proprietary functions within limited boundaries." (*Id.*, § 50077, subd. (c).) It requires a two-thirds vote of the electorate as a condition for the adoption of "special taxes" (*id.* § 50077, subd. (a)).

---

[9] Section 2215 of the Revenue and Taxation Code defines a "special district" as "any agency of the state for the local performance of governmental or proprietary functions within limited boundaries," but excepts from its terms those agencies which are "not authorized by statute to levy a property tax rate." This provision is contained in chapter 3, part 4, of division 1 of the Revenue and Taxation Code. Chapter 3, is entitled "Reimbursement for Costs Mandated by the State."

While this broad definition would appear at first blush to include LACTC, there are persuasive reasons why we should not view it as determinative of the question before us. As we have seen, *Amador* held that, although section 4 is cast in permissive terms, it is restrictive in nature in that it limits the right of local entities to adopt "special taxes" by requiring a two-thirds vote for their imposition. In enacting sections 50075 to 50077, the Legislature viewed section 4 as having an affirmative aspect as well, i.e., as affording "districts" a right to levy taxes by a two-thirds vote. These provisions were expressly intended as enabling legislation to fulfill the grant of power in section 4. Since the aim of the legislation was to broaden the rights of local entities to adopt taxes, the application of the definition contained in section 50077 to limit these rights would be unwarranted. There is nothing to indicate that the Legislature intended to withdraw from a local entity like LACTC the power to levy a tax by a majority vote if Proposition 13 did not compel such a restriction....

. . . .

... To the extent section 4 clearly requires a particular entity to obtain the consent of two-thirds of the voters, it affords the "effective" property tax relief we discussed in *Amador*. However, as we discuss above, there are strong policy reasons for holding that if, as here, the intention of the voters to require a two-thirds vote is not clear, a majority is to be deemed sufficient for the valid adoption of a "special tax."

Nor are we impressed with a suggestion that our interpretation of section 4 could result in the wholesale avoidance of the purpose of article XIIA by the Legislature, which could reorganize existing "special districts" to remove their property-taxing power or create new ones without such power, thereby allowing them to adopt a "special tax" by majority vote. We cannot assume that the Legislature will attempt to avoid the goals of article XIIIA by such a device. In any event, that problem can be dealt, with if and when the issue arises. The legislation creating LACTC and granting it the power to levy only a sales tax antedated Proposition 13 by two years. Thus, there can be no claim here that the Legislature was attempting to evade the restrictions imposed by section 4.

We hold that the sales tax in issue here was validly adopted by a majority vote and that, therefore, Richmond must take appropriate steps to implement its imposition.

Let a peremptory writ of mandate issue as prayed.

. . . .

RICHARDSON, JUSTICE, dissenting.

I respectfully dissent.

Article XIII A, section 4 of the California Constitution provides: "Cities, Counties and special districts, by a two-thirds vote of the qualified electors of such district, may impose special taxes on such district, except ad valorem taxes on real property or a transaction tax or sales tax on real property or a transaction tax or sales tax on the sale of real property within such City, County or special district."

The majority concludes that this constitutional limitation does not bar a retail transaction and use tax (sales tax) which is to be operative throughout Los Angeles County and which was approved by only 54 percent of its voters. The majority's reason is that the entity *initiating* the tax, Los Angeles County Transportation Commission (LACTC), is not a "special district" within the purview of section 4. Accordingly, the majority would sustain the tax "even if it is a 'special tax' within the meaning of the section." (*Ante*, ... p. 943 of 643 P.2d.)

....

In reaching its conclusion that LACTC is not a "special district," the majority has applied a new rule of "strict construction" of constitutional language. (*Ante,* p. 945 of 643 P.2d.) The primary feature of this new interpretive rule appears to be that any ambiguities in the constitutional provision before us must be resolved in favor of allowing local government to *evade* the clear two-thirds voter approval requirement by which the people chose to limit additional or increased tax levies by such government. Beyond labelling the constitutional restriction as "fundamentally undemocratic" (*ibid.*), the majority cites no authority for applying such a rule of strict construction within this context. I have found no such authority. . . .

....

. . . The fact that the Legislature has elected to create a separate commission to improve public transportation does not change the functional nature of the public service being rendered. Nor does the legislative action either permit or require us to ignore the obvious replacement role which LACTC's sales tax can, and doubtless will, play as a substitute for a real property tax.

What the majority opinion really tells us is that the constitutional restrictions of article XIII A, section 4 can be readily and completely avoided by the simple creation of a district which is geographically precisely coterminous with a county, but which lacks its real property taxing power. In this connection, I believe the majority is exceedingly naive when it insists that the Legislature will not be importuned successfully by other local entities to grant to them similarly easy escapes from the fiscal constraints of article XIII A. (*Ante,* . . . p. 947 of 643 P.2d.) I think such appeals are not only probable, but certain, and in large numbers. The majority has cut a hole in the financial fence which the people in their Constitution have erected around their government. Governmental entities may be expected, instinctively, to pour through the opening seeking the creation of similar revenue-generating entities in myriad forms which will be limited only by their ingenuity. "We are not to 'shut our minds' as judges to truths that 'all others can see and understand.'" (*McGovern v. City of New York* (1923) 234 N.Y. 377, 392, 138 N.E.2d 26.)

....

Equally important to a conclusion that LACTC is a "special district" within the purview of section 4 is the apparent comprehensive nature of the taxing limitation imposed by article XIII A. The two-thirds voter approval requirement has been constitutionally ordained not only for tax increases instituted by *counties, cities* and *special districts* (§ 4), but also for tax increases implemented by the *state* Legislature itself (§ 3). To recognize an otherwise undefined *residual* category of local governmental agencies, "nonspecial districts" as it were, which are free to impose new or increased taxes without the two-thirds voter approval requirement is anomalous at best. At worst, such a construction would create a loophole which would be fatal to the rule itself, thereby permitting the most flagrant flouting of the people's will by the creation of multiple "nonspecial districts" which could levy taxes willy nilly without restraint, oblivious to the constitutional command and subversive of its clear objectives.

....

I return to the overall objective of article XIII A described by the framers as assuring "effective real property tax relief" and their attempt to achieve that objective by prohibiting local imposition of substitute taxes unless approved by two-thirds of the electorate which is to be taxed. . . .

There is a direct relationship between the objective of article XIII A and the definition of "special taxes," the adoption of which is limited by section 4. Without disavowing our identification of that objective in *Amador*—and the majority does not suggest such disavowal—it is apparent that the broadest possible definition of "special taxes" would best serve that objective of tax relief. But it is not necessary within the context of this case to probe the definitional limits of "special taxes." It is patently obvious that the constitutional phrase *must* encompass the tax adopted by LACTC. The purpose of the tax in question is to generate within the geographical boundaries of Los Angeles County revenues for the improvement of public transit within that locale. Such a tax is a substitute for those revenues which could otherwise have been generated by real property taxes imposed by Los Angeles County itself *but for* the restrictions of article XIII A. To be consistent with the constitutional limitation which concededly would bar the county from imposing the new tax on its citizens without the approval of two-thirds of the county's voters, we should similarly bar the county's *surrogate*, LACTC, from accomplishing the same forbidden objective without the constitutionally requisite approval.

. . . .

Similarly, there is no basis for concluding that section 4's two-thirds voter approval requirement for "special taxes" was meant to be limited to: (1) "real property taxes," most, if not all, of which would appear to be barred expressly by section 4 . . .; (2) "special assessments" or regulatory fees, which are exacted in reasonable proportion to the cost of a specific governmental service benefitting the payor, and are not taxes at all . . .; (3) taxes imposed on specific entities or activities . . .; or (4) taxes imposed upon taxpayers which are exempt from "ordinary" taxes . . . . There is no suggestion in the language or history of article XIII A that adoption of any of these specific and limited meanings of the term "special taxes" was contemplated by the framers of the provision or the voters who adopted it. Nor, in my view, would the far-reaching purposes of article XIII A be served by construing that term in so restrictive a fashion.

Also, there is an overriding reason for interpreting the term "special taxes" in a broad and comprehensive manner. As we stressed in *Amador,* the "super-majority" two-thirds vote requirement for "special taxes" is defensible largely as the *preserver* of home rule principles. . . . Confining to a narrow category the taxes to which that requirement is applicable would seriously undermine those principles.

. . . .

Focusing not upon LACTC's characterization of itself or of its tax, but rather upon the function of government which it proposes to accomplish with the revenues from that tax, I conclude that LACTC's sales tax is constitutionally deficient. It is a "special tax" imposed by a "special district." Because it was not approved by a "two-thirds vote of the qualified electors of such district . . .," it violated article XIII A, section 4 of the California Constitution.

Comments: 1. In *Mills v. County of Trinity,* 166 Cal. Rptr. 674 (Cal. App. 1980), a county's adoption of new fees for processing subdivision, zoning and other land-use applications was challenged as constituting a "special tax" within the meaning of article XIIIA. The plaintiff maintained that section 4 of article XIIIA requiring a two-thirds affirmative vote of the electors was a prerequisite to the imposition of higher fees. The California Court of Appeals held that "the 'special tax' referred to in section 4 of article XIIIA does not embrace fees charged in connection with regulatory activities [when the] fees do not exceed the reasonable cost of providing services necessary to the activity for which the fee is charged and which are not levied for unrelated revenue purposes." *Id.* at 676. Under the holding in *Mills,* can a California municipality disaggregate all its services, charge a fee to cover each service, and escape Proposition 13?

The meaning of the term "special taxes" in section 4 of article XIIIA was again at issue in *City & County of San Francisco v. Farrell,* 648 P.2d 935 (Cal. 1982). In *Farrell,* the challenge was to an increased payroll and gross receipts tax implemented without a two-thirds affirmative vote of the electors. The California Supreme Court held that the increased payroll and gross receipts tax, the proceeds of which are placed into the city's general fund to be used for general governmental expenditures, was not a tax levied for a specific purpose, and therefore was not a "special tax" within the meaning of section 4. The court reasoned as follows:

> There can be no doubt that the term "special taxes" is ambiguous in the sense that it has been interpreted to mean different things in different contexts. . . .
>
> In deciding whether the payroll and gross receipts taxes come within the term "special taxes" in section 4, we are faced with considerations not before the court in *Amador.* We are asked to read the word "special" out of the phrase "special taxes," in violation of settled rules of construction and in the face of the language of section 3, which indicates that the drafters knew how to say "any" taxes when that is what they meant. Our choice here is not simply between acceptance of one of a number of different meanings of an ambiguous term in a statute, but between disregarding the word "special" altogether in section 4, or affording it some meaning consistent with the intent of the voters in enacting the provision. Application of the rule of strict construction of provisions which require extraordinary majorities for the enactment of legislation is particularly appropriate in these circumstances.
>
> In keeping with these principles, we construe the term "special taxes" in section 4 to mean taxes which are levied for a specific purpose rather than, as in the present case, a levy placed in the general fund to be utilized for general governmental purposes. This is a common meaning of the term.

Id. at 938, 940.

2. Other language in article XIIIA has also posed problems of interpretation. In *Carman v. Alvord,* 644 P.2d 192 (Cal. 1982), the California Supreme Court addressed the meaning of the one percent property tax limitation under Proposition 13. In *Carman,* a landowner brought a class action suit seeking refund of an ad valorem tax which the city council had assessed to defray the costs of the State Employee's Retirement System (PERS). Plaintiff claimed that the tax levy was in violation of Proposition 13 because it exceeded the one-percent-of-value limit. Plaintiff maintained that the tax was not exempt under section 1(b) of article XIIIA because PERS was not a prior "indebtedness approved by the voters." PERS charges arise new every year; therefore, plaintiff claimed that the exemption applied only to "interest and redemption charges."

The court found that the tax was exempt under section 1(b) of article XIIIA. Section 1(b) provides that: "The limitation provided for in subdivision (a) shall not apply to ad valorem taxes or special assessments to pay the interest and redemption charges on any indebtedness approved by the voters prior to the time this section becomes effective." The court held that the PERS obligation was a prior indebtedness approved by the voters in 1948. When the voters approved the plan, they authorized the special tax to fund the obligation; they approved "all indebtedness to employees, current and future." The court found that the term "indebtedness" included the contractual obligations under PERS.

3. California courts have disagreed on whether special assessments are subject to the property tax limitations of Proposition 13. In *Solvang Municipal Improvement District v. Board of Supervisors,* 169 Cal. Rptr. 391 (Cal. App. 1980) and *County of Fresno v. Malmstrom,* 156 Cal. Rptr. 777 (Cal. App. 1979), the court concluded that special assessments to service and redeem assessment bonds for local improvements, including parking lots, were not ad valorem taxes within the meaning of article XIIIA, sections 1 and 4 of the California Constitution. According to the court, Proposition 13 was directed against general governmental spending and general real property taxes. Special assessments were not designed to pay for general expenditures but rather were charges to pay local improvements that have specially benefited the affected property.

But in *In re Validity of Maintenance District No. 5A*, 186 Cal. Rptr. 276 (Cal. App. 1982), the court held that a special assessment to fund a newly created maintenance district was subject to the property tax limitation. The City of San Jose, acting under its home rule powers, established the maintenance district to operate and maintain landscaped median islands on the public streets within the district. The ordinance was patterned after a state statute authorizing local maintenance districts in which the assessments were levied on an ad valorem basis. San Jose, in an effort to avoid the Proposition 13 limitations, required assessments to be based on the proportionate size of the parcel on the theory that the estimated benefit each parcel would receive would be proportionate to its size. (See the discussion of special assessments, *supra*. The court, drawing heavily on a 1980 statute determining that assessments under the state maintenance district statute were subject to the one percent tax limitation, held that San Jose's plan also was subject to the tax limitation. The court saw no material difference between the ad valorem basis for assessment under the state code and the parcel size basis under the San Jose charter. The court concluded:

> If the City's program is validated, the effect would be to countenance evasion of the stated purpose of article XIII A "to assure effective real property tax relief." (*Amador Valley*, ...) The City would be free to draw boundaries throughout the entire city, label these areas "maintenance districts," and then levy assessments for all "local improvements" within that district. These "local improvements" would not be limited to routine street repairs and maintenance. Conceivably, the "local improvements" would include what once were general governmental services such as fire and police protection, neighborhood schools and libraries, trash collection and street light maintenance, all of which could now be said to specifically benefit the property situated within the carefully drawn boundaries of these maintenance districts.... The City would then be able to accomplish indirectly what it could not accomplish directly, namely: (1) generate revenue without being subject to the property taxation limitation contained in section 1 of article XIIIA; or (2) impose special taxes without the two-thirds vote of the electors in such district as required by section 4 of article XIII A.

Id. at 283. Is the attitude of the court in *Maintenance District* consistent with the approach of the California Supreme Court?

For an argument that the post-Proposition 13 practice of levying special assessments to finance services such as police and fire protection and to maintain facilities should be subject to the Proposition 13 tax limitation, see Note, *Police and Fire Service Special Assessments Under Proposition 13,* 16 U.S.F.L. Rev. 781 (1982).

As noted in the introductory materials to this section, Missouri adopted a constitutional amendment, popularly known as the Hancock Amendment, imposing limitations on state and local taxing powers. Like California's Proposition 13, the Hancock Amendment requires voter approval of taxation implemented above specified percentage levels. The Hancock Amendment's application to licenses and fees was one of the first challenges to the amendment's validity. The following case answers that challenge.

ROBERTS v. McNARY

Supreme Court of Missouri
636 S.W.2d 332 (1982)

Donnelly, Chief Justice.

On November 4, 1980, Missouri voters adopted an amendment to their State Constitution—Article X, §§ 16 through 24, inclusive (the Hancock Amendment). Section 22, which is pertinent here, provides in part as follows:

§ 22. [Taxation by political subdivisions, limitations—repayment of bonds]

Section 22. (a) Counties ... are hereby prohibited from levying any tax, license or fees, not authorized by law, charter or self-enforcing provisions of the constitution when this section is adopted or from increasing the current levy of an existing tax, license or fees, above that current levy authorized by law or charter when this section is adopted without the approval of the required majority of the qualified voters of that county or other political subdivision voting thereon. ...

In its proposed budget for the 1982 calendar year, St. Louis County included increases in certain fees charged for numerous county services, such as parks and building inspection. This budget, with the increased fees, was adopted by the St. Louis County Council in January 1982. On January 22, 1982, respondent Wilhelmina Roberts, a resident and taxpayer of St. Louis County, filed a declaratory judgment action seeking to prevent St. Louis County from implementing the fee increases. She alleged that the county ordinances which increased the fees violated Mo.Const. Art. X, § 22, because the increases were not submitted to the qualified voters of the county for approval. Respondent requested that the ordinances be declared unconstitutional and that an injunction be issued against their enforcement. After trial, the court granted the relief requested, and Gene McNary, County Executive, and St. Louis County have filed this appeal. This Court has jurisdiction because the validity of a provision of the State Constitution is involved. Mo.Const. Art. V, § 3.

The first point raised on appeal concerns whether the charges which St. Louis County seeks to raise, or establish, fall within the phrase "tax, license or fees" within Art. X, § 22(a). Appellants contend that the purpose of the Hancock Amendment—limitation of taxation—requires that "tax, license or fees" be read to include only those levies which seek to generate general revenue. Therefore, they argue that "user" fees or "regulatory" fees (which, it is agreed, accurately describe the fees in this case) are not governed by Art. X, § 22(a) because they support only the service for which they are collected. On the other hand, respondent's position is that a plain reading of Art. X, § 22(a) would include all licenses or fees, regardless of the use to which the funds generated are put.

Appellants have two pillars of support for their interpretaion of Art. X, § 22(a). First, the testimony of Melton D. Hancock (after whom the Amendment was named) was that the words "license or fees" were added to "tax" in § 22(a) to prevent the government from levying higher licenses and fees in order to generate general revenue to compensate for the funds lost through the tax-limiting aspect of the Amendment. The second prong of appellants' argument is that the Hancock Amendment as a whole, as shown in § 16, limits only local taxing and state taxing and spending, and therefore does not extend to "user" or "regulatory" fees because by definition they are not considered taxes.

Rules employed in construction of constitutional provisions are the same as those employed in construction of statutes, but the former are to be given a broader construction due to their more permanent character. ... Crucial words must be viewed in context and it must be assumed that words used were not intended to be meaningless. ... This Court has recognized that in construction of constitutional provisions, it should undertake to ascribe to words the meaning which the people understood them to have when they adopted the provision. *State ex inf. of Danforth v. Cason,* 507 S.W.2d 405, 408 (Mo. banc 1973). "The framers of the Constitution and the people who adopted it 'must be understood to have employed words in their natural sense, and to have intended what they have said.' This is but saying that no forced or unnatural construction is to be put

upon their language." *State ex inf. Danforth v. Cason,* 507 S.W.2d at 409. ...
The meaning of the words in the provision, as conveyed to the voters, is presumed to be their natural and ordinary meaning. ... The ordinary, and commonly understood meaning is derived from the dictionary. ... Moreover, the grammatical order and selection of the associated words as arranged by the drafters is also indicative of the natural significance of the words employed. *Id.* Of course, this Court must give due regard to the primary objectives of the provision under scrutiny as viewed in harmony with all related provisions, considered as a whole. ...

Article X, § 22(a) prohibits counties from levying any tax, license or fee not then authorized and from increasing any existing tax, license or fee. Webster's Third New International Dictionary (1965) defines these words as follows: (1) tax—"a pecuniary charge imposed by legislative or other public authority upon persons or property for public purposes: a forced contribution of wealth to meet the public needs of a government"; (2) license—"a right or permission granted in accordance with law by a competent authority to engage in some business or occupation, to do some act, or to engage in some transaction which but for such license would be unlawful"; (3) fee—"a fixed charge for admission; a charge fixed by law or by an institution for certain privileges or services; a charge fixed by law for services of a public officer."

This Court has recently spoken on two of these words:

> The term "tax" has been defined variously, but the appropriate definition for us is found in *Leggett v. Missouri State Life Ins. Co.,* 342 S.W.2d 833, 875 (Mo. banc 1960) in which we stated: "Taxes are 'proportional contributions imposed by the state upon individuals for the support of government and for all public needs.' ... Taxes are not payments for a special privilege or a special service rendered. ... Fees or charges prescribed by law to be paid by certain individuals to public officers for services rendered in connection with a specific purpose ordinarily are not taxes ... unless the object of the requirement is to raise revenue to be paid into the general fund of the government to defray customary governmental expenditures ... rather than compensation of public officers for particular services rendered. ...

Craig v. City of Macon, 543 S.W.2d 772, 774 (Mo. banc 1976).

Reading the words examined here for their ordinary and customary meanings, they present a sweeping list of the types of pecuniary charges a government makes. Quite simply, this exhibits an intent to control any such charges to the extent that the voters must approve any increase in them. Therefore, the charges which appellants seek to enact by county ordinance are governed by Art. X, § 22(a).

This is consistent with the objectives of the Hancock Amendment as clearly understood by voters—to rein in increases in governmental revenue and expenditures. The official ballot title for the Hancock Amendment specifically informed voters that the amendment "prohibits local tax or fee increases without popular vote." "[T]he Amendment ... is popularly described as 'the taxing and spending lid' amendment, words which also reflect its central purposes." *Buchanan v. Kirkpatrick,* 615 S.W.2d 6, 13 (Mo. banc 1981). Limiting the ability of counties to increase licenses or fees is certainly in harmony with the objectives of the Amendment as a whole. The judgment of the trial court on this issue must be sustained. ...

Appellants' next point deals with the relationship between the charter of St. Louis County and Mo.Const. Art. X, § 22(a). On November 6, 1979, St. Louis

County voters amended their county charter to authorize the County Council to set all charges by reposing legislative power in it in § 2.180 of the St. Louis County Charter. Against this factual backdrop, appellants argue (1) that the fee increases fall within the "authorized" exception in Art. X, § 22(a), and (2) that the fees are, in fact, approved by the voters because they voted for the amendment to the St. Louis County charter prior to adoption of the Hancock Amendment.

With respect to the first aspect of this issue, appellants contend that if a statute or charter, extant prior to adoption of the Hancock Amendment, *authorizes* a county to levy a *fee* (but no specific fee was set or levied), then after Hancock the county can impose a fee under that authority without submitting it to the voters for approval. Appellants state that the fees involved do not have a set rate or amount except that they must not "cause the receipts to substantially exceed the associated costs." They conclude that the trial court erred because the evidence established that the costs of the services exceeded the revenues obtained from the charges.

Respondent counters with a view that where the county has authority to levy a fee but no specific amount has as yet been set, the "current levy" should be viewed as being zero. Thus, the establishment of a specific fee here would require voter approval just as in any other fee increase.

Utilizing the rules of construction earlier stated and considering the facts of this case, appellants' position is without support. The specific language in Art. X, § 22(a) involved in this issue is as follows:

> Counties . . . are hereby *prohibited from levying any tax, license or fees, not authorized by law, charter or self-enforcing provisions of the constitution* when this section is adopted *or from increasing the current levy of an existing tax, license or fees* above that current levy authorized by law or charter when this section is adopted without the approval of the required majority of the qualified voters of that county . . . ." (emphasis added).

The first phrase of § 22(a) means that it does not affect any license or fee specific in amount which, although authorized at the time of the adoption of the Hancock Amendment, had not yet actually been imposed. The second phrase states that any license or fee existing [i.e., actually imposed] at the time the Hancock Amendment was adopted could not be increased without complying with § 22(a). Therefore, appellants' assertion that a county can impose a license or fee under an enabling authority which sets no specific dollar amount or rate without complying with Art. X, § 22(a) must fail. The resolution of this issue also denies appellants' argument that the voters' adoption of the 1979 amendment to the St. Louis County Charter satisfies the "voter approval" requirement in Art. X, § 22(a).

. . . .

The judgment is affirmed.

All concur.

Comments: 1. One of the ironies of the *Roberts* case is that the principal supporter for whom the amendment is named testified against the general meaning that the court ascribed to the term "license and fees." His, and County Executive McNary's, argument was that the voter approval requirement only applied to revenue generating levies and not "user" and "regulatory" charges. A major concern was that the broad construction of the terms adopted by the court would create chaos at the polls. However, the fears of local officials did not materialize. Despite record long ballots with as many as 100 local fee increases, including leaf pickup and ice skate rentals, the November 1982 elections in St.

Louis County went smoothly as voters studied crib sheets on the propositions while waiting patiently an extra 30-40 minutes to vote.

2. Like Proposition 13, the Hancock Amendment is a tax limitation provision affecting both state and local governments. It differs from Proposition 13 in the approach taken to state taxes. Proposition 13 limits the property tax rate ("one percent of full cash value"), restricts the method of determining the assessed value of real property (a maximum two percent annual increase in the "fair market value base" is allowed to reflect inflation), and requires a two-thirds vote of both houses of the legislature for any changes in state taxes designed to increase revenues. The Hancock Amendment, patterned after a recent amendment to Michigan's Constitution, article IX, §§ 25-34 (1978), approaches the problem from a different point of view—total state revenues. The general assembly is prohibited from imposing "taxes of any kind which, together with all other revenues of the state, federal funds excluded, exceed the revenue limit established in this section." Mo. Const. art. X, § 18(a). Revenue limits are to be calculated for each fiscal year, using a complicated formula that includes the total state revenues (TSR) for the base year (fiscal year 1980-1981) divided by personal income (PI) for calendar year 1979 times the calendar year prior to the calendar year in which a particular fiscal year's appropriations are being made:

Another way of stating the constitutional limit, using the tax limit for fiscal 1981-1982 as an example, is:

$$\frac{\text{Tax Limit,}}{\text{FY 1981-82}} = \text{TSR, FY 1980-81} \times \frac{\text{PI, Cal. 80}}{\text{PI, Cal. 79}}$$

Thus, the tax limit for fiscal 1981-82 is last year's (FY 80-81) TSR increased by the percentage growth in PI from calendar 1979 to calendar 1980. If PI went up by eight percent, then the tax limit is eight percent higher than the prior TSR.

Sarasohn, *Overview of Missouri Taxation* in MISSOURI TAXATION LAW AND PRACTICE § 1-11 (The Missouri Bar, 1981).

Note how the tax limit is tied to fluctuations in personal income. If personal income increased by fifteen percent in 1981 over 1979 (seven to eight percent per year), then the revenue limit for fiscal year 1982-1983 would be fifteen percent above the total state revenues for fiscal year 1980-1981.

Federal income tax policy can become a factor in evaluating limitations such as the Hancock Amendment. Missouri provides a state income tax deduction for federal income taxes. A major federal income tax reduction will substantially increase Missouri's income tax revenue without a corresponding increase in personal income. A significant change in the general economy or a substantial change in federal income tax policy could produce a situation in which the tax limit for a given fiscal year is exceeded without any new legislatively imposed new or increase in taxes. Major state revenue sources such as income and sales taxes are affected significantly by economic growth or decline. In addition, there is a significant time lag between the change in the economy and the tax limit effect. Because the tax limit is determined by personal income for the calendar year that precedes the fiscal year, and the fiscal year begins July 1, the lag is approximately one and one half years. Assume, for example, a tax limit that is eight percent higher than the prior year's total state revenue. If a sudden surge in the economy produces a twelve percent growth in personal income, a corresponding growth in state revenue will occur. As a result, the revenue limit for that year will be exceeded by four percent. The twelve percent increase in personal income will not raise the revenue limit until the following year.

If the revenue limit is exceeded by one percent or more, "the excess revenues shall be refunded pro rata based on the liability reported on the Missouri state income tax ... annual returns filed following the close of such fiscal year." § 18(b). Does this refund mechanism, which favors income taxpayers over other taxpayers, pose any constitutional problems? Assume that sales and use taxes account for about thirty percent of total state revenue in Missouri. Does this refund mechanism foreclose sales and use taxes? What administrative problems would it pose for state and local officials?

3. The emphasis the Hancock Amendment places on total state revenues is complicated by an ambiguity in the definition of that term. Article X, § 17(1) states that total state revenues "includes all general and special revenues, license[s] and fees, excluding federal funds, as defined in the budget message of the governor for fiscal year 1980-81." The definition is borrowed from the Michigan provision, § 33. However, the January 1980 budget message in Missouri did not define total state revenue (Michigan's did). Would the following items be included in total state revenues: cash balances at the beginning of the fiscal year, revenue bond proceeds, fees charged by state-supported colleges and universities? *See, generally* Sarasohn, *supra.*

4. The Hancock Amendment, in addition to limiting state revenues and expenditures and local government taxes, licenses or fees, also protects local governments from bearing increased expenditures placed upon them by the state. Article X, § 21, prevents the state from "reducing the state financed proportion of the costs of any existing activity or service required of counties or other political subdivisions."

Section 21 also prohibits the general assembly or any state agency from mandating new or increased levels of service or activity performed by local government without state funding. The Missouri Supreme Court, in *Boone County v. State,* 631 S.W.2d 321 (Mo. 1982), held that a state-mandated salary increase for tax collectors of second class counties must be funded by the state. The court found that the payment of a county tax collector's salary was an activity conducted by the county pursuant to a state mandate. The term "activity" was broadly construed to include the general functions of the county government. Accordingly, a required increase in salary was an increased level of activity, i.e., government operations. Therefore, any state-mandated increase in expenditures for that activity beyond pre-Hancock Amendment levels must be paid by the state. A complicating factor was a separate, long-standing constitutional requirement that the state set salaries for county officials. Mo. Const., art. VI, § 11. A strong dissent argued that § 21 did not apply because no new activity was required of the tax collectors. What problems are posed by the amendment and the court's construction for state budget officials and for local officials inundated by demands for salary increases (see Chapter 6)? Would an expanded view of home rule powers (see Chapter 3) permit local governments to raise salaries or would the state have an easier time imposing the increase because of the Hancock Amendment?

5. Is the St. Louis Board of Police Commissioners, created by the Missouri legislature, to govern the St. Louis police force under state statute, Mo. Ann. Stat. §§ 84.010-84.340, a "state agency" subject to the limitations of § 21? Under the statute (and a similar one for Kansas City), commissioners are appointed by the governor. The mayor is an ex officio member. The police board is made responsible for the St. Louis police force. The city is required to appropriate moneys sufficient to accommodate the annual budget for the police force that is certified as required by the board.

In *State ex rel. Sayad v. Zych,* 642 S.W.2d 907 (Mo. 1982), the board sought mandamus to order the city to appropriate all the funds requested for its 1982-1983 budget after the city refused to approve an increase, citing § 21 and *Boone County.* The court sided with the city, citing over 100 years of precedent that "the Police Commissioners are an agency of the State Government, and required to perform within a specified locality some of the most important duties of the government." *State ex rel. St. Louis Police Commissioners v. St. Louis County Court,* 34 Mo. 546, 571 (1864). In the court's view, the fact that the police board is not a part of the state budgetary process does not remove it from the § 21 limitations because § 21 applies to "any state agency." A sharply worded dissent argued in part as follows:

> The explanation and name for this creature [police board] are to be found in its history. The parent of the metropolitan police force was a municipal police force. And it continues to be a municipal police force insofar as it serves and is paid for by the City. Its final reason for being is the City, not the state as a whole in the sense that the State Highway Patrol is a servant of the whole state. And to declare that it serves a statewide purpose is only to assert a truism: that the police power inheres in the state and not in a municipal corporation. In order, however, to remove the police force from the influence of politics in a city that by the turn of the last century was the fourth largest in the United States, the General Assembly removed its control from the local political

forces. But that control was not placed in the state government. It was, instead, placed in a Board of Commissioners who by state statute are appointed by the governor but who must be local in residence. The control, thus, did not pass to the state. It was simply removed from the City by the state and placed in an independent agency. The net result is that the state does not police the City of St. Louis; but the state has dictated in precise terms how the City of St. Louis will be policed. Thus, while the formal cause of the Board is a state statute, its material, efficient and final causes are the city of St. Louis.

It is, as is urged by the Board, a hybrid agency, bearing characteristics of both local and state agency and is manifestly not a body contemplated within the Hancock Amendment. It is to remain autonomous from the influence of local political forces and because of its nature, without the contemplation of the Hancock Amendment.

The majority opinion alters the character of the St. Louis metropolitan police force and makes it a state agency for part of its appropriations, although it serves only St. Louis City and is not part of the state agency organization. That invalidates the intention of Chapter 84 of the Missouri Revised Statutes. I believe that this goes far beyond anything contemplated by the Hancock Amendment. . . .

. . . .

To meet the purpose of the Hancock Amendment head-on: The substance of this dissent would do no violence to the theory of that amendment, which is to put a lid on taxes. While the overall budget for police purposes is increased, the total budget for the citizens need not be; and, after all, it seems it is the total budget to which the Hancock Amendment is aimed.

Id. at 915-16.

Which argument is more persuasive on the state agency question? What factors should be used in deciding that question? The state agency-local government dichotomy is discussed in Chapter 3.

6. In *Oswald v. City of Blue Springs*, 635 S.W.2d 332 (Mo. 1982), the Missouri Supreme Court was faced with a question concerning voter-approved revenue bonds for the city's water and sewer system. Section 22(b) specifically exempts "taxes imposed for the payment of principal and interest on bonds or other evidences of indebtedness or for the payment of assessments on contractual obligations in anticipation of which bonds are issued which were authorized prior to the effective date of this section." In *Oswald,* the parties acknowledged that the city had the power to raise water and sewer rates to pay the principal and interest on a revenue bond issue for construction of a water treatment plant which had been approved by the voters in the spring of 1981 (post-Hancock). For this reason, the court did not have to decide whether revenue bonds are within the scope of § 22(a) or (b). The remaining question was whether the city could increase water and sewer rates to meet the costs of maintenance and operation of the physical plant itself. The court found that the city had an obligation to assure the value and marketability of the bonds through upkeep of the physical plant, and that nothing in the Hancock Amendment prohibited that.

7. The *Roberts* opinion poses some serious questions for issuers of tax-exempt revenue bonds. As noted in the *Oswald* case, § 22(b) of the Hancock Amendment clearly exempts from the referendum requirement taxes imposed to pay principal and interest on pre-Hancock bonds. But the amendment does not specifically cover post-Hancock bonds. It does require voter approval for new or increased taxes, licenses or fees. If you were bond counsel to a hospital district or an advisor to prospective purchasers of hospital revenue bonds, would the fact that a substantial portion of the revenue to pay the principal and interest on the bonds was to come from patient fees concern you? Would it make any difference if the bonds were issued by a municipality or by an independent special district pursuant to legislative authority? Would the fact that the special district did or did not have the power to tax influence your thinking? Would this issue arise if licenses and fees were not a part of the provision, as is the case in Michigan?

PROPERTY TAX RELIEF PROVISIONS

Since the property tax is a tax on nonliquid wealth, taxpayers with little or no liquid wealth are particularly vulnerable to tax increases based on fluctuating inflation rates. There are a number of alternatives to property tax limitations, including tax exemptions and abatements which provide taxpayers with some relief from property taxes.

> Circuit breakers and homestead exemptions are both formulas to make the property tax less burdensome to homeowners. Without a circuit breaker or homestead exemption, the property tax is calculated exclusively on the value of property and the tax rate.
>
> Since middle and low income people typically pay a higher portion of their total income for housing than the wealthy, the property tax is regressive. Circuit breakers — which introduce an income or ability to pay criterion into the property tax — and homestead exemptions can make it less regressive. They also can be used to stabilize property tax burdens for homeowners and renters and prevent or compensate for property tax shifts from business property onto residential property.
>
> There is no single formula for a circuit breaker. It can operate on a sliding scale, or it can be drafted to provide relief to homeowners above a certain age, below a certain income, or when taxes reach a specified percentage of income. Generally, the state pays the circuit-breaker benefit to the homeowner, either directly or through a credit against the state income tax, so that local government is not penalized for having a high number of poor or elderly. In this manner, circuit breakers can help compensate poor communities as well as poor people for the inequitable distribution of wealth.
>
> Homestead exemptions subtract a flat amount from the assessed value of the property. If a home is assessed at $20,000, a $5,000 exemption reduces the effective assessment to $15,000, and thereby cuts the tax by one-fourth. Everybody gets the same tax reduction from a homestead exemption, unlike a circuit breaker, but this is still much fairer than a Proposition 13 type cut, which gives much larger dollar reductions to high bracket taxpayers. California had a homestead exemption before Proposition 13, but its value was eroded by inflation. Ideally, homestead exemptions should be indexed to inflation. Another problem occurs when properties in some parts of the state are underassessed relative to others, since a flat exemption will give underassessed areas disproportionate benefits. In many states, older and poorer cities and neighborhoods are over-assessed relative to others. A flat homestead exemption will be of less value in these circumstances.

Conference on Alternative State and Local Policies, State and Local Tax Revolt: New Directions for the 80's, at 119 (D. Tipps ed. 1980). Review the materials on agricultural property tax abatement, *supra*. Is this form of tax relief preferable to the tax limitation imposed by Proposition 13? How would you make this evaluation?

Increased federal or state aid is another alternative to property tax limitations. Consider, for example, that many municipalities have used federal general revenue sharing funds to reduce or stabilize local property taxes. Is this method of property tax relief preferable to a property tax limitation? Gelfand, *supra*, discusses a number of other alternatives to tax limitations. He concludes:

> Only those who cling to claim that property owners still merit treatment as a privileged class can justify [tax limitations]. Intergenerational equity certainly cannot serve as the justifying principle for these constitutional real estate tax limits. Such limits protect only the *present* generation of taxpayers, who can effectively protect themselves from excessive taxation through referenda or

ordinary elections. Moreover, constitutional tax limits, like constitutional debt ceilings, reduce fiscal flexibility and undercut responsiveness to the concerns of local voters.

Id. at 591-92 (emphasis in original).

A deferred tax payment plan provides another method of relief. Under this plan, tax payments are deferred until either the property is liquified at sale or on the owner's death. One commentator has suggested that the revenues temporarily lost to the tax-collecting governmental unit may be subsidized by the sale of tax-free bonds secured by the market value of the properties. *See* Kaufman, *Inflation, Proposition 13 Fever, and Suggested Relief* in THE PROPERTY TAX REVOLT 215 (G. Kaufman & K. Rosen eds. 1981); K. BROWNING & W. JOHNSON, THE DISTRIBUTION OF THE TAX BURDEN (1979). Would such bonds meet the public purpose requirement? Would they be general obligation or revenue bonds? Would they be marketable? What if property values dropped?

Massachusetts has introduced a "renters' deduction" as part of a voter approved tax limitation measure. Framed as legislation rather than a constitutional amendment, the proposition was intended to address a host of voter dissatisfactions. Among these dissatisfactions was Massachusetts' higher than the national average property tax. The Massachusetts proposition is summarized and a substantive challenge to the renters' deduction is discussed in the following case.

MASSACHUSETTS TEACHERS ASS'N v. SECRETARY OF COMMONWEALTH

Supreme Judicial Court of Massachusetts
—— Mass.——, 424 N.E.2d 469 (1981)

WILKINS, JUSTICE.

At the November, 1980, general election, acting under the initiative process of the Constitution of the Commonwealth, the voters adopted as chapter 580 of the Acts of 1980 a tax limitation measure commonly known as Proposition 2½[4]. The plaintiffs contend that Proposition 2½ was not a proper subject of an initiative petition and that procedural requirements of the initiative process authorized by the Constitution were not adequately followed in the presentation of Proposition 2½ to the voters. They also raise before us a challenge to the constitutionality of a substantive provision of Proposition 2½, that is a challenge

---

[4] The characterization of the initiative proposal as "Proposition 2½" is a blatant colloquialism. The word "proposition" is derived from a well-known tax limitation measure submitted to the people of California in 1978 as Proposition 13. In California, matters put to popular vote are characterized as propositions. In Massachusetts, we simply call them questions.

The reference to "2½" is not based on an offbeat numbering system. Proposition 2½ was in fact the second question on the 1980 ballot. The reason for the reference to "2½" is that the principal tax limitation feature of St. 1980, c. 580, is based on the initial objective of § 1 of the act to restrict most cities' or towns' total annual assessments against their real and personal property to 2½% of the fair cash value of that property.

We shall often use the expression "Proposition 2½" in this opinion to refer either to the proposal or to the act, as the case may be.

which could have been made if Proposition 2½ had been adopted by the Legislature rather than through the initiative process.[5]

These cases are before us on a report ... by a judge of the Superior Court of the propriety of his rulings, which (a) declared that Proposition 2½ was adopted in a constitutionally adequate manner according to the procedures set forth in art. 48 of the Amendments to the Constitution of the Commonwealth, as amended by art. 74 of the Amendments, and (b) rejected the only substantive challenge to Proposition 2½ which the judge concluded was properly before him. We granted a request for an expeditious, direct appeal to this court. We agree with each of the judge's rulings challenged in this court.

....

Proposition 2½

Proposition 2½ (St.1980, c. 580) is entitled "An Act Limiting State and Local Taxation and Expenditures." Certain of its sections place limitations on the amount of tax or other revenue permitted to be collected. Thus, for example, the maximum motor vehicle excise payable to cities and towns is reduced from $66.00 to $25.00 per $1,000 of valuation. G. L. c. 60A, § 1, as amended by St.1980, c. 580, § 9. Proposition 2½ grants a tax deduction in the calculation of a taxpayer's State income tax in an amount equal to one-half of the rent paid for his or her principal place of residence. G. L. c. 62, § 3B(*a*)(9), inserted by St.1980, c. 580, § 11. A somewhat different provision limits charges and fees for goods provided or services rendered by a city, town, or other governmental agency to the "cost of furnishing such goods or providing such services." G. L. c. 59, § 20A, inserted by St.1980, c. 580, § 12.

Most significantly, Proposition 2½ places a limitation on the total taxes permitted to be assessed annually on a municipality's real or personal property. G. L. c. 59, § 21C, inserted by St.1980, c. 580, § 1. The total annual assessments of most cities and towns may not exceed 2½% of the full and fair cash valuation of their real and personal property, unless that percentage is increased by a two-thirds vote at a general election. G. L. c. 59, § 21C(1). See G. L. c. 59, § 21C(4). If a municipality exceeds 2½% "on the effective date of the enactment of [§ 21C]," the municipality need not necessarily lower its total assessments to 2½% immediately. It must reduce its assessments annually by not less than 15% of the total taxes assessed in the fiscal year of that effective date until it reaches the level of 2½%. G. L. c. 59, § 21C(2). If a municipality's total assessments were less than 2½% of the full and fair cash valuation of its property in fiscal year 1979, it must use that lesser percentage in lieu of 2½%. G. L. c. 59, § 21C(3). There is also a provision limiting increases in tax assessments in each successive year to 2½% of the preceding year's assessments but authorizing an increase in that percentage by a two-thirds vote at a general election. G. L. c. 59, § 21C(4). Also, the 2½% limitation, or any other applicable percentage limitation, may be reduced in a city or town by a majority vote at a general election. G. L. c. 59, § 21C(5).

Other portions of Proposition 2½ are concerned with freeing cities and towns from expenditures mandated by State law. Thus, the fiscal autonomy of school committees is abolished (see G. L. c. 71, §§ 16B and 34, as amended by and appearing in St.1980, c. 580, §§ 6 and 7 respectively), as is compulsory, binding arbitration of disputes involving a municipality and a collective-bargaining rep-

---

[5] This substantive challenge is to the renter's deduction, a deduction allowed, in computing a renter's State income tax liability, of one-half of the rent paid for the taxpayer's principal residence.

resentative of its police or firefighters (see St.1980, c. 580, § 10). There are extensive provisions concerned with preventing the involuntary imposition on cities and towns of certain direct service or cost obligations resulting from statutes and administrative rules or regulations. See G. L. c. 29, § 27C, inserted by St.1980, c. 580, § 2; G. L. c. 11, §§ 6 and 7, as appearing in and inserted by St.1980, c. 580, §§ 3 and 4, respectively. There is also a limitation on counties' and other government entities' charges to cities and towns. See G. L. c. 59, § 20A, inserted by St.1980, c. 580, § 12. Finally, Proposition 2½ authorizes cities and towns in certain circumstances to revoke their acceptance of certain provisions of the General Laws. See G. L. c. 4, § 4B, inserted by St.1980, c. 580, § 5.

. . . .

The Constitutionality of the Renter's Deduction

The plaintiffs challenge the constitutionality of the renter's deduction, a deduction from taxable income of fifty per cent of the rent paid by an individual who rents his principal place of residence in the Commonwealth. See St.1980, c. 580, § 11.[26] The argument is founded on two somewhat related theories: (1) the classification violates equal protection of the laws provisions of the Fourteenth Amendment to the Constitution of the United States and comparable principles expressed in the Constitution of the Commonwealth, and (2) the special classification of rent payers violates the uniformity and proportionality requirements of other provisions of the State Constitution, most particularly the requirements of uniformity set forth in art. 44 of the Amendments. Our analysis of these constitutional challenges is governed by the same principles that would govern our analysis if the measure had been adopted by the Legislature rather than through the initiative process. . . .

The plaintiffs' challenges based on a claimed violation of equal protection of the law principles are of no merit. The applicable standards in equal protection analysis under the Fourteenth Amendment to the Constitution of the United States and comparable provisions of the Constitution of the Commonwealth are well established. The essential point in that "[a] classification by a Legislature of property and persons for the purpose of taxation is not violative of . . . [the equal protection] clause of the Fourteenth Amendment so long as any basis of fact can be reasonably conceived showing that the distinction upon which it rests has a fair and rational relation to the object sought to be accomplished by the enactment, and so long as, the classification being valid, the State deals equally with all the members of the same class." *Frost v. Commissioner of Corps. & Taxation,* 363 Mass. 235, 248, 293 N.E.2d 862, appeal dismissed, 414 U.S. 803 . . . (1973), quoting from *Old Colony R. R. v. Assessors of Boston,* 309 Mass. 439, 446, 35 N.E.2d 246 (1941). A State's scope of discretion is especially wide in the field of taxation. . . . The line of cases in the Federal courts upholding this principle is

---

[26] Section 11 reads as follows:

Section 3 of Chapter 72 of the General Laws, as most recently amended by Chapter 599 of the Acts of 1977, is hereby further amended by adding after Part B (8) the following new sub-paragraph:
(9) In the case of an individual who rents his principal place of residence in the Commonwealth, an amount equal to fifty percent of such rent.

The reference to c. 72 of the General Laws is wrong. The reference should be to G.L. c. 62. Also, the reference to § 3B(8) of G.L. c. 62 should be to § 3B(a)(8) of G.L. c. 62.

lengthy. . . . The same is true of this court's cases. . . . The distinction between residential renters and non-renters is a rational one in equal protection terms. The people could easily have concluded that residential tenants should be given favored income tax treatment as a means of offsetting Federal tax advantages accorded home owners as well as State tax benefits that home owners could be expected to realize as a result of other provisions of Proposition 2½. In determining the rationality of an enactment for equal protection purposes, it is entirely appropriate to consider the effects in Massachusetts of Federal taxing measures. . . .

The plaintiffs' challenge to the renter's deduction as a violation of art. 44's requirement of uniformity is more substantial. We first discuss the relevant principles of law.

One effect of art. 44 was to withdraw from the scope of the proportionality requirement of Part II, c. 1, § 1, art. 4, whatever is rightly made subject to the income tax. . . . Thus, there is no requirement that levies on income and on property be proportional to each other. . . . In view of the diverse treatment of local property taxation within the Commonwealth, it would be impossible to achieve overall proportionality in the application of both local taxation of property and a Statewide income tax law. Article 44 does express, however, a rule of proportionality by requiring "a uniform rate throughout the Commonwealth upon incomes derived from the same class of property." See *Opinion of the Justices,* 354 Mass. 792, 794, 236 N.E.2d 882 (1968).

Turning to the issue before us, the plaintiffs argue that the uniformity required by art. 44 is destroyed by giving renters a deduction in determining their State income tax liability where home owners are given no reasonably parallel deduction, such as a deduction for local real estate taxes paid or for interest payments on mortgage obligations, or both. They point to opinions interpreting the proportionality requirement of Part II, c. 1, § 1, art. 4, to the effect that special treatment extended to a single class of taxpayer is impermissible. The plaintiffs further indicate that the renter's deduction does not fit into the pattern of exemptions that have previously been approved. See *Opinion of the Justices,* 324 Mass. 724, 731, 733, 85 N.E.2d 222 (1949), where exemptions from local property taxes are classified and discussed.

The Attorney General argues that the renter's deduction is a reasonable exemption authorized by art. 44. The "reasonable exemptions" provision of art. 44 does not authorize special treatment that undercuts the dominant requirement of uniformity in art. 44. See *Opinion of the Justices,* 354 Mass. 792, 794, 236 N.E.2d 882 (1968) (a deduction for certain political contributions not reasonable exemption or abatement under art. 44). However, "[t]he power of exemption implies to some extent the power of discrimination and of classification required by the best interests of society." *Opinion of the Justices,* 270 Mass. 593, 601, 170 N.E. 800 (1930). The only limitation on exemptions stated in art. 44 is that they be reasonable, but by implication they must not conflict with other provisions of the Constitution. . . . Exemptions from the income tax have been approved as reasonable. . . . "The Legislature surely has a considerable range of discretion within the bounds of reason . . . in establishing exemptions from the tax." *Daley v. State Tax Comm'n,* 376 Mass. 861, 865, 866, 383 N.E.2d 1140 (1978).

We reject as an adequate justification for the renter's deduction the fact that the Federal income tax law grants a residential property owner deductions for local property taxes assessed to and paid by him and for interest payments on his mortgage obligations. Further, we do not find the fact that Proposition 2½ is expected to reduce local property taxes for many home owners to be a reasonable basis for upholding the renter's deduction. While these circumstances, extraneous to the operation of the State income tax statutes, may be given some weight in the analysis of the reasonableness of the renter's deduction under art. 44, the requirement of uniformity and the reasonableness of any exemption must largely be tested and met within the scope of the income tax system itself.

Analyzing the reasonableness of the renter's deduction in relation to the operation of the Commonwealth's income tax provisions, we find reasonable justification for the deduction in the untaxed benefit, measured by the fair rental value, that a home owner receives in the use of his home. In order to reach our conclusion that the renter's deduction is reasonable, we need not decide that the fair rental value of a home owned by its occupant is income which could be subject to taxation under art. 44. It is sufficient to note that a home owner has invested assets in his home, that he derives an economic benefit from his occupancy of it, and that our income tax law does not impose any obligation on the home owner to make any tax payment on account of his receipt of that benefit.

Although practical considerations no doubt justify the failure to tax the fair rental value of residential real estate to its owner-occupant, it is clear that the home owner receives a tax-free benefit from the use of the equity in his home. If the taxpayer had invested his assets instead in securities, savings, or other property, he would expect to generate taxable income (assuming no other exemption). A person with $50,000 invested in his home pays no annual State income tax with respect to the benefit realized from that investment, whereas a home renter who also has $50,000 but invests it in stock, for example, will be taxed on the annual income from that investment.

In the absence of the renter's deduction, a rent payer is taxed on his income from the investment of his assets without the benefit of any "exemption" similar to that extended to the home owner. The renter's deduction tends to reduce the disparate treatment of the home owner and home renter in the operation of the income tax law. It has been said that the failure to tax imputed rents is a cause of inequity between home owners and renters that "might be cured by a special deduction for renters." B. I. Bittker & L. M. Stone, Federal Income Taxation 83 (5th ed. 1980). See also Note, Federal Income Tax Discrimination Between Homeowners and Renters: A Proposed Solution, 12 Ind.L.Rev. 583, 600-601 (1979); R. Goode, The Individual Income Tax 124 (Brookings Inst., rev. ed. 1976). Considering home owners' obligations to pay local real estate taxes, to maintain their premises, to pay for insurance, and to pay interest on their mortgages, the allowance of a deduction of one-half of the rent paid annually by a residential tenant appears reasonable in relation to the benefit the benefit a home owner receives from the tax-free use of his home. The command of uniformity expressed in art. 44 is at least as fully met with the renter's deduction as it was before the adoption of the renter's deduction.

Conclusion

We have considered all the challenges argued to us with respect to the rulings the judge reported for appellate review and find no error in those rulings. It is appropriate, therefore, that judgment be entered in the Superior Court declaring that Proposition $2^{1}/_{2}$ (St.1980, c. 580) was lawfully adopted through the initiative process of the Constitution of the Commonwealth and that the renter's deduction, provided for by G.L. c. 62, § 3B(a)(9), inserted by St.1980, c. 580, § 11, is, on its face, neither violative of the equal protection provisions of the

Constitution of the United States or of the Constitution of the Commonwealth, nor violative of the proportionality and uniformity requirements of the Constitution of the Commonwealth.

So ordered.

F. STATE ASSISTANCE TO LOCAL GOVERNMENTS

This discussion of local finances and borrowing has continually highlighted the growing fiscal pressures on local governments. These pressures are augmented by the substantial disparities in the revenue-raising capacity of local government units. For both of these reasons—growing financial pressures at the local level and persistent disparities in local government revenue-raising capacity—both the states and the national government have increasingly come to the rescue of local governments with programs of financial assistance for the support of local government programs. This section looks briefly at programs of financial assistance for local governments at the state level.

The financial extent of state assistance to local governments is presented in Advisory Commission on Intergovernmental Relations, State and Local Roles in the Federal System 55-58 (1982). Ninety percent of state aid to local governments in 1979 was in the form of categorical grants, practically all of which went to support local expenditures for education, highways, and public welfare. State grants for education made up about two thirds of this amount. Our focus here is on the remaining ten percent of state aid which is used for general local government support.

State financial support to some extent takes the form of state assistance for relief from local property taxes. The most popular of these programs is the so-called "circuit breaker," which provides property tax relief for elderly and low-income taxpayers in a large number of states (see *supra*). This relief is often provided by way of direct state grants to the taxpayer, thus avoiding any local losses in property tax revenue. *See* Advisory Commission on Intergovernmental Relations, Property Tax Circuit-Breakers: Current Status and Policy Issues (1975). Another growing form of state financial assistance is the payments made by some states to make up for losses in property tax revenues resulting from state-mandated tax exemptions of governmentally owned and charitable property. *See* Palmer & Shinn, *Compensatory Payment Plans in the States*, 48 St. Gov't 216 (1975).

In addition to these special property tax relief programs, several states also have general revenue sharing programs in which a portion of state revenues from selected state taxes is shared with local government units. Most of the taxes that are shared with local governments are state sales or similar taxes, although Michigan and New York share state personal income taxes with local government units. In most of these state aid programs the state allocation formula does not attempt to allocate state aid in order to achieve fiscal equalization among the local government units that are assisted, and sharing by population is the commonest form of allocation criterion in use. A compelling argument has been made that fiscal equalization should be the basis on which state aid programs should be constructed. *See* Curran & Krasniewski, *State Aid to Local Governments—What Form Should It Take?*, in 1974 Proceedings of the Sixty-Seventh Annual Conference on Taxation 218 (1975). These authors address the question of what kinds of fiscal equalization formulas should be used:

> Whenever equalization is addressed, an appropriate question is: What do we equalize? Tax burdens? Fiscal effort? Fiscal capacity? We feel that State reve-

nue sharing should be primarily directed toward equalization of local fiscal capacity. Emphasis on revenue raising ability rather than tax burden or effort achieves two ends. First, it guarantees the possibility of accomplishing what we have called a common level of service. Through unconditional State support, a "poor" local government can augment its own fiscal resources in order to bring its level of service delivery up to the common level. Second, this approach preserves local autonomy in the determination of local tax levels. If the residents of a local jurisdiction desire a package of governmental services which exceeds the common level, they may do so by increasing their own local tax burden. However, the State has no responsibility to reward such behavior. It merely insures the potential achievement of an equal level of local service.

Id. at 224.

In light of these suggestions, consider the following two state program criteria for the distribution of state financial aid:

(a) FLA. STAT. ANN. § 218.20-26. This program contains a three-factor apportionment formula for municipalities based on population as weighted by size, sales tax collections, and "the ratio of the relative local ability to raise revenues." *Id.* § 218.245. The third factor is determined as follows:

1. By dividing the per capita nonexempt assessed real and personal property valuation of all eligible municipalities by the per capita nonexempt real and personal property valuation of each eligible municipality.
2. By multiplying the population of an eligible municipality by the percentage applicable to that municipality as established under subparagraph 1.
3. By dividing the population, as recalculated to reflect the relative local ability, by the total recalculated population of all eligible municipalities in the state.

Id. § 218.245.

(b) ARIZ. REV. STAT. ANN. (state privilege tax):

After deducting from the taxes collected pursuant to this article . . . the appropriation made for expenses of the department in administering this article, the appropriation made to the department of economic security, the appropriation made to the municipalities, . . . forty per cent of the remaining amount in the account collected in each calendar month shall, . . . be credited by the state treasurer to the general fund of the state, and the other sixty per cent shall be paid by the state treasurer every calendar month to the several county treasurers of the state by averaging the following proportions:

1. The proportion that the assessed valuation used to determine secondary property taxes of each county, after deducting that part of such assessed valuation exempt from taxation at the beginning of the month for which the amount is to be paid, bears to the total assessed valuations used to determine secondary property taxes of all the counties after deducting that portion of such assessed valuations exempt from taxation at the beginning of the month for which the amount is to be paid.
2. The proportion that the tax monies collected during the calendar month within each county under this article . . . bear to the total tax monies collected under this article . . . throughout the state for the calendar month.

Id. § 42-1342. Tax-shared funds must be used first for the payment of principal and interest on outstanding county bonds and warrants before they are credited to the general county fund. *Id.* § 42-1344. There is no comparable provision for municipalities.

These formulas generally share state taxes on the basis of assessed valuation, weighted as in Florida by population. Is this a good index of fiscal capacity? Note that it does not take local needs into account, as they might be indicated by such factors as the age of the city, the extent of blight, the extent of poverty, or similar criteria. The Arizona law also distributes state sales tax revenues in part on the basis of local share of sales taxes collected. This factor appears to be based on a proportionality criterion. Could it be argued that the distribution of state funds should be inverse to the local share of sales taxes collected?

G. EXPENDITURES

This chapter has concentrated on the revenue side of state and local finances. We turn now to an examination of the spending side. Generally speaking, the types of limitations previously discussed apply to expenditures. This is particularly true of the public purpose doctrine which, as noted earlier, operates as a check on spending as well as taxation and borrowing. In addition, particular restrictions on spending that will be discussed include requirements for balanced budgets and legislative appropriations before funds can be expended.

1. STATE MANDATES

A by-product of the growing involvement of state governments in local affairs is the "baggage" that goes with any form of governmental assistance. One piece of baggage that often generates controversy because of its impact on local budgets and expenditures (cf. the Hancock Amendment discussion *supra*) is the state mandate, discussed in the following report:

ADVISORY COMMISSION ON INTERGOVERNMENTAL RELATIONS, STATE AND LOCAL ROLES IN THE FEDERAL SYSTEM 157, 162, 166-68 (1982)

Among the major friction points in state-local relations are state mandates—that is, state constitutional, legislative, executive, or administrative requirements or limitations on local government actions. Technological change, population mobility, and the rise of local fiscal emergencies, among other factors, have convinced state authorities of the need for tighter state control in some areas. Consequently, they have imposed mandates to ensure that certain important functions are performed throughout the state, that uniform standards of service prevail statewide, or that desirable social or economic goals are achieved. Often, however, they reflect state legislative inability to resist the pressures of local interest groups, particularly teachers, police, firefighters, and other employee unions. The fundamental issues are whether (and, if so, how much) state mandates shackle local governments and whether they are necessary to achieve state interests.

. . . .

Mandates may be classed in various ways. . . . An ACIR typology of *expenditure* mandates helps one to see why local governments consider them so onerous. Five major types of expenditure mandates are distinguished:

rules of the game mandates—relating to the organization and procedures of local government, e.g., the form of government, holding of local elections, and provisions of the criminal code that define crimes and call for certain punishment;

spillover mandates—dealing with new programs or enrichment of existing local government programs in highly intergovernmental areas such as education, health, welfare, hospitals, environment, and nonlocal transportation;

interlocal equity mandates—which require localities to act or refrain from acting to avoid injury to, or conflict with, neighboring jurisdictions, the areas including local land use regulations, tax assessment procedures and review, and environmental standards;

loss of local tax base mandates—where the state removes property or selected items from the local tax base, such as exemption of churches and schools from the property tax, and food and medicine from the sales tax; and

personnel benefit mandates—where the states set salary, wage levels, working conditions, or retirement benefits.

. . . .

State mandating of local governments varies among states as well as among functional activities and types of requirement and in impact. No nationwide data concerning all classes of state mandates have been collected. The most extensive were gathered in the 1976 ACIR nationwide survey of expenditure mandates in which several responsible sources in each state were surveyed. Responses indicated that in the 77 specific program areas listed, 22 states had 39 or more mandates requiring local expenditures. The most commonly mandated functions were solid waste disposal standards (45 states), special education programs (45 states), workman's compensation for local personnel other than police, fire, and education (42 states), and various provisions relating to retirement systems (35 or more states).

States with the most expenditure mandates were New York (60 out of 77 possibilities), California (52), Minnesota (51), and Wisconsin (50). The fewest expenditure mandates were imposed in border and southern states with West Virginia (8) and Alabama (11) having the least.

. . . .

Reflecting rising concern for local financial conditions and seeking to highlight the costs of proposed laws or rules, states began to attach fiscal notes to mandating legislation and to agency rules. These estimated the dollar cost to local governments of the state requirements. By 1977, a total of 22 states had attached fiscal notes to mandating legislation. In addition, Alaska's constitution established limits on mandates and California, Louisiana, Montana, and Pennsylvania provided reimbursement for the local outlays required or for revenue losses.

By the end of 1979, the number of states requiring fiscal notes had increased to 36. Of these, most had a statutory basis while others handled them through legislative rules. In addition, Maryland—which had a fiscal note law requiring the impact statements to indicate the cost of legislation to the state government only—attached local financial impact statements to legislation as a matter of practice. Mandates imposed in the administrative process by agency rules and regulations were covered in only a few states, but the number was on the rise. In addition, the State of Washington established a reimbursement procedure for programs the state transfers to localities.

Although states are far less likely to reimburse local governments for the costs of state mandates than they are to require fiscal notes, the number of states providing for reimbursement is on the rise. By the end of 1979, 13 states had provisions for compensating their local units for the costs of the requirements they imposed, although compliance was mixed. It is apparent from these figures that states have become more responsive to local difficulties in financing the actions states have imposed upon them, but, to date, there is little evidence that they have curbed their penchant to mandate.

2. THE BUDGETING PROCESS

a. Operations

ADVISORY COMMISSION ON INTERGOVERNMENTAL RELATIONS, STATE & LOCAL ROLES IN THE FEDERAL SYSTEM 121-23 (1982)

The budget is the ultimate statement of any government's policy choices. In it are set out the allocation of public resources and the locus of costs—"who gets what." Moreover, the budget serves as a major management tool. In the process of compiling it, government programs can be reviewed and evaluated, their costs assessed, the desirability of expanding, reducing, or eliminating them considered, and efforts to improve productivity and responsiveness outlined. For the Governor, it constitutes an implement for influencing the course of public policy and a major mechanism for assuring control of the state administration.

The Governor's role in the budgetary process ordinarily involves responsibility for budget preparation and submission to the legislature and for general oversight to assure budget compliance once appropriation bills have been enacted. Both on these functions are performed by subordinates for the most part, although the chief executive can make the ultimate determinations. As discussed above, the Governor has authority for preparation and submission of the budget in all but three states.

Considerable attention has been given to the budget process in recent years as efforts to upgrade governmental efficiency and effectiveness have intensified. Productivity improvement has often resulted in changes. State budget officers have employed new managerial concepts such as performance budgeting, planning-programming-budgeting systems (PPBS), management-by-objective (MBO), program budgeting, and zero-based budgeting (ZBB) toward this end.

Types of Budget Innovations

Early attempts at improving budgetary processes were directed at the development of an executive budget in order to enhance the control of the Governor over state funds. Because Governors lacked the staff to exploit the budget for other management purposes, it became a control device. General practices revolved around line-item budgeting, incrementalism, and budget execution. Listing of proposed expenditures on a line-item basis provides a detailed breakdown of the goods and services being purchased with state dollars (salaries, supplies, travel, etc.) and increases central control of expenditures. Incrementalism focuses on the margin of increase over existing appropriations, using last year's budget as a base. Budget execution, with its emphasis on keeping track of the funds, consumed most of the resources of the budget staff.

Performance Budgeting

A move to a "performance budget" began in the 1950s, following the recommendation of the Hoover Commission (Commission on Organization of the Executive Branch of the Government) that the federal budgetary process be redesigned. The commission recommended that the focus be on

> ... The general character and relative importance of the work to be done, or upon the service to be rendered, rather than upon the things acquired, such as personal services, supplies, equipment, and so on. These latter objects are, after all, only the means to an end. The all-important thing in budgeting is the work or service to be accomplished, and what that work or service will cost.

The commission's report, along with that of the "Little Hoover Commissions" established shortly thereafter in many states, gave impetus to the adoption of performance budgeting. According to Allen Schick, 33 states had adopted performance budgeting, at least to some degree, by 1971. Many of these systems were not true performance budgeting systems although they incorporated some of the concepts. They often retained elements of the old line-item practices. While the changes brought improvement to state budgeting, they failed to achieve their major aims.

PPBS

[The report describes the planning-programming-budgeting systems introduced to government by former Secretary of Defense Robert McNamara. PPBS emphasized the identification of objectives, anticipation of future implications, consideration of all pertinent costs and systematic analysis of alternative methods for achieving the objectives. After an initial surge of interest by the states, the movement lost steam because of serious difficulties in using PPBS. Its formalities, emphasis on long-term planning, and decisionmaking by executives were difficult for states where the emphasis was on year-to-year budgeting with heavy legislative involvement.—Eds.]

Zero-Base Budgeting

A new wave of innovation brought zero-base budgeting to the states. In contrast to PPBS, first used at the federal level, ZBB had its first public usage in the states. Like PPBS, it is a planning-oriented process. Beginning with the objectives to be accomplished, it attempts to develop an efficient operating plan and budget. The two major steps involved are: (1) designing and ranking packages of decisions that reflect several possible levels of activity of the organization concerned, the financial requirements needed to support each possible level of activity, and other relevant management data; and (2) establishing priorities for these decision packages. In the use of this system, line-item data can be retained.

ZBB, like other budgeting systems, has had problems. One writer termed it a fraud. Some practitioners feel that the paperwork requirements consume too much time under an annual budget cycle. More importantly, policy issues are often submerged because the process is not sufficiently effectiveness-oriented. Nevertheless, it has had enough success that states continue to adopt it.

State Usage

The hybrid budgeting systems under which most states operate make categorization almost impossible. As states adopted, then abandoned, performance budgeting, PPBS, ZBB, or parts of these systems, they were left with increasingly variegated systems, tailored to suit their own needs.

A survey of state budget officers conducted in 1977 found that, of the 40 officers responding, 33 indicated a significant change in their budgetary process over the previous ten years: Eleven replied that they had adopted PPBS/program budgeting processes; nine indicated the use of ZBB or modified ZBB systems; 12 specified that they had adopted modified systems combining elements of the others; and New York was the single state to adopt a management-by-objective system. Impacts on the budget process were set out as follows:

> An analysis of the questionnaires showed that the budget directors in these states and jurisdictions perceived *policy* impacts or changes in budgetary

emphasis as a result of the budget process change. However, operationally, the budgetary process seldom changed. For example, in the 11 PPBS/program budget states and jurisdictions, a statistically significant number of budget directors indicated a greater emphasis was being given to strategic planning and output effectiveness after the introduction of the budget change. It was further indicated that these changes in emphasis resulted in a greater centralization of budgetary decisionmaking, an improved flow of information for decisionmaking, and greater innovativeness by agencies. Yet, additional analysis of the questionnaires revealed that no statistically significant changes occurred in the recruiting patterns of the budget office nor in the functional distribution of time and effort by the budget office. Similar patterns were found for respondents classified as ZBB and modification states and jurisdictions. Consequently, as far as the budget office is concerned, it might be concluded that budget process changes were more form than substance.

Because of the difficulty of reaching definitive conclusions about the changes that had occurred, the investigators conducted case studies in nine states. These studies underscored the conclusions that budget offices in each state "continue to emphasize financial control." While the changes were aimed at focusing greater attention upon policy analysis, planning, information organization, and evaluation, this goal had been reached in only a limited number of states. Financial control remained the primary priority.

b. Capital Improvements

Planners have long argued that capital improvements decisions represent significant policy choices for local governments and should be recognized as such. A study conducted by the American Society of Planning Officials (now American Planning Association) noted the high costs of capital improvements (over $27.5 billion in 1974-1975) and the impact they can have on change in a community. Water and sewer lines, highways and schools have major secondary effects on development by serving as catalysts for private investment. American Society of Planning Officials, Local Capital Improvements and Development Management Literature Synthesis, at iv (1977). The ASPO (APA) study described capital improvements programs and projects as follows:

1. What is a Capital Improvements Program?

The National Council on Governmental Accounting has defined the capital improvements program as follows:

A plan for capital expenditures to be incurred each year over a fixed period of years to meet capital needs arising from the long-term work program or otherwise. It sets forth each project or other contemplated expenditure in which the local government is to have a part and specifies the full resources estimated to be available to finance the projected expenditures.

Capital improvements programs vary from the simple to the extremely complex, depending on the size of the governmental unit and the sophistication of the participants. The time period covered by the CIP may range from one year to 20 years; the majority cover six years. In many cases, the first year of the CIP is called the capital budget. A capital budget can generally be thought of as the link between the longer term capital improvements program and the current annual budget and appropriation process used by most governmental units. Most governmental units update the CIP annually.

[The report notes that the CIP serves as a link between planning and development, as well as a basis for estimating capital requirements, scheduling capital projects, establishing priorities, coordinating scheduling and monitoring the progress of capital projects.—Eds.]

2. *What is a Capital Improvement Project?*

The definitions of a "capital improvement project" vary between different sized governmental units and different levels of local government. A capital improvement project is most broadly defined as any major project requiring the expenditure of public funds (over and above operating expenditure of public funds) for the purchase, construction or replacement of the physical assets of the community. In most cases this includes land necessary for a project. Generally, a capital improvement project has a "useful life" of over one year and has a significant value which may be defined from $5,000 upward, depending on the size of the governmental unit. Projects may range from the costly airports, highways, and sewers and treatment plants, to hospitals, fire and police stations, parks, tennis courts, and street lights.

[The ASPO report identified a number of methods used to finance capital improvements, including current revenue (pay as you go), reserve funds, general obligation and revenue bonds (issued by the general purpose government or by special purpose authorities or districts), special assessments, tax increment financing, and state or federal grants.—Eds.]

As the ASPO report notes, capital improvement budgeting is closely related to land use planning, although the two have been viewed separately by state and local decision-makers. In recent years, a number of attempts have been made to link the budgeting process with the land use planning process. The following case considers the constitutionality of a well-known growth management plan of this type. The court's discussion of statutory authority and zoning exclusion problems has been omitted. This excerpt considers the argument that the timing of land development in accordance with a capital budget program was a taking of property.

GOLDEN v. PLANNING BOARD OF RAMAPO

Court of Appeals of New York
30 N.Y.2d 359, 285 N.E.2d 291, *appeal dismissed,* 409 U.S. 1003 (1972)

SCILEPPI, JUDGE.

. . . .

Experiencing the pressures of an increase in population and the ancillary problem of providing municipal facilities and services, the Town of Ramapo, as early as 1964, made application for grant under section 801 of the Housing Act of 1964 (78 U.S.Stat. 769) to develop a master plan. The plan's preparation included a four-volume study of the existing land uses, public facilities, transportation, industry and commerce, housing needs and projected population trends. The proposals appearing in the studies were subsequently adopted pursuant to section 272-a of the Town Law, Consol.Laws, c. 62, in July, 1966 and implemented by way of a master plan. The master plan was followed by the adoption of a comprehensive zoning ordinance. Additional sewage district and drainage studies were undertaken which culminated in the adoption of a capital budget, providing for the development of the improvements specified in the master plan within the next six years. Pursuant to section 271 of the Town Law, authorizing comprehensive planning, and as a supplement to the capital budget, the Town Board adopted a capital program which provides for the location and sequence of additional capital improvements for the 12 years following the life of the capital budget. The two plans, covering a period of 18 years, detail the capital improvements projected for maximum development and conform to the specifications set forth in the master plan, the official map and drainage plan.

Based upon these criteria, the Town subsequently adopted the subject amendments for the alleged purpose of eliminating premature subdivision and urban sprawl. Residential development is to proceed according to the provision of adequate municipal facilities and services, with the assurance that any concomitant restraint upon property use is to be of a "temporary" nature and that other private uses, including the construction of individual housing, are authorized.

The amendments did not rezone or reclassify any land into different residential or use districts, but, for the purposes of implementing the proposals appearing in the comprehensive plan, consist, in the main, of additions to the definitional sections of the ordinance, section 46-3, and the adoption of a new class of "Special Permit Uses", designated "Residential Development Use." "Residential Development Use" is defined as "The erection or construction of dwellings [on] any vacant plots, lots or parcels of land" (§ 46-3, as amd.); and, any person who acts so as to come within that definition, "shall be deemed to be engaged in residential development which shall be a separate use classification under this ordinance and subject to the requirement of obtaining a special permit from the Town Board" (§ 46-3, as amd.).

The standards for the issuance of special permits are framed in terms of the availability to the proposed subdivision plat of five essential facilities of services; specifically (1) public sanitary sewers or approved substitutes; (2) drainage facilities; (3) improved public parks or recreation facilities, including public schools; (4) State, county or town roads — major, secondary or collector; and, (5) firehouses. No special permit shall issue unless the proposed residential development has accumulated 15 development points, to be computed on a sliding scale of values assigned to the specified improvements under the statute. Subdivision is thus a function of immediate availability to the proposed plat of certain municipal improvements; the avowed purpose of the amendments being to phase residential development to the Town's ability to provide the above facilities or services.

Certain savings and remedial provisions are designed to relieve . . . potentially unreasonable restrictions. Thus, the board may issue special permits vesting a present right to proceed with residential development in such year as the development meets the required point minimum, but in no event later than the final year of the 18-year capital plan. The approved special use permit is fully assignable, and improvements scheduled for completion within one year from the date of an application are to be credited as though existing on the date of the application. A prospective developer may advance the date of subdivision approval by agreeing to provide those improvements which will bring the proposed plat within the number of development points required by the amendments. And applications are authorized to the "Development Easement Acquisition Commission" for a reduction of the assessed valuation. Finally, upon application to the Town Board, the development point requirements may be varied should the board determine that such a variance or modification is consistent with the on-going development plan.

The undisputed effect of these integrated efforts in land use planning and development is to provide an over-all program of orderly growth and adequate facilities through a sequential development policy commensurate with progressing availability and capacity of public facilities. . . .

The proposed amendments have the effect of restricting development for onwards to 18 years in certain areas. Whether the subject parcels will be so restricted for the full term is not clear, for it is equally probable that the proposed facilities will be brought into these areas well before that time. Assuming, however, that the restrictions will remain outstanding for the life of the program, they still fall short of a confiscation within the meaning of the Constitution.

An ordinance which seeks to permanently restrict the use of property so that it may not be used for any reasonable purpose must be recognized as a taking: The only difference between the restriction and an outright taking in such a case "is that the restriction leaves the owner subject to the burden of payment of taxation, while outright confiscation would relieve him of that burden". . . . An appreciably different situation obtains where the restriction constitutes a *temporary* restriction, promising that the property may be put to a profitable use within a reasonable time. The hardship of holding unproductive property for some time might be compensated for by the ultimate benefit inuring to the individual owner in the form of a substantial increase in valuation; or, for that matter, the landowner might be compelled to chafe under the temporary restriction, without the benefit of such compensation, when that burden serves to promote the public good. . . .

We are reminded, however, that these restrictions threaten to burden individual parcels for as long as a full generation and that such a restriction cannot, in any context, be viewed as a temporary expedient. The Town, on the other hand, contends that the landowner is not deprived of either the best use of his land or of numerous other appropriate uses, still permitted within various residential districts, including the construction of a single-family residence, and consequently, it cannot be deemed confiscatory. Although no proof has been submitted on reduction of value, the landowners point to obvious disparity between the value of the property, if limited in use by the subject amendments and its value for residential development purposes, and argue that the diminution is so considerable that for all intents and purposes the land cannot presently or in the near future be put to profitable or beneficial use, without violation of the restrictions.

Every restriction on the use of property entails hardships for some individual owners. Those difficulties are invariably the product of police regulation and the pecuniary profits of the individual must in the long run be subordinated to the needs of the community. . . . The fact that the ordinance limits the use of, and may depreciate the value of the property will not render it unconstitutional, however, unless it can be shown that the measure is either unreasonable in terms of necessity or the diminution in value is such as to be tantamount to a confiscation. . . . Diminution, in turn, is a relative factor and though its magnitude is an indicia of a taking, it does not of itself establish a confiscation. . . .

Without a doubt restrictions upon the property in the present case are substantial in nature and duration. They are not, however, absolute. The amendments contemplate a definite term, as the development points are designed to operate for a maximum period of 18 years and during that period, the Town is committed to the construction and installation of capital improvements. The net result of the on-going development provision is that individual parcels may be committed to a residential development use prior to the expiration of the maximum period. Similarly, property owners under the terms of the amendments may elect to accelerate the date of development by installing, at their own expense, the necessary public services to bring the parcel within the required number of development points. While even the best of plans may not always be realized, in the absence of proof to the contrary, we must assume the Town will put its best effort forward in implementing the physical and fiscal timetable outlined under the plan. Should subsequent events prove this assumption unwarranted, or should the Town because of some unforeseen event fail in its primary obligation to these landowners, there will be ample opportunity to undo the restrictions upon default. For the present, at least, we are constrained to proceed upon the assumption that the program will be fully and timely implemented. . . .

Thus, . . . the present amendments propose restrictions of a certain duration and founded upon estimate determined by fact. Prognostication on our part in upholding the ordinance proceeds upon the presently permissible inference that within a reasonable time the subject property will be put to the desired use at an appreciated value. In the interim assessed valuations for real estate tax purposes reflect the impact of the proposed restrictions. . . . The proposed restraints, mitigated by the prospect of appreciated value and interim reductions in assessed value, and measured in terms of the nature and magnitude of the project undertaken, are within the limits of necessity.

In sum, where it is clear that the existing physical and financial resources of the community are inadequate to furnish the essential services and facilities which a substantial increase in population requires, there is a rational basis for "phased growth" and hence, the challenged ordinance is not violative of the Federal and State Constitutions. Accordingly, the order appealed from should be reversed and the actions remitted to Special Term for entry of a judgment declaring section 46-13.1 of the Town Ordinance constitutional.

BREITEL, JUDGE (dissenting). [Omitted.]

Comments: 1. *Ramapo* was the first case to uphold the constitutionality of a timed growth management program based on a capital budget program. Do you agree with the court's analysis of the taking issue? Was it important to the court's decision that the entire municipality was programmed for growth during the eighteen-year capital budget period? What if only some of the municipality had been programmed for growth during this period? For an extensive consideration of growth management problems see D. MANDELKER & R. CUNNINGHAM, PLANNING AND CONTROL OF LAND DEVELOPMENT ch. 7 (1979).

2. Is *Ramapo* qualified by *Charles v. Diamond,* 360 N.E.2d 1295 (N.Y. 1977)? A village had provided sewer service, and a local ordinance required developers to connect with the village sewer system. While the village had issued a building permit to a developer who sought connection with the village system, the state environmental agency informed the developer that it could not connect to the village system until deficiencies in the system had been corrected, and likewise instructed the county health department to refuse a system connection. The developer then brought an action against the state and county agencies and the village contending that their actions amounted to an unconstitutional appropriation of its property.

While remanding the case for trial because the record had not been sufficiently developed to decide the constitutional issues, the New York highest court noted that temporary restrictions on development because of service difficulties were justified, but that permanent restrictions were not. A series of factors were identified to determine how long a restriction on development for this reason could last, including the extent of the sewer problem, the ability of the community to raise the necessary capital, and the role of the state and federal governments. An extensive delay would be justified "only if the remedial steps are of sufficient magnitude to require extensive preparations, including preliminary studies, applications for assistance to other governmental entities, the raising of large amounts of capital, and the letting of work contracts." *Id.* at 1301.

Noting that it had accepted development delays of up to eighteen years in the *Ramapo* decision, the court then noted that "the crucial factor, perhaps even the decisive one, is whether the ultimate cost of the benefit is being shared by the members of the community at large, or, rather, is being hidden from the public by the placement of the entire burden upon particular property owners." *Id.* at 1300. The court also commented in *Charles,* again citing *Ramapo,* that the municipality "must be committed firmly to the construction and installation of the necessary improvements." *Id.* at 1301.

Capital improvement budgeting is an attempt to provide an orderly basis for the provision of capital improvements consistent with revenue resources. Local governments must also meet obligations imposed under the federal Constitution's equal protection clause, which a court may apply to reorder local capital expenditures. The following case is the leading decision on the equal protection problem:

HAWKINS v. TOWN OF SHAW

United States Court of Appeals
437 F.2d 1286 (5th Cir. 1971)

TUTTLE, CIRCUIT JUDGE:

Referring to a portion of town or a segment of society as being "on the other side of the tracks" has for too long been a familiar expression to most Americans. Such a phrase immediately conjures up an area characterized by poor housing, overcrowded conditions and, in short, overall deterioration. While there may be many reasons why such areas exist in nearly all of our cities, one reason that cannot be accepted is the discriminatory provision of municipal services based on race. It is such a reason that is alleged as the basis of this action.

Appellants are Negro citizens of the Town of Shaw, Mississippi. They alleged that the town has provided various municipal services including street paving and street lighting, sanitary sewers, surface water drainage as well as water mains and fire hydrants in a discriminatory manner based on race. Appellants brought a class action seeking injunctive relief under 42 U.S.C. § 1983 against the town, the town's mayor, clerk and five aldermen. After a three-day trial, the trial court applied the traditional equal protection standard despite the presence of appellants' undisputed statistical evidence which we feel clearly showed a substantial qualitative and quantitative inequity in the level and nature of services accorded "white" and "black" neighborhoods in Shaw. The court stated:

> If actions of public officials are shown to have rested upon rational considerations, irrespective of race or poverty, they are not within the condemnation of the Fourteenth Amendment, and may not be properly condemned upon judicial review. Persons or groups who are treated differently must be shown to be similarly situated and their unequal treatment demonstrated to be *without any rational basis* or based upon an invidious factor such as race. 303 F.Supp. 1162, 1168 (N.D.Miss.1969). (Emphasis added.)

Because this court has long adhered to the theory that "figures speak and when they do, Courts listen," *Brooks v. Beto,* 366 F.2d 1, 9 (1966), ... we feel that appellants clearly made out a prima facie case of racial discrimination. The trial court thus erred in applying the traditional equal protection standard, for as this

Court and the Supreme Court have held: "Where racial classifications are involved, the Equal Protection and Due Process Clauses of the Fourteenth Amendment 'command a more stringent standard' in reviewing discretionary acts of state or local officers. *Jackson v. Godwin,* 400 F.2d 529, 537 (5th Cir., 1968)." In applying this test, defendants' actions may be justified only if they show a compelling state interest. *Loving v. Virginia,* 388 U.S. 1, . . . (1967). We have thoroughly examined the evidence and conclude that no such compelling interests could possibly justify the gross disparities in services between black and white areas of town that this record reveals.

Facts

The Town of Shaw, Mississippi, was incorporated in 1886 and is located in the Mississippi Delta. Its population, which has undergone little change since 1930, consists of about 2,500 people—1,500 black and 1,000 white residents. Residential racial segregation is almost total. There are 451 dwelling units occupied by blacks in town, and, of these, 97% (439) are located in neighborhoods in which no whites reside. That the town's policies in administering various municipal services have led to substantially less attention being paid to the black portion of town is clear.

Nearly 98% of all homes that front on unpaved streets in Shaw are occupied by blacks. Ninety-seven percent of the homes not served by sanitary sewers are in black neighborhoods. Further, while the town has acquired a significant number of medium and high intensity mercury vapor street lighting fixtures, every one of them has been installed in white neighborhoods. The record further discloses that similar statistical evidence of grave disparities in both the level and kinds of services offered regarding surface water drainage, water mains, fire hydrants, and traffic control apparatus was also brought forth and not disputed. Finally, it was alleged that this disparity was the result of a long history of racial discrimination.

Surely, this was enough evidence to establish a prima facie case of racial discrimination. The only question that remains to be examined is whether or not these disparities can possibly be justified by any compelling state interests. As we have already indicated, an examination of the record reveals they cannot. . . .

Relief

In reaching this decision and in fashioning an appropriate remedy, we are not unaware of the fundamental institutional problems involved. The need for judicially discoverable and manageable standards as well as an awareness of the distinctions between the roles played by the coordinate branches of government must, of course, be foremost in our mind. Nevertheless, having carefully considered the problems involved, we feel this case warrants judicial intervention.

The Town of Shaw, indeed any town, is not immune to the mandates of the Constitution. As Mr. Justice White noted in *Avery v. Midland County,* 390 U.S. 474 at 480 . . . (1967):

> A city, town, or county may no more deny the equal protection of the laws than it may abridge freedom of speech, establish an official religion, arrest without probable cause, or deny due process of law.

In concluding that an equal protection violation has occurred, we have not, of course, been guided by a statutory set of standards or regulations clearly defining how many paved streets or what kind of sewerage system a town like Shaw should have. We have, however, been able to utilize what we consider a most reliable yardstick—namely, the quality and quantity of municipal services provided in the white area of town. As the record reveals, this is an area which, for the most part, does not significantly differ in need or expectations from the black portion of town. Making a comparison between these two areas is hardly an insuperable judicial task. Indeed, we are dealing with some of the most basic amenities of urban life and the disparities are by no means slight.

Yet, it may also be argued that even though this court has adequate standards to determine fairly that municipal services have been allocated in a discriminatory manner, the correction of this problem is not a judicial function. We disagree. The separation of powers principle assumes that we have a system of checks and balances. In Madisonian terms, each department or power center is to act as a curb on other departments or centers. Indeed, "unless these departments be so far connected and blended, as to give to each a constitutional control over the others, the degree of separation which the maxim requires as essential to a free government, can never in practice, be duly maintained." Madison, The Federalist, No. 48. Utilizing the power vested in this court to check an abuse of state or municipal power is, in effect, consistent with the separation of powers principle.

In so doing, however, we are, by no means, the first court to exercise such power as to municipal actions. When confronted with a similar case, the court in *Hadnot v. City of Prattville,* 309 F. Supp. 967 (D.C.Ala.1970), found discrimination in the provision of various facilities in municipal parks. The court ordered the city to equalize the "equipment, facilities and services" provided in a park located in a black neighborhood with those provided in parks located in white neighborhoods. In *Gautreaux v. Chicago Housing Authority,* 304 F.Supp. 736 (N.D.Ill.1969), the court found discrimination in the administration of a public housing program and assumed a major role in implementing desegregation by issuing a comprehensive and specific order for integrating the public housing system. See also, *Kennedy Park Homes Assoc. v. City of Lackawanna,* D.C., 318 F.Supp. 669.

We feel that issuing a specific order outlining exactly how the equalization of municipal services should occur is neither necessary nor proper in the context of this case. We do require, however, that the Town of Shaw, itself, submit a plan for the court's approval detailing how it proposes to cure the results of the long history of discrimination which the record reveals. We are confident that the municipal authorities can, particularly because they so staunchly deny any racial motivation, propose a program of improvements that will, within a reasonable time, remove the disparities that bear so heavily on the black citizens of Shaw....

[The court en banc heard further argument, then reaffirmed the panel judgment. Portions of the dissenting opinion of the court en banc follow.—Eds.]

RONEY, CIRCUIT JUDGE (with whom SIMPSON and CLARK, CIRCUIT JUDGES join, dissenting):

At the outset it seems to me that we must recognize the inherent uniqueness, in the Equal Protection context, of cases involving those municipal services which require capital expenditures. The provision of municipal services to the property of residents is largely a question of priorities which our system of government conceives should be determined by elected officials responsive to the people. The daily news media well portray the difficulties every city is having in establishing such priorities. It is doubtful that any priority determination could ever be justified on the compelling interest standard as laid down by the cases which fathered the doctrine. In the provision of streets, sewers, lights, water and other facilities, given limited resources, the city simply has to start with something some place. As municipal improvements are originated, installed, repaired, improved and modernized, it is intrinsic to the process that at any given point of time services will be unequal, a condition which probably does not serve any compelling interest. While there could be no compelling state interest in starting with the provision of services in the white areas of a town with segregated neighborhoods, neither could there be a compelling state interest to start any other particular place. Even if there is a compelling reason for a given priority, it is questionable, if this is tantamount to a compelling state interest. For the law to require that the town must show a compelling interest to justify the priorities it establishes in making capital improvements simply requires the impossible. For the Courts to assume control of those priorities merely results in substituting one non-compelling list of priorities for another. . . .

[On remand, the district court ordered the Town of Shaw to formulate a plan to equalize municipal services. Following extensive negotiations between the parties, a plan was presented which was approved by the court. The plan required the Town of Shaw to establish new water mains, fire hydrants, street lights, sanitary sewer system, storm water drainage grades and ditches, and to pave more than thirty separate streets. A three-year timetable was established and the project was to be financed through general revenue sharing funds and use of eighty-five percent of the town's expected cash surplus. Inflation took its toll and project costs increased from an estimated quarter of a million dollars to approximately one half million dollars. *See generally* FORDHAM, LOCAL GOVERNMENT LAW 505-55 (1975).—Ed.]

Comments: 1. What happens if the board of aldermen refuses to implement the plan? Suppose severe cost overruns occur. If a bond issue is proposed and the people vote it down, then what? The extent of judicial power to fashion remedies that affect the legislative process is discussed in Chapter 10. *See also City of Camden v. Byrne,* 411 A.2d 462 (N.J. 1980), discussed *infra.*

2. Post-*Hawkins* developments are discussed in the following excerpt from an extensive analysis of racial discrimination in the provision of services:

Hawkins v. Town of Shaw and its progeny are simple in concept. In the *Hawkins* line of cases, blacks or some other minorities are concentrated in one or more parts of a city (or it could be a county, school district, special district, or some other local governmental entity) and whites live in other parts. The minorities present proof in court that facilities and services provided by the governmental entity in the minority areas of the city are inferior to those provided in the white areas.

. . . .

Much to the chagrin of egalitarians, however, in a seven-to-two decision, the United States Supreme Court ruled in *Washington v. Davis* [426 U.S. 229 (1976)] that racially disproportionate impact, while relevant, would not, without other evidence of a racially discriminatory purpose, invoke strict judicial scrutiny of equal protection challenges. The Court expressly disapproved of cases, such as *Hawkins,* which "rested on or expressed the view that proof of discriminatory racial purpose is unnecessary in making out an equal protection violation . . . ." Fortunately, in view of the difficulty of producing direct evidence of discriminatory intent, the Court elaborated:

[I]nvidious discriminatory purpose may . . . be inferred from the totality of relevant facts [which] may for all practical purposes demonstrate unconstitutionality because in various circumstances the discrimination is very difficult to explain on nonracial grounds.

As a result, *Hawkins* can still be read as meeting the *Davis* standard.... Whether a race case is provable or not is another question, but a statement of fact concerning unequal services and an allegation that the differences stem from racial distinctions can at least survive a motion to dismiss. Therefore, when statistics show that services to minority areas are substantially inferior to those in white areas in town, the defendant town may find itself ordered to equalize services unless it provides some explanation.

Statistics, however, are not always supportive. For example the Urban Institute conducted an empirical study in connection with a Fairfax County, Virginia case, which alleged that black neighborhoods had substandard streets. The study showed that black neighborhoods did have substandard streets but so did neighborhoods with low housing values, low population densities, and low rates of home ownership. The study concluded that when these other factors were taken into account, substandard streets and racial characteristics did not correlate in a statistically significant way.

Although discrimination on the basis of race might not be provable in court, that does not preclude a political response. The Fairfax County case was settled when the State of Virginia and Fairfax County agreed to spend an additional $1 million to improve eighty-nine roads in the county's predominantly black neighborhoods.

[Several years after the settlement, a dispute developed with black residents not party to the settlement over acquisition of rights-of-way to widen some of the streets as required to bring the streets into the Virginia secondary highway system so that the State Highway Department would be responsible for maintenance. Believing it had no authority under state law to spend funds for maintenance of roads not eligible for inclusion in the secondary highway system, the county repudiated the settlement agreement. For a history of the case, see *Fairfax Countywide Citizens Ass'n v. Fairfax County,* 571 F.2d 1299 (4th Cir. 1978), in which the court held the settlement agreement was a private contract not subject to federal jurisdiction because it had not been incorporated into the court order dismissing the case.—Eds.]

If a city spends less in minority areas than in white areas, or facilities such as parks are relatively inadequate in black areas, then a case of racial discrimination may be made out. [*Hadnot v. City of Prattville,* 309 F. Supp. 967 (M.D. Ala. 1970).] But if inputs are equal, a city is not discriminating racially just because the output is not equal, as, for example, where a public park is vandalized in the minority community. [*Beal v. Lindsay,* 468 F.2d 287, 290-91 (2d Cir. 1972).] The closing of fire stations in minority areas might be justified by showing the closing of some stations was necessitated by lowered funding and that the choice of stations to be closed was based on minimizing response time from the remaining stations. [*Towns v. Beame,* 386 F. Supp. 470, 474 (S.D.N.Y. 1974).]

Even if the court finds inequality, if steps are being taken to remedy past inequities by concentrating funds in minority areas, applying for grants for those areas, and otherwise proceeding in good faith, the court will be reluctant to give further relief. No court, for example, is likely to order the local government to divert the entire municipal budget to equalize capital facilities immediately or to issue bonds to provide capital facilities immediately. The most that a court is likely to require is a plan to spend more than an equal amount in minority areas to make up for past discrimination, leaving the details to the discretion of the local government officials so long as they proceed in good faith. If grant funds to be directed to minority areas are diverted elsewhere, the diversion can be enjoined. And the availability of general revenue sharing funds may lead a court to order their expenditure in more poorly serviced minority areas, thus speeding the process of equalization. Where services rather than facilities are involved, evidence that services were unequal in the past, but have been subsequently equalized, will not support court intervention to ensure that they continue to be provided equally. [*Burner v. Washington,* 399 F. Supp. 44, 48 (D.D.C. 1975).]

Hagman, *The Use of Boundary Lines to Discriminate in the Provision of Services by Race,* 54 J. Urb. L. 849, 865-69 (1977).

3. As Professor Hagman noted, *Washington v. Davis* made the *Hawkins* type of case much more difficult to prove but did not eliminate the possiblity of such action. Efforts continue but for the most part have been unsuccessful. See *Mlikotin v. City of Los Angeles,* 643 F.2d 652 (9th Cir. 1981) (allegation that city has not distributed services in an equal manner, without more, does not state a claim upon which relief can be granted); *Collins v. Town of Goshen,* 635 F.2d 954 (2d Cir. 1980) (no invidious discrimination in plan to provide water to a particular development by water district managed by officials elected by entire town); *Village of Riverwoods v. Untermyer,* 369 N.E.2d 1385 (Ill. 1977) (ordinance requiring connections to sanitary sewer system in one portion of village while permitting septic tanks in other portions upheld); *Bonnet v. State,* 357 A.2d 772 (N.J.L. 1976) (state system requiring counties to share costs of certain state services such as courts, prosecutors, jury commissioners, probation department, and percentage of benefits under certain welfare benefits upheld despite heavy statistical attack focusing on relatively high local tax burden in urban areas).

The court did find that a *Hawkins* case had been proved in a case brought against a small Florida city in which an ordinance in force until 1968 required blacks to live "on the south side of the railroad tracks." *Dowdell v. City of Apopka,* 698 F.2d 1181 (11th Cir. 1983). The court found a "magnitude of ... disparity" in municipal expenditures explicable only on racial grounds and a half-century pattern of decisionmaking indicating "a deliberate deprivation of services to the black community."

4. In *Town of Goshen, supra* Comment 3, plaintiffs claimed that the water service plan effectively disenfranchised them with respect to the determination of the appropriate level of municipal services. Voting rights questions have an important bearing on municipal services issues, particularly if disputes over services are seen as nothing more than questions of priority, as the dissent in *Hawkins* argued. Developments in the voting rights area are discussed in Chapter 10.

3. APPROPRIATIONS

The actual expenditure of public funds is subject to specific state control. The basic control, found in state constitutions, prohibits any withdrawal of funds from the treasury except by appropriations made by the legislative body. *Cf.* Idaho Const., art. VII, § 13. In *Leonardson v. Moon,* 451 P.2d 542 (Idaho 1969), the Idaho Supreme Court, after reviewing the cases, defined an appropriation as "(1) authority from the legislature, (2) expressly given, (3) in legal form, (4) to proper officers, (5) to pay from public monies, (6) a specified sum, and no more, and (7) for a specified purpose, and no other." *Id.* at 550.

The appropriations process is linked to the budget process, with exceptions made for emergencies declared by the governor, as noted in the following provision from the Missouri Const., art. 4, § 25:

> Until it acts on all the appropriations recommended in the budget, neither house of the general assembly shall pass any appropriation other than emergency appropriations recommended by the governor.

States typically restrict appropriations by requiring a balanced budget. The New Jersey Constitution provides

> [n]o general appropriation law or other law appropriating money for any State purpose shall be enacted if the appropriation contained therein, together with all prior appropriations made for the same fiscal period, shall exceed the total amount of revenue on hand and anticipated which will be available to meet such appropriations during such fiscal period, as certified by the Governor.

N.J. Const. art. VIII, § II, par. 2. In addition, statutes restrict the power of state officials to incur indebtedness or otherwise bind the state without an appropriation.

> No state officer, employee, board, department or commission shall contract indebtedness on behalf of the state, nor assume to bind the state, in an amount in excess of money appropriated or otherwise lawfully available. This section shall not apply to a case where a statute expressly authorizes the making of a contract or contracts for a stated maximum amount which exceeds the money appropriated or otherwise available for payments thereon.

N.Y. State Finance Law § 41.

Similar provisions in state statutes and home rule charters govern the expenditures of local governments. One of the questions that often arises is the degree of flexibility such provisions give to public officials. The following case examines that issue in the context of a home rule provision requiring the adoption of an annual operating budget:

KRAHMER v. McCLAFFERTY

Superior Court of Delaware
288 A.2d 678 (1972)

Opinion

O'HARA, JUDGE.

Plaintiff, a taxpayer of the City of Wilmington, has initiated this suit seeking a Writ of Mandamus to compel the defendants, members of The Council of the City of Wilmington ("Council"), to enact an annual operating budget ordinance in compliance with the Home Rule Charter of the City of Wilmington ("Charter"). Defendants have moved for judgment on the pleadings. For purposes of this motion the Court assumes, as it must, that all of the allegations of plaintiff's complaint are true.

The Charter, § 2-300, requires defendants to adopt, on or before May 31 of each year, an annual operating budget for the fiscal year beginning July 1 thereafter. § 2-300(2) specifically provides:

> ... shall make appropriations to [specified branches of city government] ... and for all other items which are to be met out of the revenue of the city. All appropriations shall be made in lump sum amounts and according to the following classes of expenditures for each office, department, board or commission: (a) personal services, (b) materials, supplies and equipment, (c) debt service, (d) such additional classes as the mayor shall recommend in his proposed annual budget ordinance.

In 1971 prior to the deadline Council passed an annual operating budget ordinance which, in addition to other items, provided for an appropriation of $310,564.00 for "materials, supplies and equipment". The complaint alleges that in actual fact defendants intended to spend only about $49,510.00 for materials, supplies and equipment and the balance was intended for other purposes.

The complaint further contends that the defendants, members of the majority party, proposed by this device to, in effect, hold back an appropriated fund which Council could from time to time during the fiscal year appropriate to other uses for the purposes of gaining partisan political advantage.

Prior to the passage of the budget ordinance, Council was advised by the City Solicitor that it was not empowered to create such a "contingency fund", it not having been recommended by the Mayor. Disregarding such advice, defendants proceeded to the enactment of the ordinance including within it the questioned appropriation as indicated. Subsequent thereto the Mayor vetoed the appropriation allotted for materials, supplies and equipment and returned the ordinance to Council with a message pointing out what the Mayor designated as the illegality of the action of Council. The message of the Mayor was accompanied by a written opinion of the City Solicitor supporting the Mayor's conclusion. Thereafter the defendants overrode the Mayor's veto and passed the ordinance, including the questioned item, by a two-thirds vote. It is the contention of the complaint that in view of the circumstances of the passage of this ordinance that it was a knowing and deliberate falsehood on the part of Council.

The provisions of § 2-300(2) would seem to be a clear and unequivocal direction and authorization that Council had to make *all* its appropriations at once in the annual operating budget ordinance. This conclusion is reenforced by examination of § 2-301 which provides that "the Council may not make any operating appropriations in addition to those included in the annual operating budget ordinance (with specified exceptions not here applicable)".

The obligations imposed by § 2-300 are, generally speaking, mandatory and when violated may be enforced by mandamus. 15 McQuillen, Municipal Corporations (3rd Ed. 1970); 55 C.J.S. Mandamus § 139. The defendants herein rely, however, upon the general rule that a court may not inquire into the legislative motives of a legislative body. Defendants, applying this general rule, contend that the ordinance provision itself is valid on its face and that plaintiff does not dispute this but simply contends that the motives behind the passage of the ordinance, which do not appear on its face, were invalid. Defendants rely heavily upon the decision in *Klaw v. Pau-Mar Construction Company,* 11 Terry 487, 135 A.2d 123 (1957) and *McQuail v. Shell Oil Company,* 40 Del.Ch. 410, 183 A.2d 581 (1962). In both of these decisions, involving zoning questions, our Delaware Courts have indicated that they "will not inquire into the motives of members of a municipal legislative body in order to determine the validity of an ordinance enacted by them within the scope of their admitted powers".

Balanced against these decisions is that of *Piekarski v. Smith,* 38 Del.Ch. 402, 153 A.2d 587 (1959). In the *Piekarski* case the Wilmington City Council had passed a resolution which was attacked on grounds of fraud and bad faith and the Court had the following to say with regard to both the general rule of law referred to hereinabove and the problem raised by allegations of fraud and bad faith:

> The legal basis for the contention that the resolution was adopted "in bad faith" is found in an exception to the general rule that courts will not inquire into the motives of or inducements to legislators that may influence them in the passage of acts or resolutions. . . .
> The exception is that the validity of municipal ordinances or resolutions may be attacked if fraud or bad faith is proved. This rule is recognized in Delaware, although in none of the decided cases was any fraud or bad faith found.

> The Court must here assume to be true plaintiff's contention that defendants were fully informed of the limitation of their Charter powers and deliberately set out to evade them and that in carrying out that evasion they deliberately enacted an ordinance that was not the truth. If either of these facts can be proved "fraud or bad faith" would be established.
> . . . .

The final argument of defendants is to the effect that plaintiff mistakenly relies upon the isolated language of § 2-300(2) requiring that Council must make all of its appropriations at once in the annual operating budget ordinance. Defendants argue that this narrow a restriction of Council's powers is not required by the language of subsection (2) and, in fact, is in conflict with the provisions of § 2-300(6) which reads as follows:

> The annual operating budget ordinance may be amended after its passage to authorize the transfer of items but the aggregate of the appropriations made by it may not be increased and transfer of budget items may not be made during the last four months of any fiscal year, except upon the recommendation of the mayor.

Defendants argue that subsection (6), by limiting Council's power to transfer budgetary items during the last four months of any fiscal year except upon the recommendation of the Mayor, is implicit recognition that Council has the power to make such transfers during the first eight months without such recommendation. The Court believes that defendants strain the language of subsection (6) to reach this conclusion. At most, subsection (6) merely *authorizes* a transfer of funds originally recommended by the executive. The purpose of subsection (6) is not to give broad powers to Council to manipulate the budget for improper purposes.

The Wilmington Charter is substantially copied from the Philadelphia Home Rule Charter, and the key provision of § 2-300 is identical in all material respects with the corresponding provision of the Philadelphia Charter. It is significant that in the annotations to the Philadelphia Home Rule Charter the following language is found with regard to the purpose of subsection (6):

> Subsection (6) is intended to serve as a check on the present practice of transferring items of the budget at the end of the fiscal year. Some agencies, finding at the end of the fiscal year that they have surplus funds left under certain items, have from time to time requested and received authorization from the Council for spending those surpluses for other purposes. This sub-section prohibits such transfers during the last four months of any fiscal year except upon the recommendation of the Mayor.

This Court believes that such definition of the purposes of subsection (6) is correct and that defendants' attempt to rely upon it to expand its otherwise restricted powers is incorrect.

The point of all this is that in subsection (2) Council is granted its specific powers with regard to the annual operating budget and, in fact, has clearly enunciated for it categories witthin which it may appropriate moneys. This subsection requires not only that money be appropriated for specific valid purposes but that the overall budget shall consist of *all* of the appropriations to be made. The only category within subsection (2) which would permit of something in the nature of an emergency or a contingency fund is found in sub-paragraph (d) of subsection (2) wherein appropriations may be made for "additional classes" not otherwise specifically mentioned, if the Mayor shall so recommend in his proposed annual budget ordinance. Subsection (6) merely recognizes that within this overall budget there are times and occasions when moneys allotted for a particular class and for a valid purpose therein may within the budget year be transferred to another class named in the budget. This can be done if Council should determine this is appropriate, within the first eight months of the fiscal year and if Council and the Mayor together deem it appropriate within the last four months of the fiscal year. In this effort to control budgetary juggling but at the same time permitting some leeway, this Charter provision is hardly intended as a contradiction of the mandatory requirements of subsection (2).

For the reasons herein stated this Court concludes that the plaintiff has alleged a sufficient factual basis which, if established, would form the basis for the issuance of the Writ of Mandamus requested. Having reached this conclusion it follows that defendants' motion for a judgment on the pleadings must be denied.

It is so ordered.

Comments: 1. The effect and extent of home rule authority is discussed in Chapter 3. Note how the charter acts to confine the flexibility of local officials to spend money.

2. The principal case demonstrates that the courts will enforce limitations on local government spending powers. A court may also find within its authority the power to order appropriations when it establishes that a city has a contractual obligation to provide benefits. In *Tate v. Antosh,* 281 A.2d 192 (Pa. Commw. 1971), city employees challenged the city's decision to discontinue their disability benefits. The city personnel director had advised employees that the city would make no further payments after the present fund was exhausted. After finding that the city had an obligation to the employees, the court concluded:

> [S]imply because City Council refuses to appropriate sufficient funds to effectuate payment, the City as a public employer is not relieved of its duty to follow the mandate of the arbitration panel. The appropriation of funds does not involve the performance of any illegal act on the part of the City. Unquestionably the City has the power to make appropriations for all lawful purposes as defined in its Home Rule Charter. The City can lawfully make the necessary appropriation and, where it has a mandatory duty to do so pursuant to a valid arbitration award, a court may order that duty to be performed. . . .

Would the court's decisions be the same if a state legislature were involved?

3. May a court seize funds earmarked for a municipality under a state program to replace funds lost by a statute repealing certain local taxing powers because the municipality refuses to participate in a county-mandated reassessment program? In *Essex County Board of Taxation v. City of Newark,* 353 A.2d 535 (N.J. App. Div. 1976), the court invalidated such an approach with the following analysis:

> The moneys thus to be received by the municipality are anticipated miscellaneous revenues. Under the legislative mandate embodied in the Local Budget Law (N.J.S.A. 40A:4-1 *et seq.*) such revenues may be disbursed for a particular purpose only if the governing body has theretofore made an appropriation for such purpose. The appropriation may be effected either by including it in the annual budget to be adopted by the municipality, N.J.S.A. 40A:4-3, or in authorized situations, by adopting a resolution making an "emergency" appropriation or an ordinance making a "special emergency" appropriation. Provisions authorizing emergency appropriations by resolution are set forth in N.J.S.A. 40A:4-46 *et seq.* Power to adopt ordinances making special emergency appropriations in a situation such as is here involved is to be found in N.J.S.A. 40A:4-53 which provides in pertinent part that:
>
>> A [municipality] may adopt an ordinance authorizing special emergency appropriations for the carrying out of any of the following purposes:
>>
>> a. Preparation of an approved tax map.
>>
>> b. Preparation and execution of a complete program of revaluation of real property for the use of the local assessor.
>
> The Legislature, whose function it is to declare public policy, particularly as it involves the fiscal affairs of municipalities, has made it clear that (except in situations not present in this case) municipal funds may not be disbursed for any purpose unless there has been a prior appropriation for that purpose.
>
> . . . .
>
> We are satisfied that a court may not—as the trial judge did here by authorizing seizure of moneys belonging to the municipality and ordering its application to payment of the cost of the revaluation and tax map contracts—ignore the legislatively declared public policy that an appropriation by the municipality's governing body precede any disbursement of municipal funds.
>
> . . . .
>
> The recalcitrance of members of the municipal council cannot justify ignoring the statutory mandate that there be an appropriation. As we have shown above, the trial court has full power, if it but exercise it, to compel the required appropriation to be made.

Id. at 540-41.

Likewise, in *City of Camden v. Byrne,* 411 A.2d 462 (N.J. 1980), the state legislature failed to appropriate funds to carry out the provisions of several separate tax statutes (sales and use taxes, bus franchise replacement tax, transfer inheritance tax) through which municipalities were to receive a percentage of the taxes collected. In declining to order the funds appropriated, the court ruled that the state constitutional requirement for a unitary appropriation law covering but a single fiscal year, N.J. Const., art. VIII, § II, par. 2, negated any argument that the separate statutes were self-executing as current appropriations. The court concluded that, because the power to recommend and approve appropriations was vested in the governor and the power to make specific appropriations was vested exclusively in the legislature, it had no power to order appropriations to be made. The interplay of executive, legislative and judicial roles in the appropriations process is developed in Part Two *infra.*

4. The courts have used a flexible approach in analyzing limitations on appropriation powers and have upheld specific expenditures not expressly appropriated but which fall within a more general appropriation. In *Ashley v. Rye School District,* 274 A.2d 795 (N.H. 1971), a taxpayer sought to enjoin the Rye school district and board from expending funds for salaries for teachers' aids. The taxpayer claimed that the budget committee had not appropriated funds for this purpose and as a result, the board was prohibited from making this expenditure. The court rejected the taxpayer's argument finding that a valid appropriation had been made. The court concluded that:

> One of the appropriations voted by the school district meeting was "for the support of schools, for the salaries of school district officials and agents." Clearly this was a valid appropriation and the expenditure of this money by the school board for teachers and a teacher aide was "for the support of schools" as authorized by the school district meeting. When the school board paid the salary of the teacher aide from the unencumbered surplus of the instructional salaries account it expended no money not authorized by the school district vote.
>
> ... [I]n the present case there was, strictly speaking, no transfer of one appropriation to another, but merely a transfer within the same appropriation which the district noted for school purposes. This was clearly authorized by [statute]. The action of the Budget Committee and the vote of the school district in disapproving a program of appropriating $10,511 for four teacher aides was not and, as the trial court states, "can not be interpreted as a retroactive disapproval" of the employment of a teacher aide.

Id. at 796-97.

The explosive growth of federal grants-in-aid programs, with the traditional "carrot and stick" approach of dangling federal assistance and then threatening to withdraw it if states do not comply with the wishes of Congress, has spurred a number of states to seek better control of federal funds by requiring legislative appropriation of federal federal funds before they can be expended. Questions of federalism (discussed in Chapter 8) and separation of powers are raised, as the following case indicates:

SHAPP v. SLOAN

Supreme Court of Pennsylvania
480 Pa. 449, 391 A.2d 595 (1979), *appeal dismissed sub nom. Thornburgh v. Casey,* 440 U.S. 942 (1979)

Before EAGEN, O'BRIEN, ROBERTS, POMEROY, NIX and MANDERINO, JJ.

Opinion

Manderino, Justice.

On July 7, 1976, the Governor of Pennsylvania, various cabinet officers and the Governor's Justice Commission—appellants in this case—filed a petition for review directed against the State Treasurer challenging the constitutionality of Acts 117 and 17-A of 1976. They sought a declaratory judgment holding these acts to be null and void, and a writ of mandamus and injunctive relief to compel the State Treasurer to honor requisitions properly presented for federal funds allocated to State agencies pursuant to Acts of Congress. The Governor, Attorney General and the Justice Commission asked also for a preliminary injunction to enjoin the State Treasurer from refusing to honor requisitions for payment of federal funds to the Department of Justice for salaries and operating expenses incurred by the Office of the Special Prosecutor. The General Assembly was granted permission to intervene as a respondent.

After a hearing on the request for the preliminary injunction seeking release of the Special Prosecutor's funds, the Commonwealth Court entered an order dated July 15, 1976, denying the injunction as sought but granting an injunction directing the Treasurer to issue her warrants for payment of expenses already incurred, up to the amount of federal funds allocated to that office by the Law Enforcement Assistance Administration (LEAA) through June 30, 1976 and still unexpended. This Court denied a stay of that order. The parties are now before us on cross-appeal from this order of July 15, 1976.

Appellants are also appealing from the final order of the Commonwealth Court entered on December 3, 1976, granting the State Treasurer's and General Assembly's motions for summary judgment and dismissing appellants' motions for partial summary judgment and modification of order.

From 1961 to 1975, the annual appropriations acts of the General Assembly contained a general provision appropriating grants made to the Commonwealth for various federally funded programs to the State agency involved in the programs' administration. The provision in the General Appropriations Act of 1975 was typical of these general allocations:

> In addition to the amounts appropriated by this act, all moneys received from the Federal Government, or from any other source as contributions for the programs provided herein, or as payment for services or materials furnished by one institution to another, except those collections designated as revenues, *shall be paid into the General Fund and are hereby appropriated out of the General Fund* for the purposes of the respective appropriations. (Emphasis added.)

General Appropriations Act of 1975, 1975 Act No. 8-A, § 8(b).

Although many of these General Appropriations Acts also appropriated funds for some specific programs, legislative control over the funds was, in the General Assembly's own terms, "minimal." At most, the General Assembly's actual control consisted of authorizing applications for particular federal programs and placing conditions or restrictions upon application for federal funds. The legislature did, of course, maintain exclusive control over appropriations of State matching funds and general revenue sharing.

Despite the minimal control exercised in the yearly Appropriations Acts, it is to be noted that for more than a decade the Acts clearly and unambiguously placed such federal funds into the State's General Fund, apparently without objection from the Executive.

By 1975, federal aid programs had been increasingly implemented in Pennsylvania, and federal funds accounted for approximately 25% of the total resources of the Commonwealth. The General Assembly accordingly decided to exercise over such federal funds the full control which it considers its constitutional responsibility as the branch of government entrusted with control of the state's finances.

Therefore, on June 29, 1976, following extensive study and hearings, the General Assembly enacted Act 117 over the Governor's veto. ...

In essence, Act 117 mandates that all federal funds be deposited in the General Fund without designation as a restricted or separate account, and that they be available for appropriation by the General Assembly, (§ 5, 72 P.S. § 4615). The State Treasurer is prohibited from paying out any such federal funds unless pursuant to a specific appropriation by the General Assembly. (§ 3, 72 P.S. § 4613).

Act 17-A of 1976, also in issue, is the Federal Augmentation Appropriation Act of 1976, implementing Act 117 by making the line appropriations of federal monies to the intended programs.

This controversy arose when the State Treasurer refused, in the absence of an appropriation, to disperse to the Justice Department for the office of the Special Prosecutor monies allocated to Pennsylvania by the Law Enforcement Assistance Administration (LEAA).

Appellants urge us to consider numerous arguments in support of their position, bolstered in a voluminous brief by contentions both of policy and of constitutional interpretation. Nevertheless, the conflict revolves around one basic question—the validity of Acts 117 and 17-A of 1976 under the Pennsylvania and the United States Constitutions. If the Acts in issue were constitutionally enacted, the State Treasurer was mandated by law to refuse payment of monies for which no appropriation had been made.

The appropriations power in this Commonwealth is vested in the General Assembly by Article III, Section 24 of the Pennsylvania Constitution, which provides that:

> [N]o money shall be paid out of the treasury, except on *appropriations made by law* ... but cash refunds of taxes, licenses, fees, and other charges paid or collected, but not legally due, may be paid, as provided by law, without appropriation from the fund into which they were paid on warrant of the proper officer. (Emphasis added.)

Inasmuch as Article II of the Pennsylvania Constitution gives to the General Assembly the legislative power of the Commonwealth, the above section 24 of Article III requires legislative action before money can be paid out of the treasury.

The appellants argue, however, that Acts 117 and 17-A are not constitutional exercises of the General Assembly's Article III, Section 24 power to make appropriations for funds in the state treasury. They contend that legislative authority over state funds does not extend to federal funds, and that the Acts therefore unconstitutionally expand the state legislative power. In insisting that the General Assembly's paramount power over state funds does not extend to funds "not raised under state law," appellants offer a plethora of sub-arguments to show that the Executive, rather than the legislature, has the power to control expenditure of funds which the federal government has committed to state executive officers and agencies. Thus, their argument is two-pronged: the Legislature has exceeded its Constitutional power by assuming to control funds not legally at its disposal; and in doing so, has encroached upon the rightful sphere of the executive in violation of the doctrine of Separation of Powers embodied in our Constitution.

. . . .

Appellants have failed to prove their basic premise that funds not raised under general state law are constitutionally differentiated from other funds in the State Treasury, and thus constitutionally beyond the scope of the General Assembly's authority. We can find no legal basis for the assumption that federal funds are not subject to the General Assembly's Article III, Section 24 appropriation power.

[The court held that a Pennsylvania lower court decision did not compel a different conclusion.—Eds.]

The cases relied on from foreign jurisdictions likewise fail to convince us that the legislative power of appropriation does not extend to federal funds. For example, in neither *Navajo Tribe v. Arizona Department of Administration,* 111 Ariz. 279, 528 P.2d 623 (1975) nor *Sego v. Kirkpatrick,* 86 N.M. 359, 524 P.2d 975 (1974), cited by appellants, were the grantees either officials or agencies of the state government. Neither case, then, is in point in deciding how federal funds granted directly to a state, through an agency or official of the state, shall be dispersed.

Appellants cite *MacManus v. Love,* 179 Colo. 218, 499 P.2d 609 (1972), a Colorado case, contending that federal funds received in that state may be expended by the executive branch without legislative approval. We find its reasoning completely unpersuasive. Appellants argue that the executive branch is entitled to use federal funds without legislative approval because the executive branch, or one of its officials or agencies, is the nominal recipient charged with the responsibility for administering the programs for which the funds were received. Accordingly, argue the appellants, the State Treasurer is only the custodian of the funds. That funds are designated custodial funds does not mean that legislative action approving the use of the funds is not needed. . . .

The funds which Pennsylvania receives from the federal government do not belong to officers or agencies of the executive branch. They belong to the Commonwealth. The agency or official who is authorized to apply for federal funds does so only *on behalf of* the Commonwealth. The federal grants are made to the *state,* not to a single branch of state government. See, for example, the Omnibus Crime Control and Safe Streets Act of 1968, P.L. 90-351, 82 Stat. 197, *as amended,* 42 U.S.C. 3701 et seq. (1970 and Supp.1978), which throughout its provisions makes clear that grants are to "States" (or "State and local governments"), and nowhere indicates that grants are to be made to a single branch of the state government. Appellants have cited nothing which dictates that the federal laws pursuant to which these programs are funded requires that the Pennsylvania legislature is to be by-passed.

As pointed out earlier, twenty-five percent of Pennsylvania's budget is now derived from federal funds. The logical result of appellants' argument—if the percentage were, as an example, to reach one hundred percent — would be to eliminate the need for a legislative branch of government. The federal government could simply supply federal monies to the executive branch which would proceed to administer the revenue without appropriation of any of the monies by the legislature.

It is fundamental within Pennsylvania's tripartite system that the General Assembly enacts the legislation establishing those programs which the state provides for its citizens and appropriates the funds necessary for their operation. The executive branch implements the legislation by administering the programs.

... It must do so within the requirements and restrictions of the relevant legislation, and within the amount appropriated by the legislature. The executive branch may not of its own initiative use funds appropriated for one program in carrying out another and may not spend on a program more than its designated amount. It is in this way that the doctrine of separation of powers functions.

Nothing in the federal legislation pursuant to which these funds are granted suggests that the same principles by which programs wholly state funded are operated are inapplicable to programs for which federal funds are supplied. That the executive agency or official must use federal monies within the program for which they were intended, and must provide an accounting to show that they were so used, does not lead to the conclusion that the funds are under that official's control and outside the control of the legislature. No one would suggest such a conclusion as to programs wholly initiated by the Commonwealth itself.

The programs for which these federal funds are received are intended by Congress for administration on the state level, and cover matters traditionally of state concern, such as education, law enforcement and public welfare. It is the General Assembly, not the executive branch, which has been given the constitutional power to determine what programs will be adopted in our Commonwealth and how they will be financed. Although this may be done upon the recommendations of the executive branch, the final determinations are legislative in nature. The executive's function is to carry out those programs authorized by legislation.

To hold that the Executive has control of these federal funds would permit a dual system which would result in duplication of services and obliteration of the distinctions between the separate functions and powers of these two co-equal branches of government. It would, for example, enable the Governor to use federal funds to establish and finance one system of agencies for law enforcement or education without the approval or authorization of the very body which is constitutionally empowered to set up and finance state plans for education or law enforcement. With a large portion of the state budget now provided by federal funding, the executive branch could well end up with as much legislative responsibility as the General Assembly itself. It is *that* result which we feel would "clearly and palpably" violate the doctrine of separation of powers embodied in our Constitution. The fullest efficiency can be achieved only through proper integration and coordination of all programs administered on the state level, be they federally funded, state funded or funded by matching funds. This is most logically achieved if the General Assembly retains its fiscal control while the legislature functions to put the programs into practice.

Appellants seem to fear that legislative fiscal control over federal funds amounts to legislative seizure for its own purposes. The Legislature is not free to use arbitrarily those funds which the Commonwealth has accepted pursuant to agreement with the federal government. The federal government may impose conditions and limitations upon the monies it allocates to the states and the General Assembly must stay within those guidelines or refuse the grant. Within each grant, however, there remains the necessity to establish spending priorities and to allocate the available monies. This is properly a legislative function.

Appellants have reiterated throughout their brief that it is federal policy to allow state governments as much control as possible over these federally funded programs. It cannot, therefore, be considered an encroachment upon federal supremacy that the legislature, rather than the executive, exercises the discretion granted the state government by the Congress.

We note that at least one federal committee involved with this problem has determined that state legislative control over federal funds does not contravene federal policy and is, in fact, the desirable mode of administration. The Advisory Commission on Intergovernmental Relations (ACIR), a permanent committee created by the United States Congress in 1959 to monitor the operation of the American federal system and recommend improvements, has urged state legislatures to assume greater control of federal funds coming into state governments.

In its Bulletin 76-4 of November, 1976 referred to *supra,* the commission recommended that state legislatures include all federal aid in appropriation bills, prohibit spending of federal funds over the amount appropriated by the legislature, and establish spending priorities by making the line appropriations within the program allocations. In explaining the rationale behind its recommendations, the Commission noted that the states have been accorded much more discretion in the administration of federal funds since the late 1960's, and that there has also been a sharp increase in the amounts of federal aid granted to the states. These factors suggest the need for legislative involvement in the decisions relating to the uses of these funds.

At the time of the publication of Bulletin 76-4, the ACIR was drafting model legislation for use by state legislatures intending to become more involved in the appropriating of federal funds. In more than a year and a half which has passed since the ACIR first made its recommendations in August, 1976, we have received no indication that Congress has in any way disapproved its committee's actions in advising state legislatures to increase their role in the spending of federal monies. There is no evidence before us to indicate that Congress considers such state legislative involvement an encroachment upon the supremacy of the federal government.

. . . .

JONES, former C.J., did not participate in the consideration or decision of this case.

POMEROY, J., concurs in the result.

ROBERTS, J., filed a dissenting opinion in which O'BRIEN, J., joins.

ROBERTS, JUSTICE, dissenting.

. . . .

I

. . . .

The majority's interpretation of Acts 117 and 17-A not only offends the Supremacy Clause of the United States Constitution, and makes those acts unconstitutional, but the majority's application of these acts to withhold federal funds granted to the executive for the Office of the Special Prosecutor also violates the separation of powers doctrine as this Court has applied it to Pennsylvania government. The Special Prosecutor directed the work of the 1974 Special Investigating Grand Jury probing allegations of political and official corruption in Philadelphia. Acts 117 and 17-A, as applied by the Commonwealth Court and the majority, permit the legislative branch to curtail an investigation lawfully directed by the executive under the guidance of the judiciary. This Court has held that the Legislature may not, consistent with the Pennsylvania scheme of separation of powers, by statute deny a district attorney and a legally constituted investigating Grand Jury the power to continue its investigation. *Dauphin County Grand Jury Investigation Proceedings (No. 2),* 332 Pa. 342, 348-58, 2 A.2d 802, 804-09 (1938).

By interpreting Acts 117 and 17-A to cut off federal funds to the Special Prosecutor, the majority allows the Legislature indirectly, through power over the purse, to stifle an investigation, which the Legislature may not do directly. *Id.* At the time of argument concerning the application for an injunction pending appeal in this case, November, 1976, employees of the Special Prosecutor's Office had worked for two months without compensation. The number of active investigations had dropped from nineteen to four. The staff could not continue to work without pay indefinitely, and eventually Acts 117 and 17-A, as interpreted by the Commonwealth Court and the majority, resulted in the demise of that Office and the end of its investigations. There is in reality no legally comprehensible distinction between an act of the Legislature specifically terminating an investigation begun by a prosecutor and a Grand Jury, *Dauphin County Grand Jury Investigation Proceedings (No. 2), supra,* and an act that, as here, is interpreted to shut off all funding to the Special Prosecutor and to end the functional life of the investigating Grand Jury. Either approach infringes upon those functions reserved to the executive and the judiciary. *Cf. Commonwealth ex rel. Carroll v. Tate,* 442 Pa. 45, 274 A.2d 193 (1971) (Courts must be funded to allow them to carry out their constitutional duties). Here, of course, no state funds were provided the Special Prosecutor, and federal funds granted by LEAA were withheld.

Interpreting Acts 117 and 17-A in a manner which ends the ability of a Grand Jury to function ignores "the grand jury's . . . special role in insuring fair and effective law enforcement. . . . The grand jury's investigative power must be broad if its public responsibility is adequately to be discharged." *Calandra v. United States,* 414 U.S. 338, 343-44 (1974). The Grand Jury's investigative power may not be limited or, as here, terminated by legislation which is interpreted to withhold allocated federal funds. *See* 42 U.S.C. §§ 3733, 3734. Nor will our Constitution tolerate the refusal to provide state funds to this vital arm of law enforcement. *Cf. Commonwealth ex rel. Carroll v. Tate, supra.*

Comments: 1. About half of the court decisions to date have agreed with the Pennsylvania court. For a contrary decision see, e.g., *MacManus v. Love,* 499 P.2d 609 (Colo. 1972).

The growing use of block grants since 1981 as the mechanism for dispensing federal aid has intensified the efforts of state legislatures to control the allocation of federal funds. Unlike categorical grants, most of the newer block grants go to the states directly, not to local governments, and they are dispensed with relatively few restrictions. Can an argument be made that block grants should be appropriated even in states like Colorado, which rejected earlier attempts at legislative appropriation of federal funds? These issues are discussed in Chapter 8.

2. Legislative reassertion of appropriation authority over federal grants raises both political and constitutional problems. Since separation of powers doctrine as it applies to executive power is sufficiently pliable, the political considerations affecting this appropriation issue may well influence judicial determination of the constitutional issue.

These issues are discussed in Brown, *Federal Funds and National Supremacy: The Role of State Legislatures in Federal Grant Programs,* 28 AM. U.L. REV. 279 (1979). Brown points out that most federal assistance legislation does not specify a role for state legislatures, some require utilization of the applicable state procedure for state funds, and some specify an executive role in program administration without necessarily foreclosing legislative appropriation. An example of this last category is a federal assistance statute requiring administration of the federal program by a "single state agency." This kind of limitation is common, and reflects a federal preference to avoid complexities in program administration.

Arguments for legislative appropriation of federal assistance funds include the claim that the legislature must control all of the funds available for executive expenditure in order to exercise control over the budgetary process. Another argument is that unrestrained executive use of federal funds may commit the state to programs the legislature might not have approved. Legislative authority would then be circumvented.

Executive objections to legislative appropriation rely on the federal-state executive relationship created by federal assistance legislation. "Congress enacts these programs to further national interests that currently are not being served adequately at the state level; if the states were doing what Congress wanted, no grant program would be necessary." Brown, *supra,* at 285. Another argument against legislative appropriation is that it permits political legislative interference in the federal assistance process. Legislatures, for example, "might thwart the objectives of federal grant programs through practices such as legislative screening of grant applications to be submitted by executive branch agencies." Brown, *supra,* at 287. Can it be argued that legislative screening is consistent with the legislature's responsibility to set spending priorities?

For an argument that the federal grant system should be modified to encourage state legislative participation in an oversight capacity, see Comptroller General of the United States, Federal Assistance System Should Be Changed to Permit Greater Involvement by State Legislatures (1980). The report stresses that improvements in state legislatures (annual sessions, improved staff, use of post-audit and evaluation procedures by legislative committees) and the enormous impact of federal grants on state budgets are substantial reasons for increasing the role of state legislatures in the federal grant-in-aid system.

3. Legislative appropriation of federal assistance funds also raises a federal supremacy question. In the principal case, the court found no conflict with the federal legislation. If there is a direct conflict, welfare cases such as *King v. Smith,* 392 U.S. 309 (1968), indicate that state legislation inconsistent with federal grant legislation is invalid. That case invalidated a state welfare regulation inconsistent with the federal law. What should the result be when the impact of federal legislation on the state appropriations process is unclear? Consult the federal preemption cases, *infra* Chapter 8.

4. Legislative appropriation of federal assistance funds also presents a tenth amendment problem under the United States Supreme Court's *National League* decision. *See* Chapter 8.

What if a state court holds that legislative appropriation of federal assistance funds violates the separation of powers as required by the state constitution? If the federal statute requires legislative appropriation, does it violate the tenth amendment? For an argument that it may, see Comment, *Federal Interference with Checks and Balances in State Governments: A Constitutional Limit on the Spending Power,* 128 U. PA. L. REV. 402 (1979).

Chapter 6

SERVING THE PUBLIC SECTOR: OFFICERS AND EMPLOYEES

Government employment makes up a substantial share of the nation's work force. One estimate places one out of six employees in government service. State and local government employees make up a major share of the government total, and state and local government employment has been growing faster than government employment at the federal level. Although the growth in state and local employment has slowed in recent years, the decentralization of government which appears well under way may reverse this trend. The table that follows shows state and local government employment in October 1981:

State and Local Government Employment
(in thousands)

Total	13,103
State	3,726
Local	9,377
County	1,808
Municipal	2,469
Township	386
School district	4,222
Special district	482

Source: U.S. Bureau of Census, Public Employment in 1981, at 2 (1982).

Public employees at one time served at the will of their public employers. Appointment was through political patronage, not merit, and the law placed few limitations on removal. The maxim, now generally discarded, that government employment is a privilege, not a right, sums up the state of the law in this period.

Developments in the law of public employment have radically changed these ground rules. Civil service systems apply the merit principle to the selection of government employees and place limitations on their removal. Unionization and collective bargaining now competes with the civil service system in setting the conditions of government employment.

Doctrinal developments in the United States Supreme Court also affect the freedom of government entities to set the terms of employment. The Court applies equal protection, procedural due process and free speech doctrine to limit the conditions of employment and the freedom to remove government employees. The established doctrine, that government employment is a privilege and not a right, has been substantially qualified by the Supreme Court.

Another important contemporary concern is the conduct of officers and employees while in government. Official integrity has become a salient public issue since Watergate. This issue is as important at the state and local level as it is at the federal level.

This chapter examines these contemporary issues as they affect government employment and service by officials in the public sector.

A. LIMITING ENTRY TO GOVERNMENT SERVICE

The opportunity to serve in political office or government employment carries important benefits. Competition may be great, and state and local governments may attempt to limit entry by establishing preferences, such as preferences for veterans, or by excluding certain classes of applicants. These exclusions often reflect political influences. The exclusion of aliens from employment is one example. Residency requirements are another. The following case illustrates the constitutional limitations governments face when they apply residency restrictions to government service.

WARDWELL v. BOARD OF EDUCATION

United States Court of Appeals
529 P.2d 625 (6th Cir. 1976)

Before MILLER and ENGEL, CIRCUIT JUDGES, and CHURCHILL, DISTRICT JUDGE.
WILLIAM E. MILLER, CIRCUIT JUDGE.

This appeal requires us to consider the constitutionality of a rule adopted by the Board of Education of the City of Cincinnati requiring all teachers in the Cincinnati schools hired after November 13, 1972, to establish within 90 days of employment residency within the city school district.

In December, 1972, plaintiff, Terry Wardwell, was hired to teach in the Cincinnati schools. As a condition of employment he agreed to move into the city school district pursuant to a rule announced by the school superintendent in November, 1972, that all newly-employed teachers must establish residence within the district within 30 days after employment. In January, 1973, the Board adopted the following resolution, essentially ratifying the superintendent's rule:

> RESOLVED, That any employee hired by the Cincinnati Schools after November 13, 1972 must either reside within the Cincinnati School District, or agree, as a condition of employment, to establish residency within the district within ninety days of employment. Employees who live in the district must continue to reside therein as long as they are so employed. This policy does not affect in any way personnel hired before the above date.

Plaintiff Wardwell lived outside the district but within the State of Ohio. Despite the requirement he failed to change his residence. He filed the present action in July, 1973, under 28 U.S.C. § 1343 and 42 U.S.C. § 1983, challenging the residency requirement on equal protection grounds and seeking injunctive relief and attorney's fees. No preliminary injunction was requested because enforcement of the rule had been stayed by a preliminary injunction issued by a state court. Since being hired, plaintiff Wardwell has taught at one time in a predominantly white school located within a ten minute drive from his home and later at a predominantly black school about twenty minutes from his home outside the district.

The district court denied the request for an injunction and upheld the validity of the rule, relying heavily on the Fifth Circuit's reasoning in *Wright v. City of Jackson,* 506 F.2d 900 (5th Cir. 1975).

Plaintiff argues that the Board's residency requirement infringes his constitutionally protected right to travel as defined in *Shapiro v. Thompson,* 394 U.S. 618 ... (1969), and in *Dunn v. Blumstein,* 405 U.S. 330 ... (1972), extending the protection, as he contends, to both intrastate and interstate travel and embracing as a necessary corollary the right to remain in one place.

We find no support for plaintiff's theory that the right to intrastate travel has been afforded federal constitutional protection. An examination of *Shapiro, supra, Dunn, supra,* and the Supreme Court's more recent opinion in *Memorial Hospital v. Maricopa County,* 415 U.S. 250 . . . (1974), convinces us that the aspect of the right to travel with which the Court was concerned in those cases is not involved here. It is clear that the Court was dealing with the validity of durational residency requirements which penalized recent interstate travel.[1] Such *durational* residency requirements or restrictions affecting the interstate aspect of travel will not pass constitutional muster "absent a compelling state interest."

In *Memorial Hospital,* . . . the Court at some length emphasized that *Shapiro* and the later cases were not to be construed as applying to bona fide *continuing,* as distinguished from *durational,* residency requirements when it said:

> The right of interstate travel has repeatedly been recognized as a basic constitutional freedom. Whatever its ultimate scope, however, the right to travel, was involved in only a limited sense in *Shapiro.* The Court was there concerned only with the right to migrate, "with intent to settle and abide" or, as the Court put it, "to migrate, resettle, find a new job, and start a new life." . . . Even a bona fide residence requirement would burden the right to travel, if travel meant merely movement. But, in *Shapiro,* the Court explained that "[t]he residence requirement and the one-year waiting-period requirement are distinct and independent prerequisites" for assistance and only the latter was held to be unconstitutional. . . . Later, in invalidating a durational residence requirement for voter registration on the basis of *Shapiro,* we cautioned that our decision was not intended to "cast doubt on the validity of appropriately defined and uniformly applied bona fide residence requirements." *Dunn v. Blumstein* . . . .

Our conclusion that *Shapiro* and the other right to travel cases are not applicable to intrastate travel and *continuing* employee residency requirements is supported by *Detroit Police Officers Association v. City of Detroit,* 405 U.S. 950 . . . (1972), on which the district court in this case and the Fifth Circuit in *Wright, supra,* relied. The case involved a Detroit residency requirement for policemen. The Michigan Supreme Court, applying the "rational basis test," determined that the classification bore a reasonable relationship to the object of the legislation and was therefore valid. *Detroit Police Officers Association v. City of Detroit,* 385 Mich. 519, 190 N.W.2d 97 (1971). The Supreme Court in a brief order dismissed the appeal "for want of a substantial federal question." While we do not consider it necessary to base the result in the present case primarily on *Detroit Police Officers,* we recognize that the Supreme Court's dismissal of the appeal "for want of a substantial federal question" is a decision on the merits of the case appealed. . . . We conclude that the "compelling state interest" test is the applicable test in cases involving infringement of the right to interstate travel by *durational* residency requirements. On the other hand, where, as in the present case, a *continuing* employee residency requirement affecting at most the right of intrastate travel is involved, the "rational basis" test is the touchstone to determine its validity.[3]

---

[1] The Supreme Court in *Memorial Hospital, supra* at 255-56 . . . refused to decide whether a constitutional distinction can be drawn between interstate and intrastate travel. In so doing, the Court made clear that it was only considering the infringement of the right of interstate travel which had occurred in that case.

[3] We have assumed, arguendo, that the right to travel embraces the right not to travel or to remain

We find a number of rational bases for the residency requirement of the Cincinnati School Board. The Cincinnati school superintendent testified that promulgation of the rule was based on the following conclusions: (1) such a requirement aids in hiring teachers who are highly motivated and deeply committed to an urban educational system, (2) teachers who live in the district are more likely to vote for district taxes, less likely to engage in illegal strikes, and more likely to help obtain passage of school tax levies, (3) teachers living in the district are more likely to be involved in school and community activities bringing them in contact with parents and community leaders and are more likely to be committed to the future of the district and its schools, (4) teachers who live in the district are more likely to gain sympathy and understanding for the racial, social, economic, and urban problems of the children they teach and are thus less likely to be considered isolated from the communities in which they teach, (5) the requirement is in keeping with the goal of encouraging integration in society and in the schools. These conclusions appear to us clearly to establish rational bases for the residency requirement imposed by the Cincinnati Board.

Appellant insists that the basic purpose of the residency rule is to advance "quality integrated" education and to help in eliminating racial segregation in the community and school system. The rule is not rationally related to this objective, appellant claims, because school and community integration would only be promoted by requiring teachers to live in the attendance districts of the schools at which they teach. Integration is not encouraged, it is argued, by a regulation such as the present which requires teachers to live somewhere in the district at large when the district itself contains many segregated areas. This argument overlooks the various other convincing and rational bases for adoption of the rule. Although it is possible that the rule will not materially contribute to racial integration, we consider that the numerous other legitimate objectives of the rule are wholly adequate to demonstrate that the residency classification fully comports with the rational basis test. Many other courts have recognized the importance of employees being highly committed to the area in which they work and motivated to find solutions for its problems. . . . Such commitment and motivation, it is not unreasonable to suppose, may best be fostered by requiring teachers to live and pay taxes in the place in which they are employed to work.

Other arguments against the validity of this residency requirement are advanced. First, it is said that the right to teach, which in Ohio is controlled by state law through the issuance of a teaching certificate, entitles a teacher to be considered for employment only on his merits as prescribed by statute. This right may not be withheld on constitutionally impermissible grounds. The state certification of teachers distinguishes teachers as a group from municipal employees performing other functions. We agree with appellee, however, that the possession of an Ohio certificate establishes only that a teacher has met certain minimum standards. It does not entitle him to a teaching position with any particular local school board. Local boards are free to impose additional qualifications and conditions of employment or to adopt higher standards. See Ohio Revised Code 3319.07.

Finally, appellant argues that the residency requirement is invalid because it requires newly-hired teachers to move into and remain in the district and permits those already hired to remain or move outside the district. Appellee replies that distinguishing between new teachers and teachers with experience who may have

---

in one place. Such an alleged constitutional right, however, has never been dealt with by the Supreme Court. Nor have other courts dealing with residency requirements recognized it. . . .

tenure and who did not know of the requirement when they accepted employment, is a reasonable distinction which the state is free to make. While we recognize that the limited applicability of the rule may be its most questionable feature, we do not believe that the residency requirement must fail because it does not apply to all teachers employed by the Cincinnati schools. The Supreme Court has pointed out that there is no constitutional requirement that regulations must cover every class to which they might be applied, *see United States v. Carolene Products Co.,* 304 U.S. 144 ... (1938). It has further stated that "if the classification has some reasonable basis, it does not offend the constitution simply because the classification 'is not made with mathematical nicety or because in practice it results in some inequality.'" *Dandridge v. Williams,* 397 U.S. 471, 485 ... (1970).

Affirmed.

Comments: 1. The Supreme Court's *Shapiro* decision, which is discussed in *Wardwell,* invalidated a requirement that a recipient of welfare assistance be a resident of the state for one year. This type of requirement has been called a "durational" residency requirement. The residency requirement in *Wardwell* only required that employees be "continuing" residents.

Shapiro also considered a restriction on the interstate right to travel. The durational residency requirement required residency in the state. *Wardwell* concluded that *Shapiro* had invalidated interstate but not intrastate residency requirements. These distinctions have become important in the government employee residence cases.

The Supreme Court upheld a continuing residence requirement shortly after *Wardwell* in *McCarthy v. Philadelphia Civil Service Commission,* 424 U.S. 645 (1976). The Court avoided the interstate versus intrastate distinction. In a brief per curiam opinion, it seemed to place its decision on the distinction between durational and continuing residency requirements:

[We have not] questioned the validity of a condition placed upon municipal employment that a person be a resident *at the time* of his application. In this case appellant claims a constitutional right to be employed by the city of Philadelphia *while* he is living elsewhere. There is no support in our cases for such a claim.

Id. at 646-47 (emphasis in original). *Compare Hicklin v. Orbeck,* 437 U.S. 518 (1978). The Court invalidated under the federal privileges and immunities clause a state statute requiring oil and gas lessees from the state to hire state residents. See also *People ex rel. Holland v. Bleigh Construction Co.,* 335 N.E.2d 469 (Ill. 1975), invalidating an Illinois statute requiring public works projects to employ only "Illinois laborers," defined as citizenship in the United States and one year residency in Illinois, but upholding a preference for Illinois residents.

2. The state cases that apply the federal constitution appear consistent with *McCarthy.* They strike down durational residency requirements, e.g., *Eggert v. City of Seattle,* 505 P.2d 801 (Wash. 1973). Continuing residency requirements are upheld, e.g., *Ector v. City of Torrance,* 514 P.2d 433 (Cal. 1973), *cert. denied,* 415 U.S. 935 (1974). But see *Town of Milton v. Civil Service Commission,* 312 N.E.2d 188 (Mass. 1974), upholding a hiring preference of policemen for persons who had lived in the municipality for one year. (Should police be treated differently from other municipal employees?)

The equal protection review standard applied by the courts may determine the result in these cases. The Supreme Court appears to apply the strict scrutiny equal protection review standard to durational residency requirements. Under this standard, the requirement must be justified by a "compelling" governmental interest, which the courts usually are not willing to find. Continuing residency requirements are only subject to the minimal "rational relationship" standard of equal protection review, under which courts usually uphold legislation. But see the discussion of state court equal protection review in Chapter

1, indicating that some state courts apply a more rigorous standard than the Supreme Court. Compare *Donnelly v. City of Manchester*, 274 A.2d 789 (N.H. 1971), invalidating a continuing residency requirement under state and federal equal protection doctrine, but not specifying the standard of review.

The Supreme Court applies the strict scrutiny standard when a fundamental right is restricted. The right to travel recognized by *Shapiro* is a fundamental right but the Supreme Court has not extended the right to travel doctrine. It has limited the doctrine primarily to durational restrictions that penalize the right to receive government benefits. See *Sosna v. Iowa*, 419 U.S. 393 (1975), upholding a one-year residency requirement for divorce.

3. *Wardwell* listed a number of reasons for upholding the continuing residency requirement. *See also Salt Lake City Fire Fighters Local 1645 v. Salt Lake City*, 449 P.2d 239 (Utah 1969). The court noted that the city was justified in requiring employees to live within a reasonable distance from work and to contribute through their taxes to city revenues.

Commentators have been critical of these justifications. *See* Note, *Municipal Employee Residency Requirements and Equal Protection*, 84 YALE L.J. 1684 (1975). *But see* Note, *Residency Requirements for City Employees: Important Incentives in Today's Urban Crisis*, 18 URB. L. ANN. 197 (1980). *Compare* Comment, *An Intermediate Standard for Equal Protection Review of Municipal Residence Requirements*, 43 OHIO ST. L.J. 195 (1982).

4. The alien cases provide an interesting comparison with the residency cases. The Supreme Court has applied strict scrutiny equal protection review to restrictions on aliens, but has relaxed this standard in cases considering restrictions on the employment of aliens in government service. "[C]itizenship is a relevant ground for determining membership in the political community." *Cabell v. Chavez-Salido*, 454 U.S. 432, 438 (1982). The Court continued:

> The exclusion of aliens from basic governmental processes is not a deficiency in the democratic system but a necessary consequence of the community's process for political self-definition. Self-government . . . begins by defining the scope of the community of the governed and thus of the governors as well: Aliens are by definition those outside of this community.

Id. at 439-40.

The Court then applied the two-step process adopted in *Sugarman v. Dougall*, 413 U.S. 634 (1973), to uphold statutes barring aliens from various state offices. Under the *Sugarman* tests, the Court first considers the specificity of the restriction on aliens and may strike it if overbroad. Even if sufficiently precise, the restriction on alien employment may only be applied to officers who "participate directly in the formulation, operation, or review of broad public policy" that "go to the heart of representative government." *Sugarman*, at 647. These officers included "persons holding state elective or important nonelective executive, legislative, and judicial positions." *Id.*

For additional discussion see Note, *Prohibitions on Employment Opportunities for Resident Aliens: Legislative Recommendations*, 10 FORDHAM URB. L.J. 699 (1981-1982). Are the alien employment cases relevant to a consideration of municipal residency requirements?

5. After the decision in the *Ector* case, Comment 2 *supra*, the California constitution was amended to provide that "[a] city or county . . . may not require that its employees be residents of any such city or county . . . except that such employees may be required to reside within a reasonable and specific distance of their place of employment or other designated location." Cal. Const. art. XI, § 10(b). In *Cooperrider v. San Francisco Civil Service Commission*, 158 Cal. Rptr. 801 (Cal. App. 1979), the court held that a durational residency requirement violated the constitutional provision. The court held that the provision protected the right to intrastate travel and "provided greater individual protection than the federal law."

A residency requirement may also conflict with state civil service legislation. In *Mandelkern v. City of Buffalo*, 409 N.Y.S.2d 881 (App. Div. 1978), city attorneys who wished to live outside the city challenged the validity of a continuing residency requirement. They claimed the requirement conflicted with the civil service law, which authorized removal only for misconduct or incompetence. The city intended to dismiss them from their jobs if they left the city to reside elsewhere.

The court found no conflict. The residency requirement was a qualification for employment. The civil service law prescribed the procedures for removal of an employee for delinquencies in job performance. "It has nothing to do with eligibility for employment."

A residency requirement may also violate a state constitution's "special legislation" clause if it is applied to a limited number of cities. See the *Adamowski* case, discussed in Chapter 9.

6. Residency restrictions on elective office raise additional questions because they also affect the right to vote. The most relevant Supreme Court case struck down an excessive filing fee for candidates as an impairment of the right to vote. The Court held that the fee fell "with unequal weight on voters, as well as candidates." *Bullock v. Carter,* 405 U.S. 134 (1972). Some courts interpret this and related Supreme Court cases to hold that the right to hold public office is a fundamental right whose impairment must be justified by a compelling governmental interest. *See Johnson v. Hamilton,* 541 P.2d 881 (Cal. 1975) (invalidating durational residency requirement for candidates for city office). Other courts uphold durational residency requirements, especially when applied to state offices. *Gilbert v. State,* 526 P.2d 1131 (Alaska 1974). *But see Antonio v. Kirkpatrick,* 479 F.2d 1147 (8th Cir. 1978) (ten-year residency requirement for elected state auditor invalid under rational relationship test). Would the same requirement be invalid if it applied to the governor?

What are the reasons for applying durational residency requirements to candidates for public office? The justification usually asserted is that the candidate must be familiar with the issues likely to arise in the election, and the voters must be familiar with the candidate. The residency requirement is claimed to serve these objectives. The California court decisively rejected this reasoning in *Johnson:*

> The knowledge, appreciation, and comprehension of the public issues and problems which a candidate either possesses or may reasonably be expected to acquire are so much the product of the variables of motivation, intelligence, maturity, experience, opportunity, and desire as to make any flat rule of physical residence appear immediately suspect and arbitrary.

Id. at 886. The court also took notice of increasing voter apathy, and suggested that this danger "suggests the wisdom of widening rather than narrowing the candidate options available to the public."

What about an appointive office? In *Langmeyer v. State,* 656 P.2d 114 (Idaho 1982), the court upheld a five-year durational residency requirement for appointment to a local planning commission. The court accepted the state's argument that "the durational residency requirement is rational to insure that the appointees have the opportunities to know the customs and mores of the people and a working knowledge of the local area." The court held that the traditional equal protection test was applicable.

7. State and local civil service laws commonly provide a preference for veterans, which has uniformly been upheld. The leading Supreme Court case is *Personnel Administrator v. Feeney,* 442 U.S. 256 (1979). The Court noted:

> The veterans' hiring preference ... has traditionally been justified as a measure designed to reward veterans for the sacrifice of military service, to ease the transition from military to civilian life, to encourage patriotic service, and to attract loyal and well-disciplined people to civil service occupations.

Id. at 265. How do these justifications compare with the justifications for a residency requirement?

The Court in *Feeney* rejected an argument that the statute was an unconstitutional gender classification because veterans were overwhelmingly men. The argument was that the statutory preference, though neutral on its face, in fact discriminated against women. Gender status is not a fundamental right, but the Supreme Court has applied a "middle-level" equal protection review to gender discrimination cases.

8. The constitutionality of loyalty oaths has received extensive Supreme Court consideration. The Court applies a balancing test, and has not found loyalty oaths invalid per se. It has upheld an oath requiring employees to defend the federal and state constitutions and oppose the overthrow of government by force and violence. *Cole v. Richardson,* 405 U.S. 676 (1972), *noted,* 58 CORNELL L. REV. 383 (1973). An oath violates freedom of association when it is based on membership in a disloyal organization but does not require that the employee be an active member with a specific intent to assist in achieving the aims of the organization. *Elfbrandt v. Russell,* 384 U.S. 11 (1966).

9. Powers of appointment of officers and employees are regulated at the local level by statute and home rule charters. The majority rule at the state level appears to be that the power of appointment is not exclusively a gubernatorial function. See *Leek v. Theis,* 539 P.2d 304 (Kan. 1975), upholding a statute requiring legislative confirmation of gubernatorial appointees. *Contra, Bradner v. Hammond,* 553 P.2d 1 (Alaska 1976). *See also Monier v. Gallen,* 414 A.2d 1297 (N.H. 1980) (legislature may prevent governor from creating "ad hoc" state agency through personnel appointments).

A NOTE ON FEDERAL EMPLOYMENT DISCRIMINATION LEGISLATION

Hiring, promotion and all phases of government employment are covered by legislation prohibiting discrimination in employment. The most important statutes are at the federal level, and the most important of the federal statutes is Title VII of the Civil Rights Act of 1964, 42 U.S.C. § 2000e et seq. Title VII did not apply to state and local governments until 1972. It still exempts some officers and employees, including elected officials and "an appointee on the policy-making level."

Employment discrimination also is prohibited by Section 1981 of the Civil Rights Act of 1871, 42 U.S.C. § 1981, which prohibits discrimination in the making of contracts. *See Johnson v. Railway Express Agency,* 421 U.S. 454 (1975). Other federal statutes prohibiting employment discrimination are the Equal Pay Act, 29 U.S.C. § 206(d), and the Age Discrimination in Employment Act, 29 U.S.C. § 621 et seq.

A key provision of Title VII states:

> It shall be an unlawful employment practice for an employer —
> (1) to fail or refuse to hire or to discharge any individual, or otherwise to discriminate against any individual with respect to his compensation, terms, conditions, or privileges of employment, because of such individual's race, color, religion, sex, or national origin; or
> (2) to limit, segregate, or classify his employees or applicants for employment in any way which would deprive or tend to deprive any individual of employment opportunities or otherwise adversely affect his status as an employee, because of such individual's race, color, religion, sex, or national origin.

42 U.S.C. § 2000e-2(a).

The administration of Title VII and of many of the other federal employment discrimination laws has been delegated to the Equal Employment Opportunity Commission, which has statutory enforcement powers. Title VII also authorizes suits by the Attorney General and by employees.

Test for Discrimination

The Supreme Court requires proof of discriminatory intent in suits claiming employment discrimination under the fourteenth amendment. *Washington v. Davis,* 426 U.S. 229 (1976). In this case, black applicants claimed that a qualification test administered by a local police department was discriminatory.

The Court applies a discriminatory impact test under Title VII. *Griggs v. Duke Power Co.,* 401 U.S. 424 (1971), is the leading case. The company had restricted blacks to the labor department prior to the enactment of Title VII. The company then required all employees who wanted to transfer out of that department to have either a high school diploma or achieve a passing grade on two professionally prepared aptitude tests. These requirements applied equally to white and black employees, but in operation they barred a disproportionate number of blacks from transfer.

The Court held that the requirements were invalid because they had a disproportionate impact and were not related to job performance.

> [Title VII] proscribes not only overt discrimination but also practices that are fair in form, but discriminatory in operation. The touchstone is business necessity. If an employment practice which operates to exclude Negroes cannot be shown to be related to job performance, the practice is prohibited.

Id. at 431.

Griggs also adopted a *prima facie* case rule. The employer has the burden of showing that a job requirement is related to the employment, but only after the employee has made out a *prima facie* case of discrimination by showing that the requirement selects applicants in a racial pattern significantly different from that of the pool of applicants. The employer must also show that no alternative method is available for the selection of his employees. For an application of these rules in a case holding testing requirements invalid, see *Albemarle Paper Co. v. Moody,* 422 U.S. 405 (1975).

Employment Discrimination Found Invalid

In addition to testing requirements, a number of other employment requirements have been held invalid under Title VII. In *Dothard v. Rawlinson,* 433 U.S. 321 (1977), the Court held invalid a height and weight requirement applied to prison guard applicants. The Court noted that the requirements would disqualify a significant percentage of women but only an insignificant percentage of men. The Court also held that the purpose of these requirements could be met by testing for strength. The Court did uphold a subsequently adopted rule which applied a gender-based qualification to guards required to search or engage in physical contact with persons of the opposite sex. The Court relied on a provision in Title VII permitting sex-based discrimination when it is a "bona fide occupational qualification reasonably necessary to the normal operation of that particular business or enterprise." 42 U.S.C. § 2000e-2(e).

Does a one-year durational residency requirement for public employment violate Title VII? What if blacks make up forty percent of the population of the community that has lived there for more than one year, but seventy percent of the population that has lived there for less than one year? Does the requirement discriminate against blacks?

What if the government employee claims that a discriminatory qualifying test is not applied in a discriminatory manner? This problem arose in *Connecticut v. Teal,* 102 S. Ct. 2525 (1982). Applicants for a permanent promotion to supervisor in a state agency were given a qualifying test which was found to have a discriminatory impact. The black passing rate was approximately sixty-eight percent of the white passing rate. When promotions were made, the state agency adopted an "affirmative action" program and promoted almost twice as many blacks than whites from the group that participated in the selection process. The state agency argued that the favorable treatment of blacks in the promotion process provided a "bottom line" defense to the Title VII violation, but the Court rejected this argument.

Relying on the statutory employment discrimination prohibition quoted earlier, the Court held that "[t]he statute speaks, not in terms of jobs and promotions, but in terms of *limitations* and *classifications* that would deprive any individual of employment *opportunities*." (Emphasis in original.) The Court added that "[t]he principal focus of the statute is the protection of the individual employee, rather than the protection of the minority group as a whole." The dissent suggested that state and local governments with limited funds would have to adopt a hiring quota to comply with the *Teal* decision. Why? Isn't a hiring quota a "bottom line" defense? For a full treatment of employment discrimination problems see A. SMITH, C. CRAVER & L. CLARK, EMPLOYMENT DISCRIMINATION LAW (2d ed. 1982).

B. REMOVAL FROM GOVERNMENT SERVICE: PATRONAGE AND POLITICS

The status of a government employee or official changes once that person is appointed to government service. Civil service employees are protected by civil service laws that authorize removal only for cause. Employees and officers who are not protected by civil service may serve at the pleasure of the appointing officer or may have a statutory fixed term of office.

Removal of non-civil service officers and employees initially was without constitutional restriction, a reflection of the one-time venerable rule that government service is a privilege, not a right. This rule has been substantially qualified by United States Supreme Court cases providing constitutional protection to rights of free speech and association exercised by government officers and employees.

One important set of cases in which the Court has protected these rights are the patronage cases in which officers or employees were removed for political reasons. These cases raise important questions concerning the role of political loyalty in government service. The case that follows is the Supreme Court's latest holding on this question:

BRANTI v. FINKEL
United States Supreme Court
445 U.S. 507 (1980)

MR. JUSTICE STEVENS delivered the opinion of the Court.

The question presented is whether the First and Fourteenth Amendments to the Constitution protect an assistant public defender who is satisfactorily performing his job from discharge solely because of his political beliefs.

Respondents, Aaron Finkel and Alan Tabakman, commenced this action in the United States District Court for the Southern District of New York in order to preserve their positions as assistant public defenders in Rockland County, New York. On January 4, 1978, on the basis of a showing that the petitioner public defender was about to discharge them solely because they were Republicans, the District Court entered a temporary restraining order preserving the status quo. After hearing evidence for eight days, the District Court entered detailed findings of fact and permanently enjoined petitioner from terminating or attempting to terminate respondents' employment "upon the sole grounds of their political beliefs." 457 F. Supp. 1284, 1285 (1978). The Court of Appeals affirmed in an unpublished memorandum opinion, judgment order reported at 598 F.2d 609 (CA2 1979) (table).

The critical facts can be summarized briefly. The Rockland County Public Defender is appointed by the County Legislature for a term of six years. He in turn appoints nine assistants who serve at his pleasure. The two respondents have served as assistants since their respective appointments in March 1971 and September 1975; they are both Republicans.

Petitioner Branti's predecessor, a Republican, was appointed in 1972 by a Republican-dominated County Legislature. By 1977, control of the legislature had shifted to the Democrats and petitioner, also a Democrat, was appointed to replace the incumbent when his term expired. As soon as petitioner was formally appointed on January 3, 1978, he began executing termination notices for six of the nine assistants then in office. Respondents were among those who were to be terminated. With one possible exception, the nine who were to be appointed or retained were all Democrats and were all selected by Democratic legislators or Democratic town chairmen on a basis that had been determined by the Democratic caucus.

The District Court found that Finkel and Tabakman had been selected for termination solely because they were Republicans and thus did not have the necessary Democratic sponsors:

> The sole grounds for the attempted removal of plaintiffs were the facts that plaintiffs' political beliefs differed from those of the ruling Democratic majority in the County Legislature and that the Democratic majority had determined that Assistant Public Defender appointments were to be made on political bases. 457 F. Supp., at 1293.

The court rejected petitioner's belated attempt to justify the dismissals on nonpolitical grounds. Noting that both Branti and his predecessor had described respondents as "competent attorneys," the District Court expressly found that both had been "satisfactorily performing their duties as Assistant Public Defenders." *Id.*, at 1292.

Having concluded that respondents had been discharged solely because of their political beliefs, the District Court held that those discharges would be permissible under this Court's decision in *Elrod v. Burns,* 427 U. S. 347, only if assistant public defenders are the type of policymaking, confidential employees who may be discharged solely on the basis of their political affiliations. He concluded that respondents clearly did not fall within that category. Although recognizing that they had broad responsibilities with respect to particular cases that were assigned to them, the court found that respondents had "very limited, if any, responsibility" with respect to the overall operation of the public defender's office. They did not "act as advisors or formulate plans for the implementation of the broad goals of the office" and, although they made decisions in the context of specific cases, "they do not make decisions about the orientation and operation of the office in which they work." 457 F. Supp., at 1291.

The District Court also rejected the argument that the confidential character of respondents' work justified conditioning their employment on political grounds. He found that they did not occupy any confidential relationship to the policymaking process, and did not have access to confidential documents that influenced policymaking deliberations. Rather, the only confidential information to which they had access was the product of their attorney-client relationship with the office's clients; to the extent that such information was shared with the public defender, it did not relate to the formulation of office policy.

In light of these factual findings, the District Court concluded that petitioner could not terminate respondents' employment as assistant public defenders consistent with the First and Fourteenth Amendments. On appeal, a panel of the Second Circuit affirmed, specifically holding that the District Court's findings of fact were adequately supported by the record. That court also expressed "no doubt" that the District Court "was correct in concluding that an assistant public defender was neither a policymaker nor a confidential employee." We granted certiorari, 443 U. S. 904, and now affirm.

Petitioner advances two principal arguments for reversal: [6] First, that the holding in *Elrod v. Burns* is limited to situations in which government employees are coerced into pledging allegiance to a political party that they would not voluntarily support and does not apply to a simple requirement that an employee be sponsored by the party in power; and, second, that, even if party sponsorship is an unconstitutional condition of continued public employment for clerks, deputies, and janitors, it is an acceptable requirement for an assistant public defender.

I

In *Elrod v. Burns* the Court held that the newly elected Democratic Sheriff of Cook County, Ill., had violated the constitutional rights of certain non-civil-service employees by discharging them "because they did not support and were not members of the Democratic Party and had failed to obtain the sponsorship of one of its leaders." 427 U. S., at 351. That holding was supported by two separate opinions.

Writing for the plurality, Mr. Justice Brennan identified two separate but interrelated reasons supporting the conclusion that the discharges were prohibited by the First and Fourteenth Amendments. First, he analyzed the impact of a political patronage system [7] on freedom of belief and association. Noting that in order to retain their jobs, the Sheriff's employees were required to pledge their allegiance to the Democratic Party, work for or contribute to the party's candidates, or obtain a Democratic sponsor, he concluded that the inevita-

---

[6] Petitioner also makes two other arguments. First, he contends that the action should have been dismissed because the evidence showed that he would have discharged respondents in any event due to their lack of competence as public defenders. See Mt. Healthy City Board of Ed. v. Doyle, 429 U. S. 274. The Court of Appeals correctly held this contention foreclosed by the District Court's findings of fact, which it found to be adequately supported by the record. In view of our settled practice of accepting, absent the most exceptional circumstances, factual determinations in which the district court and the court of appeals have concurred, we decline to review these and other findings of fact petitioner argues were clearly erroneous. . . .

Second, relying on testimony that an assistant's term in office automatically expires when the public defender's term expires, petitioner argues that we should treat this case as involving a "failure to reappoint" rather than a dismissal and, as a result, should apply a less stringent standard. Petitioner argues that because respondents knew the system was a patronage system when they were hired, they did not have a reasonable expectation of being rehired when control of the office shifted to the Democratic Party. A similar waiver argument was rejected in Elrod v. Burns . . . . After Elrod, it is clear that the lack of a reasonable expectation of continued employment is not sufficient to justify a dismissal based solely on an employee's private political beliefs.
. . . .

[7] Mr. Justice Brennan noted that many other practices are included within the definition of a patronage system, including placing supporters in government jobs not made available by political discharges, granting supporters lucrative government contracts, and giving favored wards improved public services. In that case, as in this, however, the only practice at issue was the dismissal of public employees for partisan reasons. . . . In light of the limited nature of the question presented, we have no occasion to address petitioner's argument that there is a compelling governmental interest in maintaining a political sponsorship system for filling vacancies in the public defender's office.

ble tendency of such a system was to coerce employees into compromising their true beliefs.[8] That conclusion, in his opinion, brought the practice within the rule of cases like *Board of Education v. Barnette,* 319 U. S. 624, condemning the use of governmental power to prescribe what the citizenry must accept as orthodox opinion.[9]

Second, apart from the potential impact of patronage dismissals on the formation and expression of opinion, MR. JUSTICE BRENNAN also stated that the practice had the effect of imposing an unconstitutional condition on the receipt of a public benefit and therefore came within the rule of cases like *Perry v. Sindermann,* 408 U.S. 593. In support of the holding in *Perry* that even an employee with no contractual right to retain his job cannot be dismissed for engaging in constitutionally protected speech, the Court had stated:

> For at least a quarter-century, this Court has made clear that even though a person has no "right" to a valuable governmental benefit and even though the government may deny him the benefit for any number of reasons, there are some reasons upon which the government may not rely. It may not deny a benefit to a person on a basis that infringes his constitutionally protected interests—especially, his interest in freedom of speech. For if the government could deny a benefit to a person because of his constitutionally protected speech or associations, his exercise of those freedoms would in effect be penalized and inhibited. This would allow the government to "produce a result which [it] could not command directly." *Speiser v. Randall,* 357 U. S. 513, 526. Such interference with constitutional rights is impermissible.
> . . . .
>
> Thus, the respondent's lack of a contractual or tenure "right" to re-employment for the 1969-1970 academic year is immaterial to his free speech claim. Indeed, twice before, this Court has specifically held that the non-renewal of a nontenured public school teacher's one-year contract may not be predicated on his exercise of First and Fourteenth Amendment rights. *Shelton v. Tucker,* [364 U. S. 479]; *Keyishian v. Board of Regents,* [385 U. S. 589]. We reaffirm those holdings here. *Id.,* at 597-598.

If the First Amendment protects a public employee from discharge based on what he has said, it must also protect him from discharge based on what he believes. Under this line of analysis, unless the government can demonstrate "an overriding interest," 427 U. S., at 368, "of vital importance," *id.,* at 362, requiring that a person's private beliefs conform to those of the hiring authority, his beliefs cannot be the sole basis for depriving him of continued public employment.

---

[8] An individual who is a member of the out-part maintains affiliation with his own party at the risk of losing his job. He works for the election of his party's candidates and espouses its policies at the same risk. The financial and campaign assistance that he is induced to provide to another party furthers the advancement of that party's policies to the detriment of his party's views and ultimately his own beliefs, and any assessment of his salary is tantamount to coerced belief. See Buckley v. Valeo, 424 U. S. 1, 19 (1976). Even a pledge of allegiance to another party, however ostensible, only serves to compromise the individual's true beliefs. Since the average public employee is hardly in the financial position to support his party and another, or to lend his time to two parties, the individual's ability to act according to his beliefs and to associate with others of his political persuasion is constrained, and support for his party is diminished. [427 U. S.,] 355-356.

MR. JUSTICE BRENNAN also indicated that a patronage system may affect freedom of belief more indirectly, by distorting the electoral process. Given the increasingly pervasive character of government employment, he concluded that the power to starve political opposition by commanding partisan support, financial and otherwise, may have a significant impact on the formation and expression of political beliefs.

[9] Regardless of the nature of the inducement, whether it be by the denial of public employment or, as in Board of Education v. Barnette, 319 U. S. 624 (1943), by the influence of a teacher over students, "[i]f there is any fixed star in our constitutional constellation, it is that no official, high or petty, can prescribe what shall be orthodox in politics, nationalism, religion, or other matters of opinion or force citizens to confess by word or act their faith therein." *Id.,* at 642. [427 U.S.,] at 356.

Mr. Justice Stewart's opinion concurring the judgment avoided comment on the first branch of Mr. Justice Brennan's analysis, but expressly relied on the same passage from *Perry v. Sindermann* that is quoted above.

Petitioner argues that *Elrod v. Burns* should be read to prohibit only dismissals resulting from an employee's failure to capitulate to political coercion. Thus, he argues that, so long as an employee is not asked to change his political affiliation or to contribute to or work for the party's candidates, he may be dismissed with impunity—even though he would not have been dismissed if he had had the proper political sponsorship and even though the sole reason for dismissing him was to replace him with a person who did have such sponsorship. Such an interpretation would surely emasculate the principles set forth in *Elrod*. While it would perhaps eliminate the more blatant forms of coercion described in *Elrod*, it would not eliminate the coercion of belief that necessarily flows from the knowledge that one must have a sponsor in the dominant party in order to retain one's job.[11] More importantly, petitioner's interpretation would require the Court to repudiate entirely the conclusion of both Mr. Justice Brennan and Mr. Justice Stewart that the First Amendment prohibits the dismissal of a public employee solely because of his private political beliefs.

In sum, there is no requirement that dismissed employees prove that they, or other employees, have been coerced into changing, either actually or ostensibly, their political allegiance. To prevail in this type of an action, it was sufficient, as *Elrod* holds, for respondents to prove that they were discharged "solely for the reason that they were not affiliated with or sponsored by the Democratic Party." 427 U. S., at 350.

II

Both opinions in *Elrod* recognize that party affiliation may be an acceptable requirement for some types of government employment. Thus, if an employee's private political beliefs would interfere with the discharge of his public duties, his First Amendment rights may be required to yield to the State's vital interest in maintaining governmental effectiveness and efficiency. *Id.*, at 366. In *Elrod*, it was clear that the duties of the employees—the chief deputy of the process division of the sheriff's office, a process server and another employee in that office, and a bailiff and security guard at the Juvenile Court of Cook County—were not of that character, for they were, as Mr. Justice Stewart stated, "nonpolicymaking, nonconfidential" employees. *Id.*, at 375.

As Mr. Justice Brennan noted in *Elrod*, it is not always easy to determine whether a position is one in which political affiliation is a legitimate factor to be considered. *Id.*, at 367. Under some circumstances, a position may be appropriately considered political even though it is neither confidential nor policymaking in character. As one obvious example, if a State's election laws require that precincts be supervised by two election judges of different parties, a Republican judge could be legitimately discharged solely for changing his party registration.

---

[11] As Mr. Justice Brennan pointed out in *Elrod*, political sponsorship is often purchased at the price of political contributions or campaign work in addition to a simple declaration of allegiance to the party. *Id.*, at 355. Thus, an employee's realization that he must obtain a sponsor in order to retain his job is very likely to lead to the same type of coercion as that described by the plurality in *Elrod*. While there was apparently no overt political pressure exerted on respondents in this case, the potentially coercive effect of requiring sponsorship was demonstrated by Mr. Finkel's change of party registration in a futile attempt to retain his position. . . .

That conclusion would not depend on any finding that the job involved participation in policy decisions or access to confidential information. Rather, it would simply rest on the fact that party membership was essential to the discharge of the employee's governmental responsibilities.

It is equally clear that party affiliation is not necessarily relevant to every policymaking or confidential position. The coach of a state university's football team formulates policy, but no one could seriously claim that Republicans make better coaches than Democrats, or vice versa, no matter which party is in control of the state government. On the other hand, it is equally clear that the Governor of a State may appropriately believe that the official duties of various assistants who help him write speeches, explain his views to the press, or communicate with the legislature cannot be performed effectively unless those persons share his political beliefs and party commitments. In sum, the ultimate inquiry is not whether the label "policymaker" or "confidential" fits a particular position; rather, the question is whether the hiring authority can demonstate that party affiliation is an appropriate requirement for the effective performance of the public office involved.

Having thus framed the issue, it is manifest that the continued employment of an assistant public defender cannot properly be conditioned upon his allegiance to the political party in control of the county government. The primary, if not the only, responsibility of an assistant public defender is to represent individual citizens in controversy with the State.[13] As we recently observed in commenting on the duties of counsel appointed to represent indigent defendants in federal criminal proceedings:

> [T]he primary office performed by appointed counsel parallels the office of privately retained counsel. Although it is true that appointed counsel serves pursuant to statutory authorization and in furtherance of the federal interest in insuring effective representation of criminal defendants, his duty is not to the public at large, except in that general way. His principal responsibility is to serve the undivided interests of his client. Indeed, an indispensable element of the effective performance of his responsibilities is the ability to act independently of the government and to oppose it in adversary litigation. *Ferri v. Ackerman,* 444 U. S. 193, 204.

Thus, whatever policymaking occurs in the public defender's office must relate to the needs of individual clients and not to any partisan political interests. Similarly, although an assistant is bound to obtain access to confidential information arising out of various attorney-client relationships, that information has no bearing whatsoever on partisan political concerns. Under these circumstances, it would undermine, rather than promote, the effective performance of an assistant public defender's office to make his tenure dependent on his allegiance to the dominant political party.[14]

---

[13] This is in contrast to the broader public responsibilities of an official such as a prosecutor. We express no opinion as to whether the deputy of such an official could be dismissed on grounds of political party affiliation or loyalty. Cf. Newcomb v. Brennan, 558 F.2d 825 (CA7 1977), cert. denied, 434 U. S. 968 (dismissal of deputy city attorney).

[14] As the District Court observed at the end of its opinion, it is difficult to formulate any justification for tying either the selection or retention of an assistant public defender to his party affiliation:

> Perhaps not squarely presented in this action, but deeply disturbing nonetheless, is the question of the propriety of political considerations entering into the selection of attorneys to serve in the sensitive positions of Assistant Public Defenders. By what rationale can it even be suggested that it is legitimate to consider, in the selection process, the politics of one who is to represent indigent

Accordingly, the entry of an injunction against termination of respondents' employment on purely political grounds was appropriate and the judgment of the Court of Appeals is

Affirmed.

Mr. Justice Stewart, dissenting.

I joined the judgment of the Court in *Elrod v. Burns,* 427 U. S. 347, because it is my view that, under the First and Fourteenth Amendments, "a nonpolicymaking, nonconfidential government employee can[not] be discharged . . . from a job that he is satisfactorily performing upon the sole ground of his political beliefs." *Id.,* at 375. That judgment in my opinion does not control the present case for the simple reason that the respondents here clearly are not "nonconfidential" employees.

The respondents in the present case are lawyers, and the employment positions involved are those of assistants in the office of the Rockland County Public Defender. The analogy to a firm of lawyers in the private sector is a close one, and I can think of few occupational relationships more instinct with the necessity of mutual confidence and trust than that kind of professional association.

I believe that the petitioner, upon his appointment is Public Defender, was not constitutionally compelled to enter such a close professional and necessarily confidential association with the respondents if he did not wish to do so.[*]

Mr. Justice Powell, with whom Mr. Justice Rehnquist joins, and with whom Mr. Justice Stewart joins as to Part I, dissenting.

The Court today continues the evisceration of patronage practices begun in *Elrod v. Burns,* 427 U. S. 347 (1976). With scarcely a glance at almost 200 years of American political tradition, the court further limits the relevance of political affiliation to the selection and retention of public employees. Many public positions previously filled on the basis of membership in national political parties now must be staffed in accordance with a constitutionalized civil service standard that will affect the employment practices of federal, state, and local governments. Governmental hiring practices long thought to be a matter of legislative and executive discretion now will be subjected to judicial oversight. Today's decision is an exercise of judicial lawmaking that, as The Chief Justice wrote in his *Elrod* dissent, "represents a significant intrusion into the area of legislative and policy concerns." *Id.,* at 375. I dissent.

---

defendants accused of crime? No "compelling state interest" can be served by insisting that those who represent such defendants publicly profess to be Democrats (or Republicans). 457 F. Supp., at 1293, n. 13.

In his brief petitioner attempts to justify the discharges in this case on the ground that he needs to have absolute confidence in the loyalty of his subordinates. In his dissenting opinion, Mr. Justice Stewart makes the same point, relying on an "analogy to a firm of lawyers in the private sector." . . . We cannot accept the proposition, however, that there cannot be "mutual confidence and trust" between attorneys, whether public defenders or private practitioners, unless they are both of the same political party. To the extent that petitioner lacks confidence in the assistants he has inherited from the prior administration for some reason other than their political affiliations, he is, of course, free to discharge them.

[*] Contrary to repeated statements in the Court's opinion, the present case does not involve "private political benefits," but public affiliation with a political party.

I

The Court contends that its holding is compelled by the First Amendment. In reaching this conclusion, the Court largely ignores the substantial governmental interests served by patronage. Patronage is a long-accepted practice that never has been eliminated totally by civil service laws and regulations. The flaw in the Court's opinion lies not only in its application of First Amendment principles, . . . but also in its promulgation of a new, and substantially expanded, standard for determining which governmental employees may be retained or dismissed on the basis of political affiliation.[2]

. . . The Court gives three examples to illustrate the standard. Election judges and certain executive assistants may be chosen on the basis of political affiliation; college football coaches may not. . . . And the Court decides in this case that party affiliation is not an appropriate requirement for selection of the attorneys in a public defender's office because "whatever policymaking occurs in the public defender's office must relate to the needs of individual clients and not to any partisan political interests." . . .

The standard articulated by the Court is framed in vague and sweeping language certain to create vast uncertainty. Elected and appointed officials at all levels who now receive guidance from civil service laws, no longer will know when political affiliation is an appropriate consideration in filling a position. Legislative bodies will not be certain whether they have the final authority to make the delicate line-drawing decisions embodied in the civil service laws. Prudent individuals requested to accept a public appointment must consider whether their predecessors will threaten to oust them through legal action.

. . . .

A constitutional standard that is both uncertain in its application and impervious to legislative change will now control selection and removal of key governmental personnel. Federal judges will now be the final arbiters as to who federal, state, and local governments may employ. In my view, the Court is not justified in removing decisions so essential to responsible and efficient governance from the discretion of legislative and executive officials.

II

. . . .

The constitutionality of appointing or dismissing public employees on the basis of political affiliation depends upon the governmental interests served by patronage. No constitutional violation exists if patronage practices further sufficiently important interests to justify tangential burdening of First Amendment rights. See *Buckley v. Valeo,* 424 U. S. 1, 25 (1976). This inquiry cannot be resolved by reference to First Amendment cases in which patronage was neither involved nor discussed. Nor can the question in this case be answered in a principled manner without identifying and weighing the governmental interests served by patronage.

---

[2] The Court purports to limit the issue in this case to the dismissal of public employees. See . . . n. 7. Yet the Court also states that "it is difficult to formulate any justification for tying either the selection or retention of an assistant public defender to his party affiliation." *Ante,* at . . . n. 14. If this latter statement is not a holding of the Court, it at least suggests that the Court perceives no constitutional distinction between selection and dismissal of public employees.

III

Patronage appointments help build stable political parties by offering rewards to persons who assume the tasks necessary to the continued functioning of political organizations. "As all parties are concerned with power they naturally operate by placing members and supporters into positions of power. Thus there is nothing derogatory in saying that a primary function of parties is patronage." J. Jupp, Political Parties 25-26 (1968). The benefits of patronage to a political organization do not derive merely from filling policymaking positions on the basis of political affiliation. Many, if not most, of the jobs filled by patronage at the local level may not involve policymaking functions. The use of patronage to fill such positions builds party loyalty and avoids "splintered parties and unrestrained factionalism [that might] do significant damage to the fabric of government." *Storer v. Brown,* 415 U. S. 724, 736 (1974).

Until today, I would have believed that the importance of political parties was self-evident. Political parties, dependent in many ways upon patronage, serve a variety of substantial governmental interests. A party organization allows political candidates to muster donations of time and money necessary to capture the attention of the electorate. Particularly in a time of growing reliance upon expensive television advertisements, a candidate who is neither independently wealthy nor capable of attracting substantial contributions must rely upon party workers to bring his message to the voters. In contests for less visible offices, a candidate may have no efficient method of appealing to the voters unless he enlists the efforts of persons who seek reward through the patronage system. Insofar as the Court's decision today limits the ability of candidates to present their views to the electorate, our democratic process surely is weakened.

Strong political parties also aid effective governance after election campaigns end. Elected officials depend upon appointees who hold similar views to carry out their policies and administer their programs. Patronage—the right to select key personnel and to reward the party "faithful"—serves the public interest by facilitating the implementation of policies endorsed by the electorate. The Court's opinion casts a shadow over this time-honored element of our system. It appears to recognize that the implementation of policy is a legitimate goal of the patronage system and that some, but not all, policymaking employees may be replaced on the basis of their political affiliation. . . . But the Court does not recognize that the implementation of policy often depends upon the cooperation of public employees who do not hold policymaking posts. As one commentator has written: "What the Court forgets is that, if government is to work, policy implementation is just as important as policymaking. No matter how wise the chief, he has to have the right Indians to transform his ideas into action, to get the job done."[13] The growth of the civil service system already has limited the ability of elected politicians to effect political change. Public employees immune to public pressure "can resist changes in policy without suffering either the loss of their jobs or a cut in their salary." [14] Such effects are proper when they follow from legislative or executive decisions to withhold some jobs from the patronage system. But the Court tips the balance between patronage and nonpatronage positions, and, in my view, imposes unnecessary constraints upon the ability of responsible officials to govern effectively and to carry out new policies.

---

[13] Peters, A Kind Word for the Spoils System, The Washington Monthly, Sept. 1976, p. 30.

[14] The Court quotes M. Tolchin & S. Tolchin, To the Victor . . . : Political Patronage from the Clubhouse to the White House 72, 73 (1971).]

Although the Executive and Legislative Branches of Government are independent as a matter of constitutional law, effective government is impossible unless the two Branches cooperate to make and enforce laws. Over the decades of our national history, political parties have furthered—if not assured—a measure of cooperation between the Executive and Legislative Branches. A strong party allows an elected executive to implement his programs and policies by working with legislators of the same political organization. But legislators who owe little to their party tend to act independently of its leadership. The result is a dispersion of political influence that may inhibit a political party from enacting its programs into law. The failure to sustain party discipline, at least at the national level, has been traced to the inability of successful political parties to offer patronage positions to their members or to the supporters of elected officials.

The breakdown of party discipline that handicaps elected officials also limits the ability of the electorate to choose wisely among candidates. Voters with little information about individuals seeking office traditionally have relied upon party affiliation as a guide to choosing among candidates. With the decline in party stability, voters are less able to blame or credit a party for the performance of its elected officials. Our national party system is predicated upon the assumption that political parties sponsor, and are responsible for, the performance of the persons they nominate for office.

In sum, the effect of the Court's decision will be to decrease the accountability and denigrate the role of our national political parties. This decision comes at at time when an increasing number of observers question whether our national political parties can continue to operate effectively. Broad-based political parties supply an essential coherence and flexibility to the American political scene. They serve as coalitions of different interests that combine to seek national goals. The decline of party strength inevitably will enhance the influence of special interest groups whose only concern all too often is how a political candidate votes on a single issue. The quality of political debate, and indeed the capacity of government to function in the national interest, suffer when candidates and officeholders are forced to be more responsive to the narrow concerns of unrepresentative special interest groups than to overarching issues of domestic and foreign policy. The Court ignores the substantial governmental interests served by reasonable patronage. In my view, its decision will seriously hamper the functioning of stable political parties.

. . . .

V

The benefits of political patronage and the freedom of voters to structure their representative government are substantial governmental interests that justify the selection of the assistant public defenders of Rockland County on the basis of political affiliation. The decision to place certain governmental positions within a civil service system is a sensitive political judgment that should be left to the voters and to elected representatives of the people. But the Court's constitutional holding today displaces political responsibility with judicial fiat. In my view, the First Amendment does not incorporate a national civil service system. I would reverse the judgment of the Court of Appeals.

Comments: 1. *Branti* places the protection of the discharged employee on first amendment rights. *Elrod v. Burns* articulated the standard of review to be applied in first amendment cases:

> It is firmly established that a significant impairment of First Amendment rights must survive exacting scrutiny.... "This type of scrutiny is necessary even if any deterrent effect on the exercise of First Amendment rights arises, not through direct governmental action, but indirectly as an unintended but inevitable result of the government's conduct ...." ... Thus encroachment "cannot be justified upon a mere showing of a legitimate state interest." ... The interest advanced must be paramount, one of vital importance, and the burden is on the government to show the existence of such interest.

Id. at 362.

One interest advanced for patronage discharge in *Elrod* was "the need to insure effective government and the efficiency of public employees." The Court rejected this argument. "The inefficiency resulting from wholesale replacement of large numbers of public employees every time political office changes hands belies this justification." *Id.* at 364.

"Preservation of the democratic process" was also advanced as a paramount interest. The Court answered that "the elimination of patronage practice . . . will [not] bring about the demise of party politics . . . . Patronage dismissals thus are not the least-restrictive alternative to achieving the contribution they may make to the democratic process." *Id.* at 369. Is Justice Powell's dissent in *Branti* a convincing answer to this argument?

What if an employee is transferred to a less responsible position, demoted, or given less demanding responsibilities? The employee may be protected if "the specific reassignment or transfer does in fact impose upon the employee such a Hobson's choice between resignation and surrender of protected rights as to be tantamount to outright dismissal." *Delong v. United States*, 631 F.2d 618, 624 (4th Cir. 1980).

How far has *Branti* modified *Elrod*? One student commentator states:

> Although policy formulation for nearly all governmental jobs has some relation to political parties, a reasonable interpretation of the *Branti* decision would make the patronage discharge of a policymaking-confidential employee invalid unless the employee's policymaking or confidential standing "directly and justifiably concerns political parties."

Case Comment, 16 SUFF. U.L. REV. 415, 425, n.42 (1982). Do you agree? *See also* Note, *Patronage Dismissals Under a First Amendment Analysis: The Aftermath of Branti v. Finkel*, 25 ST. LOUIS L.J. 189 (1981).

The plaintiff in *Branti* sued under § 1983 of the federal Civil Rights Act of 1871. For discussion of this statute see Chapter 7.

2. *Elrod* also discussed Supreme Court cases upholding the constitutionality of the Hatch Act, but concluded that they were consistent with its opinion. The Hatch Act applies to federal employees and to state and local government employees who work in programs funded by federal financial assistance. The Act once prohibited virtually all political activity. It now only prohibits government employees from becoming candidates for partisan political office or soliciting other public employees. 5 U.S.C. § 1502(a) (3). Some states have similar legislation.

The Supreme Court rejected arguments that the Hatch Act was vague and overbroad in *United Public Workers v. Mitchell*, 330 U.S. 75 (1949), and reaffirmed this holding in *United States Civil Service Commission v. National Ass'n of Letter Carriers*, 413 U.S. 548 (1973), and in *Broadrick v. Oklahoma*, 413 U.S. 601 (1973), with respect to a state Hatch Act. *Elrod* noted that the Hatch Act upheld in these cases "did serve in a necessary manner to foster and protect efficient and effective government." It added that "the activities that were restrained by the legislation involved in those cases are characteristic of patronage practices." *Id.* at 366-67. In *Letter Carriers*, the Court also stated that "it is in the best interest of the country, indeed essential, that federal service should depend upon meritorious performance rather than political service, and that the political influence of federal employees on others and on the electoral process should be limited." *Compare Fort v. Civil Service Commission*, 392 P.2d 385 (Cal. 1964) (total ban on political activities violates free speech).

Consider *McCormick v. Edwards,* 646 F.2d 173 (5th Cir. 1981). A program director of a regional law enforcement program funded with federal assistance was dismissed for participating in a political campaign for a mayoral candidate of the opposition party. The position was not in the civil service. The court held that the dismissal did not violate the program director's first amendment rights, relying on the Hatch Act cases. The court noted that a civil service employee could be dismissed under the Hatch Act for partisan political activity, and that it would be an "anomaly" not to apply this rule to non-civil service employees. Is this case consistent with *Branti?* The court in *McCormick* did not apply the strict scrutiny review called for in *Elrod*. Was this error? *Branti* also held that "the ultimate inquiry . . . is whether the hiring authority can demonstrate that party affiliation is an appropriate requirement for the effective performance of the public office involved." How should this line be drawn? In *Sweeney v. Bond,* 669 F.2d 542 (8th Cir. 1982), a new governor discharged a number of "fee agents" who belonged to the opposition party. A fee agent is authorized by statute to issue state motor vehicle licenses and collect state motor vehicle and use taxes.

The court held that the fee agents did not come under the *Elrod-Branti* holdings because they were more like independent contractors than public employees. They were not paid by the state and were not supervised by the state revenue agency. "Fee agents are traditionally looked upon as representatives of the incumbent governor. Many spend much of their time in this way and are not restricted in their active pursuit of party politics by the confines of their fee agent offices." *Id.* at 546. Should the factors listed by the court decide the patronage dismissal issue?

3. What if an employee is dismissed for political reasons and also because she was found to be incompetent? This problem is handled by the causation rule of *Mt. Healthy School District Board of Education v. Doyle,* 429 U.S. 274 (1977), which is discussed in footnote 6 of the *Branti* decision. In *Mt. Healthy,* an untenured school teacher who had engaged in misconduct on his job sent to a radio station a memorandum on teacher dress and appearance which had been circulated by his principal. The communication to the ratio station was arguably protected as free speech.

The Court adopted a "rule of causation" to avoid placing an employee "in a better position as a result of the exercise of constitutionally protected conduct than he would have occupied had he done nothing." The rule was stated as follows:

> Initially, in this case, the burden was properly placed upon respondent [the teacher] to show that his conduct was constitutionally protected, and that this conduct was a "substantial factor" — or to put it in other words, that it was a "motivating factor" in the Board's decision not to rehire him. Respondent having carried that burden, however, the District Court should have gone on to determine whether the Board had shown by a preponderance of the evidence that it would have reached the same decision as to respondent's reemployment even in the absence of the protected conduct.

Id. at 287.

The *Mt. Healthy* causation rule requires findings on difficult questions of motivation and causation, and shifts the decision-making burden to the trial court. *See Van Ootehgem v. Gray,* 628 F.2d 488 (5th Cir. 1980)(employee dismissed for protected free speech and not refusal to follow job order).

The *Mt. Healthy* rule was applied to a patronage discharge in *Tanner v. McCall,* 625 F.2d 1183 (5th Cir. 1980). When a sheriff's office changed hands politically, the new sheriff reappointed all but nineteen or twenty in an office staff of eight-five. The court found no free speech violation:

> When neutral decisional criteria are utilized by an employer, a plaintiff's case is more difficult to prove. Circumstantial evidence can be used to supply inferences of an intent to infringe constitutional rights . . . . The strength of the inference, however, depends on the strength of the circumstances . . . . In some cases, the inferences fail to ripen into proof. . . . In this case no clear statistical pattern of discrimination exists.

Id. at 1192.

See also the last sentence in footnote 14 of the majority opinion in *Branti*. The Court said that the public defender could discharge his assistants if he lacked "confidence" in them. Is this a correct statement of the law in view of *Mt. Healthy?*

4. Civil service legislation usually authorizes discharge only for cause. The cases hold that a "cause" discharge must be based on a substantial fault or shortcoming of the dismissed employee which is substantially related to his employment. *See Paulson v. Civil Service Commission,* 518 P.2d 148 (Nev. 1974)(deputy assistant chief of police did not return from leave of absence).

Is the *Elrod-Branti* patronage rule the equivalent of a discharge for cause test in view of the *Mt. Healthy* causation test? Would it make any difference in the *Paulson* case that the chief of police and mayor belonged to another political party, and that the discharge was partly based on political motives?

5. *Perry v. Sindermann,* which is discussed in *Branti,* also established that government employees may have a right to a notice and hearing on their dismissal even though they are not tenured. The employee, if not tenured, must have an "entitlement" or "expectation" in continued employment in order to claim procedural due process protections. See also the opinion by a divided Court in *Arnett v. Kennedy,* 416 U.S. 134 (1974).

6. Justice Powell's dissent in *Branti* makes the point that a patronage system is essential to the democratic political process. An article by Dean Sandalow views this problem from the perspective of the local government reform movement initiated by Progressives and Populists at the turn of the century:

> All the reforms of municipal government proposed by the Progressives were shaped by their desire to rid cities of machine politics. Machine politics was characterized by corruption, inefficiency, and the concentration of political power. The reforms were aimed at producing honesty, efficiency, and broad citizen participation in politics.

Sandalow, *The Distrust of Politics,* 56 N.Y.U.L. REV. 446, 456 (1981). Sandalow adds that "[t]he reformers' concentration on the public interest and their failure to take account of private or special interests also led them to ignore one of the most important tasks of government at every level: the management of conflict." *Id.* at 454.

Are these observations relevant to the patronage dismissal issue? Consider the following comments by the Supreme Court in *Elrod.*

> [Political patronage affects t]he free functioning of the electoral process .... Conditioning public employment on partisan support prevents support of competing political interests. Existing employees are deterred from such support, as well as the multitude seeking jobs .... Patronage thus tips the electoral process in favor of the incumbent party ....

Id. at 356. For additional discussion see Note, *Patronage Politics: Democracy's Antidote to Enforced Neutrality in Civil Service,* 6 U. DAYTON L. REV. 231 (1981).

7. The majority opinion in *Branti* suggests that political affiliation can be a consideration in hiring as well as discharge. *See* footnote 14. See also Justice Powell's dissent, footnote 2. Is this extension of the *Elrod-Branti* rule justified? How would the Supreme Court apply free speech protections to applicants for employment? Could the Court apply the fourteenth amendment protections recognized by *Sindermann?* Is judicial supervision of the hiring process through the application of constitutional protections more or less objectionable than judicial supervision of the discharge process?

8. At the state level, the governor's power to remove an officer is held not to be inherent and must rest on a specific constitutional or statutory grant under the majority rule. *State ex rel. Thompson v. Morton,* 84 S.E.2d 791 (W. Va. 1954). *But see Wilt v. Commonwealth,* 406 A.2d 1217 (Pa. Commw. 1979) (governor has inherent power to make rules for removal of management level non-civil service employees).

Statutes and constitutions may authorize gubernatorial removal of an executive officer for cause, but the courts are not clear on whether the governor's removal order is judicially reviewable, and if so, under what standards. *See State ex rel. Wehe v. Frazier,* 182 N.W. 545 (1921) (held reviewable). *Contra State ex rel. Ulrick v. Sanchez,* 255 P. 1027 (N.M. 1927) (governor's order of removal held conclusive on courts so long as one of constitutionally specified causes is assigned). In *Lunding v. Walker,* 359 N.E.2d 96 (Ill. 1976), the court, noting an "increased willingness" on the part of courts to review a governor's action, held that the cause assigned by the governor for removal of a state elections board member was reviewable by the courts because of the independent nature of that board. Both the majority and dissenting opinions discuss an amendment to the 1970 Illinois Constitution offered by Professor Netsch as delegate to the convention, and provide a detailed discussion of the governor's removal power.

C. INTEGRITY IN GOVERNMENT SERVICE: CONFLICTS OF INTEREST

Government service provides opportunities for profit and self-advantage. Apart from the obvious possibilities for corruption, kickbacks, self-dealing and the like, government service raises problems of conflict of interest that often are difficult to resolve. Especially at the local level, government officials have a personal and financial interest in the community which may be difficult to separate from their official roles. This section looks at the conflict of interest problem as one of the important issues affecting the integrity of government service.

The case and discussion that follow concentrate on the conflict of interest problem as it arises in the local land use planning and zoning process. Planning and zoning are critical issues at the local level, and play an important role in local politics. Local elections are frequently decided on the views of candidates on zoning and planning problems, especially in suburban communities. The officials who serve on planning boards and commissions may have strong personal views on planning and zoning issues. They may also belong to local organizations that have a stake in how the zoning and planning process is administered. Developers and owners of property in the community also frequently serve on local zoning and planning boards. Separating personal interest from official duty is not always an easy matter. On conflicts of interest in zoning see generally D. MANDELKER, LAND USE LAW §§ 6.64-6.67 (1982). On the problem of bribery and corruption in office see Winckler, *Drafting an Effective Bribery Statute,* 1 AM. J. CRIM. L. 210 (1972).

DANA-ROBIN CORP. v. COMMON COUNCIL

Supreme Court of Connecticut
166 Conn. 207, 348 A.2d 560 (1974)

Before HOUSE, C.J., and SHAPIRO, LOISELLE, MACDONALD and BOGDANSKI, JJ.
MACDONALD, ASSOCIATE JUSTICE.

The plaintiff, Dana-Robin Corporation, appealed to the Court of Common Pleas from the action of the defendant the common council of the city of Danbury in denying its petitions for zone changes and design approval. From the judgment dismissing the appeal, and after our grant of certification, the plaintiff has appealed to this court. The plaintiff's assignments of error, consisting primarily of challenges to the finding and conclusions of the court and its overruling of the plaintiff's claims of law, are directed for the most part at claimed procedural irregularities at both the planning commission and common council levels. The plaintiff maintains that an adverse report of the planning commission on its proposed apartment complex was improper and illegal due to the participation therein of members who should have been disqualified because of conflict of interest, dual office holding, and the unlawful participation of a new member.
. . .

The record and the finding, which is not subject to material correction, reveal the following general facts: In 1970, the plaintiff owned a fifty-five-acre tract of land zoned for single-family residences located "approximately two to four miles" from the Western Connecticut State College campus in Danbury, Connecticut. After preliminary discussions with Danbury officials and the planning commission, the plaintiff developed a plan for the construction of a 963-unit housing project on this land, consisting of four ten-story towers and terrace apartments, together with recreational and commercial facilities. The development, to to be called St. George Terrace, was designed to appeal to relatively high and middle income residents, rather than to college students.

On April 1, 1970, the plaintiff submitted three petitions to the common council, which also serves as the Danbury zoning commission. General Statutes § 8-1. The first sought an amendment to the zoning regulations to establish a new residential classification designated PA-40, which would permit high-density multiple housing. The second sought to have fifty of the fifty-five acres zoned PA-40 and the remaining five acres zoned commercial. The third petition requested specific approval to erect St. George Terrace on the plaintiff's property.

As required by General Statutes § 8-3a, the common council referred the petitions to the planning commission for an advisory report. On June 17, 1970, the planning commission voted to disapprove the petitions. Upon disapproval of a zoning proposal by the planning commission, a two-thirds vote of all the members of the common council is required to adopt the proposal. General Statutes § 8-3a .... Absent a planning commission disapproval, a simple majority vote would be sufficient for adoption. After the planning commission's action, the common council appointed a five-man committee to hold a public hearing on the petitions as permitted by General Statutes § 8-3. This hearing was held on July 13, 1970, and the committee voted four to one for approval. On September 1, 1970, the common council met to act on the petitions. Of the twenty-one members of the council, twenty were present but two disqualified themselves, and the vote was ten to eight in favor of the petitions. The moderator ruled that because two-thirds of the council's membership failed to vote in favor of the proposals, they had not been approved. On appeal to the Court of Common Pleas, the council's action was sustained.

The plaintiff first contends that the vote of disapproval by the planning commission was invalid because two of its members should have disqualified themselves because of a conflict of interest, as required by General Statutes § 8-21; that because of the invalidity of the planning commission's adverse report, only a simple majority vote of the common council was required for approval of its three petitions, and that since a majority vote was obtained by the plaintiff at the meeting on September 1, 1970, the petitions were actually approved.

One of the challenged members of the planning commission, Vincent DeFlumeri, and his mother and sister were the sole stockholders of two real estate corporations which owned and rented residential properties in Danbury. One of those corporations, Ridge Realty Corporation, owned Beaver Brook Hall, an off-campus dormitory for students who could not obtain rooms on campus. Beaver Brook Hall was located about seven-tenths of a mile from the campus. It contained forty rooms and could house eighty-one students, In 1970, however, Beaver Brook Hall was not fully occupied.

The court found that only a few of the students at Western Connecticut State College have automobiles and that only alternative housing located near the campus would make it difficult to keep Beaver Brook Hall fully occupied. As previously noted, the plaintiff's property was found to be two to four miles away from the campus, and the project was found to be designed to appeal to relatively high and middle income residents and not college students. The court also found that neither the plaintiff nor its expert witnesses ever indicated to either the planning commission or the common council that St. George Terrace would be occupied by or was planned for use by students. While some of these findings were challenged, the evidence printed in the defendant's appendix adequately supports them. The court concluded that DeFlumeri's financial interest in Beaver Brook Hall "did not disqualify him from sitting as a member of the Planning Commission since . . . [his] interests were too remote or speculative financially . . . [and not] such as to create a personal bias or prejudice."

General Statutes § 8-21 provides, in relevant part: "No member of any planning commission shall participate in the hearing or decision of the commission of which he is a member upon any matter in which he is directly or indirectly interested in a personal or financial sense." "An 'interest' has been defined as having a share or concern in some project or affair, as being involved, as liable to be affected or prejudiced, as having self-interest, and as being the opposite of distinterest." *Housing Authority v. Dorsey,* 164 Conn. 247, 252, 320 A.2d 820.

Public office is a trust conferred by public authority for a public purpose. The status of each member of the planning commission forbids him from placing himself in a position where private interests might conflict with his public duty. It is the policy of the law to keep the official so far from temptation as to ensure his unselfish devotion to the public interest. The question becomes one of public policy. The modification of zoning regulations must command the highest public confidence, since zoning restrictions limit a person's free use of his real estate for the public good. We repeatedly have held that anything which tends to weaken public confidence is against public policy. . . . The test is not whether personal interest does conflict, but whether it reasonably might conflict. . . . If a zoning authority member fails to disqualify himself despite a conflict of interest, the action of the authority in which he participates is invalid. . . .

We also have pointed out, however, that "[t]he decision as to whether a particular interest is sufficient to disqualify is necessarily a factual one and depends on the circumstances of the particular case." *Anderson v. Zoning Commission,* 157 Conn. 285, 291, 253 A.2d 16, 20. In subjecting those circumstances to careful scrutiny, courts must exercise a degree of caution. "Local governments would . . . be seriously handicapped if any conceivable interest, no matter how remote and speculative, would require the disqualification of a zoning official." *Anderson v. Zoning Commission,* supra. Here, the trial court heard the evidence presented and made the "factual" conclusion that DeFlumeri's interest was too "speculative" to require a disqualification. Since the findings relevant to that determination are supported by the evidence and in themselves amply support this conclusion, we see no reason to interfere with it.

. . . .

The other member of the planning commission whose participation the plaintiff challenges, George Valluzzo, owned a six-unit apartment house in Danbury. His wife owned two one-family rental homes as trustee for his son and daughter, respectively. His brothers also owned a few residential rental properties in Danbury. The court concluded that the Valluzzo family interests were too remote or speculative to disqualify him. To do otherwise, in our opinion, would have been to conclude that, as a matter of law, any interest in rental property must operate to disqualify a zoning official from consideration of matters concerning proposed rental property development. "If this were so, it would not only discourage but might even prevent capable men and women from serving as members of the various zoning authorities. Of course, courts should scrutinize the circumstances with great care and should condemn anything which indicates the likelihood of corruption or favoritism. They must, however, also be mindful that to abrogate a municipal action on the basis that some remote and nebulous interest may be present would be to deprive unjustifiably a municipality, in many important instances, of the services of its duly-elected or appointed officials." *Anderson v. Zoning Commission,* supra. No expert testimony was introduced to the effect that the holdings of Valluzzo conflicted with the interests of the plaintiff, nor does the record indicate that any of the Valluzzo property was in close proximity to the proposed complex. We have no basis, therefore, to interfere with the court's conclusion.

. . . .

There is no error.

In this opinion House, C. J., and Shapiro, J., concurred.

Bogdanski, Associate Justice (dissenting).

On the basis of the trial court's own finding of facts I cannot but conclude that there was error as a matter of law in holding that Vincent DeFlumeri was not disqualified to participate and vote in the planning commission's deliberations.

The trial court found the following facts: DeFlumeri owned 25 percent of Ridge Realty Corporation, with the balance of the corporation being owned by his mother and sister. Ridge Realty owned Beaver Brook Hall, which was located about seven-tenths of a mile from the campus of Western Connecticut State College. Beaver Brook Hall was an off-campus dormitory for students who could not find rooms on campus. Although it contained forty rooms, housing eighty-one students when full, DeFlumeri had been unable to fully rent Beaver Brook Hall. The rent at Beaver Brook Hall was $345 per student per semester, and a $35 breakage deposit was required. The trial court found that St. George Terrace, if approved, would not financially injure Beaver Brook Hall. But it also found that "[t]he availability of St. George Terrace may possibly alleviate the shortage of off-campus housing at Western Connecticut State College until the proposed and planned dormitories were constructed by the college."

General Statutes § 8-21 provides, in part: "No member of any planning commission shall participate in the hearing or decision of the commission of which he is a member upon any matter in which he is directly or indirectly interested in a personal or financial sense."

As a public officer, a member of a planning commission "must not be permitted to place himself in a position in which personal interest may conflict with his public duty." *Low v. Madison,* 135 Conn. 1, 8, 60 A.2d 774, 777. It is the policy of the law to keep the official so far from temptation as to ensure his unselfish devotion to the public interest. The modification of zoning regulations must command the highest public confidence. Anything which tends to weaken public confidence is against public policy. . . . The test is not whether personal interest does conflict, but whether it reasonably might conflict. . . .

In my view, the trial court failed to apply the correct legal test. The DeFlumeri family received substantial revenues from Beaver Brook Hall, but were already having difficulty keeping it fully occupied. The construction of a housing complex in Danbury, with recreational and commercial facilities, which might attract even a few students who might otherwise live in Beaver Brook Hall, was no imaginary, remote or insubstantial threat to DeFlumeri's financial interests. That DeFlumeri's vote on the planning commission may in fact have been untainted is not the relevant consideration. A personal or financial interest that reasonably might conflict suffices to require disqualification. *Kovalik v. Planning & Zoning Commission,* supra; *Mills v. Town Plan & Zoning Commission,* supra; *Low v. Madison,* supra. On the facts of this case, as a matter of law, DeFlumeri was disqualified from sitting and voting on the plaintiff's petitions. Since he failed to disqualify himself, the action of the planning commission disapproving those petitions was void. *Kovalik v. Planning & Zoning Commission,* supra.

. . . .

In this opinion LOISELLE, J., concurred.

Comments: 1. The *Danbury* case indicates that a speculative financial interest is not disqualifying, but the distinction is not always easy to draw. In *Kovalik v. Planning & Zoning Commission,* 234 A.2d 838 (Conn. 1967), a municipality amended its zoning ordinance to change the residential zoning in one half of the community from a one-acre to a two-acre lot minimum. The chairman of the zoning commission, which adopted the change, owned eight percent of the area affected by the rezoning. This interest was held disqualifying. Is this case distinguishable from *Danbury*? How would the chairman of the commission benefit from a zoning change that made the zoning on his land more, rather than less, restrictive?

Compare *Town of North Hempstead v. Village of North Hills,* 342 N.E.2d 566 (N.Y. 1975). The court found no conflict of interest in the adoption of a new zoning district even though members of the town board owned land meeting the minimum four-acre requirement for the new district.

Courts will find a disqualifying interest when the conflict is direct. Assume that a member of a planning commission contracts to sell land to a manufacturer on condition that the manufacturer obtain a zoning amendment. The commission member then votes for the amendment, which passes. *See Daly v. Town Plan & Zoning Commission,* 191 A.2d 250 (Conn. 1967)(held disqualifying).

2. Assume that an official of a local building trades union also serves on the planning commission. She votes for a zoning amendment rezoning land from residential to high-rise apartment uses. Is there a conflict of interest because members of her union might be employed in the construction of a building that might be built on the property? See *Tangen v. State Ethics Commission,* 550 P.2d 1275 (Hawaii 1976), finding no conflict of interest in a similar situation. The court noted that any impact on union members would depend "upon the intervening decisions of the landowners."

Compare *Save a Valuable Environment v. Bothell,* 576 P.2d 401 (Wash. 1978). Two members of a local chamber of commerce served on a planning commission which approved a rezoning for a shopping center. "The trial court found the shopping center would financially benefit most of the Chamber's members and that their support was crucial to the success of the application." The supreme court found a violation of an "appearance of fairness" rule which it applies to rezonings. It also rejected an argument that its holding violated rights of association protected by the free speech clause of the federal Constitution.

3. If a member of a zoning board makes statements indicating that he has prejudged a matter on which he subsequently votes, he will be disqualified. *Barbara Realty Co. v. Zoning Board of Review,* 128 A.2d 342 (R.I. 1957). This rule is an application of the usual disqualification of judicial and quasi-judicial officers for bias.

Campaign statements are another matter. Assume a candidate for city council runs on a platform to "get those mobile homes out of the city." After his election, he votes for a zoning amendment that deletes all mobile home zoning districts from the zoning ordinance. The courts find no disqualification, holding that disqualification would frustrate freedom of expression in political campaigns. *See City of Fairfield v. Superior Court,* 557 P.2d 375 (Cal. 1975). Is there a free speech issue here?

The campaign statement cases are consistent with the general rule that courts will not question the motives of members of legislative bodies. Under this view, members of a local legislative body are not subject to disqualification for bias or conflicts of interest. See *Fiser v. City of Knoxville,* 584 S.W.2d 659 (Tenn. App. 1979). Courts sometimes make an exception if fraud is shown.

4. What about lawyers? Assume that a landowner applies to the zoning board of adjustment for a variance needed to construct an office building. The board exercises quasi-judicial functions and the conflict of interest rules apply. The landowner is represented by the senior partner in a law firm. The senior partner's brother is a member of the board. Is he disqualified? *See Kremer v. City of Plainfield,* 244 A.2d 335 (N.J.L. 1978) (board member disqualified when his nephew was a partner in the firm representing the applicant).

The court in *Plainfield* emphasized that the uncle-nephew relationship was not too remote to establish a conflict of interest. It also pointed out that the nephew was not a "subordinate employee" in the firm. What if the law firm "screens" the board member's relative out of the case and does not allow him to participate in the variance application?

5. Conflict of interest and bias disqualification rules are judicially imposed, but many states have adopted conflict of interest legislation of general or limited applicability. The statute, see the *Danbury* case, may simply disqualify for "direct financial interest," leaving the definition of this term to the courts.

A model act has been proposed to apply to all conflicts of interest and has been adopted in some states. It disqualifies for "substantial financial interest," and then defines "financial interest" as:

(1) An ownership interest in a business,
(2) A creditor interest in an insolvent business, or
(3) An employment, or prospective employment for which negotiations have already begun.

A Conflict-of-Interest Act, 1 HARV. J. ON LEGIS. 68, 75 (1964).

Would this definition change the result in any of the cases discussed in these Comments? Didn't the planning commission member in *Danbury* have a disqualifying "ownership interest in a business"? The Hawaii statute applicable in the *Tangen* case contained a similar definition.

The article proposing the model act also noted that "[a] well-drawn statute should prohibit conflicts of interest which are most damaging to the standards of good government and yet not prohibit so much that competent people will be discouraged from serving." *Id.* at 69. Does the "financial interest" definition accomplish this purpose? Would you revise it? If so, how?

6. As an alternative or supplement to conflict of interest legislation, some states have followed the federal model and require financial disclosure by state and local officials. Financial disclosure laws applicable to public officials affect fundamental constitutional rights of privacy, and require a strict scrutiny review for overbreadth. *See Buckley v. Valeo,* 424 U.S. 1 (1976). The history of financial disclosure legislation in California indicates the problems which must be faced in drafting a statute that meets this constitutional requirement.

The most recent California case is *Hays v. Wood,* 603 P.2d 19 (Cal. 1979), which considered a financial disclosure law adopted through popular initiative. The court reviewed two earlier cases which considered the constitutionality of earlier similar legislation:

In [*City of Carmel-by-the-Sea v. Young,* 466 P.2d 225 (Cal. 1970)] we considered the 1969 financial disclosure law . . . and discussed the basic standards applicable to statutes of this nature. The 1969 Act required "every public officer" (§ 3700) and "each candidate" (§ 3702) for state or local public office to file, as a public record, a statement "describing the nature and extent" of each "investment" exceeding $10,000 at the time of filing of the statement (other than personal residence or recreational property). (§ 3700.) While readily accepting the validity of public disclosure as an appropriate technique, we found that the statute therein presented was too broad. We said that the law "encompass[es] indiscriminately persons holding office in a statewide agency regardless of the nature or scope of activity of the agency, as well as those whose offices are local in nature . . . ." More importantly, we noted, "No effort is made to relate the disclosure to financial dealings or assets which might be expected to give rise to a conflict of interest; that is, to those having some rational connection with or bearing" upon the actual functions of the official or his agency. . . . Rather, we observed, the 1969

Act covered, without distinction, *all* substantial commercial investments of the official, his spouse and children, regardless of their nature or location. We concluded that the law was not drawn as narrowly as possible to achieve its legitimate purpose and we invalidated it.

In 1973, the Legislature enacted a new disclosure statute designed to overcome the deficiencies of its predecessor. (§ 3600 et seq., superseded but not repealed by § 87100 et seq., hereafter the 1973 Act.) The 1973 Act applied only to candidates for, or incumbents of, certain designated high-level offices (§ 3700). As to those affected, it required disclosure of limited information about investments or real property in excess of $1,000, and of somewhat more detailed information, including identities, concerning each source of personal income (including gifts, loans, and business income) in excess of $250. Unlike the 1969 Act, the 1973 law did not require disclosure of the exact amounts of income or investment; rather, like the current Act, it called only for a statement whether each covered income or investment source exceeded $1,000 or $10,000. (*Ibid.*) Subdivision (c) of section 3700 provided that no such financial interest need be disclosed if it could not be "affected materially" by the official's public duties; under subdivision (d), only investments, income sources or property *within the official's jurisdiction* could be so affected.

In *County of Nevada v. MacMillen*, 522 P.2d 1345 [1974], we upheld the 1973 Act, finding that it sufficiently remedied the flaws which we had observed in the 1969 version. We stressed that the 1973 law went only so far as necessary to discourage actual and substantial conflicts of interest. In particular we noted that, compared with the earlier statute, it applied to a more limited group of high-level offices and required less specific information about the investments covered. Most significantly, disclosure was required only as to those investments and sources of income which might actually be expected to influence the performance of official duty....

We conclude that the present law is within the guidelines established by *City of Carmel* and *Nevada*. Like the 1973 law, application of the present Act is restricted to those designated high-level state and local offices which might reasonably be expected to have a substantial influence on public policy. With the few exceptions discussed below, the disclosure schemes of the two laws are similar. They seek appropriate information about the sources and general magnitude of financial interests which may give rise to conflicts of interest, but refrain from prying unnecessarily into their exact nature and amount.

Id. at 22, 23. Compare the California financial disclosure law with conflict of interest legislation like that considered in *Danbury*. Does conflict of interest legislation, as applied in *Danbury* and the cases considered in this Comment, *supra,* only "discourage actual and substantial conflicts of interest"? Should it? Does the constitutional right of privacy objection apply to conflict of interest legislation?

A NOTE ON POST-EMPLOYMENT RESTRICTIONS ON GOVERNMENT OFFICERS, EMPLOYERS AND ATTORNEYS

A substantial number of states have enacted restrictions on former officers and employees. The statutes usually apply only to the state government, but some apply to local governments as well. A prohibition on contracts with the state or local government is the most common restriction. Other activities prohibited include legislative lobbying, appearances before state agencies, and disclosure of confidential information.

The most common restriction is a temporary ban for a one-year or two-year period on the prohibited activities. Some of the statutes allow the prohibited activities but require notice by the former officer or employee to the state ethics commission. Another common restriction prohibits an officer or employee from accepting offers of future employment while in government service. Enforcement of these prohibitions is usually delegated to a state ethics commission, and the statutes also impose criminal and civil penalties. *See* Schmitz, A Survey of State Post-Employment Restrictions in St. Louis Univ. School of Law, "The Revolving Door"—Ethics in Government Service 39 (1980).

Like the conflict of interest statutes, the post-employment restriction statutes must define the governmental duties and responsibilities to which the restriction applies. Assume, for example, that a local government employee served as staff adviser to the local board of zoning adjustment. One month after leaving this position and entering private practice as a city planner, he seeks to represent one of his clients before the board on an application which was filed during his employment. He did not personally handle this application, but did handle many similar applications. Is he disqualifed? Consider the following statutes enacting post-employment restrictions:

> No former ... public employee shall represent a person, with or without compensation, on any matter before the governmental body with which he has been associated for one year after he leaves that body.

Pa. Stat. Ann. tit. 65, § 403(e).

> No public ... employee may represent another person for compensation before a public agency by which he ... was employed within the preceding twelve months ... concerning any matter with which ... [he] was directly concerned and in which he personally participated during his employment ... by a substantial and material exercise of administrative discretion.

Ariz. Rev. Stat. § 38-504(A).

Is the former employee disqualified under either statute? If not, are the statutes too narrowly drawn? And if so, how would you revise them to apply to this former employee in this instance?

What about government attorneys who leave government service? Apart from the state post-employment legislation, attorneys are governed by the Model Code of Professional Responsibility, which is in effect in forty-nine states. The relevant code provisions are discussed in the following excerpt:

> Disciplinary Rule 9-101(B) deals with the former government attorney's personal disqualification. That Rule reads:
>
>> A lawyer shall not accept private employment in a matter in which he had substantial responsibility while he was a public employee.

The Rule applies whether the attorney switches side in the dispute or stays on the same side of the controversy.

It is expectable that the Model Code would prohibit the attorney from switching sides and opposing the government in the very same matter in which he or she had previously represented the government. Indeed, the attorney would arguably be prohibited from doing so even if the draftsmen of the Model Code had omitted Disciplinary Rule 9-101(B). Absent that Rule, the attorney would still be bound by the general conflict-of-interest norms, that is, the Disciplinary Rules under Canon 5. The courts have consistently construed those Rules as forbidding an attorney from opposing a former client in the same or a substantially related matter. In *Emle Industries, Inc. v. Patentex, Inc.*, 478 F.2d 562 (2d Cir. 1973), Judge Kaufman, one of the most prolific writers on this subject, argued that an attorney's continuing duty of confidentiality to a former client necessitates that prohibition. Government attorneys are subject to the same prohibition under Rule 9-101(B). *United States v. Standard Oil Company*, 136 F. Supp. 345 (S.D.N.Y. 1955).

The most important difference between the prohibitions generally governing private attorneys and those for former government attorneys is that only the latter are forbidden from subsequently representing another client on the same side of the dispute. *General Motors Corporation v. City of New York*, 501 P.2d 639 (2d Cir. 1974), is a classic illustration of that difference. In the late 1950's and early 1960's, Reycraft worked in the Antitrust Division of the United States Department of Justice. While there, he was personally involved in the prosecution of *United States v. General Motors,* an antitrust suit against General Motors. In that suit, the government alleged that General Motors had attempted to monopolize the national market for the manufacture and sale of city and inter-city buses. Reycraft not only investigated the case; he drafted and signed the complaint.

Reycraft later left government employ and joined the private law firm of Caldwalader, Wickersham & Taft. That firm represented the City of New York in its antitrust suit against General Motors. Reycraft was active in litigating that suit. Like the federal government's antitrust suit against General Motors, New York's suit charged that General Motors had attempted to monopolize the bus market. Thus, Reycraft had not really switched sides in the dispute. In the present suit, he was not opposing the United States. Moreover, while a federal attorney, he had argued that General Motors' practices violated the antitrust laws; and he was urging the very same contention in the second suit. Nevertheless, the court held that his participation in the second suit ran afoul of Rule 9-101(B). Writing for the court, Judge Kaufman explained the policy justification for invoking the Rule even when the attorney remains on the same side of the legal dispute:

> The purpose behind this plain interdiction is not difficult to discern. Indeed, the City recognizes its salutary goal, as stated by the ABA Committee on Professional Ethics to be: "to avoid the manifest possibility that . . . a former Government lawyer's actions as a public legal official might be influenced by the hope of later being employed privately to uphold or upset what he had done.
> Id. at 648-49.

In other words, the restrictions on the government attorney's subsequent employment are calculated to ensure the attorney's loyalty during government service. The Rule is designed to remove the government attorney's temptation to betray the public interest to enhance his or her prospects for future private employment.

Imwinkelried, *Ethical Problems Facing Former Government Attorneys Now Practicing Land Use Law,* Newsletter of the Planning and Law Division, Am. Planning Ass'n, Vol. 5, No. 6, at 2, 4, 5 (1981).

How would the disciplinary rule apply to the hypothetical case described above? Note that the former government attorney's law firm may also be vicariously disqualified. *See* Rule 5-105(D). *See generally* Morgan, *Appropriate Limits on Participation by a Former Agency Official in Matters Before an Agency,* 1980 Duke L.J. 1.

What if a city attorney assists in drafting new zoning regulations for an historic district? After he resigns his job he represents a developer who files an application for development within the district before the city planning commission. Is the attorney disqualified under the disciplinary rule? *See Committee for Washington's Riverside Parks v. Thompson,* 451 A.2d 1177 (D.C. App. 1982) (finding no diqualification under similar circumstances). What interpretive problem under the disciplinary rule does this hypothetical case raise?

Compare the statutory restrictions on former federal government attorneys. 18 U.S.C. § 207. The attorney may not represent a party other than the United States in a matter in which he or she personally and substantially participated. Neither may the attorney, for a period of one year, make a personal appearance before a federal court, department or agency on a matter which fell within his or her official responsibilities.

D. UNIONS, STRIKES AND COLLECTIVE BARGAINING

Like private employees, government employees associate together in labor unions, bargain through their unions over the terms and conditions of their employment, and may even strike their government employers. In the private sector, labor relations are governed by the provisions of the National Labor Relations Act (NLRA) and comparable state legislation, but the national act exempts state and local governments. 29 U.S.C. § 152(2). This exemption means that labor relations in the public sector are governed by state legislation and state decisional law.

Most state courts hold that government employees may not be prohibited from joining labor unions, but do not require state and local governments to bargain with them. A prohibition on joining labor unions is usually held to violate the freedom of association protected by the first amendment. *See* Annot., 40 A.L.R.3d 728 (1971).

The law of government employee labor relations has been modified in most states by the adoption of public employee relations acts (PERA) modeled on the federal Act. The PERAs comprehensively regulate labor relations in government employment. Like the federal Act, the PERAs grant government employees the right to join or to refrain from joining a labor union. Employees are also granted the right to bargain collectively with their government employers over the terms and conditions of their employment.

The PERAs provide procedures to be followed in the exercise of these rights and these procedures also are modeled on the federal Act. The PERA indicates which government employees and employers are covered by the Act, and may be limited to local employees or to certain types of employees, such as teachers. Procedures are provided to determine the appropriate government employee unit which may organize as a labor union. Election procedures also are provided to determine which union shall act as bargaining representative. The statute also prohibits employer and union practices which interfere with an employee's exercise of his statutory rights. These practices are known as unfair labor practices.

The PERA usually creates a new state agency or designates an existing agency to administer the statute. These agencies, although they have different names, will be referred to as Public Employee Relations Boards (PERBs). Their equivalent at the national level is the National Labor Relations Board. Decisions by the PERBs are subject to limited judicial review.

The state PERAs differ in some respects from the National Labor Relations Act. Government employee strikes are usually prohibited. As an alternative to the strike, a PERA may provide other means for the settlement of disputes arising out of collective bargaining, such as fact finding, mediation or binding arbitration.

Many of the labor relations problems that arise under the PERAs are similar to those that arise in the private sector under the National Labor Relations Act. Government employee labor relations present some issues that do not arise in the private section, however, and these issues are considered in this section.

One important issue concerns the scope of collective bargaining in the public sector. Some conditions of government employment require policy decisions by government entities and are not subject to collective bargaining. Collective bargaining may also conflict with the requirements of civil service laws. Whether a collective bargaining agreement can alter civil service tenure requirements is one example.

Strikes also present a special problem in the public sector. Government employee strikes have been considered to be against the public interest, and are prohibited in most states. Government employee strikes occur despite these prohibitions, and government agencies may then seek judicial relief. Whether courts may enjoin government employee strikes requires a balancing of the employee's interest in improving his working conditions with the public's interest in preventing the disruption of government services. For a law school casebook providing full review of labor relations in the public sector and the state labor relations statutes see H. EDWARDS, R. CLARK & C. CRAVER, LABOR RELATIONS LAW IN THE PUBLIC SECTOR (2d ed. 1979).

1. THE SCOPE OF COLLECTIVE BARGAINING

CITY OF BELOIT v. WISCONSIN EMPLOYMENT RELATIONS COMMISSION

Supreme Court of Wisconsin
73 Wis. 2d 43, 242 N.W.2d 231 (1976)

FACTS

The Beloit Education Association, the exclusive collective bargaining agent for school teachers in the Beloit city school system, and the Beloit City School Board were parties to a collective bargaining agreement which expired on August 24, 1973. On February 8, 1973, the parties began negotiating a successor contract. The negotiations continued until April 25, 1973. On that date the board filed a petition with the Wisconsin Employment Relations Commission, seeking a declaratory ruling under sec. 111.70(4)(b), Stats., as to whether certain proposals submitted by the Beloit Education Association were mandatory subjects of collective bargaining under sec. 111.70(1)(d), Stats. The subjects on which such declaratory ruling was sought were as follows:

(1) the manner in which supervision and evaluation of teachers will be conducted,
(2) the structure and maintenance and availability to teachers of school district files and records,
(3) right of representation prior to reprimand, warning or discipline,
(4) whether or not "just cause" shall be the standard applied in limitation of the Board's actions with respect to renewal of individual teachers' contracts,
(5) the procedure and order of preference to be utilized in event of teacher layoffs,
(6) the treatment and disposition of problem students,
(7) class size,
(8) type and extent of in-service training to be conducted,
(9) the type and extent of reading program to be utilized,
(10) the establishment and structure of summer programs,
(11) the school calendar.

On September 11, 1974, following a hearing, the Wisconsin Employment Relations Commission issued a declaratory ruling finding certain subject matters to be matters for mandatory collective bargaining, and certain others not to be such. On September 23, 1974, the Beloit Education Association moved for reconsideration of the ruling, and, in response thereto, certain changes were made in the commission's ruling. Both parties filed petitions for review with the circuit court. On March 31, 1975, the circuit court modified the ruling of the commission and affirmed the ruling, as modified. From this judgment both parties have appealed.

. . . .

ROBERT W. HANSEN, JUSTICE.

This is an appeal by a school board and by a teachers' association from a circuit court judgment. That judgment modified and affirmed a ruling of the state employment relations commission. That ruling declared the rights of the school board as employer and of the teachers' association as collective bargaining agent under sec. 111.70(1)(d), Stats.

THE STATUTE. This statute (sec. 111.70(1)(d), Stats.), establishing the right of "collective bargaining" in the public sector in this state, provides as follows:

> (d) *"Collective bargaining" means* the performance of *the mutual obligation* of a municipal employer, through its officers and agents, and the representatives of its employes, *to meet and confer* at reasonable times, *in good faith, with respect to wages, hours and conditions of employment with the intention of reaching an agreement,* or to resolve questions arising under such an agreement. The duty to bargain, however, does not compel either party to agree to a proposal or require the making of a concession. Collective bargaining *includes the reduction of any agreement reached to a written and signed document. The employer shall not be required to bargain on subjects reserved to management and direction of the governmental unit except insofar as the manner of exercise* of such functions *affects the wages, hours and conditions of employment* of the employes. In creating this subchapter the legislature recognizes that *the public employer must exercise its powers and responsibilities to act for the government and good order of the municipality, its commercial benefit and the health, safety and welfare of the public to assure orderly operations and functions within its jurisdiction, subject to those rights secured to public employes by the constitutions of this state and of the United States and by this subchapter.* [Emphasis supplied.]

THE LIMITS. As to collective bargaining in the public sector, the italicized portions of the statute establish three categories: (1) Where collective bargaining is required; (2) where collective bargaining is permitted, but not required; and (3) where collective bargaining agreements are prohibited.[1] The obligation of the public employer to "meet and confer" and its right to agree to a policy in a "written and signed document" extends only to matters of "wages, hours and conditions of employment." Beyond such limit is the area of "subjects reserved to management and direction of the governmental unit," where the public employer may, but is not required, to "meet and confer" and may, but is not required, to agree in a "written and signed document." Beyond such limit of voluntary bargaining is the area involving the exercise of the public employer's "powers and responsibilities to act for the . . . good order of the municipality, its commercial benefit and the health, safety and welfare of the public." Here the proper forum for the determination of the appropriate public policy is not the closed session at the bargaining table. More than the bilateral input of the public employer and the employees' bargaining agent is required for deciding the appropriate public policy. Here the multilateral input of employer, employees, taxpayers, citizen groups and individual citizens is an integral part of the decision-reaching process, and bargaining sessions are not to replace public meetings of public bodies in the determination of the appropriate public policy.

---

[1] *Compare:* National Labor Relations Board v. Borg-Warner Corp. (1958), 356 U.S. 342, 348, 349 . . . .

THE PARTIES. Here we deal with collective bargaining between a local school board and a teachers' association. Both board and association are involved, not only in the collective bargaining process as statutorily defined, but also in the political process as constitutionally assured.[3] The school board is an employer under the statute, and it is also a public body of elected officials, with powers and duties for the operation of the school system in the public interest. As such employer, it must bilaterally "meet and confer" and may agree in a "written and signed document" as to matters involving "wages, hours and conditions of employment." As such public body and as to matters of school management and educational policy, it cannot be required to collectively bargain with the collective bargaining agent for its employees. The teachers' association here is a collective bargaining agent under the statute, and also a professional association of teachers concerned with matters of school system management and educational policy.[7] As such bargaining agent the association can collectively bargain with the board as to matters of "wages, hour and conditions of employment." As a professional association it may also be heard as to matters of school and educational policies, but it makes such contribution or input along with other groups and individuals similarly concerned.[8]

THE PROBLEM. The difficulty encountered in interpreting and applying sec. 111.70(1)(d), Stats., is that many subject areas relate to "wages, hours and conditions of employment," but not only to such area of concern. Many such subjects also have a relatedness to matters of educational policy and school management and operation. What then is the result if a matter involving "wages, hours and conditions of employment" also relates to educational policy or school administration? An illustration is the matter of classroom size, subsequently discussed. The number of pupils in a classroom has an obvious relatedness to a "condition of employment" for the teacher in such classroom. But the question of optimum classroom size can also be a matter of educational policy. And if a demand for lowered classroom size were to require the construction of a new school building for the reduced-in-size classes, relatedness to management and direction of the school system is obvious. Would such required result of a new building not be a matter on which groups involved, beyond school board and

---

[3] Art. X, sec. 1, Wis.Const., providing: "The supervision of public instruction shall be vested in a state superintendent and such other officers as the legislature shall direct; and their qualifications, powers, duties and compensation shall be prescribed by law. . . ."

[7] See: Smith, Edwards and Clark, Labor Relations Law in the Public Sector (Bobbs-Merrill 1974) at page 366, quoting Wellington and Winters, The Unions and the Cities (1971) at pages 21-30, the authors stating:

". . . [S]ome of the services government provides are performed by professionals—teachers, social workers, and so forth—who are keenly interested in the underlying philosophy that informs their work. . . .

"The issue is not a threshold one of whether professional public employees should participate in decisions about the nature of the services they provide. . . . The issue rather is the method of that participation."

[8] Summers, Public Employee Bargaining: A Political Perspective, 83 Yale L.J. (1974), 1156, 1195, the author stating:

To say that curriculum content is not a proper subject of bargaining does not mean that teachers have no legitimate interest in that subject or that they should not participate in curriculum decisions. It means only that the bargaining table is the wrong forum and the collective agreement is the wrong instrument. . . . [N]o organization should purport to act as an exclusive representative; the discussions should not be closed; and the decision should not be bargained for or solidified as an agreement. In addition, all of the ordinary political processes should remain open for individuals or groups of teachers to make their views known to the politically responsible officials and thus to influence the decision.

teachers' association, are entitled to have their say and input? Other courts have faced this same problem. Some limit required bargaining to matters "directly" related to "wages, hours and conditions of employment."[9] Some make the test whether the subject matter is "significantly" related to "wages, hours and conditions of employment."[10] Some make the test whether the subject "materially" affects the working conditions.[11] Commentators appear to agree that drawing the line or making the distinction is not easy.[12]

THE CONSTRUCTION. The state employment relations commission was petitioned to determine by declaratory ruling which of various proposals for bargaining were mandatorily bargainable. It responded by initially concluding that only subject matters that were *primarily* related to wages or hours or conditions of employment were mandatorily bargainable. As to such matters, the school board was *required* to "meet and confer" and collectively bargain as to demands of the teachers' association. This construction of the statute was upheld as reasonable by the reviewing court. We agree. The dictionary defines "primarily" as meaning "fundamentally." It is in this sense of the word that "primarily" is here used. What is fundamentally or basically or essentially a matter involving "wages, hours and conditions of employment" is, under the statute, a matter that is required to be bargained. The commission construed the statute to require manadatory bargaining as to (1) matters which are *primarily* related to "wages, hours and conditions of employment," and (2) the impact of the "establishment of educational policy" affecting the "wages, hours and conditions of employment." We agree with that construction.

THE APPLICATION. Having adopted the "primarily so" test as to the matters where mandatory bargaining is required by the statute, the commission proceeded to apply that test to a variety of the teachers' association demands submitted to the commission for testing. That was correct for we have here a case-by-case approach to specific situations. There was no attempt by the commission and there is none by this court to develop broad and sweeping rules that are to apply across the board to all situations. As did the commission and the reviewing court, we will now proceed to discuss the application of the "primarily so" test to each of the subject areas claimed by the teachers' association to be appropriate subjects for required bargaining.

(A) TEACHER EVALUATION. A series of proposals relating to teacher evaluation were submitted to the school board by the teachers' association as appropriate subjects for required bargaining. As to two of them, (1) who was to evaluate teacher performance, and (2) assistance to teachers whose evaluations were poor, the commission held that they did not primarily involve "wages, hours

---

[9] *See:* National Education Association v. Board of Education (1973), 212 Kan. 741, 753, 512 P.2d 426, 435, the court holding: "The key, as we see it, is how direct the impact of an issue is on the well-being of the individual teacher, as opposed to its effect on the operation of the school system as a whole." *See also:* School Dist. of Seward Education Ass'n v. School Dist. of Seward (1972), 188 Neb. 772, 784, 199 N.W.2d 752, 759.

[10] *See:* Clark County School Dist. v. Local Government Employee Management Rel. Bd. (Neb.1974), 530 P.2d 114, 118, the court holding: "[C]lass size is significantly related to wages, hours, and working conditions. . . ."

[11] *See:* Aberdeen Education Ass'n v. Aberdeen Bd. of Education, Ind. School Dist. (S.D. 1974), 215 N.W.2d 837, 841, the court holding: "It is our opinion that the term 'other conditions of employment' as used in SDCL 3-18-3 means conditions of employment which materially affect rates of pay, wages, hours of employment and working conditions . . . ."

[12] Smith, Edwards and Clark, *supra*, footnote 7, 379, quoting Perry and Wildman, The Impact of Negotiations in Public Education: The Evidence from the Schools (1970), 165-171, the authors stating: "'First, it should be noted that it is exceedingly difficult to distinguish between "educational policy" and "salaries and working conditions" where teacher bargaining is concerned.'"

and conditions of employment." As to the others,[16] involving procedures to be used in evaluation, the commission held that they did primarily relate to "wages, hours and conditions of employment." The circuit court affirmed these holdings. Obviously the area of teacher evaluation relates to "management and direction" as well as to "wages, hours and conditions of employment." However, as to the procedures followed, these matters go to the right of teachers to have notice and input into procedures that affect their job security. On the record that was before it, we uphold the conclusions reached by the commission as to teacher evaluation procedures being mandatorily bargainable.[17]

(B) TEACHER FILES. The teachers' association suggested as required bargaining matters certain proposals concerning teacher files and records.[18] The commission found these proposals to relate primarily to "wages, hours and conditions of employment," with bargaining required. The commission incorporated the rationale of its holding as to teacher evaluation, and the reviewing court affirmed, holding the purpose of keeping teacher files to be "for the purpose of evaluating teachers and may well affect their continued employment." Once again it is clear that the proposals relate to "management and direction" as well as to "wages, hours and conditions of employment." However the trial court noted that the proposals go only to those complaints or files which have effect on evaluation or continued employment. So limited, the scope of a teacher's personnel file and the right of teacher access to it would appear to relate primarily to "wages, hours and conditions of employment." At least, on the record before us, we affirm the commission holding as to teacher files and records.

(C) JUST CAUSE STANDARD. The teachers' association claimed bargaining was required under the statute as to its proposals regarding the "just cause standard" for disciplinary action against teachers.[19] The commission held that

---

[16] The proposals can be summarized as follows:

Teacher Supervision and Evaluation (1) Orientation of new teachers as to evaluative procedures and techniques, (2) Length of observation period and openness of observation, (3) Number and frequency of observations, (4) Copies of observation reports and conferences regarding same, and teachers' objections to evaluations, and (5) Notification of complaints made by parents, students and others.

[17] Clark County School Dist. v. Local Government Employee Management Rel. Bd., *supra*, footnote 10, using the "significantly related" test, stating: "... the evaluation of a teacher's performance is significantly related to a teacher's working conditions inasmuch as the evaluation affects transfer, retention, promotion and the compensation scale."

[18] The proposals can be summarized as follows:

Teacher Files and Records (1) Review of personal files and copies of contents therein, and entitlement to representation at such review, (2) Identification of obsolete matters in teacher files, and if obsolete, or otherwise inappropriate to retain, the same shall be destroyed, (3) Prior review of derogatory material and right to submit written answer thereto, the latter to be included in personal file, (4) Conclusion of final evaluation prior to severance, and exclusion of material, received after serverance or following receipt of notice or resignation or notice of "consideration of non-renewal" from teacher files, (5) Limitation on establishment of more than one file per teacher, and (6) Notification, in writing, to teacher of alleged delinquencies, indication of expected correction, and time period therefor, as well as notification of breaches of discipline, and, where possibility of termination exists, notification thereof to Beloit Education Association.

[19] The "just cause" proposals can be summarized as follows:

Just Cause Standard (1) A just cause basis prior to discharge, non-renewal, suspension, discipline, reprimand, reduction in rank or compensation, or deprivation of any professional advantage, (2) Permissible suspension with pay, (3) Charges forwarded to School Board, and copies thereof to suspended teacher, Association president, and chairman of Grievance Committee, by certified mail, and (4) Hearing on charges, together with appeal procedures.

these "just cause" proposals primarily relate to "wages, hours and conditions of employment," and mandated bargaining. The trial court affirmed this holding. As to this holding the school board does not challenge the requirement of bargaining as to a just cause for dismissal. Instead it challenges the bargain ability of renewal or nonrenewal of a teacher's contract. Outside of Milwaukee county where teachers have tenure, the state statute provides that, on or before March 15 of each year, the school board "shall give the teacher written notice of renewal or refusal to renew his contract." While there are restrictions on the right to renew, the school board contends that this statute is not consistent with required bargaining as to renewal or nonrewal of teacher contracts. The trial court found no conflict, finding the only effect of the "written notice" statute to be that "no labor agreement can alter the dates on which notice of nonrenewal is to be given, or any of its other terms." (Absent notice of nonrenewal, the contract renews itself.) We agree that such setting of a minimum procedure for notice and hearing, before a school board can decide not to rehire a teacher, does not limit or negative the right, also granted by the legislature, to teachers to collectively bargain in areas primarily related to "wages, hours and conditions of employment." On the facts before it the commission was entitled to hold that the proposals relating to the "just cause standard" were mandatorily bargainable.

(D) TEACHER LAYOFFS. The teachers' association submitted certain proposals in the field of teacher layoffs as mandatorily bargainable items.[24] As to a decrease in the number of teachers "by reason of a substantial decrease of pupil population," the association's proposal was that such layoffs be "only in the inverse order of the appointment of such teachers."[25] While the commission held all of the teacher layoff proposals to primarily relate to "wages, hours and conditions of employment," it is the proposal for seniority in case of layoffs that was challenged on review and is challenged on this appeal. The school board claims an impingement on the right of the board to determine what programs will be reduced and what staff qualifications are needed. The trial court held that nothing in the association proposal, as worded, went to what school programs were to be reduced or eliminated in case of layoff due to a decrease in pupil population. To the suggestion that "a more senior Fourth Grade athletic teacher must displace a less senior Twelfth Grade physics teacher," the trial court responded that "such an absurd result was not required." While terming it a clarification, it then modified the commission holding to require that "a reasonable clarification to that effect be inserted in the collective bargaining agreement if proposed by the School Board." As so clarified and modified, the proposals stop well short of invading the school board's right to determine the curriculum, and to retain, in case of layoff, teachers qualified to teach particular subjects in such curriculum. As so limited and modified, the proposal, we hold, is one primarily related to "wages, hours and conditions of employment," and hence required to be bargained.

---

[24] The teacher layoff proposals can be summarized as follows:

Teacher Layoffs (1) The basis for layoffs, (2) Order of recall, (3) Qualification for recall, (4) Non-loss of previous service credits, and (5) No new or substitute appointments while qualified teachers are in layoff status.

[25] The actual proposal states in part:

If necessary to decrease the number of teachers by reason of a substantial decrease of pupil population . . . [the employer] may lay off the necessary number of teachers, but only in the inverse order of the appointment of such teachers.

(E) PROBLEM STUDENTS. The teachers' association submitted as proper subjects for mandated bargaining a number of proposals involving "problem students."[27] The commission found the proposals to be "ambiguous" and divided them into two categories of student misbehavior: (1) Misbehavior that does not involve threats to physical safety (of the teachers); and (2) misbehavior of students that presents a physical threat to the teacher's safety. It then held that the first category was not mandatorily bargainable, and that the second was. The reviewing court continued this sharp distinction, upholding the commission ruling that held the portions of the association's proposals that were required bargaining subjects to be confined "strictly to student misbehavior involving physical threats to the teacher's safety." The trial court also noted a particular association proposal dealing with referral of problem students for needed counseling.[28] The trial court held that this proposal did not primarily relate to "wages, hours and conditions of employment," and held it not to be mandatorily bargainable. With the limitations set by the commission and the modification made by the reviewing court, we affirm the holding that the proposals as to problem students who present a physical threat to teacher safety are primarily related to "wages, hours and conditions of employment," and are required by the statute to be bargained.

(F) SCHOOL CALENDAR. The teachers' association suggested the school calendar as a required bargaining topic. The commission ruled that "all aspects of the school calendar" were mandatorily bargainable. The reviewing court affirmed this holding, adding that "all that is required of the employer in collective bargaining is to bargain in good faith with respect to proposals submitted by the collective bargaining agent of the employees. An agreement with respect to a particular proposal is not required." The school board challenges this finding of bargainability, relying heavily upon the case, decided prior to the enactment of sec. 111.70(1)(d), Stats., in which our court held that a school board ". . . need neither surrender its discretion in determining calendar policy nor come to an agreement in the collective-bargaining sense." However, subsequently, our court has held: "The school calendar and in-service days are subject to negotiation with the bargaining agent under sec. 111.70(2), Stats." Given this applicable ruling by this court, we affirm the trial court holding that, while the school board cannot be required to agree or concede to an association demand as to calendar days, it is required to meet, confer and bargain as to any calendaring proposal that is primarily related to "wages, hours and conditions of employment."

(G) IN-SERVICE TRAINING. A variety of proposals regarding teacher in-service training were submitted by the teachers' association as proper subjects for required bargaining.[32] With a single exception all such proposals were held

---

[27] The proposals as to problem students can be summarized as follows:

Problem Students (1) Referral of problem students to specialized personnel and others, (2) Relief of teacher responsibility with respect to problem students, (3) Consent of teacher to whom problem student is assigned, (4) Exclusion of problem student from classroom, report thereof, and consultation prior to return to classroom, (5) Teacher self-protection and report of action taken, and (6) Liability insurance coverage and compensation resulting in absence from duty from injuries in performance of teaching and related duties, with no deduction from accumulated sick leave.

[28] The particular proposal was as follows: ". . . Whenever it appears that a particular pupil requires the attention of special counselors, special teachers, social workers, law enforcement personnel, physicians or other professional persons, such students shall be referred to that particular person."

[32] The in-service training proposals included:

The afternoon of the third Thursday of each month will be designated as "in-service day." If the

by the commission not to primarily relate to "wages, hours and conditions of employment," and, therefore, not to be subject matters where bargaining is required.[33] The single exception and the only proposal in this area held to be mandatorily bargainable was the one regarding: "The number of in-service days during the school year and the day of the week such days will fall." The trial court held this proposal to be a matter of calendaring, and to be governed by the holding, heretofore upheld, as to calendar day proposals being mandatorily bargainable. We agree, noting that the decision of this court making the school calendar subject to negotiation included "in-service days" in its holding. On the record before it the commission was entitled to hold the "in-service days" proposal mandatorily bargainable.

(H) CLASSROOM SIZE. The teachers' association submitted to the commission as a subject matter requiring mandated bargaining a proposal concerning class size.[35] The commission, on the evidence before it, concluded that the size of a class is not primarily a matter of "wages, hours and conditions of employment" but is primarily a matter of basic educational policy.[36] Therefore, it concluded, "decisions on class size are permissive and not mandatory subjects of bargaining." The trial court affirmed this holding, stating that, on the basis of the evidence before it, the commission could conclude that a school board's prerogatives in making educational policy include the power to decide that class size does affect the quality of education and to set class size accordingly. The commission also held that the size of a class has an impact upon conditions of employment of teachers.[37] So it concluded that: "While the School Board has the right to unilaterally establish class size, it nevertheless has the duty to bargain the impact of the class size, as it affects hours, conditions of employment and salaries." The reviewing court also affirmed this commission holding that, while class size was not bargainable, the impact of class size upon "wages, hours and conditions of employment" was mandatorily bargainable. We affirm the trial court holding, agreeing that the commission was warranted in reaching the conclusions it did.

---

third Thursday of any given month falls on a holiday or during a vacation, another appropriate day will be substituted. The calendar for in-service days will be structured jointly by representatives of the association and the central administration. Although the in-service program will be planned to make maximum use of staff talents, outside consultants may be required. In such cases, the board agrees to pay the reasonable costs of said consultants provided that the cost does not exceed $1,000 (one thousand dollars). The time of in-service will be 12:00—4:00. Adequate time for lunch will be provided.

[33] The *WERC* memorandum stated: "However, we conclude that the type of programs to be held on such days, and the participants therein are not subjects of mandatory bargaining, since we are satisfied that such programs and the participants therein have only a minor impact on working conditions, as compared to the impact on educational policy."

[35] The proposal as to class size was as follows:

Because the pupil-teacher ratio is an important aspect of an effective educational program, the Board agrees that class size should be lowered wherever possible to meet the optimum standards of one (1) to twenty-five (25). Exceptions may be allowed in traditional large group instruction or experimental classes, where the Association has agreed in writing to exceed this standard.

[36] The *WERC* memorandum stated: "The size of a class is a matter of basic educational policy because there is very strong evidence that the student-teacher ratio is a determinant of educational quality. Therefore, decisions on class size are permissive and not mandatory subjects of bargaining."

[37] *Id.*, continuing: "On the other hand, the size of the class affects the conditions of employment of teachers. The larger the class, the greater the teacher's work load, e. g., more preparation, more papers to correct, more work projects to supervise, the probability of more disciplinary problems, etc."

(I) READING PROGRAM. The teachers' association claimed that its proposal as to a school reading program was a matter that required bargaining.[38] The commission held that the association's proposal on "reading" related primarily to educational policy,[39] and not to "wages, hours and conditions of employment." It concluded that such proposal was subject to voluntary or permissive bargaining, but that bargaining as to it was not required. The trial court affirmed this holding. The commission further held that: "If a reading program is established, which involves teachers, the impact of the same upon their wages, hours and working conditions, is a subject of mandatory bargaining." This commission ruling was not challenged on appeal, and is here set forth in the interest of completeness. We see no basis upon which it could be successfully challenged.

(J) SUMMER SCHOOL. The teachers' association sought to have declared mandatorily bargainable its proposals for the initiation of a summer school program.[40] The commission held that such proposal for initiating a summer school program related primarily to basic educational policy, and did not primarily relate to "wages, hours and conditions of employment." Therefore it concluded the proposals for a summer school were subject to permissive, but not mandatory bargaining. However the commission also held, should the school board determine unilaterally to establish a summer school session, "matters relating to wages, hours and working conditions of teachers participating in a summer school session, are subject to mandatory bargaining." This holding by the commission is not challenged by either party on appeal, and is set forth, this being an action for declaring of rights, in the interests of completeness. We find it to be entirely correct as a conclusion of law.

(K) ASSISTANCE TO TEACHERS. The teachers' association urged that the commission find mandatorily bargainable its proposals for assistance to teachers having professional difficulties.[41] The commission declined so to do, holding

---

[38] The proposal as to a reading program was as follows:

The Board and the Association agree that each child shall have the opportunity to enhance and expand reading skills necessary to allow a child to reach his optimum reading expectancy level. Therefore the Board agrees to assess the reading achievement and the native ability of each child annually. These figures shall be made available to the Association. The necessary staff, materials, and programs shall be furnished for the child found to be one or more years below his optimum reading expectancy level, to remedy his reading deficit.

[39] The *WERC* memorandum stated:

It is clear to the Commission that the Association's proposal on "reading" relates primarily to basic educational policy, and therefore concerns a matter subject to permissive, but not mandatory bargaining. The need for such a program is essentially a determination of whether the District should direct itself toward certain educational goals.

[40] The proposals for a summer program included in relevant part: (1) That a summer program be initiated; (2) that a maximum of ten teachers be employed for a period of one month at a total salary cost of $10,000; (3) that all other teachers involved receive six credits on the salary schedule; (4) all students participating to do so free of charge; (5) federal grants or aid be applied for when and if possible; (6) that the program be under the direction of the director of curriculum; and (7) that the summer workshop be for one month with hours of 8-12 and 1-4.

[41] The teacher assistance proposals were as follows:

1. Definite positive assistance shall be immediately provided to teachers upon recognition of "professional difficulties." ... 2. Beginning immediately with the conference after the classroom observation, specific appropriate direction shall be offered to guide the individual toward the solution of his particular professional problem. Suggested actions shall include at least three of the following: (a) Demonstration in an actual classroom situation (b) Direction of the teacher toward a model for emulation, allowing opportunities for observation (c) Initiation of conferences with evaluator, teacher and area coordinator or department chairmen to plan positive moves toward improvement of professional classroom performance (d) Guidance for the teacher toward profes-

instead that the proposals for teacher assistance primarily related to the management of the school system, and were not primarily or even significantly related to "wages, hours and conditions of employment." In explaining its reasons for so concluding, the commission stated in its memorandum: ". . . the proposals involving . . . assistance to teachers having professional difficulties, and the techniques to be employed in dealing with teachers found to be suffering professional difficulties, reflect efforts to determine management techniques rather than 'conditions of employment.' As such, they are not subjects of mandatory bargaining." The trial court affirmed this holding. While such assistance to teachers having professional difficulties is not unrelated to their continued employment or promotion, it is evident that the primary relatedness is to the "management and direction" of the school system. On the record before it the commission acted properly in so concluding.

. . . .

Judgment affirmed.

Comments: 1. The court in *Beloit* rather uncritically accepted the rulings of the commission on what were bargainable issues. Did the commission and the court, in your opinion, properly apply the test for bargainable issues that the court adopted? Would these issues be bargainable under the alternative tests discussed by the court?

2. The educational bargaining cases illustrate the line that must be drawn between bargaining issues that affect the teacher's employment and issues that remain subject to managerial discretion and are outside the bargaining process. Most state PERAs adopt the language of the NLRA and require bargaining over "terms and conditions" of employment. Some courts have adopted general rules to determine which issues fall within this general term. The *Beloit* case states what is probably the majority rule on the bargainability of the issues considered.

The *Beloit* case also adopted a three-part classification of bargainable issues into mandatory, permissive, and those which lie within managerial discretion and are not constitutionally delegable. A similar three-part classification applies in the private sector, but not all courts have adopted it in the public sector. These courts distinguish between issues which are bargainable and those which are not because they fall within managerial discretion.

The elusive line between what is managerial and what is bargainable raises a dilemma. Expansion of the range of bargainable issues would substantially qualify managerial authority in the public sector. Expansion of the scope of managerial authority would substantially qualify the scope of the collective bargaining process. Judicial attitudes toward the scope of bargaining in the public sector also have been influenced by the prohibition on public employees' strikes adopted by most states. Some courts believe that the scope of bargaining should be expanded to offset the strike prohibition.

How did the Wisconsin court resolve these dilemmas? Do you agree with its decision on each of the bargainable subjects it considered?

In *Blackhawk Teachers' Federation Local 2308 v. Wisconsin Employment Relations Board*, 326 N.W.2d 247 (Wis. App. 1982), the Federation asked the court to reconsider the "primary relation" test adopted in *Beloit*. The legislature had strengthened the statutory prohibition against public employee strikes after the *Beloit* case. The Federation argued that strikes had occurred though prohibited prior to the amendment, and that

---

sional growth workshops (e) Observation, continued and sustained, by the evaluator to note the day-to-day lessons and their interrelationships (f) Maintenance and expansion of the collection of professional literature with assigned reading, designed to suggest possible solutions to identified problems.

Beloit limited the scope of collective bargaining to offset the strike weapon. The court reaffirmed *Beloit,* noting that the more stringent strike prohibition "does not necessarily result in a significant increase in a municipal employer's bargaining power."

3. Consider the following alternative formulations of the line between managerial and bargainable issues and compare them with the formulation in *Beloit*:

> [N]egotiable terms and conditions of employment are those matters which intimately and directly affect the work and welfare of public employees and on which negotiated agreement would not significantly interfere with the exercise of inherent management prerogatives pertaining to the determination of governmental policy.

State v. State Supervisory Employees Ass'n, 393 A.2d 233, 239 (N.J. 1978).

> It does little good, we think, to speak of negotiability in terms of "policy," versus something which is not "policy." . . . The key, as we see it, is how direct the impact of an issue is on the well-being of the individual teacher, as opposed to its effect on the operation of the school system as a whole.

National Education Ass'n of Shawnee Mission, Inc. v. Board of Education, 512 P.2d 426, 435 (Kan. 1973).

> [T]he appropriate test . . . is to balance the element of educational policy involved against the effect that the subject has on a teacher's employment.

Sutherlin Education Ass'n v. Sutherlin School District No. 130, 548 P.2d 204, 205 (Or. App. 1976). Several courts have adopted the balancing test.

4. Some state statutes have handled the scope of bargaining problem by defining the issues which are subject to collective bargaining. In such a state, a court may view the adoption of a detailed statutory list as an expression of legislative intent to limit the scope of the bargaining process to those matters listed. *See Colonial School Board v. Colonial Affiliate,* 449 A.2d 243 (Del. 1982); *Charles City Community School District v. Public Employment Relations Board,* 275 N.W.2d 766 (Iowa 1979).

Other states have followed the example of a comparable federal executive order and have adopted legislation generally defining the scope of managerial prerogative:

> A public employer is not required to meet and negotiate on matters of inherent managerial policy, which include, but are not limited to, such areas of discretion or policy as the functions and programs of the employer, its overall budget, utilization of technology, the organizational structure and selection and direction and number of personnel.

Minn. Stat. Ann. § 179.66(1).

5. The courts have dealt with a number of bargainable scope issues in addition to those discussed in the *Beloit* case. One important issue which has arisen in times of government retrenchment is the question of layoffs. The courts have generally held that decisions over layoffs are a matter of managerial discretion. *City of Brookfield v. Wisconsin Employment Relations Commission,* 275 N.W.2d 723 (Wis. 1979). The court held that "economically motivated layoffs of public employees resulting from budgetary restraints is a matter primarily related to the exercise of municipal powers and responsibilities and the integrity of the political processes of municipal government." *Id.* at 728. *Accord Maywood Board of Education v. Maywood Education Ass'n,* 401 A.2d 711 (N.J. App. Div. 1979).

What if a university, or a school system, decides to consolidate one or more previously existing departments into one department? One court held that this decision was a matter of educational policy. *Dunellen Board of Education v. Dunellen Education Ass'n,* 311 A.2d 737 (N.J. 1973). The consolidation action did not result in the dismissal of any employee. The court noted that "[t]his step may have enabled experimental coordination of the two departments to ascertain whether their educational productivity might be increased through measures of joint activity." *Id.* at 743. What if the consolidation had resulted in the dismissal of several teachers?

Student participation in university affairs may raise a bargaining problem. Assume that a university administration wishes to adopt a program in which decisions on promotion and tenure are partly based on "teaching effectiveness," to be determined in part by student evaluations. The court held that the student input was a bargainable item in *Central Michigan University Faculty Ass'n v. Central Michigan University,* 273 N.W.2d 21 (Mich. 1978). It noted that "the procedures and criteria adopted affect the retention, tenure, and promotion of faculty members [and] are clearly matters within the employment sphere." The dissenters believed that the impact of student evaluations on employment would be minor.

6. Is a residency requirement bargainable? Recall that most courts have upheld continuing residency requirements which require that employees continue to reside in the municipality. *See* Section A. In *Detroit Police Officers Ass'n v. City of Detroit,* 214 N.W.2d 803 (Mich. 1974), the court held that a continuing residency requirement was bargainable as a "condition of employment" and was not exempted from bargaining as a "continuing recruiting requirement." The court noted that "[a] recruiting requirement, whether it is age, mental competency, physical characteristics or residency, focuses on that point in time at which a candidate for employment is hired." Do you agree with this distinction? The court also held that the residency requirement, although adopted by ordinance, could not supersede the PERA mandatory bargaining requirement. What about a durational residency requirement? *See accord City of New Haven v. Connecticut State Board of Labor Relations,* 410 A.2d 140 (Conn. 1979). *See generally* Hayford & Durkee, *Residency Requirements in Local Government Employment: The Impact of a Public Employer's Duty to Bargain,* 29 LAB. L.J. 343 (1978).

7. A collective bargaining agreement usually is signed by a state or local executive or separate agency, but the legislative body must appropriate the funds to carry out the agreement. What if the agreement calls for an eight percent pay increase but the legislature, believing it too high, appropriates only five percent? What are the executive's or agency's options?

Budgeting procedures are not easily integrated with the bargaining process. Bargaining may continue during budget preparation and beyond the budget submission date, creating problems for decision makers who must estimate the impact of a new union contract on expenditure estimates. Some of the state PERAs have impasse resolution procedures geared to the budget submission date. *See* D. STANLEY, MANAGING LOCAL GOVERNMENT UNDER UNION PRESSURE 112, 115-19 (1972).

In *City of Des Moines v. Public Employment Relations Board,* 275 N.W.2d 753 (Iowa 1979), the court held that the budget submission date was the termination date for mandated statutory impasse procedures. The court held that otherwise it would be "impossible for a political subdivision to deal effectively with its duty to formulate a budget." But cf. *Garden City Educators' Ass'n v. Vance,* 585 P.2d 1057 (Kan. 1978), holding that statutory impasse procedures could extend beyond the budget submission date. Some of the PERAs require that bargaining be completed before the budget submission date.

Assume a statute prohibits a school district from incurring an annual deficit and requires approval from a local tax board for a tax increase to avoid a deficit. A school district enters into a collective bargaining contract providing for two successive annual wage increases. It claims the second annual increase would cause a deficit and that the no-deficit statute voids the collective bargaining agreement. The tax board refused to tax increase to pay the second-year increase.

Is the collective bargaining agreement void? In a similar case, *South Bend Community School Corp. v. National Education Ass'n-South Bend,* 444 N.E.2d 348 (Ind. App. 1983), the court said that a collective bargaining contract that created a deficit would be void as beyond the school district's authority. The court refused to void the contract because the school district had not shown that the wage increase expense was the expense that caused the deficit. How could this showing be made?

8. Conflicts have arisen between the state PERAs and civil service merit legislation governing public employment. The problem arises from the merit principle which is the key element in the civil service system. The system applies the merit principle in the recruiting and selection of employees, the classification of employment positions, promotion, and discipline. Conflicts with collective bargaining arise because the employee union may seek to make these issues subject to the bargaining process.

Several states have attempted to deal with this problem by exempting all matters covered by the civil service law from the bargaining process or by exempting all or some merit-related items. In the absence of a statutory exemption, the courts must reconcile the merit system legislation with the collective bargaining legislation. Most of the decisions have not found a facial conflict between the two statutes, but have held that conditions of employment not specifically covered by the merit system legislation are subject to bargaining. *See Pacific Legal Foundation v. Brown,* 624 P.2d 1215 (Cal. 1981)(personnel board's authority to determine classifications in civil service does not include authority to determine salaries); *State v. State Supervisory Employees Ass'n,* 393 A.2d 233 (N.J. 1978)(may bargain on conditions of employment falling between minima and maxima fixed by statute).

Some courts have adopted a policy favoring either the civil service system requirements or the collective bargaining process. *Compare Laborer's International Union, Local 1029 v. State,* 310 A.2d 664 (Del. Ch. 1973), *aff'd,* 314 A.2d 919 (Del. 1974) (favoring civil service system), *with American Federation of State, County and Municipal Employees v. County of Lancaster,* 263 N.W.2d 471 (Neb. 1978)(contra).

9. There is an extensive literature on the policy issues raised by the scope of bargaining problems in the public sector. One view would limit public sector bargaining. This view distinguishes private sector bargaining, which is restrained by market competition. No such restraint exists in the public sector. Public sector bargaining may also displace the political process as the arena for making decisions. *See, e.g.,* H. WELLINGTON & R. WINTER, THE UNIONS AND THE CITIES 21-30 (1971).

Proponents of a broader scope for public sector bargaining argue that public employee unions do not have sufficient power to affect public policy decisions, and that public agency managers can make the political trade-offs required by the bargaining process. Proponents for an expanded scope of bargaining also stress that the employee status of public employees is paramount. Like private employees, they should have access to the collective bargaining process to determine their conditions of employment. *See* Wollett, *The Bargaining Process in the Public Sector: What Is Bargainable?,* 51 OR. L. REV. 177 (1971); NOTE, *The Scope of Negotiations Under the Iowa Public Employment Relations Act,* 63 IOWA L. REV. 649 (1978).

The problem of defining the scope of public policymaking discretion which is exempt from outside review arises frequently in state and local government law. Compare the discussion of discretionary governmental acts which do not attract liability in tort, see Chapter 6, and the limitation of judicial remedies against local governments to ministerial as compared with discretionary acts, see Chapter 12.

10. For additional discussion of public sector bargaining see W. GERSHENFELD, J. LOEWENBERG & B. INGSTER, SCOPE OF PUBLIC-SECTOR BARGAINING (1977)(experience in various states); M. LIEBERMAN, PUBLIC-SECTOR BARGAINING (1980); Clark, *The Scope of the Duty to Bargain in Public Employment* in LABOR RELATIONS LAW IN THE PUBLIC SECTOR 81 (A. Knapp ed. 1977); Sackman, *Redefining the Scope of Bargaining in Public Employment,* 19 B.C.L. REV. 155 (1977). *See also* Annot., 84 A.L.R.3d 242 (1978).

2. STRIKES AND STRIKE INJUNCTIONS

If bargaining fails, the strike is the strategy of last resort. Although the right to strike is conferred by statute in the private sector, the rule is the other way in the public sector. Public employees do not have a constitutional right to strike. *Anchorage Education Ass'n v. Anchorage School District,* 648 P.2d 993 (Alaska 1982). Neither are public employee strikes legal at common law. The illegality rules make enforcement of the strike ban comparatively simple, at least on the surface. Strikes are enjoinable, and strikers are subject to civil and criminal contempt for violating strike injunctions.

Most states have ratified the common law ban on government employee strikes by adopting legislation denying the right to strike. Some of this legislation carries penalties. See Nev. Rev. Stat. §§ 288.230-288.360, authorizing injunctions, union fines, union official fines and prison sentences, and dismissal or suspension of union members. Other state legislation simply adopts the common law ban without specifying remedies or penalties. This legislation raises a remedial problem, especially in connection with an injunction, which is the most effective remedy for ending a strike. Whether the illegality of a public employee strike under the statutory ban is enough for an injunction is one of the principal questions, as the following case indicates.

TIMBERLANE REGIONAL SCHOOL DISTRICT v. TIMBERLANE REGIONAL EDUCATION ASS'N

Supreme Court of New Hampshire
114 N.H. 245, 317 A.2d 555 (1974)

KENISON, CHIEF JUSTICE.

The major issue in this case is whether the presiding justice properly denied the plaintiff's petition to enjoin the defendants from engaging in or aiding and abetting a strike. The plaintiff filed the petition for injunction on February 28, 1974, and requested an immediate hearing. The Presiding Justice, *Morris*, J., assigned the case to Master Leonard C. Hardwick, Esquire, who, after several hearings and meetings on the petition, filed a report on March 11, 1974 recommending the petition be presently denied but remain on file to be brought forward on the motion of the court or of the parties. The presiding justice approved the master's report forthwith and issued a decree in accordance with the recommendation. On March 19, 1974, the plaintiff filed a motion to set aside the decree as against the law and the facts. This motion was denied by the court, subject to the plaintiff's exception, and was reserved and transferred. The following facts appear from the pleadings, reserved case, briefs and oral arguments.

The Timberlane Regional Education Association (hereinafter TREA) is the collective bargaining agent for some, if not all, of the teachers in the Timberlane Regional School District and is affiliated with the New Hampshire Education Association, whose membership consists of school teachers employed throughout the State. The TREA and the Timberlane Regional School Board (hereinafter board) agreed to meet during the spring and summer of 1973 for the purpose of negotiating a contract for the 1974-75 school year.

The board proceeded to hire a professional negotiator and delayed meeting with the TREA until July 31, 1973. The parties met throughout the fall and early winter and, by January 14, 1974, had reached a tentative agreement on approximately one-quarter of the items submitted for negotiation by the TREA. The majority of the remaining items, which included salary schedules, sick and emergency leave, teacher rights and responsibilities, teacher evaluation, academic freedom and grievance procedures, had been declared non-negotiable by the board. It became apparent that an impasse was developing in regard to these items, and the members of the TREA voted to submit their differences with the board to a mediator for resolution. The TREA contacted the Federal Mediation Service which agreed to undertake mediation if both parties so requested. The board, however, declined to accept this offer, and several other attempts to find a mutually agreeable mediator came to naught.

The parties resumed negotiations on February 15, 1974, and met again on February 18, 20 and 23. These meetings resulted in a tentative agreement on several of the remaining items, but their differences with respect to [a] great majority of these items were unresolved. During the course of negotiations on

February 23, 1974, the TREA discovered for the first time that on February 16, 1974, the board had submitted salary proposals to the budget committee, despite the fact that an agreement had not been worked out between the parties on this matter. The board then stated at the end of this session that it would go no further and declined to negotiate on the evening of February 23, or at any time on February 24, and 25, 1974.

The members of the TREA met on February 25, 1974, and voted to call for mediation because of an impasse in negotiations and to refuse to teach until mediation began. Last minute efforts to achieve compromise between the positions of the parties came to no avail, and the strike commenced on February 26, 1974. Approximately two-thirds of the teaching staff in the district did not report to work, and pickets were set up in the vicinity of the schools. The board was initially able to keep all of the schools in the district open by hiring substitute teachers, and student attendance did not drop appreciably. The board, however, was ultimately forced to shut down the Timberlane Regional High and Junior High Schools.

"[P]ublic employer collective bargaining is now an established fact at the federal level and in the majority of state and local governments. The transition from uniform disapproval to majority acceptance of public employer collective bargaining began in 1955, when New Hampshire adopted legislation [Laws 1955, 255:1 effective July 14, 1955, now RSA 31:3] authorizing town governments to engage in collective bargaining with public employee unions." Blais, State Legislative Control over the Conditions of Public Employment: Defining the Scope of Collective Bargaining for State and Municipal Employees, 26 Vand. L.Rev. 1, 2 (1973). Nevertheless, in most jurisdictions, a strike by public employees is prohibited either by statute or by judicial decision. Annot., 37 A.L.R.3d 1147 §§ 2, 3 (1971), Supp.1973). New Hampshire is no exception to this rule, for this court held in *Manchester v. Manchester Teachers Guild,* 100 N.H. 507, 510, 131 A.2d 59, 63 (1957), that such strikes are illegal under the common law of this State and characterized this prohibition as a matter of public policy solely within the province of the legislature. *See* N. Edwards, The Courts and the Public Schools 682 (1971).

We are aware of the general dissatisfaction with the effect of this prohibition on labor negotiations between government and public employees. *See, e. g.,* Anderson, The Impact of Public Sector Bargaining 1973 Wis.L.Rev. 986, 1023-25 (1973); Burton & Krider, The Role and Consequences of Strikes by Public Employees, 79 Yale L.J. 418, 437-40 (1970); Edwards, The Emerging Duty to Bargain in the Public Sector, 71 Mich.L.Rev. 885, 891-93 (1973); Foegen, A Qualified Right to Strike—in the Public Interest, 18 Lab.L.J. 90, 98-99 (1967); Kheel, Strikes and Public Employment, 67 Mich.L.Rev. 931 (1969); Wellington & Winter, Structuring Collective Bargaining in Public Employment, 79 Yale L.J. 805, 822-25 (1970). In the private sector, the right to strike is viewed as an integral part of the collective bargaining process. Anderson, Strikes and Impasse Resolution in Public Employment, 67 Mich.L.Rev. 943, 957 (1969). In the public sector, however, the denial of the right to strike has the effect of heavily weighing the collective bargaining process in favor of the government. Without legislation providing alternative methods for resolving impasses in negotiation, there is no ultimate sanction available to the public employees for compelling the good faith of the government, and as a consequence, the only recourse available to them, if they are being treated unfairly, is to terminate their employment or to engage in an illegal strike. Bernstein, Alternatives to the Strike in Public Labor Relations, 85 Harv.L.Rev. 459, 464-66 (1971); Lev, Strikes by Government Employees:

Problems and Solutions, 57 A.B.A.J. 771 (1971); *Note*: Striking a Balance in Bargaining with Public School Teachers, 56 Ia.L.Rev. 598, 599-601 (1971); *Note*: Teachers' Strikes — A New Militancy, 43 Notre Dame Lawyer 367 (1968).

It is not a proper judicial function to make policy judgments as to the merits of providing public employees with the right to strike or of developing alternative processes such as compulsory mediation or arbitration to resolve government labor disputes. For an excellent discussion of such policy matters, *see* Anderson, The Impact of Public Sector Bargaining, 1973 Wis.L.Rev. 986 (1973); Wellington & Winter, Structuring Collective Bargaining in Public Employment, 79 Yale L.J. 805 (1970). This decision must be made by the legislature. RSA ch. 98-C (Supp.1973) (Prohibiting strikes by state employees organizations where an agreement has been entered into with the State providing mediation and arbitration procedures for impasse resolution); RSA ch. 105-B (Supp.1973) (Prohibiting strikes by police organizations, but providing mediation and arbitration procedures for impasse resolution); *see* N.H. House bill 889 (1973 Session; vetoed) (Prohibiting public employee strikes but requiring the employer to bargain in good faith and providing procedure for impasse resolution); *see, e. g.,* Alas. Stat. § 23.40.200 (1972) (Granting right to strike to certain public employees, including teachers, if not detrimental to public health, safety and welfare); Hawaii Rev. Stats., § 89-12 (Supp.1973) (Authorizing strikes by public employees if there is no danger to public health and safety); Pa.Stat.Ann. Tit. 43, § 1101.1003 (Supp.1973) (Permitting strikes by public employees if collective bargaining process is exhausted and no clear or present danger to public health, safety and welfare); Vt.Stat.Ann. Tit. 16 § 2010 (Supp.1973) (Allowing strikes by teachers unless clear and present danger to a sound program of school education). *See also* Alderfer, Follow-up on the Pennsylvania Public School Strikes, 25 Lab.L.J. 161 (1974); *Note:* Teacher Negotiations in Illinois: Statutes and Proposed Reforms, 1973 U.Ill.L.F. 307 (1973).

However, in the absence of legislation, the courts are necessarily compelled to consider the problems inherent in labor relations between the government and public employees when called upon to issue an injunction to prevent an illegal strike. The injunction is an extraordinary remedy which is only granted under circumstances where a plaintiff has no adequate remedy at law and is likely to suffer irreparable harm unless the conduct of the defendant is enjoined. The availability of injunctive relief is a matter within the sound discretion of the court exercised on a consideration of all the circumstances of each case and controlled by established principles of equity. . . .

In view of the nature of this remedy, a growing number of jurisdictions have applied equitable principles to deny the government the use of an injunction against illegal strikes by teachers unless there is a showing of irreparable harm to the public. One of the first cases in formulating this new approach was *School Dist. for Holland v. Holland Educ. Ass'n,* 380 Mich. 314, 157 N.W.2d 206 (1968) in which the Michigan Supreme Court indicated that the refusal of the government to bargain in good faith would be a factor of importance in the determination of whether or not to issue an injunction. *Id.* at 327, 157 N.W.2d at 211. This position was embraced by the Rhode Island Supreme Court in *School Committee of Westerly v. Westerly Teachers Ass'n,* R.I., 299 A.2d 441, 445 (1973) which held that an injunction would not issue "unless it clearly appears from specific facts . . . that irreparable harm will result. . . ." *See* C. Nolte, Law and the School Superintendent § 7.14 (2d ed. 1971).

We are persuaded by these recent developments that it would be detrimental to the smooth operation of the collective bargaining process to declare that an injunction should automatically issue where public teachers have gone on strike. *Note*: Ohio Public Sector Labor Relations Law: A Time for Reevaluation and Reform, 42 U.Cinn.L.Rev. 679, 702-07 (1973); *see* N.E.A. Report on Strikes in 1972-73 School Year, 541 BNA Gov't Employ.Rel.Rep. D-1 thru D-3 (Feb. 11, 1974). The essence of the collective bargaining process is that the employer and the employees should work together in resolving problems relating to the employment. The courts should intervene in this process only where it is evident the parties are incapable of settling their disputes by negotiation or by alternative methods such as arbitration and mediation. *See Danville Bd. of School Directors v. Fifield*, Vt., 315 A.2d 473 (1974), reported in 547 BNA Gov't Employ.Rel. Rep. B-1 (Mar. 25, 1974). Judicial interference at any earlier stage could make the courts "an unwitting third party at the bargaining table and a potential coercive force in the collective bargaining processes." *School Committee of Westerly v. Westerly Teachers Ass'n*, R.I., 299 A.2d 441, 446 (1973). Accordingly, it is our view that in deciding to withhold an injunction the trial court may properly consider among other factors whether recognized methods of settlement have failed, whether negotiations have been conducted in good faith, and whether the public health, safety and welfare will be substantially harmed if the strike is allowed to continue. *See Levitt v. Maynard*, 105 N. H. 447, 450, 202 A.2d 478, 480 (1964); Gosseen, Labor Relations Law, 1972/73 Annual Survey of American Law, 445, 460 n. 108 (1973).

We have reviewed the master's report and the record and are satisfied that the trial court took these matters into account in denying the injunction for the present. We agree with the master's opinion that the parties had not yet exhausted the possibilities of finding compromise in the collective bargaining process at the time the injunction was refused.

Plaintiff's exception overruled.

All concurred.

Comments: 1. Although the *Timberlane* case indicates that some courts apply the traditional irreparable harm rule to strike injunctions, the majority rule is clearly the other way. The leading case adopting the majority view is *Anderson Federation of Teachers v. School City of Anderson*, 251 N.E.2d 15 (Ind. 1969). The court upheld a temporary restraining order against striking teachers, noting that all public strikes "lead to anarchy" and are "unthinkable and intolerable." In this case, a small group of teachers struck for better wages, and the schools never closed. See also the *Anchorage* case, *supra*.

More explicit policy reasons have been suggested for prohibiting public employee strikes. Two authors argued for a strike ban because market restraints are weak in the public sector where services are essential, because the public will impose pressure for a quick settlement, because other public interest groups have no comparable weapon, and because strikes distort the political process. Wellington & Winter, *Structuring Collective Bargaining in Public Employment,* 79 Yale L.J. 805, 822 (1970). For a critique of this argument see Burton & Krider, *The Role and Consequences of Strikes by Public Employees,* 79 Yale L.J. 418, 424-32 (1970).

The arguments against public employee strikes are similar to the arguments for limiting the scope of the bargaining process in the public sector. *See* Section A.1, *supra.* Is the likelihood of a strike affected by the scope of the bargaining process? Are public employees more likely to strike if the issues which can be considered in the bargaining process are extensive?

One court has held that a failure on the part of a school district to bargain in good faith weighed against the issuance of an injunction. "It has long been a basic maxim of equity that one who seeks equitable relief must enter the court with clean hands." *School District*

No. 351 Oneida County v. Oneida Education Ass'n, 567 P.2d 830 (Idaho 1977). The court also held that it was error for the trial court to issue an *ex parte* preliminary injunction. Testimony introduced in a hearing might have led to an injunction barring the strike but conditioned on good faith bargaining by the school district. Is this a good remedy?

Another factor to consider in assessing the strike issue is the role of the courts in the injunction process. The irreparable injury standard is vague and ill-defined, and allows for considerable judicial discretion. An appellate court, as in *Timberlane,* may also affirm a lower court decree, whether or not the strike is enjoined. This tendency shifts control over the strike to the trial courts with little appellate supervision.

Consider also the possibility that resort to the courts may create an adversary situation which interferes with the bargaining process and may increase militancy. *See Joint School District No. 1 v. Wisconsin Rapids Education Ass'n,* 234 N.W.2d 289, 300 (Wis. 1975). The court believed that these considerations "mitigate against the easy availability of injunctive relief." Is this a proper conclusion?

2. The disruption in public services that will be sufficient to ground an injunction based on irreparable harm is not clear. In the school strike situation, one author has listed a number of possible adverse impacts. Appleton, Standards for Enjoining Teacher Strikes: The Irreparable Harm Test and Its Statutory Analogues (unpub. M.S.N.D.). These impacts include disruption in the educational program; difficulties for students such as seniors, who may be affected by disruptions in the school schedule; work suspensions for striking teachers; interruption of collateral benefits, such as free lunches; community concerns, such as delinquency by students out of school; possible loss of state funding; and general disruption in the school calendar. Which of these impacts, singly or cumulatively, should be enough to warrant an injunction under the irreparable harm standard?

The nature of the public employment is another factor to consider. The New Hampshire Supreme Court which decided *Timberlane* upheld a strike injunction against firemen. *City of Dover v. International Ass'n of Firefighters, Local No. 1312,* 322 A.2d 918 (N.H. 1974). The court stressed that "the public health, safety and welfare ... consideration is of paramount importance with respect to public employees who perform vital functions within the community, and it is unlikely that any situation would arise wherein a court would permit firemen to curtail essential services without being enjoined." What other public employees might fall within this category? Does the scope of bargaining vary with the nature of the public employment?

3. In the private sector, the Norris-LaGuardia Act prohibits federal courts from issuing injunctions against striking employees. 29 U.S.C. §§ 101-115. The Supreme Court held this statute inapplicable to public employee strikes, reasoning that it applied only to labor disputes between "persons" having a status or relationship, and that the federal government was not a "person" under this definition. *United States v. United Mine Workers,* 330 U.S. 258 (1947). A number of states have adopted anti-injunction statutes based on the federal act, and most state courts have followed the *Mine Workers* holding. See, e.g., the *Wisconsin Rapids* case, *supra.* The Wisconsin court added that it applied a strict construction rule to statutes limiting the judicial injunctive power, and that the state had adopted a PERA which applied to public sector labor relations.

Are these arguments convincing? Note that the failure to apply the anti-injunction statute leaves the decision on strike injunctions to the courts, absent legislation dealing expressly with the public sector. Is this exercise of judicial power desirable?

4. The *Timberlane* case listed several statutes that confer a limited right to strike. One statutory innovation is illustrated by the Pennsylvania statute. It prohibits a strike injunction during statutorily regulated negotiation and mediation. If mediation and negotiation fail to produce an agreement, a strike may be enjoined if it creates "a clear and present danger or threat to the health, safety or welfare of the public." Pa. Stat. Ann. tit. 43, §§ 1101.1002, 1101.1003.

Several decisions by the intermediate Pennsylvania Commonwealth Court have construed the statute, with mixed results. The leading case is *Armstrong Education Ass'n v. Armstrong School District,* 291 A.2d 120 (Pa. Commw. 1973), in which the court set aside a strike injunction. The court held that the "danger or threat [must be] real or actual and that a strong likelihood exists that it will occur." Neither must the danger or threat "be one which is normally incident to a strike by public employees."

Compare *Philadelphia Federation of Teachers v. Ross,* 301 A.2d 405 (Pa. Commw. 1973), which upheld an injunction: "The lower court reasonably found the possibility of increased gang activity, that the existence of the strike required substantial increase in costs of police protection to public property and posed the possibility of loss of state aid to the school district." Are these disruptions "normally incident to a strike"? The court has upheld injunctions when a loss of state aid was likely because the strike made it impossible to provide a full calendar year of instruction. *Bristol Township Education Ass'n v. School District,* 322 A.2d 767 (Pa. Commw. 1974). The dissenting opinion argued that this holding equated the inability to offer a full year of instruction with the "clear and present danger" required by the statute.

Does the statutory "clear and present danger" rule differ from the "irreparable harm" rule adopted in *Timberlane*? What do you think of the Commonwealth Court's interpretation of the statute? Would you adopt a different interpretation?

5. A number of remedies are available for strikes besides strike injunctions. See the Nevada statute, *supra*. Dismissal of the striking employees is one possibility. In *Hortonville Joint School District No. 1 v. Hortonville Education Ass'n,* 426 U.S. 482 (1976), the Court found no federal due process violation when a school board dismissed teachers following a strike. The Court found no actual personal bias, and dismissed a claim of bias based on the school board's involvement "in the negotiations that preceded and precipitated the striking teachers' discharge." The Court stressed that "[s]tate law vests the governmental, or policymaking, function exclusively in the School Board." Compare the conflict of interest cases discussed in Section C, *supra*.

A private cause of action in tort against the union for strike damage is another possibility. Assume that a strike by city sanitation workers causes pollution to beaches. Municipalities in which the beaches are located then sue the striking union. For a case recognizing liability in a case of this type based on a private nuisance theory see *Caso v. District Council 37, AFSCME,* 350 N.Y.S.2d 173 (N.Y. App. Div. 1973). Members of the public might also sue as beneficiaries of a statutory strike prohibition, or as beneficiaries of the continuing employment contract between the union members and their public employer. *See* Note, *Private Damage Actions Against Public Sector Unions for Illegal Strikes,* 91 Harv. L. Rev. 1309 (1978).

A leading case rejecting a tort claim by a public employer is *Lamphere Schools v. Lamphere Federation of Teachers,* 252 N.W.2d 818 (Mich. 1977). As a policy reason for rejecting this form of relief the court noted that it would aggravate employer-employee labor relations. It would also give the public employer an unfair advantage because a striking union would face the threat of a damage suit once the strike was over. Compare *United Construction Workers v. Laburnum Construction Corp.,* 347 U.S. 656 (1954), holding that under federal preemption doctrine, the NLRA bars a private tort where the nature of the claim is such that it would impermissibly intrude into the scheme of federal regulation.

6. Los Angeles County voters, in November 1982, approved an initiative making it a county law that county workers who go on strike will be fired automatically. California law does not prohibit public employee strikes, and similar but less inclusive ordinances had previously been adopted by voters in San Diego and San Francisco. *See Strike Out!,* 69 A.B.A.J. 31 (1983). Is the Los Angeles County initiative preempted because the state has failed to prohibit public employee strikes? See Chapter 3 for a discussion of state preemption.

Chapter 7
GOVERNMENTAL LIABILITY

In recent years, citizens have achieved notable success in efforts to hold state and local governments responsible for injuries to personal and property interests resulting from governmental activity. The trend has been so pronounced that numerous governmental officials and their supporters have predicted dire consequences, including possible governmental paralysis, because of the perceived encroachment of litigators and the courts upon what had been viewed as an almost sacrosanct domain of governmental decision-making. An intense debate has developed in local government circles as a result of the courts' increased willingness to entertain complaints of the citizenry against its government.

Recent comments by two experienced specialists in local government law highlight the debate.

> In a recent case *Community Communications Company, Inc. v. City of Boulder,* [reproduced *infra*], Justice Brennan, writing for the majority, may have seriously undermined the viability of home rule in America by withdrawing from home rule municipalities the "state action" exemption to the Sherman Antitrust Act. . . .
>
> Home rule municipalities are placed in a regulatory quandary; on the one hand, police power ordinances and regulations will in all likelihood produce a barrage of antitrust court litigation, unless on the other hand municipalities are willing to return all regulatory authority to the state. . . . As it now stands, this decision has produced a chilling effect on police power regulation. If the spirit of this decision is extended . . . the century old home rule experiment, unique to America, will be crippled or destroyed. Home rule municipalities will again have to crawl back to the state legislature begging for handouts, an evil which was abolished by state constitutional amendments prohibiting special legislation. The experimental era, the Renaissance of entrusting a portion of the state's power with smaller and responsive political entities, will be over and the dark ages before home rule was initiated by Joseph Pulitzer will return.

Freilich & Carlisle, Editor's Comment, *The Community Communications Case: A Return to the Dark Ages Before Home Rule,* 14 URB. L., at v-vi (1982).

> Municipal lawyers throughout the country are expressing alarm at the fact that their clients can incur liability for substantial legal expenses when a citizen has a dispute with a unit of state or local government. This is not a new phenomenon, in that statutes in numerous states authorize taxpayers' suits, and the prevailing taxpayer is entitled to recover his fees. What is more, it may be a necessary incentive to keep state and local government from abusing a position of great power. . . .
>
> There was great harshness imposed upon the Thiboutot family by the determination of the Maine public official [*Maine v. Thiboutot*, 448 U.S. 1 (1980) (Civil rights action, 42 U.S.C. § 1983, may be brought for denial of AFDC benefits in violation of federal law)—Eds.]. The public official interpreted an extremely complicated federal statute to the detriment of many citizens of Maine. . . .
>
> While it is undoubtedly true that the attorneys' fees aspect of the *Thiboutot* rule will impose hardships on many municipalities, it is important to recognize that there is another side to the issue. The *Thiboutot* rule will also relieve severe hardships which units of local government impose upon millions of citizens through indifferent and even whimsical administration of federal laws.

Manley, *The Next Thirty Years of Civil Rights Litigation,* 13 Urb. L. 541, 549-51 (1981).

This chapter will explore the development of the trend toward governmental responsibility, from the general demise of the tort immunity doctrine through the growth of the inverse condemnation, civil rights and antitrust doctrines now being applied to citizens' disputes with their governments. In addition to the basic concepts, questions concerning appropriate remedies, including attorneys' fees and punitive damages, standards of proof, counter-measures available to cities such as malicious prosecution suits, liability insurance and other forms of risk management, as well as possible limits to statutory liability will be discussed.

A. STATE COURTS AND LEGISLATION

1. THE GOVERNMENTAL-PROPRIETARY DISTINCTION AND TORT IMMUNITY

History and Origins

Governmental tort immunity and the governmental-proprietary distinction in local government law are so closely intertwined that consideration of the origin and demise of one inevitably necessitates consideration of the other. Both were judicial inventions although each also purported to have politically and historically deep roots. The fascinating history of tort immunity and governmental-proprietary functions appears in two important legal commentaries on the doctrines.

In 1924-1928 Professor Edwin M. Borchard of the Yale Law School published a series of scholarly and influential articles on governmental tort liability covering the history, theory, evolution, judicial handling and frailties of the concept of sovereign immunity which underlay tort immunity. Borchard, *Governmental Liability in Tort,* 34 Yale L.J. 1, 129, 229 (1924-1925), 36 Yale L.J. 1, 757, 1039 (1926-1927), 28 Colum. L. Rev. 577, 734 (1928). The chief target of Professor Borchard's scholarship was tort immunity, and his articles helped to lay the foundation for the subsequent demise of the doctrine. He set the stage as follows:

> The common law and the political theory underlying both British and American constitutional law have been regarded as a bulwark of protection to the individual in his relations with the Government. The "rule of law" which Dicey and others extol is designed by judicial control to restrict within the bounds of legality the operation of the governmental machine in its contact with the citizen. Yet it requires but a slight appreciation of the facts to realize that in Anglo-American law the individual citizen is left to bear almost all the risks of a defective, negligent, perverse or erroneous administration of the State's functions, an unjust burden which is becoming graver and more frequent as the Government's activities become more diversified and as we leave to administrative officers in even greater degree the determination of the legal relations of the individual citizen. . . . [T]here is no reason why the most flagrant of the injuries wrongfully sustained by the citizen, those arising from the torts of officers, should be allowed to rest, as they now generally do, in practice if not in theory, at the door of the unfortunate citizen alone. This hardship becomes the more incongruous when it is realized that it is greatest in countries like Great Britain and the United States, where democracy is assumed to have placed the individual on the highest plane of political freedom and individual justice. . . .

The reason for this long-continued and growing injustice in Anglo-American law rests, of course, upon a medieval English theory that "the King can do no wrong," which without sufficient understanding was introduced with the common law into this country, and has survived mainly by reason of its antiquity.[2] The facts that the conditions which gave it birth and that the theory of absolutism which kept it alive in England never prevailed in this country and have since been discarded by the most monarchical countries of Europe, have nevertheless been unavailing to secure legislative reconsideration of the propriety and justification of the rule that the State is not legally liable for the torts of its officers. To be sure, we profess to ease the conscience by according the injured individual an action against the wrongdoing officer—frequently a person without pecuniary responsibility—or else, under our decentralized system of administration, by permitting an action against political subdivisions of the State and local bodies and corporations for injuries inflicted when acting in their "private" or "corporate" as distinguished from their "governmental" capacities. But no serious effort has been made to penetrate the mysticism encumbering this department of the law and to relieve it of its theological and metaphysical conceptions and misconceptions.

34 YALE L.J. at 1-2. In subsequent sections Borchard analyzed in detail the two principal legal theories by which the immunity of the state has been justified in this country: the King can do no wrong, and Justice Holmes' doctrine that the authority that makes the law is not subject to the law.[1] Borchard, 36 YALE L.J. at 17-41, 757-807.

While the broad concept of sovereign immunity is the principal underpinning of governmental immunity in this country,[2] the tort immunity of local units of government developed its own set of precedents and theories to sustain it. This immunity developed separately for quasi-corporations (counties, towns, school districts and most special districts) and municipal corporations (cities, boroughs and villages). In the case of quasi-corporations, Professor Borchard traced the source of immunity as follows:

In the United States, that immunity appears first to have been worked out in New England, [the case was *Mowrer v. Leicester,* 9 Mass. 247 (1812)—Eds.] where a court of Massachusetts relied upon the English case of *Russell v. Men of Devon.* [2 T.R. 667, 100 Eng. Rep. 359 (K.B. 1788).—Eds.] In that case, an unincorporated county was held immune from responsibility for an injury

---

[2] That this maxim was misunderstood, even by Blackstone and Coke, see the excellent monograph of Ludwik Ehrlich, Proceedings against the Crown (1921) 42-49. The maxim merely meant that the King was not privileged to do wrong. If his acts were against the law, they were *injurice* (wrongs). Bracton, while ambiguous in his several statements as to the relation between the King and the law, did not intend to convey the idea that he was incapable of committing a legal wrong. Ehrlich, *op. cit.,* 43. Indeed, there appears to have been a considerable measure of redress obtainable, though not damages. *Ibid.* 44-46.

[1] Justice Holmes' explanation of the source of the doctrine of sovereign immunity appeared in Kawananakoa v. Polyblank, 205 U.S. 349, 353 (1907), a suit involving an attempted mortgage foreclosure and sale of land, a part of which was then owned by the territory of Hawaii. In holding the territory not subject to suit without its consent, Holmes said: "A sovereign is exempt from suit, not because of any formal conception or obsolete theory, but on the logical and practical ground that there can be no legal right as against the authority that makes the law on which the right depends."

[2] The history of federal and state immunity is reviewed in, among others, Kramer, The Governmental Tort Immunity Doctrine in the United States 1790-1955, 1966 U. Ill. L.F. 795, 796-810.

arising out of a defective bridge, because it had no corporate fund or the means of obtaining one, and it seemed impracticable to permit judgment to be satisfied out of the assets of possibly a few individuals. Hence the injured individual, for practical reasons, was denied relief. Yet the only similarity between the situation in New England and the *Russell* case lay in the fact that the defendants were counties. The New England county was incorporated, had a corporate fund and the means of enlarging it by taxation and was charged by statute with the duty of keeping highways in repair. Under the authority of *Russell v. Devon,* therefore, practically no reason for immunity can be found in these circumstances to exist, yet the Massachusetts court passed judgment for the defendant on the unconvincing ground that the county was a *quasi-*corporation created by the legislature for purposes of public policy and not voluntarily, like a city, and that as a State agency it was therefore immune. This poorly reasoned decision, based upon a case which contradicts rather than sustains it, has been followed very generally in New England and has become the "common law" of the states of the United States, with few exceptions. That a quite different rule prevails with respect to municipal corporations proper, in the case of highways and bridges, and that the distinctions are curiously sustained, will be presently noted.

As the old reasons for county immunity, mentioned in the *Russell* case, disappeared in fact, new reasons had to be devised. The usual ground was public policy, but on the nature of that policy the courts cannot agree. Only a few courts have gone so far as to suggest that the county is, like the state of which it is a political subdivision, immune from suit without consent. The great majority of the courts, however, have put the immunity from substantive responsibility on the ground that the county was created for public purposes, charged with the performance of duties as an arm or branch of the state government, and cannot therefore be liable for failure or negligence in the performance of its public—sometimes even called corporate—duties. The alleged distinction in this respect between counties and municipal corporations proper is said to lie in the further fact that counties and so-called *quasi-*corporations generally are involuntary political divisions of the state organized without regard to the consent of the inhabitants, whereas municipal corporations proper, it is said, are voluntary associations organized under a franchise or charter from the State at the request and for the benefit and local advantage and convenience of the inhabitants.

34 YALE L.J. at 41-43. Borchard rejected the distinction, however:

In view of the close legal approximation between the incorporated county and the municipal corporation, it is believed that no valid ground for a distinction between the two, so far as concerns liability in tort, any longer exists. Indeed, it is believed that with the deflation of the conception of sovereignty and the realization that all political group organizations, from the smallest to the largest, are merely means adopted by the people to enable them to perform certain public services, that there is no sound reason either for differentiating their responsibility according to size or form of organization or to grant them immunity for the torts of their agents and employees.

Id. at 45.

The early history of municipal responsibility for torts, leading to the establishment of the governmental-proprietary distinction, was exhaustively documented by Professor James D. Barnett, *The Foundations of the Distinction Between Public and Private Functions in Respect to the Common-Law Tort Liability of Municipal Corporations (The Antecedents of Bailey v. City of New York),* 16 OR. L. REV. 250 (1937). Barnett found that the early English law did not generally distinguish between public and private corporations in terms of legal liability; and even though there later developed a narrow category of "crown" functions for which liability was not imposed, the liability of English "local" corporations was increasingly assimilated to that of natural persons. *Id.* at 255, 258.

There was thus in fact no good authority for a distinction between "public" and "private" corporations for the use of American courts in their early consideration of corporate tort liability. The earliest reported American case coming to attention that recognized the tort liability of a municipal corporation is *Hooe v. Alexandria*,[33] decided in 1802, in which no distinction was made between the tort liability of public and private corporations, and the city was held liable, simply as "a corporation." The later cases, until after the decision in *Bailey v. New York,* which "bifurcated" the municipal corporation in this regard, generally took this attitude, where they did not, indeed, expressly repudiate the distinction in this connection.

Id. at 259. There were a few cases during this period, notably the Dartmouth College case, *Trustees of Dartmouth College v. Woodward,* 17 U.S. (4 Wheat.) 518 (1819), that drew a distinction between public and private corporations, but principally for purposes of determining whether they were subject to legislative control. *Id.* at 254-55, 261-63. Barnett felt, however, that the doctrine of nonliability of quasi-municipal corporations undoubtedly contributed to the distinction between public and private functions of municipal corporations for purposes of tort liability. The culmination of these distinctions, according to Barnett, was the "momentus" decision in *Bailey v. Mayor of New York,* 3 Hill 531, 38 Am. Dec. 669 (N.Y. Sup. Ct. 1842). In the *Bailey* case plaintiffs sued for damage to their property caused when a dam constructed and maintained by the water commissioners of New York broke because of alleged negligence of defendants, who were apparently the mayor and council of New York. The court conceded that if the defendants were acting solely for the state in prosecuting the work, they would not be liable for the conduct of those whom they had to employ for that purpose; the doctrine of respondeat superior is not applicable. In the court's view, that was not this case.

The powers conferred by the several acts of the legislature authorizing the execution of this great work are not, strictly and legally speaking, conferred for the benefit of the public. The grant is a special, private franchise, made as well for the private emolument and advantage of the city, as for the public good. The state, in its sovereign character, has no interest in it. It owns no part of the work. The whole investment under the law and the revenue and profits to be derived therefrom, are a part of the private property of the city; as much so as the lands and houses belonging to it, situate within its corporate limits.

The argument of the defendants' counsel confounds the powers in question with those belonging to the defendants in their character as a municipal or public body—such as are granted exclusively for public purposes to counties, cities, towns, and villages, where the corporations have, if I may so speak, no private estate or interest in the grant. . . . If [the powers are] granted for public purposes exclusively, they belong to the corporate body in its public, political, or municipal character. But if the grant was for purposes of private advantage and emolument, though the public may derive a common benefit therefrom, the corporation, *quoad hoc,* is to be regarded as a private company. It stands on the same footing as would any individual or body of persons upon whom the like special franchises had been conferred: *Dartmouth College v. Woodward,* 4 Wheat. 668, 672. . . .

---

[33] 1 Cr. C. C. 90, 12 Fed. Cas. No. 6,666 (U. S. C. C. 1802). There are here no citations (in cordance with a general habit of Chief Justice Marshall, who delivered the opinion) to either

Id. at 539, 38 Am. Dec. at 671-72. Having found that the defendants were like any other private company, the court further held that the water commissioners, although appointed by the governor and senate, were acting as agents of the defendants and granted plaintiffs a new trial. (Subsequent developments in the *Bailey* case are reported in 38 Am. Dec. at 676-77.) It was the *Bailey* case which rendered

> municipal corporations liable in tort for the exercise only of its "private" as distinguished from its "public" functions. The distinction was absolutely reactionary and extremely unfortunate in that it limited the liability of municipal corporations to *one class of functions* in contradiction to the *prevailing* view (from which there was almost no dissent) that, logically and justly, applied the general principle of tort liability to all corporations alike, *without distinction of functions.* However, the doctrine, with many variations, inconsistencies, and exceptions in application, was accepted generally, although not universally, and thus became "the American doctrine" of municipal tort liability.

Barnett, *supra* at 268-69.

The dual nature of the municipal corporation—part private corporation and liable for its torts as a private corporation would be, part agent of the state and immune as the state would be—produced a large body of case law which virtually everyone, courts and commentators alike, came to describe as confused, irreconcilably in conflict, unsound, lacking in rational basis, etc.

> In the effort to distinguish governmental from corporate functions of municipal corporations, the courts have drawn in aid various criteria or justifications which seemed to them controlling or persuasive. Thus, aside from the argument derived from the sovereign immunity of the city as agent of the state, the immunity has been placed on the ground that the city derives no pecuniary benefit from the exercise of public functions; that in the performance of public governmental duties the officers are agents of the state and not of the city, and that therefore the doctrine of *respondeat superior* does not apply; that cities cannot properly perform their functions if they are made liable for the torts of their employees; that the city should not be liable for negligence in the performance of duties imposed upon it by the legislature, but only in the case of those voluntarily assumed under general powers; that in determining whether or not to undertake an act the function is governmental, but the execution of the decision in practice is corporate or ministerial; that powers exercised for the benefit of the public at large are governmental, but those conferred for its own benefit and by reason of its nature as a municipal corporation are corporate.
>
> It is believed that not one of these alleged criteria or justifications is sound, and that all of them can be found to have been denied validity in decided cases.

Borchard, *supra,* 34 YALE L.J. at 132-34.

No purpose would be served by an extensive review of the governmental-proprietary decisions. They are summarized or collected in numerous sources. *See, e.g.,* W. PROSSER, HANDBOOK OF THE LAW OF TORTS § 131, at 978-83 (4th ed. 1971); K. DAVIS, ADMINISTRATIVE LAW TREATISE § 25.07, at 463-65 (1958)[3] (both contain citations to still other sources).

English or American authorities. See also Hooe v. Alexandria, 1 Cr. C. C. 98, 12 Fed. Cas. No. 6,667 (U. S. C. C. 1802). *Cf.* Riddle v. Proprietors of the Locks & Canals on Merrimack River, 7 Mass. 169, 188, 5 Am. Dec. 35 (1810).

[3] For convenience Professor Davis' treatise and the two supplements which are in separate volumes will hereinafter be cited as follows: K. Davis, Administrative Law Treatise (1958), as Davis, 1958

How the Doctrine Was Modified

One of the more interesting modern decisions was that of Judge McGowan in *Elgin v. District of Columbia,* 337 F.2d 152 (D.C. Cir. 1964), a tort action against the District arising out of a school playground accident. The court first declined to reexamine, by less than a full court, its recent decision to leave termination of tort immunity to the legislative judgment of Congress. It turned then to the governmental-proprietary distinction, acknowledging that the inconsistencies in classifying functions as one or the other reflect "a growing conviction that a strict rule of immunity from liability has outlived its time." *Id.* at 154.

> We do think it significant that, in the traditional formularization of the opposed concepts as "governmental" and "proprietary," there has been an increasing tendency to substitute "ministerial" for "proprietary." This sounds upon our ears as the knell of the old rationale, which was stated in terms of activities customarily associated with government as compared with those ordinarily carried on by the private sector of society. This was, at best, a tangential articulation of the most sensible support to be found for the immunity grant; and the use of the word "ministerial" both elimininates any continuing utility it might have and focuses attention upon a sharper and more satisfying analysis.
>
> That analysis is more concerned with trying to distinguish between the functions performed within an area of readily recognizable governmental responsibility, than with undertaking to define precisely where the boundaries of that area lie. And, with such functions so identified and differentiated, it next inquires whether an injury inflicted as a consequence of one of such functions can be subjected to judicial redress without thereby jeopardizing the quality and efficiency of government itself. "Ministerial" connotes the execution of policy as distinct from its formulation. This in turn suggests differences in the degree of discretion and judgment involved in the particular governmental act. Where those elements are important, it is desirable that they operate freely and without the inhibiting influence of potential legal liability asserted with the advantage of hindsight. To the extent that the rule of municipal tort immunity continues to serve any useful purpose, this would appear to be that purpose; and its illumination in any given set of facts has been, and is, sought through the function-discriminating exception.

Id. at 154-55. The court acknowledged that the provision of schools is in the traditional terminology a public or governmental function and had been so held in an earlier decision. "Under the court's more recent approach, a finding that a function is 'governmental' is the beginning of the inquiry into the issue of answerability in tort, not the end of it." *Id.* at 156. The court then continued:

> In the case before us, the facts alleged in substance are that a guardrail erected by the school authorities to separate a school playground from a depressed area-way adjoining it had its protective purpose and capacity impaired because a section of it became missing; and that, although a dangerous condition was thus created, nothing was done to remedy it, nor were the required recreational activities on the playground suspended until repairs were effected. These are, we repeat, the allegations. They may or may not be established to the satisfaction of a court or jury after trial. The question before us now is not whether they are true, but whether the opportunity should have been given to prove them to be true.

Treatise; K. Davis, Administrative Law Treatise (Supp. 1970), as Davis, 1970 Supp.; K. Davis, Administrative Law of the Seventies (1976), as Davis, 1976 Supp. Professor Davis has not updated his 1976 supplement in this area.

We think it should have been. In so concluding, we accept the proposition that it is the appropriate business, and indeed the urgent responsibility, of the District of Columbia to provide and operate schools and their accompanying playgrounds. We apprehend also that the discharge of that responsibility will frequently involve the performance of functions calling for the highest degrees of discretion and judgment; and it will be time enough, when and if such claims are before us, for this court to deal with the question of the District's liability in tort for harms allegedly flowing from such functions. . . .

We are not persuaded, however, that the function of repairing broken guardrails imposes upon the District determinations of such delicacy and difficulty that its ability to furnish public education will be ponderably impaired by liability for neglect in failing to make such repairs. If "ministerial" is to be given anything like its accepted usage, it surely has patent applicability to these circumstances. If we accept, as this court has, the right of a pedestrian on a public sidewalk to get to the jury on his claim of the District's liability in negligence for permitting a depressed area alongside such sidewalk to exist unguarded . . . we do not see how we can deny the same right on the facts alleged here. From the standpoint of the school child here involved, the school playground was not only a public area which he was privileged to traverse but one in which he was affirmatively required to be at the time of his injury. In the posture which this case has before us, a remand for the purpose of permitting the complaint to be pursued in appropriate proceedings impresses us as well within the scope which this court has already given for the assertion of claims against the District of Columbia sounding in tort.

It is so ordered.

Id. at 156-57. For later developments in the District of Columbia, see *Spencer v. General Hospital,* 425 F.2d 479 (D.C. Cir. 1969), *infra.*

It was widely believed that the governmental-proprietary distinction was invented by the courts as a way to counter the harshness of the common law of immunity. Commenting on the " 'nongovernmental-governmental' " quagmire that has long plagued the law of municipal "corporations," the Supreme Court said (in a case actually arising under the Federal Tort Claims Act): "The fact of the matter is that the theory whereby municipalities are made amenable to liability is an endeavor, however awkward and contradictory, to escape from the basic historical doctrine of sovereign immunity." *Indian Towing Co. v. United States,* 350 U.S. 61, 65 (1955). Judge Dillon also believed that "[t]he distinction [between the public-governmental and the private-proprietary nature of municipal corporations] originated with the courts, to promote justice . . . in order to hold such corporations liable to private actions." 1 DILLON, MUNICIPAL CORPORATIONS 184 (5th ed. 1911). Professor Barnett's historical survey, however, would indicate that the predominant rule for municipal corporations at the time of the *Bailey* case was one of liability and that the practical effect of the distinction was to carve out an area of municipal immunity where it did not generally exist. See also *Hack v. City of Salem,* 189 N.E.2d 857 (Ohio 1963) (concurring opinion of Judge Gibson).

Nevertheless, it was undoubtedly true that the proprietary exception constituted the largest area of governmental liability for tort for many years. Dissatisfaction with the governmental-proprietary distinction, and presumably with the underlying principle of immunity, led, however, to the development of other means to achieve government responsibility for its torts.

One of the most frequently employed alternatives is the enactment by Congress and many state legislatures (whose state constitutional prohibition against special legislation does not prohibit it) of private laws compensating tort victims who cannot recover through the courts. See 3 DAVIS, 1958 TREATISE § 25.02.

One of the more famous—although perhaps not typical of private laws—was the law enacted by Congress to compensate victims of the Texas City disaster after the Supreme Court held in *Dalehite v. United States,* 346 U.S. 15 (1953), that they could not recover under the Federal Tort Claims Act, 28 U.S.C. §§ 2671-2680. Other techniques which have contributed to overcoming some of the rigors of the immunity doctrine are: laws authorizing government units to purchase liability insurance which includes a waiver of immunity (*see* 3 DAVIS, 1958 TREATISE § 25.04, at 447-49, 1970 SUPP., at 844; 1976 SUPP., at 557-59); creation of courts of claims with authority to adjudicate some or most of the claims against the state (*see* 3 DAVIS, 1958 TREATISE § 25.03, at 445-46); a considerable variety of statutes effectively waiving immunity to a greater or lesser degree for the state or local units of government, or both, including those imposing liability for particular types of torts, most commonly arising out of automobile accidents (*see* 3 DAVIS, 1958 TREATISE § 25.03, at 447); a widely adopted exception that imposes liability on municipalities for the maintenance of a nuisance even when the activity is governmental (*see* W. PROSSER, *supra* at 982-83); and the conversion of damage to property into a "taking" which is then compensable under eminent domain principles. See the discussion of inverse condemnation, *infra*.

Professor Jaffe, in quoting a 1942 article (David, *Public Tort Liability Administration: Basic Conflicts and Problems,* 9 LAW & CONTEMP. PROB. 335, 336-37 (1942)) which said that the statutes permitting liability for the defective condition of streets and for automobile cases meant that a remedy was available in ninety percent of the injury claims against municipalities, criticized the critics of sovereign immunity for not having acknowledged the substantial inroads on the doctrine made by legislation, although admittedly piecemeal. Jaffee, *Suits Against Governments and Officers: Damage Actions,* 77 HARV. L. REV. 209, 211-12 (1963). Davis had reached a consistent conclusion in his 1958 TREATISE. In assessing the impact of all of the direct and indirect inroads on immunity, he said: "Of all deserving tort claims against federal, state and local governmental units, probably far more are paid today than are unpaid, despite the persistence of the basic doctrine that the sovereign cannot be sued without consent." 3 DAVIS, 1958 TREATISE § 25.01, at 434. *See also* Van Alstyne, *Governmental Tort Liability: A Decade of Change,* 1966 U. ILL. L.F. 919. That the basic doctrine of immunity had persisted, however, even while liability was increasingly imposed through legislative initiative and limited judicial exceptions, is evident from the 1954 survey of law and practice governing tort immunity of state and local governments in all of the then forty-eight states. Leflar & Kantrowitz, *Tort Liability of the States,* 29 N.Y.U.L. REV. 1363 (1954) (see especially at 1407 the list of states classified according to the degree of liability assumed).

Abandonment of Governmental Immunity

Pathfinding decisions in Florida, Illinois and California led to a general abandonment of the tort immunity doctrine. In *Hargrove v. Town of Cocoa Beach,* 96 So. 2d 130 (Fla. 1957), the Florida Supreme Court rejected its prior decisions and held that a municipal corporation is liable for the torts of police officers under the doctrine of respondeat superior, but left open the prospect that liability would not be imposed for "legislative or judicial, or quasi-legislative or quasi-judicial functions."

In Illinois, the opportunity for reexamination of the immunity doctrine came in a suit filed against a school district by the father of a child who was severely injured, along with thirteen other children, in a school bus accident. The Illinois

Supreme Court examined many of the theories and justifications for immunity and concluded:

> We conclude that the rule of school district tort immunity is unjust, unsupported by any valid reason, and has no rightful place in modern day society.

Molitor v. Kaneland Community Unit District No. 302, 163 N.E.2d 89, 96 (Ill. 1959), *cert. denied,* 362 U.S. 968 (1960). In the course of its opinion the court spoke to the propriety of judicial abrogation of the doctrine.

> Defendant strongly urges that if said immunity is to be abolished, it should be done by the legislature, not by this court. With this contention we must disagree. The doctrine of school district immunity was created by this court alone. Having found that doctrine to be unsound and unjust under present conditions, we consider that we have not only the power, but the duty, to abolish that immunity. "We closed our courtroom doors without legislative help, and we can likewise open them." . . .
>
> We have repeatedly held that the doctrine of *stare decisis* is not an inflexible rule requiring this court to blindly follow precedents and adhere to prior decisions, and that when it appears that public policy and social needs require a departure from prior decisions, it is our duty as a court of last resort to overrule those decisions and establish a rule consonant with our present day concepts of right and justice. . . .

Id. at 96.

In *Muskopf v. Corning Hospital District,* 359 P.2d 457 (Cal. 1961), the California Supreme Court ruled that the doctrine of governmental immunity from tort liability "must be discarded as mistaken and unjust." *Id.* at 458. The suit resulted from a fall plaintiff suffered while being treated for a broken hip in a hospital run by a hospital district. Previous cases had held that hospital districts were state agencies exercising a governmental function and thus were immune from tort liability. In reaching its conclusion, the court drew heavily on the history of the development of county or local district immunity, discussed *supra,* and concluded that the immunity rule was "an anachronism, without rational basis, and has existed only by the force of inertia." *Id.* at 460.

Following the *Muskopf* decision, the California legislature enacted what amounted to a two-year moratorium on the effect of the court's holding in order to give itself time to work out a new pattern of liability and immunity. That statute was interpreted and upheld in *Corning Hospital District v. Superior Court,* 370 P.2d 325 (Cal. 1962). At the end of this period the legislature enacted a comprehensive Tort Claims Act in 1963. *See* Van Alstyne, *supra,* 1966 U. Ill. L.F. at 935-40.

By 1982, according to a note criticizing the Virginia Supreme Court for refusing to abolish the doctrine, *Freeman v. City of Norfolk,* 266 S.E.2d 885 (Va. 1980), forty-three states had either abolished municipal tort immunity or limited its scope. Note, *Municipal Tort Immunity in Virginia,* 68 Va. L. Rev. 639 n.2 (1982). Mississippi has since joined this group. *See Pruett v. City of Rosedale,* 421 So. 2d 1046 (Miss. 1982).

Activity on the tort front was not confined to the courts, however. As we have previously seen, legislation played an important role in early efforts to impose tort liability on government in selected circumstances. During the period when immunity was being successfully challenged in the courts, state legislatures continued to act—in some cases to carve out additional selected areas of liability, in some cases to enact virtually unconditional waivers of immunity, in some cases to develop a pattern combining appropriate areas of liability and immunity, after the courts had judicially abolished immunity. In reviewing the patchwork quilt, Professor Davis again provided an overall summary of the direction provided by legislative action:

> As long ago as 1946 Congress enacted the Federal Tort Claims Act. The states have been quite slow in adopting comparable legislation. Before 1970, abolition of the immunity of state and local governments came primarily from the courts. But since 1970, abolition has come much more from legislatures than from courts, and the probability seems strong that legislative action will continue to increase and judicial action to decrease.

DAVIS, 1976 SUPP. § 25.00-1. A description and citation of each state's statutory pattern is beyond our purposes in this section. Moreover, legislation is still in a state of flux in many states; as experience develops wth the modern approach of liability, presumably the legislatures, as well as the courts, will refine the new limits on the liability of government units.

Comments: 1. A majority of courts, including, of course, those which judicially abolished the doctrine of immunity, took the position that because the doctrine was judicially created, the courts were free to abandon it when it was found to cause injustice and serve no useful social purpose. Many of the courts used very strong language in condemning and then abrogating the doctrine. That suggests the question whether there are any limitations on what the legislature may do in reacting to the court's action.

Two ways in which the question might arise are seen in the decisions of Illinois and Arkansas. In Illinois, after the *Molitor* decision abolished school district immunity specifically and was generally thought to cover all local government immunity, the legislature's first response was to pass a series of bills which had the effect of restoring immunity to some local governments, authorizing the purchase of insurance by some, placing dollar limitations on the liability of others, requiring indemnification of employees by some and allowing liability to stand with respect to others. In *Harvey v. Clyde Park District,* 203 N.E.2d 573 (Ill. 1964), the court was faced with one of these statutes which reinstated total immunity for park districts. The plaintiff had been injured in a park district playground accident, and his complaint was dismissed below. The supreme court reversed, holding that the statute barring recovery against a park district, in conjunction with the others, violated the Illinois constitutional prohibition against special legislation. The case is reproduced in Chapter 9.

In Arkansas the state supreme court had abolished immunity in *Parish v. Pitts,* 429 S.W.2d 45 (Ark. 1968). In 1969 the Arkansas legislature enacted a law which declared it to be the public policy of the state that all counties, municipal corporations, school districts and other political subdivisions shall be immune from liability for damages, and no tort action shall lie against them. In *Hardin v. City of Devalls Bluff,* 508 S.W.2d 559 (Ark. 1974), the statute was challenged on constitutional grounds. The court first made it clear that the General Assembly has full authority to declare the public policy of the state with respect to tort liability. It then addressed the following constitutional provision:

> § 13. Every person is entitled to a certain remedy in the laws for all injuries or wrongs he may receive in his person, property or character; he ought to obtain justice freely, and without purchase, completely, and without denial, promptly and without delay, conformably to the laws.

Ark. Const. art. II, § 13. The court's view was that counties and municipal corporations were not liable in tort for governmental functions at the time the constitution was adopted and that the drafters therefore never contemplated that that section would guarantee redress for governmental torts. If a provision similar to § 13 were adopted after judicial abrogation of immunity, would the Arkansas court invalidate a legislative restoration of immunity?

Can you think of any other grounds on which an act restoring immunity might be challenged? For discussion see Van Alstyne, *Governmental Tort Liability: Judicial Lawmaking in a Statutory Milieu*, 15 STAN. L. REV. 163, 225-29 (1963). Compare the concurring opinion of Justice Manderino in *Ayala v. Philadelphia Board of Public Education*, 305 A.2d 877 (Pa. 1973), in which he said that "the doctrine of governmental immunity is unconstitutional as is the doctrine of sovereign immunity. No branch of government—the executive, the legislative, or the judicial branch—can deprive a citizen of proper redress for a wrong. The denial of justice in any case is not constitutionally permitted." *Id.* at 889.

2. Despite the decline in importance of the governmental-proprietary distinction in determining local government tort liability, courts continue to struggle with the concept. What, for example, is the operation of a public hospital—governmental or proprietary? What tests are used to answer the question? In *Parker v. City of Highland Park*, 273 N.W.2d 413 (Mich. 1978), the Supreme Court of Michigan adopted an "of essence to government" test to determine governmental functions and rejected the "common good of all" test in concluding that, while the operation of a hospital is a "noble undertaking" that contributes to the "common good," the modern hospital is essentially a business and is not entitled to immunity. The court was construing a statutorily revived limited immunity for governmental functions.

On the other hand, the Supreme Court of Oklahoma rejected an argument of similarity to private mental hospitals in concluding that a state mental hospital was immune because its role of protecting the public from the "harmful tendency" of its patients constituted a governmental function. *Neal v. Donahue*, 611 P.2d 1125 (Okla. 1980). The Oklahoma court also held that the purchase of professional liability insurance was not necessarily inconsistent with an employee's or officer's limited immunity from suit, and that the doctrine of sovereign immunity was not violative of the "remedy for every wrong" provision of the Oklahoma Constitution (art. II, sec. 6) nor the due process or equal protection clauses of the fourteenth amendment.

A NOTE ON THE GOVERNMENTAL-PROPRIETARY DISTINCTION IN OTHER CONTEXTS

The governmental-proprietary distinction has faded into the background as the principal determinant of local government liability in tort. Although its importance in resolving that question has diminished, the distinction has deep roots in the law of state and local government, and it has been invoked as a device for dealing with a number of other questions about the rights or obligations of municipal corporations, some of which are listed below. Given the unsatisfactory role it played in resolving the important legal and social issues of local government tort liability and given the confusion, universally acknowledged, in the judicial attempts to define what is governmental and what is proprietary, students should consider whether use of this analytical device is appropriate in each of these contexts. Was there a valid historical or other reason for invoking the distinction which renders it still useful? If not, what should replace it?

1. *Right to compensation for municipal property taken by the state.* See the Note on the Condemnation of the Property of One Governmental Unit by Another, *supra.*

2. *State control of municipal activity.* (a) State imposed tax for municipal purposes. A number of state constitutions prohibit state imposition of a tax for local, municipal, or corporate purposes. In interpreting these provisions some courts have turned to the governmental-proprietary concept developed for torts. In *People ex rel. Sanitary District v. Schlaeger*, 63 N.E.2d 382 (Ill. 1945), the imposition of the cost of elections of sanitary district commissioners upon the district was challenged. The court held that elections were governmental and the costs of elections were not incurred for "local purposes." See *State ex rel. Helena Housing Authority v. City Council,* 90 P.2d 514 (Mont. 1939), holding valid a state law which required the city to pay the costs of the Helena Housing Authority because slum clearance is a governmental function, and *State ex rel. Gebhardt v. City Council,* 55 P.2d 671 (Mont. 1936), upholding a police minimum wage law because the police function was governmental not corporate; but see *State ex rel. Kern v. Arnold,* 49 P.2d 976 (Mont. 1935), holding a state mandatory wage and hour law for firemen invalid because firemen exercise a proprietary function except while engaged in fighting a fire or going to and from the scene.

(b) State regulation of municipally owned utilities. When Indiana created a commission to regulate utility rates, it made no express provision for the regulation of the rates charged by municipal utilities. In *City of Logansport v. Public Service Commission,* 177 N.E. 249 (Ind. 1931), the court held that a municipal electric utility, because of its proprietary nature, was subject to state regulation in the same manner as a private utility. But see *Georgia Public Service Commission v. City of Albany,* 179 S.E. 369 (Ga. 1935), rejecting the Indiana court's use of the governmental-proprietary distinction.

3. *Municipal utility contracts.* Courts faced with contracts limiting the power to set the rates charged consumers by a municipal utility have sometimes turned to the governmental-proprietary distinction. The Tennessee Supreme Court upheld a contract between the city of Memphis and the Tennessee Valley Authority under which the rates charged by the city in reselling electricity which it purchased from TVA were determined by joint approval of the city and TVA. *Memphis Power & Light Co. v. City of Memphis,* 112 S.W.2d 817 (Tenn. 1937). The Tennessee court said that the city, in operating an electric utility, acted in its private or proprietary capacity and had the same power as a private corporation would have to set its rates by contract and to provide for revision of the rates only with approval of the other contracting party. That apparently did not constitute an invalid delegation of rate making power to TVA. But see *Johnson v. State,* 128 S.E.2d 651 (Ga. App. 1962), in which the court, while agreeing that a municipal corporation acted in a proprietary capacity in operating an electric distribution system and for that reason had the right to enter into a twenty-year contract for the purchase of electric energy from TVA, nevertheless held that a provision governing resale rates, which was virtually identical with that in the Tennessee case, went too far in delegating the city's discretion to set rates and was ultra vires. See also the *City of Texarkana* case, reproduced in Chapter 5.

4. *The power to contract.* A city's power to contract freely may also depend on the governmental-proprietary distinction. In *Gardner v. City of Dallas,* 81 F.2d 425 (5th Cir.), *cert. denied,* 298 U.S. 668 (1936), the court upheld a long-term contract granting to the plaintiff the exclusive right to purchase the city's wet garbage. Garbage disposal in Texas was a corporate, not a governmental, function despite the fact that the contract labeled it governmental, and the city's contract with respect to garbage disposal was said to be governed by the same rules as one made by a private corporation. By similarly denominating the operation of a municipal auditorium as proprietary and thus comparable to private functions, courts have upheld a broad discretion in the city to rent the auditorium as it chooses. *See, e.g., State v. City of Spokane,* 330 P.2d 718 (Wash. 1958) (upholding city's refusal to permit use of auditorium by ice hockey team); and *State ex rel. White v. City of Cleveland,* 181 N.E. 24 (Ohio 1932) (upholding city's refusal to permit a commercial musical promoter to lease city auditorium).

5. *The cost of relocation of utility lines.* When municipal corporations have forced the relocation of utility lines, the governmental or proprietary nature of

the municipal activity may determine which party bears the costs of relocation. In *City of New York v. New York Telephone Co.,* 14 N.E.2d 831 (N.Y. 1938), the city was forced to bear the costs of relocating telephone lines to accommodate new subway entrances because it was acting in its proprietary capacity as owner and operator of the subway. But see *New York Telephone Co. v. City of Binghamton,* 219 N.E.2d 184 (N.Y. 1966), in which the court limited the earlier holding to cases where the city chooses to operate a public utility business; here, where the relocation was caused by a subsidized housing project, the court put aside the governmental-proprietary test and returned to the common law rule which denied compensation to the utility.

In *Union Electric Co. v. Land Clearance for Redevelopment Authority,* 555 S.W.2d 29 (Mo. 1977), the Missouri Supreme Court ruled that a forced relocation of utility lines to aid an urban renewal project was an exercise of a governmental function (no relocation compensation) rather than a proprietary function, the utility's argument because the area being vacated was to be occupied by a private hotel. And in *Pacific Telephone & Telegraph Co. v. Redevelopment Agency,* 142 Cal. Rptr. 584 (Cal. App. 1978), the court rejected the governmental-proprietary test as "not a serviceable tool for decision-making" in denying a claim for the cost of relocation of utility lines because of the vacation of two streets to make way for a shopping mall. The court reasoned that the right to compensation should depend on legislative requirements or a finding of a constitutionally compensable taking or damaging of property.

6. *Antitrust liability.* In *City of Lafayette v. Louisiana Power & Light Co.,* 435 U.S. 389 (1978), discussed *infra,* the governmental-proprietary distinction was the focal point of Chief Justice Burger's swing vote. In his concurring opinion, Chief Justice Burger reasoned "there is nothing in *Parker v. Brown,* 317 U.S. 341 (1943) ("state action" is not subject to federal antitrust laws), or its progeny, which suggests that a proprietary enterprise with the inherent capacity for economically disruptive anticompetitive effects should be exempt from the Sherman Act merely because it is organized under state law as a municipality." 435 U.S. at 418.

7. The governmental-proprietary distinction has been used in still other areas, discussed elsewhere in the book, e.g., municipal rights against the state (Chapter 1); the inherent right to local self government (Chapter 3); state delegation of local control to state commissions (Chapter 3); inter-local conflicts (Chapter 4); and taxation of income from municipal activities (Chapter 5).

2. THE DISCRETIONARY-MINISTERIAL DISTINCTION

Despite the declarations concerning the demise of governmental tort immunity, the continued life of the discretionary-ministerial (nondiscretionary) distinction applied to acts of public officials suggests that governmental immunity has been modified rather than abolished.

LIPMAN v. BRISBANE ELEMENTARY SCHOOL DISTRICT

Supreme Court of California
55 Cal. 2d 224, 11 Cal. Rptr. 97, 359 P.2d 465 (1961)

GIBSON, CHIEF JUSTICE.

This action for damages was brought by plaintiff, superintendent of defendant school districts, against the district, three trustees, the county superintendent of schools and the district attorney. A demurrer to the complaint was sustained without leave to amend, and plaintiff has appealed from the ensuing judgment.

The Complaint Against the School District

It is alleged in substance against the district that the three trustees, constituting a majority of the board and acting within the scope of their official duties, maliciously engaged in a course of conduct for the purpose of discrediting plaintiff's reputation and forcing her out of her position. The asserted conduct of the trustees consisted primarily of disparaging statements made by them concerning plaintiff to various persons including district employees attending secret meetings, newspaper reporters and members of the public to the effect that she was dictatorial, operated a "rubber stamp board," was overpaid, suppressed facts from the board, tampered with minutes of board meetings, received "kickbacks" from district employees, used school employees and school time to engage in political campaigns, engaged in "shady dealings" and "cleaned up" on business transactions involving the district, and that a grand jury investigation was being made of plaintiff concerning discrepancies in construction funds. It is further alleged that the conduct of the trustees constituted a repudiation by the district of plaintiff's contract and so maligned her reputation and integrity as to prevent her from performing her duties.

In *Muskopf v. Corning Hospital District,* Cal., 11 Cal. Rptr. 89, 359 P.2d 457, we held that the rule of governmental immunity may no longer be invoked to shield a public body from liability for the torts of its agents who acted in a ministerial capacity. But it does not necessarily follow that a public body has no immunity where the discretionary conduct of governmental officials is involved. While, as pointed out in the *Muskopf* case, a governmental agent is personally liable for torts which he commits when acting in a ministerial capacity, a different situation exists with respect to discretionary conduct. Because of important policy considerations, the rule has become established that government officials are not personally liable for their discretionary acts within the scope of their authority even though it is alleged that their conduct was malicious. . . . The subjection of officials, the innocent as well as the guilty, to the burden of a trial and to the danger of its outcome would impair their zeal in the performance of their functions, and it is better to leave the injury unredressed than to subject honest officials to the constant dread of retaliation. . . .

The immunity of the agency from liability for discretionary conduct of its officials, however, is not coextensive with the immunity of the officials in all instances. . . .[4] The danger of deterring official action is relevant to the issue of liability of a public body but is not decisive of that issue. It is unlikely that officials would be as adversely affected in the performance of their duties by the fear of liability on the part of their employing agency as by the fear of personal liability. The community benefits from official action taken without fear of personal liability, and it would be unjust in some circumstances to require an individual

---

[4] [Professor Davis single out this language is very important. "The basic proposition is that a governmental unit may be liable in tort even when the officer or employee through which it acts is immune. This proposition may be sound and necessary. . . ." Davis, 1970 Supp. § 25.00, at 830. Later Davis criticized as "vulnerable to challenge" the inconsistent recommendation of the California Law Revision Commission that "[A] public entity should be immune from liability for the act or omission of its employee if the employee himself is immune from liability." See *id.* § 25.17, at 863-66 for Davis' explanation of why he considers the court's position preferable to that of the Commission. Compare Davis' praise for another recommendation of the Commission that "[a] public entity should be liable for a negligent or wrongful act or omission of its employee within the scope of his employment to the extent that the employee is personally liable for such act or omission." *Id.* § 25.17, at 863.—Eds.]

injured by official wrongdoing to bear the burden of his loss rather than distribute it throughout the community. Although it may not be possible to set forth a definitive rule which would determine in every instance whether a governmental agency is liable for discretionary acts of its officials, various factors furnish a means of deciding whether the agency in a particular case should have immunity, such as the importance to the public of the function involved, the extent to which governmental liability might impair free exercise of the function, and the availability to individuals affected of remedies other than tort suits for damages.

With respect to the complaint against the district, the acts alleged, insofar as they came within the scope of authority of the trustees, were of a discretionary character. As we shall see in discussing the complaint against the individual defendants, the trusteees were immune as to such acts. There is a vital public interest in securing free and independent judgment of school trustees in dealing with personnel problems, and trustees, being responsible for the fiscal well-being of their districts, would be especially sensitive to the financial consequences of suits for damages against the districts. It is also significant that, without holding a school district liable in tort for acts like those complained of, an employee from the outset has protection, in the form of mandamus or recovery for breach of contract, against consequences which would be among the most harmful and tangible, *i.e.*, wrongful dismissal or suspension. . . .

The district is immune from tort liability for the alleged acts of the trustees within the scope of their authority, and familiar principles of agency preclude its liability for acts outside the scope of their authority. Accordingly, the complaint does not state a cause of action in tort against the district. . . .

[In the remainder of the opinion the court held that the school district was not liable on these facts for breach of contract arising out of the same conduct. It also held that the trustees were acting within the scope of their discretionary powers and thus immune with respect to their efforts to investigate plaintiff's management of the school district, but that the complaint stated a cause of action against the individual trustees in defamation and interference with contract for those parts of their acts (gratuitous statements to the press and public about plaintiff's conduct) which were not within the scope of their employment. The judgment was affirmed as to the district and reversed as to the individual defendants.—Eds.]

Comments: 1. Several years later, the California Supreme Court returned to the discretionary-ministerial questions:

> In drawing the line between the immune "discretionary" decision and the unprotected ministerial act we recognize both the difficulty and the limited function of such distinction. As we said in *Lipman v. Brisbane Elementary School Dist.*, . . . "it may not be possible to set forth a definite rule which would determine in every instance whether a governmental agency is liable." A workable definition nevertheless will be one that recognizes that "[m]uch of what is done by officers and employees of the government must remain beyond the range of judicial inquiry" (3 Davis, Administrative Law Treatise (1958) § 25.11, p. 484); obviously "it is not a tort for government to govern" (*Dalehite v. United States* (1953) 346 U.S. 15, 57 (Jackson, J., dissenting)). Courts and commentators have therefore centered their attention on an assurance of judicial abstention in areas in which the responsibility for basic policy decisions has been committed to coordinate branches of government. Any wider judicial review, we believe, would place the court in the unseemly position of determining the propriety

of decisions expressly entrusted to a coordinate branch of government. Moreover, the potentiality of such review might even in the first instance affect the coordinate body's decision-making process.

We recognize that this interpretation of the term "discretionary" presents some difficulties. For example, problems arise in attempting to translate this concern for the court's role in the governmental structure into an applicable touchstone for decision. Our proposed distinction, sometimes described as that between the "planning" and "operational" levels of decision-making (cf. *Dalehite v. United States,* supra 346 U.S. 15, 35-36), however, offers some basic guideposts, although it certainly presents no panacea. Admittedly, our interpretation will necessitate delicate decisions; the very process of ascertaining whether an official determination rises to the level of insulation from judicial review requires sensitivity to the considerations that enter into it and an appreciation of the limitations on the court's ability to reexamine it. Despite these potential drawbacks, however, our approach possesses the dispositive virtue of concentrating on the reasons for granting immunity to the governmental entity. It requires us to find and isolate those areas of quasi-legislative policy-making which are sufficiently sensitive to justify a blanket rule that courts will not entertain a tort action alleging that careless conduct contributed to the governmental decision.

Johnson v. State, 447 P.2d 352, 360-61 (Cal. 1968) (holding that parole officer's failure to warn plaintiff of foreseeable, latent danger in accepting foster child into her home was not an exercise of a discretionary function).

2. Does the planning-operational dichotomy adopted in *Johnson v. State* clarify the issue?

In *Cairl v. State,* 323 N.W.2d 20 (Minn. 1982), the court concluded that a decision to release a mentally retarded and potentially dangerous youth for holiday home leave who subsequently set fire to an apartment building was protected by the discretionary immunity rule. Minnesota statutes expressly recognize the discretionary immunity rule. Minn. Stat. § 3.736(3)(b) and § 466.03(6). In reaching its decision, the court noted that it had accepted the planning-operational distinctions as a guide, *Larson v. Independent School District No. 314,* 289 N.W.2d 112 (Minn. 1980), but concluded that the nature of the governmental act complained of must be examined in order to avoid a "mere labeling approach." 323 N.W.2d at 23. The court focused on the nature of the decision-making process and found it met the test for protection because it involved professional evaluation of a number of complex and competing factors and was an important element in planning the patient's overall treatment program.

Most of the state statutes enacted in the wake of the movement to abrogate general governmental tort immunity took a waiver of immunity approach patterned after the Federal Tort Claims Act, 28 U.S.C. § 2671, 2680(a). However, contrary to the Federal Tort Claims Act, a number of the state statutes do not provide an exception for discretionary acts of public officials. Faced with this legislative silence, the courts have confronted the discretionary-ministerial issue, as the following case indicates:

COMMERCIAL CARRIER CORP. v. INDIAN RIVER COUNTY

Supreme Court of Florida
371 So. 2d 1010 (1979)

SUNDBERG, JUSTICE.

. . . .

Commercial Carrier Corporation v. Indian River County

Petitioner, Commercial Carrier Corporation, and its liability insurer, Merchants Mutual Insurance Company, were defendants below in an action for wrongful death arising from the collision of petitioner's tractor-trailer and decedents' automobile. The collision occurred at an unmarked intersection in Indian River County at which it is alleged there had previously been a stop sign and pavement markings governing the road upon which petitioner's vehicle was operating. Petitioner and its liability insurer filed a third-party complaint naming Indian River County and the Florida Department of Transportation (DOT) as third-party defendants. The complaint sought indemnity and contribution for the negligent failure of Indian River County to maintain the stop sign at the intersection, and for the negligent failure of the DOT to paint or replace on the pavement the word "STOP" in advance of the entrance to the intersection. Respondents filed motions to dismiss the complaint, alleging in part that (1) petitioner had failed to comply with the notice requirement of section 768.28(6), Florida Statutes (1975); (2) section 768.28 did not waive the immunity of the state or its agencies from claims for indemnity or contribution; (3) Commercial Carrier had failed to allege the breach of any duty owing to it as opposed to the public at large; and (4) petitioner had failed generally to state a cause of action. The trial court dismissed the third-party complaint, and the District Court of Appeal, Third District, affirmed.

Cheney v. Dade County

Julia Ramy filed suit against petitioner Cheney and his liability insurer for damages resulting from an intersection collision on March 14, 1975, in Dade County. Petitioner filed a third-party complaint against respondent, alleging that the county had negligently maintained a traffic light at the intersection and that this negligence was the sole cause of the accident. Petitioner pleaded alternatively that he was only passively negligent and thus entitled to indemnity.

Respondent moved to dismiss the complaint on the following grounds: (1) the complaint failed to state a cause of action because the doctrine of sovereign immunity precludes recovery against respondent; (2) petitioner failed to allege knowledge on the part of the respondent as to the malfunctioning of the traffic light; (3) petitioner failed to allege how sovereign immunity had been waived; and (4) petitioner failed to allege compliance with the notice provisions of section 768.28(6), supra. The trial court granted respondent's motion and dismissed the third-party complaint with prejudice. The District Court of Appeal, Third District, affirmed, holding that no cause of action existed for respondent's allegedly negligent act.

The operative portion of section 768.28 reads:

> (1) In accordance with section 13, Art. X, state constitution, the state, for itself and for its agencies or subdivisions, hereby waives sovereign immunity for liability for torts, but only to the extent specified in this act. Actions at law against the state or any of its agencies or subdivisions to recover damages in tort for money damages against the state or its agencies or subdivisions for injury or loss of property, personal injury, or death caused by the negligent or wrongful act or omission of any employee of the agency or subdivision while acting within the scope of his office or employment under circumstances in which the state or such agency or subdivision, if a private person, would be liable to the claimant in accordance with the general laws of this state, may be prosecuted subject to the limitations specified in this act.

A limitation upon the liability of the state and its agencies and subdivisions is expressed in section 768.28(5):

> The state and its agencies and subdivisions shall be liable for tort claims in the same manner and to the same extent as a private individual under like circumstances, but liability shall not include punitive damages or interest for the period prior to judgment. Neither the state nor its agencies or subdivisions shall be liable to pay a claim or a judgment by any one person which exceeds the sum of $50,000 or any claim or judgment, or portions thereof, which, when totaled with all other claims or judgments paid by the state arising out of the same incident or occurrence, exceeds the sum of $100,000. However, a judgment or judgments may be claimed and rendered in excess of these amounts and may be settled and paid pursuant to this act up to $50,000 or $100,000, as the case may be, and that portion of the judgment that exceeds these amounts may be reported to the legislature, but may be paid in part or in whole only by further act of the legislature.

By definition, "state agencies or subdivisions" include "the executive departments, the legislature, the judicial branch, and the independent establishments of the state; counties and municipalities; and corporations primarily acting as instrumentalities or agencies of the state, counties, or municipalities."[5] As a condition precedent to instituting an action on a claim against the state or one of its agencies or subdivisions, the claimant is required to give written notice to the appropriate agency or agencies [6] and the action must be commenced within four years after such claim accrues.[7]

The district court in *Commercial Carrier Corporation, supra,* asserting that it was unnecessary to discuss the implications of section 768.28, held that it is not actionable negligence for a governmental authority to fail to maintain a traffic control device at a given time and place. *Gordon v. City of West Palm Beach,* 321 So.2d 78 (Fla. 4th DCA 1975), among other cases, was cited as authority for the holding. In *Cheney, supra,* the same court applied the holding in *Modlin v. City of Miami Beach,* 201 So.2d 70 (Fla. 1967), and concluded that section 768.28 "does not create a liability in the State where the act complained of does not give rise to liability in the agent committing the act, because the duty claimed to be violated is a duty owed to the citizens of the state in general and is not a duty owed to a particular person or persons." 353 So.2d at 626. By importing a concept of municipal immunity from tort liability the court reasoned that no cause of action existed for the alleged wrong and, therefore, section 768.28 had no application because it was not intended to create a cause of action where none existed at common law prior to its enactment.

Respondents and amici support the decisions of the district court on several grounds. Apart from the reasoning of the court below, they maintain (1) that section 768.28 was intended to make the tort liability of the state and its political subdivisions coextensive, that liability to be measured by the scope of liability of municipal corporations at the time of enactment of the statute; (2) that there can be no tort liability under the act for essentially governmental functions because "private persons" do not perform such functions; and (3) that the acts or omissions complained of are discretionary in nature, thereby immunizing the governmental authority from liability.

---

[5] § 768.28(2), Fla.Stat. (1975).

[6] § 768.28(6), Fla.Stat. (1975).

[7] § 768.28(12), Fla.Stat. (1975).

Petitioners and other amici assert a much broader scope of operation for section 768.28, ranging from unlimited liability in tort for all acts or omissions by government to liability at least for those governmental acts and omissions at the operational level which involve no discretion. Each submits that the conduct complained of in the instant cases supports a cause of action even under a limited view of the statute.

While we are not prepared to embrace the notion that all acts or omissions by governmental authorities will subject them to liability in tort under the statute, nevertheless we conclude that the district court has ascribed much too narrow a field of operation to section 768.28. For the reasons articulated below we disapprove the decisions under review.

. . . .

Respondents' final argument poses a more difficult problem. They maintain that the acts complained of involve the exercise of discretion or judgment by governmental officials or employees and, therefore, the performance of such acts or omissions are exempt from operation of the statute. Petitioners counter with the assertion that unlike the Federal Tort Claims Act, which contains an express exception for discretionary acts,[10] no exception for such acts is expressed in the Florida statute. The implication is that our legislature had available to it the federal act, as is apparent from certain language borrowed from that legislation, and it made the conscious choice not to provide an exception for discretionary acts. While it cannot be denied that our statute contains no such exception, it does not necessarily follow that all acts or omissions by governmental officials or employees may form the basis for recovery against the governmental authority involved. The absence of a "discretionary exception" in their waiver statute has not precluded several jurisdictions from holding that certain areas of governmental conduct remain immune from scrutiny by judge or jury as to the wisdom of that conduct.

The Court of Appeals of New York in *Weiss v. Fote*, 7 N.Y.2d 579, 200 N.Y.S.2d 409, 167 N.E.2d 63 (1960), construed that state's broad waiver of immunity statute so as not to authorize an action by an injured pedestrian who alleged negligence on the part of the City of Buffalo in providing too short a "clearance interval" for the traffic signal lights at the intersection where the injury occurred. New York's statute contained no "discretionary exception"; nonetheless the court analyzed two lines of authority predating the waiver statute and concluded that certain judgmental decisions by governmental officials may not be the subject of tort liability. One line of cases rested immunity on the policy of maintaining the administration of municipal affairs in the hands of state or municipal executive officers as against the incursion of courts and juries, while the other rested the immunity on the sovereign character of the state or municipality in the performance of its governmental functions. While the latter cases lost their legal force and effect with the passage of the New York Court of Claims Act, the former retained their vitality because they were not predicated simply upon the premise that the sovereign can do no wrong. They were grounded instead upon a concept of separation of powers which will not permit the substitution of the decision by a judge or jury for the decision of a governmental body as to the reasonableness of planning activity conducted by that body. As articulated by Judge Fuld:

---

[10] 28 U.S.C. § 2680(a) (1975).

> To accept a jury's verdict as to the reasonableness and safety of a plan of governmental services and prefer it over the judgment of the governmental body which originally considered and passed on the matter would be to obstruct normal governmental operations and to place in inexpert hands what the Legislature has seen fit to entrust to experts. Acceptance of this conclusion, far from effecting revival of the ancient shibboleth that "the king can do no wrong", serves only to give expression to the important and continuing need to preserve the pattern of distribution of governmental functions prescribed by constitution and statute.

7 N.Y.2d at 586, 200 N.Y.S.2d at 413, 167 N.E.2d at 66.

The state of Washington has also implied a discretionary function exception in its waiver of immunity statute in the absence of an express exception. The case of *Evangelical United Brethren Church v. State,* 67 Wash.2d 246, 407 P.2d 440 (1965), involved a claim against the state by plaintiffs whose buildings had been destroyed by fire set by an escapee from a state-maintained juvenile correction facility. The allegations of fault on the part of the state related to (i) the maintenance of a certain "open program" (as opposed to close security) at the correction facility; (ii) assignment of the escapee to the "open program"; (iii) assignment of the escapee to a particular type work detail at the facility; and (iv) failure to timely notify local law enforcement agencies of the escape. The state responded that the decisions, acts or omissions complained of involved the exercise of administrative judgment and discretion and could not be properly characterized as tortious conduct. The court recognized that by enactment of the Washington waiver statute the legislature intended to abolish on a broad basis the doctrine of sovereign tort immunity. However, it was concluded that the statute was not as broad as it might have been written. Noting the absence of the varied exceptions found in the Federal Tort Claims Act, the court observed nonetheless that state government was liable for damages only when such damages arise out of " 'tortious conduct to the same extent as if it were a private person or corporation.' " 407 P.2d at 444. It was judged necessary to determine where, in the area of governmental processes, orthodox tort liability stops and the act of governing begins. *Id.* The court recognized that the legislative, judicial and purely executive processes of government, including discretionary acts and decisions within the framework of such processes, cannot and should not be characterized as tortious. Public policy and maintenance of the integrity of our system of government necessitate this immunity, however unwise, unpopular, mistaken or neglectful a particular decision or act might be. The rationale for this conclusion was stated thus:

> The reason most frequently assigned is that in any organized society there must be room for basic governmental policy decision and the implementation thereof, unhampered by the threat or fear of sovereign tort liability, or, as stated by one writer "Liability cannot be imposed when condemnation of the acts or omissions relied upon *necessarily* brings into question the propriety of governmental objectives or programs or the decision of one who, with the authority to do so, determined that the acts or omissions involved should occur or that the risk which eventuated should be encountered for the advancement of governmental objectives." Peck, The Federal Tort Claims Act, 31 Wash.L.Rev. 207 (1956).

Id. at 444 (emphasis in original). After reviewing the characterizations utilized by a number of courts in attempting to ferret out those acts or functions which remain immune from tort liability, the court proposed the following preliminary test:

Whatever the suitable characterization or label might be, it would appear that any determination of a line of demarcation between truly discretionary and other executive and administrative processes, so far as susceptibility to potential sovereign tort liability be concerned, would necessitate a posing of at least the following four preliminary questions: (1) Does the challenged act, omission, or decision necessarily involve a basic governmental policy, program, or objective? (2) Is the questioned act, omission, or decision essential to the realization or accomplishment of that policy, program, or objective as opposed to one which would not change the course or direction of the policy, program, or objective? (3) Does the act, omission, or decision require the exercise of basic policy evaluation, judgment, and expertise on the part of the governmental agency involved? (4) Does the governmental agency involved possess the requisite constitutional, statutory, or lawful authority and duty to do or make the challenged act, omission, or decision? If these preliminary questions can be clearly and unequivocally answered in the affirmative, then the challenged act, omission, or decision can, with a reasonable degree of assurance, be classified as a discretionary governmental process and nontortious, regardless of its unwisdom. If, however, one or more of the questions call for or suggest a negative answer, then further inquiry may well become necessary, depending upon the facts and circumstances involved.

Id. at 445. Through application of this test the first two grounds asserted for liability were determined to involve acts for which the state was immune. Although the remaining two bases for liability were not adjudged to involve immune conduct, the state was held not to be liable on standard tort principles of lack of foreseeability and causation.

Ohio has reached the same result under its waiver statute, not withstanding the absence of an express "discretionary" exception. *See Harris v. State,* 48 Ohio Misc. 27, 358 N.E.2d 639 (1976).

This concept of exemption from tort liability for the exercise of certain governmental functions bottomed on the concept of separation of powers has found expression in at least one prior decision of this Court. In *Wong v. City of Miami,* 237 So.2d 132 (Fla. 1970), merchants whose property was damaged in connection with a rally which culminated in civil disorder and plundering sued the city and Dade County for negligent handling of the rally. At the request of merchants bordering the rally area, the city increased police protection in the area. Subsequently, on order of the mayor confirmed by an order of the county sheriff, the increased police forces were removed. After the forces were removed the rally got out of hand and participants damaged the neighboring stores in excess of $100,000 before police control could be reestablished.

The plaintiffs filed suit predicated on the theory that removal of the officers was a careless and negligent act. The city responded with a motion to dismiss on the grounds that (i) no sufficient connection was alleged between withdrawal of the officers and the injuries complained of; (ii) police protection was a duty owed the public generally which would not inure to the benefit of particular private citizens; and (iii) *removal of officers was within the realm of governmental discretion.* The county moved for summary judgment. The trial court granted the motions and dismissed the complaint with prejudice. The District Court of Appeal, Third District, affirmed with one judge dissenting. The dissent, relying on *Hargrove, supra,* concluded that a special duty was demonstrated. The majority, also applying *Hargrove,* drew the opposite conclusion and cited for analogy *Steinhardt v. Town of North Bay Village,* 132 So.2d 764 (Fla. 3d DCA 1961), which dealt with the negligent provision of fire protection.

It is important to note that while this Court discharged the writ of certiorari it took issue with the aspect of the majority decision which impliedly conceded negligence on the part of the city but found it not to be actionable because of sovereign immunity:

> While sovereign immunity is a salient issue here, we ought not lose sight of the fact that inherent in the right to exercise police powers is the right to determine strategy and tactics for the deployment of those powers. In the Report of the National Advisory Commission on Civil Disorders, issued pursuant to Executive Order 11365 in 1967, the point was frequently made that police visibility was often an operative factor in the raising of tensions, and that withdrawal from an area could be a highly useful tactical tool for the relaxing of tensions in certain situations. *The sovereign authorities ought to be left free to exercise their discretion and choose the tactics deemed appropriate without worry over possible allegations of negligence.* Here officials thought it best to withdraw their officers. Who can say whether or not the damage sustained by petitioners would have been more widespread if the officers had stayed, and because of a resulting confrontation, the situation had escalated with greater violence than could have been controlled with the resources immediately at hand? If that had been the case, couldn't petitioners allege just as well that *that* [emphasis theirs] course of action was negligent?

237 So.2d at 134 (emphasis supplied). This was a clear recognition by the Court of a principle of law apart from the ancient doctrine of immunity as a simple aspect of sovereignty. It represents the distinct principle of law alluded to by Judge Fuld in *Weiss v. Fote, supra,* which makes not actionable in tort certain judgmental decisions of governmental authorities which are inherent in the act of governing.

Hence, we are persuaded by these authorities that even absent an express exception in section 768.28 for discretionary functions, certain policy-making, planning or judgmental governmental functions cannot be the subject of traditional tort liability. Like the Washington court, we recognize that the identification of these functions will in many instances be difficult. The temptation is strong to fall back on semantic labels for ease of application and seeming certainty. However, we eschew this temptation, as it surely will result in a return to the overly structured and often misleading analysis which persists in the law of municipal sovereign immunity.

A semantic test for identification of discretionary governmental functions which should continue to enjoy immunity was attempted and then disavowed in California, whose statute contains a discretionary exception. For a time, the lower appellate courts in California labored unsuccessfully to develop a dictionary definition of "discretion" which established liability for minor discretionary actions but preserved immunity for high-level decisions.[12] Disavowal of this definitional approach came in *Johnson v. State,* 69 Cal.2d 782, 73 Cal.Rptr. 240, 447 P.2d 352 (1968), where the California Supreme Court recognized that all governmental functions, no matter how seemingly ministerial, can be characterized as embracing the exercise of some discretion in the manner of their performance. Consequently, that court opted for an analysis predicated on policy considerations and adopted a test articulated in *Lipman v. Brisbane Elementary School District,* 55 Cal.2d 224, 11 Cal.Rptr. 97, 99, 359 P.2d 465, 467 (1961):

> Although it may not be possible to set forth a definitive rule which would determine in every instance whether a governmental agency is liable for discre-

---

[12] See Note, The Discretionary Function Exception to Government Tort Liability, 61 Marq. L.Rev. 163, 168 (1977).

tionary acts of its officials, various factors furnish a means of deciding whether the agency in a particular case should have immunity, such as the importance to the public of the function involved, the extent to which government liability might impair free exercise of the function, and the availability to individuals affected of remedies other than tort suits for damages.

As a tool for identifying discretionary acts under the Federal Tort Claims Act the federal courts, commencing with the decision in *Dalehite v. United States, supra,* have developed an analysis which distinguishes between decisions made at the "planning level" and those at the "operational level." Planning level functions are generally interpreted to be those requiring basic policy decisions, while operational level functions are those that implement policy.[13] *Johnson v. State, supra,* likewise employed the planning-operational distinction as an aid to isolate those discretionary functions of government which should be immune from tort liability. The *Johnson* court was not unmindful of the deficiencies inherent in such an analysis, but perceived that the lack of certainty and predictability of such approach was overridden by its emphasis on the considerations behind the rule of governmental immunity:

> We recognize that this interpretation of the term "discretionary" presents some difficulties. For example, problems arise in attempting to translate this concern for the court's role in the governmental structure into an applicable touchstone for decision. Our proposed distinction, sometimes described as that between the "planning" and "operational" levels of decision-making (cf. *Dalehite v. United States,* supra, 346 U.S. 15, 35-36 . . .), however, offers some basic guideposts, although it certainly presents no panacea. Admittedly, our interpretation will necessitate delicate decisions; the very process of ascertaining whether an official determination rises to the level of insulation from judicial review requires sensitivity to the considerations that enter into it and an appreciation of the limitations on the court's ability to reexamine it. Despite these potential drawbacks, however, our approach possesses the dispositive virtue of concentrating on the reasons for granting immunity to the governmental entity. It requires us to find and isolate those areas of quasi-legislative policy-making which are sufficiently sensitive to justify a blanket rule that courts will not entertain a tort action alleging that careless conduct contributed to the governmental decision.

73 Cal.Rptr. at 248-249, 447 P.2d at 360-61 (footnote omitted).

Alaska and Hawaii have adopted a similar construction of discretionary function immunity under their respective waiver statutes. *State v. Abbott,* 498 P.2d 712 (Alaska 1972); *Rogers v. State,* 51 Hawaii 293, 459 P.2d 378 (1969). The Utah Supreme Court cited *Johnson* in a case with substantially the same facts as *Rogers* and reached a similar conclusion. *Carroll v. State,* 27 Utah 2d 384, 496 P.2d 888 (1972). Minnesota has held that deployment of police and fire departments during riots falls within the discretionary function exception. *Silver v. City of Minneapolis,* 284 Minn. 266, 170 N.W.2d 206 (1969).

So we, too, hold that although section 768.28 evinces the intent of our legislature to waive sovereign immunity on a broad basis, nevertheless, certain "discretionary" governmental functions remain immune from tort liability. This is so because certain functions of coordinate branches of government may not be subjected to scrutiny by judge or jury as to the wisdom of their performance. In

---

[13] Although the *Dalehite* opinion suggested that implementation of policy is also immune, this premise has never been adopted by the state courts and has been limited by subsequent federal decisions. See Reynolds, The Discretionary Function Exception of the Federal Tort Claims Act, 57 Geo. L.J. 81 (1968); 61 Marq.L.Rev. at 170.

order to identify those functions, we adopt the analysis of *Johnson v. State, supra,* which distinguishes between the "planning" and "operational" levels of decision-making by governmental agencies. In pursuance of this case-by-case method of proceeding, we commend utilization of the preliminary test iterated in *Evangelical United Brethren Church v. State, supra,* as a useful tool for analysis.

Recurring, then, to the instant cases. It is apparent that the *maintenance* of a traffic signal light which is in place does not fall within that category of governmental activity which involves broad policy or planning decisions. This is operational level activity. So too is the proper *maintenance* of a traffic sign at an intersection and the proper *maintenance* of the painted letters "STOP" on the pavement of a highway. As asserted by Commercial Carrier Corporation in its brief (main brief at 17), the gravamen of that petitioner's complaint is the failure of the county and Department of Transportation to maintain existing traffic control devices which had been in place. We do not deal in these cases with the issue of whether or not, or what type of, traffic control devices should have been installed at the particular intersections. Accordingly, we express no opinion with respect to whether liability could be imposed on the governmental bodies involved for failure in the first instance to place traffic control devices at the intersections.

. . . .

Accordingly, the petitions for writ of certiorari are granted, the decisions of the District Court of Appeal, Third District, are quashed, and these consolidated cases are remanded to the district court with directions to remand to the trial court for proceedings not inconsistent with this decision.

It is so ordered.

ENGLAND, C. J., and ADKINS, HATCHETT and ALDERMAN, JJ., concur.

OVERTON, J., dissents with an opinion, with which BOYD, J., concurs.

OVERTON, JUSTICE, dissenting.

I dissent. By allowing a negligence action against the state and county for failure to properly maintain a public roadway, the majority opinion, in my view, contravenes the legislative intent and purpose of section 768.28, Florida Statutes (1975). The majority accepts the legal principle that there can be no action against the state or county unless the legislature has authorized it. Although politically this type of legal action against the state may be desirable, it is not permissible under the provisions of the statute adopted by the legislature.

The subject statute expressly provides that it applies only "under circumstances in which the state or such agency or subdivision, *if a private person,* would be liable to the claimant . . ." section 768.28(1) (emphasis added), and "The state and its agencies and subdivisions shall be liable for tort claims in the same manner and to the same extent *as a private individual under like circumstances* . . . ." section 768.28(5) (emphasis added).

The effect of the majority opinion is to allow negligence claims against the state and counties for failure to properly maintain miles of interstate and primary state and county roads. I am unable to accept the premise required by the majority that the failure to timely fix a traffic light, the failure to put a stop sign in place, and the failure to repaint "STOP" on the pavement of a highway are "circumstances" for which a "private person" would be liable. Common sense dictates that the maintenance of thousands of miles of public roadways is not the kind of activity which private individuals engage in, but is uniquely governmental in nature.

Without question, this is a perplexing and inconsistent area of the law, not only in this jurisdiction but in other jurisdictions in the nation as well. Illustrative are the decisions of the United States Supreme Court in *Dalehite v. United States,* 346 U.S. 15 . . . (1953), and *Indian Towing Co. v. United States,* 350 U.S. 61 . . . (1955). In *Dalehite,* the United States Supreme Court held that the negligence of the Coast Guard in failing to prevent a catastrophic fire by regulating the storage of a potentially explosive fertilizer and by its negligent failure to properly fight the fire after it had started was outside the parameters of the federal tort claims act. On the other hand, in *Indian Towing Co.,* the same Court, without receding from *Dalehite,* held that the negligence of the Coast Guard in the operation of a lighthouse was a proper action under the act. The majority accepts the reasoning of the United States Supreme Court in the latter decision and analogizes it to the facts in the instant cases. It is difficult, however, to reconcile *Indian Towing Co.* with *Dalehite,* and I would not use one as a basis for ascertaining the intent of the legislature in adopting section 768.28, Florida Statutes (1975).

The majority also rejects the argument that the use of funds for the maintenance of public roadways is a discretionary function and, therefore, immune from liability. This is, in my view, a legitimate contention. The availability of such funds is established by appropriation formulas, and discretionary decisions must be made as to the maintenance projects which can be accomplished with available funds. The majority opinion in effect says a judge or jury can override that discretionary decision.

For the reasons expressed, I would affirm the district court's decisions because I discern no legislative intent to allow recovery under section 768.28, Florida Statutes (1975), for the negligent maintenance of public roadways.

BOYD, J., concurs.

Comments: 1. The Florida Supreme Court has returned to the governmental immunity problem on several occasions since *Commercial Carrier.* In *Cauley v. City of Jacksonville,* 403 So. 2d 379 (Fla. 1981), the court upheld a legislatively imposed limit on the amount of money damages ($100,000) recoverable in tort against a municipality for negligent performance of operational level or proprietary functions. The court ruled that the legislature had struck a reasonable balance by broadening recovery allowable against state governmental entities generally while limiting the recovery allowable against municipalities. Chief Justice Sundberg, who authored the *Commercial Carrier* opinion, dissented on the grounds that there is "a vast difference in waiving immunity by increasing recovery from nothing to a maximum of $50,000/$100,000 [the statute applicable to state and county entities construed in *Commercial Carrier*], and 'creating' immunity by lowering recovery from full compensation to a $50,000/$100,000 limitation (municipalities apparently never enjoyed total immunity in Florida). The former is acceptable; the latter is not." *Id.* at 387.

In a series of cases decided the same day in the following year, *Department of Transportation v. Nelson,* 419 So. 2d 1071 (Fla. 1982); *Ingham v. State Department of Transportation,* 419 So. 2d 1081 (Fla. 1982); and *City of St. Petersburg v. Collom,* 419 So. 2d 1082 (Fla. 1982), the supreme court ruled that decisions concerning installation of traffic control devices, the initial plan and alignment of roads, or the improvement or upgrading of roads or intersections were basic capital improvements and judgmental, planning-level functions entitled to immunity. However, the failure to comply with statutory standards and criteria for design, construction and maintenance, and failure to warn of known dangers were operational-level activities not entitled to immunity. Once again Justice Sundberg dissented, this time because of the conviction that the court "has simply exchanged one set of result descriptive labels for another." *Id.* at 1079. Justice Sundberg argued that the planning-operational distinction articulated by the California Court in *Johnson v. State, supra,* was designed to limit discretionary acts subject to immunity to those that required basic policy decisions involving a conscious balancing of risks and advantages. The burden of proof to establish that the requisite "considered decision" had been made is on the governmental agencies involved, and that burden was not met in Justice Sundberg's opinion.

2. As the court in the principal case noted, the discretionary-ministerial distinction often is grounded in separation of powers principles that prevent "certain functions of coordinate branches of government" from being "subjected to scrutiny by judge or jury as to the wisdom of their performance." Is this another name for the governmental-proprietary distinction? Have the courts restored general governmental immunity? What about the costs to persons injured by tortious conduct of discretionary decision-makers? If the injuries are foreseeable, should the municipality be responsible? For an argument that administrative acts can be appropriately reviewed without improper judicial interference and advocating a legislative response to balance the governmental and public interests, see Note, *Municipal Tort Liability: A Legislative Solution Balancing the Needs of Cities and Plaintiffs,* 16 URB. L. ANN. 305 (1979).

3. Advocating a case-by-case analysis to determine whether the conduct in question should be exempt from liability on public policy considerations, the court in *Biloon's Electrical Service, Inc. v. City of Wilmington,* 401 A.2d 636 (Del. Super. 1979), denied recovery to the owners of a repair shop destroyed by fire during a civil disturbance. The owners argued that the destruction of their shop was the result of the city's failure to provide adequate police protection, which led to a fire battalion chief's decision to delay deployment of fire-fighting equipment. The court, in denying the claim, reasoned as follows:

> The fundamental principal, implicit or explicit, in all the cases is that a municipality cannot be held to a standard of strict liability for police and fire protection. To impose the duty of an insurer on these men and women would be to utterly ignore the difficulty and danger inherent in the tasks they are required to perform. . . . The rule is "liability" not "immunity" but exceptions to liability are necessary when public policy considerations far outweigh the value of an individual property. For instance, if under riot conditions snipers are shooting at police and firemen who respond to scenes of violence and arson, any discretionary decision to restrict municipal response to the conflagration for the purpose of saving lives must take precedence over the value of mere property. Any argument that attempts to question the merits of that decision based on a full and complete record of the exigent circumstances presented to those who made the decisions leads to an attempt to second guess executive decisions. The danger in that process is the jeopardy of impairing the governing process itself.
>
> . . . This points up the argument for non-liability in cases where fundamental tort liability was never heretofore recognized. The concept has been named foreseeability but what is suggested is that basically we are discussing "duty." Does the decision of a city to institute police and fire protection create a duty on the city running to each and every citizen to protect them from all hazards? Certainly not! Any standard less than guaranteed protection, such as the reasonableness of their actions, calls into play an examination of the public policy decisions which resulted in less than guaranteed protection. This we cannot permit.

Id. at 641-42.

4. Does the abrogation of general governmental tort immunity create a new theory of liability for municipalities or does it simply remove an available defense in certain tort actions? Many states have enacted statutes which provide liability for public employers in tort "in the same manner as a private individual under like circumstances." *See, e.g.,* Massachusetts Tort Claims Act, Mass. Gen. Laws Ann. ch. 258, § 2. In *Dinsky v. Town of Framingham,* 438 N.E.2d 51 (Mass. 1982), the court noted that governmental immunity was a defense and abrogation of that defense did not create any new theory of liability. Thus a duty from the defendant municipality to the injured plaintiff must be established.

In the enforcement of regulatory provisions such as building and housing codes, the question becomes whether municipal officials have a private duty to individual citizens distinct from their duty to the public to enforce the law. In *Dinsky*, the court adhered to the majority rule that a building code is enacted for the benefit of the public and its violation does not give rise to a private right of action. Thus, plaintiffs were denied recovery for negligent issuance of building permits where lots had not been graded properly and serious flooding developed. Exceptions have been recognized when the code itself provides a duty to private individuals. *Halvorson v. Dahl*, 574 P.2d 1190 (Wash. 1978) (housing code specifically provided that it was enacted for the benefit of the occupants of the buildings and not just the general public).

The developing minority view is expressed in *J & B Development Co. v. King County*, 631 P.2d 1002 (Wash. 1981), *noted,* 17 GONZAGA L. REV. 569 (1982). In rejecting the public duty rule, the court construed a Washington statute, with the same language as the Massachusetts statute previously noted, as requiring common law tort principles which define the scope of a duty in terms of "foreseeability" to apply to municipalities. Thus, when a county employee negligently issued a building permit without detecting a setback requirement and the permit holder was later required to relocate the foundation of a house, the county was liable in damages because "a duty owed to the public generally is a duty owed to individual members of the public." *Id.* at 1008. *See also Stewart v. Schmeider*, 386 So. 2d 1351 (La. 1980) (municipality held liable for injuries resulting from building collapse when building inspector failed to examine detailed plans before issuing building permit in violation of statute); *Coffey v. Milwaukee*, 247 N.W.2d 132 (Wis. 1976) (complaint alleging a building inspector's negligence in inspecting standpipes stated a cause of action against the municipality). For a discussion of recent developments in this field, see Carlisle, Coleman, Fontana, Moskowitz & Smith, *Testing the Limits: A Report on the Uncertainties of Government Liability in 1982,* 14 URB. L. 687, 689-97 (1982). *See also* Stone & Rinker, *Government Liability for Negligent Inspections,* 57 TUL. L. REV. 328 (1982), discussing *Stewart v. Schmeider.*

5. Punitive or exemplary damages will not be awarded against a state or municipality unless authorized by statute. The purpose of punitive damages is to inflict punishment for wrongdoing and deter similar conduct. Who would actually bear the burden if punitive damages were assessed against a state or local government? *See Chappell v. City of Springfield,* 423 S.W.2d 810 (Mo. 1968). *See also City of Newport v. Fact Concerts, Inc.,* 453 U.S. 247 (1981), discussed *infra.*

A NOTE ON THE IMMUNITY OF PUBLIC OFFICIALS

There is a split in authority on whether discretionary immunity is absolute. The general, and some say the preferred, view is that a public official is not immune from liability for damages when acting in excess of authority, or with malice or bad faith. The Supreme Court of Hawaii ruled that a nonjudicial government officer is not immune from tort liability when he has acted maliciously but it held the plaintiff to a higher than normal standard of proof (of malice) in order to afford some protection to innocent public officers. *Madeiros v. Kondo,* 522 P.2d 1269 (Hawaii 1974). In so doing, the court overruled any remaining prior rule of absolute immunity and explicitly rejected the "fictions of ministerial functions, quasi-judicial functions, inferior public officers, scope or color of authority." *Id.* at 1272. In subsequent decisions, the court held that court-appointed psychiatrists were entitled to absolute immunity as judicial officials, *Seibel v. Kemble,* 631 P.2d 173 (Hawaii 1981), but that prison guards were nonjudicial governmental officials, entitled only to the qualified privilege articulated in *Kondo, Towse v. State,* 647 P.2d 696 (Hawaii 1982). In applying the malice test of *Kondo,* the court in *Towse* (a defamation case) adopted a test of reasonable conduct (no malice if conduct was reasonable) rather than the "constitutionally based 'actual malice' test" of *New York Times v. Sullivan,* 376 U.S. 254 (1964), in finding that statements made to the press and statements in a report of a task force on state prisons were privileged.

In Pennsylvania "high public officials" enjoy absolute immunity when acting officially within the scope of their authority while lesser officials have a conditional immunity which is available when they are acting both within the scope of their authority and without malice or recklessness. *DuBree v. Commonwealth,* 303 A.2d 530 (Pa. Commw. 1973). The test of whether one is a "high" public official depends on the nature of the official duties, particularly whether they involve policymaking. In *DuBree,* the Secretary of Highways and possibly several subordinates including the district engineer and superintendent of maintenance were found to be high public officials. Public prosecutors, but not public defenders, are "high" public officials. *Barto v. Felix,* 378 A.2d 927 (Pa. Super. 1977). The court reasoned that prosecutors, in addition to their judicial function (which is shared by public defenders), perform important administrative tasks of a broad policy-making nature. The public defender, on the other hand, is concerned primarily with the clients being served.

When an official acts beyond the scope of his authority, the action is ultra vires and he will be held liable individually for resulting damages. *See* 2A C. ANTIEAU, MUNICIPAL CORPORATION LAW § 22.81 (1982). The city or state, however, will not be held liable for the ultra vires acts of its public officials. This is the general rule in state courts throughout the country. *See* 18 E. MCQUILLIN, THE LAW OF MUNICIPAL CORPORATIONS § 53.60 (3d ed. 1977).

Although the predominant view is to the contrary, some courts will apply different rules of immunity to public officials from those applied to the governmental units themselves. In *DePalma v. Rosen,* 199 N.W.2d 517 (Minn. 1972), the city of St. Paul demolished Nick DePalma's house for failure to conform to the building code. He brought suit for damages against the city and individual city council members. Because the decision to raze the building was discretionary, the council members were held to be immune from assessment of damages—even if their decision was wrong. The city, on the other hand, had failed to comply with the requirements of its code in providing a rehearing process for the aggrieved landowner. As a result, it had taken plaintiff's property without due process of law, and he was entitled to damages in the nature of a condemnation award. See, contra, *MacLeod v. City of Takoma Park,* 263 A.2d 581 (Md. 1970), rejecting an inverse condemnation theory because the razing of the plaintiff's building did not constitute a taking for public use and also denying ordinary tort damages because plaintiff failed to file a timely notice. Compare *Hermer v. City of Dover,* 215 A.2d 693 (N.H. 1965). There both the building inspector and the city were said to be immune from tort damages for the wrongful closing of a retail store by order of the building inspector since he was performing a governmental function at the time.

3. INVERSE CONDEMNATION

Courts wishing to impose liability for injurious damages arising out of governmental conduct have also developed another doctrine arising out of the taking and damaging clause of state constitutions, which require compensation to be paid when property is taken or damaged without compensation. As the following case indicates, this clause has given rise to so-called actions in reverse eminent domain or inverse condemnation, in which compensation for the taking or damaging of property can be awarded after the fact.

V.T.C. LINES, INC. v. CITY OF HARLAN

Court of Appeals of Kentucky
313 S.W.2d 573 (1957)

MOREMEN, CHIEF JUSTICE.

Appellant, V. T. C. Lines, Inc., a common carrier of passengers for hire, has its bus station and garage located across the street from a swimming pool owned and operated as a recreational facility by the city of Harlan. Appellant filed complaint in the Harlan Circuit Court and alleged that for several days in the spring of 1953, the city cleaned its swimming pool by sand-blasting it with the result that the emery dust used, settled in great quantities in and on the bus station and garage and caused damage to the working parts of the diesel engines which were used in the buses. It was explained that diesel engines do not have electrically operated ignition systems, that the motors are started by forcing air into the cylinders in large quantities so that the temperature of the air, because of the compression, becomes very hot and causes the fuel to ignite and the cylinders to fire. It was averred that the polluted air caused great wear and tear in the metal and moving parts of the automobile engines and destroyed their usefulness and life.

Appellee filed answer which set up, among other defenses, that the damages, if any, resulted from the exercise of a governmental function.

The city filed a motion for summary judgment and the court, being of the opinion that

> The ground for sustaining the motion for summary judgment is based on the proposition that the City being an arm of the state government and the acts complained of being in the nature of a governmental function and that the property claimed to have been injured being personal property and not such property that may have been condemned pursuant to section 242 of the Kentucky Constitution, the plaintiff has no cause of action against the City. *Davis v. The City of Lebanon,* 108 Ky. 688 [57 S.W. 471],

dismissed appellant's complaint.

Appellant has based its right to recover upon § 242 of the Kentucky Constitution which reads:

> Municipal and other corporations, and individuals invested with the privilege of taking private property for public use, shall make just compensation for property taken, injured or destroyed by them; which compensation shall be paid before such taking, or paid or secured, at the election of such corporation or individual, before such injury or destruction. . . .

This section, which did not appear in the Constitution of 1850, is an extension to municipalities, and others, of the limitations placed on a sovereign. It extends also to "injuring or destroying," while section 13 is confined solely to "taking." The constitutional protection against a "taking" by the sovereign state is found in section 13 of the Constitution and reads, "nor shall any man's property be taken or applied to public use without the consent of his representatives, and without just compensation being previously made to him."

We have found these sections to be self-executing and in cases where property has been appropriated, the owner, despite a lack of statutory authority, has been permitted to recover damages. A suit, which seeks to recover damages after land has been taken, has been termed "a retroactive condemnation of land." . . . And, "a condemnation [suit] in reverse." . . .

The seriousness of the question here involved arises from the fact that there are several rights which stem from the principle that private rights must yield to the general public welfare.

To understand the various rights, we must remember that in the beginning the power of a sovereign was absolute and each ruler had complete ownership of all land and complete domination over the lives and property of his subjects to the extent that he could capriciously take either. The right of eminent domain is a vestige of that despotism and was attributed to the sovereign long before this commonwealth existed.

The constitutional provisions which we have quoted are in the nature of limitations rather than grants of right because they restrict the sovereign to taking only where reimbursement is made. We have also retained recognition of the ancient sovereign immunity which denied to citizens the right to recover for deliberate or negligent acts of the sovereign.

At the same time we have recognized that that which we call police power is a separate and valid authority of the state, the only difference being that eminent domain authorizes or permits taking without the consent of the owner upon compensation being paid to him, while police power authorizes regulation and destruction of property without compensation if it promotes the general welfare of the citizens. ... This police power is harsh in execution and permits the destruction of private property in event of necessity, such as war. It is under this power that the government exercises its right of taxation.

The third theory, which our cases seem to entwine with the eminent domain and the police power theories, is that which relates to the immunity of a sovereign to answer for negligent acts committed by it, unless that immunity has been waived.

This immunity arises not in connection with eminent domain or police power, but from the primitive right, which absolute sovereigns had, to be free from the consequences of any act, and exists separate and apart from the other two theories.

All three of these subjects are based upon a primitive conception of sovereign immunity and each one, under our present development and softening of the law, should be considered distinctly. We should not borrow from the eminent domain theory of compensation for injury or damage and apply it to either of the other two premises.

It would then seem to be a simple thing, to conclude that under § 242 a recovery may be had only when property is taken for a public use and then only in cases where the property itself is of the character which may be devoted to public use. This distinction was pointed out in *T. B. Jones & Co. v. Ferro Concrete Construction Co.,* 154 Ky. 47, 156 S.W. 1060, 1062, where, in connection with § 242, it was said:

> In other words, the provision has reference to property taken under the power of eminent domain; it has no reference to property which was not taken and could not be taken under the power of eminent domain. It is not the purpose of the constitutional provision to make municipal corporations liable for all injuries to property inflicted by the negligence of their servants, irrespective of the fact that the corporation was in this work acting as an arm of the state government and discharging a governmental function.

In subsequent cases this distinction is not too clear. In *City of Louisville v. Hehemann,* 161 Ky. 523, 171 S.W. 165, L.R.A. 1915C, 747 it was held that a city, in maintaining a garbage dump in such condition that it was annoying and dangerous to the residents in the vicinity, was, under § 242, liable for injury to the property rights of a neighboring resident. In *Jefferson County v. Bischoff,* 238 Ky. 176, 37 S.W.2d 24, a recovery was allowed for damages to a neighboring home for injury to the property and for interference with its occupancy as a home by reason of the operation of a rock quarry by the county in connection with the construction and maintenance of its roads. Each of these cases apparently involves the maintenance of a nuisance, and a nuisance and an act of negligence are not always the same. But neither of these cases is predicated on the theory that private property was deliberately taken for public use and that the damage was incidental to the taking.

In *Commonwealth v. Moore,* Ky., 267 S.W.2d 531, 532, owners of property which adjoined a highway right-of-way sought damages from the commonwealth allegedly caused by the construction of a highway which destroyed appellees' tobacco crop by reason of the fact that large quantities of dust settled on the tobacco. The actual taking of land was involved from the outset because plaintiffs had voluntarily conveyed a portion of their property for a right-of-way. The court held that when property is appropriated for public use, the compensation to which a landowner is entitled embraces consequential damage to his remaining land and includes damage from the debris that was tossed upon it. The court concluded:

> It is our opinion that the damage caused to appellees was of a consequential nature incident to the prudent and proper exercise of the Commonwealth's right to use the property it acquired for highway purposes. It did not constitute a new taking of their property and consequently they should not have been permitted to recover compensation in these actions.

While this case does not recognize that the damage may have been the result of a negligent act or, for that matter, may have been the result of a nuisance created by the Department of Highways, still recovery was denied even though the act which caused the damage was a positive one which had occurred after the acquisition of the right-of-way was consummated.

It is somewhat difficult to reconcile the theory of this case with that previously announced in *Commonwealth v. Kelley,* 314 Ky. 581, 236 S.W.2d 695, 697, in which case Kelley bought a house on the south side of Highway 460. On the north side of the highway opposite Kelley's house was a ditch into which water drained from a hillside. A culvert lay under the road and emptied at the corner of Kelley's property. When there were heavy rains the water overflowed onto Kelley's property. Kelley sued for damages. There was evidence that the commonwealth had permitted the culvert to become choked with stones, branches and other materials. Even though Kelley had purchased the house after the culverts, ditches, et cetera, had been constructed, we authorized recovery and, after a discussion of sovereign immunity, said:

> The appellants argue that to show a "taking" of property, the petition must state facts from which the court may infer a total ouster from possession, or at least a substantial deprivation of all beneficial use of the land affected. It seems to us, however, that an interference with the legally protected use to which land has been dedicated, which destroys that use or places a substantial and additional burden on the landowner to maintain that use, is a "taking" of his property.

In *Department of Highways v. Corey,* Ky., 247 S.W.2d 389, 390, a case similar in fact to the *Kelley* case, we reaffirmed our position and stated:

> Unless the physical damage detailed in the testimony is of such a nature as to amount to a "taking" of property for a public purpose without just com-

pensation, for which the State's sovereign immunity from suit is waived by Sections 13 and 242 of the Constitution, Mrs. Corey was not entitled to a judgment in her favor, and her petition should have been dismissed because the State is immune to such a suit for negligence.

The petition was based on negligent construction of culverts.

In *Commonwealth v. Geary,* Ky., 254 S.W.2d 477, it was again stated that such an action which is in the nature of a trespass could be maintained although we observed that the court had traveled a somewhat circuitous route in order to justify recovery on the theory that the property had been taken without just compensation.

The distinction made in the last quotation above seems to lack a foundation because whenever property is physically damaged, it is taken to that extent and the circuitous route which we have traveled seems to lead us inevitably to the rule that whenever any property is damaged by a sovereign, whether it is the result of common acts of negligence or is related to the exercise of eminent domain or of police power, damages must be paid by the sovereign.

We have discussed at length a few of the great number of decided cases on this point because we believe the whole group discloses that this court, in most instances, has, with reluctance, enforced the rule of sovereign immunity and, at times, has seemed to accept any excuse, however sophisticated, in order to grant relief to a person who has been harmed. This indicates that we should either abandon the original premise and recede from our prior decision concerning governmental immunity or should cease to contrive artificial distinctions and decide the cases by judicial fiat.

The courts of Florida have taken a giant step in *Hargrove v. Town of Cocoa Beach, Florida,* Fla., 96 So. 2d 130. This case contains a remarkable and courageous opinion and we will quote at some length from the opinion in our discussion of the case. [In this case, discussed *supra,* the Florida court abolished the immunity doctrine.—Eds.]

It was concluded and the opinion affirmatively stated that a municipal corporation may be held liable for the torts of police officers under the doctrine of respondeat superior. However, the court specifically excepted, and did not impose liability on, a municipality in the exercise of legislative or judicial, or quasi legislative or quasi judicial, functions.

Regardless of how the majority of the personnel of this court may feel at the present time concerning whether we should follow the path marked by the Florida Court, we must recognize that we are faced with a judicial problem which results from the fact that the immunity rule (although never clearly defined) has become so imbedded in the common law of this state over the years that it has become a definite part of our mores. We must make a choice as to whether the change in such a rule should be made by the legislature or by us. The majority of the court believes that the change addresses itself to legislative discretion and that we must content ourselves only with criticism of the rule which we have created.

When we return to the facts of the instant case, we are faced with the problem of placing it in its proper category. We believe that it is not an action where our rule of "reverse eminent domain" should apply. It falls more properly into the group of cases which concern the responsibility of a city for its negligent act. We have held that maintenance of parks and recreational facilities may be classified as a governmental function and we find that the acts complained of here were the result of the negligent acts of a servant of the city while performing that function. . . . We further believe that the property destroyed was not of the type which ordinarily may be devoted to public use.

Judgment affirmed.

Comments: 1. The *V.T.C.* case indicates that the principles covering compensation in inverse condemnation (reverse eminent domain) lawsuits can rather easily be extended to situations in which the injury occurs because of the negligent acts of the local government unit. Nevertheless, most courts do not allow inverse condemnation for what they consider to be acts of negligence. Mandelker, *Inverse Condemnation: The Constitutional Limits of Public Responsibility,* 1966 Wis. L. Rev. 3, 24-28. There is no satisfactory judicial rationale for this position. "Sometimes the decisions simply say that no liability can be imposed under the constitution for single tortious acts which fall under the immunity rule. In other cases no real explanation may be given, the court may fall back on the suggestion that the injury is incidental and consequential, or it may rely on a variety of related concepts which suggest that liability cannot be imposed for acts unconnected with the construction of the improvement." *Id.* at 25. Some courts have nevertheless blurred the distinction between a non-compensable negligent act and a compensable taking. *See Holtz v. Superior Court,* 475 P.2d 441 (Cal. 1970), imposing inverse liability for any physical injury to real property proximately caused by the improvement as deliberately designed and constructed. *See also* Van Alstyne, *Inverse Condemnation: Unintended Physical Damage,* 20 Hastings L.J. 431 (1969). Some courts may also reject the argument put forward in the principal case, that inverse condemnation does not lie if the property taken or damaged cannot be devoted to a public use. *See Sutfin v. State,* 67 Cal. Rptr. 665 (Cal. App. 1968).

The Kentucky court has now receded from the *V.T.C.* case and has abandoned sovereign immunity in tort. *Haney v. City of Lexington,* 386 S.W.2d 738 (Ky. 1964). Since this is so, why is it still necessary to resort to inverse condemnation actions in that state? Consider the possibility that the measure of damages in the inverse suit may be different, and that a different statute of limitations may apply. Moreover, as inverse suits are not tortious they may not permit the assertion of defenses based on the absence of negligent conduct on the defendant's part.

2. The original position in eminent domain law was that compensation was payable only when property was physically taken and title appropriated by the public agency for public use. If property not physically taken was in some way injured or damaged by an adjacent public facility there was no compensation. Compensation began to be awarded in inverse condemnation in cases like this as soon as courts were willing to recognize that an interference with the use of land was compensable as a taking of a property right in that land. *See, e.g., Eaton v. Boston, C. & M.R.R.,* 51 N.H. 504 (1872). Moreover, governmental liability in nuisance cases like this has been long established. *See, e.g., Stein v. Highland Park Independent School District,* 540 S.W.2d 551 (Tex. Civ. App. 1976). The cases discussed in the *V.T.C.* opinion that allow inverse recovery in nuisance-like cases in which the construction of or activity on a public facility damages adjacent property are thus exceptions to the general rule that no compensation is payable for consequential damage in eminent domain. They reflect an incorporation of nuisance recovery principles into eminent domain law.

Nevertheless, as the Kentucky nuisance-based inverse cases demonstrate, the courts are divided on how far inverse recovery in this situation can be extended. Obviously, a broad extension of liability for compensation in these cases would make public agencies responsible in a wide variety of situations for indirect impacts on adjacent property. For example, suppose a school district builds an elementary school across the street from my house. The noise and congestion that the school brings reduce the value of my property. Is the school district liable? The following cases indicate the different approaches that courts have taken to this and similar problems:

City of Louisville v. Munro, 475 S.W.2d 479 (Ky. 1971). Plaintiffs brought an action in inverse condemnation alleging that the "mere establishment" of a municipal zoo adjacent to their residence had depreciated its value. Recovery was denied, the court noting that in no case had it allowed recovery in inverse condemnation "where the alleged taking, injury or interference did not have *physical* aspects." *Id.* at 482 (emphasis in original). *Accord, Evans v. Just Open Government,* 251 S.E.2d 546 (Ga. 1979) (prison). But cf. *Edwards v. Bridgeport Hydraulic Co.,* 211 A.2d 679 (Conn. 1965), construing a statute authorizing damages against a private utility company for the erection of utility structures to include the depreciation in nearby property values resulting from the construction of a water tower.

Thornburg v. Port of Portland, 376 P.2d 100 (Or. 1962). Plaintiffs sued in inverse condemnation for damage to their residence due to the noise from airplanes using the defendant's airport which flew nearby but not over their property. The court first noted that the Supreme Court has allowed recovery for noise damage in this situation when airplanes fly directly over the plaintiff's property, apparently on the ground that a continuing trespass has occurred or that an easement has been taken. *United States v. Causby,* 328 U.S. 256 (1946). Compensation should also be allowed, the court held, when the flights are near but not over the plaintiff's property.

The Oregon court then held that the subject matter of inverse condemnation is private property, and that this property right includes the right to use and enjoy land. A nuisance can therefore be a taking giving rise to an inverse condemnation action whenever it is such an invasion of the rights of the property owner that he is ousted from the enjoyment of his land. The cases on the allowability of inverse recovery in this situation are divided. *See, contra, Ferguson v. City of Keene,* 238 A.2d 1 (N.H. 1968). For discussion see Stoebuck, *Condemnation by Nuisance: The Airport Cases in Retrospect and Prospect,* 71 Dick. L. Rev. 207 (1967). *See also* Lesser, *The Aircraft Noise Problem: The Past Decade and, at Least for a While Longer, Local Liability,* 13 Urb. L. 285 (1981); *Long v. City of Charlotte,* 293 S.E.2d 101 (N.C. 1982) (reviewing basis of liability in inverse condemnation).

Northcutt v. State Road Department, 209 So. 2d 710 (Fla. App. 1968). The department constructed an expressway adjacent to plaintiffs' residence, and they claimed that shock waves, vibrations, and noise from the highway had totally destroyed the value of their property for residential purposes. Their action for inverse condemnation was dismissed, the court noting that inverse recovery lies only for physical invasions and distinguishing cases like *Thornburg* as follows:

> We think there is a substantial difference between the use of an airport by airplanes and the use of highway and access roads by motor vehicles. The noise intensity factor is different; the safety factors are different; and the use factors are different. . . . An airport may be placed at a considerable distance from a city while it is a public necessity for roads and highways to be built close to, or directly through a city . . . . [To allow plaintiffs to recover] would bring to an effective halt the construction, operation and maintenance of access roads and highways within the State of Florida.

Id. at 711. *See also Sheridan Drive-In Theatre, Inc. v. State,* 384 P.2d 597 (Wyo. 1963), denying inverse recovery to the plaintiff, who alleged that its drive-in theater had to shut down because lights from an adjacent highway interfered with its operation. *Thornburg* was distinguished because in that case there was an interference with the ordinary use of property. Here the plaintiff's use of its property was extraordinary and unusual. The court recognized that the intensity of light can amount to a nuisance if it interferes with an occupation that is no more than ordinarily sensitive to light, but that this rule will not afford protection to hypersensitive individuals or industries.

3. The applicability of inverse condemnation concepts to zoning and other land use control activities of local governments has received increased attention, although the Supreme Court refused to decide the question in two recent cases, *Agins v. Tiburon,* 447 U.S. 255 (1980) and *San Diego Gas & Electric Co. v. City of San Diego,* 450 U.S. 621 (1981). The arguments, pro and con, are generally as follows:

> Police power regulations such as zoning ordinances and other land-use restrictions can destroy the use and enjoyment of property in order to promote the public good just as effectively as formal condemnation or physical invasion of property. From the property owner's point of view, it may matter little whether his land is condemned or flooded, or whether it is restricted by regulation to use in its natural state, if the effect in both cases is to deprive him of all beneficial use of it. From the government's point of view, the benefits flowing to the public from preservation of open space through

regulation may be equally great as from creating a wildlife refuge through formal condemnation or increasing electricity production through a dam project that floods private property. Appellee [city] implicitly posits the distinction that the government intends to take property through condemnation or physical invasion whereas it does not through police power regulations. But "the Constitution measures a taking of property not by what a State says, or by what it intends, but by what it *does.*" *Hughes v. Washington,* 389 U.S. 290, 298 (1967) (STEWART, J., concurring) (emphasis in original)
. . . .

. . . .

Having determined that property may be "taken for public use" by police power regulation within the meaning of the Just Compensation Clause of the Fifth Amendment, the question remains whether a government entity may constitutionally deny payment of just compensation to the property owner and limit his remedy to mere invalidation of the regulation instead. Appellant argues that it is entitled to the full fair market value of the property. Appellee argues that invalidation of the regulation is sufficient, without payment of monetary compensation. In my view, once a court establishes that there was a regulatory "taking," the Constitution demands that the government entity pay just compensation for the period commencing on the date the regulation first effected the "taking," and ending on the date the government entity chooses to rescind or otherwise amend the regulation. This interpretation, I believe, is supported by the express words and purpose of the Just Compensation Clause, as well as by cases of this Court construing it.

San Diego Gas & Electric Co. v. City of San Diego, 450 U.S. at 653-54 (1981) (BRENNAN, J., dissenting).

We are persuaded by various policy considerations to the view that inverse condemnation is an inappropriate and undesirable remedy in cases in which unconstitutional regulation is alleged. The expanding developments of our cities and suburban areas coupled with a growing awareness of the necessity to preserve our natural resources, including the land around us, has resulted in changing attitudes toward the regulation of land use. Recognition of this historic trend is not new. The United States Supreme Court perceptively observed more than 50 years ago that with the passage of time and increased concentration of people "problems have developed, and constantly are developing, which require, and will continue to require, additional restrictions in respect of the use and occupation of private lands in urban communities. Regulations, the wisdom, necessity and validity of which, as applied to existing conditions, are so apparent, that they are now uniformly sustained, a century ago, or even half a century ago, probably would have been rejected as arbitrary and oppressive. Such regulations are sustained, under the complex conditions of our day . . . . And in this there is no inconsistency, for while the meaning of constitutional guaranties never varies, the scope of their application must expand or contract to meet the new and different conditions which are constantly coming within the field of their operation. In a changing world, it is impossible that it should be otherwise." (*Euclid v. Ambler Co.,* . . . (1926) 272 U.S. 365, 386-387.)

In the half century since *Euclid,* the foregoing abstract principles under the force of experience have coalesced into a specific functional requirement. Community planners must be permitted the flexibility which their work requires. As we ourselves have recently observed, "If a governmental entity and its responsible officials were held subject to a claim for inverse condemnation merely because a parcel of land was designated for potential public use on one of these several authorized plans, the process of community planning would either grind to a halt, or deteriorate to publication of vacuous generalizations regarding the future use of land." (*Selby Realty Co. v. City of San Buenaventura,* (1973) . . . 514 P.2d 111, 117.)

Other commentators have recognized that the utilization of an inverse condemnation remedy would have a chilling effect upon the exercise of police regulatory powers at a local level because the expenditure of public funds would be, to some extent, within the power of the judiciary. "This threat of unanticipated financial liability will intimidate legislative bodies and will discourage the implementation of strict or innovative planning measures in favor of measures which are less stringent, more traditional, and fiscally safe." (Hall, *Eldridge v. City of Palo Alto*: Aberration or New Direction in Land Use Law? (1977) 28 Hastings L.J. 1569, 1597.)

We envisage that the availability of an inverse condemnation remedy in these situations would pose yet another threat to legislative control over appropriate land-use determinations. It has been noted, that "The weighing of costs and benefits is essentially a legislative process. In enacting a zoning ordinance, the legislative body assesses the desirability of a program on the assumption that compensation will not be required to achieve the objective of that ordinance. Determining that a particular land-use control requires compensation is an appropriate function of the judiciary, whose function includes protection of individuals against excesses of government. But it seems a usurpation of legislative power for a court to force compensation. Invalidation, rather than forced compensation, would seem to be the more expedient means of remedying legislative excesses." (Fullham & Schart, Inverse Condemnation: Its Availability in Challenging the Validity of a Zoning Ordinance (1974) 26 Stan.L.Rev. 1439, 1450-51. ...)

Other budgetary consequences reveal themselves when the land use control is exercised by means of the initiative. "Legislation in the nature of zoning can be and has been enacted by the people through a direct initiative. Are the voters, through the initiative power, also to have this unwelcome power to *inadvertently* commit funds from the public treasury? The logical extension of requiring compensation for the mere enactment of a harsh zoning measure indicates that the answer would be in the affirmative. The potential for fiscal chaos would be great if this were the result." (28 Hastings L.J., supra, at p. 1598, emphasis in original.)

In combination, the need for preserving a degree of freedom in the land-use planning function, and the inhibiting financial force which inheres in the inverse condemnation remedy, persuade us that on balance, mandamus or declaratory relief rather than inverse condemnation is the appropriate relief under the circumstances.

Agins v. City of Tiburon, 598 P.2d 25, 29-31 (Cal. 1979). *See* D. MANDELKER, LAND USE LAW §§ 8.19-8.22 (1982).

B. FEDERAL LAW

So far, we have dealt with cases brought in state courts. When a citizen resorts to federal court to seek relief from state or local governmental action, or inaction, a different set of obstacles arises. The following comments are meant to alert you to possible difficulties; they are far from an exhaustive treatment of the federal court issues.

1. THE ELEVENTH AMENDMENT

The eleventh amendment reads:

The judicial power of the United States shall not be construed to extend to any suit in law or equity, commenced or prosecuted against one of the United States by citizens of another State, or by citizens or subjects of any Foreign State.

Through judicial interpretation, the amendment has been held to bar recovery against a state by its own citizens, as well as citizens of other states. *Hans v. Louisiana,* 134 U.S. 1 (1890).

Whenever money damages are to be paid from public funds in the state treasury, the eleventh amendment may preclude recovery. In *Edelman v. Jordan,* 415 U.S. 651 (1974), the Supreme Court held that the eleventh amendment barred welfare recipients from recovering retroactive monetary benefits from the state of Illinois in federal court. Contrast *Edelman* with *Ex parte Young,* 209 U.S. 123 (1908), a "watershed case" holding that the eleventh amendment did not bar an action to enjoin the attorney general of Minnesota from enforcing an unconstitutional statute. What distinguishes the remedies sought in the two cases?

Later, the Supreme Court softened the effect of *Edelman* in *Fitzpatrick v. Bitzer,* 427 U.S. 445 (1976). The Court held that the 1972 amendments to Title VII of the Civil Rights Act of 1964, authorizing federal courts to award money damages against a state government found to have discriminated in an individual's employment, did not violate the eleventh amendment. "Congress has the power to authorize federal courts to enter such an award against the State as a means of enforcing the substantive guarantees of the Fourteenth Amendment." *Id.* at 448. In *Edelman* congressional authorization was absent. The petitioners in *Fitzpatrick* were awarded back pay and attorneys' fees under the authority of the Title VII provisions.

Another means of avoiding the eleventh amendment is state waiver of the immunity, which the courts have recognized. In *Skehan v. Board of Trustees,* 669 F.2d 142 (3d Cir. 1982), the court held that an award of special damages for back pay against a state college in favor of a nontenured associate professor reinstated after successfully establishing a denial of first amendment and due process rights because of the circumstances of his dismissal was barred by the eleventh amendment. Professor Skehan had argued that the Pennsylvania Supreme Court's judicial abrogation of the doctrine of sovereign immunity, *Mayle v. Pennsylvania Department of Highways,* 388 A.2d 709 (Pa. 1978), constituted a waiver of the state's eleventh amendment immunity. The Third Circuit rejected the argument, concluding that such waiver should come only from the legislature or executive, and then only if clearly articulated, because of the potential monetary burden on the state treasury.

> More significantly, even if judicial waiver of Eleventh Amendment immunity were appropriate, we do not believe that the *Mayle* decision constitutes a waiver of such immunity. The Supreme Court has held that "[i]n deciding whether a State has waived its constitutional protection under the Eleventh Amendment, we will find waiver only where stated 'by the most express language or by such overwhelming implications from the text as [will] leave no room for any other reasonable construction.'"

Edelman v. Jordan, 415 U.S. at 673 ... (quoting *Murray v. Wilson Distilling Co.,* 213 U.S. 151 ... (1909)).

The opinion of the Pennsylvania Supreme Court in *Mayle* does not, by even the most liberal standards, constitute a clear and unequivocal waiver of Eleventh Amendment immunity. The precise question before the court in *Mayle* was whether Pennsylvania could be sued in state court for injuries suffered by the plaintiff as a result of a negligently maintained public highway. ... In reversing the lower court's dismissal of appellant's complaint based on the sovereign immunity doctrine, the Pennsylvania court expressly "abrogated" that doctrine, reasoning that since sovereign immunity in Pennsylvania was a non-constitutional doctrine that was established by judicial decisions, the state constitution did not preclude it from abolishing this judicially-created doctrine. The court further reasoned that none of the historical arguments favoring retention of the doctrine have continuing validity. Except to note that the Pennsylvania legislature had refused to ratify the Eleventh Amendment when it was proposed by Congress, the *Mayle* opinion does not discuss, either expressly or impliedly, the question of waiver of Pennsylvania's federal constitutionally-based immunity from suit in federal court. Rather, the opinion focuses on the judicially-created common law doctrine of sovereign immunity.

669 F.2d at 148-49.

2. CIVIL RIGHTS CASES: SUING GOVERNMENT AND ITS OFFICIALS UNDER THE CIVIL RIGHTS ACT OF 1871, 42 U.S.C. § 1983

Section 1983 reads as follows:

Every person who, under color of any statute, ordinance, regulation, custom or usage, of any state or territory, subjects, or causes to be subjected, any citizens of the United States or other person within the jurisdiction thereof to the deprivation of any rights, privileges, or immunities secured by the Constitution and laws, shall be liable to the party injured in an action at law, suit in equity, or other proper proceeding for redress.

One of the most significant areas of judicial activism with respect to governmental responsibility has been the application of the Civil Rights Act of 1871 to state and local governments. The breakthrough occurred in the now famous *Monell* decision of 1978 when the Supreme Court overruled its 1961 decision, *Monroe v. Pape,* 365 U.S. 167, and held that local government units were intended by Congress to be included among those persons to whom § 1983 applies:

> Local governing bodies, therefore, can be sued directly under § 1983 for monetary, declaratory, or injunctive relief where, as here, the action that is alleged to be unconstitutional implements or executes a policy statement, ordinance, regulation, or decision officially adopted and promulgated by that body's officers. Moreover, although the touchstone of the § 1983 action against a government body is an allegation that official policy is responsible for a deprivation of rights protected by the Constitutions, local governments, like every other § 1983 "person", by the very terms of the statute, may be sued for constitutional deprivations visited pursuant to governmental "custom" even though such a custom has not received formal approval through the body's official decisionmaking channels. . . .
>
> On the other hand, . . . a municipality cannot be held liable *solely* because it employs a tortfeasor or, in other words, a municipality cannot be held liable under § 1983 on a respondent superior theory.

Monell v. New York City Department of Social Services, 436 U.S. 658, 690-91 (1978).

Monell set the stage for two decisions in 1980 that significantly altered the face of local government law:

OWEN v. CITY OF INDEPENDENCE

United States Supreme Court
445 U.S. 622 (1980)

Mr. Justice Brennan delivered the opinion of the Court.
. . . .

I

The events giving rise to this suit are detailed in the District Court's findings of fact, 421 F. Supp. 1110 (WD Mo. 1976). On February 20, 1967, Robert L. Broucek, then City Manager of respondent city of Independence, Mo., appointed petitioner George D. Owen to an indefinite term as Chief of Police. In 1972, Owen and a new City Manager, Lyle W. Alberg, engaged in a dispute over petitioner's administration of the police department's property room. In March of that year, a handgun, which the records of the Department's property room stated had been destroyed, turned up in Kansas City in the possession of a felon. This discovery prompted Alberg to initiate an investigation of the management of the property room. Although the probe was initially directed by petitioner, Alberg soon transferred responsibility for the investigation to the City's Department of Law, instructing the City Counselor to supervise its conduct and to inform him directly of its findings.

Sometime in early April 1972, Alberg received a written report on the investigation's progress, along with copies of confidential witness statements. Although the City Auditor found that the police department's records were insufficient to permit an adequate accounting of the goods contained in the property room, the City Counselor concluded that there was no evidence of any criminal acts or of any violation of state or municipal law in the administration of the property room. Alberg discussed the results of the investigation at an informal meeting with several City Council members and advised them that he would take action at an appropriate time to correct any problems in the administration of the police department.

On April 10, Alberg asked petitioner to resign as Chief of Police and to accept another position within the department, citing dissatisfaction with the manner in which petitioner had managed the department, particularly his inadequate supervision of the property room. Alberg warned that if petitioner refused to take another position in the department his employment would be terminated, to which petitioner responded that he did not intend to resign.

On April 13, Alberg issued a public statement addressed to the Mayor and the City Council concerning the results of the investigation. After referring to "discrepancies" found in the administration, handling, and security of public property, the release concluded that "[t]here appears to be no evidence to substantiate any allegations of a criminal nature" and offered assurances that "[s]teps have been initiated on an administrative level to correct these discrepancies." *Id.*, at 1115. Although Alberg apparently had decided by this time to replace petitioner as Police Chief, he took no formal action to that end and left for a brief vacation without informing the City Council of his decision.

While Alberg was away on the weekend of April 15 and 16, two developments occurred. Petitioner, having consulted with counsel, sent Alberg a letter demanding written notice of the charges against him and a public hearing with a reasonable opportunity to respond to those charges. At approximately the same time, City Councilman Paul L. Roberts asked for a copy of the investigative report on the police department property room. Although petitioner's appeal received no immediate response, the Acting City Manager complied with Roberts' request and supplied him with the audit report and witness statements.

On the evening of April 17, 1972, the City Council held its regularly scheduled meeting. After completion of the planned agenda, Councilman Roberts read a statement he had prepared on the investigation. Among other allegations, Roberts charged that petitioner had misappropriated police department property for his own use, that narcotics and money had "mysteriously disappeared" from his office, that traffic tickets had been manipulated, that high ranking police officials had made "inappropriate" requests affecting the police court, and that "things have occurred causing the unusual release of felons." At the close of his statement, Roberts moved that the investigative reports be released to the news media and turned over to the prosecutor for presentation to the grand jury, and that the City Manager "take all direct and appropriate action" against those persons "involved in illegal, wrongful, or gross inefficient activities brought out in the investigative reports." After some discussion, the City Council passed Roberts' motion with no dissents and one abstention.

City Manager Alberg discharged petitioner the very next day. Petitioner was not given any reason for his dismissal; he received only a written notice stating that his employment as Chief of Police was "terminated under the provisions of Section 3.3(1) of the City Charter." Petitioner's earlier demand for a specification of charges and a public hearing was ignored, and a subsequent request by his attorney for an appeal of the discharge decision was denied by the city on the grounds that "there is no appellate procedure or forum provided by the Charter or ordinances of the City of Independence, Missouri, relating to the dismissal of Mr. Owen." App. 26-27.

The local press gave prominent coverage both to the City Council's action and petitioner's dismissal, linking the discharge to the investigation. As instructed by the City Council, Alberg referred the investigative reports and witness statements to the Prosecuting Attorney of Jackson County, Mo., for consideration by a grand jury. The results of the audit and investigation were never released to the public, however. The grand jury subsequently returned a "no true bill," and no further action was taken by either the City Council or City Manager Alberg.

II

Petitioner named the city of Independence, City Manager Alberg, and the present members of the City Council in their official capacities as defendants in this suit. Alleging that he was discharged without notice of reasons and without a hearing in violation of his constitutional rights to procedural and substantive due process, petitioner sought declaratory and injunctive relief, including a hearing on his discharge, backpay from the date of discharge, and attorney's fees. The District Court, after a bench trial, entered judgment for respondents. 421 F. Supp. 1110 (WD Mo. 1976).

The Court of Appeals initially reversed the District Court. . . .

Respondents petitioned for review of the Court of Appeals' decision. Certiorari was granted, and the case was remanded for further consideration in light of our supervening decision in *Monell v. New York City Dept. of Social Services, supra.* 438 U.S. 902 (1978). The Court of Appeals on the remand reaffirmed its original determination that the city had violated petitioner's rights under the Fourteenth Amendment, but held that all respondents, including the city, were entitled to qualified immunity from liability. 589 F.2d 335 (CA8 1978).

Monell held that "a local government may not be sued under § 1983 for an injury inflicted solely by its employees or agents. Instead, it is when execution of a government's policy or custom, whether made by its lawmakers or by those whose edicts or acts may fairly be said to represent official policy, inflicts the injury that the government as an entity is responsible under § 1983." 436 U.S., at 694. The Court of Appeals held in the instant case that the municipality's official policy was responsible for the deprivation of petitioner's constitutional rights: "[T]he stigma attached to [petitioner] in connection with his discharge was caused by the official conduct of the City's lawmakers, or by those whose acts may fairly be said to represent official policy. Such conduct amounted to official policy causing the infringement of [petitioner's] constitutional rights, in violation of section 1983." 589 F.2d, at 337.

Nevertheless, the Court of Appeals affirmed the judgment of the District Court denying petitioner any relief against the respondent city, stating:

The Supreme Court's decisions in *Board of Regents v. Roth,* 408 U.S. 564 (1972), and *Perry v. Sindermann,* 408 U.S. 593 (1972), crystallized the rule of establishing the right to a name-clearing hearing for a government employee allegedly stigmatized in the course of his discharge. The Court decided those two cases two months after the discharge in the instant case. Thus, officials of the City of Independence could not have been aware of [petitioner's] right to a name-clearing hearing in connection with the discharge. The City of Independence should not be charged with predicting the future course of constitutional law. ... We extend the limited immunity the district court applied to the individual defendants to cover the City as well, because its officials acted in good faith and without malice. We hold the City not liable for actions it could not reasonably have known violated [petitioner's] constitutional rights. *Id.*, at 338 (footnote and citations omitted).

We turn now to the reasons for our disagreement with this holding.

III

Because the question of the scope of a municipality's immunity from liability under § 1983 is essentially one of statutory construction, ... the starting point in our analysis must be the language of the statute itself. ... By its terms, § 1983 "creates a species of tort liability that on its face admits of no immunities." *Imbler v. Pachtman,* 424 U.S. 409, 417 (1976). Its language is absolute and unqualified; no mention is made of any privileges, immunities, or defenses that may be asserted. Rather, the act imposes liability upon "*every person*" who, under color of state law or custom, "subjects, or causes to be subjected, any citizen of the United States ... to the deprivation of any rights, privileges, or immunities secured by the Constitution and laws." And *Monell* held that these words were intended to encompass municipal corporations as well as natural "persons."

Moreover, the congressional debates surrounding the passage of § 1 of the Civil Rights Act of 1871, 17 Stat. 13—the forerunner of § 1983—confirm the expansive sweep of the statutory language. ...

However, notwithstanding § 1983's expansive language and the absence of any express incorporation of common-law immunities, we have, on several occasions, found that a tradition of immunity was so firmly rooted in the common law and was supported by such strong policy reasons that "Congress would have specifically so provided had it wished to abolish the doctrine." *Pierson v. Ray,* 386 U.S. 547, 555 (1967). Thus in *Tenney v. Brandhove,* 341 U. S. 367 (1951), after tracing the development of an absolute legislative privilege from its source in 16th-century England to its inclusion in the Federal and State Constitutions, we concluded that Congress "would [not] impinge on a tradition so well grounded in history and reason by covert inclusion in the general language" of § 1983. *Id.,* at 376.

Subsequent cases have required that we consider the personal liability of various other types of government officials. ...

In each of these cases, our finding of § 1983 immunity "was predicated upon a considered inquiry into the immunity historically accorded the relevant official at common law and the interests behind it." *Imbler v. Pachtman, supra,* at 421. Where the immunity claimed by the defendant was well-established at common law at the time § 1983 was enacted, and where its rationale was compatible with the purposes of the Civil Rights Act, we have construed the statute to incorporate that immunity. But there is no tradition of immunity for municipal corporations, and neither history nor policy support a construction of § 1983 that would justify the qualified immunity accorded the city of Independence by the Court of Appeals. We hold, therefore, that the municipality may not assert the good faith of its officers or agents as a defense to liability under § 1983.

A

Since colonial times, a distinct feature of our Nation's system of governance has been the conferral of political power upon public and municipal corporations for the management of matters of local concern. As *Monell* recounted, by 1871, municipalities—like private corporations—were treated as natural persons for virtually all purposes of constitutional and statutory analysis. In particular, they were routinely sued in both federal and state courts. . . . Local governmental units were regularly held to answer in damages for a wide range of statutory and constitutional violations, as well as for common-law actions for breach of contract. And although, as we discuss below, a municipality was not subject to suit for all manner of tortious conduct, it is clear that at the time § 1983 was enacted, local governmental bodies did not enjoy the sort of "good-faith" qualified immunity extended to them by the Court of Appeals.

As a general rule, it was understood that a municipality's tort liability in damages was identical to that of private corporations and individuals:

> There is nothing in the character of a municipal corporation which entitles it to an immunity from liability for such malfeasances as private corporations or individuals would be liable for in a civil action. A municipal corporation is liable to the same extent as an individual for any act done by the express authority of the corporation, or of a branch of its government, empowered to act for it upon the subject to which the particular act relates, and for any act which, after it has been done, has been lawfully ratified by the corporation. T. Shearman & A. Redfield, A Treatise on the Law of Negligence § 120, at 139 (1869) (hereinafter Shearman & Redfield).

. . . Under this general theory of liability, a municipality was deemed responsible for any private losses generated through a wide variety of its operations and functions, from personal injuries due to its defective sewers, thoroughfares, and public utilities, to property damage caused by its trespasses and uncompensated takings.

Yet in the hundreds of cases from that era awarding damages against municipal governments for wrongs committed by them, one searches in vain for much mention of a qualified immunity based on the good-faith of municipal officers. . . .

To be sure, there were two doctrines that afforded municipal corporations some measure of protection from tort liability. The first sought to distinguish between a municipality's "governmental" and "proprietary" functions; as to the former, the city was held immune, whereas in its exercise of the latter, the city was held to the same standards of liability as any private corporation. The second doctrine immunized a municipality for its "discretionary" or "legislative" activities, but not for those which were "ministerial" in nature. A brief examination of the application and the rationale underlying each of these doctrines demonstrates that Congress could not have intended them to limit a municipality's liability under § 1983.

The governmental-proprietary distinction owed its existence to the dual nature of the municipal corporation. On the one hand, the municipality was a corporate body, capable of performing the same "proprietary" functions as any private corporation, and liable for its torts in the same manner and to the same extent, as well. On the other hand, the municipality was an arm of the State, and when acting in that "governmental" or "public" capacity, it shared the immunity traditionally accorded the sovereign. But the principle of sovereign immunity— itself a somewhat arid fountainhead for municipal immunity—is necessarily nullified when the State expressly or impliedly allows itself, or its creation, to be sued. Municipalities were therefore liable not only for their "proprietary" acts, but also for those "governmental" functions as to which the State had withdrawn their immunity. And, by the end of the 19th century, courts regularly held that in imposing a specific duty on the municipality either in its character or by statute, the State had impliedly withdrawn the city's immunity from liability for the nonperformance or misperformance of its obligation. . . . Thus, despite the nominal existence of an immunity for "governmental" functions, municipalities were found liable in damages in a multitude of cases involving such activities.

That the municipality's common-law immunity for "governmental" functions derives from the principle of sovereign immunity also explains why that doctrine could not have served as the basis for the qualified privilege respondent claims under § 1983. First, because sovereign immunity insulates the municipality from unconsented suits altogether, the presence or absence of good faith is simply irrelevant. The critical issue is whether injury occurred while the city was exercising governmental, as opposed to proprietary, powers or obligations—not whether its agents reasonably believed they were acting lawfully in so conducting themselves. More fundamentally, however, the municipality's "governmental" immunity is obviously abrogated by the sovereign's enactment of a statute making it amenable to suit. Section 1983 was just a such a statute. By including municipalities within the class of "persons" subject to liability for violations of the Federal Constitution and laws, Congress—the supreme sovereign on matters of federal law—abolished whatever vestige of the State's sovereign immunity the municipality possessed.

The second common-law distinction between municipal functions—that protecting the city from suits challenging "discretionary" decisions—was grounded not on the principle of sovereign immunity, but on a concern for separation of powers. A large part of the municipality's responsibilities involved broad discretionary decisions on issues of public policy—decisions that affected large numbers of persons and called for a delicate balancing of competing considerations. For a court or jury, in the guise of a tort suit, to review the reasonableness of the city's judgment on these matters would be an infringement upon the powers properly vested in a coordinate and coequal branch of government. . . . In order to ensure against any invasion into the legitimate sphere of the municipality's policymaking processes, courts therefore refused to entertain suits against the city "either for the non-exercise of, or for the manner in which in good faith it exercises, discretionary powers of a public or legislative character." 2 Dillon [Law of Municipal Corporations] § 753, at 862 [2nd ed. 1873].

Although many, if not all, of a municipality's activities would seem to involve at least some measure of discretion, the influence of this doctrine on the city's liability was not as significant as might be expected. For just as the courts implied an exception to the municipality's immunity for its "governmental" functions, here, too, a distinction was made that had the effect of subjecting the city to liability for much of its tortious conduct. While the city retained its immunity for decisions as to whether the public interest required acting in one manner or another, once any particular decision was made, the city was fully liable for any injuries incurred in the execution of its judgment. . . . Thus municipalities remained liable in damages for a broad range of conduct implementing their discretionary decisions.

Once again, an understanding of the rationale underlying the common-law immunity for "discretionary" functions explains why that doctrine cannot serve as the foundation for a good-faith immunity under § 1983. That common-law doctrine merely prevented courts from substituting their own judgment on matters within the lawful discretion of the municipality. But a municipality has no "discretion" to violate the Federal Constitution; its dictates are absolute and imperative. And when a court passes judgment on the municipality's conduct in a § 1983 action, it does not seek to second-guess the "reasonableness" of the city's decision nor to interfere with the local government's resolution of competing policy considerations. Rather, it looks only to whether the municipality has conformed to the requirements of the Federal Constitution and statutes. As was stated in *Sterling v. Constantin,* 287 U.S. 378, 398 (1932), "When there is a substantial showing that the exertion of state power has overridden private rights secured by that Constitution, the subject is necessarily one for judicial inquiry in an appropriate proceeding directed against the individuals charged with the transgression."

. . . .

B

Our rejection of a construction of § 1983 that would accord municipalities a qualified immunity for their good-faith constitutional violations is compelled both by the legislative purpose in enacting the statute and by considerations of public policy. The central aim of the Civil Rights Act was to provide protection to those persons wronged by the " '[m]isuse of power, possessed by virtue of state law and made possible only because the wrongdoer is clothed with the authority of state law.' " *Monroe v. Pape,* 365 U.S. 167, 184 (1961) (quoting *United States v. Classic,* 313 U.S. 299, 326 (1941)). By creating an express federal remedy, Congress sought to "enforce provisions of the Fourteenth Amendment against those who carry a badge of authority of a State and represent it in some capacity, whether they act in accordance with their authority or misuse it." *Monroe v. Pape, supra,* at 172.

How "uniquely amiss" it would be, therefore, if the government itself—"the social organ to which all in our society look for the promotion of liberty, justice, fair and equal treatment, and the setting of worthy norms and goals for social conduct"—were permitted to disavow liability for the injury it has begotten. . . . A damages remedy against the offending party is a vital component of any scheme for vindicating cherished constitutional guarantees, and the importance of assuring its efficacy is only accentuated when the wrongdoer is the institution that has been established to protect the very rights it has transgressed. Yet owing to the qualified immunity enjoyed by most government officials, see *Scheuer v. Rhodes,* 416 U.S. 232 (1974), many victims of municipal malfeasance would be left remediless if the city were also allowed to assert a good-faith defense. Unless countervailing considerations counsel otherwise, the injustice of such a result should not be tolerated.

Moreover, § 1983 was intended not only to provide compensation to the victims of past abuses, but to serve as a deterrent against future constitutional deprivations, as well. See . . . *Carey v. Piphus,* 435 U.S. 247, 256-257 (1978). The knowledge that a municipality will be liable for all of its injurious conduct, whether committed in good faith or not, should create an incentive for officials who may harbor doubts about the lawfulness of their intended actions to err on the side of protecting citizens' constitutional rights. Furthermore, the threat that damages might be levied against the city may encourage those in a policymaking position to institute internal rules and programs designed to minimize the likelihood of unintentional infringements on constitutional rights. Such procedures are particularly beneficial in preventing those "systemic" injuries that result not so much from the conduct of any single individual, but from the interactive behavior of several government officials, each of whom may be acting in good faith. *Cf.* Note, Developments in the Law: Section 1983 and Federalism, 90 Harv. L. Rev. 1133, 1218-1219 (1977).

Our previous decisions conferring qualified immunities on various government officials . . . are not to be read as derogating the significance of the societal interest in compensating the innocent victims of governmental misconduct. Rather, in each case we concluded that overriding considerations of public policy nonetheless demanded that the official be given a measure of protection from personal liability. The concerns that justified those decisions, however, are less compelling, if not wholly inapplicable, when the liability of the municipal entity is at issue.

In *Scheuer v. Rhodes, supra,* at 240, The Chief Justice identified the two "mutually dependent rationales" on which the doctrine of official immunity rested:

> (1) the injustice, particularly in the absence of bad faith, of subjecting to liability an officer who is required, by the legal obligations of his position, to exercise discretion; (2) the danger that the threat of such liability would deter his willingness to execute his office with the decisiveness and the judgment required by the public good.

The first consideration is simply not implicated when the damage award comes not from the official's pocket, but from the public treasury. It hardly seems unjust to require a municipal defendant which has violated a citizen's constitutional rights to compensate him for the injury suffered thereby. Indeed, Congress enacted § 1983 precisely to provide a remedy for such abuses of official power. . . . Elemental notions of fairness dictate that one who causes a loss should bear the loss.

It has been argued, however, that revenue raised by taxation for public use should not be diverted to the benefit of a single or discrete group of taxpayers, particularly where the municipality has at all times acted in good faith. On the contrary, the accepted view is that stated in *Thayer v. Boston, supra* — "that the city, in its corporate capacity, should be liable to make good the damages sustained by an [unlucky] individual, in consequence of the acts thus done." 19 Pick., at 516. After all, it is the public at large which enjoys the benefits of the government's activities, and it is the public at large which is ultimately responsible for its administration. Thus, even where some constitutional development could not have been foreseen by municipal officials, it is fairer to allocate any resulting financial loss to the inevitable costs of government borne by all the taxpayers, than to allow its impact to be felt solely by those whose rights, albeit newly recognized, have been violated. . . .

The second rationale mentioned in *Scheuer* also loses its force when it is the municipality, in contrast to the official, whose liability is at issue. At the heart of this justification for a qualified immunity for the individual official is the concern that the threat of *personal* monetary liability will introduce an unwarranted and unconscionable consideration into the decisionmaking process, thus paralyzing the governing official's decisiveness and distorting his judgment on matters of public policy. The inhibiting effect is significantly reduced, if not eliminated, however, when the threat of personal liability is removed. First, as an empirical matter, it is questionable whether the hazard of municipal loss will deter a public officer from the conscientious exercise of his duties; city officials routinely make decisions that either require a large expenditure of municipal funds or involve a substantial risk of depleting the public fisc. . . . More important, though, is the realization that consideration of the *municipality's* liability for constitutional violations is quite properly the concern of its elected or appointed officials. Indeed, a decisionmaker would be derelict in his duties if, at some point, he did not consider whether his decision comports with constitutional mandates and did not weigh the risk that a violation might result in an award of damages from the public treasury. As one commentator aptly put it, "Whatever other concerns should shape a particular official's actions, certainly one of them should be the constitutional rights of individuals who will be affected by his actions. To criticize section 1983 liability because it leads decisionmakers to avoid the infringement of constitutional rights is to criticize one of the statute's *raisons d'être."*

IV

In sum, our decision holding that municipalities have no immunity from damages liability flowing from their constitutional violations harmonizes well with developments in the common law and our own pronouncements on official immunities under § 1983. Doctrines of tort law have changed significantly over the past century, and our notions of governmental responsibility should properly reflect that evolution. No longer is individual "blameworthiness" the acid test of liability; the principle of equitable loss-spreading has joined fault as a factor in distributing the costs of official misconduct.

We believe that today's decision, together with prior precedents in this area, properly allocates these costs among the three principals in the scenario of the § 1983 cause of action: the victim of the constitutional deprivation; the officer whose conduct caused the injury; and the public, as represented by the municipal entity. The innocent individual who is harmed by an abuse of governmental authority is assured that he will be compensated for his injury. The offending official, so long as he conducts himself in good faith, may go about his business secure in the knowledge that a qualified immunity will protect him from personal liability for damages that are more appropriately chargeable to the populace as a whole. And the public will be forced to bear only the costs of injury inflicted by the "execution of a government's policy or custom, whether made by its lawmakers or by those whose edicts or acts may fairly be said to represent official policy." *Monell v. New York City Dept. of Social Services,* 436 U.S., at 694.

Reversed.

MR. JUSTICE POWELL, with whom THE CHIEF JUSTICE, MR. JUSTICE STEWART, and MR. JUSTICE REHNQUIST join, dissenting.

. . . .

Section 1983 provides a private right of action against "any person" acting under color of state law who imposes or causes to be imposed a deprivation of constitutional rights. Although the statute does not refer to immunities, this Court has held that the law "is to be read in harmony with general principles of tort immunities and defenses rather than in derogation of them." *Imbler v. Pachtman,* 424 U.S. 409, 418 (1976). . . .

This approach reflects several concerns. First, the common-law traditions of immunity for public officials could not have been repealed by the "general language" of § 1983. . . . In addition, "the public interest requires decisions and action to enforce laws for the protection of the public." *Scheuer v. Rhodes,* 416 U.S. 232, 241 (1974). Because public officials will err at times, "[t]he concept of immunity assumes . . . that it is better to risk some error and possibly injury from such error than not to decide or act at all." *Id.,* at 242. . . . By granting some immunity to governmental actors, the Court has attempted to ensure that public decisions will not be dominated by fears of liability for actions that may turn out to be unconstitutional. Public officials "cannot be expected to predict the future course of constitutional law. . . ." *Procunier v. Navarette,* 434 U.S. 555, 562 (1978).

In response to these considerations, the Court has found absolute immunity from § 1983 suits for state legislators, . . . and prosecutors in their role as advocates for the state. . . . Other officials have been granted a qualified immunity that protects them when in good faith they have implemented policies that reasonably were thought to be constitutional. This limited immunity extends to police officers, . . . state executive officers, . . . local school board members, . . . the superintendent of a state hospital, . . . and prison officials. . . .

The Court today abandons any attempt to harmonize § 1983 with traditional tort law. It points out that municipal immunity may be abrogated by legislation. Thus, according to the Court, Congress "abolished" municipal immunity when it included municipalities "within the class of 'persons' subject to liability under § 1983." . . .

This reasoning flies in the face of our prior decisions under this statute. We have held repeatedly that "immunities 'well grounded in history and reason' [were not] abrogated 'by covert inclusion in the general language' of § 1983." *Imbler v. Pachtman, supra,* 424 U.S., at 418. . . . The peculiar nature of the Court's position emerges when the status of executive officers under § 1983 is compared with that of local governments. State and local executives are personally liable for bad-faith or unreasonable constitutional torts. Although Congress had the power to make those individuals liable for all such torts, this Court has refused to find an abrogation of traditional immunity in a statute that does not mention immunities. Yet the Court now views the enactment of § 1983 as a direct abolition of traditional municipal immunities. Unless the Court is overruling its previous immunity decisions, the silence in § 1983 must mean that the 42d Congress mutely accepted the immunity of executive officers, but silently rejected common-law municipal immunity. I find this interpretation of the statute singularly implausible.

Important public policies support the extension of qualified immunity to local governments. First, as recognized by the doctrine of separation of powers, some governmental decisions should be at least presumptively insulated from judicial review. Chief Justice Marshall wrote in *Marbury v. Madison,* 1 Cranch 137, 170 (1803), that "[t]he province of the court is . . . not to inquire how the executive or executive officers, perform duties in which they have a discretion." Marshall stressed the caution with which courts must approach "[q]uestions, in their nature political, or which are, by the constitution and laws, submitted to the executive." The allocation of public resources and the operational policies of the government itself are activities that lie peculiarly within the competence of executive and legislative bodies. When charting those policies, a local official should not have to gauge his employer's possible liability under § 1983 if he incorrectly — though reasonably and in good faith—forecasts the course of constitutional law. Excessive judicial intrusion into such decisions can only distort municipal decisionmaking and discredit the courts. Qualified immunity would provide presumptive protection for discretionary acts, while still leaving the municipality liable for bad faith or unreasonable constitutional deprivations.

Because today's decision will inject constant consideration of § 1983 liability into local decisonmaking, it may restrict the independence of local governments and their ability to respond to the needs of their communities. Only this Term, we noted that the "point" of immunity under § 1983 "is to forestall an atmosphere of intimidation that would conflict with [officials'] resolve to perform their designated functions in a principled fashion." *Ferri v. Ackerman,* 444 U.S. 193, 203-204 (1979).

The Court now argues that local officials might modify their actions unduly if they face personal liability under § 1983, but that they are unlikely to do so when the locality itself will be held liable.... This contention denigrates the sense of responsibility of municipal officers, and misunderstands the political process. Responsible local officials will be concerned about potential judgments against their municipalities for alleged constitutional torts. Moreover, they will be accountable within the political system for subjecting the municipality to adverse judgments. If officials must look over their shoulders at strict municipal liability for unknowable constitutional deprivations, the resulting degree of governmental paralysis will be little different from that caused by fear of personal liability.

In addition, basic fairness requires a qualified immunity for municipalities. The good-faith defense recognized under § 1983 authorizes liability only when officials acted with malicious intent or when they "knew or should have known that their conduct violated the constitutional norm." *Procunier v. Navarette,* 434 U.S., at 562. The standard incorporates the idea that liability should not attach unless there was notice that a constitutional right was at risk. This idea applies to governmental entities and individual officials alike. Constitutional law is what the courts say it is, and — as demonstrated by today's decision and its precursor, *Monell* — even the most prescient lawyer would hesitate to give a firm opinion on matters not plainly settled. Municipalities, often acting in the utmost good faith, may not know or anticipate when their action or inaction will be deemed a constitutional violation.

The Court nevertheless suggests that, as a matter of social justice, municipal corporations should be strictly liable even if they could not have known that a particular action would violate the Constitution. After all, the Court urges, local governments can "spread" the cost of any judgment across the local population. The Court neglects, however, the fact that many local governments lack the resources to withstand substantial unanticipated liability under § 1983. Even enthusiastic proponents of municipal liability have conceded that ruinous judgments under the statute could imperil local governments. *E.g.,* Note, Damage Remedies Against Municipalities for Constitutional Violations, 89 Harv. L. Rev. 922, 958 (1978). By simplistically applying the theorems of welfare economics and ignoring the reality of municipal finance, the Court imposes strict liability on the level of government least able to bear it. For some municipalities, the result could be a severe limitation on their ability to serve the public.

MAINE v. THIBOUTOT

United States Supreme Court
448 U.S. 1 (1980)

Mr. Justice Brennan delivered the opinion of the Court.

. . . .

I

Respondents, Lionel and Joline Thiboutot, are married and have eight children, three of whom are Lionel's by a previous marriage. The Maine Department of Human Services notified Lionel that, in computing the Aid to Families with Dependent Children (AFDC) benefits to which he was entitled for the three children exclusively his, it would no longer make allowance for the money spent to support the other five children, even though Lionel is legally obligated to support them. Respondents, challenging the State's interpretation of 42 U. S. C. § 602 (a)(7), exhausted their state administrative remedies and then sought judicial review of the administrative action in the State Superior Court. By amended complaint, respondents also claimed relief under § 1983 for themselves and others similarly situated. The Superior Court's judgment enjoined petitioners from enforcing the challenged rule and ordered them to adopt new regulations, to notify class members of the new regulations, and to pay the correct amounts retroactively to respondents and prospectively to eligible class members. The court, however, denied respondents' motion for attorney's fees. The Supreme Judicial Court of Maine, 405 A. 2d 230 (1979), concluded that respondents had no entitlement to attorney's fees under state law, but were eligible for attorney's fees pursuant to the Civil Rights Attorney's Fees Awards Act of 1976, 90 Stat. 2641, 42 U. S. C. § 1988. We granted certiorari. 444 U. S. 1042 (1980). We affirm.

II

. . . .

The question before us is whether the phrase "and laws," as used in § 1983, means what it says, or whether it should be limited to some subset of laws. Given that Congress attached no modifiers to the phrase, the plain language of the statute undoubtedly embraces respondents' claim that petitioners violated the Social Security Act.

Even were the language ambiguous, however, any doubt as to its meaning has been resolved by our several cases suggesting, explicitly or implicitly, that the § 1983 remedy broadly encompasses violations of federal statutory as well as constitutional law. . . .

. . . .

In the face of the plain language of § 1983 and our consistent treatment of that provision, petitioners nevertheless persist in suggesting that the phrase "and laws" should be read as limited to civil rights or equal protection laws. Petitioners suggest that when § 1 of the Civil Rights Act of 1871, 17 Stat. 13, which accorded jurisdiction and a remedy for deprivations of rights secured by "the Constitution of the United States," was divided by the 1874 statutory revision into a remedial section, Rev. Stat. § 1979, and jurisdictional sections, Rev. Stat. §§ 563 (12) and 629 (16), Congress intended that the same change made in § 629 (16) be made as to each of the new sections as well. Section 629 (16), the jurisdictional provision for the circuit courts and the model for the current jurisdictional provision, 28 U. S. C. § 1343 (3), applied to deprivations of rights secured by "the Constitution of the United States, or of any right secured by any law providing for equal rights." On the other hand, the remedial provision, the predecessor of § 1983, was expanded to apply to deprivations of rights secured by "the Constitution and laws," and § 563 (12), the provision granting jurisdiction to the district courts, to deprivations of rights secured by "the Constitution of the United States, or of any right secured by any law of the United States."

. . . .

... Petitioners' arguments amount to the claim that had Congress been more careful, and had it fully thought out the relationship among the various sections, it might have acted differently. That argument, however, can best be addressed to Congress, which, it is important to note, has remained quiet in the face of our many pronouncements on the scope of § 1983. Cf. *TVA v. Hill,* 437 U. S. 153 (1978).

III

[The Court then held that the Civil Rights Attorney's Fees Award Act of 1976, 42 U.S.C. § 1988, applied to statutory actions under § 1983. Since the Court had held that the statutory action was "properly brought" under § 1983, and since § 1988 made no exception for statutory § 1983 actions, the Court concluded that § 1988 "plainly" applied to this suit.—Eds.]

MR. JUSTICE POWELL, with whom THE CHIEF JUSTICE and MR. JUSTICE REHNQUIST join, dissenting.

[The dissenting opinion said in part:]

The Court's opinion does not consider the nature or scope of the litigation it has authorized. In practical effect, today's decision means that state and local governments, officers, and employees now may face liability whenever a person believes he has been injured by the administration of *any* federal-state cooperative program, whether or not that program is related to equal or civil rights.

1

Even a cursory survey of the United States Code reveals that literally hundreds of cooperative regulatory and social welfare enactments may be affected. The States now participate in the enforcement of federal laws governing migrant labor, noxious weeds, historic preservation, wildlife conservation, anadromous fisheries, scenic trails, and strip mining. Various statutes authorize federal-state cooperative agreements in most aspects of federal land management. In addition, federal grants administered by state and local governments now are available in virtually every area of public administration. Unemployment, Medicaid, school lunch subsidies, food stamps, and other welfare benefits may provide particularly inviting subjects of litigation. Federal assistance also includes a variety of subsidies for education, housing, health care, transportation, public works, and law enforcement. Those who might benefit from these grants now will be potential § 1983 plaintiffs.

No one can predict the extent to which litigation arising from today's decision will harass state and local officials; nor can one foresee the number of new filings in our already overburdened courts. But no one can doubt that these consequences will be substantial. And the Court advances no reason to believe that any Congress—from 1874 to the present day—intended this expansion of federally imposed liability on state defendants.

Comments: 1. Do you agree with the Court's conclusion in *Owen,* that the policy reasons justifying official immunity do not justify municipal immunity? Do you agree with the Court's conclusion that a municipality does not have the "discretion" to violate the federal Constitution? Does the Court also mean to hold that a municipality does not have "discretion" to violate a federal law? Why is this a reason for not recognizing municipal immunity?

2. The principal cases substantially increased potential local government liability for claims under 42 U.S.C. § 1983. A number of questions are posed concerning the effect these decisions will have on municipalities. Will municipalities begin to withdraw from litigation-generating activities such as land use regulation, law enforcement and municipal employment? Will local governments change their internal operations to minimize potential liability? To what extent will the Reagan Administration's efforts to shift control over domestic programs from federal to state and local governments (discussed in Chapter 8) affect municipal liability? For an analysis that concludes by predicting no significant withdrawal from controversial activities, little discernible change in internal operations, but extensive lobbying for greater local control over federal funds, see Goode, *The Changing Nature of Local Governmental Liability Under Section 1983*, 22 URB. L. ANN. 71 (1981). See also Peters, *Municipal Liability After Owen v. City of Independence and Maine v. Thiboutot*, 13 URB. L. 407, 443-49 (1981) (advocating a thorough review and documentation of municipal policies and administrative practices).

3. As the *Owen* case noted, questions of immunity for municipal officials have been resolved in two ways. Absolute immunity under § 1983 has been granted to judges, legislators and prosecutors, while a qualified immunity has been accorded governors and other executive officials when acting "in good faith."

In *Scheuer v. Rhodes*, 416 U.S. 232 (1974), discussed in the *Owen* case, the Supreme Court adopted a qualified immunity test for public officials acting in good faith and with reasonable grounds during the course of official conduct. In subsequent cases, the Supreme Court has amplified the "good faith and reasonable grounds" qualified immunity adopted in *Scheuer*. A two-part good faith test was adopted in *Wood v. Strickland*, 420 U.S. 308 (1975). To enjoy the qualified immunity, the official must act in accordance with constitutional rights and must have sincerely believed that he was doing right. Actions violating "clearly established" constitutional rights are not in good faith. The *Wood* test was applied to find a qualified immunity in *Procunier v. Navarette*, 434 U.S. 555 (1978) (prison official alleged to violate § 1983 by interfering with prisoner's outgoing mail). The Court has now qualified this immunity rule, and only requires proof of objective rather than subjective good faith. *Harlow v. Fitzgerald*, 102 S. Ct. 2727 (1982).

The Court adopted a new tangent in official immunity cases in *Butz v. Economou*, 438 U.S. 478 (1978). That case considered the immunity of a federal rather than a state or local official. Holding that federal officials should enjoy no greater immunity than local officials, the Court rejected an absolute immunity claim except in limited circumstances. Absolute immunity would be extended to federal officials when "essential for the conduct of the public business" and when the official was exercising a quasi-judicial, adjudicatory function. The question is whether the *Butz* holding applies to state and local government officials, and whether it modifies earlier official immunity doctrine adopted by the Supreme Court.

> Before *Economou*, most courts applied an "extent of discretion" test when considering the scope of immunity for local executive officials. The more discretion an official exercised, the broader the scope of immunity that was granted. That test was applied in a variety of ways. Courts would usually consider what branch of government employed the official and whether he had performed legislative or quasi-judicial functions. Some courts would carefully analyze the action to classify it; others would automatically attach a label to it (i.e., all building permit decisions are ministerial).

Netter, *Official Immunity Under Section 1983: The Immunity Maze*, LAND USE L. & ZONING DIG., Vol. 32, No. 2, at 3 (1980). Is it clear that immunity for discretionary actions and immunity for quasi-judicial actions are equivalent?

Some courts have wrestled with the immunity problems presented by the Supreme Court decisions. In *Centennial Land & Development Co. v. Township of Medford*, 397 A.2d 1136 (N.J.L. 1979), a developer was granted approval of his land subdivision by the local planning board, provided the local zoning board of adjustment granted a zoning variance. The zoning statute authorized the board to grant a zoning variance if hardship was shown. When the variance was denied, the developer sued under § 1983.

Applying the quasi-judicial exception adopted in *Economou,* the court engaged in a functional analysis of the procedures required by the zoning legislation. It held that "the proceedings before the respective boards here share enough of the characteristics of the judicial process to warrant an absolute privilege." *Id.* at 1141. Board members were subject to strict rules of accountability and were subject to the code of judicial conduct. Both boards were required to hold hearings on development proposals, and testimony was taken under oath and was subject to cross-examination. Board decisions must include findings of fact and conclusions of law. While noting that some cases had applied the qualified immunity rule of *Wood v. Strickland* to local officials, the court believed that "*Economou* adds a new dimension to the *Wood v. Strickland* analysis by focusing on the presence of safeguards analogous to those in the judicial system. It is this factor which dictates a different result in this case." *Id.* at 1143.

Was the court justified in applying the *Economou* doctrine to municipal officials? Is absolute official immunity necessary at the local level? In *Centennial,* the court noted that a failure to accord absolute immunity would "deter intelligent civic-minded persons from serving on municipal land use boards." *Id.* at 1140. Do you agree with this intuitive conclusion?

What about the immunity of local legislators? In *Lake Country Estates, Inc. v. Tahoe Regional Planning Agency,* 440 U.S. 391 (1979), the Court extended the absolute immunity of state legislators to the appointed members of a regional planning board created by interstate compact. The Court believed that this extension of absolute immunity was required by the "public good."

While the Supreme Court in *Lake Country Estates* reserved the question, lower federal courts have since held that local legislators also enjoy absolute immunity. *Hernandez v. City of Lafayette,* 643 F.2d 1188 (5th Cir. 1981), *cert. denied,* 455 U.S. 907 (1982). *Gorman Towers, Inc. v. Bogoslavsky,* 626 F.2d 607 (8th Cir. 1980); *Bruce v. Riddle,* 631 F.2d 272 (4th Cir. 1980). In *Gorman,* the court emphasized that alternative checks on unconstitutional conduct existed at the local level. That case was also an attack on a local zoning action. The court emphasized that an unconstitutional zoning action may be attacked directly in court, that willful violations of constitutional rights are punishable as crimes under federal law, and that local elected officials are subject to the electoral process.

How does this analysis of official immunity compare with the analysis in *Economou*? In *Centennial*? What basis is there for concluding that courts in official immunity cases under § 1983 should focus on the nature of the official action? The nature of the decision-making process? The availability of alternative checks on official conduct? Compare the discussion *supra* of the discretionary function exemption from the liability of municipal governments in tort.

4. Is a mayor who twice vetoes amendments to a zoning ordinance and, between the vetoes, refuses to sign a formal settlement terminating a state court suit after agreeing to do so absolutely immune regardless of whether the acts were taken in good faith? In *Hernandez,* discussed *supra,* the court concluded that the mayor was acting in a legislative capacity and thus entitled to absolute immunity when he vetoed the zoning amendments. *Id.* at 1193-94. The court reasoned that the mayor's veto, like the vetoes of presidents or state governors, was a part of the legislative process. "When the mayor exercises his veto power, it constitutes the policy-making decision of an individual elected official. It is as much an exercise of legislative decision-making as is the vote of a member of Congress, a state legislator, or a city councilman." *Id.* at 1194.

For an argument that some types of zoning decisions are administrative in nature, particularly those involving changes in existing zoning classifications, see *Fasano v. Board of County Commissioners,* 507 P.2d 23 (Or. 1973). In *Fasano,* the Oregon Supreme Court held that a decision to change the zoning of a thirty-two-acre tract from single-family residential to planned residential to permit construction of a mobile home park was a judicial rather than a legislative act. The court explained the distinction as follows:

> Ordinances laying down general policies without regard to a specific piece of property are usually an exercise of legislative authority, are subject to limited review, and may only be attacked upon Constitutional grounds for an arbitrary abuse of authority. On

the other hand, a determination whether the permissible use of a specific piece of property should be changed is usually an exercise of judicial authority and its propriety is subject to an altogether different test.

Id. at 26.

Is the *Fasano* rationale persuasive? If so, was *Hernandez* decided correctly? Might a "judicial" (nonlegislative) act subject the decision-making to a § 1983 suit? In *Detz v. Hoover,* 539 F. Supp. 532 (E.D. Pa. 1982), the court, in denying a motion to dismiss a civil rights complaint by a former police chief who was denied reinstatement because he had previously filed for bankruptcy, concluded that "a municipality's employment decisions, whether they regard hiring, firing or failure to reinstate, are essentially administrative in nature, notwithstanding the fact that a legislative body is the responsible decision maker." *Id.* at 534. As such, the decision-makers possessed only qualified, good-faith immunity and dismissal of a complaint alleging intentional and malicious action was not appropriate, the court concluded. Although the court refused to dismiss the complaint, it noted that the plaintiff, who alleged that he was discriminated against because he had sought protection under the Bankruptcy Act, 11 U.S.C. § 525, was not likely to prevail on the merits because "in deciding whether to hire a police officer, local governments may properly consider, as a factor, the fact that the applicant has been unable to manage his or her financial affairs." *Id.*

5. As noted in the introduction to this section, the Supreme Court in *Monell* qualified the reach of § 1983 by excluding claims of respondeat superior. However, *Monell* stated that liability may be founded on "edicts or acts" that "may fairly be said to represent official policy," 436 U.S. 658, 694, as well as on governmental custom. For a collection and analysis of the cases that have grappled with the issue of what constitutes official policy or custom, see Goode, *supra,* Comment 1. Professor Goode notes that courts have looked at the degree of authority to make a "final decision" possessed by the official, the frequency with which the act occurs, and whether or not the alleged violation constitutes more than negligence in failure to train and supervise. 22 URB. L. ANN. at 88-94. As Professor Goode notes, the courts are beginning to accept § 1983 actions based solely on negligent conduct of defendants. *Parratt v. Taylor,* 451 U.S. 527 (1981) (allegation that prison officials negligently deprived individuals of property stated a valid due process claim). *Watson v. McGee,* 527 F. Supp. 234 (S.D. Ohio 1981) (allegation that pretrial detainers at a city jail suffered smoke inhalation, lung damage and other injuries because of negligence of city officials stated a valid due process liability claim).

6. The Court in *Thiboutot* construed the Civil Rights Attorney's Fees Awards Act of 1976, 42 U.S.C. § 1988, holding that attorney's fees are available in any action brought under § 1983. Suppose suit is filed under a non-civil rights statute such as the Social Security Act alleging that state regulations deprived plaintiff of rights guaranteed by the particular statute and, as a result, that plaintiff's due process and equal protection rights were violated. After protracted negotiations, the matter is settled and a consent decree is entered favorable to the plaintiff. Should plaintiff be entitled to recover attorney's fees? In *Maher v. Gagne,* 448 U.S. 122 (1980), a companion case to *Thiboutot,* the court upheld an award of attorney's fees against the state because the constitutional claims were "sufficiently substantial" to support federal jurisdiction and plaintiff, through the consent decree, obtained sufficient relief to be deemed the "prevailing party."

Are there any limits to the award of attorney's fees under § 1983? The court in *Maher* expressly left open the question "whether a federal court could award attorney's fees against a state based (solely) on a statutory, non-civil-rights claim." 448 U.S. at 130.

Professor Goode notes the substantial impact the attorney's fees award can have on a case, and the corresponding likelihood that statutory claims will be pleaded under § 1983 routinely. In one recent case, attorneys were awarded $273,000 after a jury awarded the plaintiff $38,500. The case was complicated by a trip to the Supreme Court. 22 URB. L. ANN. at 88 n.107.

7. During the 1981 term, the Supreme Court placed some substantial limitations on the *Monell-Owen-Thiboutot* trilogy:

(a) In *City of Newport v. Fact Concerts, Inc.,* 453 U.S. 247 (1981), the Court overturned a lower court's award of punitive damages in a case involving an unsuccessful, last minute attempt by various city officials to cancel an entertainment license for a rock concert. The Court concluded that common law municipal immunity from punitive damages was well established when the Civil Rights Act of 1871 (the predecessor to § 1983) was enacted, and thus, if Congress had intended to abolish that particular immunity, it would have done so at the time. In addition, the Court reasoned that public policy considerations dictated against an award of punitive damages. Innocent taxpayers would be hurt through increased taxes or decreased public services and fully compensated plaintiffs would receive windfalls if punitive damages were awarded. *Id.* at 267. For a criticism of absolute immunity from punitive damages because of a concern that voter apathy and inadequate internal municipal controls will prevent effective control of official misconduct, see Note, *Municipal Corporations Are Immune from Exemplary Damages Under 42 U.S.C. § 1983,* 13 TEX. TECH. L. REV. 156 (1982).

The *Fact Concerts* rationale was applied to a civil rights suit claiming U.S.C. § 1981 (racial discrimination) in *Heritage Homes of Attleboro, Inc. v. Seekonk Water District,* 670 F.2d (1st Cir. 1982) (municipal water district motivated by racial considerations when it excluded a housing development was immune from punitive damages).

Should *Fact Concerts* be applied retroactively? In *Ieva v. Grabowski,* No. 81-734, slip op. (2d Cir. Dec. 30, 1981), the court of appeals reversed a punitive damages award against a city which had been found liable for allowing police officers to strike with night sticks when overcoming non-lethal resistance to arrest. At the trial, the city made no objection to the jury charge regarding punitive damages, requested no contrary instructions, and conceded the availability of punitive damages against it at trial.

(b) In *Pennhurst State School & Hospital v. Halderman,* 451 U.S. 1 (1981), reproduced *infra,* Chapter 8, the Court noted two situations in which the *Thiboutot* rule would not apply:

(1) Laws securing "rights" that also contain a comprehensive scheme of enforcement (exclusive remedies for violations); and
(2) Laws that do not secure "rights" within the meaning of § 1983.

In declining to reach the question of a private cause of action under § 1983 for claims involving the Developmentally Disabled Assistance and Bill of Rights Act, 42 U.S.C. §§ 6001-6080, the Court commented that "it is at least an open question whether an individual's interest in having a State provide the required 'assurances' (of a habilitation plan) is a 'right secured' by the laws of the United States within the meaning of § 1983," and that it is "unclear whether the express remedy contained in this Act is exclusive." *Id.* at 28. For a discussion of the comprehensiveness test, see Note, *Preclusion of Section 1983 Causes of Action by Comprehensive Statutory Remedial Schemes,* 82 COLUM. L. REV. 1183 (1982).

And in *Middlesex County Sewage Authority v. National Sea Clammers Ass'n,* 453 U.S. 1 (1981), the Court held that claims alleging damages to fishing grounds caused by discharges and ocean dumping of sewage and other wastes were not cognizable under § 1983 because the remedial devices available under the Federal Water Pollution Control Act, as amended, 33 U.S.C. § 1252 et seq., and the Marine Protection, Research, and Sanctuaries Act of 1972, 33 U.S.C. § 1401 et seq., were sufficiently comprehensive to demonstrate "not only that Congress intended to foreclose implied private actions but also that it intended to supplant any remedy that otherwise would be available under § 1983." *Id.* at 21.

(c) Claims involving questions of state and local taxation constitute one major class of potential suits under 42 U.S.C. § 1983. The administration of state property tax systems, discussed in Chapter 5, has produced innumerable disputes in recent years. To what extent should home owners whose property taxes are higher than those in neighboring communities because of deficiencies in local assessment procedures be able to obtain relief under § 1983? Assuming the facts as stated above to be true, the home owners presumably can establish a § 1983 claim based on denial of equal protection and due process of law by unequal taxation of real property. However, in *Fair Assessment in Real Estate Ass'n v. McNary,* 454 U.S. 100 (1981), the Supreme Court held that "tax payers are barred by the principle of comity from asserting § 1983 actions against the validity of state tax systems in federal courts." The Court based its decision on the conclusion that requiring state officers to respond in federal courts every time a taxpayer alleges a § 1983 claim would be contrary to "the scrupulous regard for the rightful independence of state governments which should at all times actuate the federal courts." *Id.* at 111, *quoting Matthews v. Rodgers,* 284 U.S., at 525 (1932). Although all nine justices concurred in the result, only five agreed with the application of the principle of comity to the case. Justices Brennan, Marshall, Stevens and O'Connor would have limited the case to a dismissal for failure to exhaust available administrative remedies because state court relief requires such exhaustion, viewing the majority opinion as an "unprecedented step" to "renounce jurisdiction over an entire class of damages actions brought pursuant to 42 U.S.C. §1983." *Id.* at 119.

In the previous term, the Court denied access to federal courts to Illinois taxpayers alleging a similar disparity but seeking an injunction under the Tax Injunction Act, 28 U.S.C. § 1341 because a "plain, speedy and efficient remedy may be had in the courts of [the] state." *Rosewell v. LaSalle National Bank,* 450 U.S. 503, *quoting* 28 U.S.C. § 1341.

Is the majority opinion concluding that the collection of taxes is an "integral operation" of a "traditional government function" as in *National League of Cities v. Usery,* 426 U.S. 833 (1976), Chapter 8, *infra*? Is the collection of taxes entitled to greater protection from federal court scrutiny than land use regulation or law enforcement? Should it be? *Cf. Hernandez v. City of Lafayette, supra.*

8. *Monell* and *Owen* merely held that municipalities do not have immunity under § 1983. They did not hold, of course, that municipalities are absolutely liable under § 1983 for a federal constitutional or statutory violation. Note, for example, that municipalities cannot be held liable on a simple respondeat superior theory. The following comment indicates possible defenses available to municipalities faced with potential liability in § 1983 actions:

> One level of response to *Owen* will be in the realm of substantive law. Section 1983 creates only a remedy for violation of constitutional guarantees, not new rights. Cities will seek "cover" in the element of reasonableness already inherent in those guarantees and they will seek to expand that element. There is a balancing or good-faith component in fourth amendment and eighth amendment concepts, as well as in the due process guarantees of the fifth and fourteenth amendments.
>
> . . . .
>
> Municipalities will also emphasize that there is no vicarious liability under section 1983. One person is responsible for the acts of others only if directly involved. A city, in the analysis of *Owen* and *Monell,* is only another "person." The Court emphasized in *Monell* that it is not the right of control but the fact of control that makes a city liable. In *Owen* the city had direct involvement and knowledge because it was the council's acts which created the need for a name-clearing hearing. But if the city manager had simply fired Owen, direct involvement and knowledge on the part of the council would be missing. Arguably, the city would not then be liable.
>
> *Monell* and *Owen* thus raise the question of which officials act for a city and as to what. *Monell* stated that municipal liability attaches under section 1983 only to official acts pursuant to a "policy statement, ordinance, regulations, or decision officially adopted and promulgated by that body's officers." Either acts *or* policy would be sufficient for liability. But this only refines the issue into separate questions of who may adopt policy and who may implement it. In *Owen,* there was action by the council tantamount to policy. In *Monell,* there was policy and there were acts pursuant to it. Cities may be encouraged by the poles of action and policy to steer between the two, avoiding liability by leaving action to unguided lower officials.
>
> Cities will also argue, after *Monell* and *Owen,* that the offending acts of subordinate officials were departures from policy. This raises the possibility of liability for departures so frequent or substantial as to suggest that the policy is honored only in the breach or is incapable of implementation. It may be necessary to show that the responsible city officials have *actual* knowledge of these breaches or an obligation to acquire such knowledge. The latter, in turn, raises questions as to what misconduct, how frequent and serious, and by whom, will be sufficient to create a "custom" leading to liability.

Misconduct amounting to a custom equivalent to policy within the liability framework of *Monell* implies a duty of supervision. Ordinarily, failure to supervise may be excused by ignorance or good faith, and *that,* in turn, resurrects the ghost of the argument which the city lost in *Owen.* At best, it would be resurrected only because the Court in *Owen* articulated supervision as an objection precluding a good-faith defense and it would operate only in the context where no policy existed, unlike *Owen* and *Monell.*

LaFrance, *Monell: Once More, with Feeling,* 14 CLEARINGHOUSE REV. 330, 331, 332 (1980). *See also* Levinson, *Suing Political Subdivisions in Federal Court: From Edelman to Owen,* 11 U. TOL. L. REV. 829 (1980).

9. There is an intricate relationship between the eleventh amendment and § 1983. Does the eleventh amendment protect local governments? In *Mt. Healthy City Board of Education v. Doyle,* 429 U.S. 274 (1977), the Supreme Court held that a school board was not immune from suit under the eleventh amendment because it was considered under Ohio law to be a municipal corporation or other political subdivision and not an arm of the state. Compare the Missouri Supreme Court's decision that the St. Louis Board of Police Commissioners is a state agency. *State ex rel. Sayad v. Zych,* discussed in Chapter 5.

Does *Monell* permit a suit against the state for civil rights violations? Is the state a person? See *State v. Hall,* 411 N.E.2d 366 (Ind. App. 1980), holding that states cannot be sued for monetary damages under § 1983, and citing *Meyer v. State of New Jersey,* 462 F.2d 1252 (3d Cir. 1972); *Edelman v. Jordan;* and *Monell.* For an argument that the state is a "person" for purposes of section 1983, see Note, *Amenability of States to Section 1983 Suits: Reexamining Quern v. Jordan (440 U.S. 332, 1979),* 62 B.U.L. REV. 731 (1982). Can Congress require waiver of eleventh amendment immunity? In *Sharp v. Commonwealth,* 372 A.2d 59 (Pa. Commw. 1977), the court assumed without deciding that "Congress could constitutionally bar the states and their officers from asserting immunity in suits in state courts arising out of activities within the sphere of legitimate federal regulation." *Id.* at 61. The court held that state officials did not waive their immunities by including promises in highway contracts, as a precondition to the receipt of federal aid, to comply with federal laws governing safety and health. Does *Maine v. Thiboutot* effectively overrule *Edelman v. Jordan?* Assuming the plaintiffs in *Edelman* sued for violations of the Social Security Act, couldn't that suit prevail under § 1983?

10. Is exhaustion of state administrative remedies a prerequisite to a § 1983 action? In *Patsy v. Board of Regents,* 102 S. Ct. 2557 (1982), the Supreme Court found that it was not. Petitioner filed suit under § 1983 claiming that her employer had denied her employment opportunities because of her sex and race. The district court dismissed the complaint because petitioner had not exhausted the available administrative remedies. The court of appeals remanded the case, finding that exhaustion was not required if certain conditions were met on appeal. The Supreme Court concluded that the legislative history of § 1983 supported the finding that exhaustion was not required. The Court also discussed the legislative history of 42 U.S.C. § 1997. Section 1997e carves out an exception to the general nonexhaustion rule for certain adult prisoner claims. The court noted that Congress had enacted this exception because it was well aware that exhaustion was not a general requirement under § 1983.

11. Of course, it must be remembered that *Monell, Owen* and *Thiboutot* are based on a federal statute. What Congress gives, Congress can take away. Shortly after the *Owen* and *Thiboutot* decisions were handed down, amendments were introduced to limit the scope of municipal liability under § 1983. For a study of section 1983 cases filed over a two-year period in the Central District of California which includes Los Angeles, see Eisenberg, *Section 1983: Doctrinal Foundations and an Empirical Study,* 67 CORNELL L. REV. 482 (1982). Professor Eisenberg concluded that serious confusion exists concerning section 1983 doctrine, but that the doctrinal problems do not warrant restriction of section 1983. The study found that section 1983 cases were not overwhelming the federal courts; trivial claims were not dominating district court dockets, and courts were not overseeing minute details of public institutions such as prisons.

3. FEDERAL ANTITRUST STATUTES

For years, state and local governments have operated under a judicially created "state action exemption" from federal antitrust legislation. *Parker v. Brown,* 317 U.S. 341 (1943). Blanket immunity from sanctions for anticompetitive activities was assumed by many local officials until the Supreme Court, in a 4-1-4 decision featuring five separate opinions, held that there were no "sufficiently weighty" policy considerations justifying an automatic exemption for all municipal activities independent of the exemption granted state action. *City of Lafayette v. Louisiana Power & Light Co.,* 435 U.S. 389 (1978). The divided opinions in that case left the status of local antitrust liability unclear. The Court provided clearer guidance in a subsequent decision in which a plaintiff sought to apply antitrust liability to a home rule municipality:

COMMUNITY COMMUNICATIONS CO. v. CITY OF BOULDER

Supreme Court of the United States
455 U.S. 40 (1982)

JUSTICE BRENNAN delivered the opinion of the Court.

The question presented in this case, in which the District Court for the District of Colorado granted preliminary injunctive relief, is whether a "home rule" municipality, granted by the state constitution extensive powers of self-government in local and municipal matters, enjoys the "state action" exemption from Sherman Act liability announced in *Parker v. Brown,* 317 U. S. 341 (1943).

I

Respondent city of Boulder is organized as a "home rule" municipality under the Constitution of the State of Colorado.[1] The city is thus entitled to exercise "the full right of self-government in both local and municipal matters," and with respect to such matters the City Charter and ordinances supersede the laws of the State. Under that Charter, all municipal legislative powers are exercised by an elected City Council. In 1964 the City Council enacted an ordinance granting to Colorado Televents, Inc., a 20-year, revocable, nonexclusive permit to conduct a cable television business within the city limits. This permit was assigned to petitioner in 1966, and since that time petitioner has provided cable television service to the University Hill area of Boulder, an area where some 20% of the city's population lives, and where, for geographical reasons, broadcast television signals cannot be received.

---

[1] The Colorado Home Rule Amendment, Colo. Const., Art. XX, § 6, provides in pertinent part:

The people of each city or town of this state, having a population of two thousand inhabitants . . ., are hereby vested with, and they shall always have, power to make, amend, add to or replace the charter of said city or town, which shall be its organic law and extend to all its local and municipal matters.

Such charter and the ordinances made pursuant thereto in such matters shall supersede within the territorial limits and other jurisdiction of said city or town any law of the state in conflict therewith.

. . . .

It is the intention of this article to grant and confirm to the people of all municipalities coming within its provisions the full right of self-government in both local and municipal matters. . . .

The statutes of the state of Colorado, so far as applicable, shall continue to apply to such cities and towns, except insofar as superseded by the charters of such cities and towns or by ordinance passed pursuant to such charters.

From 1966 until February 1980, due to the limited service that could be provided with the technology then available, petitioner's service consisted essentially of retransmissions of programming broadcast from Denver and Cheyenne, Wyo. Petitioner's market was therefore confined to the University Hill area. However, markedly improved technology became available in the late 1970's, enabling petitioner to offer many more channels of entertainment than could be provided by local broadcast television. Thus presented with an opportunity to expand its business into other areas of the city, petitioner in May 1979 informed the City Council that it planned such an expansion. But the new technology offered opportunities to potential competitors, as well, and in July 1979 one of them, the newly formed Boulder Communications Co. (BCC), also wrote to the City Council, expressing its interest in obtaining a permit to provide competing cable television service throughout the city.

The City Council's response, after reviewing its cable television policy, was the enactment of an "emergency" ordinance prohibiting petitioner from expanding its business into other areas of the city for a period of three months. The City Council announced that during this moratorium it planned to draft a model cable television ordinance and to invite new businesses to enter the Boulder market under its terms, but that the moratorium was necessary because petitioner's continued expansion during the drafting of the model ordinance would discourage potential competitors from entering the market.

Petitioner filed this suit in the United States District Court for the District of Colorado, and sought, *inter alia*, a preliminary injunction to prevent the city from restricting petitioner's proposed business expansion, alleging that such a restriction would violate § 1 of the Sherman Act. The city responded that its moratorium ordinance could not be violative of the antitrust laws, either because that ordinance constituted an exercise of the city's police powers, or because Boulder enjoyed antitrust immunity under the *Parker* doctrine. The District Court considered the city's status as a home rule municipality, but determined that that status gave autonomy to the city only in matters of local concern, and that the operations of cable television embrace "wider concerns, including interstate commerce ... [and] the First Amendment rights of communicators." ... Then, assuming, *arguendo,* that the ordinance was within the city's authority as a home rule municipality, the District Court considered *City of Lafayette v. Louisiana Power & Light Co.,* 435 U. S. 389 (1978), and concluded that the *Parker* exemption was "wholly inapplicable," and that the city was therefore subject to antitrust liability. ... Petitioner's motion for a preliminary injunction was accordingly granted.

On appeal, a divided panel of the United States Court of Appeals for the Tenth Circuit reversed. 630 F. 2d 704 (1980). The majority, after examining Colorado law, rejected the District Court's conclusion that regulation of the cable television business was beyond the home rule authority of the city. ... The majority then addressed the question of the city's claimed *Parker* exemption. It distinguished the present case from *City of Lafayette* on the ground that, in contrast to the municipally operated revenue-producing utility companies at issue there, "no proprietary interest of the City is here involved." ... After noting that the city's regulation "was the only control or active supervision exercised by state or local government, and ... represented the only expression of policy as to the subject matter," ... the majority held that the city's actions therefore satisfied the criteria for a *Parker* exemption .... We granted certiorari, 450 U. S. 1039 (1981). We reverse.

II

A

Parker v. Brown, 317 U. S. 341 (1943), addressed the question whether the federal antitrust laws prohibited a State, in the exercise of its sovereign powers, from imposing certain anticompetitive restraints. These took the form of a "marketing program" adopted by the State of California for the 1940 raisin crop; that program prevented appellee from freely marketing his crop in interstate commerce. *Parker* noted that California's program "derived its authority ... from the legislative command of the state," *id.*, at 350, and went on to hold that the program was therefore exempt, by virtue of the Sherman Act's own limitations, from antitrust attack:

> We find nothing in the language of the Sherman Act or in its history which suggests that its purpose was to restrain a state or its officers or agents from activities directed by its legislature. In a dual system of government in which, under the Constitution, the states are sovereign, save only as Congress may constitutionally subtract from their authority, an unexpressed purpose to nullify a state's control over its officers and agents is not lightly to be attributed to Congress." *Id.*, at 350-351.

The availability of this exemption to a State's municipalities was the question presented in *City of Lafayette, supra.* In that case, petitioners were Louisiana cities empowered to own and operate electric utility systems both within and beyond their municipal limits. Respondent brought suit against petitioners under the Sherman Act, alleging that they had committed various antitrust offenses in the conduct of their utility systems, to the injury of respondent. Petitioners invoked the *Parker* doctrine as entitling them to dismissal of the suit. The District Court accepted this argument and dismissed. But the Court of Appeals for the Fifth Circuit reversed, holding that a "subordinate state governmental body is not *ipso facto* exempt from the operation of the antitrust laws," *City of Lafayette v. Louisiana Power & Light Co.,* 532 F. 2d 431, 434 (1976) (footnote omitted), and directing the District Court on remand to examine "whether the state legislature contemplated a certain type of anticompetitive restraint," *ibid.*

This Court affirmed. In doing so, a majority rejected at the outset petitioners' claim that, quite apart from *Parker,* "Congress never intended to subject local governments to the antitrust laws." 435 U. S., at 394. A plurality opinion for four Justices then addressed petitioners' argument that *Parker,* properly construed, extended to "all governmental entities, whether state agencies or subdivisions of a State, ... simply by reason of their status as such." 435 U. S., at 408. The plurality opinion rejected this argument, after a discussion of *Parker, Goldfarb v. Virginia State Bar,* 421 U. S. 773 (1975), and *Bates v. State Bar of Arizona,* 433 U. S. 350 (1977). These precedents were construed as holding that the *Parker* exemption reflects the federalism principle that we are a Nation of *States,* a principle that makes no accommodation for sovereign subdivisions of States. The plurality opinion said:

> Cities are not themselves sovereign; they do not receive all the federal deference of the States that create them. *Parker*'s limitation of the exemption to "official action directed by a state," is consistent with the fact that the States' subdivisions generally have not been treated as equivalents of the States themselves. In light of the serious economic dislocation which could result if cities were free to place their own parochial interests above the Nation's economic goals reflected in the antitrust laws, we are especially unwilling to presume that

Congress intended to exclude anticompetitive municipal action from their reach. 435 U.S., at 412-413 (footnote and citations omitted).

The opinion emphasized, however, that the State as sovereign might sanction anticompetitive municipal activities and thereby immunize municipalities from antitrust liability. Under the plurality's standard, the *Parker* doctrine would shield from antitrust liability municipal conduct engaged in "pursuant to state policy to displace competition with regulation or monopoly public services." 435 U. S., at 413. This was simply a recognition that a State may frequently choose to effect its policies through the instrumentality of its cities and towns. It was stressed, however, that the "state policy" relied upon would have to be "clearly articulated and affirmatively expressed." *Id.*, at 410. This standard has since been adopted by a majority of the Court. *New Motor Vehicle Board of California v. Orrin W. Fox Co.*, 439 U. S. 96, 109 (1978); *California Retail Liquor Dealers Assn. v. Midcal Aluminum, Inc.*, 445 U. S. 97, 105 (1980).[14]

B

Our precedents thus reveal that Boulder's moratorium ordinance cannot be exempt from antitrust scrutiny unless it constitutes the action of the State of Colorado itself in its sovereign capacity, see *Parker,* or unless it constitutes municipal action in furtherance or implementation of clearly articulated and affirmatively expressed state policy, see *City of Lafayette, Orrin W. Fox Co.*, and *Midcal.* Boulder argues that these criteria are met by the direct delegation of powers to municipalities through the Home Rule Amendment to the Colorado Constitution. It contends that this delegation satisfies both the *Parker* and the *City of Lafayette* standards. We take up these arguments in turn.

(1)

Respondent city's *Parker* argument emphasizes that through the Home Rule Amendment the people of the State of Colorado have vested in the city of Boulder " '*every power* theretofore possessed by the legislature ... in local and municipal affairs.' " The power thus possessed by Boulder's City Council assertedly embraces the regulation of cable television, which is claimed to pose essentially local problems.[16] Thus, it is suggested, the city's cable television moratorium ordinance is an "act of government" performed by the city *acting as the State* in local matters, which meets the "state action" criterion of *Parker*.

---

[14] In *Midcal* we held that a California resale price maintenance system, affecting all wine producers and wholesalers within the State, was not entitled to exemption from the antitrust laws. In so holding, we explicitly adopted the principle, expressed in the plurality opinion in *City of Lafayette,* that anticompetitive restraints engaged in by state municipalities or subdivisions must be "clearly articulated and affirmatively expressed as state policy" in order to gain an antitrust exemption. *Midcal,* 445 U. S., at 105. The price maintenance system at issue in *Midcal* was denied such an exemption because it failed to satisfy the "active state supervision" criterion described in City of Lafayette, 435 U. S., at 410, as underlying our decision in Bates v. State Bar of Arizona, 433 U. S. 350 (1977). Because we conclude in the present case that Boulder's moratorium ordinance does not satisfy the "clear articulation and affirmative expression" criterion, we do not reach the question whether that ordinance must or could satisfy the "active state supervision" test focused upon in *Midcal.*

[16] ... For the purposes of this decision we will assume, without deciding, that respondent city's enactment of the moratorium ordinance under challenge here did fall within the scope of the power delegated to the city by virtue of the Colorado Home Rule Amendment.

We reject this argument: it both misstates the letter of the law and misunderstands its spirit. The *Parker* state-action exemption reflects Congress' intention to embody in the Sherman Act the federalism principle that the States possess a significant measure of sovereignty under our Constitution. But this principle contains its own limitation: Ours is a *"dual* system of government," *Parker,* 317 U. S., at 351 (emphasis added), which has no place for sovereign cities. As this Court stated long ago, all sovereign authority "within the geographical limits of the United States" resides either with

> the Government of the United States, or [with] the States of the Union. *There exist within the broad domain of sovereignty but these two.* There may be cities, counties, and other organized bodies with limited legislative functions, but they are all derived from, or exist in, subordination to one or the other of these. *United States v. Kagama,* 118 U. S. 375, 379 (1886) (emphasis added).

The dissent in the Court of Appeals correctly discerned this limitation upon the federalism principle: "We are a nation not of 'city-states' but of States." 630 F. 2d, at 717. *Parker* itself took this view. When *Parker* examined Congress' intentions in enacting the antitrust laws, the opinion noted: "[N]othing in the language of the Sherman Act or in its history . . . suggests that its purpose was to restrain a state or its officers or agents from activities *directed by its legislature.* . . . [And] an unexpressed purpose to nullify a *state's control over its officers and agents* is not lightly to be attributed to Congress." 317 U. S., at 350-351 (emphasis added). Thus *Parker* recognized Congress' intention to limit the state-action exemption based upon the federalism principle of limited state sovereignty. *City of Lafayette, Orrin W. Fox Co.,* and *Midcal* reaffirmed both the vitality and the intrinsic limits of the *Parker* state-action doctrine. It was expressly recognized by the plurality opinion in *City of Lafayette* that municipalities "are not themselves sovereign," 435 U. S., at 412, and that accordingly they could partake of the *Parker* exemption only to the extent that they acted pursuant to a clearly articulated and affirmatively expressed state policy, 435 U. S., at 413. The Court adopted this view in *Orrin W. Fox Co.,* 439 U. S., at 109, and *Midcal,* 445 U. S., at 105. We turn then to Boulder's contention that its actions were undertaken pursuant to a clearly articulated and affirmatively expressed state policy.

(2)

Boulder first argues that the requirement of "clear articulation and affirmative expression" is fulfilled by the Colorado Home Rule Amendment's "guarantee of local autonomy." It contends, quoting from *City of Lafayette,* 435 U. S., at 394, 415, that by this means Colorado has "comprehended within the powers granted" to Boulder the power to enact the challenged ordinance, and that Colorado has thereby "contemplated" Boulder's enactment of an anticompetitive regulatory program. Further, Boulder contends that it may be inferred, "from the authority given" to Boulder "to operate in a particular area"—here, the asserted home rule authority to regulate cable television—"that the *legislature* contemplated the kind of action complained of." (Emphasis supplied.) Boulder therefore concludes that the "adequate state mandate" required by *City of Lafayette, supra,* at 415, is present here.

But plainly the requirement of "clear articulation and affirmative expression" is not satisfied when the State's position is one of mere *neutrality* respecting the municipal actions challenged as anticompetitive. A State that allows its municipalities to do as they please can hardly be said to have "contemplated" the specific anticompetitive actions for which municipal liability is sought. Nor can those actions be truely described as "comprehended within the powers *granted*," since the term, "granted," necessarily implies an affirmative addressing of the subject by the State. The State did not do so here: The relationship of the State of Colorado to Boulder's moratorium ordinance is one of precise neutrality. As the majority in the Court of Appeals below acknowledged: "[W]e are here concerned with City action in the absence of any regulation whatever by the State of Colorado. Under these circumstances there is no interaction of state and local regulation. We have only the action or exercise of authority by the City." 630 F.2d, at 707. Indeed, Boulder argues that as to local matters regulated by a home rule city, the Colorado General Assembly is without power to act. Cf. *City of Lafayette, supra,* at 414, and n. 44. Thus in Boulder's view, it can pursue its course of regulating cable television competition, while another home rule city can choose to prescribe monopoly service, while still another can elect free-market competition: and all of these policies are equally "contemplated," and "comprehended within the powers granted." Acceptance of such a proposition—that the general grant of power to enact ordinances necessarily implies state authorization to enact specific anticompetitive ordinances—would wholly eviscerate the concepts of "clear articulation and affirmative expression" that our precedents require.

III

Respondents argue that denial of the *Parker* exemption in the present case will have serious adverse consequences for cities, and will unduly burden the federal courts. But this argument is simply an attack upon the wisdom of the long-standing congressional commitment to the policy of free markets and open competition embodied in the antitrust laws. Those laws, like other federal laws imposing civil or criminal sanctions upon "persons," of course apply to municipalities as well as to other corporate entities.[20] Moreover, judicial enforcement of Congress' will regarding the state-action exemption renders a State "no less able to allocate governmental power between itself and its political subdivisions. It means only that when the State itself has not directed or authorized an anticompetitive practice, the State's subdivisions in exercising their delegated power must obey the antitrust laws." *City of Lafayette,* 435 U. S., at 416. As was observed in that case:

> Today's decision does not threaten the legitimate exercise of governmental power, nor does it preclude municipal government from providing services on a monopoly basis. *Parker* and its progeny make clear that a State properly may ... direct or authorize its instrumentalities to act in a way which, if it did not

---

[20] ....

We hold today only that the Parker v. Brown exemption was no bar to the District Court's grant of injunctive relief. This case's preliminary posture makes it unnecessary for us to consider other issues regarding the applicability of the antitrust laws in the context of suits by private litigants against government defendants. As we said in *City of Lafayette,* "[i]t may be that certain activities which might appear anticompetitive when engaged in by private parties, take on a different complexion when adopted by a local government." 435 U. S., at 417, n. 48. Compare, *e. g.,* National Society of Professional Engineers v. United States, 435 U. S. 679, 687-692 (1978) (considering the validity of anticompetitive restraint imposed by private agreement), with Exxon Corp. v. Governor of Maryland, 437 U. S. 117, 133 (1978) (holding that anticompetitive effect is an insufficient basis for invalidating a state law). Moreover, as in *City of Lafayette, supra,* at 401-402, we do not confront the issue of remedies appropriate against municipal officials.

reflect state policy, would be inconsistent with the antitrust laws....
[A]ssuming that the municipality is authorized to provide a service on a monopoly basis, these limitations on municipal action will not hobble the execution of legitimate governmental programs. *Id.*, at 416-417 (footnote omitted).

The judgment of the Court of Appeals is reversed, and the action is remanded for further proceedings consistent with this opinion.

It is so ordered.

Justice White took no part in the consideration or decision of this case.

Justice Stevens, concurring. [Omitted.]

Justice Rehnquist, with whom The Chief Justice and Justice O'Connor join, dissenting.

[The dissent began by noting that the Court's decision would "impede, if not paralyze, local governments' efforts to enact ordinances and regulations aimed at protecting public health, safety, and welfare, for fear of subjecting the local government to liability under the Sherman Act." The dissent believed that the Court had improperly analyzed the issues in the case as a question of exemption rather than preemption. The dissent noted that preemption involved the supremacy clause and "implicates our basic notions of federalism." The Court had been reluctant to find preemption because it "treads on the very sensitive areas of federal-state relations." A preemption analysis "reconciles" the federal and state statutory schemes, and the dissent believed it was applicable under Court precedents to the antitrust liability problem at the local level.

[The dissent also considered the difficulties the Court would face in applying its holding that "a municipality may be liable under the Sherman Act for enacting anticompetitive legislation, unless it can show that it is acting simply as the 'instrumentality' of the State." The federal courts apply either a "per se" rule or a Rule of Reason in determining whether private conduct violates the antitrust act. The dissent was concerned "whether the '*per se*' rules of illegality apply to municipal defendants in the same manner as they are applied to private defendants." The dissent continued:]

Most troubling, however, will be questions regarding the factors which may be examined by the Court pursuant to the Rule of Reason. In *National Society of Professional Engineers v. United States*, 435 U. S. 679, 695 (1978), we held that an anticompetitive restraint could not be defended on the basis of a private party's conclusion that competition posed a potential threat to public safety and the ethics of a particular profession. "[T]he Rule of Reason does not support a defense based on the assumption that competition itself is unreasonable." *Id.*, at 696. *Professional Engineers* holds that the decision to replace competition with regulation is not within the competence of private entities. Instead, private entities may defend restraints only on the basis that the restraint is not unreasonable in its effect on competition or because its procompetitive effects outweigh its anticompetitive effects....

Applying *Professional Engineers* to municipalities would mean that an ordinance could not be defended on the basis that its benefits to the community, in terms of traditional health, safety, and public welfare concerns, outweigh its anticompetitive effects. A local government would be disabled from displacing competition with regulation. Thus, a municipality would violate the Sherman Act by enacting restrictive zoning ordinances, by requiring business and occupational licenses, and by granting exclusive franchises to utility services, even if the city determined that it would be in the best interests of its inhabitants to displace competition with regulation. Competition simply does not and cannot further the interests that lie behind most social welfare legislation. Although state or local enactments are not invalidated by the Sherman Act merely because they may have anticompetitive effects, ... this Court has not hesitated to invalidate such statutes on the basis that such a program would violate the antitrust laws if engaged in by private parties. ... Unless the municipality could point to an affirmatively expressed state policy to displace competition in the given area sought to be regulated, the municipality would be held to violate the Sherman Act and the regulatory scheme would be rendered invalid. Surely, the Court does not seek to require a municipality to justify every ordinance it enacts in terms of its procompetitive effects. If municipalities are permitted only to enact ordinances that are consistent with the procompetitive policies of the Sherman Act, a municipality's power to regulate the economy would be all but destroyed. ... This country's municipalities will be unable to experiment with innovative social programs. ...

On the other hand, rejecting the rationale of *Professional Engineers* to accommodate the municipal defendant opens up a different sort of Pandora's Box. If the Rule of Reason were "modified" to permit a municipality to defend its regulation on the basis that its benefits to the community outweigh its anticompetitive effects, the courts will be called upon to review social legislation in a manner reminiscent of the *Lochner* era. Once again, the federal courts will be called upon to engage in the same wide-ranging, essentially standardless inquiry into the reasonableness of local regulation that this Court has properly rejected. Instead of "liberty of contract" and "substantive due process," the procompetitive principles of the Sherman Act will be the governing standard by which the reasonableness of all local regulation will be determined. Neither the Due Process Clause nor the Sherman Act authorizes federal courts to invalidate local regulation of the economy simply upon opining that the municipality has acted unwisely. The Sherman Act should not be deemed to authorize federal courts to "substitute their social and economic beliefs for the judgment of legislative bodies, who are elected to pass laws." *Ferguson v. Skrupa,* 372 U. S. 726, 730 (1963). The federal courts have not been appointed by the Sherman Act to sit as a "superlegislature to weigh the wisdom of legislation." *Lincoln Federal Labor Union v. Northwestern Iron & Metal Co.,* 335 U. S. 525, 535 (1949).

Before this Court leaps into the abyss and holds that municipalities may *violate* the Sherman Act by enacting economic and social legislation, it ought to think about the consequences of such a decision in terms of its effect both upon the very antitrust principles the Court desires to apply to local governments and on the role of the federal courts in examining the validity of local regulation of the economy.

Comments: 1. Reread the criticism of the *Boulder* decision reproduced at the beginning of this chapter. Do you agree with it? Has the Supreme Court really told us how a state may clearly and affirmatively adopt a policy to displace competition? Must it be express? If implied, what is the basis for the implication? Review the state enabling legislation considered in Chapter 3. Does any of this legislation contain the "policy" required by the *Boulder* decision?

2. Do you agree with the dissent, that the application of the antitrust Rule of Reason may mean a return to an assertive application of substantive due process applied through the Sherman Act? The problem can arise in the exercise of local zoning and land use powers.

As exercised at the local level, the zoning power rests on statutory or home rule grounds. The statutory basis for the zoning power is broad-based, however: the Standard Zoning Enabling Act, the model act first proposed for state adoption in the 1920s and still in force in practically all the states, provides a virtually unfettered grant of the zoning power:

> For any or all of such purposes [e.g., the "general welfare" of the community] the local legislative body may divide the municipality into [zoning] districts of such number, shape and area as may be deemed best suited to carry out the purposes of this article; and within such districts it may regulate and restrict the . . . use of buildings, structures, or land.

U.S. Dep't of Commerce, A Standard Zoning Enabling Act § 2 (rev. ed. 1926).

Suppose, for example, a city refused to rezone a tract of land to permit commercial activity in a developing part of the city because of a desire to promote the downtown business district? In *Mason City Center Ass'n v. City of Mason City*, 468 F. Supp. 737 (N.D. Iowa 1979), the city entered into an agreement with downtown developers under which it agreed to deny zoning to any competing regional shopping center. The court refused to grant a motion to dismiss and denied the city an antitrust exemption.

The city claimed that the state zoning legislation provided an exemption from the federal antitrust laws. The legislation was based on the Standard Zoning Act. The court disagreed, noting that it was "somewhat fatuous to contend" that the zoning statute "inevitably reflect[ed] a state's clear and affirmative intent to displace competition." It noted that the zoning statute did not require municipalities to zone and did not require municipalities which did zone to make anticompetitive zoning decisions. In a subsequent trial of this case, the jury found against the plaintiff and the court of appeals affirmed. 671 F.2d 1146 (8th Cir. 1982). It did not discuss the lower court holding on the facts. How would you amend the zoning enabling act to provide a *Parker* exemption that would pass the *Boulder* test?

3. In *Boulder,* the Court left open the question whether active state supervision was necessary to exempt local governments from the Sherman Act, as required in *Midcal*. In *Mason City* the district court noted, in denying an exemption, that the zoning statute did not provide for a state agency to supervise local zoning. *Compare Stauffer v. Town of Grand Lake,* 1981-1 Trad. Cases (CCH) ¶ 64,029 (D. Colo. 1981). The court held that the state zoning act, which was based on the model act, *supra*, provided active state supervision. It noted that the zoning act required public notice of all zoning amendments, and that all zoning decisions were appealable to the state courts. Do you agree? *See generally* Morgan, *Antitrust and State Legislation: Standards of Immunity after Midcal,* 35 Ark. L. Rev. 453 (1982).

4. Cases like *Lafayette* and *Boulder* deal only with the problem of municipal exemption. They do not consider the question of municipal liability. Although the Sherman Act does not contain any exceptions, footnote 48 in the *Lafayette* plurality opinion suggested that there may be reasons for modifying the antitrust rules when local government activities are under scrutiny. The court was able to find potential antitrust liability in *Mason City* because there was an agreement between the city and the downtown developers. What if there is no overt agreement?

Assume the following facts: A developer obtains a rezoning to build a regional shopping center, but progress is slow because of financial difficulties. Eventually another developer appears with a proposal to build another regional shopping center at another site. The city officials are interested, because the new shopping center promises to have a major department store as a tenant. The city manager tells the second developer to go ahead and not to worry about a rezoning. The second developer then expresses concern about progress by the first developer. The city can support only one shopping center, and the developer's attorney calls the city's attorney suggesting that the first developer be "stopped." Soon thereafter the city revokes the first developer's zoning, causing it to lose a major tenant who was under consideration. The first developer fails. The city then rezones for the second developer, who successfully builds his shopping center. Is there a conspiracy?

The court thought so in a similar case, *Westborough Mall, Inc. v. City of Cape Girardeau,* 693 F.2d 733 (8th Cir. 1982), and reversed a summary judgment that had been granted to the city. The court of appeals noted that conspiracy in antitrust cases can be proved through circumstantial evidence. How much evidence is necessary? What if the facts were less outrageous than they were in the *Westborough* case?

5. Note the list of "typical local governmental actions" that municipalities in Illinois were advised might raise antitrust issues:

1. any regulatory activity, including occupational licensing and regulation;
2. the operation of sports arenas or convention centers;
3. the provision of water, electric and other utility services;
4. garbage collection;
5. transit systems, including taxis;
6. public health services;
7. airports;
8. parking lots;
9. procurement practices generally with an emphasis on public competitive bidding wherever possible;
10. industrial and commercial financing activities;
11. and last, but certainly not least, zoning.

Antitrust Do's and Don'ts, ILL. MUN. REV. 17, 19 (July 1982).

Antitrust claims have been litigated in a number of these areas, but most of the cases are pre-*Boulder.* Municipal airports present an especially interesting antitrust problem. Airports are a "natural monopoly" created under state statutory authorization, and control a number of important airport concessions including access to the airport by the airlines and ground concessions. Airport access and the number of ground concessions will depend on demand. The airport authority may also decide to limit the number of ground concessions, or to have only one. Antitrust problems may then arise. *See generally* Hart, *Antitrust Immunity for Airport Operators,* 12 TRANSP. L.J. 1 (1981).

In *Pueblo Aircraft Services, Inc. v. City of Pueblo,* 679 F.2d 805 (10th Cir. 1982), *cert. denied,* — S. Ct. — (1983), the city decided to have only one ground base operator after leases to three operators expired. The operators performed a number of aircraft refueling, maintenance and service functions. The lease was put out to competitive bidding and the unsuccessful bidder, who had previously held a ground base operator lease, sued under the federal antitrust law.

Pueblo was a home rule city, but the court recognized that it could not find antitrust immunity for this reason after *Boulder.* Instead, it looked to the statutory enabling authority for airports in Colorado and held that the statute authorized the operation of the airport as a governmental function. The city was exempt from the antitrust laws for this reason, and because the statute authorized the city to carry out an important state economic program. Is this decision consistent with *Boulder*? Does *Boulder* hold that a state may displace competition through a statute authorizing a natural monopoly?

Antitrust problems also arise in the provision of municipal services. For example, the municipality may limit its service area and exclude a developer from receiving municipal services. Or it may condition the receipt of one municipal service on the receipt of others. The cases have generally found an antitrust exemption by holding that the state statutes authorized the provision of public services on a monopolistic, anti-competitive basis, e.g., *Community Builders, Inc. v. City of Phoenix,* 652 F.2d 823 (9th Cir. 1981); *Town of Hallie v. City of Chippewa Falls,* 314 N.W.2d 321 (Wis. 1982).

6. In addition to the questions of exemption and standards for determining liability (per se versus the Rule of Reason), the question of remedies haunts state and local governments. Section 4 of the Clayton Act, 15 U.S.C. § 15 provides in part: "Any person who shall be injured . . . shall recover three fold the damages by him sustained, and the cost of suit, including a reasonable attorney's fee." The Court in *Lafayette* expressly declined to decide any question of remedy. 435 U.S. at 402.

Commentators generally have argued that public policy considerations (chilling effect on local government decision-making, enormous potential budgetary impact, possible retroactive effect) should prevent the granting of treble damages. Injunctions on the basis that a particular activity was a violation of the federal antitrust statutes would vindicate the federal policy. *See, e.g.,* Taurman, *Reflections on City of Lafayette: Applying the Antitrust "State Actions" Exemption to Local Governments,* 13 URB. L. 159 (1981); Poli, *Antitrust Treble Damages as Applied to Local Governmental Entities: Does the Punishment Fit the Defendant?,* 1980 ARIZ. ST. L.J. 411; Rose, *Municipal Activities and the Antitrust Laws After City of Lafayette,* 57 U. DET. J. URB. L. 482 (1980); Note, *The Application of Antitrust Laws to Municipal Activities,* 79 COLUM. L. REV. 518, 544-49 (1979); P. AREEDA & D. TURNER, ANTITRUST LAW 217a (1978); *The Supreme Court, 1977 Term,* 92 HARV. L. REV. 57, 277-88 (1978); Posner, *The Proper Relationship Between State Regulation and the Federal Antitrust Laws,* 49 N.Y.U.L. REV. 693 (1974).

However, Justice Blackmun sharply criticized the Court for its "nonchalance" in declining to deal with the question of remedy and its failure to come to grips with the "plainly mandatory language" of § 4 of the Clayton Act. *Lafayette,* 435 U.S. at 442-43. To date, no treble damage judgments have been entered.

7. Despite predictions of dire consequences, cities have not lost all protection from antitrust liability. One commentator noted that in the first two years after *Lafayette,* lower federal courts in fourteen reported cases split evenly on the question of local government protection under the state action doctrine. All the cases involved pretrial motions; dismissals of antitrust claims were obtained in seven and denied in seven others. Taurman, *Reflections on City of Lafayette: Applying the Antitrust "State Action" Exemption to Local Governments,* 13 URB. L. 159, 166, 170, 172-73, 176-77 (1981).

Perhaps the most realistic view is as follows:

> [T]he world of municipal officials has not been shattered by the Supreme Court's decision in *City of Lafayette.* Their world, however, is different; new legal doctrines must be learned and new legal problems must be anticipated and treated. . . . In fact, their world may be better although many municipal officials might not agree. The economic, political, and social values inherent in antitrust laws provide many social benefits and are consistent with long-standing American traditions. While attention to the competitive impact of municipal decisions may seem inconvenient to some persons, it is likely to produce governmental decisions that result in more efficient, effective, and democratic government.

Rose, *An Overview: Municipal Antitrust Liability,* 1980 ARIZ. ST. L.J. 245, 251 (1980).

Chapter 8

FEDERALISM

A. THE FEDERAL SYSTEM

That an analysis of American state and local government law includes an examination of the federal role in American governmental affairs should come as no surprise. As any student of the American governmental scene well knows, the federal government has seized on expanded judicial readings of the constitutional commerce and spending clauses to exert a profound influence in the affairs of state and local governments. Examples abound. Acting to clean up environmental pollution, Congress has legislated massive programs of air and water pollution control. These programs require a federal-state cooperative effort in the exercise of regulatory powers to abate pollution as well as in the expenditure of federal and state funds for necessary public facilities such as waste water treatment plants. Extensive federal control of the airways has, in some instances, preempted local control of local airport operations. Grant-in-aid programs of all kinds have proliferated, including narrowly targeted programs focusing on particular public facilities, such as hospitals; broader functional programs aimed at a cluster of governmental problems, such as rural and urban community development; and the virtually unrestricted revenue transfer program enacted by the federal general revenue sharing act.

This intrusion of the federal government into matters that historically have been the responsibility of state and local government has blurred the lines of governmental authority in the American federal system. Questions arise concerning the permissible extent of federal power, especially as it may affect or curtail traditional governmental roles at the state or local level.

The first section of this chapter reviews tenth amendment and federal preemption problems in the exercise of federal power over state and local governments. The next section reviews the role of the federal government in setting standards for state and local governments, either directly under the commerce clause or through the federal grant-in-aid system. A final section reviews the federal grant-in-aid system, including the general revenue sharing program and block grants.

1. TENTH AMENDMENT PROBLEMS

The scope of federal power over state and local governments, including tenth amendment problems, has been tested in a series of Supreme Court cases considering amendments to the Fair Labor Standards Act that applied that Act to state and local government units. This Act, which provides authority at the federal level to set maximum hours of work and minimum wages, is based on the federal power over interstate commerce. The accepted formulation that Congress may choose the "appropriate means to enumerated ends" reflects the position the Court takes on congressional application of that power. This point of view, for a time, sanctioned the application of the Fair Labor Standards Act to state and local governments.

In *Maryland v. Wirtz,* 392 U.S. 183 (1968), the Court upheld the extension of the federal minimum wage and maximum hours law to certain state employees. The federal law had been amended to extend to any "enterprise" engaged in commerce, and state hospital and school employees were added to the categories included within this definition. The Court upheld the extension of the enterprise concept to these employees, finding a sufficient connection with interstate commerce to justify the amendment to the statute.

The Court then turned to the state sovereignty argument, noting that the Act exempted executive, administrative, and professional employees, that the Act only regulated wages and hours, and that the Act did not affect the way in which school and hospital duties are performed. Thus the question was not "whether Congress may, under the guise of the commerce power, tell the states how to perform medical and educational functions. . . ." *Id.* at 193. Moreover, the federal government, "when acting within a delegated power, may override countervailing state interests whether these be described as 'governmental' or 'proprietary' in character." *Id.* at 195. However, the Court admitted in a footnote that Congress could not "declare a whole state an 'enterprise' affecting commerce and take over its budgeting activities." *Id.* at 196 n.27.

Then, in *Fry v. United States,* 421 U.S. 542 (1975), the Court in a brief opinion upheld the temporary Economic Stabilization Act of 1970, which imposed federal wage and salary controls on a statutory wage and salary increase enacted by the State of Ohio. Justice Rehnquist, dissenting, noted that the Tenth Amendment should be construed to mean that state "legislative authority could be superseded by Congress in many areas where Congress was competent to act, [but] Congress was nonetheless not free to deal with a State as if it were just another individual or business enterprise subject to regulation." *Id.* at 557. When the full-blown application of the Fair Labor Standards Act to state and local governments was finally tested the Court reached a different judgment.

NATIONAL LEAGUE OF CITIES v. USERY

United States Supreme Court
426 U.S. 833 (1976)

Mr. Justice Rehnquist delivered the opinion for the Court.

Nearly 40 years ago Congress enacted the Fair Labor Standards Act, and required employers covered by the Act to pay their employees a minimum hourly wage and to pay them at one and one-half times their regular rate of pay for hours worked in excess of 40 during a work week. By this act covered employers were required to keep certain records to aid in the enforcement of the Act, and to comply with specified child labor standards. This Court unanimously upheld the Act as a valid exercise of congressional authority under the commerce power in *United States v. Darby,* 312 U.S. 100 (1941), observing:

> Whatever their motive and purpose, regulations of commerce which do not infringe some constitutional prohibition are within the plenary power conferred on Congress by the Commerce Clause. *Id.,* at 115.

The original Fair Labor Standards Act passed in 1938 specifically excluded the States and their political subdivisions from its coverage. In 1974, however, Congress enacted the most recent of a series of broadening amendments to the Act. By these amendments Congress has extended the minimum wage and maximum hour provisions to almost all public employees employed by the States and by their various political subdivisions. Appellants in these cases include individual cities and States, the National League of Cities, and the National Governors' Conference; they brought an action in the District Court for the District of Columbia which challenged the validity of the 1974 amendments. They asserted in effect that when Congress sought to apply the Fair Labor Standards Act provisions virtually across the board to employees of state and municipal governments it "infringed a constitutional prohibition" running in favor of the States *as States*. The gist of their complaint was not that the conditions of employment of such public employees were beyond the scope of the commerce power had those employees been employed in the private sector, but that the established constitutional doctrine of intergovernmental immunity consistently recognized in a long series of our cases affirmatively prevented the exercise of this authority in the manner which Congress chose in the 1974 Amendments.

I

[The Court first noted the extension of the FLSA that was upheld in *Wirtz* and then proceeded to a discussion of the 1974 amendments.—Eds.]

... By its 1974 amendments, then, Congress has now entirely removed the exemption previously afforded States and their political subdivisions, substituting only the Act's general exemption for executive, administrative, or professional personnel, 29 U.S.C. § 213(a)(1), which is supplemented by provisions excluding from the Act's coverage those individuals holding public elective office or serving such an officeholder in one of several specific capacities. 29 U.S.C. § 203(e)(2)(C). The Act thus imposes upon almost all public employment the minimum wage and maximum hour requirements previously restricted to employees engaged in interstate commerce. These requirements are essentially identical to those imposed upon private employers, although the Act does attempt to make some provision for public employment relationships which are without counterpart in the private sector, such as those presented by fire protection and law enforcement personnel. See 29 U.S.C. § 207(k).

Challenging these 1974 amendments in the District Court, appellants sought both declaratory and injunctive relief against the amendments' application to them, and a three-judge court was accordingly convened pursuant to 28 U.S.C. § 2282. That court, after hearing argument on the law from the parties, granted appellee Secretary of Labor's motion to dismiss the complaint for failure to state a claim upon which relief might be granted. The District Court stated it was "troubled" by appellants' contentions that the amendments would intrude upon the States' performance of essential governmental functions. 406 F.Supp. 826. The court went on to say that it considered their contentions:

> substantial and that it may well be that the Supreme Court will feel it appropriate to draw back from the far-reaching implications of [*Maryland v. Wirtz, supra*]; but that is a decision that only the Supreme Court can make, and as a Federal district court we feel obliged to apply the *Wirtz* opinion as it stands.

We noted probable jurisdiction in order to consider the important questions recognized by the District Court. ... We agree with the District Court that the appellants' contentions are substantial. Indeed upon full consideration of the question we have decided that the "far-reaching implications" of *Wirtz*, should be overruled, and that the judgment of the District Court must be reversed.

II

It is established beyond peradventure that the Commerce Clause of Art. I of the Constitution is a grant of plenary authority to Congress. That authority is, in the words of Chief Justice Marshall in *Gibbons v. Ogden,* 9 Wheat. (22 U.S.) 1 (1824), "... the power to regulate; that is to prescribe the rule by which commerce is to be governed." *Id.*, at 196.

When considering the validity of asserted applications of this power to wholly private activity, the Court has made it clear that

> [e]ven activity that is purely intrastate in character may be regulated by Congress, where the activity, combined with like conduct by others similarly situated, affects commerce among the States or with foreign nations. *Fry v. United States,* 421 U.S. 542, 547 (1975).

Congressional power over areas of private endeavor, even when its exercise may preempt express state law determinations contrary to the result which has commended itself to collective wisdom of Congress, has been held to be limited only by the requirement that "the means chosen by [Congress] must be reasonably adapted to the end permitted by the Constitution." *Heart of Atlanta Motel, Inc. v. United States,* 379 U.S. 241 (1964).

Appellants in no way challenge these decisions establishing the breadth of authority granted Congress under the commerce power. Their contention, on the contrary, is that when Congress seeks to regulate directly the activities of States as public employers, it transgresses an affirmative limitation on the exercise of its power akin to other commerce power affirmative limitations contained in the Constitution. Congressional enactments which may be fully within the grant of legislative authority contained in the Commerce Clause may nonetheless be invalid because found to offend against the right to trial by jury contained in the Sixth Amendment, *United States v. Jackson,* 390 U.S. 570 (1968), or the Due Process Clause of the Fifth Amendment, *Leary v. United States,* 395 U.S. 6 (1969). Appellants' essential contention is that the 1974 amendments to the Act, while undoubtedly within the scope of the Commerce Clause, encounter a similar constitutional barrier because they are to be applied directly to the States and subdivisions of States as employers.[12]

This Court has never doubted that there are limits upon the power of Congress to override state sovereignty, even when exercising its otherwise plenary powers to tax or to regulate commerce which are conferred by Art. I of the Constitution. In *Wirtz,* for example, the Court took care to assure the appellants that it had "ample power to prevent . . . 'the utter destruction of the State as a sovereign political entity,'" which they feared. 392 U.S., at 196. Appellee Secretary in this case, both in his brief and upon oral argument, has agreed that our federal system of government imposes definite limits upon the authority of Congress to regulate the activities of the States as States by means of the commerce power. . . . In *Fry, supra,* the Court recognized that an express declaration of this limitation is found in the Tenth Amendment:

> While the Tenth Amendment has been characterized as a "truism," stating merely that "all is retained which has not been surrendered." *United States v. Darby,* 312 U.S. 100 (1941), it is not without significance. The Amendment expressly declares the constitutional policy that Congress may not exercise

---

[12] Mr. Justice Brennan's dissent intimates, . . . that guarantees of individual liberties are the only sort of constitutional restrictions which this Court will enforce as against congressional action. It reasons that "Congress is constituted of representatives in both the Senate and House *elected from the States.* . . . Decisions upon the extent of federal intervention under the Commerce Clause into the affairs of the States are in that sense decisions of the the States themselves." . . . Precisely what is meant by the phrase "are in that sense decisions of the States themselves" is not entirely clear from this language; it is indisputable that a common constituency of voters elects both a State's governor and its two United States Senators. It is equally indisputable that since the enactment of the Seventeenth Amendment those Senators are not dependent upon state legislators for their election. But in any event the intimation which this reasoning is used to support is incorrect. . . .

power in a fashion that impairs the States' integrity or their ability to function effectively in a federal system. . . . 421 U.S., at 547. . . .

The expressions in these more recent cases trace back to earlier decisions of this Court recognizing the essential role of the States in our federal system of government. Chief Justice Chase, perhaps because of the particular time at which he occupied that office, had occasion more than once to speak for the Court on this point. In *Texas v. White,* 7 Wall. 700, 725 (1869), he declared that "[t]he Constitution, in all its provisions, looks to an indestructible Union, composed of indestructible States." In *Lane County v. Oregon,* 7 Wall. 71 (1869), his opinion for the Court said:

> Both the States and the United States existed before the Constitution. The people, through that instrument, established a more perfect union by substituting a national government, acting, with ample power, directly upon the citizens, instead of the Confederate government which acted with powers, greatly restricted, only upon the States. But in many Articles of the Constitution the necessary existence of the States, and, within their proper spheres, the independent authority of the States, is distinctly recognized. *Id.,* at 76. . . .

Appellee Secretary argues that the cases in which this Court has upheld sweeping exercises of authority by Congress, even though those exercises pre-empted state regulation of the private sector, have already curtailed the sovereignty of the States quite as much as the 1974 amendments to the Fair Labor Standards Act. We do not agree. It is one thing to recognize the authority of Congress to enact laws regulating individual businesses necessarily subject to the dual sovereignty of the government of the Nation and of the State in which they reside. It is quite another to uphold a similar exercise of congressional authority directed not to private citizens, but to the States as States. We have repeatedly recognized that there are attributes of sovereignty attaching to every state government which may not be impaired by Congress, not because Congress may lack an affirmative grant of legislative authority to reach the matter, but because the Constitution prohibits it from exercising the authority in that manner. In *Coyle v. Smith,* 221 U.S. 559 (1911), the Court gave this example of such an attribute:

> The power to locate its own seat of government, and to determine when and how it shall be changed from one place to another, and to appropriate its own public funds for that purpose, are essentially and peculiarly state powers. That one of the original thirteen states could now be shorn of such powers by an act of Congress would not be for a moment entertained. 221 U.S., at 565.

One undoubted attribute of state sovereignty is the States' power to determine the wages which shall be paid to those whom they employ in order to carry out their governmental functions, what hours those persons will work, and what compensation will be provided where these employees may be called upon to work overtime. The question we must resolve in this case, then, is whether these determinations are "functions essential to separate and independent existence," *Coyle v. Smith, supra,* at 580, quoting from *Lane County v. Oregon, supra,* 7 Wall. at 76, so that Congress may not abrogate the States' otherwise plenary authority to make them.

In their complaint appellants advanced estimates of substantial costs which will be imposed upon them by the 1974 amendments. Since the District Court dismissed their complaint, we take its well-pleaded allegations as true, although it appears from appellee's submissions in the District Court and in this Court that resolution of the factual disputes as to the effect of the amendments is not critical to our disposition of the case.

Judged solely in terms of increased costs in dollars, these allegations show a significant impact on the functioning of the governmental bodies involved. The Metropolitan Government of Nashville and Davidson County, Tenn., for example, asserted that the Act will increase its costs of providing essential police and fire protection, without any increase in service or in current salary levels, by $938,000 per year. . . .

Increased costs are not, of course, the only adverse effects which compliance with the Act will visit upon state and local governments, and in turn upon the citizens who depend upon those governments. In its complaint in intervention, for example, California asserted that it could not comply with the overtime costs (approximately $750,000 per year) which the Act required to be paid to California Highway Patrol cadets during their academy training program. California reported that it had thus been forced to reduce its academy training program from 2,080 hours to only 960 hours, a compromise undoubtedly of substantial importance to those whose safety and welfare may depend upon the preparedness of the California Highway Patrol. . . .

Quite apart from the substantial costs imposed upon the States and their political subdivisions, the Act displaces state policies regarding the manner in which they will structure delivery of those governmental services which their citizens require. The Act, speaking directly to the States *qua* States, requires that they shall pay all but an extremely limited minority of their employees the minimum wage rates currently chosen by Congress. It may well be that as a matter of economic policy it would be desirable that States, just as private employers, comply with these minimum wage requirements. But it cannot be gainsaid that the federal requirement directly supplants the considered policy choices of the States' elected officials and administrators as to how they wish to structure pay scales in state employment. The State might wish to employ persons with little or no training, or those who wish to work on a casual basis, or those who for some other reason do not possess minimum employment requirements, and pay them less than the federally prescribed minimum wage. It may wish to offer part time or summer employment to teenagers at a figure less than the minimum wage, and if unable to do so may decline to offer such employment at all. But the Act would forbid such choices by the States. The only "discretion" left to them under the Act is either to attempt to increase their revenue to meet the additional financial burden imposed upon them by paying congressionally prescribed wages to their existing complement of employees, or to reduce that complement to a number which can be paid the federal minimum wage without increasing revenue.

This dilemma presented by the minimum wage restrictions may seem not immediately different from that faced by private employers, who have long been covered by the Act and who must find ways to increase their gross income if they are to pay higher wages while maintaining current earnings. The difference, however, is that a State is not merely a factor in the "shifting economic arrangements" of the private sector of the economy, *Kovacs v. Cooper,* 336 U.S. 77, 95 (1949) (Frankfurter, J., concurring), but is itself a coordinate element in the system established by the framers for governing our federal union.

The degree to which the FLSA amendments would interfere with traditional aspects of state sovereignty can be seen even more clearly upon examining the overtime requirements of the Act. The general effect of these provisions is to require the States to pay their employees at premium rates whenever their work exceeds a specified number of hours in a given period. The asserted reason for these provisions is to provide a financial disincentive upon using employees beyond the work period deemed appropriate by Congress. According to appellee,

> [t]his premium rate can be avoided if the [State] uses other employees to do the overtime work. This, in effect, tends to discourage overtime work and to spread employment, which is the result Congress intended. Appellee's Brief, at 43.

We do not doubt that this may be a salutary result, and that it has a sufficiently rational relationship to commerce to validate the application of the overtime provisions to private employers. But, like the minimum wage provisions, the vice of the Act as sought to be applied here is that it directly penalizes the States for choosing to hire governmental employees on terms different from those which Congress has sought to impose.

This congressionally imposed displacement of state decisions may substantially restructure traditional ways in which the local governments have arranged their affairs. Although at this point many of the actual effects under the proposed Amendments remain a matter of some dispute among the parties, enough can be satisfactorily anticipated for an outline discussion of their general import. The requirement imposing premium rates upon any employment in excess of what Congress has decided is appropriate for a governmental employee's workweek, for example, appears likely to have the effect of coercing the States to structure work periods in some employment areas, such as police and fire protection, in a manner substantially different from practices which have long been commonly accepted among local governments of this Nation....

Our examination of the effect of the 1974 amendments, as sought to be extended to the States and their political subdivisions, satisfies us that both the minimum wage and the maximum hour provisions will impermissibly interfere with the integral governmental functions of these bodies. We earlier noted some disagreement between the parties regarding the precise effect the amendments will have in application. We do not believe particularized assessments of actual impact are crucial to resolution of the issue presented, however. For even if we accept appellee's assessments concerning the impact of the amendments, their application will nonetheless significantly alter or displace the States' abilities to structure employer-employee relationships in such areas as fire prevention, police protection, sanitation, public health, and parks and recreation. These activities are typical of those performed by state and local governments in discharging their dual functions of administering the public law and furnishing public services. Indeed, it is functions such as these which governments are created to provide, services such as these which the States have traditionally afforded their citizens. If Congress may withdraw from the States the authority to make those fundamental employment decisions upon which their systems for performance of these functions must rest, we think there would be little left of the States' "separate and independent existence." *Coyle, supra.* Thus, even if appellants may have overestimated the effect which the Act will have upon their current levels and patterns of governmental activity, the dispositive factor is that Congress has attempted to exercise its Commerce Clause authority to prescribe minimum wages and maximum hours to be paid by the States in their capacities as sovereign governments. In so doing, Congress has sought to wield its power in a fashion that would impair the States' "ability to function effectively [with]in a federal system," *Fry, supra,* 421 U.S., at 547. This exercise of congressional authority does not comport with the federal system of government embodied in the Constitution. We hold that insofar as the challenged amendments operate to directly displace the States' freedom to structure integral operations in areas of traditional governmental functions, they are not within the authority granted Congress by Art. I, § 8, cl. 3.[17]

III

One final matter requires our attention. Appellee has vigorously urged that we cannot, consistently with the Court's decisions in *Wirtz, supra,* and *Fry, supra,* rule against him here. It is important to examine this contention so that it will be clear what we hold today, and what we do not.

With regard to *Fry*, we disagree with appellee. There the Court held that the Economic Stabilization Act of 1970 was constitutional as applied to temporarily freeze the wages of state and local government employees. The Court expressly noted that the degree of intrusion upon the protected area of state sovereignty was in that case even less than that worked by the amendments to the FLSA which were before the Court in *Wirtz*. The Court recognized that the Economic Stabilization Act was "an emergency measure to counter severe inflation that threatened the national economy," 421 U.S., at 548.

We think our holding today quite consistent with *Fry*. The enactment at issue there was occasioned by an extremely serious problem which endangered the well-being of all the component parts of our federal system and which only collective action by the National Government might forestall. The means selected were carefully drafted so as not to interfere with the States' freedom beyond a very limited, specific period of time. The effect of the across-the-board freeze authorized by that Act, moreover, displaced no state choices as to how governmental operations should be structured nor did it force the States to remake such choices themselves. Instead, it merely required that the wage scales and employment relationships which the States themselves had chosen be maintained during the period of the emergency. Finally, the Economic Stabilization Act operated to reduce the pressures upon state budgets rather than increase them. These factors distinguish the statute in *Fry* from the provisions at issue here. The limits imposed upon the commerce power when Congress seeks to apply it to the States are not so inflexible as to preclude temporary enactments tailored to combat a national emergency. "[A]lthough an emergency may not call into life a power which has never lived, nevertheless emergency may afford a reason for the exertion of a living power already enjoyed." *Wilson v. New,* 243 U.S. 332, 348 (1917).

With respect to the Court's decision in *Wirtz*, we reach a different conclusion. Both appellee and the District Court thought that decision required rejection of appellants' claims. Appellants, in turn, advance several arguments by which they seek to distinguish the facts before the Court in *Wirtz* from those presented by the 1974 amendments to the Act. There are undoubtedly factual distinctions between the two situations, but in view of the conclusions expressed earlier in this opinion we do not believe the reasoning in *Wirtz* may any longer be regarded as authoritative.

Wirtz relied heavily on the Court's decision in *United States v. California,* 297 U.S. 175 (1936). The opinion quotes the following language from that case:

---

[17] We express no view as to whether different results might obtain if Congress seeks to affect integral operations of state governments by exercising authority granted it under other sections of the Constitution such as the Spending Power, Art. I, § 8, cl. 1 or § 5 of the Fourteenth Amendment.

"[We] look to the activities in which the states have traditionally engaged as marking the boundary of the restriction upon the federal taxing power. But there is no such limitation upon the plenary power to regulate commerce. The state can no more deny the power if its exercise has been authorized by Congress than can an individual." 297 U.S., at 183-185. 392 U.S., at 198.

But we have reaffirmed today that the States as States stand on a quite different footing than an individual or a corporation when challenging the exercise of Congress' power to regulate commerce. We think the dicta [18] from *United States v. California,* simply wrong.[19] Congress may not exercise that power so as to force directly upon the States its choices as to how essential decisions regarding the conduct of integral governmental functions are to be made. We agree that such assertions of power if unchecked, would indeed, as Mr. Justice Douglas cautioned in his dissent in *Wirtz,* allow "the National Government [to] devour the essentials of state sovereignty," 392 U.S., at 205, and would therefore transgress the bounds of the authority granted Congress under the Commerce Clause. While there are obvious differences between the schools and hospitals involved in *Wirtz,* and the fire and police departments affected here, each provides an integral portion of those governmental services which the States and their political subdivisions have traditionally afforded their citizens. We are therefore persuaded that *Wirtz* must be overruled.

The judgment of the District Court is accordingly reversed and the case is remanded for further proceedings consistent with this opinion.

So ordered.

Mr. Justice Blackmun, concurring.

The Court's opinion and the dissents indicate the importance and significance of this case as it bears upon the relationship between the Federal Government and our States. Although I am not untroubled by certain possible implications of the Court's opinion—some of them suggested by the dissents—I do not read the opinion so despairingly as does my Brother Brennan. In my view, the result with respect to the statute under challenge here is necessarily correct. I may misinterpret the Court's opinion, but it seems to me that it adopts a balancing approach, and does not outlaw federal power in areas such as environmental protection, where the federal interest is demonstrably greater and where state facility compliance with imposed federal standards would be essential. . . . With this understanding on my part of the Court's opinion, I join it.

Mr. Justice Brennan, with whom Mr. Justice White and Mr. Justice Marshall join, dissenting.

The Court concedes, as of course it must, that Congress enacted the 1974 amendments pursuant to its exclusive power under Art. I, § 8, cl. 3, of the Constitution "To regulate Commerce . . . among the several States." It must therefore be surprising that my Brethren should choose this Bicentennial year

---

[18] The holding of United States v. California, 297 U.S. 175 (1936), as opposed to the language quoted in the text, is quite consistent with our holding today. There California's activity to which the congressional command was directed was not in an area that the States have regarded as integral parts of their governmental activities. It was, on the contrary, the operation of a railroad engaged in "common carriage by rail in interstate commerce. . . ." 297 U.S., at 182. . . .

[19] Mr. Justice Brennan's dissent leaves no doubt from its discussion, . . ., that in its view Congress may under its commerce power deal with the States as States just as they might deal with private individuals. We venture to say that it is this conclusion, rather than the one we reach, which is in the words of the dissent a "startling restructuring of our federal system . . . ." . . . Even the Government, defending the 1974 Amendments in this Court, does not take so extreme a position.

of our independence to repudiate principles governing judicial interpretation of our Constitution settled since the time of Chief Justice John Marshall, discarding his postulate that the Constitution contemplates that restraints upon exercise by Congress of its plenary commerce power lie in the political process. For 152 years ago Chief Justice Marshall enunciated that principle to which, until today, his successors on this Court have been faithful.

> [T]he power over commerce ... is vested in Congress as absolutely as it would be in a single government, having in its constitution the same restrictions on the exercise of the power as are found in the constitution of the United States. *The wisdom and the discretion of Congress, their identity with the people, and the influence which their constituents possess at elections, are ... the sole restraints on which they have relied, to secure them from its abuse. They are the restraints on which the people must often rely solely, in all representative governments. Gibbons v. Ogden,* 9 Wheat. 1, 197 (1824) (emphasis added).
>
> ....

Only 34 years ago, *Wickard v. Filburn,* 317 U.S. 111, 120 (1942), reaffirmed that "[a]t the beginning Chief Justice Marshall ... made emphatic the embracing and penetrating nature of [Congress' commerce] power by warning that effective restraints on its exercise must proceed from political rather than from judicial processes."

My Brethren do not successfully obscure today's patent usurpation of the role reserved for the political process by their purported discovery in the Constitution of a restraint derived from sovereignty of the States on Congress' exercise of the commerce power. ...

My Brethren thus have today manufactured an abstraction without substance, founded neither in the words of the Constitution nor on precedent. An abstraction having such profoundly pernicious consequences is not made less so by characterizing the 1974 amendments as legislation directed against the "States *qua* States." ... Of course, regulations that this Court can say are not regulations of "commerce" cannot stand, *Santa Cruz Fruit Packing Co. v. NLRB,* 303 U.S. 453, 466 (1938), and in this sense "[t]he Court has ample power to prevent ... 'the utter destruction of the State as a sovereign political entity.'" *Maryland v. Wirtz,* 392 U.S. 183, 196 (1968). But my Brethren make no claim that the 1974 amendments are not regulations of "commerce"; rather they overrule *Wirtz* in disagreement with historic principles that *United States v. California, supra,* reaffirmed: "[W]hile the commerce power has limits, valid general regulations of commerce do not cease to be regulations of commerce because a State is involved. If a State is engaging in economic activities that are validly regulated by the Federal Government when engaged in by private persons, the State too may be forced to conform its activities to federal regulation." 392 U.S., at 196-197. Clearly, therefore, my Brethren are also repudiating the long line of our precedents holding that a judicial finding that Congress has not unreasonably regulated a subject matter of "commerce" brings to an end the judicial role. "Let the end be legitimate, let it be within the scope of the constitution, and all means which are appropriate, which are plainly adapted to that end, which are not prohibited, but consist with the letter and spirit of the constitution, are constitutional." *McCulloch v. Maryland, supra,* 4 Wheat. at 421.

The reliance of my Brethren upon the Tenth Amendment as "an express declaration of [a state sovereignty] limitation," ... not only suggests that they overrule governing decisions of this Court that address this question but must astound scholars of the Constitution. ...

Today's repudiation of this unbroken line of precedents that firmly reject my Brethren's ill-conceived abstraction can only be regarded as a transparent cover for invalidating a congressional judgment with which they disagree. The only analysis even remotely resembling that adopted today is found in a line of opinions dealing with the Commerce Clause and the Tenth Amendment that ultimately provoked a constitutional crisis for the Court in the 1930's. *E.g., Carter v. Carter Coal Co.,* 298 U.S. 238 (1936); *United States v. Butler,* 297 U.S. 1 (1936); *Hammer v. Dagenhart,* 247 U.S. 251 (1918). See Stern, The Commerce Clause and the National Economy, 1933-1946, 59 Harv.L.Rev. 645 (1946). We tend to forget that the Court invalidated legislation during the Great Depression, not solely under the Due Process Clause, but also and primarily under the Commerce Clause and the Tenth Amendment. It may have been the eventual abandonment of that overly restrictive construction of the commerce power that spelled defeat for the Court-packing plan, and preserved the integrity of this institution, *id.*, at 682, ... but my Brethren today are transparently trying to cut back on that recognition of the scope of the commerce power. My Brethren's approach to this case is not far different from the dissenting opinions in the cases that averted the crisis. ...

That no precedent justifies today's result is particularly clear from the awkward extension of the doctrine of state immunity from federal taxation—an immunity conclusively distinguished by Mr. Justice Stone in *California,* and an immunity that is "narrowly limited" because "the people of all the states have created the national government and are represented in Congress," *Helvering v. Gerhardt,* 304 U.S. 405, 416 (1938) (Stone, J.)—to fashion a judicially enforceable restraint on Congress' exercise of the commerce power that the Court has time and again rejected as having no place in our constitutional jurisprudence. "[W]here [Congress] keeps within its sphere and violates no express constitutional limitation it has been the rule of this Court, going back almost to the founding days of the Republic, not to interfere." *Katzenbach v. McClung,* [379 U.S. 294, 305 (1954)—Eds.] . . . .

Also devoid of meaningful content is my Brethren's argument that the 1974 amendments "displace[ ] State policies." ... The amendments neither impose policy objectives on the States nor deny the States complete freedom to fix their own objectives. My Brethren boldly assert that the decision as to wages and hours is an "undoubted attribute of state sovereignty," ... and then never say why. Indeed, they disclaim any reliance on the costs of compliance with the amendments in reaching today's result. . . . This would enable my Brethren to conclude that, however insignificant that cost, any federal regulation under the commerce power "will nonetheless significantly alter or displace the States' abilities to structure employer-employee relationships." [8] This then would mean that, whether or not state wages are paid for the performance of an "essential" state function (whatever that may mean), the newly discovered state sovereignty constraint could operate as a flat and absolute prohibition against congressional regulation of the wages and hours of state employees under the Commerce Clause. The portent of such a sweeping holding is so ominous for our constitutional jurisprudence as to leave one incredulous. . . .

---

[8] My Brethren's reluctance to rely on the cost of compliance to invalidate this legislation is advisable. "Such matters raise not constitutional issues but questions of policy. They relate to the wisdom, need, and effectiveness of a particular project. They are therefore questions for the Congress not the courts." Oklahoma ex rel. Phillips v. Guy F. Atkinson Co., [313 U.S. 508, 527—Eds.]. . . .

My Brethren do more than turn aside longstanding constitutional jurisprudence that emphatically rejects today's conclusion. More alarming is the startling restructuring of our federal system, and the role they create therein for the federal judiciary. This Court is simply not at liberty to erect a mirror of its own conception of a desirable governmental structure. If the 1974 amendments have any "vice," . . . my Brother STEVENS is surely right that it represents "merely . . . a policy issue which has been firmly resolved by the branches of government having power to decide such questions." . . . It bears repeating "that effective restraints on . . . exercise [of the Commerce power] must proceed from political rather than from judicial processes." *Wickard v. Filburn, supra,* 317 U.S., at 120.

It is unacceptable that the judicial process should be thought superior to the political process in this area. Under the Constitution the judiciary has no role to play beyond finding that Congress has not made an unreasonable legislative judgment respecting what is "commerce." My Brother BLACKMUN suggests that controlling judicial supervision of the relationship between the States and our National Government by use of a balancing approach diminishes the ominous implications of today's decision. Such an approach, however, is a thinly veiled rationalization for judicial supervision of a policy judgment that our system of government reserves to Congress.

Judicial restraint in this area merely recognizes that the political branches of our Government are structured to protect the interests of the States, as well as the Nation as a whole, and that the States are fully able to protect their own interests in the premises. Congress is constituted of representatives in both Senate and House *elected from the States.* The Federalist No. 45, at 311-312 (J. Cooke ed. 1961) (J. Madison); The Federalist No. 46, at 317-318 (J. Cooke ed. 1961) (J. Madison). Decisions upon the extent of federal intervention under the Commerce Clause into the affairs of the States are in that sense decisions of the States themselves. Judicial redistribution of powers granted the National Government by the terms of the Constitution violates the fundamental tenet of our federalism that the extent of federal intervention into the State's affairs in the exercise of delegated powers shall be determined by the States' exercise of political power through their representatives in Congress. See Wechsler, The Political Safeguards of Federalism: The Role of the States in the Composition and Selection of the National Government, 54 Col.L.Rev. 543 (1954). There is no reason whatever to suppose that enacting the 1974 amendments Congress, even if it might extensively obliterate state sovereignty by fully exercising its plenary power respecting commerce, had any purpose to do so. Surely the presumption must be to the contrary. Any realistic assessment of our federal political system, dominated as it is by representatives of the people *elected from the States,* yields the conclusion that it is highly unlikely that those representatives will ever be motivated to disregard totally the concerns of these States. The Federalist No. 46, *supra,* at 319. Certainly this was the premise upon which the Constitution, as authoritatively explicated in *Gibbons v. Ogden,* was founded. Indeed, though the States are represented in the National Government, national interests are not similarly represented in the States' political processes. Perhaps my Brethren's concern with the judiciary's role in preserving federalism might better focus on whether Congress, not the States, is in greater need of this Court's protection.
. . .

A sense of the enormous impact of States' political power is gained by brief reference to the federal budget. The largest estimate by any of the appellants of the cost impact of the 1974 amendments—one billion dollars—pales in comparison with the financial assistance the States receive from the Federal Government. In fiscal 1977 the President's proposed budget recommends $60.5 billion in federal assistance to the States, exclusive of loans. Office of Management and Budget, Special Analyses: Budget of the United States Government, Fiscal Year 1977, p. 255. Appellants complain of the impact of the amended FLSA on police and fire departments, but the 1977 budget contemplates outlays for law enforcement assistance of $716 million. *Id.*, at 258. Concern is also expressed about the diminished ability to hire students in the summer if States must pay them a minimum wage, but the Federal Government's "summer youth program" provides $400 million for 670,000 jobs. *Ibid.* Given this demonstrated ability to obtain funds from the Federal Government for needed state services, there is little doubt that the States' influence in the political process is adequate to safeguard their sovereignty....

We are left then with a catastrophic judicial body blow at Congress' power under the Commerce Clause. Even if Congress may nevertheless accomplish its objectives—for example by conditioning grants of federal funds upon compliance with federal minimum wage and overtime standards, cf. *Oklahoma v. United States Civil Service Comm'n,* 330 U.S. 127, 144 (1947)—there is an ominous portent of disruption of our constitutional structure implicit in today's mischievous decision. I dissent.

MR. JUSTICE STEVENS, dissenting. [Omitted.]

Comments: 1. Justice Brennan suggested at the close of his dissent that the *Oklahoma* case was still good law. Congress has regularly enacted scores of federal programs offering federal grants-in-aid to states and local governments which require the recipient governments to meet a specified set of federal statutory conditions in order to receive federal financial assistance. For example, Congress regularly requires state and local governments to pay prevailing rates of wages to employees of private contractors who work on projects receiving federal aid. Justice Brennan apparently meant that Congress could likewise condition federal grants with a requirement that states and localities receiving these grants adhere to the federal Fair Labor Standards Act. Silence in the majority opinion on this point raises the question whether or not the *Oklahoma* case is still good law.

At issue in the *Oklahoma* case were the provisions of the federal Hatch Act, which denies federal funds to any state or local government if an employee in a program supported by federal funds engages in political activity. The Court there held that the tenth amendment does not deprive Congress of the authority to adopt all means for the exercise of a power granted to the federal government that are "appropriate and plainly adapted" to the granted power. "The end sought by Congress through the Hatch Act is better public service by requiring those who administer funds for national needs to abstain from active political partisanship." *Id.* at 143.

The majority opinion in *National League of Cities* indicated that Congress does not have the authority to regulate the states as states. Note, however, the pervasiveness of the Hatch Act prohibition, which applies to any state agency receiving federal funding. Could an argument be made that attaching the Hatch Act prohibition to all federal grants is equally a regulation of the states as states considering the pervasiveness of this requirement in state government?

With the principal case compare *Town of Arlington v. Board of Conciliation & Arbitration,* 352 N.E.2d 914 (Mass. 1976), in which the Massachusetts court upheld a statute creating a labor mediation board authorized to mediate labor disputes with municipalities. The statute was upheld although it applied to home rule cities, and although the awards made by the board were made binding on these cities. Why is a state court able to reach a decision obviously at odds with the principles announced in the *National League of Cities* case? See the materials on state preemption, *supra* Chapter 3, Section D.

2. Whether or not Congress has the authority to override state sovereignty through the enactment of legislative mandates applicable to state and local governments will also depend on the federal power under which the legislation is enacted. In *Fitzpatrick v. Bitzer,* 427 U.S. 445 (1976), the Court considered amendments to the Civil Rights Act of 1964 in which Congress authorized federal courts to award damages to private individuals against state governments found to have subjected them to employment discrimination. An eleventh amendment objection was made to the amendment, on the ground that Congress did not have the power to override the state immunity conferred by that amendment. The Court disagreed, noting that the Civil Rights Act had been passed to implement the fourteenth amendment to the federal Constitution, and that this amendment, in section 5, explicitly states: "The Congress shall have power to enforce, by appropriate legislation, the provisions of this article." The Court stated:

> There can be no doubt that [our cases have] sanctioned intrusions by Congress, acting under the Civil War Amendments, into the judicial, executive, and legislative spheres of autonomy previously reserved to the States. The legislation considered in each case was grounded on the expansion of Congress' powers—with the corresponding diminution of state sovereignty—found to be intended by the Framers and made part of the Constitution upon the States' ratification of those Amendments, a phenomenon aptly described as a "carv[ing] out" in *Ex parte Virginia* [100 U.S. 339 (1880)].

Id. at 455-56. *Ex parte Virginia* upheld the arrest and indictment of a state judge under a federal criminal statute prohibiting the exclusion on the basis of race of any citizen from service on a state court jury.

Compare *Hopkins Federal Savings & Loan Ass'n v. Cleary,* 296 U.S. 315 (1935), holding unconstitutional a federal statute authorizing a state building and loan association to convert to a federal association without the consent of the state that created it. The Court held that the federal statute was "an unconstitutional encroachment upon the reserved powers of the states," citing the tenth amendment. *Id.* at 335. It noted that it was not concerned with the exercise of federal power under the commerce clause. *Id.* at 338.

3. Numerous questions have been raised concerning how the *National League of Cities* rule should be applied to congressional commerce power legislation. In *Hodel v. Virginia Surface Mining & Reclamation Ass'n* 452 U.S. 264 (1981), the Supreme Court posed a three-part test:

> It should be apparent from this discussion that in order to succeed, a claim that congressional commerce power legislation is invalid under the reasoning of *National League of Cities* must satisfy *each* of three requirements. First, there must be a showing that the challenged statute regulates the "States as States." ... Second, the federal regulation must address matters that are indisputably "attribute[s] of state sovereignty." ... And third, it must be apparent that the States' compliance with the federal law would directly impair their ability "to structure integral operations in areas of traditional governmental functions."

Id. at 287-88.

In *Hodel,* the Court held that "steep-slope" provisions of the 1977 Surface Mining Control and Reclamation Act, 30 U.S.C. § 1201 et seq., which require coal operators to return sites to their "approximate original contour," do not regulate "states as states" but rather regulate the activities of private individuals and businesses. The Court characterized the Surface Mining Act as a "program of cooperative federalism" in which the states may regulate, albeit within limits established by the federal government.

In *United Transportation Union v. Long Island Railroad,* 102 S. Ct. 1349 (1982), the Court upheld national regulation of a state-owned railroad by applying the three-part test of *Hodel* and concluding that operation of a railroad is not an integral part of a state's function. Long Island Railroad Company and the employees' union had failed to reach agreement after conducting bargaining negotiations. Before a cooling off period expired, the Union sought a declaratory judgment in federal court that the dispute was covered by the Railway Labor Act, 45 U.S.C. § 151 et seq., rather than by New York's Taylor Law which prohibits unions from striking. After the President intervened and imposed another sixty-day cooling off period, the railroad filed suit in state court seeking an injunction of the impending strike. Before the state court acted, the district court found that the railroad was a carrier subject to the Railway Labor Act. *United Transportation Union v. Long Island Railroad,* 509 F. Supp. 1300 (E.D.N.Y. 1980). The court of appeals reversed, finding that operation of the railroad was an "integral state governmental function and that the federal Act displaced 'essential governmental decisions' involving that function." *United Transportation Union v. Long Island Railroad,* 634 F.2d 19 (3d Cir. 1980).

The Supreme Court reversed, stressing that there was no justification for a rule which would allow the states, by acquiring functions previously performed by the private sector, to erode federal authority in areas traditionally subject to federal statutory regulation. The Court emphasized that federal regulation provides uniformity and efficiency in the railway system. The Court also stressed the balance between federal and state roles in regulation and pointed out that the state had acquired the railroad in full awareness of the federal regulation. The Court held that federal regulation of railroads which are involved in interstate transport does not impair the state's ability to function as a state.

The Court concluded as follows:

> Just as the Federal Government cannot usurp traditional state functions, there is no justification for a rule which would allow the States, by acquiring functions previously performed by the private sector, to erode federal authority in areas traditionally subject to federal statutory regulation. Railroads have been subject to comprehensive federal regulation for nearly a century.

Id. at 102 S. Ct. at 1355.

In a third case construing commerce power legislation, *Federal Energy Regulatory Commission v. Mississippi,* 102 S. Ct. 2126 (1982), the Court upheld the Public Utility Regulatory Policies Act of 1978 (PURPA), 16 U.S.C. §§ 2601 et seq., which requires state utility regulatory commissions to "consider" the adoption and implementation of specific "rate design" and regulatory standards, against tenth amendment challenges. In a 5-4 decision, the Court ruled that the mandatory consideration provisions "simply establish requirements for continued state activity in an otherwise pre-emptible field." *Id.* at 2142.

In a biting dissent, Justice O'Connor declared:

> Application of these principles to the present case reveals the Tenth Amendment defects in Titles I and III. Plainly those titles regulate the "States as States." While the statute's ultimate aim may be the regulation of private utility companies, PURPA addresses its commands solely to the States. Instead of requesting private utility companies to adopt lifeline rates, declining block rates, or the other PURPA standards, Congress directed state agencies to appraise the appropriateness of those standards. It is difficult to argue that a statute structuring the regulatory agenda of a state agency is not a regulation of the "State."
>
> I find it equally clear that Titles I and III address "attribute[s] of state sovereignty." Even the Court recognizes that "the power to make decisions and to set policy is what gives the State its sovereign nature." . . . The power to make decisions and set policy, however, embraces more than the ultimate authority to enact laws; it also includes the power to decide which proposals are most worthy of consideration, the order in which they should be taken up, and the precise form in which they should be debated. PURPA intrudes upon all of these functions. It chooses twelve proposals, forcing their consideration even if the state agency deems other ideas more worthy of immediate attention. In addition, PURPA hinders the agency's ability to schedule consideration of the federal standards. Finally, PURPA specifies, with exacting detail, the content of the standards that will absorb the agency's time.
>
> If Congress routinely required the state legislatures to debate bills drafted by congressional committees, it could hardly be questioned that the practice would affect an attribute of state sovereignty. PURPA, which sets the agendas of agencies exercising delegated legislative power in a specific field, has a similarly intrusive effect.
>
> . . . .
>
> I do not believe, moreover, that Titles I and III of PURPA are less intrusive than preemption. When Congress preempts a field, it precludes only state legislation that conflicts with the national approach. The States usually retain the power to complement congressional legislation, either by regulating details unsupervised by Congress or by imposing requirements that go beyond the national threshold. Most importantly, after

Congress preempts a field, the States may simply devote their resources elsewhere. This country does not lack for problems demanding legislative attention. PURPA, however, drains the inventive energy of state governmental bodies by requiring them to weigh its detailed standards, enter written findings, and defend their determinations in state court. While engaged in these congressionally mandated tasks, state utility commissions are less able to pursue local proposals for conserving gas and electric power. The States might well prefer that Congress simply impose the standards described in PURPA; this, at least, would leave them free to exercise their power in other areas.

Federal preemption is less intrusive than PURPA's approach for a second reason. Local citizens hold their utility commissions accountable for the choices they make. Citizens, moreover, understand that legislative authority usually includes the power to decide which ideas to debate, as well as which policies to adopt. Congressional compulsion of state agencies, unlike preemption, blurs the lines of political accountability and leaves citizens feeling that their representatives are no longer responsive to local needs.

The foregoing remarks suggest that, far from approving a minimally intrusive form of federal regulation, the Court's decision undermines the most valuable aspects of our federalism. Courts and commentators frequently have recognized that the fifty States serve as laboratories for the development of new social, economic, and political ideas. This state innovation is no judicial myth. When Wyoming became a State in 1890, it was the only State permitting women to vote. That novel idea did not bear national fruit for another thirty years. Wisconsin pioneered unemployment insurance, while Massachusetts initiated minimum wage laws for women and minors. After decades of academic debate, state experimentation finally provided an opportunity to observe no-fault automobile insurance in operation. Even in the field of environmental protection, an area subject to heavy federal regulation, the States have supplemented national standards with innovative and far-reaching statutes. Utility regulation itself is a field marked by valuable state invention. PURPA, which commands state agencies to spend their time evaluating federally proposed standards and defending their decisions to adopt or reject those standards, will retard this creative experimentation.

Id. at 2147-48, 2151-52.

4. Commentators have been critical of the three-prong *Hodel* test. *See, e.g.,* LaPierre, *The Political Safeguards of Federalism Redux: Intergovernmental Immunity and the States as Agents of the Nation,* 60 WASH. U.L.Q. 779 (1982):

Notwithstanding the superficial allure of an enumerated test, the *Hodel* three-prong test is an intellectual sham because it does not resolve the basic issues left unanswered in *NLC* [*National League of Cities.*—Eds.] It does not define the states' role in the federal system nor does it establish a principled basis for judicial intervention in the national political process. *Hodel* teaches only that the Court now believes that some particular language of the *NLC* plurality opinion is especially pertinent.

In addition to the mere invocation of talismanic words from *NLC* and the failure to resolve the basic issues raised by *NLC,* the *Hodel* test is marred by three other defects. First, prong number one rules out any state autonomy limit on national authority to regulate private activity. Although the Court expressly held that *NLC* does not limit Congress' power to regulate private activity, it did not explain why the states' interests in regulating private activity are any less important than the interests protected under the test from national interference. Second, the *Hodel* test does not settle the question whether *NLC* provides absolute immunity for certain, specific state activities or whether the validity of national regulations as applied to the states is to be determined by balancing national and state interests. The third prong of the test suggests that traditional state functions enjoy absolute immunity from regulations established under the commerce power, but *Hodel* also approved a balancing test by stating that some national interests may justify "state submission" even if the three-prong test for immunity is satisfied. Since the Court concluded that the first prong was not satisfied because the statute regulated private activity, it did not interpret or apply the language quoted from *NLC* and provided no guidelines for identifying either protected state functions or for balancing national and state interests. Finally, *Hodel* recognized Congress' power to employ the states as its agents by upholding one of the means by which Congress induces the states to enforce national standards governing private activity. The Court, however, did not apply its new test to this question of Congress' power to require the affirmative exercise of state authority over private activity. The Court did not explain why its three-prong test of Congress' power to diminish state autonomy by regulating the states did not also apply to the question of Congress' power to employ the states as

the nation's agents. Nor did it formulate any alternative, principled test of this power.
Id. at 895-96.

Professor LaPierre concluded that the Court in *United Transportation Union* reached the right result for the wrong reason. Simply concluding that the operation of a railroad is not a traditional state function provides no principled basis for reconciling *National League* (Congress cannot regulate states as employers by establishing wage and hour standards) with *United Transportation Union* (Congress can regulate states as employers by authorizing employees of a state-owned railroad to strike). What criteria should be used to determine the proper application of federalism principles in resolving conflicts over Congress's power to regulate states? Is the question simply one of balancing state and national interests? If so, what are those interests and how should they be balanced? *See* LaPierre, at 1014-17.

Professor LaPierre advocates use of the theory of political accountability in the operation of the national political process. Decisions by Congress represent the political choice of the nation and should be given preference over choices at the state level because the national political process assures full participation by the electorate in the allocation of political authority. He argues that the political checks involved in the impact of national policy on private activity and the imposition of administrative and financial costs on the national electorate make Congress politically accountable. These political checks insure that decisions to regulate state and local government, as well as private activity, are the products of a national majority and thus consistent with the interest of the framers of the Constitution. He argues that *National League* should be overruled because there is no basis for judicial intervention in the political process when the decisions are the product of a national majority, even though state autonomy may be diminished. On the other hand, the requisite political checks are not present in situations where regulations or taxes are applied solely to the states, where national authority is delegated to state officers, agencies or political subdivisions, in excess of or contrary to their state law authority and where statutes mandate state enforcement of national regulations. Thus, judicial intervention to invalidate these activities is both warranted and necessary.

Is Professor LaPierre's theory persuasive? Realistic? Will the national electorate respond effectively so that the political checks he describes will influence congressional action? What about Justice O'Connor's concern about preserving the states as laboratories of innovation?

In his excellent article, Professor LaPierre discusses several recent commentaries on *National League. See, e.g.,* J. CHOPER, JUDICIAL REVIEW AND THE NATIONAL POLITICAL PROCESS 171-259 (1980) (federalism questions should be non-justiciable); Kaden, *Politics, Money, and State Sovereignty: The Judicial Role,* 79 COLUM. L. REV. 847 (1979) (the states' role as a source of political liberty provides basis for determining limits on national authority); Michelman, *States' Rights and States' Roles: Permutations of "Sovereignty" in National League of Cities v. Usery,* 86 YALE L.J. 1165 (1977); Tribe, *Unraveling National League of Cities: The New Federalism and Affirmative Rights to Essential Government Services,* 90 HARV. L. REV. 1065 (1977) (both Michelman and Tribe argue that *National League of Cities* should be interpreted as an individual rights decision and the states' role in providing constitutionally guaranteed social services to their citizens should be protected from national interference); Stewart, *Pyramids of Sacrifice? Problems of Federalism in Mandating State Implementation of National Environmental Policy,* 86 YALE L.J. 1196 (1977) (advocating broad national power over the states). *See also* Note, *Taking Federalism Seriously: Limiting State Acceptance of National Grants,* 90 YALE L.J. 1694 (1981); Note, *Federal Grants and the Tenth Amendment: "Things As They Are" and Fiscal Federalism,* 50 FORDHAM L. REV. 130 (1981).

In addition to its power under the commerce clause, the federal government regulates activities by imposing conditions on the receipt of federal assistance. Congressional activity in this sphere is governed by the spending clause of the

Constitution. Important *National League of Cities* questions arise, as the following case indicates.

WALKER FIELD v. ADAMS

United States Court of Appeals
606 F.2d 290 (10th Cir. 1979)

Before HOLLOWAY, DOYLE and MCKAY, CIRCUIT JUDGES.
HOLLOWAY, CIRCUIT JUDGE.

Plaintiff-appellant Walker Field Public Airport Authority ("Walker Field") brings this appeal from a dismissal of its suit against the Secretary of Transportation and others. The suit challenged the lawfulness of defendants' actions in seeking to require the County of Mesa and the City of Grand Junction, Colorado, to join the Walker Field Authority in assuming obligations for improvement of Walker Field airport for which the Federal Government offered to make a Grant Agreement. The action was dismissed for "failure to state a claim for relief within the jurisdiction of the court."

Since the complaint and action were dismissed for such defects in the complaint, we turn to the facts as alleged in that pleading and to a discussion of the general background of the controversy.

I

The Airport and Airway Development and Revenue Act of 1970, as amended, 49 U.S.C. Secs. 1701-1742 (1976) (the "Act"), provides for the expansion and improvement of the Nation's airport and airway system. Financing for these improvements is largely, although not exclusively, provided by airport and airway user charges imposed by the Act. The charges collected are paid into the Airport and Airway Trust Fund, 49 U.S.C. Sec. 1742(b) (1976), from which they are returned to individual airports under, *inter alia,* the terms of project grant agreements, 49 U.S.C. Sec. 1714(a) (1976).

The complaint avers that on September 23, 1976, Walker Field, a political subdivision of the State of Colorado formed under the Colorado Public Airport Authority Law, Colo. Rev. Stat. Secs. 41-3-101 — 41-3-108 (1973), for the purpose of acquiring and improving airports submitted to the Federal Aviation Administration ("FAA") a Project Application for financial assistance under the Act for the construction of fire bays, fencing and a taxiway for the Walker Field airport. The estimated cost of the project was $690,480.00 (I R. 4). No other agency submitted an application.

On January 4, 1977, Edward G. Tatum, Chief of the Denver Airport District Office of the FAA transmitted an "Offer" to Walker Field, Mesa County, and the City of Grand Junction as joint sponsors of the proposed project ("joint sponsors"). The "Offer" was made on and subject to, *inter alia,* the following condition (I R. 16):

> 16. The FAA in tendering this Grant Offer on behalf of the United States recognizes the existence of a Co-sponsorship Agreement between the City of Grand Junction, Mesa County, and Walker Field, Colorado, Public Airport Authority, entered into between the parties on August 14, 1972. By acceptance of this Grant Offer said parties assume their respective obligations as set forth in said Co-sponsorship Agreement. It is understood and agreed that said agreement will not be amended, modified or terminated without prior written approval of the FAA.

On January 10, 1977, Walker Field executed a Grant Acceptance thereby agreeing to all of the terms and conditions which had been added to the Offer. Subsequently on January 17 and 19, respectively, the Board of County Commissioners of Mesa County and the City Council of the City of Grand Junction adopted resolutions, (I R. 18-21), adverting to the Offer, declaring that they had not made application for a grant and declining to assume, on behalf of their citizens, the obligations of sponsorship under the Grant Agreement.

. . . .

Walker Field's complaint alleged that . . . if the Act is construed to permit the defendants to impose such conditions, such power would be in excess of that granted the Federal Government by the Constitution and that such power to manipulate the States and their political subdivisions with respect to authority reserved to them would violate the concept of immunities between the United States and the several States. . . .

Third, we will consider constitutional arguments pressed by Walker Field and the State of Colorado as amicus based on *National League of Cities v. Usery* . . . . In essence it is argued that if there is such discretion to compel the County of Mesa and the City of Grand Junction to join as co-sponsors for the project, then such discretion would be contrary to the Tenth Amendment's provision that powers not delegated to the United States by the Constitution, nor prohibited by it to the States, are reserved to the States or to the people. More specifically the amicus argues that the challenged actions of defendants violate the constitutional doctrine of intergovernmental immunities, that it was the State's policy in the Public Airport Authority Act, C.R.S. 1973, 41-3-102, to finance and operate airport facilities on a self-paying basis "without the incurrence of an indebtedness by the State of Colorado, or by any of its [other] political subdivisions . . .", and that the Secretary has no power to negate that State policy by forcing a City and County to co-sponsor an airport authority program. . . .

We do not agree. Unless barred by some controlling constitutional prohibition, the Federal Government may impose the terms and conditions upon which its money allotments to the States shall be disbursed and any state law or regulation inconsistent with the federal terms and conditions is to that extent invalid. *See King v. Smith,* 392 U.S. 309, 333 n.34 . . .; *Stiner v. Califano,* 438 F. Supp. 796, 800 (W.D. Okl.). We feel that the terms and conditions imposed here do not ". . . . operate to directly displace the States' freedom to structure integral operations in areas of traditional governmental functions." *National League of Cities v. Usery,* 426 U.S. 833, 852, . . .; *City of Macon v. Marshall,* 439 F. Supp. 1209, 1216-17 (M.D. Ga.); *Stiner v. Califano, supra,* 438 F. Supp. at 800 n. 4. Since there are no direct, mandatory terms and conditions imposed, and since the State and its agencies can avoid completely the structuring of their relationships or assuming the obligations stipulated by the Secretary by declining the grants, we feel that there is no violation of the constitutional limitation relied on. *See City of Macon v. Marshall, supra,* 439 F. Supp. at 1217. It may be that some conditions imposed under the spending power of Congress would exceed constitutional limits, but we see no such violation here. Thus we are not convinced that the constitutional arguments or *National League of Cities* demonstrate any invalidity in the Secretary's actions.

In sum, we agree with the conclusions reached by the trial court for the reasons stated. The remaining arguments of Walker Field and the amicus have been considered but they require no further discussion. Considering all the claims of error, we must hold that the ruling of the trial court was correct and its judgment is affirmed.

McKay, Circuit Judge, dissenting:

Had it *required* the City of Grand Junction and the County of Mesa to incur financial risks for an airport project, Congress would clearly have operated to "directly displace the States' freedom to structure integral operations in areas of traditional governmental functions." *National League of Cities v. Usery,* 426 U.S. 833, 852. . . . City and county funds would necessarily have been diverted from other essential governmental activities, an effect expressly condemned in *National League of Cities.* . . . Even more starkly, the congressional mandate would have operated on the very structure of the state's subdivisions — requiring union in a continuing Co-Partnership Agreement — and would have imposed financial obligations directly contrary to an express Colorado policy. It would, that is, have "displace[d] state policies regarding the manner in which [the States] will structure delivery of those governmental services which their citizens require," *id.* at 847 . . ., and have impaired Colorado's "ability to function effectively in a federal system." *Id.* at 852, *quoting Fry v. United States,* 421 U.S. 542, 547 n.7 . . . (1975).

National League of Cities was of course dealing with federally mandated programs, and by footnote reserved to another day an express reexamination of the limits, if any, on federal stipulations appended to the exercise of spending power. . . . This court's citations to the spending power cases in distinguishing the instant case from *National League of Cities* is flawless as those cases appear to read. But the cases themselves suggest that these broad principles and sweeping language do not imply unlimited license to effect federal will through use of the spending power. Those cases stand today in essentially the same posture as the Commerce Clause cases before *National League of Cities* was decided. While certainly not a license to disregard prior authority, the Supreme Court's footnote does suggest that a logical reexamination of the spending power cases is not precluded. At the very least, *National League of Cities* suggests that we should be watchful for "whatever may be the limits of [the power to fix the terms on which money allotments may be disbursed to the states]." *Lau v. Nichols,* 414 U.S. 563, 569, . . . (1974). Taking that cue, I do not believe that the sweeping import of the cited cases can be sustained anymore than was *Maryland v. Wirtz,* 392 U.S. 183, . . . (1968), the eight year old case overturned in *National League of Cities.* . . . Since it is clear that the federally mandated alteration of state government function in this case is precisely the kind condemned in *National League of Cities,* the principal logical distinction between the cases, if any, must be bottomed on the fiction that the spending power cases involve a freedom of choice which is not available under the mandated programs condemned in *National League of Cities.* The time has long since passed when the mere formality of choice should satisfy constitutional requirements.

This court should not ignore the practical financial needs of present day state governments. Those needs may well have ended the freedom of choice once inherent in such conditional grants. Few, if any, states or state subdivisions can now supply adequate services without the benefit of federal largesse. The possibility of refusing federal grants is often only apparent, not real. Particularly after a state has poured significant funding into a program or facility (*e.g.,* the erection of an airport) and attendant local expectations have grown, the state can hardly decline the federal aid necessary to maintain and improve that facility. When grants have risen to this level of necessity, attached conditions must withstand close constitutional scrutiny similar to that applied in *National League of Cities* to direct regulation of state governmental structure. The federally imposed requirements here fail to survive that scrutiny.

The Supreme Court has repeatedly expressed its concern with preserving the "essentials of state sovereignty," *National League of Cities,* 426 U.S. at 855 . . ., *quoting Maryland v. Wirtz,* 392 U.S. 183 . . . (1968) (Douglas, J., dissenting), a concern this court should not minimize. That concern has been manifested in a broad range of cases, which go far beyond direct regulation, the Commerce Clause, and the other particular issues of *National League of Cities. See, e.g., Paul v. Davis,* 424 U.S. 693 . . . (1976); *Rizzo v. Goode,* 423 U.S. 362 . . . (1976); *Younger v. Harris,* 401 U.S. 37 . . . (1971).

The Civil War Amendments were designed to insure that states are subject to federal power insofar as they fail to provide the protections of individual liberty mandated by the Bill of Rights. To that degree the prior understanding of federalism was modified by subsequent amendments. However, the concept of diversified power, as a check on the loss of individual liberty that would be inherent in one central government of unlimited power, remains vigorous. The essence of that constitutional concept is that there must be institutional encumbrances on government intrusion into individual liberty as well as restraints on direct and discrete intrusions. These constitutional concerns about restraints on governmental power through institutional structure are grounded not only in the Tenth Amendment but also in the "structural assumptions of the Constitution as a whole." L. TRIBE, AMERICAN CONSTITUTIONAL LAW 301 (1978).

Indeed, the cases cited in the majority opinion do not themselves mandate unlimited exercise of federal spending power. At no time has the Supreme Court suggested that *any* federal government exercise of any constitutional power is immune from the constraints of other constitutional provisions. *See, e.g., Lau v. Nichols,* 414 U.S. 563 . . . (1974); *Ivanhoe Irrigation Dist. v. McCracken,* 357 U.S. 275, 295 . . . (1958) (conditions must be "reasonable"); *King v. Smith,* 392 U.S. 309, 333 n.34 . . . (1968) ("unless based on some controlling constitutional prohibition"). The requirements of federalism provide such constraints, even when Congress is exercising powers that are otherwise plenary. *National League of Cities v. Usery.* . . .

This is not to suggest that the concept of federalism proscribes all conditions which might be attached to spending power legislation, even some conditions which might run afoul of *National League of Cities* broadly construed. As the concept immunizes the states from some federal intrusion, so the spending power itself obligates responsible disbursal of funds collected through federal power. It is inevitable that the states' desires to be immunized from federal stipulations will conflict with the responsible exercise of the spending power. Where those two constitutional concepts come into conflict some balancing must be employed. Such a conflict exists in the instant case. The duty of Congress to insure solvent management of the federal funds might require the states to make financial or governmental structural alterations which strictly speaking would run afoul of the standards set in *National League of Cities.* It is not suggested that Congress may not require some assurance of financially responsible participation by local units seeking federal tax collecting benefits. However, the concepts of institutional integrity embodied in the federal structure and so strongly reaffirmed in *National League of Cities* are sufficiently important to require, at a minimum, that the federal program employ the least intrusive method which will satisfy its responsible spending duties and that the stipulation be relevant to the primary purpose of the spending proposal. If the spending power is not confined in such a manner, then *National League of Cities* would become a silly and useless exercise. In this case no alternatives were offered. The state was given no opportunity to propose viable alternatives, but rather the

Secretary's designee indulged in precisely the kind of rigid mandate employed in *National League of Cities* sans the fictitious opportunity to reject the financial enticement.

Our recent satisfactory encounters with federal leadership in the area of explicit constitutional guarantees of individual liberties may well have beguiled us into subordinating in our minds the significance of the individual protection embodied in a division of authority. This case presents a prime opportunity to examine the scope, restraints and divisions of the exercise of power among constitutionally acknowledged institutions of government. The exercise of federal power in this case goes beyond the scope of its properly delegated authority and offends the restraints embodied in the concept of federalism. The result of effectively implementing the restraints embodied in that concept well may be a determination by Congress to forgo major spending projects if prohibited from imposing some favored but unconstitutional conditions. That, of course, would be the intended fruit of federalism, a restraint on the arrogation of federal power to the unreasonable detriment of state viability. This case should be reversed.

Comments: 1. The application of *National League* to federal grant-in-aid programs remains a major unresolved issue of critical importance to state and local governments. Most federal courts follow the majority opinion in the principal case and adopt the "option" theory to find no tenth amendment violation. What is the basis for the "balancing" test urged by Judge McKay in his dissenting opinion? Is it consistent with the plurality opinion in *National League*? With Justice Blackmun's concurring opinion?

In its *Federal Energy Regulatory Comm'n* decision, discussed *supra*, the Supreme Court said it "has recognized that valid federal enactments may have an effect on state policy — and may, indeed, be designed to induce state action in areas that otherwise would be beyond Congress's regulatory authority," citing *Oklahoma v. Civil Service Comm'n*, discussed *supra*. It is the majority opinion in *Walker Field* consistent with this interpretation of *Oklahoma?*

2. Other lower federal courts have upheld legislation enacted under the federal spending power that requires modifications in local government structure and authority. In *Montgomery County v. Califano*, 449 F. Supp. 1230 (D. Md. 1978), *aff'd*, 599 F.2d 1048 (4th Cir. 1979), a tenth amendment challenge was brought against the National Health Planning and Resources Development Act. That Act requires the designation of local Health Service Agencies with the authority, in part, to approve or disapprove local government applications for federal funding. The county contended that the Act "deprives state and local governments of any real responsibility or control over planning and regulation of local health services and thereby offends the Tenth Amendment." *Id.* at 1243. The county also claimed that the Act gave the agencies "unprecedented" authority to regulate in an area previously subject to state and local supervision. *Id.* The court rejected the tenth amendment challenge and commented in part:

> The Act imposes no civil or criminal penalties on such states or their officials. While the withholding of federal funds in some instances may resemble the imposition of civil or criminal penalties and while economic pressure may threaten such havoc to a state's well-being as to cause the federal legislation to cross the line which divides inducement from coercion, that line is not crossed in this case. Nor does the Act displace local initiative with federal directives. The Act mandates essentially a cooperative venture among the federal government and state and local authorities. It erects a health planning apparatus in which national guidelines are applied at the local level through newly created agencies manned by area residents, some or many of whom will be local elected officials. The Act appears carefully drawn to disperse widely the authority over health planning.

Id. at 1247.

In view of this case and the principal case, what conditions on local governments imposed under federal grant legislation might a federal court find unconstitutional? *See also North Carolina ex rel. Morrow v. Califano,* 445 F. Supp. 532 (E.D.N.C. 1977), *aff'd,* 435 U.S. 962 (1978) (federal statute upheld that required state certification of need for health care facilities).

3. Consider *New Hampshire Department of Employment Security v. Marshall,* 616 F.2d 240 (1st Cir.), *appeal dismissed & cert. denied,* 449 U.S. 806 (1980). This case was a challenge to the federal unemployment insurance law. State participation in the federal unemployment insurance program is not compelled. The federal legislation levies an unemployment insurance tax on private employers, but ninety percent of the tax is remitted if the employers make contributions to a state unemployment insurance fund. The federal government also makes administrative grants to the states. Faced with these inducements, all states have decided to participate in the program.

In this case, a challenge was brought to amendments to the federal law extending the unemployment insurance program to previously uncovered state and local government employees and employees of nonprofit schools. The court noted that *National League* was based in part on tenth amendment and in part on "impairment of state sovereignty" grounds. It then addressed the "state sovereignty" argument and held:

> Unlike the effect of the wage and hour standards in *Usery*, we do not think that this evidence establishes that extending coverage to the employees of New Hampshire and its political subdivisions will "significantly alter or displace" the ability of New Hampshire "to structure employer-employee relationships in such areas as fire prevention, police protection, sanitation, public health and parks and recreation." *National League of Cities v. Usery,* 426 U.S. at 851. . . . [The statute] does not set the wage rates or affect hours worked. All it does is insure unemployment benefits for state employees. Its administration is entirely within the control of the state. *See Pearce v. Wichita County,* 590 F.2d 128 (5th Cir. 1979), and *Marshall v. City of Sheboygan,* 577 F.2d 1 (7th Cir. 1978), in which the Equal Pay Act was upheld as constitutional under the commerce clause on the grounds that, unlike the minimum wage provisions condemned in *Usery*, the provisions of the Equal Pay Act did not impermissibly interfere with the states' employment scheme.

Id. at 248.

Do you agree with this analysis? There was evidence in the case that the cost to the state of compliance with the amendments would range between $330,000 and $1,100,000. Is this evidence relevant to the constitutional issue? If so, why? The same result was reached by the District of Columbia Circuit in *County of Los Angeles v. Marshall,* 631 F.2d 767 (D.C. Cir. 1980), in which over 1,200 plaintiffs, including state and local governments unsuccessfully challenged the 1976 unemployment compensation amendments.

For discussion of the status of federal grant-in-aid legislation under *National League* see LaPierre, *supra,* at 823-65; Comment, *Toward New Safeguards on Conditional Spending: Implictions of National League of Cities v. Usery,* 26 AM. U.L. REV. 726 (1977).

EQUAL EMPLOYMENT OPPORTUNITY COMMISSION v. WYOMING

United States Supreme Court
103 S. Ct. 1054 (1983)

JUSTICE BRENNAN delivered the opinion of the Court.

Under the Age Discrimination in Employment Act of 1967, . . . 29 U.S.C. § 621 *et seq.* . . . (ADEA or Act), it is unlawful for an employer to discriminate against any employee or potential employee on the basis of age, except "where age is a bona fide occupational qualification reasonably necessary to the normal operation of the particular business, or where the differentiation is based on reasonable factors other than age." The question presented in this case is whether Congress acted constitutionally when, in 1974, it extended the definition of "employer" under § 11(b) of the Act to include state and local governments. The United States District Court for the District of Wyoming, in an enforcement action brought by the Equal Employment Opportunity Commission (EEOC or Commission), held that, at least as applied to certain classes of state workers, the extension was unconstitutional. 514 F. Supp. 595 (1981). The Commission filed a direct appeal under 28 U. S. C. § 1252, and we noted probable jurisdiction. 454 U. S. 1140 (1982). We now reverse.

I

Efforts in Congress to prohibit arbitrary age discrimination date back at least to the 1950s. During floor debate over what was to become Title VII of the Civil Rights Act of 1964, amendments were offered in both the House and the Senate to ban discrimination on the basis of age as well as race, color, religion, sex, and national origin. These amendments were opposed at least in part on the basis that Congress did not yet have enough information to make a considered judgment about the nature of age discrimination, and each was ultimately defeated. . . . Title VII did, however, include a provision . . . which directed the Secretary of Labor to "make a full and complete study of the factors which might tend to result in discrimination in employment because of age and of the consequences of such discrimination on the economy and individuals affected," and to report the results of that study to Congress. That report was transmitted approximately one year later. . . .

In 1966, Congress directed the Secretary of Labor to submit specific legislative proposals for prohibiting age discrimination. . . . The Secretary transmitted a draft bill in early 1967, . . . and the President, in a message to Congress on older Americans, recommended its enactment and expressed serious concern about the problem of age discrimination . . . . Congress undertook further study of its own, and Committees in both the House and the Senate conducted detailed hearings on the proposed legislation. . . .

The Report of the Secretary of Labor, whose findings were confirmed throughout the extensive fact-finding undertaken by the Executive Branch and Congress, came to the following basic conclusions: (1) Many employers adopted specific age limitations in those States that had not prohibited them by their own anti-discrimination laws, although many other employers were able to operate successfully without them. (2) In the aggregate, these age limitations had a marked effect upon the employment of older workers. (3) Although age discrimination rarely was based on the sort of animus motivating some other forms of discrimination, it was based in large part on sterotypes unsupported by objective fact, and was often defended on grounds different from its actual causes. (4) Moreover, the available empirical evidence demonstrated that arbitrary age lines were in fact generally unfounded and that, as an overall matter, the performance of older workers was at least as good as that of younger workers. (5) Finally, arbitrary age discrimination was profoundly harmful in at least two ways. First, it deprived the national economy of the productive labor of millions of individuals and imposed on the governmental treasury substantially increased costs in unemployment insurance and federal Social Security benefits. Second, it inflicted on individual workers the economic and psychological injury accompanying the loss of the opportunity to engage in productive and satisfying occupations.

The product of the process of fact-finding and deliberation formally begun in 1964 was the Age Discrimination in Employment Act of 1967. The preamble to the Act emphasized both the individual and social costs of age discrimination.

The provisions of the Act as relevant here prohibited various forms of age discrimination in employment, including the discharge of workers on the basis of their age. Section 4(a), 29 U. S. C. § 623(a). The protection of the Act was limited, however, to workers between the ages of 40 and 65, . . . raised to age 70 in 1978 . . . . Moreover, in order to insure that employers were permitted to use neutral criteria not directly dependent on age, and in recognition of the fact that even criteria that are based on age are occasionally justified, the Act provided that certain otherwise prohibited employment practices would not be unlawful "where age is a bona fide occupational qualification reasonably necessary to the normal operation of the particular business, or where the differentiation is based on reasonable factors other than age." Section 4(f)(1), 29 U. S. C. § 623(f)(1).

The ADEA, as originally passed in 1967, did not apply to the Federal Government, to the States or their political subdivisions, or to employers with fewer than 25 employees. In a report issued in 1973, a Senate committee found this gap in coverage to be serious, and commented that "[t]here is . . . evidence that, like the corporate world, government managers also create an environment where young is sometimes better than old." Senate Special Committee on Aging, Improving the Age Discrimination Law, 93rd Cong., 1st Sess., 14 (Comm. Print 1973) . . . . In 1974, Congress extended the substantive prohibitions of the Act to employers having at least 20 workers, and to the Federal and State Governments.

II

Prior to the district court decision in this case, every federal court that considered the question upheld the constitutionality of the 1974 extension of the Age Discrimination in Employment Act to state and local workers as an exercise of Congress's power under either the Commerce Clause or § 5 of the Fourteenth Amendment.

This case arose out of the involuntary retirement at age 55 of Bill Crump, a District Game Division supervisor for the Wyoming Game and Fish Department. Crump's dismissal was based on a Wyoming statute that conditions further employment for Game and Fish Wardens who reach the age of 55 on "the approval of [their] employer." Crump filed a complaint with the EEOC, alleging that the Game and Fish Department had violated the Age Discrimination in Employment Act. After conciliation efforts between the Commission and the Game and Fish Department failed, the Commission filed suit in the District Court for the District of Wyoming against the State and various of its officials seeking declaratory and injunctive relief, back pay, and liquidated damages on behalf of Mr. Crump and other similarly situated.

The District Court, upon a motion by the defendants, dismissed the suit. It held that the Age Discrimination in Employment Act violated the doctrine of Tenth Amendment immunity articulated in *National League of Cities v. Usery,* . . . at least insofar as it regulated Wyoming's employment relationship with its game wardens and other law enforcement officials. . . . The District Court also held, citing *Pennhurst State School v. Halderman,* 541 U. S. 1 (1981), that the application of the ADEA to the States could not be justified as an exercise of Congress's power under § 5 of the Fourteenth Amendment because Congress did not explicitly state that it invoked that power in passing the 1974 amendments. . . .

III

The appellees have not claimed either in the District Court or in this Court that Congress exceeded the scope of its affirmative grant of power under the Commerce Clause in enacting the ADEA.... Rather, the District Court held and appellees argue that, at least with respect to state game wardens, application of the ADEA to the States is precluded by virtue of external constraints imposed on Congress's commerce powers by the Tenth Amendment.

A

National League of Cities v. Usery struck down Congress's attempt to extend the wage and hour provisions of the Fair Labor Standards Act to state and local governments. *National League of Cities* was grounded on a concern that the imposition of certain federal regulations on state governments might, if left unchecked, "allow 'the National Government [to] devour the essentials of state sovereignty' ".... It therefore drew from the Tenth Amendment an "affirmative limitation on the exercise of [congressional power under the Commerce Clause] akin to other commerce power affirmative limitations contained in the Constitution." ... The principle of immunity articulated in *National League of Cities* is a functional doctrine, however, whose ultimate purpose is not to create a sacred province of state autonomy, but to ensure that the unique benefits of a federal system in which the States enjoy a "separate and independent existence," ... not be lost through undue federal interference in certain core state functions.

Hodel v. Virginia Surface Mining & Reclamation Assn., Inc., ... summarized the hurdles that confront any claim that a state or local governmental unit should be immune from an otherwise legitimate exercise of the federal power to regulate commerce:

> [I]n order to succeed, a claim that congressional commerce power legislation is invalid under the reasoning of *National League of Cities* must satisfy *each* of three requirements. First, there must be a showing that the challenged statute regulates the "States as States." Second, the federal regulation must address matters that are indisputably "attribute[s]" of state sovereignty." And third, it must be apparent that the State's compliance with the federal law would directly impair their ability "to structure integral operations in areas of traditional governmental functions."

... Moreover,

> Demonstrating that these three requirements are met does not ... guarantee that a Tenth Amendment challenge to congressional commerce power action will succeed. There are situations in which the nature of the federal interest advanced may be such that it justifies state submission.

... The first requirement — that the challenged federal statute regulate the "State as States" — is plainly met in this case.[10] The second requirement — that the

---

[10] It is worth emphasizing, however, that it is precisely this prong of the *National League of Cities* test that marks it as a specialized immunity doctrine rather than a broad limitation on federal authority. As we made clear in *Hodel,*

> A wealth of precedent attests to congressional authority to displace or pre-empt state laws regulating *private* activity affecting interstate commerce when these laws conflict with federal law.... Although such congressional enactments obviously curtail or prohibit the States' prerogatives to make legislative choices respecting subjects the States may consider important, the Supremacy Clause permits no other result....

federal statute address an "undoubted attribute of state sovereignty" — poses significantly more difficulties.[11] We need not definitively resolve this issue, however, nor do we have any occasion to reach the final balancing step of the inquiry described in *Hodel,* for we are convinced that, even if Wyoming's decision to impose forced retirement on its game wardens does involve the exercise of an attribute of state sovereignty, the Age Discrimination in Employment Act does not "directly impair" the State's ability to "structure integral operations in areas of traditional governmental functions."

B

The management of state parks is clearly a traditional state function. . . . As we have already emphasized, however, the purpose of the doctrine of immunity articulated in *National League of Cities* was to protect States from federal intrusions that might threaten their "separate and independent existence." . . . Our decision as to whether the federal law at issue here directly impairs the States' ability to structure their integral operations must therefore depend, as it did in *National League of Cities* itself, on considerations of degree. . . . We conclude that the degree of federal intrusion in this case is sufficiently less serious than it was in *National League of Cities* so as to make it unnecessary for us to override Congress's express choice to extend its regulatory authority to the States.

In this case, appellees claim no substantial stake in their retirement policy other than "assur[ing] the physical preparedness of Wyoming game wardens to perform their duties." . . . Under the ADEA, however, the State may still, at the very least, assess the fitness of its game wardens and dimiss those wardens whom it reasonably finds to be unfit. Put another way, the Act requires the State to achieve its goals in a more individualized and careful manner than would otherwise be the case, but it does not require the state to abandon those goals, or to abandon the public policy decisions underlying them. . . .

Perhaps more important, appellees remain free under the ADEA to continue to do *precisely what they are doing now,* if they can demonstrate that age is a "bona fide occupational qualification" for the job of game warden. . . . Thus, in distinct contrast to the situation in *National League of Cities,* . . . even the state's discretion to achieve its goals *in the way it thinks best* is not being overridden entirely, but is merely being tested against a reasonable federal standard.

---

[11] *National League of Cities* held that "there are attributes of sovereignty attaching to every state government which may not be impaired by Congress" and that "[o]ne undoubted attribute of state sovereignty is the States' power to determine the wages which shall be paid to those whom they employ in order to carry out their governmental functions, what hours those persons will work, and what compensation will be provided where those employees may be called upon to work overtime." . . . Precisely what it meant by an "undoubted attribute of state sovereignty" is somewhat unclear, however, and our subsequent cases applying the *National League of Cities* test have had little occasion to amplify on our understanding of the concept.

A State's employment relationship with its workers can, under certain circumstances, be one vehicle for the exercise of its core sovereign functions. In *National League of Cities,* for example, the power to determine the wages of government workers was tied, among other things, to the exercise of the State's public welfare interest in providing jobs to persons who would otherwise be unemployed . . . . Moreover, some employment decisions are so clearly connected to the execution of underlying sovereign choices that they must be assimilated into them for purposes of the Tenth Amendment. See *id.,* at 850 (relating power to determine hours of government workers to unimpeded exercise of State's role as provider of emergency services). See generally *id.,* at 851 (stressing importance of state autonomy as to *"those* fundamental employment decisions *upon which their systems for performance of* [their dual functions of administering the public law and furnishing public services] *must rest"*) (emphasis added). But we are not to be understood to suggest that every state employment decision aimed simply at advancing a generalized interest in efficient management — even the efficient management of traditional state functions — should be considered to be an exercise of an "undoubted attribute of state sovereignty."

Finally, the Court's concern in *National League of Cities* was not only with the effect of the federal regulatory scheme on the particular decisions it was purporting to regulate, but also with the potential impact of that scheme on the States' ability to structure operations and set priorities over a wide range of decisions.... Indeed, *National League of Cities* spelled out in some detail how application of the federal wage and hour statute to the States threatened a virtual chain reaction of substantial and almost certainly unintended consequential effects on state decisionmaking.... Nothing in this case, however, portends anything like the same wide-ranging and profound threat to the structure of State governance.

The most tangible consequential effect identified in *National League of Cities* was financial: forcing the States to pay their workers a minimum wage and an overtime rate would leave them with less money for other vital state programs. The test of such financial effect as drawn in *National League of Cities* does not depend, however, on "particularized assessments of actual impact," which may vary from State to State and time to time, but on a more generalized inquiry, essentially legal rather than factual, into the direct and obvious effect of the federal legislation on the ability of the States to allocate their resources.... In this case, we cannot conclude from the nature of the ADEA that it will have either a direct or an obvious negative effect on state finances. Older workers with seniority may tend to get paid more than younger workers without seniority, and may by their continued employment accrue increased benefits when they do retire. But these increased costs, even if they were not largely speculative in their own right, might very well be outweighed by a number of other factors: Those same older workers, as long as they remain employed, will not have to be paid any pension benefits at all, and will continue to contribute to the pension fund. And, when they do retire, they will likely, as an actuarial matter, receive benefits for fewer years than workers who retire early.[15] Admittedly, as some of the *amici* point out, the costs of certain state health and other benefit plans would increase if they were automatically extended to older workers now forced to retire at an early age. But Congress, in passing the ADEA, included a provision specifically disclaiming a construction of the Act which would require that the health and similar benefits received by older workers be in all respects identical to those received by younger workers....

The second consequential effect identified in *National League of Cities* was on the States' ability to use their employment relationship with their citizens as a tool for pursuing social and economic policies beyond their immediate managerial goals. See, *e. g.*, 426 U. S., at 848 (offering jobs at below the minimum wage to persons who do not possess "minimum employment requirements"). Appellees, however, have claimed no such purposes for Wyoming's involuntary retirement statute. Moreover, whatever broader social or economic purposes could be imag-

---

[15] Appellees argue that prohibiting involuntary retirement at age 55 will somehow interfere with the State's ability to "enable those law enforcement officers who, due to the rigors of their occupations, cannot work beyond 55 to retire with a maximum [pension] benefit." ... They do not, of course, suggest that anything in the Age Discrimination in Employment Act forbids the state from continuing to provide maximum pension benefits to game wardens who retire at age 55. Rather, they claim that eliminating mandatory retirement will require the State to "balance [its pension] fund periodically based upon the number of employees who remained in service beyond 55," and that this would require "the complete restructing of the benefit program." Frankly, we do not see how the State's financial ability to provide maximum benefits to game wardens who retire at age 55 would be anything but helped by eliminating the involuntary retirement of workers eligible to receive those maximum benefits. Cf. National League of Cities v. Usery, ... (distinguishing Economic Stabilization Act from Fair Labor Standards Act on basis that former "operated to reduce the pressures upon state budgets rather than increase them").

ined for this particular Wyoming statute would not, we are convinced, bring with them either the breadth or the importance of the state policies identified in *National League of Cities*.[17]

IV

The extension of the ADEA to cover state and local governments, both on its face and as applied in this case, was a valid exercise of Congress's powers under the Commerce Clause. We need not decide whether it could also be upheld as an exercise of Congress's powers under § 5 of the Fourteenth Amendment. The judgment of the District Court is reversed, and the case is remanded for further proceedings consistent with this opinion.

So ordered.

[The dissenting opinion and the concurring opinion of Justice Stevens are omitted.—Eds.]

Comment: Is *National League* overruled? After the *Wyoming* decision, what federal legislation is likely to violate the tenth amendment?

In note 17 of the *Wyoming* decision the Court refers to the "well-defined federal interest in the legislation." Is this another qualification on *National League?* Does the Court mean that a "well-defined federal interest" can overcome an assertion that the tenth amendment is violated because a federal statute infringes on "indisputable" attributes of state sovereignty?

2. SUPREMACY: PREEMPTION AND BORROWING OF POWER

Nothing in the tenth amendment prevents the federal government from preempting state and local legislation through the supremacy clause, Article VI, clause 2 of the federal Constitution. This clause provides that the Constitution and all laws enacted pursuant thereto shall be the supreme law of the land.

Federal preemption presents questions quite similar to the questions presented by the state preemption of local ordinances, which is considered in Chapter 3, but there are differences. Federal legislative powers, unlike state legislative powers, are based on specific grants of power in the federal Constitution. For this reason, federal legislation is more programmatic than state legislation. It generally addresses itself to a specific program area and enacts for that program a sweeping and comprehensive federal regulatory scheme. In addition, the administration of this programmatic federal legislation is always delegated to a federal administrative agency that exercises more administrative discretion than its state counterparts.

For all of these reasons, preemption issues arising out of federal legislation may turn as much on the context of federal constitutional powers as on the specifics of the legislation at hand. Moreover, the comprehensive and programmatic reach of federal legislation, and the availability of extensive legislative

---

[17] Even if the minimal character of the federal intrusion in this case did not lead us to hold that the ADEA survives the third prong of the *Hodel* inquiry, it might still, when measured against the well-defined federal interest in the legislation, require us to find that the nature of that interest "justifies state submission." We note, incidentally, that the strength of the federal interest underlying the Act is not negated by the fact that the federal government happens to impose mandatory retirement on a small class of its own workers.... Once Congress has asserted a federal interest, and once it has asserted the strength of that interest, we have no warrant for reading into the ebbs and flows of political decisionmaking a conclusion that Congress was insincere in that declaration, and must from that point on evaluate the sufficiency of the federal interest as a matter of law rather than of psychological analysis.

histories at the federal level, makes the federal legislative purpose at the same time more discoverable and more expansive.

Just as in the state cases dealing with the same problem, many of the federal cases considering problems of federal preemption become mired in the specifics of the federal legislative program as it affects the state or local enactment. Nevertheless, cases arise in which there has been no explicit coverage of the subject area to which the state legislation or the local ordinance applies. The case that follows, which deals with potentially conflicting federal and state regulation of immigrant labor, is in this category. The section continues with examples of preemption problems arising under federal statutes that contain explicit preemption provisions, and closes with a related problem, the extent to which localities may borrow regulatory power from federal statutes.

DeCANAS v. BICA

United States Supreme Court
424 U.S. 351 (1976)

Mr. Justice Brennan delivered the opinion of the Court.

California Labor Code § 2805(a) provides that "No employer shall knowingly employ an alien who is not entitled to lawful residence in the United States if such employment would have an adverse effect on lawful resident workers." The question presented in this case is whether § 2805(a) is unconstitutional either because it is an attempt to regulate immigration and naturalization or because it is pre-empted under the Supremacy Clause, Art. VI, cl. 2, of the Constitution, by the Immigration and Nationality Act, 8 U.S.C. § 1101 *et seq.* (INA), the comprehensive federal statutory scheme for regulation of immigration and naturalization.

Petitioners, who are immigrant migrant farmworkers, brought this action pursuant to § 2805(c) against respondent farm labor contractors in California Superior Court. The complaint alleged that respondents had refused petitioners continued employment due to a surplus of labor resulting from respondents' knowing employment, in violation of § 2805(a), of aliens not lawfully admitted to residence in the United States. Petitioners sought reinstatement and a permanent injunction against respondents' wilful employment of illegal aliens.[2] The Superior Court, in an unreported opinion, dismissed the complaint, holding "that Labor Code 2805 is unconstitutional . . . [because] [i]t encroaches upon, and interferes with, a comprehensive regulatory scheme enacted by Congress in the exercise of its exclusive power over immigration. . . ." The California Court of Appeal, Second Appellate District, affirmed, 40 Cal. App. 3d 976, 115 Cal. Rptr. 444 (1974). The Court of Appeal held that § 2805(a) is an attempt to regulate the conditions for admission of foreign nationals, and therefore unconstitutional because, "in the area of immigration and naturalization, congressional power is exclusive." . . . The Court of Appeal further indicated that state regulatory power over this subject matter was foreclosed when Congress, "as an incident of national sovereignty," enacted the INA as a comprehensive scheme governing all aspects of immigration and naturalization, including the employment of aliens, and "specifically and intentionally declined to add sanctions on employers to its

---

[2] We assume *arguendo* in this opinion, in referring to "illegal aliens," that the prohibition of § 2805(a) only applies to aliens who would not be permitted to work in the United States under pertinent federal laws and regulations. Whether that is the correct construction of the statute is an issue that will remain open for determination by the state courts on remand. See Part III, *infra*.

control mechanism." *Ibid.*[4] The Supreme Court of California denied review. We granted certiorari, 422 U.S. 1040 (1975). We reverse.

I

Power to regulate immigration is unquestionably exclusively a federal power. ... But the Court has never held that every state enactment which in any way deals with aliens is a regulation of immigration and thus *per se* pre-empted by this constitutional power, whether latent or exercised. For example, *Takahashi v. Fish & Game Comm'n,* 334 U.S. 410, 415 (1948), and *Graham v. Richardson,* 403 U.S. 365, 372-373 (1971), cited a line of cases that upheld certain discriminatory state treatment of aliens lawfully within the United States. Although the "doctrinal foundations" of the cited cases, which generally arose under the Equal Protection Clause, ... "were undermined in *Takahashi,*" see *In re Griffiths,* 413 U.S. 717, 718-722 (1973), *Graham v. Richardson, supra* at 372-375, they remain authority that, standing alone, the fact that aliens are the subject of a state statute does not render it a regulation of immigration, which is essentially a determination of who should or should not be admitted into the country, and the conditions under which a legal entrant may remain. Indeed, there would have been no need, in cases such as *Graham, Takahashi,* or *Hines v. Davidowitz,* 312 U.S. 52 (1941), even to discuss the relevant congressional enactments in finding pre-emption of state regulation if all state regulation of aliens was *ipso facto* regulation of immigration, for the existence *vel non* of federal regulation is wholly irrelevant if the Constitution of its own force requires pre-emption of such state regulation. In this case, California has sought to strengthen its economy by adopting federal standards in imposing criminal sanctions against state employers who knowingly employ aliens who have no federal right to employment within the country; even if such local regulation has some purely speculative and indirect impact on immigration, it does not thereby become a constitutionally proscribed regulation of immigration that Congress itself would be powerless to authorize or approve. Thus, absent congressional action, § 2805 would not be an invalid state incursion on federal power.

II

Even when the Constitution does not itself commit exclusive power to regulate a particular field to the Federal Government, there are situations in which state regulation, although harmonious with federal regulation, must nevertheless be invalidated under the Supremacy Clause. As we stated in *Florida Lime & Avocado Growers, Inc. v. Paul,* 373 U.S. 132, 142 (1963):

> federal regulation ... should not be deemed preemptive of state regulatory power in the absence of persuasive reasons — either that the nature of the regulated subject matter permits no other conclusion, or that Congress has unmistakably so ordained.

In this case, we cannot conclude that pre-emption is required either because "the nature of the subject matter [regulation of employment of illegal aliens] permits no other conclusion," or because "Congress has unmistakably so ordained" that result.

---

[4] H.R. 982, now pending in Congress, would amend 8 U.S.C. § 1324(a) to provide a penalty for knowingly employing an alien not lawfully admitted to the United States. [Would the enactment of this bill preempt the California law, which also imposes a peanlty?—Eds.]

States possess broad authority under their police powers to regulate the employment relationship to protect workers within the State. Child labor laws, minimum and other wages laws, laws affecting occupational health and safety, and workmen's compensation laws are only a few examples. California's attempt in § 2805(a) to prohibit the knowing employment by California employers of persons not entitled to lawful residence in the United States, let alone to work here, is certainly within the mainstream of such police power regulation. Employment of illegal aliens in times of high unemployment deprives citizens and legally admitted aliens of jobs; acceptance by illegal aliens of jobs on sub-standard terms as to wages and working conditions can seriously depress wage scales and working conditions of citizens and legally admitted aliens; and employment of illegal aliens under such conditions can diminish the effectiveness of labor unions. These local problems are particularly acute in California in light of the significant influx into that State of illegal aliens from neighboring Mexico. In attempting to protect California's fiscal interests and lawfully resident labor force from the deleterious effects on its economy resulting from the employment of illegal aliens, § 2805(a) focuses directly upon these essentially local problems and is tailored to combat effectively the perceived evils.

Of course, even state regulation designed to protect vital state interests must give way to paramount federal legislation. But we will not presume that Congress, in enacting the INA, intended to oust state authority to regulate the employment relationship covered by § 2805(a) in a manner consistent with pertinent federal laws. Only a demonstration that complete ouster of state power—including state power to promulgate laws not in conflict with federal laws—was "the clear and manifest purpose of Congress" would justify that conclusion. *Florida Lime & Avocado Growers, Inc. v. Paul, supra,* at 146, quoting *Rice v. Sante Fe Elevator Corp.,* 331 U.S. 218, 230 (1947). Respondents have not made that demonstration. They fail to point out, and an independent review does not reveal, any specific indication in either the wording or the legislative history of the INA that Congress intended to preclude even harmonious state regulation touching on aliens in general, or the employment of illegal aliens in particular.[6]

Nor can such intent be derived from the scope and detail of the INA. The central concern of the INA is with the terms and conditions of admission to the country and the subsequent treatment of aliens lawfully in the country. The comprehensiveness of the INA scheme for regulation of immigration and naturalization, without more, cannot be said to draw in the employment of illegal aliens as "plainly within ... [that] central aim of federal regulation." *San Diego Unions v. Garmon,* 359 U.S. 236, 244 (1959). This conclusion is buttressed by the fact that comprehensiveness of legislation governing entry and stay of aliens was to be expected in light of the nature and complexity of the subject. "Given the

---

[6] Of course, state regulation not congressionally sanctioned that discriminates against aliens lawfully admitted to the country is impermissible if it imposes additional burdens not contemplated by Congress:

> The Federal Government has broad constitutional powers in determining what aliens shall be admitted to the United States, the period they may remain, regulation of their conduct before naturalization, and the terms and conditions of their naturalization. See Hines v. Davidowitz, 312 U.S. 52, 66. Under the Constitution the states are granted no such powers; *they can neither add to nor take from the conditions lawfully imposed by Congress upon admission, naturalization and residence* of aliens in the United States or the several states. State laws which impose discriminatory burdens upon the entrance or residence of *aliens lawfully within* the United States conflict with this constitutionally derived federal power to regulate immigration, and have accordingly been held invalid. Takahashi v. Fish & Game Commission, 334 U.S. 410, 419 (emphasis supplied). ...

complexity of the matter addressed by Congress in ... [the INA], a detailed statutory scheme was both likely and appropriate, completely apart from any questions of pre-emptive intent." *New York Department of Social Services v. Dublino,* 413 U.S. 405, 415 (1973).

It is true that a proviso to 8 U.S.C. § 1324, making it a felony to harbor illegal entrants, provides that "employment (including the usual and normal practices incident to employment) shall not be deemed to constitute harboring." But this is at best evidence of a peripheral concern with employment of illegal entrants, and *San Diego Unions v. Garmon,* 359 U.S., at 243, admonished that "due regard for the presuppositions of our embracing federal system, including the principle of diffusion of power not as a matter of doctrinaire localism but as a promoter of democracy, has required us not to find withdrawal from the States of power to regulate where the activity regulated was a merely peripheral concern of the [federal regulation]. ..."

Finally, rather than evidence that Congress "has unmistakably ... ordained" exclusivity of federal regulation in this field, there is evidence in the form of the 1974 amendments to the Farm Labor Contractor Registration Act, 7 U.S.C. § 2041 *et seq.*, that Congress intends that States may, to the extent consistent with federal law, regulate the employment of illegal aliens. Section 2044(b) authorizes revocation of the certificate of registration of any farm labor contractor found to have employed "an alien not lawfully admitted for permanent residence, or who has not been authorized by the Attorney General to accept employment." Section 2045 prohibits farm labor contractors from employing "an alien not lawfully admitted for permanent residence or who has not been authorized by the Attorney General to accept employment." Of particular significance to our inquiry is the further provision that "This chapter and the provisions contained herein are *intended to supplement State action* and compliance with this chapter shall not excuse anyone from compliance with *appropriate State law and regulation.*" *Id.*, § 2051 (emphasis supplied). Although concerned only with agricultural employment, the Farm Labor Contractor Registration Act is thus persuasive evidence that the INA should not be taken as legislation by Congress expressing its judgment to have uniform federal regulations in matters affecting employment of illegal aliens and therefore barring state legislation such as § 2805(a).

Hines v. Davidowitz, 312 U.S. 52 (1941), and *Pennsylvania v. Nelson,* 350 U.S. 497 (1956), upon which respondents rely, are fully consistent with this conclusion. *Hines* held that Pennsylvania's Alien Registration Act was pre-empted by the federal Alien Registration Act. *Nelson* held that the Pennsylvania Sedition Act was pre-empted by the federal Smith Act. Although both cases relied on the comprehensiveness of the federal regulatory schemes in finding pre-emptive intent, both federal statutes were in the specific field which the States were attempting to regulate, while here there is no indication that Congress intended to preclude state law in the area of employment regulation. And *Nelson* stated that even in the face of the general immigration laws, States would have the right "to enforce their sedition laws at times when the Federal Government has not occupied the field and is not protecting the entire country from seditious conduct." 350 U.S., at 500. Moreover, in neither *Hines* nor *Nelson* was there affirmative evidence, as here, that Congress sanctioned concurrent state legislation on the subject covered by the challenged state law. Furthermore, to the extent those cases were based on the predominance of federal interest in the fields of immigration and foreign affairs, there would not appear to be a similar federal interest in a situation in which the state law is fashioned to remedy local problems, and operates only on local employers, and only with respect to individuals whom the Federal Government has already declared cannot work in this country. Finally, the Pennsylvania statutes in *Hines* and *Nelson* imposed burdens on aliens lawfully within the country that created conflicts with various federal laws.

III

There remains the question whether, although the INA contemplates some room for state legislation, § 2805(a) is nevertheless unconstitutional because it "stands as an obstacle to the accomplishment and execution of the full purposes and objectives of Congress" in enacting the INA. *Hines v. Davidowitz, supra* 312 U.S., at 67; *Florida Lime & Avocado Growers, Inc. v. Paul, supra* 373 U.S., at 141. We do not think that we can address that inquiry upon the record before us. The Court of Appeal did not reach the question in light of its decision, today reversed, that Congress had completely barred state action in the field of employment of illegal aliens. Accordingly, there are questions of construction of § 2805(a) to be settled by the California courts before a determination is appropriate whether, as construed, § 2805(a), "can be enforced without impairing the federal superintendence of the field" covered by the INA. *Id.*, at 142.

For example, § 2805(a) requires that to be employed an alien must be "entitled to lawful residence." In its application, does the statute prevent employment of aliens who, although "not entitled to lawful residence in the United States," may under federal law be permitted to work here? Petitioners conceded at oral argument that, on its face, § 2805(a) would apply to such aliens and thus unconstitutionally conflict with federal law. They point, however, to the limiting construction given § 2805(a) in Administrative Regulations promulgated by the California Director of Industrial Relations. California Administrative Code, Title 8, part 1, c. 8, art. 1, § 16209 defines an alien "entitled to lawful residence" as follows: "An alien entitled to lawful residence shall mean any non-citizen of the United States who is in possession of a Form I-151, Alien Registration Receipt Card, or any other document issued by the United States Immigration and Naturalization Service which authorizes him to work." *Dolores Canning Co. v. Howard*, 40 Cal. App. 3d 673, 677 n. 3, 115 Cal. Rptr. 435, 436 n. 3 (1974). Whether these regulations were before the Superior Court in this case does not appear, and the Court of Appeal found § 2805(a) unconstitutional without addressing whether it conflicts with federal law. Obviously it is for the California courts to decide the effect of these administrative regulations in construing § 2805(a), and thus to decide in the first instance whether and to what extent, see n. 5, *supra* § 2805 as construed would conflict with the INA or other federal laws or regulations. It suffices that this Court decide at this time that the Court of Appeal erred in holding that Congress in the INA precluded any state authority to regulate the employment of illegal aliens.

The judgment of the Court of Appeal is reversed and the case is remanded for further proceedings not inconsistent with this opinion.

It is so ordered.

Reversed and remanded.

MR. JUSTICE STEVENS took no part in the consideration or decision of this case.

Comments: 1. In *Hines v. Davidowitz,* which is discussed in the principal case, the Court summarized the law of federal preemption as follows:

> This Court, in considering the validity of state laws in the light of treaties or federal laws touching the same subject, has made use of the following expressions: conflicting; contrary to, occupying the field; repugnance; difference; irreconcilability; inconsistency; violation; curtailment; and interference. But none of these expressions provides an infallible constitutional test or an exclusive constitutional yardstick. In the final analysis, there can be no one crystal clear, distinctly marked formula. Our primary function is to determine whether, under the circumstances of this particular case, Pennsylvania's law stands as an obstacle to the accomplishment and execution of the full purposes and objectives of Congress.

Id. at 67. Does the thrust of this quotation indicate that the Court might have been able to reach a contrary opinion in *Bica*? Consider that control over immigration is vested in Congress by the Constitution, and indeed is an exclusive federal power. Was the Court perhaps misled because the California statute, in form, was not a regulation of immigration? The Court's characterization of the California statute as one dealing with a "local" concern is interesting considering that labor markets in the United States are not insular, and in view of *Edwards v. California,* 314 U.S. 160 (1941). In *Skafte v. Rorex,* 553 P.2d 830 (Colo. 1976), the Colorado court, on the authority of *Bica,* found no federal preemption of a state statute denying aliens the right to vote in school elections.

2. The United States Supreme Court has continued its reluctance to invalidate state legislation not directly in conflict with or expressly preempted by federal legislation. In *Exxon Corp. v. Governor of Maryland,* 437 U.S. 117 (1978), the Court upheld a Maryland statute requiring, in part, uniform application of temporary price reductions granted by oil producers and refiners to all retail service stations they supplied, regardless of localized competitive conditions. Appellant oil companies alleged this provision violated § 2(b) of the Clayton Act, which permits price discrimination in good faith to meet local competition.

The Court recognized a conflict existed between the state statute and the policy favoring competition found in the federal antitrust laws, but refused to find preemption. The conflict was hypothetical, since there were no clear conflicts between the federal and state law. The Court also feared a finding of preemption based upon the state statute's adverse effect on competition could logically lead to the effective destruction of state economic regulation.

In *Philadelphia v. New Jersey,* 437 U.S. 617 (1978), the Court upheld, against a supremacy clause challenge, a New Jersey statute prohibiting importation of liquid or solid waste into the state. Although it struck down the statute as violative of the commerce clause, the Court ruled that Congress had neither expressly nor implicitly preempted the field of interstate waste transportation. The Court found express provision in the Solid Waste Disposal Act, 42 U.S.C. § 6901 et seq., for continued state control over waste management. *See also New York Telephone Co. v. New York Labor Department,* 440 U.S. 519 (1979) (congressional silence in enacting the National Labor Relations Act created an inference that the states can make policy determinations regarding unemployment benefits for striking workers).

When federal legislation contains an explicit preemption provision, or when Congress manifests a clear purpose to preempt, the Supreme Court has invoked the supremacy clause to strike the state statute even when the federal law encroaches upon a field traditionally controlled by the states. *See Jones v. Rath Packing Co.,* 430 U.S. 519 (1977). *Accord Douglas v. Seacoast Products, Inc.,* 431 U.S. 265 (1977).

In *Ray v. Atlantic Richfield Co.,* 435 U.S. 151 (1978), the Court found certain requirements of the state of Washington Tanker Law preempted by direct conflict with the purpose and intent of the federal Ports and Waterways Safety Act of 1972 (PWSA), 33 U.S.C. § 1221 et seq., 46 U.S.C. § 391a. The Tanker Law regulated oil tanker design, size, and movement within Puget Sound. Oil refiners and shippers brought suit alleging preemption by the PWSA. At issue were three operative provisions of the Washington law requiring: (1) that all tankers exceeding a minimum weight carry state-licensed pilots while navigating the Sound; (2) that no tanker exceeding a maximum weight enter the Sound; and (3) that tankers below the maximum weight enter only if they either meet certain design safety standards or use tug escorts.

The Court noted the similarity of purpose in both the federal and state statutes. Each sought to ensure vessel safety and protect the marine environment against oil spillage. In examining the operative provisions individually, the Court found that each was preempted. The pilotage licensing requirement was preempted in part by conflict with an express directive in the PWSA. The Court found the state's ban on tankers exceeding a maximum weight preempted by the PWSA's legislative history and actions by the Secretary of Transportation. The legislative history showed Congress desired a single decision-maker, "someone with an overview of all the possible ramifications of the regulation of oil tankers ... [acting] only after balancing all of the competing interests," to promulgate all regulations concerning tanker size. *Id.* at 177. The Secretary had promulgated a "vessel-traffic-control system" for the Sound which contained only limited restrictions on supertanker operation. This failure to ban the large tankers by the federal decision-maker charged with authority to do so precluded the state from enforcing its size limitation.

On the design safety standards issue, the Court stated:

> This statutory pattern shows that Congress, insofar as design characteristics are concerned, has entrusted to the Secretary the duty of determining which oil tankers are sufficiently safe to be allowed to proceed in the navigable waters of the United States. This indicates to us that Congress intended uniform national standards for design and construction of tankers that would foreclose the imposition of different or more stringent state requirements. In particular, as we see it, Congress did not anticipate that a vessel found to be in compliance with the Secretary's design and construction regulations and holding a Secretary's permit, or its equivalent, to carry the relevant cargo would nevertheless be barred by state law from operating in the navigable waters of the United States on the ground that its design characteristics constitute an undue hazard.
>
> ... [T]he mere fact that a vessel has been inspected and found to comply with the Secretary's vessel safety regulations does not prevent a State or city from enforcing local laws having other purposes, such as a local smoke abatement law. ... But in none of the relevant cases sustaining the application of state laws to federally licensed or inspected vessels did the federal licensing or inspection procedure implement a substantive rule of federal law addressed to the object also sought to be achieved by the challenged state regulation. *Huron Portland Cement Co. v. Detroit,* for example, made it plain that there was "no overlap between the scope of the federal ship inspection laws and that of the municipal ordinance ..." there involved. [362 U.S.] at 446 .... The purpose of the "federal inspection statutes [was] to insure the seagoing safety of vessels ... to affor[d] protection from the perils of maritime navigation," while "[b]y contrast, the sole aim of the Detroit ordinance [was] the elimination of air pollution to protect the health and enhance the cleanliness of the local community." *Id.*, at 445 ....
>
> Here, we have the very situation that *Huron Portland Cement Co. v. Detroit* ... put aside. Title II [of the PWSA] aims at insuring vessel safety and protecting the marine environment; and the Secretary must issue all design and construction regulations that he deems necessary for these ends, after considering the specified statutory standards. The federal scheme thus aims precisely at the same ends as does ... the Tanker Law. Furthermore, under the PWSA, after considering the statutory standards and issuing all design requirements that in his judgment are necessary, the Secretary inspects and certifies each vessel as sufficiently safe to protect the marine environment and issues a permit or its equivalent to carry tank-vessel cargoes. Refusing to accept the federal judgment, however, the State now seeks to exclude from Puget Sound vessels certified by the Secretary as having acceptable design characteristics, unless they satisfy the different and higher design requirements imposed by state law. The Supremacy Clause dictates that the federal judgment that a vessel is safe to navigate United States waters prevail over the contrary state judgment.
>
> Enforcement of the state requirements would at least frustrate what seems to us to be the evident congressional intention to establish a uniform federal regime controlling the design of oil tankers....

Id. at 163-66. *See generally* Comment, *Environmental Law: A Reevaluation of Federal Pre-Emption and the Commerce Clause,* 7 FORDHAM URB. L.J. 649 (1979).

3. How far does a finding of preemption extend? For example, does federal preemption of state regulation of radiation hazards, see *Pacific Legal Foundation v. State Energy Resources Conservation & Development Commission,* 659 F.2d 903 (9th Cir. 1981), affect a common law tort action for damages resulting from discharge of non-radioactive water into waterways by a nuclear power plant? In *Van Dissel v. Jersey Power & Light Co.,* 438 A.2d 563 (N.J. App. Div. 1981), riparian landowners brought suit against the owner of a nuclear power plant claiming that temperature changes in water caused by the processes of the nuclear plant had created a warm water environment allowing for the proliferation of shipworms which, in turn, destroyed wooden docks, appurtenances and other structures extending into the waterways. Plaintiffs claimed that the exclusive federal regulatory jurisdiction over radiological hazards did not deprive them of their state tort claims for non-radiological damages. Holding the claim preempted by federal law, the court found that the change in water temperature was directly related to the cooling system. The radioactive waste disposal system was found to be an integral part of the cooling system. Since the cooling system was authorized and approved by a federal agency, the plaintiffs' assertion of state tort claims was an impermissible interference with the radioactive waste discharge system.

A NOTE ON THE BORROWING OF FEDERAL SUBSTANTIVE POWERS BY STATE AND LOCAL GOVERNMENTS

As Congress continues to enact new substantive programs it places new substantive responsibilities on states and local governments that may take some time for state legislatures to pick up, either in state legislation authorizing state programs or authorizing local regulatory, participatory and other activities. A question arises whether state and local governments can "borrow" substantive powers contained in federal grant-in-aid or other legislation.

This issue arose in extensive litigation over the authority of the City of Tacoma, Washington, to build a hydroelectric power dam. In the first case, *Washington v. Federal Power Commission,* 207 F.2d 391 (9th Cir. 1953), the state challenged a license granted to the city by the Commission to construct the dam. Section 9(b) of the Federal Power Act provided that license applicants must demonstrate to the Commission that they had complied with applicable state requirements. The state pointed out that the city had not complied with various state requirements, including a twenty-five-foot height limit and a requirement for a water diversion permit.

The court upheld the Commission:

> The rationale of the objectors' contentions has already been considered and rejected by the Supreme Court in *First Iowa Hydro-Elec. Co-op. v. Power Commission,* 1946, 328 U.S. 152 . . . . In that case the United States Supreme Court analyzed § 9 (b) in the light of an Iowa statute which prohibited the building or maintaining of a dam on any navigable stream of the State of Iowa without a permit from the Executive Council of the State. In order to obtain a State permit, an applicant was required to comply with State regulation of the project. The Supreme Court held that the Iowa licensing provisions were in direct conflict with the Federal Power Act, and that if a State license were a "condition precedent to securing a federal license for the same project under the Federal Power Act . . . the Executive Council of Iowa [would possess] a veto power over the federal project. Such a veto power easily could destroy the effectiveness of the Federal Act." . . . Indeed, if § 9 (b) were construed to require compliance with state laws in every instance, it would make every application to the Federal Power Commission subject to state control in direct contradiction to the Congressional mandate that the project be subject to "the judgment of the Commission." Therefore, the Supreme Court concluded, § 9 (b) does not in itself require compliance with state law; it only empowers the

Commission to require such evidence of compliance with state law as, in the Commission's judgment, would be "appropriate to effect the purposes of a federal license on the navigable waters of the United States." ...

The Commission in our case acted within the scope of its discretion in not requiring Tacoma to show compliance with the laws of the State of Washington regulating the construction of dams in Washington, because compliance with those laws would have prevented the development of the Cowlitz Project; and in the opinion of the Commission of the Cowlitz Project was "best adapted to a comprehensive plan" for the development of a concededly navigable stream. The Federal Government's Constitutional authority to regulate commerce and navigation includes the "power to control the erection of structures in navigable waters," *United States v. Appalachian Power Co.*, 1940, 311 U.S. 377, 405. The Federal Government's power over navigable waters is superior to that of the state. ...

The objectors further contend that Tacoma, as a creature of the State of Washington, cannot act in opposition to the policy of the State or in derogation of its laws.

Again, we turn to the *First Iowa* case, *supra*. There, too, the applicant for a federal license was a creature of the state and the chief opposition came from the state itself. Yet, the Supreme Court permitted the applicant to act inconsistently with the declared policy of its creator, and to prevail in obtaining a license.

Consistent with the *First Iowa* case, *supra* we conclude that the state laws cannot prevent the Federal Power Commission from issuing a license or bar the licensee from acting under the license to build a dam on a navigable stream since the stream is under the dominion of the United States. However, we do not touch the question as to the legal capacity of the City of Tacoma to initiate and act under the license once it is granted. There may be limitations in the City Charter, for instance, as to indebtedness limitations. Questions of this nature may be inquired into by the Commission as relevant to the practicability of the plan, but the Commission has no power to adjudicate them.

Id. at 396-97.

This case was appealed to the United States Supreme Court, which denied certiorari. 347 U.S. 936 (1954).

In the meantime, independent litigation was started in the state courts of Washington to validate the bond issue required for the project. Here the state raised, for the first time, the point that the city, in order to carry out its project, would need to condemn state-owned land which was being used for a fish hatchery, and that statutory authority to condemn the state's property had not been conferred on the city. In *City of Tacoma v. Taxpayers of Tacoma*, 307 P.2d 567 (Wash. 1957), the court held:

> There remains the subsidiary question: can a municipal corporation of this state be endowed, by Federal legislation, with power to condemn state-owned lands previously dedicated to a public use, in the absence of power and capacity so to act under state statutes; or, specifically, can the city of Tacoma receive the power and capacity to condemn state-owned lands previously dedicated to a public use, from the license issued to it by the Federal Power Commission in the absence of such power and capacity under state statutes?

> This is not a question of the right of the Federal government to control all phases of activity on navigable streams, nor a question of its power, under the Federal Power Act, to delegate that right. It only questions the capacity of a municipal corporation of this state to act under such license when its exercise requires the condemnation of state-owned property dedicated to a public use.
> ....

In the instant case, the subject matter—the inherent inability of the city to condemn state lands dedicated to a public use—does not present a question of *state statutory prohibition;* it presents a question of *lack of state statutory power* in the city. It does not present a Federal question; it presents a question peculiarly within the jurisdiction of the state of Washington.

The Federal government may not confer corporate capacity upon local units of government beyond the capacity given them by their creator, and the Federal Power Act, as we read it, does not purport to do so.

If it be held that the Federal government may endow a state-created municipality with powers greater than those given it by its creator, the state legislature, a momentous and novel theory of constitutional government has been evolved that will eventually relegate a sovereign state to a position of impotence never contemplated by the framers of our Constitutions, state and Federal.

Id. at 576-77.

The Supreme Court reversed and remanded. 357 U.S. 320 (1958). It held that the question whether the federal license had delegated federal eminent domain power to the city was foreclosed by the Ninth Circuit decision, *supra,* and that the attack on the bond validation was impermissibly collateral.

Professor LaPierre, *supra,* at 1032, states that this litigation is "best interpreted as confined to the question of the validity of state law restrictions that apply equally to public and private licensees of the FPC and national authority to preempt these restrictions." He states that these cases do not address the question of national power to supplement state law. He also cites *Washington Public Power Supply System v. Pacific Northwest Power Co.,* 217 F. Supp. 481 (D. Or. 1963), *vacated,* 332 F.2d 87 (9th Cir. 1964). This case held that when a state law did not authorize a municipality to construct hydroelectric facilities outside the state, this authority could not be conferred by an FPC license.

B. FEDERAL STANDARDS FOR STATE AND LOCAL PROGRAMS

1. IN GENERAL

Much like its counterparts at the state level, federal statutes preempting state and local legislation also legislate standards to which state and local regulations must conform. State and local air pollution emission control legislation, for example, must contain emission limitations at least as stringent as those adopted under the federal law. Federal legislation, again like its state counterparts, may also provide explicit standards for program implementation which state and local governments must meet. In some instances these federal standards are attached to federal programs of financial assistance, and compliance with federal standards is a condition to the continuing receipt of federal aid. In other instances the federal legislation may be enacted pursuant to federal interstate commerce or other powers, and compliance with federal standards is mandated through this exercise of congressional authority.

Federal legislative standards can fall equally on state or local governments, or on both. An example of a federal program imposing legislative standards on local governments is the Housing and Community Development Act of 1974, 42 U.S.C. § 5301 et seq. (1976, subsequently amended, 1981), which replaces earlier urban renewal and related federal programs and imposes broadly phrased restrictions on the community development projects for which federal assistance available under this program may be used. An important component of the local effort in this program is the locally prepared Housing Assistance Plan, which must be prepared by the recipient local government and which indicates how that government will meet its lower income housing need.

An example of a federal program principally related to state government is the massive program of federal aid for highways, 23 U.S.C. § 101 et seq. (1970, subsequently amended, 1978). This program provides extensive federal grants for a state-constructed and state-operated program of interstate, primary, secondary, and urban highways. The agency charged with the implementation of this program at the state level is the state highway agency. The federal-aid highway program has elements that require the participation of both regional agencies and local governments, as in the regional transportation planning process.

A cursory review of the many federal programs that impose standards on state and local governments would only confuse the enterprising student. We focus therefore, on the mental health program as a program in which state and local roles had been established and which the federal government later entered. This program presents a fascinating case study of the legal problems that arise when the federal government decides to influence the content of state and local compliance. Particular attention will be given to programs affecting mentally retarded persons institutionalized in state facilities receiving federal finacial assistance. This is an area of widespread public interest in which the controversies attendant on affective regulation have only been partially resolved.

It may also be helpful to briefly outline two other federal statutory programs that illustrate federal attempts to influence state regulatory action consistent with federal statutory requirements:

Coordinated National Recreational Boating Safety and Facilities Improvement Program

This program was enacted, as the congressional declaration of policy and purpose states, "to improve boating safety and facilities and to foster greater development, use, and enjoyment of all the waters of the United States." Congress encouraged the states, the boating industry and the boating public to participate in "the development, administration, and financing of a national recreational boating safety and facilities improvement program." 46 U.S.C. § 1451 (Supp. IV 1980).

The statute provides federal assistance for state programs, and the following section contains the state program requirements:

(a) The Secretary, in accordance with this section and such regulations as he may promulgate, may allocate and distribute funds from the fund to any State that has an accepted State recreational boating safety and facilities improvement program, if the State demonstrates to his satisfaction that—

...

(2) funds distributed will be used to develop and administer a State recreational boating safety and facilities improvement program containing the minimum requirements set forth in subsection (b), (c), or (d) of this section;

...

(4) the program submitted by that State designates a State lead authority or agency, which would implement or coordinate the implementation of the State recreational boating safety and facilities improvement program supported by Federal financial assistance in that State. ...

(b) The Secretary shall accept a State recreational boating safety program, and such program shall be eligible to receive funds ... if such program includes —

(1) a vessel numbering system, either approved or administered by the Secretary under this chapter;

(2) a cooperative boating safety assistance program with the Coast Guard in that State;

(3) sufficient patrol and other activity to insure adequate enforcement of applicable State boating safety laws and regulations; and

(4) an adequate State boating safety education program.

(c) The Secretary shall accept a State recreational boating facilities improvement program, and such program shall be eligible to receive funds . . . if such program includes—

(1) a complete description of recreational boating facility improvement projects to be undertaken by the State; and

(2) consultation with State officials responsible for the statewide comprehensive outdoor recreation plan required by the Land and Water Conservation Fund Act of 1965 and for any program developed under the Coastal Zone Management Act of 1972.

(d) Any State may, at its election, submit a combined program to the Secretary for the improvement of recreational boat safety and the improvement of recreational boating facilities in that State. . . .

§ 1475.

Do you agree that there is a "national interest" in boating safety at the state level? How intrusive on state authority is the federal statute? Does it raise a *National League of Cities* problem?

Section 1475(a)(3) of the boating act requires state matching funds. Some federal grant-in-aid legislation contains a "maintenance of effort" provision. The recipient state or local government is prohibited from using any of its federal grant to replace state or local funds previously used for the program. *See, e.g.,* Clean Air Act § 7405(b). What is the purpose of this provision? Does it raise a tenth amendment problem?

Clean Air Act

Federal requirements for state air quality programs are contained in the Clean Air Act. 43 U.S.C. §1857 et seq. (1970), now classified as 42 U.S.C. § 7401 et seq. (1980). At the state level, the states are required to adopt a state air quality implementation plan, and the federal statute specifies its contents. 42 U.S.C. § 7410. Most of these implementation plan requirements are substantive in nature, but the federal law also requires the states to provide the "necessary assurances that the State will have adequate personnel, funding, and authority to carry out" the implementation plan required by the federal law. § 7410(a)(2)(F). This latter requirement is potentially far-reaching. For example, it requires the states to adopt the necessary legislation at the state level to implement federal program requirements. This statute provides as well for a federal-state partnership, as state implementation plans are subject to review and approval by the federal Environmental Protection Agency (EPA). Difficult questions arise concerning the nature of the review and disapproval authority that EPA can exercise. Federal financial assistance for state air quality programs is available under this Act and presumably the federal agency can withhold federal aid from noncomplying states. What else may the federal agency do when reviewing state implementation plans? The "assurances" provision quoted above appears to present especially difficult problems of administration.

EPA's administration of this provision in its implementation plan review procedures was considered in *NRDC v. EPA,* 478 F.2d 875 (1st Cir. 1973). At that time, EPA regulations required a "description" of the resources available and needed by the state in order to carry out its plan. This language incorporated EPA's conception of the assurances provision, and it was attacked in this case. The court upheld the regulation:

> At first glance, a description does not seem to inspire confidence or provide certainty that the state will have adequate personnel, funding and authority to carry out its plan. Yet given the mechanics of state-federal relations, it is difficult to imagine what sort of guarantee the current Rhode Island executive or legislature could give the E.P.A. to insure that adequate resources would be devoted to the plan. Petitioner speaks of a "commitment ... to use all reasonable efforts to obtain these resources from the legislature or from other programs.... The Governor [should] give his assurance that he will do everything possible to obtain adequate resources, including filing special acts before the state legislature, or if necessary making available the necessary resources from other programs under his control." Such assurances might have a symbolic effect; however, they would have little more, since a governor or even a present session of the legislature cannot make binding commitments on behalf of their successors, nor would such representations seem to be enforceable.
>
> We believe that Congress has left to the [EPA] Administrator's sound discretion determination of what assurances are "necessary." The Administrator has required the states to describe their resources, doubtless reasoning that review of such an inventory is the best practical "assurances" he can obtain.... The "necessary assurances" clause seems to us to call less for rhetoric than for the Administrator's reasoned judgment as to the adequacy of resources.

Id. at 883-84. What else might the EPA Administrator have required? The court rejected the notion that EPA should have required a "best efforts" assurance from the governor. For discussion of the Clean Air Act see D. CURRIE, AIR POLLUTION: FEDERAL LAW AND ANALYSIS (1981).

2. MENTAL DISABILITY

Prior to 1963, state and local governments assumed primary responsibility for the care of the mentally ill and mentally disabled, spending more than twice as much as the federal government. As inadequacies in state mental health systems became apparent, the federal government established a commission to study and prepare a national mental health care plan. After a six-year study, the Joint Commission on Mental Illness and Health concluded that: "Federal support is necessary to assist in the creation of community health services but such Federal support should be so tailored as not to result in the Federal Government assuming the traditional responsibility of the states, localities and medical profession for the care and treatment of the mentally ill." H.R. Rep. No. 694, 88th Cong., 1st Sess. 2 (1963).

This section examines the federal mental health program, concentrating on the care of the mentally retarded as a program in which the role of the federal government in setting standards for state compliance was eventually decided by the Supreme Court. A brief history of this program will help put this decision in perspective.

In response to the Joint Commission study, Congress adopted the Mental Retardation Facilities and Community Mental Health Centers Construction Act of 1963, 42 U.S.C. § 2661 et seq. 1964 (reclassified with amendments at 42 U.S.C. § 6000 et seq. (1976)). Passage of the Act marked the beginning of extensive federal involvement in the field. Congress designed the Act to provide a program of federal, state and local cooperation. Through the program, Congress hoped to expand the facilities available for the care of the mentally retarded and to provide better treatment by increasing funds for research. Title I of the 1963 Act, although modified through the years, still provides the basis for legislation concerning the mentally retarded and developmentally disabled.

The central purpose of the Act was the authorization of federal financial assistance for the construction of research centers, facilities and mental health centers, and for the training of teachers. Under Title I of the Act, Congress appropriated $20 million over a three-year period for federal matching funds for up to 75% of the construction costs for research centers and facilities and $22.5 million over a three-year period to pay a maximum of 75% of the construction costs of college or university-associated facilities. Congress also appropriated $27.5 million over a two-year period for formula grants to be allocated among the states to pay $33^1/_3$ to $66^2/_3$ of the construction costs of public and other nonprofit facilities. The Act also provided application processes, regulations, state plan requirements, and the standards for approval of state plans. The Act authorized the Secretary of Health, Education and Welfare, now the Secretary of Health and Human Services, to appropriate the funds among the states on the basis of: (1) population; (2) extent of a state's needs for facilities; and (3) the state's financial needs. 42 U.S.C. § 2672 (1964). Under Section 133 of Title I, the Secretary would proscribe "the kind of services needed to provide adequate services for mentally retarded persons residing in the State ... and [would proscribe] that the State plan shall provide adequate facilities for the mentally retarded to furnish needed services for persons unable to pay thereof ...." 42 U.S.C. § 2673 (1964).

Although Congress originally designed the grant programs to assist the states with construction costs, amendments to the Act broadened the scope of grant coverage. The House Reports on the Developmentally Disabled Assistance and Bill of Rights Act of 1975 contain a discussion of the present function of the formula grant programs:

> The state formula grant program represented a new, innovative approach to the provision of services to a population such as that with developmental disabilities. The program included: (1) Federal support for a wide area of diversified services which could be provided as necessary to the disabled and provided for the combined use of funds under the program and other state programs in order to facilitate the development of comprehensive and integrated services. (2) Development of new and innovative programs to fill gaps in existing services and to expand the reach of such services to new groups of individuals. (3) Responsibility at the state level for developing strategies for the successful implementation of the program. (4) Requiring a state developmental disabilities council to guide the program which was to be broadly representative of state and local agencies and consumers interested in developmental disabilities. (5) Flexibility of allowing the states to distribute their funds under the program as appropriate among both several state agencies and several different functions including planning, administration, construction and services.

H.R. Rep. No. 58, 94th Cong., 1st Sess. 2 (1975). Through amendments to the Act, Congress has extended the grant program to cover costs of initiating and implementing programs, and costs of planning and services. The amendments which have most substantively changed the 1963 Act and which are of concern here are the amendments of 1970 and 1975.

In October 1970, Congress passed the Developmental Disabilities Services and Facilities Construction Amendments, 42 U.S.C. §§ 2671-2677 (1970). The principal purpose of the amendments was to extend for three years the existing programs of grants for construction and staffing of facilities, to expand coverage of the Act to include persons suffering from other neurological handicapping conditions, and to include programs designed to provide for other developmental disabilities. The amendments also provided for federal assistance for comprehensive planning and services. A new section in the amendments authorized grants to cover administration and operating costs of demonstration facilities and interdisciplinary training programs.

In 1975, Congress passed the Developmentally Disabled Assistance and Bill of Rights Act, 42 U.S.C. § 6000 et seq. (1976), which the following case discusses. Although the Act extended the 1963 provisions which were still in effect, it also provided a two-year substantive revision. A central change was the creation of a new special project authority and a new 30% earmark of state allotment for projects of national significance. The Act also required states to spend a certain percentage of their allotment for deinstitutionalization programs. Besides including the new section 111 (codified at 42 U.S.C. § 6010) which the Supreme Court discusses in the following case, the 1975 Act also included section 113 which provides that:

> [t]he Secretary shall require as a condition to a State receiving an allotment under part C for a fiscal year ending before October 1, 1977, that the State provide the Secretary satisfactory assurances that not later than such date (1) the State will have in effect a system to protect and advocate the rights of persons with developmental disabilities, and (2) such system will (A) have the authority to pursue legal, administrative, and other appropriate remedies to insure the protection of the rights to such persons who are receiving treatment, services or habilitation to persons with developmental disabilities. . . .

42 U.S.C. § 6012. Under the 1963 Act and the amending acts, the Secretary is authorized to approve state plans and to withhold payments if he finds that a state has not complied with the provisions of its state plan.

The preceding discussion raises a number of questions. Did Congress wish to improve state care but without expressly mandating such improvement as part of the statute? What if improvement is not forthcoming after receipt of funds? What if Congress does mandate, as it did in *Oklahoma v. United States Civil Service Commission, supra*? What is the remedy? The following case discusses these issues:

PENNHURST STATE SCHOOL & HOSPITAL v. HALDERMAN
Supreme Court of the United States
451 U.S. 1 (1981)

JUSTICE REHNQUIST delivered the opinion of the Court.

At issue in these cases is the scope and meaning of the Developmentally Disabled Assistance and Bill of Rights Act of 1975, 89 Stat. 486, as amended, 42 U.S.C. § 6000 *et seq.* (1976 ed. and Supp. III). The Court of Appeals for the Third Circuit held that the Act created substantive rights in favor of the mentally retarded, that those rights were judicially enforceable, and that conditions at the Pennhurst State School and Hospital (Pennhurst), a facility for the care and treatment of the mentally retarded, violated those rights. For the reasons stated below, we reverse the decision of the Court of Appeals and remand the cases for further proceedings.

I

The Commonwealth of Pennsylvania owns and operates Pennhurst. Pennhurst is a large institution, housing approximately 1,200 residents. Seventy-five percent of the residents are either "severely" or "profoundly" retarded—that is, with an IQ of less than 35—and a number of the residents are also physically handicapped. About half of its residents were committed there by court order and half by a parent or other guardian.

In 1974, respondent Terri Lee Halderman, a minor retarded resident of Pennhurst, filed suit in the District Court for the Eastern District of Pennsylvania on behalf of herself and all other Pennhurst residents against Pennhurst, its superintendent, and various officials of the Commonwealth of Pennsylvania responsible for the operation of Pennhurst. The additional respondents (hereinafter, with respondent Halderman, referred to as respondents) in these cases—other mentally retarded persons, the United States, and the Pennsylvania Association for Retarded Citizens (PARC)—subsequently intervened as plaintiffs. PARC added several surrounding counties as defendants, alleging that they were responsible for the commitment of persons to Pennhurst.

As amended in 1975, the complaint alleged, *inter alia,* that conditions at Pennhurst were unsanitary, inhumane, and dangerous. Specifically, the complaint averred that these conditions denied the class members due process and equal protection of the law in violation of the Fourteenth Amendment, inflicted on them cruel and unusual punishment in violation of the Eighth and Fourteenth Amendments, and denied them certain rights conferred by the Rehabilitation Act of 1973, 87 Stat. 355, as amended, 29 U. S. C. § 701 *et seq.* (1976 ed. and Supp. III), the Developmentally Disabled Assistance and Bill of Rights Act, 42 U. S. C. § 6001 *et seq.* (1976 ed. and Supp. III), and the Pennsylvania Mental Health and Mental Retardation Act of 1966, Pa. Stat. Ann., Tit. 50, §§ 4101-4704 (Purdon 1969). In addition to seeking injunctive and monetary relief, the complaint urged that Pennhurst be closed and that "community living arrangements"[1] be established for its residents.

The District Court certified a class consisting of all persons who have been or may become residents of Pennhurst. After a 32-day trial, it issued an opinion, reported at 446 F. Supp. 1295 (1977), making findings of fact and conclusions of law with respect to the conditions at Pennhurst. Its findings of fact are undisputed: Conditions at Pennhurst are not only dangerous, with the residents often physically abused or drugged by staff members, but also inadequate for the "habilitation" of the retarded.[2] Indeed, the court found that the physical, intellectual, and emotional skills of some residents have deteriorated at Pennhurst....

The District Court went on to hold that the mentally retarded have a federal constitutional right to be provided with "minimally adequate habilitation" in the "least restrictive environment," regardless of whether they were voluntarily or

---

[1] "Community living arrangements" are smaller, less isolated residences where retarded persons are treated as much as possible like nonretarded persons.

[2] There is a technical difference between "treatment," which applies to curable mental illness, and "habilitation," which consists of education and training for those, such as the mentally retarded, who are not ill. This opinion, like the opinions of the courts below, will use the terms interchangeably.

involuntarily committed.... The court also held that there existed a constitutional right to "be free from harm" under the Eighth Amendment, and to be provided with "nondiscriminatory habilitation" under the Equal Protection Clause.... In addition, it found that § 504 of the Rehabilitation Act of 1973, 29 U. S. C. § 794, and § 201 of the Pennsylvania Mental Health and Mental Retardation Act of 1966, Pa. Stat. Ann., Tit. 50, § 4201 (Purdon 1969), provided a right to minimally adequate habilitation in the least restrictive environment.

Each of these rights was found to have been violated by the conditions existing at Pennhurst. Indeed, the court held that a large institution such as Pennhurst could not provide adequate habilitation.... It thus ordered that Pennhurst eventually be closed, that suitable "community living arrangements" be provided for all Pennhurst residents, that plans for the removal of residents from Pennhurst be submitted to the court, that individual treatment plans be developed for each resident with the participation of his or her family, and that conditions at Pennhurst be improved in the interim. The court appointed a Special Master to supervise the implementation of this order....

The Court of Appeals for the Third Circuit substantially affirmed the District Court's remedial order. 612 F. 2d 84 (1979) (en banc). Unlike the District Court, however, the Court of Appeals sought to avoid the constitutional claims raised by respondents and instead rested its order on a construction of the Developmentally Disabled Assistance and Bill of Rights Act ....[3] It found that §§ 111 (1) and (2) of the Act ... 42 U. S. C. § 6010(1) and (2), the "bill of rights" provision, grant to mentally retarded persons a right to "appropriate treatment, services, and habilitation" in "the setting that is least restrictive of ... personal liberty." The court further held that under the test articulated in *Cort v. Ash*, 422 U.S. 66, 78 (1975), mentally retarded persons have an implied cause of action to enforce that right.... Because the court found that Congress enacted the statute pursuant to both § 5 of the Fourteenth Amendment and the spending power, it declined to consider whether a statute enacted pursuant to the spending power alone "could ever provide the predicate for private substantive rights." ... As an alternative ground, the court affirmed the District Court's holding that Pennhurst residents have a state statutory right to adequate "habilitation."

The court concluded that the conditions at Pennhurst violated these federal and state statutory rights. As to relief, it affirmed the order of the District Court except insofar as it ordered Pennhurst to be closed. Although the court concluded that "deinstitutionalization is the favored approach to habilitation" in the least restrictive environment, it did not construe the Act to require the closing of large institutions like Pennhurst.... The court thus remanded the case to the District Court for "individual determinations by the court, or by the Special Master, as to the appropriateness of an improved Pennhurst for each such patient" and instructed the District Court or the Master to "engage in a presumption in favor of placing individuals in [community living arrangements.]" ...

Three judges dissented. Although they assumed that the majority was correct in holding that Pennhurst residents have a right to treatment under the Act and an implied cause of action under the Act to enforce that right, they disagreed that the Act imposed a duty on the defendants to provide the "least restrictive treatment" possible. The dissent stated that "the language and structure of the Act, the relevant regulations, and the legislative history all indicate that the States

---

[3] As originally enacted in 1975, the definition of "developmentally disabled" included mental retardation. § 6001 (7) (A) (i). As amended in 1978, however, a mentally retarded individual is considered developmentally disabled only if he satisfies various criteria set forth in the Act. ...

may consider their own resources in providing less restrictive treatment." ... It did not believe that the general findings and declarations contained in a funding statute designed to encourage a course of conduct could be used by the federal courts to create absolute obligations on the States.

We granted certiorari to consider petitioners' several challenges to the decision below. ... Petitioners first contend that 42 U. S. C. § 6010 does not create in favor of the mentally retarded any substantive rights to "appropriate treatment" in the "least restrictive" environment. Assuming that Congress did intend to create such a right, petitioners question the authority of Congress to impose these affirmative obligations on the States under either its spending power or § 5 of the Fourteenth Amendment. Petitioners next assert that any rights created by the Act are enforceable in federal court only by the Federal Government, not by private parties. Finally, petitioners argue that the court below read the scope of any rights created by the Act too broadly and far exceeded its remedial powers in requiring the Commonwealth to move its residents to less restrictive environments and create individual habilitation plans for the mentally retarded. Because we agree with petitioners' first contention— that § 6010 simply does not create substantive rights—we find it unnecessary to address the remaining issues.

II

We turn first to a brief review of the general structure of the Act. It is a federal-state grant program whereby the Federal Government provides financial assistance to participating States to aid them in creating programs to care for and treat the developmentally disabled. Like other federal-state cooperative programs, the Act is voluntary and the States are given the choice of complying with the conditions set forth in the Act or forgoing the benefits of federal funding. ... The Commonwealth of Pennsylvania has elected to participate in the program. The Secretary of the Department of Health and Human Services (HHS), the agency responsible for administering the Act, has approved Pennsylvania's state plan and in 1976 disbursed to Pennsylvania approximately $1.6 million. Pennhurst itself receives no federal funds from Pennsylvania's allotment under the Act, though it does receive approximately $6 million per year in Medicaid funds.

The Act begins with an exhaustive statement of purposes. 42 U. S. C. § 6000 (b)(1) .... The "overall purpose" of the Act, as amended in 1978, is:

> [*T*]*o assist* [the] states to assure that persons with developmental disabilities receive the care, treatment, and other services necessary to enable them to achieve their maximum potential through a system which coordinates, monitors, plans, and evaluates those services and which ensures the protection of the legal and human rights of persons with developmental disabilities. (Emphasis supplied.)

As set forth in the margin, the "specific purposes" of the Act are to "assist" and financially "support" various activities necessary to the provision of comprehensive services to the developmentally disabled. § 6000 (b)(2) ....

The Act next lists a variety of conditions for the receipt of federal funds. Under § 6005, for example, the Secretary "as a condition of providing assistance" shall require that "each recipient of such assistance take affirmative action" to hire qualified handicapped individuals. Each State, in turn, shall "as a condition" of receiving assistance submit to the Secretary a plan to evaluate the services provided under the Act. § 6009. Each State shall also "as a condition" of receiving assistance "provide the Secretary satisfactory assurances that each program . . . which receives funds from the State's allotment . . . has in effect for each developmentally disabled person who receives services from or under the program a habilitation plan." § 6011(a) . . . . And § 6012 (a) . . . conditions aid on a State's promise to "have in effect a system to protect and advocate the rights of persons with developmental disabilities."

At issue here, of course, is § 6010, the "bill of rights" provision. It states in relevant part:

> Congress makes the following findings respecting the rights of persons with developmental disabilities:
> (1) Persons with developmental disabilities have a right to appropriate treatment, services, and habilitation for such disabilities.
> (2) The treatment, services, and habilitation for a person with developmental disabilities should be designed to maximize the developmental potential of the person and should be provided in the setting that is least restrictive of the person's personal liberty.
> (3) The Federal Government and the States both have an obligation to assure that public funds are not provided to any institutio[n] . . . that—(A) does not provide treatment, services, and habilitation which is appropriate to the needs of such person; or (B) does not meet the following minimum standards . . . .

Noticeably absent from § 6010 is any language suggesting that § 6010 is a "condition" for the receipt of federal funding under the Act. Section 6010 thus stands in sharp contrast to §§ 6005, 6009, 6011, and 6012.

The enabling parts of the Act are the funding sections. 42 U. S. C. §§ 6061-6063. . . . Those sections describe how funds are to be allotted to the States, require that any State desiring financial assistance submit an overall plan satisfactory to the Secretary of Health and Human Services, and require that funds disbursed under the Act be used in accordance with the approved state plan. To be approved by the Secretary, the state plan must comply with several specific conditions set forth in § 6063. It, *inter alia,* must provide for the establishment of a State Planning Council, § 6063(b)(1), and set out specific objectives to be achieved under the plan, § 6063 (b)(2)(A) . . . . Services furnished under the plan must be consistent with standards prescribed by the Secretary, §§ 6063 (b)(5)(A) (i) . . ., and be provided in an individual manner consistent with § 6011, § 6063 (b)(5)(B). . . . The plan must also be supported by assurances that any program receiving assistance is protecting the human rights of the disabled consistent with § 6010, § 6063 (b)(5)(C) . . . . Each State must also require its State Planning Council to serve as an advocate of persons with developmental disabilities. § 6067 . . . .

The Act further provides procedures and sanctions to ensure state compliance with its requirements. The Secretary may, of course, disapprove a state plan, § 6063(c). If a State fails to satisfy the requirements of § 6063, the Secretary may terminate or reduce the federal grant. § 6065 . . . . Any State dissatisfied with the Secretary's disapproval of the plan, or his decision to terminate funding, may appeal to the federal courts of appeals. § 6068. No other cause of action is recognized in the Act.

III

As support for its broad remedial order, the Court of Appeals found that 42 U. S. C. § 6010 created substantive rights in favor of the disabled and imposed an obligation on the States to provide, at their own expense, certain kinds of treatment. The initial question before us, then, is one of statutory construction: Did Congress intend in § 6010 to create enforceable rights and obligations?

A

In discerning congressional intent, we necessarily turn to the possible sources of Congress' power to legislate, namely, Congress' power to enforce the Fourteenth Amendment and its power under the Spending Clause to place conditions on the grant of federal funds. . . .

Although this Court has previously addressed issues going to Congress' power to secure the guarantees of the Fourteenth Amendment, . . . we have had little occasion to consider the appropriate test for determining when Congress intends to enforce those guarantees. Because such legislation imposes congressional policy on a State involuntarily, and because it often intrudes on traditional state authority, we should not quickly attribute to Congress an unstated intent to act under its authority to enforce the Fourteenth Amendment. . . . The case for inferring intent is at its weakest where, as here, the rights asserted impose *affirmative* obligations on the States to fund certain services, since we may assume that Congress will not implicitly attempt to impose massive financial obligations on the States.

Turning to Congress' power to legislate pursuant to the spending power, our cases have long recognized that Congress may fix the terms on which it shall disburse federal money to the States. . . . Unlike legislation enacted under § 5, however, legislation enacted pursuant to the spending power is much in the nature of a contract: in return for federal funds, the States agree to comply with federally imposed conditions. The legitimacy of Congress' power to legislate under the spending power thus rests on whether the State voluntarily and knowingly accepts the terms of the "contract." . . . There can, of course, be no knowing acceptance if a State is unaware of the conditions or is unable to ascertain what is expected of it. Accordingly, if Congress intends to impose a condition on the grant of federal moneys, it must do so unambiguously. . . . By insisting that Congress speak with a clear voice, we enable the States to exercise their choice knowingly, cognizant of the consequences of their participation.

Indeed, in those instances where Congress has intended the States to fund certain entitlements as a condition of receiving federal funds, it has proved capable of saying so explicitly. . . . We must carefully inquire, then, whether Congress in § 6010 imposed an obligation on the States to spend state money to fund certain rights as a condition of receiving federal moneys under the Act or whether it spoke merely in precatory terms.

B

Applying those principles to these cases, we find nothing in the Act or its legislative history to suggest that Congress intended to require the States to assume the high cost of providing "appropriate treatment" in the "least restrictive environment" to their mentally retarded citizens.

There is virtually no support for the lower court's conclusion that Congress created rights and obligations pursuant to its power to enforce the Fourteenth Amendment. The Act nowhere states that that is its purpose. Quite the contrary, the Act's language and structure demonstrate that it is a mere federal-state funding statute. The explicit purposes of the Act are simply "to assist" the States through the use of federal grants to improve the care and treatment of the mentally retarded. § 6000 (b) . . . . Nothing in either the "overall" or "specific" purposes of the Act reveals an intent to require the States to fund new, substantive rights. Surely Congress would not have established such elaborate funding incentives had it simply intended to impose absolute obligations on the States.

Respondents nonetheless insist that the fact that § 6010 speaks in terms of "rights" supports their view. Their reliance is misplaced. . . . Contrary to respondents' assertion, the specific language and the legislative history of § 6010 are ambiguous. We are persuaded that § 6010, when read in the context of other more specific provisions of the Act, does no more than express a congressional preference for certain kinds of treatment. It is simply a general statement of "findings" and, as such, is too thin a reed to support the rights and obligations read into it by the court below. The closest one can come in giving § 6010 meaning is that it justifies and supports Congress' appropriation of money under the Act and guides the Secretary in his review of state applications for federal funds. . . . As this Court recognized in *Rosado v. Wyman,* [397 U. S. 397, 413 (1970)] "Congress sometimes legislates by innuendo, making declarations of policy and indicating a preference while requiring measures that, though falling short of legislating its goal, serve as a nudge in the preferred directions." This is such a case.

The legislative history buttresses our conclusion that Congress intended to encourage, rather than mandate, the provision of better services to the developmentally disabled. The House Committee believed the purpose of the Act was simply to continue an existing federal grant program, designed to promote "effective planning by the states of their programs, initiation of new, needed programs, and filling of gaps among existing efforts." H. R. Rep. No. 94-58, pp. 6, 8-9 (1975). Indeed, as passed by the House, the Act contained no "bill of rights" provision whatsoever. The Committee instead merely "applauded" the efforts of others to secure rights for the developmentally disabled. *Id.,* at 7.

. . . .

In sum, nothing suggests that Congress intended the Act to be something other than a typical funding statute. Far from requiring the States to fund newly declared individual rights, the Act has a systematic focus, seeking to improve care to individuals by encouraging better state planning, coordination, and demonstration projects. Much like the Medicaid statute considered in *Harris v. McRae,* 448 U. S. 297 (1980), the Act at issue here "was designed as a cooperative program of shared responsibilit[ies], not as a device for the Federal Government to compel a State to provide services that Congress itself is unwilling to fund." *Id.,* at 309.

There remains the contention of the Solicitor General that Congress, acting pursuant to its spending power, conditioned the grant of federal money on the State's agreeing to underwrite the obligations the Court of Appeals read into § 6010. We find that contention wholly without merit. As amply demonstrated above, the "findings" in § 6010, when viewed in the context of the more specific provisions of the Act, represent general statements of federal policy, not newly created legal duties.

The "plain language" of § 6010 also refutes the Solicitor General's contention. When Congress intended to impose conditions on the grant of federal funds, as in §§ 6005, 6009, 6011, 6012, 6063, and 6067, it proved capable of doing so in clear terms. Section 6010, in marked contrast, in no way suggests that the grant of federal funds is "conditioned" on a State's funding the rights described therein. The existence of explicit conditions throughout the Act, and the absence of conditional language in § 6010, manifest the limited meaning of § 6010. . . .

. . . .

The fact that Congress granted to Pennsylvania only $1.6 million in 1976, a sum woefully inadequate to meet the enormous financial burden of providing "appropriate" treatment in the "least restrictive" setting, confirms that Congress must have had a limited purpose in enacting § 6010. When Congress does impose affirmative obligations on the States, it usually makes a far more substantial contribution to defray costs. *Harris v. McRae, supra.* It defies common sense, in short, to suppose that Congress implicitly imposed this massive obligation on participating States.

Our conclusion is also buttressed by the rule of statutory construction established above, that Congress must express clearly its intent to impose conditions on the grant of federal funds so that the States can knowingly decide whether or not to accept those funds. That canon applies with greatest force where, as here, a State's potential obligations under the Act are largely indeterminate. It is difficult to know what is meant by providing "appropriate treatment" in the "least restrictive" setting, and it is unlikely that a State would have accepted federal funds had it known it would be bound to provide such treatment. The crucial inquiry, however, is not whether a State would knowingly undertake that obligation, but whether Congress spoke so clearly that we can fairly say that the State could make an informed choice. In this case, Congress fell well short of providing clear notice to the States that they, by accepting funds under the Act, would indeed be obligated to comply with § 6010. Not only does § 6010 lack conditional language, but it strains credulity to argue that participating States should have known of their "obligations" under § 6010 when the Secretary of HHS, the governmental agency responsible for the administration of the Act and the agency with which the participating States have the most contact, has never understood § 6010 to impose conditions on participating States. Though Congress' power to legislate under the spending power is broad, it does not include surprising participating States with postacceptance or "retroactive" conditions.

. . .

. . . .

In sum, the court below failed to recognize the well-settled distinction between Congressional "encouragement" of state programs and the imposition of binding obligations on the States. *Harris v. McRae,* 448 U. S. 297 (1980). Relying on that distinction, this Court in *Southeastern Community College v. Davis,* 442 U. S. 397 (1979), rejected a claim that § 504 of the Rehabilitation Act of 1973, which bars discrimination against handicapped persons in federally funded programs, obligates schools to take affirmative steps to eliminate problems raised by an applicant's hearing disability. Finding that "state agencies such as Southeastern are only 'encourage[d] . . . to adopt and implement such policies and procedures,'" *id.,* at 410 (quoting the Act), we stressed that "Congress understood [that] accommodation of the needs of handicapped individuals may require affirmative action and knew how to provide for it in those instances where it wished to do so." *Id.,* at 411. Likewise in this case, Congress was aware of the need of developmentally disabled persons and plainly understood the difference, financial and otherwise, between encouraging a specified type of treatment and mandating it.

....

VI

Congress in recent years has enacted several laws designed to improve the way in which this Nation treats the mentally retarded. The Developmentally Disabled Assistance and Bill of Rights Act is one such law. It establishes a national policy to provide better care and treatment to the retarded and creates funding incentives to induce the States to do so. But the Act does no more than that. We would be attributing far too much to Congress if we held that it required the States, at their own expense, to provide certain kinds of treatment. Accordingly, we reverse the principal holding of the Court of Appeals and remand for further proceedings consistent with this opinion.

Reversed and remanded.

JUSTICE BLACKMUN, concurring in part and concurring in the judgment. [Omitted.]

Justice White, with whom JUSTICE BRENNAN and JUSTICE MARSHALL join, dissenting in part.

....

In essence, the Court concludes that § 6010 of the Act so-called "Bill of Rights" section, merely serves to establish guidelines which States should endeavor to fulfill, but which have no real effect except to the extent that the Secretary of Health and Human Services chooses to use the criteria established by § 6010 in determining funding under the Act. In my view, this reading misconceives the important purposes Congress intended § 6010 to serve. That section, as confirmed by its legislative history, was intended by Congress to establish requirements which participating States had to meet in providing care to the developmentally disabled. The fact that Congress spoke in generalized terms rather than the language of regulatory minutia cannot make nugatory actions so carefully undertaken.

....

Comments: 1. The contract theory introduced by the Court in federal-state funding programs (requiring all conditions placed by Congress on the receipt of federal funds to be clear and unambiguous) represents an apparent limitation of the Court's willingness to permit Congress to fix the terms for receipt of federal money. The leading case of *Oklahoma v. United States Civil Service,* 330 U.S. 127 (1947), discussed in *National League of Cities, supra,* and the notes following, upheld congressional conditions on federal grants-in-aid under the Hatch Act (limiting political activity) so long as the conditions were appropriate and plainly adapted to a permitted end. Did the "bill of rights" provision of the Developmentally Disabled Assistance and Bill of Rights Act meet this test? For a discussion, see Note, *Pennhurst State School and Hospital v. Halderman: Back to the Drawing Board for the Developmentally Disabled,* 60 N.C.L. REV. 1119 (1982).

2. Of course, the contract theory has its limitations. The Court made much of the notion of "unfair surprise" in *Pennhurst.* Such a limitation would hardly be applicable in a case where the facts did not admit of unfair surprise or otherwise indicate an actual agreement was struck. But can *Pennhurst* be read as a major eleventh amendment statement requiring strong evidence that states have waived the prerogatives of sovereignty before they can be subjected to onerous grant conditions? If so, would the "clear statement" of intent to require waiver as a condition to receipt of federal aid have to be contained in the statute itself? Would legislative history suffice? Could "interpreting" or "implementing" regulations issued by the executive branch constitute the "clear statement"? For an argument favoring the eleventh amendment interpretation of *Pennhurst* and limiting the power to impose onerous regulations to statutory language, see Baker, *Making the Most of Pennhurst's "Clear Statement" Rule,* 31 CATH. U.L. REV. 439 (1981).

3. Note the interpretation by the Court of the "least restrictive environment" standard. 42 U.S.C. § 6010(2). Is the Court's acceptance of the argument that "least restrictive environment" is synonymous with deinstitutionalization persuasive?

4. The question whether federal reimbursement, or lack thereof, for state expenditures determines the state responsibility for incurring the expenditure was litigated in *Harris v. McRae,* 448 U.S. 297 (1979), the "Hyde Amendment" case. The Hyde Amendment had been enacted annually since 1976 to limit severely the use of federal funds to reimburse states under the Medicaid program, Title XIX of the Social Security Act, for the cost of abortions. Plaintiffs, in addition to raising first and fifth amendment constitutional challenges, argued that the Hyde Amendment did not remove the obligations of states participating in the Medicaid program to fund all medically necessary abortions.

This argument was based on a statutory requirement that participating states agree to provide financial assistance to the "categorically needy" (persons eligible for assistance under the Aid to Families with Dependent Children program, 42 U.S.C. § 601 et seq. and the Supplemental Security Income program, 42 U.S.C. § 1381 et seq.) with respect to five general areas of medical treatment: (1) inpatient hospital services; (2) outpatient hospital services; (3) other laboratory and X-ray services; (4) skilled nursing facilities services, periodic screening and diagnosis of children, and family planning services; and (5) services of physicians. Participating states must receive approval of a state Medicaid plan. States are not required to fund all possible medical treatment falling within the five categories but must establish in their plans reasonable standards for detemining the extent of medical assistance to be given. Participating states receive reimbursement from the federal government for a major portion of the cost of the medical assistance provided under the approved plan. In concluding that states are not obligated to fund medically necessary abortions because of the denial of reimbursement under the Hyde Amendment, the Supreme Court characterized the Medicaid program as a "system of cooperative federalism" for sharing responsibility for the costs of health services.

> Thus, if Congress chooses to withdraw federal funding for a particular service, a State is not obliged to continue to pay for that service as a condition of continued federal financial support of other services. This is not to say that Congress may not now depart from the original design of Title XIX under which the Federal Government shares the financial responsibility for expenses incurred under an approved Medicaid plan. It is only to say that, absent an indication of contrary legislative intent by a subsequent Congress, Title XIX does not obligate a participating State to pay for those medical services for which federal reimbursement is unavailable.

Id. at 309.

5. As a result of *Pennhurst,* developmentally disabled persons must look to sources other than § 6010 of the Developmentally Disabled Act to obtain redress for improper and inadequate conditions in mental institutions. Two possible approaches are the due process clause of the fourteenth amendment and Title I of the 1973 Rehabilitation Act (29 U.S.C. § 701 et seq.)

In *Youngberg v. Romeo,* 102 S. Ct. 2452 (1982), respondent sued under 42 U.S.C. § 1983 claiming that the officials at Pennhurst Hospital had violated her son's rights under the eighth and fourteenth amendments. She alleged that the officials had failed to institute appropriate preventive procedures, and that the doctors restrained her son for prolonged periods. While her son was in Pennhurst, he was injured more than sixty times by his own violence and the violent reactions of others toward him.

The district court instructed the jury that only if they found defendants "deliberately indifferent to the serious medical [and psychological] needs" of the son, could they find that the hospital had violated his eighth and fourteenth amendment rights. The court of appeals, in reversing a verdict for the defendants, held that the eighth amendment was not the appropriate remedy for determining the rights of the involuntarily committed. Instead, the court found that the fourteenth amendment provided the basis for their rights. The court held that the involuntarily committed have liberty interests in freedom of movement, in personal liberty, and in habilitation designed to treat their retardation. The court found that only an "overriding non-punitive" state interest could limit the liberty interests of the patients. *Romeo v. Youngberg,* 644 F.2d 147, 157-58 (3d Cir. 1980).

The Supreme Court, in affirming the court of appeals' decision, addressed respondent's claim to safe conditions and freedom from bodily restraint and concluded that the due process clause of the fourteenth amendment protected those interests. However, the Court found that in some circumstances restraint may be necessary. Under those circumstances, the Court must balance the individual's liberty interest against the societal demands to determine if the nature of the restraint violated due process. The Court addressed respondent's claim of a constitutional right to "minimal adequate habilitation" and found that the son did have a constitutional right to reasonable training to insure safety and freedom from restraint, but that the Court must give deference to the hospital's determination on what is "reasonable" training. 102 S. Ct. 2452, 2459-61 (1982).

In *Ryans v. New Jersey Commission for the Blind & Visually Impaired,* 542 F. Supp. 841 (D.N.J. 1982), the court considered whether Title I of the Rehabilitation Act of 1973, which entitles handicapped individuals to certain rehabilitative services and benefits, and the circumstances under which it was passed, indicated a congressional intent to permit handicapped individuals to assert a private right of action under the Act. The court found that the structure of the Act, the legislative history, and the Act's provisions for administrative remedies indicated that Congress did not intend to provide a judicial remedy. Even though the Court concluded that Title I did not implicitly create a private right of action, it found that a plaintiff may be allowed to enforce the Act's provisions under 42 U.S.C. § 1983.

As noted in Chapter 7, the Supreme Court has limited the availability of § 1983 remedies. Under *Pennhurst* and *Middlesex County,* the Court will not recognize a § 1983 remedy if the federal statute creates no enforceable rights, or if Congress intended to create an exclusive remedy in the statute. Therefore, if the Court allows a plaintiff to bring a § 1983 suit, it will have to establish that the Act does create specific rights and obligations, and that the plaintiff's exhaustion of administrative remedies will insure no conflict between congressional intent and the institution of a § 1983 suit.

The lower court's decision in *Pennhurst* that the state had an obligation to provide treatment rested in part on the Pennyslvania Mental Health and Mental Retardation Act of 1966, Pa. Stat. Ann., Tit. 50, §§ 4101-4704 (1969 & 1982 Supp.). The Supreme Court, in its remand, stated that it was "unclear" whether state law provides an independent and adequate ground to support the lower court's decision. In the following case, the Pennsylvania Supreme Court construed the state statute.

IN RE SCHMIDT

Supreme Court of Pennsylvannia
494 Pa. 86, 429 A.2d 631 (1981)

NIX, JUSTICE.

Appellant, County of Allegheny, petitioned the Court of Common Pleas for the involuntary commitment of respondent, Joseph Schmidt, to an appropriate facility. Appellee, Commonwealth of Pennsylvania, intervened as a party-respondent and presented testimony to establish that the state-operated facility known as Western Center would not be an appropriate facility as required by the Mental Health and Mental Retardation Act of 1966 (hereinafter referred to as the Act).... 50 P.S. § 4406. The trial court concluded that respondent was a mentally retarded individual requiring a closely supervised structured residential program.

The county was ordered to "develop a practical life management plan" setting forth "in detail the type of residential placement appropriate for [respondent] with a placement appropriate for his needs." The county was given a six-month period in which to complete the placement of respondent in an appropriate facility meeting his needs. The trial court further ordered that during the six-month period, but no longer, respondent was to be temporarily committed to the state-operated institution known as Western Center, even though that institution was not an appropriate facility for respondent. The court en banc expressed the hope that, "If Joseph receives an appropriate placement that meets his needs, . . . the time might come when placement at Western Center will in fact be appropriate." This appeal by the county followed.

Respondent is an adult male who at the age of eight was placed by the Court of Common Pleas, upon the petition of respondent's family, in a privately operated residential school for mentally retarded children. Respondent resided and received treatment for the following fourteen years at this school which was under contract with the county to provide such care. He is able to walk, although he frequently moves around on his hands and knees. He can use a scoop dish to feed himself but still requires much assistance. He is unable to discriminate between edible and inedible objects and, although not toilet trained, he is toilet regulated. The school found that as respondent grew into a husky, muscular young man, it was unable channel his physical energy and curiosity and was unable to provide the constant supervision respondent required. The county attempted unsuccessfully to find other suitable placement for respondent. It was at this point, after fourteen years of assuming the responsibility, that appellant county petitioned for respondent's commitment to an appropriate state facility.

Evidence established that Western Center was not an appropriate facility for respondent since its staff-patient ratio was 1:14. Respondent's previous school found that it could not adequately treat respondent in a 1:7 staff-patient ratio. Testimony at the hearing established that in order for respondent to receive the training he needs to reduce dependency, respondent must be in a setting with a 1:3 staff-patient ratio. Respondent was, however, temporarily committed to Western Center, since there was no alternative placement available to the trial court.

Neither is there any real dispute between the county and the state that (1) the county does not presently have a program that will meet respondent's needs; and (2) Western Center does not presently have a program to meet respondent's needs. The actual controversy between the county and the state is which of them is legally obligated to assume the responsibility for providing the proper care for respondent. The county argues that the trial court should have placed upon the state the responsibility of providing appropriate care. The state, on the other hand, argues that the trial court's order should be affirmed because it is the county's responsibility to provide the proper care for respondent.

We start the inquiry with the realization that the mentally retarded are in no way responsible for their dependency, and that society's concern for their welfare should not be grudgingly or reluctantly given. We also recognize that this is not a question of which governmental unit will ultimately bear the financial cost of the services required. The basic issue is which governmental unit has the responsibility to assume the initiative in locating and developing the appropriate placement. The court below determined that it was the county's responsibility; for the reasons that follow, we cannot agree.

We are not here concerned with the legitimacy of the deprivation of the liberty of an individual that may be occasioned by residential placement. ... This Commonwealth has committed itself to a rejection of the former view that indiscriminate institutionalization was the panacea for the resolution of the problems presented by citizens who were not self-sufficient because of mental retardation. ... 50 P.S. § 7102 .... We also embrace the view that a mentally retarded person shall not be determined to require involuntary residential placement unless the degree of retardation shows an inability to provide for the most basic personal needs and provision for such needs is not available and cannot be developed or provided for in the existing home or in the community in which the individual resides.

Our question here is somewhat different. Here there is no question that residential care will be required for the long-term care of Joseph Schmidt, even under the most favorable prognosis. This is not an instance where there is a possiblity of a less structured placement than those made available by existing state facilities. To the contrary, the available state facility is inadequately structured for respondent's present needs and the anticipated objective of the court below is to provide him with the skills to cope with life in a setting such as Western Center. The question to be decided here is under existing statutory law which governmental unit, i.e., the state or county, has the responsibility to locate or develop the long-term residential program required by respondent.

The responsibilities and duties of the state are set forth in Art. II of the Act. Specifically, § 201(1) of the Act, 50 P.S. § 4201(1), states that it shall be the duty of the state "to assure within the State the availability and equitable provision of adequate ... mental retardation services for all persons who need them, ..." Subsection (4) further requires the state to "adopt State-wide plans for the operation of all State operated facilities ... and to assign to each facility or portion thereof, such duties for the care of the mentally disabled, as the secretary shall prescribe." Section 202(b) of the Act, 50 P.S. § 4202(b), authorizes the state through the Department of Public Welfare (department) "to establish, extend, operate and maintain additional facilities and provide ... mental retardation services therein."

In counter distinction to the obligation and responsibilities of the state the Act describes in Art. III the obligations and responsiblities of the counties. Specifically, § 301(d) of the Act, 50 P.S. § 4301(d), provides that:

... it shall be the duty of local authorities in cooperation with the department to insure that the following mental health and mental retardation services are available:

(1) Short term inpatient services other than those provided by the State.
(2) Outpatient services.
(3) Partial hospitalization services.
(4) Emergency services twenty-four hours per day which shall be provided by, or available within at least one of the types of services specified heretofore in this paragraph.
(5) Consultation and education services to professional personnel and community agencies.
(6) Aftercare services for persons released from State and County facilities.
(7) Specialized rehabilitative and training services including sheltered workshops.

(8) Interim care of mentally retarded persons who have been removed from their homes and who having been accepted, are awaiting admission to a State operated facility.

(9) Unified procedures for intake for all county services and a central place providing referral services and information.

Paragraph (e) of section 301 of the Act, 50 P.S. § 4301, grants the power to local authorities to establish certain enumerated services and programs beyond those mandated under paragraph (d).

It is evident that the dichotomy sought to be achieved under the Act was intended to separate and yet coordinate state-county responsibilities to insure the availability of adequate mental retardation services for all of the residents of the states in need of such services. The state, through the department, was given the responsibility for the overall supervision and control of the program. Read together, § 201(1), (4) of the Act, 50 P.S. § 4201(1)(4), and 202(b) of the Act, 50 P.S. § 4202(b), impose the duty and grant the authority to ensure adequate services for the mentally retarded. Under § 201(1) of the Act, 50 P.S. § 4201(1), the state has the obligation to provide adequate mental health services and the department is charged with the duty to implement that obligation. The direction in § 201(4) of the Act, 50 P.S. § 4201(4), limited by the clause, "as the secretary shall prescribe" must be read in context with the obligations the department is by law required to discharge. The secretary is obligated to prescribe that which is necessary for the implementation of the State's responsibility in this area. The authorization in § 202(b) of the Act, 50 P.S. § 4202(b), provides an additional grant of power which is to be used when required to meet the obligation placed upon the state.

In comparison, the duties assigned to counties are not all encompassing. The counties have been charged under § 301(d) of the Act, 50 P.S. § 4301(d), to provide short term care as well as rehabilitative and supportive services. The county's insistence in this lawsuit upon an interpretation which would limit its function to providing "interim" care for the mentally retarded has justifiably engendered strong disagreement from appellee and the court below. Under the clear language of § 301(d) of the Act, 50 P.S. § 4301(d), there was a greater responsibility reposed in the county than merely providing services to ameliorate the situation until a state placement could be arranged. See § 301(d)(2), (3), (6) and (7) of the Act, 50 P.S. § 4301(d)(2), (3), (6) and (7). We fully agree with the court below that the legislative scheme was designed to require the county to provide those supportive services where they would eliminate the necessity of institutionalization, even where those services would be required on a long term basis.

With the acceptance of the principle of "normalization" and the resultant legislation, it is clear that the restrictive view urged by the county as to its obligations in the area is out of step. The concept of normalization envisions that the mentally retarded person and his or her family shall have the right to live a life as close as possible to that which is typical for the general population. Consistent with this concept is the requirement that the least restriction consistent with adequate treatment and required care shall be employed.

The doctrine of least restrictive alternative was first articulated by Chief Judge Bazelon in *Lake v. Cameron,* 364 F.2d 657 (D.C.Cir.1966) and subsequently adopted as a constitutional requirement in a series of commitment and treatment related cases.

These regulations make it clear that the legislative grant of power to the counties under § 301(e)(3) of the Act, 50 P.S. § 4301(e)(3), empowering them to establish additional services and programs "designed to prevent . . . the necessity of admitting or committing the mentally disabled to a facility" was intended to be utilized by the counties to minimize the necessity of institutionalization. It was more than a mere grant of power to be used at the county's option. The power of the department to issue the regulations in question and to require the counties to assume the responsibilities set forth therein was clearly within the purview of section 201 of the Act, 50 P.S. § 4201, which charges the department to create a comprehensive and coordinate program in conjunction with the county governments. Moreover, any question as to the legislative recognition of the concept of normalization and the adoption of the doctrine of least restrictive alternatives in matters relating to the mentally retarded has been removed by the enactment of the Mental Health Procedures Act, Act of 1976, . . . 50 P.S. § 7101.

While we agree with the rejection by the court below of the narrow role urged by the county for its participation and obligations in the area of mental retardation, we cannot agree that the county is responsible in this instance for the care of Joseph Schmidt. In this case the need for institutionalization can neither be prevented or minimized. Joseph Schmidt will unquestionably require long term residential placement. There is no less restrictive alternative available for the county to provide. To the contrary, the available state facility is inadequate because it does not provide a sufficiently structured environment for Joseph. The concept of normalization is not a consideration in the placement of Joseph.

It is the state's responsiblity to find a placement for Joseph with a staff-patient ratio suitable to his needs. The state will not be allowed to ignore that responsibility and that obligation by stating that an appropriate facility is not immediately available. Section 201(1) of the Act, 50 P.S. § 4201(1), requires the state to provide *adequate* mental retardation services for persons in need of them. Joseph Schmidt has clearly demonstrated his need and the State must respond to it.

Accordingly, the decree of the court below is reversed and the matter is remanded for further proceedings consistent herewith.

Comments: 1. The principal case illustrates a common facet of American social welfare programs—the decentralization of certain services, in this case short-term care, outpatient services, emergency facilities and after-care services. Read together, *Pennhurst* and *Schmidt* provide a picture of a typical social welfare program: the state with the basic authority and responsibility, the federal government providing a carrot (public funds) and a stick ("conditions" and "incentives"), with local government (in this case the county) delegated a piece of the action with varying degrees of authority, responsibility and assistance. Is this the most efficient way to provide a given public service? The most effective?

2. Following *Schmidt,* the Third Circuit took up *Pennhurst* on remand and concluded that the Pennsylvania statute, as construed by *Schmidt,* provided adequate support for the district court's decision that mentally retarded persons have a right to treatment in the least restrictive environment.

> The resolution in *Schmidt* resulted from the Pennsylvania Supreme Court's conclusion that where long term institutional care is in fact the least restrictive means of habilitation, institutionalization is permissible and the state is obliged to provide it. Our prior holding that individual determinations must be made for each member of the class is entirely consistent with the holding that Joseph Schmidt must be provided a place in a state facility.
>
> But unlike *Schmidt,* we have before us numerous class members who the court found should not be in Pennhurst. For these the court ordered that suitable community living

arrangements be provided, and enjoined the county defendants from recommending future commitments to Pennhurst without an individual determination that a community living arrangement or other less restrictive environment would be suitable. These holdings are also consistent with the *Schmidt* opinion . . . .

The defendants urge that because the *Schmidt* case did not present any issue of funding of proper care, it should not be regarded as controlling. . . . Except that this is a class action, however, we are not persuaded that there is any essential difference in the posture of the *Schmidt* case and this. As in this case, the County attempted to limit its responsibility to petitioning for the commission of mentally retarded persons to a state residential facility. The *Schmidt* court made clear that the Pennsylvania law imposed the obligation on both levels of government to provide habilitation in that environment providing the least restriction on personal liberty consistent with habilitation. . . .

. . . There is no suggestion in the *Schmidt* opinion that this order would be qualified by the necessity for appropriations. . . . On this record we, like the Supreme Court of Pennsylvania, must assume that the Pennsylvania legislature intends compliance with its statutes.

Halderman v. Pennhurst State School & Hospital, 673 F.2d 645-47 (3d Cir.) (en banc), *cert. granted,* 102 S. Ct. 2956 (1982).

3. What remedy is available when a state agency violates conditions contained in a federal grant legislation, or when a state law or regulation is inconsistent with the federal legislation? In *Pennhurst,* the Court noted:

[R]elief may well be limited to enjoining the Federal Government from providing funds to the Commonwealth. . . . [W]e have [also] affirmed lower court decisions enjoining a State from enforcing any provisions which conflict with federal law in violation of the Supremacy Clause. . . . In still other cases, we have struck down state laws without addressing the form of relief.

Id. at 29. The Court concluded that the relief question posed "difficult questions" and did not consider them because they had not been considered by the court of appeals.

See also *King v. Smith,* 392 U.S. 309 (1968), in which the Court invalidated an Alabama welfare assistance regulation which violated the federal law under which aid was made available for state assistance programs. The Court said:

There is of course no question that the Federal Government, unless barred by some controlling constitutional provision, may impose the terms and conditions upon which its money allotments to the States shall be disbursed, and that any state law or regulation inconsistent with such federal terms and conditions is to that extent invalid.

Id. at 333. Does the *King v. Smith* remedy or the remedies suggested in *Pennhurst* raise tenth amendment problems?

Professor LaPierre, *supra,* at 861-62, believes that a federal decision to withhold aid is not an "interference with a state's political decisionmaking process," but that "preemption of state law that conflicts with a condition of a national grant cuts deeply into the state's political decisionmaking process." What is the basis for this distinction? Is it consistent with the Supreme Court's decision in the *Federal Energy Regulatory Comm'n* case, *supra*?

4. *National League of Cities* questions, *supra,* may turn on the organizational structure established by state and local governments to carry out a particular function. A common approach in the mental health field is the use of community-based nonprofit corporations to perform services under contract with a state agency. Is an employee of such an organization entitled to minimum wages under the Fair Labor Standards Act? In *Williams v. Eastside Mental Health Center, Inc.,* 669 F.2d 671 (11th Cir. 1982) *(appeal pending),* the court reversed a lower court holding that the center was exempt from the minimum wage law under *National League of Cities.*

The determinative fact in this case is simply that the entity with which we are dealing is not a state or a political subdivision of a state as defined by the Court in *Usery* and in other cases involving similar issues. Eastside Mental Health Center is not the State of Alabama, nor is it an agency or department of the State of Alabama. Indeed no party contends otherwise.

Moreover as it currently exists under Alabama state law, Eastside is not a public agency or corporation. As was noted earlier, the Center is incorporated as a non-profit institution ..., rather than as a public corporation under ... the Alabama Code. The Center is in fact distinct from many of the other community mental health centers operating in the State of Alabama in precisely this regard. For whatever reason, Alabama did not elect to operate Eastside as a state institution with state employees; instead it set up a not for profit corporation with a separate, independent board of directors to administer it. Whatever may have been the state's reason for doing it this way, it must live with the consequences. It cannot claim an immunity based on a condition which it itself sought to avoid.

Here, then, lies the greatest difference between *Usery* and the facts of this case. Here we are concerned with application of the FLSA wages paid by a not for profit corporation which operates by contract with a public corporation of the State of Alabama and by contract with other entities. There is thus no impact on the state in its relation with its own employees. Thus, the FLSA does not affect the "States as States."

. . . .

For purposes of the sovereignty issue before us, Eastside is thus best characterized as a private, non-profit corporation, licensed in the State of Alabama to perform the services of a community mental health center, and carrying out such services by means of ordinary contracts with various state and local agencies and institutions. It is thus analogous to a normal nonprofit institution in its basic corporate structure, while at the same time analogous to a private business doing contracting work for the state in its basic business operations.

Id. at 678-79. The court also held, with one judge dissenting on this point, that the provision of mental health services is not an "integral" function triggering the *National League of Cities* exemption no matter what form the delivery mechanism takes because the service affects a limited class of persons and not the state as a whole. Is this consistent with the political accountability theory espoused by Professor LaPierre, *supra?*

5. The interplay of federal and state law is such that, while the Constitution is the supreme law of the land and is often viewed as the controlling document in civil rights litigation, cases arise in which state law may provide greater substantive and procedural rights than federal law. In remanding a challenge to a state practice of forcibly administering antipsychotic drugs to mental patients involuntarily committed to state institutions, the Supreme Court commented:

[I]t is distinctly possible that Massachusetts recognizes liberty interests of persons adjudged incompetent that are broader than those protected directly by the Constitution of the United States. Compare *Roe III,* [421 N.E.2d 40 (Mass. 1981)] (protected liberty interest in avoiding unwanted treatment continues even when a person becomes incompetent and creates a right of incompetents to have their "substituted judgment" determined) with *Addington v. Texas,* 441 U.S. 418, 429-430 (1979) (because a person "who is suffering from a debilitating mental illness" is not "wholly at liberty," and because the complexities of psychiatric diagnosis "render certainties virtually beyond reach," "practical considerations" may require "a compromise between what it is possible to prove and what protects the rights of the individual"). If the state interest is broader, the *substantive* protection that the Constitution affords against the involuntary administration of antipsychotic drugs would not determine the actual substantive rights and duties of persons in the State of Massachusetts.

Procedurally, it also is quite possible that a Massachusetts court, as a matter of state law, would require greater protection of relevant liberty interests than the minimum adequate to survive scrutiny under the Due Process Clause. Compare *Roe III,* ... ("We have ... stated our preference for judicial resolution of certain legal issues arising from proposed extraordinary medical treatment. ...") with *Youngberg v. Romeo,* ... ("[T]here certainly is no reason to think judges or juries are better qualified than appropriate professionals in making [treatment] decisions."), and with *Parham v. J.R.,* [442 U.S. 584 (1979)] (Courts must not "unduly burden[ ] the legitimate efforts of the States to deal with difficult social problems. The judicial model for fact-finding for all constitutionally protected interests, regardless of their nature, can turn rational decisionmaking into an unmanageable enterprise."). Again on this hypothesis state law would be dispositive of the procedural rights and duties of the parties to this case.

Finally, even if state procedural law itself remains unchanged by *Roe III,* the federally mandated procedures will depend on the nature and weight of the *state* interests, as well as the individual interests, that are asserted. To identify the nature and scope of state interests that are to be balanced against an individual's liberty interests, this Court may look to state law. . . . Here we view the underlying state law predicate for weighing asserted state interests as being put into doubt, if not altered, by *Roe III.*

Mills v. Rogers, 102 S. Ct. 2442, 2450-51 (1982).

C. THE FEDERAL GRANT-IN-AID SYSTEM

1. IN GENERAL

It is commonly accepted that federal grants-in-aid are used by the federal government to influence policy-making by state and local governments. Since this is so, it is important to note the growing importance of federal financial assistance to these governments. In 1954, federal assistance amounted to 11.4 per cent of state and local government general revenue from their own sources. By 1981, the federal contribution was at an estimated 28.3% after peaking at 31.7% in 1978. Advisory Commission on Intergovernmental Relations, Significant Features of Fiscal Federalism, 1979-1980 Edition 161 (1980).

The following selection indicates the structure of the federal grant-in-aid programs:

ADVISORY COMMISSION ON INTERGOVERNMENTAL RELATIONS, CATEGORICAL GRANTS: THEIR ROLE AND DESIGN 5-6 (1978)

A Typology of Federal Grants

The federal grant-in-aid system now consists of three general types of grants: categorical grants, block grants, and general revenue sharing.

Categorical grants can be used only for a specifically aided program and usually are limited to narrowly defined activities. Legislation generally details the parameters of the program and specifies the types of funded activities. However in some cases . . . the specific activities may be determined by administrators.

This study identifies four types of categorical grants: formula grants, project grants, formula-project grants (combining various aspects of both grant types), and open-end reimbursement grants. This classification is based chiefly on an analysis of the means of distributing the funds available to carry out approved activities and focuses on the degree to which the process fosters competition among potential recipients and vests discretion in federal administrators.

When grant funds are allocated among recipients according to factors specified within enabling legislation or administrative regulations, the grant is considered a formula grant. Project grants are non-formula in nature—potential recipients submit specific, individual applications in the form and at the times indicated by the grantor. The formula-project categorical grant uses a mixture of fund allocation means; distribution takes place in two stages—the first involves state area allocations governed by a statute or regulation formula, and the second entails project applications and discretionary awards. Open-end reimbursement grants—often regarded as formula grants—are characterized by an arrangement wherein the federal government is committed to reimbursing a specified proportion of state-local program costs, thus eliminating competition among recipients as well as the need for an allocation formula.

The second of the tripartite components of the present federal grant system is the block grant. It may be defined as a grant that is given chiefly to general purpose governmental units in accordance with a statutory formula for use, largely at the recipient's discretion, in a variety of activities within a broad functional area. Fundable activities are more numerous than for a categorical grant and fewer conditions constraining recipients' discretion in funds spending are attached.

The third component of the federal grant system is general revenue sharing (GRS), under which funds are distributed by formula with few or no limits on the purposes for which they may be spent and few if any restrictions on the procedures by which they are spent.

. . . .

The differentiation of the three types of grants (and among the four kinds of categoricals) thus reflects varying combinations of three characteristics:

1. The range of federal administrator's funding discretion. At one extreme no such discretion exists because grant funds are distributed by an entitlement formula with a legislative prescribed matching ratio. At the opposite extreme, the federal administrator has wide latitude in awarding project grants among many competing eligible recipients.

2. The range of recipient discretion concerning aided activities. Such discretion is greatest in the case of GRS and most constrained in certain project grants, wherein the scope of permitted activities is narrowly specified, sometimes to a particular facility or experimental program.

3. The type, number, detail, and scope of grant program conditions. These conditions, such as planning, fiscal management, administrative organization, and performance standards requirements, determine the degree of federal intrusiveness in the recipient's conduct of the grant-aided activity.

The proliferation of categorical grants and the program conditions they place on state and local governments have led to complaints that they place a heavy burden on state and local agencies that administer these grants. The flavor of these complaints is captured in the following excerpts from a report prepared in the President's Executive Office in 1975, and which reflects the situation at that time:

EXECUTIVE OFFICE OF THE PRESIDENT, STRENGTHENING PUBLIC MANAGEMENT IN THE INTERGOVERNMENTAL SYSTEM 9-10, 12 (1975)

While acknowledging the necessity for Federal funding and technical assistance in delivering domestic programs to citizens in their jurisdiction, many State and local elected officials also view it as a burden on their own capacity to govern. . . .

The Committee heard repeated complaints along these lines from State and local leaders. If their cooperation is desired in carrying out national objectives, it would appear vital to determine whether these opinions reflect inbuilt conflicts that might be avoided. In general, their complaints center on three characteristics of the design and administration of categorical assistance: (1) fragmentation, (2) administrative inflexibility, and (3) the bypassing of their authority. . . .

Fragmentation. Nearly 80 per cent of Federal assistance to State and local government is delivered through specific purpose or categorical grant programs. These number about 1,100 and are administered by 54 agencies. In the health area alone, for instance, the State or local manager is faced with a choice of 230 programs administered by 10 agencies. There are 23 just for facility planning and construction; 22 for narcotics addiction and drug abuse.

This proliferation of programs, the Comptroller General of the United States said, causes State and local government "substantial problems" when they "attempt to identify, obtain and use Federal assistance to meet their needs." ...

Administrative Inflexibilities. State and local officials have long complained of "red tape" in Washington, but a recent review of Federal assistance by the Comptroller General added up to an across-the-board indictment of the delivery system, citing inadequate grant disseminating information, complex and varying application and administrative processes and "narrowness and restrictiveness" in program guidelines. ...

The reasons for conflicts between local priorities and Federal administrative guidelines have nothing to do with malintentions. Most Federal categorical programs, at the time of their design, were intended to achieve specific national purposes and hence carried detailed administrative prescriptions as to how those purposes were to be achieved. Many, in fact, have been achieved. But it is now generally recognized that overly detailed administrative regulations in many areas not only fail to achieve their purposes but fail precisely because of the burdens they place on State and local management.

In other words, the Federal mission agencies, by reason of their legislative mandates, have concentrated on the accomplishment of specific operational or service responsibilities. State and local governments have been viewed as mere instruments of national policy.

The result has been the development of a network of regulations that serves individual program needs. But when these come together at the State and local levels, the resulting mix has an enormous and often adverse impact on local priorities. ...

Bypassing of State and local elected officials. Federal agencies rountinely channel domestic assistance to non-governmental and special-purpose agencies as well as to government agencies at the State and local level. ...

The special-purpose agencies (for housing, water supply, resource conservation, etc.) created by Federal funding have added to the fragmentation of local government in metropolitan and rural areas, often weakened its accountability to citizens, and generally undermined the management position of its elected executive officials.

One county in Ohio, for instance, must deal with the following independent, Federally funded organizations: a three-county Resource Conservation and Development District, a nine-county Economic Development District, and a twelve-county areawide health planning district.

Even though locally elected officials may be members of or be represented on private or intergovernmental bodies, these organizations are still largely beyond their effective control.

In the case of Federal assistance that is directed to departments or agencies under their control, the bypassing of elected officials takes subtler forms. Federal program managers tend to relate to State and local department and agency heads and staffs in vertical lines. This relationship creates "bureaucracies ... within the State and local governments" that are "outside the scope of these governments, to the point where it is impossible for a mayor and a city council to make a realistic policy," according to Allen E. Pritchard, Jr., former executive vice-president of the National League of Cities.

The National Governors' Conference also has noted the tendency of State level officials to form interest group associations around narrow functional bases. These each relate to some entity in Washington and there is "frequent extensive in-fighting and maneuvering between them."

One effect of Federal programming that creates quasi-independent organizations within or without State and local government is that it builds demands for matching resources, or in some cases, the assumption, on short notice, of full fiscal responsibility if Federal funding is suddenly terminated or delayed.

This has led Mayor Janet Hayes of San Jose, California to term Federal (as well as State) assistance to localities as the "shift and shaft programs" in which the higher level of government shifts responsibilities on to the city and then fails to provide the funds. The effect is to make local fiscal management subject to the whims of outside funding.

See also the Summary of Recommendations of the National Governors' Association advocating consolidation of grant-in-aid programs to ease problems of duplication and excessive administrative requirements, reprinted in *Hearings on the State and Local Fiscal Assistance Act of 1972 Before a Subcomm. of the House Comm. on Government Operations*, 96th Cong., 2d Sess. 440 (1980).

The enactment of block grants which consolidate several categorical grants is an effort at the federal level to delegate more responsibility to state and local governments and to build up their governing capacity. Whether state and local governments have or can develop that capacity has produced some skepticism, as the following comments indicate:

PRESSMAN, POLITICAL IMPLICATIONS OF THE NEW FEDERALISM, in FINANCING THE NEW FEDERALISM 37-38 (W. Oates ed. 1975)

One reason for skepticism about . . . aggressive behavior on the part of local governments is rooted in the frequent critical observations about "local government capacity." Although this term is frequently used in a technical sense—meaning weakness in personnel, planning, and management—a number of studies have deplored local governments' political inadequacies as well. Effective action at the local level can be hampered by the absence of institutions with extensive formal powers, by the lack of a strong and coherent system of parties and groups, and by timid behavior on the part of elected leaders.

Federal funds can provide additional resources to local leaders, and politically adept local executives have been able to use those resources to their own advantage. But, . . . the ability to utilize new federal resources varies among local communities and local leaders. Recent analyses of federal programs have shown that weaknesses in local political systems can create obstacles to the effective use of federal funds. The [federal government] cannot abolish the problem of local political capacity. Because of the tendency on the part of many local officials to try to avoid conflict and minimize their own responsibilities, we should not be too ready to assume that such officials will welcome the disappearance of federal guidelines. After all, guidelines provide an excellent scapegoat for local leaders who wish to avoid being held responsible for what may be an unpopular act. Even aggressive mayors can benefit from the opportunity to say that "the feds are making me do it" in backing a controversial cause. . . . Federal guidelines, though much maligned in the rhetoric of local officials, do provide those same officials with an excuse to refuse to make concessions to other local actors. Thus, binding guidelines can actually provide leaders with an increased measure of freedom in the local arena. No wonder the abolition of guidelines is less than unanimously supported by mayors.

Similar concerns have been expressed about the capabilities of state governments, which are discussed in Chapter 1. State and local experience under a conventional categorical grant program, the federal mental health program, is discussed *supra*. Experience under the newer forms of federal assistance that delegate substantially more responsibility to the states is discussed in the sections on general revenue sharing and block grants that follow. *See generally* Sandalow, *Federal Grants and the Reform of State and Local Government* in FINANCING THE METROPOLIS 175-80 (J. Credine ed. 1970).

2. THE GENERAL REVENUE SHARING PROGRAM

Background

Categorical grant programs contain programmatic and administrative requirements as a condition to the receipt of federal aid, and are intended to implement the statutory purposes for which Congress authorized financial assistance. To provide financial aid to state and local governments without the limitations attached to categorical grants, Congress in 1972 enacted the State and Local Fiscal Assistance Act, better known as the General Revenue Sharing Act. Unlike the categorical federal aid programs, general revenue sharing puts over six billion dollars annually in state and local coffers, to be spent at state and local discretion with a minimum of federal control.

The leading exponents of the concept of revenue sharing were Walter W. Heller, who proposed it when he served as chairman of the President's Council of Economic Advisors in 1964, and Joseph A. Pechman, director of economic studies at the Brookings Institution, who was appointed by President Johnson as chairman of a task force to develop a proposal.[1] Heller's concept is more fully described in W. HELLER, NEW DIMENSIONS OF POLITICAL ECONOMY ch. 3 (1966). Because the version enacted by Congress in 1972 differed in several significant respects from its source, it is worth noting the essence of Heller's concept:

> The core of the revenue-sharing plan is the regular distribution of a specified portion of the federal individual income tax to the state primarily on the basis of population and with next to no strings attached or, at least, no hamstrings attached. This distribution would be over and above existing and future conditional grants.

Heller, *A Sympathetic Reappraisal of Revenue Sharing* in REVENUE SHARING AND THE CITY 6 (H. Perloff & R. Nathan eds. 1968). Heller believed that this form of revenue sharing would come closest to serving what he believed should be the goals of any new approach to supplying federal funds to the states:

> Ideally, any new plan or approach should supply funds in ways that will

---

[1] The idea of federal revenue sharing was not new, but its realization can be said to date from the Heller-Pechman proposals. A brief historical perspective is given in O. Stolz, Revenue Sharing; Legal and Policy Analysis 2-9 (1974).

—not only relieve immediate pressures on state-local treasuries, but make their revenues more responsive to economic growth;
   —build up the vitality, efficiency, and fiscal independence of state-local governments;
   —increase the progressivity of our federal-state-local tax system;
   —reduce economic inequalities and fiscal disparities among the states;
   —stimulate state and local tax efforts;
   —ensure that the plight of local, and especially urban, governments will be given full weight.

Id. at 5-6. By 1967, incidentally, Heller's reappraisal of the pass-through question had led him to conclude that the revenue sharing formula should explicitly require a minimum pass-through from the states to local governments. *Id.* at 32-37.

This section explores some of the conceptual and legal problems that are raised by the general revenue sharing program. When studying these materials, consider whether the objectives of the program as originally conceived by Heller were implemented in the way he intended.

The Statute

As originally enacted in 1972, the General Revenue Sharing program, 31 U.S.C. § 1221 et seq. (1976 & Supp. III 1979), distributed to state and local governments funds, called "entitlements," based on a complex formula designed to take into consideration state population, general tax effort and relative income. In 1976, an alternative formula was developed to include urban population and low-income population as additional factors. The funds could be used for what the act called "priority expenditures," which amounted to a list of most operating expenditures of local governments, except education and welfare. In addition, the funds could be used for "ordinary and necessary capital expenditures as authorized by law." This provision was virtually impossible to enforce, as local governments could simply place general revenue funds in one of the statutory categories and use the funds freed up by this process for expenditures not authorized by the statute. In only one case was this kind of transfer struck down, and in that instance the fund transfer was transparently blatant. *Mathews v. Massell,* 356 F. Supp. 291 (N.D. Ga. 1973) (city of Atlanta used funds freed up to give rebate on water charges). *See generally* Comment, *The Revenue Sharing Act of 1972; United and Untraceable Dollars from Washington,* 10 HARV. J. ON LEGIS. 176 (1973). The congressional response to these problems was to remove the limitations on spending entirely in 1976.

Of the amount allocated to a particular state, two thirds was to be reallocated to local units of general government (counties and municipalities, but not special districts) under complex statutory formulae contained in § 108 of the Act, and one third was to be retained by the state.

Enforcement of the nondiscrimination provisions, 31 U.S.C. § 1242, was severely criticized. *See* United States Comm'n on Civil Rights, The Federal Civil Rights Enforcement Effort—1974, Vol. IV: To Provide Fiscal Assistance (1975); *Hearings on Civil Rights Aspects of General Revenue Sharing Before the Subcomm. on Civil and Constitutional Rights of the House Comm. on Judiciary,* 94th Cong., 1st Sess. (1975). The problem is that the pervasive distribution of general revenue sharing money has exposed local governments with long-standing discriminatory employment and service availability practices to charges that they are in violation of the civil rights provisions of the general revenue sharing law. From the discussion so far it is clear that this leverage is enormous. Revenue sharing is so important at the local level that local governments simply cannot refuse revenue sharing funds.

The 1976 amendments considerably strengthened the enforcement procedures. Originally the Act simply authorized the Treasury Secretary, who is responsible for the administration of the Act, to notify the governor of the state of any noncompliance with the nondiscrimination provision. The governor was then to attempt to secure compliance, and if he was not able to do so the matter could be referred to the U.S. Attorney General for appropriate action. The Act now provides for a variety of administrative, judicial, and agency hearings on noncompliance, places time limits on the duty of the Secretary to send notices of noncompliance, and authorizes the suspension of general revenue sharing funds unless a compliance agreement is executed or the notice of termination is successfully challenged. The U.S. Attorney General may now bring an action under this section in his own right, and the Secretary is authorized to enter into cooperation agreements with other state and federal agencies, presumably including civil rights agencies, to investigate noncompliance with the nondiscrimination provisions.

A follow-up study of civil rights problems after the 1976 amendments reported that the amendments have had a positive impact. More information was available to determine the status of pending cases; effective administrative sanctions, including withholding of funds, had been developed; and major settlements had been obtained in Baltimore, Mobile and San Francisco requiring the elimination of barriers to municipal employment by minorities. However, substantial deficiencies continued, primarily in delays in processing complaints, case backlog, reluctance to apply sanctions, failure to monitor settlements and premature closing of cases. *Testimony of William L. Taylor & Morton H. Sklar, Center for National Policy Review, Catholic University Law School, Hearings on the State and Local Fiscal Assistance Act of 1972 Before a Subcomm. of the House Comm. on Government Operations,* 96th Cong., 2d. Sess. 597, 601-13 (1980).

The general revenue sharing legislation was extended for three additional years in the closing days of the Carter Administration. Act of Dec. 28, 1980, Pub. L. No. 96-604, 94 Stat. 3516. The only major change in the legislation was a change in state entitlements. States were omitted in fiscal 1981. They were included for fiscal 1982 and 1983, but would have to give up an equivalent amount in their categorical grant assistance to receive general revenue sharing.

This change in the legislation reflected an ongoing debate over state participation in the program. Changes in the comparative fiscal situation of federal, state and local governments prompted the congressional decision to limit the state role. Most important were the surpluses acquired by many state governments, the rapid increase in state tax revenues, tax cuts by state legislatures, and the call by some states for a constitutional convention to consider an amendment requiring a balanced federal budget. These factors are outlined in the following statement by the then Assistant Director of the Advisory Commission on Intergovernmental Relations. His statement reflects the federal, state and local fiscal situation at that time:

STATEMENT BY JOHN SHANNON, ASSISTANT DIRECTOR, ADVISORY COMMISSION ON INTERGOVERNMENTAL RELATIONS, in Revenue Sharing with the States, Hearing Before the Subcomm. on the City, House Comm. on Banking, Finance and Urban Affairs, 96th Cong., 1st Sess. 53, 54-57 (1979)

The original case for including the states as well as the localities in the federal revenue sharing program rested on three major arguments.

1. *A Federal Aid Flexibility Rationale.* The proliferation of narrow purpose federal aids to states and localities has caused a hardening of the categories. Federal revenue sharing would build a much needed element of flexibility into the federal aid system.

2. *The Fiscal Equalization Justification.* Federal revenue sharing would reduce somewhat the fiscal disparities between the rich and the poor states and between the have and the have not localities within each state.

3. *A Fiscal Mismatch Justification.* The supporters of revenue sharing repeatedly pointed to the fact of a fiscal imbalance—that the revenue cream was rising to the federal level while the bulk of major domestic expenditure responsibilities remain at state and local levels. Thus, federal revenue sharing was needed to redress this fiscal mismatch that favored the federal fisc.

The first two arguments for a general revenue sharing program involving state and local governments have lost none of their validity. Both states and localities have made good use of the fiscal flexibility of general revenue sharing funds. Also, although the fiscal equalization effect of revenue sharing is quite mild as among states, it is quite significant as among communities within states and within metropolitan areas. Central cities, for example, ordinarily receive far more on a per capita basis than do their affluent suburban neighbors.

The justification of fiscal mismatch, however, is now open to question. While it is still generally agreed that localities remain the low men on the fiscal totem pole, evidence of fiscal deterioration at the federal level and marked fiscal improvement at the state level challenges the federal-state component of the fiscal mismatch argument.

Federal Fiscal Deterioration

Several factors have now combined to take a good share of the wind out of the federal fiscal sails.

1. Congress is running into increasing resistance in its efforts to raise social security taxes to cover the vast expansion in social security benefits. It may soon be forced to dip into federal general funds to pay for social security benefits or develop a new federal tax source.

2. The strength of the federal government's number one revenue producer, the income tax, is being sapped as it must now perform an increasing number of non-revenue chores—repeatedly Congress has had to cut this tax in order to spur the economy, offset inflation-induced tax increases, and compensate for social security tax hikes.

3. Unlike the 50's and 60's, the federal government can no longer shift resources from defense to non-defense functions. Defense outlays have dropped from almost 14 percent of GNP in 1954 to $6^{1}/_{2}$ percent by 1979.

4. The fear of double-digit inflation is making it increasingly difficult for the federal government to paper over the revenue short falls by means of deficit financing.

5. On the expenditure side, the federal government has assumed responsibility for financing an increasing share of the programs with the fastest growth—income maintenance for the elderly and poor; and the health care costs for the elderly, the poor, and the near poor. In addition, the federal government has presided over the explosive growth of federal aid to states and localities.

Strengthened State Position

The relative position of the states within our federal system has grown significantly over the last two decades. This marked improvement is reflected by the following facts.

1. States have more balanced revenue systems—today 37 states make use of both the personal income tax and the general sales tax as compared to only 19 states in 1960.

2. State-local tax systems are less regressive—twenty-nine states now partially shield home owners from property tax overload situations through state financed circuit-breakers. More than half of the sales tax states now remove much of the regressive sting from the sales tax with food and drug exemptions or with income tax credits.

3. As a group, the states have now clearly forged ahead of local governments on the tax front. In 1963, the states were raising about $1 for each $1 raised by local governments. Now the states are raising $1.40 for each $1 collected at the local level.

4. This striking state revenue advance is due in no small measure to the remarkable performance of the state personal income tax—the fastest growing revenue source in our intergovernmental system. The performance of the state personal income tax is also making it increasingly difficult for state policymakers to argue that the federal government has "preempted" the income tax field.

5. In "good times," most states no longer have to rely on politically painful tax rate increases now that their revenue systems are much more responsive to economic growth, both real and inflationary. As indicated by the ACIR's latest survey, state tax officials believe that the net 1978 increase in state revenues came wholly from inflation and real economic growth, without any increase attributable to legislative change.

Comments: 1. The fiscal situation in the states soon deteriorated. Many states used up accumulated surplus between 1981 and 1982, a change produced by declining federal assistance and a prolonged recession. They faced the prospect of increased taxes, reduced expenditures, or both in order to avoid the deficits which are prohibited by practically all state constitutions. In the Reagan Administration, Congress also enacted a substantial cut in the federal income tax and increased defense spending. Huge deficits in federal spending resulted. How do these changes affect Shannon's analysis?

2. A number of factors must be considered in evaluating the 1980 change in the general revenue sharing legislation. Available estimates indicate that the states have passed through from fifteen to forty percent of their general revenue sharing funds to local governments. A very high proportion of this pass-through assistance has gone to local school districts as an attempt to compensate for the omission of school districts from the general revenue sharing program. It also reflects the increasing tendency of state governments to finance a larger share of local school expenditures. This change, in some states, reflects state court decisions requiring equalization of school expenditures. See Chapter 10.

Whether the states, as a group, will be fiscally healthy is another question. See the discussion in Chapter 5, *supra*. State revenues increase largely because of the income tax, which is income elastic and produces higher revenues during periods of inflation without increases in tax rates. The elasticity of the state income tax also means that it is highly vulnerable in periods of recession, when incomes fall. At the local level, the widespread adoption of stringent limitations on the property tax can be expected to reduce local government revenues in some states. This development is discussed in Chapter 5. Whether the federal government should accept the responsibility to make up revenue deficiencies produced by state-imposed tax limitations raises an obvious political question.

3. The 1980 amendments did not revise the revenue sharing formulas. Attempts to devise formulas more responsive to need have proved difficult. *See* Stanfield, *Playing Computer Politics with Local Aid Formulas,* 9 NAT'L J. 1977 (1978). An attempt to develop a formula placing greater emphasis on poverty, for example, was found to shift funds from Frostbelt to Sunbelt states, where incomes are lower. It quickly lost political support. *Id.* at 1980. "Even far-fetched factors can sometimes produce desired results.... [A]n experiment ... applied such irrelevant numbers as annual rainfall and January temperatures to 25 large cities and found they would have received roughly the same revenue sharing money as under the actual formula." *Id.* at 1979.

In addition, a study by the Advisory Commission on Intergovernmental Relations compared per capita state and local revenue sharing receipts with a composite stress index developed by the commission. The study found that per capita receipts matched well with state and local stress factors. The stress index measures public welfare burden, family tax burden, personal income growth and per capita personal income. *See* Stanfield, *Revenue Sharing Survived This Year, But 1980 May Be a Different Story,* 11 NAT'L J. 1331 (1979). For mathematic formulas expressing the present statutory distribution formulas see Comptroller General of the U.S., *How Revenue Sharing Formulas Distribute Aid: Urban-Rural Implications* (1980).

General revenue sharing must be reenacted in 1984. As of this writing, its retention is expected.

4. The distributive impact of the general revenue sharing program produced some surprises, as indicated in an extensive study published in 1975. R. NATHAN, A. MANVEL & S. CALKINS, MONITORING REVENUE SHARING (1975). The program at that time favored the states with high tax effort and low tax capacity, and to this extent compensated for interstate differences in tax capacity. The program still fell short of compensating in full for these differences, primarily because of the modest scale of the general revenue sharing program as compared with total state and local finances. *Id.* at 92-93.

Within states, the statutory formula distributed more aid to the smaller rather than the larger metropolitan areas. Average income is much higher in metropolitan areas, and this distribution occurred because the within-state allocation formula has a low-income factor which is counted twice in the allocation criteria. *Id.* at 100-01. Within metropolitan areas, the larger cities tended to do better than their suburbs. *Id.* at 133-34. What do these findings indicate about the objectives served by general revenue sharing as compared with the expectations of its original sponsors as described *supra*?

Some of the statutory allocation formulas also are deceptive. The statute includes population in the county area allocation formula, for example, but this factor is not determinative. In fact, this allocation factor reduces to Adjusted Taxes divided by the square of Per Capita Income. The allocation factors are discussed in the *Madison County* case, which is reproduced *infra*.

5. The repeal of the priority spending categories in 1976 makes it difficult to determine how state and local governments use general revenue sharing funds, but a survey by the U.S. Conference of Mayors provides some indication. Of the 97 cities surveyed, 36 used these funds to support their overall operating budget, 23 used them for capital improvements, and about one third used them for fire and police services. A minority of the cities used general revenue sharing funds for social services such as health and recreation. *Hearings on the State and Local Fiscal Assistance Act of 1972 Before a Subcomm. of the House Comm. on Government Operations,* 96th Cong., 2d Sess. 295 (1980). These cities also indicated the adjustments that would have to be made if general revenue sharing were eliminated. Two thirds indicated they would have to reduce or eliminate services, one third anticipated a need to raise taxes, and a number indicated they would have to delay or eliminate capital improvements or lay off city workers.

What do these findings indicate about the function of general revenue sharing? About local "capacity"? Note that many of the uses to which cities put general revenue sharing funds are not supported by federal categorical grants.

Even though the general revenue sharing program is a 100%, non-matching entitlement program, federal law is not the sole determinant of questions concerning how the funds may be used, as the following case indicates.

STATE EX REL. CONGER v. MADISON COUNTY

Supreme Court of Tennessee
581 S.W.2d 632 (1979)

Opinion

HENRY, CHIEF JUSTICE.

The principal issue before the Court is whether Federal Revenue Sharing Funds allocated to a county and, by its Quarterly Court, transferred to the County School Fund, must be apportioned with a special school district within the county under § 49-605, T.C.A.[1] The Trial Judge responded in the affirmative; the Court of Appeals in the negative; we agree with the Court of Appeals.

A preliminary issue, but one of pivotal importance, is whether such funds may be used by a county for school purposes.

We hold that they may.

I

History of the Lawsuit

This action was instituted on August 24, 1977 in the Circuit Court at Jackson by the three Commissioners of the City of Jackson, who, by virtue of their office constitute the School Board of the City of Jackson, which maintains its own school system, operating wholly within the city.

Named as parties defendant were Madison County, the County Judge, the County Trustee, and the surety on the Trustee's official bond.

The complaint alleges, and the trial judge found, that during the early part of 1977 the Quarterly Court of Madison County appropriated to the Madison County General Purpose School Fund, for maintenance and operating purposes, the sum of $201,476.00 from Federal Revenue Sharing Funds, and that this sum was not apportioned with the City of Jackson.

It is further averred and established by the proof that the Quarterly Court, in its budget for the fiscal year ending in 1978, appropriated from Federal Revenue Sharing Funds to the Madison County School System the sum of $565,822.51, accompanied by a stated intention that those funds would not be apportioned in accordance with the City's view of the mandate of § 49-605, T.C.A. These funds also were appropriated for maintenance and operation.

The trial court held that apportionment was required under § 49-605, T.C.A., and should have been accomplished by using the average daily attendance (ADA) computations. The ADA ratio between the two systems indicated that the City of Jackson's share was 48.561537% and that of Madison County, 51.438427%.

---

[1] The apportionment provision is now codified in § 49-614, T.C.A., which contains new acronyms, e. g., WFTEADA (weighted full-time equivalent average daily attendance), in place of ADA. Section 49-602, *et seq.* contains the statutory provisions relating to the State Foundation Program, and was derived from Chapter 289, Acts of 1977. References in this opinion are to § 49-605, T.C.A., as it appears in main Volume 9, T.C.A.

From these figures, the Trial Judge found that it would have required a total appropriation of $391,683.82 to validate the appropriation to the Madison County System. This would have resulted in an apportionment of $190,207.82 to the City of Jackson. Therefore, he awarded judgment against Madison County in this amount.

. . . .

The Court of Appeals, in a brief opinion, held that § 49-605, T.C.A. "has no application to funds received by Madison County under the State and Local Fiscal Assistance Act of 1972, as amended."

We examine these divergent legal conclusions.

II

Federal Revenue Sharing Act [3]

We think an orderly consideration of this action must start with the Federal Revenue Sharing Act.

This act was designed to return to state and local communities revenue collected by the federal government for use "according to their own perceived demands and objectives and not those of the federal government." *Carolina Action v. Simon,* 389 F.Supp. 1244, 1248 (M.D.N.C.1975).

It should be noted at the outset that, in its original form, the act restricted the use of these federal funds to "priority expenditures." Education was not an enumerated permitted use. See 31 U.S.C. § 1222. This section was repealed by Pub.L. 94-488, § 3(a), 90 Stat. 2341, October 3, 1976.

The statutory scheme of distribution is somewhat cumbersome and tends to be confusing. It is not required that we deal with it in detail. The allocation among states is determined by 31 U.S.C. § 1225.

The amount allocated to each state is divided one-third to the state government and two-thirds to local governments, 31 U.S.C. § 1226, on the basis of a formula derived from the Act. The two-thirds allocated to local governments is distributed on the basis of a formula reflected in 31 U.S.C. § 1227. Generally speaking, the local government share is allocated to county areas on the basis of the ratio that the population of the county, multiplied by the general tax effort factor of that county area, multiplied by the relative income factor, bears to the sum of that figure for all county areas in the state. 31 U.S.C. § 1227(a).

The county area share is divided between the county and all municipalities of the county. The allocation to a county government is on the basis of the ratio the adjusted taxes of the county government bears to the adjusted taxes of the county government and all other units of local government located in the county area. 31 U.S.C. § 1227(b)(1).

The remaining funds are then allocated among the municipalities (in Tennessee) located in the county area. 31 U.S.C. § 1227(b)(2). As a result, the municipalities within a county area *collectively* receive their allocations in the same manner as do counties. The allocation *among* the municipalities is based upon a formula taking into consideration population, general tax effort, and relative income. 31 U.S.C. § 1227(b)(2).

Attached hereto as an Appendix is a flow chart designed to show generally the distribution of these funds. It is included solely to clarify this opinion, and should

---

[3] The correct title of this law is the "State and Local Fiscal Assistance Act of 1972." We elect to use the popular name.

only be used for that purpose. The details of the various formulae and other factors not shown in this appendix are set forth in Chapter 24, Title 31, U.S.C.

As will be seen by this narration and by reference to the appendix, the City of Jackson has already received an allocation of Federal Sharing Funds, wholly separate and apart from those received by Madison County. The entitlement of all governmental units is determined by computer and the distributions are made directly to the local governments from the Federal Sharing Office in Washington, D. C. May the City of Jackson receive a portion of the funds allocated to the county?

Federal statutes alone do not provide the answer. In order to qualify for the federal funds, a county or municipality

> ... must establish ... to the satisfaction of the Secretary that—
> . . . .
> (4) it will provide for the expenditure of amounts received under subchapter I of this chapter only in accordance with the laws and procedures applicable to the expenditure of its own revenues. 31 U.S.C. § 1243(a)(4)

Thus, the answer to the question presented in this action lies in the statutes of the State of Tennessee.

III

Source, Use, and Nature of County Funds

Federal Revenue Sharing Funds are not earmarked for any specific purpose. Upon their receipt by a county, they become subject to appropriation and use by the Quarterly Court.

In attempting to clarify the nature and permissible use of these funds, our statutory law is not particularly helpful. For instance, § 5-801, T.C.A., undertakes to inventory all sources of county revenue. It reads:

> County revenue is derived from taxes on polls, property, privileges, litigation, merchants, peddlers; from strays, fines and forfeitures, as below [see Section 5-802 through 5-805], and from money remaining unclaimed more than two (2) years in clerks' offices.

It is obvious that this statute is hopelessly out of date and that Federal Revenue Sharing Funds, now a major source of county revenue, do not fit into any of the listed classifications.

There is, however, another statute, not cited by the principal parties, but relied upon by the Surety on the Trustee's bond, which we consider to be highly significant. Section 5-924, T.C.A. reads as follows:

> All funds from whatever source derived, including but not limited to taxes, county aid funds, *federal funds,* and fines, which are to be used in the operation and respective programs of the various departments, commissions, institutions, boards, offices, and agencies of county governments shall be appropriated to such use by the county legislative bodies. (Emphasis supplied)

It should be noted that this statute, as originally enacted in 1959 did not include federal funds. By Chapter 615 of the Public Acts of 1976 the original language was changed by adding the words "federal funds." No other change was made. Section 49-605, however, was not amended.

It would seem clear that the Quarterly Court of Madison County had the authority, under this statute, to appropriate Federal Revenue Sharing Funds to use in the operation and maintenance of the school system. Indeed, independent of this statutory authorization, it would seem that the Quarterly Court had the authority to place these revenues in any of the County's funds, including the school fund.

There is, however, a line of cases that at least superficially tends to indicate a contrary result.

In *State ex rel. Davidson County Board of Education v. Pollard,* 124 Tenn. 127, 136 S.W. 427 (1910), the question presented to the Court was whether a county court had the authority to make an appropriation out of the general fund of a county for school purposes. Responding in the negative, the Court held that

> county purposes are of two kinds, general county purposes and special county purposes, and that moneys raised by taxation for special county purposes cannot be used for a general county purpose, and that money raised for general county purposes cannot be used for a special county purpose. 124 Tenn. 130-131, 38 S.W. at 428.

The Court quoted with approval the following language from *Kennedy v. Montgomery County,* 98 Tenn. 165, 179, 38 S.W. 1075, 1079 (1897):

> The taxpayers of every county have a right to know for what purpose they are being taxed, and also to know that taxes collected from them for any special purpose are applied to such purpose, and not to some other, at the discretion of county officials, and according to their ideas of public policy or expediency. *The law does not provide for the mixing of special and ordinary funds, nor the supplementing of one by the other by county officials.* (Emphasis in original). 124 Tenn. at 135, 136 S.W. at 429.

The *Pollard-Kennedy* rationale was followed in *Board of Commissioners of Union City v. Obion County,* 188 Tenn. 666, 222 S.W.2d 7 (1949). In that case it appeared that the county had paid a bonus to teachers in the county schools, and had funded it by a transfer from the "General Fund" to the "School Fund." Pointing out that the general fund "had been levied and collected for specific county purposes," the Court held that "[t]he mere fact that . . . the money was passed through the elementary school fund prior to its disbursement . . . did not change the nature of the money or make it legally a part of the elementary school fund." Therefore, the Court held it "remained a part of the County's 'General Fund' " and could not be diverted. . . .

An equally strong case is *State ex rel. Baird v. Wilson County,* 212 Tenn. 619, 371 S.W.2d 434 (1963). In that case the County Quarterly Court had diverted money from the county general fund for elementary school purposes. Relying upon *Obion County, supra* and *State, ex rel. Cope v. Davidson County,* 198 Tenn. 24, 277 S.W.2d 396 (1955), (fund derived from special tax for teacher transportation was in reality a means for increasing salaries without making a devise with the City of Nashville) the Court said:

> Both the *Obion County* case and the *Davidson County* case clearly state that funds derived from taxes levied for one purpose, when transferred by the Quarterly County Court to the school fund, do not become a part of the funds to which transferred. The unauthorized and *ultra vires* resolution of the County Court diverting funds from the legitimate purpose for which the tax to produce such funds had been levied does not change the nature of the fund or make it legally a part of the fund to which it is thus wrongfully transferred. 212 Tenn. at 626, 371 S.W.2d at 438.

If we hold these cases to be applicable, it would logically follow that Federal Revenue Sharing Funds may not be used for the maintenance and operation of public schools in the county, and that such a use would be an unauthorized diversion. Pursuant to such a holding the county would have to transfer the funds to the County General Fund and there could be no apportionment.

Such a holding would frustrate the purpose of the act, which is to permit local governments to "spend these funds according to their own perceived demands and objectives." Further, it would be contrary to § 5-924, T.C.A. which provides, *inter alia,* that "[a]ll . . . federal funds . . . which are to be used [for various county purposes] shall be appropriated to such use by the county legislative bodies."

Finally, such a holding would contradict common sense and, in effect, make these funds unusable for any purpose. It must be borne in mind that these are not conventional county revenues raised by conventional tax levies. They are Federal Sharing Funds, and their use must lie in the sound judgment and discretion of the county government.

The cases noted above involve the unauthorized diversion of conventional tax revenues raised for specific and itemized purposes. Therefore our courts consistently and correctly have held that tax revenues raised for stated public purposes may not be diverted. Federal Revenue Sharing Funds, however, are not derived from county tax levies and collected for designated purposes.

We, therefore, hold that Federal Revenue Sharing Funds may be allocated for school purposes.

Nothing in our recent case of *City of Harriman v. Roane County,* 553 S.W.2d 904 (Tenn. 1977) alters this conclusion. In that case we were dealing with conventional county revenues, expenditure of which is governed by state statutory and decisional law. We held that the proceeds of the wholesale beer tax could not lawfully be appropriated to school purposes "without specific statutory authorization," 553 S.W.2d at 907, and that although the second half of the retail sales tax proceeds could be so used, they must be apportioned in accordance with § 49-605, T.C.A.

Again, in the instant case we do not deal with conventional state or county revenues, but with funds that come to local governments with the restriction that they will be expended "in accordance with the laws and procedures applicable to the expenditure of its own revenues." 31 U.S.C. § 1243(a)(4). There is no Tennessee law that precludes the use of these funds for any legitimate county purpose.

IV

Apportionment

The remaining question is whether these funds must be apportioned with the City of Jackson. We respond in the negative.

Section 49-605, T.C.A. provides, in pertinent part as follows:

> For each school system there shall be levied for current operation and maintenance not more than one school tax for all such grades as may be included in the local school program. Each system shall place in one separate school fund all school revenues for current school operation purposes *received from the state, county, and other political subdivisions, if any.* . . . All school funds for current operation and maintenance purposes collected by any county, [except for transportation tax levy funds] shall be *apportioned* by the county trustee *among the county, city, and special school districts therein* on the basis of the average daily attendance maintained by each, during the current school year. (Emphasis supplied.)

By its very phraseology, this statute cannot be applicable to Federal Revenue Sharing Funds, the source of which is the Federal Government. Money received from the Federal Government obviously is not received from a state, county, or other political *subdivision*. The political facts of life are that the Federal Government is in no sense a "political subdivision."

The apportionment provision for "[a]ll school funds for current operation and maintenance purposes collected by any county" simply refers to all funds collected or received from the state, county, or other political subdivision. It adds nothing to the scope and extent of the definition of the funds embraced within the statute.

Section 49-605, T.C.A. embraces all funds received from the state, raised by local taxation, or derived from appropriate bond issues. It is inapplicable to Federal Revenue Sharing Funds, which may or may not be used for school purposes.

We, therefore, hold that a county's share of Federal Revenue Sharing Funds, allocated to the County School Fund, is not subject to the provisions of § 49-605, T.C.A. and, therefore need not be apportioned among the special school districts of a county.

This result not only is dictated by the language of the statute, but is commanded by considerations of equity and fundamental fairness. Under the formula heretofore discussed, the City of Jackson has already received its fair share of Federal Revenue Sharing Funds. This suit represents an effort to encroach upon the County's share. If we were to hold in the City's favor, the County would have to pay the City the sum of $190,207.82 as a result of having appropriated $201,476.00 to the School Fund, leaving a net gain of $11,268.18. This would be unconscionable.

. . . .

[The opinion contains charts indicating how general revenue sharing funds are distributed under the federal statutory formula and how they were distributed in this case.—Eds.]

The pie has already been sliced; we are not willing to slice it again.

Section 49-605, T.C.A. came into existence long before Revenue Sharing came upon the scene. If the conclusions we reach are not in the public interest, the General Assembly should be requested to scrutinize § 49-605, T.C.A. in the light of the distribution of federal funds to the local governments of Tennessee.

Affirmed.

FONES, J., concurs with opinion. [Omitted.]

COOPER and HARBISON, JJ., concur.

BROCK, J., dissents with opinion. [Omitted.]

Comments: 1. The principal case raises the issue of state control over federal funds coming into the state. During the 1970s, the Pennsylvania legislature took the lead in asserting control over federal grants-in-aid.

In *Lynn v. Commonwealth Department of Public Welfare,* 391 A.2d 1093 (Pa. Commw. 1978), the court considered whether plaintiff was entitled to a refund of funds that the Pennsylvania Department of Public Welfare had collected as reimbursement for interim assistance that it had given the plaintiff. Plaintiff had received the assistance before she applied for assistance benefits granted under Title XVI of the Social Security Act, 41 U.S.C. §§ 1381-1385. Plaintiff had signed an agreement with the department authorizing the Secretary of Health, Education and Welfare to make the first assistance payment to the Pennsylvania Department and authorizing the Department to collect reimbursement for the assistance. Instead of sending the first payment to the Department, the Secretary sent the payment to plaintiff. After the Department collected its reimbursement from her, plaintiff filed a petition for refund.

The court found that plaintiff was not entitled to a refund because, in § 1383(g)(1), Congress had provided that the Secretary, upon agreement with an individual, could reimburse participating states out of benefits in the amount of the interim assistance. The court concluded that, in § 1383(g)(1), Congress had created an exception to § 407 which prohibits the states from using legal process in obtaining public assistance reimbursement.

The Advisory Commission on Intergovernmental Relations reports that over three fourths of the states now exercise some control over federal grants, with at least eight actively appropriating the funds received. Advisory Commission on Intergovernmental Relations, State and Local Roles in the Federal System 55 (1982) citing Pound, *The State Legislatures,* BOOK OF THE STATES, 1980-81, 82 (The Council of State Governments 1980). *See also* Comptroller General of the U.S., Federal Assistance System Should Be Changed to Permit Greater Involvement by State Legislatures (1981). For a discussion of the appropriations process, see Chapter 5, *supra*.

2. In addition to seeking to establish control over federal funds coming into their jurisdictions, states have used their positions as managers of federal programs and as conduits for the channeling of funds to local governments to add requirements of their own to federal-local programs. The Advisory Commission on Intergovernmental Relations study cited above notes a greater tendency to add procedural requirements rather than performance standards.

> Experience in the administration of the federal Outdoor Recreation Programs provides an example of the addition of state requirements. A 1980 study of their operations in Virginia, Massachusetts, and Wisconsin found that state administrators in all three require local officials to submit copies of cancelled checks, contracts, bidding proposals, and other documents, so they can maintain desk audit capability at the state level, before reimbursing them for their outlays. This apparently is the result of the imposition on state administrators of the responsibility for misspent federal funds mandated by Office of Management and Budget Circular A-102. Neither the [federal] Land and Water Conservation Act, establishing the program, nor the federal guidelines adopted to implement it, imposes such a requirement. According to a Virginia official, the materials and desk-audit capability are necessary because "there is no federal definition of source documentation."
>
> This expression of motivation for the increased requirements corresponds with the assessment of James Q. Wilson in his book, *Politics of Regulation* (1980). He comments that:
>
>> Critics of regulatory agencies notice [the] proliferation of rules and suppose it is the result of "Imperialistic" or expansionist instincts of bureaucratic organizations. I am struck more by the defensive threat-avoiding, scandal-minimizing instincts of these agencies.

Advisory Commission on Intergovernmental Relations, State and Local Roles in the Federal System 195 (1982).

3. A third significant effect of the proliferation of federal programs has been the imposition on the states of direct management responsibilities. The Advisory Commission study describes some typical examples:

> One of the most notable impositions comes in the *National Health Planning Act of 1974,* [42 U.S.C. §§ 300o-300s (1976)] which requires states to designate a health planning and development agency (HPDA) to undertake the planning stipulated under the act as well as to administer the required "certificate of need" program. Moreover, states must establish state health coordinating councils charged with approving state plans, reviewing all applications for federal grants for health care, and advising HPDAs. The penalty for noncompliance is the cutoff of all health funding under a variety of health programs. Equally stringent provisions are found in *The Education of All Handicapped Children Act,* [20 U.S.C. §§ 1401-1411 (1976)] which specifies that the state education agency shall have responsibility for seeing that all other state, as well as local, agencies carry out the provisions of the act. These two impositions are only illustrative

of the many management functions required of states by federal statutes. The inclusion of this kind of mandate in federal grant legislation is new. The grant statutes, even in the 1960s, did not contain such extensive detail in regard to state agency organization, composition, and relationships with other units.

Id. at 200-01.

3. BLOCK GRANTS

In addition to the general revenue sharing program, the Nixon Administration saw the adoption of compromise block grant programs in manpower, community development and social services. These programs were added to earlier block grant programs adopted for public health and criminal justice in the 1960s.

Block grant consolidations also were pressed in the Reagan Administration, which saw the adoption of several block grant programs in the Omnibus Budget Reconciliation Act of 1981. This Act, which is codified throughout the United States Code, ushered in the first reduction in size of the federal grant-in-aid system since the major expansion in federal activity began in the Roosevelt Administration. It also signaled a possible sea change in the system for managing domestic programs, with responsibility for establishing priorities and choosing among alternatives shifting more and more to the states from the federal government.

More than seventy-five categorical grant programs were consolidated into nine major block grants, seven of which were new and two revisions of existing programs. The block grants are for Community Development (small cities and rural areas); Elementary and Secondary Education; Preventive Health and Health Services (revision); Alcohol, Drug Abuse and Mental Health; Maternal and Child Health Services; Primary Care; Social Services (revisions); Community Services, and Low-Income Home Energy Assistance. Each of the block grant consolidations also carried a reduction in federal funding.

The Elementary and Secondary Education block grant was typical. It consolidated thirty-seven categorical grant programs but reduced federal funding. It contained no restrictions on funding activities or grant eligibility. States were required to pass through at least eighty percent of the block grant to local education agencies on the basis of enrollment adjusted for the number of higher cost children. The Secretary of Education was required to approve the criteria used for the local pass through. An annual evaluation of program effectiveness was required beginning in federal fiscal year 1984. The block grants are summarized in Advisory Commission on Intergovernmental Relations, Intergovernmental Perspective, Vol. 8, No. 1, at 8-11 (1982).

Block grants were defined by Congress in the following manner:

(b) For purposes of this chapter—

(1) block grant funds are funds which are received for a program—

(A) which provides for the direct allocation of funds to States only, except for the allocation of funds for use by the Federal agency administering the program; and

(B) which provides funds that may be used at the discretion of the State, in whole or in part, for the purpose of continuing to support activities funded, immediately before the date of the enactment of this Act, under programs the authorizations of which are discontinued by this Act and which were funded, immediately before such date of the enactment, by Federal Government allocations to units of local government or other eligible entities, or both; and

(2) "State" includes the District of Columbia and any territory or possession of the United States.

Omnibus Budget Reconciliation Act, 31 U.S.C. § 1243 (1981).

In the following excerpt from the Legislative History of the Omnibus Budget Reconciliation Act of 1981, the Senate Committee on Labor and Human Resources discussed the block grant concept. The discussion was contained in a justification and explanation of the Committee's actions concerning the health services block grant as part of the budget reconciliation process, authorized by Title III of the Congressional Budget and Impoundment Control Act of 1974, 31 U.S.C. §§ 1321-1332. As noted by the Senate Budget Committee in its report recommending passage of the Omnibus Budget Reconciliation Act of 1981, "[r]econciliation permits the Congress to consider many spending reductions in one bill, while reserving to the individual committees the power to make recommendations for reductions in laws within their respective jurisdictions." S. Rep. No. 139, 97th Cong., 1st Sess. 2 (1981).

SENATE REPORT NO. 139, 97th Cong., 1st Sess. 868-72 (1981)

Justification—Health Block Grants and Other Health Programs

. . . .

B. The Block Grant Approach

The Committee believes the block grant is the appropriate vehicle for continuing needed health care assistance and preventive health care activities while at the same time reducing overall expenditures and alleviating the problems engendered by categorical programs. In a report released in 1977, the Advisory Commission on Intergovernmental Relations observed that the block grant appears to be the best-suited instrument of assistance if the goals are decentralization, economy and efficiency, generalist control, and coordination. Those are precisely the goals of this Committee.

. . . .

... In its 1977 report on block grants, the Advisory Commission on Intergovernmental Relations recommended that Congress use the block grant as the preferred instrument of providing Federal financial assistance to State and local governments in cases where:

(1) A cluster of functionally related categorical programs has been in existence for some time;
(2) The broad functional area to be covered is a major component of the recipient's traditional range of services and direct funding;
(3) Heavy support for those recipient services that the Congress determines also to have national significance is intended;
(4) No more than mild fiscal stimulation of recipient outlays is sought;
(5) A modest degree of innovative undertakings is anticipated;
(6) Program needs are widely shared both geographically and jurisdictionally; and
(7) A high degree of consensus over general purposes exists among the Congress, the Federal administering agency and recipients.

The Committee finds that in great part these elements are present in the case of the programs that would be replaced by the block grant programs under the Committee proposal.

The Committee bills for health services and preventive health services are designed to address the problems of inflexibility, lack of coordination, redundance, and uncertainty with respect to funding that have been experienced in the categorical grant system. The bills authorize a program of block grants to the States, to replace a group of existing categorical programs, for the provision of specified health services and preventive health services. No matching of funds is required, and the allocation would be based on the amounts distributed under the current programs in fiscal year 1981, reduced by about 20 to 25 percent. Assistance would be subject to the nondiscrimination provisions now applicable under title I of the Housing and Community Development Act of 1974. Federal requirements for detailed State plans and lengthy reports would be eliminated. Audit requirements of the Intergovernmental Cooperation Act would be observed, but efforts to avoid duplicative audit activities would be encouraged. States would be able to use grant funds only for those services specifically authorized, except for a limited authority to transfer monies between blocks.

Under the Committee bills each State would receive a grant that could be used to provide any of the services now authorized by the categorical grant programs specified. The amount each State receives would bear the same ratio to the total appropriation as the total amount allotted to the State for fiscal year 1981 under the replaced programs bears to the total amount allotted for that year to all States for those programs. Beginning with fiscal year 1982, appropriations of $850 million for health services and $194 million for preventive health services would be authorized for each of 4 fiscal years (thru fiscal year 1985). In effect, this means that each State would receive 75 to 80 percent of its 1981 allotment for the consolidated programs. The Committee believes that the reduction will be offset by a decrease in administrative costs and by a more efficient delivery of services.

The Committee has included provisions designed to encourage the accountability of the States in administering the block grants under the proposed program and at the same time to insure a more equitable allocation. Many Members of Congress, as well as State officials and representatives of groups with an interest in the programs that will be replaced, have expressed the fear that State administrators would emphasize certain services at the expense of others. Indeed, many have been concerned that some areas might be neglected altogether. To insure that in each State the allocation decisions will appropriately reflect the real health needs of the State, the Committee bill requires that, after fiscal year 1982, the State legislature hold public hearings on the allocation of funds under the grant. The Committee envisions that both through the forum of open hearings and discussion, and through the debates and votes of elected representatives, the public and the various affected interests would have an opportunity to be heard.

. . . .

As is clear, the Committee intends that States be provided with the broadest possible latitude in the use of block grant funds and be free from all but the most minimal and necessary federal administrative and regulatory direction. Nonetheless the expenditure of federal funds, as with all contracting relationships, must be accompanied by some accountability that funds are not misdirected or fraudulently used. The Secretary is specifically empowered to withhold funds, but only if the State has misused funds by a substantial and serious failure to carry out its assurances and the requirements of the statute. Such withholding cannot be made for minor or insubstantial deviations or without adequate notice and opportunity for a public hearing to be conducted within the affected state and at which all interested parties are represented.

The Secretary and the Comptroller General are both directed to undertake investigations to assure State compliance with the statutory and auditing requirements of the block grants. It is not contemplated that it will be necessary for investigations to be extensive or far-reaching except when specific circumstances require it. The Committee expects such investigations to be primarily operated within a State and that state officials will not be compelled to come to Washington, D.C. or regional offices to explain their programs. States will have to "open their books" to such investigations but may not be required to produce voluminous responses; or produce or compile information in a new form or if not readily available. This provision should not be interpreted to bar reasonable investigative requests, but should stop unreasonable requests and "fishing" expeditions.

Comments: 1. In an attempt to derive some degree of uniformity from a legislative process that involved numerous congressional committees and subcommittees, Title XVII was added to the Act. It requires states to prepare reports and hold public hearings on the use of block grant funds, provide access for the Comptroller General to applicable books and records, and conduct financial and compliance audits of block grant funds. An interesting limitation to the uniformity provisions is that they apply only "to the extent that such funds may be used at the discretion of the State as described in subsection (b)(1)(B)." 31 U.S.C. § 1243 (1981) (the definition of block grant funds) From your reading of the definition, is it clear which programs would not be subject to the Title XVII reporting and auditing requirements?

2. Increasing congressional hostility to a perceived overreaching on the part of the federal bureaucracy (and possibly the courts) is evident throughout the Act. For example, in the Alcohol, Drug Abuse and Mental Health Services block grant, a long subsection extending over two pages and covering thirteen separate certifications the governor must make with the annual application ends with the proviso: "The Secretary may not prescribe for a state the manner of compliance with the requirements of this subsection." 42 U.S.C. § 300w-4 (1981). And, in the section requiring specific annual reports (to be established by the Secretary after consultation with the states and the Comptroller General) to determine whether funds were expended properly, to describe the activities of the state and to establish a record of the purposes, recipients and progress toward achieving the purposes for the block grant expenditures, Congress provided that the Secretary "may not establish reporting requirements which are burdensome." 42 U.S.C. § 300w-5 (a)(2) (1981). Finally, in the section directing the Secretary to withhold funds after complaint, investigation and public hearing from any state not using its allotment in accordance with the state certification or the requirements of the block grant program, Congress closed with the restriction that the "Secretary may not withhold funds . . . for a minor failure to comply." 42 U.S.C. § 300w-6(a)(4) (1981). To whom does the state turn for guidance on compliance with these requirements? What is a burdensome requirement? What is a minor failure to comply? Who is to make those decisions?

3. As the 1981 block grants were implemented, a major intergovernmental issue was the effect of "crosscutting" requirements on the new block grants. Crosscutting regulations are described by the Advisory Commission on Intergovernmental Regulations:

> Most regulations associated with grant programs are specific to one program or project. However, numerous crosscutting requirements exist, that apply to all federal assistance programs, even to General Revenue Sharing (GRS), which was intended to be entirely discretionary with the recipient government. Depending on how one counts, from 34 to 59 regulations apply to all federal grant programs. These include: (1) prohibitions against use of the funds for lobbying; (2) restrictions on use of the funds for debt retirement; (3) compliance with the prevailing wage standards under the *Davis-Bacon Act;* (4) requirements for citizen participation; (5) restrictions against discrimination in recruitment and employment against various sectors of the popu-

lation including minorities, women, various ethnic groups, the handicapped, and others; (6) prohibitions against discrimination by subcontractors; and (7) restrictions on discrimination in the provision of municipal services.... The U.S. Office of Management and Budget reports that of the 37 crosscutting regulations involving socioeconomic factors, 32 are based in public law and five in executive orders.

Advisory Commission on Intergovernmental Relations, State and Local Roles in the Federal System 58 (1982).

Regulations issued by some federal agencies did not include all of the crosscutting requirements. For example, interim regulations of the Department of Health and Human Services were "silent on most of the crosscutting regulations and specifically include only crosscutting regulations on civil rights: the prohibitions on discrimination for race, color, national origin, sex, handicap, age, and religion." Advisory Commission on Intergovernmental Relations, Intergovernmental Perspective, Vol. 8, No. 2, at 4 (1982). Is there a remedy here? To what extent does *Pennhurst* raise questions about crosscutting regulations? *See* Baker, *Making the Most of Pennhurst's "Clear Statement" Rule,* 31 CATH. U.L. REV. 439, 447 (1981).

4. The impact on state and local governments will be a major concern as the 1981 block grants are implemented. Many of the superseded categorical grants provided funds directly to local governments or nonprofit agencies. One of the features of the block grants is the reliance on the states to establish priorities and distribute funds. How local governments will fare remains to be seen, but it is clear that local governments will be taking a greater interest in proceedings in state houses. One of the purposes of Title XVII, discussed in Comment 1, *supra,* was to insure that former recipients of categorical grants do not get frozen out of the block grant process. Are you confident that Title XVII will be effective in this regard?

Consider the experience under the education block grant, which is explained *supra*. One of the programs folded into the block grant was the program authorized by the Emergency School Aid Act, which had funded school desegregation programs since 1972. The desegregation program took up twenty-eight percent of the funds appropriated in 1981 for all of the programs brought within the block grant. Desegregation aid could not be used for busing, but only for voluntary efforts to end the isolation of minority students and improve their education. Only 330 of the many thousands of school districts received desegregation aid in 1981. Funds appropriated for the block grant have declined substantially, and cities receiving most of the desegregation aid have suffered. The City of St. Louis block grant was only $708,000 in 1982. It received $12.4 million in desegregation aid in 1981.

Desegregation aid is only one of several programs that must be funded by the block grant, and the states determine how the grant is passed through to cities:

> Even though the desegregation program constituted a major share of the funds before consolidation, all program objectives must be weighed in parceling out the block grant funds. California and New York fashioned formulas that would have given cities the same proportion of emergency aid funds that they had before the program was merged. The [U.S.] Education Department rejected those formulas because they were not constructed according to the five factors spelled out in the block grant.

Stanfield, *No Solution,* 15 NAT'L J. 128 (1983). What does this experience indicate about the problem of federal control under block grants? Is there a solution to the "no solution"?

5. Passage of the first phase of the Reagan Administration's plan to restructure the federal grants-in-aid system and introduction of the second phase (a proposed Medicaid-welfare swap between the federal government and the states and a turnback of about thirty-five federal programs to the states) has ushered in a constitutional debate of major proportions. What is the appropriate use of the congressional spending power? What limits on this power are posed by the enumeration of delegated powers under Article 1, section 8 of the Constitution? Does Congress have the power to provide federal funds to states and localities without imposing federal policy strings? For an article exploring those questions and arguing that block grants must pass a national purpose test in the same way that categorical grants must do, see Cole, *The Federal Spending Power and Unconditional and Block Grants to State and Local Governments,* 16 CLEARINGHOUSE REV. 616 (1982).

When Congress reconvened in January 1983, the Reagan Administration introduced a much scaled-down version of its original "second phase" plan. Congress does not seem interested.

PART TWO

INTRA-GOVERNMENTAL DISTRIBUTION OF POWER

The foundation stones of the United States constitutional system of government rest on a separation of powers that is both vertical and horizontal. In the vertical structure of American government, the national government is one of delegated powers, and all powers not so delgated are reserved to the states by the tenth amendment to the federal Constitution. The third or local layer of government in what is essentially a tri-partite structure lacks a federal constitutional base but has been a firm fixture of American government from the beginning and is recognized and regulated in most state constitutions. Much of Part I of the casebook relates, directly or indirectly, to legal relations, conflicts, and divisions of power among the vertical elements of American government.

Horizontally, American government at national and state levels has a tri-partite structure while local governments less frequently do. This separation of powers among the legislative, executive, and judicial branches of government is continuously being challenged in state and local government decision making and in legal disputes, even when it is not obvious or acknowledged. These intra-governmental distributions of power are the underlying concern of Part II of the casebook. An analysis of these problems leads into an examination of the role played by each of the branches, and of the points at which their interaction affects the course of state and local government decision making.

Neither tenet, that the state governments are the reservoir of all powers not specifically delegated elsewhere, and that governmental powers are divided among three separate and equal branches, is as strong or well defined as its frequent reiteration would suggest. Possibly neither was intended to be taken as an absolute by those who wrote these principles into the federal and state constitutions. But it is still impossible to sort out the issues of intra-governmental power in state and local government without knowing what kinds of authority may be exercised by each of the branches of government and subject to what limitations. The materials in this part of the casebook relate to this question. It may first be helpful to reproduce a summary of the purpose of the separation of powers doctrine, recently restated by the United States Supreme Court which expresses the less than absolute formulation of the doctrine that has been suggested here:

> We do not think appellants' arguments based upon Art. II, § 2, cl. 2, of the Constitution may be so easily dismissed as did the majority of the Court of Appeals. Our inquiry of necessity touches upon the fundamental principles of the Government established by the Framers of the Constitution, and all litigants and all of the courts which have addressed themselves to the matter start on common ground in the recognition of the intent of the Framers that the powers of the three great branches of the National Government be largely separate from one another.
>
> James Madison, writing in the Federalist No. 47, defended the work of the Framers against the charge that these three governmental powers were not *entirely* separate from one another in the proposed Constitution. He asserted that while there was some admixture, the Constitution was nonetheless true to

Montesquieu's well-known maxim that the legislative, executive, and judicial departments ought to be separate and distinct:

> The reasons on which Montesquieu grounds his maxim are a further demonstration of his meaning. "When the legislative and executive powers are united in the same person or body," says he, "there can be no liberty, because apprehensions may arise lest *the same* monarch or senate should *enact* tyrannical laws to execute them in a tyrannical manner." Again: "Were the power of judging joined with the legislative, the life and liberty of the subject would be exposed to arbitrary control, for *the judge* would then be *the legislator*. Were it joined to the executive power, *the judge* might behave with all the violence of *an oppressor*." Some of these reasons are more fully explained in other passages; but briefly stated as they are here, they sufficiently establish the meaning which we have put on this celebrated maxim of this celebrated author.
>
> Yet it is also clear from the provisions of the Constitution itself, and from the Federalist Papers, that the Constitution by no means contemplates total separation of each of these three essential branches of Government. The President is a participant in the lawmaking process by virtue of his authority to veto bills enacted by Congress. The Senate is a participant in the appointive process by virtue of its authority to refuse to confirm persons nominated to office by the President. The men who met in Philadelphia in the summer of 1787 were practical statesmen, experienced in politics, who viewed the principle of separation of powers as a vital check against tyranny. But they likewise saw that a hermetic sealing off of the three branches of Government from one another would preclude the establishment of a Nation capable of governing itself effectively.

Buckley v. Valeo, 424 U.S. 1, 120-21 (1976) (emphasis in original).

Chapter 9

THE STATE LEGISLATURE

Part I established that the state legislatures have plenary power, except as limited by particular provisions of the state constitution. *See* Chapter 1. For example, state constitutions frequently place some fiscal limits on state legislatures, as noted in Chapter 5. This chapter examines additional constitutional limitations on state legislation. One of these limitations prohibits special legislation and determines the way in which state legislatures may make legislative policy: they may enact general, not special laws. This limitation has been applied to prevent state legislatures from adopting legislation limited to a single local government or to a class of local governments that the courts consider too narrow.

A second limitation discussed in this chapter is the prohibition on the delegation of legislative power. This limitation prevents the legislature from delegating policy-making authority to state and local agencies, and to the courts, although most courts do not apply the delegation of power limitation to delegations to local governments.

These two limitations help to define the state legislature's role as one of the coordinate branches of government. The legislature must make policy; it cannot delegate policy making. The legislature must also make policy for the entire state; it may not make policy selectively for individual units of local government within the state.

A. SPECIAL LEGISLATION

Constitutional prohibitions on special legislation arose out of legislative abuses in the late nineteenth century in the enactment of legislation limited to a single local government unit. These local laws conferred special powers on the affected unit, altered its form of government, or restricted or limited its powers in some way. To prevent these practices, states amended their constitutions to forbid the enactment of special legislation.

The special legislation provision of the Illinois Constitution of 1870, which is interpreted in the Illinois decisions reproduced in this section, is typical: "The general assembly shall not pass local or special laws in any of the following enumerated cases." The provision then lists a number of "cases," including "regulating county and township affairs" and "incorporating cities, towns or villages." The all-encompassing "case," which is contained in many state constitutions and which applies to most special legislation problems, is the last: "In all other cases where a general law can be made applicable, no special law shall be enacted." Ill. Const. art. IV, § 22 (1870). The special legislation provision of the new 1970 Illinois Constitution is reproduced in Comment 1 following the *Maloney* case, *infra*.

The special legislation prohibition covers any attempt at subject matter classification in legislation, and is not limited solely to the problem of municipal classification. Both functions of the special legislation prohibition are considered here.

In many states, local governments are divided into several classes according to population size, often with a single class reserved for the largest city in the state.

Legislation is then enacted limited to a single class of local governments, or to one or more classes. In addition to this system of prior classification, legislation is often enacted which is limited to a single local government or a group of local governments, again usually through population classifications. The effect of both practices is a confusing mixture of (1) legislation made variously applicable to each of the separately defined classes of local governments, and (2) scattered enactments, each of which is applicable to a differently defined group of local governments.

Constitutional prohibitions on special legislation take several forms:

> One type of provision forbids special legislation as to certain listed subjects [such as] the incorporating of cities and towns [and] regulating the affairs of municipalities and other local units . . . . A second type of provision commonly declares that all general laws shall have uniform application throughout the state and that no special law shall be passed where a general law could be made applicable . . . . A third type of provision merely requires that special legislation must undergo a specified procedure before it is considered, or at least before it is passed, by the state legislature.

O. REYNOLDS, LOCAL GOVERNMENT LAW 86-87 (1982). *See also* J. WINTERS, STATE CONSTITUTIONAL LIMITATIONS ON SOLUTIONS OF METROPOLITAN AREAS PROBLEMS (1962).

Special legislation problems are heavily litigated. Almost all legislation classifies in some way, and is subject to attack as special legislation. The cases are seldom principled, even within a single state. Questions also arise because of the kinship of the special legislation prohibition with the equal protection clause. Both constitutional limitations restrict arbitrary lawmaking.

Whether the special legislation prohibition is still necessary or desirable is debatable. Special legislation can resolve legislative controversy by limiting a statute to a single city or group of cities. Moreover, metropolitan areas may require special legislative attention, and the special legislation prohibition can invalidate legislation designed to address the problems of those areas. Yet the prohibition does prevent heavy-handed meddling in local government affairs, and it probably requires the state legislature at least to reflect before acting on classes of cities rather than all of them.

The materials that follow use a series of special legislation cases from Illinois to illustrate the special legislation prohibition. A group of cases from one state can illustrate the development of special legislation doctrine, as influenced by continually shifting views of the special legislation prohibition on the state supreme court. When reading these cases, keep in mind that the Illinois constitution did not have an equal protection clause until 1970. The special legislation prohibition provided a substitute. Cases since the adoption of the 1970 constitution have tended to merge equal protection and special legislation doctrine, as the materials will indicate.

Comments: 1. The application of the special legislation prohibition raises a number of threshold questions. One question is whether the constitutional provision raises justiciable questions. The problem arises under constitutional provisions stating that the legislature may not pass a special law when a general law "can be made applicable." Some constitutional provisions expressly state that the question of general law applicability is a judicial question, while some provide that the legislature shall make this determination. *Compare* Ala. Const. art. IV, § 105 (justiciable), *with* Va. Const. art. IV, § 15 (contra). Some courts read this provision to apply only when a general law on the subject has been enacted. They may still uphold a special law if the general law is incomplete or not exhaustive. *See Hedrick v. County Court,* 172 S.E.2d 312 (W. Va. 1970). Other courts read the provision to mean that a special law is invalid if the subject is amenable to treatment by a general law.

Courts apply the usual presumption of constitutionality to laws claimed to be special, but the presumption is not absolute. State courts are more willing than the federal courts to disregard the presumption if they believe that the special legislation prohibition has been violated. For discussion see C. SANDS & M. LIBONATI, LOCAL GOVERNMENT LAW §§ 3.24, 3.27 (1981).

2. Another question that often arises under special legislation is whether the classification adopted by the legislation is an open one for which other local governments can qualify though not presently included. If it is closed, the classification will be held invalid. This problem is manipulated under statutes creating a general set of classifications for local governments by simply adjusting the population limits upward as municipalities grow, a legislative practice that most courts have chosen to ignore. See also *Bopp v. Spainhower,* 519 S.W.2d 281 (Mo. 1975), upholding a special law authorizing a sales tax for transportation purposes. The law applied in part to a first-class county operating under a charter and not containing a city or part of a city over 400,000 inhabitants. Jackson County would have qualified except that it contained a first class city with a population over 500,000. The sales tax had to be imposed within six months after the effective date of the act, and the court noted that by that time the population of the first class city in Jackson County "could have been reduced to less than 400,000. This could have occurred by reason of war or an extensive fire or an epidemic of serious proportions or other unforeseen disaster." *Id.* at 285.

Courts usually hold that a class is closed if it is based on previously existing conditions which do not allow local governments to move from one class to another. *See State ex rel. Douglas v. Marsh,* 300 N.W.2d 181 (Neb. 1980) (state revenue sharing). Compare *Hotel Dorset Co. v. Trust for Cultural Resources,* 385 N.E.2d 1284 (N.Y. 1978), upholding a law providing special tax advantages for cultural institutions. The law, as drafted, appeared to apply only to the Museum of Modern Art. The court relied heavily on the presumption of constitutionality, and noted that there had been no proof that other cultural institutions could not qualify.

Special laws are often adopted which are applicable only to the largest governmental unit in the state, such as the largest city, county or metropolitan area. These special laws may reflect the political influence of the legislative delegation from that government unit or area. The following case illustrates this problem:

GACA v. CITY OF CHICAGO

Supreme Court of Illinois
411 Ill. 146, 103 N.E.2d 617 (1952)

BRISTOW, JUSTICE.

This appeal, involving the constitutionality of section 1-15 of the Revised Cities and Villages Act, (Ill. Rev. Stat. 1949, chap. 24, par. 1-15,) comes direct from superior court of Cook County. On March 29, 1949, appellee, John Gaca, filed suit against appellant, the city of Chicago, to recover the sum of $2300 which represented the amount of a judgment obtained against him by Mary and Edward Mallory in the superior court of Cook County, by reason of their having been falsely arrested. Appellee's right to recovery in this action is predicated upon the foregoing statutory enactment, the pertinent provision being: "In case any injury to the person or property of another is caused by a member of the police department of a municipality having a population of 500,000 or over, while the member is engaged in the performance of his duties as policeman, and without the contributory negligence of the injured person or the owner . . ., the municipality in whose behalf the member of the municipal police department is performing his duties as policeman shall indemnify the policeman for any judgment recovered against him as the result of such injury, except where the injury results from the wilful misconduct of the policeman."

The appellant, the city of Chicago, filed its amended motion to strike, alleging that the statute involved is unconstitutional and void because it contravenes section 22 of article IV of the constitution of the State of Illinois, S.H.A. The trial court, ruling adversely to this claim, entered judgment for the plaintiff and against the city in the sum of $2300 and costs. The defendant stood on its motion to strike.

The statute under consideration undertakes indemnification for injuries to person or property caused by Chicago policemen, who, in the course of their employment, injure another. Injuries resulting from the wilful misconduct of policemen are excepted. It is contended by appellant that this statute is violative of section 22 of article IV of the constitution in that it constitutes a special or local law granting a special privilege and is special legislation applying only to the city of Chicago.

The purpose of section 22 of article IV of the constitution of this State, prohibiting special laws and granting special privileges, is to prevent the enlargement of the rights of one or more persons and the impairment of, or discrimination against, the rights of others. . . .

Let us quote from appellant's brief so that we may have clearly defined their contentions made upon this subject: "Indemnifying policemen for judgments rendered against them while engaging in a performance of their duties, has no relation to large concentrations of population, organized crime or congested traffic. . . . The fact that some individuals are policemen in Springfield and Evanston, and others are policemen in Chicago, affords no ground for denying indemnity to the policemen of Springfield or Evanston and granting an indemnity to the policemen of Chicago; it affords no ground for granting to Springfield or Evanston an immunity from indemnity while placing on the citizenry of Chicago the financial responsibility to indemnify its policemen. In maintaining law and order within their territorial limits, all municipalities are agents of the State, performing an identical governmental function, and all should receive the same treatment at the hands of the Legislature."

The following principles of law have [been] announced by this court, which should provide for us a guide in resolving this question. Establishing classifications is primarily a legislative function, and judicial interference is never warranted except for the purpose of ascertaining whether the legislative action is clearly unreasonable. A classification will suffice as a basis for legislation if such classification is based on a rational difference of situation or condition found to exist in the persons or objects upon which the classification rests. Before a court can interfere with the legislative judgment in this case, it must be able to say that there is no fair reason for the law which would not require with equal force its extension to other cities of smaller population which are not affected. . . . The legislative classification need not be so broad and comprehensive as to include all the evils which might possibly be brought within its terms. Nor need the classification be scientific, logical, or consistent, provided it is not arbitrary and rests upon a reasonable basis. . . . Legislation is not special or local because it relates to only one city where the classification, based on population, has a reasonable relation to the purposes and objects of a statute and where the General Assembly could reasonably have concluded that there was a difference of situations and conditions between cities of 500,000 or more and those in cities of smaller populations. . . .

Furthermore, we must bear in mind that there is a presumption that the General Assembly and its committees did their duty, and that they acted conscientiously in making a survey of the conditions prevailing in Chicago and other municipalities in the State before they enacted the present legislation. Quite analogous to the situation presented to us on this appeal was that involved in *People v. Kastings,* 307 Ill. 92, 138 N.E. 269, 273. That case considered legislation which required indemnity bonds as a condition precedent to the issuance of licenses to operate taxicabs in a city having more than the population specified in the statute, namely, 100,000. At the time of the passage of that statute Chicago was the only city in Illinois with a population in excess of that figure. This court in that case judicially noticed the difference caused by density and concentration of population in traffic conditions and situations in Chicago, as contrasted with smaller cities, and then said "that there is much greater probability of injury to persons and property in the streets of such cities than in the streets of smaller cities." Compelling is the force of the language employed by this court in that case, which appears applicable to our present situation: "The act is not special or local legislation within the meaning of the Constitution, because it is limited in its application to cities having a population of 100,000 or more. In Illinois there were no cities having a population of more than 100,000 people when this legislation was enacted except Chicago, but the act may apply to any city that shall hereafter have more than 100,000 population. We may take judicial notice of the fact that in cities of more than 100,000 people, like Chicago, the streets and highways are much more congested by pedestrians and various other travelers and by traffic, and that there is much greater probability of injury to persons and property in the streets of such cities than in the streets of smaller cities. There is no objection to the legislation by reason of the fact that at present Chicago is the only city to which this legislation applies, if there is any reasonable basis for such classification. Under the stipulated facts in this case Chicago has 2,700,000 more population than any other city in Illinois. The greater the danger the greater the necessity for police regulation. It is a fact that greater danger exists in cities of greater population, and that is the very reason for basing the classification on population in this state, and it is sustainable, we think, without question. It is within the power of the Legislature to classify cities on the basis of population, and enact laws applicable to each class, where there is a reasonable basis for the classification in view of the objects and purposes to be accomplished by the legislation. ..."

There is little, if any, difference between the indemnity of a taxicab company for payment of judgments for injuries to person and property arising from the negligence of the taxi drivers and requiring the city wherein the taxicabs are operated to provide the same indemnity for injuries to person and property arising from the negligence of drivers of police vehicles. ...

A complete support for our conclusions in this cause can be found in the cases of *Littell v. City of Peoria,* 374 Ill. 344, 29 N.E.2d 533, 538, and *People ex rel. Moshier v. City of Springfield,* 370 Ill. 541, 19 N.E.2d 598. Therein the court had before it two legislative acts involving a minimum wage of policemen and firemen. It provided for specified minimum wages to employees in municipalites of 10,000 or more population but less than 25,000 and higher wages in municipalities having a population of 25,000 but less than 150,000. Those cases passed upon the constitutionality of each of those acts and passed upon the same questions as are presenented here. In upholding the validity of the Policemen's Minimum Wage Act in the *Littell* case, the court said: "The purpose of the act and the extent to which there has been an exercise of the police power cannot be determined solely from an evaluation of the personal benefits accruing to those engaged in police work in the city of Peoria. It must be determined from the character of service police officers are required to render in behalf of the State in the preservation of peace and order. As heretofore pointed out, police protection is a matter of general concern to the whole State. Failure to detect and check crime in the more populous centers might leave the remainder of the State a prey to disorder and violence. The legislature could well conclude that the risk attendant upon the duties of a police officer, the hours that he is subject to call and the general character of service he is required to render, demanded special consideration and that a higher wage would result in securing greater efficiency in the service and more securely protect the peace and order of the whole State."

It would appear, therefore, that this court placed its sanction upon the legislative determination that the hazards and risks of police work were greater in a city of 10,000 to 25,000 than in a smaller community and likewise greater in cities of 25,000 to 150,000 than in those in the category of 10,000 to 25,000 population.

Relieving the policemen of the city of Chicago of the burden of carrying public liability insurance, which is the effect of section 1-15, indirectly increases their wages. When we consider the high rates in Chicago, as compared with other parts of the State, this saving is no small item. We are asked by the appellants to hold that the legislature transcended its power in providing, by this indirect method, an improvement in the salaries of policemen in that city.

We must constantly be on our guard to prevent a substitution of judicial discretion for legislative judgment. In considering the reasonableness of the classification made by the General Assembly, courts will not attempt to assert their judgment as against the judgment of the General Assembly, nor refuse to uphold legislation merely on the ground that their judgment in this regard differs from that of the General Assembly. The question of classification, as we have said heretofore, is distinctly within the province of the legislature, and this has never been a judicial question except for the purpose of ascertaining whether the legislative action is clearly unreasonable.

Was the legislature, therefore, in the instant case, unreasonable in giving the policemen of Chicago additional security because their problems are essentially different from those of policemen in other cities of Illinois? We do not think that it was unreasonable for the General Assembly to conclude that a policeman's job in the city of Chicago is fraught with hazards uncommon to any other city in Illinois. The people of the State of Illinois are vitally interested in law enforcement in the city of Chicago. By increasing the wages and the security of members of their police department an improvement in the personnel of that law-enforcement agency will surely follow. Preliminary to the passage of the present legislation it must be presumed that some committee of the legislature made a conscientious study and survey of conditions in Chicago to find out if this legislation was warranted. This investigation would doubtless reveal congestion in travel, both pedestrian and vehicular, causing an uncommon number of automobile accidents; blight and slum areas; areas of unassimilated foreign elements where crimes are bred and protection is offered fleeing criminals; skid rows where poverty, crime and general disrespect for the law abounds; narcotic rings, hoodlums, gangsters, and racketeers that kill with sawed-off shotguns, all of which pose problems on Chicago that are not found in other parts of Illinois.

In this case, a judgment was entered against Gaca as a result of a charge of false arrest. In small towns an alert policeman has a wide acquaintance, and knows practically everyone living in his territory. The chances of his making a mistake in identification are negligible, but the danger of arresting some innocent person in a congested metropolitan area is ever-present. Under the instant law, a metropolitan policeman will not be deterred or restrained in the performance of his duty by the knowledge that, if he makes a mistake, he may be called upon to pay a substantial judgment.

Counsel for appellant also make a contention that because of this law, the tort liability of a policeman will be different in Chicago than in other cities. All that section 1-15 requires is that a municipality of 500,000 or more shall indemnify the policemen for any judgment recovered, while in small localities the policemen must bear the expense of such protection. It does not change the general tort liability of a policeman. ...

For the reasons heretofore assigned, the judgment of the superior court is affirmed.

Judgment affirmed.

SCHAEFFER and HERSHEY, JJ., dissenting.

By a long line of decisions the rule has been established that legislation which classifies municipalities upon the basis of population violates the constitutional prohibition against special legislation unless the classification bears a reasonable relation to the objectives which the legislation seeks to accomplish. ... Here the objective sought to be accomplished is the indemnification of police officers for judgments rendered against them because of nonwilful injuries inflicted in the performance of their duties. The question is whether a classification which restricts the application of the statute to the city of Chicago, alone, is reasonably related to that objective.

The factors relied upon by the majority to sustain the statute are (1) heavier and more congested traffic in Chicago, (2) the relatively wide acquaintance of a policeman in a small town and the resulting diminished likelihood of false arrests due to mistaken identification, and (3) a generalized group of social conditions which are said to exist in Chicago but not elsewhere in the State.

In support of the first of these grounds, traffic congestion, reliance is placed upon *People v. Kastings,* 307 Ill. 92, 138 N.E. 269, which sustained a statute requiring indemnity bonds as a condition to the issuance of taxicab licenses in cities with a population of more than 100,000. That case would be in point if the statute before us were confined to indemnification of police officers for injuries due to the operation of automobiles. But it falls far short of the mark when it is relied upon to sustain a statute which imposes a duty to indemnify for *all* negligent conduct of police officers, whether or not that conduct involves the use of an automobile.

The opinion also makes the point that there is less likelihood of false arrests due to mistaken identity in small towns, because an alert policeman in a small town knows practically everyone in his community. There are many municipalities in the State with respect to which that statement is true, although the argument begins to lose reality well before it reaches Evanston, (73,030), Springfield, (80,832), Rockford, (92,503) and Peoria, (111,523). But false arrests do not typically result from mistaken identity. The person arrested is ordinarily the person intended to be arrested. No reported false-arrest case in Illinois has been found which involved an arrest of one person when another was intended to be arrested. Nor is it clear that the arresting policeman is liable in such a situation. The question does not appear to have arisen in Illinois, and there is no unanimity of opinion in those jurisdictions which have passed upon it. ...

Perhaps the majority's enumeration of social conditions which exist in Chicago and not in other parts of Illinois is such obvious hyperbole as not to warrant discussion. Because it seems to be seriously advanced, however, it may be noted that not all of the slum and blighted areas of Illinois are in Chicago. . . . Nor have "hoodlums, gangsters, and racketeers" afflicted Chicago alone. . . . The records of the United States courts deny the statement that narcotic rings are peculiar to Chicago. Reports of the Administrator of the Federal Courts, Table D3. With the exception of traffic conditions, the asserted differences between Chicago and the other cities of the State, which are relied upon to sustain the statute, are either nonexistent or irrelevant.

The majority opinion quotes from *Littell v. City of Peoria,* 374 Ill. 344, 29 N.E.2d 533, which sustained the validity of a statute fixing minimum wages of policemen according to population classifications. But in that case the court expressly refrained from discussing the objection raised in this case, saying, 374 Ill. at page 350, 29 N.E.2d at page 538: "Defendant's contention that the act is special legislation and violates section 22 of article 4 of the Constitution is answered in *People [ex rel. Moshier] v. City of Springfield,* supra." In the *City of Springfield* case, 370 Ill. 541, 548, 19 N.E.2d 598, 602, where the question now before us was considered, the court sustained the Firemen's Minimum Wage Act against attack under section 22 of article IV because "The difference in the cost of living, and in the hazards of the occupation, in municipalities within the two classifications in the act, and in those not embraced within its terms, furnishes a reasonable basis . . . for such a classification. It bears a direct relation to the object and purpose of the legislation."

Of course differences in the cost of living between large and small cities are directly related to the salaries to be paid to policemen and firemen, and so are differences in the hazards of the occupation. But the differnces which will sustain the present classification must be those which relate to the obligation imposed upon the taxpayers of a single municipality to indemnify its policemen for the "nonwilful" injuries they inflict in the performance of their duties.

Apparently relying on the minimum wage cases, the majority would support this legislation upon the ground that this statute indirectly brings about "an improvement in the salaries of policemen in that city." Reference is made to relieving policemen of the burden of carrying public liability insurance, and to higher rates charged for such insurance in Chicago than in other parts of the State. Here again, however, the argument carries only far enough to reach cases involving automobile accidents, and falls far short of meeting the expanded scope of the present statute. Moreover, there is a vast difference between a statute fixing minimum wages in terms of population classifications which correlate with differences in living costs, and a statute which arbitrarily increases police salaries in a single city, without relation to any relevant consideration. The version of the statute suggested in the majority opinion underscores the serious question which exists under section 10 of article IX of the constitution, which prohibits the General Assembly from imposing taxes upon municipal corporations for corporate purposes. That is the question which the majority does not discuss. In our opinion this constitutional objection is important; it should be squarely faced, and the grounds which underlie the ruling of the majority should be explicitly stated.

Municipalities have not heretofore been liable for the unlawful or negligent acts of policemen in the performance of their duties. . . . The policeman, however, has been individually liable for his tort, notwithstanding he commits it while engaged in the performance of a governmental function. . . . These rules of law are altered by the present statute so that the taxpayers of a single city are required to indemnify policemen for damages caused by their negligence. No similar obligation is placed upon the taxpayers of any other municipality, although the duties performed by municipal policemen are identical throughout the State.

The imposition upon the taxpayers of a single city of a financial burden from which the taxpayers of all other cities in the State are free can be sustained only if the discrimination is warranted by circumstances related to the legislative purpose. Such circumstances, in our opinion, do not exist.

Comments: 1. Is the objection to the statute considered in the *Gaca* case based on the propriety of the population standard as applied to the subject matter of the legislation, on the reasonableness of the population classification that was adopted, or on both aspects of the statute? Is there also a hint in the dissenting opinion that the vice of the statute was its improper modification of tort law?

2. The *Gaca* case deals with a commonly enacted legislative classification that singles out the largest municipality in the state for special treatment. While the cases tend to uphold this kind of classification, they are not uniform. Subsequent treatment in Illinois of legislative classifications limited to Chicago is illustrative:

In *People ex rel. Adamowski v. Wilson,* 170 N.E.2d 605 (Ill. 1960), the court considered a statute which limited to Chicago a requirement that persons appointed to municipal office be qualified electors of the city and residents of the city for at least one year prior to their appointment or election. The court (opinion by Schaefer, J.) struck down the statute as special legislation. It noted:

> The legislative classification can be sustained only upon the assumption that a city with a population of more than 200,000 will always have a sufficient number of residents and electors who have the precise technical training and knowledge that is needed, and who are available to serve as municipal officers.
>
> But the kind of knowledge and technical training with which the statute is concerned is not centered exclusively in the largest cities. To make the point it is necessary to refer only to the University of Illinois, located in Champaign, which has a population of less than 60,000, and to Northwestern University, located in Evanston.

Id. at 612. Is the *Adamowski* case consistent with the *Gaca* decision?

Compare People ex rel. County of Du Page v. Smith, 173 N.E.2d 485 (Ill. 1961). A water supply, drainage, sewage, pollution and flood control act was applicable to counties contiguous to another county having a population of one million or more. The act was applicable only to five counties contiguous to Cook County, in which Chicago is located. In upholding the act the court noted that sewage and pollution control problems are more critical in "rapidly growing counties contiguous to a large and heavily populated metropolitan area." The court took notice of the population of Cook County, the overflow into adjoining counties, and the rapid increase in the growth of those counties in recent years. See also *Latham v. Board of Education,* 201 N.E.2d 111 (Ill. 1964).

3. Legislative classifications limited to the largest local government unit in the state have provoked a substantial amount of litigation. The following decisions from states other than Illinois are illustrative:

Board of Education v. Board of Education, 472 S.W.2d 496 (Ky. 1971). The court invalidated a statute, limited to counties containing cities of the first class, which provided a special procedure for transferring areas from one school district to another:

> It may be conceded that the size and the growth of the population in counties containing cities of the first class may necessitate the transfer of adjacent areas from one school district to another more frequently than elsewhere but the fact that the problem arises more often does not of itself indicate that the general law enacted to deal with the problem is inadequate. Granted also that the magnitude of problems encountered in settling the terms of the transfer is greater, yet there is no showing that the administrative machinery for settling the terms of the transfer through the office of the Superintendent of Public Instruction and the State Board of Education as provided by the general law is inadequate.

Id. at 500.

State ex rel. City of Charleston v. Bosely, 268 S.E.2d 590 (W. Va. 1980). A statute authorized the two largest cities in the state to levy a hotel tax and to use the proceeds of the tax to fund bonds for the construction of convention centers. The legislation was invalidated under a constitutional provision providing that "in no case shall a special act be passed, where a general law can be made applicable."

The court noted that the special legislation provision was an equal protection clause which prohibited arbitrary classifications, and held:

> What possible rational reason could the legislature have had for sanctioning such a classification? It cannot be that municipal growth and development are of particular interest only to cities with populations of 50,000 or more. It is in the interest of every community, perhaps more so in the case of our smaller municipalities, to stimulate economic growth. It cannot be that our urban centers have an exclusive interest in bringing in conventions, attractions and public events which promote tourism.

Id. at 596.

The courts have usually upheld statutes limited to the largest metropolitan area in the state which authorize the formation of a metropolitan government or the establishment of a metropolitan district or authority. *See, e.g., Dwyer v. Omaha-Douglas Public Building Commission,* 195 N.W.2d 236 (Neb. 1972) (joint building authority); *Frazer v. Carr,* 360 S.W.2d 449 (Tenn. 1962) (metropolitan government); *Municipality of Metropolitan Seattle v. City of Seattle,* 357 P.2d 863 (Wash. 1960) (metropolitan district).

4. The purpose of the legislation as related to the classification adopted plays an important role in special legislation cases. This issue was important in *Gaca*. Compare the following cases:

Atlantic City Parking Authority v. Atlantic County, 434 A.2d 676 (N.J.L. 1981). A statute authorized the "governing body of any county in which is located a municipality in which casino gaming is authorized" to establish a transportation authority. The statute was applicable only to Atlantic County. The court rejected a special legislation objection. "The court finds that a sufficient nexus exists between the presence of casino gaming in Atlantic City and the transportation problems created thereby.... [T]ransportation is the most immediate collateral problem related to casino gaming." *Id.* at 684.

Jackson Redevelopment Authority v. King, Inc., 364 So. 2d 1104 (Miss. 1978). The court upheld a statute authorizing the urban renewal authority of the largest city in the state to condemn land for a public parking facility. "We hold that the legislature's classification of cities with populations over 100,000 to meet the parking problems created by their large population is valid, and this classification is reasonable and germane to the subject matter of the legislation."

City of Los Angeles v. City of Artesia, 140 Cal. Rptr. 684 (Cal. App. 1977). The court upheld a statute which required the county to charge municipalities contracting for county services made available to the municipalities on contract. The statute was limited to Los Angeles County. As a "possible reasonable basis for the statute" the court noted the "unmatched complexity" of local government in the county. It also noted that the statute limited service charges to the incremental cost of the service. This limitation would encourage the consolidation of police forces in a heavily populated urban county where there was a higher incidence of crime.

Avis Rent-A-Car System, Inc. v. Romulus Community Schools, 254 N.W.2d 555 (Mich. 1977). A statute authorizing the taxation of concessions at airports and limited to the largest county in the state was invalidated as special legislation. "We do not see a reasonable relationship between the withdrawing of a tax exemption from airport concessions and the size of the county where the airport is located."

Can you reconcile these cases? On what basis does a court decide whether the purpose of the classification is related to the regulation? Does this decision require a form of judicial policy-making?

5. Legislative classifications may be more difficult to uphold when they are drafted to apply only to the second largest city or county in the state, or to the second tier of cities and counties, and exclude the largest city. In *Elias v. City of Tulsa,* 408 P.2d 517 (Okla. 1965), a statute conferring extraterritorial zoning power applied only to Tulsa, the second largest city in the state, excluding Oklahoma City, the largest city. It was held invalid as special legislation, the court noting that urban problems within the purview of zoning increase rather than decrease with city size. Compare *Williams v. Starr*, 534 P.2d 29 (Okla. App. 1975), upholding planning enabling legislation applicable to counties containing less than 100,000 inhabitants and a city with a population of 5,000 or more. The court noted that the act applied to at least three counties in southwestern Oklahoma, and that to apply the "*Elias* principle" it must be shown "that there exists no legitimate relationship between the objective of the legislation and the restrictive classification adopted." *Id.* at 30.

See also *Frost v. City of Chattanooga*, 488 S.W.2d 370 (Tenn. 1972), invalidating an annexation statute applicable only to that city and excluding larger cities in the state. The court noted that the statute was not drafted to "create a class of municipalities who had similar annexation-taxation problems with fringe population areas." *Id.* at 372. Compare *Pinchback v. Stephens*, 484 S.W.2d 327 (Ky. 1972), upholding a city-county merger statute excluding counties containing a city of the first class. The exclusion was proper because in the excluded counties the merger problems "are more complex by reason of the size of the population and its apportionment among the various local governmental units." *Id.* at 330. No facts were introduced to support this assertion.

6. A statute may narrowly define the class of cities to which it applies. This type of statute usually is invalidated. In *Strickland v. Richmond County*, 254 S.E.2d 844 (Ga. 1979), a statute applicable to all counties between a population of 145,000 and 165,000 provided that no company providing water or sewerage services could increase its rates without the approval of the governing body of the county. The court could not see "why the customers of a water company in counties of the particular size stated are more in need of this price control and approval than in larger or smaller counties." *But see, e.g., City of Walnut Creek v. Silveira*, 306 P.2d 453 (Cal. 1957), upholding a statute applicable to cities with a population of 4,000 or less, constituting less than one seventh of the total population of the city and the unincorporated urban area within a radius of three miles.

7. Many of these cases suggest the political controversies that underlie the enactment of special legislation. Legislators from outlying areas of the state may resist enabling legislation applicable statewide which provides the authority for a controversial governmental program even though its adoption is not mandated. The existence of legislative authority for the program provides the legal basis for local mobilization of support to get the program adopted at the local level. Attempts to limit the legislation authorizing urban renewal projects in Kansas to Kansas City, the second largest city in the state, illustrate this tendency. *See Redevelopment Authority v. State Corporation Commission*, 236 P.2d 782 (Kan. 1951) (invalidating law when limited to cities between 125,000 and 150,000); *State ex rel. Fatzer v. Redevelopment Authority*, 269 P.2d 484 (Kan. 1954) (same, law applicable to cities with population in excess of 125,000 with townsites more than ninety years old). In both of these cases the effect of the classification was to limit the law to Kansas City. The law was finally upheld when it was amended to apply to all cities with a population of more than 75,000 and covered the three largest cities in the state, although some cities with old townsites were excluded. *State ex rel. Fatzer v. Urban Renewal Agency*, 296 P.2d 656 (Kan. 1956).

Statewide enabling legislation for controversial programs can be made more palatable when a local referendum is required. Special legislation problems are created if the largest cities in the state are excluded from the referendum requirement. This exclusion has been upheld, *Isaacs v. Oklahoma City*, 437 P.2d 229 (Okla. 1966), *cert. denied*, 389 U.S. 825 (1967); *City of Kansas City v. Robb*, 332 P.2d 520 (Kan. 1958). The Kansas referendum exclusion case came after the law had been extended to the three largest cities. The court noted that urban renewal was more urgent in the larger cities, which could not afford the expense and delay of a referendum. It also pointed out that more controversy over the selection of urban renewal areas might be expected in smaller communities.

Like the equal protection clause, the special legislation prohibition places limitations on subject matter classification in state legislation. Some state courts hold that the two constitutional provisions impose identical requirements. *See City of Los Angeles, supra.* The following cases illustrate the application of the special legislation provision to substantive subject matter classifications.

HARVEY v. CLYDE PARK DISTRICT

Supreme Court of Illinois
32 Ill. 2d 60, 203 N.E.2d 573 (1965)

SCHAEFER, JUSTICE.

This action was instituted on behalf of William Harvey, a minor, to recover damages for injuries alleged to have been caused by the negligence of the defendant, Clyde Park District, in maintaining its playground facilities. The complaint alleged that as a result of defendant's negligence, the plaintiff was thrown to the ground while using a children's slide. The defendant moved to dismiss the complaint upon the ground that it was immune from liability by reason of section 12.1 of the Park District Code, which provides: "Any park district shall not be liable for any injuries to person or property, or for the death of any person heretofore or hereafter caused by or resulting from the negligence of its agents, servants, officers or employees in the operation or maintenance of any property, equipment or facility under the jurisdiction, control or custody of the park district, or otherwise occasioned by the acts or conduct of such agents, servants, officers or employees." Ill. Rev. Stat. 1963, chap. 105, par. 12.1-1.

The circuit court sustained the motion to dismiss and the plaintiff has appealed directly to this court, contending that the statute is unconstitutional because it is special legislation in violation of section 22 of article IV of the Constitution of Illinois S.H.A., and also because it violates section 19 of article II of that Constitution, which provides: "Every person ought to find a certain remedy in the laws for all injuries and wrongs which he may receive in his person, property or reputation . . . ."

This court's decision in *Molitor v. Kaneland Community Unit District No. 302,* 18 Ill. 2d 11, 163 N.E.2d 89, 86 A.L.R. 2d 469 held that the school district was liable for damages arising from the negligent operation of a school bus. The reasons that prompted the court to reject the school district's claim of immunity in that case, however, applied equally to other areas of municipal immunity, and before and after the *Molitor* decision became final in December of 1959, the General Assembly enacted numerous statutes relating to municipal tort liability.

The legislation thus adopted established the following pattern: Forest preserves, park districts and the Chicago Park District are not liable for negligence . . . . There is no general provision granting immunity to municipalities—cities, villages and incorporated towns. The substance of earlier provisions relating to liability in specific situations has, however, been retained. Municipalities are liable for injuries caused by the negligent operation of motor vehicles by firemen and volunteer firemen. Municipalities having a population in excess of 500,000 must completely indemnify policemen for their nonwilful torts; other municipalities must indemnify them to the extent of $50,000. Municipalities are liable for damage to property caused by the removal, destruction or vacation of a building as unsafe or unsanitary under certain circumstances. In specified cases municipalities having a population in excess of 5,000 are liable for damage occasioned by mob violence.... The negligent tort liability of private schools and of school districts generally is limited to $10,000.... The Board of Education of the City of Chicago, however, is required to insure its employees, thus apparently permitting unlimited recovery.... Counties are not liable for negligence; however, they must indemnify sheriffs and deputy sheriffs to the extent of $50,000, for losses occasioned by nonwilful torts.... The liability of county superintendents of highways is limited to $10,000.... But township and district highway commissioners are fully liable for neglect of duty.... Drainage districts are liable for negligent torts, but the district commissioners are absolved of personal liability.... Counties, township and district highway commissioners, school districts, and townships are authorized to purchase liability insurance for their agents, employees and officers.... These governmental units are thus apparently given unrestricted freedom to determine for themselves whether or not they will be liable for negligence.

While the common-law doctrine of municipal immunity from tort liability, as it had existed prior to the *Molitor* case, was judicially created, the sovereign immunity of the State has a constitutional basis. Section 26 of article IV of the constitution provides that "The state of Illinois shall never be made defendant in any court of law or equity." Nevertheless the General Assembly has, for practical purposes, eliminated the sovereign immunity of the State by granting jurisdiction to the court of claims over "All claims against the State for damages in cases sounding in tort, in respect of which claims the claimants would be entitled to redress against the State of Illinois, at law or in chancery, if the State were suable, ... provided, that an award for damages in a case sounding in tort shall not exceed the sum of $25,000 to or for the benefit of any claimant. The defense that the State ... is not liable for the negligence of its officers, agents, and employees in the course of their employment shall not be applicable to the hearing and determination of such claims." Ill. Rev. Stat. 1963, chap. 37, par. 439.8.

It is in the light of this statutory pattern that the plaintiff argues that the statute which purports to bar a recovery in this case violates the prohibition against special legislation contained in section 22 of article IV of the constitution of Illinois. That section provides: "The general assembly shall not pass local or special laws in any of the following enumerated cases ... granting to any corporation, association or individual any special or exclusive privilege, immunity or franchise whatever."

The determinative question under section 22 of article IV is whether the statutory classification is rational. (See *e.g. People ex rel. Adamowski v. Wilson*, 20 Ill. 2d 568, 170 N.E.2d 605.) The circumstance that the alleged arbitrary discrimination results from a statutory pattern rather than from a single statute has not barred consideration of claims of violation of the equal protection clause of the 14th amendment to the Constitution of the United States, ... and we see no reason why that circumstance should bar the plaintiff's claim of discrimination in this case. Nor is it significant that the quoted provision of section 22 of article IV has been held inapplicable to municipal corporations generally, and park districts in particular. ... For more is involved here than just the classification of governmental units. Those persons who are injured by the negligence of particular governmental units are also classified, and section 22 of article IV prohibits the granting of "special or exclusive" privileges to individuals. "This provision prevents the enlargement of the rights of one or more persons in discrimination against the rights of others." *Marallis v. City of Chicago*, 349 Ill. 422, 427, 182 N.E. 394, 396, 83 A.L.R. 1222.

Many of the activities that frequently give rise to tort liability are common to all governmental units. The operation of automobiles is an obvious example. From the perspective of the injured party, or from the point of view of ability to insure against liability for negligent operation, there is no reason why one who is injured by a park district truck should be barred from recovery, while one who is injured by a city or village truck is allowed to recover, and one injured by a school district truck is allowed to recover only within a prescribed limit. And to the extent that recovery is permitted or denied on an arbitrary basis, a special privilege is granted in violation of section 22 of article IV.

. . . .

So far as the present case is concerned, cities and villages, park districts, school districts and forest preserve districts, as well as the State itself, all maintain recreational facilities that are available for public use. If the child involved in the present case had been injured on a slide negligently maintained in a park operated by a city or village there is no legislative impediment to full recovery. If the child involved in the present case had been injured on a slide negligently maintained by a school district, or by the sovereign State, limited recovery is permitted. But if the child had been injured on a slide negligently maintained by a forest preserve district, or, as was actually the case, by a park district, the legislature has barred recovery. In this pattern there is no discernible relationship to the realities of life. We hold, therefore, that the statute relied upon by the defendant is arbitrary, and unconstitutionally discriminates against the plaintiff.

From this decision it does not follow that no valid classifications for purposes of municipal tort liability are possible. On the contrary it is feasible, and it may be thought desirable, to classify in terms of types of municipal function, instead of classifying among different governmental agencies that perform the same function. Capacity to distribute some kinds of risks through insurance may be thought to be a relevant consideration. Under the Federal Tort Claims Act, which waives the sovereign immunity of the United States, there are numerous exceptions, perhaps the most important of which relates to discretionary acts. (28 U.S.C. § 2680.) The recent California legislation carves out numerous areas of nonliability, the most important of which also relates to discretionary acts. (See Cobey, The New California Tort Liability Statutes, 1 Harv. J. Legis. 16 (1964).) These illustrations do not exhaust the possibilities.

The judgment of the circuit court of Cook County is reversed, and the cause is remanded to that court with directions to overrule the motion to dismiss.

Reversed and remanded, with directions.

MALONEY v. ELMHURST PARK DISTRICT

Supreme Court of Illinois
47 Ill. 2d 367, 265 N.E.2d 654 (1970)

CULBERTSON, JUSTICE.

This is an appeal from an order of the circuit court of Du Page County granting judgment on the pleadings in favor of defendant park district in an action seeking damages for personal injuries sustained by plaintiff, a minor, while he was playing in defendant's park facility. The constitutionality of a statute being involved, plaintiff's appeal from the trial court's judgment comes directly to this court. See our Rule 302, Ill. Rev. Stat. 1969, c. 110A, § 302, 43 Ill. 2d R. 302.

The complaint alleges in substance that while plaintiff was playing on an "artificial hill" in Elmhurst Park, he fell and was severely injured. It is claimed that the defendant negligently allowed the hill to be and remain in a dangerous condition in that no fencing was provided around the hill, it was ungraded, and that rocks and other debris were allowed to remain thereon. As a proximate result of the defendant's negligence as thus averred, plaintiff fell and sustained injury. Defendant filed an answer to the complaint denying its substantive allegations, and subsequently filed a motion for judgment on the pleadings on the ground that under a provision of the Local Governmental and Governmental Employees Tort Immunity Act (Ill. Rev. Stat. 1965, ch. 85, par. 3—106), local governmental entities could not be held liable for personal injury resulting from conditions existing in parks, playgrounds or open areas employed for recreational purposes in the absence of their willful and wanton negligence in causing the injury. Plaintiff thereupon filed a motion to amend his complaint to allege willful and wanton negligence, which motion was allowed. However, plaintiff subsequently filed a motion contesting the constitutionality of the provision of the Immunity Act in question, and asked that the order allowing the amendment of his complaint be vacated. The trial court vacated such order, and, after noting plaintiff's election to stand upon the allegations of the original complaint, entered judgment on the pleadings in favor of the defendant and against plaintiff. This appeal ensues.

Section 3—106 of the Local Governmental and Governmental Employees Tort Immunity Act here in question provides as follows: "Neither a local public entity nor a public employee is liable for an injury where the liability is based on the existence of a condition of any public property intended or permitted to be used as a park, playground or open area for recreational purposes unless such local entity or public employee is guilty of willful and wanton negligence proximately causing such injury." Ill. Rev. Stat. 1965, ch. 85, par. 3—106.

Plaintiff, relying principally upon our decision in *Harvey v. Clyde Park District,* 32 Ill. 2d 60, 203 N.E.2d 573, asserts that the quoted legislation is violative of section 22 of article IV of the Illinois constitution, S.H.A., as special legislation affecting a classification scheme bearing "no discernible relationship to the realities of life." . . . It is further maintained that the legislation at issue deprives plaintiff of a remedy to which he is constitutionally entitled under section 19 of article II of the State constitution. We disagree. In *Harvey,* we held that a statute purporting to immunize park districts from tort liability while allowing it to attach to other governmental entities in similar circumstances and when they were performing similar functions amounted to invalid special legislation. . . .

The statute in question here applies equally to all local governmental entities, and comes into operation only where liability of a particular governmental entity is sought to be predicated upon the existence of a condition of public property maintained by it and intended or permitted to be used as a park, playground or open area for recreational purposes. By enactment of this statute the General Assembly has encouraged the development of and maintenance of parks, playgrounds, and other open areas to be used for recreational purposes in a manner which is in no way arbitrary, capricious or unreasonable. The wisdom of the legislation is a matter outside the purview of this court's inquiry, for as we observed in *Du Bois v. Gibbons,* 2 Ill. 2d 392, 399, 118 N.E.2d 295, 300, "There is always a presumption that the General Assembly and its committees acted conscientiously and did their duty in making a survey of the conditions prevailing in the municipalities of the State before enacting the classification legislation and the result will never be nullified by this court on the ground that its judgment might differ from that of the General Assembly. Only if it can be said that the classification is clearly unreasonable and palpably arbitrary will the courts act to hold the classifying enactment invalid."

We hold that the statute in question, in the context in which it is here attacked, is valid. Plaintiff's complaint being based upon charges of ordinary negligence, the circuit court properly entered judgment on the pleadings in favor of defendant, and the judgment must thus be, and is, affirmed.

Judgment affirmed.

Comments: 1. Recent developments in Illinois are indicated by the following cases:

Grace v. Howlett, 283 N.E.2d 474 (Ill. 1972) (opinion by Schaefer, J.). This case invalidated the state's no-fault insurance law, in part because it provided different benefit levels to injured parties depending on whether the automobile causing the injury was insured. It also exempted rented and other vehicles from the provisions of the law requiring liability insurance. The court relied on the more general form of the special legislation prohibition, which in the 1970 Illinois Constitution, art. IV, § 13, provides that "The General Assembly shall pass no special or local law when a general law is or can be made applicable [which is] a matter for judicial determination." An equal protection clause was included in the 1970 constitution by this time, and the court noted that while this and the special legislation prohibition "cover much of the same terrain, they are not duplicates. . . ." *Id.* at 479. It then added:

> Unless this court is to abdicate its constitutional responsibility to determine whether a general law can be made applicable, the available scope for legislative experimentation with special legislation is limited, and this court cannot rule that the legislature is free to enact special legislation simply because "reform may take one step at a time." . . .
>
> There are many purposes for which the obvious differences between private passenger automobiles, buses, taxicabs, trucks and other vehicles would justify different legislative treatment. But the determination of the amount to be recovered by persons injured by those vehicles and the conditions governing that recovery is not one of those purposes. What was true of the municipal tort liability statutes involved in *Harvey v. Clyde Park District* . . . is true here; those classified are those who suffer the accidental injuries as well as those who inflict them.

Id. Note that these statutory exemptions were not part of the Illinois no-fault scheme. No-fault legislation has been upheld when the legislation did not contain exemptions of this type. *See Montgomery v. Daniels,* 340 N.E.2d 444 (N.Y. 1975).

Delany v. Badame, 274 N.E.2d 353 (Ill. 1971). An attack was lodged against the Illinois guest statute, requiring a guest to show that the motorist was wilfully and wantonly negligent before a recovery for injuries could be sustained. It was argued that the statute violated that part of the Illinois special legislation prohibition forbidding grants of a special privilege or immunity to individuals. The statute was upheld and the *Harvey* case distinguished because the guest statute did not preclude a cause of action but simply changed the degree of fault necessary for recovery. In *Grace v. Howlett, supra,* the *Delany* case was in turn distinguished because "the legislature could rationally have found relevant differences in the circumstances under which the various voluntary relationships of host and guest were created which justified the imposition of differing standards of care." *Id.* at 479-80.

Anderson v. Wagner, 402 N.E.2d 560 (Ill. 1979). A statute provided a special limitation period for medical malpractice suits against physicians and hospitals. The court rejected an argument that the statute was invalid as special legislation, and reviewed the changes made in the 1970 constitution in the special legislation prohibition.

Recommendations to the constitutional convention had suggested inclusion of an equal protection clause, a suggestion which was adopted. The previous constitution did not have this clause. These recommendations also distinguished between "real" special legislation, which had been considered under the special legislation clause, and "nonreal" special legislation, which was general legislation challenged on equal protection grounds. "Real" special legislation was no longer thought to be a problem.

The court held that the special legislation prohibition contained in the 1970 constitution clarified the scope of judicial review in special legislation cases but did not alter the established definitions of what is "general" and "special." The court then noted that it had applied the special legislation and equal protection tests interchangeably, whether or not the case presented a "real" special legislation problem. These tests required judicial deference to the legislative classification. Commenting on *Grace v. Howlett* and the *Harvey* decision, the court noted that both cases had applied the equal protection standard.

For a criticism of the recent Illinois cases see Karasik, *Equal Protection of the Law Under the Federal and Illinois Constitutions: A Contrast in Unequal Treatment*, 30 DE PAUL L. REV. 263 (1981). The author claims that the Illinois cases have been inconsistent. He urges a return to activist judicial review in special legislation cases, as in *Grace v. Howlett*.

2. Not all courts apply the special legislation prohibition to "nonreal" classifications. See *Stephens v. Snyder Clinic Ass'n,* 631 P.2d 222 (Kan. 1981), holding that the special legislation prohibition only requires geographic uniformity.

Neither is the distinction between equal protection and special legislation requirements always clear, even when the special legislation prohibition is applied to all types of classifications. In *Brann v. State,* 424 A.2d 699, 704 (Me. 1981), the court said:

> Unlike the equal protection clause, the special legislation clause does not call for an inquiry into the rights or the existence of similarly situated persons. As long as there is no violation of the equal protection clause, validity under the special legislation clause does not depend on unique facts or highly unusual circumstances.

Compare *Illinois Polygraph Society v. Pelicano,* 414 N.E.2d 458, 462, 463 (Ill. 1980):

> Special legislation confers a special benefit or exclusive privilege on a person or a group of persons to the exclusion of others similarly situated . . . . It arbitrarily, and without a sound, reasonable basis, discriminates *in favor* of a select group . . . . [E]qual protection . . . consists of arbitrary and invidious discrimination *against* a person or a class of persons. (Emphasis in original.)

Equal protection law, at least at the federal level, is also marked by the development of "tiers" of judicial review. The Supreme Court applies a strict "compelling interest" standard of equal protection review when fundamental rights are affected, for example. The state courts have not always adopted the Supreme Court's tiered standards, but generally apply a stricter equal protection review even when fundamental rights are not affected. Have the state courts developed "tiers" of judicial review in the special legislation cases? Should they? What is the effect of the presumption of constitutionality applied by many state courts in the special legislation cases?

3. The courts have applied the special legislation prohibition to invalidate a number of statutes classifying "persons" for differential treatment. See *Cities Service Co. v. Governor,* 431 A.2d 663 (Md. 1981). A statute prohibited producers or refiners of petroleum products from operating retail gasoline service stations, but exempted "mass merchandisers." The exemption was narrowly drawn to apply to one retail store chain. The court invalidated the exemption as special legislation.

See also *Wilson v. City of Waynesville,* 615 S.W.2d 640 (Mo. App. 1981). A city ordinance required an airport limousine service to take on and discharge passengers at only one location in the city. The ordinance did not apply to taxicabs. The court invalidated the ordinance as special legislation. Note the anticompetitive effects of the statute and ordinance invalidated in these cases, and compare the *Pastor* case in Chapter 1.

4. Justice Levin of the Michigan Supreme Court, who then sat on the court of appeals, suggested in an important dissenting opinion that the ban on special legislation should be more stringently enforced. *Bankhead v. McEwan,* 192 N.W.2d 289, 292 (Mich. App. 1971), *aff'd,* 198 N.W.2d 414 (Mich. 1972). A statute was upheld which provided for boards of tenant affairs in public housing projects but was limited to cities of one million or more, a class that applied only to Detroit. Levin distinguished between "(a) legislation concerning governmental operations and functions, (b) legislation providing for economic regulation of business, and (c) legislation establishing or concerning individual rights and prerogatives," and noted that "where individual rights are involved, the needs of the citizen are less likely to vary significantly from one community to another." *Id.* at 299-300. Levin would have found the statute at hand unconstitutional as special legislation because it enlarged on and created new rights in public housing tenants. How would Levin classify the *Harvey* and *Maloney* cases, *supra*, and the cases discussed in the comments following those opinions?

B. DELEGATION OF POWER

[The doctrine of delegation] is concerned with the sources of policy, with the crucial joinder between power and broadly based democratic responsibility, bestowed and discharged after the fashion of representative government. Delegation without standards short-circuits the lines of responsibility that make the political process meaningful.

Bickel, *The Constitution and the War, Commentary,* July 1972, at 52.

The delegation of power limitation on state and local legislation is as well entrenched in constitutional jurisprudence as its basis and origins are obscure. No express provision in the federal or state constitutions explicitly forbids the delegation of legislative power. The doctrine is usually attributed to other principles and concepts such as the separation of governmental powers, the common law maxim of *delegata potestas non potest delegari* (a power that is originally delegated may not be redelegated), due process, or the principle of government by representative assembly. *See* Freedman, *Review: Delegation of Power and Institutional Competence,* 43 U. CHI. L. REV. 307, 310 (1976).

The Supreme Court has not invalidated a statute on delegation of power grounds for over forty years, but Justice Rehnquist revived the doctrine in his dissent in *Industrial Union Department v. American Petroleum Institute,* 448 U.S. 607 (1980). Justice Rehnquist sees three "important functions" served by the nondelegation doctrine:

[I]t ensures to the extent consistent with orderly governmental administration that important choices of social policy are made by Congress, the branch of our government most responsive to the popular will .... Second, the doctrine guarantees that, to the extent Congress finds it necessary to delegate authority, it provides the recipient of that authority with an "intelligible principle" to guide the exercise of the delegated discretion .... Third, and derivative of the second, the doctrine ensures that courts charged with reviewing the exercise of delegated legislative discretion will be able to test that exercise against ascertainable standards.

Id. at 685-86.

In the State Courts

The nondelegation doctrine is alive and well in the state courts. Delegation of power objections are frequently made to state and local legislation, although a review of the state cases indicates that most delegations are upheld. State delegation cases are common, but the decisions are unprincipled. Except for the conclusion that some state courts more frequently invalidate delegations of power than others, a principled basis for the application of delegation of power doctrine is difficult to find.

Most state courts find a proper delegation of power if the legislation provides adequate standards. *Howe v. City of St. Louis,* 512 S.W.2d 127 (Mo. 1974), provides the traditional formulation of the standards test. The court upheld a city ordinance authorizing the city's council on human relations to restrict real estate solicitation intended to create racial turnover. The court pointed out that a legislative body "may provide a regulation in general terms," may define areas in which regulations may be imposed, and may empower an administrative agency to "ascertain the facts" in applying legislation. "Arbitrary discretion" may not be conferred, but an exception exists for "police regulations for the protection of the public morals, health, safety, or general welfare." In this area, "it is impracticable to fix standards without destroying the flexibility necessary to enable the administrative officials to carry out the legislative will."

The Procedure Alternative

A number of critics believe that standard setting does not serve a useful purpose, that standards are often vague, and that courts uphold them anyway. Professor Kenneth Davis is the best-known proponent of this point of view. Davis appears to make two arguments to support his position. One is that "[s]afeguards are usually more important than standards, although both may be important. The criterion for determining the validity of a delegation should be the totality of the protection against arbitrariness, not just the one strand having to do with statutory standards." K. DAVIS, ADMINISTRATIVE LAW TEXT 44 (3d ed. 1972). There is growing support in the state decisions for the Davis position. *See, e.g., Blue Cross v. Ratchford,* 416 N.E.2d 614 (Ohio 1980) (citing cases).

Davis also rejects the standard-setting requirement because he doubts that legislatures will be willing to undertake this task. He argues that the best hope is to require the specification of standards by the administrative agency charged with the function of administering the statute. This argument means that a statute delegating administrative implementation powers with no standards at all would be acceptable. Davis also argues that there are times when the legislature does not really know what standards to adopt, or when political pressure makes it impossible to adopt standards. In these situations, the job of standard formulation will have to be done by the agency. K. DAVIS, DISCRETIONARY JUSTICE: A PRELIMINARY INQUIRY 46, 49, 50 (1969).

For a somewhat contrary position see Wright, Book Review, 81 YALE L.J. 575, 584-86 (1972). Judge Wright argues that administrative agencies may actually be more vulnerable than Congress to political pressures that prevent a resolution of policy conflicts. Should the agency be able to resolve these conflicts, policy-making would be displaced from the democratically responsible decision-making body.

1. DELEGATION TO ADMINISTRATIVE AGENCIES AND OFFICIALS

Reasons for a greater attachment to the standards doctrine in the state courts are not hard to discover, although they may not be articulated in judicial opinions. In many states, state administrative agencies are clearly not the equal of their federal counterparts in staffing and professionalization, even though the problems they must address are certainly no simpler. State agencies may not have the expertise or the resources to carry out the extensive rule-making on a variety of fronts on the order that Davis contemplates. At the municipal level, the problem is even more serious.

State courts may also be concerned about the substantive areas into which state and municipal agencies and officials intrude. Professor Jaffe makes this point. When writing about the delegation doctrine in the state courts he noted that:

It is when delegated power affects the use of real property or the practice of a profession that the judicial nerve tingles. The doctrine of delegation is then likely to be invoked against delegations which because of an uncertainty of standards (in phrase or fact) encourage undetectable discrimination or subjective notions of policy.

L. JAFFE, JUDICIAL CONTROL OF ADMINISTRATIVE ACTION 77 (abr. student ed. 1965). The federal government does not intrude in these areas. Political distance may also be a factor. National administrative agencies are certainly not immune from pressure, but the closer contacts that state and local agencies have with those they regulate do provide the opportunity for more insidious kinds of personal pressures. These pressures, in turn, lead to the arbitrary actions that courts seek to control through application of the standards requirement.

State delegation of power cases are difficult to catalog, although one author has attempted a catalog of eleven "practical considerations" that motivate the state court decisions. 1 F. COOPER, STATE ADMINISTRATIVE LAW 73-91 (1965). Along with Jaffe, Cooper notes the tendency toward stricter scrutiny when property interests are concerned, and also notes the opposite trend in cases considering statutes containing significant powers over public health, safety, or morals. Somewhat echoing the Davis analysis, Cooper also notes a trend toward the acceptance of broad delegations of power when the scope of judicial review is sufficiently broad to "re-examine factual determinations and questions as to the fairness of the administrative procedure." *Id.* at 81.

Another attempt at categorizing the delegation of power cases is provided by Merrill, *Standards—A Safeguard for the Exercise of Delegated Power*, 47 NEB. L. REV. 469 (1968). Professor Merrill divides legislative standards as follows: (1) Standards containing specific prescriptions, such as a provision that a licensee may be disciplined "who has been convicted in a court of competent jurisdiction"; (2) Standards providing a "reasonably detailed portraiture of legislative purpose," which leave the administrator a substantial degree of freedom but whose intent may be ascertained from the purpose of the act, such as a provision authorizing uniform standards of purity in food; (3) imprecise standards that gain clarity from being confined to a limited subject matter, such as a provision requiring professional competence as the basis for the issuance of an occupational license; and (4) imprecise words that acquire legal significance such as a "reasonableness" standard. Merrill also notes that imprecise words can be aided by analogous statutes and can be made specific through administrative action. *Id.* at 479-89.

A few courts have attempted a principled statement of the judicial view that finds no improper delegation of power if adequate standards are provided. The following case is a recent attempt at such a statement:

STOFER v. MOTOR VEHICLE CASUALTY CO.

Supreme Court of Illinois
68 Ill. 2d 361, 369 N.E.2d 875 (1977)

CLARK, JUSTICE.
This is a consolidated, direct, interlocutory appeal pursuant to our Rules . . .

from decisions of the circuit court of Cook County holding sections 397 and 401 of the Insurance Code of 1937 (Ill. Rev. Stat. 1975, ch. 73, pars. 1009, 1013) invalid on the grounds that the power thereby granted the Director of Insurance to prescribe uniform insurance contracts (including contractual limitations on the time within which suits may be brought against the insurer by the insured) violated the separation of governmental branches and powers mandated by section 1 of article II of our constitution (Ill. Const. 1970, art. II, sec. 1). We reverse, because we conclude that the powers thus exercised by the Director of Insurance are of the type which the legislature could (and did) properly lodge in an executive officer.

Section 397 of the Insurance Code of 1937 ... provides:

> The Director of Insurance shall promulgate such rules and regulations as may be necessary to effect uniformity in all basic policies of fire and lightning insurance issued in this State, to the end that there be concurrency of contract where two or more companies insure the same risk.

Section 401 ... further provides:

> The Director ... shall have the power
> (a) to make reasonable rules and regulations as may be necessary for making effective such laws.

Pursuant to that authority, the Director had promulgated Rule 23.01, which prescribed "the Standard Policy for fire and lightning insurance of the State of Illinois" and prohibited the making, issuance, and delivery of insurance contracts and policies which did not conform to the standard policy.

The standard policy includes the following clause:

> No suit or action on this policy for the recovery of any claim shall be sustainable in any court of law or equity unless all of the requirements of this policy shall have been complied with, and unless commenced within twelve months next after inception of the loss.

The plaintiffs in these two actions, Robert Stofer and Joseph Fox, and the defendant insurance companies entered into temporary contracts of fire insurance ("binders") which incorporated the above-quoted standard clause.

Stofer allegedly suffered a loss on October 29, 1972. On December 18, 1972, Stofer submitted a written claim to his insurer, accompanied by a sworn statement of "proof of loss." On May 22, 1973, the insurer rejected the claim, and on November 5, 1973, Stofer filed suit against his insurer in the circuit court of Cook County. As an affirmative defense, the insurance company pleaded the expiration of the 12-month period provided for such suits in the contract.

Fox's insured property allegedly was exposed to shock waves from a nearby explosion on March 6, 1972, and collapsed on June 13, 1972. Fox's insurers rejected his claim on or about October 2, 1972, and Fox filed suit against them on December 3, 1973. Fox's insurers raised the same affirmative defense as was raised against Stofer.

The circuit court struck the affirmative defense in each case on the ground that the 12-month limitation on the time for bringing suit following a loss had been prescribed by the Director of Insurance pursuant to an unconstitutional delegation of authority to him by the legislature. The circuit court consolidated the cases and rendered the findings necessary to certify the constitutional question for interlocutory appeal ..., and we granted the insurance companies' motion for direct appeal to this court pursuant to our Rule 302(b).

....

We now address the constitutional question. The separation of powers and branches of government raises extremely complex and subtle questions about the nature and function of government itself. . . .

Fox and Stofer argue that, while it may be clear that the Director can promulgate reasonable regulations to effectuate the legislature's desire to provide "concurrency of contract" and while the legislature itself could have enacted a uniform one-year limit on the time for actions against the insurer under the contract, the legislature could not give the Director the power to prescribe such a limit. They reason that limiting a person's access to judicial remedies is a "legislative act" which only can be done by statute and not by regulation, and that, even if it could be done by regulation, the enabling statute does not set forth sufficient standards to cabin the administrator's discretion in promulgating such a regulation.

We hold that the legislature may delegate to the Director the power to prescribe a uniform insurance contract containing a clause limiting the time during which actions may be brought by the insured against his insurer. This term is but another provision of the standard policy, one of many that may effectively bar relief to the insured.

We no longer find the legislative-act administrative-act distinction helpful to a reasoned analysis of the separation of powers and branches of government mandated by our constitution in the context of statutes enabling administrators to promulgate regulations prescribing rights and duties under a comprehensive regulatory statute. Rather, we think this case may be more appropriately analyzed under the second issue presented by Fox and Stofer, *i. e.*, whether the legislature provided sufficient guidance to limit the powers granted the Director.

Many of our early cases adhere to the notion that administrative rule making basically is interstitial, interpolating among the standards set by the legislature to fill in details and create a comprehensive regulatory scheme. . . . Subsequent experience, however, with the administrative regulation of highly complex and technical subjects leads us to conclude that the administrative task necessarily differs substantially from the traditional model. In determining to regulate a particularly complex subject, the legislature frequently intends only to eliminate a particular class of abuse from an otherwise lawful and valuable activity. In many cases, it simply is impractical for legislators to become and remain thoroughly apprised of the facts necessary to determine which aspects of that activity are harmful and how they might be modified. . . . In most cases, therefore, the administrator's task is not merely to interpolate among broadly stated legislative prohibitions, but, rather, to extrapolate from the broad language of his enabling statute, and, using the regulatory tools given him by the legislature, to deal with the problems which the legislature sought to address.

To require the legislature continually to determine the specific actions which ought to be prohibited and those which ought to be required would be to render the regulation of many matters hopelessly inefficient. Yet the demands of administrative efficiency are not dispositive of the mandate of our constitution. A structure which enables government to serve its citizens more efficiently also may enable it to oppress them more efficiently. The separation of powers and branches of government mandates a distribution of authority which may, on occasion, impede one of the branches in attempting to address a particular problem. This impediment is necessary, however, to impede the abuse of power by any one particular branch acting alone.

At least one commentator thus views the question of separation of powers as being limited to preventing the oppression of one branch of government by another. (*See* 1 F. Cooper, State Administrative Law 16 (1965).) We find that analysis inadequate. It is not enough that the other branches of government remain unimpeded in their ability to remedy an abuse of power by the offending branch. Rather, the requirement of affirmative authority from more than one branch of government is itself an important protection against the misguided acts of a particular bureaucracy. . . . It is for this reason that our earlier cases emphasized the need for intelligible legislative standards to guide administrative rule making. . . .

Without sufficient statutory directions against which to compare administrative regulations, the mere existence of judicial review is not a meaningful safeguard against administrative abuses. "The law is not a 'brooding omnipresence in the sky,' . . . and it cannot be drawn from there like nitrogen from the air." (*Textile Workers Union v. Lincoln Mills* (1957), 353 U.S. 448, 465 . . . (Frankfurter, J., dissenting, and quoting Justice Holmes' dissent in *Southern Pacific Co. v. Jensen* (1917), 244 U.S. 205, 222 . . .).) Thus, unless found in the statute, the restraints which the judiciary is to apply to safeguard against the abuse of discretion in administrative rule making simply do not exist. . . .

Accordingly, we find that the view which has developed through the decisions of this court in recent years requires that the legislature, in delegating its authority provide sufficient identification of the following:

(1) The *persons* and *activities* potentially subject to regulation;
(2) the *harm* sought to be prevented; and
(3) the general *means* intended to be available to the administrator to prevent the identified harm.

We recognize that the term "sufficient identification" itself is not free from ambiguity and will have to receive additional content from its application to particular facts and circumstances. The following principles should guide such applications: (1) The legislature must do all that is practical to define the scope of the legislation, *i. e.*, the persons and activities which may be subject to the administrator's authority. This effort is necessary to put interested persons on notice of the possibility of administrative actions affecting them. . . . Of course, the complexity of the subject sought to be regulated may put practical limitations upon the legislature's ability to identify all of the forms the activity may take. . . . (2) With regard to identifying the harm sought to be prevented, the legislature may use somewhat broader, more generic language than in the first element. It is sufficient if, from the language of the statute, it is apparent what types of evil the statute is intended to prevent. . . . (3) Finally, with regard to the means intended to be available, the legislature must specifically enumerate the administrative tools (*e.g.*, regulations, licenses, enforcement proceedings) and the particular sanctions, if any, intended to be available. If sanctions are provided, the legislature also must provide adequate standards and safeguards such as judicial review of the imposition of those sanctions. . . . In the instant case, we find that the rule-making authority provided in sections 397 and 401 of the Insurance Code meets the test which we have today articulated, because the legislature has adequately identified both the harm sought to be remedied and the means intended to be available to prevent such harm. (The scope of the regulation is not at issue.)

First, the legislature has indicated that it intended to prevent a chaotic proliferation of disparate fire insurance policies. But that is not all. Indeed, had the legislature left the Director completely free to promulgate a "reasonable" uniform fire insurance policy, we would have serious doubts as to the constitutionality of such uncabined discretion. ... We find, however, that the legislature has provided substantial additional standards defining the harm sought to be prevented and thereby limiting the Director's discretion. Section 143(2) of the Insurance Code (Ill. Rev. Stat. 1971, ch. 73, par. 755(2)) provided in part:

> The Director shall require the filing of all policy forms issued by any company transacting the kind or kinds of business enumerated in Classes 2 and 3 [fire insurance] of section 4. He may require, in addition thereto, the filing of any generally used riders, endorsements, application blanks and other matter incorporated by reference in any such policy or contract of insurance. Companies that are members of an organization, bureau or association may have the same filed for them by organization, bureau or association. If the Director shall find from an examination of any such policy form, rider, endorsement, application blank or other matter incorporated by reference in any such policy so filed that *it violates any provision of this Code, contains inconsistent, ambiguous or misleading clauses, or contains exceptions and conditions that will unreasonably or deceptively affect the risks that are purported to be assumed by the policy,* he shall order the company or companies issuing such forms to discontinue the use of the same. (Emphasis added.)

The policies governed by section 143 inevitably incorporate the underlying contract. The Director's discretion under sections 397 and 401 in promulgating that contract thus is limited by the terms of section 143. The requirements that the terms be consistent, unambiguous, and not contain "exceptions or conditions that will unreasonably or deceptively affect the risks that are purported to be assumed by the policy" are affirmative requirements of fairness to and protection of the persons who purchase insurance. These standards identify the harm sought to be prevented in terms not unlike those which we have found adequate on several previous occasions. (*Cf., e.g., People v. Avery* (1977), 67 Ill. 2d 182, 9 Ill. Dec. 645, 367 N.E.2d 79 (standards for designating controlled substances); *Hill v. Relyea* (1966), 34 Ill. 2d 552, 556, 216 N.E.2d 795, 797 (discharge of mental patients "as the welfare of such person and the community may require"); *Board of Education v. Page* (1965), 33 Ill. 2d 372, 376, 211 N.E.2d 361, 363 ("specifications for the minimum requirements ... which will conserve the health and safety of the pupils"); *People ex rel. Colletti v. Pate* (1964), 31 Ill. 2d 354, 359, 201 N.E.2d 390, 393 ("diminution of sentences on account of good conduct"); *City of Evanston v. Wazau* (1936), 364 Ill. 198, 204, 4 N.E.2d 78, 79 ("sufficiency of the equipment required by this act for safe operation on public highways").) We therefore hold that the legislature has sufficiently identified both the harm sought to be prevented by the Director's rule-making power and the means (standard terms which comply with section 143) intended to be available to remedy that harm.

For the foregoing reasons, the orders of the circuit court of Cook County striking the insurance companies' affirmative defense are reversed, and the causes are remanded to the circuit court of Cook County for further proceedings not inconsistent with this opinion.

Reversed and remanded.

The distinction between making and applying policy often is far from clear. The following case, from a state court which frequently invalidates legislation as an unconstitutional delegation of power, provides an example of a statute found to have delegated policy-making responsibilities:

DEPARTMENT OF BUSINESS REGULATION v. NATIONAL MANUFACTURED HOUSING FEDERATION, INC.

Supreme Court of Florida
370 So. 2d 1132 (1979)

BOYD, JUSTICE.

This appeal is from a judgment of the Circuit Court of the Second Judicial Circuit, in and for Leon County. It comes directly to us because the trial court, in announcing its judgment, declared a state law invalid. Art. V, § 3(b)(1), Fla.Const. The proceeding was begun when the appellees sought declaratory and injunctive relief from the effect of chapter 77-49, Laws of Florida. The action was defended by the governor, the attorney general, and the Department of Business Regulation. The plaintiffs based their claim for relief upon three grounds: that the statute unlawfully delegates legislative authority; that it deprives mobile home park owners of property without due process of law; and that it constitutes a denial of equal protection of the laws. In its order enjoining implementation of the statute, the court declared it unconstitutional on the first two grounds stated. The court did not address the equal protection argument.

Section 1 of the act contains a recitation of legislative findings and a statement of the purposes of the enactment:

> The Legislature finds that there exists an emergency in rental accommodations in mobile home parks. The Legislature further finds that this condition, coupled with the inordinate expense of relocating a mobile home causes tenants in such parks to be placed in an unequal bargaining position with respect to increases in charges imposed by the owners or managers of such parks. The Legislature further finds that this inequality can only be alleviated by the enactment of reasonable legislative restraints which provide both a reasonable return [on] a park owner's investment and a safeguard to tenants against exorbitant rental or service charges.

To accomplish this purpose, section 4 of the act creates the State Mobile Home Tenant-Landlord Commission to regulate rental increases in mobile home parks. The commission is placed within the Department of Business Regulation.

Section 8 sets out the essence of the regulatory scheme. Subsection (1) provides that if a park owner proposes a charge increase, in the form of an increase in rent or service charges or a decrease in service, "in any calendar year in excess of the net United States Department of Labor Consumer Price Index increases since the last rental increase," then, upon petition of fifty-one percent of the park tenants the commission is required to act. It is to hold a hearing to determine whether the charge increase is "unconscionable or not justified under the facts and circumstances of the particular situation." Subsection (2) provides a list of certain costs that may be passed on to the tenants if they are reasonable and justified. Subsection (3) provides that by November 1 of the year preceding a charge increase, the park owner must notify the tenants of the proposed amount of any increase. Without notice no increase is to be allowed.

Section 9, subsection (1), requires that the hearings be held in accordance with chapter 120, Florida Statutes (1977), the Administrative Procedure Act, and gives the commission the power to rule on a contested charge increase in one of four ways. It shall require the owner "to either reduce the rental or service charges to a rate set by the commission, to continue rental or service charges as they existed under the former lease or agreement, to increase the rental or service charges to a rate set by the commission or to increase the rental or service charges" to the rate proposed by the owner.

Section 9, subsection (2), gives the commission power to adopt rules governing its proceedings and directs the commission to adopt rules providing that increases collected but subsequently held to be unauthorized "shall be either returned to the tenants or credited toward future rental charges."

Section 11 permits appeal of the decisions of the commission to circuit court. An increase approved by the commission, however, is to be paid by the tenant. If the increase is overturned on appeal, it is to be returned or credited. If the park owner appeals, then the proposed charge, even if disapproved by the commission, must be paid but is to be deposited in the court registry. The court is authorized to make disbursements of such funds to the park owner pending the appeal if the owner is in danger of suffering hardship, such as losing the premises.

The commission, under the legislative plan, is to be composed of seven members, including two mobile home park owners or operators, two mobile home park tenants, and three members of the general public.

For the following two reasons, we hold that the circuit court was correct in ruling that chapter 77-49 is unconstitutional.

The court held that subsections (1)(a) and (2)(a) of section 83.784, Florida Statutes (1977), unlawfully delegate legislative power to an administrative body. As was made abundantly clear by our decision in *Askew v. Cross Key Waterways,* [372 So. 2d 913 (Fla. 1978)], announced in an opinion by Justice Sundberg, the doctrine against delegation of legislative power is of continuing vitality in Florida. We held that the legislature must take heed of article II, section 3, Florida Constitution, which provides: "The powers of the state government shall be divided into legislative, executive and judicial branches. No person belonging to one branch shall exercise any powers appertaining to either of the other two branches unless expressly provided herein." The opinion explained why strict adherence to the above constitutional admonition is imperative:

> A corollary of the doctrine of unlawful delegation is the availability of judicial review. In the final analysis it is the courts, upon a challenge to the exercise or nonexercise of administrative action, which must determine whether the administrative agency has performed consistently with the mandate of the legislature. When legislation is so lacking in guidelines that neither the agency nor the courts can determine whether the agency is carrying out the intent of the legislature in its conduct, then, in fact, the agency becomes the lawgiver rather than the administrator of the law.

Askew v. Cross Key Waterways . . . .

The interests of a mobile home park owner and a mobile home park tenant necessarily compete. Similar to the posture of a buyer and seller in the commercial arena, a mobile home park tenant has as his goal affordable living accommodations, while a park owner endeavors to maximize his profits. Rent control legislation seeks a balance between these competing interests by stabilizing rentals under emergency conditions in order to prevent extortionate increases in rent resulting from housing shortages, while at the same time allowing landlords a fair and equitable return upon their investments. *City of Miami Beach v. Forte Towers, Inc.*, 305 So.2d 764, 767 (Fla.1974) (Dekle, J., concurring specially). Because of the fundamental nature of these concerns and the pervasiveness of mobile home living in Florida, the point where rent control legislation strikes this balance is undoubtedly of great public moment.

The criteria for determining the validity of rental or service charge increases in subsections (1)(a) and (2)(a) of section 83.784 are constitutionally defective because they charge the commission with the fundamental legislative task of striking this balance between mobile home park owner and mobile home park tenant, without any meaningful guidance. *See Askew v. Cross Key Waterways* .... The subsections provide:

> (1)(a) Upon petition of 51 percent of the tenants of any dwelling units in a mobile home park who will be subject to a rental or service charge increase or a decrease in services in any calendar year in excess of the net United States Department of Labor Consumer Price Index increases since the last rental increase, the commission shall hold a hearing at the mobile home park or at such other facility selected by the commission, so long as it is reasonably accessible to all parties, at a date to be set by the commission, to determine whether or not the rental or service charge increase or a decrease in services is so great as to be unconscionable or not justified under the facts and circumstances of the particular situation.
>
> ....
>
> (2)(a) The increased costs to the owner of a mobile home park attributable to:
>   1. Increases in utility rates;
>   2. Property taxes;
>   3. Fluctation [*sic*] in property value;
>   4. Governmental assessments;
>   5. Cost of living increases attributable to and relevant to incidental services, normal repair, and maintenance; and
>   6. Capital improvements not otherwise promised or contracted for may be passed on to the tenants or prospective tenants in the form of increased rental or service charges if such increases are reasonable and justified under the facts and circumstances of the particular case.

The terms "unconscionable or not justified under the facts and circumstances" in (1)(a), and the terms "reasonable and justified under the facts and circumstances of the particular case" in (2)(a), are not accompanied by any standards or guidelines to aid a court or administrative agency in ascertaining the true legislative intent underlying the act. The legislature may have wanted to afford the word "unconscionable" in (1)(a) a liberal construction, so as to circumscribe narrowly a park owner's ability to pass on costs to tenants beset by inflation. As written, the act gives no hint whether this is a correct interpretation. It is thus left to the "unbridled discretion or whim" of the commission to formulate basic legislative policy. ...

Moreover, "unconscionability" is a term which has meaning in the context of an equitable proceeding in our courts between two adverse parties. A chancellor sitting in equity is guided in the exercise of his discretion in this regard by sound principles of law which have been articulated and applied on a case-by-case basis over a long period of time during the development of our rich common law heritage. ... No such guiding principles are supplied by the legislature here. Furthermore, the joining of that term with the phrase "or not justified under the facts and circumstances of the particular situation" makes the legislative standard even more nebulous.

In *Sarasota County v. Barg,* this Court invalidated portions of the act creating the Manasota Key Conservation District. Employing language similar to that contained in section 83.784, the act prohibited "undue or unreasonable dredging, filling or disturbance of submerged bottoms," as well as "unreasonable destruction of natural vegetation." In finding the above provisions violative of article II, section 3, Florida Constitution, the Court stated:

> The Act does not contain any standards or guidelines to aid any court or administrative body in interpreting these terms. The determination of what conduct falls within the proscription of these ambiguous provisions is left to the unbridled discretion of those responsible for applying and enforcing the Act. This amounts to an unrestricted delegation of legislative authority . . . .

302 So.2d at 742. *See also City of Miami Beach v. Fleetwood Hotel, Inc.,* 261 So.2d 801 (Fla.1972).

. . . .

The judgment of the circuit court is affirmed.

Comments: 1. Both the Illinois and Florida cases consider regulations which govern contractual relationships in which one of the contracting parties has a bargaining disadvantage. Insurance policyholders cannot easily bargain over the terms of an insurance contract. Mobile home park spaces are in short supply. The owner of the park has a bargaining advantage.

The Florida court decided that the adjustment of this bargaining relationship required a clear expression of legislative policy. The Illinois court allowed the state agency to adjust the bargaining relationship without a clear expression of legislative policy. What considerations might underlie these differences in the judicial approach to delegation of power?

The Florida legislation authorized an adjustment in rental charges if they were "unconscionable." This term is a legal word of art which has acquired meaning through judicial interpretation. Consult Professor Merrill's delegation categories, as explained *supra.* Would he uphold this delegation of power as falling within one of his categories? Why?

2. The Florida statute contained elaborate procedures for the determination and review of rental charges, yet the Florida court apparently rejected the Davis theory and did not consider their availability when deciding the delegation issue. Compare the court's treatment of a similar delegation problem in *Cottrell v. City & County of Denver,* 636 P.2d 703 (Colo. 1981).

A charter amendment authorized the water board to set water rates, taking into account the usual utility costs, "including those reasonably required for the anticipated growth of the Denver metropolitan area." The court held that traditional nondelegation doctrine had not been effective in protecting individuals against "the unnecessary and uncontrolled exercise of [delegated] discretionary power." The court then reformulated the delegation of power test, incorporating the Davis view:

> [T]he test is not simply whether the delegation is guided by standards, but whether there are sufficient statutory standards and safeguards and administrative standards and safeguards, in combination, to protect against unnecessary and uncontrolled exercise of discretionary power. The guiding consideration is whether these constraints are sufficient to insure that administrative action will be rational and consistent in the first instance and that subsequent judicial review of that action is available and will be sufficient.

Id. at 709. The court upheld the statute. Would it uphold the delegation of power in the Florida mobile home case? *See also Westervelt v. National Resources Commission,* 263 N.W.2d 564 (Mich. 1978).

3. Occupational licensing also affects important social interests, as the state or local license controls entry into an occupation. Some courts strike down licensing standards they consider open to abuse in the licensing process. In *Harrington & Co. v. Tampa Port Authority,* 358 So. 2d 168 (Fla. 1978), the court invalidated a statute authorizing the authority to grant stevedore licenses "as it may deem necessary, having due regard to the business of the port and harbor." It held that the statute did not provide "clear and specific guidelines" to prevent the arbitrary selection of stevedores. Would the statute be unconstitutional as a violation of due process because it was anticompetitive? *See* Chapter 10.

Compare Watchmaking Examining Board v. Husar, 182 N.W.2d 257 (Wis. 1971). The court upheld a statute providing for state licensing of watchmakers:

> [T]he purpose [of the statute] is clearly to protect the consumer from incompetent or unethical persons who hold themselves out to practice the trade of watchmaking. The statute itself sets forth the requirements as to training and experience necessary to obtain a certificate to engage in the trade. The Board is specifically delegated power to make rules and regulations for the definition of the standards of workmanship and skill. The exercise of the power is hedged about with numerous procedural safeguards.

Id. at 262.

Some courts are even more lenient. See *Levine v. Whalen,* 349 N.E.2d 821 (N.Y. 1976), upholding a state hospital licensing statute. The court rejected a delegation of power objection by relying on a legislative statement of policy that the intent of the law was "to provide for the protection and promotion of the health of the inhabitants of the area."

4. *Adoption by reference.* Legislatures sometimes attempt to provide adequate standards by incorporating by reference the provisions of private model codes or standards or by incorporating other statutes or administrative regulations. This practice raises objections that legislative power has unconstitutionally been delegated to a private agency.

This technique is sometimes used in licensing legislation. In *Gumbhir v. Kansas State Board of Pharmacy,* 618 P.2d 843 (Kan. 1980), a statute provided that a pharmacist must be a graduate of a school of pharmacy accredited by the American Council on Pharmaceutical Education. The court found an unconstitutional delegation of power. It distinguished statutes requiring lawyers to be graduates of an accredited law school because the licensing of attorneys was "an inherent power of the courts in the administration of justice." Why is this a distinction?

The same problem arises when a statute or ordinance provides for the adoption of private national fire and safety codes. The delegation is upheld if the statute contains adequate standards. See *City of Warren v. State Construction Code Commission,* 239 N.W.2d 640 (Mich. App. 1976). The statute provided that the state construction code should consist of nationally recognized codes and standards "as the commission deems appropriate." *Accord Johnson v. Roberts,* 236 S.E.2d 737 (S.C. 1977). Compare cases invalidating statutes and ordinances requiring compliance with private national codes with no option to vary the code provisions. See *Agnew v. City of Culver City,* 304 P.2d 788 (Cal. App. 1956). For discussion see Liebmann, *Delegation to Private Parties in American Constitutional Law,* 50 IND. L.J. 650 (1975).

Incorporation of a private code by reference also is invalidated when incorporation is given a prospective effect. Any changes made in the private code are incorporated without further legislative action. See *Hillman v. Northern Wasco County People's Utility District,* 323 P.2d 664 (Or. 1958), incorporating any changes made in a private code. The court noted that the private code was a compromise between conflicting interests, and could not "blindly" be accepted in advance.

Courts may reach the same result when other statutes are incorporated by reference, such as federal statutes. See *Lee v. State,* 635 P.2d 1282 (Mont. 1981), which considered the fifty-five mile per hour speed limit mandated by federal legislation. The statute mandated the state attorney general to adopt a speed limit "not less than that required by federal law." The court held that "[a] more blatant handover of the sovereign power of this state to the federal jurisdiction is beyond our ken."

Neither may legislation incorporate by reference a determination by a federal agency. *State v. Rodriguez,* 379 So. 2d 1084 (La. 1980). The state agency was to list a substance as a "controlled dangerous substance" if it was so classified by the federal drug agency. *Accord Wallace v. Commissioner of Taxation,* 232 N.W.2d 894 (Minn. 1971) (federal definition of tax terms). The cases allow incorporation of a federal agency definition if incorporation is limited to the definition at the time the state statute was enacted. *State v. Julson,* 202 N.W.2d 149 (N.D. 1972).

Some courts allow prospective incorporation of federal agency regulations if "rationally related" to the statutory purpose. *See East Suburban Press v. Township of Penn Hills,* 397 A.2d 1263 (Pa. Commw. 1979). A statute limited legal advertising to newspapers eligible for second class mailing privileges under United States Postal Service regulations. The court held that the federal regulation accomplished a different purpose. The federal agency regulated postal operations. The state statute regulated advertising.

Some courts find an improper delegation because they believe that the subject matter of the delegation is inherently political. The following case illustrates this point of view:

MILLER v. COVINGTON DEVELOPMENT AUTHORITY

Supreme Court of Kentucky
539 S.W.2d 1 (1976)

PALMORE, JUSTICE.

This is a test suit to determine whether two acts of the 1974 General Assembly are valid. They are ch. 131, the Local Development Authority Act, and ch. 132, the Tax Increment Act, which have been placed in the statutes as KRS 99.610-99.680 and KRS 99.750-99.770, respectively. We find them both invalid.

Section 1 of the Local Development Authority Act states as its legislative policy "the preservation and revitalization of historically or economically significant local areas" in first and second-class cities and counties operating under the urban county form of government, "while at the same time accommodating necessary and desirable central city and suburban growth."

The LDA Act creates an independent local agency consisting of the mayor or his designee as an ex officio nonvoting member and seven commissioners appointed by the mayor, with the approval of the governing body of the municipality, for staggered four-year terms. KRS 99.625.

Among the "public and essential governmental functions" it is expressly empowered to exercise is the threshold act of establishing a development plan fixing the boundaries of a project area and designating the "character and extent of the public and private land ownership and uses proposed within the area." This plan must be "made available for public inspection," after which the LDA may among other things proceed to acquire any or all real or personal property within the project area, to clear any or all improvements or cause them to be renovated, to develop and construct residential housing for persons and families of lower income, to subdivide, sell, lease, exchange, encumber or otherwise dispose of any of the property "at its fair cash value," notwithstanding the cost of its acquisition, for uses consistent with the development plan. None of this requires approval by the municipal governing body.

With regard to its funds (a principal source of which is provided by the Tax Increment Act, discussed hereinafter), the LDA has these powers (among others) within the jurisdiction of its municipal area for the purposes of developing the project area or areas, all without prior approval of the local governing body.

(1) To make, participate in or acquire loans for construction, development or rehabilitation of residential housing projects if it determines that such loans are not available from private lenders "upon reasonably equivalent terms and conditions;"

(2) To insure the payment of loans made by other lenders for those purposes if it determines that such insurance is not available from private insurers "upon reasonably equivalent terms and conditions;"

(3) To *make grants* (that is, as we construe it, to donate, or give away) to builders, developers and owners of residential housing for the development, construction, rehabilitation or maintenance of residential housing as it "shall deem important for a proper living environment, all on such terms and conditions" as it may deem appropriate;

(4) To consent to modifications in the rate of interest, times of payment, or any other terms of loans and agreements relating to residential housing projects to which it is a party;

(5) To construct residential housing for persons and families of lower income, and to construct, through lessees, industrial buildings pursuant to KRS 103.200-103.285;

(6) To acquire, establish and operate, lease or sublease residential housing for persons and families of lower income, and to contract to assume the rights, powers, obligations and duties of any local housing authority or similar agency of the federal, state, city or urban county government;

(7) To make periodic *grants* to reduce principal and interest payments on mortgages or rentals payable by persons and families "of low income;"

(8) To borrow or accept funds from any source and, in that respect, to "include in any contract for financial assistance with the federal, state, city or urban-county government *any conditions which the federal, state, city or urban-county government may attach to its financial aid"* not inconsistent with the purposes of the LDA Act (emphasis added); and

(9) To issue revenue bonds payable solely out of the revenues of the project, including tax increments released to the LDA pursuant to the Tax Increment Act.

The Tax Increment Act is less complex. Its fundamental provision is that any taxing district, including school districts, may contract to "release" to the LDA, for a period up to 25 years, not less than 50% or more than 95% of all ad valorem tax revenues received from a development or project area in excess of those received from the same area in the last year before its establishment.

Obviously these two statutes have the constructive public purpose of enabling urban governments to attempt the revitalization of decaying "inner cities." The theory on which the hypothecation of future ad valorem tax revenues is justified is that in the long run the taxing districts will be repaid in the form of a greatly enhanced tax base and that the increased revenues ("increments") meanwhile released to the LDA and used by it to create this enhancement are revenues that would not have existed otherwise. We find no fault in the purpose or in the theory, but for the reasons that follow it is our opinion that each of the acts transcends the limits of the Kentucky Constitution.

We need not encumber our opinion with an excruciating analysis of what this and other courts have said in cases involving similar problems with different facts. Counsel for all parties are familiar with all the broad principles and ancient shibboleths of constitutional law, and recognize that each new application comes down to a matter of degree and calls for a value judgment. In this case the burden of casting that judgment rests finally on the seven elected members of this court.

We mention the word "elected" because it is appropriate to our assessment of the LDA Act. It is a fundamental proposition that a legislative body should not and ordinarily cannot divest itself of a legislative power. A state legislature may delegate legislative powers to cities because a state constitution gives it that right. Cf. Const. § 156. If, however, a state legislature purports to authorize a city to pass such powers on to an administrative agency, it attempts to authorize something it cannot do itself. For that reason cities cannot be so authorized, notwithstanding the legislature's constitutional prerogative of prescribing the bounds of their powers. If there is one essential characteristic inherent in legislative power, it is that such power must be exercised by an elected representative or representatives of the people, and not by a person, persons or agency created or designated by those representatives. Therein, we think, lies the major flaw of the LDA Act. It authorizes the agency to exercise choices that the people are entitled to have exercised by their elected representatives.

In other instances too numerous to recount, delegations of authority have been upheld on the theory that the legislative body has prescribed standards or safeguards that so confine the administrative body's powers that it can be said that they do not exceed the scope of mere details in the execution. In our judgment they are not so confined here, nor do we have the safeguard of a long-established administrative agency such as a state highway department or department of education, with a track record of experience and expertise in a well-recognized field. Nor, indeed, are the powers delegated to the LDA confined to matters so involved or so beyond the technical competence of a legislative body that it would be unrealistic not to vest them in an administrative agency.

Take for example the very first choice the LDA is required to make, the choice of an area. By what legislative criteria is the agency restricted in arriving at this vital decision? Only by its own notions of whether the area is economically or historically "significant." Considering the emphasis placed by the remaining provisions of the Act upon revitalization of the area by means of "development," one might reasonably conclude that the "historical" aspect of this two-headed criterion is of dubious practical importance, and we so regard it. The real thrust of the Act is toward economic development. What then is to characterize an area as "economically significant?" Indeed, is there any real estate, or any area, within a city that is *not* "economically significant?" And if there are certain areas of a city that can be classified as depressed and dying, and for that reason subjected to radical cosmetic surgery, what is to prevent the elected representatives of that city either from determining its boundaries themselves or from prescribing some tangible formulae or criteria by which it is to be done, and is there any practical reason why that responsibility should be shifted to another layer of officialdom that is not directly responsible to the electorate? We think these questions go to the heart of the delegability question, and the answer is that there is no substantial reason for the ultimate choice not to be made by the legislative body, as it must be made, for example, in the case of zoning or urban renewal. Certainly it does not appear to be justified in terms of "the practical needs of effective government." Cf. *Butler v. United Cerebral Palsy of Northern Kentucky, Inc.,* Ky., 352 S.W.2d 203, 208 (1961).

The constitutional authority of any administrative agency to make a final decision on any question that lies within the authority of the direct representatives of the electorate to decide owes its existence to one of two pragmatic factors. Either, as in the instance of activities usually labeled "ministerial," the matters decided are not of sufficient public importance or impact to warrant the day-to-day attention of "the boss" (the legislative body) or, if they are of such importance, for some practical reason or reasons identifiable by the exercise of common sense they cannot be effectively handled by the legislative body itself. In theory if not in fact, the major administrative agencies that conduct substantial segments of government today live by virtue of the latter supposition. Since, however, this basis for administrative authority runs counter to the idea of unfettered democratic choice, and removes the exercise of discretion one step beyond that which is contemplated by representative government through elected legislators, we think that sound jurisprudence must confine it to instances of clear necessity.[9] It is understandable that the federal Congress cannot survey the boundaries for national parks or choose the sites of federal buildings, nor could a state legislature be expected to make such decisions directly. Within the much smaller bounds of a city or county, however, the problem is not so formidable, and the question of necessity may not result in the same answer.

It is for the broad reason that the LDA Act unnecessarily empowers a legislative choice to be delegated away that we hold it invalid under Const. §§ 27, 28. We do not reach the due process and other arguments leveled at the Act, nor do we pass on the validity of the various grants of authority heretofore mentioned for the purpose of illustrating the great scope of discretionary power vested in the administrative agency by the statute. . . .

[The court then invalidated the tax increment financing portion of the law, holding that school taxes could only be spent for school purposes under the constitution. Nor could ad valorem taxes constitute a special fund to be pledged to the payment of municipal bonds. For more on tax increment financing see Chapter 4.—Eds.]

The judgment is reversed.

All concur.

Comments: 1. The *Cross Key Waterways* case, which is discussed in the Florida mobile home decision reproduced *supra*, is another case in which a court found that inherent policy decisions had been delegated. A statute authorized a state agency to designate areas of critical state concern. One provision allowed the designation of areas having a "significant" impact on environmental resources or major public facilities. Local land use controls within these areas must conform to policies adopted by the state agency. The court invalidated the statutory designation authority.

What troubled the court was the delegation to the administrative agency of the power to make the "fundamental and primary policy" decision implicit in designating critical areas. This decision, the court held, was a legislative function. The critical areas legislation was defective because it placed in the hands of the administrative agency "the fundamental legislative task of determining which geographic areas and resources are in greatest need of protection." The legislation also was invalid for not establishing designation priorities among the environmental and natural resource areas of the state.

Note that the critical area legislation displaced local land use control authority by authorizing a state agency to adopt land use policies for critical areas. The Florida Court of Appeal relied on this reallocation of authority as a reason for holding the delegation invalid. It believed that the legislation was an attempt to correct local land use programs which did not sufficiently consider the environment, and that state legislation which corrected this neglect required more precise standards.

---

[9] "The purpose of the nondelegation doctrine should no longer be either to prevent delegation or to require statutory standards; the purpose should be the much deeper one of protecting against *unnecessary and uncontrolled discretionary power*." (Emphasis added.) Davis, Administrative Law Text (3d ed., 1972), § 2.08.

Other courts have upheld comparable legislation providing similar standards for state agency regulation of development in environmental areas, e.g., *Toms River Affiliates v. Department of Environmental Protection,* 355 A.2d 679 (N.J. App. Div. 1979). The supreme court in *Cross Keys* distinguished this legislation because it applied to circumscribed geographic areas. Do you agree with the distinction?

For discussion see Note, *Florida's Adherence to the Doctrine of Nondelegation of Power,* 7 FLA. ST. U.L. REV. 541 (1979). The critical area legislation has been amended to provide more detailed designation criteria and legislative review of designations. Fla. Stat. Ann. § 380.05.

2. What would the result have been in the *Covington* case if the legislation had authorized the council to delegate the controverted powers to the authority? This question was presented in *Indiana University v. Hartwell,* 367 N.E.2d 1090 (Ind. App. 1977). A delegation of power challenge was brought to state legislation authorizing local civil rights commissions. The statute authorized the local legislative council, by ordinance, to delegate to the commission "such powers ... as may be deemed necessary or appropriate to implement its purpose and objectives." The delegation of power was held unconstitutional. The court noted that

> the legislature has, unwittingly or not, arrayed the full panorama of powers of the State and has given any city, town, or county uncontrolled discretion to select in smorgasbord fashion those powers "deemed necessary and appropriate" to implement the purpose and objective of the Civil Rights Act and to vest a local commission agency with such selected powers.

Id. at 1093. It concluded that "[s]o long as there exists residual statutory authority to usurp powers constitutionally reserved to the three departments of the State, the statute is constitutionally defective." *Id.* at 1094. The court did not believe that the expertise of the agency constituted "an acceptable substitute for the imposition of express standards where this is a delegation of discretionary powers." *Id.*

Do the concerns expressed in the *Indiana University* case reflect the concerns expressed in the *Covington* case? Would the court in *Stofer* have upheld this statute? Are the court decisions in the *Indiana University* and *Covington* cases influenced by the nature of the power delegated? *See State ex rel. Wagner v. St. Louis County,* 604 S.W.2d 592 (Mo. 1980) (legislature may delegate power to agency to exercise power of eminent domain to acquire areas approved by local legislative body).

2. DELEGATION TO THE JUDICIARY

This topic is covered in Chapter 2.

3. DELEGATION TO LOCAL GOVERNMENTS

STATE EX REL. CITY OF CHARLESTON v. COGHILL
Supreme Court of Appeals of West Virginia
156 W. Va. 877, 207 S.E.2d 113 (1973)

NEELY, JUSTICE:

This is an original action in mandamus in which the City of Charleston, a municipal corporation of the State of West Virginia, seeks to require its clerk, Kenneth L. Coghill, to publish a certain notice inviting proposals from all persons interested in purchasing or leasing space included in a proposed off-street parking facility in Charleston. Respondent Coghill was authorized and directed to perform this duty by resolution No. 228-73 which was adopted by the Charleston City Council on April 2, 1973.

The respondent clerk has refused to publish the notice upon the ground that Chapter 8, Article 16, Section 4a of the Code of West Virginia, 1931, which gives authority to municipal corporations to construct motor vehicle parking facilities, is unconstitutional. If Code, 8-16-4a is constitutional, then the City Clerk has a nondiscretionary legal duty to publish the notice as directed by the council. The purpose of this litigation is to test the validity under the State and Federal Constitutions of the enabling legislation, Code 8-16-4a, in order to facilitate the preparation of plans and orderly financing for a project in Charleston. . . .

The respondent clerk first maintains that the Legislature's delegation of authority to a municipal corporation to determine the amount of space in a public parking facility which will be leased or sold for private business, commercial, or charitable uses is an unconstitutional delegation of legislative power. While noticing that respondent's position finds its source in the well known constitutional principle that a legislature may not abdicate its legislative power, it has also long been established law that a legislature may delegate legislative powers to municipal corporations as to matters of purely local concern. . . . This Court said in Syllabus pt. 1 of *West Virginia Water Service Company v. Cunningham,* 143 W.Va. 1, 98 S.E.2d 891 (1957):

> "Under the police power of the State, the Legislature has power to provide for the protection of the safety, health, morals, and general welfare of the public, and may delegate such powers to municipalities created by it" [Pt. 1 Syllabus, *Hayes v. The Town of Cedar Grove,* 126 W.Va. 828, 30 S.E.2d 726], *State ex rel. Bibb v. Chambers, Mayor, etc.,* 138 W. Va. 701, pt. 6 syl., 77 S.E.2d 297.

This Court, therefore, holds that the Legislature is entitled to delegate power to a municipal corporation to determine the appropriate mix of public and private uses of a public parking facility, subject to the constitutional limits on the municipality's discretion which will be further discussed in this opinion.

Comments: 1. The court then went on to discuss these constitutional limits, first implying that the delegation of power objection in this context was not serious. While the law as stated by the principal case appears to be well established, why does the delegation of legislative power to a local government stand on a different footing than the delegation of that power to an administrative agency, or to the judiciary? Consider the following analysis in *Territory of Hawaii ex rel. County of Oahu v. Whitney,* 17 Hawaii 174 (1905):

> This brings us to the question of the principles upon which the question should be solved. It is a fundamental rule that delegated power cannot be delegated. This applies to legislatures as well as to other bodies. Legislative power delegated to legislatures cannot be delegated to other persons or bodies. There is, however, an exception to this maxim as well established as the maxim itself. This exception arises by implication from the immemorial practice which has recognized the propriety of vesting in municipal organizations certain powers of local regulation over matters in which the persons within such organizations are especially interested and in regard to which they are supposed to be especially competent to judge. . . . The implication is that in delegating to legislatures the legislative power the people could not have intended to prevent the further delegation by the legislatures of certain police and other powers of a local nature which had always been exercised by municipal corporations and the exercise of which by the local communities acting through such corporations has been regarded as one of the fundamental features of the American and English systems of government.

Id. at 177-78. The court upheld a delegation of legislative power to the county.

For other cases upholding delegations of power to municipalities see *Richards v. City of Muscatine,* 237 N.W.2d 48 (Iowa 1975) (authority to issue tax increment urban renewal bonds); *Local 1485, American Federation of Teachers v. Yakima School District No. 7,* 447 P.2d 593 (Wash. 1968) (collective bargaining).

Does the court's analysis in the Hawaii case provide a satisfactory explanation for the exception? Could it be that the reason lies in the inapplicability of separation of powers doctrine to state-local relationships? Or does the explanation lie somewhere in accepted notions of plenary state power over local governments? Consult Chapter 1.

2. Courts may avoid a decision on the applicability of the nondelegation doctrine to municipalities by construing the applicable statute to impose sufficient standards. In *J.M. Mills, Inc. v. Murphy,* 352 A.2d 661 (R.I. 1976), the court considered a challenge to the state wetlands act, which conferred concurrent authority over wetlands on local governments and on the director of the state Department of Natural Resources. While reserving decision on the application of the nondelegation doctrine to municipalities, the court held that the statute imposed a "best public interest" test on municipal decisions to authorize changes in wetlands. It found that these standards were sufficient. To answer a contention that the statute was so vague that it authorized unconstitutional restrictions on wetlands, the court held that a limitation that municipalities would not exercise their delegated powers in a manner that violated constitutional rights was inherent in the statutory delegation of power. *See also State v. Boynton,* 379 A.2d 994 (Me. 1977).

3. What if the legislature simply authorizes a municipality to impose "any taxes on cigarettes, cigars or smoking tobacco such as the legislature has or would have power and authority to impose"? Acting under this delegation of authority, the City of New York enacted regulations requiring tax differentials in the city cigarette tax, which reflected differences in tar and nicotine content, to be passed on to purchasers. *People v. Cook,* 312 N.E.2d 452 (N.Y. 1974). The delegation was upheld, the court noting that the state legislature had ample authority to enact a similar requirement. No mention was made of possible delegation of power objections.

4. Although the courts may not apply the nondelegation rule to delegations to local governments, they have adopted another rule that limits these delegations. Two local governments may not exercise the same powers over the same territory at the same time. The rule has been applied to prohibit the organization of special districts within the limits of incorporated municipalities. *See State ex rel. Flaxel v. Chandler,* 175 P.2d 448 (Or. 1946).

When local governments attempt to exercise competing powers over the same territory, the courts apply a variety of rules to avoid conflict. The powers may be found not to conflict. *In re Sandia Conservancy District,* 259 P.2d 557 (N.M. 1953) (organization of conservancy district). Priority may also be given to the local government which first exercises jurisdiction. *Edwards v. Housing Authority,* 19 N.E.2d 741 (Ind. 1939). Neither may the rule apply when one of the local governments is exercising proprietary functions. *Public Utility District v. Town of Newport,* 228 P.2d 766 (Wash. 1951).

5. Are there any alternatives to aggressive enforcement of the nondelegation doctrine at the state level? Consider the following:

> A large number [of states] have established legislative oversight committees to review state agency regulations. The powers of these committees range from the purely advisory to the clearly substantive, including the power to suspend specific regulations. The presence or absence of such oversight is relevant to determining just how much authority has actually been delegated: the greater the continuing legislative involvement in the administrative process, the less justified is any charge of legislative abdication.

Developments in the Law—The Interpretation of State Constitutional Rights, 95 HARV. L. REV. 1324, 1492 (1982).

Some state courts have invalidated legislation authorizing legislative vetoes of administrative rules. *State ex rel. Barker v. Manchin,* 279 S.E.2d 622 (W. Va. 1981). Does this restriction affect the argument in the *Developments* article?

Chapter 10

THE ROLE OF THE JUDICIARY

A. IN ORDINARY STATE AND LOCAL GOVERNMENT ISSUES: LICENSING AND REGULATION

State and local governments engage in a wide variety of business and economic regulation, notably occupational licensing. Because much of this legislation is by definition restrictive of individuals or businesses, it is frequently subjected to challenge on state or federal constitutional grounds. At an earlier period, the Supreme Court regularly called upon substantive due process to strike down state legislation regulating for social and economic purposes. One of the leading cases of that era, *New State Ice Co. v. Liebmann*, 285 U.S. 262 (1932), for example, held invalid on fourteenth amendment due process grounds a state statute which required a license based on public need to engage in the business of distributing ice. The Court's attitude toward the fourteenth amendment was shifting when it decided *Nebbia v. New York*, 291 U.S. 502 (1934), upholding a New York statute which authorized a state agency to fix the retail price of milk. By 1955 the shift was complete. In *Williamson v. Lee Optical Co.*, 348 U.S. 483 (1955), the Court upheld an Oklahoma statute which, among other restrictions, prohibited opticians from duplicating or fitting lenses without a prescription from an optometrist or ophthalmologist and from advertising the sale of eyeglasses. In doing so, the Court said:

> The Oklahoma law may exact a needless, wasteful requirement in many cases. But it is for the legislature, not the courts, to balance the advantages and disadvantages of the new requirement.... But the law need not be in every respect logically consistent with its aims to be constitutional. It is enough that there is an evil at hand for correction, and that it might be thought that the particular legislative measure was a rational way to correct it.
>
> The day is gone when this Court uses the Due Process Clause of the Fourteenth Amendment to strike down state laws, regulatory of business and industrial conditions, because they may be unwise, improvident, or out of harmony with a particular school of thought.

Id. at 487-88. Equal protection challenges to regulatory legislation took a similar course of abstention. In *Friedman v. Rogers*, 440 U.S. 1 (1979), the Court rejected an equal protection challenge to the Texas Optometry Act which required four of six members of the state licensing board to be members of an association whose membership excluded the plaintiff, a licensed optometrist.

> We stated the applicable constitutional rule for reviewing equal protection challenges to local economic regulations such as § 2.02 in *New Orleans v. Dukes*, 427 U. S. 297, 303 (1976).
>
> "When local economic regulation is challenged solely as violating the Equal Protection Clause, this Court consistently defers to legislative determinations as to the desirability of particular statutory discriminations. Unless a classification trammels fundamental personal rights or is drawn upon inherently suspect distinctions such as race, religion, or alienage, our decisions presume the constitutionality of the statutory discriminations and

require only that the classification challenged be rationally related to a legitimate state interest."

Id. at 17.

Despite its reluctance to invoke the fourteenth amendment against restrictive economic practices, the Court has shown an increasing willingness to challenge them on other grounds. In two cases the Court invalidated under the first amendment state-sanctioned prohibitions on business advertising: *Virginia State Board of Pharmacy v. Virginia Citizens Consumer Council,* 425 U.S. 748 (1976) (Virginia statute prohibiting advertising of prescription drug prices); *Bates v. State Bar,* 433 U.S. 350 (1972) (court-imposed restraint on advertising by lawyers). *Cf. Friedman v. Rogers,* 440 U.S. 1 (1979) (upholding state ban on use of trade name in practice of optometry).

The Court may have abandoned substantive due process in reviewing economic regulation but not procedural due process. In *Gibson v. Berryhill,* 411 U.S. 564 (1973), the Court agreed that members of an optometry licensing board were so tainted with personal pecuniary interest that they could not constitutionally conduct hearings in the pending license revocation proceedings. *But cf. Withrow v. Larkin,* 421 U.S. 35 (1975).

The "state action" doctrine in antitrust law still protects most state-imposed anticompetitive practices. See, e.g., *Bates v. State Bar, supra,* where the advertising ban on lawyers, invalidated on first amendment grounds, was held not subject to attack under the Sherman Act because state-imposed. The applicability of antitrust laws to state and local action is covered in Chapter 7. But where the anticompetitive practice of a professional group is found not to be protected by state action, the Supreme Court has invalidated it. *Goldfarb v. Virginia State Bar,* 421 U.S. 773 (1975) (minimum fee schedule of bar associations violates Sherman Act); *National Society of Professional Engineers v. United States,* 435 U.S. 679 (1978) (society's prohibition of competitive bidding by members violates Sherman Act).

There is a growing interest in applying some form of public scrutiny to professions which self-regulate even though it may be recognized that some professional activities are unique and not suitable to uncritical antitrust application. One proposal to resolve the conflict would distinguish the organizational activities (such as setting fees and soliciting clients) from the technical quality of professional training and services. The former would be subjected to antitrust review; the latter is generally appropriate for self-regulation. *See* Kissam, *Antitrust Law, The First Amendment and Professional Self-Regulation of Technical Quality,* in REGULATING THE PROFESSIONS 155 (R. Blair & S. Rubin eds. 1980).

In the state courts, as Chapter 1 indicated, the judicial attitude toward substantive due process oversight of licensing and regulation has not been the same. In a leading article written a generation ago, one commentator noted that the state courts had continued to take a more restrictive view of state powers to regulate business, and generally had not followed the permissive lead of the United States Supreme Court. Paulsen, *The Persistence of Substantive Due Process in the States,* 34 MINN. L. REV. 91 (1950). Subsequent analyses of state court decisions conclude that while the picture is mixed, substantive due process continues to live on in state court decisions involving economic regulation. *See, e.g.,* Comment, *Substantive Due Process in the States Revisited,* 18 OHIO ST. L.J. 384 (1957); Hetherington, *State Economic Regulation and Substantive Due Process of Law,* 53 NW. U.L. REV. 13, 226 (1958); Howard, *State Courts and Constitutional Rights in the Day of the Burger Court,* 62 VA. L. REV. 873, 879-91 (1976); Note,

State Economic Substantive Due Process: A Proposed Approach, 88 Yale L.J. 1487 (1979).

The doctrine's role specifically with respect to occupational licensing, which is the principal focus of this section, is also mixed. It is by now relatively rare for a court to deny to a state altogether the police power right to license and regulate a particular occupation. See Note, *Due Process Limitations on Occupational Licensing,* 59 Va. L. Rev. 1097, 1099 n.14 (1973), and the cases following in this section. But even where the power to license and regulate is upheld, that result may follow a closer scrutiny than the Supreme Court would deem appropriate; and it is not infrequent that particular aspects of a licensing scheme are invalidated in the state courts.

It can be argued that it is appropriate for state courts to be more assertive than the federal judiciary in subjecting regulatory statutes to substantive due process. One author who has taken that position pointed out that much of this legislation results from the efforts of economic pressure groups who are in a position to focus their efforts on state legislatures to bring about the enactment of laws which further their own rather than the public interest.

> In such a situation the only remedy of those whose interests are adversely affected and who for one reason or another are unable to assert sufficient political pressure to protect their interests before the legislature, is in the courts and in the constitutional doctrines of substantive due process and equal protection. Judicial invalidation of such legislation may be technically anti-democratic, but it can hardly be called frustration of the popular will in any meaningful sense.

Hetherington, *supra,* at 249. He then notes that "[s]tate courts, since their precedents are not of national authority, may better adapt their decisions to local economic conditions and needs.... Local variations in economic conditions [thus] may justify varying local standards of economic due process." *Id.* at 250. Such a result would also permit courts to be more responsive to the almost unrelenting assault on the purpose and effect of occupational licensing that has been forthcoming in popular and scholarly publications in recent decades. One of those critics, Professor Walter Gellhorn, summed up the case against occupational licensing as follows:

> The line between the common weal and one's own is not always easily drawn. But occupational licensing has typically brought higher status for the producer of services at the price of higher costs to the consumer; it has reduced competition; it has narrowed opportunity for aspiring youth by increasing the costs of entry into a desired occupational career; it has artificially segmented skills so that needed services, like health care, are increasingly difficult to supply economically; it has fostered the cynical view that unethical practices will prevail unless those entrenched in a profession are assured of high incomes; and it has caused a proliferation of official administrative bodies, most of them staffed by persons drawn from and devoted to furthering the interests of the licensed occupations themselves.
>
>   Moreover — and this is a point largely unnoticed — members of ethnic minorities are systematically discouraged from becoming licensees by irrelevant requirements.

Gelhorn, *The Abuse of Occupational Licensing,* 44 U. Chi. L. Rev. 6, 16-18 (1976).

The two decisions that follow illustrate opposing state court views toward the licensing of watchmaking, an occupation for which licensing requirements might be thought to be unnecessary:

WATCHMAKING EXAMINING BOARD v. HUSAR

Supreme Court of Wisconsin
49 Wis. 2d 526, 182 N.W.2d 257 (1971)

This is an appeal from a judgment of the circuit court for Waukesha county which declared that ch. 125, Stats., regulating the watchmaking trade is unconstitutional. The Watchmaking Examining Board (hereafter the Board) commenced an action for declaratory judgment against Lyle C. Husar, alleging that the defendant held himself out as a watchmaker in Brookfield, Wisconsin, that he engaged in watch repairing for profit, and that he had never obtained a certificate of registration. The complaint asked for a declaration that the defendant was engaged in watchmaking and asked that the defendant be restrained from such further activity.

The defendant admitted all allegations of the complaint. He contended, however, that ch. 125, Stats., was unconstitutional in that it was an improper exercise of the state's police power.

Subsequent to the joining of issue, the parties stipulated that the only question to be tried was the constitutionality of ch. 125, Stats. It was agreed that, in the event the statute were found constitutional, further trial might be necessary in regard to certain provisions of the Administrative Code, particularly sec. Watch 1.08, which regulates the terms of apprenticeship.

Following a stipulation of facts, the cause was submitted to the trial court on briefs. The trial judge, in an extensive memorandum decision, concluded that ch. 125, Stats., was an unconstitutional exercise of the police power, which deprived the defendant of property without due process of law. He also held that the chapter unconstitutionally delegated legislative power to the administrative board. Judgment was thereupon entered dismissing the complaint of the Board. The Board has appealed from the judgment.

. . . .

HEFFERNAN, JUSTICE.

It is well established in this state that the police power may be properly exercised to limit certain substantial rights of citizens if, in the reasonable legislative judgment, the conduct of individuals must be controlled to protect the general welfare of the community. In the case of *State ex rel. Saveland Park Holding Corp. v. Wieland* (1955), 269 Wis. 262, 267, 69 N.W.2d 217, we quoted with approval the following statement of the New York Court of Appeals in *Wulfsohn v. Burden* (1925), 241 N.Y. 288, 298, 150 N.E. 120, 122:

> "The [police] power is not limited to regulations designed to promote public health, public morals, or public safety, or to the suppression of what is offensive, disorderly, or unsanitary, but extends to so dealing with conditions which exist as to bring out of them the greatest welfare of the people by promoting public convenience or general prosperity."

In a series of opinions since *Saveland,* we have explained the scope of the state's police power and the nature of the public interest that may invoke its exercise.

In *Chicago & North Western Ry. Co. v. La Follette* (1969), 43 Wis.2d 631, 169 N.W.2d 441, we reviewed some of the criteria which are to be used in determining whether the exercise of police power is unconstitutional. Therein, we pointed out that a statute is presumed to be constitutional and that a heavy burden is placed upon one challenging the constitutionality of a police-power statute. The court's function in such a challenge is not to weigh evidence in the traditional sense, but only to determine whether there is any reasonable basis for the legislative enactment. Nor will this court strike down legislation on the basis of its belief that the statute is good or bad or wise or unwise. If there is any reasonable basis for the exercise of police power by the legislature, the court must uphold the right of the legislature to act.

Chapter 125, Stats., regulates the rights of citizens to engage in a legitimate phase of private enterprise. Statutory enactments and administrative rules have been established to implement these regulations.

Section 125.04, Stats., provides that applicants shall be examined for certification by the Board. Applicants are to be "of good moral character, at least 20 years of age and possess such training and experience as the board shall by rule determine."

Section 125.05, Stats., provides that the examination:

> ... shall be confined to such knowledge, practical ability and skill as is essential in the proper repairing of watches, and shall include an examination of theoretical knowledge of watch construction and repair, and also a practical demonstration of the applicant's skill in manipulation of watchmaker's tools.

Section 125.07, Stats., provides for the registration of apprentice watchmakers.

Pursuant to the statutes, the Board has adopted certain rules. One of them is Watch 1.10 Examination (1), which provides that the examinee will be furnished a 17-jewel watch in need of repair, and he will then be obliged to fit a balance staff, true the hairspring, adjust the escapement, and make all needed repairs. Certain other skills are also required to be demonstrated. In addition, he is required to submit to an examination consisting of 50 questions pertaining to the theory of construction and repair of the modern watch.

Watch 1.08 Applicant's affidavit provides that an applicant for certification file certain affidavits, including evidence of the completion of an apprenticeship of four years or its equivalent in school training and practical experience.

These enactments are presumptively constitutional, and the burden of showing that they are unreasonable and bear no relationship to the public interest rests upon the defendant in this case. If there is any reasonable basis for the exercise of the legislative power, we are obliged to uphold the enactment.

The statutes provide that the applicant must be of good moral character, be twenty years of age, and possess the training and experience required to perform watchmaking skills in the manner prescribed by the Board. A certificate showing the attainment of these standards is required to be placed in the watchmaker's place of business.

From the face of the statute, it is obvious that the legislature sought to protect the public from fraud and incompetence in the field of watchmaking and watch repair. The legislature could reasonably have reached that conclusion and decided that the statute provided a method of protecting the public welfare. The legislature may well have believed that, because of the complexity of watch repair and watchmaking, the average citizen would be at the mercy of the watchmaker when he takes his timepiece in for repair. It would not be difficult for a watchmaker, either by design or by negligent omission, to replace parts which were not in need of repair, to use defective or substandard parts in his repair work, to create latent defects in the watch mechanism, or even to charge for repairs that were, in fact, never made. It is impossible for the average customer to determine whether he has been dealt with fairly and whether the watchmaker has conformed with minimum standards.

The legislature might well have concluded that, in view of these facts, the public could be protected only by the examination of watchmakers and the establishment of standards calculated to insure that workmanlike standards were lived up to. It could well have concluded that it was in the interest of the public to take steps to insure that only men of professional training, of high skills and competence, and of suitable moral character enter and remain in the trade. The legislature could reasonably have assumed that the ordinary contractual obligations which the customer and the watchmaker enter into were insufficient to assure protection of the general welfare. In *State ex rel. Hickey v. Levitan* (1926), 190 Wis. 646, 656, 210 N.W. 111, 114, we said, "The prevention of fraud is a subject in which the public at large is vitally interested." The protection of the consumer from abuses that might occur as a result of incompetent or unethical practices by watchmakers falls within the scope of the police power which the legislature could employ to regulate the watchmaker trade for the general welfare.

In oral argument, it was pointed out that there was no showing that there were widespread abuses that required the enactment of an all-pervasive system of state regulation. This, of course, goes to the burden of proof, which is not upon the state but upon the party seeking to upset the constitutionality of the statute. The defendant has failed to assume that burden.

In oral argument, it was also pointed out that [there] were other areas of free enterprise which were obviously of much more concern to the general welfare than watchmaking. The licensing of automobile repairmen was cited as an area in which state regulation, in regard to competence and ethical practices, would serve a far greater need than the licensing of watchmakers. This court, however, has frequently taken the position that the police power need not be exercised to eliminate all abuses, and that the legislature may selectively exercise its power. The fact that the legislature has failed to enact regulations in an area where they are arguably required does not vitiate the exercise of such power in another field where it reasonably considers regulation necessary. Inasmuch as the record is devoid of a showing that no public interest is served by the watchmaker's code and the legislature could reasonably have concluded that the public interest was served, we declare ch. 125, Stats., a constitutional enactment....

[The court then held that the statute did not unconstitutionally delegate legislative power to the Board. The delgation holding is discussed in Chapter 9, *supra*. — Eds.]

STATE EX REL. WHETSEL v. WOOD

Supreme Court of Oklahoma
207 Okla. 193, 248 P.2d 612 (1952)

HALLEY, VICE CHIEF JUSTICE.

This action involves the constitutionality of the Watchmaking Act of 1945, being Secs. 771-782, inclusive, Title 59, O.S.1951.

The State of Oklahoma, ex rel. the County Attorney of Pittsburg County, seeks a permanent injunction restraining Thomas S. Wood, Jr., from practising watchmaking in Oklahoma without first having obtained a license or certificate of registration as a watchmaker from the Oklahoma Board of Examiners in Watchmaking....

It was alleged that the defendant never had been licensed by the Board to practise watchmaking in this State, nor had he applied for or obtained a certificate of registration as an apprentice, but that he had publicly represented himself as being a qualified watchmaker and had practised watchmaking for compensation in Pittsburg County, and would continue to do so unless restrained, all in violation of the above law and to the irreparable damage and injury of the public, and especially of persons who patronize him, and to the damage and injury of persons lawfully engaged in watchmaking, rendering them insecure in their property and thus constituting a public nuisance; that the conduct of the defendant would endanger the health and safety of others, and that the plaintiff was without adequate remedy at law.

Defendant demurred to the petition generally, and also upon the ground that ... the Watchmaking Act is void in that it deprives defendant of inherent rights, privileges and immunities guaranteed by the State and Federal Constitutions in numerous particulars....

The court sustained the demurrer upon the ground that the Act sought to be enforced by this action is unconstitutional and void. The plaintiff declined to plead further and judgment was entered for the defendant.

. . . .

Plaintiff alleges that the first question to be determined is whether the State has the right to regulate watchmaking under what is termed the "police power" of the sovereign state. The defendant contends that the principal question involved is whether or not the manner of regulation provided by the Act invades the constitutional rights of the defendant. The term "police power" was aptly defined by this court in *Ex parte Tindall,* 102 Okl. 192, 229 P. 125, 126, as follows:

> The police power is an attribute of sovereignty, inherent in every sovereign state, and not deprived from any written Constitution nor vested by grant of any superior power.
>
> The term "police power" comprehends the power to make and enforce all wholesome and reasonable laws and regulations necessary to the maintenance, upbuilding, and advancement of the public weal and protection of the public interests.

The Watchmaking Act provides that in the future, an applicant must have served an apprenticeship of four years or its equivalent, as determined by the Board, before he is eligible for a license. This apprenticeship must be served under a licensed watchmaker and with his consent. This provision has the effect of placing in the hands of those holding a license the power to limit the number of those allowed to engage in watchmaking in Oklahoma, and clearly tends toward creating a monopoly.

Sec. 2 of the Act provides that no one shall engage in watchmaking for profit or compensation without first obtaining a license in the manner therein provided. In *State ex rel. Short v. Riedell,* 109 Okl. 35, 233 P. 684, 691, 42 A.L.R. 765, this court held the Accountancy Act of 1917 unconstitutional because of a similar provision as to accountants. In the body of that opinion it was said:

> The effect of the act is that in a growing, expanding, and lucrative field of usefulness of accountants, power is given a board in which accountants have control, to restrict their number, and tends toward a monopoly. It deprives those desiring an audit the right of contract in matters purely a private con-

cern, and deprives accountants not certified of the enjoyment of the gains of their own industry guaranteed to them by the Bill of Rights, in that it denies to them the right to follow the occupation for which they have qualified themselves by the expenditure of time and toil. . . .

The holding in the *Riedell* case, supra, has been approved by this court in several later cases, including *Cornell v. McAlister,* 121 Okl. 285, 249 P. 959. A review of our decisions upholding laws regulating certain classes of business shows that they are based generally upon a finding that the business or calling is affected with a public interest. . . . While watchmaking is an important calling, it is not such a business as affects the public health, safety and welfare.

The Watchmaking Act clearly prohibits one who may be fully qualified by years of training and experience from following his chosen craft and forces him to seek some other work or trade, thus depriving him of the fruits of his own industry, as guaranteed by Art. II, Sec. 2 of the Oklahoma Constitution. The provisions of the Act are unreasonable, arbitrary, and discriminatory, and are not designed to promote the general welfare or contribute to the public morals, health, or safety. The Act vests in the Board powers to make rules and regulations which may deny some citizens their inherent right to earn their livelihood in a private field of work, thus depriving them of a valuable property right without due process of law.

We have been cited to no case involving the regulation of watchmakers; but we have read with considerable interest the case of *State v. Ballance,* 229 N.C. 764, 51 S.E.2d 731, 7 A.L.R.2d 407, where the Supreme Court of North Carolina had under consideration a statute regulating the occupation of photography. That court . . . held that the Act was unconstitutional. We quote from that opinion [229 N.C. 764, 51 S.E.2d 735]:

> It is undoubtedly true that the photographer must possess skill. But so must the actor, the baker, the bookbinder, the bookkeeper, the carpenter, the cook, the editor, the farmer, the goldsmith, the horseshoer, the horticulturist, the jeweler, the machinist, the mechanic, the musician, the painter, the paper-hanger, the plasterer, the printer, the reporter, the silversmith, the stonecutter, the storekeeper, the tailor, the watchmaker, the wheelwright, the woodcarver, and every other person successfully engaged in a definitely specialized occupation, be it called a trade, a business, an art, or a profession. Yet, who would maintain that the legislature would promote the general welfare by requiring a mental and moral examination preliminary to permitting individuals to engage in these vocations merely because they involve knowledge and skill?

. . . .

This [ALR — Eds.] note shows that the supreme courts of Arizona, Florida, Georgia, Hawaii, North Dakota, Tennessee, and Virginia have passed on this question as to photographers. There is no more excuse for requiring a watchmaker to pass a test as to his technical qualifications than for requiring a photographer to pass such a test.

The judgment of the trial court is affirmed.

ARNOLD, C. J., and CORN, DAVISON, JOHNSON and O'NEAL, JJ., concur.

GIBSON and BINGAMAN, JJ., dissent.

Comments: 1. Despite the general trend toward upholding licensing statutes, courts occasionally invalidate one, particularly when the anticompetitive purpose is clear. In *Schroeder v. Binks,* 113 N.E.2d 169 (Ill. 1953), the court, although conceding the general power of the state to regulate plumbers, struck down a statute providing for the licensing of plumbers and requiring any aspiring plumber to first serve an apprenticeship under a master plumber. The court held that the statute gave too much control over access to the profession to master plumbers, and took judicial notice that the skills necessary to carry on the plumbing trade could as easily be learned in an educational institution. For discussion see Struve, *The Less-Restrictive-Alternative Principle and Economic Due Process.* 80 HARV. L. REV. 1463, 1470-73 (1967). Illinois subsequently amended its statute to provide that any approved plumbing course could be substituted for an apprenticeship. *Id.* at 1473. Later, in *People v. Johnson,* 369 N.E.2d 898 (Ill. 1977), the court held that the educational alternative available at that time was "illusory" and, until further refined, did not save the act.

In *Ohio Motor Vehicle Dealer's & Salesmen's Licensing Board v. Memphis Auto Sales,* 142 N.E.2d 268 (Ohio App. 1957), the court invalidated under the fourteenth amendment and the state constitution a statute limiting dealers' licenses to those dealers enfranchised by the manufacturer. *Compare Plantation Datsun, Inc. v. Calvin,* 275 So. 2d 26 (Fla. App. 1973), holding constitutional a licensing statute authorizing the state agency to deny a license to a motor vehicle dealer in "any community or territory" where existing dealers in the same make "are providing adequate representation." Three existing Datsun dealers in the same county protested a new dealership; the court gave short shrift to the constitutional objections.

A court which is hostile to and wishes to invalidate a licensing law may also hold that the licensing standards contained in the law are an unconstitutional delegation of power. For a discussion of delegation problems see Chapter 9. A decision invalidating licensing standards will at least force the legislature to constrain the discretion of the licensing board by adopting more specific licensing criteria.

In *State ex rel. Grand Bazaar Liquors, Inc. v. City of Milwaukee,* 313 N.W.2d 805 (Wis. 1982), the court held invalid as an arbitrary exercise of the police power and a denial of equal protection a city liquor license ordinance which required that applicants for a Class A license (for sale of packaged liquor off-the-premises) receive at least fifty percent of their income from liquor sales, thus effectively prohibiting grocery stores from selling liquor. The court said that the ordinance had no rational relationship to its purported objectives of limiting the number of liquor licenses and encouraging adherence to the liquor laws.

2. On the other hand, courts continue to uphold regulatory laws and licensing statutes applicable to occupations which are of doubtful harm to the public health and safety. *See, e.g., Illinois Polygraph Society v. Pellicano,* 414 N.E.2d 458 (Ill. 1980) (detection of deception licensing statute upheld even though it mandated use of polygraph rather than other deception detection devices); *Johnson v. Elkin,* 263 N.W.2d 123 (N.D. 1978) (certificate of public convenience and necessity to engage in house moving business); *Homes Unlimited, Inc. v. City of Seattle,* 561 P.2d 1089 (Wash. App. 1977) (ordinance regulating rental information agencies upheld except for fee provision; trial court had found effect of ordinance was to put agencies out of business); *cf. Rees v. Department of Real Estate,* 142 Cal. Rptr. 789 (Cal. App. 1977) (similar business of furnishing rental information to prospective tenants held subject to real estate licensure law; statute as construed not so overbroad as to violate due process or equal protection); *but see Anderson v. Department of Real Estate,* 155 Cal. Rptr. 307 (Cal. App. 1979) (court accepted conclusions of *Rees* but held extension of real estate licensure act to "advance fee rental agents" violated first amendment protection of commercial speech); *C & H Enterprises, Inc. v. Commissioner of Motor Vehicles,* 355 A.2d 247 (Conn. 1974) (license to engage in business of operating auto wrecker which was dependent, in turn, on license as auto repairer); *Union Mutual Life Insurance Co. v. Emerson,* 345 A.2d 504 (Me. 1975) (licensing of elevator mechanics upheld against equal protection challenge); *Williams v. State,* 514 S.W.2d 772 (Tex. Civ. App. 1974) (licensing of water well drillers upheld against unconstitutional delegation charge).

Some states require licenses for guide dog trainers (California), tattoo artists (Hawaii), foresters (Oklahoma), taxidermists (Wisconsin), and hunting guides (Wyoming). *See* Council of State Governments, Occupations and Professions Licensed by the States, Puerto Rico and The Virgin Islands 7-8 (1968), for a more complete listing of the range of occupations subject to licensing.

3. Even where courts uphold the state's right to license and regulate a business or occupation, they may be willing to invalidate a particular provision in the regulatory scheme that they deem unduly restrictive or unfair. In recent years, more decisions have taken this approach than have invalidated the right to license at all. Many of these cases have involved licensing in the beauty care field:

Grassman v. Minnesota Board of Barber Examiners, 304 N.W.2d 909 (Minn. 1981). Licensed barbers were prohibited from employing more than two apprentices and were subjected to closing hour requirements and trade area regulations; cosmetologists were not similarly regulated. The court held that it violated equal protection to apply different regulations to two essentially similar trades. *But cf. Laufenberg v. Cosmetology Examining Board,* 274 N.W.2d 618 (Wis. 1979), where the court upheld different requirements for barbers and cosmetologists, in part because the record was insufficient for it to consider the constitutional challenges.

Thorne v. Roush, 261 S.E.2d 72 (W. Va. 1979). The court invalidated on state substantive due process and equal protection grounds a provision in the barber licensing act which required a twelve-month apprenticeship. The petitioner had completed her schooling (financed by the federal Comprehensive Employment & Training Act) and passed the competency exam but was unable to secure employment as an apprentice "junior barber." The court, describing it as a restraint of trade, noted that the provision required no showing that the apprenticeship contributed to professional competence and that it appeared to do no more than provide a labor pool to be exploited by previously licensed practitioners.

Christiaan's, Inc. v. Chobanian, 373 A.2d 160 (R.I. 1977). The court struck down the statute which prohibited hairdressers and cosmeticians from performing for males the same services they performed for females. It noted that, whether analyzed in equal protection or due process terms, every court except one had invalidated similar restrictions.

Baffoni v. State, 373 A.2d 184 (R.I. 1977). The court struck down a requirement that electrolysists must complete a course of study under the supervision of a licensed Rhode Island electrologist, commenting that it could "see no relation between the knowledge necessary to practice electrolysis and the location at which the knowledge is obtained." *Id.* at 189.

4. Because the statutes and ordinances that we are dealing with in this section are forms of economic regulation, courts invariably invoke the rational relation standard when reviewing constitutional challenges. *See Husar, supra.* While state courts are more questioning than are federal courts, it is still a tough standard to meet; and not surprisingly courts frequently uphold practices whose anticompetitive effect, and sometimes purpose, seem apparent. Not surprisingly, also, many of these decisions appear in the health care fields. See, e.g., *Addiego v. State,* 394 A.2d 179 (N.J. Super. 1978), upholding a requirement that certain procedures which the complaining dentists considered were mechanical and did not require skill be performed only by a licensed dentist rather than by a dental auxiliary; *J.G. Cryan v. State,* 583 P.2d 1122 (Okla. Crim. App. 1978), upholding a requirement that a dental laboratory technician have a work authorization from a licensed dentist before performing any work. Both of these cases involve one form of the "monopolization" effect in occupational licensing.

Another form of monopolization exists when the regulatory scheme creates a hierarchy of persons within a particular profession and requires anyone below the highest level to practice only through a person who is the "first-class citizen." For example, in the dental field, in addition to dentists there are dental hygienists, dental assistants, and dental technicians. However, only the licensed dentists may deal directly with the public. Regardless of the competence of dental hygienists or dental technicians to perform certain services, they are not permitted to deal directly with the public and must offer their services through the dentist. Such requirements deny the public a choice between different types of services and deprive the public of the benefits of competition that would occur from the increased number of persons offering particular services. Moreover, it gives the "first-class" professional the right to control the price at which the other persons' services are sold.

Rose, *Occupational Licensing: A Framework for Analysis,* 1979 ARIZ. ST. L.J. 189, 197. See also *People ex rel. Illinois State Dental Society v. Sutker,* 395 N.E.2d 14 (Ill. App. 1979) (Illinois dental licensing act held to apply to dental technician whose entire business was repair and duplication of dentures for out-of-state customers by mail order).

In *Maceluch v. Wysong,* 680 F.2d 1062 (5th Cir. 1982), a Texas statute was upheld which requires graduates of osteopathic medical schools to identify themselves by "D.O." (rather than "M.D.") even though there is no substantial difference in educational content or clinical skills between accredited medical schools except that students at osteopathic schools are required to take courses in manipulative therapy which students at medical schools do not take. The court expressed sympathy for the osteopaths' plight but concluded:

> This court does not sit *de novo* as a legislative body, nor will it do so under the cloak of equal protection. A federal court decree is clean, swift, and difficult to overturn. Its powers attract those who have lost in the rough and tumble of legislative politics, but its power is undemocratic and antimajoritarian. Accordingly, the rationale for the exercise of judicial power requires, at the least, that the "constitutional" interest impinged by the legislature be one traceable to the Constitution. The Court has no veto. That belongs to the governor. And saying it is the Constitution that vetoes does not make it so.

Id. at 1069-70. See also *McCoy v. Commonwealth Board of Medical Education & Licensure,* 391 A.2d 723 (Pa. 1978), upholding a statute mandating doctors to carry medical malpractice insurance although nurses, chiropractors and dentists were not required to carry it.

5. Courts may limit the reach of a licensing statute by implying a self-help exception. In *City Council v. Naturile,* 345 A.2d 363 (N.J. Super. 1975), the court held that a property owner building a home for himself could not be denied city permits because he was not a licensed electrician or plumber. To do so would infringe his property rights. The city's interest in protecting the public could be accommodated through its right to inspect and approve the work done. Cf. *City & County of San Francisco v. Pace,* 132 Cal. Rptr. 151 (Cal. App. 1976), upholding a provision prohibiting a nonresident owner of two small residential buildings from doing electrical work on his property without a license although resident homeowners were excepted from the requirement.

Courts may also affect the reach of a licensing law by how narrowly or broadly they interpret the statutory definition of the licensed occupation. Compare *Florida Real Estate Commission v. McGregor,* 336 So. 2d 1156 (Fla. 1976), holding the state real estate license law unconstitutional as applied to a group of part-time employees of a corporate real estate company who were selling repossessed properties, with *Whitaker v. Arizona Real Estate Board,* 548 P.2d 841 (Ariz. App. 1976), holding appellant's rental information service fell within the statutory definition of real estate broker. Additional cases dealing with the rental service business are discussed in Comment 2, *supra.*

When a licensing statute is first enacted, the question arises as to whether or not it should be applied to those who have been engaged in the occupation for some time. Typically, the statute exempts existing practitioners from having to meet the requirements applicable to new applicants. This exemption is known as a "grandfather" clause, and its constitutionality is considered in the following case.

INDEPENDENT ELECTRICIANS & ELECTRICAL CONTRACTORS' ASS'N v. NEW JERSEY BOARD OF EXAMINERS OF ELECTRICAL CONTRACTORS

Supreme Court of New Jersey
54 N.J. 466, 256 A.2d 33 (1969)

The opinion of the court was delivered by
HALL, J.

....

Initially a license could have been obtained in either of two ways. The first, which still exists, is by passing an examination given by the Board "to establish the competence and qualification of the applicant to perform and supervise the various phases of electrical contracting work," N.J.S.A. 45:5A-9(b), which examination "shall cover such matters as the provisions of nationally recognized electrical installation safety standards and the theoretical and practical application of the same encountered in electrical work," N.J.S.A. 45:5A-12. To be admitted to the examination, an applicant "shall have been employed or engaged in the business of electrical construction and installation or have equivalent practical experience for a period of not less than 5 years preceding the time of such application, or shall otherwise establish to the satisfaction of the board that [he] has the necessary educational background and experience to qualify to take the examination for a license." N.J.S.A. 45:5A-9(b).

The second method of obtaining a license — by far the most utilized to date (although the opportunity to take advantage of it has now expired) — is under the "grandfather" clause, N.J.S.A. 45:5A-10. This section provides that "any person who has been employed or engaged in the business of electrical contracting in this State for a period of at least 6 years prior to the effective date of this act, and whose principal business for at least 2 years immediately preceding making of application . . . shall have been that of electrical contractor, shall be granted a license without examination; provided application should be made to the board on or before July 1, 1963 [later administratively extended for several months, we understand] and satisfactory proof is presented to said board of the applicant's fitness to engage in such business." The "satisfactory proof" included a description of the applicant's experience in the electrical contracting business and the listing of representative electrical contracts performed by him.

....

The third area we desired further exploration of related to the "grandfather" clause. N.J.S.A. 45:5A-10. This provision, it will be recalled, directed that, upon application prior to July 1, 1963, any person would be granted a license without examination if he had been employed or engaged in the electrical contracting business for at least six years prior to the effective date of the act and his "principal business" for the two years immediately preceding application had been that of electrical contractor. Section 10 further provided that the applicant must satisfy the Board of his fitness to engage in the electrical contracting business by describing his experience therein and by listing representative contracts he performed.

The additional proofs adduced, which to some extent refined our initial impressions of the actual operation of the clause (48 N.J. at 418-419, 226 A.2d 169), indicated that the Board received approximately 4,000 applications for licensure under it, of which 3,000 were granted, accounting for the vast majority of the present number of licensees. For the most part, a license would be granted where the Board, on the basis of its members' knowledge of the electrical contracting business, determined that the jobs listed on the face of the papers submitted were sufficiently representative and evidenced the requisite experience. All but one of the Board members were connected with some aspect of the industry. In some cases, additional written information was requested, outside investigation was conducted, or the applicant was called before the Board to furnish further details orally.

There was no proof that the Board issued "grandfather" licenses to unqualified persons. Plaintiffs' principal position is that the two year "principal business" requirement constituted an unconstitutional denial of equal protection because competent electrical contractors, who were regularly employed in other pursuits and operated their businesses only on a part-time basis, were refused licenses without examination, although licenses were granted without a test to those no more qualified who were full-time electrical contractors.

It is not contended, nor could it well be, that all "grandfather" clauses are discriminatory and invalid. Such provisions are a practical necessity when a profession or trade is initially licensed and are based on the legislatively permissible assumption that those who have been engaged in the occupation for some time previous are therefore sufficiently qualified to continue in it without having to pass an examination.... See Annot.: "Construction of 'grandfather clause' of statute or ordinance regulating or licensing business or occupation," 4 A.L.R.2d 667 (1949).

We think it is equally plain that the Legislature has, under fundamental principles, an especially wide discretion in determining what requirements it will impose in such a clause.... It can, for example, admit without examination all employed or engaged in the trade at the effective date of the law. Thus, our State Plumbing Licensing Law of 1968 ... directs, without more, the issuance of a master plumber's license without examination to any person employed or engaged in the plumbing business for five years.... Or it can be more restrictive. As the New York Court of Appeals said in *Wasmuth v. Allen*, ... 200 N.E.2d, at 760: "Nothing turns on the circumstance that the Legislature excused under the grandfather clause some and not others from passing the basic subject test."

We are therefore of the view that the "grandfather" clause under review does not, on its face, deny plaintiffs equal protection because it requires one's "principal business" for the two years preceding application to have been that of electrical contractor. The Legislature was entitled to conclude that such a provision would afford greater assurance to the public of competency in modern techniques for the safe laying out, supervising, and carrying through of diverse electrical work. While the clause could conceivably have been as effective from the standpoint of the public's safety if "grandfathering" had been authorized based solely on experience, regardless of the amount of a man's working time spent in the electrical contracting business, such is a matter of wisdom and policy exclusively within the legislative province....

Comments: 1. The equal protection issue inherent in a grandfather clause was addressed by the Supreme Court in *City of New Orleans v. Dukes,* 427 U.S. 297 (1976). The city enacted an ordinance prohibiting pushcart vendors in the Vieux Carre, or French Quarter, but exempting from the prohibition any vendors who had continually operated their business within the Quarter for a period of eight years prior to the enactment of the ordinance. The Court rejected an equal protection challenge, relying on the abstention approach which the Court now consistently takes toward economic regulations. Addressing the court of appeals' conclusion that the grandfather clause in this case failed even the rationality test, the Court said:

It is suggested that the "grandfather provision," allowing the continued operation of some vendors was a totally arbitrary and irrational method of achieving the city's purpose. But rather than proceeding by the immediate and absolute abolition of all pushcart food vendors, the city could rationally choose initially to eliminate vendors of more recent vintage. This gradual approach to the problem is not constitutionally impermissible. . . .

. . . The city could reasonably decide that newer businesses were less likely to have built up substantial reliance interests in continued operation in the Vieux Carre and that the two vendors which qualified under the "grandfather clause" — both of which had operated in the area for over 20 years rather than only eight — had themselves become part of the distinctive character and charm that distinguishes the Vieux Carre. We cannot say that these judgments so lack rationality that they constitute a constitutionally impermissible denial of equal protection.

Id. at 305.

2. The grandfather clause continues to provoke litigation. *See, e.g., Commercial Fisheries Entry Commission v. Apokedak,* 606 P.2d 1255 (Alaska 1980) (upholding against federal and state equal protection challenges a form of grandfather right which permitted fishermen currently operating to continue although the entry of others was severely limited; the court noted that grandfather clauses have generally withstood equal protection challenges); *Richardson v. Brunelle,* 398 A.2d 838 (N.H. 1979) (grandfather clause in the nurses' licensing statute is rational because it protects the rights of those previously licensed and ensures continuity of nursing services); *State ex rel. Grand Bazaar Liquors v. City of Milwaukee,* 313 N.W.2d 805 (Wis. 1982) (no rational basis for a grandfather provision for grocery store liquor licensees); *Packer v. Board of Behavioral Science Examiners,* 125 Cal. Rptr. 96 (Cal. App. 1975) (court refused to imply a grandfather clause in the marriage, family and child counseling licensing act); *Garono v. State Board of Landscape Architects,* 298 N.E.2d 565 (Ohio 1973) (grandfather clause requiring registration before a certain date held not to deny due process to plaintiff who applied after the date in view of adequate notice provisions).

3. Although grandfather clauses are typically included and almost always upheld, isn't there a fundamental contradiction in their inclusion? In enacting restricted entry regulatory schemes, states and cities are acting pursuant to their police power: the premise is that the licensing standards — educational requirements, experience, examination, good moral character, etc. — are necessary to protect the public health or safety. If the police power justification is valid, why isn't it equally necessary to apply the same standards to those already engaged? Could a legislature forego a grandfather clause, or is it constitutionally required? See *City of Louisville v. Coulter,* 197 S.W. 819 (Ky. 1917), upholding the absence of a grandfather clause in the plumbers licensing act:

The purpose of the act was to protect the public generally from incapacity, ignorance, want of skill, or fraud in those who, to engage in the actual work of plumbing with safety to the health of the people, must have skill and technical knowledge not possessed by the public generally, and in granting such legislation the Legislature was entirely within its authority; and if those who, because they were plumbers at the time the law was enacted or had been engaging in the business for several years, were incompetent to be safely trusted to do plumbing, should be exempted from the operations of the law, the purpose of the law would not be attained. If one who was engaged in plumbing at the time the law was enacted, or had been for several years theretofore, was competent to be entrusted with such work with safety to the public, he could easily undergo the examination and obtain the certificate; if incompetent to do the work of plumbing with safety to the public, he should be restrained until he becomes so.

Id. at 823.

A NOTE ON LICENSING BOARDS AND ADMINISTRATION

As we have seen, courts now generally uphold the right of the state to enact occupational licensing laws; and they review and occasionally invalidate a particular provision of the licensing statute or implementing rules which is indefensibly restrictive. Most licensing statutes also establish a board to administer the act.

> The dual role of most licensing boards is a matter of the utmost importance. On the one hand boards serve as gatekeepers to determine the qualifications and competence of applicants. On the other, they must see that standards are adhered to by practitioners and, when necessary, adjudicate disputes between the public and members of the regulated occupation [or, in some cases, between warring factions of the regulated occupations — Eds.]. Given the composition of the boards [typically, all or a substantial majority are licensed members of the occupation they preside over — Eds.], it is almost impossible for them to function effectively as both licensing and enforcement agencies.

B. SHIMBERG, B. ESSER & D. KRUGER, OCCUPATIONAL LICENSING: PRACTICES AND POLICIES 14-15 (1973). In addition to the dual, and often conflicting functions of the boards, their procedures were described in one report as a "due process nightmare," *Licensing Boards Under Fire,* NAT'L L.J. Feb. 18, 1980, at 1-2.

Recognition of these problems, combined with the frequent complaint that we are over-licensed in the first place, has led courts to review the administration of the licensing statutes more carefully and in some cases require higher standards of fairness. *See* Note, *Due Process Limitations on Occupational Licensing,* 59 VA. L. REV. 1097, 1118-29 (1973). This development has been assisted by the demise of the right-privilege distinction in United States Supreme Court jurisprudence. Until recently, occupational licenses have been treated as privileges, and for this reason subject to the state's plenary regulatory power. *See, e.g., Barsky v. Board of Regents,* 347 U.S. 442 (1954) (upholding suspension of physician's license when physician convicted of contempt of Congress). The right-privilege distinction appears to have been abandoned in cases like *Schware v. Board of Bar Examiners,* 353 U.S. 232, 239 n.5 (1957), striking down a refusal of a state to allow a law graduate to take a bar examination because he lacked good moral character. *See Due Process Limitations, supra,* at 1100-03.

With respect to the make-up of licensing boards, the Supreme Court has rejected due process and equal protection challenges based on membership from the regulated profession. In *Friedman v. Rogers,* 440 U.S. 1 (1979), an optometrist objected that four of the six members of the Texas Optometry Board were required by statute to be members of an association whose membership was limited to "professional" optometrists. Plaintiff, a "commercial" optometrist (the difference was in their methods of doing business; both groups had to meet the same licensing standards), maintained that this requirement resulted in subjecting him to regulation by a board dominated by a hostile faction. The Court held that the requirement was "related reasonably to the state's legitimate purpose of securing a Board that will administer the Act faithfully." *Id.* at 17. The Court acknowledged that plaintiff has "a constitutional right to a fair and impartial hearing in any disciplinary proceeding conducted against him by the Board" *(id.* at 18), but none was pending.

In two earlier cases, the Court did address the issue of fairness in disciplinary proceedings before a licensing board. In *Gibson v. Berryhill,* 411 U.S. 564 (1973) (discussed briefly *supra),* the Court found that members of the Alabama optometric board had such a possible personal pecuniary interest in the outcome of proceedings against the plaintiff-optometrists (apparently commercial optometrists, as in *Friedman v. Rogers)* that the board could not constitutionally conduct hearings on the revocation of their licenses. Personal interest was claimed because the disciplinary action was aimed at revoking the licenses of optometrists who were employed by business corporations, nearly half of all those in the state. The board members were all in private practice and would presumably pick up the business abandoned by plaintiffs if their licenses were revoked. The Court specifically did not pass on the question of the "extent to which an administrative agency may investigate and act upon the material facts of a case and then, consistent with due process, sit as an adjudicative body to determine those facts finally" *(id.* at 579 n.17) — an issue which, the Court noted, "has occasioned some divergence of views among federal courts." Subsequently, the Court addressed that issue in a case in which a doctor objected that the combination of investigative and adjudicatory functions in the Wisconsin Medical Examining Board violated his due process rights. *Withrow v. Larkin,* 421 U.S. 35 (1975). Although acknowledging that "special facts and circumstances" may dictate a contrary finding, the Court concluded that the investigative-adjudicative combination did not constitute a due process violation in this case.

The membership or method of selection of licensing boards has been successfully challenged in some state court actions, although not necessarily on equal protection grounds. See, e.g., *Rogers v. Medical Ass'n,* 259 S.E.2d 85 (Ga. 1979), holding that the requirement that appointees to the state Board of Medical Examiners must come from a list of nominees submitted by the Medical Association was an unconstitutional delegation of the appointing power to a private organization; but cf. *Humane Society of the United States v. New Jersey State Fish & Game Council,* 362 A.2d 20 (N.J. 1976), upholding against various constitutional challenges the requirement that nine of eleven members of the Fish & Game Council be recommended by designated private associations. *See also Serian v. State,* 297 S.E.2d 889 (W. Va. 1982) (optometrists may be appointed to state optometry licensing board).

American Motor Sales Corp. v. New Motor Vehicle Board, 138 Cal. Rptr. 594 (Cal. App. 1977), held violative of due process the Board's power to adjudicate disputes between car dealers and manufacturers in the face of the statutory requirement that four of nine members be dealers and lack of any similar requirement for manufacturers. The court relied heavily on *Gibson v. Berryhill, supra,* and distinguished cases holding that a licensing agency may constitutionally be composed of members of the occupation licensed:

> The Board erroneously equates the issue before us with that involved in cases which hold that a licensing or regulatory agency may constitutionally be composed in whole or in part of members of the business or profession regulated.... We have no quarrel with such holdings. Indeed who can better judge the qualifications to practice of a doctor of medicine (as one example), or his adherence to ethical standards of the medical profession, than other doctors of medicine? Whatever incidental economic benefit doctors may gain by disciplining other doctors is not of constitutional proportion; their training, technical knowledge, and experience give them the necessary expertise to make such judgments, while prima facie these are lacking in lay persons.

Id. at 598-99.

Bayside Timber Co. v. Board of Supervisors, 97 Cal. Rptr. 431 (Cal. App. 1971), held unconstitutional a state forest practice act under which forest practice rules were set by boards of timber owners. The court noted that: "It is an age-old principle of our law that no man should judge or otherwise officially preside over disputed matters in which he has a pecuniary interest." *Id.* at 439. The court also noted that the invalidity was compounded in this case because no standards were provided for the adoption of forest practice rules. Challenges have also been made to the fairness of the examinations utilized in licensing, but generally without success. *See, e.g., Thompson v. Schmidt,* 601 F.2d 305 (7th Cir. 1979); *Ponzio v. Anderson,* 499 F. Supp. 407 (N.D. Ill. 1980).

Comments: Just as criticisms of occupational licensing have run the gamut from inadequate enforcement to due process nightmares to unjustified proliferation, so also have proposals for reforming the system. Consider the following possible reforms. To what aspect of the criticism is each directed; is it likely to alleviate the concerns about licensing?

a. Eliminate some of the confusion, inconsistency and inefficiency caused by the presence of separate bureaucracies by centralizing administration of all licensing in one agency or board. The licensing statutes would be made uniform with respect to structure and procedures — with appropriate allowance for any special requirements of a particular occupation. *See, A Model Professional and Occupational Licensing Act,* 5 HARV. J. ON LEGIS. 67 (1967); SHIMBERG, ESSER & KRUGER, *supra,* at 226-27. Centralization would also facilitate codification of procedures and the development of a body of written decisions to provide precedents in disciplinary proceedings. Would it make sense to vest all of the adjudicatory authority in a single board?

b. In the enforcement (disciplinary) component of licensing, separate the investigative and adjudicative functions. This might be done by placing the adjudicative role in a single agency (as suggested above), although given the number of occupations licensed, all of them with disciplinary proceedings, the caseload could be staggering. Another way would be to assign disciplinary cases to hearing officers appointed by the state attorney general, perhaps followed by administrative appeal to a professional appeal board. *See* SHIMBERG, ESSER & KRUGER, *supra,* at 228-29; Rose, *supra,* at 207. One disadvantage of this approach might be the absence of technical knowledge if the hearing officers and board were predominantly lawyers. That could be overcome in various ways, however.

c. Reduce educational requirements and reliance on written exams, which are major entry barriers set up in almost all licensing acts. See S. Dorsey, The Occupational Licensing Queue (Center for Study of American Business, Work Paper No. 34, 1978), a study showing that written exams work against entry into licensed occupations by the less educated, the less formally trained, and minorities. Dorsey shows that in a nonprofessional trade, at least, there is no particular correlation between written scores and ability to pass a practical examination. He suggests, at the least, improving the quality of the written exam; preferably, requiring only a practical examination. *Id.* at 26. Is the current movement to require continuing education in the professions and some occupations consistent or inconsistent with Dorsey's findings?

d. Require public members on all licensing boards in order to provide adequate representation of the "public interest." California has moved the farthest in this direction. Most of its licensing boards have some public members, including the State Bar Board of Governors; and a significant number now have a majority of public members. H. SCHUTZ, L. MUSOLF & L. SHEPARD, REGULATING OCCUPATIONS IN CALIFORNIA: THE ROLE OF PUBLIC MEMBERS ON STATE BOARDS 5 (1980). To date, the experience with public members in California has been inconclusive. See also SHIMBERG, ESSER & KRUGER, *supra,* at 230-31, suggesting, as an alternative or addition to public members, a state agency representative who is more likely to be "technically competent" and not as "readily bypassed."

e. An increasing number of states require both sunrise and sunset review of licensing. Under "sunrise" review, the legislature attempts to restrain itself by institutionalizing procedures to be followed before it enacts any new licensing scheme. In Illinois, for example, the Regulatory Reform Act of 1979 requires a select committee to review proposals for new regulation and report to the legislature, including implementing legislation if it decides to recommend legislation. The statutory criteria for evaluating whether regulation of an occupation is necessary for protection of the public health, safety and welfare are:

(a) Whether the unregulated practice of a profession or occupation may significantly harm or endanger the public health, safety and welfare and whether the potential for harm is easily recognizable and not remote or dependent upon tenuous argument;

(b) Whether the practice of a profession or occupation requires specialized skill or training and whether the public clearly needs and will benefit by assurances of initial and continuing professional or occupational ability;

(c) Whether the regulation would or does have the effect of directly or indirectly increasing the costs of any goods and services and, if so, whether such increase is or would be more harmful to the public than the harm which might result from the absence of regulation;

(d) Whether the regulatory process would or does significantly reduce competition in the field and, if so, whether such reduction is or would be more harmful to the public than the harm which might result from the absence of regulation; and

(e) Whether the citizens of the State are or may be effectively protected by other means.

Ill. Rev. Stat. ch. 127, § 1953.

Under "sunset" review (now adopted in some thirty-four states), the regulatory acts are automatically repealed unless the legislature, usually following review by a special committee or independent study group, affirmatively acts to continue or modify the affected licensing statute. In Illinois, for example, the Regulatory Agency Sunset Act scheduled thirty-five licensing and regulatory acts for repeal between 1981 and 1989 under the sunset procedures. Ill. Rev. Stat. ch. 127, § 1901 et seq. Sunset and sunrise legislation is still relatively new, and it is not yet clear what impact it will have.

f. Increase federal supervision or control over state occupational licensing activities, either through an agency such as the Federal Trade Commission (which has expressed great interest from time to time) or through antitrust enforcement. *See* Rubin, *The Legal Web of Professional Regulation,* in REGULATING THE PROFESSIONS *supra,* at 39-43; SHIMBERG, ESSER & KRUGER, *supra,* at 211, 240-49. See also the antitrust discussion at the beginning of this section.

g. Replace licensing with a less restrictive system such as registration or certification. In registration, all practitioners of the trade must register with a state agency which has supervisory authority over them, but registrants are not required to meet any preconditions of education, experience, or ability. In certification, the applicants must meet minimum standards and they are then entitled to practice as, for example, a certified public accountant. Noncertified practitioners are equally free to offer their services, and very likely at a lower price, but without the special designation. *See* Rubin, *supra,* at 112-14; Gellhorn, *The Abuse of Occupational Licensing, supra,* at 26-27. Another less restrictive alternative would be enactment of a statute, without licensing, which prohibited designated unprofessional practices and provided civil penalties for violation. In some cases the public can be protected by regulating the business establishment — a restaurant or grocery store — without licensing the workers. *See* Rose, *supra,* at 191; SHIMBERG, ESSER & KRUGER, *supra,* at 222.

Reforms within the existing structure of licensing are largely dependent on the will of state legislatures, which have been slow to respond. Does that suggest that the courts should play a more vigorous role in policing regulatory licensing, whether the inquiry be equal protection, delegation, antitrust, or substantive or procedural due process?

B. IN MAJOR POLICY DECISIONS

1. REAPPORTIONMENT AND VOTING RIGHTS

No area of the law in recent history has brought the courts into a more direct supervisory role over states and local governments than that of voting rights. At least since the Supreme Court's reapportionment decisions in the early 1960s, there has been an explosion of litigation challenging not only the validity of representative districts but also the voting patterns established by states and local governments for a wide array of other activities in which they engage. The developments in this area are by no means settled or complete. The materials that follow will, however, illustrate how the courts have been drawn into the voting rights issues and how they have responded.

We begin with the principles laid down in the reapportionment[1] cases and then trace the courts' attempts to apply them to the local level of government where the tremendous variety in form and function make those principles not easily applicable. We then examine the question of who is entitled to vote on uniquely local issues such as annexation and conclude with a note on the quality of representation — an issue that underlies most of the voting rights developments.

a. The One Person-One Vote Principle in Legislative Apportionment

When the Supreme Court decided *Baker v. Carr* in 1962 (369 U.S. 186), it authorized federal court intervention in matters of legislative apportionment for the first time. *Baker v. Carr* was the culmination of a long and tortuous history [2] of attempts in federal and state courts to obtain judicial review of malapportioned congressional and state legislative districts. The Court itself had slammed the door on such attempts sixteen years earlier when Justice Frankfurter, in refusing review of unequal congressional districts in Illinois, had admonished that "[c]ourts ought not to enter this political thicket." *Colegrove v. Green,* 328 U.S. 549, 556 (1946). But in *Baker v. Carr* the Court put aside Justice Frankfurter's warning and marched full speed ahead into the political thicket, holding that a fourteenth amendment equal protection challenge to state legislative districting was clearly within the subject matter jurisdiction of the federal courts, and that it was not a nonjusticiable political question.

Two years after the Supreme Court opened the door to federal court supervision, it announced the standards by which state legislative districting would be tested.[3] In *Reynolds v. Sims,* 377 U.S. 533 (1964), the Court held:

> We hold that, as a basic constitutional standard, the Equal Protection Clause requires that the seats in both houses of a bicameral state legislature must be apportioned on a population basis. Simply stated, an individual's right to vote for state legislators is unconstitutionally impaired when its weight is in a substantial fashion diluted when compared with votes of citizens living in other parts of the State.

---

[1] "*Apportionment* is the distribution of legislative seats among previously defined territorial or other units entitled to representation while *districting* establishes the precise geographical boundaries of a territorial constituency." Silva, The Population Base for Apportionment of the New York Legislature, 32 Fordham L. Rev. 1, 3 (1963). The term "reapportionment" has, since Baker v. Carr, become widely used to embrace either or both parts of the process, and will be so used here.

[2] That history is reviewed in, inter alia, Baker v. Carr, 369 U.S. 186, 232-37 (majority opinion), and in parts of Justice Frankfurter's dissent, 369 U.S. at 266 et seq.; R. Dixon, Democratic Representation 99-118 (1968); Bickerstaff, Reapportionment by State Legislatures: A Guide for the 1980's, 34 Sw. L.J. 607, 609-12 n.32 (1980).

[3] Actually, the Court decided two important cases in the interim which pointed in the direction of what followed: Gray v. Sanders, 372 U.S. 368 (1963), invalidating Georgia's county unit system of counting votes in a primary election for statewide offices; Wesberry v. Sanders, 376 U.S. 1 (1964), holding that article I, § 2 of the Constitution, which requires that representatives in Congress be chosen "by the People of the several States," means that "as nearly as is practicable one man's vote in a congressional election is to be worth as much as another's." 376 U.S. at 7-8.

Id. at 568. This was the one man- (subsequently, person) one vote standard. In explaining how it arrived there, the Court said:

> The right to vote freely for the candidate of one's choice is of the essence of a democratic society, and any restrictions on that right strike at the heart of representative government. And the right of suffrage can be denied by a debasement or dilution of the weight of a citizen's vote just as effectively as by wholly prohibiting the free exercise of the franchise.

Id. at 555.

> [T]he fundamental principle of representative government in this country is one of equal representation for equal numbers of people, without regard to race, sex, economic status, or place of residence within a State.

Id. at 560-61.

> Legislators represent people, not trees or acres. Legislators are elected by voters, not farms or cities or economic interests. As long as ours is a representative form of government, and our legislatures are those instruments of government elected directly by and directly representative of the people, the right to elect legislators in a free and unimpaired fashion is a bedrock of our political system. It could hardly be gainsaid that a constitutional claim had been asserted by an allegation that certain otherwise qualified voters had been entirely prohibited from voting for members of their state legislature. And, if a State should provide that the votes of citizens in one part of the State should be given two times, or five times, or 10 times the weight of votes of citizens in another part of the State, it could hardly be contended that the right to vote of those residing in the disfavored areas had not been effectively diluted.

Id. at 562.

The Court acknowledged that "[m]athematical exactness or precision is hardly a workable constitutional requirement" *(id.* at 577); and it avowed an intent to permit consideration of some additional factors, especially the integrity of political subdivisions. In every case, however, the additional considerations were qualified by . . . so long as the resulting apportionment does not significantly dilute the equal population principle.

Reynolds v. Sims was one of six decisions handed down on that historic day in 1964, invalidating the legislative apportionment schemes of Alabama, New York, Maryland, Virginia, Delaware and Colorado. What followed was one of the great constitutional dramas of the century. To meet the one person-one vote edict, lawsuits were filed in many states which usually resulted in overturning the existing apportionment; state constitutions were amended and, in some cases, conventions held to correct constitutional schemes which did not measure up; in some states, a tug of war developed between federal and state courts, or between the state legislature and the courts, federal and state. In all, it was estimated that virtually every state in the country had to redistrict one or both of its houses, and in some cases the map was actually drawn by a court. The process of redistricting was repeated following the 1970 Census. Council of State Governments, Reapportionment in the Seventies 3-4 (1973).

The extent to which the Court would permit deviation from strict population equality was in doubt for some time, in part because the Court did not clearly distinguish between congressional and state legislative districting. From a series of cases decided through the 1970s, however, a pattern emerged although the edges of the pattern were not precise. The Court would apply a strict standard of mathematical equality to federal congressional districts, permitting "only the limited population variances which are unavoidable despite a good-faith effort to achieve absolute equality, or for which justification is shown." *Kirkpatrick v. Preisler,* 394 U.S. 526, 531 (1969)(5.97% maximum percentage deviation [4] held not satisfactorily justified); *White v. Weiser,* 412 U.S. 783 (1973)(4.13% maximum deviation invalidated).

With respect to state legislative districts, however, the Court would tolerate larger population discrepancies so long as, in the words of *Reynolds v. Sims,* they "are based on legitimate considerations incident to the effectuation of a rational state policy," 377 U.S. at 579.

As the Court addressed particular districting plans, it developed what appeared to be a three-tiered approach, spelled out in *Gaffney v. Cummings,* 412 U.S. 735 (1973). Some population variations are too great to be justified by any state interest and are, at the least, presumptively invalid — e.g., the *Reynolds v. Sims* cases, *Swann v. Adams,* 385 U.S. 440 (1967)(maximum deviation of 33.55% for house districts and 25.65% for senate districts); *Whitcomb v. Chavis,* 403 U.S. 124 (1971)(maximum deviation of 24.78% for house districts, 28.20% for senate districts). In other cases, the Court noted, specifically citing *Mahan v. Howell* (410 U.S. 315 (1973)), "population deviations among districts may be sufficiently large to require justification but nonetheless be justifiable and legally sustainable." *Gaffney,* 412 U.S. at 745. In *Mahan,* the Court upheld Virginia's house districts, which had a maximum deviation of 16.4%, on the basis of Virginia's rational state policy which sought to maintain the integrity of political subdivision boundaries. That objective was important because the Virginia legislature had the power to enact local legislation for those political subdivisions. The third tier, in *Gaffney* itself, is those "minor deviations from mathematical equality among state legislative districts [that] are insufficient to make out a prima facie case of invidious discrimination under the Fourteenth Amendment so as to require justification by the State." 412 U.S. at 745. In *Gaffney* the maximum deviations were 7.83% for house districts, 1.8% for senate districts; and in *White v. Regester,* 412 U.S. 766 (1973), decided the same day on the same grounds, the house districts had a maximum deviation of 9.9% and an average deviation of 1.82%.

It should be noted that the Supreme Court has been emphatic in decreeing that a court-ordered plan, as opposed to a legislatively enacted one, "must ordinarily achieve the goal of population equality with little more than *de minimis* variation." *Chapman v. Meier,* 420 U.S. 1, 27 (1975). Accord *Connor v. Finch,* 431 U.S. 407 (1977). While the population variances in those two cases (20.14% in *Chapman,* 16.5% and 19.3% in *Connor)* were of a magnitude to shift the burden of justification to the state even in a legislative apportionment, the Court was clear that the range of departure is considerably narrower in a court-ordered plan.

The intrusion of the federal courts into state legislative apportionment was also responsible (with a strong assist from resentment over the Supreme Court's school prayer and desegregation decisions) for inspiring a campaign in the 1960s

---

[4] The maximum deviation is the sum of the deviation from the ideal district of the most and the least populous districts. While this index is the most common one used to express population inequality in reapportionment cases, the Court has also on occasion in state legislative cases paid attention to the average deviation from the ideal district. *See, e.g.,* White v. Regester, 412 U.S. 755, 764 (1973).

which, if it had been successful, would not only have greatly curtailed the role of the courts in matters of legislative apportionment, but would also have constituted one of the most significant realignments in the distribution of judicial and legislative power in the history of this country. The campaign was to amend the United States Constitution either through congressional action or through use of the procedure in Article V by which two thirds of the states may apply to Congress to call a convention to amend the Constitution. One of the early proposed so-called "states' rights" amendments would have prohibited federal judicial power over the apportionment of state legislatures; another would have revised the procedure for amending the Constitution; and a third would have created a Court of the Union, composed of the state supreme court chief justices, with power to review and reverse decisions of the United States Supreme Court "relating to the rights reserved to the states or to the people."

The states' rights resolutions eventually faded, and later activity, including the congressional action led by Senator Everett Dirksen of Illinois, concentrated on an amendment which in its most common version would have permitted one house of a state legislature to be apportioned on factors other than population alone if approved by referendum. All of these efforts failed. For a history of the amendment campaigns, see R. DIXON, DEMOCRATIC REPRESENTATION 385-435 (1968). The text of the states' rights resolutions is set out in *Amending the Constitution to Strengthen the States in the Federal System,* 36 STATE GOV'T 10 (1963).

Whether viewed legally or politically, the one person-one vote mandate had significant impact. It did thrust courts into the "political thicket," and in some cases a federal court actually drew, or assumed responsibility for adopting, the boundaries of state legislative districts. The political impact has proved to be more elusive. It is fairly certain that one person-one vote reduced the influence of rural interests in state legislatures and increased urban and suburban representation (the latter being perhaps the major beneficiary of reapportionment). The result probably has been a somewhat greater urban, as well as suburban, character to the legislative work product, but it is not something easily measured. For discussion of attempts to measure, see, e.g., R. DIXON, DEMOCRATIC REPRESENTATION 577-81 (1968); Symposium, *Democratic Representation and Apportionment: Quantitative Methods, Measures and Criteria,* 219 ANNALS, N.Y. ACADEMY OF SCIENCE, Part V, 246-356 (1973); Hanson & Crew, *The Policy Impact of Reapportionment,* 8 LAW & SOC'Y REV. 69 (1973); Y. H. CHO & G. FREDERICKSON, MEASURING THE EFFECTS OF REAPPORTIONMENT IN THE AMERICAN STATES (1976), summarized in Cho & Frederickson, *The Effects of Reapportionment: Subtle, Selective, Limited,* 63 NAT'L CIV. REV. 357 (1974).

b. Application of "One Person-One Vote" to Local Governments

While the courts were struggling with the many issues that arose out of one person-one vote, the question was posed as to whether its dictates would apply to local units of government. The answer came in the following case:

AVERY v. MIDLAND COUNTY

United States Supreme Court
390 U.S. 474 (1968)

MR. JUSTICE WHITE delivered the opinion of the Court.

Petitioner, a taxpayer and voter in Midland County, Texas, sought a determination by this Court that the Texas Supreme Court erred in concluding that selection of the Midland County Commissioners Court from single-member districts of substantially unequal population did not necessarily violate the Fourteenth Amendment. We granted review, 388 U.S. 905 (1967), because application of the one man, one vote principle of *Reynolds v. Sims,* 377 U.S. 533 (1964), to units of local government is of broad public importance. We hold that petitioner, as a resident of Midland County, has a right to a vote for the Commissioners Court of substantially equal weight to the vote of every other resident.

Midland County has a population of about 70,000. The Commissioners Court is composed of five members. One, the County Judge, is elected at large from the entire county, and in practice casts a vote only to break a tie. The other four are Commissioners chosen from districts. The population of those districts, according to the 1963 estimates that were relied upon when this case was tried, was respectively 67,906; 852; 414; and 828. This vast imbalance resulted from placing in a single district virtually the entire city of Midland, Midland County's only urban center, in which 95% of the county's population resides.

The Commissioners Court is assigned by the Texas Constitution and by various statutory enactments with a variety of functions. According to the commentary to Vernon's Texas Statutes, the court:

> is the general governing body of the county. It establishes a courthouse and jail, appoints numerous minor officials such as the county health officer, fills vacancies in the county offices, lets contracts in the name of the county, builds roads and bridges, administers the county's public welfare services, performs numerous duties in regard to elections, sets the county tax rate, issues bonds, adopts the county budget, and serves as a board of equalization for tax assessments.

The court is also authorized, among other responsibilities, to build and run a hospital, Tex. Rev. Civ. Stat. Ann., Art. 4492 (1966), an airport, *id.,* Art. 2351 (1964), and libraries, *id.,* Art. 1677 (1962). It fixes boundaries of school districts within the county, *id.,* Art. 2766 (1965), may establish a regional public housing authority, *id.,* Art. 1269k, § 23a (1963), and determines the districts for election of its own members, Tex. Const., Art. V, § 18.

Petitioner sued the Commissioners Court and its members in the Midland County District Court, alleging that the disparity in district population violated the Fourteenth Amendment and that he had standing as a resident, taxpayer, and voter in the district with the largest population. Three of the four commissioners testified at the trial, all telling the court (as indeed the population statistics for the established districts demonstrated) that population was not a major factor in the districting process. The trial court ruled for petitioner. It made no explicit reference to the Fourteenth Amendment, but said the apportionment plan in effect was not "for the convenience of the people," the apportionment standard established by Art. V, § 18, of the Texas Constitution. The court ordered the defendant commissioners to adopt a new plan in which each precinct would have "substantially the same number of people."

[The Texas Court of Civil Appeals reversed the District Court, but the Texas Supreme Court reversed the Court of Civil Appeals. — Eds.]

In *Reynolds v. Sims, supra* the Equal Protection Clause was applied to the apportionment of state legislatures. Every qualified resident, *Reynolds* determined, has the right to a ballot for election of state legislators of equal weight to the vote of every other resident, and that right is infringed when legislators are elected from districts of substantially unequal population. The question now before us is whether the Fourteenth Amendment likewise forbids the election of local government officials from districts of disparate population. As has almost every court which has addressed itself to this question, we hold that it does.

The Equal Protection Clause reaches the exercise of state power however manifested, whether exercised directly or through subdivisions of the State.

> Thus the prohibitions of the Fourteenth Amendment extend to all action of the State denying equal protection of the laws; whatever the agency of the State taking the action.... *Cooper v. Aaron,* 358 U.S. 1, 17 (1958).

Although the forms and functions of local government and the relationships among the various units are matters of state concern, it is now beyond question that a State's political subdivisions must comply with the Fourteenth Amendment. The actions of local government *are* the actions of the State. A city, town, or county may no more deny the equal protection of the laws than it may abridge freedom of speech, establish an official religion, arrest without probable cause, or deny due process of law.

When the State apportions its legislature, it must have due regard for the Equal Protection Clause. Similarly, when the State delegates lawmaking power to local government and provides for the election of local officials from districts specified by statute, ordinance, or local charter, it must insure that those qualified to vote have the right to an equally effective voice in the election process. If voters residing in oversize districts are denied their constitutional right to participate in the election of state legislators, precisely the same kind of deprivation occurs when the members of a city council, school board, or county governing board are elected from districts of substantially unequal population. If the five senators representing a city in the state legislature may not be elected from districts ranging in size from 50,000 to 500,000, neither is it permissible to elect the members of the city council from those same districts. In either case, the votes of some residents have greater weight than those of others; in both cases the equal protection of the laws has been denied.

That the state legislature may itself be properly apportioned does not exempt subdivisions from the Fourteenth Amendment. While state legislatures exercise extensive power over their constituents and over the various units of local government, the States universally leave much policy and decisionmaking to their governmental subdivisions. Legislators enact many laws but do not attempt to reach those countless matters of local concern necessarily left wholly or partly to those who govern at the local level. What is more, in providing for the governments of their cities, counties, towns, and districts, the States characteristically provide for representative government — for decisionmaking at the local level by representatives elected by the people. And, not infrequently, the delegation of power to local units is contained in constitutional provisions for local home rule which are immune from legislative interference. In a word, institutions of local government have always been a major aspect of our system, and their responsible and responsive operation is today of increasing importance to the quality of life of more and more of our citizens. We therefore see little difference, in terms of the application of the Equal Protection Clause and of the principles of *Reynolds v. Sims,* between the exercise of state power through legislatures and its exercise by elected officials in the cities, towns, and counties.

We are urged to permit unequal districts for the Midland County Commissioners Court on the ground that the court's functions are not sufficiently "legislative." The parties have devoted much effort to urging that alternative labels — "administrative" versus "legislative" — be applied to the Commissioners

Court. As the brief description of the court's functions above amply demonstrates, this unit of local government cannot easily be classified in the neat categories favored by civics texts. The Texas commissioners courts are assigned some tasks which would normally be thought of as "legislative," others typically assigned to "executive" or "administrative" departments, and still others which are "judicial." In this regard Midland County's Commissioners Court is representative of most of the general governing bodies of American cities, counties, towns, and villages.[7] One knowledgeable commentator has written of "the states' varied, pragmatic approach in establishing governments." R. Wood, in Politics and Government in the United States 891-892 (A. Westin ed. 1965). That approach has produced a staggering number of governmental units — the preliminary calculation by the Bureau of the Census for 1967 is that there are 81,304 "units of government" in the United States — and an even more staggering diversity. Nonetheless, while special-purpose organizations abound and in many States the allocation of functions among units results in instances of overlap and vacuum, virtually every American lives within what he and his neighbors regard as a unit of local government with general responsibility and power for local affairs. In many cases citizens reside within and are subject to two such governments, a city and a county.

The Midland County Commissioners Court is such a unit. While the Texas Supreme Court found that the Commissioners Court's legislative functions are "negligible," 406 S.W.2d, at 426, the court does have power to make a large number of decisions having a broad range of impacts on all the citizens of the county. It sets a tax rate, equalizes assessments, and issues bonds. It then prepares and adopts a budget for allocating the county's funds, and is given by statute a wide range of discretion in choosing the subjects on which to spend. In adopting the budget the court makes both long-term judgments about the way Midland County should develop — whether industry should be solicited, roads improved, recreation facilities built, and land set aside for schools — and immediate choices among competing needs.

The Texas Supreme Court concluded that the work actually done by the Commissioners Court "disproportionately concern[s] the rural areas," 406 S.W.2d, at 428. Were the Commissioners Court a special-purpose unit of government assigned the performance of functions affecting definable groups of constituents more than other constituents, we would have to confront the question whether such a body may be apportioned in ways which give greater influence to the citizens most affected by the organization's functions. That question, however, is not presented by this case, for while Midland County authorities may concentrate their attention on rural roads, the relevant fact is that the powers of the Commissioners Court include the authority to make a substantial number of decisions that affect all citizens, whether they reside inside or outside the city limits of Midland. The Commissioners maintain buildings, administer welfare services, and determine school districts both inside and outside the city. The taxes imposed by the court fall equally on all property in the county. Indeed, it

---

[7] Midland County is apparently untypical in choosing the members of its local governing body from districts. "On the basis of available figures, coupled with rough estimates from samplings made of the situations in various States, it appears that only about 25 percent of . . . local government governing boards are elected, in whole or in part, from districts or, while at large, under schemes including district residence requirements." Brief for the United States as Amicus Curiae 22, n. 31, filed in Sailors v. Board of Education, 387 U.S. 105 (1967), and the other 1966 Term local reapportionment cases.

may not be mere coincidence that a body apportioned with three of its four voting members chosen by residents of the rural area surrounding the city devotes most of its attention to the problems of that area, while paying for its expenditures with a tax imposed equally on city residents and those who live outside the city. And we might point out that a decision not to exercise a function within the court's power — a decision, for example, not to build an airport or a library, or not to participate in the federal food stamp program — is just as much a decision affecting all citizens of the county as an affirmative decision.

The Equal Protection Clause does not, of course, require that the State never distinguish between citizens, but only that the distinctions that are made not be arbitrary or invidious. The conclusion of *Reynolds v. Sims* was that bases other than population were not acceptable grounds for distinguishing among citizens when determining the size of districts used to elect members of state legislatures. We hold today only that the Constitution permits no substantial variation from equal population in drawing districts for units of local government having general governmental powers over the entire geographic area served by the body.

This Court is aware of the immense pressures facing units of local government, and of the greatly varying problems with which they must deal. The Constitution does not require that a uniform straitjacket bind citizens in devising mechanisms of local government suitable for local needs and efficient in solving local problems. Last Term, for example, the Court upheld a procedure for choosing a school board that placed the selection with school boards of component districts even though the component boards had equal votes and served unequal populations. *Sailors v. Board of Education,* 387 U.S. 105 (1967). The Court rested on the administrative nature of the area school board's functions and the essentially appointive form of the scheme employed. In *Dusch v. Davis,* 387 U.S. 112 (1967), the Court permitted Virginia Beach to choose its legislative body by a scheme that included at-large voting for candidates, some of whom had to be residents of particular districts, even though the residence districts varied widely in population.

The *Sailors* and *Dusch* cases demonstrate that the Constitution and this Court are not roadblocks in the path of innovation, experiment, and development among units of local government. We will not bar what Professor Wood has called "the emergence of a new ideology and structure of public bodies, equipped with new capacities and motivations...." R. Wood, 1400 Governments, at 175 (1961). Our decision today is only that the Constitution imposes one ground rule for the development of arrangements of local government: a requirement that units with general governmental powers over an entire geographic area not be apportioned among single-member districts of substantially unequal population.

The judgment below is vacated and the case is remanded for disposition not inconsistent with this opinion.

It is so ordered.

[The Court's decision was 5-3 with Justice Marshall not participating. Of the three dissenters, Justices Harlan, Fortas and Stewart, only Justice Harlan would decline to apply equal protection and *Reynolds v. Sims* to local governments at all. Justice Harlan believed that the application of the one person-one vote rule to Midland County would discriminate against its rural residents. The county government performed more functions in the area of the county outside Midland City than it did within the city limits. Each rural resident had a greater interest in county government than each city dweller, yet the majority decision allowed no consideration of the greater "stake" of the rural residents.

[Justice Harlan also believed that the majority decision would inhibit the formation of metropolitan governments. Suburban residents would be reluctant to join metropolitan governments unless their interests were accommodated by a relaxation of the rule that required apportionment on the basis of population. — Eds.]

Comments: 1. In *Avery* the Supreme Court extended the fourteenth amendment principle of one person-one vote to local units "with general governmental powers over an entire geographic area." At the same time the Court acknowledged the "staggering" number and diversity of local governments in this country. It might have added that there is also a staggering number of elections at the local level with varying configurations. While the litigation involving state legislative reapportionment turned largely on satisfying the *Reynolds v. Sims* standard of equality of representation, in the local government arena the courts have had to struggle with the additional questions of which units and which elections are subject to one person-one vote. But, first, is an even more preliminary question.

One year before its decision in *Avery,* the Court had confronted one of the unique elements in local government: not all decisions nor all decision makers are subjected to the elective process. How does the fourteenth amendment handle that?

The Court faced this question in *Sailors v. Board of Education,* 387 U.S. 105 (1967). Suit was brought claiming that a county board of education was unconstitutionally constituted. The members of the county board were not elected by popular vote, but by delegates from local school boards, who were popularly elected. The Court found no constitutional violation:

> We find no constitutional reason why state or local officers of the nonlegislative character involved here may not be chosen by the governor, by the legislature, or by some other appointive means rather than by an election.

Id. at 108. Noting that the selection method in this case was "basically appointive rather than elective," the Court said: "We need not decide at the present time whether a State may constitute a local legislative body through the appointive rather than the elective process. We reserve that question for other cases." *Id.* at 109-10.

With the *Sailors* case compare *Hadley v. Junior College District,* 397 U.S. 50 (1970). The metropolitan Kansas City junior college district was formed by the consolidation of eight separate school districts following referendum approval. One of the districts, Kansas City, contained approximately sixty percent of the school-age population but under the statutory formula was entitled to only three of the six trustees. Residents of the Kansas City school district claimed that the apportionment violated their fourteenth amendment rights under *Avery.*

The Court first held that the powers of the district, while not as broad as those exercised by Midland County in *Avery,* included "important governmental functions" which were general enough and had "sufficient impact" to justify application of the *Avery* principle. Moreover, the Court said, constitutional protection of voting power should not turn on the purpose of election. "If one person's vote is given less weight through unequal apportionment, his right to equal voting participation is impaired just as much when he votes for a school board member as when he votes for a state legislator." 397 U.S. at 55. Finally, the Court rejected the argument that apportionment should turn on the distinction between elections for legislative officials and administrative officers. The distinction was not judicially manageable.

> We therefore hold today that as a general rule, whenever a state or local government decides to select persons by popular election to perform governmental functions, the Equal Protection Clause of the Fourteenth Amendment requires that each qualified voter must be given an equal opportunity to participate in that election.

Id. at 56. The Court reaffirmed that "there might be some case in which a State elects certain functionaries whose duties are so far removed from normal governmental activities and so disproprotionately affect different groups that a popular election in compliance with *Reynolds* . . . might not be required" (*id.* at 56), but this is not such a case.

2. Why was the school board in *Hadley* subject to one person-one vote while the school board in *Sailors* was not? Is there any basis for distinguishing them in terms of their functions or powers? If, as the Court suggests in *Hadley*, the determining factor is no longer the purpose of the election but rather the fact of election, why would not the election of judges from districts be subject to one person-one vote? Is it enough to say that judges do not perform governmental functions? *See Wells v. Edwards,* 409 U.S. 1095 (1973). Three dissenting Justices, White, Douglas and Marshall, maintained that judges "most certainly" perform governmental functions and probably should be subject to one person-one vote. For discussion, see R. DIXON, DEMOCRATIC REPRESENTATION 559-64 (1968).

3. Courts which have considered the issue have concluded that appointed officers are not subject to one person-one vote. *See, e.g., Burton v. Whittier Regional Vocational Technical School District,* 587 F.2d 66 (1st Cir. 1978). A Massachusetts law authorized the creation of regional school districts with a governing board that was either elected, appointed, or a combination of both. In this case, the plan called for the board to be appointed. The City of Haverhill, with forty-one percent of the population of the district, was entitled to only two representatives on a board of thirteen. The voters of Haverhill had approved the plan in a referendum. The court rejected an equal protection claim based on the fact that some regional districts had an elected board while this one was appointed. It also rejected a one person-one vote challenge to the apportionment of the board although acknowledging that the board had some legislative powers. The court felt that *Hadley* had cast doubt on the validity of the legislative-administrative distinction of *Sailors,* and that the key was the fact of appointment rather than election. *Accord, Rosenthal v. Board of Education,* 385 F. Supp. 223 (E.D.N.Y 1974), *aff'd,* 420 U.S. 985 (1975); *People ex rel. Younger v. County of El Dorado,* 487 P.2d 1193 (Cal. 1971).

4. Is the effect of the Court's decision in *Hadley*, as the dissent suggests, to discourage any metropolitan consolidation of local units of government, at least where one unit is dominant? Would the eight school districts in *Hadley* have combined if they knew that Kansas City would control the Board? Don't the Court's decisions encourage the use of appointive rather than elective boards in such situations?

In *Sailors* the Court did not attempt to answer the question of "when a State must provide for the election of local officials." Is it clear that Missouri could have provided for an appointive board in *Hadley*? What about the Midland County Commissioners Court in *Avery*? *See Citizens to Save Our Land v. McKee Creek Watershed Conservancy District,* 347 N.E.2d 41 (Ill. App. 1975) (holding that district a special purpose government whose trustees perform essentially nonlegislative functions and may therefore be appointed).

5. In *Hadley* it was a "built-in" bias in the apportionment formula, more than the population variance itself, that the Court found offended *Reynolds.* The formula made it virtually impossible to achieve equal representation. In *Abate v. Mundt,* 403 U.S. 182 (1971), the Court upheld a county board legislative apportionment despite a total deviation of 11.9% in part because it "does not contain a built-in bias tending to favor particular political interests or geographic areas." *Id.* at 187. The Court relied also on the long history in the New York county involved of the functional interrelationship between the county level and its constituent towns — which was responsible for the population inequality. The Court emphasized the special circumstances of the *Abate* apportionment but also noted that the characteristics of local governments permitted "slightly greater percentage deviations" than are tolerated for congressional or state legislative districts. *Id.* at 185.

In *Avery* the Court left open the question of whether one person-one vote would apply to a special purpose unit of government with functions "affecting definable groups of constituents more than other constituents" (390 U.S. at 484). That question was addressed in the following case:

SALYER LAND CO. v. TULARE LAKE BASIN WATER STORAGE DISTRICT

United States Supreme Court
410 U.S. 719 (1973)

Mr. Justice Rehnquist delivered the opinion of the Court.

This is another in the line of cases in which the Court has had occasion to consider the limits imposed by the Equal Protection Clause of the Fourteenth Amendment on legislation apportioning representation in state and local governing bodies and establishing qualifications for voters in the election of such representatives.... We are here presented with the issue expressly reserved in *Avery* ... :

> Were the [county's governing body] a special-purpose unit of government assigned the performance of functions affecting definable groups of constituents more than other constituents, we would have to confront the question whether such a body may be apportioned in ways which give greater influence to the citizens most affected by the organization's functions. 390 U. S., at 483-484.

The particular type of local government unit whose organization is challenged on constitutional grounds in this case is a water storage district, organized pursuant to the California Water Storage District Act, Calif. Water Code § 39000 *et seq.*...

[The Court then described the importance to California, as well as other western states, of obtaining and controlling an adequate water supply for agriculture and other uses. To respond to this need, state and federal resources were utilized to construct major dams; but for less costly projects, the California legislature authorized the creation of a number of local instrumentalities, including water storage districts. — Eds.]

Appellee district consists of 193,000 acres of intensively cultivated, highly fertile farm land located in the Tulare Lake Basin. Its population consists of 77 persons, including 18 children, most of whom are employees of one or another of the four corporations that farm 85% of the land in the district.

Such districts are authorized to plan projects and execute approved projects "for the acquisition, appropriation, diversion, storage, conservation, and distribution of water...." Calif. Water Code § 42200 *et seq.* Incidental to this general power, districts may "acquire, improve, and operate" any necessary works for the storage and distribution of water as well as any drainage or reclamation works connected therewith, and the generation and distribution of hydroelectric power may be provided for.[4] ... They may fix tolls and charges for the use of water and collect them from all persons receiving the benefit of the water or other services in proportion to the services rendered.... The costs of the projects are assessed against district land in accordance with the benefits accruing to each tract held in separate ownership.... And land that is not benefited may be withdrawn from the district on petition....

Governance of the districts is undertaken by a board of directors.... Each director is elected from one of the divisions within the district....

It is the voter qualification for such elections that appellants claim invidiously discriminates against them and persons similarly situated. Appellants are

---

[4] There is no evidence that the appellee district engages in the generation, sale, or distribution of hydroelectric power.

landowners, a landowner-lessee, and residents within the area included in the appellee's water storage district. They brought this action under 42 U. S. C. § 1983, seeking declaratory and injunctive relief in an effort to prevent appellee from giving effect to certain provisions of the California Water Code. They allege that §§ 41000 [5] and 41001 [6] unconstitutionally deny to them the equal protection of the laws guaranteed by the Fourteenth Amendment, in that only landowners are permitted to vote in water storage district general elections, and votes in those elections are apportioned according to the assessed valuation of the land. A three-judge court was convened pursuant to 28 U. S. C. § 2284, and the case was submitted on factual statements of the parties and briefs, without testimony or oral argument. A majority of the District Court held that both statutes comported with the dictates of the Equal Protection Clause, and appellants have appealed that judgment directly to this Court under 28 U. S. C. § 1253.

. . . .

We therefore turn now to the determination of whether the California statutory scheme establishing water storage districts violates the Equal Protection Clause of the Fourteenth Amendment.

I

It is first argued that § 41000, limiting the vote to district landowners, is unconstitutional since nonlandowning residents have as much interest in the operations of a district as landowners who may or may not be residents. Particularly, it is pointed out that the homes of residents may be damaged by floods within the district's boundaries, and that floods may, as with appellant Ellison, cause them to lose their jobs. Support for this position is said to come from the recent decisions of this Court striking down various state laws that limited voting to landowners, *Phoenix v. Kolodziejski,* 399 U. S. 204 (1970), *Cipriano v. City of Houma,* 395 U. S. 701 (1969), and *Kramer v. Union School District,* 395 U. S. 621 (1969).

In *Kramer,* the Court was confronted with a voter qualification statute for school district elections that limited the vote to otherwise qualified district residents who were either (1) the owners or lessees of taxable real property located within the district, (2) spouses of persons owning qualifying property, or (3) parents or guardians of children enrolled for a specified time during the preceding year in a local district school.[5] Without reaching the issue of whether or not a State may in some circumstances limit the exercise of the franchise to those primarily interested or primarily affected by a given governmental unit, it was held that the above classifications did not meet that state-articulated goal since they excluded many persons who had distinct and direct interests in school meeting decisions and included many persons who had, at best, remote and indirect interests. . . .

---

[5] Calif. Water Code § 41000 provides:
"Only the holders of title to land are entitled to vote at a general election."
[6] Calif. Water Code § 41001 provides:
"Each voter may vote in each precinct in which any of the land owned by him is situated and may cast one vote for each one hundred dollars ($100), or fraction thereof, worth of his land, exclusive of improvements, minerals, and mineral rights therein, in the precinct."
5 [Plaintiff was a bachelor living with his parents. Although he paid state and federal taxes, he had no vote. On the other hand, as the Court noted, an unemployed uninterested young man who paid no taxes but rented an apartment was entitled to vote. See 395 U.S. at 632 n.15. — Eds.]

Similarly, in *Cipriano v. City of Houma, supra,* decided the same day, provisions of Louisiana law which gave only property taxpayers the right to vote in elections called to approve the issuance of revenue bonds by a municipal utility were declared violative of the Equal Protection Clause since the operation of the utility systems affected virtually every resident of the city, not just the 40% of the registered voters who were also property taxpayers, and since the bonds were not in any way financed by property tax revenue.... And the rationale of *Cipriano* was expanded to include general obligation bonds of municipalities in *Phoenix v. Kolodziejski, supra.* It was there noted that not only did those persons excluded from voting have a great interest in approving or disapproving municipal improvements, but they also contributed both directly through local taxes and indirectly through increased rents and costs to the servicing of the bonds....

Cipriano and *Phoenix* involved application of the "one person, one vote" principle to residents of units of local governments exercising general governmental power, as that term was defined in *Avery v. Midland County....* *Kramer* and *Hadley v. Junior College District,* ... extended the "one person, one vote" principle to school districts exercising powers which,

> while not fully as broad as those of the Midland County Commissioners, certainly show that the trustees perform important governmental functions within the districts.... 397 U. S., at 53-54.

But the Court was also careful to state that:

> It is of course possible that there might be some case in which a State elects certain functionaries whose duties are so far removed from normal governmental activities and so disproportionately affect different groups that a popular election in compliance with *Reynolds, supra,* might not be required.... *Id.,* at 56.

We conclude that the appellee water storage district, by reason of its special limited purpose and of the disproportionate effect of its activities on landowners as a group, is the sort of exception to the rule laid down in *Reynolds* which the quoted language from *Hadley, supra,* and the decision in *Avery, supra,* contemplated.

The appellee district in this case, although vested with some typical governmental powers, has relatively limited authority. Its primary purpose, indeed the reason for its existence, is to provide for the acquisition, storage, and distribution of water for farming in the Tulare Lake Basin.[8] It provides no other general public services such as schools, housing, transportation, utilities, roads, or anything else of the type ordinarily financed by a municipal body.... There are no towns, shops, hospitals, or other facilities designed to improve the quality of life within the district boundaries, and it does not have a fire department, police, buses, or trains....

Not only does the district not exercise what might be thought of as "normal governmental" authority, but its actions disproportionately affect landowners. All of the costs of district projects are assessed against land by assessors in proportion to the benefits received. Likewise, charges for services rendered are

---

[8] Appellants strongly urge that districts have the power to, and do, engage in flood control activities. The interest of such activities to residents is said to be obvious since houses may be destroyed and, as in the case of appellant Ellison, jobs may disappear. But ... any flood control activities are incident to the exercise of the district's primary functions of water storage and distribution.

collectible from persons receiving their benefit in proportion to the services. When such persons are delinquent in payment, just as in the case of delinquency in payments of assessments, such charges become a lien on the land.... In short, there is no way that the economic burdens of district operations can fall on residents *qua* residents, and the operations of the districts primarily affect the land within their boundaries.

Under these circumstances, it is quite understandable that the statutory framework for election of directors of the appellee focuses on the land benefited, rather than on people as such. California has not opened the franchise to all residents, as Missouri had in *Hadley, supra,* nor to all residents with some exceptions, as New York had in *Kramer, supra.* The franchise is extended to landowners, whether they reside in the district or out of it, and indeed whether or not they are natural persons who would be entitled to vote in a more traditional political election. Appellants do not challenge the enfranchisement of nonresident landowners or of corporate landowners for purposes of election of the directors of appellee. Thus, to sustain their contention that all residents of the district must be accorded a vote would not result merely in the striking down of an exclusion from what was otherwise a delineated class, but would instead engraft onto the statutory scheme a wholly new class of voters in addition to those enfranchised by the statute.

We hold, therefore, that the popular election requirements enunciated by *Reynolds, supra,* and succeeding cases are inapplicable to elections such as the general election of appellee Water Storage District.

II

Even though appellants derive no benefit from the *Reynolds* and *Kramer* lines of cases, they are, of course, entitled to have their equal protection claim assessed to determine whether the State's decision to deny the franchise to residents of the district while granting it to landowners was "wholly irrelevant to achievement of the regulation's objectives," *Kotch v. River Port Pilot Comm'rs,* 330 U. S. 552, 556 (1947). No doubt residents within the district may be affected by its activities. But this argument proves too much. Since assessments imposed by the district become a cost of doing business for those who farm within it, and that cost must ultimately be passed along to the consumers of the produce, food shoppers in far away metropolitan areas are to some extent likewise "affected" by the activities of the district. Constitutional adjudication cannot rest on any such "house that Jack built" foundation, however. The California Legislature could quite reasonably have concluded that the number of landowners and owners of sufficient amounts of acreage whose consent was necessary to organize the district would not have subjected their land to the lien of its possibly very substantial assessments unless they had a dominant voice in its control. Since the subjection of the owners' lands to such liens was the basis by which the district was to obtain financing, the proposed district had as a practical matter to attract landowner support. Nor, since assessments against landowners were to be the sole means by which the expenses of the district were to be paid, could it be said to be unfair or inequitable to repose the franchise in landowners but not residents. Landowners as a class were to bear the entire burden of the district's costs, and the State could rationally conclude that they, to the exclusion of residents, should be charged with responsibility for its operation. We conclude, therefore, that nothing in the Equal Protection Clause precluded California from limiting the voting for directors of appellee district by totally excluding those who merely reside within the district.

III

Appellants assert that even if residents may be excluded from the vote, lessees who farm the land have interests that are indistinguishable from those of the landowners. Like landowners, they take an interest in increasing the available water for farming and, because the costs of district projects may be passed on to them either by express agreement or by increased rentals, they have an equal interest in the costs.

Lessees undoubtedly do have an interest in the activities of appellee district analogous to that of landowners in many respects. But in the type of special district we now have before us, the question for our determination is not whether or not we would have lumped them together had we been enacting the statute in question, but instead whether "if any state of facts reasonably may be conceived to justify" California's decision to deny the franchise to lessees while granting it to landowners. *McGowan v. Maryland,* 366 U. S. 420, 426 (1961).

. . . .

IV

The last claim by appellants is that § 41001, which weights the vote according to assessed valuation of the land, is unconstitutional. They point to the fact that several of the smaller landowners have only one vote per person whereas the J. G. Boswell Company has 37,825 votes, and they place reliance on the various decisions of this Court holding that wealth has no relation to resident-voter qualifications and that equality of voting power may not be evaded. . . .

Appellants' argument ignores the realities of water storage district operation. Since its formation in 1926, appellee district has put into operation four multi-million-dollar projects. The last project involved the construction of two laterals from the Basin to the California State Aqueduct at a capital cost of about $2,500,000. Three small landowners having land aggregating somewhat under four acres with an assessed valuation of under $100 were given one vote each in the special election held for the approval of the project. The J. G. Boswell Company, which owns 61,665.54 acres with an assessed valuation of $3,782,220 was entitled to cast 37,825 votes in the election. By the same token, however, the assessment commissioners determined that the benefits of the project would be uniform as to all of the acres affected, and assessed the project equally as to all acreage. Each acre has to bear $13.26 of cost and the three small landowners, therefore, must pay a total of $46, whereas the company must pay $817,685 for its part.[10] Thus, as the District Court found, "the benefits and burdens to each landowner . . . are in proportion to the assessed value of the land." . . . We cannot say that the California legislative decision to permit voting in the same proportion is not rationally based.

Accordingly, we affirm the judgment of the three-judge District Court and hold that the voter qualification statutes for California water storage district elections are rationally based, and therefore do not violate the Equal Protection Clause.

---

[10] . . . [S]mall landowners are protected from crippling assessments resulting from district projects by the dual vote which must be taken in order to approve a project. Not only must a majority of the votes be cast for approval, but also a majority of the voters must approve. In this case, about 189 landowners constitute a majority and 189 of the smallest landowners in the district have only 2.34% of the land.

Affirmed.

MR. JUSTICE DOUGLAS, with whom MR. JUSTICE BRENNAN and MR. JUSTICE MARSHALL concur, dissenting. [Omitted.]

Comments: 1. In *Associated Enterprises, Inc. v. Toltec Watershed Improvement District,* 410 U.S. 743 (1973), decided the same day, the Court similarly rejected an equal protection challenge to the referendum by which the watershed district was created. Voting was limited to landowners, weighted according to acreage.

2. The limits of the Court's *Avery-Hadley-Salyer* exception were tested in *Ball v. James,* 451 U.S. 355 (1981), a 5-4 decision with Justices White, Brennan, Marshall and Blackmun dissenting. In that case the challenge was to the system by which directors of the Salt River Project Agricultural Improvement and Power District are elected — the franchise being limited to otherwise qualified voters who own land within the District in proportion to the number of acres owned. The Court majority upheld the voting scheme, applying the two-pronged test of *Salyer* "whether the purpose of the district is sufficiently specialized and narrow and whether its activities bear on landowners so disproportionately as to distinguish the district from those public entities whose more general governmental functions demand application of the *Reynolds* principle." *Id.* at 362. Once it found that the district met those tests, the voting scheme need only bear a reasonable relation to its statutory objectives rather than satisfying the more stringent compelling state interest standard. *Id.* at 371 and 364-65 n.8.

The Court itself acknowledged significant differences between the Salt River District and the Tulare District involved in *Salyer.* In contrast to Tulare, Salt River covered half the population of the state, including large parts of Phoenix (Arizona); it was one of the largest suppliers of electric power in the state; about forty percent of the water it delivered went for urban or other nonagricultural purposes; some ninety-eight percent of the district's revenues came from sales of electricity, not water; and all outstanding bonds for capital improvements were being serviced with revenues from the sale of power. Nevertheless, the Court still found that "these distinctions do not amount to a constitutional difference." The district did not "exercise the sort of governmental powers that invoke the strict demands of *Reynolds.*" The Court also concluded that even the district's water functions, the primary reason for its creation, were relatively narrow and did not transform the essentially business enterprise character of the district. Finally, neither the existence nor the size of the district's electric power business affected the legality of the property-based voting scheme. In the Court's view, the relationship between the nonvoting residents purchasing electricity and the district was that of consumer and the business enterprise from whom they buy.

In his concurring opinion, Justice Powell admitted that "it may be difficult to decide when experimentation and political compromise have resulted in an impermissible delegation of those governmental powers that generally affect all of the people to a body with a selective electorate." But, he felt, "state legislatures, responsive to the interests of all the people, normally are better qualified to make this judgment than federal courts." *Id.* at 373.

The dissenters, in addition to concluding that the Salt River District did not satisfy the two tests of *Salyer* and was thus subject to strict scrutiny, also returned to the original suggestion in *Avery* that one person-one vote might not apply strictly to special purpose districts, and offered their own explanation of what was meant: "Thus, even assuming that the landowners are more directly affected, *Avery* suggests that there may be situations where total exclusion is unconstitutional, but where the exact one-person, one-vote rule does not apply. The Court's decision today ignores the possibility of some alternative plan and instead sanctions an unjustifiable total exclusion." *Id.* at 376-77 n.2.

For discussion of *Ball v. James* see De Young, *Governing Special Districts: The Conflict Between Voting Rights and Property Privileges,* 1982 ARIZ. ST. L.J. 419.

3. *Hill v. Stone,* 421 U.S. 289 (1975), combined elements of a restricted franchise and the requirement of concurrent majorities (see *Lockport v. Citizens for Community Action,* 430 U.S. 259 (1977), *infra).* The city of Ft. Worth conducted an election to authorize the issuance of bonds to finance transportation improvements and the construction of a city library. In accordance with Texas law, local bond elections were conducted under a dual box system. Those persons who had "rendered" property for taxation cast their votes in one box ("rendering" meant the listing of property — real, personal, or mixed, of any value, however small — with the tax assessor, whether or not taxes were paid on the property); all other registered voters voted in a separate box. To be approved, the bond issue must receive a majority vote in the renderers' box and a majority vote in both boxes combined.

As the Court noted: "The effect of the dual box procedure was that the non-renderers could help defeat a bond issue, but they could not help pass it." *Id.* at 293 n.3. The library bonds were approved by a majority of all the voters but failed to receive a majority in the renderers' box and therefore lost. The Court held the voting scheme violative of equal protection under the *Kramer, Cipriano* and *Phoenix* decisions (which are discussed in *Salyer, supra).* Ft. Worth's election did not qualify as a special interest election, and the state's attempted justification did not satisfy the compelling state interest test.

4. At this point, the student might pause to review the Court's decisions already noted. Can you follow the constitutional thread running through these voting rights cases? Consider for example, the following additional questions:

a. Why is the operation of a junior college system *(Hadley)* more of a governmental function than supplying water and power to almost half the population of Arizona *(Ball v. James)*?

b. If the water and electricity services provided by the Salt River District in *Ball v. James* had been provided instead by, say, a county, could the county limit the franchise in a bond authorization to property owners in proportion to the value of their property? Conversely, if the utility in *Cipriano* had been operated by a special district rather than by the municipality, would *Sawyer* and *Ball v. James* permit the bond referendum to be limited to property owners?

c. If a separate unit of government operates the mass transit system for a large metropolitan area, is the election of its governing board subject to one person-one vote? Any difference if, instead, it provides sewage disposal?

Note that in *Sailors* and *Hadley* the fourteenth amendment issue was presented in a form akin to that of the more "traditional" one person-one vote cases — equality of voting power in the selection of their governing authority. In *Salyer* and its circle of cases, the one person-one vote issue is posed in a different form — denial of the right to vote at all in a local government election and, to a lesser degree, dilution due to the weighting of votes.

5. Courts attempting to apply the *Salyer* exception have reached differing results. In *Johnson v. Lewiston Orchards Irrigation District,* 584 P.2d 1646 (Idaho 1978), a non-property owning resident of Lewiston challenged the Idaho statutes which limited to property owners the right to vote in an election for directors, or any other election involving the district, most of which was located within the city boundaries. The district furnished both domestic water (sixty-six percent of revenues) and irrigation water (thirty-four percent of revenues). The district also owned a park and swimming pool, which were operated by the city, and was authorized to, but did not, provide garbage disposal service. The court invalidated the voting restriction, concluding that the circumstances were more like those in *Phoenix v. Kolodziejski* (property ownership requirement for voting on general obligation bond issue) than in *Salyer.* This district, with its responsibility for domestic water supply, did not fall within the special interest exception of *Salyer,* the court concluded. The *Johnson* decision was one of two cited by the dissenting Justice in *Ball v. James* as having correctly interpreted and applied the *Salyer* test. The other was *Choudhry v. Free,* 552 P.2d 438 (Cal. 1976), in which the court invalidated the requirement that a director of the Imperial Irrigation District, the largest such district in the state, be a "freeholder." There were no property qualifications for voting either in the election to create the district or for the directors; the only restriction was that the directors themselves be freeholders. The court invoked strict scrutiny and distinguished *Salyer.* Would either of these cases be decided the same way after *Ball v. James*?

At least one court concluded that *Ball v. James* broadened the exception of *Salyer* so much that it reversed itself. In *In re Esler v. Walters,* 437 N.E.2d 1090 (N.Y. 1982), the New York court had previously held that the *Salyer* exception did not operate to save a statute requiring that voters in an election to create a water district be landowners. In this case the question was the validity of a landowner requirement to vote in an election to consolidate water districts. The court held that the voting limitation was valid because "it is now clear from the Supreme Court's decision in the *Ball* case that the question is not whether those entitled to vote are the only ones affected by the operations of this type of special public entity, but whether the effect on them is disproportionately greater than on those claiming an equal right to vote...." *Id.* at 1094.

c. Voting Rights in Local Elections

In most of the cases previously considered there was a continuing electoral relationship involving, broadly defined, the selection of government representatives — *e.g.,* the election of county commissioners *(Avery),* school board members *(Hadley, Kramer),* special district directors *(Salyer, Ball v. James).* That was not true in every case, however: *Cipriano, Phoenix v. Kolodziejski* and *Hill v. Stone* each involved a single bond issue referendum, albeit pursuant to statutes which were applicable to other similar elections. And in *Associated Enterprises v. Toltec* the challenged voting restriction occurred in the election creating the district — although the Supreme Court applied the same analysis as it had to the election of directors in *Salyer,* decided the same day. For this reason, all of the voting rights cases should be considered as a spectrum, however blurred it may be at times.

Nevertheless, the issues are not identical, nor are the results, when the right to vote is claimed in a peculiarly local government setting — such as annexation or incorporation, and certain other "one shot" elections that occur at the local level. We explore some of those cases now, and begin with a review of *Hunter v. City of Pittsburgh, supra,* Chapter 2. Recall that in *Hunter* the annexation (technically, consolidation) of Allegheny by Pittsburgh was approved over the negative vote of the residents of Allegheny, the Court rejecting two federal constitutional claims made by the plaintiff-citizens of Allegheny: impairment of obligation of contract between the city and the plaintiffs that they were to be taxed only for the purposes of that city; and denial of due process by subjecting the residents of Allegheny to the burden of additional taxation resulting from the consolidation. The plaintiffs did not fashion an equal protection challenge to the voting scheme, and the Court did not directly pass on its validity. The Court did note, however, the plaintiffs' argument that "[t]he manner in which the right of due process of law has been violated ... is that the method of voting on the consolidation prescribed in the act has permitted the voters of the larger city to overpower the voters of the smaller city, and compel the union without their consent and against their protest." 207 U.S. at 177.

In the following case the Court considered the validity of a dual or concurrent vote majority in a local government election:

TOWN OF LOCKPORT v. CITIZENS FOR COMMUNITY ACTION AT THE LOCAL LEVEL, INC.

United States Supreme Court
430 U.S. 259 (1977)

Mr. Justice Stewart delivered the opinion of the Court.

New York law provides that a new county charter will go into effect only if it is approved in a referendum election by separate majorities of the voters who live in the cities within the county, and of those who live outside the cities. A three-judge Federal District Court held that these requirements violate the Equal Protection Clause of the Fourteenth Amendment. We noted probable jurisdiction of this direct appeal from the District Court's judgment under 28 U. S. C. § 1253. 426 U. S. 918.

I

County government in New York has traditionally taken the form of a single-branch legislature, exercising general governmental powers. General governmental powers are also exercised by the county's constituent cities, villages, and towns. The allocation of powers among these subdivisions can be changed, and a new form of county government adopted, pursuant to referendum procedures specified in Art. IX of the New York Constitution and implemented by § 33 of the Municipal Home Rule Law. Under those procedures a county board of supervisors may submit a proposed charter to the voters for approval. If a majority of the voting city dwellers and a majority of the voting noncity dwellers both approve, the charter is adopted.

In November 1972, a proposed charter for the county of Niagara was put to referendum. The charter created the new offices of County Executive and County Comptroller, and continued the county's existing power to establish tax rates, equalize assessments, issue bonds, maintain roads, and administer health and public welfare services. No explicit provision for redistribution of governmental powers from the cities or towns to the county government was made. The city voters approved the charter by a vote of 18,220 to 14,914. The noncity voters disapproved the charter by a vote of 11,594 to 10,665. A majority of those voting in the entire county thus favored the charter.

The appellees, a group of Niagara County voters, filed suit pursuant to 42 U. S. C. § 1983 in the United States District Court for the Western District of New York, seeking a declaration that the New York constitutional and statutory provisions governing adoption of the charter form of county government are unconstitutional, and an order directing the appropriate New York officials to file the Niagara County charter as a duly enacted local law....

[The prior proceedings resulted in a district court holding that the concurrent majority requirement violated equal protection. — Eds.]

In the case before us the District Court, though recognizing that "the precise issue here presented appears to be one of first impression," concluded that the rule of *Reynolds v. Sims,* controlled its resolution. "Reasoning by analogy," the court held, in short, that the dual-majority requirement of New York law "is unconstitutional because it violates the one man, one vote principle." 386 F. Supp., at 7. In assessing the correctness of the District Court's judgment it is thus appropriate to begin by recalling the basic rationale of the decisions of this Court in which that principle was first developed and applied.

The rationale is, at bottom, so simple as to be almost self-evident. Beginning with *Reynolds v. Sims, supra,* cases in which the principle emerged involved challenges to state legislative apportionment systems that gave "the same number of representatives to unequal numbers of constituents."... The Court concluded that in voting for their legislators, all citizens have an equal interest in representative democracy, and that the concept of equal protection therefore requires that their votes be given equal weight....

The equal protection principles applicable in gauging the fairness of an election involving the choice of legislative representatives are of limited relevance, however, in analyzing the propriety of recognizing distinctive voter interests in a "single-shot" referendum. In a referendum, the expression of voter will is direct, and there is no need to assure that the voters' views will be adequately represented through their representatives in the legislature. The policy impact of a referendum is also different in kind from the impact of choosing representatives — instead of sending legislators off to the state capitol to vote on a multitude of issues, the referendum puts one discrete issue to the voters. That issue is capable, at least, of being analyzed to determine whether its adoption or rejection will have a disproportionate impact on an identifiable group of voters. If it is found to have such a disproportionate impact, the question then is whether a State can recognize that impact either by limiting the franchise to those voters specially affected or by giving their votes a special weight. This question has been confronted by the Court in two types of cases: those dealing with elections involving "special-interest" governmental bodies of limited jurisdiction, and those dealing with bond referenda.

The Court has held that the electorate of a special-purpose unit of government, such as a water storage district, may be apportioned to give greater influence to the constitutent groups found to be most affected by the governmental unit's functions. *Salyer Land Co. v. Tulare Water Dist.*, 410 U. S. 719. But the classification of voters into "interested" and "noninterested" groups must still be reasonably precise, as *Kramer v. Union School Dist.*, 395 U. S. 621, demonstrates. The Court assumed in that case that the voting constituency in school district elections could be limited to those "primarily interested in school affairs," *id.,* at 632, but concluded that the State's classification of voters on the asserted basis of that interest was so imprecise that the exclusion of otherwise qualified voters was impermissible.

In the bond referenda cases, the local government had either limited the electoral franchise to property owners, or weighted property owners' votes more heavily than those of nonproperty owners by using a "dual box" separate-majority approval system quite similar to the one at issue in the present case. *Cipriano v. City of Houma,* 395 U. S. 701; *Phoenix v. Kolodziejski,* 399 U. S. 204; *Hill v. Stone,* 421 U. S. 289.

In the *Cipriano* case, involving revenue bonds, it was apparent that all voters had an identity of interest in passage of the bond issue, and limitation of the electoral franchise to "property taxpayers" was, plainly, invidiously discriminatory. The other two cases, however, involved general obligation bonds. There, as in *Salyer* and *Kramer,* the validity of the classification depended upon whether the group interests were sufficiently different to justify total or partial withholding of the electoral franchise from one of them. In support of the classifications, it was argued that property owners have a more substantial stake in the adoption of obligation bonds than do nonproperty owners, because the taxes of the former directly and substantially fund the bond obligation. The Court rejected that argument for limiting the electoral franchise, however, noting that nonproperty owners also share in the tax burden when the tax on rental property or commercial businesses is passed on in the form of higher prices. Although the interests of the two groups are concededly not identical, the Court held that they are sufficiently similar to prevent a state government from distinguishing between them by artificially narrowing or weighting the electoral franchise in favor of the property taxpayers.[13]

---

[13] We have held, however, that a referendum voting scheme that can be characterized in math-

These decisions do not resolve the issues in the present case. Taken together, however, they can be said to focus attention on two inquiries: whether there is a genuine difference in the relevant interests of the groups that the state electoral classification has created; and, if so, whether any resulting enhancement of minority voting strength nonetheless amounts to invidious discrimination in violation of the Equal Protection Clause.

III

The argument that the provisions of New York law in question here are unconstitutional rests primarily on the premise that all voters in a New York county have identical interests in the adoption or rejection of a new charter, and that any distinction, therefore, between voters drawn on the basis of residence and working to the detriment of an identifiable class is an invidious discrimination. If the major premise were demonstrably correct — if it were clear that all voters in Niagara County have substantially identical interests in the adoption of a new county charter, regardless of where they reside within the county — the District Court's judgment would have to be affirmed under our prior cases. *Cipriano v. City of Houma, supra.* That major premise, however, simply cannot be accepted. To the contrary, it appears that the challenged provisions of New York law rest on the State's identification of the distinctive interests of the residents of the cities and towns within a county rather than their interests as residents of the county as a homogeneous unit. This identification is based in the realities of the distribution of governmental powers in New York, and is consistent with our cases that recognize both the wide discretion the States have in forming and allocating governmental tasks to local subdivisions, and the discrete interests that such local governmental units may have *qua* units....

General-purpose local government in New York is entrusted to four different units: counties, cities, towns, and villages. The State is divided into 62 counties; each of the 57 counties outside of New York City is divided into towns, or towns and one or more cities. Villages, once formed, are still part of the towns in which they are located. The New York Legislature has conferred home rule and general governmental powers on all of these subdivisions, and their governmental activities may on occasion substantially overlap. The cities often perform functions within their jurisdiction that the county may perform for noncity residents; similarly villages perform some functions for their residents that the town provides for the rest of the town's inhabitants. Historically towns provided their areas with major social services that more recently have been transferred to counties; towns exercise more regulatory power than counties; and both towns and counties can create special taxing and improvement districts to administer services. See 13 New York Temporary State Commission on the Constitutional Convention, Local Government 20 (1967).

Acting within a fairly loose state apportionment of political power, the relative energy and organization of these various subdivisions will often determine which one of them in a given area carries out the major tasks of local government. Since the cities have the greatest autonomy within this scheme, changes serving to strengthen the county structure may have the most immediate impact on the functions of the towns as deliverers of government services. *Id.,* at 19.

---

ematical terms as giving disproportionate power to a minority does not violate the Equal Protection Clause, there being no discrimination against an identifiable class. Gordon v. Lance, 403 U.S. 1....

The provisions of New York law here in question clearly contemplate that a new or amended county charter will frequently operate to transfer "functions or duties" from the towns or cities to the county, or even to "abolish one or more offices, departments, agencies or units of government." Although the 1974 Charter does not explicitly transfer governmental functions or duties from the towns to Niagara County, the executive-legislative form of government it provides would significantly enhance the county's organizational and service delivery capacity, for the purpose of "greater efficiency and responsibility in county government." Niagara County Charter, 1972. The creation of the offices of County Executive and Commissioner of Finance clearly reflects this purpose. Such anticipated organizational changes, no less than explicit transfers of functions, could effectively shift any pre-existing balance of power between town and county governments toward county predominance. In terms of efficient delivery of government services, such a shift might be all to the good, but it may still be viewed as carrying a cost quite different for town voters and their existing town governments from that incurred by city voters and their existing city governments.

The ultimate question then is whether, given the differing interests of city and noncity voters in the adoption of a new county charter in New York, those differences are sufficient under the Equal Protection Clause to justify the classifications made by New York law. . . . If that question were posed in the context of annexation proceedings, the fact that the residents of the annexing city and the residents of the area to be annexed formed sufficiently different constituencies with sufficiently different interests could be readily perceived. The fact of impending union alone would not so merge them into one community of interest as constitutionally to require that their votes be aggregated in any referendum to approve annexation. Cf. *Hunter v. Pittsburgh,* 207 U. S. 161. Similarly a proposal that several school districts join to form a consolidated unit could surely be subject to voter approval in each constituent school district.

Yet in terms of recognizing constituencies with separate and potentially opposing interests, the structural decision to annex or consolidate is similar in impact to the decision to restructure county government in New York. In each case, separate voter approval requirements are based on the perception that the real and long-term impact of a restructuring of local government is felt quite differently by the different county constituent units that in a sense compete to provide similar governmental services. Voters in these constituent units are directly and differentially affected by the restructuring of county government, which may make the provider of public services more remote and less subject to the voters' individual influence.

The provisions of New York law here in question no more than recognize the realities of these substantially differing electoral interests. Granting to these provisions the presumption of constitutionality to which every duly enacted state and federal law is entitled, we are unable to conclude that they violate the Equal Protection Clause of the Fourteenth Amendment.

For the reasons stated in this opinion the judgment is reversed.

It is so ordered.

THE CHIEF JUSTICE concurs in the judgment.

Comments: 1. Note the Court's oblique reference to *Hunter*. Does Justice Stewart mean to say that Pennsylvania could have required separate majorities in Allegheny and in Pittsburgh for approval of the consolidation? Could the state have permitted annexation of Allegheny without any vote at all among residents of Allegheny, (a) following adoption of a resolution by the Pittsburgh city council, or (b) following a successful referendum in Pittsburgh? Could it have required concurrent majorities consisting of (a) majority approval in both cities aggregated, plus (b) majority approval either in Allegheny, or in Pittsburgh? If the New York statute in *Lockport* failed to provide for concurrent majorities, would the Court invalidate it? What is the difference among these various combinations?

2. Given the number of local government boundary change elections provided for in this country, it is not surprising that the courts have had to face a variety of challenges in voting requirements. In resolving a particular challenge, a court may be guided to its decision by first determining which set of Supreme Court precedents is applicable which, in turn, determines whether it invokes strict scrutiny-compelling state interest, or the more traditional rational relationship standard of equal protection analysis. For discussion, see Note, *State Restrictions on Municipal Elections: An Equal Protection Analysis,* 93 Harv. L. Rev. 1491 (1980).

Almost every local government organization also involves several sets of interests or interested parties, as the court seemed to recognize in *Lockport*. Do the courts clearly identify those interests and give them adequate recognition? Or is that the role of the courts?

Adams v. City of Colorado Springs, 308 F. Supp. 1397 (D. Colo.), aff'd, 399 U.S. 901 (1970), is a leading pre-*Lockport* case upholding an annexation voting scheme. An annexation statute denied the right to vote when territory to be annexed had over two-thirds contiguity with the annexing city, but provided for a vote when the territory to be annexed had between one-sixth and two-thirds contiguity. The court held that the Supreme Court's voting rights cases did not apply. The important factor in those cases was "that the franchise was granted to one group of persons to the detriment of another group." The court upheld the statute as a reasonable classification under the equal protection clause. Denying the right to vote when the annexed area has over two-thirds contiguity with the annexing city was proper because "the interrelationship between the two areas is or can be so close that the city should be allowed to annex despite the unwillingness of the residents of the annexed territory."

Curtis v. Board of Supervisors, 501 P.2d 537 (Cal. 1972), is a leading decision which invalidated a statute restricting the right to vote in municipal incorporations. The statutory scheme was complicated, but in essence it allowed landowners representing fifty-one percent of the assessed valuation of land included within a proposed incorporation to block the incorporation by filing a protest. The court held that the Supreme Court's voting rights cases applied because the statutory right of protest touched upon and burdened the right to vote. The strict scrutiny "compelling interests" standard of the voting rights cases was not met because landowners did not have an interest sufficient to justify their right to block an election. All residents, not just landowners, had a "substantial interest" in the governmental powers which would be exercised by a newly incorporated municipality.

Adams and *Curtis* suggest that voting rights may differ by area but not by land ownership. What about nonresidents? Do they have an interest in the governmental affairs of a neighboring city? The following case considers this question:

HOLT CIVIC CLUB v. CITY OF TUSCALOOSA
United States Supreme Court
439 U.S. 60 (1978)

Mr. Justice Rehnquist delivered the opinion of the Court.

Holt is a small, largely rural, unincorporated community located on the northeastern outskirts of Tuscaloosa, the fifth largest city in Alabama. Because the community is within the three-mile police jurisdiction circumscribing Tuscaloosa's corporate limits, its residents are subject to the city's "police [and] sanitary regulations." Ala. Code § 11-40-10 (1975). Holt residents are also subject to the criminal jurisdiction of the city's court, Ala. Code § 12-14-1 (1975), and to the city's power to license businesses, trades, and professions, Ala. Code § 11-51-91 (1975). Tuscaloosa, however, may collect from businesses in the police jurisdiction only one-half of the license fee chargeable to similar businesses conducted within the corporate limits. *Ibid.*

In 1973 appellants, an unincorporated civic association and seven individual residents of Holt, brought this statewide class action in the United States District Court for the Northern District of Alabama, challenging the constitutionality of these Alabama statutes. They claimed that the city's extraterritorial exercise of police powers over Holt residents, without a concomitant extension of the franchise on an equal footing with those residing within the corporate limits, denies residents of the police jurisdiction rights secured by the Due Process and Equal Protection Clauses of the Fourteenth Amendment. . . . We now conclude that appellants' constitutional claims were properly rejected.

. . . .

II

Appellants' amended complaint requested the District Court to declare the Alabama statutes unconstitutional and to enjoin their enforcement insofar as they authorize the extraterritorial exercise of municipal powers. Seizing on the District Court's observation that "[appellants] do not seek extension of the franchise to themselves," appellants suggest that their complaint was dismissed because they sought the wrong remedy.

The unconstitutional predicament in which appellants assertedly found themselves could be remedied in only two ways: (1) the city's extraterritorial power could be negated by invalidating the State's authorizing statutes or (2) the right to vote in municipal elections could be extended to residents of the police jurisdiction. We agree with appellants that a federal court should not dismiss a meritorious constitutional claim because the complaint seeks one remedy rather than another plainly appropriate one. . . . But while a meritorious claim will not be rejected for want of a prayer for appropriate relief, a claim lacking substantive merit obviously should be rejected. We think it is clear from the pleadings in this case that appellants have alleged no claim cognizable under the United States Constitution.

A

Appellants focus their equal protection attack on § 11-40-10, the statute fixing the limits of municipal police jurisdiction and giving extraterritorial effect to municipal police and sanitary ordinances. Citing *Kramer v. Union Free School Dist.,* 395 U. S. 621 (1969), and cases following in its wake, appellants argue that the section creates a classification infringing on their right to participate in municipal elections. The State's denial of the franchise to police jurisdiction residents, appellants urge, can stand only if justified by a compelling state interest.

[The Court discussed the *Kramer, Cipriano* and *Phoenix* cases. — Eds.]

Appellants also place heavy reliance on *Evans v. Cornman,* 398 U. S. 419 (1970). In *Evans* the Permanent Board of Registry of Montgomery County, Md., ruled that persons living on the grounds of the National Institutes of Health (NIH), a federal enclave located within the geographical boundaries of the State, did not meet the residency requirement of the Maryland Constitution. Accordingly, NIH residents were denied the right to vote in Maryland elections. This Court rejected the notion that persons living on NIH grounds were not residents of Maryland:

> Appellees clearly live within the geographical boundaries of the State of Maryland, and they are treated as state residents in the census and in determining congressional apportionment. They are not residents of Maryland only if the NIH grounds ceased to be a part of Maryland when the enclave was created. However, the "fiction of a state within a state" was specifically rejected by this Court in *Howard v. Commissioners of Louisville,* 344 U. S. 624, 627 (1953), and it cannot be resurrected here to deny appellees the right to vote. *Id.,* at 421-422.

Thus, because inhabitants of the NIH enclave were residents of Maryland and were "just as interested in and connected with electoral decisions as they were prior to 1953 when the area came under federal jurisdiction and as their neighbors who live off the enclave," *id.,* at 426, the State could not deny them the equal right to vote in Maryland elections.

From these and our other voting qualifications cases a common characteristic emerges: The challenged statute in each case denied the franchise to individuals who were physically resident within the geographic boundaries of the governmental entity concerned. See, *e. g., Hill v. Stone,* 421 U. S. 289 (1975) (invalidating provision of the Texas Constitution restricting franchise on general obligation bond issue to *residents* who had "rendered" or listed real, mixed, or personal property for taxation in the election district).... No decision of this Court has extended the "one man, one vote" principle to individuals residing beyond the geographic confines of the governmental entity concerned, be it the State or its political subdivisions. On the contrary, our cases have uniformly recognized that a government unit may legitimately restrict the right to participate in its political processes to those who reside within its borders. See, *e. g., Dunn v. Blumstein,* 405 U. S. 330, 343-344 (1972); *Evans v. Cornman, supra,* at 422; *Kramer v. Union Free School Dist.,* 395 U. S., at 625.... Bona fide residence alone, however, does not automatically confer the right to vote on all matters, for at least in the context of special interest elections the State may constitutionally disfranchise residents who lack the required special interest in the subject matter of the election. See *Salyer Land Co. v. Tulare Lake Basin Water Storage Dist.,* 410 U. S. 719 (1973); *Associated Enterprises, Inc. v. Toltec Watershed Improvement Dist.,* 410 U. S. 743 (1973).

Appellants' argument that extraterritorial extension of municipal powers requires concomitant extraterritorial extension of the franchise proves too much. The imaginary line defining a city's corporate limits cannot corral the influence of municipal actions. A city's decisions inescapably affect individuals living immediately outside its borders. The granting of building permits for high rise apartments, industrial plants, and the like on the city's fringe unavoidably contributes to problems of traffic congestion, school districting, and law enforcement immediately outside the city. A rate change in the city's sales or ad valorem tax could well have a significant impact on retailers and property values in areas bordering the city. The condemnation of real property on the city's edge for construction of a municipal garbage dump or waste treatment plant would have obvious implications for neighboring nonresidents. Indeed, the indirect extraterritorial effects of many purely internal municipal actions could conceivably have a heavier impact on surrounding environs than the direct regulation contemplated by Alabama's police jurisdiction statutes. Yet no one would suggest that nonresidents likely to be affected by this sort of municipal action have a constitutional right to participate in the political processes bringing it about. And unless one adopts the idea that the Austinian notion of sovereignty, which is presumably embodied to some extent in the authority of a city over a police jurisdiction, distinguishes the direct effects of limited municipal powers over police jurisdiction residents from the indirect though equally dramatic extraterritorial effects of purely internal municipal actions, it makes little sense to say that one requires extension of the franchise while the other does not.

Given this country's tradition of popular sovereignty, appellants' claimed right to vote in Tuscaloosa elections is not without some logical appeal.... The line heretofore marked by this Court's voting qualifications decisions coincides with the geographical boundary of the governmental unit at issue, and we hold that appellants' case, like their homes, falls on the farther side.

B

Thus stripped of its voting rights attire, the equal protection issue presented by appellants becomes whether the Alabama statutes giving extraterritorial force to certain municipal ordinances and powers bear some rational relationship to a legitimate state purpose. *San Antonio Independent School Dist. v. Rodriguez,* 411 U. S. 1 (1973). "The Fourteenth Amendment does not prohibit legislation merely because it is special, or limited in its application to a particular geographical or political subdivision of the state." *Fort Smith Light Co. v. Paving Dist.,* 274 U. S. 387, 391 (1927). Rather, the Equal Protection Clause is offended only if the statute's classification "rests on grounds wholly irrelevant to the achievement of the State's objective." *McGowan v. Maryland,* 366 U. S. 420, 425 (1961); *Kotch v. Board of River Port Pilot Comm'rs,* 330 U. S. 552, 556 (1947).

Government, observed Mr. Justice Johnson, "is the science of experiment," *Anderson v. Dunn,* 6 Wheat. 204, 226 (1821), and a State is afforded wide leeway when experimenting with the appropriate allocation of state legislative power. This Court has often recognized that political subdivisions such as cities and counties are created by the State "as convenient agencies for exercising such of the governmental powers of the State as may be entrusted to them." *Hunter v. Pittsburgh,* 207 U. S. 161, 178 (1907).... In *Hunter v. Pittsburgh,* the Court discussed at length the relationship between a State and its political subdivisions, remarking: "The number, nature and duration of the powers conferred upon [municipal] corporations and the territory over which they shall be exercised rests in the absolute discretion of the State." 207 U. S., at 178. While the broad statements as to state control over municipal corporations contained in *Hunter* have undoubtedly been qualified by the holdings of later cases such as *Kramer v. Union Free School Dist., supra,* we think that the case continues to have substantial constitutional significance in emphasizing the extraordinarily wide latitude that States have in creating various types of political subdivisions and conferring authority upon them.[7]

---

[7] In this case residents of the police jurisdiction are excluded only from participation in municipal

The extraterritorial exercise of municipal powers is a governmental technique neither recent in origin nor unique to the State of Alabama. See R. Maddox, Extraterritorial Powers of Municipalities in the United States (1955). In this country 35 States authorize their municipal subdivisions to exercise governmental powers beyond their corporate limits. Comment, The Constitutionality of the Exercise of Extraterritorial Powers by Municipalities, 45 U. Chi. L. Rev. 151 (1977). Although the extraterritorial municipal powers granted by these States vary widely, several States grant their cities more extensive or intrusive powers over bordering areas than those granted under the Alabama statutes.[8]

In support of their equal protection claim, appellants suggest a number of "constitutionally preferable" governmental alternatives to Alabama's system of municipal police jurisdictions. For example, exclusive management of the police jurisdiction by county officials, appellants maintain, would be more "practical." From a political science standpoint, appellants' suggestions may be sound, but this Court does not sit to determine whether Alabama has chosen the soundest or most practical form of internal government possible. Authority to make those judgments resides in the state legislature, and Alabama citizens are free to urge their proposals to that body. See, *e. g., Hunter v. Pittsburgh,* 207 U. S., at 179. Our inquiry is limited to the question whether "any state of facts reasonably may be conceived to justify" Alabama's system of police jurisdictions, *Salyer Land Co. v. Tulare Lake Basin Water Storage Dist.,* 410 U. S., at 732, and in this case it takes but momentary reflection to arrive at an affirmative answer.

The Alabama Legislature could have decided that municipal corporations should have some measure of control over activities carried on just beyond their "city limit" signs, particularly since today's police jurisdiction may be tomorrow's

---

elections since they reside outside of Tuscaloosa's corporate limits. This "denial of the franchise," as appellants put it, does not have anything like the far-reaching consequences of the denial of the franchise in Evans v. Cornman, 398 U. S. 419 (1970). There the Court pointed out that "[i]n nearly every election, federal, state, and local, for offices from the Presidency to the school board, and on the entire variety of other ballot propositions, appellees have a stake equal to that of other Maryland residents." *Id.,* at 426. Treatment of the plaintiffs in *Evans* as nonresidents of Maryland had repercussions not merely with respect to their right to vote in city elections, but with respect to their right to vote in national, state, school board, and referendum elections.

[8] Municipalities in some States have almost unrestricted governmental powers over surrounding unincorporated territories....

By setting forth these various state provisions respecting extraterritorial powers of cities, we do not mean to imply that every one of them would pass constitutional muster. We do not have before us, of course, a situation in which a city has annexed outlying territory in all but name, and is exercising precisely the same governmental powers over residents of surrounding unincorporated territory as it does over those residing within its corporate limits. See Little Thunder v. South Dakota, 518 F. 2d 1253 (CA8 1975). Nor do we have here a case like Evans v. Cornman, *supra,* where NIH residents were subject to such "important aspects of state powers" as Maryland's authority "to levy and collect [its] income, gasoline, sales, and use taxes" and were "just as interested in and connected with electoral decisions as . . . their neighbors who live[d] off the enclave." 398 U. S., at 423, 424, 426.

Appellants have made neither an allegation nor a showing that the authority exercised by the city of Tuscaloosa within the police jurisdiction is no less than that exercised by the city within its corporate limits. The minute catalog of ordinances of the city of Tuscaloosa which have extraterritorial effect set forth by our dissenting Brethren, . . . is as notable for what it does not include as for what it does. While the burden was on appellants to establish a difference in treatment violative of the Equal Protection Clause, we are bound to observe that among the powers *not* included in the "addendum" to appellants' brief referred to by the dissent are the vital and traditional authorities of cities and towns to levy ad valorem taxes, invoke the power of eminent domain, and zone property for various types of uses.

annexation to the city proper. Nor need the city's interests have been the only concern of the legislature when it enacted the police jurisdiction statutes. Urbanization of any area brings with it a number of individuals who long both for the quiet of suburban or country living and for the career opportunities offered by the city's working environment. Unincorporated communities like Holt dot the rim of most major population centers in Alabama and elsewhere, and state legislatures have a legitimate interest in seeing that this substantial segment of the population does not go without basic municipal services such as police, fire, and health protection. Established cities are experienced in the delivery of such services, and the incremental cost of extending the city's responsibility in these areas to surrounding environs may be substantially less than the expense of establishing wholly new service organizations in each community.

Nor was it unreasonable for the Alabama Legislature to require police jurisdiction residents to contribute through license fees to the expense of services provided them by the city. The statutory limitation on license fees to half the amount exacted within the city assures that police jurisdiction residents will not be victimized by the city government.

"Viable local governments may need many innovations, numerous combinations of old and new devices, great flexibility in municipal arrangements to meet changing urban conditions." *Sailors v. Board of Education,* 387 U. S., at 110-111. This observation in *Sailors* was doubtless as true at the turn of this century, when urban areas throughout the country were temporally closer to the effects of the industrial revolution. Alabama's police jurisdiction statute, enacted in 1907, was a rational legislative response to the problems faced by the State's burgeoning cities. Alabama is apparently content with the results of its experiment, and nothing in the Equal Protection Clause of the Fourteenth Amendment requires that it try something new.

. . . .

Affirmed.

MR. JUSTICE STEVENS, concurring. [Omitted.]

MR. JUSTICE BRENNAN, with whom MR. JUSTICE WHITE and MR. JUSTICE MARSHALL join, dissenting.

. . . .

. . . The Court rests [today's] holding on the conclusion that "a government unit may legitimately restrict the right to participate in its political processes to those who reside within its borders." The Court thus insulates the Alabama statutes challenged in this case from the strict judicial scrutiny ordinarily applied to state laws distributing the franchise. In so doing, the Court cedes to geography a talismanic significance contrary to the theory and meaning of our past voting-rights cases.

There is no question but that the residents of Tuscaloosa's police jurisdiction are governed by the city. Under Alabama law, a municipality exercises "governing" and "lawmaking" power over its police jurisdiction. *City of Homewood v. Wofford Oil Co.,* 232 Ala. 634, 637, 169 So. 288, 290 (1936). Residents of Tuscaloosa's police jurisdiction are subject to license fees exacted by the city, as well as to the city's police and sanitary regulations, which can be enforced through penal sanctions effective in the city's municipal court. See *Birmingham v. Lake,* 243 Ala. 367, 372, 10 So. 2d 24, 28 (1942). The Court seems to imply, however, that residents of the police jurisdiction are not governed enough to be included within the political community of Tuscaloosa, since they are not subject to Tuscaloosa's powers of eminent domain, zoning, or ad valorem taxation. . . . But this position is sharply contrary to our previous holdings. . . .

The residents of Tuscaloosa's police jurisdiction are vastly more affected by Tuscaloosa's decisionmaking processes than were the plaintiffs in either *Kramer* or *Cipriano* affected by the decisionmaking processes from which they had been unconstitutionally excluded....

The criterion of geographical residency relied upon by the Court is of no assistance in this analysis. Just as a State may not fracture the integrity of a political community by restricting the franchise to property taxpayers, so it may not use geographical restrictions on the franchise to accomplish the same end. This is the teaching of *Evans v. Cornman*. . . . Residents of Tuscaloosa's police jurisdiction are assuredly as "interested in and connected with" the electoral decisions of the city as were the inhabitants of the NIH enclave in the electoral decisions of Maryland. True, inhabitants of the enclave lived "within the geographical boundaries of the State of Maryland," but appellants in this case similarly reside within the geographical boundaries of Tuscaloosa's police jurisdiction. They live within the perimeters of the city's "legislative powers." . . .
. . . .

Appellants' equal protection claim can be simply expressed: The State cannot extend the franchise to some citizens who are governed by municipal government in the places of their residency, and withhold the franchise from others similarly situated, unless this distinction is necessary to promote a compelling state interest. No such interest has been articulated in this case. Neither Tuscaloosa's interest in regulating "activities carried on just beyond [its] 'city limit' signs," . . . nor Alabama's interest in providing municipal services to the unincorporated communities surrounding its cities, . . . are in any way inconsistent with the extension of the franchise to residents of Tuscaloosa's police jurisdiction. Although a great many States may presently authorize the exercise of extraterritorial lawmaking powers by a municipality, and although the Alabama statutes involved in this case may be of venerable age, neither of these factors, as *Reynolds v. Sims*, 377 U. S. 533 (1964), made clear, can serve to justify practices otherwise impermissible under the Equal Protection Clause of the Fourteenth Amendment.

Comments: 1. If the plaintiffs in Tuskegee *(Gomillion)* had a right to vote in a city in which they didn't live, why shouldn't the plaintiffs in Tuscaloosa have a right to vote in a city to whose jurisdiction they are more subject than were the *Gomillion* plaintiffs to Tuskegee? Isn't the Court incorrect when it says that the common characteristic to all of its voting rights cases was the fact of residence? What is the difference between the majority's residence factor and the dissent's "political community" concept? Would the Court's decision have been the same if the complaining nonresidents in *Holt* were black? For discussion see Comment, *The Constitutionality of the Exercise of Extraterritorial Powers by Municipalities,* 45 U. Chi. L. Rev. 151 (1977).

Even if nonresidents of a municipality have no right to participate generally in municipal elections, could it be argued that a nonresident should be permitted to vote on a specific issue that affects her directly? *See Kollar v. City of Tucson,* 319 F. Supp. 482 (D. Ariz. 1970), *aff'd,* 402 U.S. 967 (1971) (nonresident user of city water service denied right to vote in revenue bond referendum despite probable effect on water rates).

In *Moorman v. Wood,* 504 F. Supp. 467 (E.D. Ky. 1980), the court reviewed a Kentucky statute which authorized any city to annex a contiguous part of another city, following voter approval of the residents of the annexation area. Only they were permitted to vote on the annexation. In this case two small cities moved to annex portions of the larger adjacent city of Covington. Plaintiffs, who were residents of part of Covington not being annexed, contended that the statute violated equal protection because it did not permit all the citizens of Covington to vote on what amounted to deannexation of part of their city. The court, in upholding the statute, said that annexation elections were "special interest" elections, subject to the less stringent equal protection analysis. It concluded that this statute, however, satisfied the compelling state interest as well as the rational basis standard. Because of the bitter, prolonged annexation battles in that area, the legislature had a compelling interest in seeking a quick, decisive way to settle annexation disputes. It chose the method of voting rather than one which would permit a balancing of all interests; and it chose to limit the vote to residents of the area being annexed. The court rejected plaintiffs' argument that all residents of Covington must be given the right to vote because they are substantially affected. Paraphrasing the *Holt* majority's comment that the argument proves too much, the court pointed out that "[m]any persons other than residents of the annexation areas have a substantial interest at least equal to that of the citizens of Covington in the outcome of these annexations" — for example, a nonresident who works and pays a payroll tax to the city, or a nonresident property owner. Since it is not possible to permit everyone affected by an annexation election to vote, the court felt, limiting the vote to residents of the annexation area satisfies a compelling state interest. The court also noted that an annexation election is a "single-shot" referendum where, unlike the choice of legislative representatives, it is easier to determine the impact on identifiable groups of voters. The Kentucky court was also clearly influenced by, in its view, the desirability of entrusting "these dificult policy problems of local government" to state legislatures to resolve, not the federal courts.

2. *Holt* and *Lockport* suggest that the outcome in a voting rights case depends on the level of equal protection review applied by the Court. Do these cases mean that the minimal equal protection review standard must now be applied to all voting cases in which there are geographic classifications?

The California Supreme Court thought not in *Fullerton Joint Union High School District v. State Board of Education,* 654 P.2d 168 (Cal. 1982). The Yorba Linda elementary school district was completely surrounded by two "unified" school districts. Unified districts provide both elementary and high school education. Students from the Yorba Linda district traveled across the adjacent districts to attend high school in the Fullerton district. The state board approved a reorganization plan to detach the Yorba Linda district from the Fullerton district and to constitute Yorba Linda as a unified district which would also offer high school education. The board exercised its statutory discretion to call an election on its reorganization proposal, but limited the election to residents of the Yorba Linda district. The court held that the exclusion of voters in the Fullerton district violated equal protection.

The court applied strict scrutiny equal protection review. It distinguished *Lockport,* reading that case as holding that a state can require concurrent majorities in different areas in a single-issue referendum. "But nothing in *Lockport* endorses measures which deny the vote entirely to residents of one of the areas, nor permits such measures to escape strict judicial scrutiny." The court also distinguished *Holt,* holding that "it holds only that distinctions which coincide with the boundaries of the governmental entity concerned, and exclude no one physically resident within those boundaries, do not require strict scrutiny." Do you agree with this reading of those decisions?

The court then considered whether a compelling state interest justified the exclusion of voters in the Fullerton district from the election. It found none. It did not believe that Fullerton voters could be excluded because they were numerous and their self-interest in preventing the detachment of the Yorba Linda district would "swamp" the less numerous voters in that district. The court did say that they might find a compelling state interest if uninterested voters were excluded "in order to protect the interests of persons vitally concerned." Can you give an example of an election to which this justification might constitutionally apply?

An opinion which dissented on the voting rights issue castigated the majority for misreading *Holt* and *Lockport.* This justice also believed that the majority was influenced by a concern that the reorganization proposal would have "an adverse impact on school integration." The facts indicated that the Fullerton district would be more segregated if the reorganization proposal were approved.

On the same day, the California Supreme Court upheld an annexation statute providing for an election only in the area to be annexed if at least twenty-five percent of the voters or twenty-five percent of the owners of the assessed value of land in the area protested. *Citizens Against Forced Annexation v. Local Agency Formation Commission,* 654 P.2d 193 (Cal. 1982). An election also was required in the annexing municipality if the assessed value of land in the annexed area equalled one half or more of the assessed value of land in the annexing city, or if the voters in the annexed area equalled one half or more of the voters in the annexing municipality. The statutory provision requiring an election only in the annexed area applied in this case. The court said:

> We conclude that the state's interest in carrying out a policy of planned, orderly community development under the guidance of the local agency formation commissions, and in particular its interest in avoiding the creation or perpetuation of islands of unwanted, unincorporated territories, is of compelling importance. That interest cannot be achieved if residents of the [annexing] city or their elected representatives have the power to reject an annexation endorsed by the commission and approved by the residents of the affected territory.

Id. at 202. Is this decision consistent with *Fullerton?* For a discussion of the California Local Agency Formation Commissions see Chapter 3.

3. Consider the following additional variants of the voting rights problem in boundary change cases.

a. *The statute entirely denies the right to vote. Berry v. Bourne,* 588 F.2d 422 (4th Cir. 1978). One of the optional methods of annexation in South Carolina provided that when a petition is filed signed by seventy-five percent of the freeholders in a contiguous area requesting annexation, the city council may complete the annexation simply by adopting a resolution. In this case, registered voters in the area to be annexed claimed a violation of equal protection because they were denied the right to vote on the issue. The court rejected the claim, basing its decision squarely on *Hunter v. Pittsburgh,* whose broad affirmation of state legislative power over annexation was, in the court's judgment, subject to only one exception: challenges resting on racial discrimination. None of the voting rights cases (*Cipriano* and *Kramer* are cited) was in point because there was no election provided for here.

Accord Citizens Committee to Oppose Annexation v. City of Lynchburg, 400 F. Supp. 68 (W.D. Va.), *modified on other grounds,* 528 F.2d 816 (4th Cir. 1975), *appeal denied,* 423 U.S. 1043 (1976). The *Lynchburg* case arose in Virginia, which is unique in delegating annexation decisions entirely to the courts. In *Berry v. Bourne,* on the other hand, the annexation was carried out unilaterally by the annexing city council. It might be argued that voters of the annexing city participate in annexation through their election of members of the council, while the annexees, who did not vote for members of the governing board of the annexing city, were unconstitutionally denied the right to participate equally in the annexation decision. This approach was suggested in Note, *The Right to Vote in Municipal Elections,* 88 HARV. L. REV. 1571, 1599 (1975). The court in *Berry v. Bourne* noted that suggestion and dismissed it: "Such an argument is supported by no authority and appears to us to be an extreme exercise in preciosity and without merit." 588 F.2d at 425.

With *Berry v. Bourne,* compare *Hayward v. Clay,* 573 F.2d 187 (4th Cir.), *cert. denied,* 439 U.S. 959 (1978), in which the court invalidated another method of annexation provided by South Carolina. There the annexation was initiated by petition signed by fifteen percent of the freeholders in the area seeking annexation. In order to become effective, the proposed annexation must be approved by a majority of the freeholders in the annexation area, and also by a majority of the registered voters in the annexation area and the annexing city, counted together. In this case the two elections were held simultaneously; the registered voters in both areas approved the proposal, but the freeholders in the annexation area did not approve. The court invalidated the freeholder requirement, relying heavily on *Hill v. Stone* and noting that *Hunter* did not overcome the need to conform to the Constitution with respect to voting rights.

For other courts agreeing with the Fourth Circuit that there is no constitutional right to vote on an annexation, see *Adams v. Colorado Springs, supra.*

b. *The right to vote is extended to some, but not all interests. Millis v. Board of County Commissioners,* 626 P.2d 652 (Colo. 1981). The plaintiffs, out-of-state owners of vacation houses in a water district created following a referendum vote of 27-21, contended that the Colorado statute denied them equal protection because it excluded out-of-state owners from voting on any district matters, including creation of the district, while Colorado residents who owned property within the district but did not live there were permitted to vote. The court held the provision valid under Colorado's equal protection guarantee (the federal constitutional claims had been disposed of in a prior suit). Applying a rational relationship standard, the court said that there were good reasons to give Colorado residents a greater voice in the district because they were more likely to be concerned about the environment, urban development and adequate water supply. As for including in the franchise Colorado property owners who did not live in the district, the court summarily concluded that it was not for it to determine whether this was the best classification possible.

Note that in the California *Curtis* case, *supra,* the interests accommodated in the boundary change proceeding were, in a sense, reversed. It was the nonresident, largely corporate, landholders who had the power to protest and thereby block the incorporation while nearby nonresidents who did not own land but may well have been affected by the incorporation had no means to express their views. Is their interest comparable to the out-of-state property owners in *Millis?* See 88 HARV. L. REV. at 1595-96.

In *Texfi Industries, Inc. v. City of Fayetteville,* 269 S.E.2d 142 (N.C. 1980), the annexation statute under scrutiny provided for a referendum in the annexation area if fifteen percent of the voters signed a petition requesting it. The area in question was entirely commercial and industrial; there were no natural residents and so no way to activate the election procedure. The plaintiffs, corporate "residents" of the annexation area, objected that the statute gave resident voters but not corporations the right to vote on the proposed annexation. The court rejected a strict scrutiny test, noting that a corporation has no fundamental right to vote on an annexation, and upheld the statute under the rationality test.

In *Kelley v. Mayor & Council,* 327 A.2d 748 (Del. 1974), the problem was not exclusion of a voter group but, in a sense, over-inclusion. In an annexation election, every non-property owning voter in the annexation area got one vote, and every corporation, firm, and individual owning real estate within the area was entitled to one vote per $100 of assessed valuation. The court invoked strict scrutiny to sustain an equal protection challenge to this weighted voting scheme, holding that the *Salyer* exception did not extend to a unit of general local government such as a city.

In an unusual twist to the accommodation of interests, the Alabama Supreme Court set aside an annexation election in which the boundaries of the territory to be annexed had admittedly been drawn to exclude those voters who were opposed to the annexation. *City of Birmingham v. Community Fire District,* 336 So. 2d 502 (Ala. 1976). The court quoted *Kramer* to the effect that absent a compelling state interest, qualified voters may not be excluded from an election unless their stake in the outcome is substantially smaller than that of the ones allowed to vote.

c. *Access to initiate the boundary change procedure is restricted.* As *Berry v. Bourne, supra,* illustrates, a number of state statutes provide that the annexation (and incorporation) process is initiated by the filing of a petition signed by a designated portion of those affected. The process is then completed in any one of several different ways — e.g., acceptance by resolution of the governing board of the annexing unit, election, or court review. Not infrequently, the petition must be signed by a stated percentage of the property owners or freeholders in the area to be annexed and, in some cases, the percentage is measured by the value of the property as well as the number of property owners. Clearly, if these percentages are high enough, this requirement enables the favored group to prevent a boundary change which others who are affected by it may favor — particularly if it is the only method provided for initiating the change. For discussion, see 88 HARV. L. REV. at 1604-09. Consider, for example, the incorporation involved in the *Curtis* case. If, instead of the protest procedure, the petition requirement for initiating the incorporation had been fifty-one percent of the landowners by assessed valuation, the same group whose protest blocked the incorporation could have achieved the same result. Several courts have addressed this issue. In *Torres v. Village of Capitan,* 582 P.2d 1277 (N.M. 1978), the New Mexico statute permitted annexation of contiguous property upon the filing of a petition signed by the owners of a majority of acres in the area proposed to be annexed. There was no provision for an election, and the process apparently was completed by acceptance by the city council. The court upheld the procedure, reasoning that petitioning for annexation is not a fundamental voting right and therefore not subject to strict scrutiny. It noted respectable authority to the contrary, citing *Curtis.*

Accord Doenges v. City of Salt Lake City, 614 P.2d 1237 (Utah 1980) (annexation initiated by petition signed by majority of property owners, owning at least one third of the property in value); *Township of Jefferson v. City of West Carrollton,* 517 F. Supp. 417 (S.D. Ohio 1981) (the signing of a petition to annex is not a voting rights issue but only a condition precedent to bringing the matter before the county commission which makes the decision).

d. *Voters in the annexation area and in the annexing city are permitted to vote on the annexation, but their votes are aggregated.* In *Capella v. City of Gainesville,* 377 So. 2d 658 (Fla. 1979), the court rejected a constitutional challenge to aggregated voting, relying in part on *Hunter. Accord Wall v. Board of Elections,* 250 S.E.2d 408 (Ga. 1978).

e. *Voting in special district elections is limited to property owners.* Courts reach different conclusions in applying the *Salyer* tests to the exclusion of nonproperty owners from elections involving special districts. *See supra* and *compare Chesser v. Buchanan,* 568 P.2d 39 (Colo. 1977) (Moffat Tunnel Improvement District meets *Salyer* tests), *with In re Extension of Boundaries of Glaize Creek Sewer District,* 574 S.W.2d 357 (Mo. 1978) (sewer district election does not fall within *Salyer* exception).

f. *An election is required either in the annexing city or the area to be annexed, but not in both.* Annexation statutes commonly provide for an election to be held in the area to be annexed, following adoption by the governing body of the annexing city of a resolution or ordinance proposing the annexation. While the voters of the annexing city do not have a direct vote on the issue, it can be argued that their interests are reflected in the vote of their elected representatives. In *Murphy v. Kansas City,* 347 F. Supp. 837 (W.D. Mo. 1972), residents of the annexing city could vote on the issue because annexation was accomplished by means of an amendment to the city charter. Residents of the area to be annexed, however, had no vote. The court rejected their equal protection claim, relying principally on *Hunter.*

A NOTE ON THE QUALITY OF REPRESENTATION

In the course of state legislative and local government reapportionment litigation, as well as in the myriad of related voting rights cases, it became evident that equal voting power for equal numbers of people — the primary goal of *Reynolds* and one person-one vote — was only the beginning. More subtle challenges were mounted to legislative apportionment plans which brought to the surface issues of fair representation, or the quality of representation.

Frequently, but not invariably, the issues arose where there were allegations of racial or ethnic discrimination: often at-large voting or multimember districts were the pattern. Many of these cases would undoubtedly have been brought in any event (e.g., *Gomillion),* but enactment by Congress of the Voting Rights Act of 1965 added an incentive as well as a statutory procedure for attacking racial malapportionment and inequality of representation.

It is beyond the limitations of this casebook to explore in detail the complex, fascinating and murky legal corners of fair representation. Only a few major developments affecting local governments will be noted. A simple example will illustrate the problem. Assume a large city governed by a city council of ten members. The population of the city is sixty percent white, forty percent black, both groups living in relatively segregated areas. If the council is elected from single-member districts, the minority black population might well elect four representatives — depending, of course, on how the district lines are drawn and other factors. If, on the other hand, the council members are elected at large — and racial bloc voting occurs — the black population could find itself with no representation on the council. There is no violation of one person-one vote in the at-large election: every voter has equal voting power. But every group does not have equal representation of its interests.

Challenges to at-large voting or multimember districts (which have similar effects) have been before the courts on many occasions. Their status is far from resolved, but the Supreme Court has offered some guidelines. Multimember districts are not per se unconstitutional, and it must be shown that they unconstitutionally operated to dilute or cancel the voting strength of racial or political elements. *Whitcomb v. Chavis,* 403 U.S. 124 (1971). Where that showing is made, the court may invalidate their use and order single-member districts. *White v. Regester,* 412 U.S. 755 (1973) (state legislative multimember districts effectively excluded blacks and Mexican-Americans from access to the political process). Where the reapportionment plan is court-ordered rather than initiated by a legislative body, single-member districts are to be preferred absent unusual circumstances. *Chapman v. Meier,* 420 U.S. 1 (1975) (state legislature); *East Carroll Parish School Board v. Marshall,* 424 U.S. 636 (1976) (county governing board).

Most of the cases dealing with the validity of multimember districts and at-large voting were triggered by a reapportionment of state legislative or local governing body districts. The plans were then reviewed under fourteenth amendment equal protection standards or pursuant to § 5 of the Voting Rights Act of 1965, 42 U.S.C. § 1973c, in the case of the states and parts thereof which are required to preclear any changes in voting or election laws with the Attorney General or the federal court in the District of Columbia. *See Allen v. State Board of Elections,* 393 U.S. 544 (1969); *Georgia v. United States,* 411 U.S. 526 (1973); *City of Port Arthur v. United States,* 103 S. Ct. 530 (1982). In *City of Rome v. United States,* 446 U.S. 156 (1980), the Court confirmed that § 5 requires preclearance of changes made in the at-large method of electing members of the Rome, Georgia, city commission which were found to have the effect of abridging the voting rights of black residents. The Court also reaffirmed that § 5 outlaws voting practices that are discriminatory either in purpose or in effect, whether or not the fifteenth amendment, under which Congress acted, reaches effect as well as intent.

The trigger does not work, however, for the large number of local governments, particularly municipalities, which have had an at-large voting system in place for some time. One study reported that 63.7% of the cities reporting used at-large voting; the number was even higher (67.4%) for cities between 25,000 and 50,000 population; and only in cities over 500,000 was the ward system dominant (68.8%). 1979 Municipal Year Book 99. *See* Note, *Tracking the Court Through a Political Thicket: At-Large Election Systems and Minority Vote Dilution,* 23 URB. L. ANN. 227, 230 n.17 (1982). The in-place at-large elections in these municipalities can, however, be challenged under the fourteenth and fifteenth amendments as well as under § 2 of the Voting Rights Act, 42 U.S.C. § 1973. Unlike § 5 (the preclearance provision), § 2 is not limited to the "covered" jurisdictions, most of them in the south, which had a history of discrimination. Section 2 prohibits any voting practice which denies or abridges the right to vote on account of race, color, or language (added in 1975).

The scope of § 2 was significantly restricted by the Supreme Court's 1980 decision in *City of Mobile v. Bolden,* 446 U.S. 55. At issue was the validity under the fourteenth and fifteenth amendments and § 2 of the Voting Rights Act of Mobile's long established system of electing all three members of the governing commission at large. Since 1911, when the at-large system was established, no black had ever been elected to the city commission. A deeply divided Court rejected the challenge. A majority of the Justices apparently agreed that the fourteenth amendment requires discriminatory intent in a racial voting dilution case, but one of that "majority," Justice White, dissented, because in his view the totality of facts supported an inference of purposeful discrimination. That is the standard of *White v. Regester,* and "[t]he Court's decision is flatly inconsistent with *White v. Regester." Id.* at 94. A plurality of the Court held that purposeful discrimination is also an essential ingredient in a fifteenth amendment challenge; that same plurality apparently would also hold that the fifteenth amendment protects only "pure" voting rights, i.e., access to the ballot, but does not extend to dilution cases such as this. The Voting Rights Act claim was disposed of quickly: Section 2 of the Act tracks the fifteenth amendment and adds nothing to the claim under that amendment.

Congress, which had under consideration extension of the Voting Rights Act, parts of which were due to expire in August 1982, rejected the *Mobile* plurality opinion as a "marked departure" from preexisting law in requiring discriminatory intent in fifteenth amendment and § 2 dilution cases. To underscore its point, Congress revised § 2 to read as follows:

> Sec. 2. (a) No voting qualification or prerequisite to voting or standard, practice, or procedure shall be imposed or applied by any State or political subdivision in a manner which results in a denial or abridgement of the right of any citizen of the United States to vote on account of race or color, or in contravention of the guarantees set forth in section 4(f)(2), as provided in subsection (b).
>
> (b) A violation of subsection (a) is established if, based on the totality of circumstances, it is shown that the political processes leading to nomination or election in the State or political subdivision are not equally open to participation by members of a class of citizens protected by subsection (a) in that its members have less opportunity than other members of the electorate to participate in the political process and to elect representatives of their choice. The extent to which members of a protected class have been elected to office in the State or political subdivision is one circumstance which may be considered: *Provided,* That nothing in this section establishes a right to have members of a protected class elected in numbers equal to their proportion in the population.

Voting Rights Act Amendments of 1982, Pub. L. No. 97-205, § 3, 96 Stat. 134, approved June 29, 1982. The Senate report explained:

> The "results" standard is meant to restore the pre-*Mobile* legal standard which governed cases challenging election systems or practices as an illegal dilution of the minority vote. Specifically, subsection (b) embodies the test laid down by the Supreme Court in *White.* [*White v. Regester.* —Eds.]

S. Rep. No. 97-147, 97th Cong., 2d Sess. 27, reprinted in [1982] U.S. Code Cong. & Ad. News 205.

Curiously, just two days after the Voting Rights Act extension was approved, the Supreme Court held, in a case similar to *Mobile,* that the at-large election of county commissioners in Burke County, Georgia, was "maintained for the purpose of denying blacks equal access to the political processes in the county." *Rogers v. Herman Lodge,* 102 S. Ct. 3272 (1982). The decision (by a clear majority of six Justices) rested on the fourteenth amendment alone; the Court declined to pass on the fifteenth amendment claim or on § 2 of the Voting Rights Act. While the majority opinion purported to be consistent with its prior rulings requiring specific intent, it clearly approved the use of non-direct circumstantial evidence to support the finding. The fact that Justice White wrote the majority opinion, having dissented in *Mobile,* further suggests that the Court returned to the standard of *White v. Regester,* at least for fourteenth amendment purposes.

One of the preeminent scholars of the reapportionment saga, the late Professor Robert G. Dixon, Jr., once complained that: "It [the Court] has centered on something called 'equality'; it has never come to grips with 'representation' "; and " 'Equal population' districting is an objective concept. But it has no necessary relation to any particular quality of political *representation."* Dixon, *The Warren Court Crusade for the Holy Grail of "One Man-One Vote,"* 1969 SUP. CT. REV. 227, 268. The question might well be asked whether it is properly the Court's role to define the elusive concept of fair representation.

The literature on fair representation is extensive. *See, e.g.,* REPRESENTATION AND REDISTRICTING ISSUES Part II (B. Grofman, A. Lijphart, R. McKay & H. Scarrow eds. 1982); Clinton, *Further Explorations in the Political Thicket: The Gerrymander and the Constitution,* 59 IOWA L. REV. 1 (1973); Note, *Tracking the Court Through a Political Thicket: At-Large Election Systems and Minority Vote Dilution,* 23 URB. L. ANN. 227 (1982); Comment, *Racial Vote Dilution in Multimember Districts: The Constitutional Standard After Washington v. Davis,* 76 MICH. L. REV. 694 (1978); Comment, *Constitutional Challenges to Gerrymanders,* 45 U. CHI. L. REV. 845 (1978); Comment, *Challenges to At-Large Election Plans: Modern Local Government on Trial,* 47 U. CIN. L. REV. 64 (1978); Note, *Group Representation and Race Conscious Apportionment: The Roles of States and the Federal Courts,* 91 HARV. L. REV. 1847 (1978); Note, *United Jewish Organizations v. Carey and the Need to Recognize Aggregate Voting Rights,* 87 YALE L.J. 571 (1978).

2. SCHOOL FINANCE

The school finance reform movement which began in the late 1960s and early 1970s focused a spotlight on more issues of fundamental importance to state and local government than perhaps any other dispute in recent history: the priority of universal public education; the responsibility of the public schools (what should we expect of them); where "control" of the schools should rest; where the financial obligation for the public school system should rest; the most appropriate tax package to pay for state and local government; inequities in the incidence of the property tax and the assessment practices on which it is based; and, finally, the extent to which the courts should intervene to help resolve major issues of public policy.

The search for a rational system of financing public education was not itself new.[6] For a variety of reasons, however, in the late 1960s the search acquired an

---

[6] Important contributions were made by E. Cubberley, School Funds and Their Apportionment (1905); G. Strayer & R. Haig, Financing of Education in the State of New York (1923); P. Mort, W. Reusser & J. Polley, Public School Finance (3d ed. 1960); C. Benson, The Economics of Public Education (1961).

intensity that has led to the involvement of almost every group with an intellectual or action-oriented interest: educators, economists, as well as taxpayers, political scientists, lawyers, politicians, the courts. Books, articles in professional journals and law review analyses — too numerous to cite — have been written on one or another of the issues.

While it is difficult to select only a few, among the more influential writings in terms of the legal challenge to school finance were: Horowitz, *Unseparate But Unequal — The Emerging Fourteenth Amendment Issue in Public Education*, 13 U.C.L.A. L. REV. 1147 (1966) (concerned primarily with inequalities between individual schools in advantaged and disadvantaged areas within a school district); Horowitz & Neitring, *Equal Protection Aspects of Inequalities in Public Education and Public Assistance Programs from Place to Place Within a State*, 15 U.C.L.A. L. REV. 787 (1968); A. WISE, RICH SCHOOLS, POOR SCHOOLS (1968), based on his earlier article, *Is Denial of Equal Educational Opportunity Constitutional?* 13 ADMR'S NOTEBOOK 2 (U. Chi. 1965), and his unpublished doctoral dissertation at the University of Chicago, The Constitution and Equality: Wealth, Geography and Educational Opportunity (1967) (the 1965 article was probably the first published challenge to school financing as a violation of equal protection); J. COONS, W. CLUNE & S. SUGARMAN, PRIVATE WEALTH AND PUBLIC EDUCATION (1970) [hereinafter cited as J. COONS et al., PRIVATE WEALTH], and their earlier article, *Educational Opportunity: A Workable Test for State Financial Structures,* 57 CALIF. L. REV. 305 (1969); THE QUALITY OF INEQUALITY: SUBURBAN AND URBAN PUBLIC SCHOOLS (C. Daly ed. 1968) (papers presented at a conference at the University of Chicago Center for Policy Study).

What differentiated the more recent period of concern for the cost and availability of public school education from the others was the involvement of the courts. By the late 1960s great issues of public policy were not just debated; they were taken to court. The efforts to develop constitutional theories to challenge the existing structure of school finance, it is fair to say, contributed greatly both to the ferment for change and to a broader understanding of the nature and impact of that system.

Beginning in 1968 — the year when suits were filed in Michigan, Illinois, Virginia, Texas and California, challenging the constitutional validity of those states' school finance systems — the courts have been deeply involved in the school finance movement. Whether or not they should be and what demands that participation may place on them are among the questions which students should consider as they review the materials that follow.

First, it is necessary to describe how the schools were — and, to a considerable extent, still are — financed. The two dominant characteristics were: (1) heavy reliance on the locally based property tax and (2) distribution of state aid to school districts by means of what is termed the foundation plan.

(1) *Source of funds.* The federal, state and local levels of government all contribute to the cost of public education in the United States. Their respective proportions and the sources of the funds are shown in the following estimates for the school year 1971-72, which was at the beginning of the school finance reform movement.

ESTIMATED PUBLIC SCHOOL REVENUE AND NONREVENUE RECEIPTS, BY LEVEL OF GOVERNMENT AND SOURCE, 1971-72 SCHOOL YEAR

Thousand of Dollars

Level of government and source	Amount	Percent from source	Percent of total
Local, total	28,033.0	100.0	54.7
Property taxes	23,000.0	82.0	44.9
Other taxes	469.4	1.7	0.9
Fees and charges	1,895.8	6.8	3.7
Borrowing	2,667.8	9.5	5.2
State, total	19,877.8	100.0	38.8
Sales taxes	9,477.7	47.7	18.5
Income taxes	4,940.5	24.9	9.6
Other taxes	2,720.3	13.7	5.3
Miscellaneous, fees, and other	2,739.3	13.8	5.4
Federal, total	3,305.7	100.0	6.5
Personal income tax	1,990.0	60.2	3.9
Corporate income tax	690.9	20.9	1.3
Other	624.8	18.9	1.2
All levels	51,216.5		100.0

Source: R. REISCHAUER & R. HARTMAN, REFORMING SCHOOL FINANCE, at 6 (1973).

Even before the activity of the 1970s, the local share of school funding had declined substantially over the years, due to increased state aid and the enactment of federal aid programs, particularly the Elementary and Secondary Education Act of 1965.

PERCENTAGE OF FUNDS ALLOCATED TO PUBLIC SCHOOLS BY LEVEL OF GOVERNMENT . . . VARIOUS YEARS, 1929-30 TO 1969-70 SCHOOL YEARS

Level of government or state	1929-30	1939-40	1949-50	1959-60	1965-66	1969-70
Percentage of funds allocated to public schools						
Local	82.7	67.9	57.3	56.5	53.0	52.7
State	17.0	30.3	39.8	39.1	39.1	40.7
Federal	0.3	1.8	2.9	4.4	7.9	6.6
All levels	100.0	100.0	100.0	100.0	100.0	100.0
Percentage of total allocations derived from state sources						
Idaho	7.7	10.7	23.5	27.6	39.1	43.2
Delaware	87.9	84.4	83.5	82.5	79.7	70.6
Iowa	4.3	1.1	19.1	12.0	12.5	30.1
New Mexico	21.8	45.3	86.0	74.4	63.5	62.7
Oklahoma	10.6	34.0	56.5	27.7	27.9	40.8
Wyoming	27.1	4.3	42.0	47.5	39.2	25.4

Id. at 5. The local share has declined still further as a result of legislative changes in the following decade (*see* Note on Legislative Response, *infra*). The percentage distribution within individual states varies greatly from a low for the local contribution of 2.6% (Hawaii) to a high of 88.7% (New Hampshire).

As these tables indicate, the largest single source of revenue for schools was the property tax. That was an important factor in the movement for reform. In addition to its role in financing education, the property tax was also the major source of locally raised revenue for the other major services provided at the local level of government. It had, moreover, long been the most unpopular form of taxation in the minds of taxpayers[7] and many economists. Its visibility is undoubtedly one reason; another is the widely held view that the property tax is regressive: that is, the burden is disproportionate to one's rung on the economic ladder.[8] Given the fact that over fifty-five percent of property tax collections go to the schools, it was not difficult to postulate that genuine property tax relief required a change in the method of financing public education.

(2) *Forms of state aid.* The second common denominator in school financing was the means by which state aid was distributed to local school units. (In most states the unit is a separate school district; in some, however, the schools are operated by a municipality or another unit of local government.) Curiously enough for a reform movement having as its objective equality of educational opportunity,[9] the major existing plan for dispensing state aid — against which the reform was mounted — was itself designed to equalize.

In order to provide perspective on state aid to schools, Professors Coons, Clune and Sugarman, with appropriate editorializing, described the conditions in which it developed:

The Original Compromise in Public Education

By the turn of the century the pattern of American life had already been deeply affected by the industrial revolution. One crucial consequence was the dramatic variation in wealth between geographic regions. As a secondary and less visible result, the then fledgling institution of locally financed public education was in danger of being turned into an engine for oppression of the poor, as pernicious in its effects as the exclusive private education of earlier days which it had begun to replace. Localism by itself already was failing spectacularly to provide the needed solution.

. . . .

In order to appreciate the first state aid movements that consolidated in about 1906, we must examine briefly the early character of public education and the clash of philosophies in which it was born. The spirit of that clash is difficult to recreate. For us today the appellation "public" may suggest merely the contrast with "private"; it does not necessarily suggest the nineteenth-century perspective that "public" meant for all the people and not merely the privileged few. Even seeing this does not expose the precise character of the struggle; it is hard to set aside our preoccupation today with the parochial-public school contrast. The real issue in the nineteenth century common school movement was the finance question: in short, taxes. The great school debate concerned whether it was moral, right, democratic, and constitutional to make schools a function of government, thereby forcing nonconsenting, nonusing taxpayers to support them.

Prior to the great reform, education was a private affair for both rich and poor. The elite went to truly private schools and the poor were left essentially with the charity school (financed by the rich) and the rate-bill school (the rate-bill was a tuition-like device which "taxed" the parents of attending chil-

---

[7] That perception has changed in recent years. According to the Advisory Commission on Intergovernmental Relations' annual poll, the property tax was considered the worst (that is, least fair) tax in five of the ten years in which the poll was conducted beginning in 1972. In the four most recent years, however, (1979-82) the federal income tax has moved into first place: In 1982 it ranked first in thirty-six percent of the responses; the local property tax, first in thirty percent. ACIR, Changing Public Attitudes on Government and Taxes 4 (1982).

[8] For an analysis of the "revisionist" view of this proposition, see, e.g., H. Aaron, Who Pays the Property Tax? (1975).

[9] In this context "equality of educational opportunity" is used in the sense of equal inputs which, generally, though not inevitably, translates into equal expenditures per pupil. That this is not the only definition of the expression is elaborated by Arthur Wise in Rich Schools, Poor Schools, see *supra*.

dren).... What was urgently needed was a redistribution of educational resource, from taxpayers without school children to those with and from rich to poor. A true tax, a general tax, was called for; education, to the reformers, had to become a public function.

From the outset the change was resisted by property owners whose steady counter-force was reflected in the shape and implementation of the reforms, which were grudging and gradual. One of the first concessions by state governments was to permit local communities to organize schools which would have the power to tax consenting residents.... The first crisp and meaningful step was to permit localities to organize districts to tax nonconsenting adults; and finally, of course, to *require* the districts to be organized and to commence taxing.

What is instructive in this process is the unwillingness of the state government to assume the function of education. The reformers' plea was made directly to the state — the entity with power to organize a school system; but the response came in the form of delegation of primary responsibility to the smallest possible local unit — first the individual and then the local community. This vigorous buck-passing was in substantial degree ideological at root. Education was thought to be the sphere of the individual and every related act of government a potential intrusion. Pressed to take on the function of education, but strongly opposed by powerful citizens espousing an individualistic philosophy, the legislatures sought and found the smallest workable unit for the task — a solution perhaps dictated by subsidiarity.[10]

At that point, the systems stabilized in a compromise between subsidiarity and equality — a compromise that was expressed in the balance of the school districts' relative autonomy on one hand and its duty to educate all children on the other. Given a relative uniformity of wealth and population distribution, the system was tolerable. Economic revolution swiftly turned the compromise into a Frankenstein.

....

... The result was that many localities found themselves wholly unable to finance adequate education.

The extent of this underfinancing can be seen from statistics gathered by this century's first great reformer, Ellwood P. Cubberley.[16] Poor districts were forced to tax their wealth at many times the rate of rich districts but gleaned only a fraction of what their neighbors produced with a lighter burden. According to the custom of the early part of this century, when funds dried up the poor districts simply closed their meager schools....

The reformers who have come forward in this century ... have succeeded in evoking modest steps by state governments toward the ideal of redistributing educational resources. Their solutions are always measures superimposed upon the old system, the new commitment of the state coming in the form of state aid, generally gathered from statewide taxes, to supple-

---

[10] ["Subsidiarity," as used by the authors, embraces the "principle that government should ordinarily leave decision-making and administration to the smallest unit of society competent to handle them." *Id.* at 14. — Eds.]

[16] Cubberley was both an eminent historian of education and a theoretician of educational finance. His work in the area of state aid to education was conintued by Paul R. Mort and his associates. See E. P. Cubberley, Public Education in the United States: A Study and Interpretation of American Educational History (Boston, 1919); Readings in Public Education in the United States: A Collection of Sources and Readings to Illustrate the History of Educational Practice and Progress in the United States (Boston, 1934); and the frequently cited *School Funds*. [Cited *supra*. — Eds.]

ment the revenues of localities unable to support adequate public schools on their own.

J. Coons et al., Private Wealth, *supra,* at 45-51 (most footnotes omitted).

Indeed, the authors noted: "The story of public education for the first sixty-nine years of the twentieth century is not one of basic reform, but merely that of increasing marginal state aid to local schools." *Id.* at 46. The two principal formulas that were designed to improve the capacity of school districts, especially poorer ones, to provide education were the flat grant and the foundation plan. It was Ellwood Cubberley who advocated the flat grant early in this century. The name is a fairly accurate description: the state pays to the school district a set amount per unit of measure, which could be per classroom, or per teacher, but more commonly, as the plan grew, was per pupil in average daily attendance (ADA). The second and more famous of the plans was that proposed by G. Strayer and R. Haig for use in New York. It is variously known as the foundation plan, the Strayer-Haig formula, or, by many states, as their equalization aid. By the time the school finance reform movement became active, the Strayer-Haig formula, frequently combined with a flat grant, was the method of distributing state aid in most states including Illinois and California whose plans were at issue in the *McInnis* and *Serrano* cases, *infra.* There were of course many variations — probably no two states had identical formulas — but even in states which did not have a pure Strayer-Haig (Texas, for example, which was the subject of the *Rodriguez* case, *infra),* the effect on the availability of school funds in local school districts was substantially the same. That effect will appear in the cases reported below.

In simplified form, the foundation plan works as follows. The state sets a foundation level, which is the minimum expenditure guaranteed to every school district. Assume that it is $500 for every pupil in average daily attendance (ADA) and that this state also includes in its formula a flat grant of $50 per pupil in ADA. In order to qualify for state aid, the school district is required to impose a minimum property tax rate of 10 mills, or $1 per $100 of assessed valuation (AV). (In some cases the rate is assumed for computational purposes.) Now assume two school districts: District A has an assessed valuation (AV) of $10,000 per pupil in ADA (computed by dividing the total district AV of $10 million by the number of pupils, 1000, in ADA); District B has an AV of $50,000 per pupil in ADA. The formula would produce these results:

District A

$10,000 AV per pupil	
Qualifying tax rate raises	$100 in local funds
State flat grant adds	50
	150
Foundation level guarantees	$500
	-150
State equalization aid	$350
Total available at qualifying rate	= $500

District B

$50,000 AV per pupil
Qualifying tax rate raises $500 in local funds
State flat grant adds   50
                                                                                $550
District B receives no equalization aid
Total available at qualifying rate   = $550

Next assume both districts choose to impose a 20 mill tax rate, 10 mills in excess of the qualifying rate:

District A

Qualifying tax rate raises	$100
plus flat grant	50
plus equalization	350
Additional property tax of 10 mills raises	100
Total available to spend	$600

District B

Qualifying tax rate raises	$500
plus flat grant	50
Additional property tax rate of 10 mills raises	500
Total available to spend	$1050

Note these characteristics of the formula: the foundation plan has some equalizing effect under the figures used in the example; the flat grant adds nothing to District A's state aid because it is effectively absorbed in the equalization aid; at identical tax rates above the minimum qualifying rate, District A falls farther behind District B in the amount of funds raised, or, to reverse the equation, District B can spend more with less effort. While some states imposed maximum tax rates on school districts, they normally were in excess of the qualifying rate, and, in any event, could usually be overriden by referendum.

Two additional points should be noted. First, a number of states recognized that some groups of students cost more to educate than others and that there are geographical cost differentials. These differences might be addressed either in separate categorical grant programs (e.g., for special education or compensatory education) or by weighting the formula to produce a higher yield (e.g., for high school students). The add-ons, however, were not generally designed to relate to the variances in district wealth. Second, while interdistrict disparities vary among the states, those used in the example are by no means the extremes either in district wealth or in expenditures — as the cases reported below will show.

a. *McInnis* and Educational Needs

McINNIS v. SHAPIRO

United States District Court
293 F. Supp. 327 (N.D. Ill. 1968), aff'd sub nom.
McInnis v. Ogilvie, 394 U.S. 322 (1969)

DECKER, DISTRICT JUDGE.
This is a suit filed by a number of high school and elementary school students

attending school within four school districts of Cook County, Illinois, on behalf of themselves and all others similarly situated challenging the constitutionality of various state statutes dealing with the financing of the public school system.

Plaintiffs claim that these statutes violate their fourteenth amendment rights to equal protection and due process because they permit wide variations in the expenditures per student from district to district, thereby providing some students with a good education and depriving others, who have equal or greater educational need. Plaintiffs claim to be members of this disadvantaged group.

To correct this inequitable situation, they seek a declaration that the statutes are unconstitutional and a permanent injunction forbidding further distribution of tax funds in reliance on these laws.

The defendants are state officials charged with the administration of the legislation which allegedly permits this discrimination.

A three-judge district court was convened pursuant to 28 U.S.C. §§ 2281 and 2284. Defendants then moved to dismiss the complaint (1) for lack of jurisdiction and (2) for failure to state a cause of action.

We conclude that we have jurisdiction. After examining the complaint, and studying the extensive briefs filed by the respective parties as well as the brief of the *amici curiae,* we further conclude that no cause of action is stated for two principal reasons: (1) the Fourteenth Amendment does not require that public school expenditures be made only on the basis of pupils' educational needs,[4] and (2) the lack of judicially manageable standards makes this controversy nonjusticiable. After explaining the structure of the existing Illinois legislation, this opinion will discuss these two conclusions in detail.

. . . .

II. The Financing of Illinois' Public Schools

The General Assembly has delegated authority to local school districts to raise funds by levying a tax on all property within the district. In addition, the school districts may issue bonds for constructing and repairing their buildings. Legislation limits both the maximum indebtedness and the maximum tax rate which localities may impose for educational purposes. In 1966-67, the approximately 1300 districts had roughly $840 per pupil with which to educate their students, of which about 75% came from local sources, 20% was derived from state aid, and 5% was supplied by the federal government. Since the financial ability of the individual districts varies substantially, per pupil expenditures vary between $480 and $1,000. . . . [A] state common school fund supplements each district's local property tax revenues, guaranteeing a foundation level of $400 per student. The common school fund has two main components: (1) a flat grant to districts for each pupil, and (2) an equalization grant awarded to each district which levies a minimum property tax rate.[8] The equalization grant is calculated on the assumption that the district only assesses the minimum rate. Total reve-

---

[4] While the complaining students repeatedly emphasize the importance of pupils' "educational needs," they do not offer a definition of this nebulous concept. Presumably, "educational need" is a conclusory term, reflecting the interaction of several factors such as the quality of teachers, the students' potential, prior education, environmental and parental upbringing, and the school's physical plant. Evaluation of these variables necessarily requires detailed research and study, with concomitant decentralization so each school and pupil may be individually evaluated. . . .

[8] Over 97% of the districts qualify for the equalization grant. The flat grant, accounting for about one-third of the state aid, is now $47 per elementary student and $54.05 per high school pupil.

nues from the state common school fund account for about 15% — 18% of all districts' income.

The local tax revenue per student which is necessarily generated by the preceding minimum rate is added to the flat grant per pupil. If this sum is less than $400, the difference is the equalization grant. Therefore, every district levying the minimum rate is assured of at least $400 per child. On the other hand, if a locality desires to tax itself more heavily than the minimum rate, it is not penalized by having the additional revenue considered before determination of the equalization grant. Since the hypothetical calculation uses the same tax rate for all localities, the assumed revenue per child depends upon the total assessed property value in a district and the number of students. Thus, the equalization grant tends to compensate for variations in property value per pupil from one district to another.

Finally, numerous special programs, both state and federal, supply about 10% of the districts' revenues. This "categorical aid" is allocated for particular purposes such as bus transportation or assistance to handicapped and disadvantaged children. Plaintiffs do not challenge these programs, conceding that they are rationally related to the educational needs of the students.

III. The Fourteenth Amendment: Equal Protection and Due Process

The underlying rationale of the complaint is that *only* a financing system which apportions public funds according to the educational needs of the students satisfies the Fourteenth Amendment.[11] Plaintiffs assert that the distribution of school revenues to satisfy these needs should not be limited by such arbitrary factors as variations in local property values or differing tax rates.

Clearly, there are wide variations in the amount of money available for Illinois' school districts, both on a per pupil basis and in absolute terms. Presumably, students receiving a $1000 education are better educated than those acquiring a $600 schooling. While the inequalities of the existing arrangement are readily apparent, the crucial question is whether it is unconstitutional. Since nearly three-quarters of the revenue comes from local property taxes, substantially equal revenue distribution would require revamping this method of taxation, with the result that districts with greater property values per student would help support the poorer districts.

A. Social Policy

While the state common school fund tends to compensate for the variations in school districts' assessed valuation per pupil, variation in actual expenditures remains approximately 3.0 to 1, 2.6 to 1, and 1.7 to 1 for elementary, high school and unit districts respectively. Though districts with lower property valuations usually levy higher tax rates, there is a limit to the amount of money which they can raise, especially since they are limited by maximum indebtedness and tax

---

[11] Although plaintiffs stress the alleged denial of equal protection, they seek relief resembling substantive due process. Surely, quality education for all is more desirable than uniform, mediocre instruction. Yet if the Constitution only commands that all children be treated equally, the latter result would satisfy the Fourteenth Amendment. Certainly, parents who cherish education are constitutionally allowed to spend more money on their children's schools, be it by private instruction or higher tax rates, than those who do not value education so highly. Thus, the students' goal is presumably a judicial pronouncement that each pupil is entitled to a minimum level of educational expenditures, which would be significantly higher than the existing $400.

rates. Plaintiffs argue that state statutes authorizing these wide variations in assessed value per student are irrational, thus violating the due process clause. Moreover, under the equal protection clause, the students contend that the importance of education to the welfare of individuals and the nation requires the courts to invalidate the legislation if potential, alternative statutes incorporating the desirable aspects of the present system can also achieve substantially equal per pupil expenditures.

Illustrating how the school financing could be improved, plaintiffs suggest two alternatives: (1) all students might receive the same dollar appropriations, or (2) the state could siphon off all money in excess of $ X per pupil which was produced by a given tax rate, in effect eliminating variations in local property values while leaving the districts free to establish their own tax rate.

Without doubt, the educational potential of each child should be cultivated to the utmost, and the poorer school districts should have more funds with which to improve their schools. But the allocation of public revenues is a basic policy decision more appropriately handled by a legislature than a court. To illustrate, the following considerations might be relevant to a financing scheme: state-wide variations in costs and salaries, the relative efficiency of school districts, and the need for local experimentation.

. . . .

In the instant case, the General Assembly's delegation of authority to school districts appears designed to allow individual localities to determine their own tax burden according to the importance which they place upon public schools. Moreover, local citizens must select which municipal services they value most highly. While some communities might place heavy emphasis on schools, other may cherish police protection or improved roads. The state legislature's decision to allow local choice and experimentation is reasonable, especially since the common school fund assures a minimum of $400 per student.

Plaintiffs stress the inequality inherent in having school funds partially determined by a pupil's place of residence, but this is an inevitable consequence of decentralization. The students also object to having revenues related to property values, apparently without realizing that the equalization grant effectively tempers variations in assessed value by using a hypothetical calculation. Furthermore, the flat grants and state and federal categorical aid reduce the school's dependence on local taxes. . . .

IV. Lack of Judicially Manageable Standards

Even if the Fourteenth Amendment required that expenditures be made only on the basis of pupils' educational needs, this controversy would be nonjusticiable. While the complaint does not present a "political question" in the traditional sense of the term, there are no "discoverable and manageable standards" by which a court can determine when the Constitution is satisfied and when it is violated.

The only possible standard is the rigid assumption that each pupil must receive the same dollar expenditures. Expenses are not, however, the exclusive yardstick of a child's educational needs. Deprived pupils need more aid than fortunate ones. Moreover, a dollar spent in a small district may provide less education than one used in a large district. As stated above, costs vary substantially throughout the state. The desirability of a certain degree of local experimentation and local autonomy in education also indicates the impracticability of a single, simple formula. Effective, efficient administration necessitates decentralization so that local personnel, familiar with the immediate needs, can administer the school system. As new teaching methods are devised and as urban growth demands changed patterns of instruction, the only realistic way the state can adjust is through legislative study, discussion and continuing revision of the controlling statutes. Even if there were some guidelines available to the judiciary, the courts simply cannot provide the empirical research and consultation necessary for intelligent educational planning....

Plaintiffs have assumed that requiring expenditures to be related to the needs of the students will result in better education for deprived students without a corresponding decrease in the quality of education now offered by the affluent districts. The more money the latter districts must supply to the former, however, the less incentive the well-to-do will have to raise their tax rates. If the quality of good public schools declines, affluent children have the option to attend private schools, thus completely eliminating the need for the wealthy to raise taxes.

V. Conclusion

The present Illinois scheme for financing public education reflects a rational policy consistent with the mandate of the Illinois Constitution. Unequal educational expenditures per student, based upon the variable property values and tax rates of local school districts, do not amount to an invidious discrimination. Moreover, the statutes which permit these unequal expenditures on a district to district basis are neither arbitrary nor unreasonable.

There is no Constitutional requirement that public school expenditures be made only on the basis of pupils' educational needs without regard to the financial strength of local school districts. Nor does the Constitution establish the rigid guideline of equal dollar expenditures for each student.

Illinois' General Assembly has already recognized the need for additional educational funds to provide all students a good education. Furthermore, the legislative School Problems Commission assures a continuing and comprehensive study of the public schools' financial problems. If other changes are needed in the present system, they should be sought in the legislature and not in the courts. Plaintiffs have stated no grounds for judicial relief, and this cause must be dismissed.

b. *Serrano* **and District Wealth**

SERRANO v. PRIEST

Supreme Court of California
5 Cal. 3d 584, 96 Cal. Rptr. 601, 487 P.2d 1241 (1971)

SULLIVAN, JUSTICE.

We are called upon to determine whether the California public school financing system, with its substantial dependence on local property taxes and resultant wide disparities in school revenue, violates the equal protection clause of the Fourteenth Amendment. We have determined that this funding scheme invidiously discriminates against the poor because it makes the quality of a child's education a function of the wealth of his parents and neighbors. Recognizing as we must that the right to an education in our public schools is a fundamental interest which cannot be conditioned on wealth, we can discern no compelling state purpose necessitating the present method of financing. We have concluded, therefore, that such a system cannot withstand constitutional challenge and must fall before the equal protection clause.

Plaintiffs, who are Los Angeles County public school children and their parents, brought this class action for declaratory and injunctive relief against certain state and county officials charged with administering the financing of the California public school system. Plaintiff children claim to represent a class consisting of all public school pupils in California, "except children in that school district, the identity of which is presently unknown, which school district affords the greatest educational opportunity of all school districts within California." Plaintiff parents purport to represent a class of all parents who have children in the school system and who pay real property taxes in the county of their residence.

Defendants are the Treasurer, the Superintendent of Public Instruction, and the Controller of the State of California, as well as the Tax Collector and Treasurer, and the Superintendent of Schools of the County of Los Angeles. The county officials are sued both in their local capacities and as representatives of a class composed of the school superintendent, tax collector and treasurer of each of the other counties in the state.

The complaint sets forth three causes of action. The first cause alleges in substance as follows: Plaintiff children attend public elementary and secondary schools located in specified school districts in Los Angeles County. This public school system is maintained throughout California by a financing plan or scheme which relies heavily on local property taxes and causes substantial disparities among individual school districts in the amount of revenue available per pupil for the districts' educational programs. Consequently, districts with smaller tax bases are not able to spend as much money per child for education as districts with larger assessed valuations.

It is alleged that "As a direct result of the financing scheme . . . substantial disparities in the quality and extent of availability of educational opportunities exist and are perpetuated among the several school districts of the State. . . . [Par.] The educational opportunities made available to children attending public schools in the Districts, including plaintiff children, are substantially inferior to the educational opportunities made available to children attending public schools in many other districts of the State. . . ." The financing scheme thus fails to meet the requirements of the equal protection clause of the Fourteenth Amendment of the United States Constitution and the California Constitution in several specified respects.

In the second cause of action, plaintiff parents, after incorporating by reference all the allegations of the first cause, allege that as a direct result of the financing scheme they are required to pay a higher tax rate than taxpayers in many other school districts in order to obtain for their children the same or lesser educational opportunities afforded children in those other districts.

. . . .

Plaintiffs pray for: (1) a declaration that the present financing system is unconstitutional; (2) an order directing defendants to reallocate school funds in order to remedy this invalidity; and (3) an adjudication that the trial court retain jurisdiction of the action so that it may restructure the system if defendants and the state Legislature fail to act within a reasonable time.

All defendants filed general demurrers to the foregoing complaint asserting that none of the three claims stated facts sufficient to constitute a cause of action. The trial court sustained the demurrers with leave to amend. Upon plaintiffs' failure to amend, defendants' motion for dismissal was granted.... An order of dismissal was entered ... and this appeal followed.

Preliminarily we observe that in our examination of the instant complaint, we are guided by the long-settled rules for determining its sufficiency against a demurrer. We treat the demurrer as admitting all material facts properly pleaded, but not contentions, deductions or conclusions of fact or law....

I

We begin our task by examining the California public school financing system which is the focal point of the complaint's allegations. At the threshold we find a fundamental statistic — over 90 percent of our public school funds derive from two basic sources: (a) local district taxes on real property and (b) aid from the State School Fund.[2]

By far the major source of school revenue is the local real property tax. Pursuant to article IX, section 6 of the California Constitution, the Legislature has authorized the governing body of each county, and city and county, to levy taxes on the real property within a school district at a rate necessary to meet the district's annual education budget. (E.D. Code, § 20701 et seq.) The amount of revenue which a district can raise in this manner thus depends largely on its tax base — i. e., the assessed valuation of real property within its borders. Tax bases vary widely throughout the state; in 1969-1970, for example, the assessed valuation per unit of average daily attendance of elementary school children ranged from a low of $103 to a peak of $952,156 — a ratio of nearly 1 to 10,000....

The other factor determining local school revenue is the rate of taxation within the district. Although the Legislature has placed ceilings on permissible district tax rates (§ 20751 et seq.), these statutory maxima may be surpassed in a "tax override" election if a majority of the district's voters approve a higher rate. (§ 20803 et seq.) Nearly all districts have voted to override the statutory limits. Thus the locally raised funds which constitute the largest portion of school revenue are primarily a function of the value of the realty within a particular school district, coupled with the willingness of the district's residents to tax themselves for education.

Most of the remaining school revenue comes from the State School Fund pursuant to the "foundation program," through which the state undertakes to supplement local taxes in order to provide a "minimum amount of guaranteed support to all districts...." (§ 17300.) With certain minor exceptions, the foundation program ensures that each school district will receive annually, from state or local funds, $355 for each elementary school pupil (§§ 17656, 17660) and $488 for each high school student. (§ 17665.)

The state contribution is supplied in two principal forms. "Basic state aid" consists of a flat grant to each district of $125 per pupil per year, regardless of the releative wealth of the district. (Cal. Const., art. IX, § 6, par. 4; Ed. Code, §§ 17751, 17801.) "Equalization aid" is distributed in inverse proportion to the wealth of the district.

To compute the amount of equalization aid to which a district is entitled, the State Superintendent of Public Instruction first determines how much local

---

[2] California educational revenues for the fiscal year 1968-1969 came from the following sources: local property taxes, 55.7 percent; state aid, 35.5 percent; federal funds, 6.1 percent; miscellaneous sources, 2.7 percent....

property tax revenue would be generated if the district were to levy a hypothetical tax at a rate of $1 on each $100 of assessed valuation in elementary school districts and $.80 per $100 in high school districts. (§ 17702.) To that figure, he adds the $125 per pupil basic aid grant. If the sum of those two amounts is less than the foundation program minimum for that district, the state contributes the difference. (§§ 17901, 17902.) Thus, equalization funds guarantee to the poorer districts a basic minimum revenue, while wealthier districts are ineligible for such assistance.

An additional state program of "supplemental aid" is available to subsidize particularly poor school districts which are willing to make an extra local tax effort. An elementary district with an assessed valuation of $12,500 or less per pupil may obtain up to $125 more for each child if it sets its local tax rate above a certain statutory level. A high school district whose assessed valuation does not exceed $24,500 per pupil is eligible for a supplement of up to $72 per child if its local tax is sufficiently high. (§§ 17920-17926.)

Although equalization aid and supplemental aid temper the disparities which result from the vast variations in real property assessed valuation, wide differentials remain in the revenue available to individual districts and, consequently, in the level of educational expenditures.[9] For example, in Los Angeles County, where plaintiff children attend school, the Baldwin Park Unified School District expended only $577.49 to educate each of its pupils in 1968-1969; during the same year the Pasadena Unified School District spent $840.19 on every student; and the Beverly Hills Unified School District paid out $1,231.72 per child. . . . The source of these disparities is unmistakable: in Baldwin Park the assessed valuation per child totaled only $3,706; in Pasadena, assessed valuation was $13,706; while in Beverly Hills, the corresponding figure was $50,885 — a ratio of 1 to 4 to 13. . . . Thus, the state grants are inadequate to offset the inequalities inherent in a financing system based on widely varying local tax bases.

Furthermore, basic aid, which constitutes about half of the state educational funds . . . actually widens the gap between rich and poor districts. . . . Such aid is distributed on a uniform per pupil basis to all districts, irrespective of a district's wealth. Beverly Hills, as well as Baldwin Park, receives $125 from the state for each of its students.

For Baldwin Park the basic grant is essentially meaningless. Under the foundation program the state must make up the difference between $355 per elementary child and $47.91, the amount of revenue per child which Baldwin Park could raise by levying a tax of $1 per $100 of assessed valuation. Although

---

[9] Statistics compiled by the legislative analyst show the following range of assessed valuations per pupil for the 1969-1970 school year:

	Elementary	High School
Low	$103	$11,959
Median	19,600	41,300
High	952,156	349,093

Per pupil expenditures during that year also varied widely:

	Elementary	High School	Unified
Low	$407	$722	$612
Median	672	898	766
High	2,586	1,767	2,414

under present law, that difference is composed partly of basic aid and partly of equalization aid, if the basic aid grant did not exist, the district would still receive the same amount of state aid — all in equalizing funds.

For Beverly Hills, however, the $125 flat grant has real financial significance. Since a tax rate of $1 per $100 there would produce $870 per elementary student, Beverly Hills is far too rich to qualify for equalizing aid. Nevertheless, it still receives $125 per child from the state, thus enlarging the economic chasm between it and Baldwin Park. See Coons, Clune & Sugarman, Educational Opportunity: A Workable Constitutional Test for State Financial Structures (1969) 57 CAL. L. REV. 305, 315.

II

[In Part II the court rejected plaintiffs' claim that the school financing scheme violated the California constitutional provision requiring the legislature to provide for a system of free common schools. — Eds.]

III

Having disposed of these preliminary matters, we take up the chief contention underlying plaintiffs' complaint, namely that the California public school financing scheme violates the equal protection clause of the Fourteenth Amendment to the United States Constitution.[11]

As recent decisions of this court have pointed out, the United States Supreme Court has employed a two-level test for measuring legislative classifications against the equal protection clause. "In the area of economic regulation, the high court has exercised restraint, investing legislation with a presumption of constitutionality and requiring merely that distinctions drawn by a challenged statute bear some rational relationship to a conceivable legitimate state purpose. [Citations.]

"On the other hand, in cases involving 'suspect classifications' or touching on 'fundamental interests,' [fns. omitted] the court has adopted an attitude of active and critical analysis, subjecting the classification to strict scrutiny. [Citations.] Under the strict standard applied in such cases, the state bears the burden of establishing not only that it has a *compelling* interest which justifies the law but that the distinctions drawn by the law are *necessary* to further its purpose." . . .

---

[11] The complaint also alleges that the financing system violates article I, sections 11 and 21, of the California Constitution. Section 11 provides: "All laws of a general nature shall have a uniform operation." Section 21 states: "No special privileges or immunities shall ever be granted which may not be altered, revoked, or repealed by the Legislature; nor shall any citizen, or class of citizens, be granted privileges or immunities which, upon the same terms, shall not be granted to all citizens." We have construed these provisions as "substantially the equivalent" of the equal protection clause of the Fourteenth Amendment to the federal Constitution. . . . Consequently, our analysis of plaintiffs' federal equal protection contention is also applicable to their claim under these state constitutional provisions.

A

Wealth as a Suspect Classification

In recent years, the United States Supreme Court has demonstrated a marked antipathy toward legislative classifications which discriminate on the basis of certain "suspect" personal characteristics. One factor which has repeatedly come under the close scrutiny of the high court is wealth....

Plaintiffs contend that the school financing system classifies on the basis of wealth. We find this proposition irrefutable. As we have already discussed, over half of all educational revenue is raised locally by levying taxes on real property in the individual school districts. Above the foundation program minimum ($355 per elementary student and $488 per high school student), the wealth of a school district, as measured by its assessed valuation, is the major determinant of educational expenditures. Although the amount of money raised locally is also a function of the rate at which the residents of a district are willing to tax themselves, as a practical matter districts with small tax bases simply cannot levy taxes at a rate sufficient to produce the revenue that more affluent districts reap with minimal tax efforts.... For example, Baldwin Park citizens, who paid a school tax of $5.48 per $100 of assessed valuation in 1968-1969, were able to spend less than half as much on education as Beverly Hills residents, who were taxed only $2.38 per $100....

Defendants vigorously dispute the proposition that the financing scheme discriminates on the basis of wealth. Their first argument is essentially this: through *basic* aid, the state distributes school funds equally to all pupils; through *equalization* aid, it distributes funds in a manner beneficial to the poor districts. However, state funds constitute only one part of the entire school fiscal system. The foundation program partially alleviates the great disparities in local sources of revenue, but the system as a whole generates school revenue in proportion to the wealth of the individual district.

Defendants also argue that neither assessed valuation per pupil nor expenditure per pupil is a reliable index of the wealth of a district or of its residents. The former figure is untrustworthy, they assert, because a district with a low total assessed valuation but a miniscule number of students will have a high per pupil tax base and thus appear "wealthy." Defendants imply that the proper index of a district's wealth is the total assessed valuation of its property. We think defendants' contention misses the point. The only meaningful measure of a district's wealth in the present context is not the absolute value of its property, but the ratio of its resources to pupils, because it is the latter figure which determines how much the district can devote to educating each of its students.[14]

But, say defendants, the expenditure per child does not accurately reflect a district's wealth because that expenditure is partly determined by the district's tax

---

[14] Gorman Elementary District in Los Angeles County, for example, has a total assessed valuation of $6,063,965, but only 41 students, yielding a per pupil tax base of $147,902. We find it significant that Gorman spent $1,378 per student on education in 1968-1969, even more than Beverly Hills....

We realize, of course, that a portion of the high per-pupil expenditure in a district like Gorman may be attributable to certain costs, like a principal's salary, which do not vary with the size of the school. On such expenses, small schools cannot achieve the economies of scale available to a larger district. To this extent, the high per-pupil spending in a small district may be a paper statistic, which is unrepresentative of significant differences in educational opportunities. On the other hand, certain economic "inefficiencies," such as a low pupil-teacher ratio, may have a positive educational impact. The extent to which high spending in such districts represents actual educational advantages is, of course, a matter of proof....

rate. Thus, a district with a high total assessed valuation might levy a low school tax, and end up spending the same amount per pupil as a poorer district whose residents opt to pay higher taxes. This argument is also meritless. Obviously, the richer district is favored when it can provide the same educational quality for its children with less tax effort. Furthermore, as a statistical matter, the poorer districts are financially unable to raise their taxes high enough to match the educational offerings of wealthier districts. . . . Thus, affluent districts can have their cake and eat it too: they can provide a high quality education for their children while paying lower taxes. Poor districts, by contrast, have no cake at all.

Finally, defendants suggest that the wealth of a school district does not necessarily reflect the wealth of the families who live there. The simple answer to this argument is that plaintiffs have alleged that there is a correlation between a district's per pupil assessed valuation and the wealth of its residents and we treat these material facts as admitted by the demurrers.

More basically, however, we reject defendants' underlying thesis that classification by wealth is constitutional so long as the wealth is that of the district, not the individual. We think that discrimination on the basis of district wealth is equally invalid. The commercial and industrial property which augments a district's tax base is distributed unevenly throughout the state. To allot more educational dollars to the children of one district than to those of another merely because of the fortuitous presence of such property is to make the quality of a child's education dependent upon the location of private commercial and industrial establishments.[16] Surely, this to rely on the most irrelevant of factors as the basis for educational financing. . . .

We turn now to defendants' related contention that the instant case involves at most de facto discrimination. We disagree. Indeed, we find the case unusual in the extent to which governmental action is the cause of the wealth classifications. The school funding scheme is mandated in every detail by the California Constitution and statutes. Although private residential and commercial patterns may be partly responsible for the distribution of assessed valuation throughout the state, such patterns are shaped and hardened by zoning ordinances and other governmental land-use controls which promote economic exclusivity. . . . Governmental action drew the school district boundary lines, thus determining how much local wealth each district would contain. . . .

B

Education as a Fundamental Interest

But plaintiffs' equal protection attack on the fiscal system has an additional dimension. They assert that the system not only draws lines on the basis of wealth but that it "touches upon," indeed has a direct and significant impact upon, a

---

[16] Defendants contend that different levels of educational expenditure do not affect the quality of education. However, plaintiffs' complaint specifically alleges the contrary, and for purposes of testing the sufficiency of a complaint against a general demurrer, we must take its allegations to be true.

Although we recognize that there is considerable controversy among educators over the relative impact of educational spending and environmental influences on school achievement (compare Coleman, et al., Equality of Educational Opportunity (U.S. Office of Ed. 1966) with Guthrie, Kleindorfer, Levin & Stout, Schools and Inequality (1971); see generally Coons, Clune & Sugarman, *supra*, 57 Cal. L. Rev. 305, 310-311, fn. 16), we note that the several courts which have considered contentions similar to defendants' have uniformly rejected them. . . .

"fundamental interest," namely education. It is urged that these two grounds, particularly in combination, establish a demonstrable denial of equal protection of the laws. To this phase of the argument we now turn our attention.

. . . .

... Plaintiffs' contention — that education is a fundamental interest which may not be conditioned on wealth — is not supported by any direct authority.

We, therefore, begin by examining the indispensable role which education plays in the modern industrial state. This role, we believe, has two significant aspects: first, education is a major determinant of an individual's chances for economic and social success in our competitive society; second, education is a unique influence on a child's development as a citizen and his participation in political and community life. [The remainder of the court's opinion concluding that education is a fundamental interest is omitted. — Eds.]

C

The Financing System Is Not Necessary to Accomplish a Compelling State Interest

We now reach the final step in the application of the "strict scrutiny" equal protection standard — the determination of whether the California school financing system, as presently structured, is necessary to achieve a compelling state interest.

The state interest which defendants advance in support of the current fiscal scheme is California's policy "to strengthen and encourage local responsibility for control of public education." (Ed. Code, § 17300.) We treat separately the two possible aspects of this goal: first, the granting to local districts of effective decision-making power over the administration of their schools; and second, the promotion of local fiscal control over the amount of money to be spent on education.

The individual district may well be in the best position to decide whom to hire, how to schedule its educational offerings, and a host of other matters which are either of significant local impact or of such a detailed nature as to require decentralized determination. But even assuming arguendo that local administrative control may be a compelling state interest, the present financial system cannot be considered necessary to further this interest. No matter how the state decides to finance its system of public education, it can still leave this decision-making power in the hands of local districts.

The other asserted policy interest is that of allowing a local district to choose how much it wishes to spend on the education of its children. Defendants argue: "[I]f one district raises a lesser amount per pupil than another district, this is a matter of choice and preference of the individual district and reflects the individual desire for lower taxes rather than an expanded educational program, or may reflect a greater interest within that district in such other services that are supported by local property taxes as, for example, police and fire protection or hospital services."

We need not decide whether such decentralized financial decision-making is a compelling state interest, since under the present financing system, such fiscal freewill is a cruel illusion for the poor school districts. We cannot agree that Baldwin Park residents care less about education than those in Beverly Hills solely because Baldwin Park spends less than $600 per child while Beverly Hills spends over $1,200. As defendants themselves recognize, perhaps the most accurate reflection of a community's commitment to education is the rate at which its citizens are willing to tax themselves to support their schools. Yet by that standard, Baldwin Park should be deemed far more devoted to learning than Beverly Hills, for Baldwin Park citizens levied a school tax of well over $5 per $100 of assessed valuation, while residents of Beverly Hills paid only slightly more than $2.

In summary, so long as the assessed valuation within a district's boundaries is a major determinant of how much it can spend for its schools, only a district with a large tax base will be truly able to decide how much it really cares about education. The poor district cannot freely choose to tax itself into an excellence which its tax rolls cannot provide. Far from being necessary to promote local fiscal choice, the present financing system actually deprives the less wealthy districts of that option. . . .

[The court additionally rejected defendants' arguments that equal protection would require the same test of inequality to be applied to all tax-supported public services (if it is to be applied here), and that *McInnis* had already decided the applicability of equal protection to school financing. Finally, the court sustained the second and third causes of action, which basically sought the same finding of constitutionality as the first. — Eds.]

In sum, we find the allegations of plaintiffs' complaint legally sufficient and we return the cause to the trial court for further proceedings. We emphasize, that our decision is not a final judgment on the merits. We deem it appropriate to point out for the benefit of the trial court on remand (see Code Civ. Proc. § 43) that if, after further proceedings, that court should enter final judgment determining that the existing system of public school financing is unconstitutional and invalidating said system in whole or in part, it may properly provide for the enforcement of the judgment in such a way as to permit an orderly transition from an unconstitutional to a constitutional system of school financing.

. . . .

By our holding today we further the cherished idea of American education that in a democratic society free public schools shall make available to all children equally the abundant gifts of learning. . . .

The judgment is reversed and the cause remanded to the trial court with directions to overrule the demurrers and to allow defendants a reasonable time within which to answer.

WRIGHT, C.J., and PETERS, TOBRINER, MOSK and BURKE, JJ., concur.

MCCOMB, Justice (dissenting). [Omitted.]

Comments: 1. Following remand and an extensive trial covering 62 court days, Judge Jefferson of the Los Angeles County Superior Court again held that California's school funding was unconstitutional. Unpublished opinion, Super. Ct., L.A. County No. 938,254, Apr. 10, 1974. (Significant portions of the trial court's findings of fact, conclusions of law and judgment order are described in the subsequent supreme court opinion, 557 P.2d 929, 936-40.) On December 30, 1976, the California Supreme Court, in a 4 to 3 decision, affirmed, holding that the trial court had correctly interpreted and applied the first *Serrano* decision. The court acknowledged that the intervening decision of the United States Supreme Court in *San Antonio Independent School District v. Rodriguez* (the text of which follows) undercut the federal equal protection claim, but it noted that the *Serrano* complaint also rested on state equal protection grounds. Again applying a strict scrutiny test, the court repeated that "(1) discrimination in educational opportunity on the basis of district wealth involves a suspect classification, and (2) education is a fundamental interest." *Serrano v. Priest,* 557 P.2d 929, 951 (Cal. 1976) (hereinafter the 1971 decision will be referred to as *Serrano;* the 1976 decision, as *Serrano II*). Before the second round of *Serrano* decisions, the California legislature enacted two bills, SB 90 and AB 1267, which made significant changes in the state school financing program but did not, as the California Supreme Court noted, alter the basic concept. The new laws retained the foundation program, including the flat grant, but almost doubled the foundation level, thus substantially increasing the revenues available to poorer districts. The new laws also imposed limits on the rate at which revenues, and therefore expenditures, could increase from local property taxation under a formula intended to permit low-expenditure districts to catch up in time — a device called "convergence." However, the revenue limits could be overriden with voter approval, and it was this feature, more than any other, which the California court said perpetuated the ability of the affluent districts to increase their local spending for education in a manner which poorer districts with a low assessed valuation could not as a practical matter match. Interdistrict disparities thus were not effectively eliminated, and the California system failed to meet the constitutional standard "because it renders the educational opportunity available to the students of this state a function of the taxable wealth per ADA of the districts in which they live." *Id.* at 953.

2. With the advent of Proposition 13 in 1978, school districts were severely limited in the amount of local funds that could be raised for education. In the first years following adoption, the state, which had a surplus in excess of five billion dollars, used that surplus to make up lost revenues for local governments, particularly school districts. Changes were also made in the method of funding schools. More for this reason than because of *Serrano,* the state's share of the cost of elementary and secondary education rose from 35.5% (at the time of *Serrano*) to more than 68% in 1981-82. Much of this bail-out state funding was distributed in accordance with what the school district was spending prior to Proposition 13 — so that it tended to perpetuate disparities among districts. Nevertheless, the range of disparity in expenditure has been narrowed compared with pre-*Serrano.* That trend is consistent with Judge Jefferson's order which effectively required that disparities in expenditure among districts be reduced to less than $100 by 1980-81. The extent to which there has been compliance with the court judgments is the subject of continuing litigation. The case was reopened in December 1979 upon complaint of the plaintiffs that the current system has not sufficiently eliminated the wealth-related disparities in expenditures, a claim which the state defendants deny. The matter is currently pending. Lawyers Comm. for Civil Rights Under Law, Update on State-Wide School Finance Cases 4-5 (1982). *See* Chapter 5 for a discussion of Proposition 13.

A NOTE ON REMEDIAL ALTERNATIVES

Neither *Serrano* nor the other decisions which followed in the immediate wake of *Serrano* came to grips with the question of what type of relief would be acceptable following a declaration that their school finance system was unconstitutional. Apart from the fact that *Serrano* was decided on a motion to dismiss and had to be sent back for trial, the court's theory of invalidity — fiscal neutrality [11] — is essentially a negative test: it says what may not be done but not what must be done. There was some initial confusion, especially in the media, about the impact of *Serrano,* primarily a hasty and inaccurate conclusion that it

---

[11] The closest the California Supreme Court came to formulating its test of invalidity was in the opening paragraph: "We have determined that this funding scheme invidiously discriminates against the poor because it makes the quality of a child's education a function of the wealth of his parents and neighbors." 487 P.2d at 1244. While the court did not so acknowledge, it was clear that it had adopted the Coons-Clune-Sugarman principle which the authors denominated Proposition 1: "the quality of public education may not be a function of wealth other than the total wealth of the state." J. Coons et al., Private Wealth at 304. That standard is also identified as fiscal neutrality.

sounded the death knell for the property tax as a source of school funding. Thereafter, both the proponents and opponents of *Serrano* agreed that there was a range of alternatives that apparently would satisfy the court's fiscal neutrality standard. While subsequent legal developments have shifted the focus (*see infra*), the list of available alternatives is essentially the same, at least in response to a *Serrano*-type decision.

District power equalizing. The most discussed of the alternatives was district power equalization (DPE), in part no doubt because it was the invention of the same group who advanced the *Serrano* fiscal neutrality standard.[12] Professors Coons, Clune and Sugarman defined their concept: "A power equalizing system of state aid is one that leaves subunits free to select levels of spending for education while giving each unit equal power to do so." J. Coons et al., Private Wealth, at 202. A simple table illustrates how it works — where E (Effort) is the rate at which the district chooses to tax itself and O (Offering) is the available expenditure guaranteed for that level of effort with the state making up any deficiency not raised by local taxation and recapturing any excess when the tax rate produces more than the given expenditure level:

E	O
1 percent	400 per weighted ADA pupil
1½	600
2	800
2½	1,000
3	1,200

Id. at 205. The essence of DPE is that it guarantees equal resources for equal effort; it does not require equal expenditure per pupil. For this reason, some of its critics claimed that it was more concerned with taxpayers than with school children. *See, e.g.,* Goldstein, *Interdistrict Inequalities in School Financing: A Critical Analysis of Serrano v. Priest and Its Progeny,* 120 U. Pa. L. Rev. 504, 512 n.28 (1972).

For a fascinating analysis of the fiscal equity impacts of the DPE proposal, see Inman & Rubinfeld, *The Judicial Pursuit of Local Fiscal Equity,* 92 Harv. L. Rev. 1662 (1979). The authors also consider the full market value tax assesment and *Hawkins v. Shaw* service equalization reforms discussed in Chapter 5.

Full state funding. The second major line of response to *Serrano* was to propose that the state assume total responsibility for raising and distributing the funds for education, abandoning the local property tax for that purpose and substituting either a statewide property tax or other state level taxes. The form of distribution would remain to be determined. The state aid might go to the districts on an equal dollars per pupil basis although the *Serrano* test clearly does not require that. So long as disparities in district wealth are eliminated, nothing in *Serrano* would prevent additional spending that relates to higher costs, whether it be program or geographic differences. Among the proponents of full

---

[12] While the particulars of DPE were the intellectual invention of Coons, Clune and Sugarman, its equalization principle was not new, as the authors acknowledge. Both Paul Mort and Charles Benson had proposed equalization schemes which are analyzed in J. Coons et al., Private Wealth, at ch. 5. Under "percentage equalization" the state equalizes that percentage of the local budget which the district's relative poverty prevents it from raising. With the "resource equalizer" every district is guaranteed resources (*i.e.,* assessed valuation per capita) equal to that of the average district; if its AV is below the average (and only those below that level would receive grants), the state equalizes the deficiency in revenues at a given tax rate. *See* C. Benson, The Cheerful Prospect 90-93 (1965).

state funding was Michelson, *Reform Through State Legislatures, What Is a "Just" System for Financing Schools? An Evaluation of Alternative Reforms,* 38 LAW & CONTEMP. PROBS. 436, 457-58 (1974).

Other alternatives. Among the other alternatives proposed were: redraw school district boundaries to achieve a greater equality of property wealth (*see* Justice Marshall's dissent in *Rodriguez, infra,* 411 U.S. at 130-31 n.98); remove commercial, industrial and mineral property (which are the primary advantages of property rich districts) from the local property base and tax them at the state or perhaps a regional level; retain the essential structure of existing programs but greatly increase the foundation level and eliminate the flat grant, see Schoettel, *Judicial Requirements for School Finance and Property Tax Redesign: The Rapidly Evolving Case Law,* 25 NAT'L TAX J. 455, 462-63 (1972).

Undoubtedly the most far-reaching proposal to restructure school finance is the voucher system. The proposal can take many different forms, but its basic purpose is to encourage competition and choice among public and private schools by providing vouchers to parents with which they can purchase education for their children at any school of their choice. The concept has been around for some time. Professor Milton Friedman, the conservative "Chicago School" economist, has been the leading modern advocate of vouchers. *See, e.g.,* M. FRIEDMAN, CAPITALISM AND FREEDOM 85-98 (1962).

The *Serrano* developments, as well as general dissatisfaction with the state of public education, brought renewed interest, and a voucher system has been a more frequently debated financing alternative in recent years. Among the proponents have been Professors Coons and Sugarman, who also played a prominent role in developing the legal theories for *Serrano. See* Coons & Sugarman, *Family Choice in Education: A Model State System for Vouchers* (Cal. Institute of Govt'l Studies 1971); *see also* 59 CALIF. L. REV. 321 (1971); S. Sugarman, *Family Choice: The Next Step in the Quest for Equal Educational Opportunity?,* 1974 LAW & CONTEMP. PROBS. 513; J. COONS & S. SUGARMAN, EDUCATION BY CHOICE: THE CASE FOR FAMILY CONTROL (1978).

The March 1982 Conference on Challenges to Urban and Suburban Education in the 1980s, held at Pace University Law School, featured several presentations dealing with vouchers, which are reprinted in The Urban Lawyer. Rebell, *Educational Voucher Reform: Empirical Insights from the Experience of New York's Schools for the Handicapped,* 14 URB. LAW. 441 (1982); Coons, *Educational Alternatives for the 1980's: Common Schools and the Commoner,* 5 URB. LAW. 77 (1983); Fishman, *Family Choice: An Idea Whose Time Has Come and Gone?,* 15 URB. LAW. 113 (1983). Again, California seems to be the center of voucher activity, and attempts continue to be made through the initiative to place a voucher proposal on the ballot. *See* Stanfield, *The School Finance Revolution — More Help for Taxpayers Than Schools,* 11 NAT'L J. 1935 (1979).

c. *Rodriguez* and Local Control

Following the *Serrano* decision, plaintiffs surged into the courts to challenge their states' school financing systems. Suits alleging that heavy reliance on the local property tax to fund the schools violated state and federal equal protection guarantees were filed in at least twenty-two states within two years after *Serrano.* While most of these cases were still pending, the Supreme Court addressed the fourteenth amendment challenge to school financing in *Rodriguez,* which follows:

SAN ANTONIO INDEPENDENT SCHOOL DISTRICT v. RODRIGUEZ

Supreme Court of United States
411 U.S. 1 (1973)

Mr. Justice Powell delivered the opinion of the Court.

This suit attacking the Texas system of financing public education was initiated by Mexican-American parents whose children attend the elementary and secondary schools in the Edgewood Independent School District, an urban school district in San Antonio, Texas. They brought a class action on behalf of school children throughout the State who are members of minority groups or who are poor and reside in school districts having a low property tax base. Named as defendants were the State Board of Education, the Commissioner of Education, the State Attorney General, and the Bexar County (San Antonio) Board of Trustees. The complaint was filed in the summer of 1968 and a three-judge court was impaneled in January 1969. In December 1971 the panel rendered its judgment in a *per curiam* opinion holding the Texas school finance system unconstitutional under the Equal Protection Clause of the Fourteenth Amendment.[5] The State appealed, and we noted probable jurisdiction to consider the far-reaching constitutional questions presented. 406 U. S. 966 (1972). For the reasons stated in this opinion, we reverse the decision of the District Court.

I

. . . .

Until recent times, Texas was a predominantly rural State and its population and property wealth were spread relatively evenly across the State. Sizeable differences in the value of assessable property between local school districts became increasingly evident as the State became more industrialized and as rural-to-urban population shifts became more pronounced. The location of commercial and industrial property began to play a significant role in determining the amount of tax resources available to each school district. These growing disparities in population and taxable property between districts were responsible in part for increasingly notable differences in levels of local expenditure for education.

In due time it became apparent to those concerned with financing public education that contributions from the Available School Fund [a state fund whose primary resources were a state property tax and public lands set aside for school support — Eds.] were not sufficient to ameliorate these disparities. . . . [T]he Fund was providing only $46 per student by 1945.

Recognizing the need for increased state funding to help offset disparities in local spending and to meet Texas' changing educational requirements, the state legislature in the late 1940's undertook . . . [a study which led to adoption of] the Texas Minimum Foundation School Program. Today, this Program accounts for approximately half of the total educational expenditures in Texas.

The Program calls for state and local contributions to a fund earmarked specifically for teacher salaries, operating expenses, and transportation costs. The State, supplying funds from its general revenues, finances approximately

---

[5] 337 F. Supp. 280. The District Court stayed its mandate for two years to provide Texas an opportunity to remedy the inequities found in its financing program. The court, however, retained jurisdiction to fashion its own remedial order if the State failed to offer an acceptable plan. *Id.*, at 286.

80% of the Program, and the school districts are responsible — as a unit — for providing the remaining 20%. The districts' share, known as the Local Fund Assignment, is apportioned among the school districts under a formula designed to reflect each district's relative taxpaying ability.... The district, in turn, finances its share of the Assignment out of revenues from local property taxation....

Today every school district [in addition imposes] a property tax from which it derives locally expendable funds in excess of the amount necessary to satisfy its Local Fund Assignment under the Foundation Program....

The school district in which appellees reside, the Edgewood Independent School District, has been compared throughout this litigation with the Alamo Heights Independent School District. This comparison between the least and most affluent districts in the San Antonio area serves to illustrate the manner in which the dual system of finance operates and to indicate the extent to which substantial disparities exist despite the State's impressive progress in recent years. Edgewood is one of seven public school districts in the metropolitan area. Approximately 22,000 students are enrolled in its 25 elementary and secondary schools. The district is situated in the core-city sector of San Antonio in a residential neighborhood that has little commercial or industrial property. The residents are predominantly of Mexican-American descent: approximately 90% of the student population is Mexican-American and over 6% is Negro. The average assessed property value per pupil is $5,960 — the lowest in the metropolitan area — and the median family income ($4,686) is also the lowest. At an equalized tax rate of $1.05 per $100 of assessed property — the highest in the metropolitan area — the district contributed $26 to the education of each child for the 1967-1968 school year above its Local Fund Assignment for the Minimum Foundation Program. The Foundation Program contributed $222 per pupil for a state-local total of $248. Federal funds added another $108 for a total of $356 per pupil.[32]

Alamo Heights is the most affluent school district in San Antonio. Its six schools, housing approximately 5,000 students, are situated in a residential community quite unlike the Edgewood District. The school population is predominantly "Anglo," having only 18% Mexican-Americans and less than 1% Negroes. The assessed property value per pupil exceeds $49,000, and the median family income is $8,001. In 1967-1968 the local tax rate of $.85 per $100 of valuation yielded $333 per pupil over and above its contribution to the Foundation Program. Coupled with the $225 provided from that Program, the district was able to supply $558 per student. Supplemented by a $36 per-pupil grant from federal sources, Alamo Heights spent $594 per pupil.

Although the 1967-1968 school year figures provide the only complete statistical breakdown for each category of aid, more recent partial statistics indicate that the previously noted trend of increasing state aid has been significant....

[In a footnote the Court noted that the effect of the state's allocation formula was to grant a district like Alamo Heights, which was already spending at a higher level, more state aid than Edgewood; and in this respect it was similar to other states' "anti-equalizing" formulas. Despite this, the Court, said state aid did significantly reduce the disparity in resources between the two districts. — Eds.]

---

[32] While federal assistance has an ameliorating effect on the difference in school budgets between wealthy and poor districts, the District Court rejected an argument made by the State in that court that it should consider the effect of the federal grant in assessing the discrimination claim. 337 F. Supp., at 284. The State has not renewed that contention here.

Despite these recent increases, substantial interdistrict disparities in school expenditures found by the District Court to prevail in San Antonio and in varying degrees throughout the State [38] still exist. And it was these disparities, largely attributable to differences in the amounts of money collected through local property taxation, that led the District Court to conclude that Texas' dual system of public school financing violated the Equal Protection Clause....

Texas virtually concedes that its historically rooted dual system of financing education could not withstand the strict judicial scrutiny that this Court has found appropriate in reviewing legislative judgments that interfere with fundamental constitutional rights or that involve suspect classifications. If, as previous decisions have indicated, strict scrutiny means that the State's system is not entitled to the usual presumption of validity, that the State rather than the complainants must carry a "heavy burden of justification," that the State must demonstrate that its educational system has been structured with "precision," and is "tailored" narrowly to serve legitimate objectives and that it has selected the "less drastic means" for effectuating its objectives, the Texas financing system and its counterpart in virtually every other State will not pass muster....

II

The District Court's opinion does not reflect the novelty and complexity of the constitutional questions posed by appellees' challenge to Texas' system of school financing. In concluding that strict judicial scrutiny was required, that court relied on decisions dealing with the rights of indigents to equal treatment in the criminal trial and appellate processes, and on cases disapproving wealth restrictions on the right to vote. Those cases, the District Court concluded, established wealth as a suspect classification. Finding that the local property tax system discriminated on the basis of wealth, it regarded those precedents as controlling. It then reasoned, based on decisions of this Court affirming the undeniable importance of education, that there is a fundamental right to education and that, absent some compelling state justification, the Texas system could not stand.

We are unable to agree that this case, which in significant aspects is *sui generis,* may be so neatly fitted into the conventional mosaic of constitutional analysis under the Equal Protection Clause. Indeed, for the several reasons that follow, we find neither the suspect-classification nor the fundamental-interest analysis persuasive.

A

The wealth discrimination discovered by the District Court in this case, and by several other courts that have recently struck down school-financing laws in other States, is quite unlike any of the forms of wealth discrimination heretofore reviewed by this Court. Rather than focusing on the unique features of the alleged discrimination, the courts in these cases have virtually assumed their findings of a suspect classification through a simplistic process of analysis: since, under the traditional systems of financing public schools, some poorer people

---

[38] The District Court relied on the findings presented in an affidavit submitted by Professor Berke of Syracuse. His sampling of Texas school districts demonstrated a direct correlation between the amount of a district's taxable property and its level of per-pupil expenditure. But his study found only a partial correlation between a district's median family income and per-pupil expenditures. The study also shows, in the relatively few districts at the extremes, an inverse correlation between percentage of minorities and expenditures. [The table is omitted.—Eds.]

receive less expensive educations than other more affluent people, these systems discriminate on the basis of wealth. This approach largely ignores the hard threshold questions, including whether it makes a difference for purposes of consideration under the Constitution that the class of disadvantaged "poor" cannot be identified or defined in customary equal protection terms, and whether the relative — rather than absolute — nature of the asserted deprivation is of significant consequence. Before a State's laws and the justifications for the classifications they create are subjected to strict judicial scrutiny, we think these threshold considerations must be analyzed more closely than they were in the court below.

The case comes to us with no definitive description of the classifying facts or delineation of the disfavored class. Examination of the District Court's opinion and of appellees' complaint, briefs, and contentions at oral argument suggests, however, at least three ways in which the discrimination claimed here might be described. The Texas system of school financing might be regarded as discriminating (1) against "poor" persons whose incomes fall below some identifiable level of poverty or who might be characterized as functionally "indigent," or (2) against those who are relatively poorer than others, or (3) against all those who, irrespective of their personal incomes, happen to reside in relatively poorer school districts. Our task must be to ascertain whether, in fact, the Texas system has been shown to discriminate on any of these possible bases and, if so, whether the resulting classification may be regarded as suspect.

The precedents of this Court provide the proper starting point. The individuals, or groups of individuals, who constituted the class discriminated against in our prior cases shared two distinguishing characteristics: because of their impecunity they were completely unable to pay for some desired benefit, and as a consequence, they sustained an absolute deprivation of a meaningful opportunity to enjoy that benefit. . . . [The Court's review of its precedents is omitted. — Eds.]

Only appellees' first possible basis for describing the class disadvantaged by the Texas school-financing system — discrimination against a class of definably "poor" persons — might arguably meet the criteria established in these prior cases. Even a cursory examination, however, demonstrates that neither of the two distinguishing characteristics of wealth classifications can be found here. First, in support of their charge that the system discriminates against the "poor," appellees have made no effort to demonstrate that it operates to the peculiar disadvantage of any class fairly definable as indigent, or as composed of persons whose incomes are beneath any designated poverty level. Indeed, there is reason to believe that the poorest families are not necessarily clustered in the poorest property districts. A recent and exhaustive study of school districts in Connecticut concluded that "[i]t is clearly incorrect . . . to contend that the 'poor' live in 'poor' districts. . . . Thus, the major factual assumption of *Serrano* — that the education financing system discriminates against the 'poor' — is simply false in Connecticut." [53] Defining "poor" families as those below the Bureau of the

---

[53] Note, A Statistical Analysis of the School Finance Decisions: On Winning Battles and Losing Wars, 81 Yale L.J. 1303, 1328-1329 (1972).

[The Yale Note, in turn, was sharply criticized by two educational economists who found it "incorrect in its statistical inferences and in most of its theoretical analysis", Grubb & Michelson, Public School Finance in a Post-*Serrano* World, 8 Harv. Civ. Lib.-Civ. Rights L. Rev. 550, 552 (1973).

[Consider whether the Court's attempt to define wealth discrimination meets the theoretical contentions of the *Serrano*-type challenge.

Census "poverty level," the Connecticut study found, not surprisingly, that the poor were clustered around commercial and industrial areas — those same areas that provide the most attractive sources of property tax income for school districts. Whether a similar pattern would be discovered in Texas is not known, but there is no basis on the record in this case for assuming that the poorest people — defined by reference to any level of absolute impecunity — are concentrated in the poorest districts.

Second, neither appellees nor the District Court addressed the fact that, unlike each of the foregoing cases, lack of personal resources has not occasioned an absolute deprivation of the desired benefit. The argument here is not that the children in districts having relatively low assessable property values are receiving no public education; rather, it is that they are receiving a poorer quality education than that available to children in districts having more assessable wealth. Apart from the unsettled and disputed question whether the quality of education may be determined by the amount of money expended for it, a sufficient answer to appellees' argument is that, at least where wealth is involved, the Equal Protection Clause does not require absolute equality or precisely equal advantages. Nor, indeed, in view of the infinite variable affecting the educational process, can any system assure equal quality of education except in the most relative sense. Texas asserts that the Minimum Foundation Program provides an "adequate" education for all children in the State [b]y providing 12 years of free public-school education, and by assuring teachers, books, transportation, and operating funds. . . .

For these two reasons — the absence of any evidence that the financing system discriminates against any definable category of "poor" people or that it results in the absolute deprivation of education — the disadvantaged class is not susceptible of identification in traditional terms.

As suggested above, appellees and the District Court may have embraced a second or third approach, the second of which might be characterized as a theory of relative or comparative discrimination based on family income. Appellees sought to prove that a direct correlation exists between the wealth of families within each district and the expenditures therein for education. That is, along a continuum, the poorer the family the lower the dollar amount of education received by the family's children.

The principal evidence adduced in support of this comparative-discrimination claim is an affidavit submitted by Professor Joel S. Berke of Syracuse University's Educational Finance Policy Institute. . . .

Some assert that only by defining the class in terms of personal poverty can a doctrinal link be forged with judicial precedent. Perhaps this is so, but, if it were thought necessary as a doctrinal matter to employ personal wealth in the legal standard, I would prefer to argue as follows: Wealth is the capacity to purchase a specific good; here that good is education. Wealth, however, must be defined differently for purposes of private and public education. One buys private education with private wealth; he is education-poor in the private market when his personal income is inadequate to afford tuition. One buys public education only with public money; he is education-poor in the public market if his school district is poor. In the case of public education, personal wealth and district wealth are *identical,* because the only wealth a family has available for the purchase of public education is that of its school district. If a family's district is poor, that district is poor insofar as its ability to purchase public education is concerned. Analytically it is hard to know what else could be meant by "personal" poverty in relation to the purchase of public education. So far as proof of the constitutional violation is concerned, it is proper literally to identify district poverty with personal poverty.

Coons, Recent Trends in Science Fiction: *Serrano* Among the People of Number, 6 J. Law & Ed. 23, 38 (1977). *See also* Clune, Wealth Discrimination in School Finance, 68 Nw. U.L. Rev. 651 (1973). — Eds.]

Professor Berke's affidavit is based on a survey of approximately 10% of the school districts in Texas. His findings, ... show only that the wealthiest few districts in the sample have the highest median family incomes and spend the most on education, and that the several poorest districts have the lowest family incomes and devote the least amount of money to education. For the remainder of the districts — 96 districts composing almost 90% of the sample — the correlation is inverted, *i.e.,* the districts that spend next to the most money on education are populated by families having next to the lowest median family incomes while the districts spending the least have the highest median family incomes. It is evident that, even if the conceptual questions were answered favorably to appellees, no factual basis exists upon which to found a claim of comparative wealth discrimination.

This bring us, then, to the third way in which the classification scheme might be defined — *district* wealth discrimination. Since the only correlation indicated by the evidence is between district property wealth and expenditures, it may be argued that discrimination might be found without regard to the individual income characteristics of district residents. Assuming a perfect correlation between district property wealth and expenditures from top to bottom, the disadvantaged class might be viewed as encompassing every child in every district except the district that has the most assessable wealth and spends the most on education. Alternatively, as suggested in MR. JUSTICE MARSHALL's dissenting opinion, ... the class might be defined more restrictively to include children in districts with assessable property which falls below the statewide average, or median, or below some other artificially defined level.

However described, it is clear that appellees' suit asks this Court to extend its most exacting scrutiny to review a system that allegedly discriminates against a large, diverse, and amorphous class, unified only by the common factor of residence in districts that happen to have less taxable wealth than other districts. The system of alleged discrimination and the class it defines have none of the traditional indicia of suspectness: the class is not saddled with such disabilities, or subjected to such a history of purposeful unequal treatment, or relegated to such a position of political powerlessness as to command extraordinary protection from the majoritarian political process.

We thus conclude that the Texas system does not operate to the peculiar disadvantage of any suspect class. But in recognition of the fact that this Court has never heretofore held that wealth discrimination alone provides an adequate basis for invoking strict scrutiny, appellees have not relied solely on this contention. They also assert that the State's system impermissibly interferes with the exercise of a "fundamental" right and that accordingly the prior decisions of this Court require the application of the strict standard of judicial review. ...

B

In *Brown v. Board of Education,* 347 U.S. 483 (1954), a unanimous Court recognized that "education is perhaps the most important function of state and local governments." *Id.* at 493. What was said there in the context of racial discrimination has lost none of its vitality with the passage of time:

> Compulsory school attendance laws and the great expenditures for education both demonstrate our recognition of the importance of education to our

democratic society. It is required in the performance of our most basic public responsibilities, even service in the armed forces. It is the very foundation of good citizenship. Today it is a principal instrument in awakening the child to cultural values, in preparing him for later professional training, and in helping him to adjust normally to his environment. In these days, it is doubtful that any child may reasonably be expected to succeed in life if he is denied the opportunity of an education. Such an opportunity, where the state has undertaken to provide it, is a right which must be made available to all on equal terms. *Ibid.*

. . .

Nothing this Court holds today in any way detracts from our historic dedication to public education. We are in complete agreement with the conclusion of the three-judge panel below that "the grave significance of education both to the individual and to our society" cannot be doubted. But the importance of a service performed by the State does not determine whether it must be regarded as fundamental for purposes of examination under the Equal Protection Clause. . . .

. . . It is not the province of this Court to create substantive constitutional rights in the name of guaranteeing equal protection of the laws. Thus, the key to discovering whether education is "fundamental" is not to be found in comparisons of the relative societal significance of education as opposed to subsistence or housing. Nor is it to be found by weighing whether education is as important as the right to travel. Rather, the answer lies in assessing whether there is a right to education explicitly or implicitly guaranteed by the Constitution. . . .

Education, of course, is not among the rights afforded explicit protection under our Federal Constitution. Nor do we find any basis for saying it is implicitly so protected. As we have said, the undisputed importance of education will not alone cause this Court to depart from the usual standard for reviewing a State's social and economic legislation. It is appellees' contention, however, that education is distinguishable from other services and benefits provided by the State because it bears a peculiarly close relationship to other rights and liberties accorded protection under the Constitution. Specifically, they insist that education is itself a fundamental personal right because it is essential to the effective exercise of First Amendment freedoms and to intelligent utilization of the right to vote. . . .

Even if it were conceded that some identifiable quantum of education is a constitutionally protected prerequisite to the meaningful exercise of either right, we have no indication that the present levels of educational expenditure in Texas provide an education that falls short. Whatever merit appellees' argument might have if a State's financing system occasioned an absolute denial of educational opportunities to any of its children, that argument provides no basis for finding an interference with fundamental rights where only relative differences in spending levels are involved and where — as is true in the present case — no charge fairly could be made that the system fails to provide each child with an opportunity to acquire the basic minimal skills necessary for the enjoyment of the rights of speech and of full participation in the political process.

. . . .

. . . In one further respect we find this a particularly inappropriate case in which to subject state action to strict judicial scrutiny. The present case, in another basic sense, is significantly different from any of the cases in which the Court has applied strict scrutiny to state or federal legislation touching upon constitutionally protected rights. Each of our prior cases involved legislation which "deprived," "infringed," or "interfered" with the free exercise of some such fundamental personal right or liberty. . . . Every step leading to the establishment of the system Texas utilizes today — including the decisions permitting localities to tax and expend locally, and creating and continuously expanding state aid — was implemented in an effort to *extend* public education and to improve its quality. Of course, every reform that benefits some more than others may be criticized for what it fails to accomplish. But we think it plain that, in substance, the thrust of the Texas system is affirmative and reformatory and, therefore, should be scrutinized under judicial principles sensitive to the nature of the State's efforts and to the rights reserved to the States under the Constitution.

C

[In this section the Court noted that its decision to reject the strict scrutiny test was supported by additional considerations: 1. The Court has traditionally deferred to state legislatures on the subject of how states choose to raise and disburse state and local tax revenues because the Court lacks expertise and the requisite familiarity with local problems; 2. The Court also lacks specialized knowledge in the area of educational policy, leading it to avoid "premature interference with the informed judgments made at the state and local level." "On even the most basic questions in this area the scholars and educational experts are divided. Indeed, one of the major sources of controversy concerns the extent to which there is a demonstrable correlation between educational expenditures and the quality of education — an assumed correlation underlying virtually every legal conclusion drawn by the District Court in this case." *Id.* at 42-43; 3. The Court should be cautious where the principles of federalism are involved and "it would be difficult to imagine a case having a greater potential impact on our federal system than the one now before us." *Id.* at 44. "These same considerations are relevant to the determination whether that [Texas] system, with its conceded imperfections, nevertheless bears some rational relationship to a legitimate state purpose. It is to this question that we next turn our attention." *Id.* — Eds.]

III

[In part III the Court described in somewhat more detail the Texas school finance system; *see* part I, *supra*. It pointed out that every district supplements the foundation grant but the local supplements vary greatly due principally to differences in property wealth. The Court noted:

> In large measure, these additional local revenues are devoted to paying higher salaries to more teachers. Therefore, the primary distinguishing attributes of schools in property-affluent districts are lower pupil-teacher ratios and higher salary schedules.

Id. at 46. In a footnote the Court elaborated on this point:

> ... the extent to which the quality of education varies with expenditure per pupil is debated inconclusively by the most thoughtful students of public education. While all would agree that there is a correlation up to the point of providing the recognized essentials in facilities and academic opportunities, the issues of greatest disagreement include the effect on the quality of education of pupil-teacher ratios and of higher teacher salary schedules ... There appear to be few empirical data that support the advantage of any particular pupil-teacher ratio or that document the existence of a dependable correlation between the level of public school teachers' salaries and the quality of their classroom instruction....

Id. at 47, n. 101. After noting that the Texas plan was based on Strayer-Haig efforts to accommodate the competing forces of a guaranteed statewide minimum educational program and preservation of local participation, the Court continued: — Eds.]

The Texas system of school finance is responsive to these two forces. While assuring a basic education for every child in the State, it permits and encourages a large measure of participation in and control of each district's schools at the local level. In an era that has witnessed a consistent trend toward centralization of the functions of government, local sharing of responsibility for public education has survived. . . .

Appellees do not question the propriety of Texas' dedication to local control of education. To the contrary, they attack the school-financing system precisely because, in their view, it does not provide the same level of local control and fiscal flexibility in all districts. Appellees suggest that local control could be preserved and promoted under other financing systems that resulted in more equality in educational expenditures. While it is no doubt true that reliance on local property taxation for school revenues provides less freedom of choice with respect to expenditures for some districts than for others, the existence of "some inequality" in the manner in which the State's rationale is achieved is not alone sufficient basis for striking down the entire system. . . . It is also well to remember that even those districts that have reduced ability to make free decisions with respect to how much they spend on education still retain under the present system a large measure of authority as to how available funds will be allocated. They further enjoy the power to make numerous other decisions with respect to the operation of the schools. The people of Texas may be justified in believing that other systems of school financing, which place more of the financial responsibility in the hands of the State, will result in a comparable lessening of desired local autonomy. That is, they may believe that along with increased control of the purse strings at the state level will go increased control over local policies.

Appellees further urge that the Texas system is unconstitutionally arbitrary because it allows the availability of local taxable resources to turn on "happenstance." They see no justification for a system that allows, as they contend, the quality of education to fluctuate on the basis of the fortuitous positioning of the boundary lines of political subdivisions and the location of valuable commercial and industrial property. But any scheme of local taxation — indeed the very existence of identifiable local governmental units — requires the establishment of jurisdictional boundaries that are inevitably arbitrary. It is equally inevitable that some localities are going to be blessed with more taxable assets than others. Nor is local wealth a static quantity. Changes in the level of taxable wealth within any district may result from any number of events, some of which local residents can and do influence. For instance, commercial and industrial enterprises may be encouraged to locate within a district by various actions — public and private.

Moreover, if local taxation for local expenditures were an unconstitutional method of providing for education then it might be an equally impermissible means of providing other necessary services customarily financed largely from local property taxes, including local police and fire protection, public health and hospitals, and public utility facilities of various kinds. We perceive no justification for such a severe denigration of local property taxation and control as would follow from appellees' contentions. It has simply never been within the constitutional prerogative of this Court to nullify statewide measures for financing public services merely because the burdens or benefits thereof fall unevenly depending upon the relative wealth of the political subdivisions in which citizens live.

In sum, to the extent that the Texas system of school financing results in unequal expenditures between children who happen to reside in different districts, we cannot say that such disparities are the product of a system that is so irrational as to be invidiously discriminatory.... One also must remember that the system here challenged is not peculiar to Texas or to any other State. In its essential characteristics, the Texas plan for financing public education reflects what many educators for a half century have thought was an enlightened approach to a problem for which there is no perfect solution. We are unwilling to assume for ourselves a level of wisdom superior to that of legislators, scholars, and educational authorities in 50 States, especially where the alternatives proposed are only recently conceived and nowhere yet tested. The constitutional standard under the Equal Protection Clause is whether the challenged state action rationally furthers a legitimate state purpose or interest.... We hold that the Texas plan abundantly satisfies this standard.

IV

In light of the considerable attention that has focused on the District Court opinion in this case and on its California predecessor, *Serrano v. Priest,* 5 Cal. 3d 584, 487 P.2d 1241 (1971), a cautionary postscript seems appropriate. It cannot be questioned that the constitutional judgment reached by the District Court and approved by our dissenting Brothers today would occasion in Texas and elsewhere an unprecedented upheaval in public education. Some commentators have concluded that, whatever the contours of the alternative financing programs that might be devised and approved, the result could not avoid being a beneficial one. But, just as there is nothing simple about the constitutional issues involved in these cases, there is nothing simple or certain about predicting the consequences of massive change in the financing and control of public education. Those who have devoted the most thoughtful attention to the practical ramifications of these cases have found no clear or dependable answers and their scholarship reflects no such unqualified confidence in the desirability of completely uprooting the existing system.

The complexity of these problems is demonstrated by the lack of consensus with respect to whether it may be said with any assurance that the poor, the racial minorities, or the children in overburdened core-city school districts would be benefited by abrogation of traditional modes of financing education. Unless there is to be a substantial increase in state expenditures on education across the board — an event the likelihood of which is open to considerable question [111] — these groups stand to realize gains in terms of increased per-pupil expenditures only if they reside in districts that presently spend at relatively low levels, *i.e.,* in those districts that would benefit from the redistribution of existing

---

[111] Any alternative that calls for significant increases in expenditures for education, whether financed through increases in property taxation or through other sources of tax dollars, such as income and sales taxes, is certain to encounter political barriers. At a time when nearly every State and locality is suffering from fiscal undernourishment, and with demands for services of all kinds burgeoning and with weary taxpayers already resisting tax increases, there is considerable reason to question whether a decision of this Court nullifying present state taxing systems would result in a marked increase in the financial commitment to education.... In Texas, it has been calculated that $2.4 billion of additional school funds would be required to bring all schools in that State up to the present level of expenditure of all but the wealthiest districts — an amount more than double that currently being spent on education....

resources. Yet, recent studies have indicated that the poorest families are not invariably clustered in the most impecunious school districts. Nor does it now appear that there is any more than a random chance that racial minorities are concentrated in property-poor districts. Additionally, several research projects have concluded that any financing alternative designed to achieve a greater equality of expenditures is likely to lead to higher taxation and lower educational expenditures in the major urban centers, a result that would exacerbate rather than ameliorate existing conditions in those areas.

These practical considerations, of course, play no role in the adjudication of the constitutional issues presented here. But they serve to highlight the wisdom of the traditional limitations on this Court's function. The consideration and initiation of fundamental reforms with respect to state taxation and education are matters reserved for the legislative processes of the various States, and we do no violence to the values of federalism and separation of powers by staying our hand. We hardly need add that this Court's action today is not to be viewed as placing its judicial imprimatur on the status quo. The need is apparent for reform in tax systems which may well have relied too long and too heavily on the local property tax. And certainly innovative thinking as to public education, its methods, and its funding is necessary to assure both a higher level of quality and greater uniformity of opportunity. These matters merit the continued attention of the scholars who already have contributed much by their challenges. But the ultimate solutions must come from the lawmakers and from the democratic pressures of those who elect them.

Reversed.

[JUSTICE STEWART wrote a separate concurring opinion. JUSTICE WHITE wrote a dissenting opinion, concurred in by JUSTICES DOUGLAS and BRENNAN, in which he would invalidate the Texas plan because it bore no rational relationship to the legitimate state purpose of maximizing local initiative and choice. — Eds.]

MR. JUSTICE MARSHALL, with whom MR. JUSTICE DOUGLAS concurs, dissenting.

[Justice Marshall described the majority's holding as "a retreat from our historic commitment to equality of educational opportunity"; and he had no difficulty in finding that "the schoolchildren of property-poor districts constitute a sufficient class for our purposes." With respect to the relationship between money spent and educational quality, he acknowledged that the authorities disagree as to its significance, but

> [i]t is an inescapable fact that if one district has more funds available per pupil than another district, the former will have greater choice in educational planning than will the latter. In this regard, I believe the question of discrimination in educational quality must be deemed to be an objective one that looks to what the State provides its children, not to what the children are able to do with what they receive. That a child forced to attend an underfunded school with poorer physical facilities, less experienced teachers, larger classes, and a narrower range of courses than a school with substantially more funds — and thus with greater choice in educational planning — may nevertheless excel is to the credit of the child, not the State.

Id. at 83-84.

[In addressing the constitutional questions, Justice Marshall argued for a balanced approach to equal protection analysis rather than either of the "neat categories" of strict scrutiny or mere rationality, for the fundamentality of education, and for recognition of the invidiousness of the group wealth classification created by the state in this case. He noted that the only justification offered was local control, which he found to be, on this record, an excuse rather than a justification.

[Finally, Justice Marshall denied that invalidation of the Texas scheme would mean either the end of a local control of education or the elimination of the property tax as a source of educational funding. All it would end would be interdistrict wealth discrimination. In his conclusion Justice Marshall commented:

> The Court seeks solace for its action today in the possibility of legislative reform. The Court's suggestions of legislative redress and experimentation will doubtless be of great comfort to the schoolchildren of Texas's disadvantaged districts, but considering the vested interests of wealthy school districts in the preservation of the status quo, they are worth little more. The possibility of legislative action is, in all events, no answer to this Court's duty under the Constitution to eliminate unjustified state discrimination.

Id. at 132. — Eds.]

d. State Constitutional Challenges: Thorough and Efficient

The Supreme Court's decision in *Rodriguez* briefly slowed the momentum for achieving school finance reform through the courts. It clearly precluded a fourteenth amendment challenge; and it initially discouraged state equal protection challenges because state constitutional provisions are commonly, although not invariably, interpreted consistently with the federal counterpart. After *Rodriquez,* federal or state courts in at least twenty states dismissed actions patterned generally on the *Serrano-Rodriguez* theory although not all those courts accepted every aspect of the Court's analysis in *Rodriguez. See, e.g., Olsen v. Oregon,* 554 P.2d 139 (Or. 1976) (upholding Oregon's school finance system on a balancing test, which was neither strict scrutiny nor rational relation).

As it turned out, however, the reform movement was far from dead. The New Jersey Supreme Court pointed the way by invalidating that state's school finance system under a state constitutional provision which required:

> The Legislature shall provide for the maintenance and support of a thorough and efficient system of free public schools for the instruction of all the children in the State.

N.J. Const. art. VIII, § 4, ¶ 1. In *Robinson v. Cahill,* 303 A.2d 273 (N.J. 1973), *cert. denied sub nom. Dickey v. Robinson,* 414 U.S. 976 (1973), a decision handed down only two weeks after *Rodriguez,* the New Jersey court rejected a state equal protection claim but held that the funding system (similar to *Serrano* with even heavier reliance on local property taxes) did not satisfy the state's obligation to provide a "thorough and efficient" system of schools. Unlike the negative fiscal neutrality theory of *Serrano,* the New Jersey court's decision required it to confront the problem of defining a positive constitutional mandate for equal educational opportunity. The task was not easy for the court nor for the legislative and executive branches. During a three-year period the state supreme court handed down six opinions or orders,[13] culminating in an order which briefly closed down the entire state common school system until the New Jersey legislature finally bowed to the court's will and enacted a major tax and

---

[13] Robinson v. Cahill, *supra* (Robinson I); 306 A.2d 65, *cert. denied sub nom.* Dickey v. Robinson, 414 U.S. 976 (1973) (Robinson II); 335 A.2d 6 (1975) (Robinson III); 351 A.2d 713 (N.J.), *cert. denied sub nom.* Klein v. Robinson, 423 U.S. 913 (1975) (Robinson IV); 355 A.2d 129 (1976) (Robinson V); 358 A.2d 457 (1976) (Robinson VI). A seventh decision resulted in dissolution of the injunction which closed the schools, 360 A.2d 400 (1976).

school reform package — by a one vote margin. The package included enactment, for the first time in New Jersey's history, of a state income tax, which many considered to be the only revenue source sufficient to fund the Public School Education Act, passed by the legislature to comply with *Robinson,* and to provide some property tax relief.

It is fair to say that by the time of the sixth *Robinson v. Cahill,* the court had spent as much time in reinterpreting what it had held in *Robinson I,* and debating important separation of powers issues as in defining a thorough and efficient education. The dilemma which the court faced as a result of the failure of the other branches to put into effect a school program that would satisfy the constitutional mandate was described by one of the dissenting justices (Justice Mountain) in *Robinson VI,* the decision in which the court enjoined further expenditure of public funds to support the schools. He commented:

> Underlying the question of school financing — with which the series of *Robinson* opinions has been chiefly concerned — exists a far more important issue of constitutionalism: to what extent, if at all, should courts affirmatively intrude to rectify perceived instances of unconstitutional conduct which under our system of government should be corrected by one or other of the political branches of government — the executive or legislative. This is the issue we face here. This Court decided in *Robinson I,* . . . that the system of financing public education in this state violated *Article* 8, § 4, 1 of the New Jersey Constitution. . . . The Constitution places the obligation directly upon the *Legislature.* It is not diffused between or among two or more of the branches of government as are many constitutional obligations; it is imposed squarely upon one of the political branches.
>
> It is the view of a majority of this Court that to this date there has not been legislative compliance with the constitutional mandate. The Court therefore faces the serious dilemma as to whether it should take further action to bring about compliance or stay its hand. Resolving the problem is not easy. This whole question as to the affirmative duty — if such it be — of the judiciary to compel compliance by other branches of government with requirements that have been determined by the judiciary to be necessitated by the Constitution, has been described by an eminent authority as "the next great challenge of American constitutionalism." Cox, *The Role of the Supreme Court in American Government* (1976) 98.
>
> . . . .
>
> Examined abstractly, powerful arguments can be presented to sustain each of the opposing viewpoints. In support of judicial restraint it may be pointed out that judicial activism, of the kind in which the majority has now engaged, generally results in violating accepted notions as to the doctrine of the separation of powers. . . .
>
> Secondly, such judicial activism removes from the legislative body, which has been elected by the people, the opportunity to resolve the problem and gives that power to a small group of persons who have not been popularly elected. . . .
>
> In the third place the intrusion of the judiciary — regardless of alleged provocation — into areas of legislative or executive competence and concern places in serious jeopardy what has been called the Court's "power of legitimacy." . . .
>
> Fourthly, the task of enforcement may often be beyond the competence of the Court for lack of supportive resources. . . .
>
> Finally, . . . [t]he Court may often be unable to view the governmental problem in its entirety and as a whole. For instance, in the case before us the obvious effort of the Court is to compel the raising of a very large amount of money and seeing that it is allocated to educational needs. Worthy as is this purpose,

it takes no account of any number of other public needs of which the Legislature is acutely aware. Welfare, public health, needed renovation and construction of public facilities including correctional institutions, mass transit and essential increases in the wages and salaries of public employees, to name but a few, are also very worthy purposes. But revenues have some finite limit; there is a point beyond which taxpayer endurance cannot be expected to continue. If the judiciary seeks satisfactorily to resolve the problem before it, may not competing needs be forced to go unmet? The Legislature can, as it customarily does, take account of *all* public obligations, and allocate funds accordingly.

On the other hand it is pointed out that unless the courts will act, no one will act. This may or may not be true in a particular case, but the argument has much merit. On its face, at least, there seems no good reason why the citizens of the State should be asked to forego a constitutional right because of governmental inaction. Resort to the ballot box is a last and often ineffectual remedy.

. . . .

Consideration of the present case in the light of what has been abstractly stated above, convinces me that the action taken by the majority is most unfortunate. The Court has resorted to the equitable remedy of injunction. I have grave misgivings as to the wisdom of this step. This is no ordinary injunction. Its effect will be and is intended to be coercive. It is hoped that by threatening to close the schools this Court will induce the Legislature to raise and appropriate for educational purposes some very large sum of money. Thus the Court is indirectly commanding that a tax be imposed. But the taxing power is legislative and cannot be exercised by the judiciary. Should it seek to do indirectly what all readily admit it cannot do directly? It seems to be agreed that in all probability the money can only be raised by imposing an income tax throughout the state. Should the Court throw its great weight and influence in the scales, upon an issue so deeply controversial which has thus far met consistent legislative rejection? Of course the Legislature may, for whatever reason, fail to respond in the manner the majority must anticipate it will. What would happen then?

358 A.2d at 460-62.

Comments: 1. For further discussion of the New Jersey litigation, see, e.g., R. LEHNE, THE QUEST FOR JUSTICE (1978); Berke & Sinkin, *Developing a "Thorough and Efficient" School Finance System: Alternatives for Implementing Robinson v. Cahill,* 3 J.L. & EDUC. 337 (1974); Tractenberg, *Robinson v. Cahill: The "Thorough and Efficient" Clause,* 38 LAW & CONTEMP. PROBS. 312 (1974); Note, *Robinson v. Cahill: A Case Study in Judicial Self-Legitimization,* 8 RUT.-CAM. L.J. 508 (1977); Note, *School Finance Reform: Robinson v. Cahill,* 13 URB. L. ANN. 139 (1977).

In 1981, a new suit was filed on behalf of children in four urban school districts, claiming that the unconstitutional defects of New Jersey's school funding had not been corrected and that the disparities in resources and expenditures were even greater than under the prior scheme. That suit, *Abbott v. Burke,* is pending in the Superior Court, Chancery Division, of Mercer County.

2. In *Robinson VI* both the majority and dissenting Justice Mountain quoted from Professor Archibald Cox's published lectures on the Supreme Court, A. Cox, THE ROLE OF THE SUPREME COURT IN AMERICAN GOVERNMENT (1976). Cox's thesis is that the Warren Court revised the Supreme Court's role from one of negative contribution to public policy to one in which the Court imposed affirmative duties for reform on the political branches of government. In support of this thesis Cox cited the school desegregation and reapportionment decisions and, as an example of the attempt (albeit unsuccessful) to use the courts to obtain equal public benefits, school finance which he described as "[t]he most ambitious effort to use the Constitution to reform on-going State programmes by imposing new affirmative duties." *Id.* at 92. In sympathizing with the United States

Supreme Court's hesitancy to enter the morass of school finance, Professor Cox speculated:

> It would be hardly surprising if some legislature failed to act out of stubbornness, inability to reach a consensus among its members, or a despairing willingness, as in some reapportionment cases, to dump its problems upon the court. Surely the risk was sufficient for the Supreme Court to ask itself, "If some legislature fails to act, what happens next?"
>
> What *would* happen next? It is no answer to say, "Shut down the schools and the legislature will do its duty." But are federal courts all over the country to decide the policy questions, levy the taxes, and distribute the revenues? Not to act would be to acknowledge judicial futility. To act would be to adopt a tax and fiscal policy for the State. It might even become necessary to set up the machinery to make the policy effective. In addition to questions of competency, those of legitimacy would surely arise. Even in the case of legislative default, does a federal court — usually a single judge — have legitimate power to levy taxes on a people without their consent, and to decide where and how public money shall be spent? Nor would this be the end of the road. There is obvious risk of a collision arising between the court and the political authorities at some subsequent date if the court is forced to act and the legislature thereafter chooses a different programme.

Id. at 95-96. Are Professor Cox's concerns unique to the federal courts? Does the history of New Jersey's school finance litigation (which is not ended yet) support or deny Cox's apparent call for caution (although not necessarily forbearance)?

A NOTE ON STATE CONSTITUTIONAL CHALLENGES

Undaunted by *Rodriguez* and perhaps spurred on by *Robinson v. Cahill* as well as *Serrano,* challengers have continued to seek invalidation of their states' school finance systems — with mixed results.[14] In the cases after *Rodriguez,* the constitutional basis for the challenge was either a state equal protection clause or a constitutional provision such as New Jersey's "thorough and efficient," or both.[15] While many of the cases pursued the fiscal neutrality theory of *Serrano,* a number of them pushed beyond that theory even to the point of seeking or requiring (as the New Jersey court purported to do) that the state define and fund a program that meets an affirmative standard of equal educational opportunity. One analyst has identified three complaints running through the litigation of this period: (1) unfairness due to the differential tax wealth of school districts; (2) unfairness due to inadequate recognition of the different costs or needs of the districts; (3) inadequate level of funding of education generally. Andersen, *State School Finance Litigation,* 14 URB. LAW. 583, 585 (1982). See also Education Commission of the States, School Finance Reform in the States: 1980, at 6-7, noting that litigants now argue that expenditures can be related neither to property wealth, nor to household income, municipal overburden, education overburden nor local taxpayer referenda; additionally, that positive standards have been developed in some cases which require the state to implement an affirmative duty.

The major state supreme court decisions are noted below. Litigation is still pending in a number of states. *See generally* Note, *Judicial Control of the Purse — School Finance Litigation in State Courts,* 28 WAYNE L. REV. 1393 (1982).

---

[14] In the period beginning with *Serrano* school finance litigation has proceeded in some 30 states. These developments are reported in Lawyers' Comm. for Civil Rights Under Law, School Finance Project, Update on State-Wide School Finance Cases: 1972, 1974, 1976, 1977, 1978, 1980, 1982.

[15] The state constitutional provisions of 34 states guaranteeing a free public education in language comparable to New Jersey's "thorough and efficient" are collected in Levin, Current Trends in School Finance Reform Litigation: A Commentary, 1977 Duke L.J. 1099, 1103 n.18.

States Upholding the School Finance System

Shofstall v. Hollins, 515 P.2d 590 (Ariz. 1973). The Arizona Supreme Court rejected plaintiffs' argument that the disparities in school district wealth caused by a traditional school finance plan violated the Arizona constitution, specifically, art. XI, § 1, which provides that the legislature "shall enact such laws as shall provide for the establishment and maintenance of a general and uniform public school system." Although holding that education is a fundamental right, the court found that there existed a uniform free educational system throughout the state. In evaluating that system the court required only that it be "rational, reasonable and neither discriminatory nor capricious." *Id.* at 592. Arizona's school finance system met those standards.

Thompson v. Engelking, 537 P.2d 635 (Idaho 1975). The court rejected both a state equal protection claim and one based on the Idaho constitutional provision making it the duty of the legislature "to establish and maintain a general, uniform and thorough system of public free common schools." The Idaho court was reluctant to become a super-legislature, "legislating in a turbulent field of social, economic and political policy." *Id.* at 640. It declined to follow the lead of *Robinson v. Cahill,* noting that "Idaho precedent, dealing with the responsibilities and duties of the various levels of government in our own educational system, requires a different conclusion from that reached by the New Jersey court in analyzing their constitution." *Id.* at 651.

Olsen v. Oregon, 554 P.2d 139 (Or. 1976). The court held Oregon's system not violative of state equal protection or the constitutional provision requiring a "uniform and general system of Common schools."

Danson v. Casey, 399 A.2d 360 (Pa. 1979). The court rejected a challenge by Philadelphia school parents that was based not on the disparities among districts, but on a somewhat ill-defined theory that the state's school finance system failed to provide their children with a thorough and efficient education and denied them equal educational opportunity. The plaintiffs' principal objection seemed to be that the Philadelphia schools did not receive adequate funds, from state and local sources, to maintain "a normal program of educational services."

Board of Education of City School District v. Walter, 390 N.E.2d 813 (Ohio 1979), *cert. denied,* 444 U.S. 1015 (1980). The Ohio court upheld that state's school finance system under both the state equal protection clause and the "thorough and efficient" provision. Particularly interesting in the Ohio case is the fact that the funding mechanism under attack was a variation of district power equalizing. It was termed "equal yield for equal effort" and "[i]ts objective is to equalize the property wealth based upon which the school districts raise operating revenue through the levy of voter-approved taxes so that school districts receive the same number of dollars per pupil in basic state aid plus local revenue for each mill up to 30 mills." *Id.* at 816. There were, in addition, hold-harmless provisions and direct grants for specialized programs.

The court applied a rational relation standard to the equal protection claim, holding that strict scrutiny was "inappropriate" because "[t]his case is more directly concerned with the way in which Ohio has decided to collect and spend state and local taxes than it is a challenge to the way in which Ohio educates its children." *Id.* at 819. Local control was a rational basis for supporting Ohio's system of financing education. With respect to the thorough and efficient clause, the court disagreed with the appellate court that the trial court had overstepped its power in holding that the school finance system violated that clause. It was a justiciable issue, but courts should be circumspect and deferential when reviewing legislative judgments. The court then concluded that the equal yield formula was sufficient to assure an adequate education and that the legislature had not abused its discretion. The dissenting opinion illustrates the shift in approach that has occurred since the *Serrano* fiscal neutrality principle. While referring to wide disparities in funding, the dissent was clearly more concerned with the "meager financial resources" and "emaciated proceeds" which the Ohio statutes made available to the schools. *Id.* at 827, 828.

McDaniel v. Thomas, 285 S.E.2d 156 (Ga. 1981). The court upheld Georgia's system, rejecting both the state equal protection challenge and that based on the state constitutional requirement that the "provision of an adequate education . . . shall be a primary obligation" of the state. The court read the adequate education provision to require a generalized minimum education, which apparently was satisfied, but held that it was for the legislature to give content to the term "adequate" beyond that mimimum. On the equal protection claim, the court noted that "[i]n terms of equalization the system is a poor one. However, the system does bear some rational relationship to legitimate state purposes [local control — Eds.] and is therefore not violative of state equal protection." *Id.* at 168. The legislature had enacted a district power equalization program but had not funded it.

Lujan v. Colorado State Board of Education, 649 P.2d 1005 (Colo. 1982). The Colorado Supreme Court, reversing the district court, upheld the state's school finance system under the state equal protection guarantee and under the provision requiring the general assembly to "provide for the establishment and maintenance of a thorough and uniform system of free public schools." Most of the opinion was devoted to determining whether education was a fundamental right in Colorado and whether wealth was a suspect classification. Neither qualified. A traditional rational basis test was applied and local control provided the legitimate state purpose.

In its rejection of a suspect classification, the court was influenced in part by its conclusion that "suspectness" in this case was dependent on showing a correlation between low-income residents and low-property wealth districts; there was no evidence to show a satisfactory statistical correlation, according to the court. In addressing the status of education as a fundamental right, the court rejected the explicit-implicit test enunciated by the Supreme Court in *Rodriguez* and held that education, while "vital," was not such a fundamental interest as to warrant strict scrutiny. This part of its analysis was similar to that of other courts which have rejected the fundamentality of education. The Colorado court, however, appeared to believe that acceptance of the position that education was a fundamental right inevitably led it also to accept equality of expenditures.

> Appellees [instead] argue that we should accept, amidst a raging controversy, that there is a direct correlation between school financing and educational quality and opportunity. We refuse, however, to venture into the realm of social policy under the guise that there is a fundamental right to education which calls upon us to find that equal educational opportunity requires equal expenditures for each school child. Even if we were to accept appellees' contention, we would, nonetheless, refuse to adopt their *a priori* argument whereby a lack of complete uniformity in school funding between all of the school districts of Colorado necessarily leads to a violation of the equal protection laws in this state.

Id. at 1018.

Similarly, in rejecting the claim based on the "thorough and uniform" clause, the court again seemed to believe that it was being asked to mandate equal expenditures.

We find that Article IX, Section 2 of the Colorado Constitution is satisfied if thorough and uniform educational opportunities are available through state action in each school district. While each school district must be given the control necessary to implement this mandate at the local level, this constitutional provision does not prevent a local school district from providing additional educational opportunities beyond this standard. In short, the requirement of a "thorough and uniform system of free public schools" does not require that educational expenditures per pupil in every school district be identical.

Id. at 1025.

Although the state school aid formula contained a form of district equalization, the overall scheme, as the court acknowledged, rested in part on property values, resulting in variances in the amounts raised and spent per pupil among the school districts. See *id.* at 1013-14. The extent of the disparities was not referred to in the majority opinion, but was spelled out in the dissenting opinion of Justice Lohr, quoting from the trial court's findings. The dissent's point was that the school finance system operated in such a way as to lock in the inability of the low-wealth districts to improve their funding capacity. Given these factors, could it be argued that the majority opinion did not correctly address the constitutional argument?

States Invalidating the School Finance System

Horton v. Meskill, 376 A.2d 359 (Conn. 1977). The court invalidated Connecticut's school finance system under the state's equal rights and equal protection provisions, finding that education was a fundamental right and applying a strict scrutiny standard. The court left to the legislature the duty of fashioning a constitutional system, noting that many options were available and that absolute equality was not required. At the time of suit, Connecticut relied very heavily on local property tax funding for the schools (seventy percent), and the bulk of state aid (over eighty percent) was distributed in the form of flat grants.

Seattle School District No. 1 v. State, 585 P.2d 71 (Wash. 1978). Under a state constitutional provision which makes it "the paramount duty of the state to make ample provision for the education of all children," the court held that the state had a mandatory duty to "make ample provision for the 'basic education' of our resident children through a general and uniform system supported by dependable and regular tax sources." *Id.* at 97. This obligation was not met by a funding system under which a significant portion of school funds (25.6% statewide; 37.7% in the Seattle district) was provided by special excess levies — local taxes which were dependent on voter approval. That system, which was not a "dependable and regular tax source" (*id.* at 99) was unconstitutional, although the court would permit the use of special levies to fund enrichment programs which go beyond the basic education. Absent the special excess levies, the court held, the state system of funding did not comply with the constitutional mandate for the children of the Seattle district.

The court made clear that it was for the legislature to define the content of basic education and to determine a sufficient level of funding (without reliance on special excess levies), and it allowed the legislature until July 1981 for compliance. The court's decision effectively overruled *Northshore School District No. 417 v. Kinnear,* 530 P.2d 178 (Wash. 1974), an earlier and unsuccessful attack on the state's school funding system which was based on the disparities resulting from inequality in assessed valuation. Justice Rosellini (a former governor), joined by two other members of the court, filed a strong dissent in the *Seattle* case, decrying that the majority had usurped the legislative function of making public policy decisions on educational levels and allocation of funds.

Beyond providing broad constitutional guidelines, the majority decision in *Seattle* purported to leave entirely to the legislature the responsibility to define the substantive content of a "basic education" and to make ample provision for funding it. Compare *Pauley v. Kelly, infra* where the West Virginia courts also decided that the constitution imposed an affirmative duty to provide a "thorough and efficient" education. In that case, the courts went on to define in exquisite detail what that educational offering should include and also ordered changes in the property taxation system. One commentator has suggested that the *Seattle* majority might not have deferred as much to legislative discretion as it claimed, at least with respect to the funding system. "[But], in fact, the opinion substantially limited the range of legislative choice. To begin with, the majority opinion removed from possible legislative choice any system with significant local control over funding levels. No legislative plan can meet the Stafford [majority—Eds.] requirements that is not essentially a fully state funded plan." Andersen, *School Finance Litigation — The Styles of Judicial Intervention,* 55 WASH. L. REV. 137, 153 (1979).

For subsequent action in Washington, see *Seattle School District No. 1 v. State,* 647 P.2d 25 (Wash. 1982). The legislature had enacted the Basic Education Act of 1977 and had "fully funded" it in the 1981 appropriations. Due to a state fiscal crisis, the Governor by executive order had insituted across-the-board cuts, including education. In this decision a majority of the court refused to enjoin the Governor's action on traditional injunctive relief grounds, commenting that the petitioners have not shown "that they have a clear legal right to a particular dollar amount of funding." *Id.* at 26.

Pauley v. Kelly, 255 S.E.2d 859 (W. Va. 1979). The court reversed dismissal of the complaint, holding that the presence of a "thorough and efficient "clause in the state constitution demonstrated that education was a fundamental right and that state equal protection thus required that any discriminatory classification be subjected to strict scrutiny. In a decision that is unique among the school finance cases, the court exhaustively traced the history and interpretation of "thorough and efficient" clauses in state constitutions and arrived at a definition by which the lower court was to test West Virginia's system on remand:

> We may now define a thorough and efficient system of schools: It develops, as best the state of education expertise allows, the minds, bodies and social morality of its charges to prepare them for useful and happy occupations, recreation and citizenship, and does so economically.
>
> Legally recognized elements in this definition are development in every child to his or her capacity of (1) literacy; (2) ability to add, subtract, multiply and divide numbers; (3) knowledge of government to the extent that the child will be equipped as a citizen to make informed choices among persons and issues that affect his own governance; (4) self-knowledge and knowledge of his or her total environment to allow the child to intelligently choose life work — to know his or her options; (5) work-training and advanced academic training as the child may intelligently choose; (6) recreational pursuits; (7) interests in all creative arts, such as music, theatre, literature, and the visual arts; (8) social ethics, both behavioral and abstract, to facilitate compatibility with others in this society.
>
> Implicit are supportive services: (1) good physical facilities, instructional materials and personnel; (2) careful state and local supervision to prevent waste and to monitor pupil, teacher and administrative competency.

Id. at 877.

The court added that if the existing educational system was found not to meet those high equality standards, the trial court must also ascertain that the failure did not result from inefficiency and failure (by the school districts) to follow existing statutes. Accompanying the remand was a detailed listing of the issues, witnesses, and facts which the trial court was to consider, covering not only school funding and management, but also the property tax assessment system. Following remand and an extensive trial, on May 11, 1982, Judge Arthur Recht of the Circuit Court of Kanawha County issued his opinion, holding that the West Virginia school finance system violated the "thorough and efficient" and equal protection clauses of the state constitution. The opinion is unreported but is summarized in Lawyers Committee for Civil Rights Under Law, School Finance Project, Update on State-wide School Finance Cases 36-39 (1982). The court defined in detail the standards necessary to provide a thorough and efficient education (curriculum, staff, facilities, instructional materials and equipment, health, transportation, etc.), and held that they were not being met in the property-poor districts. The court also criticized the taxing authorities' failure to enforce the constitutionally required equal and uniform taxation of property. The court called upon the legislature "to completely re-construct the entire system of education in West Virginia," and he stated his intention to appoint a commissioner (later modified to an advisory committee) to develop a master plan which would meet the high quality educational system which the constitution required. Judge Recht's decision has not been appealed.

Washakie County School District No. One v. Herschler, 606 P.2d 310 (Wyo.), cert. denied, 449 U.S. 824 (1980). The court without trial invalidated Wyoming's school finance system under the state equal protection clause, relying heavily on the *Serrano* theory. Although the court invoked equality of financing as its objective, it made clear that it was not requiring that each school district receive exactly the same number of dollars per pupil, a course that would not take into account special problems and special needs. An earlier related decision is *Sweetwater County Planning Committee for the Organization of School Districts v. Hinkle,* 491 P.2d 1234 (Wyo. 1971).

One of the most important and interesting of the recent school finance decisions was that of New York's highest court in part because it dealt directly with two issues particularly acute to urban school systems: municipal overburden and disproportionately higher educational costs. The issue of municipal overburden was raised in some of the earlier cases, including *Robinson v. Cahill* where the court made clear in *Robinson V* that the state funding plan must be prepared to deal with districts whose fiscal incapacity is due to municipal overburden. It has been a point of frequent discussion in the literature. In the New York case it was also extensively tried and was a major factor in the lower courts' holding of unconstitutionality. The court of appeals' disposition of this and the urban high-cost issue, as well as the equal protection claim, appears in the following opinion.

BOARD OF EDUCATION, LEVITTOWN UNION FREE SCHOOL DISTRICT v. NYQUIST

Court of Appeals of New York
57 N.Y.2d 27, 439 N.E.2d 359, 453 N.Y.S.2d 643 (1982),
appeal dismissed, 103 S. Ct. 775 (1983)

Opinion of the Court

JONES, JUDGE.
The present amalgam of statutory prescriptions for State aid to local school

districts for the maintenance and support of public elementary and secondary education does not violate the equal protection clause of either the Federal or the State Constitution nor is it unconstitutional under the education article of our State Constitution.

This declaratory judgment action challenging the State's provisions for financing our public schools is prosecuted by two groups, representing different constituencies and mounting attacks based on different predicates. The original plaintiffs by which the action was instituted in 1974 are the boards of education of 27 school districts located at various sites in the State and 12 students of public schools located in some of those districts. The intervenors, whose participation in the action was agreed to by the original parties, are the boards of education, officials, resident taxpayers, and students of the Cities of New York, Buffalo, Rochester and Syracuse, together with a federation of parent and parent-teacher associations in the City of New York. Defendants are the Commissioner of Education, the University of the State of New York, the State Comptroller and the Commissioner of Taxation and Finance of the State of New York.

It is the contention of the original plaintiffs (who are "property-poor" school districts) that the system for financing public schools presently in effect in this State (as principally set forth in Education Law, § 2022 [provision for local district financing]; and § 3602 [apportionment of State aid]) by which funds raised by locally imposed taxes are augmented by allocations of State moneys in accordance with a variety of formulas and grants, violates the equal protection clauses of both the State and the Federal Constitutions and the education article of our State Constitution because that system results in grossly disparate financial support (and thus grossly disparate educational opportunities) in the school districts of the State. The intervenors, representing interests in school districts located in four of the largest cities in the State, also assert violations of the same State and Federal constitutional provisions as the result of circumstances said to be peculiar to cities which they contend place them in a position comparable to that of property-poor districts. Included in these circumstances, they assert, are special financial burdens borne by cities in four categories: (1) demands on municipal budgets (from which local funds for education are secured) for noneducation needs peculiar to cities ("municipal overburden"), (2) diminished purchasing power of the municipal education dollar, (3) significantly greater student absenteeism (with a resulting adverse effect both because of added operational costs and because State aid is largely allocated on the basis of average daily attendance), and (4) larger concentrations in cities of pupils with special educational needs, all four of which may be comprehended within the term "metropolitan overburden". These factors are said to result in greatly disparate educational opportunities available to children in the cities' public schools when compared to the offerings of some of the school districts not located within cities.

Succinctly stated, it is the gravamen of the complaint of the original plaintiffs (and the findings of the courts below provide factual support for their argument) that property-rich districts have an ability to raise greater local tax revenue enabling them to provide enriched educational programs beyond the fiscal ability of the property-poor districts. The intervenors argue that although they are not disadvantaged in their ability to raise gross revenue from local sources, in consequence of the economic factors of metropolitan overburden the net effective economic ability of the city districts falls well below that of noncity districts (and the factual determinations made below support their argument). Both then assert that State aid as presently granted serves to perpetuate, and even to exacerbate, these disparities.

. . . .

After an extended nonjury trial which produced 23,000 pages of transcript and 400 exhibits, the Justice presiding issued a judgment declaring that the State's public school finance system violates both the equal protection clause (art. I, § 11) and the education article (art. XI, § 1) of the State Constitution and, as to the cities whose interests are represented by the intervenors, the equal protection clause (14th Amdt., § 1) of the Federal Constitution as well.... The Appellate Division, by a divided court, modified the judgment of the trial court; while concurring in the determination that the provisions of the State Constitution had been violated, the appellate court rejected the conclusion that the intervenors had also established a violation of the Federal Constitution.... We now modify the order of the Appellate Division and direct that judgment be entered declaring that the present admixture of statutory provisions for State aid to local school districts, considered in connection with the existing system for local financing, is constitutional under the equal protection clause of the Federal Constitution and under both the equal protection clause and the education article of the State Constitution.

At the outset it is appropriate to comment briefly on the context in which the legal issues before us arise. Although New York State has long been acknowledged to be a leader in its provision of public elementary and secondary educational facilities and services, and notwithstanding that its per pupil expenditures for such purposes each year are very nearly the highest in the Nation,[2] it must be recognized that there are nonetheless significant inequalities in the availability of financial support for local school districts, ranging from minor discrepancies to major differences, resulting in significant unevenness in the educational opportunities offered.[3] These disparities may properly be ascribed in some respects to the wide variances between the property assessment bases on which local district taxes are imposed.[16] Similarly, it may be accepted that the four major cities represented by the intervenors, by reason of the factors encompassed in metropolitan overburden, are forced to provide instructional services and facilities of a lesser quantity, variety, and quality than those provided in some other school districts. No claim is advanced in this case, however, by either the original plaintiffs or the intervenors that the educational facilities or services provided in the school districts that they represent fall below the State-wide minimum standard of educational quality and quantity fixed by the Board of Regents; their attack is directed at the existing disparities in financial resources which lead to educational unevenness above that minimum standard.

The determination of the amounts, sources, and objectives of expenditures of public moneys for educational purposes, especially at the State level, presents issues of enormous practical and political complexity, and resolution appropriately is largely left to the interplay of the interests and forces directly involved and indirectly affected, in the arenas of legislative and executive activity. This is of the very essence of our governmental and political polity. It would normally

---

[2] For the year 1981-1982 there was expended $9.6 billion for public elementary and secondary education, $4 billion of State aid (the largest single item in the State budget) and $5.6 billion raised by local taxes. [At the time of trial fifty-five percent of educational funds came from local sources; forty percent, from the state; the remainder from federal aid. — Eds.]

[3] We are assuming that there is a significant correlation between amounts of money expended and the quality and quantity of educational opportunity provided.

[16] For example, the disparity in property wealth ranged from $412,370 per pupil on a weighted average daily attendance to $8,884, a ratio of 46 to 1. When the extremes were eliminated, the ratio was still more than 4 to 1. The disparity in operating expenditures per pupil ranged from $4,215 to $936. Additional disparities were elaborated in the lower court opinions, *Levittown,* 408 N.Y.S.2d 606, 615-17 (Sup. Ct. 1978), 443 N.Y.S.2d 843, 849-50 (App. Div. 1981). — Eds.

be inappropriate, therefore, for the courts to intrude upon such decision-making.... With full recognition and respect, however, for the distribution of powers in educational matters among the legislative, executive and judicial branches, it is nevertheless the responsibility of the courts to adjudicate contentions that actions taken by the Legislature and the executive fail to conform to the mandates of the Constitutions which constrain the activities of all three branches. That because of limited capabilities and competences the courts might encounter great difficulty in fashioning and then enforcing particularized remedies appropriate to repair unconstitutional action on the part of the Legislature or the executive is neither to be ignored on the one hand nor on the other to dictate judicial abstention in every case. In the discharge of our judicial responsibility in this case, recognizing the existence of the very real disparities of financial support as found by the lower courts, we nonetheless conclude that such disparities do not establish that there has been a violation of either Federal or State Constitution.[4]

[The court first rejected the original plaintiffs' fourteenth amendment claim on the authority of *Rodriguez*. — Eds.]

With respect to the intervenors' position in this litigation, not *in haec verba* put before or considered by the Supreme Court in *San Antonio*, that metropolitan overburden is an unequalizing force which must be remedied by compensating increases in State aid to city school districts, a response is found in the opinion by Justice Hopkins at the Appellate Division, which observes that the cited inequalities existing in cities are the product of demographic, economic, and political factors intrinsic to the cities themselves, and cannot be attributed to legislative action or inaction. While unquestionably education faces competition in the contest for municipal dollars from other forms of public service for which nonmunicipal school districts bear no responsibility, municipal dollars flow into the cities' treasuries from sources other than simply real property taxes — sources similarly not available to nonmunicipal school districts. The disbursement of the funds received from real estate taxes and such other sources and the decisions as to how they shall be allocated are decisions to be made by municipal governmental bodies. In the words of Justice Hopkins: "It is beyond the power of this court in this litigation to determine whether the appropriations of the intervenor-plaintiffs have been wisely directed or reasonably applied, or whether their budgets are fairly divided in terms of priority of need between the competing services, such as police, fire, health, housing and transportation, and it is, equally, beyond the power of the court to determine whether the resources of the intervenor-plaintiffs can otherwise be employed so that their educational needs can be met."... Accordingly, we conclude that, applying the rational basis

---

[4] Although worded in terms of a challenge to the State's system for financing public education including both financial support generated by real property taxation within the local district and that received from the State in the form of State aid, we interpret the assault to be primarily focused on asserted constitutional infirmities in the provisions for State aid. No argument is advanced, for instance, that the legislature should realign local school district boundaries to assure property-equal districts or that some other revenue-generating means should be substituted for local district real property taxation. Indeed, we have some doubt as to the jurisprudential prudence (assuming that our court would have jurisdiction to do so) of issuing any blanket declaration of unconstitutionality as to the entire system for financing public education, composed as it is of a combination of local and State-wide factors, economic and political — if for no reason other than the great difficulty of fashioning practical remedies or of implementing any such declaration.... Challenges to the provisions made by the Legislature for appropriation and allocation of State aid to local school districts in the light of the present geographical boundaries of such districts fixed by legislative action and of legislative authorization for local district real property taxation, do present justiciable issues which call for judicial resolution.

test, the intervenors have failed to demonstrate denial of equal protection under the Federal Constitution.

We turn then to the claims of both original plaintiffs and intervenors that, whatever may be determined with respect to the equal protection clause of the Federal Constitution, a violation of the comparable provision of our State Constitution (art. I, § 11) has been demonstrated — the conclusion reached by both courts below. Our attention must first be directed to identification of the standard appropriate to the subject now before us (financial support for public education) for examination as to whether there has been a violation of our constitutional mandate of equal protection. . . . The Appellate Division, declining to apply the measurement of strict scrutiny that had been employed by the trial court and under which the trial court had found the education finance system invalid, concluded that the intermediate or more careful scrutiny test described in *Alevy v. Downstate Med. Center of State of N. Y.*, 39 N.Y.2d 326, 384 N.Y.S.2d 82, 348 N.E.2d 537 was properly to be employed — justifying this decision by its conclusion that the right to education in this State "represents an important constitutional interest". . . . The choice of that intermediate standard, under which the appellate court also found the system invalid, cannot be sustained however, both for the previously recited reasons articulated in the *San Antonio* case and in face of our decision in *Matter of Levy*, 38 N.Y.2d 653, 382 N.Y.S.2d 13, 345 N.E.2d 556, app. dsmd. *sub nom. Levy. v. City of New York*, 429 U.S. 805, . . . reh. den. 429 U.S. 966. . . . In *Levy* we expressly held that rational basis was the proper standard for review when the challenged State action implicated the right to free, public education. Nothing in the present litigation impels a departure from that decision, made as it was with full recognition of the existence in our State Constitution of the education article (art. XI).

The circumstance that public education is unquestionably high on the list of priorities of governmental concern and responsibility, involving the expenditures of enormous sums of State and local revenue, enlisting the most active attention of our citizenry and of our Legislature, and manifested by express articulation in our State Constitution, does not automatically entitle it to classification as a "fundamental constitutional right" triggering a higher standard of judicial review for purposes of equal protection analysis. Thus, in *Matter of Bernstein v. Toia*, 43 N.Y.2d 437, 402 N.Y.S.2d 342, 373 N.E.2d 238, where the concern was public assistance to the needy — clearly a matter of significant interest, provision for which is similarly included in our State Constitution [5] (art. XVII, § 1) — we employed the rational basis test as the proper standard for review. The more careful scrutiny standard has been applied when the challenged State action has resulted in intentional discrimination against a class of

---

[5] The inclusion in our State Constitution of a declaration of the Legislature's obligation to maintain and support an educational system is not to be accorded the same significance for purposes of equal protection analysis as would a counterpart reference to education in the Federal Constitution. The two documents are drafted from discretely different constitutional perspectives. The Federal Constitution is one of delegated powers and specified authority; all powers not delegated to the United States or prohibited to the States are reserved to the States or to the people (U.S.Const., 10th Amdt.). Great significance accordingly is properly attached to rights guaranteed and interests protected by express provision of the Federal Constitution. By contrast, because it is not required that our State Constitution contain a complete declaration of all powers and authority of the State, the references which do appear touch on subjects and concerns with less attention to any hierarchy of values, and the document concededly contains references to matters which could as well have been left to statutory articulation (e.g., provision for superintendence and repair of canals, art. XV, § 3, scarcely to be classified a fundamental constitutional right on any view).

persons grouped together by reason of personal characteristics, the use of which called into question the propriety of the particular classifications....

No classification of persons is present in the case now before us, in which the claimed unequal treatment is among school districts resulting from disparity as to revenue available for educational purposes in consequence of unequal tax bases or unequal demands on local revenue. The claim is of discrimination between property-poor and property-wealthy school districts. No authority is cited to us, however, that discrimination between units of local government calls for other than rational basis scrutiny.

Our inquiry is therefore only whether there has been demonstrated the absence of a rational basis for the present school financing system, premised as it is on local taxation within individual school districts with supplemental State aid allocated in accordance with legislatively approved formulas and plans. Addressing the submissions of the original plaintiffs, our conclusion is that there has not been such a showing, and that the justification offered by the State — the preservation and promotion of local control of education — is both a legitimate State interest and one to which the present financing system is reasonably related.

Under the existing system the State is divided into more than 700 local school districts, each of which varies from the others and, from time to time, varies within itself, in greater or lesser degree, as to number of pupils and value of assessable real property, as well as with respect to numerous other characteristics, including personal wealth of its taxpayers. Outside the cities in the State (in which school funding is a part of the total municipal fiscal process), funds for the support of the education program offered in the schools of a district are raised through the imposition of local taxes following voter authorization based on approval of a budget prepared and submitted by an elected board of education, reflecting the instructional program (within standards fixed by the State) perceived by the local board of education to be responsive to the needs and desires of the community. By way of assuring that a basic education will be provided and that a uniform, minimum expenditure per pupil will occur in each district, the Legislature has long provided for payment of supplementing State aid such that presently $1,885 per pupil (and, by a weighting computation, larger amounts for particular types of pupils) is available for education in each district. Throughout the State, voters, by their action on school budgets, exercise a substantial control over the educational opportunities made available in their districts; to the extent that an authorized budget requires expenditures in excess of State aid, which will be funded by local taxes, there is a direct correlation between the system of local school financing and implementation of the desires of the taxpayer.

It is the willingness of the taxpayers of many districts to pay for and to provide enriched educational services and facilities beyond what the basic per pupil expenditure figures will permit that creates differentials in services and facilities. Justification for a system which allows for such willingness was recognized by the Supreme Court of the United States in *San Antonio School Dist. v. Rodriguez*, 411 U.S. 1, 48, n. 102.... Any legislative attempt to make uniform and undeviating the educational opportunities offered by the several hundred local school districts — whether by providing that revenue for local education shall come exclusively from State sources to be distributed on a uniform per pupil basis, by prohibiting expenditure by local districts of any sums in excess of a legislatively fixed per pupil expenditure, or by requiring every district to match the per pupil expenditure of the highest spending district by means of local taxation or by means of State aid (surely an economically unrealistic hypothesis)

— would inevitably work the demise of the local control of education available to students in individual districts. . . .

The State-wide $360-per-pupil flat grant provided by State aid legislation is immune from attack under the equal protection clause, for on its face there is no inequality in this per pupil distribution of State aid which is allocated to all school districts without differentiation. Nor does the fact that the "save harmless" or special aid grants accrue to the benefit of only those districts which stand to suffer identified harm by reason of changing property values or of diminishing pupil registration serve to invalidate the school financing system. In addition to the fact that only a minimal amount of State aid is distributed under this category, we cannot say that there is no rational basis for the Legislature's selection of districts subject to these impacts as those for whom alleviating relief is appropriate and for its provision for such relief so long as the relief is uniformly available to school districts falling within the classifications.

As to the intervenors, their contentions that they are denied equal protection under the State Constitution must be rejected for the same reasons that their comparable claims under the Federal Constitution are rejected. . . .

Finally, we consider the claim, upheld by all the Judges below, that the present school financing system violates the education article (art. XI, § 1) of our State Constitution. It is there required that "[t]he legislature shall provide for the maintenance and support of a system of free common schools, wherein all the children of this state may be educated."

It is significant that this constitutional language — adopted in 1894 at a time when there were more than 11,000 local school districts in the State, with varying amounts of property wealth offering disparate educational opportunities — makes no reference to any requirement that the education to be made available be equal or substantially equivalent in every district. Nor is there any provision either that districts choosing to provide opportunities beyond those that other districts might elect or be able to offer be foreclosed from doing so, or that local control of education, to the extent that a more extensive program were locally desired and provided, be abolished. What appears to have been contemplated when the education article was adopted at the 1894 Constitutional Convention was a State-wide system assuring minimal acceptable facilities and services in contrast to the unsystematized delivery of instruction then in existence within the State. Nothing in the contemporaneous documentary evidence compels the conclusion that what was intended was a system assuring that all educational facilities and services would be equal throughout the State. The enactment mandated only that the Legislature provide for maintenance and support of a system of free schools in order that an education might be available to all the State's children. There is, of course, a system of free schools in the State of New York. The Legislature has made prescriptions (or in some instances provided means by which prescriptions may be made) with reference to the minimum number of days of school attendance, required courses, textbooks, qualifications of teachers and of certain nonteaching personnel, pupil transportation, and other matters. If what is made available by this system (which is what is to be maintained and supported) may properly be said to constitute an education, the constitutional mandate is satisfied.

Interpreting the term education, as we do, to connote a sound basic education, we have no difficulty in determining that the constitutional requirement is being met in this State, in which it is said without contradiction that the average per pupil expenditure exceeds that in all other States but two. There can be no dispute that New York has long been regarded as a leader in free public education. Because decisions as to how public funds will be allocated among the several services for which by constitutional imperative the Legislature is required to make provision are matters peculiarly appropriate for formulation by the legislative body (reflective of and responsive as it is to the public will), we would be reluctant to override those decisions by mandating an even higher priority for education in the absence, possibly, of gross and glaring inadequacy — something not shown to exist in consequence of the present school financing system.

For the reasons stated,[9] the order of the Appellate Division should be modified, without costs, to direct that the judgment of Supreme Court be modified by substituting for the declarations that the State's school financing system violates the equal protection clause and the education article of the State Constitution a declaration that the present statutory provisions for allocation of State aid to local school districts for the maintenance and support of elementary and secondary public education are not violative of either Federal or State Constitution.

FUCHSBERG, JUDGE (dissenting).

[The dissent concluded that New York's school financing system violated both of the state constitutional provisions. A substantial part of the dissent recited the findings of the lower courts describing the impact of that system, first, on the large cities with their disproportionately large number of pupils with special educational needs and their municipal overburden, and, second, on the property poor districts.—Eds.]

Comments: 1. The underlying thesis of the intervening plaintiffs (the four large cities of New York, Buffalo, Rochester and Syracuse) was that the state aid formula failed to measure the true capacity of large urban school districts to finance public education. This was so for several reasons.

> It is the contention of the intervenors that the inexorable costs of providing a large number of non-educational services reduced the amount of revenue derived from real property taxation and available to finance education. It is this need to provide those non-educational municipal services which is called "municipal overburden" and which the "property per child" state aid standard does not adequately take into account.

408 N.Y.S.2d at 620. The findings made by the lower courts in support of this theory were detailed. For example, the four intervening cities spent twenty-eight percent of their local taxes for schools while jurisdictions outside of those cities spent forty-five percent; in New York City, excluding federal and state aid, the non-educational expenditure per capita was $401.06 while in the rest of the state it was $183.17. 408 N.Y.S.2d at 621.

---

[9] The dissent illustrates the very great, and perhaps understandable, temptation to yield to a result-oriented resolution of this litigation. Universal acceptance of the central role of education in our society today is unquestioned.

The dissenter, however, misapprehends the issue before us on this appeal. It is not whether education is of primary rank in our hierarchy of societal values; all recognize and support the principle that it is. It is not whether there are great and disabling and handicapping disparities in educational opportunities across our State, centered particularly in our metropolitan areas; many recognize and decry this state of affairs. The ultimate issue before us is a disciplined perception of the proper role of the courts in the resolution of our State's educational problems, and to that end, more specifically, judicial discernment of the reach of the mandates of our State Constitution in this regard. The expostulation of the dissenter, and the urgings of those who would alleviate the existing disparities of educational opportunity, are properly to be addressed to the Legislature for its consideration and weighing in the discharge of its obligation to provide for the maintenance and support of our State's educational system. Primary responsibility for the provision of fair and equitable educational opportunity within the financial capabilities of our State's taxpayers unquestionably rests with that branch of our government. . . .

A second reason why the state aid formula failed to measure their capacity was "educational overburden." In part, the objection was that the use of average daily attendance to distribute state aid penalized large urban districts which have higher absenteeism. More critically, they contended, their schools had the greatest concentrations of children with special and high cost needs. Again, the findings of the lower courts were extensive and dramatic. For example, New York City in 1980-81 had fifty-one percent of the schoolchildren with special educational needs, thirty-three percent of the total public school enrollment and only twenty-nine percent of the state's operating aid. 443 N.Y.S.2d at 851. Moreover, the costs for teachers' salaries and other normal services were considerably higher in the large urban cities. 408 N.Y.S.2d at 624. This combination of factors led one commentator to conclude:

> From every point of view, the big cities [in New York] are the worst off under the present school funding system. Their school funding capacity is no better than that of the property poor districts, yet at greater tax rates they end up with even less state and local operating funds than many of the original plaintiffs in the *Levittown* case.

Silard, Presentation on *Levittown* Ruling to Conference on Challenges to Urban and Suburban Education in the 1980's: Ensuring Equitable and Efficient Public Education in a Pluralist Society (March 1982, Pace Univ. L. Sch.).

Given these additional factors, did the court of appeals' opinion adequately address the intervening plaintiffs' arguments? Is there a difference in theory of constitutional dimensions between the two sets of plaintiffs? Are the intervening plaintiffs really arguing that the constitution requires that funding for education be geared to needs? If so, have we come full circle from *McInnis v. Shapiro, supra*?

2. Even before the New York Court of Appeals' rejection of the municipal overburden and educational overburden theories, their soundness had been questioned by some. Professor Andersen commented:

> Many believe there is no logic in increasing *school* aid to a district merely because residents of the district face high *welfare* or *police* costs. The logical cure for that, say the critics, is state subventions in aid of welfare or police. The court [New York Supreme Court — Eds.] briefly referred to defendants' witnesses on this matter. Defendants could not, of course, contest the fact that noneducational expenses were higher in large cities. But they did urge that any extra noneducational tax burden in urban areas was within the control of local taxpayers; such taxpayers should not be allowed to choose higher quality municipal services and then, complaining about municipal overburden, ask for additional state school aid. Plaintiffs responded by urging that increased expenses in urban areas were not a matter of choice, but were instead required by the very nature of urban life.
>
> The court agreed with plaintiffs that these expenses were "inexorable," and concluded that the witnesses for the state failed to show how a city could avoid present levels of noneducational expenses. That plainly is a difficult burden to impose on a defendant, and it is not at all clear how it could ever be met. Moreover, such a showing is not logically dispositive of the issue to be decided: whether *school* monies should be increased because of higher *police* costs.

Andersen, *School Finance Litigation — The Styles of Judicial Intervention,* 55 WASH. L. REV. 137, 161-62 (1979). He also quoted a letter to the New York Times written by one of the defense witnesses in *Levittown,* Dean Dick Netzer of the Graduate School of Public Administration of New York University:

> Public-finance ecomomists are close to unanimous in considering the "municipal overburden" argument to be without merit. If cities have high non-school costs because they are saddled with fiscal responsibility for welfare, pay high salaries and fringe benefits to non-school employees or choose to engage in a host of marginal activities, then those problems should be addressed directly, by state assumption of welfare costs, tough collective bargaining, better management, or whatever. It makes no sense to increase *school aid* to offset deficiencies in welfare finance or city budgeting.

Id. With respect to the educational overburden argument, Professor Andersen noted:

> Closely related to the overburden argument is the court's acceptance of the existence and relevance of increased costs of education in urban areas and of the increased cost

of educating urban pupils. As indicated above, plaintiffs showed that significantly higher per pupil costs were incurred in urban school systems. The accuracy of this proof is not easy to contest, though some of it will be arguably impressionistic. Even where the numbers are firm, however, their meanings are disputable. Higher costs may reflect increased costs of doing business in urban areas, as the court found, or may merely reflect higher program quality levels — a cause for greater spending that is not necessarily something the state should be compelled to subsidize. Higher teacher salaries may reflect the unattractiveness of urban areas for teachers, or may be caused, as some allege, by a district's unwillingness to battle teacher unions. That urban districts have greater concentrations of poor and minority students may mean, as the *Levittown* court found, that urban districts need more educational resources, or it may mean, as some witnesses testified that state grants-in-aid of welfare should be increased. Indeed, to the extent that the state treasury is finite and claims for education and welfare are therefore mutually exclusive, the court's requirement that educational spending be increased in urban areas could result in lower welfare spending in those areas — not an obvious victory for urban areas with their relatively high proportion of welfare recipients and their relatively low proportion of public school students....

Id. at 162-63.

3. The response in New York state to the need for school finance reform following the two lower court decisions but immediately prior to the Court of Appeals decision is described in Gaeta, *Solutions to the School Finance Inequities Posed by the Levittown Decision*, 14 Urb. Law. 603 (1982); Christiansen & Gifford, *Building Towards School Finance Reform in New York State: Problems, Progress, and Prospects*, 14 Urb. Law. 619 (1982).

A NOTE ON THE LEGISLATIVE RESPONSE TO *SERRANO, RODRIGUEZ* AND THEREAFTER

Since the Supreme Court decision in *Rodriguez*, the course of the school finance reform movement in the courts has been checkered, as the preceding materials reveal. The *"Serrano* movement" was not confined to the courts, however, and perhaps had its greatest impact on state legislatures. The California decision had brought to the forefront of public debate an issue that had been festering for many years: the inequities that the established pattern of school finance created, both in tax burden and in expenditure capability. It was also widely believed — until *Rodriguez* — that the *Serrano* position, or a variation thereof, would prevail. As a result a number of state legislatures began to tackle the problem of revising their systems of funding public education. In the 1972-73 legislative year at least eleven states substantially revised their school aid programs. *See* Grubb, *The First Round of Legislative Reforms in the Post-Serrano World,* 38 Law & Contemp. Probs. 459 (1974) [hereinafter cited as Grubb]. If the school finance litigation did not make new constitutional law in more than a handful of states, it certainly helped to make new statutory law in a large number of states.

Study commissions were created in all of the states, and their deliberations and reports contributed to the pressure for change. A list of state studies is found in A. Stauffer, Major School Finance Changes in 1973, app. 1 (Education Commission of the States, 1973).

The most famous of the state reports was the three-volume Fleischmann Report for New York, N.Y. State Commission on the Quality, Cost and Financing of Elementary and Secondary Education, Final Report (1972), which recommended that New York adopt full state funding, to be financed in part by a statewide property tax. The President's Commission on School Finance also recommended "that State governments assume responsibility for financing substantially all of the non-Federal outlays for public elementary and secondary education, with local supplements permitted up to a level not to exceed 10 percent of the State allocation," and further that "[s]tate budgetary and allocation criteria include differentials based on educational need." President's Commission on School Finance, Schools, People & Money, at xiii (1972). Several states mounted an all-out assault on the property tax as the foundation for school financing. In Colorado, Michigan and Oregon, for example, proposals were submitted to the voters which would have eliminated the local property tax as a source of educational revenue. Despite the presumed public revolt against property taxes which gave impetus to the school finance reform movement, the proposals were all rejected.

Just as *Rodriguez* did not halt school finance reform at the judicial level, it also did not stop attempts at legislative reform. *See, e.g.,* Grubb, *supra;* National Conference of State Legislatures, SCHOOL FINANCE REFORM: A LEGISLATORS' HANDBOOK (J. Callahan & W. Wilken eds. 1976) [hereinafter cited as National Conference of State Legislatures], reporting on eighteen states which had enacted legislative reforms by the close of 1975. That activity has continued to this day although not at the frenzied pace of the early post-*Serrano* years. In the first wave of legislative response, several characteristics began to emerge.

Most of the states which revised their school aid programs during that period incorporated some form of district power equalizing, often in the form of a guaranteed tax base per pupil. Only a few states followed the Coons-Clune-Sugarman district power equalizing principle to the end by providing for "recapture", sometimes called negative aid. With recapture, a property wealthy district must remit to the state, for eventual redistribution, the excess revenues which its larger tax base produced at the given tax rate. Montana was one of the few states to incorporate this device. *See State ex rel. Woodahl v. Straub,* 520 P.2d 776 (Mont.), *cert. denied,* 419 U.S. 845 (1974). At issue was the validity of Montana's new taxing system for the support of public schools. The effect of the system was to impose a uniform statewide property tax and to require counties which raised funds in excess of the amount needed to fund the foundation program to remit the excess to the state to be used to support the foundation program in other counties — a form of "recapture." The court found that provision objectionable because it was a state tax levied for the benefit of the state as a whole, even though some areas may derive more benefit from it.

The Wisconsin negative aid classifications were challenged as a violation of various state constitutional provisions and of the fourteenth amendment's equal protection and due process guarantees. In *Buse v. Smith,* 247 N.W.2d 141 (Wis. 1976), the court, emphasizing the right of local school districts to spend for the support of educational opportunities beyond the state mandated level — a right said to be founded in the constitution — held that Wisconsin's negative aid payments violated the constitutional rule of uniform taxation. In so holding, the court equated negative aid payments with the local property tax which is the source of the payments. The rule of uniformity apparently also requires uniform and equal distribution of tax proceeds: that rule, the court said, was violated by a system under which one school district (negative aid) must levy a tax for the benefit of another (positive aid) district. The reasoning of the majority (three judges dissented) is difficult to follow. *See* Comment, *State Constitutional Restrictions on School Finance Reform,* 90 HARV. L. REV. 1528 (1977).

Another departure from pure district power equalizing that most reform states adopted was authority to override by referendum the tax rate or spending limitations imposed. This authority permits wealthy districts to continue to reap the benefits of their richer property tax base. *See* Grubb, at 467. On the other hand, a number of states attempted to address several major criticisms of the *Serrano* fiscal neutrality approach: that it did not make provision for the fact that some students are more costly to educate than others and that some regions are more expensive; and that the large cities (which are usually not the poorest in property wealth) [17] might actually lose aid despite their added costs. By the use of categorical grants or weighted formulas, revised state plans made additional aid available for such factors as compensatory education, bilingual education, special education, municipal overburden and other geographic differentials. Those programs are summarized in National Conference of State Legislatures, at 6-7, chs. 2 and 3; Grubb, at 466, 468.

Finally, one characteristic common to all of the reform states was that the state share of total school costs increased significantly after adoption of the revised school finance plan. Because increased state aid itself helps to reduce district disparities, "it may well be that increases in the level of state aid will be the most significant aspect of the new school finance legislation." Grubb, at 465.

The changes that were being made in school finance often did not satisfy the challengers, however, and in a number of later court cases, in addition to California's *Serrano II,* the school financing scheme under challenge had already incorporated some changes which themselves were responses to the demand for greater "equity." Undoubtedly one reason for the continuing confrontation is the difficulty of agreeing as to the "equitable" goal of school finance reform. For a study which attempts to define and measure "equity," both for children who receive educational services and for taxpayers who pay for those services, see A. ODDEN, R. BERNE & L. STIEFEL, EQUITY IN SCHOOL FINANCE (Education Commission of the States, 1979).

After a decade of school finance reform, some of the early trends continued, others took form. The Education Commission of the States, which has both reported on and contributed to the "movement," summarized the impact of legislative developments as follows:

> During the past 10 years, half of the states modified their school finance systems. Toward the end of the 1970s, research was undertaken to analyze the impacts of those modifications in order to determine whether the objectives of these programs were being achieved. Numerous studies of individual states have been completed. Typically, these charted the progress of school finance systems over time; however, few studies have compared the states to one another. Those studies that did compare the states found that greater progress was made in reducing the relationship between school district expenditure levels and school district wealth than in reducing the disparity among districts in their expenditure levels. This may simply reflect the fact that in the early part of the 1970s a primary objective of policymakers was to deal with property tax related problems. Studies have also shown that school finance reform led to increased expenditures for education in general and most of the new funds were not used to increase teacher salary levels. Finally, school finance reform has directed funds to districts with special needs, such as large proportions of pupils in need of compensatory education.

A. ODDEN & J. AUGENBLICK, SCHOOL FINANCE REFORM IN THE STATES: 1981, at 41 (Education Commission of the States). One measurable change during the

---

[17] A number of studies have noted that the property tax base in central cities is sometimes higher per pupil than the state average. *See, e.g.,* B. Levin, T. Muller, W. Scanlon & M. Cohen, Public School Finance: Present Disparities and Fiscal Alternatives 13 (Urban Institute, 1973): "With the exception of Detroit, central cities in this study have consistently higher per pupil property values, in part because of the presence of a larger commercial-industrial base than other types of districts within the state; on the other hand, they generally have lower per capita income than suburban districts." In connection with the latter point, the Urban Institute Study also noted that state aid formulas which use an income measure of fiscal capacity benefit central cities and rural areas more than a formula based on property wealth. *Id.* at 19-20.

decade resulting from the increased state contribution to school funding was a shift in the share of total funding coming from each level of government. Measured by revenue receipts by government source, the shares were:

	Federal	State	Local
1968-69	7.3%	40.7%	52.0%
1980-81	9.0%	49.7%	41.4%

Source: Advisory Commission on Intergovernmental Relatings, State and Local Finances, Significant Features 1967 TO 1970, at 45 (1969); Significant Features of Fiscal Federalism 1980-81, at 27 (1981).

The Education Commission 1981 report also identified six major characteristics of school finance reforms enacted during that period:

Expanded General Aid

General operating equalization aid programs have been broadened and strengthened. Districts low in property wealth per pupil have usually become eligible for much more state aid than districts richer in property wealth per pupil. This has usually happened by "leveling up" less wealthy or lower spending districts rather than by redistributing funds from rich to poor districts....

Three types of specific formulas have been used in the efforts to enhance equalization goals.... Some states have enacted higher level foundation programs. Under these finance plans, the state guarantees a minimum level of per pupil revenues. Each local district may supplement that foundation amount. The amount of supplementation is often restricted by state law....

Other states have enacted formulas designed to reward equal local effort with equal revenues per pupil; these plans have been called district power equalization, guaranteed tax base, guaranteed yield, resource equalizer or percentage equalizing....

Several states have added power equalizing components on top of higher level foundation programs so that above the foundation expenditure level, districts are guaranteed similar revenues per pupil at similar tax rates....

As a result of strengthening general aid formulas, state funding has consistently risen. In nearly every state that has enacted a school finance reform, the state not only increased the total dollars that it allocated for elementary/secondary education, but also increased the percent of public school revenues coming from state sources. School finance reform has brought forth increased state support of public schools.

Increased Equity

School finance reforms have increased the equity of state school finance structures. Irrespective of the method chosen, school finance reforms have reduced expenditure per pupil disparities per se, and have been even more effective in diminishing the link between expenditures per pupil and local school district property wealth.... While there had been concern that power equalization types of programs might accomplish the latter but not the former goal, the overall results indicate that progress on both fronts has been made in states that have implemented school finance reforms.... It also appears that school finance reform states have made significantly greater advances in improving the equity of their school financing systems that have states that have not passed school finance reforms....

Expanded Measures of Fiscal Capacity

New methods have been developed to expand the measure of fiscal capacity of local school districts beyond just property wealth per pupil.... Income is likely to be a more important factor as states and school districts seek new sources of revenue for education. A number of states currently return a portion of state collected income taxes to school districts in proportion to amounts collected....

Special Pupil Needs

The states have dramatically expanded their role in providing high cost programs for various special pupil populations. They have expanded the number of programs they support and have increased the level of support for such programs [as handicapped aid, compensatory education, bilingual education — Eds.]

Special District Needs

Additional formula adjustments and factors have been designed to assist school systems with particular district related characteristics. Additional state aid has been allocated for sparsely populated districts, districts with one room rural schools, districts with a very small pupil population, low wealth districts with very high tax rates, urban districts with "municipal overburdening" conditions, districts facing relatively high prices for educational resources, and districts with declining enrollments. Michigan, for example, allocates additional state aid to school districts in which the noneducation tax rate exceeds the statewide average by more than 25 percent. New York State is investigating the impact of municipal overburden since it was a specific issue raised in the *Levittown* court suit. Florida uses a cost-of-living index to adjust state aid distributions to local school districts....

Tax and Spending Limitations

Tax and spending limitations have been incorporated directly into new school finance formulas or into revised rules and regulations in nearly two-thirds of the states. While most of these limitation measures have emergency clauses or other mechanisms that permit some discretion in the application of strict limitations, most school districts in the country nevertheless have constraints on their ability to increase expenditures, budgets or property tax rates....

... While in the extreme, [these] tax or expenditure limitations can have devastating effects on educational programs, they have contributed, in their less extreme forms, to improving the equity of school finance systems.

Id. at 1-5. *See also* Jordan & McKeown, *Equity in Financing Public Elementary and Secondary Schools* in SCHOOL FINANCE POLICIES AND PRACTICES 79 (J. Guthrie ed. 1980).

A NOTE ON THE COST-QUALITY ISSUE AND EQUALITY OF EDUCATIONAL OPPORTUNITY

One of the important and most controversial issues in the school finance debate is also the least understood and even at this date, resolved: does money buy equality of educational opportunity? The underlying premise in the school finance cases, particularly those tried on equal protection grounds, is that disparities in district wealth (measured by assessed valuation) create disparities in expenditure per pupil which in turn deny equal educational opportunity to those pupils who live in the poorer districts and are thus deprived of even the opportunity for equality of expenditure.

Even the cases tried on a theory that goes beyond the *Serrano* wealth disparity theory assumed the importance of available dollars to the quality or equality of educational opportunity. But it was a premise. The question was: have students been deprived of educational opportunity because fewer dollars were spent on their education; is there a relationship between expenditures (cost) and quality? Indeed, how is quality measured? Is it measured by dollars spent (inputs), as the school finance reform theorists seem to assume, or by achievement scores (outputs), or by some other index of educational outcome?

> Not so many years ago, educators measured the "quality" of a school by the resources which went into the school, not by the quality of the students who came out of it. The most ambitious attempt to do this systematically was that of Paul Mort (1946), who established a set of criteria of a good school, most of which were indicated by the resources that could be provided by outlays from the board of education. They included such things as increased school library facilities, smaller pupil-teacher ratios, and nonteaching professional support staffs.
>
> In the 1960s, with the initiation of large-scale surveys of students in national samples of schools (especially in . . . the Equal Educational Opportunity Survey), attention began to shift from resource inputs to the outcomes of education, and in particular to achievement in basic verbal and mathematical skills. . . .
>
> But this shift of attention to the outcomes of education did not bring with it an avalanche of new information about the ways in which schools bring about achievement in cognitive skills. Instead, the most striking result was that variations in schools made considerably less difference in a child's achievement than did variations in that child's family background. An almost equally significant result was that in general, those resources that had been regarded as measures of a school's quality showed little or no detectable relation to achievement, thus raising doubts about the assumptions that had been held concerning a school's quality.
>
> These results have discouraged those who view schooling as a powerful equalizer of opportunity. They even cast doubt on the belief that schools are effective institutions of learning. . . .
>
> . . . .
>
> More optimistic results have been noted in several recent studies. . . .

J. COLEMAN, T. HOFFER & S. KILGORE, HIGH SCHOOL ACHIEVEMENT xxv-xxvi (1982).

The study to which the authors refer, and the event that gave the greatest impetus to the cost-quality dispute was the publication in 1966 for the Office of Education, U.S. Department of Health, Education and Welfare, of the Coleman Report; J. Colman Equality of Educational Opportunity (1966). The principal author of the 1966 report was also one of the authors of the 1982 study, which is a comparison of public, Catholic and private schools at the high school level and their effect on achievement. It was the Coleman report, however, which was the focal point of the dispute. Among the hundreds of statistical tables and findings in this complex report, which was designed chiefly to survey educational opportunities of minorities, was the following:

> Of the many implications of this study of school effects on achievement, one appears to be of overriding importance. This is the implication that stems from the following results taken together:
>   1. The great importance of family background for achievement;
>   2. The fact that the relation of family background to achievement does not diminish over the years of school;
>   3. The relatively small amount of school-to-school variation that is not

accounted for by differences in family background, indicating the small independent effect of variations in school facilities, curriculum, and staff upon achievement;

4. The small amount of variance in achievement explicitly accounted for by variations in facilities and curriculum;

5. Given the fact that no school factors account for much variation in achievement, teachers' characteristics account for more than any other — taken together with the results ... which show that teachers tend to be socially and racially similar to the students they teach;

6. The fact that the social composition of the student body is more highly related to achievement, independently of the student's own social background, than is any school factor;

7. The fact that attitudes such as a sense of control of the environment, or a belief in the responsiveness of the environment, are extremely highly related to achievement, but appear to be little influenced by variations in school characteristics.

Taking all these results together, one implication stands out above all: That schools bring little influence to bear on a child's achievement that is independent of his background and general social context; and that this very lack of an independent effect means that the inequalities imposed on children by their home, neighborhood, and peer environment are carried along to become the inequalities with which they confront adult life at the end of school. For equality of educational opportunity through the schools must imply a strong effect of schools that is independent of the child's immediate social environment, and that strong independent effect is not present in American schools.

Id. at 325.

The suggestion that expenditures on education (at least above some minimum level) had little bearing on student achievement was carried forward in some of the papers that grew out of a Harvard faculty seminar on the Coleman survey, ON EQUALITY OF EDUCATIONAL OPPORTUNITY (F. Mosteller & D. Moynihan eds. 1972) and in another reappraisal of the Coleman data by Christopher Jencks, concerned primarily with economic inequality, C. JENCKS, INEQUALITY, A REASSESSMENT OF THE EFFECT OF FAMILY AND SCHOOLING IN AMERICA (1972). Others took sharp issue with the Coleman methodology or conclusions, or both. *See, e.g.,* Bowles & Levin, *The Determinants of Scholastic Achievement — An Appraisal of Some Recent Evidence,* 3 J. HUMAN RESOURCES 3, 17 (1968). Evidence tending to show a relationship between cost and quality, based on California studies, was also introduced in the *Serrano* trial (*see Serrano v. Priest,* Cal. Super. Ct., April 10, 1974). The dispute was lively.[18]

The President's Commission on School Finance concluded:

The relationship between cost and quality in education is exceedingly complex and difficult to document. Despite years of research by educators and economists, reliable generalizations are few and scattered. What is clear is that when parents, with the means to do so, choose their children's schools, the ones they select, whether public or private, usually cost more to operate than the

---

[18] Summaries of the social science research are found in Schoettle, The Equal Protection Clause in Public Education, 71 Colum. L. Rev. 1355, 1378-88 (1971); McDermott & Klein, The Cost-Quality Debate in School Finance Litigation: Do Dollars Make a Difference?, 38 Law & Contemp. Probs. 415, 423-54 (1974) (calls attention to weaknesses of using standardized achievement tests to evaluate effectiveness of school programs and expenditures). For a highly readable account of the social science dispute and some of the personalities involved, see Hodgson, Do Schools Make a Difference?, The Atlantic, March 1973, at 35.

school they reject. There are exceptions, of course, where costs are relatively low and parent satisfaction high, or conversely other schools where costs are high and satisfaction nonexistent. And there are numerous examples of schools where increases in per pupil costs have been accompanied by no discernible improvement in educational quality.

. . . .

Reason would seem to dictate that there must be fruitful ways to spend money to improve schools, to equalize educational opportunity and to produce quality education for children. The fact that research has revealed no sure means for improving schools should surprise no one. The truth is that educational research itself is only beginning to come to grips with the complexity of the total teaching and learning process.

. . . .

Encouraging more research into needs, methods, and possible solutions may seem like counseling patience to a person trapped in a burning building. That is certainly not our intention. But we do not agree with those who argue that money is the remedy for virtually all the ills of our educational system.

With all that, we recognize that money builds schools, keeps them running, pays their teachers, and, in crucial if not clearly defined ways, is essential if children are to learn. . . .

President's Commission on School Finance, Schools, People & Money (1972) at x-xi.

That the educators and social scientists have not resolved the cost-quality dispute does not necessarily eliminate a separate question: in a law suit challenging the constitutionality of disparities in school funds, what is necessary to be proved about the relation between cost and quality, and how is it to be proved? The approach utilized by the plaintiffs in the trial of *Serrano v. Priest* has been described by the chief trial attorney and the expert education witness for the plaintiffs:

Basically, we believe that a negative inputs or expenditures standard of equal educational opportunity should be adopted. An inputs standard defines and evaluates educational opportunities in terms of the programs, services, and facilities made available to children, and thus is a "school concept" of educational opportunities. Inputs are chosen because the focus is upon what the state provides to the child, not on what the child does with what the state provides him, as that is beyond the power of the school to control. The word "quality" should perhaps be avoided, for that connotes an attribute that goes beyond opportunity, beyond what the school itself provides.

. . . .

Proof of the input-opportunity relationship in the affirmative case should be limited to demonstrating existing inequalities in inputs and to presenting testimony of school personnel on the educational consequences of input disparities. Social science research evidence should be avoided during the affirmative case and held for rebuttal, a strategy consistent with the notion that output research is not relevant to equal protection analysis. Input evidence should alone establish a prima facie case of inequality of educational opportunity. Plaintiffs should prevail where no social science evidence is offered to rebut the input-opportunity relationship or where such evidence is deemed legally irrelevant.

The cost-quality relationship may also be regarded as admitted, because of the conduct of the state in encouraging spending above the foundation plan, and the testimony of state and local defendants that expenditures beyond the foundation program can be important educationally if spent wisely. Assertions by the defendants regarding the value of local control also represent an admission on the cost-quality issue, for the very concept of local control presupposes a relationship between cost and educational quality.

Where social science research evidence is offered in school finance litigation to rebut the input-opportunity relationship, and that evidence is accepted by the trial court in resolving the cost-quality issue, the burden of proof can be shifted to defendants who are challenging the legislative declaration of fact underlying the entire financing structure, that is, that money matters. In effect, in school finance litigation plaintiffs are contending that there are no rational bases for those explicit and implicit statutory declarations. If the state is to be permitted to question what should be viewed as legislative factual determinations, then the burden of proof in such an inquiry should properly rest with the party challenging the validity of such statutes.

McDermott & Klein, *The Cost-Quality Debate in School Finance Litigation: Do Dollars Make a Difference?*, 38 LAW & CONTEMP. PROBS. 415, 433-35 (1974).

Discussion of the cost-quality issues in the decided cases after *Serrano* has not been extensive. The Supreme Court, noting that the cost-quality controversy had received considerable attention, said only: "Indeed, one of the major sources of controversy concerns the extent to which there is a demonstrable correlation between educational expenditures and the quality of education — an assumed correlation underlying virtually every legal conclusion drawn by the District Court in this case." *Rodriguez,* 411 U.S. at 42-43. Because the Court rejected the plaintiffs' constitutional claim, it did not have to resolve the "correlation controversy."

State courts which have similarly denied constitutional challenges typically dismiss the issue with brief notice, if indeed they refer to it at all. *See, e.g., Lujan* (Colorado), 649 P.2d at 1018, *supra*. The dissent scolded the majority, pointing out that any disagreement about the cost-quality relationship was resolved by the trial court's factual finding that the level of expenditure per pupil is directly related to the ability to provide educational quality, *id.* at 1035-36. *Danson v. Casey* (Pa.), *supra:* "Even appellants recognize, however, that expenditures are not the exclusive yardstick of educational quality, or even of educational quantity." 399 A.2d at 366; *Thompson v. Engelking* (Idaho), *supra;* one of the court's principal reasons for not wanting to "venture into the realm of social policy," 537 P.2d at 642, was that plaintiff's argument rested on the assumption that the quality of education varies directly with the amount of funds expended — a premise subject to considerable debate.

An exception was *McDaniel v. Thomas* (Georgia), *supra,* where the court rejected the constitutional challenges even though it had specifically found: "The evidence in this case establishes beyond doubt that there is a direct relationship between a district's level of funding and the educational opportunities which a school district is able to provide its children." 285 S.E.2d at 160. The court noted that the funding disadvantages were reflected in the quality of instructional staffs, employee benefits, student-teacher ratios, curriculum offerings, availability of textbooks, library books, instructional aids, counseling, extra-curricular activities, etc. Despite these findings, the court applied an undemanding rational relation test and upheld the funding system. In *Levittown* (New York), *supra,* the court of appeals chose to assume a correlation between money spent and quality of educational opportunity but went on to reject the constitutional claims. The trial court, which held the other way, made extensive findings on the "significant consequences of disparities in expenditures," 408 N.Y.S.2d at 617.

Even in the decisions invalidating school finance systems, the discussion may not be extensive. In *Robinson v. Cahill,* although the justices later got into disputes over inputs vs. outputs vs. other standards of measuring quality, the court's conclusion in the basic opinion was brief and straightforward:

> There was testimony with respect to the correlation between dollar input per pupil and the end product of the educational process. Obviously equality of dollar input will not assure equality in educational results. There are individual and group disadvantages which play a part. Local conditions, too, are telling, for example, insofar as they attract or repel teachers who are free to choose one community rather than another. But it is nonetheless clear that there is a significant connection between the sums expended and the quality of the educational opportunity. And of course the Legislature has acted upon that premise in providing State aid on formulas designed to ameliorate in part the dollar disparities generated by a system of local taxation. Hence we accept the proposition that the quality of educational opportunity does depend in substantial measure upon the number of dollars invested, notwithstanding that the impact upon students may be unequal because of other factors, natural or environmental.

303 A.2d at 277. In *Washakie County School District* (Wyoming), *supra*, the court having found a fundamental right and a suspect class, apparently shifted the burden of proof on all issues to the state defendants and found that they were not persuasive in unlinking financial resources and educational quality. It continued:

> While we would agree that there are factors other than money involved in imparting education, those factors are not easy of measurement and comparison. There is some general disagreement over the degree to which money counts. However, the legislature has here set up a system which fosters and predetermines great disparities in spending. It would be unacceptable logic to deduce that the wealthy counties are squandering their money merely from the fact the poorer counties are getting along just fine and providing an adequate education on the lesser amounts per child they have. For the state and the wealthy districts to put forth the assertion that money is not everything is making just such an argument. Money for school district operations, except for the foundation fund operation and perhaps some federal funds, is not distributed upon the basis of need for quality education. Equality of dollar input is manageable. There is no other viable criterion or test that the appellees show to exist, and our exploration of the subject has resulted only in discovery of a quagmire of speculation, so slippery that it evades any secure grasp for judicial decision making. It is nothing more than an illusion to believe that the extensive disparity in financial resources does not relate directly to quality of education.

606 P.2d at 334. In *Horton v. Meskill* (Connecticut), *supra*, the court reviewed a list of criteria for evaluating the quality of education and concluded:

> In most cases, the optimal version of these criteria is achieved by higher per pupil operating expenditures, and because many of the elements of a quality education require higher per pupil operating expenditures, there is a direct relationship between per pupil school expenditures and the breath and quality of educational programs.

376 A.2d at 368. In the *Seattle School District* case (Washington), *supra*, it was the dissenting justice who reviewed the trial testimony on "the relationship between money and the quality of a child's education," 585 P.2d at 121. He noted:

> Amazingly, all three [educational — Eds.] experts agreed on the most important point: there is no scientific proof of a positive relationship between student achievement levels and various types of input, such as expenditures per pupil, student-teacher ratios, and staff salaries.

Id. The dispute continues.

Chapter 11

THE CHIEF EXECUTIVE

This chapter considers the chief executive — the mayor and the governor. Because the separation of powers principle does not generally apply to local governments, most of the interesting law on executive power has arisen at the state level. This chapter concentrates on the executive power of the governor, and examines his role in the law-making process. The first section considers the validity and use of gubernatorial executive orders. A second section considers the gubernatorial veto as it is applied in the legislative process.

A. EXECUTIVE ORDERS

The Executive Order is not authorized nor even acknowledged in the United States Constitution or the constitutions of the states — except for a few relatively recent and limited references in state constitutions. Yet the practice of chief executives in issuing what came to be known as executive orders or proclamations has existed from the earliest days of the Republic at the federal level and very likely also at the state level — although the recorded history of gubernatorial executive orders is sparse.

The terms executive order and proclamation do not have established meaning, form, or subject matter: the range encompasses such diverse uses as a proclamation establishing Be Kind to Animals Week, a proclamation declaring the results of an election, a memorandum requesting executive offices to conserve energy, an order requiring state offices to close one hour early in winter to conserve energy, an order authorizing collective bargaining for public employees, and an order requiring state agencies to enforce a policy of nondiscrimination by government contractors.

A congressional staff study of presidential executive orders and proclamations described them as follows:

> Executive orders and proclamations are directives or actions by the President. When they are founded on the authority of the President derived from the Constitution or statute, they may have the force and effect of law.
>
> There is no law or even Executive order which attempts to define the terms "Executive order" or "proclamation". In the narrower sense Executive orders and proclamations are written documents denominated as such. . . .
>
> Executive orders are generally directed to, and govern actions by, Government officials and agencies. They usually affect private individuals only indirectly.
>
> Proclamations in most instances affect primarily the activities of private individuals.
>
> Since the President has no power or authority over individual citizens and their rights except where he is granted such power and authority by a provision in the Constitution or by statute, the President's proclamations are not legally binding and are at best hortatory unless based on such grants of authority.

House Comm. on Government Operations, Executive Orders and Proclamations: A Study of a Use of Presidential Powers, 85th Cong., 1st Sess. I (Comm. Print 1957). In a brief history of presidential orders and proclamations the staff study reported that no one knows exactly how many executive orders have been issued, in large part because a majority of orders were never deposited with the Department of State, and the numbering of orders was not instituted until 1907. Estimates of unnumbered orders range from 15,000 to 50,000. With enactment of the Federal Register Act in 1935, however, executive orders and proclamations were required to be numbered and filed with Division of Federal Register. *Id.* at 35-41.

There is still little information readily available about the number and content of executive orders and proclamations issued by state governors. A few states now require that executive orders be maintained or filed as public records, but statutes which go beyond that to attempt to define and otherwise regulate their use are still rare. The Maryland statute is more detailed than most:

§ 15CA. Definition.

(a) In this subtitle, the following words have the meanings indicated.
(b) *"Executive order"* means
(1) A written order, proclamation, or directive issued over the Governor's signature:
(i) Pursuant to Article II, § 24 of the Constitution; [executive reorganization]
(ii) Pursuant to §§ 3A, 14A, or 15B of this article; [relates to secretarial orders, codes of ethics and emergency powers]
(iii) In the exercise of authority granted to the Governor by § 15C of this article or by any other law dealing with organization of the executive branch, both within and between departments, units and agencies of that branch;
(iv) Establishing a task force, board, commission, committee or advisory or study unit; or
(v) Promulgating rules of conduct or procedure, or guidelines for State employees, State agencies, or persons dealing with them or subject to their jurisdiction or control;
(2) A proposal, order, or directive of the secretary of a principal department, changing the organization, placement, or name of a unit of State government within the secretary's jurisdiction and approved in writing by the Governor; and
(3) An amendment, modification, or revocation of any of the above.

Md. Ann. Code art. 41, § 15CA. The statute also provides for an index of executive orders in the office of the Secretary of State, and for the publication of executive orders that affect statutes in the session laws and state code. *Id.,* §§ 15CC, 15CE.

A survey of state governors conducted by the Iowa Law Review in 1964 did not produce overall figures but did suggest considerable variance among the states in the extent of use as well as the form and content of executive orders. The responses also suggested that many states confined the use to ceremonial proclamations and "perfunctory and mandatory statutory requirements." Note, *Gubernatorial Executive Orders as Devices for Administrative Direction and Control,* 50 IOWA L. REV. 78, 97 n.109 (1964).

From the perspective of executive-legislative separation of powers, the major uses of executive orders might be classified in terms of the extent to which the governor's action can be said to be purely executive or to involve elements of law making. The following classification may be helpful.

1. Ceremonial proclamations, in which the governor designates a group, an individual or a cause to be honored, for example, Senior Citizens Week. The largest number of gubernatorial proclamations and orders is of this type. Normally it has no legal impact — unless the proclamation "triggers a holiday," as it might in the case of a day of mourning. *See* Note, *Gubernatorial Executive Orders, supra,* at 82-83.

2. Directives relating to internal administrative matters. For example, the governor issues an order requiring that state employees observe the 55-mile-per-hour speed limit in state cars in order to conserve fuel. This exercise of a governor's authority to administer executive agencies under his jurisdiction would normally be unquestioned.

3. Executive orders creating committees to investigate and advise the governor on personnel practices or computer utilization within the executive department. The creation of the committee would seem to fall within the governor's prerogatives, but the expenditure of state funds for that purpose might be questioned unless the governor had an unrestricted contingency fund.

4. Executive orders and proclamations in which the governor's action affects persons or events outside of his own executive departments but is specifically authorized, or in some cases mandated, by statute or constitution. An example might be a statute empowering the governor to call a special election to fill vacancies. Because the governor's action is specifically authorized, the order or proclamation is not objectionable on grounds the governor usurped legislative authority. The statute might be challenged, however, on grounds that the legislature invalidly delegated its legislative powers.

5. Executive orders or proclamations in which the chief executive makes policy decisions which, whatever the governor's claimed source of authority, the legislature would ordinarily make. These decisions may be essentially administrative or they may affect third persons. In either case, they pose the issue of what is the scope of the governor's lawmaking power?

See also Comment, *Executive Orders of the Wisconsin Governor,* 1980 Wis. L. Rev. 333.

1. GOVERNOR'S POWERS OF ADMINISTRATION: REORGANIZATION

MARTIN v. CHANDLER

Court of Appeals of Kentucky
318 S.W.2d 40 (1958)

Cullen, Commissioner.

Robert R. Martin, Superintendent of Public Instruction of Kentucky, brought action against the Governor, the Commissioner of Finance, and the State Treasurer, seeking a permanent injunction against the carrying out of an executive order of the Governor which ordered that the functions, personnel and funds of the Property Utilization Division of the Department of Education be transferred to the Department of Finance. Judgment was entered dismissing the complaint and Martin has appealed.

The Property Utilization Division, functioning as an organizational unit of the Department of Education, with a substantial personnel, has been carrying out in Kentucky the program of distributing federal surplus property under Title 40, § 484, U.S.C.A. The history of this division, and of the federal statute, is of some significance.

Under the original Surplus Property Act of 1944 (1944, c. 479, Public Law 457, 58 Stat. 765) provision was made for distribution of surplus property appropriate or suitable for education or health uses, to "any State or local government, or to any nonprofit educational or charitable organization." In 1945, in order to enable Kentucky participation in the program, the then Governor, by executive order, created a "State Educational Agency for Surplus Property," composed of ten persons appointed by the Governor, which was directed to function "subject to the approval of the State Board of Education." It appears that the appointed members of the agency did not serve for any substantial period of time, no subsequent appointments were made, and the Department of Education, as such, assumed administration of the surplus property distribution program. In 1948, in the general appropriation act (1948, c. 2), there was included in the appropriations to the Department of Education the following item:

(e) *Surplus Property.* For ordinary recurring expenses of operation, of which $10,000.00 shall be used as a revolving fund,
1948-1949 . . . . $30,000.00

In 1950 the federal act was amended . . . to provide, among other things, that distribution could be made by the federal administrator directly to tax-supported or nonprofit educational or health institutions, or "to State departments of education or health for distribution to such tax-supported and nonprofit . . . institutions . . .; except that in any State where another agency is designated by State law for such purpose such transfer shall be made to said agency for such distribution within the State." In Kentucky, the Department of Education continued to administer the program, and to act as the sole state agency for distribution purposes. In 1954 and 1956 appropriations (in the form of revolving funds) were made by the legislature to the Department of Education for the surplus property program. Early in 1956, in an order of the Superintendent of Public Instruction reorganizing the Department of Education, a Division of Property Utilization was designated within the department, and this order was approved by the Commissioner of Finance and the Governor in accordance with KRS 12.030.

In July, 1956 the federal act was again amended . . . . Under this amendment it was provided . . . that:

> No such property shall be transferred for use within any State except to the State agency designated under State law for the purpose of distributing, in conformity with the provisions of this subsection, all property allocated under this subsection for use within such State.

The 1956 amendment also authorized distribution of surplus property for civil defense purposes, in addition to the former purposes of education and health.

Following the 1956 amendment the State Department of Education through its Division of Property Utilization, continued to administer the surplus property program in Kentucky. In 1958 a revolving fund appropriation was made to the Department of Education for the "Division of Property Utilization (Surplus Property)." . . . Then, on September 2, 1958, the Governor issued the executive order now in question. That order reads as follows:

Secretary of State
Commonwealth of Kentucky
    By virtue of the authority vested in me as Governor of the Commonwealth of Kentucky by Chapter 12 of the Kentucky Revised Statutes, and for greater economy of operation and administrative convenience, I hereby authorize and order, effective as of this date, that all property, officers and employees held by or employed by the Department of Education for use in carrying out property utilization functions and all appropriation balances to the credit of the Department of Education expressly earmarked for use in carrying out property utilization be transferred to the Department of Finance for use in carrying out the purposes of said property utilization organization.
    Executive Order number 383, dated December 28, 1945, is hereby superseded and revoked.

The executive order of 1945, referred to in the last sentence of the 1958 order, is the one hereinbefore referred to, in which a "State Educational Agency for Surplus Property" was created.

. . . .

We conceive of two reasons why the argument is not sustainable that since the surplus property division was created initially by executive order, it can be transferred by executive order. The first reason is that the function of handling the disposition of surplus federal property was not vested in a division of the Department of Education by the executive order of 1945, but rather in a special agency which was to function "subject to the approval of the State Board of Education." The distribution function appears to have come to be exercised by the Department of Education, and the surplus property division to have developed, simply as a result of the nonfunctioning and ultimate disappearance of the designated special agency. The second reason is that, even if it should be considered that the division was created by the executive order of 1945, the Governor has no inherent or implied authority to revoke or retract a completed executive act. . . .

. . . .

The primary argument of the appellees is based on the premise that the surplus property division in the Department of Education was never created by law and has no valid existence. Even if we were to accept this premise, we could not reach the conclusion, contended for by the appellees, that the Governor therefore has the power to vest the distribution function in some other agency. The Governor has only such powers as are vested in him by the Constitution and the statutes enacted pursuant thereto. . . . Basically, his power is to execute the laws, not to create laws.

If the Department of Finance had statutory authority to perform the function of handling the distribution of federal surplus property, for health, education and civil defense purposes, the Governor clearly would have power to authorize that department to establish a subordinate division to administer the function. But the statute relied upon, KRS 42.060, does not give any such authority. The Department of Finance is not set up to perform functions of education, health or civil defense, but is strictly a financial administration agency.

While KRS 12.030 authorizes the Commissioner of Finance, with the approval of the Governor, to permit any department head to "create" subordinate units, we do not conceive this to mean that these officers can vest in a department a *function* of government that the department is not authorized by statute to perform.

In any event, we do not accept the premise that the surplus property division as an administrative unit of the Department of Education has no valid existence. As we view it, the legal status of the division depends upon whether the state has made a valid election to engage in the distribution of federal surplus property as a function of state government, and has validly designated the agency to handle this function.

It must be conceded that the legislature has not, by express, formal language, stated that Kentucky shall engage in the function of surplus property distribution, nor has it by such language authorized or directed the Department of Education to perform this function. However, the fact is that since 1945 the state has engaged in the performance of this function through the Department of Education, and the legislature repeatedly has made appropriations to the Department of Education for this function.

We think it is not unreasonable to say that when the legislature has appropriated funds for the performance of a particular function, this constitutes a valid legislative election that the state engage in the function. Likewise, when the appropriations have been made to a designated divisional unit of an administrative department, which has factual existence, this would seem to be a sufficient designation of the unit as the agency to perform the function. There is no problem about the sufficiency of the defining of the scope of the function, because that is fully taken care of by the federal act.

It is true that the scope of the surplus property program was expanded by the 1956 federal act, but the appropriation made by the 1958 Kentucky legislature, to the "Division of Property Utilization (Surplus Property)," must be considered as authorizing the functions provided for by the federal act as amended.

Since we are upholding the validity of the existence of the surplus property division as a unit of our state government, it will be obvious that we consider the division to be a "State agency designated under State law" within the meaning of the 1956 federal act.

It is our ultimate conclusion that the executive order of September 2, 1958, is invalid, and that the plaintiff below is entitled to the relief prayed for.

The judgment is reversed, with directions to enter judgment granting a permanent injunction as prayed for in the complaint as amended.

BIRD and EBLEN, JJ., concur in the result. [Omitted.]

ATTORNEY GENERAL OF CALIFORNIA

Opinion No. 62-13
40 Op. Att'y Gen. 145 (1962)

The Honorable Edmund G. Brown, Governor of the State of California, has requested an opinion on the following questions:

Does the Governor have authority by executive action to establish the Business and Commerce Agency and thereafter assign the Department of Insurance to the agency; and, further, may the Governor delegate his supervisory power over the Department of Insurance to the Business and Commerce Agency?

The conclusions are:

The Governor, as chief executive of the state, has authority to establish, by executive action, the Business and Commerce Agency and designate an administrator thereof, and may assign the Department of Insurance to such non-statutory agency. However, the Governor may not delegate his discretionary supervisory powers over the Department of Insurance to the Administrator of the Business and Commerce Agency.

Analysis

The Legislature, during the 1961 regular session, enacted Statutes 1961, chs. 2037 and 2073, which provide for a partial reorganization of the state government, as suggested by the Governor in his statement to the Legislature February 13, 1961. These statutes, which became effective October 1, 1961, created four agencies; namely, Resources, Health and Welfare, Youth and Adult Corrections, and the Highway Transportation Agency. Each of these agencies is headed by an administrator appointed by the Governor. On October 1, 1961, the Governor, by executive action, created four more agencies in an interim arrangement until the Legislature could take action to complete the Governor's basic plan of state governmental reorganization. These are called: Revenue and Management; Employment Relations; Public Safety; and Business and Commerce. The Governor assigned various departments, boards, and commissions with related programs to the different non-statutory agencies. To complete such interim reorganization, the Governor also assigned other boards and commissions to the statutory agencies.

The Governor designated the Savings and Loan Commissioner as administrator of the Business and Commerce Agency. The Business and Commerce Agency consists of fourteen state departments, boards, and commissions, one of which is the Department of Insurance. The Insurance Commissioner has questioned the legality of the Governor's action of October 1, 1961, establishing the four non-statutory agencies. . . .

. . . [I]t is clear that the Governor is the state's chief magistrate and executive officer in whom is vested the supreme executive power of the state. . . . It is his primary duty to execute the laws of this state and conduct the executive business, both civil and military, of the state. The Governor is also required to supervise the official conduct of all executive and ministerial officers and see that all offices are filled and their duties performed. Further, the Governor need not personally attend to the enforcement and execution of the laws, but can provide therefor by appropriate executive officers. . . .

It is readily apparent that the intent and purpose of the Governor's action establishing the non-statutory agencies was to provide an interim vehicle to assist him in expediting the executive business of the state. The non-statutory agencies are set up on an informal basis and dependent upon the cooperation of the non-statutory administrator and the various department heads within the agency. There is nothing illegal or irregular in the Governor's establishing such a form of liaison between himself and the several department heads of the state; nor is there anything improper in the Governor's designating a department head as an administrator of such non-statutory agencies at no extra expense to the state. [The administrator received no salary in that capacity, and apparently the Business and Commerce Agency expended no funds in its own name.—Eds.]

In general, the basic functions, duties, and responsibilities of departments, boards, and commissions are unchanged as a result of the reorganization whether such department, board, or commission is assigned to a particular agency by statute, Stats. 1961, chs. 2037, 2073, or by executive action. . . .

Where a department, board, or commission is assigned to an agency by executive action, the agency administrator is merely a coordinator for all such departments, boards, and commissions. The administrator also advises and consults with the Governor on agency matters and acts as a liaison between the different departments, boards, and commissions assigned to the agency and the Governor. Further, a department, board, or commission is not divested of any of its authority to make rules and regulations, issue permits, and formulate general policy by the reorganization, whether it be statutory or by executive action. As before stated, the duties, functions, and responsibilities conferred upon a department, board or commission remain unchanged.

The agency administrator does not have the authority to annul, amend, revise, or modify any legal action of a department, board, or commission any more so than the Governor himself does. Any supervisory powers the Governor possessed with respect to the various state department heads prior to the reorganization, whether by statute or executive action, were neither increased nor diminished by the reorganization. There is no necessity to herein delineate the scope of the relationship that exists between the Governor and the various departments, boards, and commissions. It should also be noted that the Governor does not have the right to delegate his supervisory powers with respect to discretionary functions; however, he does have the power to coordinate and to make more efficient the executive department of the state government. An executive reorganization which requires various department heads to coordinate the activities of their departments through a coordinator, as in the instant case, does not constitute a delegation of the Governor's supervisory power.

It is apparent from the various documents submitted to this office in connection with the governmental reorganization that the Governor, in establishing the non-statutory agencies, has not attempted to usurp any of the powers or duties of the Legislature or of any of the department heads.

Comments: 1. Do the Kentucky and California opinions indicate where the line is drawn between the governor's authority to arrange the executive bureaucracy to his liking and the point at which he is no longer executing but rather creating the law? In *Martin v. Chandler* does the court mean to say that absent the long history of administration of surplus property by the Department of Education, the governor still would not have been able to assign that function to the Department of Finance? If so, is the result that the Superintendent of Public Instruction has greater authority than the governor?

2. The executive order and administrative reorganization have developed a close relationship over the years, especially at the presidential level. For many years, Congress has authorized the President to initiate changes in administrative structure which can be defeated by a vote of disapproval in either house of Congress. Reorganization Act of 1949, 5 U.S.C. § 901 et seq. A brief history of the federal experience is set forth in J. KALLENBACH, THE AMERICAN CHIEF EXECUTIVE 382-87 (1966). The constitutionality of federal reorganization acts has been sustained in *Isbrandtsen-Moller Co. v. United States,* 14 F. Supp. 407 (S.D.N.Y. 1936), *aff'd on other grounds,* 300 U.S. 139 (1937); *Swayne & Hoyt v. United States,* 18 F. Supp. 25 (D.D.C. 1936), *aff'd on other grounds,* 300 U.S. 297 (1937); *FTC v. Gibson,* 460 F.2d 605 (5th Cir. 1972) (court rejected as frivolous challenge to Reorganization Act of 1949 as unlawful delegation of legislative powers of Congress to President).

3. At the state level, a governor's power to effect administrative reorganization may be very important. Typically, the governor's control of the executive department is circumscribed by the presence of independently elected state officials, with whom he shares executive power, and a large number of departments, boards and agencies, which make efficient management difficult. If the structure of the executive department is left entirely to legislative action, needed changes are likely to be slow in coming and piecemeal in approach. A few states have enacted statutes similar to the federal reorganization acts, empowering the governor to issue executive orders reorganizing executive agencies, which become effective in a specified number of legislative days unless disapproved by either or both houses of the legislature. Challenges to the constitutional validity of these statutes, chiefly on separation of powers grounds, have been raised in several states with varying results.

New Hampshire. Opinion of the Justices, 83 A.2d 738 (N.H. 1959), holding the New Hampshire statute did not unconstitutionally delegate legislative power to the governor: the governor's power is to submit reorganization plans to the legislature, but it is only the legislature's action or inaction which determines whether they become law. However, the court found that the sections requiring a concurrent resolution of both houses to disapprove plans violated the constitutional provisions for separate action by each house. The dissent would uphold the statutes as a valid delegation of legislative power.

New Jersey. Brown v. Heymann, 297 A.2d 572 (N.J. 1972), holding the Executive Reorganization Act of 1969 a valid delegation of legislative power with sufficient standards and limitations on the governor's action. The Act did not "threaten the security against aggregated power which the separation-of-powers doctrine was designed to provide." *Id.* at 10, 297 A.2d at 577.

Oklahoma. Op. of the Att'y Gen. No. 75-253 (1975; unpublished) declaring the Oklahoma reorganization statute violated the separation of powers provisions of the Oklahoma constitution to the extent it vested "law making" authority in the governor to amend or repeal existing statutes. The statute also was said to be contrary to specific constitutional procedures for enactment of a law, such as the requirement that every bill receive the favorable vote of a majority of members elected to each house, and to the constitutional provisions for initiative and referendum.

Compare Brown v. Barkley, 628 S.W.2d 616 (Ky. 1982). The governor issued an executive order transferring functions of the Department of Agriculture to a new agency. The Department was headed by a Commissioner of Agriculture designated by the constitution to be elected by popular vote. The court held that the reorganization act, which authorized the governor to reorganize "statutory administrative department[s]," did not apply to agencies headed by constitutionally elected officers. Neither did the governor have the constitutional power to order the reorganization. The court noted that, because constitutionally elected officers were elected by the people, "they are not answerable to the supervision of anyone else."

4. The governor's executive power may also protect agencies created by executive order from legislative review. In *Opinion of the Justices,* 392 A.2d 125 (N.H. 1978), a "sunset" law providing for the termination of state agencies exempted agencies "required" by the state constitution. The court held that the exemption included agencies created by gubernatorial executive order, noting that the governor had issued these orders under "his executive power to administer, coordinate, plan, direct, and provide an effective mechanism for the fulfillment of his constitutional functions and duties."

5. In order to assure that the governor will have an important role to play in administrative reorganization, the Model State Constitution provides:

> The legislature shall by law prescribe the functions, powers and duties of the principal departments and of all other agencies of the state and may from time to time reallocate offices, agencies and instrumentalities among the principal departments, may increase, modify, diminish or change their functions, powers and duties and may assign new functions, powers and duties to them; but the governor may make such changes in the allocation of offices, agencies and instrumentalities, and in the allocation of such functions, powers and duties, as he considers necessary for efficient administration. If such changes affect existing law, they shall be set forth in executive orders, which shall be submitted to the legislature while it is in session, and shall become effective, and shall have the force of law, sixty days after submission, or at the close of the session, whichever is sooner, unless specifically modified or disapproved by a resolution concurred in by a majority of all the members.

National Municipal League, Model State Constitution, § 5.06 (1963). For similar provisions see Alaska, art. 3, § 23; California, art. 5, § 6 (authorizes legislature to authorize governor to initiate reorganization); Kansas, art. 1, § 6; Illinois, art. 5, § 11; Maryland, art. 2, § 24; Michigan, art. 5, § 2; North Carolina, art. 3, § 5; South Dakota, art. 4, § 8. The validity of the Kansas executive reorganization provision was challenged and upheld in *Vansickle v. Shanahan,* 511 P.2d 223 (Kan. 1973). The court, in an interesting opinion that traced the sources of the doctrine of separation of powers, held that the guaranty clause of the United States Constitution is justiciable, and that separation of powers is inherent in a representative form of government. It acknowledged that the executive reorganization provision of the Kansas constitution vests in the governor "a limited share of legislative power to make law, subject to legislative veto, but the legislative and executive departments are not destroyed, nor are their powers or authority materially curtailed. . . . [T]he legislature still has power to reorganize the executive department as it may see fit, subject to the governor's veto. . . ." *Id.* at 243-44.

6. *In re Di Brizzi,* 101 N.E.2d 464 (N.Y. 1951). The governor issued an executive order creating the New York State Crime Commission to investigate the relationship of organized crime and state and local governments. Acting on the basis of a World War I statute, which authorized the attorney general at the request of the governor to inquire into matters concerning the public peace, the governor's order requested the attorney general to pursue the investigation through the State Crime Commission. A witness subpoenaed

to testify before the Commission claimed the governor had no statutory authority to create a Commission with subpoena power. The court agreed there was no statutory authority for creation of the Commission, implying that the governor could not act without that authority. The court upheld the investigation and subpoena, however, on the basis of the "public peace" statute. If the governor is constitutionally responsible for faithful execution of the laws, why is it not within his power to create a device to aid him? Could the governor create a commission by executive order to investigate wrong-doing within executive departments? With subpoena power?

7. The effect on important public policy decisions of separating the governor from control of executive departments, whether desirable or not, can be seen in *State Highway Commission v. Haase*, 537 P.2d 300 (Colo. 1975). The governor of Colorado opposed a segment of the federal interstate system proposed for the metropolitan Denver area and directed the head of the state Department of Highways not to submit necessary documents to the federal Department of Transportation to assure federal funding. The state Highway Commission, on the other hand, directed the chief engineer of the Division of Highways to make the submissions. The Highway Commission, previously an independent commission with broad powers over the highway program of the state, was transferred intact to the Department of Highways by a legislative reorganization plan. The court held that the Commission nevertheless continued to exercise powers independently of the head of the Highway Department and that the governor had no authority to prevent the state's application for federal funding on the interstate route. The court noted in passing that the statutes required the Commission's budget to be submitted to the governor for approval and that he might still refuse to approve a budget containing funds for the interstate road. *See also State ex rel. S. Monroe & Son Co. v. Baker,* 147 N.E. 501 (Ohio 1925). The court held that the governor could not by executive order require directors of highways and finance to reject low bids on highway projects, even though both were executive officers appointed by the governor and at least one was subject to removal by the governor. The court's reasoning was that executive officials are not deputies of the governor but possess powers and independent judgment beyond his control.

2. GOVERNOR'S POWER TO MAKE POLICY THROUGH EXECUTIVE AGENCIES

The governor may be under political pressure to use his executive order authority to make policy in areas of concern in which the legislature has not acted, or has not acted to his satisfaction. The governor may use his authority over executive agencies to establish policies that supplement existing legislation. Ethics in government and nondiscrimination are two areas in which governors have attempted to make policy through executive orders. The case that follows is one judicial response to this attempted exercise of executive authority.

RAPP v. CAREY

Court of Appeals of New York
44 N.Y.2d 157, 375 N.E.2d 745 (1978)

Opinion of the Court

BREITEL, CHIEF JUDGE.

Defendants, the Governor and the State Board of Public Disclosure, appeal from the Appellate Division's unanimous affirmance of an order granting summary judgment to plaintiffs, State employees, and declaring the Governor's Executive Order No. 10.1 (9 NYCRR 3.10) unconstitutional. The disputed order purports to require a wide range of State employees within the executive branch to file multidetailed personal financial statements with the Board of Public Disclosure, and to abstain from various political and business activities.

The issue is whether under the State Constitutions the Governor may, by executive order, without benefit of authorizing legislation, mandate on State employees, many not subject to removal by the Governor, the filing of financial disclosure statements, and the abstention from activities not prohibited by statute. Not at issue is the wisdom of requiring such statements and prohibiting the proscribed activities, or the hardly doubted power to impose such requirements by appropriate legislation.

There should be an affirmance. Neither in the Constitution nor in the statutes is there express or implied authority for the Governor to exact of State employees compliance with the requirements of Executive Order No. 10.1. Nor does the Governor's order merely implement existing legislation relating to conflicts of interest. The order reaches beyond that, and assumes the power of the Legislature to set State policy in an area of concededly increasing public concern.

The executive order was promulgated by the Governor on October 22, 1976. Paragraph II, which requires annual filing of a financial disclosure statement, prohibits service in political party office, and regulates outside employment and activity, applies to the following employees: (1) employees of the executive department and other State departments and agencies headed by gubernatorial appointees or nominees (a) whose annual State salary is at least $30,000; or (b) who hold nonsecretarial, nonclerical positions classified as managerial or confidential; and (2) members of the governing bodies of State entities, if the member is appointed or nominated by the Governor and receives more than $15,000 per year in compensation from the State. Paragraph III, which also requires filing of a financial disclosure statement, but does not contain the same prohibitions on outside activity, applies to members of governing bodies of State entities, if the member is appointed by the Governor and receives State compensation with amounts to no more than $15,000. The State Board of Public Disclosure, first established by the Governor in Executive Order No. 10 (9 NYCRR 3.10), an earlier more limited attempt to regulate potential conflicts of interest, was continued to administer the new executive order.

The agencies purportedly covered by the executive order are not confined to the executive department, a department that is but one of many in the executive branch. It also extends to other State departments and many so-called independent agencies, such as public authorities, over which the Governor had no general control or powers of supervision or operation.

On November 1, 1976, the State board directed covered employees to complete financial disclosure statements and return them to the board by December 1. This action was brought by covered employees to have the order declared unconstitutional and to enjoin its enforcement. Special Term granted the requested relief, and a unanimous Appellate Division affirmed.

Not at issue is the constitutionality of a statute requiring financial disclosure by public employees and officers. It was implied, necessarily, that a statute to that effect would be valid in *Evans v. Carey,* ... 359 N.E.2d 983....

. . . .

The executive power of the State, vested in the Governor, is broad (see N.Y. Const., art. IV, §§ 1, 3; Executive Law, arts. 2, 3). In his capacity to oversee, even beyond his responsibility to operate, the Governor may investigate the management and affairs of any department, board, bureau, or commission of the State (Executive Law, § 6). This investigatory power, which includes the power to subpoena witnesses, as well as to require the production of books and papers, and which authorizes the Governor to delegate the investigatory function to persons appointed by him for that purpose, permits the Governor to exercise considerable vigilance, but not necessarily direction, in protecting against conflicts of interest. The Constitution and statutes thus recognize explicitly the need for and the power in the Governor to oversee, but again not necessarily to direct, the administration of the various entities in the executive branch.

The Governor may also direct the Attorney-General to inquire into matters "concerning the public peace, public safety and public justice" (Executive Law, § 63, subd. 8). Implementation of this power is illustrated by Governor Dewey's creation in 1951 of the New York State Crime Commission to investigate the relationship between organized crime and State government....

There are, however, limits to the breadth of executive power. The State Constitution provides for a distribution of powers among the three branches of government.... This distribution avoids excessive concentration of power in any one branch or in any one person. Where power is delegated to one person, the power is always guided and limited by standards. In fact, even the Legislature is powerless to delegate the legislative function unless it provides adequate standards.... Without such standards there is no government of law, but only government by men left to set their own standards, with resultant authoritarian possibilities.

Defendants cite numerous instances, reaching far back into the State's history, in which the Governor has acted by "executive order", although not usually so denominated. But, until 1950, none of those orders had any rule-making component. They were emergency measures later submitted to the Legislature for ratification, actions taken pursuant to an unchallenged constitutional or statutory power of the Governor, or proclamations without significant legal effect.... After 1950, there were a number of different types of orders which were seemingly cast in a rule-making mold, but were repetitive of existing legislation as to standards and implemented the enforcement of those standards by voluntary arrangements, directions for co-ordination or the interposition of mediatory bodies (see, e. g., Executive Order Establishing Code of Fair Practices, 1960 Public Papers of Governor Nelson A. Rockefeller, p. 1130; Executive Order for Resolution of Employee Complaints, 1950 Public Papers of Governor Thomas E. Dewey, p. 613). Assuming they were valid, as they undoubtedly were in large measure, the order in this case goes beyond any of them.

It is true that in this State the executive has the power to enforce legislation and is accorded great flexibility in determining the methods of enforcement (see N.Y. Const., art. IV, § 3). But he may not, as was recently said of the Mayor of the City of New York, "go beyond stated legislative policy and prescribed a remedial device not embraced by the policy" *(Matter of Broidrick v. Lindsay,* ... 350 N.E.2d 595, 597). And, as noted in the *Broidrick* case, decided unanimously by this court, the flexibility allowed the executive in designing an enforcement mechanism depends upon the nature of the problem to be solved.... Where it would be practicable for the Legislature itself to set precise standards, the executive's flexibility is and should be quite limited.

Defendants seek to justify the executive order as an implementation of section 74 of the Public Officers Law. That statute, called a code of ethics for State officers and employees, provides guidelines designed to eliminate substantial conflicts of interest between State duties and private interests. Together with section 73 of the Public Officers Law, which, as opposed to guidelines, contains absolute rules and proscriptions, section 74 constitutes the legislative policy of the State in the conflict of interest area.

Crucial is the contrast between sections 73 and 74, enacted together in 1954.... In section 73 the Legislature enacted a blanket prohibition of conduct by State employees thought to be detrimental to State interests. The prohibited conduct and the employees to which each prohibition applies are carefully described. In addition, subdivision 6 of the statute mandates public disclosure of a circumscribed category of investments by certain State employees and officers. Thus, in section 73 the Legislature demonstrated its ability and readiness to proscribe specified transactions peculiarly vulnerable to conflicts of interest, transactions in "definable areas on which there should be no disagreement" (Governor's Memorandum on Approval, 1954 Public Papers of Governor Thomas E. Dewey, pp. 304, 305).

Section 74 is a different type of statute. Designed to cover "areas where distinctions are close, and the differences between right and wrong not always easily ascertainable, [it] establish[es] broad standards of conduct, leaving to advisory committees the process of developing a body of rules and precedents on the basis of continuing experience and trial and error" *(id.)*.

As Mr. Justice Harold J. Hughes succinctly stated at Special Term in holding the executive order invalid, first quoting from the declaration of legislative intent accompanying enactment of section 74, . . . " 'Government is and should be representative of all the people who elect it, and some conflict of interest is inherent in any representative form of government. Some conflicts of material interests which are improper for public officials may be prohibited by legislation. Others may arise in so many different forms and under such a variety of circumstances, that it would be unwise and unjust to proscribe them by statute with inflexible and penal sanctions which would limit public service to the very wealthy or the very poor. For matters of such complexity and close distinctions, the legislature finds that a code of ethics is desirable to set forth for the guidance of state officers and employees the general standards of conduct to be reasonably expected of them' . . . [t]he inflexible proscriptions of the Executive Order are clearly at variance with this declaration of legislative intent" *(Rapp v. Carey,* 88 Misc.2d 428, 431, 390 N.Y.S.2d 573, 575). In short, this order is not an implementation of section 74; it is a nullification of it — a nullification, however benevolent in purpose, without benefit of legislative action.

The challenged order presumes to prohibit service in political party office by all State employees covered by paragraph II, not just by the small group of officials of high rank named in subdivision 8 of section 73 of the Public Officers Law. The order, again without any apparent statutory authority, would also prohibit, except on permission of the Board of Public Disclosure, all types of privately compensated employment by State employees. That the dual loyalties engendered by this dual employment may rightly be condemned is not the issue. The crux of the matter is the determination by the Legislature, implicit in its enactment of the code of ethics, that the existence of conflicts in these areas is to be determined on a case-by-case basis, not by use of blanket prohibitions.

None of this is to say that the Governor may not require that his appointees, serving at his will, abstain from transactions or business associations that potentially conflict with State duties. The Governor is, of course, free to regulate the business activities of employees serving at his pleasure. The same cannot be said, however, of employees who have civil service tenure, or even gubernatorial appointees who serve for fixed terms. These employees may not be removable except for cause, and are thus not subject to summary dismissal by the Governor. The challenged executive order exceeds the Governor's power of appointment and reaches employees who could be neither directly appointed nor summarily dismissed by the Governor. As to these employees, the Governor is without power to impose the strictures contained in the executive order.

The restriction on political activities is particularly troublesome. While the restriction on the merits would be supported by many or even most, it involves a broad question of policy, hardly resolvable by other than the representatively elected lawmaking branch of government, the Legislature.

The out-of-State cases relied upon by defendants are not on point. True, in *Illinois State Employees Assn. v. Walker,* 57 Ill.2d 512, 315 N.E.2d 9, cert. den. sub nom. *Troopers Lodge No. 41 v. Walker,* 419 U.S. 1058, ... the Illinois Supreme Court upheld the Governor's power to issue an executive order requiring financial disclosure statements. But that holding rested squarely on the Illinois Constitution which provided that all "holders of state offices and all members of a Commission or Board created by this Constitution shall file a verified statement of their economic interests, as provided by law". ... No similar provision may be found in the Constitution or statutes of this State.

Shapp v. Butera, 22 Pa.Cmwlth. 229, 348 A.2d 910 involved the status under the Pennsylvania "Right to Know Act" of financial disclosure statements filed pursuant to an executive order issued by the Governor. The Commonwealth Court of Pennsylvania, in concluding that the statements filed were not subject to public examination, inspection, and copying, noted that "[t]he financial statements requested by the Governor had no more legal effect than a request by the Governor to have birthday greetings sent to him" (*id.,* p. 237, 348 A.2d p. 914). By contrast, the present executive order was designed to be mandatory, not merely an invitation to voluntary compliance.

In *Opinion of Justices,* N.H., 360 A.2d 116 the New Hampshire Supreme Court sustained a resolution adopted by the Governor and council to the extent that the resolution stated a policy prohibiting employment of elective officials in the executive branch, but struck down provisions restricting the right of elective officials to do business with the State. The court concluded "[h]owever desirable comprehensive legislation in the area of conflict of interest may be, the enactment of such legislation is the prerogative and responsibility of the legislature and not of the executive" (N.H., 360 A.2d, p. 122).

The sister State cases, therefore, present problems different from the ones created by the instant executive order. Moreover, they do not and could not bear significantly on the issue in this case, arising as it does under this State's particular constitutional and statutory provisions. The sister State cases are useful principally to show how other States have reacted to the use of executive orders in the conflict of interest area, and as such, they are either inconclusive, or largely supportive of the general principles here discussed.

The crux of the case is the principle that the Governor has only those powers delegated to him by the Constitution and the statutes. On the principle, there is general agreement. ... There should be no less agreement on application of the principle to the facts of this case. On no reasonable reading of the Constitution, the Executive Law, or the relevant provisions of the Public Officers Law can the Governor's exercise of legislative power, exemplified in the executive order, be sustained.

Under our system of distribution of powers with checks and balances, the purposes of the executive order however desirable, may be achieved only through proper means. No single branch of government may assume a power, especially if assumption of that power might erode the genius of that system. The erosion need not be great. "Rather should we be alive to the imperceptible but gradual increase in the assumption of power properly belonging to another department" (*People v. Tremaine,* 252 N.Y. 27, 57, 168 N.E. 817, 827 [concurring opn. per Crane, J.]).

... The Governor's objective may be achieved by obtaining the requisite legislation. Critical, however, is that any difficulty or even impossibility of obtaining legislation through the constitutionally prescribed mechanisms may not be made a source of executive lawmaking power where none otherwise exists.

Accordingly, the order of the Appellate Division should be affirmed, with costs.

COOKE, JUDGE (dissenting in part).

I respectfully dissent.

The power and position of the Governor of the State of New York should not be thwarted by a declaration that his order is unconstitutional and invalid — either as a matter of law or State policy. Executive power of the State is vested constitutionally in the Governor and by statute he is authorized at any time to examine and investigate the management and affairs of any department, board, bureau or commission of the State. The Governor was empowered within this framework, therefore, to issue the order requiring applicable officers and employees of the State to file financial statements, the exercise of this power being consistent with and in implementation of the State code of ethics. Far from nullifying and completely counteracting the force and effectiveness of the code of ethics, the order in this respect would implement its provisions and thus breathe life into the legislative scheme. When acting in the exercise of his executive powers, as in this respect, the Governor of the State should be immune from judicial interference....

As a matter of law, as head of the executive department, the Governor is authorized to regulate the activities of those officers and employees functioning wholly within that department. From the standpoint of policy alone, it would be anomalous indeed to hold the Governor responsible for the faithful execution of the laws, if at the same time he is refused control over the human agencies whom he must necessarily employ for that purpose.

Executive Order No. 10.1 represents an attempt by the Governor to provide a framework pursuant to which he might ascertain whether certain State officers and employees (hereafter referred to as "employees") are abiding by high ethical standards required of them in the performance of their duties. That order, to the extent that it is grounded on powers conferred expressly or by necessary implication either by the Constitution or by statute, thereby voicing the will of the people or the Legislature, should be upheld and enforced.

....

I. Executive Department Officers and Employees

As chief executive officer of the State, the Governor functions in a dual capacity. His primary responsibilities, as delineated in the Constitution, include the power to make recommendations to the Legislature, the duty to approve or veto legislative enactments and the requirement that he "take care that the laws are faithfully executed" (N.Y.Const., art IV, §§ 3, 7). Although an equal partner with the legislative and judicial branches of the government, the Governor, as head of the executive department, bears sole responsibility with respect to the oversight and internal functioning of that department (N.Y.Const., art. IV, § 1; Executive Law, § 30). In acting upon that responsibility, the Governor may promulgate any rules and regulations he determines are necessary to ensure the efficient operation of the executive department....

Thus, by virtue of the authority vested in him as chief of the executive department of the State government, the Governor possesses both the power and the duty to regulate the eligibility for employment and the conditions to be met for continued employment of persons within that department.... So long as the Governor confines the scope of the order to employees wholly within the executive department ... and the scope of the order is not violative of any specific constitutional proscriptions ... neither the legislative nor judicial branches are free to interfere, "it being a basic part of the organic law that each department should be free from interference, in the discharge of its own functions and peculiar duties, by either of the others"....

Thus, insofar as Executive Order No. 10.1 regulates the activities of State employees whose duties are confined wholly within the executive department, its promulgation represents an exercise of the Governor's ancillary powers to effectuate the proper workings of that department. The Governor has not only the right to ascertain whether conflicts of interest or unethical behavior exist in his department, he has an affirmative duty to assure that none of his subordinates responsible for execution of executive duties are tainted by outside interests which would undermine his responsibility to "take care that the laws are faithfully executed" (N.Y.Const., art. IV, § 3). Should the Governor fail in this duty, he may be impeached. Apart from impeachment, the electorate may refuse to grant him another term of office. The Governor's reputation and honor are unmistakably intertwined with the ability to do those things that his constitutional duties require. His control over those subordinates he must employ should not be circumscribed by the judiciary under the guise of a separation of powers inquiry.

II. Financial Disclosure by Covered Officers and Employees

Whereas the power of the Governor to promulgate Executive Order No. 10.1 with respect to employees in the executive department arises from his position as head of that department of government, a different analysis is necessary with respect to application of the order to nonexecutive employees. Ours is a system in which governmental powers are distributed among three branches — the executive, legislative and judicial. This separation of governmental powers, however, does not inflexibly ordain that the functions of each branch of government be kept wholly and entirely separate and distinct; rather "[t]he true meaning is, that the whole power of one of these departments should not be exercised by the same hands which possess the whole power of either of the other departments" (Story's Constitution [5th ed], p. 393; see, also, Madison, The Federalist, No. XLVII, p. 268). The validity of Executive Order No. 10.1, then, is dependent upon a showing that it was promulgated to effectuate the provisions of the Constitution or an act of the Legislature.... Absent this afore-mentioned showing of purpose, the act of the Governor would be tantamount to legislation by executive fiat, a clear violation of the separation of powers doctrine....

It is therefore necessary to examine the statutory scheme evidenced by the prohibition against conflicts of interest (Public Officers Law, § 73) and the code of ethics (Public Officers Law, § 74) in order to ascertain whether Executive Order No. 10.1 does in fact usurp legislative prerogatives. Section 73 of the Public Officers Law, forbidding certain enumerated conflicts of interest, was enacted in recognition of an express desire to guarantee that the governmental process not be subverted by official corruption and inefficiency, as well as the necessity of the "maintenance in public affairs of moral and ethical standards which are worthy and warrant the confidence of the people." (Message from

Governor Dewey to the Legislature, Jan. 6, 1951). At the same time, it was recognized that it would be nothing less than a Sisyphean task for the Legislature to identify and proscribe all conflicts of interest in the myriad settings in which they might arise . . . , thus necessitating the establishment of a code of ethical standards for all State employees in the performance of their duties (Public Officers Law, § 74).

Accordingly, in a preamble to the code of ethics the Legislature recognized that because improper conflicts "may arise in so many different forms and under such a variety of circumstances", that it was not only impractical but "unwise and unjust to proscribe them by statute with inflexible and penal sanctions" and that "[f]or matters of such complexity and close distinctions, the legislature finds a code of ethics is desirable to set forth for the guidance of state officers and employees the general standards of conduct to be reasonably expected of them" (L.1954, ch. 696, § 1). Of necessity, then, the code of ethics is couched in broad, general terms. . . . On the other hand of course, there is no language in the code which would lead to the conclusion that the Legislature intended to exclusively occupy the field of governmental ethics. Indeed, the Legislature explicitly recognized that it was necessary that the code be implemented in a manner consistent with its purpose. It is in such a context that executive enforcement of a general legislative statement is proper. . . . Here, the disclosure sought by the Governor is consistent with the policies underlying the ethics legislation and should be upheld. . . . In short, there is no going "beyond stated legislative policy", but rather adherence to it. . . .

While separation of powers is one of the principal features of our Constitution, it is the plain duty of that branch of government which is called upon to interpret the laws of this State to avoid slavish formalisms which serve only to ossify the executive without any corresponding benefit. Clearly, the function of making the laws is peculiar to the Legislature. But that is not to say that whenever the Legislature speaks on a particular subject, that subject is perforce removed from the scope of executive power. Rather, the answer is that there are some fields that are peculiar to the legislative branch, some peculiar to the executive, and others common to both. The duty of fixing the moral tone of State government and of ensuring that public servants conform their official conduct to those standards is a responsibility shared coextensively by all branches.

It is beyond cavil that the office of the Governor was deliberately fashioned as one necessarily imbued with power and independence. It is equally obvious that the framers of our Constitution did not intend to create an office in which an autocratic incumbent might arrogate any power unto himself at any time. But neither was it intended that the Governor be an automaton, constitutionally impotent to exercise the powers bestowed upon him — this being especially important at a time when, due to the events of recent years, the people demand that their public servants be free from even the barest trace of the taint of impropriety. Here, the Legislature has provided merely the bare framework within which the Governor may accomplish this task. Executive action, insofar as validly supplied by Executive Order No. 10.1, is necessary to complete it and adapt it to present day realities.

The Constitution does not denominate the Governor as merely an agent of the Legislature; nor does it ennoble him as the powerless titular head of the State. Rather the Governor is the agent of the People of the State of New York, deriving his power from them and directly responsible to them. Taken collectively, the provisions in the Constitution, providing that the Governor shall take care that the laws are faithfully executed and that the executive power shall be vested in the Governor, conclusively demonstrate that his is the office to which the people look for integrity in State government. The fact that the Legislature has perfunctorily addressed the subject does not of necessity preclude further executive action. Indeed, that the Legislature has recognized that conflicts of interest by those in State government should be avoided and that these conflicts arise in myriad settings indicates that it is incumbent that the Governor take steps to combat these conflicts and the attendant official corruption they might engender. There is no cause to fear executive tyranny so long as the laws are being faithfully executed. Certainly there is no basis for fear of executive usurpation of legislative prerogatives when the Governor acts, as he did in this case, to further the workings of a program which the Legislature itself recognized as incapable of statutory completion.

JASEN, JUDGE (dissenting). [Omitted.]

GABRIELLI, JONES and WACHTLER, JJ., concur with BREITEL, C. J.

COOKE, J., dissents in part and votes to modify in a separate opinion.

JASEN, J., dissents and votes to reverse in another opinion.

FUCHSBERG, J., taking no part.

Order affirmed.

Comments: 1. The majority and dissenting opinions state different philosophies on the scope of executive authority. In your opinion, which is correct? Does the dissenting opinion rely entirely on legislative authority to uphold the executive order? If not, where does the dissent find this authority?

The majority opinion states that the governor may require appointees serving at his will to "abstain from transactions or business associations that potentially conflict with State duties." Why may the governor issue an executive order prohibiting this type of conduct, but not the conduct proscribed in the executive order at issue in the case?

In a portion of the dissent which is omitted, Judge Cooke notes that the court had sustained the constitutionality of a financial disclosure requirement. *Evans v. Carey,* 359 N.E.2d 983 (N.Y. 1976). The court rejected a right of privacy objection to the Executive Order considered in *Rapp. See also* Chapter 6. Do you suppose that this decision influenced the majority in *Rapp* to hold that the executive order was unauthorized?

2. With the principal case, compare *Kenny v. Byrne,* 365 A.2d 211 (N.J. App. Div. 1976), aff'd mem., 383 A.2d 428 (N.J. 1978). Governor Byrne issued an executive order requiring all employees of the executive branch to file financial disclosure statements. The court held that the contention that the executive order was beyond the governor's "constitutional powers" was "manifestly without merit." It added:

> The Governor is vested with the executive power of the State. . . . As head of the Executive Branch of government he has the duty and power to supervise all employees in each principal department of that branch . . . . Of necessity, this includes the inherent power to issue directives and orders by way of implementation in order to insure efficient and honest performance by those state employees within his jurisdiction.

Id. at 215. The court also noted that the "objective of the 1947 [state] Constitution was the creation of a strong executive." Is this purpose relevant to the governor's executive order authority? Does the New Jersey court successfully answer the arguments put forward in the principal case for not upholding the governor's authority to issue a similar order?

3. For a case striking down an executive order requiring state suppliers and state-regulated businesses to provide a statement of political contributions, see *Buettell v. Walker,* 319 N.E.2d 502 (Ill. 1974). The court held, without discussion, that the authority to issue the executive order did not fall within the governor's constitutional executive authority. Like many state constitutions, the Illinois Constitution provides that "[t]he Governor shall have the supreme executive power, and shall be responsible for the faithful execution of the laws." Art. XIII, § 2.

Does the *Buettell* case mean that the chief executive has no authority, in the absence of a statute, to set conditions on the persons with whom the state does business? Is there a difference between: (a) adoption by the executive department of a pre-qualification procedure for prospective suppliers, one part of which is the disclosure of political contributions, and (b) rejection by an executive agency of the low bid submitted by a prospective supplier who failed to file a list of political contributions? Does *Buettell* mean that the governor or treasurer — whichever official has custody of state funds — could not condition placement of those funds on a prior agreement by the banks seeking deposits: (a) that they would not discriminate on grounds of race or sex in employment practices or in the granting of loans and mortgages; (b) that they would not engage in "redlining" (the practice of refusing to make mortgages or home improvement loans in a deteriorating neighborhood)?

4. What if the legislature creates a commission to investigate the ethics, including the campaign finances, of executive employees? In *Parcell v. State,* 620 P.2d 834 (Kan. 1980), the legislature created a Governmental Ethics Commission to investigate both the legislative and executive branches. The Commission was empowered to investigate violations of the Campaign Finance Act and to report violations to the state attorney general or the appropriate county or district attorney. The Commission had no means to enforce compliance with its findings. Six members of the Commission were appointed by the legislature and the governor appointed the remaining five.

The court upheld the act creating the Commission, finding that it was a cooperative rather than a coercive exercise of legislative power. The division of appointment power ensured "fair consideration" in Commission investigations. What if the Commission also had enforcement powers?

5. *Nondiscrimination.* In the 1960s, a number of state governors issued executive orders, typically denominated a Code of Fair Practices, which were intended to strengthen the state's nondiscrimination policy. Some provisions of the Code reaffirmed the policy that state services, employment and financial aid were to be administered on a nondiscriminatory basis. Many of them also sought to address the issue of discrimination by occupations and businesses licensed by the state, or by contractors doing business with the state.

In *Opinion of Attorney General* (Indexed Letter 63-86, July 24, 1963, unpublished), an executive order was held to be valid which established racial discrimination as a ground for the revocation of state licenses. The attorney general ruled that the order "would be valid where the statutes governing the license in question could be construed to authorize racial discrimination as a grounds for discipline or, in the absence of such authorization, where the Constitution requires nondiscrimination." He noted that some licensing statutes, for example, authorized disciplinary action for "conduct unbecoming a member of a profession in good standing."

Compare *Opinion of the Attorney General,*48 Md. Op. Att'y Gen. 72 (1963). The attorney general ruled that the governor could "correct" discrimination by a state board in granting licenses. "In the absence of legislation," he could not order license suspension or revocation because a licensee discriminated in her work or practice. The executive order prohibited discrimination by any state-licensed business or profession, and the attorney general found that it could not be applied in the second circumstance he mentioned.

The nondiscrimination opinions consider the extent to which the governor, by executive order, may enlarge on state legislation. In *Chang v. University of Rhode Island,* 375 A.2d 925 (R.I. 1977), the governor by executive order extended the state Fair Employment Practices Act to nonprofit educational institutions. The Act expressly excluded such institutions.

In holding the executive order invalid, the court relied on the much-cited analysis of presidential executive power in Justice Jackson's concurring opinion in *Youngstown Sheet & Tube Co. v. Sawyer,* 343 U.S. 579, 634 (1952). Justice Jackson noted that the President may act according to express or implied congressional authorization. He may act in the absence of a congressional grant or denial of authority. He may also adopt measures incompatible with congressional authority, but in these cases the presidential exercise of power must be carefully scrutinized for it is at its "lowest ebb."

The court in *Chang* held that the executive order in that case fell within the third category. Because the legislature had excluded nonprofit educational institutions from the Act, the executive order could be "supported only if regulation of the university's employment practices was exclusively within the executive domain and beyond the control of the legislature." That was not the case, as the state constitution had reserved the control of education to the legislature, which had delegated control over state educational institutions to a state board of regents.

See also *Fullilove v. Carey,* 406 N.Y.S.2d 888 (N.Y. App. Div. 1978), *aff'd,* 424 N.Y.S.2d 183 (1979). The governor issued an executive order requiring state contractors to adopt affirmative action plans. State legislation permitted but did not require such plans. The court held the order invalid. Would the court in *Fullilove* agree or disagree with the California attorney general's opinion, *supra?* Can the two executive orders be distinguished? Do the cases indicate that the improved sophistication and coverage of state nondiscrimination acts limit the scope of executive authority?

6. *Local executive orders.* At the local government level, executive authority to adopt executive orders is governed by statute or, in the case of home-rule governments, by the home-rule charter. In *County Executive v. Doe,* 436 A.2d 459 (Md. 1981), the county executive issued an order prohibiting abortions in county owned or operated hospitals except when necessary to save the life of the mother. The court held that the order was unauthorized by the charter. It noted that the charter had created a "system of county government in which the executive branch and the legislative branch were separate and distinct." The executive was in charge of general administration, but the council was authorized to assign duties and responsibilities to executive branch agencies. Acting under this authority, the council had created a Department of Hospitals and Health Services with responsibility for a "comprehensive health care program for the county." The court held:

> The County Executive is bound by the Charter to direct, supervise and control the implementation of the Council's allocation of duties and functions to these agencies as part of his responsibility to faithfully execute the laws enacted by the County Council. The vesting of this power in the County Executive does not, however, constitute a grant of unbridled authority permitting him to usurp, nullify or supersede, at his pleasure, functions and duties committed by law to other executive branch officers, or to refuse to observe existing laws enacted by the Council.

Id. at 463.

The court cited *Rapp v. Carey,* reproduced *supra.* Is that case relevant? Isn't the division of power established by the Prince George's County charter similar to the distribution of power established by state constitutions between the governor and legislature? If so, shouldn't there be an implied power in the county executive to specify the obligations and responsibilities of county agencies? Why should the establishment of the county health department by the council abrogate this power?

B. VETO POWERS

The veto power of the chief executive is often described as an exception to the separation of powers doctrine, but that characterization is accurate only if separation of powers is taken as an absolute in American government, which it is not. In both cases — the doctrine and the exception — the source is the same: the constitution.[1] Clearly, however, the veto thrusts the chief executive into the

---

[1] Many of the first state constitutions did not authorize an executive veto. According to Frank Prescott's study, however, by 1812 eight of the 18 states provided for it and thereafter no new state except West Virginia (which has since adopted it) entered the union without some form of executive veto. Prescott, The Executive Veto in American States, 3 W. Pol. Q. 98, 98-100 (1950). North Carolina is the only state which has no gubernatorial veto.

legislative process by giving him the power to deny approval to bills enacted by the legislature. While the power is conditional in the sense that the legislature is constitutionally entitled to override the executive's action, in practice gubernatorial vetoes are overriden in a small percentage of the cases. There are various reasons for this: The difficulty of assembling an extraordinary majority, which most states require, to overturn the governor; the opportunity for the legislature to reconsider an issue in a less charged atmosphere; and the fact that many vetoes may reflect technical errors or other matters about which there is no real dispute. A major practical reason is that state legislatures have tended to complete a large proportion of their business at the close of the session and then adjourn either sine die or for a long recess, thereby effectively foreclosing the opportunity to override subsequent vetoes.

The veto powers available to most state governors are more varied and more sophisticated than the presidential veto. Under Article I, § 7, the president is limited to approving or disapproving a bill in its entirety, or to withholding action and thereby achieving the same result as disapproval when the adjournment of Congress prevents return of the bill (the pocket veto). The latter has the additional advantage to the president that Congress has no power to attempt to override the veto.

In addition to the general veto power similar to the president's, which all states except North Carolina provide, and the pocket veto,[2] some 43 state governors have the power to veto items, or parts, or sections of a bill, usually limited to appropriations; a small number of governors (eight by constitutional grant, one by court decision) have the power to reduce appropriations; and seven state constitutions authorize the power of executive amendment or amendatory veto, which permits the governor to return a bill to the legislature with recommended changes.[3] The gubernatorial veto power is also strengthened in a number of states by the requirement that bills be confined to a single subject, and in a few states, by the additional requirement that appropriation bills be confined to the subject of appropriations. Where these provisions exist, they will reduce the legislative practice of attaching an unacceptable "rider" to a bill which the executive is compelled to sign. The president's veto does not enjoy this protection.

Because the veto power gives the executive an essentially negative weapon to be wielded in the midst of the legislative process, it is perhaps not surprising that it has generated a number of conflicts which the courts are called upon to resolve. In terms of the balance of powers between the executive and the legislature, the most interesting and important of these cases arise from disputes over the scope and availability of the item veto.

---

[2] A recent study of the pocket veto found that "19 of the 20 [state] jurisdictions retaining some form of pocket veto have limited the power to *sine die* adjournments or diluted their provisions vis-à-vis the federal clause." Comment, The Veto Power and Kennedy v. Simpson: Burning a Hole in the President's Pocket, 69 Nw. U.L. Rev. 587, 618 (1974).

[3] *See* Council of State Governments, The Book of the States 1976-77, at 70-71. The texts of the 50 state constitutions are compiled in Columbia Univ. Legislative Drafting Research Fund, Constitutions of the United States, National and State (2d ed.).

WELDEN v. RAY

Supreme Court of Iowa
229 N.W.2d 706 (1975)

[The vetoed items designated as "lined out" have been italicized in the decision. — Eds.]

UHLENHOPP, JUSTICE. This appeal involves vetoes of qualifications which the legislature imposed upon appropriations.

In Senate File 540, the Sixty-Fifth General Assembly of Iowa appropriated funds to the Iowa Commission on Alcoholism. Section 2, with the vetoed language lined out, provides:

There is appropriated from the general fund of the state for the biennium beginning July 1, 1973 and ending June 30, 1975, for the Iowa commission on alcoholism, the following amounts, or so much thereof as may be necessary, to be used in the manner designated: . . .

For purposes of carrying out the provisions of section one hundred twenty-three A point eight (123A.8) and chapter one hundred twenty-three B (123B) of the Code relating to the treatment of alcoholism, subject to the approval of the governor, *the following amount not more than fifteen percent of which may be allocated to any one local alcoholism unit or facility:*

[1973-1974]	[1974-1975]
$500,000	$500,000

. . . .

In House File 780, the General Assembly appropriated funds to the office for planning and programming and the office for economic opportunity. Section 1, with the vetoed language lined out, provides in part: . . .

[Only one of the appropriations included in Section 1 is reproduced here. — Eds.]

    4. For salaries, support, maintenance, and miscellaneous purposes for the state building code; *however, in no event, shall this include more than three additional employees:*

[1973-1974]	[1974-1975]
$120,310	$124,810

[Additional vetoes similar to those quoted are omitted. — Eds.]

Plaintiffs commenced this action claiming that the vetoes we have set out do not come within the purview of the 1968 item-veto amendment to the Iowa Constitution. That amendment states:

> The Governor may approve appropriation bills in whole or in part, and may disapprove any item of an appropriation bill; and the part approved shall become a law. Any item of an appropriation bill disapproved by the Governor shall be returned, with his objections, to the house in which it originated, or shall be deposited by him in the office of the Secretary of State in the case of an appropriation bill submitted to the Governor for his approval during the last three days of a session of the General Assembly, and the procedure in each case shall be the same as provided for other bills. Any such item of an appropriation bill may be enacted into law notwithstanding the Governor's objections, in the same manner as provided for other bills.

The trial court upheld the vetoes, and plaintiffs appealed.

The appeal presents four principal questions: whether the power to appropriate is essentially legislative in character, whether the power to veto includes the power not only to nullify but also to alter, whether the separate-and-severable doctrine applies in this situation, and whether the *Brady* rule controls here. . . .

I. Appropriating as a Legislative Function.

The appropriation of money is essentially a legislative function under our scheme of government. The classic statement of the doctrine followed throughout the country was made in a Mississippi decision, *Colbert v. State*, 86 Miss. 769, 775, 39 So. 65, 66:

> Under all constitutional governments recognizing three distinct and independent magistracies, the control of the purse strings of government is a legislative function. Indeed, it is the supreme legislative prerogative, indispensable to the independence and integrity of the Legislature, and not to be surrendered or abridged, save by the Constitution itself, without disturbing the balance of the system and endangering the liberties of the people. The right of the Legislature to control the public treasury, to determine the sources from which the public revenues shall be derived and the objects upon which they shall be expended, to dictate the time, the manner, and the means, both of their collection and disbursement, is firmly and inexpugnably established in our political system. This supreme prerprogative of the Legislature, called in question by Charles I., was the issue upon which Parliament went to war with the King, with the result that ultimately the absolute control of Parliament over the public treasury was forever vindicated as a fundamental principle of the British Constitution. The American commonwealths have fallen heirs to this great principle, and the prerogative in question passes to their Legislatures without restriction or diminution, except as provided by their Constitutions, by the simple grant of the legislative power.

... Inherent in the power to appropriate is the power to specify how the money shall be spent. ...

All legislative appropriations are qualified to a degree; the legislature does not appropriate money without stating how the funds shall be used. Sometimes the qualification is general: "For salaries, support, maintenance and miscellaneous purposes." 65 G.A. ch. 9, § 1(1) (appropriation to department of justice). Sometimes the qualification is more specific: "to be used for aid to school districts for development and the conduct of programs, services and activities of vocational education through secondary schools." 65 G.A. ch. 10, § 1(3) (appropriation for vocational education). In either event, the qualification states how and for what purposes the money may be expended.

The qualification may be affirmative in form: "Salaries of nine legal assistants." 65 G.A. ch. 1, § 1(48) (appropriation for supreme court law clerks). Or it may be couched in the negative: "not more than one thousand five hundred sixty [positions] are to be filled at any one time." 65 G.A. ch. 117, § 1(1) (area offices and county services of social services department). No difference in substance exists between affirmative and negative qualifications; both are restrictions upon the appropriations.

Each of the provisions vetoed in the acts before us was a condition or restriction, affirmative or negative, upon the purpose or use of the money appropriated. In imposing the conditions or restrictions, the legislature exercised the authority which is inherent in its power to appropriate.

We do not suggest that the legislature may, under the guise of a qualification upon an appropriation, violate the separation of powers by invading the Governor's authority to exercise executive functions. . . . Obviously, for example, the legislature could not constitutionally make an appropriation to a department conditional upon the Governor's appointing a specified individual to be head of the department. Such a provision would contravene § 1 of article III of our constitution, quite apart from the matter of a veto. We have no such provision here. The qualifications in these bills were within the legislative domain; they did not invade the Governor's powers.

II. Nullify vs. Alter.

Involved in this case is the basic nature of "veto" — whether the concept of veto includes power to alter. If a governor may veto a legislatively-imposed qualification upon an appropriation but let the appropriation itself stand, he may alter and thus, in fact, legislate — notwithstanding that our constitution states, "The Legislative authority of this State shall be vested in a General Assembly." Iowa Const. Art. III, § 1 (Legislative Department).

The authorities hold that an attempted veto of a qualification on an appropriation is not within the scope of the item veto. The leading case is another Mississippi decision, *State ex rel. Teachers and Officers of Industrial Institute and College v. Holder,* 76 Miss. 158, 23 So. 643. Section 73 of the legislative article of the Mississippi Constitution, like our item-veto amendment, permits veto of "part" of an appropriation bill. In *Holder* the Mississippi Supreme Court held:

> Every bill of the character in question has three essential parts: The purpose of the bill, the sum appropriated for the purpose, and the conditions upon which the appropriation shall become available. Suppose a bill to create a reformatory for juvenile offenders, or to build the capitol, containing all necessary provisions as to purpose, amount of appropriation, and conditions; may the governor approve and make law of the appropriation, and veto and defeat the purpose or the conditions or both, whereby the legislative will would be frustrated, unless the vetoed purposes or conditions were passed by a two-thirds vote of each house? This would be monstrous. The executive action alone would make that law which had never received the legislative assent. And after all, and despite pragmatic utterances of political doctrinaires, the executive, in every republican form of government, has only a qualified and destructive legislative function, and never creative legislative power. If the governor may select, dissent, and dissever, where is the limit of his right? Must it be a sentence or a clause or a word? Must it be a section, or any part of a section, that may meet with executive disapprobation? May the governor transform a conditional or a contingent appropriation into an absolute one, in disregard and defiance of the legislative will? That would be the enactment of law by executive authority without the concurrence of the legislative will, and in the face of it. The true meaning of section 73 is that an appropriation bill made up of several parts (that is, distinct appropriations), different, separable, each complete without the other, which may be taken from the bill without affecting the others, which may be separated into different parts complete in themselves, may be approved, and become law in accordance with the legislative will, while others of like character may be disapproved, and put before the legislature again, dissociated from the other appropriations. To allow a single bill, entire, inseparable, relating to one thing, containing several provisions all complementary of each other, and constituting one whole, to be picked to pieces, and some of the pieces approved, and others vetoed, is to divide the indivisible; to make of one, several; to distort and prevent legislative action, and by veto make a two-thirds vote necessary to preserve what a majority passed, allowable as to the entire bill, but inapplicable to a unit composed of diverse complementary parts, the whole passed because of each. 76 Miss. at 181-182, 23 So. at 645.

[The court cited and quoted from decisions in other states consistent with the Mississippi holding that the governor may not veto conditions or restrictions in an appropriation bill while permitting the appropriation itself to stand. — Eds.]

We thus hold that if the Governor desires to veto a legislatively-imposed qualification upon an appropriation, he must veto the accompanying appropriation as well....

Since each of the clauses involved in the acts before us is a qualification upon the particular appropriation, the Governor could not let the appropriation stand yet nullify the condition upon which the legislators gave their consent to the expenditure.

III. Separate and Severable Provisions.

We would have a different case if the clauses involved here came under the rule relating to separate, severable provisions on which appropriations were not dependent for passage by the legislature. We had such a severable section in *State ex rel. Turner v. Iowa State Highway Comm'n,* 186 N.W.2d 141 (Iowa). The act involved there appropriated funds for the highway commission. 63 G.A. ch. 30. Section 4 of the act then provided, "No moneys appropriated by this Act shall be used for capital improvements, but may be used for overtime pay of employees involved in technical trades." Section 5 provided, "The permanent resident engineers' offices presently established by the state highway commission shall not be moved from their locations, however, the commission may establish not more than two temporary resident engineers' offices within the state as needed." The appropriation did not appear dependent upon inclusion of § 5 in the bill. We held § 5 separate and severable and subject to separate veto under the Governor's authority to veto part of an appropriation bill. But we were careful to distinguish § 4 from § 5. We stated:

> It should be noted section 5 places no prohibition against the use of any moneys appropriated by the act for the moving of permanent resident engineers' offices presently established by the defendant commission. *Had such language as used in section 4 been employed in section 5 we are impelled to the view that section 5 would have in such case been a proviso or condition upon the expenditure of the funds appropriated,* but lacking such phraseology it obviously is not. 186 N.W. 2d at 150 (italics added).

....

The clauses involved in the instant case were integral parts of the appropriations themselves, quite different from § 5 of the act involved in the Iowa State Highway Commission case.

IV. Brady Rule.

We would also have a different case had the legislature attempted to evade the item-veto amendment by the device of a lump-sum appropriation followed by subdivisions calling for the expenditure of the lump sum in specified amounts for named purposes. See *People ex rel. State Board of Agriculture v. Brady,* 277 Ill. 124, 115 N.E. 204. The legislature contended in *Brady* that the governor could not item-veto one of the subdivisions without vetoing the lump sum, *as the subdivisions constituted qualifications upon the appropriation of the lump sum.* The Illinois Supreme Court held otherwise, however, saying to hold that the whole bill was one item would constitute a legislative evasion of the governor's authority to veto distinct items....

The legislative device of a lump-sum appropriation with subdivisions unconstitutionally invades the item-veto authority of a governor, just as the gubernatorial device of the veto of a qualification on an appropriation unconstitutionally invades the lawmaking authority of a legislature. But the problem of the *Brady* case is not presented by the appropriation acts before us. None of these acts appropriates a lump sum followed by a breakdown of that sum into smaller amounts for specific purposes....

The clauses involved in the case at bar are lawful qualifications upon the respective appropriations. They are not separate, severable provisions. The legislature did not evade the Governor's item-veto authority by the lump-sum device. The attempted vetoes by the Governor are beyond the scope of the item-veto amendment and are of no effect.

Reversed.

All Justices concur except HARRIS and REYNOLDSON, JJ., who dissent.

HARRIS, JUSTICE (dissenting).

I dissent in the belief an affirmance is clearly demanded by our holding in *State ex rel. Turner v. Iowa State Highway Commission,* 186 N.W.2d 141 (Iowa 1971) (hereinafter *Highway Commission).* And I am convinced the majority rejects the sounder view of item veto as a limited legislative function given the executive branch of state government as a developed part of an over-all scheme of checks and balances. In all respect, I submit it offends both the rule of stare decisis and the promise of better and more effective state government to seize on dictum in *Highway Commission* in order to retreat from its clear holding. Regrettably we thereby readopt a 19th century view of separation of state governmental powers which is wholly inadequate for the current needs of effective government.

I. Item veto should be interpreted in the light of the obvious and simple truth that no branch of government can function in any capacity without expenditure of public funds. Therefore under the better view an item veto power is given at least in part to provide for carefully limited executive participation in appropriation matters. Under the majority view the item veto is rendered quite meaningless....

III. It is important also to remember the item veto amendment was not worded so as to make it a second class provision of our constitution. The amendment was adopted by the people out of their desire to adjust the healthy tension between the legislative and executive branches of our state government. We can assume the people must have considered the tension to have theretofore been out of balance. No one disputes the "purse string power" of the legislature. But the power invested in any branch of government by our constitution is subject to other express provisions. Article III, § 1, Iowa Constitution. The item veto amendment is such an express provision and should not be rendered impotent on the claim its exercise infringes a right of another branch of government. The item veto provision is inscribed in the same constitution by which the people organize all three branches of government....

....

IV. Finally I believe the majority opinion is wrong in renouncing *Highway Commission's* definition of separability. The trial court rightly described the proper rule:

> ... [T]he Governor's power of item veto extends at least to provisions which are separable from an appropriation bill. Clearly, separability means that the vetoed provisions and the remainder of the bill contain ideas and concepts

capable of standing on their own. The idea and concept of the provision which is vetoed must be in some manner complete in itself, as must the remainder of the bill. Viewed in this light, the vetoed provisions and the remainder of the bills here in question in each case contain two separate, and therefore separable, ideas. They contain appropriations for specified purposes, and directions that funds not be used for other specified purposes.

I do not believe the Governor's authority as recognized in *Highway Commission* should be barred by specific draftsmanship in drawing the bill. Specific draftsmanship is the practice of scrambling the words which express a complete and otherwise separable legislative idea throughout an appropriation bill. . . .

Under the majority opinion an item veto can be exercised only at sufferance of the legislature. The power to exercise it would arise only in the unlikely event an appropriation bill would be so carelessly drafted as to omit the litany which the majority holds converts a distinct legislative idea into a purpose or proviso. The check given by the people to the executive branch is thereby surrendered to the very branch the people intended to be checked.

I would affirm.

REYNOLDSON, J., joins this dissent.

STATE EX REL. KLECZKA v. CONTA

Supreme Court of Wisconsin
82 Wis. 2d 679, 264 N.W.2d 539 (1978)

HEFFERNAN, JUSTICE.

. . . .

[The gubernatorial veto provision of the Wisconsin Constitution provides in part:

Appropriation bills may be approved in whole or in part by the governor, and the part approved shall become law, and the part objected to shall be returned [to the legislature for reconsideration] in the same manner as provided for other bills.

Wis. Const., art. V, § 10. — Eds.]

The petitioners' contentions are directed principally to the partial vetoes of the Governor of secs. 51 and 53 of the enrolled bill. Sec. 51 of the enrolled bill created sec. 71.095 of the Wisconsin Statutes to provide in part as follows:

(1) Every individual filing an income tax statement may designate that their income tax liability be increased by $1 for deposit into the Wisconsin Election Campaign Fund for the use of eligible candidates under s. 11.50.

Acting Governor Schreiber exercised his partial veto by lining out the words, "that their income tax liability be increased by," and the words, "deposit into." The section as changed by the partial veto reads:

(1) Every individual filing an income tax statement may designate $1 for the Wisconsin Election Campaign Fund for the use of eligible candidates under s. 11.50.

It is conceded that the bill as enrolled would require taxpayers to "add on" to their tax liabilities the sum of $1 if they wished that sum to go the campaign fund. As changed by the Governor's partial veto, a taxpayer instead elects to designate that the sum of $1 be "checked off" or expended from the state general funds for the purposes of the Election Campaign Fund.

The parties have stipulated that the change made in sec. 51 will result in approximately $600,000 in tax funds being expended directly for political purposes per annum. Under the bill as passed by the Legislature, only the sum which taxpayers agreed to have added to their tax liability would have been used for political purposes. Under the provisions of sec. 51 as partially vetoed, the sums used for political purposes will come out of general tax revenues.

The change in sec. 53 was made by the veto of the portion which provided:

(1) Section 71.095 of the statutes, as created by this act, shall apply to all individual income tax returns for any calendar year or corresponding fiscal year which commences not more than 6 months preceding the effective date of this act, and to each calendar year or corresponding fiscal year thereafter.

It is alleged by the Attorney General that the partial veto of sec. 53 accelerated the effective date of the bill by one year.

. . . .

. . . [T]he question remains whether the words excised were appropriately removed by partial veto.

The words removed had the effect of replacing taxpayers' voluntary add-on to their personal tax liabilities the sum of $1 for political purposes, with an election by the taxpayer to direct that $1 be paid out of general funds and general tax revenues.

The additional charge to the general fund is estimated to be $600,000 per annum. This the petitioners claim created an appropriation where none existed before. Implicit in the petitioners' argument and explicit in the argument of the Attorney General is the additional argument that *voluntary* contributions were a proviso or condition upon which the appropriation depended and that such proviso or condition was *ipso facto* inseverable from the appropriation itself.

The petitioners acknowledge that the Legislature cannot, by a statement incorporated in the legislation, frustrate the Governor's partial-veto power by declaring that certain portions of a bill are inseverable. In that respect, the petitioners are correct. Severability, petitioners acknowledge, is the test of the partial-veto power. Petitioners concede that what is severable may be excised from the legislation by the Governor's partial veto.

The petitioners correctly assert that severability must be determined, not as a matter of form, but as a matter of substance. The brief of the petitioners argues that a partial veto which would make an appropriation where none existed before is not a severable change.

. . . [W]e conclude that, for a Governor to exercise a partial veto, the bill must, as it comes to the Governor, contain an appropriation. The principal thrust of the petitioners is based on the assumption that this bill contained no appropriation when it reached the Governor. We have concluded that assumption is incorrect. The bill clearly provided for an appropriation of funds obtained by a voluntary add-on option afforded a taxpayer. Those funds were then appropriated for election purposes by the bill.

Hence, it is incorrect, under the facts, for the petitioners to assert that the bill as altered by the Governor created an appropriation where none existed before. The Governor's veto left the appropriation untouched. Rather, it affected the source from which the appropriated funds were to be derived. Accordingly, to conclude, as the petitioners would have us do, that this bill is inseverable because it created an appropriation where none existed before is patently incorrect.

Severability is indeed the test of the Governor's constitutional authority to partially veto a bill, but the test of severability is that established by the Wisconsin court and not by courts which operate under a different constitution. . . .

Three major Wisconsin cases have discussed the power of the Governor to partially veto a bill under the authority of art. V, sec. 10: *State ex rel. Wisconsin Telephone Co. v. Henry,* 218 Wis. 302, 260 N.W. 486 (1935); *State ex rel. Martin v. Zimmerman,* 233 Wis. 442, 289 N.W. 662 (1940); *State ex rel. Sundby v. Adamany,* 71 Wis.2d 118, 237 N.W.2d 910 (1976).

Each of these cases emphasizes that the power of the Governor to approve or disapprove a bill "in part" is a far broader power than that conferred upon Governors under the partial-veto provisions of most state constitutions. In most instances, the power of the Governor is confined to the excision of appropriations or items in an appropriation bill.

The *Henry* case, *supra,* extensively discussed the distinction between the Wisconsin Constitution and other state constitutions which give a more limited power to the Governor. The *Henry* case sanctioned the Governor's exercise of the partial veto of appropriations, general legislation, and other parts of an appropriation bill which did not contain specific appropriations. The court concluded that any portion of an appropriation bill was severable and could be excised so long as it left, in respect to "the parts approved, as they were in the bill . . . a complete, entire, and workable law." . . .

In the *Henry* case, one of the provisions vetoed by the Governor was the express statement of the legislative intent. The court acknowledged that the powers conferred on the Governor by the Constitution in respect to the partial veto were broad indeed. It stated:

> It may well be that sec. 10, art. V, Wisconsin Constitution, was not intended to empower the Governor, in vetoing parts of an appropriation bill, to dissever or dismember a single piece of legislation which is not severable, or so as to leave merely provisions which are not a complete or fitting subject for a separate enactment by the Legislature. Although that may not have been intended, there is nothing in that provision which warrants the inference or conclusion that the Governor's power of partial veto was not intended to be as coextensive as the Legislature's power to join and enact separable pieces of legislation in an appropriation bill. As the Legislature can do that in this state, there are reasons why the governor should have a coextensive power of partial veto, to enable him to pass, in the exercise of his *quasi*-legislative function, on each separable piece of legislation or law on its own merits. (at 314-15, 260 N.W. at 492).

Accordingly, the court in *Henry* stated that the Governor's power to disassemble legislation by the partial veto was as broad as the Legislature's power initially to join the legislation into a single bill. It put but one limitation on the Governor's power, and that is that the remainder after partial veto be a "complete, entire, and workable law." It found in *Henry* that the part approved by the Governor constituted, independently of the disapproved portions, a complete, entire, and workable law.

In the subsequent case of *Martin, supra,* the rationale of *Henry* was followed. . . .

The workable-law test was reemphasized in *Sundby, supra.* . . .

We conclude that the test of severability has clearly and repeatedly been stated by this court to be simply that what remains be a complete and workable law. The power of the Governor to dissassembly the law is coextensive with the power of the Legislature to assembly its provisions initially.

This conclusion in respect to severability is consistent with the Legislature's own declaration. In sec. 990.001(11), Stats., the Legislature stated, "The provisions of the statutes are severable. The provisions of any session law are severable. . . ."

While that legislative declaration is concerned primarily with the construction and effect of legislation which may be in part defective, it evinces a general legislative purpose to give force to portions of legislation which survive a constitutionally authorized nullification, whether that nullification be by the courts or by the Governor.

In the present case it is undisputed that what remained after the Governor's partial veto is a complete, entire, and workable law. As such, it is severable and reflects the proper exercise of the partial-veto power conferred on the Governor by the Constitution of the state.

In addition, the cases decided by this court have repeatedly pointed out that, because the Governor's power to veto is coextensive with the legislature's power to enact laws initially, a governor's partial veto may, and usually will, change the policy of the law. . . .

Thus, the fact that the Acting Governor's partial veto in the instant case changed the policy of the legislation from that of encouraging add-ons to a taxpayer's personal liability to that of imposing a charge on the general fund does not lead to the conclusion that the veto power was unconstitutionally exercised. It reflected a change of policy which the Governor had the authority to make under the Constitution because his authority is coextensive with the authority of the Legislature to enact the policy initially.

It should be borne in mind, of course, that the very section of the Constitution which gives to the Governor the authority to change policy by the exercise of a partial veto also gives the final disposition and resolution of policy matters to the Legislature. The Governor's changed policy can ultimately remain in effect only if the Legislature acquiesces in a partial veto by its refusal or failure to override the Governor's objections.

There remains yet another facet of the authority of the Governor to exercise a partial-veto power that should be explored. It is urged by the petitioners and by the Attorney General that provisos and conditions of an appropriation may not be severed from the appropriation itself. It is argued that, even when a workable bill remains after the exercise of the partial veto, the fulfilment of that test alone does not make what remains a properly severable and independent bill. The position of the antagonists to the Governor's partial veto in this case is that, whenever an appropriation is made on the basis of a legislatively established proviso or condition, the provisos themselves may not be separately vetoed, but the entire appropriation, including the provisos, must be excised by the Governor.

In the instant case it is argued that the appropriation of moneys for political purposes was conditioned by the Legislature upon the voluntary contribution to be made by taxpayers and that proviso or condition is inseverable from the appropriation itself.

The conclusion urged by the petitioners and the Attorney General reasonably could be reached from the dicta of Wisconsin cases. We are satisfied, however, that those pronouncements are dicta only and, more importantly, have no relevance to interpretation of the partial-veto provisions of the Wisconsin Constitution.

In *Henry, supra,* the first case to come before the court on the partial veto, petitioners therein relied upon *State ex rel. Teachers and Officers v. Holder,* 76 Miss. 158, 23 So. 643 (1898). . . . [This case is discussed in *Welden v. Ray,* reproduced *supra.* — Eds.]

No provision of art. V, sec. 10, of the Constitution limits the Governor's authority to veto appropriations because of any legislatively imposed conditions.

The alleged limitation arises from the language of *Henry*. The source of the dicta which has led to the contention of the petitioners is apparent from the text of *Henry*. *Henry* relies upon the Mississippi case of *Holder, supra,* for the contention that the governor's partial-veto power cannot be exercised when there are legislatively imposed provisos or conditions on an appropriation. The *Holder* case itself, however, cites no authority for a general proposition that a governor cannot veto a proviso or condition to an appropriation. It should be noted that, although the Mississippi Constitution is similar to the Wisconsin Constitution in that it provides that the governor may veto "parts" of an appropriation bill, another portion of the Mississippi Constitution, sec. 69, specifically provides that the legislature has the power to set conditions under which appropriated money is to be paid. This is a constitutional provision which has no counterpart in the Wisconsin Constitution. Sec. 69 may well justify in *Holder* the language in respect to "conditions," for in Mississippi the governor apparently may not veto a proviso or a condition to an appropriation. That concept, however, finds no support in the Wisconsin Constitution.

. . . .

The dicta, in reliance upon *Holder,* which appears in *Henry* and in subsequent Wisconsin cases, does not correctly state the Wisconsin law. Under the Wisconsin Constitution, the governor may exercise his partial-veto power by removing provisos and conditions to an appropriation so long as the net result of the partial veto is a complete, entire, and workable bill which the legislature itself could have passed in the first instance.

Unlike the fact situation in *Henry,* the Acting Governor vetoed what is arguably a condition which the Legislature had placed on the appropriation. By so doing, he changed the policy of the law as envisaged by the legislature. He caused the general fund to be charged with an obligation which the Legislature did not anticipate; and also, it is contended, he accelerated the effective date of the bill. These are policy changes, legislative in nature, which the Constitution authorized him to make.

The bill was an appropriation bill. What remained after the Governor's partial veto was a complete, entire, and workable bill. As such it was severable from the legislative package of the enrolled bill. The Acting Governor compiled with the constitutional mandates by timely and appropriately messaging his objections to the house of the Legislature in which the bill originated. He made an appropriate return of the vetoed legislation as the Constitution contemplates it. We accordingly hold that Acting Governor Schreiber constitutionally exercised the power of partial veto as conferred upon governors of Wisconsin by art. V, sec. 10, of the Constitution.

. . . .

CONNOR T. HANSEN, JUSTICE (concurring in part, dissenting in part). [Omitted.]

Comments: 1. Compare the gubernatorial veto provisions in the Iowa, Wisconsin and Mississippi constitutions. Do they really explain the results in the cases? Does the court's decision in *Welden v. Ray* preclude almost any gubernatorial vetoes of appropriations? Does the Wisconsin court's decision in *Conta* make gubernatorial vetoes practically immune from attack? Is there a middle ground? For discussion of vetoes in Wisconsin, see Harrington, *The Propriety of the Negative — The Governor's Partial Veto Authority,* 60 MARQ. L. REV. 865 (1977).

2. Consider this situation. For reasons of economy and policy, e.g., he does not believe in large custodial institutions located far from population centers, the governor announces a program to phase out two of the state's antiquated mental health hospitals. Legislators from the areas in which the institutions are located, responding to the fears of residents that the closing will have a negative effect on the economy of the area, enlist the support of their colleagues in the legislature to oppose the governor's program. In the appropriations for the mental health department, the legislature attaches a proviso that none of the amounts appropriated in that act may be used for any purpose in connection with the closing of the named institutions or any other institutions within the department's jurisdiction. Would the Iowa and Wisconsin courts permit the governor to item veto that provision on the ground that it is unnecessary, unwise and violates the separation of powers by infringing on his executive authority? Would it make any difference if before the action above, the legislature had passed a separate bill prohibiting the governor from closing any institution, the bill was vetoed, and the legislature was not able to override the veto?

3. Can the legislature in the guise of attaching conditions to appropriations in fact write new substantive law, thereby depriving the governor of the opportunity to express approval or disapproval of those provisions? The provision in a number of state constitutions which limits every bill to one subject and its stricter counterpart, limiting appropriation bills to the subject of appropriations, is designed in part to protect the integrity of the gubernatorial veto; but it does not serve that purpose if the added matter is read as a condition on the appropriation and not subject to the item veto. Is the difference between a condition and a separate item all that clear? How would you analyze the vetoes noted below?

a. The legislature appropriated $688,800 to the State Personnel Board with the qualification, vetoed by the governor, that the funds could not be spent for promulgating or filing rules, policies or plans which would have significant financial impact. See *State ex rel. Sego v. Kirkpatrick,* 524 P.2d 975, 983 (N.M. 1974).

b. In the appropriation to the institutions of higher education, the legislature included a provision, vetoed by the governor, that in the event actual revenues to the universities exceeded the amounts appropriated from six named funds and state department of finance could approve expenditures of the excess. *Id.* at 984-85. Cf. *People ex rel. Kirk v. Lindberg,* 320 N.E.2d 17 (Ill. 1974).

c. The legislature appropriated $1.1 million to the office of administration "For Capitol Building Renovation (West Side)." The governor vetoed out the words West Side. See *State ex rel. Cason v. Bond,* 495 S.W.2d 385 (Mo. 1973).

d. The appropriation to the attorney general's office for operating expenses contained language, specifically declared by the legislature to be an integral part of the appropriation and not a separate item, which provided that the appropriation was also available to permit the secretary of state to hire independent counsel to defend certain law suits. The governor vetoed that provision. See *State ex rel. Brown v. Ferguson,* 291 N.E.2d 434 (Ohio 1972).

4. A variation of the condition versus separate item issue is presented by the practice of lump sum appropriations, which has given rise to considerable litigation. To illustrate: the legislature appropriates $2 million to the state personnel department, to be used for the following purposes: $1 million for in-service training programs for state employees; $500,000 for tuition and other expenses of state employees on authorized leave to seek additional education; $500,000 for advertising and other expenses in connection with state recruitment of employees.

Can the governor item veto the $500,000 allocation for recruitment expenses: is it a separate item of appropriation, susceptible to item veto, or simply a condition as to how the $2 million appropriation is to be spent? If the latter, hasn't the legislature found a way effectively to abrogate the governor's item veto by lumping appropriations in large categories with the itemization or breakdown cast as conditions? What are the limits of the legislature's power to lump-sum appropriate: could it appropriate the entire operating budget of the executive agencies in one lump sum?

The New York courts have made clear that the answer to this question is no. They have read that state's constitution as requiring the governor and the legislature to itemize appropriations, but permitting lump sums where itemization is impracticable. *People v. Tremaine,* 21 N.E.2d 891 (N.Y. 1939). In *Tremaine* the court disapproved of lump sum appropriations for an entire department or bureau.

The decisions on availability of the governor's veto on lump sum appropriations are not easy to reconcile. *E.g., In re Opinion of the Justices,* 2 N.E.2d 789 (Mass. 1936). The legislature appropriated $100,000 for payment of extraordinary expenses and other expenditures (a kind of contingency fund requested by the governor) but added the condition that not less than $50,000 be reserved for a specified purpose, not less than $10,000 be reserved for entertainment of the president and other distinguished guests, and not more than $5,000 be transferred to certain other items of appropriation. The governor vetoed the language allocating the appropriation among specified purposes. The court held the governor's attempted veto a nullity; it was an attempt to enlarge the legislature's appropriation by removing the restrictions imposed on the use of the items appropriated. *Id.* at 791. In Massachusetts the governor has the power to reduce appropriations as well as to item veto them. Should this weigh in the decision? *See Brown v. Firestone,* 382 So. 2d 654 (Fla. 1980) (interpreting veto provision in 1968 state constitution as overruling earlier case *contra*).

Compare *Reardon v. Riley,* 76 P.2d 101 (Cal. 1938); *Railroad Commission v. Riley,* 82 P.2d 394 (Cal. 1938); *Pomeroy v. Riley,* 82 P.2d 697 (Cal. 1938). In the three California cases the court permitted the governor to veto language which required that a stated part of the appropriation was to be used for a specified purpose, but it held that the entire amount appropriated was available for expenditure. Does this result change the character of the veto from a negative weapon into an affirmative law-making power?

5. As many of the above cases suggest, the form in which appropriation bills are drawn frequently renders the item veto useless. The governor is faced with the choice, for example, of approving what he may believe to be an inflated appropriation for personal services in an agency or vetoing the entire item and leaving the agency without any funds for salaries. Modern budgeting practices have encouraged the use of broader categories of appropriation. In somewhat less than one-fifth of the states, the power to reduce appropriations is granted to the governor by constitution. Where it is not authorized, the courts have almost always rejected the governor's attempt to reduce an appropriation as an act of creative lawmaking, inconsistent with separation of powers. *See, e.g., Mills v. Porter,* 222 P. 428 (Cal. 1924) (court suggested that if legislature had appropriated more than available revenues, governor could veto entire bill and call legislature into special session); *Wood v. State Administrative Board,* 238 N.W. 16 (Mich. 1931); *contra Commonwealth v. Barnett,* 48 A. 976 (Pa. 1901) (legislature had, however, violated spirit of constitutional requirement of single subject by passing lump sum appropriation).

6. The item veto is usually authorized only in connection with appropriations. A question then arises whether the bill on which the item veto is used is an appropriations bill. With the *Conta* opinion's ruling on this point, compare *In re Opinion of the Justices,* 212 N.E.2d 562 (Mass. 1965). The court held that the annual county funding bill, though denominated an "appropriation," was not an appropriation as that term was used in the veto provision in the constitution. The court held that the bill was more in the nature of an authorization to counties to raise and expend funds, and did not directly appropriate state funds from the state treasury. *Accord Opinion of the Justices,* 210 A.2d 852 (Del. 1965) (bill provided formula for appropriations to school districts but did not appropriate money). Is the bill in the *Conta* case distinguishable?

When the governor's attempt to exercise item veto power has been held invalid, what is the status of the resulting bill? Some courts hold that the improperly exercised veto is ineffectual and the entire bill becomes law, including the vetoed part. *See, e.g., State ex rel. Turner v. Iowa Highway Commission,* 186 N.W.2d 141 (Iowa 1971); *State ex rel. Cason v. Bond, supra* Comment 3. Others hold that the failure of the veto results in failure of the entire bill. *Opinion of the Justices,* 306 A.2d 720, 723 (Del. 1973); *State ex rel. Finnegan v. Dammann,* 264 N.W. 622 (Wis. 1936). The reason most often assigned for the differing results is the difference in the constitutional language covering executive vetoes. Generally, in the first group of states, the constitution provides that a bill becomes law unless the governor takes affirmative action to veto all or part of it; the ineffective veto is thus ignored. In the second group, a bill does not become law unless approved by the governor within certain time limits: the governor not having approved all of the bill, it fails. Can either or both of these explanations be said confidently to reflect the governor's probable intent? Does it make any difference why the governor misjudged the scope of his power: e.g., the bill was not an appropriation bill; the language vetoed was found to be a condition, not a separate item, etc.?

7. In the separation of powers lexicon, the amendatory veto presents the most interesting challenge. While differing in detail among the seven states which have adopted it, typically the amendatory or conditional veto permits the governor to return a bill to the legislature with specific recommendations for change which would make the bill acceptable to him. The legislature may adopt the governor's recommended changes or reenact the bill, by the same vote required for initial passage. The bill then returns to the governor for his approval or certification that the legislature's action was in accordance with his proposals. The legislature generally has the option of treating the governor's action as an outright veto and moving to override it in the usual manner. See *Application of McGlynn*, 155 A.2d 289 (N.J. App. Div. 1955).

The extent of the amendatory veto is not clear. In Illinois it may be used for more than technical amendments. *Compare People ex rel. Klinger v. Howlett*, 278 N.E.2d 84 (Ill. 1972) (suggesting that the governor may not substitute an entirely new bill), *with People ex rel. City of Canton v. Crouch*, 403 N.E.2d 242 (Ill. 1980) (upholding numerous substantive amendments to a tax increment financing act). For a discussion of the amendatory veto in Illionis and other states, see Comment, *The Illinois Amendatory Veto*, 11 J. Mar. J. Prac. & Proc. 415 (1978). Studies indicate that most amendatory vetoes have been accepted by the legislature. *See* J. Kallenbach, The American Chief Executive 365-66 (1966).

Washington allows the governor to veto sections or items in any bill. Wash. Const. art. III, § 12. In *Cascade Telephone Co. v. Tax Commission*, 30 P.2d 976 (Wash. 1934), the court upheld a veto from an excise tax levy bill of a section requiring certain taxpayers to pass the tax on to their customers. The dissent objected that the governor's veto had completely reversed the legislative intent: the legislature taxed *A;* the governor taxed *B*. *Compare Washington Ass'n of Apartment Ass'ns v. Evans*, 564 P.2d 788 (Wash. 1977) (invalidating vetoes of substantive provisions in landlord-tenant bill).

8. May a court review a gubernatorial veto? For a fascinating opinion in which a court did review a gubernatorial veto under 28 U.S.C. § 1983 to determine whether it was so arbitrary and capricious that it violated plaintiff's due process rights, see *Saffioti v. Wilson*, 392 F. Supp. 1335 (S.D.N.Y. 1975). If the governor's veto message were essentially non-informational, as many are (i.e., I veto this bill because it is not in the best interests of the state), how would the court apply a standard of arbitrary and capricious? Could the plaintiff subpoena the notes and records of the governor or his aides? Could the governor be subpoenaed to testify? As to what? What kind of relief could the court grant?

9. *Local vetoes.* At the local level, the executive veto is exercised subject to legislative provisions or home rule charters. In *County Commissioners v. County Executive*, 296 N.W.2d 621 (Mich. App. 1980), the county executive vetoed resolutions calling for the withdrawal of the county from a regional transportation authority. State legislation authorized the veto of any ordianance or resolution. The court upheld the veto, rejecting a suggestion that the resolution was not subject to veto because "it had regional implications." The court held that "the resolution itself could only bind Oakland County and would not operate beyond its boundaries," even though it might have an indirect inter-county effect.

A NOTE ON EXECUTIVE IMPOUNDMENT

Executive impoundment of legislative appropriations led to dramatic confrontations between the President and Congress which culminated in the Nixon Administration. Although numerous lawsuits were brought challenging President Nixon's impoundment of appropriated funds, the only case that reached the Supreme Court was decided on statutory grounds. See *Train v. City of New York,* 420 U.S. 35 (1975), holding that the impoundment was unauthorized by statute, and not reaching the constitutional question.

The executive impoundment issue also has arisen at the state level. An understanding of the constitutional issues presented first requires a definition. The term "impoundment" does not have an accepted meaning, and may be defined narrowly or broadly:

> In its broadest context, impoundment occurs whenever the President spends less than Congress appropriates for a given period. Impoundment may be temporary or permanent, but in most cases it enjoys statutory support and no constitutional issue emerges.

Fisher, *Funds Impounded by the President: The Constitutional Issue,* 38 GEO. WASH. L. REV. 124 (1969).

> Impoundment in its broadest sense includes any type of executive action which effectively precludes the obligation or expenditure of any part of budget authority. It does not include presidential action which is in strict compliance with discretion invested in the executive branch by the Congress.

Mikva & Hertz, *Impoundment of Funds — The Courts, the Congress, and the President: A Constitutional Triangle,* 69 Nw. U.L. REV. 335, 337 (1974). *Accord* Note, *The Likely Law of Executive Impoundment,* 59 IOWA L. REV. 50, 55-56 (1973).

The scattered state decisions on executive impoundment have not been receptive. In *West Side Organization Health Services Corp. v. Thompson,* 391 N.E.2d 392 (Ill. App. 1978), *rev'd as moot,* 404 N.E.2d 208 (Ill. 1980), the governor vetoed a line item appropriation for drug treatment services, reducing the appropriation by $100,000. The legislature overrode the veto and the governor then directed a withholding of the same amount for budgetary reasons.

The court held that the constitution conferred no inherent impoundment authority on the governor. The constitution contained explicit provisions for the control of state finance, authorized borrowing to cover deficits, and conferred a specific veto authority to reduce line item appropriations. The court concluded that the legislature had "the ultimate authority to determine both the level and allocation of public spending," and that the governor had "no express authority by the constitution to reserve appropriated funds in frustration of the General Assembly's expressed intent." *Id.* at 402.

The New York court reached the same conclusion in *County of Oneida v. Berle,* 404 N.E.2d 133 (N.Y. 1980). The legislature added $14 million dollars to the governor's recommendation for sewage treatment works reimbursement to local governments, but the governor directed withholding of $7 million of that amount for fiscal reasons. The New York court also noted that explicit budgetary procedures had been provided by the constitution, holding that the executive was "required to implement policy declarations of the Legislature, unless vetoed or judicially invalidated." The governor had not attempted to veto the increased appropriation.

The governor also argued that the power to impound was authorized by his implicit constitutional obligation to maintain a balanced budget. The court found no such obligation, concluding that in its absence the governor "can hardly possess implied power unilaterally to 'reduce' a lawful appropriation."

An intermediate position was adopted in *Opinion of the Justices,* 376 N.E.2d 1217 (Mass. 1978). The court found no inherent executive authority to impound, holding that it was the function of the legislature to determine social goals and priorities. Noting that the "activity of spending money is essentially a legislative task," the court then advised that:

> the Governor be allowed some discretion to exercise his judgment not to spend money in a wasteful fashion, provided that he has determined reasonably that such a decision will not compromise the achievement of underlying legislative purposes and goals.

Id. at 1223. The court also advised that a proposed law authorizing the legislature by resolution to release the governor from expending an entire appropriation was unconstitutional. Such a resolution would modify a previously enacted appropriation bill and would circumvent the constitutional authority of the governor to veto appropriation acts.

The state impoundment cases appear impressed that the fiscal checks and balances provided by state constitutions are sufficient, and that fiscal control by the governor should be exercised through the veto power. Is this conclusion consistent with the judicial view of separation of powers and gubernatorial authority as expressed in the cases reproduced and discussed in this chapter? Is there any reason for implying gubernatorial authority to exercise impoundment powers? Can you think of any reasons, other than fiscal, for exercising this power? Would they influence your view of executive impoundment at the state level?

Chapter 12
CITIZEN CONTROL OF GOVERNMENTAL ACTION

Opportunities for the review and supervision of governmental action have been stressed throughout this casebook. In this country, this supervisory role is primarily exercised by the courts. This chapter looks at the judicial procedures that allow litigants to seek judicial review of state and local government action. A final section considers the initiative and referendum process, which provides an alternative electoral method through which citizens can participate in state and local government decision making.

A. THROUGH THE COURTS

Citizen access to the courts to review state and local government action is by no means always guaranteed or universal. State agencies are subject to the judicial review provisions of state administrative procedure acts, where they have been adopted. Some states make these acts applicable to local governments, and judicial review is expressly provided by some statutes conferring authority on local governments, such as taxation and zoning laws.

If statutory judicial review is not available, a litigant seeking to challenge a local government action must use the judicial review opportunities provided by what are called the extraordinary or "high prerogative" writs. This section reviews the use of these writs to review local government actions, and closes with a review of the important question of taxpayer standing to sue. For an excellent review of this subject, see Bruff, *Judicial Review in Local Government Law: A Reappraisal,* 60 MINN. L. REV. 669 (1976).

An important and distinctive characteristic of the extraordinary writs must first be noted. The writs are similar to the early private causes of action. Rember that litigants could not simply sue, for example, in tort. The plaintiff had to select a cause of action that would allow recovery for the damage he had suffered. If the litigant selected the wrong cause of action, he was out of court.

The extraordinary writs operate in much the same way. The court first decides whether the writ selected by the plaintiff is the appropriate writ to review the local government action he has challenged. If the plaintiff selected the correct writ, the court then proceeds to a consideration of the merits of his action. If the plaintiff did not select the correct writ, he is usually (but not always) out of court. The decision on what writ to use is thus very important in actions against local governments. Incidentally, the writ of mandamus may be an exception to this rule. In mandamus cases, the court usually decides the merits of the action when it considers whether the writ is appropriate. The next section indicates why this is so.

1. MANDAMUS

CARTWRIGHT v. SHARPE
Supreme Court of Wisconsin
40 Wis. 2d 494, 162 N.W.2d 5 (1968)

This is an appeal by the School Board of Joint School District #1, Fond du Lac county, from a judgment which ordered the issuance of a peremptory writ of mandamus directing the school board to furnish transportation for the school children of the petitioner and other school children residing in the city of Fond du Lac who lived more than two miles from and attended St. Mary's Springs Academy, a parochial high school.

Joint School District #1, Fond du Lac county, consists of the city of Fond du Lac and parts of several adjacent townships. The board of education for the district consists of seven members elected at large from the district. An appropriating authority approves the school budget and levies the school tax. The appropriating authority consists of the members of the city council of Fond du Lac and the town chairman of the several towns.

The school district operates a high school, two junior high schools and several elementary schools located in the city of Fond du Lac, and several elementary schools in the district but outside the city of Fond du Lac. There are 10 elementary parochial schools within the district, all of them located in the city, and two parochial high schools, one within the city (Winnebago Lutheran Academy) and one outside the city (St. Mary's Springs Academy).

St. Mary's Springs Academy is located about two miles from the city limits of Fond du Lac, at the junction of State Trunk Highway 23 and County Trunk K. Highway 23 is the route from Fond du Lac to St. Mary's Springs. It is a well traveled state trunk highway without a sidewalk or other special provision for pedestrians. The school has about 650 students; 392 of them reside in the city of Fond du Lac and more than two miles from the school. Approximately 400 additional students live in the city and more than two miles from their schools, public or private.

Prior to the ratification of the school bus constitutional amendment, art. I, sec. 23, Wis. Const., bus transportation was provided for only those public school students who resided outside of the city of Fond du Lac and more than two miles from their schools. After the constitutional amendment and enabling legislation, bus transportation was provided for all students, both public and parochial, who lived outside the city and more than two miles from their schools.

On August 14, 1967, the petitioner, Theodore C. Cartwright, who had two children of high school age and who were enrolled at St. Mary's Springs Academy, appeared before the school board and filed a petition with 4,000 signatures requesting that the school district provide transportation for the students who lived in the city of Fond du Lac and attended St. Mary's Springs Academy. On August 21st, at a special meeting, the board voted "enthusiastically" to support the request that funds be placed in the budget for transportation of city students. On September 25, 1967, the school board adopted a recommended budget which included $48,200 for the transportation of city students who lived more than two miles from their schools. It was expected that 392 city students would be transported to St. Mary's Springs Academy and 400 to other schools in the city, including parochial schools.

On October 9, 1967, the school board adopted a resolution to the effect that the district provide this transportation through the city bus service "provided funds are made available in the 1968 budget." The city bus company was about to cease its operations and so notified the school board. The board authorized negotiations with the Johnson Bus Company "pending the outcome of the budget hearing on November 20th."

The total budget proposed by the school board to the appropriating authority was $5,992,598.

At the budget hearing the appropriating authority cut the proposed budget as recommended by the school board in the amount of $200,000 without reference to any specific item in the budget.

The school board then met to recalculate its budget to comply with the $200,000 reduction. Among the items which were eliminated or altered to stay within the authorized budget was the $48,200 for transportation of all students who resided within the city.

As a result no transportation was provided for any of the students who lived in the city and more than two miles from their schools, whether they be public or parochial, and transportation was provided for all students who lived outside the city and more than two miles from their schools, whether they were public or parochial. Children in the St. Mary's Springs Academy area (outside the city) living more than two miles from their schools were transported to both public and parochial schools, but students who lived in the city were not transported to St. Mary's Springs Academy.

The petitioner then applied to the circuit court for Fond du Lac county for an alternative writ of mandamus to compel the school district to transport his children and the other children residing in Fond du Lac to and from St. Mary's Springs Academy.

The circuit court found for the petitioner and by a judgment directed a peremptory writ of mandamus to issue requiring school board members to "make arrangements for the furnishing of transportation on or before March 15, 1968, to the children of the petitioner and other city resident pupils living more than two miles from St. Mary's Springs Academy."

The school board appeals.

. . . .

BEILFUSS, JUSTICE.

Prior to 1967 it was not constitutionally permissible, in Wisconsin, for a public school district to provide transportation for children attending parochial or private schools, although it was mandatory in some instances and permissible in others to provide transportation for students attending public schools.

In 1967, by virtue of the mandate of a state-wide referendum, the Wisconsin constitution was amended to provide:

> Art. I, sec. 23. "*Transportation of school children.* Nothing in this constitution shall prohibit the legislature from providing for the safety and welfare of children by providing for the transportation of children to and from any parochial or private school or institution of learning."

Pursuant to authority provided by the constitutional amendment, the legislature did elect to provide for the transportation of children to any parochial or private school by amending the existing statutes for public school transportation so as to provide for transportation for students attending private or parochial schools and public schools upon a reasonably uniform basis.

This enabling legislation was created by chs. 68 and 313, Laws of 1967. Section 1 of ch. 68 provides:

> *Purpose.* The intent of this act is to provide for the safety and welfare of children by providing for their transportation to and from public and private schools.

The controlling statutes as they now exist became effective in January, 1968, and are as follows:

121.54(1). Subsections (2) and (6) and s. 121.57 do not apply to pupils who reside in cities, except that where annual or special meeting of a common school district or a union high school district, or the school board of a city school district or unified school district determines to provide transportation for such pupils, state aid shall be paid in accordance with s. 121.58 and there shall be reasonable uniformity in the transportation furnished pupils who reside in cities as between pupils attending public and private schools.

121.54(2) (a) Except as provided in sub. (1), every school board shall provide transportation to and from public school for all pupils who reside in the school district 2 miles or more from the nearest public school they are entitled to attend.

121.54(2) (b) 1. Except as provided in sub. (1), the school board of each school district shall provide transportation to and from the school he attends for each pupil residing in the school district who attends any elementary grade, including kindergarten, or high school grade, comparable to any grade offered by such school district, at a private school located 2 miles or more from his residence, if such private school is the nearest available private school which the pupil may reasonably choose to attend and is situated within the school district. . . .

It is the position of the respondent-petitioner that sec. 121.54(2) (b) 1, Stats., requires that the school board provide transportation for his children to St. Mary's Springs Academy because they reside more than two miles from the school and it is the nearest parochial school that they may reasonably choose to attend. It is the contention of the appellant-school board that by virtue of sec. 121.54(1) it is optional with the school board whether students who reside in the city and more than two miles from school will be transported, and that if transportation is furnished to the petitioner's children transportation must be furnished to all other children, public or parochial, who reside in the city and are more than two miles from their school, and to do otherwise would violate the statute in that transportation would not be reasonably uniform as to pupils of public and private schools.

Before discussing the principal issue, namely the construction of the statutes in question, it may be well to define the scope of the writ of mandamus. In *Menzl v. City of Milwaukee* (1966), 32 Wis. 2d 266, at pp. 275-276, 145 N.W.2d 198, at p. 203, this court stated that mandamus was a discretionary writ and added:

"Mandamus is a summary, drastic, and extraordinary writ issued in the sound discretion of the court. Although classed as a legal remedy, mandamus is equitable in its nature and its issuance is generally controlled by equitable principles. The rights of the public and of third persons may be considered."

"The [trial] court has discretion as to the issuing of a writ of *mandamus* directed to a public officer. The order of the court will not be reversed except for abuse of such discretion." *State ex rel. New Strand Theatre Co. v. Common Council of City of Racine* (1930), 201 Wis. 423, 425, 230 N.W. 60, 61.

Moreover, it is an abuse of discretion for a court to compel action through mandamus when the officer's duty is not clear and unequivocal and requires the exercise of the officer's discretion. . . . But it is equally well settled that a writ of mandamus will issue to enforce the performance of plain imperative duties of a ministerial character imposed on executive agencies. . . . Furthermore, it is the proper remedy to compel public officers to perform their clearly prescribed statutory duty. . . .

Mandamus is not the proper remedy to control the acts of governmental bodies when acting within the scope of their legal powers. . . . Nor can mandamus be used to compel specific action by a municipal body or officer where such action is discretionary. . . .

The basic issue is whether under the law and the facts of this case is it a mandatory obligation of the school district to provide transportation of the in-city students (all of whom live more than two miles from the school) to St. Mary's Springs Academy. If the determination by the school board is discretionary rather than mandatory it is clear the petitioner cannot obtain the desired relief by means of mandamus.

The respondent-petitioner relies upon sec. 121.54(2) (b) 1, Stats., which provides the more than two-mile standard for children attending private schools and the overall safety and welfare of children provision of the intent of the legislative act (ch. 68, Laws of 1967), and the constitutional amendment (Art. I, sec. 23, Wis. Const.).

The appellant-school board asserts that sec. 121.54(2) (b) 1, Stats., by its own specific terms, is subject to sec. 121.54(1), which makes it optional with the school board as to whether children who reside in the city will be provided transportation and if transportation is provided it must be reasonably uniform as to all children who reside in the city, both as to public and private students.

From a literal reading of these statutes (set forth above), there is no question from language which is plain and unambiguous that the "over two mile" provision for mandatory transportation does not "apply to pupils who reside in cities" except where the school board "determines" to provide such transportation.

Both the appellant-school board and respondent-petitioner cite authorities in support of their construction of the statute. The school board cites the familiar rule that when a statute is plain and unambiguous no interpretation is necessary; and that a court may not review matters outside the statutory language to determine its meaning, nor can the court add language to a statute to obtain a desired result — such is prohibited judicial legislation.

The petitioner-respondent cites authorities to the effect that even though the language of a statute may be plain and unambiguous, if to give the statute its apparent meaning would result in an absurdity or obscure the legislative purpose the court may look to the history of the legislation to find the real intent of the legislature and may substitute the right word for one clearly wrong if need be.

For many years, the "over two miles" and city option statutes have existed in almost identical form as they do today. The important change provided by the constitutional amendment and the enabling legislative acts was to provide that where transportation is furnished, either mandatory or permissive, it must be on a reasonably uniform basis to children attending either public or private schools.

It is true that the safety and welfare of the children were the laudable motivating factors of the transportation statutes. There is no reason to suspect that these factors were not relied upon by the legislature before the enactment of the constitutional amendment and the enabling legislation of the present statutes. What the constitutional amendment and the enabling legislation accomplished was to provide that the same consideration of safety and welfare should apply to public and private students alike....

[The court then held that the classifications provided by the statute were reasonable. — Eds.]

Judgment directing the issuance of the writ of mandamus is reversed.

HALLOWS, CHIEF JUSTICE (dissenting). [Omitted.]

Comments: 1. The school transportation problem again came before the Wisconsin Supreme Court in *Morrissette v. De Zonia,* 217 N.W.2d 377 (Wis. 1974). This case again involved a joint school district, that is, the district covered the city and adjoining territory outside the city limits. In this case the district refused to provide transportation for any middle or high school students living more than two miles away from the school. Litigants in the case were public school children and their parents who met this standard and who lived in the district but outside the city limits.

Recall that school transportation is not mandatory for pupils living in the city. In this case the district claimed that a statute, not considered in the *Cartwright* case, justified its refusal to provide transportation. That statute provided that "Territory outside a city which is joined with city territory in the formation of a city school district is attached to the city for school purposes." Therefore, the district argued, pupils living outside the city limits but within the school district resided in the city for purposes of the school transportation statute, with the result that the district could decide within its discretion whether or not to provide transportation for them. Consult again the statutes quoted in the *Cartwright* case.

The court did not accept the school district's argument, holding that the statute "attaching" the extraterritorial portions of the school district to the city for school purposes did not make the pupils residing in the extraterritorial portions of the district "residents" of the city for purposes of the school transportation law. In doing so, the court relied on the fact that the legislature by statute had reversed the result of the *Cartwright* case soon after that decision. It did so by making an exception to the discretionary option to provide school transportation to pupils living in cities in the case of "pupils who reside in cities [if] . . . the school they attend is located outside the city but within the boundaries of the school district." Why is this statutory change relevant to the decision in the *Morrissette* case?

This statutory analysis was necessary to the decision for, as the supreme court noted:

> The trial court here misunderstands the necessity for a clear and unequivocal duty before mandamus will lie to compel performance of that duty. The court apparently felt that if construction and statutory interpretation were necessary to determine whether a mandatory duty existed under the facts, then mandamus would not lie even after such interpretation revealed the nature of the action sought to be compelled. . . . Because one has to resolve apparently conflicting statutory provisions to arrive at the nature of the duty sought to be compelled by mandamus does not mean that mandamus will not lie once that determination is made.

Id. at 379.

Why would mandamus be an appropriate remedy in *Morrissette* but not in *Cartwright?* What determines whether an act is ministerial-mandatory or discretionary? Could mandamus be used to compel a voting registrar to permit married women to register to vote in their maiden names? *See Custer v. Bonadies,* 318 A.2d 639 (Conn. Supp. 1974). The court first interpreted the Connecticut statutes to mean that a married woman may register in her maiden name and then granted mandamus, noting that the obligation of registrars to register as a voter any applicant who possesses the statutory qualifications under his or her own legal name was ministerial and not discretionary. There was no discretion in the statutes to refuse registration to anyone meeting these requirements.

2. Courts may often rely on "shall provide" language in a statute to find a mandatory duty to take some action. This result may be reached even when it is a question of appropriating funds, usually considered a discretionary responsibility. Thus in *People ex rel. Younger v. County of El Dorado,* 487 P.2d 1193 (Cal. 1971), the California attorney general brought an original action in the state supreme court for a writ of mandamus to compel two California counties to pay to the (Lake) Tahoe Regional Planning Agency their share of the funds necessary to support the Agency's activities. This agency had been created pursuant to statutes enacted by the states of California and Nevada under the terms of a congressionally approved interstate compact. The writ was allowed to issue and the court noted:

In the instant case, there is a clear duty imposed by law upon the counties. As already noted, section 66801, article VII, subdivision (a) provides that "[e]ach county in California *shall pay* the sum allotted to it by the agency from any funds available therefor . . . ." (Italics added.) The statute confers no discretion upon the counties; they must pay the sum apportioned to them.

There is also a beneficial right in the People of the State of California to compel the counties to perform their duty. The unique scenic attributes which the Agency must preserve are enjoyed not only by the residents of the region but also by large numbers of the state's general citizenry. Failure of respondent counties to provide funds for the Agency at once impairs the functioning of that body and disturbs the harmony and effectiveness of interstate relations. The state, as a party to the interstate Compact, and as an entity which contributes funds to the Agency, has an important interest in securing the success of the Agency.

Finally, by issuing the alternative writ, we have necessarily determined that there is no adequate remedy in the ordinary course of law and that this case is a proper one for the exercise of our original jurisdiction.

Id. at 1199.

See also United Mine Workers of America v. Miller, 291 S.E.2d 673 (W. Va. 1982). The court granted a writ of mandamus to compel the director of the state department of mines to allow miners to accompany state inspectors during mine inspections. The statute stated that "authorized representatives of the miners . . . shall be given an opportunity to accompany" inspectors during inspections. The court held that the word "shall" in the absence of language showing a contrary intent should be afforded a "mandatory connotation." It also noted that it had enlarged the scope of mandamus "especially where there is an urgent question of public policy."

3. While mandamus may compel the performance of a clear, ministerial duty, it is not available to direct the exercise of a discretionary duty in a particular manner. In *Edelstein v. Ferrell,* 295 A.2d 390 (N.J.L. 1972), a member of a voter registration drive sought to mandamus the county superintendent of elections to hold increased off-premises registration, particularly in minority areas. The applicable statute provided that the superintendent "shall receive the application for registration of all eligible voters who shall personally appear for registration during office hours at the office of the commissioner . . . or at such other place or places as may from time to time be designated by him . . . for registration." The court first defined "ministerial" as follows:

If a statute imposes a command to act or the performance of a positive duty in compliance with defined standards, the matter is ministerial and mandamus would be available to compel obedience.

Id. at 396.

The court found the choice of registration locations to be within the superintendent's discretion. Since he had exercised his discretionary authority in scheduling off-premises registration, and there was no showing that he had abused his discretion, mandamus was inappropriate. "All the plaintiff has shown is that she thinks Ferrell should have performed his statutory duty differently." *Id.* Does the statute impose a duty to conduct at least some off-premises registration? If the superintendent refused to take any registrations off-premises would an action in mandamus lie to require him to do so?

4. In some cases, mandamus may be used to force an official to take action within discretionary limits. A Mississippi court stated this rule as follows:

The proper function of mandamus is to supply a remedy for inaction on the part of an official or commission to whom it is directed. . . . It can direct an official or commission to perform its official duty or to perform a ministerial act, but it cannot project itself into the discretionary function of the official or the commission. Stated differently, it can direct action to be taken, but it cannot direct the outcome of the mandated function.

Hinds County Democratic Executive Committee v. Muirhead, 259 So. 2d 692, 694 (Miss.), *cert. denied,* 409 U.S. 852 (1972).

Moreover, when a public official acts in an arbitrary or capricious fashion, constituting an abuse of discretion, mandamus may issue to review that action. In *Haymart v.*

Freiberger, 498 S.W.2d 590 (Mo. App. 1973), the county superintendent of schools refused to reassign several children to a closer school in another district under a statute which provided that the superintendent "shall assign" the pupils to the other school district when it is "more accessible." The children attended the Mokane school, twenty-three miles from home, and wanted to transfer to the Fulton schools, about five miles away.

> All of the evidence in this case disclosed that in addition to the proximity of the Fulton schools, other factors operated to make the Fulton schools more accessible in the broad sense of that term. Conceding that accessibility is not solely a matter of geography does not alter the fact in this case, that the children's ability to utilize all the services of the school was impaired if they were required to attend the Mokane School and that there was uncontroverted evidence that the road hazard would be greater, not only as to the distance and time involved, but as to the quality of the roads they would travel if they attended the Mokane School. Thus, considering all the factors, the Mokane School is clearly less accessible than the Fulton schools. A contrary finding by the Superintendent based on the evidence adduced at the trial would very likely be so clearly arbitrary and capricious that it would be an abuse of discretion and permit the court's intervention on that ground.
>
> The Superintendent's own testimony affords an even stronger basis for a finding of an abuse of discretion. Her testimony refers only to "distance," and that factor, considered alone, definitely establishes that the Fulton schools are more accessible. Her admission that she considered it improper to change the pupils because of "elections" clearly demonstrates a failure to exercise a discretion, even under the broadest possible definition of "accessible." The failure to reassign cannot be supported on the ground of a discretion lawfully exercised and must be held to be arbitrary, capricious and unreasonable.

Id. at 593.

In an Iowa case, *Charles Gabus Ford v. Iowa State Highway Commission,* 224 N.W. 2d 639 (Iowa 1974), the state highway commission denied the plaintiffs access to a frontage road, after previously representing to them that access could be obtained. The court found that the commission had exercised its discretion in an arbitrary and capricious manner. In view of the fact that the commission was aware of the legitimate purpose for which access was requested, the court found a writ of mandamus compelling defendant to grant the access was properly ordered.

5. Courts in mandamus cases apply the usual rule, that the writ will not issue if another remedy is adequate, but the rule is not absolute. In *State ex rel. Brown v. City of Canton,* 414 N.E.2d 412 (Ohio 1980), the attorney general sought a writ of mandamus to compel the city to comply with a fluoridation order. The court issued the writ. It held that a mandatory injunction was not an adequate remedy because it was extraordinary. The statutory civil penalties that were available were not an adequate remedy because a similar remedy had not been successful in compelling earlier compliance with the order.

6. Courts customarily will not interfere with legislative bodies by issuing mandamus to influence the enactment of legislation. In an action brought against the Lincoln city council to compel it to repeal a zoning ordinance and reenact an earlier one, the Nebraska Supreme Court stated one reason for this judicial restraint as follows:

> Obviously the action of the members of the legislative body of the city is a matter of discretion and is not the subject of mandatory control by the courts.

Kurth v. Lincoln, 76 N.W.2d 924, 926 (Neb. 1956).

Compare Commonwealth ex rel. Carroll v. Tate, 274 A.2d 193 (Pa.), *cert. denied,* 402 U.S. 974 (1971). The judges of the Court of Common Pleas of Philadelphia County brought a mandamus action to compel the mayor and city council of Philadelphia to appropriate additional funds necessary for the administration of the court. The Pennsylvania Supreme Court affirmed the mandamus order, holding that the judicial branch of government has "the inherent power to determine and compel payment of those sums of money which are reasonable and necessary to carry out its mandated responsibilities, and its powers and duties to administer Justice, if it is to be in reality a co-equal, independent Branch of our government." *Id.* at 197.

Courts refrain from interfering with state as well as local legislative bodies. The act of legislating is inherently discretionary at both levels. Is there an additional reason why courts might be averse to intervening in the state legislative process? *See Jones v. Packel,* 342 A.2d 434 (Pa. Commw. 1975), and *Kevelin v. Jordan,* 396 P.2d 585 (Cal. 1964).

Compare the situation in which a state statute requires the enactment of a local ordinance. Is the act of legislating still discretionary? In *Taylor v. Abernathy,* 222 A.2d 863 (Pa. 1966), a state statute required municipalities to adopt pension plans for retired police and firemen. Mandamus was used to compel the local council to provide such a plan, leaving the amounts and recipients of the benefits to their discretion. In a similar vein, mandamus was used to compel the city council to enact an ordinance fixing maximum working hours for city employees when the city charter mandated implementation of such a policy. *Cleveland ex rel. Neelon v. Locher,* 266 N.E.2d 831 (Ohio 1971).

Once legislation is enacted, mandamus may be used to compel its enforcement. At this point the object of the writ is generally an executive, not a legislative body. *See, e.g., City of Miami Beach v. Sunset Islands 3 & 4 Property Owners Ass'n,* 216 So. 2d 509 (Fla. App. 1969) (building inspector required to enforce the zoning ordinance). Is there an argument for prosecutorial discretion?

What if the voters submit an initiative measure to the council with a request to submit it to popular vote? The council refuses, claiming the measure is unconstitutional, and the voters bring a writ of mandamus to compel submission to a vote. Can the court refuse to issue the writ if it also believes that the statute is unconstitutional? See *State ex rel. Althouse v. City of Madison,* 255 N.W.2d 449 (Wis. 1977), holding no, because otherwise the court would have to render an advisory opinion on the constitutionality of the initiative. As the court noted, the cases are divided on this point.

7. When a court is averse to issuing a coercive decree such as mandamus against public officials, it may decide to treat the action as one for declaratory relief. In *People ex rel. Hopf v. Barger,* 332 N.E.2d 649 (Ill. App. 1975), mandamus was sought to compel the city officials of Wheaton to comply with the Open Meetings Act after they held a closed meeting on a proposed annexation agreement. Although the Open Meetings Act itself provides for mandamus when the act is not complied with, Ill. Ann. Stat., ch. 102, § 43, the court found the remedy inappropriate; it could not affect a meeting which had already been held. "As a general rule, the writ will not issue to compel a useless act or to decide questions which no longer exist merely to establish precedent." *Id.* at 654. Further, mandamus will not issue to regulate the "general course of official conduct," or to enforce "the performance of official duties generally." To the extent that the writ sought to compel general compliance with the Act, it was inappropriate. The court went on to treat the case as proper for declaratory or injunctive relief, as the issues presented — among them, the constitutionality of the Act — were of substantial public interest.

A NOTE ON MANDAMUS AGAINST THE CHIEF EXECUTIVE

The law is settled that when a governor exercises discretionary or political powers he is not subject to mandamus or injunction, absent an abuse of discretion. *Brouillard v. Governor & Council,* 323 A.2d 901 (N.H. 1974); *State ex rel. Armstrong v. Davey,* 198 N.E. 180 (Ohio 1935) (governor's discretion in setting the date for a special election precluded mandamus). *Compare State ex rel. West Virginia Board of Education v. Miller,* 168 S.E.2d 820 (W. Va. 1969) (mandamus issued when finance commissioner, pursuant to gubernatorial approval, refused to approve payment of salary for new university position).

The courts disagree on whether mandamus will lie against a governor in the exercise of his ministerial or mandatory duties. Those favoring mandamus follow the view that the writ will issue when the duty is clearly ministerial, no discretion is involved, and there is no alternative remedy to protect individual rights. *Willits v. Askew,* 279 So. 2d 1 (Fla. 1973) (mandamus to issue state warrant in payment of tort judgment against state agency); *Blalock v. Johnston,* 185 S.E.

51 (S.C. 1936) (mandamus to appoint a tax collector on the recommendation of a majority of the General Assembly).

Mandamus may issue to compel the governor to exercise his discretion. See *Rock v. Thompson*, 426 N.E.2d 891 (Ill. 1981). State senators sought an original writ of mandamus in the supreme court in which they sought to compel the governor to convene the senate to elect a president. They claimed that the president elected by the senate had been improperly elected, the court agreed, and the writ issued.

Those courts holding that mandamus will not lie to compel action by a governor take the view that judicial inquiry into the nature of an act as political or ministerial is itself an interference with the separation of powers. *Kelly v. Curtis*, 287 A.2d 426 (Me. 1972); *Rice v. Draper*, 93 N.E. 821 (Mass. 1911); *State ex rel. Robb v. Stone*, 25 S.W. 376 (Mo. 1894), later qualified to read that mandamus will not lie against the governor when it would interfere with the exercise of executive duty and discretion; *People ex rel. Sutherland v. Governor*, 29 Mich. 320 (1874). See Annot., 105 A.L.R. 1124 (1936), and Fairlie, *The State Governor*, 10 MICH. L. REV. 458 (1912), for a review of early cases on both sides of the issue.

Following the rationale that it is not the nature of the office but rather the nature of the duty which determines the propriety of the order, see *Marbury v. Madison*, 5 U.S. (1 Cranch) 137 (1803), the principles invoked to review mandamus against a governor may apply as well to other offices of the executive branch. *State ex rel. Sayre v. Moore*, 59 N.W. 755 (Neb. 1894) (state auditor); *Burton v. Furman*, 20 S.E. 443 (N.C. 1894) (same).

Mandamus has also issued against a mayor in the exercise of his ministerial duties. *Elk City v. Johnson*, 537 P.2d 1215 (Okla. 1975) (to issue a proclamation on the result of a city election); *People ex rel. City of Salem v. McMackin*, 291 N.E.2d 807 (Ill. 1972) (to sign authorized bonds and lease agreement). *Compare State ex rel. Patterson v. Tucker*, 519 S.W.2d 22 (Mo. 1975) (denied); *Firemen's Pension & Relief Fund v. Sudduth*, 276 So. 2d 727 (La. 1973) (same).

The exercise of discretion does not necessarily foreclose judicial review of a governor's actions. An abuse of discretion or the protection of personal rights may result in judicial intervention. In *Sterling v. Constantin*, 287 U.S. 378 (1932), the Supreme Court held a governor subject to federal process to protect rights secured by the constitution, and affirmed an injunction restraining the governor from using military and executive orders to restrict plaintiff's oil production. *Accord Strutwear Knitting Co. v. Olson*, 13 F. Supp. 384 (D. Minn. 1936) (governor had the right and duty to call out the National Guard during a labor dispute, but no right to use the Guard to close plaintiff's plant); *State v. McPhail*, 180 So. 387 (Miss. 1938) (governor's actions in ordering out the National Guard were reviewable at the insistence of someone whose private property rights were affected; court upheld the governor's order calling out the Guard to aid in the enforcement of liquor and gambling laws). *See also State ex rel. Cason v. Bond*, 495 S.W.2d 385 (Mo. 1973) (mandamus granted to review governor's veto of appropriation bill).

2. PROHIBITION

FAMILY COURT v. DEPARTMENT OF LABOR & INDUSTRIAL RELATIONS

Court of Chancery of Delaware
320 A.2d 777 (1974)

[Note that this was not an action for a writ of prohibition. The action was for declaratory judgment and injunction before the Delaware Chancery Court; law and equity are still divided in that state. Nevertheless, the court had to decide, in denying the action, whether prohibition provided an adequate alternative legal remedy. In reaching this conclusion the court necessarily had to consider the elements of the prohibition writ. — Eds.]

Opinion and Order on Motion to Dismiss

QUILLEN, CHANCELLOR:

This is an action for declaratory judgment and injunctive relief brought by The Family Court of the State of Delaware (Family Court). The respondent is the Department of Labor (Department), an agency of the State of Delaware; and Council #81, American Federation of State, County, and Municipal Employees AFL-CIO (Council 81) is an intervening respondent. The issue presented is whether the Department has the jurisdiction under 19 Del. C., Ch. 13 to certify a bargaining representative for public employees with which a branch of the State Judiciary must collectively bargain.

The facts are not in dispute. On December 17, 1973, Council 81 filed a petition with the Governor's Council on Labor asking that a hearing be held for the purpose of certifying itself as the exclusive bargaining representative for certain classifications of employees of the Family Court. 29 Del. C. § 8514 (d). Anticipating the voluntary withholding of official action pending the resolution of this lawsuit, this Court denied temporary relief as requested by the petitioner. An administrative hearing was held at which the petition was accepted with the following exclusions: Judges, Judges' personal secretaries, court administrators, their personal secretaries, chief clerks of the court, all casual employees not employed more than 90 days, and all others not included specifically. Although the petitioner does not object in principle to collective bargaining, it has challenged the jurisdiction of the Department on two grounds. First, the petitioner contends that a branch of the State Judiciary is not a "public employer" as that term is defined at 19 Del. C. § 1301. Second, the petitioner contends that, if 19 Del. C., Ch. 13 is applicable to the Family Court, it is an unconstitutional invasion on the powers of the Chief Justice under Article IV, § 13 of the State Constitution, Del. C. Ann. At the suggestion of the Court the Secretary of the Department of Labor has held in abeyance the determination of the bargaining unit pending the outcome of this litigation.

Initially, I must consider whether the petitioner has an adequate remedy at law in the form of a writ of prohibition as the respondents contend. If such a remedy exists, this Court lacks the jurisdiction to determine the merits of this case. 10 Del. C. § 342. In effect, the respondents have moved to dismiss the complaint.

. . . .

Although the Superior Court may issue a writ of prohibition to an inferior court, the question arises whether such a writ may issue to an administrative body such as the Department of Labor. In *Knight v. Haley, supra* 6 W. W. Harr. at 374, 176 A. at 464, Chief Justice Layton stated that a writ of prohibition may issue to a "tribunal, possessing judicial powers." This phrase is certainly of broad scope and could reasonably be taken to include administrative bodies exercising judicial or quasi-judicial functions. But the question has not been expressly determined by any Delaware case brought to the Court's attention....

The general rule in other jurisdictions is that a writ of prohibition may issue to an inferior administrative body where that body is performing a judicial or quasi-judicial function.... Of particular application to our situation is *In re First Congressional District Election,* 295 Pa. 1, 144 A. 735 (1928) where it was held that:

> "The writ of prohibition lies from a superior court, not only to inferior judicial tribunals, but also to inferior ministerial tribunals, possessing incidentally judicial powers, and known as quasi-judicial tribunals."... This writ is very generally used in other jurisdictions ... it is an ancient common-law process employed by the Court of King's Bench in the exercise of its supervisory powers over subordinate tribunals ... and the Supreme Court of Pennsylvania is possessed of the common-law powers of the Court of King's Bench, except where such powers have been taken from us by constitutional or statutory provisions. 295 Pa. at 13, 144 A. at 739.

Thus, the Pennsylvania Court held that the power to issue a writ of prohibition to an administrative body was inherited from the common law courts of England. In *Rash v. Allen,* [1 Boyce 444, 455-56, 76 A. 370, 374-75 (1910) — Eds.] ... it was held that the Superior Court of Delaware was possessed of the same jurisdiction and powers as were the English courts of King's Bench, Common Pleas, and Exchequer.... I regard the holding of *In re First Congressional District Election* as stating a principle of law equally applicable in Delaware as it is in Pennsylvania. Thus, since the function exercised by the Department in the present case is of a quasi-judicial nature, a writ of prohibition may issue. See *Hathaway Bakeries, Inc. v. Labor Relations Commission,* 316 Mass. 136, 55 N.E.2d 254 (1944) where a writ of prohibition was issued to a Labor Relations Commission which had assumed jurisdiction to hear and decide a question of certification.

The question now becomes is this legal remedy an adequate one? If it is, its existence will deprive this court of jurisdiction.... It has been held that to be adequate the legal remedy must be available as a matter of right.... The legal remedy must be full, fair and complete.... And it must be as practical to the ends of justice and to its prompt administration as the remedy in equity....

It is with these principles in mind that the current situation must be judged. A writ of prohibition is an extraordinary legal remedy, the issuance of which rests within the sound discretion of the Court. Like the writs of mandamus, certiorari, and quo warranto, it is termed prerogative writ....

In evaluating the sufficiency of the legal remedy, prerogative writs are somewhat awkward because of their own equitable nature. But such writs, despite their prerogative nature, are capable of affording complete and adequate relief to a petitioner, and, if such is the case, resort may not be had to a court of equity....

Under certain circumstances the writ of prohibition is available as a matter of right:

> While the writ should be used with caution and only in cases of great necessity, and not in doubtful cases, yet narrow, technical rules should not govern its use; nor should the scope of the remedy be abridged, as it is better to prevent the exercise of unauthorized power than to be driven to the correction of error after it has been committed.... It is a discretionary writ in a sense that it will not issue where the facts do not appear to justify the resort to such remedy, as where there is another adequate remedy available, or where the

question of jurisdiction is doubtful; but where it is clear that the court whose action is sought to be prohibited has no jurisdiction of a cause originally, or in some collateral matter arising therein, a party who has objected seasonably to the jurisdiction and has no other remedy is entitled to the writ as a matter of right. *Knight v. Haley,* . . . [6 W. W. Harr. 366, 374-375, 176 A. at 461, 464-465 — Eds.].

The availability of an appeal is an important factor in determining this right. In the case at bar, the statute does not provide the petitioner with a remedy by way of an appeal from a decision of the Department. . . . Moreover, such a remedy evidently is not constitutionally required. . . . The right to have such a question reviewed by way of a petition for a writ of prohibition often depends upon the inadequacy of ordinary appellate review. . . . Furthermore, it has been held that, where no right of an appeal exists, prohibition will lie to bar the lower court. . . .

It therefore appears to this Court that petitioner has a right to a writ of prohibition, assuming of course that he can successfully establish the absence of jurisdiction in the Department. The right exists because the petitioner has asserted that the respondent is acting in excess of its jurisdictional power and because the petitioner has no remedy at law either by way of appeal or by any other legal remedy.

The next question is whether petitioner's legal remedy is full, fair, and complete, and as practical to the administration of justice as the remedy in equity. Petitioner's sole objection to the administrative proceedings is jurisdictional, and it is the thrust of his petition that the Department has attempted to assume power over matters not legally within its cognizance. It is for the cure of such objections that prohibition is peculiarly appropriate. . . .

The Court finds somewhat disturbing the prospect that the respondent, an administrative agency, may potentially decide questions of its jurisdiction and not be subject to judicial scrutiny. If the remedy at law in the present case were unsure or uncertain, or burdened with procedural difficulties, this Court would retain jurisdiction. However, it seems clear to this Court that if the respondent is correct as to his interpretation of . . . [the statute] he will be entitled to a writ of prohibition as a matter of right. . . . Moreover, the remedy of prohibition can include the complete relief necessary to resolve the jurisdictional question presented "according to principles that govern injunctions in equity." . . . In particular, the law court may issue an alternative or temporary writ of prohibition in order to preserve the existing status of the proceeding until it has determined whether a permanent writ should be granted. . . . At common law, a writ of prohibition could issue immediately but if the point was "too nice and doubtful to be decided merely upon a motion," then the party applying for the writ would be directed to file a declaration and the case would proceed to a further hearing. II Sharswood, Blackstone's Commentaries, pp. 111-112 (1859) (The Commentaries were originally published between 1765 and 1770. I Sharswood, *supra* A Memoir of Sir William Blackstone, p. xiv). The same result can be described by the immediate issuance of a rule to show cause staying the proceedings in the tribunal below until the return of the rule and a decision as to whether the rule should be made absolute or discharged. . . . It is also apparent that petitioner's appellate rights will afford it a full and complete review of the Superior Court's decision, and that this review will concern itself with substance and will not be frustrated by matters of mere form. . . .

. . . .

I conclude that the Court of Chancery has no jurisdiction in this case. The case is therefore dismissed subject to plaintiff's right to transfer the case to the Superior Court under 10 Del. C. § 1901. The status quo shall be maintained until the matter is presented to the Superior Court or 5:00 P.M. on May 6, 1974 whichever occurs first. It is so ordered.

Comments: 1. Prohibition is the converse of mandamus; the former prohibits action, the latter orders it. While mandamus most commonly issues to compel the performance of a ministerial act, prohibition is limited to excesses of a judicial nature and will not lie to prevent ministerial action. *See, e.g., Giacopelli v. Clymer,* 521 S.W.2d 196 (Mo. App. 1975) (writ will not issue to prohibit county clerk from administering oath for county legislators).

2. Prohibition lies to prohibit an illegal exercise of jurisdiction, not an abuse of discretion in the exercise of jurisdiction. With the principal case, compare *Milford School District v. Whitley,* 401 A.2d 951 (Del. Super. 1979). The district sought a writ of prohibition claiming that the state secretary of labor had improperly determined the appropriate bargaining unit for the district's custodial staff. The court held that the secretary had the authority to make the determination. The writ of prohibition could not be used to review the merits of the secretary's decision, even though the district claimed the secretary had abused his discretion.

3. The key to the propriety of the writ of prohibition is the exercise of a judicial or quasi-judicial function. In defining the scope of "judicial" or "quasi-judicial," a court effectively sets the limits of its power to intervene in a proceeding. The plaintiff in *State ex rel. Greenberg v. Florida State Board of Dentistry,* 297 So. 2d 628 (Fla. App. 1974), received a subpoena to appear before the Board of Dentistry for an unrevealed purpose under threat of contempt. She had never been party to a proceeding before the Board and had never applied for a license to practice dentistry. There was some oral indication that the subpoena was to compel her to give an account of a newspaper article she had written about the Board. Such a nonspecific investigation was clearly beyond the Board's statutory authority. The court issued a writ of prohibition to stop the proceedings.

> [A] citizen may not be held in contempt, and thereupon punished, upon failing or refusing to obey any subpoena, process or order of respondent or any other administrative agency until after he or she shall have first been afforded an opportunity for a hearing before a court of competent jurisdiction *and* until after that court shall have ordered obedience to such subpoena, process or order of such administrative agency, *and* such court order shall have been disobeyed....
>
> It is shocking, indeed frightening, to the delicate sensibilities of anyone schooled in the American concept of constitutional rights to ponder the possibilities or probabilities which could result from power vested in an appointed administrative board, not responsible to the electorate, authorizing it to require by subpoena, under threat of contempt, a citizen to appear before it for an unspecified purpose in an undesignated proceeding to give evidence or testimony in an unidentified cause for unspecified reasons. Such shock or fright is elevated to sheer horror when one learns, as is alleged in the affidavit filed in this cause in support of the suggestion, that the "proceeding" is in secret behind closed doors with the press and citizenry excluded, and conducted not by the board but one member thereof. Shades of star chamber!

Id. at 632, 636. Was the court concerned with the nature of the investigation, or the use of subpoena and contempt? Why didn't the court simply quash the subpoena? Could a writ of prohibition issue against a legislative body carrying on the same type of activities?

Compare *Greenberg* with *State ex rel. Turner v. Earle,* 295 So. 2d 609 (Fla. 1974). A circuit judge sought to prohibit the judicial qualifications commission from investigating him for alleged misconduct during a prior term. The Florida Supreme Court found that prohibition was inappropriate because the Commission was an investigative body. "Since the Commission lacks the power essential to judicial or quasi-judicial tribunals either to reach a final decision or to implement that decision, prohibition is an inappropriate remedy, sub judice." *Id.* at 611.

Compare McGinley v. Hynes, 412 N.E.2d 376 (N.Y. 1980). A hospital employee subpoenaed to testify in a hospital fraud investigation by the public prosecutor brought a writ of prohibition against the investigation. While holding that no "bright, clear line" could be drawn between the two functions, the court held that the prosecutor exercised executive functions when investigating crimes but quasi-judicial functions when prosecuting crimes. *Compare Hatley v. Lium,* 231 A.2d 647 (Vt. 1967) (*contra,* when prosecuting criminal charge).

In *Nicholson v. State Commission on Judicial Conduct,* 409 N.E.2d 818 (N.Y. 1980), a writ of prohibition was sought against an investigation of campaign misconduct. The plaintiff claimed that the investigation had a "chilling effect" on her first amendment rights. The court held that if "indeed the investigation impermissibly chills the exercise of these rights, the commission would be acting in excess of power and prohibition would be the appropriate remedy." *Id.* at 822.

Some courts have taken the view that the investigation of the conduct of public officials is of a judicial nature and thus subject to prohibition. A typical case is *State v. Lombardo,* 143 S.E.2d 535 (W. Va. 1965), finding a police civil service commission hearing on the suspension of a policeman to be judicial. The dissent argued that the proceeding was purely administrative, and could not be otherwise, as the commission was an administrative body. *See also City of Macon v. Anderson,* 117 S.E. 753 (Ga. 1923) (city council proceedings instituted for the removal of a member of the board of water commissioners constituted judicial action).

4. As usual, prohibition will not lie when an adequate remedy lies by way of an appeal. *See In re State Board of Professional Ethical Misconduct,* 444 N.Y.S.2d 736 (App. Div. 1981). Prohibition also lies, as usual, when the remedy by way of an appeal is inadequate. In *Silverbrook Cemetery Co. v. Department of Finance,* 444 A.2d 267 (Del. Super. 1982), the company challenged a property tax assessment in a prohibition action. The court held that it had "demonstrated that it will incur unreasonable delay and expense in being required to participate in an assessment hearing and, thereafter, appealing an assessment ruling on the theory that the action was a nullity." *Id.* at 269. If this is so, why is an appeal ever adequate?

5. Would you characterize the following actions as judicial or quasi-judicial in nature? The issuance or revocation of a license — compare *Citizens Council Against Crime v. Bjork,* 529 P.2d 1072 (Wash. 1975), *with Boswell v. Board of Medical Examiners,* 293 P.2d 424 (Nev. 1956); a medical inquest — *Mohrhusen v. McCann,* 215 N.W.2d 560 (Wis. 1974); action of election officials in placing the names of candidates on the ballot — *compare State ex rel. Gralike v. Walsh,* 483 S.W.2d 70 (Mo. 1972), *with O'Neill v. Kallsen,* 24 N.W.2d 715 (Minn. 1946); the levy of taxes — *Aronoff v. Franchise Tax Board,* 383 P.2d 409 (Cal. 1963).

3. QUO WARRANTO

As indicated in the following cases, the writ of quo warranto is commonly used to challenge the right to public office and the propriety of annexation or municipal incorporation. How are these functions similar?

STATE EX REL. CAIN v. KAY

Supreme Court of Ohio
38 Ohio St. 2d 15, 309 N.E.2d 860 (1974)

HERBERT, JUSTICE.

A single issue needs to be resolved in this case: Can an individual claimant bring an action in quo warranto to determine by what authority the respondent claims right and title to the office of chairman of the state central committee of a political party?

Quo warranto is a high prerogative writ of an extraordinary nature.... Its provenance was in early English common law, where its function was to safeguard the public interests by protecting the right of the crown against the unlawful usurpation of governmental prerogatives. A proceeding in the nature of quo warranto was an action by the crown inquiring by what authority a claimant of any office or franchise supported his claim. Eventually, the right to bring the action was extended to individual claimants for the purpose of questioning the authority of one claiming title to an office, the individual claimant's and the state's interests being, in such a case, considered commensurate.... However, the writ remained essentially a means to be employed principally by the crown to question unlawful intrusion into government interests.

In Ohio, the writ of quo warranto is treated as a civil action and is used chiefly to question the authority of claimants asserting right and title to public offices or corporate franchises.... Sections 2 and 3 of Article IV of the Constitution of Ohio confer original jurisdiction in quo warranto upon the Supreme Court and the Courts of Appeals.... The procedure to be employed in an action in quo warranto is contained in R.C. Chapter 2733. Although R.C. 2733.06 supports the right of an individual claimant to bring an action in quo warranto to question title to a public office, quo warranto has retained its common-law character as a means "... to be employed to shield the sovereignty of the state from invasion and to prevent the abuse of corporate powers." *State v. Dayton Traction Co.* (1901), 64 Ohio St. 272, 280, 60 N.E. 291, 292. The right to bring an action in quo warranto remains, as at common law, a right of the state, and, except where title to a public office is involved, the use of quo warranto remains in the state or its officers....

When a claimant institutes a quo warranto proceeding pursuant to R.C. 2733.06, he must show not only that he is entitled to the office and that the office is unlawfully held by the respondent in the action, but also that the office is a "public office" for purposes of quo warranto.... R.C. 2733.06 does not define "public office," and the definitions developed in this court and others are numerous, varied, and not wholly consistent. *E.g., State ex rel. Bricker v. Gessner* (1935), 129 Ohio St. 290, 195 N.E. 63 (membership on a county charter commission constitutes a public office); *State ex rel. Stanton v. Callow* (1924), 110 Ohio St. 367, 143 N.E. 717 (county building commissioners are not public officers); *State ex rel. Godfrey v. O'Brien* (1917), 95 Ohio St. 166, 115 N.E. 25 (members of county board of revision are public officers); *Palmer v. Zeigler* (1907), 76 Ohio St. 210, 81 N.E. 234 (county infirmary superintendent is not a public officer); *State ex rel. Atty. Genl. v. Jennings* (1898), 57 Ohio St. 415, 49 N.E. 404 (firemen, other than the chief of the department, are not public officers). These cases indicate that judicial development of a definition of "public office" which would be all-inclusive and would serve without fault in all situations has been an elusive goal. However, the general principles that should guide the determination were perhaps best articulated in *State ex rel. Atty. Genl. v. Jennings, supra* at page 424, 49 N.E. at page 405:

> It will be found ... that the most general distinction of a public office is, that it embraces the performance by the incumbent of a public function delegated to him as a part of the sovereignty of the state.... "An office, such as to properly come within the legitimate scope of an information in the nature of *quo warranto,* may be defined as a public position, to which a portion of the sovereignty of the county, either legislative, executive, or judicial, attaches for the time being, and which is exercised for the benefit of the public."

In *State ex rel. Hayes v. Jennings* (1962), 173 Ohio St. 370, 182 N.E.2d 546, this court held that members of a county central committee of a political party held public offices, by virtue of the authority vested in them by R.C. 305.02(B) to fill vacancies in certain offices held by members of the party. In *Hayes,* it was the delegation by statute of one of the sovereign functions of government, to be exercised for the public benefit, to the county central committeemen that outweighed the traditional reluctance of the court to interfere in the internal affairs of political parties. Political parties are basically voluntary associations of persons who act together principally for party and community purposes. Courts should defer to the appropriate party tribunals established by the members for the resolution of internal disputes of the party. For purposes of quo warranto, it is only where party officers assume duties affecting activities beyond the sphere of the internal affairs of the party and exercise official powers that are part of the sovereign functions of the state, properly exercisable for the public benefit, that the courts will intercede. See *State ex rel. Hayes v. Jennings, supra.*

Unlike members of a county central committee, the chairman of a state central committee is not authorized by statute to assume duties or to exercise official powers that involve the sovereign functions of government. His duties and powers extend only to the bounds of the political party and are exercisable only with respect to the internal affairs of the party. Hence, the office of chairman of the state central committee of a political party is not a public office, and is not amenable to quo warranto. In this respect, it should be noted that the case at bar does not present the question of whether members of the state central committee of a political party are public officers for purposes of quo warranto. See R.C. 3513.31; *Hayes, supra.* We are concerned here only with the position of chairman of the state central committee, a post filled through election by the committee members. Disputes concerning such position are properly resolvable within the internal structure of the party and before the appropriate party tribunals.

It was error for the Court of Appeals to entertain appellee's complaint in quo warranto. Accordingly, the judgment of the Court of Appeals is reversed and the cause is dismissed.

Judgment reversed.

PEOPLE EX REL. GORDON v. CITY OF NAPERVILLE

Appellate Court of Illinois
30 Ill. App. 3d 521, 332 N.E.2d 204 (1975)

SEIDENFELD, PRESIDING JUSTICE:

The relators appeal from an order denying them leave to file a complaint in *quo warranto* which sought to challenge the authority of the City of Naperville to annex territory under an annexation agreement. The Attorney General and the State's Attorney on request had refused to act and the relators proceeded in their own right.

The relators contend that the complaint alleged sufficient grounds for *quo warranto* relief based upon their allegations that the provisions of a city ordinance purporting to require a developer to dedicate land for park, recreation or school use as a condition to the approval of a subdivision is invalid. They argue that the invalidity of the ordinance also renders invalid the annexation and the agreement in which the developers consented to the land donations. They claim as an additional basis for *quo warranto* relief that the annexation agreement was unlawfully entered into by the city with the trustee, Chicago Title & Trust Company, for the reason that there was no disclosure of the names of the beneficiaries of the trust as required by Ill. Rev. Stat. 1973, ch. 102, par. 3.1.

The city responds that the application for the extraordinary writ of *quo warranto* was properly denied within the trial court's sound discretion because the relators did not have sufficient private interest to bring the action in their own right and because the complaint sought to test the manner in which annexation was effectuated rather than the city's authority to annex.

We first consider whether relators possess the necessary interest or standing to proceed in *quo warranto*. The petitioners allege that they are "citizens of the State of Illinois and the owners and taxpayers of real estate located in both the City of Naperville and in the County of DuPage...." They further allege:

16. The Trustee in the instant annexation is being required to make an illegal contribution which is recoverable by it to the detriment and expense of the Petitioners and all the other taxpayers of the City of Naperville, the Naperville Park District, and Community Unit School District Number 203, in spite of its promises and agreements disclaiming any such future intentions. Such an agreement places the Petitioners and all the other taxpayers of the City of Naperville, the Naperville Park District, and the Community Unit School District Number 203 in jeopardy for additional taxation because, where or not the Trustee ever attempts to secure a return of his donations made under the Annexation Agreement, the liability on the part of the City of Naperville, The Naperville Park District, and the Community Unit School District Number 203 to return said monies is established as a matter of law.

17. By virtue of the fact that the Petitioners and all other taxpayers of the City of Naperville, the Park District of Naperville, and Community Unit School District Number 203 are, have been, and will be subjected to an increased tax burden, obligation and liability, the Annexation Agreement and the Ordinance authorizing the Annexation are and should be declared by this Court to be null and void.

It is clear that *quo warranto* is the only proper remedy to attack proceedings by which territory has been annexed to a municipality.... Section 2 of the Quo Warranto Act provides, as material here, that the proceedings may be brought "by any citizen having an interest in the question on his own relation..." (Ill. Rev. Stat. 1971, ch. 112, par. 10). The fact that a relator's interest is that of a taxpayer does not necessarily exclude a finding that he has a sufficient interest to proceed in *quo warranto* if he can allege facts from which it may be concluded that the challenged action has a direct, substantial and adverse tax effect upon him.... The taxpayer may have a sufficient interest to sustain *quo warranto* if he shows a high probability or certainty that the challenged action will result in an increase in his taxes. *People ex rel. Hamer v. Board of Education* (1971), 132 Ill.App.2d 46, 49, 267 N.E.2d 1.

The Relators argue that they have a sufficient interest on the basis of their allegations that the trustee in the annexation here is being required to make an illegal contribution which the trustee can recover, creating a high probability or certainty that the petitioners' taxes will be increased in the future because of the obligation to pay for the land, valued at $344,950. The city argues, however, that the mere allegation that certain situations might at some future date increase the tax burden imposed upon the relators does not establish a "personal and substantial interest" in the contested annexation. It claims that the relators' argument is speculative and based on the unwarranted assumptions that the city, as a *bona fide* home rule unit under the 1970 Constitution, has no authority to enter into the agreement, and also upon the assumption that the owner will not honor the agreement when it is to his own advantage to do so in developing the site, and on the further assumption that the city if faced with the problem of paying for the donated land or returning it will opt to levy taxes to pay for the land, rather than return it to the donor.

Categorizing "public" and "private" rights which are often not mutually exclusive is difficult, but essential, in reviewing *quo warranto* proceedings. (See *People ex rel. McCarthy v. Firek,* 5 Ill.2d 317, 323, 125 N.E.2d 637.) In *Firek,* allegations by the relators, who were voters, taxpayers and owners of real estate within a sanitary district, that the district, which had been dissolved, had continued to levy taxes and to carry on its affairs in the same manner as before the dissolution proceedings were held to demonstrate the required interest. In *People v. Village of Buffalo Grove* (1967), 85 Ill.App.2d 382, 229 N.E.2d 401, the relator was the private utility company operating public sewerage and water works in the Village of Buffalo Grove and sought to challenge by *quo warranto* the municipality's creation and financing by revenue bonds of a public water works and sewerage system to service property annexed to the Village. Allegations that the relator had installed oversized pipes in the anticipation of serving any territory to be annexed to the village which would become valueless and that there was a possibility that the whole system would interfere with the relator's water and sewer system were held insufficient to state a private interest.[1] . . .

Finally, in *People ex rel. Hamer v. Board of Education,* 132 Ill.App.2d 46, 267 N.E.2d 1, *supra,* we found that a taxpayer who alleged that the school district's practice of issuing tax anticipation warrants when there were available funds resulted in additional tax liability had stated the necessary interest to apply for *quo warranto.*

Here, the relators do not allege that they are owners of or residents of the property included in the annexed territory. . . . They do not allege that annexation will definitely result in an increase in the taxes that they will pay. . . . Nor do they allege that the public officials had either threatened or become obligated to pay out public funds for an unlawful purpose. . . . They merely speculate that in the future the donation by the subdivider will be declared illegal and withdrawn and that then the city may decide to buy the donated property and pay for it out of public funds. They do not allege that the city is threatening to incur liabilities or is becoming liable for the expenditure of any public funds which could result in an increase in taxes. The petition for leave to file *quo warranto* is not a "full, positive and convincing" demonstration of the interest of the relator . . . nor does it show that there is a high probability or certainty that the challenged action will result in an increase in relator's taxes. . . .

We therefore conclude that the relators have not shown a sufficient interest to maintain the *quo warranto* and that for this reason alone the dismissal of their application by the trial court was proper.

We therefore will not discuss the denial of the application on its merits. The judgment of the trial court denying relators leave to file a complaint in *quo warranto* is affirmed.

Affirmed.

---

[1] Cf. Price v. City of Mattoon (1936), 364 Ill. 512, 4 N.E.2d 850, holding that a taxpayer had no standing to enjoin the carrying out of an ordinance that the purchase of a water supply system and filtration plant to be financed solely out of revenues of the utility system and not out of tax levies, even though it was alleged that in some future contingency the city might be required to make up a deficit in public funds even though it was not so indebted. Compare the case at bar with Bowes v. City of Chicago (1954), 3 Ill. 2d 175, 120 N.E.2d 15, holding that when public officials threaten to pay out public funds for the alleged unlawful purpose of a proposed filtration plant taxpayers do have a right to seek to enjoin action which would result in immediate liability and use of taxpayers' funds.

Comments: 1. Quo warranto is often used to test the right to public office and oust any usurpers. At early common law, the function of the writ was to protect the crown from the unlawful usurpation of government office or franchise. Quo warranto remains essentially a "public" action, usually brought by a representative of the state, such as the attorney general or the county attorney. The right to bring the action has generally been extended by statute to individuals claiming title to the office.

In *State ex rel. Anaya v. McBride,* 539 P.2d 1006 (N.M. 1975), the attorney general of New Mexico brought an action in quo warranto challenging the constitutionality of the appointment of a district judge. Prior to his appointment, the judge had served as a state legislator. During his legislative term, the emoluments for district judges were increased. The New Mexico constitution provides:

> No member of the legislature shall, during the term for which he was elected, be appointed to any civil office in the state, nor shall he within one year thereafter be appointed to any civil office created, or the emoluments of which were increased during such term.

N.M. Const. art. IV, § 28. The majority of the court found that the appointment violated this constitutional provision and entered a judgment of ouster against Judge McBride. The dissent argued that quo warranto was strictly a statutory proceeding in New Mexico, and that the complaint failed to meet the technical statutory requirements of alleging the name of the person rightfully entitled to the office. He claimed that the extreme nature of the remedy necessitated strict adherence to the statute. The majority responded to this argument as follows:

> One of the primary purposes of quo warranto is to ascertain whether one is constitutionally authorized to hold the office he claims, whether by election or appointment, and we must liberally interpret the quo warranto statutes to effectuate that purpose.

Id. at 1009. They noted that the state, through the attorney general, is an indispensable party plaintiff to a quo warranto action. "The reason for this requirement, of course, is that: '... a private person cannot have the writ to adjudicate his title to an office, and, indeed, the proceeding in the nature of a quo warranto goes only to removing the intruder, and no further.'" *Id.,* quoting from *De Vigil v. Stroup,* 110 P. 830, 832 (N.M. 1910). If the person claiming title to the office were a necessary party, actions such as this, where there was no identifiable claimant, could never be brought.

2. Quo warranto has more potential as a judicial remedy if it is extended to private litigants and if it can be used to challenge the legality of a governmental action. As the principal case indicates, courts will not allow private quo warranto suits unless they find that the private plaintiff has standing. This limitation was explained in *People ex rel. Turner v. Lewis,* 432 N.E.2d 665 (Ill. App. 1982).

Plaintiff was a democratic committeeman and central committee chairman. He brought a quo warranto action to challenge title to a local office. The court held an individual did not having standing to challenge a public wrong:

> The interests which a citizen may have are not peculiar to that person as an individual but are interests which are held in common to every citizen and resident of the community. If citizenship was sufficient ... [for standing] it would follow that every citizen and resident would have an equal right to the use of the writ.

Id. at 668.

Not all courts allow quo warranto to challenge the use of a governmental power. In *State ex rel. Wagner v. St. Louis County Port Authority,* 604 S.W.2d 592 (Mo. 1980), quo warranto was brought to challenge the state port authority act. The court held that quo warranto could be used to challenge the state's authority to delegate the power of eminent domain and whether the act served a public purpose. Quo warranto could not be used to challenge an exercise of the power of eminent domain. Does the principal case fall in either category?

3. In most jurisdictions, a "public office" must be involved for the writ to properly issue in cases challenging the right to office. This question was decisive in *State ex rel. Cain v. Kay, supra.* Quo warranto has been held to be the proper remedy to contest the right to the office of mayor, *State v. Jones,* 219 P.2d 706 (Kan. 1950); city councilman, *Commonwealth ex rel. Parks v. Wherry,* 152 A. 846 (Pa. 1930); sheriff, *Ferzacca v. Freeman,* 216 N.W. 469 (Mich. 1927); and state supreme court judge, *State v. Crawford,* 295 P.2d 174 (Or. 1956).

4. At common law quo warranto was the only means to contest the results of an election. Now there are statutory and constitutional provisions for election contests. The question often arises whether these provisions preclude or supplement the remedy of quo warranto. *Compare Walker v. Junior,* 24 So. 2d 431 (Ala. 1945), with *State ex rel. Abercrombie v. District Court,* 24 P.2d 265 (N.M. 1933). The two proceedings differ in purpose. An election contest allows the unsuccessful candidate to lay claim to the office while quo warranto is brought on behalf of the public to determine whether the office is properly held. For further distinctions, see *Tiegs v. Patterson,* 318 P.2d 588 (Idaho 1957).

5. Most state constitutions contain provisions that each house of the state legislature shall judge the qualifications and election of its own members. In the face of such a constitutional mandate, would you expect quo warranto to be an available remedy? The general view is that such constitutional provisions vest the legislature with the sole power to judge the qualifications of its members, leaving the judiciary with no jurisdiction to decide such issues. In *State v. Hickey,* 475 S.W.2d 617 (Mo. 1972), the attorney general of Missouri brought an action in quo warranto to oust a state representative who had moved his residence from the district where he was elected. The constitution, art. III, § 18, provided that "[e]ach house shall be the judge of the qualifications, election, and returns of its own members; may determine the rules of its own proceedings . . . and, with the concurrence of two-thirds of all members elect, may expel a member . . . ." The court held that it had no jurisdiction.

> We conclude that the universally accepted interpretation of provisions such as Article III, § 18, has been that state legislative bodies are given the sole right to determine the qualifications of their members, and that this is a continuing power, giving not only the right to decide whether a member shall be seated originally, but also whether the member becomes disqualified during his period of office and as a result vacates his office.
>
> By adopting Article III, § 18, the people have placed in the legislative body the power of determining the qualifications of members of the general assembly. . . . Only the people may change that provision. We cannot, and must not, undertake to amend such constitutional provision by judicial interpretation. To do so would violate Article II, § 1 of the Missouri Constitution, relating to separation of powers.

Id. at 621, 622. *Accord Lund ex rel. Wilbur v. Pratt,* 308 A.2d 554 (Me. 1973) (defendant's title as state representative was immune from judicial attack).

Would you expect the same result at the local level? In *State ex rel. Repay v. Fodeman,* 300 A.2d 729 (Conn. Sup. 1972), quo warranto was found to be the proper remedy to oust an alderman who moved away from his ward, thereby becoming disqualified to hold office. What if the city charter provided that the city council was to be the sole judge of the qualifications of its members? Could quo warranto be used to oust a councilman wrongfully holding office? This point was argued by the defendant alderman in *Fodeman* to no avail.

The federal Constitution, article I, § 5, similarly provides that each house shall be the judge of the qualifications, elections and returns of its own members. For a case decided under this provision, see *Laxalt v. Cannon,* 80 Nev. 588, 397 P.2d 466 (1964). *See also Powell v. McCormack,* 395 U.S. 486 (1969).

Compare Bond v. Floyd, 385 U.S. 116 (1966). A black Georgia legislator was refused a seat in the state House of Representatives because of statement he had made opposing the Vietnam war. While the exclusion was allegedly based on a determination that the legislator could not properly take the oath to support the constitution, the Supreme Court took jurisdiction to determine whether the exclusion violated the first amendment and held affirmatively on this ground.

6. Particularly in annexation cases, a dispute often arises over who may properly bring the action. Apart from a representative of the state, standing to sue in quo warranto is statutory and may vary from state to state. In Illinois, private individuals may challenge an annexation in their own right if they have sufficient interest in the question. As shown in *People ex rel Gordon v. City of Naperville, supra,* private litigants must show that they are owners or residents of property in the annexed territory, or that the annexation would result in increased taxes. *See People ex rel. McCarthy v. Firek,* 125 N.E.2d 637 (Ill. 1955). In *People ex rel. Brooks v. Lisle,* 321 N.E.2d 65 (Ill. App. 1974), the court found that a city, as representative of its people, was not a proper party plaintiff to assert a "public" right under the Quo Warranto Act in challenging the annexation of territory outside its municipal boundaries; nor did the city qualify as a citizen with a private interest on its own relation. *See* Ill. Ann. Stat. ch. 112, § 10. *Compare People ex rel. Des Plaines v. Village of Mt. Prospect,* 331 N.E.2d 373 (Ill. App. 1975), in which the city of Des Plaines brought an action in quo warranto challenging a Mt. Prospect annexation of property already claimed to have been annexed by Des Plaines. While Des Plaines' annexation which Mt. Prospect had, in turn, challenged was invalidated on the merits, no objection was made to its standing to maintain the action. In the opinion the court also called attention to a distinction between the common law writ and the statutory version of quo warranto: at common law only the defendant's rights, not the relator's title, could be adjudicated; the statutory modifications permitted the court to determine the rights of all parties to the proceeding. In this case it meant that the court could adjudicate the validity of both annexations.

Under the Kansas quo warranto statute, a private individual cannot maintain an action questioning the validity of proceedings extending the corporate limits of a city. Such actions may be brought only by the state's representatives. *Babcock v. Kansas City,* 419 P.2d 882 (Kan. 1966).

7. Quo warranto is also used to test the validity of local government organization and incorporation. *See, e.g., Gifford v. State ex rel. Lilly,* 525 S.W.2d 250 (Tex. Civ. App. 1975); *City of Orlando v. Orange County,* 309 So. 2d 16 (Fla. App. 1975), aff'd, 327 So. 2d 7 (1976). The principles are fundamentally the same whether the action is brought to challenge annexation or incorporation. *See generally* Mandelker, *Municipal Incorporation on the Urban Fringe: Procedures for Determination and Review,* 18 LA. L. REV. 628 (1958).

8. Unless otherwise provided by statute, quo warranto is generally treated as an exclusive remedy when it is adequate to resolve the issues at hand. When a judge challenged the appointment of his successor to the bench by injunctive relief, the court dismissed his complaint, stating that quo warranto was the exclusive means of determining if an individual was unlawfully holding office. *McCamant v. City & County of Denver,* 501 P.2d 142 (Colo. App. 1972). *Accord Saenz v. Lackey,* 522 S.W.2d 237, 240 (Tex. 1975) (injunction not a proper remedy once an individual is in office).

Similarly, quo warranto is the proper remedy to attack a completed annexation once the municipality exercises control over the territory. An action for declaratory relief in such circumstances has been held improper. *Homeowners v. Countryside Sanitary District,* 246 N.E.2d 494 (Ill. 1969). *Compare San Ysidro Irrigation District v. Superior Court,* 365 P.2d 753 (Cal. 1961). The court held that the city could maintain an action for declaratory relief to seek an adjudication that an irrigation district was dissolved when annexed to the city, notwithstanding the availability of quo warranto.

Prior to completion of an annexation, mandamus has been found to be a proper mode of attack, *American Distilling Co. v. Sausalito,* 213 P.2d 704 (Cal. 1950). *Compare Julian v. City of Liberty,* 427 S.W.2d 300 (Mo. 1968), in which the court found an injunction action appropriate to attack an annexation attempted under an invalid ordinance. The court reasoned as follows:

> This action constitutes no challenge to the *power* of the city to annex unincorporated areas, by compliance with provisions of the applicable law. The challenge is to the *manner* of the attempted *exercise* of its right to annexation, and its attempt to exercise municipal authority in territory which has not been annexed by lawful procedure.

Id. at 302 (emphasis in opinion). Is this a meaningful distinction?

9. A city may acquire de facto jurisdiction over an area by providing it with municipal services over a long period of time. In such cases, a quo warranto action challenging the annexation of the area may be dismissed as against the public interest. *People ex rel. Knaus v. Village of Hinsdale,* 250 N.E.2d 309 (Ill. App. 1969). The village had provided municipal services including zoning, storm services, police and fire protection, and had levied real estate taxes and issued building permits to the area for over forty years. The court reversed a judgment ousting the village: "[W]e can perceive no benefit that would result from cutting off from the city the territory in question after the many years of peaceful union without objection." *Id.* at 313.

Compare the situation in which ouster is sought against a public office holder. The Supreme Court of Missouri held that laches would not be permitted to bar a proceeding in quo warranto brought by the state to oust an official for misconduct. "The nature of the proceeding and the inherent public interest preclude the application of that doctrine." *State v. Orton,* 465 S.W.2d 618, 621 (Mo.), *cert. denied,* 404 U.S. 852 (1971).

4. INJUNCTION

BECHAK v. CORAK

Supreme Court of Pennsylvania
414 Pa. 522, 201 A.2d 213 (1964)

ROBERTS, JUSTICE.

Andrew J. Bechak and John F. Wright, Jr., taxpayers and residents of Beaver County, for themselves and others similarly situated, filed a complaint in equity against James E. Ross, Samuel M. McCune and Eli G. Corak, County Commissioners of Beaver County, James F. Tress, County Controller, and Russel Milnes, County Treasurer. The complaint alleges that the County Commissioners, since the beginning of their terms of office to the present [1963], have been reimbursed, from public funds, $150 per month for individual travel expenses, alleged to have been incurred within the county, without submitting itemized accountings or vouchers supporting the expenditures, and that the Commissioners have received public moneys as reimbursement for travel expenses outside Beaver County, also without accounting for same.

The complaint alleges further that James F. Tress, Controller, has received $125 monthly from public funds for travel within the county without filing an accounting for these expenses or producing valid receipts.

None of these payments, it is alleged, may be made to the County Commissioners or the Controller without a proper statement detailing the expenses and justifying payment.

As to the County Treasurer, the complaint alleges that although he filed a monthly expense voucher for mileage traveled within Beaver County and received reimbursement from public funds, there exists no authority in law for such expenditure or reimbursement to a County Treasurer.

The period covered by the complaint is January, 1960, to the then current year, 1963.

The relief sought is an injunction restraining the Commissioners and Controller from authorizing and approving lump sum expenses for themselves without an accounting of travel expenses incurred, supported by receipts. The complaint also seeks the appointment of an auditor to determine the exact amounts paid under the questioned procedure. Finally, the complaint asks that the court direct the Commissioners and Controller to repay all funds received by them as monthly lump sum payments and that they, together with the Treasurer, be surcharged for the payments they authorized to be made to the Treasurer.

Defendant officials filed preliminary objections to the complaint, asserting the lack of equitable jurisdiction and the availability of an adequate statutory remedy by way of an appeal from the Annual Report of the Controller.

Before argument was heard on the preliminary objections, the taxpayers filed a petition for a preliminary injunction to restrain the officials from continuing the practices alleged in the complaint. The petition further requested an order directing that the salaries of defendants and any other money due them during the balance of their terms of office be placed in escrow to set off the possible surcharges due the county because of the described practices.

The petition for preliminary injunction came on for hearing on September 21, 1963, before the Honorable Burton R. Laub of the Sixth Judicial District, specially presiding. At that time, the court also heard argument on the preliminary objections.

At the hearing, defendants questioned plaintiffs' standing as property owners and taxpayers. By their preliminary objections, defendants admitted all well pleaded allegations of fact in the complaint, including the averments that plaintiffs are duly qualified residents and taxpayers. . . .

The court below concluded that the preliminary objections were well taken as to the period prior to January 1, 1963, and dismissed the action as to these prior years. The court dismissed the objections as to the then current year and permitted defendants to file an answer. The court refused the request that the salaries and other sums due the officials be placed in escrow, but ordered the issuance of a preliminary injunction upon plaintiffs' filing a bond, as provided in Pa.R.C.P. 1531(b) (1), 12 P.S. Appendix, in the sum of $3,000.

Defendants filed two appeals: one from the grant of the preliminary injunction and one from the dismissal of the preliminary objections and the sustaining of plaintiffs' right to proceed in equity.

Plaintiffs did not file the required bond, and the preliminary injunction did not issue. Appellees moved to quash the appeal from the grant of the preliminary injunction, which motion was granted by this Court. The only issue now before our Court is whether equity has jurisdiction to enjoin county officials from committing and continuing improper or illegal conduct.

The County Code provides that county commissioners shall be allowed their expenses, necessarily incurred and actually paid in the discharge of their official duties or in the performance of any service, office, or duty imposed upon county commissioners. Act of Aug. 9, 1955, P.L. 323, § 507, 16 P.S. § 507. Similarly, the county controller is allowed expenses by Section 607 of the Code, 16 P.S. § 607.

We agree with the court below that equity has jurisdiction in this matter and that the complaint states a cause of action. It is clear that the practices alleged in the complaint are contrary to law. . . .

[The court then held that the county commissioners and controller could not be reimbursed for expenses without submission of itemized accountings, and that there was no authority at all to reimburse the county treasurer for expenses. — Eds.]

It then remains to be determined whether, in this instance, equitable jurisdiction *should* be exercised to afford the relief sought. We are of the opinion that court of equity clearly should exercise its power to act in such circumstances as here have been described.

Appellants rely upon the Act of March 21, 1806, P.L. 558, § 13, 46 P.S. § 156, which provides:

In all cases where a remedy is provided, or duty enjoined, or anything directed to be done by any act or acts of assembly of this commonwealth, the directions of the said acts shall be strictly pursued, and no penalty shall be inflicted, or anything done agreeably to the provisions of the common law, in such cases, further than shall be necessary for carrying such act or acts into effect.

In view of this act, appellants contend that the remedy by way of appeal from the Annual Report of the Controller for the year 1963 is a complete and adequate statutory remedy which precludes the exercise of equitable jurisdiction over the subject matter. We conclude, as did the court below, that the statutory remedy is not adequate to prevent present or prospective violations of the law.

The hearing judge quite properly determined:

> Defendants would have us extend the Act of 1806 to apply to current matters, requiring plaintiffs to abide the filing of the next controller's report before finding a remedy. With this we cannot agree. That act does not prohibit the interference of equity to enjoin improper and illegal conduct while it is actually in progress, nor does it prevent equity from following through with appropriate incidental relief where necessary. In *Adler v. Philadelphia,* 397 Pa. 660, 664, 156 A.2d 852, the Supreme Court reiterated what is said before in *Downing v. [Erie City] School District,* 360 Pa. 29, 33, 61 A.2d 133, that: "Equity will intervene to restrain acts of municipal authorities which are contrary to positive law or amount to bad faith or constitute a violation of public duty." Again, in *Zeigenfuse v. Boltz,* 401 Pa. 365, 372, 164 A.2d 663, it said: "The general equity jurisdiction of the courts of common pleas of the Commonwealth by virtue of Section 13, of the Act of June 16, 1836, P.L. 784, 17 P.S. § 282, embraces the power to prevent or restrain the commission or continuance of acts contrary to law and prejudicial to the interests of the community, or the rights of individuals."
>
> It would be startlingly egregious to learn that once it has been shown that a public officer is being paid funds to which he is not entitled, or that public funds are being disbursed in lump sums without itemization or voucher, equity cannot step in to restrain such practices, at least until final hearing. While lump sum payments of expenses without itemization are improper merely and not necessarily illegal or fraudulent, the same cannot be said of payments made without any authority of law. Of course, in the final disposition of this litigation the commissioners and controller will be permitted, so far as they are able, from books or memoranda kept by them, to itemize and justify the expenses which were paid to them. But if such itemization cannot be supplied, the payments cannot be sustained and there must be a surcharge. All of this was indicated in Susquehanna Auditor's Report, supra [118 Pa. Super.] p. 54, [180 A. 148]. Therefore, since the possibility exists of money due the county both from past and future acts in 1963, it is imperative that lump sum payments must be stopped. It is no answer that the county would be entitled to a money judgment if a successful appeal was later maintained as to 1963; recoupment of improper items permitted to be paid would, at least, be problematical. Nor is it any answer that the commissioners, by recent resolution, have discontinued the practices which heretofore obtained. That resolution, like its predecessors, can be altered at any meeting.

Our review of the entire record satisfies us that the chancellor has justly and wisely adjudicated the issues and questions presented.

Decree affirmed. Costs on appellants.

BRENT v. CITY OF DETROIT

Court of Appeals of Michigan
27 Mich. App. 628, 183 N.W.2d 908 (1970)

J. H. GILLIS, PRESIDING JUDGE.

Plaintiffs appeal from a summary judgment issued by the lower court in favor of defendant. Plaintiffs, property owners, complaint prayed for injunctive relief against defendant City to prevent it from building an outdoor swimming pool in Palmer Park near plaintiffs' property. A temporary restraining order was issued. At the "show cause" hearing the court dissolved the restraining order and entered summary judgment for defendant. Plaintiffs' complaint was dismissed because it failed to state a cause of action upon which relief could be granted. GCR 1963, 117.2 (1).

Plaintiffs allege that construction of the proposed swimming pool on the site selected by defendant will constitute a public nuisance. Plaintiffs argue that there are more suitable sites for the swimming pool elsewhere in the park area.

Defendant testified that a public meeting was held on the pool situs before the City's Common Council, and plaintiffs' objections were heard. As a result of that meeting, the original situs was moved to a new location, over 400 feet from plaintiffs' nearest property.

It has been a long-standing rule in Michigan that the judiciary will not interfere in the discretionary acts of municipal governments, absent fraud or a clear abuse of discretion. The Michigan Supreme Court articulated this judicial attitude when they said:

> So long as the power to govern the city and control its affairs is vested by the people in local municipal officers in pursuance of law, neither this court nor any other may assume to dictate the local governmental policy of the municipality. The power and authority is vested in the commission to govern as its discretion dictates so long as its action is not contrary to law or opposed to sound public policy. So long as the city commission acts within the limits prescribed by law, the court may not interfere with its discretion. The judiciary is not charged with supervisory control over the exercise of governmental functions by the city commission. . . . It is not the business of courts to act as city regulators and, unless the authority of the representatives of the citizens . . . has been illegally exercised, their action cannot be interfered with merely because it may not seem to other persons to have been as wise as it ought to have been. *Veldman v. City of Grand Rapids* (1936), 275 Mich. 100, 111, 112, 265 N.W. 790, 794. . . .

Courts are reluctant to enjoin anticipatory nuisances absent a showing of actual nuisance or the strong probability of such result. . . . *Falkner v. Brookfield* (1962), 368 Mich. 17, 117 N.W.2d 125. This has been true with proposed uses of children's playgrounds and park areas. See Annotation, 32 A.L.R.3d 1127. It is especially true in cases where anticipatory nuisance claims have been leveled against proposed municipal swimming pool sites. . . .

Michigan law is replete with applications of the equity maxim that:

> Equity, as a rule, will not interfere in advance of the creation of a nuisance where the injury is doubtful or contingent, and anticipated merely from the use to which the property is to be put. *Plassey v. S. Lowenstein & Son* (1951), 330 Mich. 525, 529, 48 N.W.2d 126, 128.

See also: *Warren Township School District v. City of Detroit* (1944), 308 Mich. 460, 14 N.W.2d 134 (proposed use of nearby property as airport); *Village of St. Clair Shores v. Village of Grosse Pointe Woods* (1947), 319 Mich. 372, 29 N.W.2d

860 (apprehension that use of beach as municipal park will pollute the waters of plaintiff village); *Foster v. County of Genesee* (1951), 329 Mich. 665, 46 N.W.2d 426 (proposed use of nearby property as animal shelter); *Brown v. Shelby Township* (1960), 360 Mich. 299, 103 N.W.2d 612 (proposed use of nearby property as automobile race track); *Falkner v. Brookfield, supra* (proposed use of nearby property as an automobile junk yard); *Oak Haven Trailer Court, Inc. v. Western Wayne County Conservation Association* (1966), 3 Mich. App. 83, 141 N.W.2d 645 (proposed use of nearby property by a gun club), and cases cited therein.

This is not to say that such swimming pool is forever insulated from becoming a nuisance. However, plaintiffs have pleaded nothing at this time which indicates that increased noise, traffic and parking problems will necessarily result with its construction.

> [T]o secure an injunction against a neighbor's prospective use of his property, *more must be shown than the mere possibility or even probability of harm resulting from that use. Commerce Oil Refining Corp. v. Miner* (CA 1, 1960), 281 F.2d 465, 474. (Emphasis supplied.)

Therefore, the order entered in the circuit court granting summary judgment to defendant is affirmed. Costs to defendant.

Comments: 1. In *Hames v. Polson,* 215 P.2d 950, 955 (Mont. 1950), the Montana court said: "That public bodies and public officers may be restrained by injunction from proceeding in violation of law, to the prejudice of the public, or to the injury of individual rights, cannot be questioned." In that case the city park board was enjoined from diverting publicly owned property to private uses. Only illegal or unauthorized acts that are not discretionary, however, may be enjoined. In *Marston v. Superior Court,* 507 P.2d 971, 972 (Ariz. 1973), the court said: "[A] public officer may not be enjoined from performing his official acts except in instances in which he is acting illegally or in excess of the powers conferred upon him by law." An injunction was issued which would have the effect of preventing the county recorder from administering an unauthorized test which unreasonably delayed the appointment of deputy registrars.

Although discretionary action may not be enjoined, an abuse of discretion is an illegal act subject to injunction. *See City of Huntsville v. Smartt,* 409 So. 2d 1353 (Ala. 1982). Is review for abuse of discretion really a form of review "on the merits"?

2. The *Bechak* case demonstrates a common example of improper official behavior which is challenged by injunction — the misuse of public funds. It is commonly held that injunctions are proper to prevent the illegal expenditure of public monies. In *Moshier v. City of Romulus,* 220 N.W.2d 37 (Mich. App. 1974), local taxpayers successfully enjoined the city from spending public funds for the maintenance of a private road. In an Arkansas case, 23 members of the General Assembly sought to enjoin payment of a state university professor's salary because he was a member of "a communistic organization," the Progressive Labor Party. Under state statute, anyone who was a member of a communistic organization was ineligible for state employment. The court found that the complaint stated a cause of action under the "illegal exaction" section of the state constitution (art. 16, § 13), stating, "It has long been held a court of equity has jurisdiction to enjoin payment of public funds in violation of law." *Cooper v. Henslee,* 522 S.W.2d 391, 394 (Ark. 1975). It nevertheless dissolved the lower court injunction and dismissed the complaint because the statute proscribing state employment on the basis of communist affiliation violated the first amendment of the federal Constitution.

Note that this use of the injunction can provide a useful way to challenge a municipality's authority. *See Anderson v. City of Boston,* 380 N.E.2d 628 (Mass. 1980). Taxpayers successfully enjoined a municipality from expending funds to influence the result of a state referendum, holding it did not have this authority. For additional discussion of taxpayer suits brought to enjoin the expenditure of public funds, see the next section.

An illegal use of public funds is not the only kind of illegality that can be enjoined. *See O'Fallon Development Co. v. City of O'Fallon,* 389 N.E.2d 679 (Ill. App. 1979). A shopping center developer brought an action challenging the display of its emblem on a water tower. The court held that the tower had been conveyed by easement to the city, so that the display was not an illegal use of private property. It then granted the injunction because it held that the display of the emblem was an improper use of public property for a private purpose.

3. As the *Brent* case indicates, equity principles will often lead a court to deny an injunction for anticipatory conduct by governmental units. Thus in *Nueces County Drainage & Conservation District No. 2 v. Bevly,* 519 S.W.2d 938 (Tex. Civ. App. 1975), plaintiff sued to enjoin the enlargement of an existing drainage ditch by the district, claiming that the enlargement would flood his land and thus would constitute an illegal and enjoinable taking under the Texas constitution. The court refused the injunction, noting that injury to property of this kind was compensable as a constitutional damaging rather than a taking, and that plaintiff had an adequate remedy at law for any resulting damage. The court also commented:

> Injunctions may be denied even in cases where irreparable injury is shown and where no adequate remedy at law exists, if it is reasonably clear that the injury or damage to the party who seeks the relief will be much less if the writ is refused than that which would result to the party restrained if the relief be granted.

Id. at 947. It then noted that the ditch extension was necessary to prevent serious flooding in the city of Robstown, which had resulted in damage to the public streets requiring substantial repairs. An injunction would result "in public inconvenience to a large number of persons not parties to the suit which is disproportionate to the damage ... suffered by [plaintiff]." *Id.* at 949. Is it clear in this and in the *Brent* case that plaintiffs necessarily will be awarded damages or compensation for any injury resulting from the public improvement? Consult the materials on inverse condemnation, *supra.*

For a case denying injunctive relief for anticipatory conduct outside the injury to property situation, see *Borom v. City of St. Paul,* 184 N.W.2d 595 (Minn. 1971). Plaintiffs as taxpayers sought an injunction restraining the city from entering into contracts with any contractors who discriminated on the basis of race, creed, or color in the hiring or recruitment of common or skilled labor. No specific instances of discrimination were alleged. Their suit was dismissed, the court noting in part that adequate legal remedies were available to anyone establishing discrimination by a contractor under the state nondiscrimination law and a comparable city ordinance. What advantages might there be to possible victims of discrimination from a blanket injunction order in a situation such as this? There have been complaints that state and local nondiscrimination agencies have been singularly ineffective in enforcing these statutes. Assuming lack of effective enforcement could be shown, what relief might be open to a litigant by way of injunction? Mandamus?

4. In the *Bechak* case, the lower court's issuance of a preliminary injunction was conditioned on plaintiff's filing a bond with the court for $3,000. The Pennsylvania rule applied by the court follows:

> (b) Except when the plaintiff is the Commonwealth of Pennsylvania, a political subdivision or a department, board, commission, instrumentality or officer of the Commonwealth or of a political subdivision, a preliminary or special injunction shall be granted only if
>
> (1) the plaintiff files a bond in an amount fixed and with security approved by the court, naming the Commonwealth as obligee, conditioned that if the injunction is dissolved because improperly granted or for failure to hold a hearing, the plaintiff shall pay to any person injured all damages sustained by reason of granting the injunction and all legally taxable costs and fees, or
>
> (2) the plaintiff deposits with the prothonotary legal tender of the United States in an amount fixed by the court to be held by the prothonotary upon the same condition as provided for the injunction bond.

Pa.R.Civ. P. 1531. Note that all governmental units are exempt from the requirement when they are parties plaintiff.

In federal courts, Rule 65(c) of the Federal Rules of Civil Procedure provides in part:

> (c) Security. No restraining order or preliminary injunction shall issue except upon the giving of security by the applicant, in such sum as the court deems proper, for the payment of such costs and damages as may be incurred or suffered by any party who is found to have been wrongfully enjoined or restrained. No such security shall be required of the United States or of an officer or agency thereof.

Fed. R. Civ. P. 65(c).

Although these bond requirements may serve to deter frivolous lawsuits, they can also be a substantial deterrent to bringing legitimate injunctive action against government officials and units. As indicated by the rules cited, the amount of the bond is often within the discretion of the trial judge.

5. As a general rule, a court cannot enjoin the enactment of legislation when to do so would interfere with legislative discretion and decisions. Four exceptions to this rule were set out in *Town of Pleasant Prairie v. City of Kenosha,* 226 N.W.2d 210 (Wis. 1975): when the governing body has no power to act legislatively on the subject; when the act is not legislative, but ministerial; when it goes beyond the realm of authorized powers to invade individual property; and when public funds are misused. In this case the town had sought an injunction to prevent the city from enacting a zoning ordinance affecting a particular piece of property on the ground that the area in which the property was located had improperly been annexed to the city. The court found none of the exceptions applicable and therefore denied the injunction as an attempt to restrain the legislative discretion of a municipal body. Explaining why it had declined to enjoin the borough from final passage of an ordinance (which it subsequently declared invalid), a New Jersey court stated: "A court cannot prohibit a legislative branch from meeting and passing an ordinance." *Ringwood Solid Waste Management Authority v. Borough of Ringwood,* 328 A.2d 258, 260 (N.J. Super. 1974). *Accord Real Estate Development Co. v. City of Florence,* 327 F. Supp. 513 (E.D. Ky. 1971).

Once legislation is passed, injunction becomes the proper remedy to enjoin enforcement if the legislation or its implementation is alleged to be invalid. In *Kane v. Fortson,* 369 F. Supp. 1342 (N.D. Ga. 1973), the court enjoined enforcement of Georgia's voter registration statutes insofar as they operated to deny a married woman domiciled in Georgia the right to register and vote in Georgia. The statutes in question raised an irrebuttable presumption that a married woman's domicile and residence was that of her husband. In *Bright v. Baesler,* 336 F. Supp. 527 (E.D. Ky. 1971), state and county officials were enjoined from seeking additional proof of domicile from university students seeking to register to vote which they did not require of nonstudents. In *Boyd v. Board of Trustees,* 303 N.E.2d 444 (Ill. App. 1973), customers of a water district successfully sought an injunction restraining the district from terminating their water service because they refused to pay their bills in cash. The court found the district's regulation requiring payment of all bills in cash for one year after the customer's personal check was dishonored for insufficient funds to be unreasonable.

6. As in all injunction actions, general principles governing equitable relief must also be met: that there is no adequate remedy at law and that irreparable injury will result if the relief is denied. Thus in *Cahill v. Board of Education,* 444 A.2d 907 (Conn. 1982), a teacher who claimed she was illegally discharged was denied an injunction because she had an adequate remedy at law for damages.

The separation of powers doctrine restricts the relief courts can grant in injunction actions against municipalities. In *Lap v. Thibault,* 348 So. 2d 622 (Fla. App. 1977), the court held that:

> The doctrine of separation of powers must restrict the judicial branch of government, when faced, as here, with the question of issuing a mandatory injunction to require a municipality to file legal action to recover city property, to a determination of whether the municipality's action involves illegality of a palpable abuse of authority amounting to illegality or is fraudulent or clearly oppressive.

In view of this limitation, how effective will injunctive relief be? This problem is troublesome in zoning litigation. A landowner who secures a judicial decree invalidating a zoning restriction as applied to her property may not, in most jurisdictions, secure judicial relief compelling a rezoning to allow her proposed use. *See* D. MANDELKER, LAND USE LAW §§ 8.16-8.18 (1982). If the municipality then rezones to a slightly more favorable use, but one which still prevents the landowner from going forward with her development, she must then file another court action. A few states now allow courts to provide affirmative relief that compels the necessary rezoning. *Id.*

5. TAXPAYER STANDING

A litigant who challenges state or local government action in court must have standing, a link between the personal claim and the challenged action that is sufficiently concrete to convince a court that the litigant is entitled to judicial review. Standing is provided in some of the forms of action considered so far, as in quo warranto actions, and in some of this litigation the litigant has also had a direct interest in the outcome of the proceeding. Members of the general public may also wish to challenge governmental action in cases in which they do not have a personal stake in the outcome but seek judicial relief for what they consider to be illegal or improper governmental action. They may do so in what are known as taxpayer's suits, usually brought by way of an injunction against the challenged action, or may alternatively appeal or challenge that action in their status as citizen members of the general public. This kind of action raises what are known as "standing" questions: does the litigant have standing in court to prosecute his suit? Because the interest asserted by the litigant as taxpayer or citizen may be tenuous, an initial question is whether it is sufficient and tangible enough to warrant the court's taking jurisdiction of the controversy.

Standing questions have been intensively considered in the federal courts, where they have spawned a difficult and complex body of law. Here we concentrate on taxpayer standing in the state courts, where the absence of federal constitutional requirements for a case and controversy and the closer connections between taxpayers and their state and local governments have made litigation based on taxpayer status easier to prosecute.

A taxpayer's suit challenges governmental action on the basis of direct or indirect injury to public funds raised by taxes. One might ask why taxpayer standing is allowed at all, since the actual pecuniary injury to the taxpayer is usually negligible, and the connection between any injury and the alleged illegal act is tenuous at best. Commentators suggest that the real basis for granting taxpayer standing is the recognition of a general cause of action to test the legality of governmental acts which otherwise might remain unreviewable:

> Taxpayers' litigation seems designed to enable a large body of the citizenry to challenge governmental action which would otherwise go unchallenged in the courts because of the standing requirement. Such litigation allows the courts, within the traditional notion of "standing," to add to the controls over public officials inherent in the elective process the judicial validity of their acts. Taxpayers' suits also extend the uniquely American concept of judicial review of legislative action by allowing minorities ineffective at the ballot box to invalidate statutes or ordinances on constitutional grounds.

Davis, *Taxpayers' Suits: A Survey and Summary,* 69 YALE L.J. 895, 904 (1960). *See also Bledsoe v. Watson,* 30 Cal. App. 3d 105, 106 Cal. Rptr. 197 (1973).

The taxpayers' suit is a representative suit, filed by a taxpayer on behalf of all similarly situated taxpayers. He can challenge a wrongful official action which pertains directly or indirectly to the use of public funds because his taxes will thereby be illegally used or increased. On the municipal level, the typical analogy likens city officials to trustees of the municipal corporation. Taxpayers, as cestuis que trust, may sue for a breach of that trust. Their interest in the "corporation" is objectively demonstrated by their tax contributions.

Arguments against allowing taxpayer standing fall into three main categories: (a) multiplicity of suits will result so that both the court system and governmental operation is hampered; (b) the balance of power is upset in favor of the judiciary if it is to review executive and legislative action at the whim of a taxpayer; and (c) taxpayer suits generally are not justiciable because no real adversary context can be achieved where no significant injury is demonstrable. These arguments are discussed and answered in Judge Fuld's dissent in the following case:

ST. CLAIR v. YONKERS RACEWAY, INC.

Court of Appeals of New York
13 N.Y.2d 72, 192 N.E.2d 15 (1963)

BURKE, JUDGE.

The simple question presented on this appeal is whether the complaint was properly dismissed on the ground that appellant lacks legal capacity to sue.

The appellant, who allegedly placed small wagers — $18 in all — at racetracks of several of the corporate defendants, brought this suit to have the difference paid to the State between the amount of the payments made to the State by such racetracks at the tax rates reduced by an amendment of the Pari-Mutuel Revenue Law ... and the amount which the State would have obtained under the tax rates in effect prior to the effective date of that amendment, and to require payment in the future at the old rates. The respondents, joined by the Attorney-General, moved to dismiss the complaint on the ground that appellant lacked standing to dispute the constitutionality of the amendment. . . .

[The majority opinion dismissed the suit on the basis of established New York precedent disallowing taxpayer suits to challenge state expenditures. Standing is allowed only to those "personally aggrieved . . ., and then only if the determination of the grievance requires a determination of constitutionality." The opinion quoted from an earlier case which had noted that it was the function "of the judicial department of government to declare the law in the determination of the individual rights of the parties," and that the assumption of jurisdiction in any other case would be an interference with another department of government. The opinion then continued: — Eds.]

This concept was later advanced by Mr. Justice Black in *Perkins v. Lukens Steel Co.*, 310 U.S. 113, 132, when he said: "Our decision that the complaining companies lack standing to sue does not rest upon a mere formality. We rest it upon reasons deeply rooted in the constitutional divisions of authority in our system of Government and the impropriety of judicial interpretations of law at the instance of those who show no more than a mere possible injury to the public."

The judgment appealed from should be affirmed, without costs.

FULD, JUDGE (dissenting).

The plaintiff, seeking to prevent the alleged misapplication of more than $42,000,000, sues as a citizen and taxpayer for a judgment declaring that section 45-a of the Pari-Mutuel Revenue Law (added by L. 1956, ch. 837) McK. Unconsol. Laws § 8020, violates the constitutional prohibition against the expenditure of public funds to private parties (N.Y. Const. art. VII, § 8). The courts below dismissed the complaint and we are called upon to decide whether this State shall continue to be one of the very few remaining jurisdictions to adhere to the rule that a citizen-taxpayer, who cannot show any direct or personal injury, lacks standing to challenge allegedly unconstitutional expenditures of state moneys.

Although the rule is one which judicially formulated, has been applied by this court for more than 100 years (see, e.g., *Doolittle v. Supervisors of Broome County,* 18 N.Y. 155; ... *Schieffelin v. Komfort,* 212 N.Y. 520, 106 N.E. 675 ...) it has not only been sharply criticized by authoritative writers on the subject ... but rejected by the courts of many jurisdictions....

[Included in the commentary cited by the court was 3 Davis, Administrative Law Treatise 245 (1958) and Jaffe, Standing to Secure Judicial Review: Public Actions, 74 Harv. L. Rev. 1265 (1961). — Eds.]

At the present time, virtually every state, either by decision or by statute — New York, by section 51 of the General Municipal Law, Consol. Laws, c. 24 — permits taxpayers to challenge *local* action and at least 34 states clearly sanction taxpayers' suits at the state level, that is, actions by state taxpayers challenging state action; indeed, only two states — New York and New Mexico — squarely prohibit such actions.... "This trend", it has been said, "reflects the absence of significant reasons for distinguishing municipal taxpayers' suits, permitted practically everywhere, from their state counterparts. True, the taxpayer's contribution to the state treasury may be a lesser percentage of the total than his municipal tax payments, and his interest in state affairs might therefore be said to be more remote. But no overriding considerations — such as the need for executive flexibility on the national level in foreign affairs and defense — make review of state action less desirable than review of the affairs of local government." (Note, Taxpayers' Suits, 69 Yale L.J. 895, 902.)

Of this there can be no possible doubt. The State has a vital concern, its People a deep interest, in seeing to it that the provisions of our Constitution are enforced, and unconstitutional expenditures of state funds prevented. Neither logic nor policy demands that the judiciary stay its hand and dismiss the action simply because the proceeding happens to be initiated by a vigilant and civic-minded taxpayer following official inaction. It hardly seems consonant with the Constitution itself that the enforcement of its provisions should have to turn on the meaning ascribed to it by members of the executive or administrative branch of government or on whether they choose to assert themselves.

It is self-evident that the denial of standing to a taxpayer will in most instances prevent any challenge to an expenditure of state funds as violative of the Constitution. The suggestion in the opinion of the majority that the Attorney-General and other state officials may be relied upon to attack the constitutional validity of state legislation is both unreal in fact and dubious in theory. As to the Attorney-General, for example, it would seem more appropriate to his office that he defend a statute's constitutionality when it is challenged than initiate an attack of his own.... Certainly, our Constitution does not entrust the determination of constitutionality to the executive branch of the government. But, in any event, if there is an official who is authorized to act and he declines to assert the invalidity of the statute, or otherwise raise that issue, the question whether the expenditures made pursuant to the statute's provisions violate the State Constitution will never be subjected to judicial scrutiny.

The Constitution is a People's document and the hypothesis that a citizen-taxpayer has no "interest" in state expenditures is little more than a legal fiction. It cannot be squared with the generally accepted doctrine that a taxpayer on the municipal level — where the issues are rarely of comparable importance — does possess the requisite "direct and immediate" interest to warrant his bringing an action to challenge the expenditure of municipal funds. (*Com. of Massachusetts v. Mellon,* 262 U.S. 447, 486, ... supra.) And, beyond that, as the Illinois Supreme Court declared in a case involving the alleged misappropriation of state moneys, the taxpayers' "ownership of such funds and their liability to replenish the public treasury for the deficiency," which might be occasioned by their misuse, should be deemed sufficient to supply the essential basis for standing. *(Turkovich v. Board of Trustees of Univ.,* 11 Ill.2d 460, 464, 143 N.E.2d 229.)

Little is to be gained by extended discussion of the few arguments which have been put forward to support perpetuation of the rule denying standing to taypayers on the state level, and I consider briefly but two of them.

Less than persuasive is the claim that the court's assumption of jurisdiction in these suits in the face of inaction by the executive branch of government charged with the responsibility of preventing the waste of public funds "would be an interference by one department of government with another." *(Schieffelin v. Komfort,* ... supra.) Fundamental to our form of government is the principle that determination of the constitutionality of legislation is essentially a judicial function. And, this being so, it is difficult to understand how it may be said that a court, in making such a determination, would be interfering with another branch of government, or usurping the latter's powers simply because it acts in a case initiated by a taxpayer. In brief, litigation such as this calls upon the courts to assess the constitutional validity of legislation, not to supervise the acts of another branch of government.

Nor do I find any basis for the concern — expressed in the *Doolittle* case ... and elsewhere — that opening the doors of the court to taxpayers would cause a flood of actions by officious meddlers. If there ever was reason for such a fear, it has been completely dispelled by the experience not only of the many jurisdictions where taxpayers' suits on the state level have long been sanctioned but, indeed, of our own State of New York under the statute permitting municipal taxpayers to challenge the action of local officials (General Municipal Law, § 51). The New Jersey high court accurately appraised the situation when many years ago it observed that "The general indifference of private individuals to public omissions and encroachments, the fear of expense in unsuccessful and even in successful litigation, and the discretion of the court, have been, and doubtless will continue to be, a sufficient guard to these public officials against too numerous and unreasonable attacks." *(Ferry v. Williams,* 41 N.J.L. 332, 339; see Davis, Standing to Challenge Governmental Action, 39 Minn. L. Rev. 354, 430.) The courts undoubtedly can be relied upon to discourage and prevent baseless taxpayers' suits by insisting that the action pose an issue of general public importance; that it involve an actual bona fide controversy, not one which is feigned; that all interested parties be represented; that there be no other remedy available; and that the public officials vested with authority to bring an action shall have refused to so so. All of these conditions have been met in the case before us.

In sum — although the Legislature could, of course, remove the taxpayer's disability at a stroke, enforcement of the Constitution should not depend upon the will of the legislative branch any more than on that of the executive. The apathy of the average citizen concerning public affairs has often been decried; under the court-made rule now reaffirmed, it is being compelled. I would change the rule.

The judgment appealed from should be reversed and the motion to dismiss the complaint denied.

DYE, JUDGE (dissenting). [Omitted.]

Comments: 1. For criticism of this decision, see Quirk, *Standing to Sue in New York,* 47 ST. JOHN'S L. REV. 429 (1973). By statute, New York allows taxpayer suits against municipal officers, but forbids suits against state officers unless the party asserts a "personally aggrieved" status. The argument often made to justify this distinction is that the municipal taxpayer has an especially close relationship to municipal affairs, that it is like the relationship of a stockholder to his corporation. On this basis a municipal taxpayer would have the interest necessary to attack the illegal use of corporate funds and property. This distinction is widely criticized. Jaffe, *Standing to Secure Judicial Review: Public Actions,* 74 HARV. L. REV. 1265, 1295 (1961).

New York has now retreated somewhat from its holding in *St. Clair.* In *Boryszewski v. Brydges,* 334 N.E.2d 579 (N.Y. 1975), taxpayers brought an action challenging the constitutionality of the legislative executive and retirement plan and budget statutes providing lump sum payments to legislators in lieu of expenses. Standing was granted and the court noted:

> We are satisfied that the time has now come when the judicially formulated restriction on standing (which we recognize has had a venerable existence) should be modified to bring our State's practice with respect to review of State legislative action into conformity not only with the practice in the majority of other States but also with the procedural standing of taxpayers to challenge local actions (General Municipal Law, § 51). We are now prepared to recognize standing where, as in the present case, the failure to accord such standing would be in effect to erect an impenetrable barrier to any judicial scrutiny of legislative action. In the present instance it must be considered unlikely that the officials of State government who would otherwise be the only ones having standing to seek review would vigorously attack legislation under which each is or may be a personal beneficiary. Moreover, it may even properly be thought that the responsibility of the Attorney-General and of other State officials is to uphold and effectively to support action taken by the legislative and executive branches of government. As Judge Fuld wrote generally in *St. Clair* ... "The suggestion ... that the Attorney-General and other state officials may be relied upon to attack the constitutional validity of state legislation is both unreal in fact and dubious in theory". His estimate of the situation has been verified in the years since *St. Clair.*
>
> Where the prospect of challenge to the constitutionality of State legislation is otherwise effectually remote, it would be particularly repellant today, when every encouragement to the individual citizen-taxpayer is to take an active, aggressive interest in his State as well as his local and national government, to continue to exclude him from access to the judicial process — since *Marbury v. Madison,* 1 Cranch [5 U.S.] 137, 2 L.Ed. 60, the classical means for effective scrutiny of legislative and executive action. The role of the judiciary is integral to the doctrine of separation of powers. It is unacceptable now by any process of continued quarantine to exclude the very persons most likely to invoke its powers.

Id. at 581. How does the court's discretion to refuse standing under this formulation compare with the court's discretion to refuse jurisdiction when relief is sought under one of the extraordinary writs?

2. Some state courts have liberalized standing requirements in suits against the state, recognizing that otherwise no judicial challenge would be possible. In *Cunningham v. Exon,* 276 N.W.2d 213 (Neb. 1979), a taxpayer brought a declaratory judgment action challenging an amendment to the state constitution. The court granted standing. "[I]f the amendment ... cannot be challenged by a citizen and taxpayer unless and until he has a special pecuniary interest or injury different from that of the public generally, it is entirely possible that no one may have standing to challenge it." *Id.* at 216. *See also McKee v. Likins,* 261 N.W.2d 566 (Minn. 1977) (challenge to state administrative rule on medicaid assistance). *Contra Parks v. Alexander,* 608 S.W.2d 881 (Tenn. App. 1980) (constitutional amendment). Should suits challenging constitutional amendments be distinguished?

In *Common Cause v. State*, 455 A.2d 1 (Me. 1983), the court held that state taxpayers had standing to challenge the use of state general obligation bonds to finance a port development. Plaintiff claimed this use of the bonds was not public purpose spending and violated the state's constitutional "lending of credit" provision. *See* Chapter 5. The court adopted policy reasons for granting standing to state taxpayers similar to those advanced by the dissent in *St. Clair*. Should standing be more readily granted to a taxpayer who claims a violation of a state constitutional limitation on fiscal powers? The court noted in a footnote that state taxpayers should be given standing even if they have not shown that the misconduct they challenge will increase their tax burden.

3. State courts are universally more liberal than federal courts in allowing taxpayer standing to challenge government action. Since *Frothingham v. Mellon*, 262 U.S. 447 (1923), in which the Supreme Court held that a federal taxpayer had no standing to test the constitutionality of federal expenditures, federal courts have distinguished the status of state and federal taxpayers. In *Frothingham* the Court said that the interest of a local taxpayer in the disposition of municipal funds is direct and immediate, like the stockholder's interest in the corporation. In contrast, the interest of a federal taxpayer in federal monies is "shared with millions" and thus too remote to qualify for the traditional federal court requirements of standing. This distinction has been sharply criticized by commentators and by some members of the judiciary. Davis, *Standing to Challenge Governmental Action*, 30 MINN. L. REV. 353 (1955); Comment, *New York and the Non-Hohfeldian Plaintiff Taxpayers: Standing to Sue in the State*, 36 ALB. L. REV. 203 (1971). In a later case, *Doremus v. Board of Education*, 342 U.S. 429 (1952), the Court used the federal test of direct, pecuniary injury to disallow standing to a state taxpayer attacking public expenditures used to support religious practices in public schools.

Flast v. Cohen, 392 U.S. 83 (1968), relaxed the *Frothingham* restrictions on standing. *Flast* was a federal taxpayer suit for a declaratory judgment against monetary support of sectarian schools. The Court, rather than using language requiring a financial injury to plaintiffs, outlined a two-part nexus test for standing: Standing would be granted to a federal taxpayer only if he alleged the unconstitutionality of congressional action under the taxing and spending clause, and then only if he could show that the congressional action challenged was in violation of those constitutional provisions that operate to restrict the exercise of the taxing and spending power.

The Supreme Court has strictly limited *Flast v. Cohen*. Federal taxpayers do not have standing to assert "generalized grievances" against the federal government. A federal taxpayer's standing to sue must be based on an act of Congress under the constitutional taxing and spending power. *See Valley Forge Christian College v. Americans United for Separation of Church & State, Inc.*, 454 U.S. 464 (1982) (no standing to challenge transfer of surplus government property).

The most general and widely recognized basis for taxpayer standing in state courts is a challenge to the misuse or expenditure of public funds. In these cases a distinction must be made between the personal interest of the litigant in the outcome of the action and his interest as a member of the public at large in the proper and legal expenditure of public funds consistent with constitutional and statutory requirements. The following case raises these problems.

BLAIR v. PITCHESS

Supreme Court of California
5 Cal. 3d 258, 96 Cal. Rptr. 42, 486 P.2d 1242 (1971)

SULLIVAN, JUSTICE.

In this case we are called upon to determine whether California's claim and delivery law (Code Civ. Proc., §§ 509-521) violates the Fourth, Fifth and

Fourteenth Amendments to the United States Constitution and sections 13 and 19 of article I of the Constitution of the State of California.

Originally enacted in 1872, the claim and delivery law establishes a procedure by which the "plaintiff in an action to recover the possession of personal property may, at the time of issuing the summons, or at any time before answer" require the sheriff, constable or marshal of a county to take the property from the defendant. (§§ 509, 511.) To initiate the procedure, the plaintiff must file his complaint, obtain the issuance of a summons, and file an affidavit stating that he owns or is entitled to possession of the property, that the defendant is wrongfully detaining the property and that the property has not been taken for a tax, assessment or fine, or been seized under an attachment or execution. The affidavit must also set forth the alleged cause of the wrongful detention of the property and the actual value of the property. (§ 510.) In addition, the plaintiff must file an undertaking of two or more sufficient sureties for double the value of the property. (§ 512.)

The defendant may except to the plaintiff's sureties (§ 513) or require return of the property by filing an undertaking similar to that required of the plaintiff. (§§ 514, 515.) After the sheriff seizes the property, he must deliver it to the plaintiff upon payment of his fees and necessary expenses (§§ 518, 521), and he must file the undertaking, affidavit and other relevant documents with the clerk of the court in which the action is pending (§ 520). Finally if the property is within a building or inclosure the sheriff must publicly demand its delivery, and if it is not voluntarily delivered "he must cause the building or inclosure to be broken open, and take the property into his possession; and, if necessary, he may call to his aid the power of his county." (§ 517.)

Plaintiffs, who are residents and taxpayers of the County of Los Angeles, brought this action against the county and its sheriff, marshal, and deputy sheriff, and against the constable of the Malibu Justice Court to secure an injunction restraining defendants from executing the provisions of the claim and delivery law. Plaintiffs contend that the claim and delivery law is unconstitutional and that, by expending the time of county officials in executing its provisions, defendants are illegally expending county funds....

After considering the declarations, the points and authorities and arguments of counsel, the trial court granted plaintiffs' motion for summary judgment. Judgment was entered in favor of plaintiffs and the court issued a permanent injunction restraining defendants and their employees from (1) taking any personal property under color of claim and delivery law unless the defendant is first given a hearing on the merits of the case, and (2) entering any private place to search for and seize any personal property under color of claim and delivery law unless prior thereto probable cause is established before a magistrate. Defendants appeal from the judgment.

We first consider defendants' contention that plaintiffs had no standing to maintain the action and that consequently the trial court's judgment was advisory in nature. As we noted above, plaintiffs bring their suit under section 526a, which authorizes actions by a resident taxpayer against officers of a county, town, city, or city and county to obtain an injunction restraining and preventing the illegal expenditure of public funds. The primary purpose of this statute, originally enacted in 1909, is to "enable a large body of the citizenry to challenge governmental action which would otherwise go unchallenged in the courts because of the standing requirement." (Comment, Taxpayers' Suits: A Survey and Summary (1960) 69 Yale L.J. 895, 904.)

California courts have consistently construed section 526a liberally to achieve this remedial purpose. Upholding the issuance of an injunction, we have declared that it "is immaterial that the amount of the illegal expenditures is small or that the illegal procedures actually permit a saving of tax funds." (*Wirin v. Parker* (1957) 48 Cal. 2d 890, 894, 313 P.2d 844, 846.) Nor have we required that the unlawfully spent funds come from tax revenues; they may be derived from the operation of a public utility or from gas revenues.... A unanimous court in *Wirin v. Horrall* (1948) 85 Cal. App. 2d 497, 504-505, 193 P.2d 470, 474, held that the mere "expending [of] the time of the paid police officers of the city of Los Angeles in performing illegal and unauthorized acts" constituted an unlawful use of funds which could be enjoined under section 526a.... (See also *Vogel v. County of Los Angeles* (1967) 68 Cal. 2d 18, 64 Cal. Rptr. 409, 434 P.2d 961.)

We have even extended section 526a to include actions brought by nonresident taxpayers.... In *Crowe v. Boyle* (1920) 184 Cal. 117, 152, 193 P. 111, 125, we stated: "In this state we have been very liberal in the application of the rule permitting taxpayers to bring a suit to prevent the illegal conduct of city officials, and no showing of special damage to a particular taxpayer has been held necessary."

Moreover, we have not limited suits under section 526a to challenges of policies or ordinances adopted by the county, city or town. If county, town or city officials implement a state statute or even the provisions of the state Constitution, an injunction under section 526a will issue to restrain such enforcement if the provision is unconstitutional.... Indeed, it has been held that taxpayers may sue *state* officials to enjoin such officials from illegally expending state funds.... We have even permitted taxpayers to sue on behalf of a city or county to recover funds illegally expended....

It is clear that the present action was properly brought under section 526a. Plaintiffs have alleged, and by their affidavits have established, that they are residents and taxpayers of the County of Los Angeles.... It appears from the complaint that plaintiffs seek to enjoin defendants, who admittedly are county officials, from expending their own time and the time of other county officials in executing claim and delivery process. If the claim and delivery law is unconstitutional, then county officials may be enjoined from spending their time carrying out its provisions (*Wirin v. Horrall, supra* ...) even though by the collection of fees from those invoking the provisional remedy the procedures actually effect a saving of tax funds. (*Wirin v. Parker, supra* ....)

Defendants argue nevertheless that, even if the instant action fulfills the requirements of section 526a, it was not properly cognizable by the trial court because it does not present a true case or controversy. They point out that there "is no allegation that the plaintiffs were or may be parties to a claim and delivery action." Defendants also contend that as sheriff and marshal, respectively, they merely carry out ministerial functions in executing claim and delivery process and have, therefore, no real interest adverse to plaintiffs. They cite our recent statement that, "[t]he rendering of advisory opinions falls within neither the functions nor the jurisdiction of this court. [Citations.]" (*People ex rel. Lynch v. Superior Court* (1970) 1 Cal. 3d 910, 912, 83 Cal. Rptr. 670, 671, 464 P.2d 126, 127.) They also draw our attention to the long series of United States Supreme Court decisions which have elaborated on the case or controversy requirement.

We do not find those cases applicable here, for we conclude that if an action meets the requirements of section 526a, it presents a true case or controversy. As we noted before, the primary purpose of section 526a was to give a large body of citizens standing to challenge governmental actions. If we were to hold that such suits did not present a true case or controversy unless the plaintiff and the defendant each had a special, personal interest in the outcome, we would drastically curtail their usefulness as a check on illegal government activity. Few indeed are the government officers who have a personal interest in the continued validity of their officials acts.

Furthermore, it has never been the rule in this state that the parties in suits under section 526a must have a personal interest in the litigation. We specifically stated in *Crowe v. Boyle, supra* ... that "no showing of special damage to the particular taxpayer has been held necessary." In *Wirin v. Parker, supra* ... the plaintiff had no more immediate interest in enjoining the illegal wiretaps conducted by the police department than his status as a resident taxpayer. Similarly, in *Vogel v. County of Los Angeles, supra,* ... the defendant county officials who administered the loyalty oath to new county officials and employees certainly had no personal interest in the continued use of that oath. In both *Wirin* and *Vogel* the plaintiff prevailed, and no suggestion is found in either opinion that the cases failed to present a true case or controversy.

As the extensive briefs in this case demonstrate, taxpayers have a sufficiently personal interest in the illegal expenditure of funds by county officials to become dedicated adversaries. In the same manner, the interest of government officials in continuing their programs is sufficient to guarantee a spirited opposition. There is no danger in such circumstances that the court will be misled by the failure of the parties adequately to explore and argue the issues. We are satisfied that an action meeting the requirements of section 526a thereby presents a true case or controversy.

. . . .

Comments: 1. Because specific injury was traditionally required before relief could be granted by a court of equity, courts have responded differently in deciding whether injury to the taxpayer as a member of the class of taxpayers is sufficient to confer standing, or whether a more direct personal interest must be shown. With the principal case compare *Tabor v. Moore,* 503 P.2d 736 (Wash. 1972). Taxpayers attacked local police procedures under which persons arrested without warrants were held on open charges, and which were alleged to violate constitutional rights and to involve the illegal expenditure of public funds. Because the taxpayers had failed to show a direct, special or pecuniary interest in the outcome of the action, the court applied the Washington rule which, in these instances, requires a prior demand on the attorney general to institute the suit before the taxpayer action can be brought. As no such request had been made, standing was denied.

Some courts require a pecuniary loss to the taxpayer or injury to the public before they will allow a taxpayer suit. In *Dail v. City of Phoenix,* 624 P.2d 877 (Ariz. App. 1980), the court disallowed a taxpayer suit challenging the purchase of a water system. The evidence did not show an expenditure of city tax funds, and the system had been self-supporting for some time. *Accord Henderson v. McCormick,* 215 P.2d 608 (Ariz. 1950) (city automobile sold to highest bidder even though violation of state conflict of interest law alleged); *Tucson Community Development & Design Center, Inc. v. City of Tucson,* 641 P.2d 1298 (Ariz. App. 1981) (use of federal funds for redevelopment project); *Altman v. City of Lansing,* 321 N.W.2d 707 (Mich. App. 1982) (same). The courts believed that federal funds were not local funds. Is that correct? Doesn't the receipt of federal funds release local revenues for other purposes?

Some courts, however, stress that the public injury stems from the mere fact of *misuse* of public funds (whatever the actual pecuniary result of their mishandling) rather than from a misuse which leads necessarily to depletion of the public treasury. Thus, in the principal case the court cited *Wirin v. Parker,* 313 P.2d 844 (Cal. 1957), in which the court held that injunctive relief was proper even if the challenged acts resulted in a saving of public funds. In *Howard v. City of Boulder,* 290 P.2d 237 (Colo. 1955), taxpayers were allowed to challenge the method of electing city councilmen in an injunctive and declaratory relief action without alleging pecuniary loss. Even the jurisdictions which do purport to require a showing of special damage to the tax fund often relax that requirement.

See also *City of Wilmington v. Lord,* 378 A.2d 635 (Del. 1977). The court allowed a taxpayer suit to challenge the building of a water tower in a city park. The court held that "[t]he improper use of publicly held property is sufficiently analogous to the improper use of public money." *Id.* at 638.

If some pecuniary loss or injury is alleged, the amount is irrelevant. In *Gordon v. Mayor & City Council,* 267 A.2d 98 (Md. 1970), for example, a taxpayer was allowed to maintain a taxpayer's suit to challenge the receipt by a private, but municipally supported, library of a collection of books on the ground that the transfer would in fact require the taxpayer to assume the costs of preserving the collection.

Statutes may also define the injury requirement in very general terms. Cal. Code Civ. Proc. § 526a provides in part that:

An action to obtain a judgment, restraining and preventing any illegal expenditure of, waste of, or injury to, the estate, funds, or other property of a county, town, city or city and county of the state, may be maintained against any officer thereof, or any agent, or other person, acting in its behalf, either by a citizen resident therein, or by a corporation, who is assessed for and is liable to pay, or, within one year before the commencement of the action, has paid, a tax therein.

2. In some cases the loss or injury to the public entity is either nonexistent or so tenous that it is clear that the court, in allowing standing, has converted the taxpayer's suit into a general suit for citizens' relief. Thus in *Illinois Broadcasting Co. v. City of Decatur,* 238 N.E.2d 261 (Ill. App. 1968), plaintiff broadcasting company brought suit to determine the validity of a city ordinance franchising a community antenna television company (CATV). The court granted standing in a brief paragraph, noting that public funds would have to be spent in the implementation and enforcement of the ordinance. Didn't the plaintiff have a personal interest in the outcome of this litigation? If so, should (or would) this be enough to confer standing? Contra *Green v. Cox Cable of Omaha, Inc.,* 327 N.W.2d 603 (Neb. 1982) (council member challenged grant of cable franchise). See *Belford v. City of New Haven,* 364 A.2d 194 (Conn. 1975), refusing to entertain a taxpayer's suit to enjoin the city from constructing an olympic size rowing course and other facilities on public park land. The court noted that the plaintiff in cases like this had to establish either that the governmental action challenged would result in an increase in his taxes or would in some other fashion cause him irreparable injury.

In other cases there has been no pecuniary injury of any kind. *See, e.g., People ex rel. Newdelman v. Swank,* 264 N.E.2d 794 (Ill. App. 1970), in which a plaintiff as resident and taxpayer was allowed to bring suit in mandamus and declaratory judgment challenging the refusal of the state welfare department to grant one-month security deposits to welfare recipients, as required by law. Since the taxpayer was not a welfare recipient she did not have to exhaust her administrative remedies before the state welfare agency before bringing suit. The court noted the rule in Illinois that even though citizens may not have their legal rights affected by the failure of public officials to carry out their duties, nevertheless, as members of the general public, they had the right to insist that public officials carry out their legal duties.

3. The zoning cases appear to be in a different category. The model state zoning act conferred standing on taxpayers, but only a minority of states have adopted this provision. D. MANDELKER, LAND USE LAW § 8.2 (1983). In the absence of a statutory provision, most courts deny standing to taxpayers to challenge zoning actions. The courts reach this conclusion even though the action is brought against a local agency, such as a housing authority, which proposes to use public funds for a housing project. See *Bell v. Planning & Zoning Commission,* 391 A.2d 154 (Conn. 1978). What is the reason for the distinction? The courts might believe that zoning regulations only injure physically proximate landowners, and that taxpayers who do not own land located near the proposed land use do not have a sufficiently specific injury to confer standing. Is this distinction supportable?

4. Other aspects of the taxpayer's suit might also be briefly noted. The court in *Blair* gave an extremely liberal reading to the statute, but other courts have held that the statutory remedy is not exclusive and that the taxpayer may also sue at common law or in equity. *See, e.g., Eagle Nest Corp. v. Carroll,* 37 N.Y.S.2d 716 (Sup. Ct.), *rev'd on other grounds,* 38 N.Y.S.2d 599 (App. Div. 1952). The action challenged must not be discretionary. If the action is taken to implement a discretionary power, it follows that no injunction may issue even though extremely poor judgment was used.

Laches or estoppel may sometimes defeat a taxpayer suit if the court finds that there has been acquiescence in the conduct, or if the taxpayer is suing on a municipal cause of action and the municipality would be estopped to sue. However, courts usually look at the merits of most taxpayer suits before they give weight to defenses.

Although New York statutes allow taxpayer actions at the municipal level, an additional statutory requirement limits standing to those taxpayers who have paid at least $1,000 in taxes. N.Y. Gen. Mun. Laws § 51. This requirement raises a constitutional due process question, as it limits taxpayer access to the courts on the basis of the amount of tax paid, even though courts generally do not look to amount of injury in granting standing.

Another requirement in many state statutes is a bond. This requirement has been challenged on constitutional due process grounds, but has been upheld. *State ex rel. Haberkorn v. DeKalb Circuit Court,* 241 N.E.2d 62 (Ind. 1968). *See* Annot., 89 A.L.R.2d 333 (1963) for other cases upholding the bond requirement. If the bond is not made at the time the complaint is filed, courts are fairly liberal in allowing it to be posted *nunc pro tunc. Id.* at 343-45.

Statutes sometimes provide that a portion of the amount recovered by a taxpayer's action be awarded to the plaintiff. See, for example, Okla. Stat. Ann. tit. 62 § 373, which awards one half the money and one half the value of property recovered as a result of the suit to the plaintiff.

A NOTE ON THE STANDING OF CITIZENS AND CITIZEN ORGANIZATIONS

Conceptually more difficult problems are presented when an individual or an organization asserts standing to challenge governmental action, not on the basis of a taxpayer interest in monitoring public expenditure but simply to challenge the constitutionality or legality of the action in question. There is no general right of public access to the courts to vindicate the interest of the general public in the proper and legal conduct of public affairs. The litigant must demonstrate some personal interest in the issue at hand before he can successfully proceed in court, and must also be affected in some way by the action which is being challenged.

These tests, known at the federal level as the zone of interest and injury in fact tests, generally state the law of standing in this situation. The Supreme Court has now extended the injury requirement to include more than economic or tangible harm, *Sierra Club v. Morton,* 405 U.S. 727 (1972) (environmental organization challenged federal permit for resort in national forest). The Supreme Court also holds that the injury of which the plaintiffs complain must be capable of being redressed by judicial relief. *See Warth v. Seldin,* 422 U.S. 490 (1975). The Court denied standing to individuals and organizations who challenged a suburban exclusionary zoning ordinance. None of the plaintiffs owned property in the community, and the court denied standing because invalidation of the zoning ordinance would not necessarily lead to the construction of lower income housing that would remedy the suburb's exclusionary zoning pattern. *See* Sager, *Insular Majorities Unabated: Warth v. Seldin and Eastlake v. Forest City Enterprises, Inc.,* 91 Harv. L. Rev. 1373 (1978).

Much of federal standing law, such as the injury in fact requirement, is based on the case and controversy requirement in Article III of the United States

Constitution. The Supreme Court holds that this requirement imposes a constitutional minimum on standing to sue. Constitutional overtones are missing in state court standing cases because state constitutions do not usually contain similar requirements. State courts apply standing rules in the exercise of their prudential powers to take jurisdiction of non-justiciable controversies. It was no doubt this difference in the basis for state court jurisdiction led one writer to comment in an early treatise that standing in state courts "has caused comparatively little trouble." 2 F. COOPER, STATE ADMINISTRATIVE LAW 538 (1965).

This conclusion is questionable. Some state courts have lagged behind the federal courts in their willingness to grant standing to litigants other than taxpayers. See *United States Steel Corp. v. Save Sand Key, Inc.,* 303 So. 2d 9 (Fla. 1974) (citizen group may not enjoin interference with public rights to beach). Neither is state standing law as articulate and well-developed as standing law in the Supreme Court, although some would claim that Supreme Court standing law is a mystery that few understand.

Penn Parking Garage v. City of Pittsburgh, 346 A.2d 269 (Pa. 1975), is a leading case adopting lenient standing rules. Plaintiffs were individuals subject to a newly levied tax on parking lots and parking operators who challenged the legality of the tax. Standing was granted. The case came to the court under a statute allowing an "appeal" by "aggrieved taxpayers" against any tax levied for the first time.

Although the case could have been treated as a taxpayer's suit, the court took the opportunity to liberalize the state's standing rules. Earlier the court had held that a party to be "aggrieved" must have a direct, immediate, and pecuniary interest in the litigation and that this interest must be substantial. Explaining this requirement, the court now held that an interest is substantial if it has some substance; there must be some discernible adverse effect to the interest of the plaintiff other than the interest of all citizens. The requirement for a pecuniary interest was dropped. An interest is direct if the action complained of causes some harm to the alleged interest. However, the interest must be immediate. The court interpreted this requirement to mean that there must be some causal connection between the interest and the action challenged. This connection would grow less as the causal connection grows more remote. The court also appeared to hold that the necessary causation would be found if the interest asserted is within the zone of interest protected by the statute, a rule similar to the federal standing rule. It cited, among other cases, *Gismondi Liquor License Case,* 186 A.2d 448 (Pa. Super. 1962) (neighbors may challenge grant of liquor license as neighborhood welfare among factors to be considered in granting license).

Some state courts have applied the liberalized federal standing rules in environmental cases. See *In re Lappie,* 377 A.2d 441 (Me. 1977), adopting the "private attorney general" rationale of *Sierra Club, supra,* and holding that an abutting landowner had standing to challenge a state permit for a waste disposal facility. *See also State v. Lewis,* 559 P.2d 630 (Alaska), *cert. denied,* 432 U.S. 901 (1977). The court relied on *Sierra Club* to grant standing to citizens challenging the constitutionality of a major land exchange which plaintiffs claimed would result in large financial losses to the state.

Some state courts have also adopted liberal standing rules in exclusionary zoning cases. See *Stocks v. City of Irvine,* 170 Cal. Rptr. 724 (Cal. App. 1981), expressly rejecting *Warth v. Seldin, supra* to hold that nonresidents had standing to challenge an exclusionary zoning ordinance. *Accord Home Builders League v. Township of Berlin,* 405 A.2d 381 (N.J. 1979).

Organizational standing in state courts is more problematic. *Sierra Club, supra* held that organizations had standing to challenge actions creating environmental harm when their members suffered injury in fact from the governmental action. The Supreme Court liberalized organizational standing requirements in *Hunt v. Washington State Apple Advertising Commission,* 432 U.S. 333 (1977). If its members have standing to sue, an organization may sue in their behalf if the interests it seeks to protect are germane to its purposes, and neither the claim asserted nor the relief requested requires participation of the members of the organization in the lawsuit.

The state courts are not always as lenient. In Pennsylvania, despite the holding in *Penn Parking, supra,* the intermediate Commonwealth Court denied standing to a taxpayer organization that challenged a state expenditure. *Concerned Taxpayers v. Commonwealth,* 382 A.2d 490 (Pa. Commw. 1978). The court did not allow the organization "to attain standing by claiming injury to the taxpayer status of its individual members." *See also Save Sand Key, supra.*

The zoning cases illustrate a trend in the other direction. *Residents of Beverly Glen, Inc. v. City of Los Angeles,* 109 Cal. Rptr. 724 (Cal. App. 1973), relied on *Sierra Club* to grant standing to a neighborhood organization that challenged a planned development claimed to be environmentally harmful and inconsistent with a comprehensive plan. The court held that the members of the organization were "directly and adversely affected by the governmental action involved." The New Jersey Supreme Court granted standing to a civil rights organization to challenge a suburban exclusionary zoning ordinance in the leading case of *Southern Burlington County NAACP v. Township of Mt. Laurel [I],* 336 A.2d 713 (N.J.), *appeal dismissed & cert. denied,* 423 U.S. 808 (1975).

Are there any trends in the standing cases? The courts appear more lenient on standing when important public interests are at stake, such as environmental harm and exclusionary zoning. This tendency indicates a direct relationship between a court's willingness to grant standing and the importance (or severity) of the harm claimed to be suffered. Do you agree with this view?

B. THROUGH INITIATIVE AND REFERENDUM

Beginning with the turn of the century, many states began to adopt constitutional and statutory provisions authorizing the initiative and referendum process at both state and local levels. This reform reflected the dominant populism of that period, which favored a variety of changes that would return the management of government to the people, as well as serious concern over the domination of state legislatures by interest groups and lobbyists. Today almost all of the states have constitutional provisions authorizing the referendum at the state level, most of which also authorize referendums at the local level, while about half of the states authorize the initiative process both for state and local government. The initiative or referendum may be available for constitutional amendments, for state legislation or local ordinances, or both. They are used more extensively in some states than others, and tend to be used rather more frequently in the west coast states. For a summary of these initiative and referendum provisions for state legislation, see COUNCIL OF STATE GOVERNMENTS, THE BOOK OF THE STATES: 1978-1979, at 48-50 (1978).

As applied to the legislative process, an initiative measure is a voter-initiated piece of legislation which in some states is placed directly on the ballot following submission of a petition carrying the required number of voter signatures. If the initiative is passed, the measure becomes law. Under a variant of this process the legislative body is first given an opportunity to accept or reject the measure before the election is held. A referendum is an election on a legislative measure which is called after the legislative body has taken action on a legislative proposal. The legislation may again be taken to the electorate following the submission of the requisite petition, or the legislative body may itself propose that a referendum be held. The vote on an initiative or referendum measure may take place at a special election or at a regularly scheduled election depending on the governing statute.

While in some parts of the country the initiative and referendum have become institutionalized as part of the political process, elsewhere interest in this technique has waxed and waned. An extensive use of the initiative and referendum process would of course have a substantial impact on state and local legislative policy-making, and would act as a constraint on the ability of state and local governments to legislate policy in a large number of legislative areas. Not uncommonly, recourse to both procedures becomes more frequent as sensitive political issues are pressed on legislative bodies for decision. Recently, for example, the initiative and referendum have been used to block the construction of low-income housing projects in communities or to achieve other community purposes that are protectionist in nature.

To a large extent the issues surrounding the use of the initiative and referendum at the state level are similar to those that are also present at the local level. Nevertheless, the special characteristics of local governments as governmental units dependent on a delegation of power from the state have created some special problems in connection with the use of the initiative and referendum at the local level that demand consideration. The next case illustrates the problems that can arise.

NORLUND v. THORPE

District Court of Appeal of California
34 Cal. App. 3d 672, 110 Cal. Rptr. 246 (1973)

Draper, Presiding Justice.

This proceeding in mandamus presents an issue not passed upon to date — is the resolution of a city council ordering annexation of uninhabited territory subject to a referendum by the voters of the annexing city? The strongest argument advanced by the City of Napa against this right of referendum is that annexation of territory by a city is a matter of statewide concern and that the Legislature has specifically delegated the annexation power to the legislative bodies of the cities, thus excluding any right of the city electorate. We cannot accept that argument.

On August 7, 1972, the city council of Napa adopted Resolution 6076, approving annexation of some 99 acres known as the Longwood Ranch. Only two days later, certified copy of the resolution was filed by the Secretary of State and certificate of filing issued. On September 5, 1972, petitioner here and others (an alleged total of 4111) filed a petition seeking submission of the annexation resolution to vote of the people of the city in a referendum. The city council, also on September 5, refused to file the referendum petition. Petition for writ of mandate, filed October 5, sought to compel the city clerk to examine the petition and to certify the number of qualified electors signing it and, if the requisite percentage had signed, to compel the city council to call an election. Respondents, the city clerk, and members of the city council, demurred. The demurrer was sustained without leave to amend, and petitioners sought mandate here.

A city has no inherent right to annex territory. Since such authority is not provided by the constitution, it follows that all municipal authority in this field stems from state legislation. It is only in this very general sense that annexation of territory by a city is a matter of "statewide concern." The same is true of many, if not all, powers exercised by cities. Even a charter city holds home rule powers only after its charter is approved by the Legislature. The general subject of annexation by cities is, of course, a matter of statewide concern, but no one annexation by a particular city can be so denominated. It is difficult to imagine that Napa's annexation of a comparatively small area is a matter of public concern in San Diego, Crescent City, or Sacramento.

Of course, a city cannot, either by council action or vote of the electorate, exceed the limitations upon annexation enacted by the Legislature. Thus the council cannot ignore a protest filed by a county as owner of land within the area proposed to be annexed ... nor can a city annex land in another county.... Upon a distinct ground, a city cannot enter a field which has been preempted by state legislation....

But these rules, although they undoubtedly show that annexation is a power derived from the state, do not in any way suggest that the Legislature, by the statutes providing for annexation of uninhabited territory, intended to vest all power in the city legislative bodies and to exclude the people's right of referendum. This is emphasized by reference to the former constitutional provision (Art. 4, § 1) which "further reserved to the electors of each ... city and town" the referendum power. It is hard to believe that the annexation act, adopted long before this constitutional provision was modified, intended to eliminate, by legislation alone, the very power which the constitution granted to city voters.

There is no historical reason to attribute to the Legislature an intent to eliminate the right of referendum by voters of the annexing city. When the annexation act was adopted, as for decades before, growth was an overwhelming aim of cities and their voters. Bigness was considered a virtue in itself, and there is no suggestion that any legislator even considered the possibility of any voter's dissent from expansion of his own city. The heretofore unheard of opposition to bigness has only recently tended to surface. There is no reason to attribute to the Legislature's occasional reference to the legislative body of a city as a deliberate determination to bar referendum within the annexing city.

Moreover, the statute specifically provides (Gov. Code, § 35310.1) that "[a] resolution approving or disapproving the annexation shall be considered the same as an ordinance referred to in other sections of this article." Thus the resolution approving annexation could not become effective until 30 days after its adoption. (Elec. Code, § 4050.) A prime purpose of deferment of the effective date of ordinances is to preserve the right of referendum. It is reasonably inferable from section 35310.1 that the Legislature, far from seeking to limit the annexing power to the several city councils, affirmatively intended to preserve the voters' referendum right.

Annexation is not a legislative function so intermingled with quasi-judicial and administrative functions that the latter render it an improper subject for referendum....

The annexation resolution is subject to referendum. Let writ of mandate issue directing the city clerk to examine the referendum petition and to certify the number of registered electors who have properly signed that petition. If that number meets the required percentage, respondent city council is directed to order the holding of an election thereon.

Harold C. Brown, J., concurs.

Caldecott, Associate Justice (dissenting).

I dissent.

This annexation was pursuant to the Annexation of Uninhabited Territory Act of 1939 (Gov. Code, § 35300 et seq.): "uninhabited territory" being territory in which fewer than twelve registered voters reside. (Gov. Code, § 35303.) Petitioner is not challenging the procedure by which the city council approved Resolution No. 6076, the annexation resolution, but seeks only to have the resolution submitted to a referendum vote. The city council, however, rejected the referendum petition on the basis of the city attorney's advice that Resolution No. 6076 was not a proper subject for referendum.

Article IV, section 1 of the Constitution of California provides "[t]he legislative power of this State is vested in the California Legislature which consists of the Senate and Assembly, but the people reserve to themselves the power of initiative and referendum." The power of initiative and referendum, thus, is a power reserved to the people, not a granted power. . . . Such legislative powers will be liberally construed to uphold the power wherever reasonable. . . . There are, however, necessary limitations upon the application of the initiative and referendum. As stated in *Newsom v. Board of Supervisors,* 205 Cal. 262, 271, 270 P. 676, 680, "[a] determination that direct legislation was not intended to apply to all actions of subordinate governmental bodies involving in part the exercise of the legislative function is not new in this state." In line with this policy the courts have held that the right to initiative and referendum does not apply where the action is administrative or executive, as distinguished from legislative (*Simpson v. Hite,* 36 Cal. 2d 125, 222 P.2d 225); where the act is special or local in its nature (*Hopping v. Council of City of Richmond,* 170 Cal. 605, 150 P. 977); if an essential governmental function would be seriously impaired (*Geiger v. Board of Supervisors,* 48 Cal. 2d 832, 313 P.2d 545); and when, in a matter of statewide concern, the Legislature has specifically delegated authority to the local governing board (*Mervynne v. Acker,* 189 Cal. App. 2d 558, 11 Cal. Rptr. 340). It is with this last circumstance that we are particularly concerned in the present case.

The Supreme Court in *People v. City of Long Beach,* 155 Cal. 604, 610, 102 P. 664, 667, stated: ". . . the annexation of territory to a city is not a municipal affair, within the meaning of section 6 [article 11 of the Constitution], but is a matter pertaining to the state at large and within its general powers and functions, and hence, that the general law upon that subject controls." . . .

In *Mervynne v. Acker, supra,* the court discussed the problem of whether the Legislature had delegated to the local governing board of the city as distinguished from the voters the power to establish parking meter zones. In *Mervynne,* the city council had enacted ordinances providing for parking meters. An initiative petition proposing an ordinance to repeal the parking meter ordinances was submitted to the city. The city refused to process the petition on the ground that the proposed ordinance to repeal was not a proper subject for initiative. Vehicle Code section 22508, under which the city council had enacted the ordinance, provides "[l]ocal authorities [which term is defined in Veh. Code, § 385 to mean the legislative body of a city or municipality] may by ordinance provide for the establishment of parking meter zones, ..." The court held that the Legislature by the careful wording of section 22508, literally and specifically, delegated the power over parking meter traffic regulation to the city council, stating at page 562 of 189 Cal. App. 2d at page 343 of 11 Cal. Rptr. that "[w]hen, in a matter of statewide concern, the state Legislature has specifically delegated a particular authority to the governing board, our courts have uniformly held that the initiative processes do not ordinarily apply."

In the matter of annexation the Legislature has specifically delegated the authority to the governing board of a city. As the governing board, in an annexation proceeding, exercises state power, not authority granted by the city charter, it is not unreasonable to preclude the people of a single city from exercising the power of initiative and referendum in a matter which is of statewide concern.

It is interesting to note that since the *Mervynne* decision, Vehicle Code section 22508 has been amended to provide "[a]ny ordinance adopted pursuant to this section establishing a parking meter zone or fixing rates of fees for such a zone shall be subject to local referendum processes in the same manner as if such ordinance dealt with a matter of purely local concern." If the Legislature had intended to preserve the right of referendum to the electors of the city in annexation matters, an amendment to the Annexation of the Uninhabited Territory Act of 1939, similar to that found in Vehicle Code section 22508, could have been adopted.

Petitioner maintains that Elections Code section 4050 and *Guerrieri v. City of Fontana,* 232 Cal. App. 2d 417, 42 Cal. Rptr. 781, citing Government Code section 36937, provide that ordinances take effect 30 days after final passage and that these sections imply a legislative intent that initiative and referendum process applies to all ordinances except those specifically excepted. There is no question that if all ordinances went into effect immediately the effectiveness of direct legislation would be greatly impaired. The function of these sections, however, is limited to defining the effective date of an ordinance and they do not in themselves provide authority for the application of the initiative.

For the reasons stated above I would deny the writ.

Comments: 1. The principal case indicates that state legislatures may place substantial limits on the exercise of the initiative and referendum power even though that power is constitutionally conferred. Given the breadth of the constitutional grant, how can the courts justify a state statute which limits that power?

The California decisions cited by the dissent in the principal case also illustrate some of the judicial limitations that have been placed on the initiative and referendum in that state. They appear to reflect limitations widely adopted in other states having the initiative and referendum process. The exception for acts of special and local concern was stated as dictum in the *Hopping* case and has since been confined primarily to public improvements that affect only a part of the municipality. Apparently the theory is that the improvement is not a matter of general concern to the entire electorate, but no attempt is made to explain why, if the matter is appropriate for legislative action at all, it is excluded from the initiative and referendum procedure.

In the *Geiger* case, the court held that no referendum could be held on a local sales and use tax. Although the opinion relied in part on a construction of the state constitutional provision authorizing referendums, the court also noted that the referendum could not be used to disrupt local government operations by interfering with their fiscal powers and policies. Is this exception too broadly stated? What about an initiative measure proposing that a municipality spend public funds to acquire a park site?

Note also that state statutes and municipal ordinances proposed for initiative must meet the usual requirements imposed on legislation, including the requirement that there be no improper delegation of power. *See Kugler v. Yocum,* 445 P.2d 303 (Cal. 1968), holding that a proposed ordinance providing that firemen's salaries in the city should be no less than the average of those in an adjoining larger city and in an adjoining county was not an unlawful delegation of power. The dissent held that the ordinance would limit the future exercise of legislative power by the city and so violated a "fundamental" principle of municipal law. *Compare Bagley v. City of Manhattan Beach,* 553 P.2d 1140 (Cal. 1976) (as city had no power to delegate the fixing of wages to an arbitration board whose decision would be binding, that power could not be conferred by initiative).

2. How to determine whether a matter is one of statewide concern that forecloses an initiative or referendum is not always clear. In *Friends of Mount Diablo v. County of Contra Costa,* 139 Cal. Rptr. 469 (Cal. App. 1977), the court held that an action by a county board of supervisors approving a substantial reorganization of special districts was a statewide matter not subject to referendum. *Norlund* was distinguished because it was a single annexation. "[T]he chaotic condition of heterogenous districts throughout the state was and is a matter of concern to the entire commonwealth."

For a case following *Norlund,* see *McKee v. City of Louisville,* 616 P.2d 969 (Colo. 1980). *Compare Gibbs v. City of Napa,* 130 Cal. Rptr. 382 (Cal. App. 1976). The court held that once a municipality creates a redevelopment agency, the agency "becomes a state agency when acting in redevelopment matters." Why? Is it the dependent special district character of the agency or the function that requires this conclusion?

In *In re Certain Petitions for a Binding Referendum,* 381 A.2d 1217 (N.J. App. Div. 1977), an initiative referendum was filed to repeal certain provisions of a local traffic ordinance. The court held that the initiative referendum was not available. It relied on state legislation to find a statewide policy on traffic management, and held that this policy indicated that the state transportation department and municipalities formed a "collaborative team to subserve not only purely local interests but those of contiguous areas as well .... State participation assures these broader functions." Does this holding mean that the initiative and referendum is foreclosed in all areas of statewide concern?

3. In some states, the state legislature may not delegate the referendum power to a majority of the voters unless authorized to do so by the constitution. *People ex rel. Thomson v. Barnett,* 176 N.E. 108 (Ill. 1931). For constitutional provisions conferring the power of direct legislation by way of initiative and referendum, see, e.g., Colo. Const. art. V, § 1; Mo. Const. art. 3, §§ 49-53; Ohio Const. art. II, §§ 1-1(g); Wash. Const. amend. 7, amending Art. II, § 1. Most of these provisions are in the form contained in the California constitution, quoted in the dissent in the principal case, and provide that the power is a power "reserved" to the people rather than a power granted to them. The constitution may also allow the state legislature to confer the power on municipalities. *See* 5 E. McQuillin, Municipal Corporations §§ 16.49-59 (3d ed. rev. 1981). The Ohio constitution, art. II, indicates the limits sometimes put on the exercise of the initiative and referendum power:

§ 1(e). The powers defined herein as the "initiative" and "referendum" shall not be used to pass a law authorizing any classification of property for the purposes of levying different rates of taxation thereon or of authorizing the levy of any single tax on land or land values or land sites at a higher rate or by a different rule than is or may be applied to improvements thereon or to personal property.

§ 1(f). The initiative and referendum powers are hereby reserved to the people of each municipality on all questions which such municipalities may now or hereafter be authorized by law to control by legislative action; such powers shall be exercised in the manner now or hereafter provided by law.

Constitutional initiative and referendum provisions also commonly provide the procedures to be used in exercising these powers. The exercise of the initiative and referendum power must be strictly within the constitutional provisions. *See City of Scottsdale v. Superior Court,* 439 P.2d 290 (Ariz. 1968), holding that the constitutional provision conferred no power on the city voluntarily to submit a zoning amendment to referendum.

4. Notice that the Ohio constitution explicitly adopts the limitation, adopted by way of interpretation in the principal case, that the initiative and referendum at the local level may only be employed for matters which municipalities are "authorized by law" to control. In addition, the power of initiative and referendum is often explicitly limited by statutory or constitutional provisions, e.g., Ohio Const. art. II, § 1 (d), to exclude certain types of legislation, such as emergency measures and appropriations for ordinary and common government expenditures. *See generally* Annot., 100 A.L.R.2d 314 (1965). The emer-

gency exception enables the legislature to respond immediately whenever the public health, safety or welfare is endangered without waiting for popular approval. The mere declaration of an emergency by the municipality may not, however, effectively exempt the ordinance from referendum; the status of the legislation as an emergency measure may be subject to judicial review. In *State ex rel. Gray v. Martin,* 189 P.2d 637 (Wash. 1948), the city authorized the acquisition of land for a municipal airport and air navigation station and characterized the project as "a public emergency." The court found no public emergency within the statutory exception and held the ordinance subject to referendum.

The appropriations exception is designed to prevent political interference with the funding of state and local government. In *State ex rel. Card v. Kaufman,* 517 S.W.2d 78 (Mo. 1974), a proposed ordinance which would have required firemen's salaries to be not less than those of a neighboring municipality was held to be within the appropriations exception and therefore not a proper subject for the initiative procedure. The constitutional provision prohibited the use of the initiative for the appropriation of money other than new revenues created and provided by the initiative proposal. Mo. Const. art. 3, § 51.

In *Lawrence v. Beermann,* 192 Neb. 507, 222 N.W.2d 809 (1974), state legislation which established and funded a system of increased state aid to public schools was held not to be within the appropriations exception, Neb. Const. art. III, § 3, and was therefore subject to referendum. One commentator has suggested that any future innovative funding measures which may be subject to referendum must be carefully drafted to fall within the now-narrowed appropriations exception. See 54 NEB. L. REV. 393 (1975).

5. For discussion of the initiative and referendum see Note, *Constitutional Restraints on Initiative and Referendum,* 32 VAND. L. REV. 1143 (1979); Comment, *Limitations on Initiative and Referendum,* 3 STAN. L. REV. 497 (1951).

As the dissenting opinion briefly indicated in the principal case, another limitation on the initiative and referendum is its unavailability when the action proposed is deemed to be administrative rather than legislative, a limitation implied from the fact that the power which is to be exercised is legislative. The following case illustrates the problem in a different but equally controversial context.

RAUH v. CITY OF HUTCHINSON

Supreme Court of Kansas
223 Kan. 514, 575 P.2d 517 (1978)

HOLMES, JUSTICE:

This action was filed by plaintiff-appellant, Charles E. Rauh, to restrain the Hutchinson, Kansas, City Commission from taking action on two ordinances providing for the issuance of industrial revenue bonds to finance Cargill, Inc. in the improvement and expansion of the former Barton Salt Plant. In addition to the restraining order, plaintiff prayed for a determination whether the proposed ordinances were legislative or administrative in character and therefore within the purview of the initiative and referendum statute, K.S.A. 12-3013.

While the factual situation is relatively simple, the pleadings, procedural steps taken to date, record, arguments and contentions of the parties require a rather detailed resume.

Originally, Cargill, Inc. was not a party to this action but, following the decision of the district court, was allowed to intervene for purposes of appeal. Sometime between 1971 and October, 1974, Cargill purchased the salt plant, which apparently was old and in need of extensive repairs and remodeling. In October,

1974, Cargill approached the city commission about issuing industrial revenue bonds to finance major plant improvements and expansion. On October 29, 1974, the commission adopted resolution # 1637 in which it found that issuance of five million dollars of industrial revenue bonds would be in furtherance of the statutory purposes set forth in K.S.A. 12-1740 to 12-1749, inclusive, and would promote the welfare of the community. This resolution was not published as required under K.S.A. 12-3007 for an ordinance. No further action was taken by Cargill or the city to implement the issuance of the bonds until March, 1976, when Cargill announced plans to ask the city commission to approve the application for bonds. It appears to be undisputed that the delay by Cargill in requesting the city to proceed was due to an unfavorable bond market between the fall of 1974 and late winter, 1976. Plaintiff appeared at the next city commission meeting on March 30, 1976, protesting the use of industrial revenue bonds for Cargill. On April 13, 1976, plaintiff again appeared before the commission to advise that petitions, under the initiative and referendum statute (K.S.A. 12-3013), seeking the enactment of an ordinance declaring that no bonds be issued under resolution # 1637, were being circulated to the electors of the city and would be filed with the city clerk. At the same meeting the city attorney advised the commission that inasmuch as the proposed ordinances to implement the issuance of bonds were administrative, the petitions were also administrative in nature and the ordinance proposed by the petitions would not be subject to the initiative and referendum statutes.

Cargill prepared two ordinances, # 6519 and # 6520, which were placed on first reading by the commission on May 25, 1976. These ordinances were designed to implement the issuance of the $5,000,000.00 in bonds as originally contemplated in the resolution of 1974. Following the first reading of the ordinances plaintiff filed an action in the district court and obtained a temporary restraining order preventing the city commission from acting further on the proposed ordinances. The matter was heard on the merits on June 8, 1976, at which time the court found in favor of the defendants. The court specifically found that the Cargill ordinances presented to the commission were administrative and not legislative and plaintiff's requested ordinance was not subject to K.S.A. 12-3013. Plaintiff failed to post the required bond to keep the restraining order in effect pending appeal and the commission proceeded with the issuance of the bonds. Plaintiff has taken this appeal from the orders and findings of the trial court.

Plaintiff raises a number of issues on appeal and the defendants and intervenor raise various defenses. The basic question before this court, however, is whether the action of the city commission in adopting ordinances # 6519 and # 6520 was legislative, which would submit the ordinance requested by petitioner to an election under K.S.A. 12-3013, or was it administrative, which, by the express terms of the statute, would exclude the requested ordinance from election.

The use of industrial revenue bonds by municipalities and other governmental bodies has been a relatively recent development, which has become increasingly popular since the early 1950s. Revenue bonds, as such, have long been utilized to promote the construction or expansion of public utilities, or other similar ventures, where the facility is publicly owned through the governmental entity and the primary purpose is one of public use and necessity. The use of revenue bonds for the purposes of furthering private enterprise is another matter.

The possibility that some procedure similar to industrial revenue bonds might someday be used to promote private enterprise in Kansas was foreseen over a century ago when, in 1874, Justice Miller, speaking for the United States Supreme Court, stated:

> If these municipal corporations, which are in fact subdivisions of the State, and which for many reasons are vested with quasi legislative powers, have a fund or other property out of which they can pay the debts which they contract, without resort to taxation, it may be within the power of the Legislature of the State to authorize them to use it in aid of projects strictly private or personal, but which would in a secondary manner contribute to the public goods; . . . *Savings and Loan Association v. Topeka,* 87 U.S. 455, 460, 20 Wall. 655, 659.

The distinguishing feature of all revenue bonds, whether for a municipally owned public purpose or for private enterprise, is that the bonds ordinarily are not a general financial obligation of the governmental body and its taxpayers, but are payable from the income or revenue generated by the particular facility. In Kansas, by statute, industrial revenue bonds and the interest thereon can never be paid as a general obligation of the city nor may they be payable in any manner by taxation (K.S.A. 12-1743).

The events speculated upon by Justice Miller in 1874 came to pass in 1961 when the Kansas Legislature, recognizing the potential of the use of industrial revenue bonds, passed a comprehensive act authorizing their use by cities. This act was in addition to existing revenue bond statutes. The provisions of the act are found in K.S.A. 12-1740 to 12-1749, inclusive, and amendments. The purpose of the act, as set forth in K.S.A. 12-1740, is:

> Purpose of 12-1740 to 12-1749. It is hereby declared that the purpose of this act shall be to promote, stimulate and develop the general economic welfare and prosperity of the state of Kansas through the promotion and advancement of physical and mental health, industrial, commercial, agricultural, natural resources and of recreational development in the state; to encourage and assist in the location of new business and industry in this state and the expansion of existing business and health development; and to promote the economic stability of the state by providing greater employment opportunities, diversification of industry and improved physical and mental health, thus promoting the general welfare of the citizens of this state by authorizing all cities of the state to issue revenue bonds, the proceeds of which shall be used only to purchase or construct, maintain and equip buildings and acquire sites therefor and to enlarge or remodel buildings and equip the same, for agricultural, commercial, hospital, industrial and manufacturing facilities and to enter into leases or lease-purchase agreements with any person, firm or corporation for said facilities.

K.S.A. 1977 Supp. 12-1741 provides that any city shall have power to issue revenue bonds for the purposes indicated in 12-1740 providing the governing body declares that the facility would promote the welfare of the city and further provides certain restrictions as to location of the proposed facilities. It also provides that the city shall have the power to enter into leases and lease-purchase agreements for the facilities. K.S.A. 12-1742 sets forth details concerning such leases and lease-purchase agreements and for the disposition of any monies received by the city in lieu of taxes.

K.S.A. 12-1743 provides:

> Nothing in this act shall be so construed as to authorize or permit any city to make any contract or to incur any obligation of any kind or nature except such as shall be payable solely out of the rentals from such facilities. *Such cities may issue bonds payable solely and only from the revenues derived from such*

facilities. Such bonds may be issued in such amounts as may be necessary to provide sufficient funds to pay all the costs of purchase or construction of such facility, including site, engineering and other expenses, together with interest.

Bonds issued under the provisions of this act are declared to be negotiable instruments, shall be executed by the mayor and clerk of the city, and shall be sealed with the corporate seal of the city. *The principal and interest of said bonds shall be payable solely and only from the special fund herein provided for such payments, and said bonds shall not in any respect be a general obligation of such city, nor shall they be payable in any manner by taxation.* All details pertaining to the issuance of such bonds and the terms and conditions thereof shall be determined by ordinance of the city. (Emphasis added)

K.S.A. 12-1744 provides the city may pledge the facility and the net earnings therefrom to the payment of the bonds and provides for the establishment of a sinking fund. K.S.A. 1977 Supp. 12-1744a through d provide the procedure for issuance of the bonds, filing of notices and details with the Kansas securities commissioner, findings to be made by the commissioner, provisions for filing a certificate evidencing the issuance of the bonds and sanctions against the members of the governing body of the city in the event of failure to comply with the notice and filing requirements. K.S.A. 12-1745 sets certain limitations on the amount of bonds which may be issued. K.S.A. 12-1746 exempts the bonds and all income or interest therefrom from all state taxes except inheritance taxes. K.S.A. 12-1747 defines the term revenue bonds, provides again that they shall not be general obligations of the city, shall not contain the recitals set forth in K.S.A. 10-112 (under the general bond law) and sets forth specific recitals which shall be included. K.S.A. 12-1748 provides for the construction of the terms of the act. K.S.A. 12-1749 makes the act supplemental and cumulative to other existing laws. K.S.A. 1977 Supp. 12-1749a provides for refunding of any bonds issued under the act.

Following enactment of the original act in 1961, its constitutionality was challenged and upheld by this court in *State, ex rel. v. City of Pittsburg,* 188 Kan. 612, 364 P.2d 71 (1961). Amendments which have been made to the act since 1961 are such that the discussion in *State, ex rel. v. City of Pittsburg,* supra, remains pertinent and for those interested in a detailed analysis of the constitutional aspects of the act, we would refer them to that opinion.

The initiative and referendum statute, K.S.A. 12-3013, provides a procedure whereby a city's electors may place legislative action of the city governing body before a vote of the people. The statute specifically exempts administrative ordinances from its operation.

With the foregoing rather verbose statement of the facts and background in this case, we turn to the issue at hand.

Were the original Cargill ordinances # 6519 and # 6520 legislative or administrative?

This court has recently set forth certain guidelines for determining whether an action is legislative or administrative in character in *City of Lawrence v. McArdle,* 214 Kan. 862, 522 P.2d 420 (1974). The first four paragraphs of the syllabus state:

1. The operation of the initiative and referendum statute is to be confined with a considerable degree of strictness to measures which are quite clearly and fully legislative and not principally executive or administrative.

2. One crucial test for determining that an ordinance is administrative or legislative is whether the ordinance is one making a new law or one executing a law already in existence. Permanency and generality of application are two additional key features of a legislative ordinance.

3. Acts constituting a declaration of public purpose and making provisions for ways and means of its accomplishment may be generally classified as calling for the exercise of legislative power. Acts dealing with only a small segment of an overall policy question are generally of an administrative character.

4. Decisions which require specialized training and experience in municipal government and intimate knowledge of the fiscal and other affairs of a city in order to make a rational choice may properly be characterized as administrative, even though they may also be said to involve the establishment of policy.

The distinction between legislative and administrative enactments is treated at some length in 5 *McQuillin, Mun. Corp. (3rd Ed.)* § 16.55, pp. 211-214:

§ 16.55 — Legislative or administrative measures. The power of initiative or referendum usually is restricted to legislative ordinances, resolutions, or measures, and is not extended to executive or administrative action, although a city charter may dispense with this distinction. It has been said, however, that *if the subject is one of statewide concern in which the legislature has delegated decision-making power, not to the local electors, but to the local council or board as the state's designated agent for local implementation of state policy, the action receives an "administrative" characterization, hence is outside the scope of the initiative and referendum.*

Actions relating to subjects of a permanent and general character are usually regarded as legislative, and those providing for subjects of a temporary and special character are regarded as administrative. In this connection an ordinance which shows an intent to form a permanent rule of government until repealed is one of permanent operation. Obviously, details which are essentially of a fluctuating sort, due to economic or other conditions, cannot be set up in and by an ordinance to be submitted to the vote of the people.

The test of what is a legislative and what is an administrative proposition, with respect to the initiative or referendum, has further been said to be whether the proposition is one to make new law or to execute law already in existence. *The power to be exercised* is legislative in its nature if it prescribes a new policy or plan; whereas, it *is administrative in its nature if it merely pursues a plan already adopted by the legislative body itself, or some power superior to it.* Similarly, an act or resolution constituting a declaration of public purpose and making provision for ways and means of its accomplishment is generally legislative as distinguished from an act or resolution which merely carries out the policy or purpose already declared by the legislative body. (Emphasis added)

The industrial revenue bond act is comprehensive and complete and sets forth the legislative policy and purposes in K.S.A. 12-1740. The balance of the act specifies the powers, restrictions and procedure to be utilized by the governing body of the city in exercising its administrative functions to carry out that policy. The act specifies no particular form in which the city shall make the necessary declaration that the proposed facility would promote the welfare of the city. The initial resolution and the subsequent ordinances enacted by the City of Hutchinson would appear to satisfy the statutory requirements to put the administrative procedure contemplated by the statutes into operation.

K.S.A. 12-1743, which provides in part:

All details pertaining to the issuance of such bonds and the terms and conditions thereof shall be determined by ordinance of the city

grants the governing body of the city broad discretionary powers in the exercise of its administrative functions.

In *State, ex rel. v. Urban Renewal Agency of Kansas City,* 179 Kan. 435, 296 P.2d 656, there was a constitutional attack upon the urban renewal act which authorized cities to set up and carry out urban renewal projects. While not directly in point, one argument raised against the statute was that it constituted an unlawful delegation of legislative power. We stated at page 440, 296 P.2d at 661:

> We think it clear that while the legislature cannot delegate its constitutional power to make a law, it can make a law which delegates the power to determine some fact or state of things upon which such law shall become operative. In other words, the legislature may enact general provisions but leave to those who are to act certain discretion in "filling in the details," so to speak, provided, of course, it fixes reasonable and definite standards which govern the exercise of such authority.

In the case at bar the legislature has enacted the broad general provisions and policy and delegated to the city the administrative function of "filling in the details" under reasonable and definite standards as contained in the act itself.

If the legislature had intended that industrial revenue bonds under K.S.A. 12-1740, *et seq.,* be subject to initiative and referendum it could have included such provisions in the act. Voluminous legislation has done so. One has only to make a cursory examination of the various bond statutes now in existence to find that in many, if not most, instances legislation authorizing bonds either requires an election in the first instance or provides for one upon the filing of protest petitions. (See, for example, Municipal Airfields, K.S.A. 3-113, *et seq.;* County Airports, K.S.A. 3-301, *et seq.;* Industrial Development Bonds, K.S.A. 12-3801, *et seq.;* Public Utilities, K.S.A. 12-801, *et seq.;* General Improvements, K.S.A. 12-6a15; Libraries, K.S.A. 12-1221; Swimming Pools and Golf Courses, K.S.A. 13-13,101; ad infinitum.)

One may question the reasoning behind the legislature's action in not providing such procedures under K.S.A. 12-1740, *et seq.* However, a close examination of the statutes may provide an answer. The statutes themselves contain strong and binding safeguards for the public. *The obligations for payment of the bonds and interest thereon shall not in any respect be payable as a general obligation of the city nor shall they be payable in any manner from taxation. The bonds are payable solely and only from the revenues derived from the facilities financed.* (K.S.A. 12-1743)

42 Am.Jur.2d, Initiative and Referendum, Sec. 12, states:

> Generally, an enactment originating a permanent law or laying down a rule of conduct or course of policy for the guidance of citizens or their officers or agents is purely legislative in character and referable, while an enactment which simply puts into execution previously declared policies or previously enacted laws is administrative or executive in character and not referable. *If an act carries out an existing policy of a legislative body, it is administrative whether the policy came into existence in an enactment of the body itself, in the organic law creating the body, or in an enactment of a superior legislative body.* (Emphasis added)

An examination of the cases and legal authorities will disclose that the determination of whether a municipality has acted in its legislative or administrative capacity is indeed difficult and by no means consistent. Each case must be determined on its particular facts and even then there is no unanimity of opinion. Action based on one set of facts will be considered legislative in one jurisdiction while the same or similar action may be considered administrative in a different jurisdiction.

Considering the broad general policy and the comprehensive nature of the industrial revenue bond act and applying the criteria set forth in *City of Lawrence v. McArdle,* supra, we find that the acts of the governing body of the City of Hutchinson in the adoption of ordinances # 6519 and # 6520 were administrative in character and not subject to contest by election under K.S.A. 12-3013.

In view of the conclusion reached it is not necessary to consider the other points and contentions raised by the parties.

The judgment is affirmed.

Comments: 1. The rule that an initiative or referendum may be had only on legislative, as distinguished from administrative, acts is well established. In the *Rauh* case, a delegation of power to the municipality was relied on by the court to hold that the power was administrative. How power is delegated also is relevant to whether a particular matter is of statewide rather than local concern, as the *Norlund* case, *supra,* illustrates. Do these two limitations overlap, or does the legislative-administrative distinction require a different inquiry? Since municipalities always exercise delegated power, would all of their actions in the exercise of these powers be administrative? What about home rule municipalities?

With the principal case compare *Reagan v. City of Sausalito,* 26 Cal. Rptr. 775 (Cal. App. 1962), holding that a city's resolution to acquire a park was a legislative act subject to referendum. The court held that a statutory delegation of a discretionary power to acquire the land did not make the referendum procedure inapplicable.

2. The legislative-administrative distinction is about as elusive as any of the other two-way classifications that typify local government law, such as the governmental-proprietary distinction. Many courts applying the legislative-administrative distinction in initiative and referendum cases concentrate on the nature of the policy decision rather than the nature of the statutory delegation. The following cases are illustrative. When reviewing these cases, consider whether the criteria for legislative as compared with administrative decisions, as established in the *Rauh* case, are of any assistance.

Concerned Citizens v. Pantalone, 444 A.2d 200 (N.J. App. Div. 1982). An initiative ordinance was proposed to repeal a borough ordinance imposing a beach fee. The court held that an initiative was proper. "[W]e have a local question of a basic policy nature. The issue is long-term in effect. It cannot be fairly deemed highly technical in nature." *Id.* at 205.

City of Aurora v. Zwerdlinger, 571 P.2d 1074 (Colo. 1977). The court held that an increase in utility rates was an administrative action not subject to referendum. It stated that "acts that are necessary to carry out existing legislative policies and purposes or which are properly characterized as executive are administrative." It then held that financial decisions required in the management and maintenance of a utility were administrative. Why is a beach fee distinguishable? *See also Dieruf v. City of Bozeman,* 568 P.2d 127 (Mont. 1977) (ordinance assessing benefits for off-street parking facility is administrative).

Moore v. School Committee, 378 N.E.2d 47 (Mass. 1978). The court held that a decision to close a school was legislative because it was a "policy determination." "Before voting to close and consolidate, the school committee weighed the costs of the closing on the pupils and community against the economic savings and other gains to be realized." *Id.* at 50. Isn't a similar cost-benefit calculus struck for every governmental decision?

State ex rel. Becker v. Common Council, 305 N.W.2d 178 (Wis. App. 1981). Voters proposed as an initiative a "no confidence" resolution in the chief of police. Again quoting McQuillin, see the *Rauh* case, the court held that the resolution covered an administrative matter. The local Board of Fire and Police Commissioners had exclusive authority over the removal of personnel, and the initiative was an attempt to "usurp the administrative function of the Board."

3. Courts sometimes hold that an initiative or referendum conflicts with required statutory procedures and obligations. In *Atlantic City Housing Action Coalition v. Deane*, 437 A.2d 918 (N.J.L. 1981), an initiative was filed to require the city to begin the urban redevelopment process. The court held that an initiative was not available because it conflicted with the urban redevelopment statute. The statute required the municipality to first determine that an area was blighted. It must then adopt a redevelopment plan, having first obtained the recommendations of its planning board on land use, transportation and other planning problems. The initiative would bypass this statutory procedure. "[T]he legislature would [not] intend the possibility of fragmentation or disruption of such a comprehensive redevelopment process . . . by isolated and uncoordinated actions of the local electorate via the initiative process." *Id.* at 922. *Accord City of Hitchcock v. Longmire*, 572 S.W.2d 122 (Tex. Civ. App. 1978) (annexation referendum).

Was it important in the *Atlantic City* case that the right to an initiative was conferred by statute, and in the *Hitchcock* case that the right to referendum was conferred by charter? *See Associated Homebuilders v. City of Livermore*, 557 P.2d 473 (Cal. 1976) (constitutional grant of initiative overrides statutory zoning procedures).

4. What if a referendum or initiative election is held, and the initiative or referendum passes? Is judicial review possible? Cases have been brought in federal court challenging referenda that blocked lower income housing projects, but they have not been successful. *See Ranjel v. City of Lansing*, 417 F.2d 321 (6th Cir. 1969), *cert. denied*, 397 U.S. 980, *petition for rehearing denied*, 397 U.S. 1059 (1970).

In *Arnel Development Co. v. City of Costa Mesa*, 620 P.2d 565 (Cal. 1980), an initiative was filed to repeal a rezoning ordinance for moderate income housing. The supreme court held that a rezoning was a legislative act and that an initiative was proper. The initiative passed and an action was brought to invalidate it. *Arnel Development Co. v. City of Costa Mesa*, 178 Cal. Rptr. 723 (Cal. App. 1981).

The court of appeal held the initiative invalid. It held that a zoning ordinance adopted by initiative was subject to the same grounds for invalidation as an ordinance adopted by a municipality. No change in conditions or circumstances justified the initiative repealer, which was adopted for the "sole and specific purpose" of blocking the housing development. Neither did the initiative accommodate a regional interest in the provision of moderate-income housing which the California Supreme Court had previously recognized.

5. In the absence of special limiting constitutional provisions, either the legislative body or the people through the initiative and referendum process can amend or repeal legislation enacted by the other. See the extensive discussion in Annot., 33 A.L.R.2d 1118 (1965). However, in order to restrict the power of the legislative body to nullify any legislation enacted by the people through the power of initiative or referendum, constitutional, statutory or charter provisions may require that such legislation may be repealed or amended only by a vote of the electorate. *See, e.g., State ex rel. Pike v. Bellingham*, 48 P.2d 602 (Wash. 1935); *cf. Davis v. City of Seattle*, 355 P.2d 354 (Wash. 1960); Trautman, *Initiative and Referendum in Washington: A Survey*, 49 WASH. L. REV. 55 (1973). The restriction on subsequent legislative action may be limited to a specific time period after enactment of an ordinance by initiative or referendum. *See, e.g., Reagan v. City of Sausalito, supra* (statutory one-year prohibition). Limitations on the repeal or amendment of ordinances enacted by initiative or referendum, while serving the general purpose of safeguarding the decision of the people from being overruled by the legislative body, also impose high political and social costs by shielding such legislation from the normal legislative process. *See* Note, *The California Initiative Process: A Suggestion for Reform*, 48 S. CAL. L. REV. 922, 942 (1975).

A NOTE ON THE CONSTITUTIONALITY OF THE REFERENDUM IN THE FEDERAL COURTS

An initiative or referendum procedure held valid in state court may still be subject to challenge in federal court as a violation of the federal Constitution. Chapter 10 considered objections that referendum procedures violated voting rights protected by the federal Constitution. The U.S. Supreme Court also has considered other constitutional objections to state and local initiative and referendum procedures. Some of these objections raised claims of racial discrimination:

Hunter v. Erickson, 393 U.S. 385 (1969). The city of Akron, Ohio, enacted a fair housing ordinance that prohibited discrimination in the sale or rental of housing. After plaintiff filed a complaint under the ordinance the city charter was amended to require a referendum on any ordinance of this type. The city also had a long-standing referendum procedure under which a referendum could be had on almost any city ordinance following the filing of a petition by ten per cent of the electors.

The charter provision mandating a referendum on fair housing ordinances was held unconstitutional, as it was "an explicitly racial classification treating racial housing matters differently from other racial and housing matters." *Id.* at 389. The Court noted that while the law applied on its face to both majority and minority groups its "impact" fell on the minority. *Id.* at 391. Because the mandatory referendum was based on a racial classification, it bore a heavier burden of justification than other classifications. It was not justified by "insisting that a State may distribute legislative power as it desires and that the people may retain for themselves the power over certain subjects . . . [as there is a violation of] the Fourteenth Amendment." *Id.* at 392.

James v. Valtierra, 402 U.S. 137 (1971). The decision was written by Justice Black, who had dissented in *Hunter.* This case considered the validity of an amendment to the California state constitution that mandated a referendum on all local public housing projects. These projects are built by local agencies and governments and receive federal subsidies. The Court upheld the California constitutional amendment in a brief opinion distinguishing *Hunter* because California procedure "requires referendum approval for any low-rent public housing project, not only for projects which will be occupied by a racial minority." There was no support in the record for "any claim that a law seemingly neutral on its face is in fact aimed at a racial minority." *Id.* at 141.

Justice Black chose not to examine the impact of the amendment, which arguably fell disproportionately on minority groups such as blacks who make up a large number of the tenants in public housing projects. He seemed to reject this line of analysis by commenting that "a lawmaking procedure that 'disadvantages' a particular group does not always deny equal protection." *Id.* at 142. Nor would the Court analyze governmental structures to determine whether they disadvantaged "any of the shifting and diverse groups that make up the American people." *Id.* The dissent would have invalidated the California mandatory referendum as a suspect classification based on poverty status. The *Valtierra* case thus represents a refusal by the Supreme Court, acknowledged or not, to extend to the referendum issue its holdings that, in other areas of concern, a classification based on poverty is constitutionally suspect. *See, e.g., Harper v. Virginia Board of Elections,* 383 U.S. 663 (1966) (state and local governments may not discriminate against the poor in exercise of voting rights by requiring them to pay a poll tax).

Justice Black also noted that California had extensively provided for mandatory referenda on a variety of subjects. He found a justification for mandating the referendum in this case because localities in which public housing projects are located might be subject to large expenditures for public services needed by these projects. In a footnote, Black noted that public housing projects were exempt by federal law from local property taxation and that in-lieu payments required as a substitute for local taxation were ordinarily less than the taxes that otherwise would have been levied.

City of Eastlake v. Forest City Enterprises, 426 U.S. 668 (1976). The city charter of Eastlake was amended to require that all zoning amendments be submitted to the voters in a referendum and approved by fifty-five percent of those voting. The Court found no violation of due process. There was no improper delegation of legislative power as a referendum is not such a delegation. "In establishing legislative bodies, the people can reserve to themselves the power to deal directly with matters which might otherwise be assigned to the legislature." *Id.* at 672. There was no problem of delegation without standards, as this doctrine only applies to the delegation of power by legislative bodies to regulatory agencies. Property owners whose zoning changes are rejected by the electorate may always bring an action in state court challenging the constitutionality of the zoning restriction. Support for the decision was found in *Valtierra,* in which Justice Black characterized the referendum procedure as an example of "devotion to democracy." 402 U.S. at 141. The Court also noted that the state court had characterized the zoning amendment as legislative. *Id.* at 673.

Washington v. Seattle School District No. 1, 102 S. Ct. 3187 (1982). The district had adopted a school desegregation plan that included mandatory busing. State voters then adopted a statute by initiative that prohibited school boards from requiring any student to attend a school which was not geographically nearest or next to his place of residence. The statute contained a number of exceptions that allowed school boards to assign students away from their neighborhood school for virtually all purposes except racial desegregation.

The Court held the initiative unconstitutional. Applying *Hunter,* it held that "the political majority may generally restructure the political process to place obstacles in the path of everyone seeking to secure the benefits of governmental action. But a different analysis is required when the State allocates governmental power non-neutrally, by explicitly using the racial nature of a decision to determine the decisionmaking process." *Id.* at 3195. Although the initiative was facially neutral, the Court was convinced that it "was effectively drawn for racial purposes," and was "condemned" by *Hunter.* "The initiative removes the authority to address a racial problem — and only a racial problem — from the existing decisionmaking body, in such a way as to burden minority interest." *Id.* at 3197.

Compare *Crawford v. Board of Education,* 102 S. Ct. 3211 (1982), decided the same day. The Court upheld an amendment to the California constitution adopted by referendum that limited court-ordered busing for school desegregation purposes to cases in which a federal court would order busing to remedy a fourteenth amendment violation.

After *Eastlake,* a racial discrimination objection to an initiative or referendum based on the fourteenth amendment appears most likely to succeed. If the initiative or referendum is "facially neutral" because it does not discriminate on its face, the question is whether proof of racial discrimination turns on proof of "disparate" racial impact or racial motivation. After *Hunter* and *Valtierra* and before *Seattle,* the Supreme Court held in *Washington v. Davis,* 426 U.S. 229 (1976), that "disparate impact" was not enough to prove a fourteenth amendment racial discrimination claim and that proof of racial motivation was necessary when legislation was facially neutral. Addressing this problem in *Seattle*, the Court said:

> [W]hen the political process or the decisionmaking process used to *address* racially conscious legislation — and only such legislation — is singled out for peculiar and disadvantageous treatment, the governmental action plainly "rests on 'distinctions based on race.'" (Emphasis in original.)

Id. at 3203.

The Court also distinguished *Hunter* from *Washington v. Davis*. "[T]he charter amendment at issue in *Hunter* dealt in explicitly racial terms with legislation designed to benefit minorities 'as minorities,' not legislation intended to benefit some larger group of underprivileged citizens among whom minorities were disproprotionately represented." Does the holding in *Seattle* effectively insulate the referendum procedure in *Eastlake* from a racial discrimination objection? The referendum procedure in *Valtierra*? If so, what is needed to make the *Hunter* rule applicable?

Index

A

AD VALOREM PROPERTY TAX.
Administration, p. 213.
Assessments.
  Differential assessments and classifications, p. 224.
  Fractional assessments, p. 216.
  Special assessments and special benefit taxation, p. 238.
Central city economics, p. 215.
Constitutional limitations.
  Note on the constitutionality of differential property tax assessment, p. 228.
Expenditure and tax limitations, p. 311.
Fractional assessments, p. 216.
Generally, p. 211.
Increment financing, p. 232.
Limitations upon, p. 311.
Relief provisions, p. 339.
Special assessments and special benefit taxation, p. 238.
Trends in property tax collections, p. 213.
Urban development and land use, p. 214.

AIR POLLUTION.
Clean air act, p. 535.

ANNEXATION.
Discrimination.
  Racial discrimination, p. 63.
Generally, p. 52.
Judicial review, p. 41.
Local government.
  Generally, p. 41.
  Standards, p. 55.
Racial discrimination, p. 63.

ANTITRUST LAW.
Federal antitrust statutes.
  Governmental liability, p. 484.

APPEALS.
Judicial review.
  Local government incorporations, p. 41.

APPORTIONMENT.
Courts.
  One person-one vote principle in legislative apportionment, p. 635.
  Powers of courts, p. 632.
Reapportionment.
  Power of courts, p. 632.

APPROPRIATIONS.
Budgeting process, p. 361.
Local government, p. 361.
State governments, p. 361.

ASSESSMENTS.
Ad valorem property tax.
  Differential assessments and classifications, p. 224.
  Fractional assessments, p. 216.
  Special assessments and special benefit taxation, p. 238.
Differential assessments and classifications, p. 224.
Fractional assessments, p. 216.
Special assessments and special benefit taxation, p. 238.

B

BLOCK GRANTS.
Federal grants-in-aid.
  See FEDERAL GRANTS-IN-AID.

BOND ISSUES.
Borrowing generally, p. 273.
Commercial development bond financing, p. 283.
Debt limitations, p. 294.
General obligations bond, p. 274.
Industrial bond financing, p. 283.
Industrial development bonds, p. 289.
  Small issue bonds, p. 290.
Pollution facilities bond financing, p. 283.
Revenue bonds, p. 278.
Tax equity and fiscal responsibility act of 1982, p. 288.
Tax exempt obligations, p. 288.
Types of issues, p. 273.

BOUNDARY COMMISSIONS.
Local government.
Creation, p. 71.

BUDGETING PROCESS.
Appropriations, p. 361.
Capital improvements, p. 351.
Operations, p. 349.
Performance budgeting, p. 349.
Types of budget innovations, p. 349.
Zero-base budgeting, p. 350.

C

CAPITAL IMPROVEMENTS.
Local government, p. 351.
State government, p. 351.

CITIES.
Central city economics, p. 215.
Local government.
See LOCAL GOVERNMENT.

CITIZEN CONTROL OF GOVERNMENTAL ACTION.
Generally, p. 767.

CLEAN AIR ACT, p. 535.

COLLECTIVE BARGAINING.
Public officers and employees, p. 406.
Scope, p. 407.

COMMERCE CLAUSE.
Constitutional limitations, p. 210.

COMMISSIONS.
Boundary commissions.
Creation by local governments, p. 71.

CONDEMNATION.
Interlocal conflicts, p. 161.
Inverse condemnation, p. 455.

CONFLICTS OF INTEREST.
Public officers and employees, p. 397.

CONSOLIDATION.
Local government, p. 173.

CONSTITUTIONAL LIMITATIONS.
Ad valorem property tax.
Note on the constitutionality of differential property tax assessment, p. 228.
Commerce clause, p. 210.
Courts.
Education.
State constitutional challenges, p. 706.

CONSTITUTIONAL LIMITATIONS —Cont'd
Due process.
Fiscal problems, p. 193.
Equal protection.
Fiscal problems, p. 193.
Federal system.
Tenth amendment problems, p. 495.
Fiscal problems, p. 190.
Due process, p. 193.
Equal protection, p. 193.
Governmental liability.
The eleventh amendment, p. 463.
Home rule issue, p. 101.
Initiative, p. 822.
Legislative power.
Grant versus limitation, p. 16.
Local authority, p. 8.
Local government.
Status, p. 29.
Transfer of function, p. 172.
State authority, p. 8.
Status of local government, p. 29.
Taxation, p. 193.
Public purpose, p. 201.

COUNTIES.
See LOCAL GOVERNMENT.

COURTS.
Apportionment.
One person-one vote principle in legislative apportionment, p. 635.
Powers of courts, p. 632.
Reapportionment, p. 632.
Citizen control of governmental action, p. 767.
Constitutional limitations.
Education.
State constitutional challenges, p. 706.
Education.
Cost-quality issue and equality of educational opportunity, p. 724.
Fundamental interests, p. 686.
Generally, p. 680.
Remedial alternatives, p. 689.
Injunctions.
Use against chief executive, p. 789.
Judicial review, p. 41.
Licensing and regulation.
Ordinary state and local government issues, p. 617.
Local government.
Licensing and regulation, p. 617.
Mandamus, p. 767.

COURTS—Cont'd
  Prohibition.
    Use against chief executive, p. 776.
  Quo warranto.
    Use against chief executive, p. 781.
  Reapportionment.
    Powers of courts, p. 632.
  School finance, p. 670.
  Schools.
    Cost-quality issue and equality of educational opportunity, p. 724.
    Education as a fundamental interest, p. 686.
    Remedial alternatives, p. 689.
  Standing.
    A note on the standing of citizens and citizen organizations, p. 805.
  State governments.
    Licensing and regulation, p. 617.
  Taxpayer standing, p. 796.
  Voting rights.
    Local elections, p. 652.
    Local governments.
      Application of one person-one vote to local governments, p. 638.
    Powers of courts, p. 632.
  Wealth as a suspect classification, p. 685.

D

DEBT FINANCING.
  See BOND ISSUES.

DELEGATION, DOCTRINE OF.
  State legislatures, p. 598.

DILLON'S RULE, p. 83.

DISCRIMINATION.
  Annexation.
    Racial discrimination, p. 63.
  Education.
    Cost-quality issue and equality of educational opportunity, p. 724.
  Equal protection, pp. 193, 318.
  Governmental liability.
    Civil rights cases.
      Suing government and governmental officials under the civil rights act, p. 464.
  Public officers and employees.
    Federal employment discrimination legislation, p. 382.
  Voting rights act.
    Annexation, p. 63.

DISTRICTS.
  Special districts.
    Development, p. 65.
    Nature and functions, p. 65.
    Organization, p. 66.

DOCTRINE OF DELEGATION.
  State legislatures, p. 598.

DUE PROCESS.
  Fiscal problems, p. 193.
  State legislatures.
    Limitation on powers, p. 16.
  Taxation, p. 193.

E

EDUCATION.
  Courts.
    Cost-quality issue and equality of educational opportunity, p. 724.
    Fundamental interests, p. 686.
    Generally, p. 680.
    Remedial alternatives, p. 689.
  Discrimination.
    Cost-quality issue and equality of educational opportunity, p. 724.
  School finance issues, p. 670.

ELEVENTH AMENDMENT.
  Governmental liability, p. 463.

EMINENT DOMAIN.
  Local government.
    Condemnation of the property of one governmental unit by another, p. 161.
  Inverse condemnation, p. 455.

EMPLOYEES.
  See PUBLIC OFFICERS AND EMPLOYEES.

EQUAL PROTECTION.
  Discrimination.
    See DISCRIMINATION.
  Fiscal problems, p. 193.
  Taxation, p. 193.
    Limitations upon taxation, p. 318.

EXPENDITURES.
  Budgeting process.
    See BUDGETING PROCESS.
  State and local finances.
    Generally, p. 347.

F

FEDERAL GRANTS-IN-AID.
Advisory commission on intergovernmental relations, categorical grants; their role and design, p. 555.
Block grants, p. 572.
Federal fiscal deterioration, p. 562.
Generally, p. 555.
The general revenue sharing program.
Background, p. 559.
Generally, p. 559.
Statutory provisions, p. 560.

FEDERAL SYSTEM.
Constitutional limitations.
Tenth amendment problems, p. 495.
Governmental liability.
See GOVERNMENTAL LIABILITY.
Local government.
Borrowing of federal substantive powers by state and local governments, p. 531.
Supremacy; preemption and borrowing of power, p. 523.
Tenth amendment problems, p. 495.
Standards for state and local programs.
Generally, p. 533.
State governments.
Borrowing of federal substantive powers by state and local governments, p. 531.
Supremacy; preemption and borrowing of power, p. 523.
Tenth amendment problems, p. 495.

FEDERAL VOTING RIGHTS ACT.
Racial discrimination in annexations, p. 63.

FEES.
Taxation.
See TAXATION.
User charges and other taxes, p. 262.

FINANCE.
Bond issues.
See BOND ISSUES.
Budgeting process.
See BUDGETING PROCESS.
State and local finance.
Generally, p. 185.
State assistance to local governments.
Generally, p. 345.

FISCAL PROBLEMS.
Constitutional limitations, p. 190.

FISCAL PROBLEMS—Cont'd
Due process, p. 193.
Equal protection, p. 193.

FISCAL TRENDS, p. 185.

G

GOVERNMENTAL INTEGRATION.
Generally, p. 153.

GOVERNMENTAL LIABILITY.
Federal law.
Actions against government and government officials, p. 464.
Civil rights cases, p. 464.
Federal antitrust statutes, p. 484.
Generally, p. 463.
The eleventh amendment to the United States constitution, p. 463.
Generally, p. 427.
Immunity of public officers and employees, p. 454.
State courts and legislation.
Abandonment of governmental immunity, p. 435.
Inverse condemnation, p. 455.
Public officials.
Immunity, p. 454.
The discretionary-ministerial distinction, p. 440.
The governmental-proprietary distinction and tort immunity, p. 428.

GOVERNORS.
Executive orders, p. 731.
Impoundment.
Executive impoundment, p. 765.
Injunctions, p. 789.
Mandamus.
A note on mandamus against the chief executive, p. 775.
Powers.
Administration; reorganization, p. 733.
Policies made through executive agencies, p. 740.
Veto powers, p. 750.
Prohibition, p. 776.
Quo warranto, p. 781.
Veto powers, p. 750.

GRANTS.
Federal grants-in-aid.
See FEDERAL GRANTS-IN-AID.

H

HOME RULE.
  Autonomy of local governments.
    Home rule v. non-home rule states, p. 113.
  Imperio states, p. 103.
  Legislative plenary power rule, p. 101.
  State legislatures.
    Imperio states, p. 103.
    Legislative home rule, p. 121.

I

IMMUNITY.
  Liability.
    Governmental liability.
      See GOVERNMENTAL LIABILITY.
  Public officers and employees, p. 454.

IMPERIO STATES, p. 103.

IMPOUNDMENT.
  Governors.
    Executive impoundment, p. 765.
  Mayors.
    Executive impoundment, p. 765.

INCOME TAX.
  Limitations upon, p. 311.
  Local income taxes, p. 258.

INCORPORATION.
  Generally, p. 52.
  Local government.
    Generally, p. 41.
  Statutory requirements, p. 52.

INITIATIVE.
  Constitutional limitations, p. 822.
  Generally, p. 808.

INJUNCTIONS.
  Governors, p. 789.
  Mayors, p. 789.
  Strikes, p. 419.
    Public officers and employees, p. 419.

INTERGOVERNMENTAL COOPERATION.
  Condemnation, p. 161.
    Inverse condemnation, p. 455.
  Constitutional authority, p. 164.
  Generally, p. 163.
  Statutory authority, p. 164.

INTERLOCAL CONFLICT.
  Generally, p. 153.
  Zoning ordinances, p. 155.

INVERSE CONDEMNATION, p. 455.

J

JUDICIAL REVIEW.
  Annexation, p. 41.
  Local government incorporation, p. 41.

JUDICIARY.
  See COURTS.

L

LEGISLATIVE POWER.
  Grant versus limitation, p. 16.

LEGISLATURES.
  See STATE LEGISLATURES.

LIABILITY.
  Governmental liability.
    See GOVERNMENTAL LIABILITY.

LOCAL GOVERNMENT.
  Ad valorem property tax.
    See AD VALOREM PROPERTY TAX.
  Annexation.
    Generally, p. 41.
    Standards, p. 55.
  Appropriations, p. 361.
  Autonomy.
    Home rule as compared to non-home rule states, p. 113.
  Autonomy problems, p. 79.
  Bond issues.
    See BOND ISSUES.
  Boundary commissions.
    Creation, p. 71.
  Capital improvements, p. 351.
  Citizen participation, p. 178.
  City-county consolidation, p. 163.
  Consolidation, p. 173.
  Constitutional limitations.
    Transfer of function, p. 172.
  Constitutional status, p. 29.
  Councils of government, p. 173.
    Voluntary councils, p. 181.
  Courts.
    Licensing and regulation, p. 617.
  Dillon's rule, p. 83.
  Discretionary authority, p. 130.
  Eminent domain.
    Condemnation of the property of one governmental unit by another, p. 161.
    Inverse condemnation, p. 455.
  Expenditure of limitations, p. 311.

LOCAL GOVERNMENT—Cont'd
Expenditures.
  Appropriations, p. 361.
  Budgeting process.
    Capital improvements, p. 351.
    Generally, p. 349.
    Operations, p. 349.
  Generally, p. 347.
  Limitations, p. 311.
  State mandates, p. 347.
Federal grants-in-aid, p. 555.
Federalism, p. 173.
Federal standards for local
    government programs.
  Clean air act, p. 535.
  Generally, p. 533.
  Mental disability, p. 536.
Federal system.
  Borrowing of federal substantive
    powers by state and local
    governments, p. 531.
  Supremacy; preemption and
    borrowing of power, p. 523.
  Tenth amendment problems, p. 495.
Federative governments, p. 174.
Finance.
  Ad valorem property tax.
    See AD VALOREM PROPERTY
      TAX.
  Bond issues.
    See BOND ISSUES.
  Income tax.
    See INCOME TAX.
  State assistance to local
    governments.
    Generally, p. 345.
  Taxation.
    See TAXATION.
Governmental integration.
  Consolidation, federalism and
    councils of government, p. 173.
  Cooperation and transfer of
    function, p. 163.
  Interlocal conflict, p. 153.
Home rule issue, p. 101.
  Imperio states, p. 103.
Income tax.
  See INCOME TAX.
Incorporation.
  Generally, p. 41.
Integration of local governments.
  Generally, p. 153.
Interlocal conflict.
  Generally, p. 153.

LOCAL GOVERNMENT—Cont'd
Interlocal cooperation, p. 163.
  Constitutional authority, p. 164.
  Statutory authority, p. 164.
Judicial review.
  Incorporation, p. 41.
Legislative home rule, p. 121.
Liability.
  See GOVERNMENTAL LIABILITY.
Mayors.
  Generally, p. 731.
  Veto powers, p. 750.
Neighborhood government and citizen
    participation, p. 178.
Powers.
  Dillon's rule, p. 83.
  Discretionary authority, p. 130.
  Generally, p. 79.
  Preemption by state.
    Standards, p. 131.
  Transfer of function, p. 172.
Preemption by state.
  Standards, p. 131.
Public officers and employees.
  See PUBLIC OFFICERS AND
    EMPLOYEES.
Regional agencies, p. 181.
Regulatory programs.
  State standards, p. 150.
State legislatures.
  Delegation of powers, p. 612.
State preemption and standards, p.
    131.
Statutory powers, p. 83.
Structure, p. 25.
Taxation.
  See TAXATION.
Transfer of function, p. 172.
Veto powers.
  Mayor, p. 750.

M

MANDAMUS.
Generally, p. 767.
Governors.
  A note on mandamus against the
    chief executive, p. 775.

MAYORS.
Executive orders, p. 731.
Impoundment.
  Executive impoundment, p. 765.
Injunctions, p. 789.

MAYORS—Cont'd
Mandamus.
A note on mandamus against the chief executive, p. 775.
Powers.
Veto powers, p. 750.
Prohibition, p. 776.
Quo warranto, p. 781.
Veto powers, p. 750.

MUNICIPAL CORPORATIONS.
See LOCAL GOVERNMENT.

O

ORDERS.
Executive orders, p. 731.
Mandamus, p. 767.
Prohibition, p. 776.
Quo warranto, p. 781.

P

PREEMPTION.
Report of the California commission on the law of preemption, p. 148.
State preemption and standards, p. 131.

PROHIBITION.
Generally, p. 776.

PROPERTY TAX.
See AD VALOREM PROPERTY TAX.

PUBLIC OFFICERS AND EMPLOYEES.
Chief executives.
Generally, p. 731.
Collective bargaining, p. 406.
Scope, p. 407.
Conflicts of interest, p. 397.
Discrimination.
Federal employment discrimination legislation, p. 382.
Entry to government service.
Limiting, p. 376.
Executive officers.
Veto powers, p. 750.
Governors.
Generally, p. 731.
Immunity, p. 454.
Integrity in government service.
Conflicts of interest, p. 397.
Generally, p. 397.
Limiting entry to government service, p. 376.

PUBLIC OFFICERS AND EMPLOYEES—Cont'd
Mayors.
Generally, p. 731.
Post-employment restrictions on government officers, employers and attorneys, p. 403.
Removal from government service.
Generally, p. 384.
Patronage and politics, p. 384.
Serving the public sector.
Generally, p. 375.
Strikes.
Injunctions, p. 419.
Unions, p. 406.
Veto powers, p. 750.

Q

QUO WARRANTO, p. 781.

R

RACIAL DISCRIMINATION.
See DISCRIMINATION.

REAL ESTATE TAX.
See AD VALOREM PROPERTY TAX.

REAPPORTIONMENT.
Courts.
Powers of courts, p. 632.
One person-one vote principle in legislative apportionment, p. 635.

REFERENDUM.
Constitutional limitations.
A note on the constitutionality of the referendum in the federal courts, p. 822.
Generally, p. 808.

REFORM OF STATE GOVERNMENT, p. 6.

REVENUE BONDS, p. 278.
Bond issues.
See BOND ISSUES.

REVENUES.
See TAXATION.

REVENUE SHARING.
Federal grants-in-aid, pp. 559, 560.

S

SALES TAX.
  Ad valorem property tax.
    See AD VALOREM PROPERTY TAX.
  Alternative to ad valorem property tax, p. 271.

SCHOOLS.
  Courts.
    Cost-quality issue and equality of educational opportunity, p. 724.
    Education as a fundamental interest, p. 686.
    Remedial alternatives, p. 689.
  Discrimination.
    Cost-quality issue and equality of educational opportunity, p. 724.
  Finance issues, p. 670.

SPECIAL DISTRICTS.
  Development, p. 65.
  Nature and functions, p. 65.
  Organization, p. 66.

SPECIAL LEGISLATION.
  State legislatures, p. 581.

STATE GOVERNMENT.
  Appropriations, p. 361.
  Budget process.
    Generally, p. 349.
  Capital improvements, p. 351.
  Constitutional limitations, p. 8.
  Courts.
    Licensing and regulation, p. 617.
  Expenditures.
    Appropriations, p. 361.
    Budgeting process, p. 349.
      Capital improvements, p. 351.
      Operations, p. 349.
    Generally, p. 347.
    Mandates, p. 347.
  Federal grants-in-aid, p. 555.
  Federal standards for state programs.
    Clean air act, p. 535.
    Generally, p. 533.
    Mental disability, p. 536.
  Federal system.
    Borrowing of federal substantive powers by state and local governments, p. 531.
    Supremacy; preemption and borrowing of power, p. 523.
    Tenth amendment problems, p. 495.
  Governors.
    Generally, p. 731.

STATE GOVERNMENT—Cont'd
  Governors—Cont'd
    Veto powers, p. 750.
  Liability.
    See GOVERNMENTAL LIABILITY.
  Local government.
    Budgeting process.
      Generally, p. 349.
    Generally.
      See LOCAL GOVERNMENT.
  Local regulatory programs.
    Standards, p. 150.
  Preemption.
    Report of the California commission on the law of preemption, p. 148.
  Preemption and standards, p. 131.
  Public officers and employees.
    See PUBLIC OFFICERS AND EMPLOYEES.
  Reform, p. 6.

STATE LEGISLATURES.
  Delegation of power, p. 598.
    Administrative agencies and officials, p. 599.
  Delegation of powers.
    Judicial powers, p. 612.
    Local governments, p. 612.
  Doctrine of delegation, p. 598.
  Due process.
    Limitation on powers, p. 16.
  Home rule, p. 101.
    Imperio states, p. 103.
    Legislative home rule, p. 121.
    Plenary power rule, p. 101.
  Legislative power.
    Grant versus limitation, p. 16.
  Local government.
    Delegation of powers, p. 612.
  Powers.
    Grant versus limitation, p. 16.
  Quality of representation, p. 667.
  Special legislation, p. 581.

STRIKES.
  Injunctions, p. 419.
    Public officers and employees, p. 419.
  Public officers and employees.
    Injunctions, p. 419.

T

TAXATION.
  Ad valorem property tax.
    Administration, p. 213.

TAXATION—Cont'd
  Ad valorem property tax—Cont'd
    Central city economics, p. 215.
    Constitutional limitations.
      Note on constitutionality of differential property tax assessment, p. 228.
    Differential assessments and classifications, p. 224.
    Expenditure and tax limitations, p. 311.
    Fractional assessments, p. 216.
    Generally, p. 211.
    Increment financing, p. 232.
    Relief provisions, p. 339.
    Sales tax.
      Alternative to ad valorem property tax, p. 271.
    Special benefit taxation, p. 238.
    Trends in property tax collections, p. 213.
    Urban development and land use, p. 214.
  Bond issues.
    See BOND ISSUES.
  Commerce clause, p. 210.
  Constitutional limitations, p. 192.
    Note on constitutionality of differential property tax assessment, p. 228.
    Public purpose, p. 201.
  Differential assessments and classifications.
    Ad Valorem property tax, p. 224.
  Due process, p. 193.
  Equal protection, p. 193.
    Limitations upon taxation, p. 318.
  Fiscal trends, p. 185.
  Fractional assessments.
    Ad valorem property tax, p. 216.
  Income tax.
    Local income taxes, p. 258.
  Limitations upon, p. 311.
  Miscellaneous taxes, p. 262.
  Public purpose, p. 201.
  Relief provisions.
    Ad valorem property tax, p. 339.
  Sales tax.
    Alternative to ad valorem property tax, p. 271.
  Special benefit taxation.
    Ad valorem property tax, p. 238.

TAXATION—Cont'd
  Tax equity and fiscal responsibility act of 1982, p. 288.
  User charges and other taxes, p. 262.

TENTH AMENDMENT.
  Problems, p. 495.

TORTS.
  Governmental liability.
    State courts and legislation.
      The governmental-proprietary distinction and tort immunity, p. 428.
    Immunity of public officers and employees, p. 454.

U

UNIONS.
  Public officers and employees, p. 406.
    Strikes.
      Injunctions, p. 419.

V

VETO POWERS, p. 750.

VOTING RIGHTS.
  Courts.
    Local elections, p. 652.
    Local governments.
      Application of one person-one vote to local governments, p. 638.
    Powers of courts, p. 632.
  Local elections, p. 652.
  Racial discrimination in annexations, p. 63.

W

WRIT OF MANDAMUS.
  Generally, pp. 767, 775.

WRIT OF PROHIBITION.
  Generally, p. 776.

WRIT OF QUO WARRANTO.
  Generally, p. 781.

Z

ZERO-BASE BUDGETING, p. 350.

ZONING.
  Condemnation, p. 161.
  Ordinances.
    Interlocal conflict, p. 155.
    Statutory authority, p. 164.